ART HISTORY

REVISED EDITION **VOLUME ONE**

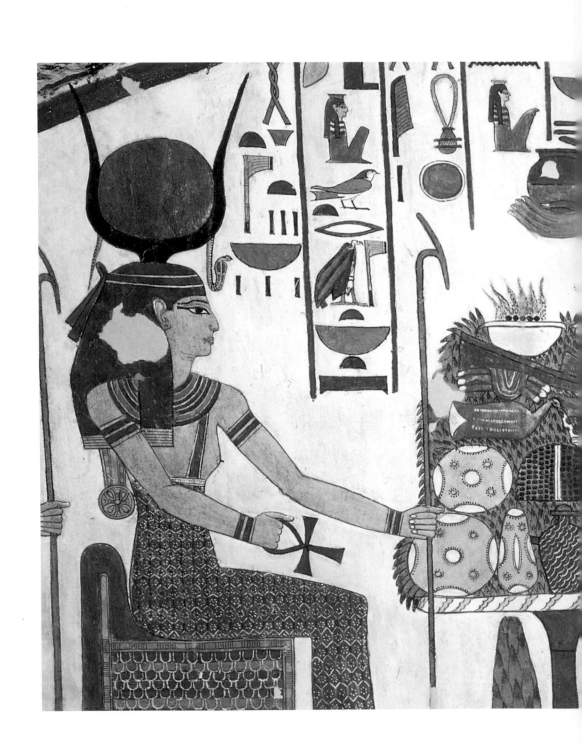

ART HISTORY

Marilyn Stokstad

REVISED EDITION VOLUME ONE

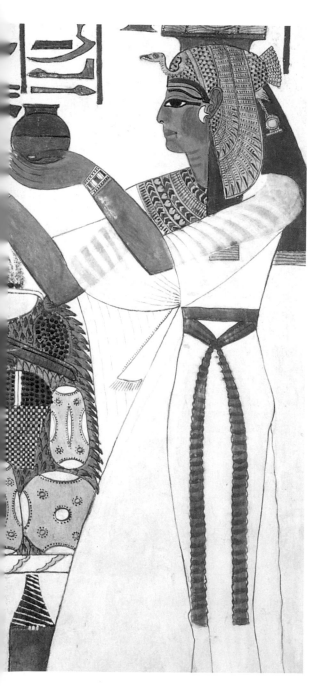

with the collaboration of Bradford R. Collins
and with chapters by Stephen Addiss, Chu-tsing Li,
Marylin M. Rhie, and Christopher D. Roy

Harry N. Abrams, Inc., Publishers

DEDICATED TO MY SISTER, KAREN L.S. LEIDER, AND MY NIECE, ANNA J. LEIDER

Project management and editorial direction: *Julia Moore*
Project consultation: *Jean Smith*
Developmental editing: *Ellyn Childs Allison, Sabra Maya Feldman, Mark Getlein, James Leggio,*
     Sheila Franklin Lieber, Jean Smith, Elaine Banks Stainton
Design, art direction, and production: *Lydia Gershey, with Yonah Schurink of Communigraph*
Photo editing, rights and reproduction: *Lauren Boucher, Jennifer Bright, Helen Lee, Catherine Ruello,*
     Janice Ackerman, Diana Gongora Pilar
Maps and timelines: *York Production Services*
Illustration: *John McKenna*
Project editing: *Jungha Oh*
Indexing: *Peter and Erica Rooney*

Library of Congress Cataloging-in-Publication Data

Stokstad, Marilyn, 1929–
     Art history / Marilyn Stokstad: in collaboration with Bradford R. Collins: with chapters by Stephen
Addiss . . . [et al.]. – Rev. ed.
          p.   cm.
     Includes bibliographical references and index.
     ISBN 0–8109–1991–5 (Abrams hardcover set). —ISBN 0–13–082583–2 (Prentice Hall hardcover).
     ISBN 0–13–082581–6 (paperback, Vol. 1). —ISBN 0–13–082582–4 (paperback, Vol. 2).

     1. Art—History.   I. Collins, Bradford R., 1942–   . II. Addiss, Stephen, 1935–   .   III. Title.
N5300.S923   1999
709—dc21   98–25873
                                                                                            CIP

Printed and bound in Japan

Harry N. Abrams, Inc.
100 Fifth Avenue
New York, NY 10011
www.abramsbooks.com

Pages 2–3: Queen Nefertari Making an Offering to Isis, wall painting in the tomb of Nefertari, Valley of the Queens, near Deir el-Bahri. Dynasty 19, c. 1279–1212 BCE

On the chapter-opening pages: 34–35, Stonehenge (detail of fig. 1-21); 60–61, gold crown from Kalhu (detail of fig. 2-25); 90–91, Great Pyramids, Giza (detail of fig. 3-10); 126–127, *Landscape,* Thera (detail of fig. 4-18); 150–151, *Marshals and Young Women,* from the Parthenon (detail of fig. 5-48); 220–221, *The Unswept Floor,* mosaic (detail of fig. 6-70); 286–287, *Anastasis,* fresco, Istanbul (detail of fig. 7-52); 336–337, *muqarnas* dome, the Alhambra (detail of fig. 8-12); 364–365, Cave Temple of Shiva, Elephanta (detail of fig. 9-20); 394–395, *Admonitions of the Imperial Instructress* (detail of fig., 10-10); 420–421, Scene from *The Tale of Genji* (detail of fig. 11-13); 442–443, Maya vessel (detail of fig. 12-12); 464–465, *The Herders' Village,* wall painting, Algeria (detail of fig. 13-1); 478–479, Purse cover, from Sutton Hoo burial ship (detail of fig. 14-7); 506–507, *Dream of Henry I, Worcester Chronicle* (detail of fig. 15-28); 544–545, *Shrine of the Three Kings* (detail of fig. 16-56)

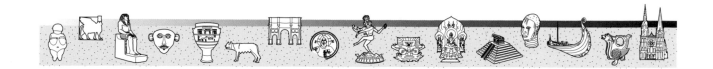

Brief Contents

Preface to the First Edition

I have been privileged to teach art history for nearly four decades. Over that time I have become persuaded that our purpose in the introductory course should not be to groom scholars-to-be but rather to nurture an educated, enthusiastic public for the arts. I have also come to believe that we are not well-enough served by the major introductory textbooks presently available, all of which originated two or more generations ago. What is needed is a new text for a new generation of teachers and students, a text that balances formalist traditions with the newer interests of contextual art history and also meets the needs of a diverse and fast-changing student population. In support of that philosophy I offer *Art History*.

I firmly believe students should *enjoy* their art history survey. Only then will they learn to appreciate art as the most tangible creation of the human imagination. To this end we have sought in many ways to make *Art History* a sensitive, accessible, engaging textbook.

We have made *Art History* contextual, in the best sense of the term. Throughout the text we treat the visual arts not in a vacuum but within the essential contexts of history, geography, politics, religion, and culture; and we carefully define the parameters—social, religious, political, and cultural—that either constrained or liberated individual artists.

***Art History* is both comprehensive and inclusive.** Our goal has been to reach beyond the West to include a critical examination of the arts of other regions and cultures, presenting a global view of art through the centuries. We cover not only the world's most significant paintings and works of sculpture and architecture but also drawings, photographs, works in metal and ceramics, textiles, and jewelry. We have paid due respect to the canon of great monuments of the history of art, but we also have treated artists and artworks not previously acknowledged. We have drawn throughout on the best and most recent scholarship, including new discoveries (the prehistoric cave paintings in the Ardèche gorge in southern France, for example) and new interpretations of well-known works. And, bearing in mind the needs of undergraduate readers, we have sought wherever feasible to discuss works on view in many different museums and collections around the United States, including college and university museums.

No effort has been spared to make this book a joy to read and use—in fact, to make it a work of art in itself. Chapter introductions set the scene for the material to come, frequently making use of contemporary references to which readers can easily relate. While the text carries the central narrative of *Art History*, set-off boxes present interesting and instructive material that enriches the text. A number of thought-provoking boxes focus on such critical issues as "the myth of 'primitive' art" and the way the titles given to works of art may affect our perception of them. Other boxes provide insights into contextual influences, such as women as art patrons, the lives of major religious leaders, and significant literary movements. **Elements of Architecture** boxes explicate basic architectural forms and terminology.

Technique boxes explore how artworks have been made, from prehistoric cave paintings to Renaissance frescoes to how a camera works. **Maps and timelines** visually place artworks in time and space, and time scales on each page let readers know where they are within the period each chapter covers. A **Parallels** feature in every chapter presents comparative information in tabular form that puts the major events and artworks discussed in that chapter in a global context. Finally, *Art History* includes **an unprecedented illustration program** of some 1,350 photographs—more than half in full color and some not published before—as well as hundreds of original line drawings (including architectural plans and cutaways) that have been created specifically for this book.

In addition, a complete ancillary package, including slide sets, CD-ROM, videodisc, videos, a student Study Guide, and an Instructor's Resource Manual with Test Bank, accompanies *Art History*.

***Art History* represents the joint effort of a distinguished team of scholars and educators.** Single authorship of a work such as this is no longer a viable proposition: our world has become too complex, the research on and interpretation of art too sophisticated, for that to work. An individual view of art may be very persuasive—even elegant—but it remains personal; we no longer look for a single "truth," nor do we hold to a canon of artworks to the extent we once did. An effort such as this requires a team of scholar-teachers, all with independent views and the capability of treating the art they write about in its own terms and its own cultural context. The overarching viewpoint—the controlling imagination—is mine, but the book would not have been complete without the work of the following distinguished contributing authors:

Stephen Addiss, Tucker Boatwright Professor in the Humanities at the University of Richmond, Virginia

Bradford R. Collins, Associate Professor in the Art Department, University of South Carolina, Columbia

Chu-tsing Li, Professor Emeritus at the University of Kansas, Lawrence

Marylin M. Rhie, Jessie Wells Post Professor of Art and Professor of East Asian Studies at Smith College

Christopher D. Roy, Professor of Art History at the University of Iowa in Iowa City

Finally, the book would not have been possible without the substantial efforts of Marion Spears Grayson, an independent scholar with a Ph.D. from Columbia University who previously taught at Tufts University and Rice University. Her refinements and original contributions greatly enhanced the overall presentation. The book has also benefited greatly from the invaluable assistance and advice of scores of other scholars and teachers who have generously answered my questions, given their recommendations on organization and priorities, and provided specialized critiques.

Preface to the Revised Edition

I want to thank my many friends and colleagues for welcoming *Art History* into their lives and their classrooms. I knew I wanted a new textbook for my students, but I had no idea how widespread that same desire was. In the three years since Abrams and Prentice Hall introduced *Art History*, it has exceeded all our hopes for its acceptance.

In light of the success of the original edition, you may ask why we have brought out a revision so soon. One of the reasons, in fact, is that the original edition has proved more than strong enough to make practicable this revision in a relatively short time. The changes are of two kinds: small **improvements of content and expression, and substantive changes to chapters on three periods of Western art: Renaissance, Baroque and Rococo, and Modernism.** To be exact, **Chapters 1 through Chapter 16 contain eighty-six changes,** and all but a few of these are in chapters on the Western tradition.

Of the thirteen chapters between Chapters 17 and 29, seven have been rethought and reorganized. We addressed the only consistent criticism of the original edition—that Giotto was confined to the Gothic chapter—by treating him in this edition within the context of both Italian Gothic art (in Chapter 16) and as the early Renaissance giant he was (in Chapter 17). To rework chapters on the modern period, my excellent collaborator, Bradford R. Collins, contributed the entire story by beginning with Neoclassicism and Romanticism (Chapter 26) and revisiting and rewriting the chapters he had written for the original edition: Chapters 27, 28, and 29. In the process, more than fifty works of art were changed and as many more were moved around in order to make the narrative of the nineteenth and twentieth centuries more coherent than ever.

Our old friend **"popular demand" brought in a few canonical works.** I too found it impossible to teach twentieth-century art without Picasso's *Guernica* and Wright's Fallingwater. And I apologize to all the saints and sinners of the sixteenth century for my original treatment of Titian: *The Pesaro Madonna* is here now (and *Isabella d'Este* stays).

I hope you all will enjoy this edition and, as you have done so generously and graciously over the last three years, will continue to share your comments and suggestions with me.

Acknowledgments to the First Edition

Writing and producing this book has been a far more challenging undertaking than any of us originally thought it would be. Were it not for the editorial and organizational expertise of Julia Moore, we never would have pulled it off. She inspired, orchestrated, and guided the team of editors, researchers, photo editors, designers, and illustrators who contributed their talents to the volume you now hold. Paul Gottlieb and Bud Therien convinced me to undertake the project, and with Phil Miller were unfailingly supportive throughout its complex gestation. A team of developmental editors led by David Chodoff at Prentice Hall and Jean Smith at Abrams refined the final manuscript to make it clear and accessible to students. Special thanks are due to Ellyn Childs Allison, Sheila Franklin Lieber, and Steve Rigolosi for their careful developmental work during the crucial early stages; to Mark Getlein for his extraordinary care in developing the chapters on Asian and African art; and to Gerald Lombardi for his work on the chapters on Western art since the Renaissance. Photo researchers Lauren Boucher, Jennifer Bright, Helen Lee, and Catherine Ruello performed miracles in finding the illustrations we needed—and, because of their zeal in finding the best pictures, sometimes helped us see what we wanted. John McKenna's drawings have brought exactly the right mix of information, clarity, and human presence to the illustration program. Special thanks also to Nancy Corwin, who was an essential resource on the history of craft, and to Jill Leslie Furst for her assistance on the chapters on the art of Pacific cultures and the art of the Americas. Designer Lydia Gershey and associate Yonah Schurink have broken new ground with their clear and inviting design and layout. Alison Pendergast, marketing manager, contributed many helpful insights as the book neared completion. My research assistants at the University of Kansas, Katherine Giele, Richard Watters, and Michael Willis, have truly earned my everlasting gratitude.

Every chapter has been read by one or more specialists: Barbara Abou-El-Haj, SUNY Binghamton; Jane Aiken, Virginia Polytechnic; Vicki Artimovich, Bellevue Community College; Elizabeth Atherton, El Camino College; Ulku Bates, Columbia University; Joseph P. Becherer, Grand Rapids Community College; Janet Catherine Berlo, University of Missouri, St. Louis; Roberta Bernstein, SUNY Albany; Edward Bleiberg, University of Memphis; Daniel Breslauer, University of Kansas; Ronald Buksbaum, Capital Community Technical College; Petra ten-Doesschate Chu, Seton Hall University; John Clarke, University of Texas, Austin; Robert Cohon, The Nelson-Atkins Museum of Art; Frances Colpitt, University of Texas, San Antonio; Lorelei H. Corcoran, University of Memphis; Ann G. Crowe, Virginia Commonwealth University; Pamela Decoteau, Southern Illinois University; Susan J. Delaney, Mira Costa College; Walter B. Denny, University of Massachusetts, Amherst; Richard DePuma, University of Iowa; Brian Dursam, University of Miami; Ross Edman, University of Illinois, Chicago; Gerald Eknoian, DeAnza State College; Mary S. Ellett, Randolph-Macon College; James D. Farmer, Virginia Commonwealth University; Craig Felton, Smith College; Mary F. Francey, University of Utah; Joanna Frueh, University of Nevada, Reno; Mark Fullerton, Ohio State University; Anna Gonosova, University of California, Irvine; Robert Grigg; Glenn Harcourt, University of Southern California; Sharon Hill, Virginia Commonwealth University; Mary Tavener Holmes, New York City; Paul E. Ivey, University of Arizona; Carol S. Ivory, Washington State University; Nina Kasanof, Sage Junior College of Albany; John F. Kenfield, Rutgers University; Ruth Kolarik, Colorado College; Jeffrey Lang, University of Kansas; William A. Lozano, Johnson County Community College; Franklin Ludden, Ohio State University; Lisa F. Lynes, North Idaho College; Joseph Alexander MacGillivray, Columbia University; Janice Mann, Wayne State University; Michelle Marcus, The

Metropolitan Museum of Art; Virginia Marquardt, University of Virginia; Peggy McDowell, University of New Orleans; Sheila McNally, University of Minnesota; Victor H. Miesel, University of Michigan; Vernon Minor, University of Colorado, Boulder; Anta Montet-White, University of Kansas; Anne E. Morganstern, Ohio State University; William J. Murnane, University of Memphis; Lawrence Nees, University of Delaware; Sara Orel, Northeast Missouri State University; John G. Pedley, University of Michigan; Elizabeth Pilliod, Oregon State University; Nancy H. Ramage, Ithaca College; Ida K. Rigby, San Diego State University; Howard Risatti, Virginia Commonwealth University; Ann M. Roberts, University of Iowa; Stanley T. Rolfe, University of Kansas; Wendy W. Roworth, University of Rhode Island; James H. Rubin, SUNY Stony Brook; John Russell, Columbia University; Patricia Sands, Pratt Institute; Thomas Sarrantonio, SUNY New Paltz; Diane G. Scillia, Kent State University; Linda Seidel, University of Chicago; Nancy Sevcenko, Cambridge, Massachusetts; Tom Shaw, Kean College; Jan Sheridan, Erie Community College; Anne R. Stanton, University of Missouri, Columbia; Thomas Sullivan, OSB, Benedictine College (Conception Abbey); Janis Tomlinson, Columbia University; the late Eleanor Tufts; Dorothy Verkerk, University of North Carolina, Chapel Hill; Roger Ward, The Nelson-Atkins Museum of Art; Mark Weil, Washington University, St. Louis; Alison West, New York City; Randall White, New York University; and David Wilkins, University of Pittsburgh.

Others who have tried to keep me from errors of fact and interpretation—who have shared ideas and course syllabi, read chapters or sections of chapters, and offered suggestions and criticism—include: Janet Rebold Benton, Pace University; Elizabeth Gibson Broun, National Museum of America Art; Robert G. Calkins, Cornell University; William W. Clark, Queens College, CUNY; Jaqueline Clipsham; Alessandra Comini, Southern Methodist University; Susan Craig, University of Kansas; Charles Cuttler; University of Iowa; Ralph T. Coe, Santa Fe; Nancy Corwin, University of Kansas; Patricia Darish,University of Kansas; Lois Drewer, Index of Christian Art; Charles Eldredge, University of Kansas; James Enyeart, Eastman House, Rochester; Ann Friedman, J. Paul Getty Museum; Mary D. Garrard, American University; Walter S. Gibson, Case Western Reserve University; Stephen Goddard, University of Kansas; Paula Gerson; Dorothy Glass, SUNY Buffalo; the late Jane Hayward, The Cloisters, The Metropolitan Museum of Art; Robert Hoffmann, The Smithsonian Institution; Luke Jordan, University of Kansas; Charles Little, The Metropolitan Museum of Art; Karen Mack, University of Kansas; Richard Mann, San Francisco State University; Bob Martin, Haskel Indian Nations University; Amy McNair, University of Kansas; Sara Jane Pearman, The Cleveland Museum of Art; Michael Plante, H. Sophie Newcomb Memorial College; John Pultz, University of Kansas; Virginia Raguin, College of the Holy Cross; Pamela Sheingorn, Baruch College, CUNY; James Seaver, University of Kansas; Caryle K. Smith, University of Akron; Walter Smith, University of Akron; Lauren Soth, Carleton College; Linda Stone-Ferrier, University of Kansas; Michael Stoughton, University of Minnesota; Elizabeth Valdez del Alamo, Montclair State College; and Ann S. Zielinski, SUNY Plattsburgh.

Finally, the book was class tested with students under the direction of these teachers: Fred C. Albertson, University of Memphis; Betty J. Crouther, University of Mississippi; Linda M. Gigante, University of Louisville; Jennifer Haley, University of Nebraska, Lincoln; Cynthia Hahn, Florida State University; Lawrence R. Hoey, University of Wisconsin, Milwaukee; Delane O. Karalow, Virginia Commonwealth University; Charles R. Mack, University of South Carolina, Columbia; Brian Madigan, Wayne State University; Merideth Palumbo, Kent State University; Sharon Pruitt, East Carolina State University; J. Michael Taylor, James Madison University; Marcilene K. Wittmer, University of Miami; and Marilyn Wyman, San Jose State University.

A Final Word

As each of us develops a genuine appreciation of the arts, we come to see them as the ultimate expression of human faith and integrity as well as creativity. I have tried here to capture that creativity, courage, and vision in such a way as to engage and enrich even those encountering art history for the very first time. If I have done that, I will feel richly rewarded.

Marilyn Stokstad
Spring 1995

Acknowledgments to the Revised Edition

Many people reviewed the original edition of *Art History* and helped with the changes and revisions to the Revised Edition. By period, they are Jean Middleton James, the entire text; Judith Oliver (Colgate University), the European Middle Ages; Edward Olszewski (Case Western Reserve University) and Edward Eglinski (The University of Kansas), Renaissance and Baroque; David Cateforis (The University of Kansas) and Grace Flam (Salt Lake City Community College), modern art and architecture; and Marta Braun (Ryerson Polytechnic University), photography.

Others whose comments were especially helpful include James Adams (Manchester College), Anthony Alofsin (University of Texas at Austin), Sara Blick (Kenyon College), Larry Beck, Nancy Corwin (Tulane University), Stephen Goddard (The University of Kansas), Wendy Kindred (University of Maine at Fort Kent), Aileen Laing (Sweet Briar College), and Amy Ogata (Cleveland Institute of Art).

Many of those acknowledged in the original edition assisted with the Revised Edition, especially Robert Calkins, Robert Cohon, Susan Craig, Charles Cuttler, Charles Eldredge, Eileen Fry, Walter Gibson, Dorothy Glass, Charles Little, Bob Martin, Amy McNair, Anta Montet-White, Sara Orel, Sarajane Pearman, John Pultz, Pamela Sheingorn, James Seaver, Linda Stone-Ferrier, Elizabeth Valdez del Alamo, Roger Ward, and Ann Zielinski.

Again, thanks to my wonderful editor at Abrams, Julia Moore, and to those who worked with her so competently, Jean Smith and Jungha Oh. Photo researchers Diana Pilar Gongora and Janice Ackerman have my gratitude, and so do Lydia Gershey and Yonah Schurink, designers extraordinary.

Marilyn Stokstad
Lawrence, Kansas
June 1998

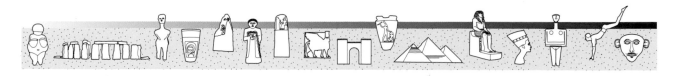

Contents

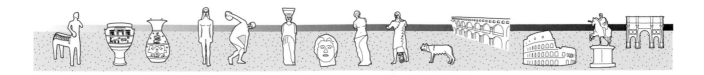

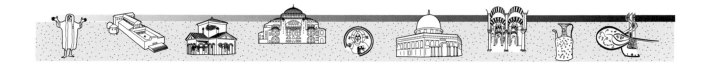

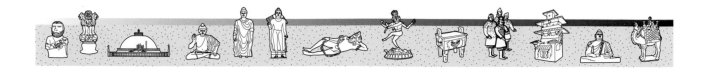

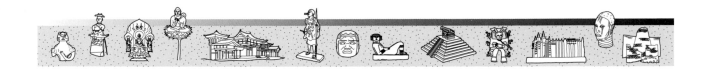

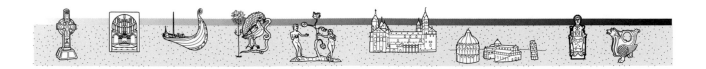

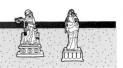

Introduction

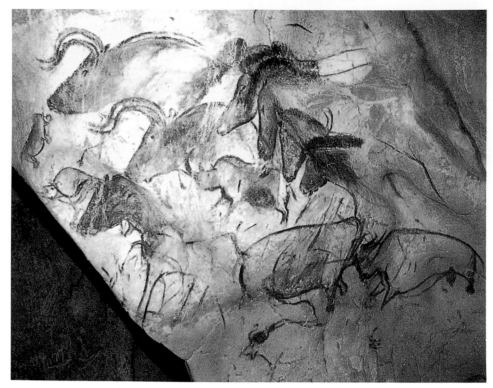

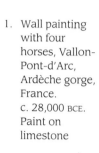

1. Wall painting with four horses, Vallon-Pont-d'Arc, Ardèche gorge, France. c. 28,000 BCE. Paint on limestone

I stood in front of that exquisite panel with the four horses' heads and . . . I was so overcome that I cried. It was like going into an attic and finding a da Vinci [painting]. Except that this great [artist] was unknown." With these words Jean Clottes, an eminent French authority on prehistoric cave art, described viewing one of the 300 breathtakingly beautiful paintings just discovered in a huge limestone cavern near the Ardèche River in southern France (Marlise Simons, "In a French Cave, Wildlife Scenes from a Long-Gone World," *The New York Times*, January 24, 1995, page C10).

These remarkable animal images, fixed in time and preserved undisturbed in their remote cavern, were created some 30,000 years ago (fig. 1). That such representations were made at all is evidence of a uniquely human trait. And what animals are painted here? When were they painted, and how have they been preserved? Why were the paintings made, and what do they tell us about the people who made them? All these questions—what is depicted, how, when, why—are subjects of art history. And, because *these* magnificent images come from a time before there were written records, they provide the best information available not just about early humans' art but also about their reality.

ART AND REALITY

What is art? And what is reality? Especially today, why should one draw or paint, carve or model, when an image can be captured with a camera? In a nineteenth-century painting, *Interior with Portraits* (fig. 2), by the American artist Thomas LeClear, two children stand painfully still while a photographer prepares to take their picture. The paintings and sculpture that fill the studio have been shoved aside to make way for a new kind of art—the photograph. As the photographer adjusts the lens of his camera, we see his baggy pants but not his head. Is LeClear suggesting that the painter's head (brain and eye) is being replaced by the lens (a kind of mechanical brain and eye) of the camera? Or even that the artist and the camera have become a single recording eye? Or is this painting a witty commentary on the nature of reality? Art history leads us to ask such questions.

LeClear's painting resembles a snapshot in its record of studio clutter, but LeClear made subtle changes in what he saw. Using the formal elements of painting—the arrangement of shapes and colors—he focused attention on the children rather than on the interesting and distracting objects that surround them. Light falls on the girl and boy and intensifies the brilliant coral and green of the cloth on the floor. Softer coral shades in the curtain and the upholstered chair

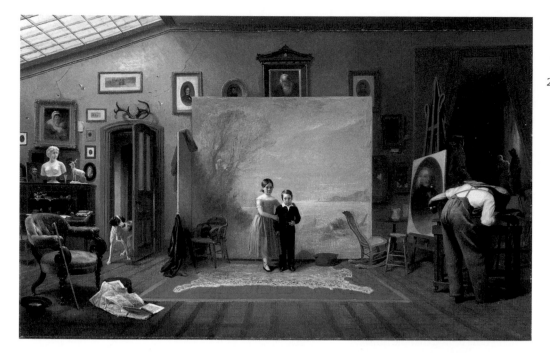

2. Thomas LeClear. *Interior with Portraits*. c. 1865. Oil on canvas, 25⅞ x 40½" (65.7 x 102.9 cm). National Museum of American Art, Smithsonian Institution, Washington, D.C. Museum purchase made possible by the Pauline Edwards Bequest

frame the image, and the repeated colors balance each other. LeClear also reminds us that art is an illusion: the photograph will show the children in a vast landscape with a rug and animal skin, but the painting reveals that the landscape is just a two-dimensional painted backdrop and the rug and animal skin just slightly worn, painted cloth. These observations make us realize that the painting is more than a portrait; it is also a commentary on the artist as a creator of illusions.

Certainly there is more to this painting—and to most paintings—than one first sees. We can simply enjoy *Interior with Portraits* as a record of nineteenth-century America, but we can also study the history of the painting to probe deeper into its significance. Who are the children? Why was their portrait painted? Who owned the painting? The answers to these questions lead us to further doubts about the reality of this seemingly "realistic" work.

Thomas LeClear worked in Buffalo, New York, from 1847 to 1863. The painting, which is now in the National Museum of American Art in Washington, D.C., once belonged to the Sidway family of Buffalo. Family records show that the girl in the painting, Parnell Sidway, died in 1849; the boy, her younger brother James Sidway, died in 1865 while working as a volunteer fire fighter. Evidence suggests that the painting was not made until the 1860s, well after Parnell's death and when James was a grown man—or possibly after his death, too. LeClear moved to New York City in 1863, and the studio seen in the painting may be one he borrowed from his son-in-law there. Another clue to the painting's date is the camera, which is a type that was not used before 1860. The Sidway children, then, could never have posed for this painting. It must, instead, be a memorial portrait, perhaps painted by LeClear from a photograph. In short, this image of "reality" cannot be "real." Art historical research reveals a story entirely different from what observation of the painting alone suggests.

This new knowledge leads us to further speculations on the nature of art. The memorial portrait, with its re-creation of vanished childhood, is a reflection on life and death. In

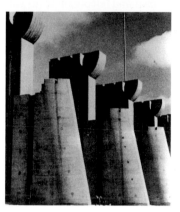 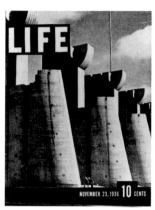

3. Margaret Bourke-White. *Fort Peck Dam, Montana*. 1936

4. First cover, *Life* magazine, November 23, 1936

this context, the ambiguities we noticed before—the contrast between the reality of the studio and the unreal landscape on the cloth in the background, the juxtaposition between the new medium of photography and the old-fashioned, painted portrait on an easel—take on deeper significance. LeClear seems to be commenting on the tension between nature and art, on art and reality, and on the role of the artist as a recording eye and controlling imagination.

But what about the reality of photographs? Today the camera has become a universal tool for picture making. Even though we know that film can be manipulated and photographs made to "lie," we generally accept that the camera tells the truth. We forget that in a photograph a vibrant, moving, three-dimensional world has been immobilized, reduced to two dimensions, and sometimes recorded in black and white.

Photographs can be powerful works of art. In the 1930s and 1940s people waited as eagerly for the weekly arrival of *Life* magazine, with its photojournalism and photo essays, as people do today for their favorite television program. An extraordinary photographer of that time was Margaret Bourke-White, whose photograph of Peck Dam (fig. 3), used on the cover of the first issue of *Life* in 1936 (fig. 4), made a dramatic social-political statement about the role of government. In the depths of the economic depression of the 1930s, public works like the dam in the picture, which controlled floods and provided electric power, gave people hope for a better life. Bourke-White's photograph is a symbol of the power of technology and engineering over nature. It seems to equate the monumental grandeur of the dam with the architectural marvels of the past—Egyptian pyramids, the Roman Colosseum, medieval European castles. The arrangement of elements in the image reflects techniques that had been perfected by artists over the centuries: the repetition of simple forms, a steady recession into space, and a dramatic contrast of light and dark. Two red bands with bold white lettering turn the photograph into a handsome piece of **graphic design**, that is, a work in which art and design, typography, and printing are brought together to communicate a message.

Bourke-White's skillful capturing of the powerful dam reminds us that the camera is merely a mechanical tool for making records until an artist puts it to use. Anyone who has ever taken a snapshot of a friend only to find that the finished picture includes unnoticed rubbish and telephone wires will recognize the importance of the human brain's ability to filter and select. But an artist's vision can turn the everyday world into a superior reality—perhaps simply more focused or intense, certainly more imaginative.

We can easily understand a photograph of a dam, the imagery in a painting of a nineteenth-century artist's studio is not too strange to us, and even prehistoric animal paintings in a cave have a haunting familiarity. Other works, however, present a few more challenges. The fifteenth-century painting *The Annunciation,* by Jan van Eyck (fig. 5), is an excellent example of how some artists try to paint more than the eye can see and more than the mind can grasp. We can enjoy the painting for its visual characteristics—the drawing, colors, and arrangement of shapes—but we need the help of art history and information about the painting's cultural context if we want to understand it fully. Jan van Eyck (1390–1441) lived in the wealthy city of Bruges, in what is now Belgium, in the first half of the fifteenth century. The painting seems to be set in Jan van Eyck's own time in a church with stone walls and arches, tile floor, wooden roof, stained-glass windows, and wall paintings. The artist has so carefully recreated the colors and textures of every surface that he convinces us of the truth of his vision. Clearly something strange and wonderful is happening. We see a richly robed youth with splendid multicolored wings interrupting a kneeling young woman's reading. The two figures gesture gracefully upward toward a dove flying down streaks of gold. Golden letters float from their lips, forming the Latin words that mean "Hail, full of grace" and "Behold the handmaiden of the Lord." But only if we know something about the symbols, or **iconography**, of Christian art does the subject of the painting become clear. The scene is the Annunciation, the moment when the angel Gabriel tells the Virgin Mary that she will bear the Son of God, Jesus Christ (recounted in the New Testament of the Christian Bible, Luke 1:26–38). All the details have a meaning. The dove symbolizes the Holy Spirit. The white lilies are symbols of Mary. The one stained-glass window of God (flanked by wall paintings of Moses) is

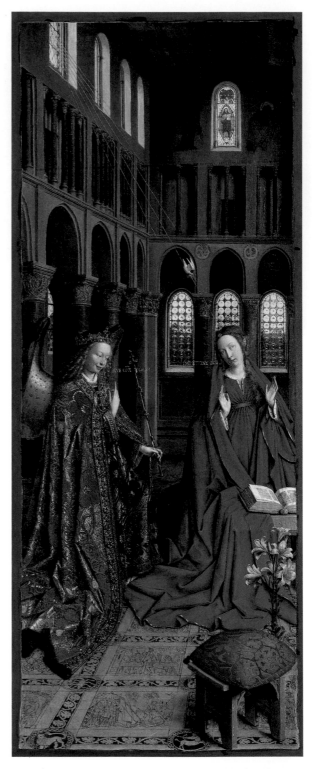

5. Jan van Eyck. *The Annunciation.* c. 1434–36. Oil on canvas, transferred from panel, painted surface 35³⁄₈ x 13⁷⁄₈" (90.2 x 34.1 cm). National Gallery of Art, Washington, D.C. Andrew W. Mellon Collection 1937.1.39

juxtaposed with the three windows enclosing Mary (representing the Trinity of Father, Son, and Holy Spirit), and this contrast suggests that a new era is about to begin. The signs of the zodiac in the floor tiles indicate the traditional date of the Annunciation, March 25. The placement of the figures in a much later architectural setting is quite unreal, however.

Art historians explain that Jan van Eyck not only is representing a miracle but also is illustrating the idea that Mary is the new Christian Church.

Art historians learn all they can about the lives of artists and those close to them. Seeking information about Jan van Eyck, for example, they have investigated his brother Hubert, Jan's wife, Margaret, and his chief patron, the duke of Burgundy. They are also fascinated by painting techniques—in this case the preparation of the wood panel, the original drawing, and the building of the images in transparent oil layers. The history of the painting (its **provenance**) is important too—its transfer from wood panel to canvas, its cleaning and restoration, and its trail of ownership. The painting, given by American financier Andrew W. Mellon to the National Gallery of Art in Washington, D.C., was once owned by Tsar Nicholas I of Russia.

In this book we study the history of art around the world from earliest times to the present. Although we treat Western art in the most detail, we also look extensively at the art of other regions. The qualities of a work of art, the artist who made it, the patron who paid for it, the audiences who have viewed it, and the places in which it has been displayed—all are considered in our study of art's history.

ART AND THE IDEA OF BEAUTY

For thousands of years people have sought to create objects of beauty and significance—objects we call art—that did more than simply help them survive. The concept of beauty, however, has found expression in a variety of **styles**, or manners of representation. The figure from Galgenburg, Austria, made more than 33,000 years ago, illustrates an **abstract** style (fig. 6). Its maker simplified shapes, eliminated all but the essentials, and emphasized the underlying human forms. An equally abstract vision of woman can be seen in Kitagawa Utamaro's *Woman at the Height of Her Beauty* (fig. 7). This late-eighteenth-century Japanese work, printed in color from a **woodblock**, or image carved out of a block of wood, is the creation of a complex society regulated by convention and ritual. The woman's dress and hairstyle defy the laws of nature. Rich textiles turn her body into a pattern, and pins hold her hair in elaborate shapes. Utamaro renders the patterned silks and carved pins meticulously, but he depicts the woman's face with a few sweeping lines. The elaboration of surface detail to create ornamental effects combined with an effort to capture the essence of form is characteristic of abstract art.

Two of the other works we have looked at so far—LeClear's *Interior with Portraits* and Jan van Eyck's *Annunciation*—exemplify a contrasting style known as **realism**. Realistic art, even if it represents an imagined or supernatural subject, has a surface reality; the artists appear, with greater or lesser accuracy, to be recording exactly what they see. Realistic art, as we have noted, can carry complex messages and be open to individual interpretation.

Realism and abstraction represent opposite approaches to the representation of beauty. In a third style, called **idealism**, artists aim to represent things not as they are but as they ought to be. In ancient Greece and Rome artists made intense observations of the world around them and then subjected

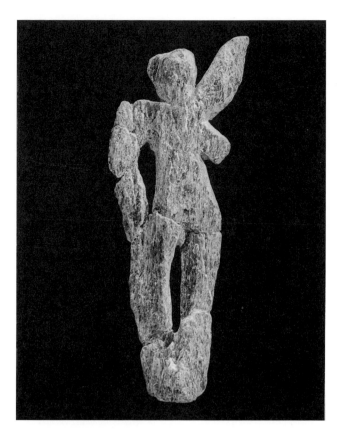

6. Human figure, found at Galgenburg, Austria. c. 31,000 BCE. Stone, height 3" (7.4 cm). Naturhistorisches Museum, Vienna

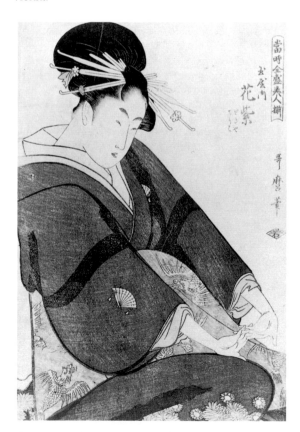

7. Kitagawa Utamaro. *Woman at the Height of Her Beauty*. Mid-1790s. Color woodblock print, 15⅛ x 10" (38.5 x 25.5 cm). Spencer Museum of Art, University of Kansas, Lawrence

William Bridges Thayer Memorial

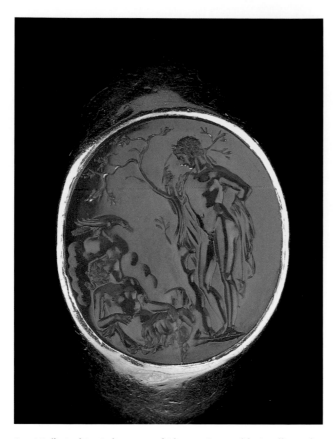

8. Attributed to Aulos, son of Alexas. Gem with Apollo and Cassandra. 40–20 BCE. Gold with engraved carnelian, ring 1³/₈ x 1" (3.4 x 2.5 cm), gem ¹³/₁₆ x ³/₄" (1.9 x 2.1 cm). The Nelson-Atkins Museum of Art, Kansas City, Missouri

Purchase: Acquired through the generosity of Mr. and Mrs. Robert S. Everitt (F93-22)

Apollo fell in love with Cassandra, and although she rejected him he gave her a potent gift—the ability to foretell the future, symbolized by the raven. To show his disappointment, the frustrated Apollo added a spiteful twist to his gift—no one would believe Cassandra's prophetic warnings. Today, doom-sayers are still called Cassandras, and ravens are associated with prophecy.

their observations to mathematical analysis to define what they considered to be perfect forms. Emphasizing human rationality, they eliminated accidents of nature and sought balance and harmony in their work. Their sculpture and painting established ideals that have inspired Western art ever since. The term *Classical,* which refers to the period in ancient Greek history when this type of idealism emerged, has come to be used broadly (and with a lowercase *c*) as a synonym for the peak of perfection in any period.

Classical idealism can pervade even the smallest works of art. About 2,000 years ago a Roman gem cutter known as Aulos added the opulence of imperial Rome to the ideals of Classical Greece when he engraved a deep-red, precious stone with the figures of the tragic princess Cassandra and the Greek god Apollo (fig. 8). Cassandra sleeps by rocky cliffs and a twisting laurel tree that suggest the dramatic natural setting of Delphi, Greece, a site sacred to Apollo. The god leans on the laurel tree, also sacred to him, with his cloak draped loosely and gracefully behind him. Apollo and Cassandra have the strong athletic bodies and regular facial features that charac-

terize Classical art, and their graceful poses and elegant drapery seem at the same time ideally perfect and perfectly natural. These beautiful figures and their story of frustrated love were not meant to be seen in a museum (a *museum* literally is the home of Apollo's Muses, the goddesses of learning and the arts). The carved gem was set in a gold finger ring and would have been constantly before its wearer's eyes. This sculpture reminds us that exceptional art can come in any size and material and can be intended for daily personal use as well as for special, occasional contemplation.

The flawless perfection of Classical Idealism could be dramatically modified by artists more concerned with emotions than pure form. The calm of Cassandra and Apollo contrasts with the melodramatic representation of a story from the ancient Greek legend of the Trojan War. The priest Laocoön (fig. 9), who attempted to warn the Trojans against the Greeks, was strangled along with his two sons by serpents. Heroic and tragic, Laocoön represents a good man destroyed by forces beyond his control. His features twist in agony, and the muscles of his superhuman torso and arms extend and knot as he struggles. This sculpture, then at least sixteen centuries old, was rediscovered in Rome in the 1500s, and it inspired artists such as Michelangelo to develop a heroic style. Through the centuries people have returned again and again to the ideals of Classical art. In the United States official sculpture and architecture often copy Classical forms, and even the National Museum of American Art is housed in a Greek-style building.

How different from this ideal of physical beauty the perception and representation of spiritual beauty can be. A fifteenth-century bronze sculpture from India represents Punitavati, a beautiful and generous woman who was deeply devoted to the Hindu god Shiva (fig. 10). Abandoned by her greedy husband because she gave food to beggars, Punitavati offered her beauty to Shiva. Shiva accepted her offering, turning her into an emaciated, fanged hag. According to legend, Punitavati, with clanging cymbals, provides the music for Shiva as he dances the cosmic dance of destruction and creation that keeps the universe in motion. To the followers of Shiva, Punitavati became a saint called Karaikkalammaiyar. The bronze sculpture, although it depicts the saint's hideous appearance, is nevertheless beautiful both in its formal qualities and in its message of generosity and sacrifice.

Some works of art defy simple categories, and artists may go to extraordinary lengths to represent their visions. The art critic Robert Hughes called James Hampton's (1909–1964) *Throne of the Third Heaven of the Nations' Millennium General Assembly* (fig. 11) "the finest piece of visionary art produced by an American." Yet this fabulous creation is composed of discarded furniture, flashbulbs, and all sorts of trash tacked together and wrapped in aluminum and gold foil and purple paper. The primacy of painting, especially oil painting, is gone. Hampton's inspiration, whether divine or not, knows no bounds. He worked as a janitor to support himself while, in a rented garage, he built his monument to Jesus. In rising tiers, thrones and altars are prepared for Jesus and Moses, the New Testament at the right, the Old Testament at the left. Everything is labeled and described, but Hampton invented his own language and writing system to express his vision. Although his language is still not fully

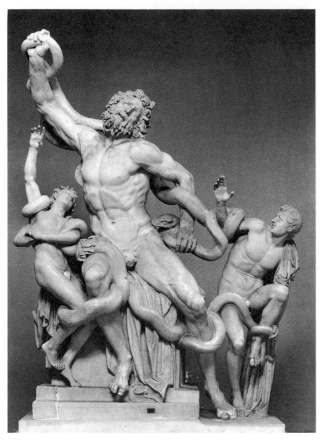

9. Hagesandros, Polydoros, and Athanadoros of Rhodes. *Laocoön and His Sons*, perhaps the original of the 2nd or 1st century BCE or a Roman copy of the 1st century CE. Marble, height 8' (2.44 m). Musei Vaticani, Museo Pio Clementino, Cortile Ottagono, Rome

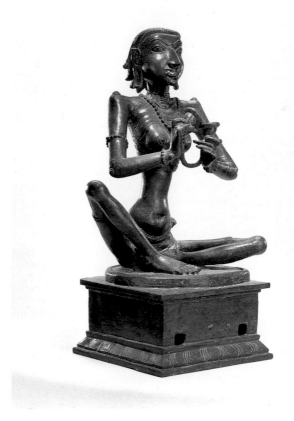

10. *Punitavati* (*Karaikkalammaiyar*), Shiva saint, from Karaikkal, India. 15th century. Bronze, height 16¼" (41.3 cm). The Nelson-Atkins Museum of Art, Kansas City, Missouri
Purchase: Nelson Trust (33-533)

understood, its major source is the Bible, especially the Book of Revelation. On one of many placards he wrote his artist's credo: "Where there is no vision, the people perish" (Proverbs 29:18).

These different ideas of art and beauty remind us that as viewers we enter into an agreement with artists, who, in turn, make special demands on us. We re-create works of art for ourselves as we bring to them our own experiences. Without our participation they are only hunks of stone or metal or pieces of paper or canvas covered with ink or colored paints. Artistic styles change with time and place. From extreme realism at one end of the spectrum to entirely non-representational art at the other, artists have worked with varying degrees of realism, idealism, and abstraction. The challenge for the student of art history is to discover not only how but why these changes have occurred and ultimately what of significance can be learned from them, what meaning they carry.

ARTISTS

We have focused so far on works of art. What of the artists who make the art? Biologists have pointed out that human beings are mammals with very large brains and that these large brains demand stimulation. Curious, active, inventive humans constantly look, taste, smell, and listen. They invent fine arts, fine food, fine perfume, and fine music. They play games, invent rituals,

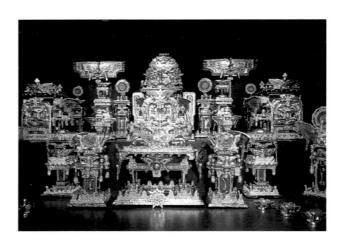

11. James Hampton. *Throne of the Third Heaven of the Nations' Millennium General Assembly*. c. 1950–64. Gold and silver aluminum foil, colored Kraft paper, and plastic sheets over wood, paperboard, and glass, 10'6" x 27' x 14'6" (3.2 x 8.23 x 4.42 m). National Museum of American Art, Smithsonian Institution, Washington, D.C.

and speculate on the nature of things, on the nature of life. They constantly communicate with each other, and some of them even try to communicate with the past and future.

We have seen that some artists try to record the world as they see it, and they attempt to educate or convince their viewers with straightforward stories or elaborate symbols.

Others create works of art inspired by an inner vision. Like the twentieth-century American Georgia O'Keeffe (fig. 12) they attempt to express in images what cannot be expressed in words. An organized religion such as Christianity or Buddhism may motivate them, but the artists may also divorce themselves from any social group and attempt to record personal visions or intense mystical experiences. These inner visions may spring from entirely secular insights, and the artist's motivation or intention may be quite different from the public perception of her or his art.

Originally, artists were considered artisans, or craftspeople. The master (and sometimes the mistress) of a workshop was the controlling intellect, the organizer, and the inspiration for others. Utamaro's color woodblock prints, for example, were the product of a team effort. In the workshop Utamaro drew and painted pictures for his assistants to transfer to individual blocks of wood. They carved the lines and color areas, covered the surface with ink or colors, then transferred the image to paper. Since ancient times artists have worked in teams to produce great buildings, paintings, and stained glass. The same spirit is evident today in the complex glassworks of American Dale Chihuly. His team of artist-craftspeople is skilled in the ancient art of glassmaking, but Chihuly remains the controlling mind and imagination. Once created, his pieces are transformed whenever they are assembled. Thus each work takes on a new life in accordance with the mind, eye, and hand of each owner-patron. Made in the 1990s, *Violet Persian Set with Red Lip Wraps* (fig. 13) has twenty separate pieces whose relationship to each other is determined by the imagination of the assembler. Like a fragile sea creature of the endangered coral reefs, the glass is vulnerable to thoughtless depredation, yet it is timeless in its reminder of primeval life. The purple captures light, color, and movement for a weary second. Artists, artisans, and patrons unite in an ever-changing individual yet communal act of creation.

About 600 years ago, artists in western Europe, especially in Italy, began to think of themselves as divinely inspired creative geniuses rather than as team workers. Painters like Guercino (Giovanni Francesco Barbieri, 1591–1666) took the evangelist Luke as their model, guide, and protector—their patron saint. People believed that Saint Luke had painted a portrait of the Virgin Mary holding the Christ Child. In Guercino's painting *Saint Luke Displaying a Painting of the Virgin* (fig. 14), the saint still holds his palette and brushes while an angel holds the painting on the easel. A book, a quill pen, and an inkpot decorated with a statue of an ox (a symbol for Luke) rest on a table behind the saint, reminders that he wrote one of the Gospels of the New Testament. The message Guercino conveys is that Saint Luke is a divinely inspired and endowed artist and that all artists share in this inspiration through their association with their patron saint.

Even the most inspired artists had to learn their trade through study or years of **apprenticeship** to a master. In his painting *The Drawing Lesson* (fig. 15), Dutch artist Jan Steen (1626–1679) takes us into an artist's studio where an apprentice watches his master teaching a young woman. The woman has been drawing from a sculpture because women then were not permitted to work from live nude models.

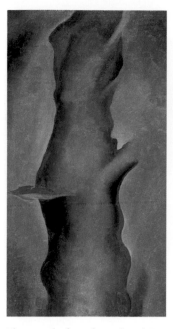

12. Georgia O'Keeffe. *Portrait of a Day, First Day.* 1924. Oil on canvas, 35 x 18" (89 x 45.8 cm). Spencer Museum of Art, University of Kansas, Lawrence
Gift of the Georgia O'Keeffe Foundation

The year before she painted *Portrait of a Day, First Day,* O'Keeffe wrote, "One day seven years ago [I] found myself saying to myself—I can't live where I want to—I can't go where I want to—I can't even say what I want to— School and things that painters have taught me even keep me from painting as I want to. I decided I was a very stupid fool not to at least paint as I wanted to and say what I wanted to when I painted as that seemed to be the only thing I could do that didn't concern anybody but myself—that was nobody's business but my own. . . I found that I could say things with color and shapes that I couldn't say in any other way—things that I had no words for. Some of the wise men say it is not painting, some of them say it is" (cited in *Alfred Stieglitz Presents One Hundred Pictures: Oils, Watercolors, Pastels, Drawings by Georgia O'Keeffe, American*, The Anderson Galleries, New York, exhibition brochure, January 29–February 10, 1923).

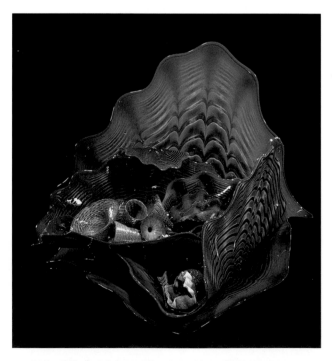

13. Dale Chihuly. *Violet Persian Set with Red Lip Wraps.* 1990. Glass, 26 x 30 x 25" (66 x 76.2 x 63.5 cm). Spencer Museum of Art, University of Kansas, Lawrence
Peter T. Bohan Acquisition Fund

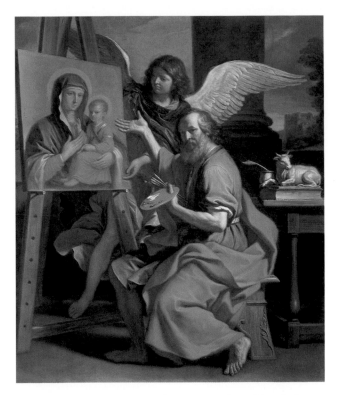

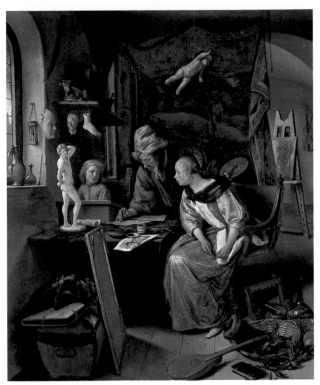

14. Guercino. *Saint Luke Displaying a Painting of the Virgin*. 1652–53. Oil on canvas, 7'3" x 5'11" (2.21 x 1.81 m). The Nelson-Atkins Museum of Art, Kansas City, Missouri Purchase (F83-55)

15. Jan Steen. *The Drawing Lesson*. 1665. Oil on wood, 19³/₈ x 16¹/₄" (49.3 x 41 cm). The J. Paul Getty Museum, Malibu, California

Plaster reproductions hang on the wall and stand on the shelf, and a carved boy-angel has been suspended from the ceiling in front of a large tapestry. The painter holds his own palette, and we see his painting set on an easel in the background. Like Thomas LeClear's painting of the photographer's studio, *The Drawing Lesson* is a valuable record of an artist's equipment and workplace, including such things as the musical instruments, furniture, glass, ceramics, and basketry used in the seventeenth century.

The painting is more than a realistic **genre painting** (scene from daily life) or **still life** (an arrangement of objects). *The Drawing Lesson* is also an **allegory**, or symbolic representation of the arts. The objects in the studio symbolize painting, sculpture, and music. The sculpture of the ox on the shelf is more than a bookend; as we have already seen, it symbolizes Saint Luke, the painters' patron saint. The basket in the foreground holds not only the woman's fur muff but also a laurel wreath, a symbol of Apollo and the classical tribute for excellence.

ARTISTS AND ART HISTORY Artists draw on their predecessors in ways that make each work a very personal history of art. They build on the works of the past, either inspired by or reacting against them, but always challenging them with their new creations. The influence of Jan Steen's genre painting, for example, can be seen in Thomas LeClear's *Interior with Portraits,* and Guercino's *Saint Luke* is based on an earlier **icon**—or miraculous image—he had seen in his local church. In his 1980–1990 *Vaquero* (Cowboy), Luis Jimenez revitalizes a sculptural form with roots in antiquity, the equestrian monument, or statue of a horse and rider (fig. 16).

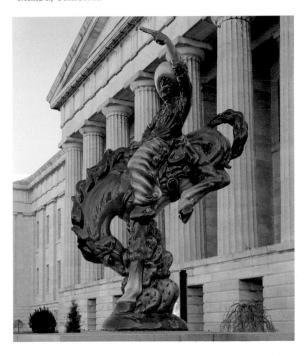

16. Luis Jimenez. *Vaquero*. Modeled 1980, cast 1990. Cast fiberglass and epoxy, height 16'6" (5.03 m). National Museum of American Art, Smithsonian Institution, Washington, D.C.

This white-hatted, gun-slinging bronco buster whoops it up in front of the stately, classical colonnade of the Old Patent Building (now the National Museum of American Art, the National Portrait Gallery, and the Archives of American Art). The Old Patent Office was designed in 1836 and finished in 1867. One of the finest Neoclassical buildings in the United States and the site of Abraham Lincoln's second inaugural ball, it was supposed to be destroyed for a parking lot when it was acquired by the Smithsonian in 1958.

Vaquero also reflects Jimenez's Mexican and Texan heritage and his place in a tradition of Hispanic American art that draws on many sources, including the art of the Maya, Aztec, and other great Native American civilizations, the African culture of the Caribbean Islands, and the transplanted art of Spain and Portugal.

Equestrian statues have traditionally been stately symbols of power and authority, with the rider's command over the animal emblematic of human control over lesser beings, nature, and the passions. Jimenez's bucking bronco turns this tradition, or at least the horse, on its head. Rather than a stately symbol of human control, he gives us a horse and cowboy united in a single exuberant and dynamic force. Located in front of the National Museum of American Art, the work can be seen as a witty satire on Washington, D.C.'s bronze monuments to soldiers. At the same time, it reminds us that real *vaqueros* included hard-working African Americans and Hispanic Americans who had little in common with the cowboys of popular fiction.

In his work, Jimenez has abandoned traditional bronze and marble for fiberglass. He first models a sculpture in a plastic paste called plasticine on a steel armature; then he makes a fiberglass mold, from which he casts the final sculpture, also in fiberglass. The materials and processes are the same as those used to make many automobile bodies, and as with automobiles, the process allows an artist to make several "originals." After a sculpture is assembled and polished, it is sprayed with the kind of acrylic urethane used to coat the outside of jet airplanes. Jimenez applies colors with an airbrush and coats the finished sculpture with three more layers of acrylic urethane to protect the color and emphasize its distinctive, sleek, gleaming surface. *Vaquero* is true public, popular art. It appeals to every kind of audience from the rancher to the connoisseur.

When artists appropriate and transform images from the past the way Jimenez appropriated the equestrian form, they enrich the **aesthetic** vocabulary of the arts in general. *Vaquero* resonates through the ages with associations to cultures distant in time and place that give it added meaning. This kind of aesthetic free-for-all encourages artistic diversity and discourages the imposition of a single correct or canonical (approved) approach or point of view. In the jargon of our time, no medium is *privileged*, and no group of artists is *marginalized*.

ART AND SOCIETY

The visual arts are among the most sophisticated forms of human communication, at once shaping and shaped by the social context in which they find expression. Artists are often interpreters of their times. They can also be enlisted to serve social ends in forms that range from heavy-handed propaganda to the more subtle persuasiveness of Margaret Bourke-White's photographs for *Life* magazine. From the priests and priestesses in ancient Egypt to the representatives of various faiths today, religious leaders have understood the value of the visual arts in educating people about doctrine and in reinforcing their faith. Especially beginning in the eleventh century in western Europe, architecture and sculpture provided settings for elaborate rites and inspiring and instructive art. At the Cathedral of Santiago de Compostela in north-

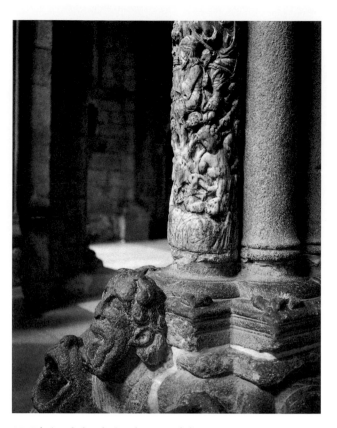

17. *Pórtico de la Gloria*. Photograph by Joan Myers. 1988
Tradition required that pilgrims to the Cathedral of Santiago de Compostela place their fingers in the tendrils of the carved Tree of Jesse as they asked Saint James's blessing on arrival in the church. Millions of fingers have worn away the carving, leaving a rich patina of age. The twefth-century sculpture still inspires twentieth-century artists such as photographer Joan Myers.

western Spain, which shelters the tomb of Saint James, the marble of the central portal has been polished and the twelfth-century sculpture have been worn down by the touch of pilgrims' fingers (fig. 17).

Marxist art historians once saw art as an expression of great social forces rather than of individual genius, but most people now agree that neither history and economics nor philosophy and religion alone can account for the art of a Rembrandt or Michelangelo. The same applies to extraordinary "ordinary" people, too, who have created powerful art to satisfy their own inner need to communicate ideas. In Lucas, Kansas, in 1905, Samuel Perry Dinsmoor, a visionary populist, began building his Garden of Eden (fig. 18). By 1927 he had surrounded his home with twenty-nine concrete trees ranging from 8 to 40 feet high. He filled the branches with figures that told the biblical story of the Creation and the Expulsion from the Garden of Eden under the ever-present—and electrified—Eye of God. Adam and Eve succumb to the serpent; Cain strikes down Abel. Evil and death enter the world as creatures attack each other. In Dinsmoor's modern world, people defend themselves through their right to vote. Under the protection of the Goddess of Liberty draped in an American flag, a man and woman literally cut down big business with a saw labeled "ballot." Dinsmoor communicated his ideas forcefully and directly through haunting imagery. At dusk his electric

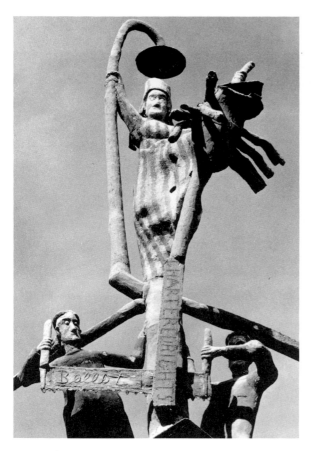

18. Samuel Perry Dinsmoor. *Goddess of Liberty and the Destruction of the Trusts by the Ballot.* Garden of Eden, Lucas, Kansas. 1905–32. Painted concrete and cement, over-lifesize

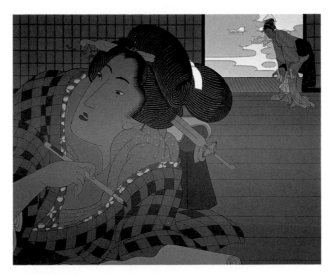

19. Roger Shimomura. *Diary* (Minidoka Series #3) 1978. Acrylic on canvas, 4'11⅞" x 6'1/16" (1.52 x 1.83 m). Spencer Museum of Art, University of Kansas, Lawrence

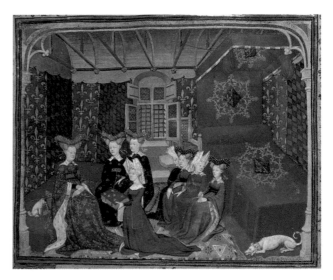

20. *Christine Presenting Her Book to the Queen of France.* 1410–15. Tempera and gold on vellum, image approx. 5½ x 6¾" (14 x 17 cm). The British Library, London MS. Harley 4431, folio 3

light bulbs—his repeated "Ever-Seeing Eye of God"—illuminate the concrete and cement figures with an unearthly glow.

Not all art with social impact is public on the scale of a pilgrimage church or a half-acre concrete Garden of Eden. Artists like Roger Shimomura turn painting and prints into powerful statements. American citizens of Japanese ancestry were forcibly confined in internment camps during World War II. Shimomura based his 1978 painting *Diary* (fig. 19) on his grandmother's record of the family's experience in an internment camp in Idaho. Shimomura painted his grandmother writing while he (the toddler) and his mother stand by an open door—a door that opens on a barbed-wire-enclosed compound. In his painting Shimomura has combined two formal traditions, the Japanese art of color woodblock prints (see fig. 7) and American Pop Art to create a personal style that expresses his own dual culture as it makes a powerful political statement.

ARTISTS AND PATRONS

Rare, valuable, beautiful, and strange things appeal to human curiosity. People who are not artists "use" art, too. They have collected special objects since prehistoric times when people buried the dead with necklaces of fox teeth. Collections of "curiosities" were passed along from one generation to the next, gaining luster or mysterious power with age. Art enhanced the owners' prestige, created an aura of power and importance, and impressed others. Many collectors truly love works of art. When collectors study diligently, they become scholars; when their expertise turns to questions of refined evaluation, they become what we call **connoisseurs**.

The patrons of art constitute a very special kind of audience for the artist. Patrons provide economic support for art and vicariously participate in its creation. In earlier periods artists depended on the patronage of individuals and the institutions they represented. An early-fifteenth-century painting shows the French writer Christine de Pisan presenting her work to the queen of France (fig. 20). Christine was a patron, too, for she hired painters and scribes to copy, illustrate, and decorate her books. She especially admired the painting of a woman artist named Anastaise, considering her work unsurpassed in the city of Paris, which she believed had the world's best painters of miniatures.

When a free market developed for art works, artists became entrepreneurs. In a painting by the seventeenth-

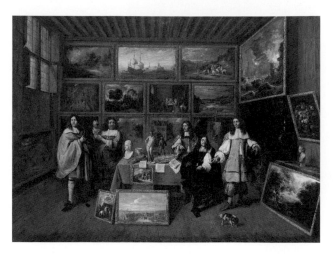

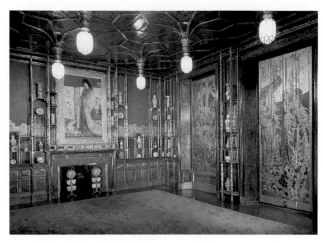

21. Gillis van Tilborch. *Cabinet d'Amateur with a Painter.* c. 1660–70. Oil on canvas, 38¼ x 51" (97.15 x 129.54 cm). Spencer Museum of Art, University of Kansas, Lawrence

22. James McNeill Whistler. *Harmony in Blue and Gold.* The Peacock Room, northeast corner, from a house owned by Frederick Leyland, London. 1876–77. Oil paint and metal leaf on canvas, leather, and wood, 13'11⅞" x 33'2" x 19'11½" (4.26 x 10.11 x 6.83 m). Freer Gallery, Smithsonian Institution, Washington, D.C. (04.61)

century Flemish painter Gillis van Tilborch, an artist and an art dealer display their wares to patrons, who examine the treasures brought before them (fig. 21). Paintings cover the walls, and sculpture and precious objects stand on the table and floor. The painting provides a fascinating catalog of the fine arts of the seventeenth century and the taste of seventeenth-century connoisseurs.

Relations between artists and patrons are not always so congenial as Tilborch portrayed them. Patrons can change their minds about a commission or purchase or fail to pay their bills. Such conflicts can have simple beginnings and unexpected results. In the late nineteenth century the Liverpool shipping magnate Frederick Leyland asked James McNeill Whistler, an American painter living in London, what color to paint the shutters in the dining room where he planned to hang Whistler's painting *The Princess from the Land of Porcelain*. The room had been decorated with expensive embossed and gilded leather and finely crafted shelves to show off Leyland's Asian porcelain collection. Whistler was inspired by the Japanese theme of his own painting as well as the porcelain, and he was also caught up in the wave of enthusiasm for Japanese art sweeping Europe. He painted the window shutters with splendid turquoise, blue, and gold peacocks. Then, while Leyland was away, he painted the entire room (fig. 22), replacing the gilded leather on the walls with turquoise peacock feathers. Leyland was shocked and angry when he saw the results. Whistler, however, memorialized the confrontation with a painting of a pair of fighting peacocks on one wall of the room. One of the peacocks represents the outraged artist, and the other, standing on a pile of coins, represents the incensed patron. The Peacock Room, which Whistler called *Harmony in Blue and Gold*, is an extraordinary example of total design, and Leyland did not change it. The American collector Henry Freer, who sought to unite the aesthetics of East and West, later acquired the room and donated it on his death to

a museum in the Smithsonian Institution in Washington, D.C., where it can now be appreciated by all. Today museums are the primary collectors and preservers of art.

THE KEEPERS OF ART: MUSEUMS From time immemorial people have gathered together objects that they considered to be precious, objects that were made of valuable material or that conveyed the idea of power and prestige. The curators, or keepers of such collections, assisted patrons in obtaining the best pieces. The idea of what is best and what is worth collecting and preserving varies from one generation to another. Yesterday's popular magazine (see fig. 4) is today's example of fine photography and graphic design.

An art museum can be thought of in two ways: as a scholarly research institute where curators care for and study their collections and teach new scholar-curators, and as a public institution dedicated to exhibiting and explaining the collections. The first university art museum in the United States was established in 1832 at Yale University. Today museums with important research and educational functions are to be found in many universities and colleges, and museums with good collections are widespread. One does not have to live in a major population center to experience wonderful art. Of the twenty-six works illustrated in this chapter, eleven are located near the author in Kansas and Missouri, and four of these are in a single university museum. No one would assert that Kansas is the art capital of the world; the point is that encounters with the real objects are not out of most people's range. And no matter how faithful the quality of reproductions in a book or a slide or a monitor showing an image from a CD-ROM, there is no substitute for a "live interview" with an actual work of art or architecture.

The display of art is a major challenge for curators. Art must be put on public view in a way that ensures its safety

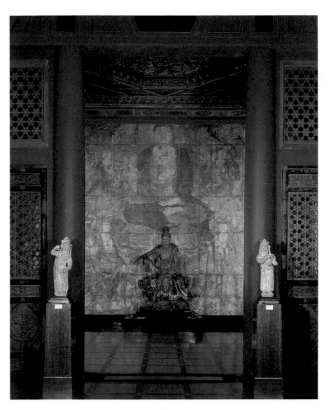

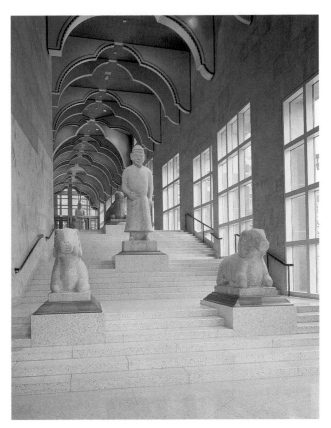

23. *The Water and Moon Kuan-yin Bodhisattva*. Northern
Sung or Liao dynasty, 11th–12th century. Wood with
paint, height 7'11" (2.41 m). Mural painting, 14th century;
wooden screens, 17th century. The Nelson-Atkins
Museum of Art, Kansas City, Missouri
Purchase: Nelson Trust (34.10)

24. Robert Venturi and Denise Scott-Brown. Stair Hall with
Ming dynasty tomb figures, Seattle Art Museum. 1986–91

and also enhances its qualities and clarifies its significance.
The installation of Chinese sculpture at the Nelson-Atkins
Museum of Art in Kansas City (fig. 23) and at the Seattle Art
Museum (fig. 24) illustrate two imaginative approaches to
this challenge.

A polychromed and gilded wooden bodhisattva, or
enlightened being, in the Nelson-Atkins Museum of Art sits
majestically in front of a mural painting of the Buddha. The
sculpture and painting are exceptional in their own right,
and together they form a magnificent ensemble, placed in a
re-created temple setting with screens from the seventeenth
century. The curators successfully established an environment that recalls the religious context of the art, subtly
emphasizes its importance, and provides it with a measure
of security.

The Seattle Art Museum had different problems to solve.
Their carved-stone Chinese tomb figures had stood outdoors
in a park for years. Weather-beaten and moss-covered, they
had been almost ignored. The new Seattle Art Museum,
designed by Robert Venturi and Denise Scott-Brown and finished in 1991, had a monumental stairwell that united the
museum interior with the steep city street outside. The figures were cleaned, restored, and placed on the stairs like
welcoming guardians for the galleries above. Set under colorful festive arches, they provide a monumental and semi-

serious contrast to the witty, theatrical, and "irreverent"
architecture—the museum coffee shop interrupts their stately
procession—and serve as an appropriate symbol for a city
that prides itself as a link between East and West.

"I KNOW WHAT I LIKE"

Our involvement with art may be casual
or intense, naive or sophisticated. At
first we may simply react instinctively
to a painting or building or photograph,
but this level of "feeling" about art—"I
know what I like"—can never be fully satisfying.

Opinions as to what constitutes a work of art change
over time. Impressionist paintings of the late nineteenth century, now among the most avidly sought and widely collected,
were laughed at when first displayed. They seemed rough
and unfinished—merely "impressions"—rather than the careful depictions of nature people then expected to see. Impressionist painters like Claude Monet in his *Boulevard des
Capucines, Paris* (fig. 25) tried to capture in paint on canvas
the reflected light that registers as color in human eyes.
Rather than carefully drawing forms he knew to exist—the
branches and leaves of trees, dark-clothed figures—he recorded immediate visual sensations with flecks of color. The
rough texture provides a two-dimensional interest that is
quite independent of the painting's subject. The mind's eye

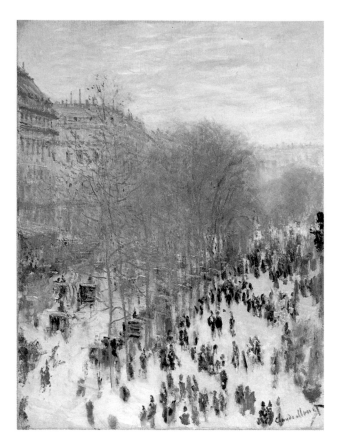

25. Claude Monet. *Boulevard des Capucines, Paris*. 1873–74. Oil on canvas, 31¼ x 23¼" (79.4 x 59.1 cm). The Nelson-Atkins Museum of Art, Kansas City, Missouri

Purchase: the Kenneth A. and Helen F. Spencer Foundation Acquisition Fund (F72-35)

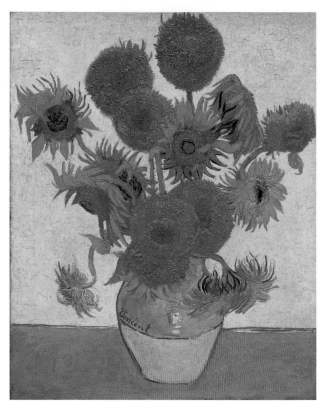

26. Vincent van Gogh. *Sunflowers*. 1888. Oil on canvas, 36¼ x 28¾" (92.1 x 73 cm). The National Gallery, London

interprets the array of colors as the solid forms of nature, suddenly perceiving the coral daubs in the lower right, for example, as a balloon man. When the critic Louis Leroy reviewed this painting the first time it was exhibited, he sneered: "Only, be so good as to tell me what those innumerable black tongue-lickings in the lower part of the picture represent?" (*Le Charivari*, April 25, 1874). Today we easily see a street in early spring filled with horse-drawn cabs and strolling men and women. In this magical moment the long-dead artist and the live viewers join to re-create nineteenth-century Paris.

Art history, in contrast to art criticism, combines the formal analysis of works of art—concentrating mainly on the visual elements in the work of art—with the study of the works' broad historical context. Art historians draw on biography to learn about artists' lives, social history to understand the economic and political forces shaping artists, their patrons, and their public, and the history of ideas to gain an understanding of the intellectual currents influencing artists' work. They also study the history of other arts—including music, drama, literature—to gain a richer sense of the context of the visual arts. Every sculpture or painting presents a challenge. Even a glowing painting like Vincent van Gogh's *Sunflowers* (fig. 26), of 1888, to which we may react with spontaneous enthusiasm, forces us to think about art, as well as feel and admire it.

Our first reaction is that *Sunflowers* is a joyous, colorful painting of a simple subject. But this is far more than a bunch of flowers in a simple pot in a sunlit room. Art history makes us search for more. The surface of the painting is richly built up—van Gogh laid on the thick oil paint with careful calculation. The brilliant yellow ground that looks flat in a reproduction in fact resembles a tightly woven basket or textile, so deliberately and carefully placed are the small brushstrokes. The space is suggested simply—by two horizontal stripes, two bands of gold different in intensity and separated by just the slightest blue line, the color of maximum contrast. Here, in fact, there is no space, no setting; we imagine a table, a sun-filled room. But did van Gogh see a pot of flowers on a windowsill, against the blazing, shimmering heat and light of the true sun? Van Gogh had a troubled life, and that knowledge makes us reflect on the possible meaning of the painting to him—for the painting, despite its brightness, reflects something ominous, a foreboding of the artist's loneliness and despair to come.

As viewers we participate in the re-creation of a work of art, and its meaning changes from individual to individual, from era to era. Once we welcome the arts into our life, we have a ready source of sustenance and challenge that grows, changes, mellows, and enriches our daily experience. No matter how much we study or read about art and artists, eventually we return to the contemplation of the work itself, for art is the tangible evidence of the ever-questing human spirit.

Starter Kit

This is a very basic primer of concepts and working assumptions used in the study of art history—a quick reference guide for this entire book and for encounters with art in general.

What Art Is

A work of art may be described in basic, nonphilosophical terms as having two components: FORM and CONTENT. It is also distinguished by STYLE, MEDIUM, and PERIOD.

FORM. Referring to purely visual aspects of art and architecture, form includes LINE, COLOR, TEXTURE, SPATIAL QUALITIES, and COMPOSITION. These various attributes are often referred to as FORMAL ELEMENTS.

Line is an element—usually drawn or painted—that defines SHAPE with a more-or-less continuous mark. The movement of the viewer's eyes over the surface of the work of art may follow a path determined by the artist and so create imaginary lines, or LINES OF FORCE.

Color has several attributes. These include HUE, VALUE, and INTENSITY.

> HUE is what we think of when we hear the word *color*. Red, yellow, and blue are the PRIMARY COLORS because other colors (SECONDARY COLORS of orange, green, and purple) can be created by mixing (combining) them. Red, orange, and yellow are known as warm colors; and green, blue, and purple as cool colors.
>
> VALUE is the relative degree of lightness or darkness in the range from white to black and is created by the amount of light reflected from an object's surface. A dark green has a deeper value than a light green, for example, and light gray has a lighter value than dark gray.
>
> INTENSITY is the degree of brightness or dullness of color. For this reason, the word *saturation* is synonymous with *intensity*.

Texture is the tactile quality of a surface. It is perceived and described with words like *smooth*, *polished*, *satiny*, *rough*, *coarse*, or *oily*. Texture takes two forms: the texture of the actual surface of the work of art and the implied (imaginary) surface of the object the artist is representing.

Spatial qualities include MASS, VOLUME, and SPACE.

> MASS and VOLUME are properties of three-dimensional objects. They take up space.
>
> SPACE may be three-dimensional and actual, as with sculpture and architecture, or may be represented in two dimensions. Unfilled space is referred to as NEGATIVE SPACE; solids are referred to as POSITIVE SPACE.

Composition is the organization, or arrangement, of form in a work of art.

> PICTORIAL DEPTH (SPATIAL RECESSION) is a specialized aspect of composition in which the three-dimensional world is

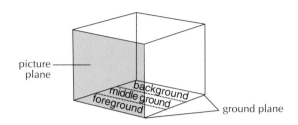

27. Diagram of picture space

represented in two dimensions in paintings and drawings. Artists have used many methods to depict objects as seeming to recede from the two-dimensional surface, called the PICTURE PLANE. The area "behind" the picture plane is called the PICTURE SPACE and conventionally contains three "zones": FOREGROUND, MIDDLE GROUND, and BACKGROUND (fig. 27). Perpendicular to the picture plane, forming the "floor" of the space, is the GROUND PLANE.

Various techniques for conveying a sense of pictorial depth have been preferred by artists in different cultures and at different times (fig. 28).

CONTENT. Content is a less specific aspect of a work of art than is form. There is also less agreement as to what content is. Content includes SUBJECT MATTER, which quite simply is what is represented, even when that consists strictly of lines and formal elements—lines and color without recognizable subject matter, for example. Content includes the IDEAS contained in a work. When used inclusively, the term *content* can embrace the social, political, and economic contexts in which a work was created, the intention of the artist, the reception of the beholder (the AUDIENCE) to the work, and ultimately the meaning in the work of art.

The study of the "what" of subject matter is ICONOGRAPHY. ICONOLOGY has come to mean the study of the "why" of subject matter.

STYLE. Understandably, specialized terminology is used to describe style in art history. Expressed very broadly, style is the combination of form and content characteristics that make a work distinctive.

Representational and **nonrepresentational style** (also called NONOBJECTIVE) refer to whether the subject matter is or is not recognizable.

Linear describes the style in which an artist uses line as the primary means of definition. When shadows and shading or modeling and highlights dominate, the style may be called PAINTERLY. Architecture and sculpture may be linear or painterly.

Realistic, naturalistic, and **idealized** are often-found descriptions of style. REALISM is the attempt to depict objects as they are in actual, visible reality. NATURALISM is a style of depiction in which the physical appearance of the rendered image in nature is the primary inspiration. A work in a naturalistic style resembles the original but not with the same exactitude

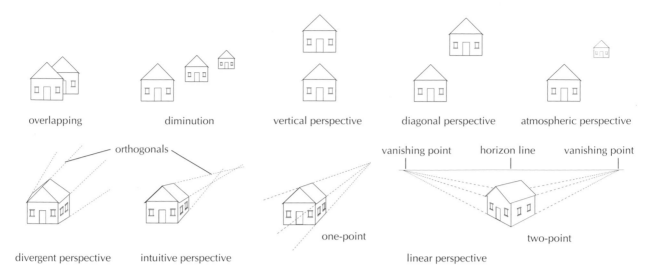

overlapping   diminution   vertical perspective   diagonal perspective   atmospheric perspective

orthogonals

vanishing point   horizon line   vanishing point

one-point

two-point

divergent perspective   intuitive perspective   linear perspective

28. Pictorial devices for depicting recession in space

Among the simpler devices are OVERLAPPING, in which partially covered elements are meant to be seen as located behind those covering them, and DIMINUTION, in which smaller elements are meant to be perceived as being farther away than larger ones. In VERTICAL and DIAGONAL PERSPECTIVE, elements are stacked vertically or diagonally, with the higher elements meant to be perceived as deeper in space. Another way of suggesting depth is through ATMOSPHERIC PERSPECTIVE, which depicts objects in the far distance with less clarity than nearer objects, often in bluish gray hues, and treats the sky as paler near the horizon. For many centuries DIVERGENT PERSPECTIVE, in which forms widen slightly and lines diverge as they recede in space, was used by East Asian artists. INTUITIVE PERSPECTIVE, such as that in some late medieval European art, uses the opposite: forms become more narrow and lines converge the farther away they are from the viewer, approximating the optical experience of spatial recession. LINEAR PERSPECTIVE, also called SCIENTIFIC, MATHEMATICAL, ONE-POINT, or Renaissance perspective, is an elaboration and standardization of intuitive perspective and was developed in fifteenth-century Italy. It uses mathematical formulas to construct illusionistic images in which all elements are shaped by imaginary lines called ORTHOGONALS that converge in one or more VANISHING POINTS on a HORIZON LINE. Linear perspective is the system that most people in Euro-American cultures think of as perspective. Because it is the visual code they are accustomed to reading, they accept as "truth" the distortions it imposes, including FORESHORTENING, in which, for instance, the soles of the feet in the foreground are the largest element of a figure lying on the ground.

and literalness as a work in a realistic style. IDEALIZATION strives for perfection that is grounded in prevailing values of a culture. Classical Greek sculpture is an example of art that is both naturalistic and idealized. ABSTRACTION is the stylistic opposite of the last three styles, because the artist makes forms that do not depict observable objects—often with the intention of extracting the essence of an object or idea. Much prehistoric art is abstract in this way. EXPRESSIONISTIC style appeals to the subjective responses of the beholder, often through exaggeration of form and expression.

MEDIUM. What is meant by medium (here we have used the plural *mediums*, to distinguish the word from the press *media*) is the material from which a given object is made. Even broader than medium is the distinction between two-dimensional, three-dimensional, mixed-medium, and ephemeral arts.

Two-dimensional arts include painting, drawing, the graphic arts, and photography.

Three-dimensional arts are sculpture, architecture, and many ornamental and practical arts.

Mixed medium includes categories such as collage and assemblage, in which the two-dimensional surface is built up from elements that are not painted, such as pieces of paper or metal or garments.

Ephemeral arts include such chiefly modern categories as performance art, earthworks, cinema, video art, and computer art, all of which have a central temporal aspect in that the artwork is viewable for a finite period of time and then disappears forever, is in a constant state of change, or must be replayed to be experienced.

Painting includes wall painting and fresco, illumination (decoration of books with paintings), panel painting (paintings on wood panels), miniature painting, handscroll and hanging scroll painting, and easel painting.

Drawings may be sketches (quick visual notes for larger drawings or paintings); studies (more carefully drawn analyses of details or entire compositions); drawings as complete artworks in themselves; and cartoons (full-scale drawings made in preparation for work in another medium, such as fresco).

Graphic arts are the printed arts—images that are reproducible and that traditionally include woodcut, engraving, etching, drypoint, and lithography.

Still photographs are a two-dimensional art.

Sculpture is a three-dimensional work of art that is carved, modeled, or assembled. Carved sculpture is reductive in the sense that the image is created by taking material away.

TECHNIQUE

Lost-Wax Casting

The lost-wax casting process (also called *cire perdue*, the French term) has been used for many centuries. It probably started in Egypt. By 200 BCE the technique was known in China and ancient Mesopotamia and was soon after used by the Benin peoples in Africa. It spread to ancient Greece sometime in the sixth century BCE and was widespread in Europe until the eighteenth century, when a piece-mold process came to predominate. The usual metal is bronze, an alloy of copper and tin, or sometimes brass, an alloy of copper and zinc.

The progression of drawings here shows the steps used by Benin sculptors. A heat-resistant "core" of clay—approximating the shape of the sculpture-to-be (and eventually becoming the hollow inside the sculpture)—was covered by a layer of wax about the thickness of the final sculpture. The sculptor carved the details in the wax. Rods and a pouring cup made of wax were attached to the model. A thin layer of fine, damp sand was pressed very firmly into the surface of the wax model, and then model, rods, and cup were encased in thick layers of clay. When the clay was completely dry, the mold was heated to melt out the wax. The mold was then turned upside down to receive the molten metal, which for the Benin was brass, heated to the point of liquification. The cast was placed in the ground. When the metal was completely cool, the outside clay cast and the inside core were broken up and removed, leaving the cast brass sculpture. Details were polished to finish the piece of sculpture, which could not be duplicated because the mold had been destroyed in the process.

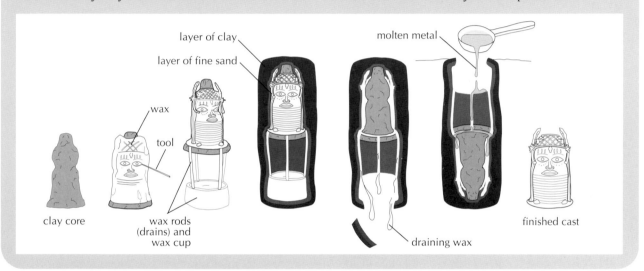

layer of clay · layer of fine sand · wax · tool · molten metal · clay core · wax rods (drains) and wax cup · draining wax · finished cast

Wood and stone sculpture, large and small, is carved sculpture because the material is not malleable. Modeled sculpture is considered additive, meaning that the object is built up from a material such as clay that is soft enough to be molded and shaped. Metal sculpture is usually cast (see "Lost-Wax Casting," above) or is assembled by welding or similar means of joining.

Sculpture is either FREESTANDING (sculpture in the round) or in RELIEF, which means projecting from the surface of which it is a part. Relief may be HIGH RELIEF, with parts of the sculpture projecting far off the background, or LOW RELIEF, in which the projections are only slightly raised. SUNKEN RELIEF, found mainly in Egyptian sculpture, is imagery carved into the surface, with the highest part of the relief being the flat surface.

Architecture is three-dimensional and highly spatial, and it is closely bound up with developments in technology and materials. An example of the relationship among technology, materials, and function is how space is spanned (see "Elements of Architecture," page 32).

Buildings are represented by a number of two-dimensional schematic drawings, including plans, elevations, sections, and cutaways (fig. 29). PLANS are imaginary slices through a building at approximately waist height. Everything below the slice is drawn as if looking straight down from above. ELEVATIONS are exterior sides of a building as if seen from a moderate distance but without any perspective dis-

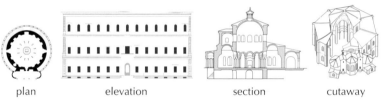

plan · elevation · section · cutaway

29. Diagrammatic drawings of buildings

tortion. SECTIONS are imaginary vertical slices from top to bottom through a building that reveal elements "cut" by the slice. CUTAWAY DRAWINGS show both inside and outside elements from an oblique angle.

Other mediums. Besides painting, drawing, graphic arts, photography, sculpture, and architecture, works of art are made in the mediums of ceramic and glass, textile and stitchery, metalwork and enamel, and many other materials. Today anything—even "junk," the discards of society—can be turned into a work of art.

PERIOD. A word often found in art historical writing, *period* means the historical era from which a work of art comes. It is good practice not to use the words *style* and *period* interchangeably. Style is the sum of many influences and characteristics, including the period of its creation. An example of good usage is: "an American house from the Colonial period built in the Georgian style."

ELEMENTS OF ARCHITECTURE

Space-Spanning Construction Devices

Gravity pulls on everything, presenting great challenges to the need to cover spaces. The purpose of the spanning element is to transfer weight to the ground. The simplest space-spanning device is post-and-lintel construction, in which uprights are spanned by a horizontal element. However, if not flexible, a horizontal element over a wide span breaks under the pressure of its own weight and the weight it carries.

Corbeling, the building up of overlapping stones, is another simple method for transferring weight to the ground. Arches, round or pointed, span space. Vaults, which are essentially extended arches, move weight out from the center of the covered space and down through the corners. The cantilever is a variant of post-and-lintel construction. When concrete is reinforced with steel or iron rods, the inherent brittleness of cement and stone is then overcome because of metal's flexible qualities. The concrete can then span much more space and bear heavier loads. Suspension works to counter the effect of gravity by lifting the spanning element upward. Trusses of wood or metal are relatively lightweight spanners but cannot bear heavy loads. Large-scale modern construction is chiefly steel frame and relies on steel's properties of strength and flexibility to bear great loads. The balloon frame, an American innovation, is based in post-and-lintel principles and exploits the lightweight, flexible properties of wood.

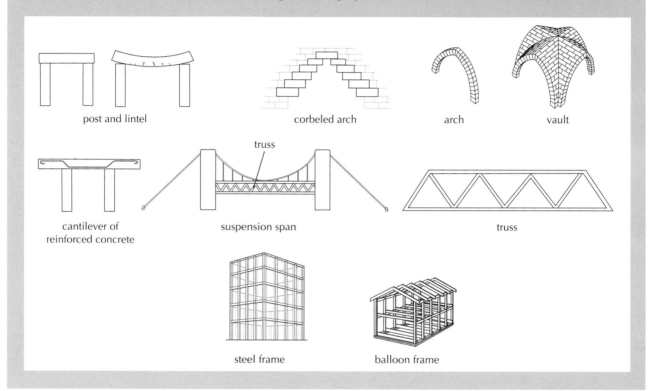

post and lintel   corbeled arch   arch   vault

truss

cantilever of reinforced concrete   suspension span   truss

steel frame   balloon frame

What Art History Is

Art history is a humanistic field of inquiry that studies visual culture. Increasingly, art history seeks to understand the role of visual culture in societies around the world and to learn more about the people and cultures who created the individual artworks through close yet multidimensional study of the art itself. Art history embraces many different approaches to visual culture. CONTEXTUAL ART HISTORY seeks to place and understand art as one expression of complex social, economic, political, and religious influences on the culture and the individuals within it. FORMALISM, or FORMAL ANALYSIS, examines and analyzes the formal elements of works of art, in and of themselves. The most traditional approach is CONNOISSEURSHIP, the almost intimate appreciation and evaluation of works of art for their intrinsic attributes, including genuineness and quality. Connoisseurship necessarily involves AESTHETICS, a branch of philosophy concerned with the nature of beauty and taste. This book combines contextual art history and formal analysis, while acknowledging other approaches.

Museums

When you visit a museum, you need no special preparation, but planning can enhance your enjoyment. Several museum resources can help you as you study the works of art there. Publications such as exhibition catalogs and museum handbooks have entries on the artworks. Postcards are an inexpensive way to take an image home.

Museum behavior is simple common sense: don't do anything that endangers the art or interferes with other people's enjoyment of it. In the galleries take a quick look around to get a sense of what is there before going back to look more carefully at individual works that attract you. You can be systematic or selective. When you approach a work of art, look at it and think about it before you read the label. You may not see the same works of art that you have studied in this book, but you will see pieces that relate to both the ideas and the artworks presented in *Art History*. Reading about art—whether in books, in catalogs, or on museum labels—should supplement, not substitute for, looking at works of art.

Use Notes

The various features of this book reinforce each other, helping the reader to become comfortable with terminology and concepts specific to art history.

Introduction and Starter Kit The Introduction is an invitation to the pleasures of art history. The Starter Kit that follows the Introduction is a highly concise primer of basic concepts and tools. The outside margins of the Starter Kit pages are tinted to make them easy to find.

Captions There are two kinds of captions in this book: short and long. Short captions identify information specific to the work of art or architecture illustrated:

> artist (when known)
> title or descriptive name of work
> date
> original location (if moved to a museum or other site)
> material or materials a work is made of
> size (height before width) in feet and inches, with
>   centimeters and meters in parentheses
> present location

The order of these elements varies, depending on the type of work illustrated. Dimensions are not given for architecture, for most wall painting, or for architectural sculpture. Some captions have one or more lines of small print below the identification section of the caption that gives museum or collection information. This is rarely required reading.

Long captions contain information of many kinds that complements the main text.

Definitions of Terms You will encounter the basic terms of art history in three places:

IN THE TEXT, where words appearing in **boldface** type are defined, or glossed, at the first use; some terms are explained more than once, especially those that experience shows are hard to remember.

IN BOXED FEATURES on technique and other subjects and in Elements of Architecture boxes, where labeled drawings and diagrams visually reinforce the use of terms.

IN THE GLOSSARY at the end of the volume, which contains all the words in **boldface** type in the text and boxes. The Glossary begins on page G1, and the outside margins are tinted to make the Glossary easy to find.

Maps, Timelines, Parallels, and Time Scales At the beginning of each chapter is a map with all the places mentioned in the chapter. Above the map, a timeline runs from the earliest through the latest years covered in that chapter. Small drawings of major artworks in the chapter are sited on the map at the places from which they come and are placed on the timelines at the times of their creation. In this way these major works are visually linked in time and place.

Parallels, a table near the beginning of every chapter, uses the main chapter sections to organize artistic and other events "at home and abroad." The Parallels offer a selection of simultaneous events for comparison without suggesting that there are direct connections between them.

Time scales appear in the upper corners of pages, providing a fast check on progress through the period.

Boxes Special material that complements, enhances, explains, or extends the text is set off in three types of tinted boxes. Elements of Architecture boxes clarify specifically architectural features, such as "Space-Spanning Construction Devices" in the Starter Kit (page 32). Technique boxes (see "Lost-Wax Casting," page 31) amplify the methodology by which a type of artwork is created. Other boxes treat special-interest material related to the text.

Bibliography The Bibliography, at the end of this book beginning on page B1, contains books in English, organized by general works and by chapter, that are basic to the study of art history today, as well as works cited in the text.

Dates, Abbreviations, and Other Conventions This book uses the designations BCE and CE, abbreviations for "before the Common Era" and "Common Era," instead of BC ("before Christ") and AD ("Anno Domini," "the year of our Lord"). The first century BCE is the period from 99 BCE to 1 BCE; the first century CE is from the year 1 CE to 99 CE. Similarly, the second century BCE is the period from 199 BCE to 100 BCE; the second century CE extends from 100 CE to 199 CE.

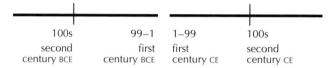

100s	99–1	1–99	100s
second	first	first	second
century BCE	century BCE	century CE	century CE

Circa ("about" or "approximately") is used with dates, spelled out in the text and abbreviated to "c." in the captions, when an exact date is not yet verified.

An illustration is called a "figure," or "fig." Figure 6-70 is the seventieth numbered illustration in Chapter 6. Figures 1 through 29 are in the Introduction and the Starter Kit. There are two types of figures: photographs of artworks or of models, and line drawings. The latter are used when a work cannot be photographed or when a diagram or simple drawing is the clearest way to illustrate an object or a place.

When introducing artists, we use the words *active* and *documented* with dates—in addition to "b." (for "born") and "d." (for "died"). "Active" means that an artist worked during the years given. "Documented" means that documents link the person to the date.

Accents are used for words in Spanish, Italian, French, and German only.

With few exceptions, names of museums and other cultural bodies in Western European countries are given in the form used in that country.

Titles of Works of Art Most paintings and sculpture created in Europe and the United States in the last 500 years have been given formal titles, either by the artist or by critics and art historians. Such formal titles are printed in italics. In other traditions and cultures, a single title is not important or even recognized. In this book we use formal titles of artworks in cases where they are established and descriptive titles of artworks where titles are not established. If a work is best known by its non-English title, such as Manet's *Dejeuner sur l'Herbe* (*Luncheon on the Grass*), the original language precedes the translation.

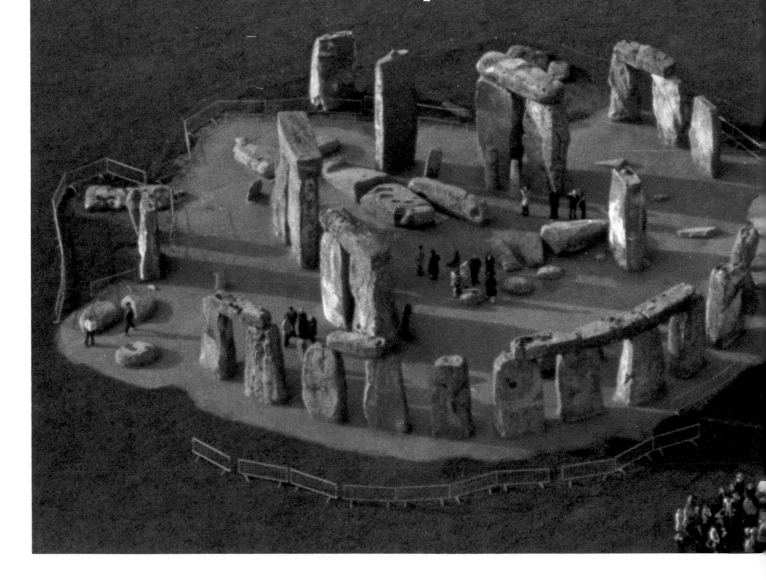

CHAPTER 1

Prehistory and Prehistoric Art in Europe

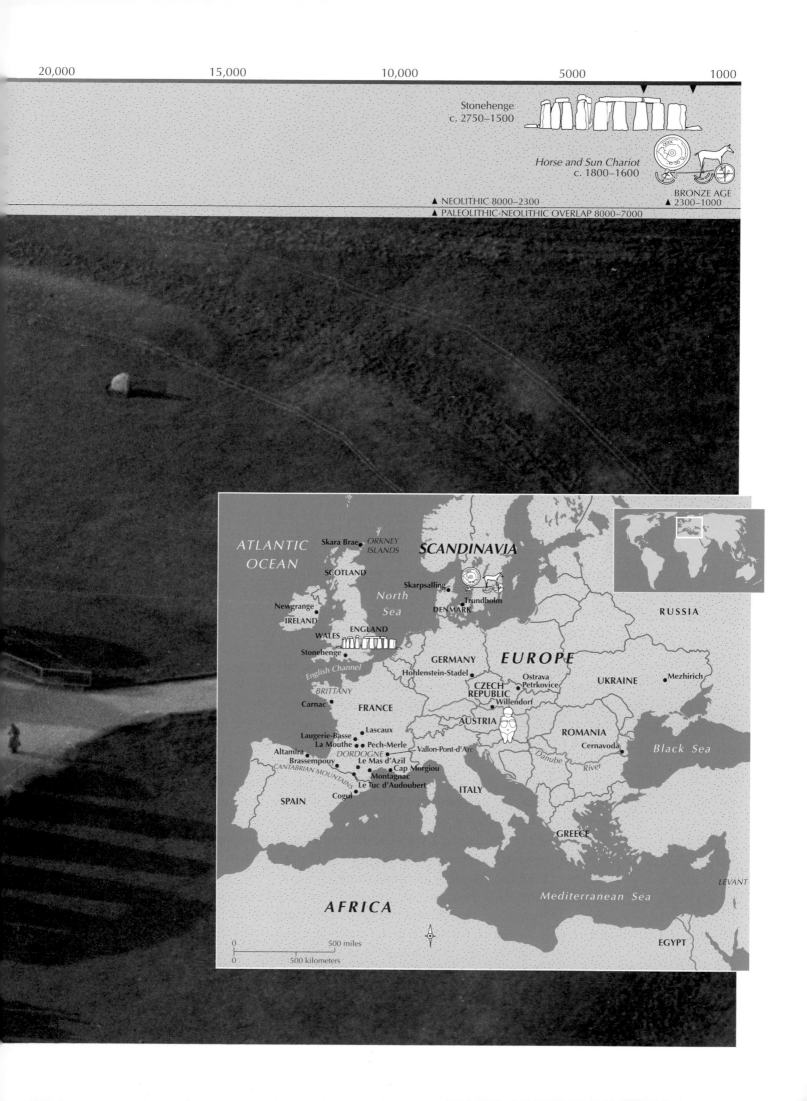

20,000   15,000   10,000   5000   1000

Stonehenge
c. 2750–1500

Horse and Sun Chariot
c. 1800–1600

BRONZE AGE
▲ 2300–1000

▲ NEOLITHIC 8000–2300
▲ PALEOLITHIC-NEOLITHIC OVERLAP 8000–7000

ATLANTIC
OCEAN

Skara Brae   ORKNEY
              ISLANDS

SCANDINAVIA

SCOTLAND

Skarpsalling

North
Sea

Trundholm

DENMARK

RUSSIA

Newgrange

IRELAND

WALES   ENGLAND

Stonehenge

English Channel

GERMANY   EUROPE

Hohlenstein-Stadel

Ostrava
Petrkovice

CZECH
REPUBLIC

Willendorf

UKRAINE   • Mezhirich

BRITTANY

Carnac

FRANCE

AUSTRIA

Laugerie-Basse   Lascaux
La Mouthe   Pech-Merle
DORDOGNE   Vallon-Pont-d'Arc
Altamira   Brassempouy   Le Mas d'Azil
CANTABRIAN MOUNTAINS   Cap Morgiou
              Montagnac
              Le Tuc d'Audoubert

ROMANIA

Cernavoda

Black Sea

Danube   River

SPAIN   Cogul

ITALY

GREECE

Mediterranean Sea

LEVANT

AFRICA

EGYPT

0   500 miles
0   500 kilometers

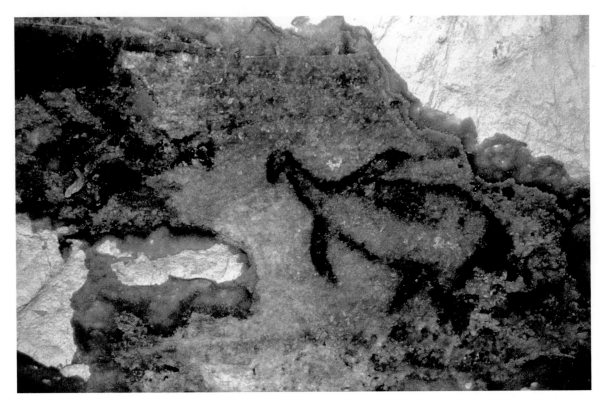

1-1. *Auk,* Cosquer cave, Cap Morgiou, France. c. 16,500 BCE. Charcoal and manganese dioxide on limestone

In July 1991, divers at Cap Morgiou, France, set out to explore what appeared to be a small cave with an entrance 121 feet below the surface of the Mediterranean. After swimming through a narrow, rising tunnel for nearly 600 feet, they suddenly bobbed up into a cavern above sea level. Looking around, they found to their amazement that the cavern walls were decorated with animal images and human handprints. The French explorers, led by diving instructor Henri Cosquer, had discovered a cave filled with prehistoric paintings in a region where no such paintings had been found before. Some of them, like the image of a playful auk, a seabird that became extinct in the Mediterranean about 150 years ago (fig. 1-1), simply delight the modern viewer. But more important, the paintings are the work of artists who recorded the interests and values of prehistoric peoples living on a hillside near what was then the edge of the sea.

Prehistory includes all of human existence before the emergence of writing. Long, long before that defining moment, people were carving objects, painting images, and creating shelters and other structures. These works of prehistoric art and architecture are fascinating in part because they are so supremely beautiful and in part because of what they disclose about the people who made them.

Prehistoric art is therefore of interest not only to art historians, but also to archeologists and anthropologists, for whom the art is only one clue—along with fossils, pollens, and other finds—to an understanding of early human life and culture. Because the sculpture, paintings, and structures that survive are only the tiniest fraction of what was created over such a long span of time, conclusions and interpretations drawn from them have to be quite theoretical, making prehistoric art one of the most speculative areas of art history.

THE PALEOLITHIC PERIOD

Archeological evidence indicates that the earliest upright human species came into being 4.4 million years ago in Africa. How and when modern humans evolved is the subject of lively debate, but anthropologists now agree that the hominids called *Homo sapiens* ("wise humans") appeared about 200,000 years ago and that the species to which we belong, *Homo sapiens sapiens*, evolved about 120,000 to 100,000 years ago. Modern humans spread across Asia, into Europe, and finally to Australia and the Americas. The results of the most recently developed dating techniques suggest that this vast movement of people took place much earlier than anthropologists had thought possible, mainly between 100,000 and 20,000 years ago. Not only did these early modern humans have the ability to travel great distances, but as the introduction to the galleries of the National Museum of Natural History in Washington, D.C., notes, they had "aesthetic spirit and questing intellect." This book presents the tangible record of that uniquely human "aesthetic spirit."

Systematic study of ancient remains began only about 200 years ago. Struck by the wealth of stone tools, weapons, and figures found at ancient living sites, those first scholars named the whole period of early human development the "Stone Age." Today's researchers divide the Stone Age into three major periods: the Paleolithic (from the Greek *paleo-*, "old," and *lithos*, "stone"), the Meso-lithic (Greek *meso-*, "middle"), and the Neolithic (Greek *neo-*, "new"). The Paleolithic period is itself divided into three phases, Lower, Middle, and Upper, reflecting their relative position in excavated strata, or layers. The Upper Paleolithic period in Europe began between 42,000 and 37,000 years ago and lasted until the end of the Ice Age, about 9000–8000 BCE. Much of northern Europe was covered by glaciers in the transitional period between the Upper Paleolithic and Neolithic and therefore presents few human traces from the period, which corresponds to the Mesolithic in other parts of the world. With the gradual retreat of the ice, people from the Near East migrated onto the continent between about 11,000 and 8,000 years ago, bringing the beginnings of Neolithic culture with them. Although the precise dates for these periods vary from place to place, the divisions are useful as we examine developments in the arts. This chapter presents the prehistoric art of Europe; later chapters consider the prehistoric art of other continents and cultures.

In the Upper Paleolithic period, very long before the development of writing, our early ancestors created another form of communication: the visual arts. Many examples of sculpture, painting, architecture, and other arts have survived the long passage of time to move us, challenge us, and provide us with insights into the lives and beliefs of their makers. Nevertheless, it is nearly impossible to determine what "art" communicated to the people who experienced it in such early times, or what values its creators attached to it.

36,000 BCE 1000 BCE

PARALLELS

Years	Period	Prehistoric Europe	World
c. 40,000–8000 BCE	Upper Paleolithic	*Lion-Human*; *Woman from Willendorf*; mammoth-bone shelters; cave paintings	**70,000–8000 BCE** Ice Age
			11,500–10,000 BCE Wooden buildings in South America (Chile); first pottery vessels (Japan); dogs domesticated; bow and arrow
c. 8000–7000 BCE	Paleolithic-Neolithic overlap		
c. 8000–2300 BCE	Neolithic	End of Ice Age; plants domesticated; Skara Brae settled; megalithic tombs; unfired clay vessels; Stonehenge; megalithic figures	**8000–1000 BCE** Plants domesticated, animal husbandry (Near East, Southeast Asia, the Americas); potter's wheel (Egypt); development of metallurgy (Near East); earliest pictographs (Sumer); development of writing (China, India); Great Pyramids at Giza (Egypt); *Stela of Hammurabi* (Babylonia)
c. 2300–1000 BCE	Bronze Age	*Horse and Sun Chariot*	

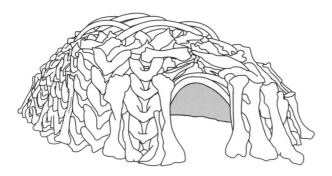

1-2. Reconstruction drawing of mammoth-bone house from Ukraine. c. 16,000–10,000 BCE

The Beginning of Architecture

People have always found ingenious ways of providing themselves with shelter. It was always possible to occupy the mouth of a cave or to fashion a hut or tent next to a protective cliff. Traditionally, *architecture* has been a term applied to the enclosure of spaces with at least some aesthetic intent, and some would object to its use in connection with such improvisations. But building even the simplest of shelters requires a degree of imagination and planning deserving of the name "architecture."

In the Upper Paleolithic period, people in some regions were building shelters that were far from simple. Circular or oval huts of light branches and hides might measure as much as 15 to 20 feet in diameter. (Modern tents to accommodate six people vary from 10-by-11-foot ovals to 14-by-7-foot rooms.) Some peoples colored their floors with powdered ocher, a naturally occurring iron ore ranging in color from yellow to red to brown. Most activities were centered on the inside fire pit, or hearth; it was there that food was prepared and tools and utensils were fashioned. Larger dwellings might have had more than one hearth and other spaces set aside for different uses—working stone, making clothing, sleeping, and dumping refuse.

Well-preserved examples of Upper Paleolithic dwellings in Russia and Ukraine reveal the great ingenuity of peoples living in those less-hospitable northern regions. To meet the need for solid, weatherproof shelter in the treeless grasslands, these builders created settlements of up to ten houses using the bones of the woolly mammoth, a kind of elephant now extinct (fig. 1-2). One of the best-preserved mammoth-bone villages, discovered in Mezhirich, Ukraine, dates from 16,000–10,000 BCE. Most of its houses were from 13 to 26 feet in diameter, and the largest one measured 24 by 33 feet and was cleverly constructed of dozens of mammoth skulls, shoulder blades, pelvis bones, jawbones, and tusks. The long, curving tusks made excellent roof supports and effective arched door openings. The bone framework was probably covered with animal hides and turf. Inside the dwelling, archeologists found fifteen small hearths that still contained ashes and charred bones left by its final occupants.

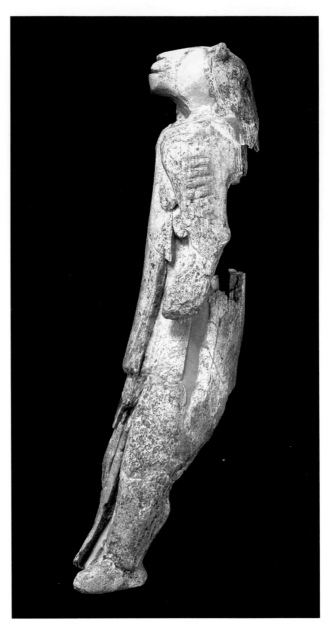

1-3. *Lion-Human*, from Hohlenstein-Stadel, Germany. c. 30,000–26,000 BCE. Mammoth ivory, height 11⅝" (29.6 cm). Ulmer Museum, Ulm, Germany

Small Sculpture

The earliest known works of sculpture are small figures, or figurines, of people and animals and date from about 32,000 BCE. Thousands of such figures in bone, ivory, stone, and clay have been found across Europe and Asia.

A human figure carved from a piece of mammoth ivory nearly a foot tall—much larger than most early figurines—was found broken into numerous fragments at Hohlenstein-Stadel, Germany (fig. 1-3). At first it appeared that its head had been lost, but when one of the excavators placed the head from what was thought to be another figurine atop the reassembled body, it was found to be a perfect fit. Astonishingly, the head in question represented some species of cat. Was this lively, powerful figure intended to represent a person wearing

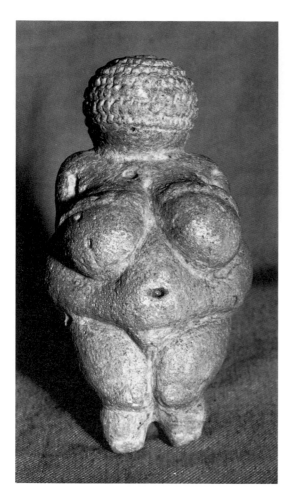

1-4. *Woman from Willendorf*, Austria. c. 22,000–21,000 BCE. Limestone, height 4³/₈" (11 cm). Naturhistorisches Museum, Vienna

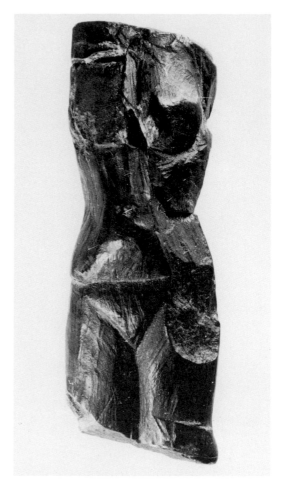

1-5. *Woman from Ostrava Petrkovice*, Czech Republic. c. 23,000 BCE. Hematite, height 1³/₄" (4.6 cm). Archeological Institute, Brno

a lion mask and taking part in some ritual? Or is this a portrayal of some imagined creature, half human and half beast? The inability to identify and interpret the figures portrayed in the art of this early period is frustrating. Some conclusions about the material existence of prehistoric people can be drawn from the available evidence—their physical appearance, their diet, tools, and types of dwellings. It is even possible to guess something of their social organization and attitudes toward each other. But it is much more difficult to form any notion of their intellectual and spiritual life. One of the few things that can be said conclusively about the *Lion-Human* is that it took sophisticated thinking to create such a creature never seen in nature. With considerable technical skill, a gifted artist from as long as 30,000 years ago managed to produce a work that still inspires wonder.

Animals and unclothed women are the subjects of most of the small sculpture from the Upper Paleolithic period. The most famous female figure from the period was discovered near Willendorf, Austria. The *Woman from Willendorf* (fig. 1-4) dates from about 22,000–21,000 BCE and is a mere 4³/₈ inches tall. Carved from limestone and originally colored with red ocher, the figure is composed of rounded shapes that convey stability, dignity, and permanence—and incidentally make the work seem

much larger than it actually is. The sculptor has carved the stone in such a way as to convey the body's fleshiness, exaggerating its female attributes by giving it pendulous breasts, a big belly with deep navel, wide hips, and solid thighs. The gender-neutral parts of the body—the face, the arms, the legs—have been reduced to mere vestiges.

Another carved figure found in what is now the Czech Republic, the *Woman from Ostrava Petrkovice*, presents an entirely different perception of the female form (fig. 1-5). It is less than 2 inches tall and dates from about 23,000 BCE. Archeologists excavating an oval house stockpiled with flintstone and rough chunks of hematite, the iron oxide ore powdered to make ocher pigment, discovered the figure next to the hearth. Someone at the house had apparently picked up one of the pieces of hematite and shaped it into the figure of a youthful, athletic woman in an animated pose, with one hip slightly raised and a knee bent as if she were walking.

The hematite woman is so beautiful that one longs to be able to see her face. Perhaps it resembled the one preserved on a fragment from another female figure found in France. This is a tiny head in ivory known as the *Woman from Brassempouy* (fig. 1-6), which dates from about 22,000 BCE. The person who carved it was

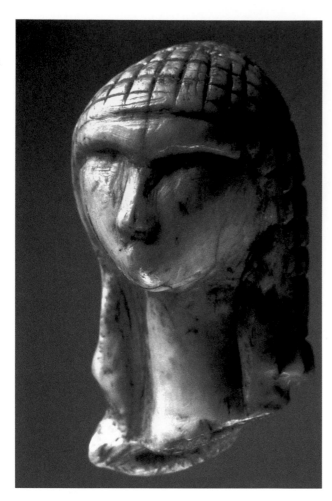

1-6. *Woman from Brassempouy*, Grotte du Pape, Brassempouy, Landes, France. c. 22,000 BCE. Ivory, height 1¼" (3 cm). Musée des Antiquités Nationales, St.-Germain-en-Laye

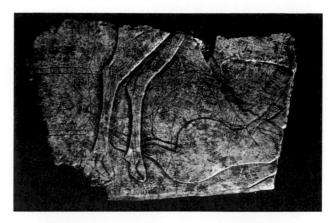

1-7. *Pregnant Woman and Deer* (?), from Laugerie-Basse, France. c. 14,000–10,000 BCE. Engraved reindeer antler, 2½ x 4" (6.7 x 10.5 cm). Musée des Antiquités Nationales, St.-Germain-en-Laye

concerned solely with those contours necessary to identify the piece as a human head—an egg shape atop a graceful neck, a wide nose, and a strongly defined browline suggesting deep-set eyes. The cap of shoulder-length hair is decorated with a grid pattern perhaps representing curls or braiding. This is an example of **abstraction**: the reduction of shapes and appearances to basic forms that do not faithfully reproduce those of the thing represented.

Instead of copying a specific person's face detail by detail, the artist provided only those features common to all of us. This is what is known as a memory image, one that relies on the generic shapes and relationships that readily spring to mind at the mention of a specific object—in this case the human head. Although it is impossible to know what motivated the artist to carve them in just this way, the simplified planes of the tiny face from Brassempouy appeal to our twentieth-century taste for abstraction. Intentionally or not, with this figure some prehistoric artist managed to communicate something essentially human. Even isolated from any cultural context, its human presence shines across the millennia.

Because so many of the surviving human figures from the period are female, some scholars have speculated that prehistoric societies were matriarchal, or dominated by women. Others believe that these female figures, many of them visibly pregnant, are a reflection of the religious notions of these early people. They suggest that early religion was chiefly concerned with perpetuating the familiar cycles of nature, thereby ensuring the continuing life of people, animals, and vegetation, and that these female figurines were created as fertility symbols. Quite likely, the *Woman from Willendorf,* the *Woman from Brassempouy,* and other Upper Paleolithic figures like them did have such a function (see "The Power of Naming," opposite). But they can also be interpreted as representations of actual women, as expressions of ideal beauty, as erotic images, as ancestor figures, or even as dolls meant to help young girls learn women's roles. Given the diversity of ages and physical types represented, it is possible that they were any or all of these.

Such self-contained, three-dimensional pieces are examples of **sculpture in the round**. Prehistoric carvers also produced **relief sculpture** in stone, bone, and ivory. In relief sculpture the surrounding material is carved away to a certain depth, forming a background that sets off the figure. A fine example of portable relief carving from the Upper Paleolithic is a 4-inch fragment of reindeer antler, dating from about 14,000–10,000 BCE, that reveals a new complexity in both subject matter and technique (fig. 1-7). On the side shown, a large deer or bison stands over a reclining woman who is unmistakably pregnant. The carver observed and rendered the slender woman's enlarged abdomen quite accurately. To emphasize the figures' contours, which are carved in very **low relief**, the artist used both **U**- and **V**-shaped gouges along with a technique called **beveling**—cutting at an angle—to create more-pronounced shadows. Also, by interrupting the lines of the woman's legs to make way for those of the deer, the artist created the illusion of space, with one figure realistically positioned behind the other. The woman wears bracelets on her raised left arm and also possibly a necklace, reflecting the delight human beings have taken in adorning themselves since very early times. As early as 35,000 years ago, they made ornamental beads from shells, teeth, bone, ivory, and stone, and at least 23,000 years ago they buried their dead with bits of finery like headbands and necklaces.

THE POWER OF NAMING

Words are only symbols for ideas. But the very words we invent—or our ancestors invented—reveal a certain view of the world and can shape our thinking. Early people recognized quite clearly the power of words and names. In the Old Testament, God gave Adam dominion over the animals (Genesis 1:28) and allowed him to name them: ". . . whatever the man called each of them, that would be its name. The man gave names to all the cattle, all the birds of the air, and all the wild animals" (Genesis 2:19–20). Today, we still exert the power of naming when we select a name for a baby, call a friend by a complimentary nickname, or use demeaning words to dehumanize those we dislike.

Our ideas about a work of art can also be affected by names, even the ones used in a caption in a book. Before the twentieth century, many works of art had no "names." Names were eventually supplied by the works' owners or by scholars writing about them. The names thus attached to works may express the cultural prejudices of those responsible for them or of the times generally.

An excellent example of such distorting prejudice is provided by the names early scholars gave to the hundreds of small prehistoric statues of women they found. The first of these to be discovered (see fig. 1-4) was promptly dubbed the "Venus of Willendorf" after the place where it had been found. Venus was the Roman goddess of love and beauty, and the use of her name for the newly discovered figure sent a message that this figure was associated with religious belief, that it represented an ideal of womanhood, and that it was one of a long line of images of "classical" feminine beauty. In no time, the majority of such sculptures from the Upper Paleolithic came to be known as "Venus figures." The name was repeated so often that even scholars began to assume that these had to be fertility figures and mother goddesses. In fact, they probably were, although there is no absolute proof that the sculptures had religious significance or were imputed to have supernatural powers. What if these simply represent obese women?

Our ability to understand and interpret works of art creatively is easily compromised by distracting labels. Even knowing that the figure was once labeled the "Venus of Willendorf" influences the way we look at it. The tradition of a name, no matter how wrongheaded, makes it extremely difficult to challenge accepted belief. Calling a prehistoric figure a "woman" instead of "Venus" frees us to think about it in new and different ways.

Cave Art

About 30,000 years ago, art in Europe entered a rich and sophisticated phase. Many of the images painted on the walls of caves in southern France and northern Spain were painted between circa 28,000 and 10,000 BCE. The earliest known site of prehistoric cave paintings in Europe was discovered in December 1994 near Vallon-Pont-d'Arc in southern France—a tantalizing trove of hundreds of animal and bird paintings (see fig. 1). The caves in question must have had a special meaning, because people returned to them time after time over many generations, in some cases over thousands of years. These subterranean galleries were not used as living quarters, but the evidence of artifacts and footprints suggests that they were gathering places where the social bond was somehow reaffirmed and strengthened. It may be that people congregated in them to celebrate initiation rites or the sealing of social alliances—just as we gather today for baptisms, bar mitzvahs, weddings, funerals, or town meetings.

The most dramatic of these cave images are paintings of grazing, running, or resting animals. Among the animals represented are the wild horse, the bison, the mammoth, the bear, the panther, the owl, deer, aurochs (extinct ancestors of oxen), the woolly-haired rhino, and the wild goat, or ibex. Also included are occasional people, both male and female, many handprints, and hundreds of geometric markings such as grids, circles, and dots. The paintings of animals in the Cosquer cave at Cap Morgiou (see fig. 1-1) were created about 16,500 BCE, but the first of the handprints found there date from long before, as early as 25,000 BCE. In other caves, painters

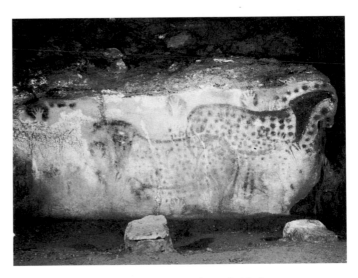

1-8. *Spotted Horses and Human Hands*, Pech-Merle cave, Dordogne, France. c. 16,000 BCE. Paint on limestone, length approx. 11'2" (3.4 m)

worked not only in large caverns but also far back in the smallest chambers and recesses, many of which are almost inaccessible today. Small stone lamps found in such caves (see fig. 1-15) indicate that they worked in the dim flicker of light from burning animal fat. Occasional small holes have been found carved into a cave's rock walls. These may have been used to anchor the scaffolding needed for painting the cave's high ceilings and walls.

A cave site at Pech-Merle, in France, appears to have been used and abandoned several times over a period of 5,000 years. Images of animals, handprints, and nearly

600 geometric symbols have been found in thirty different parts of the underground complex. The earliest artists to work in the cave, some 18,000 years ago, specialized in painting horses (fig. 1-8). All of their horses have small, finely detailed heads, heavy bodies, massive extended necks, and legs tapering to almost nothing at the hooves. The horses were then overlaid with bright red circles. Some interpreters see these circles as ordinary spots on the animals' coats, but others see them as magic rock weapons hurled at the painted horses in a ritual meant to assure success in the hunt.

The handprints on the walls at Pech-Merle and other cave sites were almost certainly not idle graffiti or accidental smudges but were intended to communicate something. Some are positive images made by simply coating the hand with color pigment and pressing it against the wall. Others are negative images: the surrounding space rather than the hand shape itself is painted. Negative images were made by placing the hand with fingers spread apart against the wall, then spitting or spraying paint around it with a reed blowpipe—an artist's tool found in such caves. Most of the handprints are small enough to be those of women or even children, yet footprints preserved in the mud floors at other caves show that they were visited by people of all sizes. A series of giant aurochs at Pech-Merle, painted in simple outlines without color, has been dated to a later period, about 15,000 BCE. Sometime afterward, other figures were created near the mouth of the cave by **incising**, or scratching lines into the walls' surface. Thanks to rapid advances in laboratory analysis techniques, it is only a matter of time until all prehistoric wall paintings can be dated more precisely.

The first cave paintings attributed to the Upper Paleolithic period were those discovered at Altamira, near Santander in the Cantabrian Mountains of northern

TECHNIQUE

PREHISTORIC WALL PAINTING

In a dark cave in France, working by the light of a flickering lamp fueled with animal fat, an artist places charcoal in his mouth, chews it, diluting it with saliva and water, then spews it out against the wall, using his hand as a stencil. The artist is Michel Lorblanchet, a cave archeologist. He is showing us how the original artists at Pech-Merle created their magnificent paintings. Other archeologists use sophisticated scientific techniques to analyze the color pigments they used to date their works, but Lorblanchet, inspired by his research on the cave painting of Australian aboriginals, seeks to re-create the actual experience of those early painters.

Having successfully reproduced a smaller painting of animals in 1979, Lorblanchet turned to the best-known and most complex of the Pech-Merle paintings, the one of the spotted horses. He first made a light sketch in charcoal, then painted the horses' outlines using the spitting technique described above. By turning himself into a human spray can, he can produce clear lines on the rough stone surface much more easily than he could with a brush. To create the line of a horse's back, with its clean upper edge and blurry lower one, he simply blew pigment below his hand; to capture its angular rump, he placed his hand vertically against the wall, holding it slightly curved; to produce the sharpest lines, such as those of the upper hind leg and tail, he placed his hands side by side and blew between them. The forelegs and the hair on the horses' bellies he executed with finger painting, and to create a stencil for the dense, round spots he punched a hole in a piece of leather. In some places he chose to blow a thicker pigment through a reed, in others he applied it with a brush made by chewing the end of a twig.

Lorblanchet had painted his first panel in less than two hours; thirty-two hours were needed to reproduce the spotted horses. The fact that he could execute such a work in a relatively short time tends to confirm that a single artist—perhaps with the help of an assistant to mix pigments and tend the lamp—created the original. It has also been noted that all of the handprints are the same size. The main pigments used in the original were ochers for the reds and manganese dioxide for the blacks. Since manganese dioxide is poisonous if swallowed, Lorblanchet worked with charcoal. Jean Clottes, who has studied the composition of pigments used in cave painting in France and contributed a great deal toward their accurate dating, has determined that pigments used in a given region remained fairly consistent but that the "recipe" for the medium—the precise mix of saliva, water, and other liquids used to bind them—varied over time and from place to place.

Scientists are now very close to pinning down exactly when a given cave painting was executed, and imaginative archeologists like Lorblanchet are showing us how they were done. Although we may never know just what these paintings meant to the artists who produced them, the very process of creating them must have been rich with significance. Lorblanchet puts it quite eloquently: "Human breath, the most profound expression of a human being, literally breathes life onto a cave wall" (*Archeology*, November–December 1991, page 30).

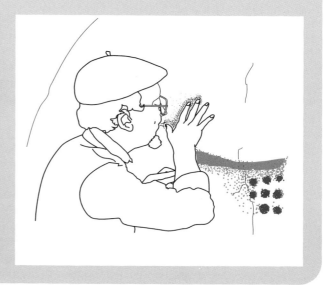

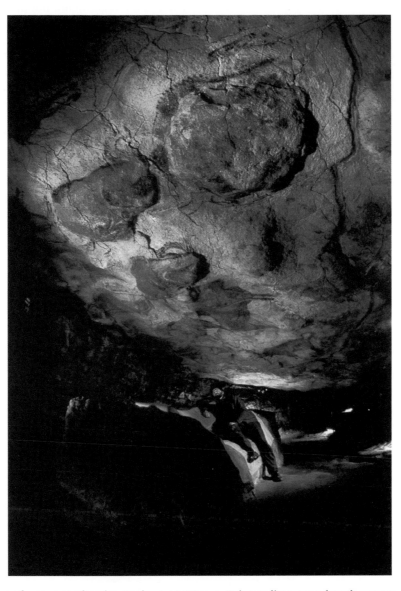

1-9. *Bison*, on the ceiling of a cave at Altamira, Spain. c. 12,000 BCE. Paint on limestone, length approx. 8'3" (2.5 m)

No one knew of the existence of prehistoric cave painting until one day in 1879, when a young girl exploring with her father on the family estate in Altamira crawled through a small opening in the ground and found herself in a cave chamber whose ceiling was covered with painted animals. Her father searched the rest of the cave, then told authorities about the remarkable find. Few people believed that these amazing works could have been done by "primitive" people, and the scientific community declared the paintings a hoax. They were accepted as authentic only in 1902, after many other cave paintings, drawings, and engravings had been discovered at other spots in northern Spain and in France.

Spain. They were recently determined to have been created about 12,000 BCE. The Altamira artists painted the bodies of their animals over and around natural irregularities in the cave's walls and ceilings to create sculptural effects. To produce the herd of bison on the ceiling of the main cavern (fig. 1-9), they used rich red and brown ochers to paint the large areas of the animals' shoulders, backs, and flanks, then added the details of the legs, tails, heads, and horns in black and brown. They must have observed the bison herd with great care in order to capture the distinctive appearance of the beasts.

The best-known cave paintings are those found in 1940 at Lascaux, in the Dordogne region of southern France. These have been dated to about 15,000–13,000 BCE (fig. 1-10). The Lascaux artists also used the contours of the rock as part of their compositions (fig. 1-11). They painted cows, bulls, horses, and deer along natural ledges, where the smooth, white limestone of the ceiling and upper wall meets a rougher surface below. The animals appear singly, in rows, face to face, tail to tail, and even painted on top of one other. As in other caves, their most characteristic features have been emphasized. Horns, eyes, and hooves are shown as seen from the front, yet heads and bodies are rendered in profile. Even when their poses are exaggerated or distorted, the animals are full of life and energy, and the accuracy in the drawing of their silhouettes, or outlines, still astonishes us.

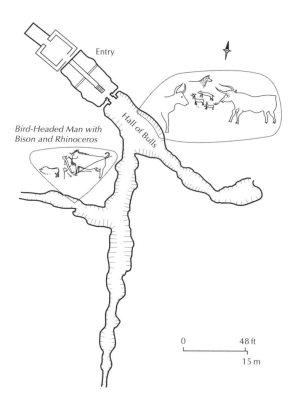

1-10. Plan of Lascaux caves, Dordogne, France

One scene at Lascaux is unusual not only because it includes a human figure but also because it is the only painting in the cave complex that seems to tell a story (fig. 1-12). It was discovered on a wall at the bottom of a 16-foot shaft containing spears and a stone lamp. A figure who could be a hunter, highly stylized but recognizably male and wearing a bird's-head mask, appears to be lying on the ground. A great bison looms above him. Below him lie a staff, or baton, and a spear thrower—a device that allowed hunters to throw farther and with greater force—the outer end of which has been carved in the shape of a bird. The long, diagonal line slanting across the bison's hindquarters is a spear. The bison has been disemboweled and will soon die. To the left of the cleft in the wall is a woolly rhinoceros—possibly the bison's slayer.

What is this scene really telling us? Why did the artist portray the man as only a sticklike figure when the bison was rendered with such accurate detail? It may be that the painting illustrates a myth or legend regarding the death of a hero. Perhaps it illustrates an actual event. Or it might depict the vision of a shaman. Shamans were—and still are—people thought to have special powers, an ability to foretell events and assist their people through contact with spirits. They typically make use of trance

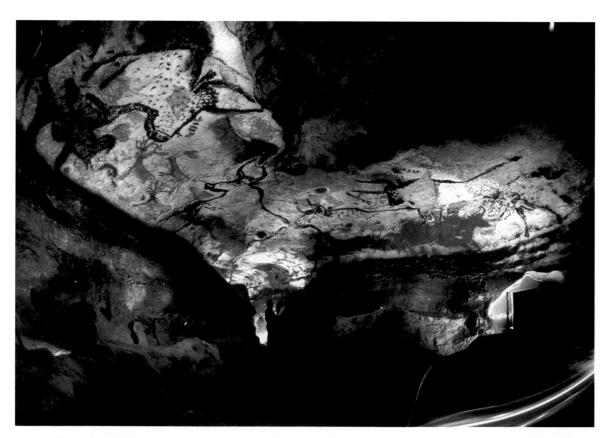

1-11. Hall of Bulls, Lascaux caves. c. 15,000–13,000 BCE. Paint on limestone

Discovered in 1940 and opened to the public after World War II, the prehistoric "museum" at Lascaux soon became one of the most popular tourist sites in France. Too popular, for the many visitors sowed the seeds of the paintings' destruction in the form of heat, humidity, exhaled carbon dioxide, and other insidious contaminants from the outside world. The cave was closed to the public in 1963, so that conservators might battle with an aggressive fungus that had attacked the paintings. Eventually they won, but instead of reopening the site, the authorities created a facsimile of it. Visitors at what is called Lascaux II may now view copies of the painted scenes without harming the precious originals.

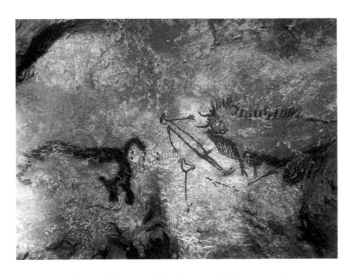

1-12. *Bird-Headed Man with Bison and Rhinoceros*, Lascaux caves. Paint on limestone, length approx. 9' (2.75 m)

states, in which they claim to receive communications from their spirit guides. The images they use to record their visions tend to be abstract, incorporating geometric figures and combinations of human and animal forms such as the bird-headed man in this scene from Lascaux or the lion-headed figure discussed above (see fig. 1-3). Some scholars have interpreted the horses with red dots on them at Pech-Merle as a shamanistic combination of natural and geometric forms. Shamans have claimed that the dots make the spirits' images permanent.

Caves were sometimes adorned with relief sculpture as well as paintings. In some instances, an artist simply heightened the resemblance of a natural projecting rock to a familiar animal form. Other reliefs were created by **modeling**, or shaping, the damp clay of the cave's floor. An excellent example of such work in clay from about 13,000 BCE is preserved at Le Tuc d'Audoubert, in the Dordogne region of France. Working with the clay underfoot, some early sculptor created two bison leaning against a ridge of rock (fig. 1-13). A third, smaller bison lies on the

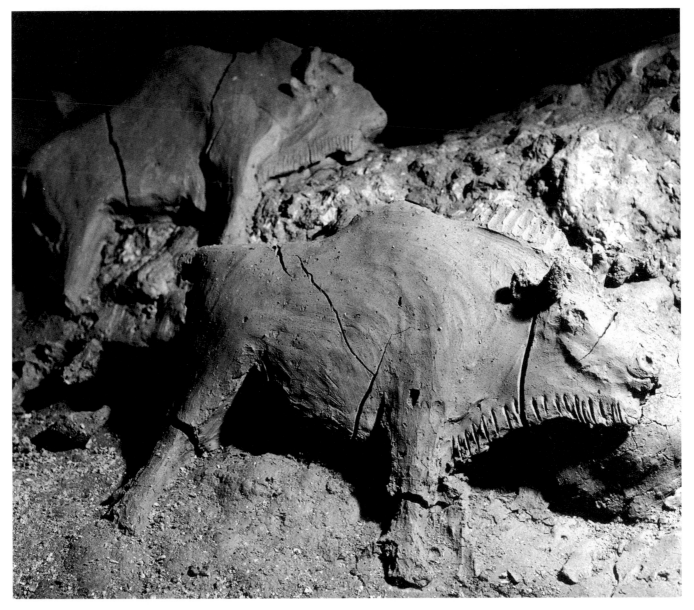

1-13. *Bison*, Le Tuc d'Audoubert, Ariège, France. c. 13,000 BCE. Unbaked clay, length 25" (63.5 cm) and 24" (60.9 cm)

cave floor. Although these beasts are modeled in very **high relief**, they display the same conventions as earlier painted ones, with emphasis on the broad masses of the meat-bearing flanks and shoulders. To make the animals even more lifelike, their creator engraved short parallel lines below their necks to represent their shaggy coats. Numerous small footprints found in the clay floor of this cave must have been left by young people, suggesting that initiation rites may well have been performed here.

The prehistoric artists who worked in caves must have felt that their art would be of some specific benefit to their communities. Perhaps Upper Paleolithic cave art was the product of rituals intended to gain the favor of supernatural forces. If so, its significance may have had less to do with the finished painting than with the very act of creating it.

THE MEANING OF PREHISTORIC CAVE PAINTINGS

What motivated people 30,000 or even 15,000 years ago to paint thousands of images of humans and animals on the walls of caves? During the last hundred years, anthropologists and art historians have devised countless theories to explain prehistoric art, but these often tell us as much about the theorizers and their times as they do about the art itself. For all their useful insights, scholars still have not fully explained the meaning of these images.

The idea that human beings have an inherent desire to decorate themselves and their surroundings—that an "aesthetic sense" is somehow innate to the human species—found ready acceptance in the nineteenth century. That was the century in which some artists promoted the idea of "art for art's sake," and many believed that people created works of art for the sheer love of beauty. Scientists agree that human beings have an aesthetic impulse and take pleasure in pursuing nonpractical activities, but the effort and organization required to accomplish the great paintings of Lascaux indicate that their creators were motivated by more than simple pleasure.

Early in the twentieth century, scholars rejected the idea of art for art's sake as a romantic notion. Led by Salomon Reinach, who believed that art fulfills a social function and that aesthetics are culturally relative, they proposed that prehistoric cave paintings might be products both of totemistic ceremonies, rites performed to strengthen the bonds within specific clans, and of increase ceremonies, or attempts to enhance the fertility of the animals on which people depended for food. In 1903 Reinach proposed that cave paintings were expressions of "sympathetic magic." Encountered in many societies to this day, sympathetic magic relies on two principal assumptions: first, that things that look the same can have a physical influence on each other, and second, that things once in contact continue to act upon each other even at great distances. In the case of cave paintings, it may have been thought that producing a picture of a bison lying down would make sure that hunters found their prey asleep, or that ritual killing of the picture of a bison would ensure the hunters' triumph over the beast itself.

In the early 1920s, Abbé Henri Breuil took these ideas somewhat further and concluded that cave paintings were early forms of religious expression. Convinced that caves were used as places of worship and the settings for initiation rites, he interpreted them as aids in rituals and in instruction.

In the second half of the twentieth century, scholars have tended to base their interpretations on rigorous scientific method and current social theory. Leading French scholars such as André Leroi-Gourhan and Annette Laming-Emperaire dismissed the "hunting magic" theory, noting that analysis of debris from human settlements revealed that the animals used most frequently for food were not the ones traditionally portrayed in cave art. Influenced by structuralist theories, these same scholars discovered that cave images were often systematically organized, with different animals predominating in different areas of the cave.

Although they disagreed on details, Leroi-Gourhan and Laming-Emperaire concluded that the cave images are definitely meaningful pictures. As Laming-Emperaire put it, the paintings "might be mythical representations . . . they might be the concrete expression of a very ancient metaphysical system . . . they might be religious, depicting supernatural beings. They might be all these at one and the same time . . ." (Annette Laming-Emperaire, *La signification de l'art rupestre paléolithique*, 1962, pages 236–237). She felt certain that horses, bison, and women suggested "calm, peace, harmony," and were "concerned with love and life."

Ongoing research continues to discover new cave images and correct earlier errors of fact or interpretation. A restudy of the Altamira cave in the 1980s led Leslie G. Freeman to conclude that there artists had faithfully represented a herd of bison during the mating season, with females occupying the center space and males standing at the outside to defend the herd. Instead of being dead, asleep, or disabled—as earlier observers had supposed—the bison on the ground are simply "dust wallowing," common behavior during the breeding season. All in all, Freeman concluded that the great ceiling mural is simply a depiction of what hunters actually might have seen in late summer.

The recent discovery of paintings in the cave at Cap Morgiou reminds us how great a role chance plays in our endeavors. Meanwhile, rigorous scientific experimentation and the development of new dating techniques have enhanced our ability to place prehistoric artifacts in time with greater accuracy (see "How Early Art Is Dated," page 49). Anthropological studies have extended our knowledge of the cultures out of which cave art emerged. The study of cave painting is a rapidly changing field. It is altogether appropriate that curators at the National Museum of Natural History in Washington, D.C., chose to place over their ever-changing exhibit illustrating early human culture a prominent label reading "What's New."

Portable Art

An aesthetic sense and the ability to pose and solve problems are among the characteristics unique to human beings. That these characteristics were richly developed in very early times is evident from Paleolithic artifacts of all kinds. The most common tools and utensils of the period are not only functional but also portable works of art.

A spear thrower from Le Mas d'Azil in southwestern France (fig. 1-14) is a splendid example. It is about a foot long and made of antler. Geometric patterns decorate its shaft. The functional hook at the end takes the form of a young ibex in the process of giving birth.

Driven by the ever-present need to assure an adequate supply of food, early hunters devised an ingenious way to increase the range of their spears. All that was required was a stick with a notch or socket on one end. Balancing a spear atop the stick with the end of the shaft seated in the stick's socket, they could then swing their arm in a great arc, giving the spear much greater momentum before setting it in flight. They often carved the notched ends of such spear throwers into images of animals. We do not know whether these animals represented some sort of personal or family emblem serving to identify the thrower's owner or were intended to assure the hunter's triumph over the prey. The young ibex on this spear thrower could simply reflect the hunter's hope of finding the animal standing still. It may be that the carver of this hunting implement was honoring the forces of regeneration that are so powerfully manifest at the moment a new life enters the world. In any case, the carver's sharp observation of nature and skillful rendering of the birthing doe created a practical object that we readily appreciate today—in an age no longer in need of spear throwers—as an elegant work of art.

Prehistoric lamps provide another example of objects that were both functional and aesthetically pleasing. Some are carved in simple abstract shapes admirably designed to hold oil and wicks and to be easily portable. Others were adorned with engraved images, like one found at La Mouthe, France (fig. 1-15). The creator of this lamp decorated its bowl with the image of an ibex. The animal's distinctive head is shown in profile, its sweeping horns reflecting the curved outline of the lamp itself.

Objects like the ibex lamp were made by people whose survival, up until about 10,000 years ago, depended upon their skill at hunting animals and gathering wild grains and other edible plants. But a change was already under way that would alter human existence forever.

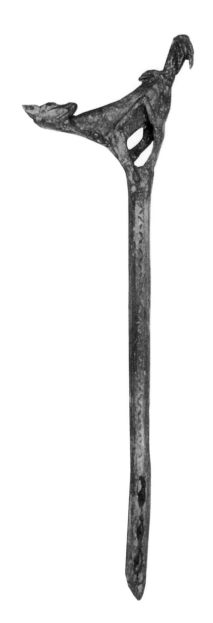

1-14. Ibex-headed spear thrower, from Le Mas d'Azil, Ariège, France. 16,000–9000 BCE. Carved antler, length 11⁵/₈" (30 cm). Musée de la Préhistoire, Le Mas d'Azil

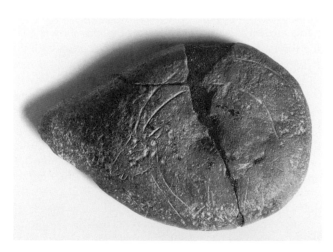

1-15. Lamp with ibex design, from La Mouthe cave, Dordogne, France. 15,000–13,000 BCE. Engraved stone, 6³/₄ x 4³/₄" (17.2 x 12 cm). Musée des Antiquités Nationales, St.-Germain-en-Laye

THE NEOLITHIC PERIOD

In modern times, advances in medicine, transportation, weapons, and communication have abruptly changed human life over the span of just a few generations. Many thousands of years ago, change came much more slowly. The warming of the climate that brought an end to the Ice Age was so gradual that the people of the time could not have known it was occurring, yet it altered life as dramatically as any changes that have come since. The retreating glaciers exposed large temperate regions, and rising ocean levels changed the shorelines of continents, in some places making islands of major land masses. It was in this period, for example, about 6000 BCE, that the land bridge connecting England with the rest of Europe disappeared beneath the waters of what are now known as the North Sea and the English Channel. Europe became covered with grassy plains supporting new edible plants and forests that lured great herds of animals, such as deer, farther and farther northward. At the same time, the people in these more-hospitable regions were finding ways to enhance their chances of survival. The bow and arrow was invented and became the weapon of choice for hunters. Bows were easier to carry and much more accurate at longer range than spears and spear throwers. Dugout boats came into use, opening up new areas for fishing and hunting. With each such advance the overall standard of living improved.

The changing environment led to a new way of life. Although still essentially hunters and gatherers, people began domesticating animals and working the land to cultivate plants. As they gained greater control over their food supply, they no longer had to move around as before but could establish settled communities. None of these changes occurred overnight. Between 10,000 and 5,000 years ago, peoples in the Levant—the lands along the eastern shore of the Mediterranean—began domesticating wild grasses, developing them into more-productive grains such as wheat. In this same period, the people of Southeast Asia learned to grow millet and rice and those in the Americas began to cultivate the bottle gourd and eventually corn. Dogs probably first joined with human hunters more than 11,000 years ago, and cattle, goats, and other animals were later domesticated along with plants. Large numbers of people became farmers, living in villages and producing more than enough food to support themselves—thus freeing some people in the village to attend to other communal needs. Over time these early societies became increasingly complex. Although the majority may still have been involved in the production of food, others specialized in political and military affairs, still others in matters of religion. The new farming culture gradually spread across Europe, reaching Spain and France by 5000 BCE. Farmers in the Paris region were using plows by 4000 BCE.

These fundamental changes in the prehistoric way of life mark the beginning of the Neolithic period. These shifts occurred in some regions sooner than others. To determine the onset of the Neolithic in a specific region, archeologists look for the evidence of three conditions: an organized, ongoing system of agriculture; animal husbandry, or the maintenance of herds of domesticated animals; and permanent, year-round settlements. By the end of the period, villages had increased in size, trading had been developed between distant regions, and advanced building technology had led to the construction of some of the world's most awe-inspiring architectural monuments.

Rock-Shelter Art

The period of transition between Paleolithic and Neolithic culture saw the rise of a distinctive art combining schematic images—simplified, diagrammatic renderings—and geometric forms with depictions of people and animals engaged in everyday activities. Artists of the time preferred to paint and engrave such works on easily accessible, shallow rock shelters. In style, technique, and subject matter, these rock-shelter images are quite different from those found in Upper Paleolithic cave art. The style is abstract, and the technique is often simple line drawing, with no addition of color. Paintings from this period portray striking new themes: people are depicted in energetic poses, whether engaged in battle, hunting, or possibly dancing. They are found in many places near the Mediterranean coast but are especially numerous, beginning about 6000 BCE, in a region located in northeastern Spain.

At Cogul, near Lérida in Catalonia, the large surfaces of a rock shelter are decorated with elaborate narrative scenes involving dozens of relatively small figures—men, women, children, animals, even insects (fig. 1-16). These date from between 4000 and 2000 BCE (see "How Early Art Is Dated," opposite). No specific landscape features are indicated, but occasional painted patterns of animal tracks give the sense of a rocky terrain, like that of the surrounding barren hillsides. In the detail shown here, a number of women are seen gracefully strolling or standing about, some in pairs holding hands. The women's small waists are emphasized by large, pendulous breasts. They wear skirts with scalloped hemlines revealing large calves and sturdy ankles, and all of them appear to have shoulder-length hair. The women stand near several long-horned cattle. These animals are larger than others appearing above, as though the artist wished to suggest a recession of the landscape into the distance, where other cattle, the Spanish ibex, red deer, and a pig can be seen grazing.

The manner in which this representation of distance has been created is a significant change in Upper Paleolithic painting. A pair of ibexes visible just above the cattle as well as a dog in the foreground are shown leaping forward with legs fully extended. This pose, called a flying gallop, has been used to indicate speed in a running animal from prehistory to the present.

In other paintings at the site, not shown here, some women seem to be looking after children while others carry baskets, gather food, and work the earth with digging sticks. It is easy to imagine that these paintings served solely as a record of daily life. They must have had some greater significance, however, for like other earlier cave paintings they were repainted many times over the centuries.

Because rock shelters were so accessible, people no doubt continued to visit these art sites long after their original purpose had been forgotten. At Cogul, in fact, there are inscriptions in Latin and an early form of Spanish left by Roman-era visitors—2,000-year-old graffiti intermingled with the much more ancient paintings.

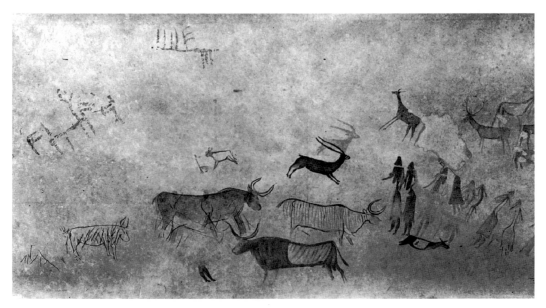

1-16. *Women and Animals*, facsimile of detail of rock-shelter painting in Cogul, Lérida, Spain. c. 4000–2000 BCE. Museo Arqueológico, Barcelona

HOW EARLY ART IS DATED

When the first Upper Paleolithic cave paintings were discovered at Altamira, Spain, in 1879, they were promptly rejected as forgeries by the Lisbon Congress on Prehistoric Archeology. Seven years later, it was shown that similar paintings discovered in France were indeed thousands of years old because a layer of mineral deposits had built up on top of them. Since those first discoveries, archeologists have developed increasingly sophisticated ways of dating such finds. During the twentieth century, archeologists have primarily used two approaches to determine an artifact's age. **Relative dating** relies on the chronological relationships among objects in either a single excavation or several sites. If archeologists have determined, for example, that pottery types A, B, and C follow each other chronologically at one site, they can apply that knowledge to another site; even if "type B" is the only pottery present, it can be assigned a relative date. **Absolute dating** aims to determine a precise span of calendar years in which an artifact was created. Arriving at even approximate absolute dates for prehistoric sculpture, painting, and architecture is extremely difficult.

Dating a work of art is easiest if the site at which it is discovered has not been disturbed. Archeologists have developed painstaking methods by which they can record each find at a given "dig" by its area, the layer (or stratum) in which it was found, and its relationship to other artifacts and preset markers.

Radiometric dating measures the degree to which radioactive materials have disintegrated and is the most accurate of several methods of absolute dating. One of the earliest radiometric methods developed is still used for dating organic (plant or animal) materials—including some of the pigments used in cave paintings. It measures a carbon isotope called radiocarbon, or carbon-14. Another measures potassium-argon ratios. The carbon-14 content in a living organism is constantly being replenished. When the organism dies, it stops absorbing carbon-14 and starts to lose its store of it. Experiments over the years have determined the rates at which most types of dead organic matter lose their radiocarbon. Under the right circumstances, the amount of carbon-14 remaining in an artifact made of an organic material can tell us how long ago the organism died. This method has serious drawbacks for dating works of art, however. Using carbon-14 dating on a carved antler or wood sculpture shows only when the animal died or the tree was cut down, not when the artist created the work, which could have been centuries later. Also, some part of the object must be destroyed to conduct this kind of test—something rarely desirable in a work of art. For this reason, researchers frequently test organic materials found in the same context as the work of art rather than the work itself.

Radiocarbon dating is most accurate for materials no more than 30,000 to 40,000 years old. Potassium-argon dating, which measures the decay of a radioactive potassium isotope into a stable isotope of argon, an inert gas, is most reliable with materials more than a million years old. For the long span of time for which neither method is very reliable, two newer techniques have been used in reports since the mid-1980s. Thermoluminescence dating measures the irradiation of the crystal structure of a material such as flint or pottery and the soil in which it is found, determined by the luminescence produced when a sample is heated. Electron spin resonance techniques involve a magnetic field and microwave irradiation to date a material such as tooth enamel and its surrounding soil.

Recent experiments have helped to date cave paintings with increasing precision. Twelve different radiocarbon-analysis series have determined that the animal images in the Cosquer cave are definitely 18,500 years old, the handprints 27,000 years old. Jean Clottes's analysis of pigments used in other caves in France has shown that different generations of painters used different "recipes" when mixing their paints, a finding that further improves attempts to date particular cave paintings.

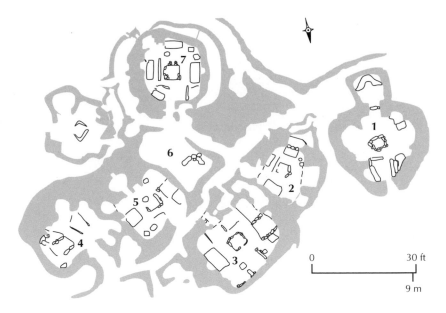

1-17. Plan, village of Skara Brae, Orkney Islands, Scotland. c. 3100–2600 BCE

Architecture

As people adopted a settled, agricultural way of life, they began to build large structures to serve as .dwellings, storage spaces, and shelters for their animals. In Europe, timber had become abundant after the disappearance of the glaciers, and Neolithic people, like their Paleolithic predecessors, continued to construct buildings out of wood and other plant materials. People clustered their dwellings in villages and eventually larger towns, and outside their settlements, they built tombs and ritual centers so huge that they still have the power to fill us with awe.

Dwellings and Villages. A northern European village frequently consisted of only three or four long timber buildings, each of them housing forty-five to fifty people. These houses might be up to 150 feet long, and they included large granaries, or storage space for the harvest, a necessity in agricultural communities. The structures were rectangular, with a row of posts down the center supporting a ridgepole, a long horizontal beam against which the slanting roof poles were braced. Their walls were probably made of what is known as wattle and daub, branches woven in a basketlike pattern, then covered with mud or clay. They were most likely roofed with thatch, some plant material such as reeds or straw tied over a framework of poles. Similar structures can still be seen today in some regions, serving as animal shelters or even dwellings.

Around 4000 BCE, Neolithic settlers began to locate their communities at sites most easily defended, near rivers, on plateaus, or in swamps. For additional protection, they also frequently surrounded them with wooden walls, earth embankments, and ditches.

A Neolithic settlement has been excellently preserved at Skara Brae, in the Orkney Islands off the northern coast of Scotland (fig. 1-17). This one happens to

have been constructed of stone, an abundant building material in this austere, treeless landscape. A huge prehistoric storm buried this seaside village under a layer of sand. Another freak storm brought it to light again in 1850. The ruins thus exposed to view present a vivid picture of Neolithic life in the far north. Among the utensils found in these Orkney structures are stone cooking pots, a whalebone basin, a stone mortar for grinding, and pottery with incised decoration. Comparison of these artifacts with objects from sites farther south and laboratory analysis of the village's organic refuse date the settlement at Skara Brae to about 3100–2600 BCE, indicating that it lay buried for well over 4,000 years.

The village consists of a compact cluster of dwellings linked together by covered passageways. Each of the houses is in the shape of a square with rounded corners. The largest one measures 20 by 21 feet, the smallest 13 by 14 feet. Their walls were formed of layers of flat stones, with each layer, or **course**, projecting slightly inward over the one below. This type of construction is called **corbeling**. In some structures such inward-sloping walls come together at the top in what is known as a **corbel vault**, but at Skara Brae they stopped short of meeting, and the remaining open space was covered with hides or turf. There are smaller corbel-vaulted rooms within the main walls of some of the houses that may have been used for storage. One room, possibly a latrine, has a drain leading out under its wall.

The houses of Skara Brae were well equipped with space-saving built-in furniture. In the room shown (fig. 1-18), a large rectangular hearth with a stone seat at one end occupies the center of the space. Rectangular stone beds, some of them engraved with simple ornaments, stand against the walls on each side of the hearth. These boxlike beds would probably have been filled with heather "mattresses" and covered with warm furs. In the left corner is a sizable storage niche built into the thick outside wall. Smaller storage niches were provided over

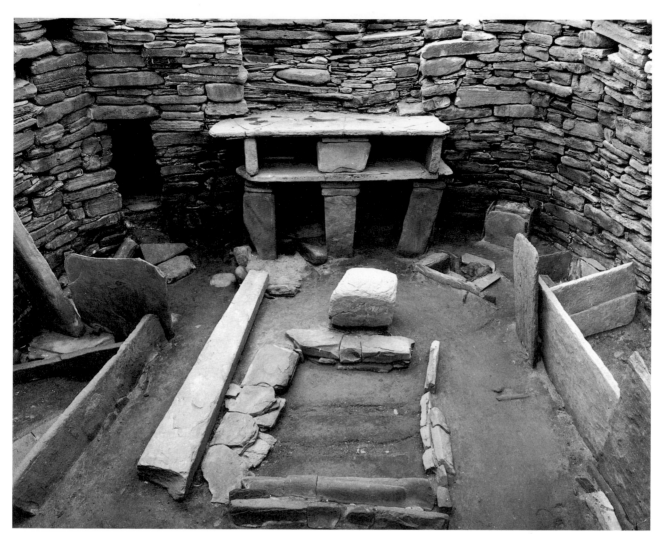

1-18. House interior, Skara Brae (house 7 in fig. 1 17)

each of the beds. Stone tanks lined with clay to make them watertight are partly sunk into the floor. These were probably used as containers for live bait, for it is clear that the people at Skara Brae were skilled fisherfolk.

On the back wall is a two-shelf cabinet that is a splendid example of what is known as **post-and-lintel construction.** In this structural system, two or more vertical elements (posts) are used to support a bridging horizontal one (lintel). The principle has been used throughout history, not only for structures as simple as these shelves but also in huge stone monuments like Stonehenge (see fig. 1-23) and the temples of Egypt (Chapter 3) and Greece (Chapter 5).

Ceremonial and Tomb Architecture. In western and northern Europe, Neolithic people commonly erected ceremonial structures and tombs using huge stones. In some cases they had to transport these great stones over long distances. The monuments thus created are examples of what is known as megalithic architecture, the descriptive term derived from the Greek word roots for large (mega-) and stone (lithos). Architecture formed of such massive elements testifies to a more complex, stratified society than any encountered before. Only strong leaders could have assembled and maintained the required labor force. Skilled engineers were needed to devise methods for shaping, transporting, and aligning the stones. Finally, powerful religious figures must have been involved, identifying the society's need for such structures and dictating their design. The accomplishments of the builders of these monuments are all the more impressive considering the short life expectancy of the time. It was uncommon for anyone to survive past the age of thirty. As one anthropologist has noted, these imposing structures were the work of teenagers.

Elaborate megalithic tombs first appeared in the Neolithic period. Some were built for single burials, others as mausoleums consisting of multiple burial chambers. The simplest type of megalithic tomb was the **dolmen,** built on the post-and-lintel principle. The tomb chamber was formed of huge upright stones supporting one or more tablelike rocks, or **capstones.** The structure was then mounded over with smaller rocks and dirt to form what is called a **cairn.** A more imposing structure was the **passage grave,** which was entered by one or more narrow, stone-lined passageways into a large room at the cairn's center (see "Elements of Architecture," page 53).

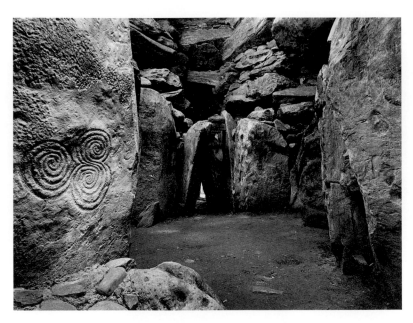

1-19. Tomb interior with corbeling and engraved stones, Newgrange,
Ireland. c. 3000–2500 BCE

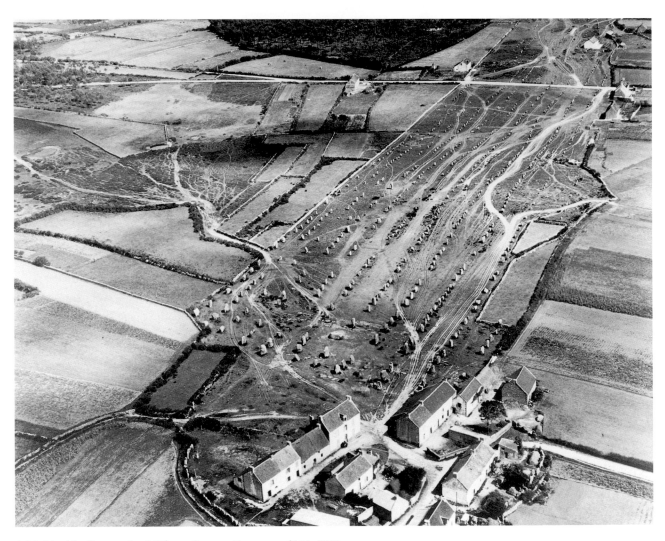

1-20. Menhir alignments at Ménec, Carnac, France. c. 4250–3750 BCE

One legend of Celtic Brittany explains the origin of the Carnac menhirs quite graphically. It relates that a defeated army retreating toward the sea found no ships waiting to carry it to safety. When the desperate warriors turned around and took up their battle stations in preparation for a fight to the death, they were miraculously transformed into stone. Another legend claims that the stones were invading Roman soldiers who were "petrified" in their tracks by a local saint named Cornely.

ELEMENTS OF ARCHITECTURE
Dolmen and Passage Grave

The **dolmen** was made up of a **post-and-lintel** frame of large, stone slabs "roofed" with one or more **capstones**, then mounded over with dirt and smaller stones called a **cairn**. This construction created a small, fully enclosed burial chamber.

Today, most dolmens are exposed, giving the erroneous impression that they were built as open-air graves.

The **passage grave** was a burial chamber, also covered over by an earth-and-pebble cairn, that was entered through a long, slab-lined passageway or passageways. The central space was sometimes segmented into several chambers and usually held multiple burials.

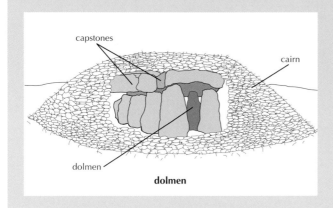

dolmen

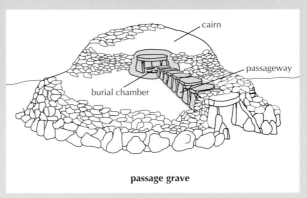

passage grave

At Newgrange, in Ireland, an elaborate passage grave (fig. 1-19) was discovered in a cairn that originally stood some 44 feet tall and measured about 280 feet in diameter. The mound was built of sod and river pebbles and was set off by a circle of decorated standing stones around its perimeter. Its passageway, 62 feet long and lined with standing stones, leads into a three-part chamber with a corbeled vault rising to a height of 19 feet. The stones at the entrance and along the passageway are engraved with linear designs, mainly rings, spirals, and diamond shapes. These patterns must have been marked out using strings or compasses, then carved by pecking at the rock surface with tools made of antlers. Such large and richly decorated structures did more than honor the distinguished dead; they were truly public architecture that fostered communal pride and a group identity. As is the case with the elaborate mausoleums and funerary monuments being built today, their function was both practical and symbolic.

Many megalithic structures were not tombs at all but ritual centers that must have attracted the people of an entire region. In the Carnac district on the south coast of Brittany, in France, thousands of **menhirs**, or single vertical megaliths, were set up sometime between 4250 and 3750 BCE. Over 3,000 of them still stand in a two-mile stretch near Ménec (fig. 1-20). Each of these squared-off stones weighs several tons. They were placed in either circular patterns known as **cromlechs** or straight rows known as **alignments**. There are thirteen rows of alignments, their stones graduated in height from about 3 feet on the eastern end to upward of 13 feet toward the west. The east-west orientation of the alignments suggests some connection to the movement of the sun. Neolithic farming peoples, whose well-being depended on a recurring cycle of sowing, growing, harvesting, and fallow

seasons, would have had every reason to worship the sun and do all they could to assure its regular motion through the year. The menhirs at Carnac may well have marked off an established procession route for large groups of people celebrating public rites. It is also possible that they were points of reference for careful observation of the sun, moon, and stars.

Of all the megalithic monuments in Europe, the one that has stirred the imagination of the public most strongly is Stonehenge, on Salisbury Plain in southern England (figs. 1-21, 1-22, 1-23). A **henge** is a circle of stones or posts, often surrounded by a ditch with built-up embankments. Laying out such circles with accuracy would have posed no particular problem. Their architects likely relied on the human compass, a simple but effective surveying method that persisted well into modern times. All that is required is a length of cord either cut or knotted to mark the desired radius of the circle. A person holding one end of the cord is stationed in the center; a co-worker, holding the other end and keeping the cord taut, steps off the circle's circumference.

Stonehenge is not the largest such circle from the Neolithic period, but because it was repeatedly reworked to incorporate new elements, it is one of the most complicated megalithic sites. It must have had, or developed, an extraordinary importance in its region. It is the product of at least four major building phases between about 2750 and 1500 BCE. In the earliest stage, its builders dug a deep, circular ditch, placing the excavated material on the inside rim to form an embankment more than 6 feet high. Digging through the turf, they exposed the chalk substratum characteristic of this part of England, thus creating a brilliant white circle about 330 feet in diameter. An "avenue" from the henge toward the northeast led well outside the embankment to a pointed sarsen megalith—sarsen is a

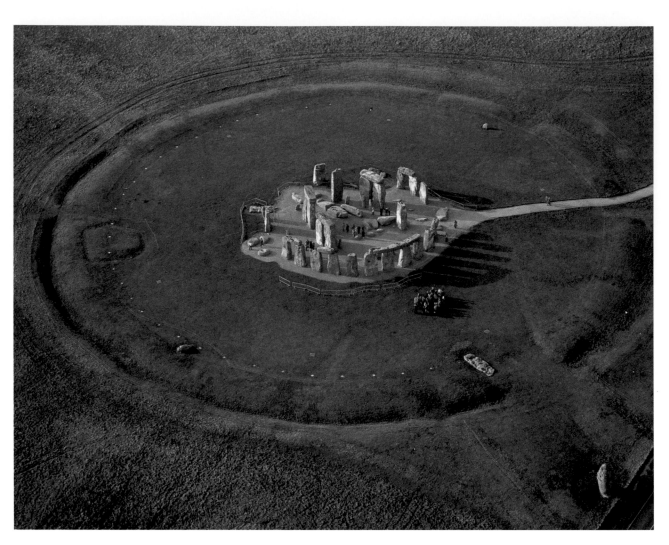

1-21. Stonehenge, Salisbury Plain, Wiltshire, England. c. 2750–1500 BCE

gray sandstone—brought from a quarry 23 miles away. Today, this so-called heel stone, tapered toward the top and weighing about 35 tons, stands about 16 feet high. The ditches and embankments bordering the approach avenue were constructed somewhat later, at the same time as the huge megalithic monument we see today.

By about 2100 BCE, Stonehenge included all of the internal elements reflected in the drawing shown here (fig. 1-22). Dominating the center was a horseshoe-shaped arrangement of five sandstone trilithons, or pairs of upright stones topped by lintels. The one at the middle stood considerably taller than the rest, rising to a height of 24 feet, and its lintel was more than 15 feet long and 3 feet thick. This group was surrounded by the so-called sarsen circle, a ring of sandstone uprights weighing up to 50 tons each and standing 20 feet tall. This circle, 106 feet in diameter, was capped by a continuous lintel. The uprights were tapered slightly toward the top, and the gently curved lintel sections were secured by mortise and tenon joints, a conical projection from one piece fitting into a hole in the next. Just inside the sarsen circle was once a ring of bluestones—worked blocks of a bluish dolerite found only in the mountains of southern Wales, 150 miles away. Why the builders of Stonehenge felt it necessary to use specifically this type of stone is one of

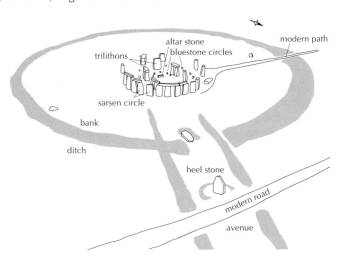

1-22. Diagram of Stonehenge, showing elements discussed here

the many mysteries of Stonehenge. Clearly the stones were highly prized, for centuries later, about 1500 BCE, they were reused to form a smaller horseshoe inside the trilithons that encloses the so-called altar stone.

Whoever stood at the exact center of Stonehenge on the morning of the summer solstice 4,000 years ago would have seen the sun rise directly over the heel stone (fig. 1-23). The observer could then warn people that the

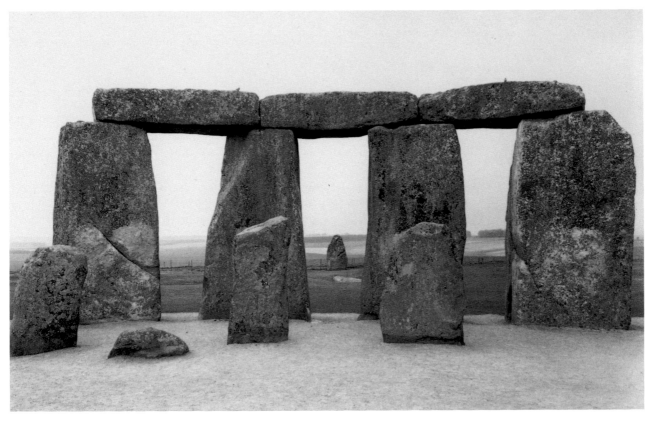

1-23. *Within Circle, Looking Toward Heel Stone, Stonehenge, 1967.* Photograph by Paul Caponigro

Caponigro, a great enthusiast of megalithic architecture, spent twenty years photographing prehistoric structures all over Europe. He admirably captures the harmonious grace and simplicity of Stonehenge by positioning his camera directly above the large "altar stone" at the heart of the complex and aiming it toward the heel stone outside the monument's perimeter. It is from this spot that a dawn visitor to the site at the time of the summer solstice can see the sun rise directly over that distant marker.

sun's strength would shortly begin to wane, that the days would grow shorter and the nights cooler until the country was once more gripped by winter.

Through the ages, many theories have been advanced to explain Stonehenge. (Most of these explanations say more about the times in which they were put forward than about Stonehenge.) In the Middle Ages, it was thought that the monument had been built by Merlin, the magician of the King Arthur legend. Later, the site was incorrectly associated with the religious practices of the Druids. It continues to challenge the ingenuity of scholars even today. Because its orientation is clearly related to the movement of the sun, some think it may have been a kind of observatory, with the help of which prehistoric astronomers could track any number of cosmic events. Anthropologists suspect that the structure was an important site for major public ceremonies, possibly planting or harvest rituals. Whatever its original function may have been, Stonehenge continues to fascinate the public. Crowds of people still gather there at midsummer to thrill to its mystery. Why such megalithic structures were built may never be discovered, but the technology developed for building them was a major advance, one that made possible, among other things, a new kind of sculpture.

Sculpture and Ceramics

Having learned how to cut and transport massive blocks of stone, Neolithic sculptors were capable of carving large, freestanding stone figures. Their menhir statues, dating from between 3500 and 2000 BCE, stood 3 to 4 feet high, and all were carved in a similar way. Elements of the human figure reduced to near-geometric forms were incised on all four sides of a single upright block. Faces were usually suggested by a vertical ridge for the nose and a horizontal one for the browline. Rarely is there any indication of a mouth. Incised linear patterns on the sides and backs of such figures have been interpreted as ribs and backbones, but it is possible that they were meant to represent elements of ritual costume or body painting. A typical menhir statue is the one of a woman found in Montagnac, in southern France (fig. 1-24). The face is composed of a straight nose, a heavy, continuous brow, and protruding eyes. Above the browline is something resembling a headband. What first appears to be a square jaw and wide, rectangular mouth is actually the outline of a piece of jewelry, probably a necklace with a single bead at the center. The woman's hands are raised to cover her breasts, so that each of her arms has the shape of the letter **U**. A belt encircles her waist. Some

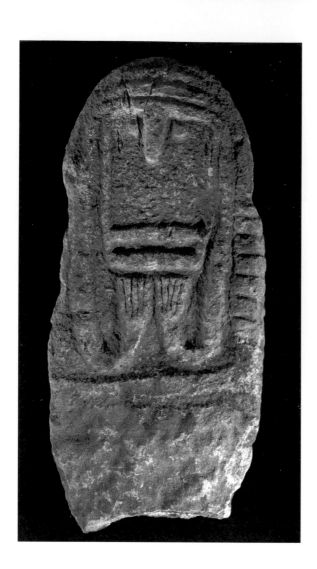

1-24. Menhir statue of a woman, from Montagnac, France. c. 2000 BCE. Limestone, height approx. 33" (85 cm). Muséum d'Histoire Naturelle et Préhistoire, Nîmes

figures of women have no arms or hands—only breasts and a necklace. Men often carry weapons.

In southern France, solitary menhir statues have been discovered on wooded hills and sometimes near tombs or villages. Set on hilly sites, they may have served as "guardians" and signposts for travelers making their way to sacred places. Those in the vicinity of tombs may have been "guardians of the dead." Some female figures found near dwellings are thought to have been household protectors.

Besides working in stone, Neolithic artists also commonly used clay. Their ceramics, whether figures of people and animals or vessels, display a high degree of technical skill and aesthetic imagination. This art required a different kind of conceptual leap. In the sculpture previously discussed, artists created their work out of an existing substance, such as stone, bone, or wood. To produce ceramic works, artists had to combine certain substances with clay—bone ash was a common addition— then subject the objects formed of that mixture to high heat for a period of time, thus creating an entirely new material. Among the ceramic figures discovered at a pottery-production center in the Danube River valley at Cernavoda, Romania, are a seated man and woman who form a most engaging pair (fig. 1-25).

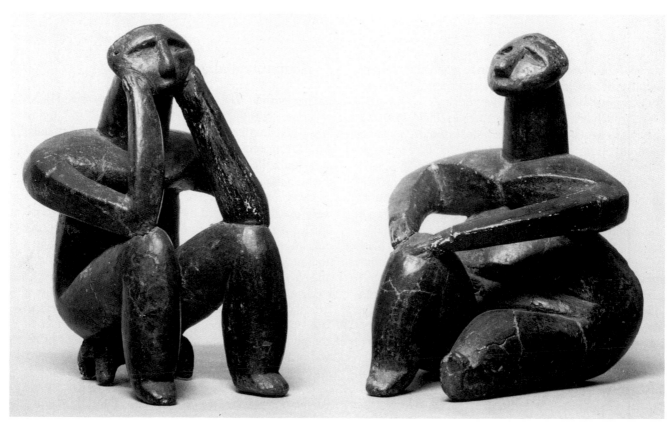

1-25. Figures of a man and a woman, from Cernavoda, Romania. c. 4000–3500 BCE. Ceramic, height 4¹/₂" (11.5 cm). National Museum of Antiquities, Bucharest

TECHNIQUE

POTTERY AND CERAMICS

The terms *pottery* and *ceramics* may be used interchangeably—and often are, which causes some confusion. The word *ceramics* came into use only in the nineteenth century. Because it covers all baked-clay wares, *ceramics* is technically a more inclusive term than *pottery*.

Pottery is all baked-clay **ware** except porcelain, which is at the "high end" of ceramic technology. Raw clay becomes a porous pottery when heated to at least 500° centigrade. It then holds its shape permanently and will not disintegrate in water. Fired at 800° centigrade, pottery is technically known as earthenware. When subjected to temperatures between 1200° and 1400°, certain stone elements in the clay vitrify, or become glassy, and the result is a stronger type of ceramics called stoneware.

Pottery vessels can be formed in several ways. It is possible, though difficult, to raise up the sides from a ball of raw clay. Another method is to coil long rolls of soft, raw clay, stack them on top of each other to form a container, and then smooth them by hand. A third possibility is to simply press the clay over an existing form, a dried gourd for example. By about 4000 BCE, Egyptian potters had developed the potter's wheel, a round, spinning plat-form on which it is relatively simple to produce a uniformly shaped vessel in a very short time.

The potter's wheel appeared in the ancient Near East about 3250 BCE and in China about 3000 BCE. After a pot is formed, it is allowed to dry completely before it is fired. For proper firing, the temperature must be maintained at a relatively uniform level. Low-fired prehistoric pottery is art made at the hearth, but special ovens for firing pottery, called **kilns**, have been discovered at prehistoric sites in Europe dating from as early as 32,000 BCE.

Fragments of low-fired ceramics are the most common artifacts found in excavations of prehistoric settlements. Pottery is relatively fragile, and new vessels are constantly in demand to replace broken ones. Moreover, pottery disintegrates very, very slowly. Pottery fragments, or **potsherds**, serve as a major key in dating lost cultures and reconstructing their living and trading patterns. One of the first ways of decorating pottery was simple incising—scratching lines into the surface of the clay before it was left to dry. By the dawn of the Bronze Age, about 2300 BCE, vessels were produced in a wide variety of specialized forms and decorated with great finesse.

The artist who made them shaped their bodies out of simple cylinders of clay but managed to pose them in ways that make them seem very true to life. The woman, spread-hipped and big-bellied, sits directly on the ground, her hands placed on her raised knee. The man hunkers on a low perch, holding his head in his hands and seemingly lost in contemplation—or at least trying to think, for he looks perplexed. It is easy to imagine the pair next to their hearth, the worker and the worrier. No aura of sacred purpose surrounds these two, despite the fact that they had accompanied their owner to the grave.

One of the unresolved puzzles of prehistory is why people in Europe did not produce pottery vessels much earlier. They understood how to make clay figures as hard as stone by firing them in an oven at high temperatures as early as 32,000 BCE. Yet it was not until about 7000 BCE that they began making vessels using the same technique—some 3,000 years after the first appearance of such vessels in Japan, for instance. Some anthropologists argue that clay is a medium of last resort for vessels. Compared to hollow gourds, wooden bowls, or woven baskets, clay vessels are heavy and quite fragile, and firing them requires a very high level of expertise.

Excellence in ceramics depends upon the degree to which a given vessel combines domestic utility, visual beauty, and fine execution (see "Pottery and Ceramics," above). Much of the surviving Neolithic pottery is so exemplary in this regard that it has been difficult to select only one or two examples for inclusion here. A group of bowls from Denmark, made in the third millennium BCE, provides only a hint of the extraordinary achievements of Neolithic artists working in clay (fig. 1-26). Taking their

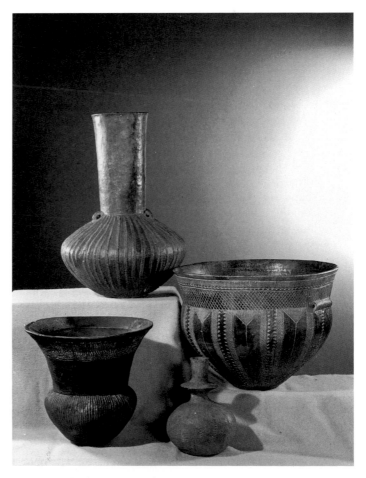

1-26. Vessels, from Denmark. c. 3000–2000 BCE. Ceramic, heights range from 5¾" to 12¼" (14.5 to 31 cm). National Museum, Copenhagen

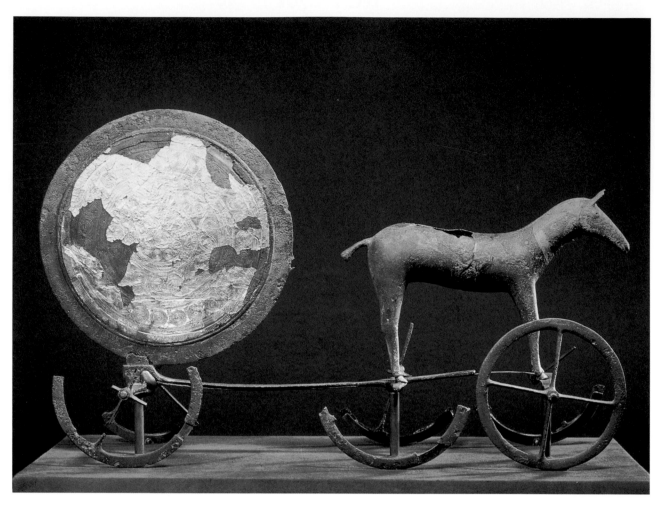

1-27. *Horse and Sun Chariot*, from Trundholm, Zealand, Denmark. c. 1800–1600 BCE. Bronze, length 23¼" (59.2 cm). National Museum, Copenhagen

forms from baskets and bags, the earliest pots were round and pouchlike and had built-in loops so that they could be suspended on cords. The earliest pieces in the illustration are the globular bottle with a collar around its neck (bottom center), a form perhaps inspired by eggs or gourd containers, and the flask with loops (top). Even when potters began making pots with flat bottoms that could stand without tipping, they often added hanging loops as part of the design. Some of the ornamentation of these pots, including hatched engraving and stitchlike patterns, seems to reproduce the texture of the baskets and bags that preceded ceramics as containers. It was also possible to decorate clay vessels by impressing stamps into their surface or scratching it with sticks, shells, or toothed implements. Many of these techniques appear to have been used to decorate the flat-bottomed vase with the wide, flaring top (bottom left), a popular type of container that came to be known as a funnel beaker.

The large engraved bowl (center right), found at Skarpsalling, is considered to be the finest piece of northern Neolithic pottery yet discovered. The potter lightly incised its sides with delicate linear patterns, then rubbed white chalk into them so that they would stand out against the dark body of the bowl—a technique similar to the one called **niello**, used to enhance linear designs incised in metal. Much of the finest art to survive from the Neolithic period is the work of potters; it is an art of the oven and the hearth.

THE BRONZE AGE

Neolithic culture persisted in northern Europe until about 2000 BCE. Metals made their appearance in the region about 2300. In southern Europe and the Aegean, copper, gold, and tin had been mined, worked, and traded even earlier (Chapter 4). Exquisite objects made of bronze—an alloy, or mixture, of tin and copper—are frequently found in the settlements and graves of early northern farming communities, especially in Britain and Scandinavia, where major mining and smelting centers developed. The period that follows the introduction of metalworking is commonly called the Bronze Age.

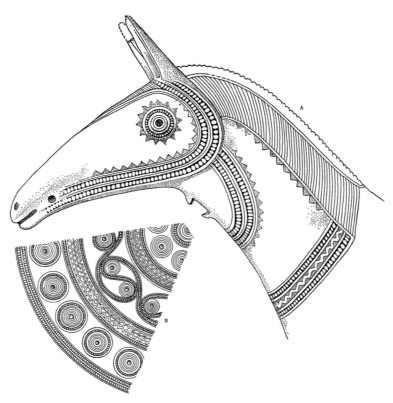

1-28. Schematic drawing of incised designs on unseen side of the *Horse and Sun Chariot* from Trundholm

A remarkable sculpture from the Bronze Age in Scandinavia depicts a wheeled horse pulling a cart laden with a large, upright disk commonly thought to represent the sun (fig. 1-27). The work dates from between 1800 and 1600 BCE and was discovered at what is now Trundholm, in Denmark. Horses had been domesticated in Ukraine by about 4000 BCE, but the first evidence of wheeled chariots and wagons designed to exploit the animals' strength dates from about 2000 BCE. Rock engravings in northern Europe show the sun being drawn through the sky by either an animal or a bird. These may be an indication that there was a widespread sun cult in the region, with special ritual practices. The Trundholm horse and sun cart could have been rolled from place to place in a ritual reenactment of the sun's passage across the sky.

The valuable materials from which the sculpture was made and the great attention devoted to its details attest to its importance. The horse, cart, and sun disk were cast in bronze. After two faults in the casting had been repaired, the horse was given its surface finish, and its head and neck were incised with ornamentation (fig.

1-28). Light striking its eyes turned them into tiny suns. Elaborate and very delicate designs were engraved on its collar and harness. The bronze sun disk, cast in two pieces, was engraved with concentric rings filled with zigzags, circles, spirals, and loops. A thin sheet of beaten gold was then applied to one of the bronze disks and pressed into the incised patterns. Finally, the disks were sealed together by means of an encircling metal band. The patterns on the horse tend to be geometric and rectilinear, but those of the sun disk are continuous and curvilinear, suggestive of the movement of the sun itself.

Much of what we know about prehistoric peoples is based on the art they produced—from the smallest carvings to menhir statues, from cave paintings to household wares. Progress continues to be made toward an understanding of when and how these works were created. We may never know *why* some of them were made. But the remote eras into which they afford us glimpses seem strangely familiar. The sheer artistry and immediacy of the images left by these very early ancestors connect us to them as surely as the earliest written records link us to those who came later.

Ain Ghazal figure
c. 7000–6000

▲ EARLY NEOLITHIC 9000　　　　　　　　　　　▲ ELAM 7000–600

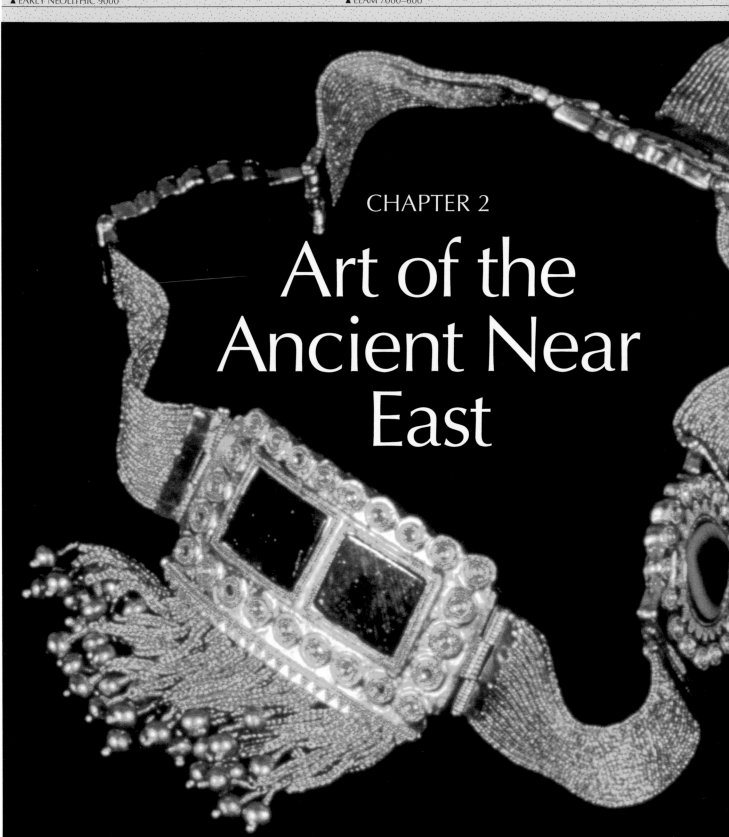

CHAPTER 2

Art of the Ancient Near East

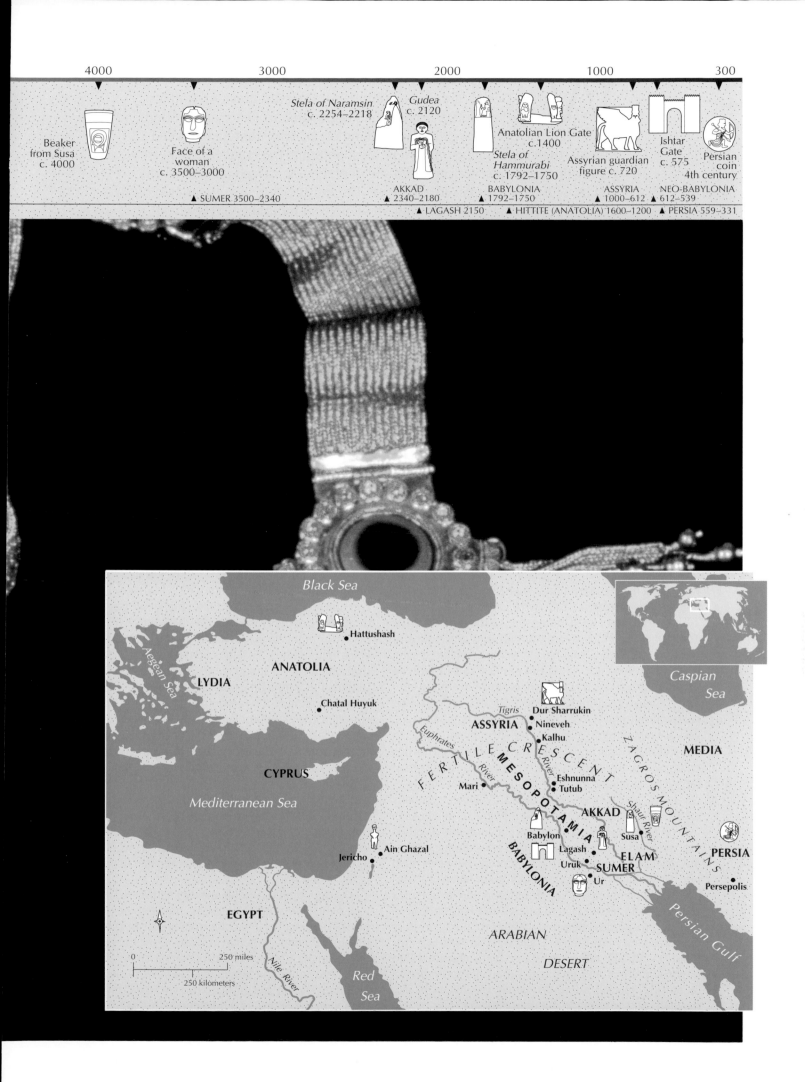

4000   3000   2000   1000   300

Beaker
from Susa
c. 4000

Face of a
woman
c. 3500–3000

Stela of Naramsin
c. 2254–2218

Gudea
c. 2120

Anatolian Lion Gate
c.1400

Stela of
Hammurabi
c. 1792–1750

Assyrian guardian
figure c. 720

Ishtar
Gate
c. 575

Persian
coin
4th century

▲ SUMER 3500–2340

AKKAD
▲ 2340–2180

BABYLONIA
▲ 1792–1750

ASSYRIA
▲ 1000–612

NEO-BABYLONIA
▲ 612–539

▲ LAGASH 2150   ▲ HITTITE (ANATOLIA) 1600–1200   ▲ PERSIA 559–331

Black Sea

Hattushash

ANATOLIA

LYDIA

Chatal Huyuk

Aegean Sea

Caspian
Sea

Tigris

Dur Sharrukin

ASSYRIA

Nineveh

Kalhu

MEDIA

Euphrates

F E R T I L E   C R E S C E N T

Z A G R O S   M O U N T A I N S

CYPRUS

Mediterranean Sea

River

M E S O P O T A M I A

River

Mari

Eshnunna

Tutub

AKKAD

Shaur River

Jericho

Ain Ghazal

Babylon

Lagash

Susa

ELAM

PERSIA

BABYLONIA

Uruk

SUMER

EGYPT

Ur

Persepolis

Nile River

ARABIAN

DESERT

Persian Gulf

0   250 miles

250 kilometers

Red
Sea

When allied forces in the Persian Gulf region launched Operation Desert Storm in January 1991, their air attack on Iraq provoked an outcry from archeologists and art historians around the world. The bombs were not just falling on an army that had invaded Kuwait; they were falling on ancient Mesopotamia, the cradle of Western civilization, the most concentrated site of archeological remains on earth, places with fabled names like Nineveh, Ur, and Babylon. As one archeologist noted, "Almost all of Iraq is an archeological mound . . . . There are half a million archeological sites from all periods. About 40,000 or 50,000 of them are considered quite important. Between 100 and 200 of them were ancient capital cities" (William H. Honan, "Attacks on Iraq Worry and Divide Archeologists," *The New York Times,* February 9, 1991). Some of the most important of these ancient sites have not yet been located; others have been found but not excavated. Ironically, the great "archeological mound" is formed of accumulated layers of vanquished and vanished cultures, for people have been fighting over this area almost since the first settlements formed there.

THE FERTILE CRESCENT

Well before settled farming communities arose in Europe and Egypt, agriculture emerged in the ancient Near East in an area long referred to as the Fertile Crescent. Geographically, the ancient Near East encompasses Anatolia (roughly modern Turkey), Mesopotamia (Iraq today), and Persia (Iran). The "crescent" rose along the Mediterranean coast through modern Jordan, Israel, Lebanon, and Syria, arched into central Turkey, and descended along the fertile plains of the Tigris and Euphrates rivers through Iraq and a slice of western Iran to the Persian Gulf. Neolithic culture began here about 9000 BCE, when the earliest settled farming communities arose, first in the hills above rivers and later in river valleys. Farming spread from this region to the east and northwest and reached Europe by about 5000 BCE. Mesopotamia's relatively harsh climate, prone to both drought and flood, may have contributed to this change, as early agriculturists cooperated to construct large-scale systems for controlling their water supply.

In the Near East, agricultural villages gradually evolved into cities, which anthropologists distinguish from villages as having a large population and a settled area clearly separated from its rural surroundings. Trade among distant communities increased. Between 4000 and 3000 BCE, a major cultural shift took place in Mesopotamia. Beginning in southern Mesopotamia, complex societies with hierarchies of priests and kings began to appear. Prosperous cities and their surrounding territory developed into city-states, each with its own government. Eventually these city-states were absorbed into larger kingdoms and empires. Urban life gave rise to increasing specialization. To satisfy the needs of city dwellers and to provide goods for export, city people began to develop skills besides those for farming. Workshops for milling flour and making bricks, pottery, cloth, carpets, and metalware sprang up, and the construction of temples and palaces kept builders and artists busy.

The peoples of the ancient Near East were polytheistic; they worshiped numerous gods and goddesses, attributing to them power over human activities and the forces of nature. The importance of the various deities depended on the area of life they controlled. Each city had one special protective deity, and people believed the dominance of the city depended on its deity's being more powerful than the gods and goddesses of surrounding cities. The names of deities changed over time and as they spread from language to language. For example, Inanna, the Sumerian goddess of fertility, love, and war, was equivalent to the Babylonians' Ishtar, the Egyptians' Isis, the Greeks' Aphrodite, and the Romans' Venus.

A class of religious specialists emerged to control rituals and sacred sites. Large **temple complexes**—clusters of religious, administrative, and service buildings—developed in each city as centers of worship and also as thriving businesses. The religious establishment administered substantial property, received a portion of the harvest, and engaged in various other commercial ventures. Religious and political power were closely interrelated, and both women and men had religious and political authority.

Mesopotamia's wealth and agricultural resources, as well as its few natural defenses, made its peoples vulnerable to repeated invasions from hostile neighbors and to internal conflicts between rivals. Over the centuries, the balance of power in Mesopotamia shifted between north and south and between local powers and outside invaders. The earliest group to rise was the Sumerians in the southern region. For a brief period they were eclipsed by the Akkadians, their neighbors to the north. When

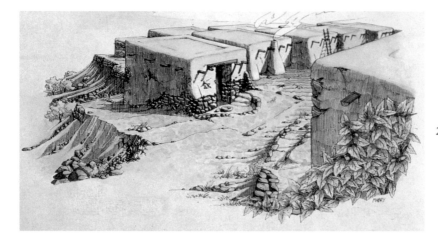

2-1. Reconstruction drawings of houses at Ain Ghazal, Jordan. c. 7200–5000 BCE

The top drawing shows one anthropologist's view of what the village looked like; below are four stages of construction.

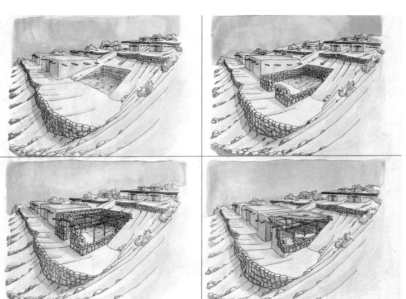

invaders from farther north in turn conquered the Akkadians, the Sumerians regained power locally. The Babylonians were the next to ascend to dominance in the south. Later, the center of power shifted to the Assyrians in the north, then back again to Babylonia, called Neo-Babylonia. Throughout this time, important cultural centers arose outside the margins of Mesopotamia as well, such as the Hittite kingdom in Anatolia, Elam on the plain between the Tigris River and the Zagros Mountains to the east, and Persia, east of Elam. Beginning in the sixth century BCE, the Achaemenid Persians, a nomadic people from the mountains of modern-day Iran, forged an empire that included not only Mesopotamia but the entire Near East and beyond.

The art produced in the ancient Near East was undoubtedly influenced by these broad political events. Interior and exterior trade relations, which determined the exchange of styles, techniques, and materials, had a greater impact on it, however, as did the dictates and needs of religion. The evolution of political and religious powers, specialization of roles, and cultural blending through trade and conquest that culminated in the mighty Persian Empire had begun thousands of years earlier, when people had begun to come together in the first Neolithic cities.

EARLY NEOLITHIC CITIES

Jericho, one of the earliest cities in the Near East, is located in the West Bank territory at the site of a natural spring where humans have lived for nearly 12,000 years. Here, as throughout the ancient Near East, where wood and stone were scarce, people turned to the earth beneath their feet for construction materials. From the ninth millennium BCE on, they molded bricks out of clay, then hardened them in the sun. These "mud bricks" were quite durable in the dry climate and provided sturdy, well-insulated shelter. Sometime between 8000 and 7000 BCE, Jericho was home to about 2,000 people living in mud-brick houses protected by a stone wall 5 feet thick and 12 to 17 feet high. The site covered 6 acres, an enormous size for its time.

An even larger Neolithic city was discovered accidentally during road construction just outside Amman, Jordan, in 1981. Ain Ghazal ("spring of the gazelles"), dated from about 7200 to 5000 BCE, occupied 30 acres on a slope that was laboriously shaped into terraces stabilized by stone retaining walls. Its houses had double stone walls with a core of dirt and pebbles, probably sealed with a layer of mud (fig. 2-1). On the interior, regularly spaced wood posts supported roof beams, which are believed to have been

PARALLELS

Dominant Culture	Years	Near East	World
Early Neolithic	c. 9000 BCE	Jericho; Ain Ghazal; Chatal Huyuk	
Elam	c. 7000–600 BCE		
			4000–3000 BCE Potter's wheel (Egypt)
Sumer	c. 3500–2340 BCE	Earliest pictographs; wheeled carts; potter's wheel; White	
	c. 2150–2030 BCE	Temple ziggurat; bronze tools and weapons; *Gilgamesh* epic	**3000–2000 BCE** World population about 100 million; hieroglyphic writing (Egypt); potter's wheel (China); first pottery in Americas (Ecuador); Stonehenge (England); Pyramids at Giza (Egypt)
Akkad	c. 2340–2180 BCE		
Lagash	c. 2150 BCE		
			2000–1000 BCE
Babylonia	c. 1792–1750 BCE	*Stela of Hammurabi*	Shang dynasty (China); Olmec civilization (Mesoamerica)
Hittite (Anatolia)	c. 1600–1200 BCE	Iron tools and weapons	
Assyria	c. 1000–612 BCE		**1000–336 BCE**
Neo-Babylonia	c. 612–539 BCE	Ishtar Gate	First Olympian Games (Greece); birth of Siddhartha Gautama, founder of Buddhism (Nepal); Parthenon (Greece);
Persia	c. 559–331 BCE	Persepolis built; Alexander the Great conquers Persia	Alexander the Great becomes king of Macedonia

covered by thickly woven branches and grasses sealed with mud. The lower walls, support posts, and floors were covered with plaster, a mixture of burned limestone ash and sand that dried quickly into a hard, water-resistant surface. These houses must have resembled the adobe pueblos that native peoples of the American Southwest began to build more than 7,000 years later.

Rather than expand the city beyond the safety and convenience of the original terraces, the people of Ain Ghazal met their growing need for space by reworking existing houses—dividing large rooms into smaller ones, adding storage pits, and enlarging hearths. As in other Neolithic settlements, the family dead were buried in graves below the floors around the hearths. Evidence from these graves suggests that infant mortality was high but that about a fifth of the population lived to be older than fifty.

Among the objects recovered from Ain Ghazal are plaster containers and painted plaster figures up to 3 feet tall (fig. 2-2). Sculptors molded the figures by applying wet plaster to frames of twigs and grasses bound together in the shape of the human form. Inset cowrie shells formed the eyes, and small dots of the black, tarlike substance bitumen—which Near Eastern artists used frequently—formed the pupils. These statues may have been related to ancestor worship, possibly practiced at this and other nearby early Neolithic sites. Because the figures show individual characteristics, they seem to memorialize particular people. The feet of one figure, for example, have six toes, more likely a deliberate representation of a rare genetic trait than a slipup by the sculptor.

Although agriculture appears to have been the economic mainstay of these new permanent communities, other specialized activities, such as manufacturing and trade, were also important. Chatal Huyuk, a sizable city in Anatolia occupied from about 6500 to 5500 BCE, developed a thriving trade in obsidian, a rare, black volcanic glass that was used from Paleolithic into modern times for making sharp blades.

The inhabitants of Chatal Huyuk lived in densely clustered single-story buildings grouped around shared courtyards, which were used as garbage dumps. The cities were easy to defend because they had no streets or open plazas and were protected with continuous, unbroken exterior walls. People moved around by crossing from rooftop to rooftop, entering houses through openings in their roofs. Many of the interior spaces were elaborately decorated and are assumed to be shrines. Walls

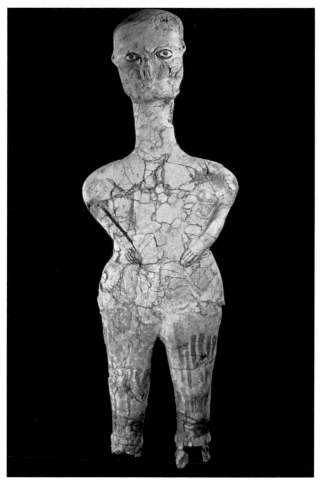

2-2. Figure, from Ain Ghazal, Jordan. c. 7000–6000 BCE. Clay plaster with cowrie shell, bitumen, and paint, height approx. 35" (90 cm). National Museum, Amman, Jordan

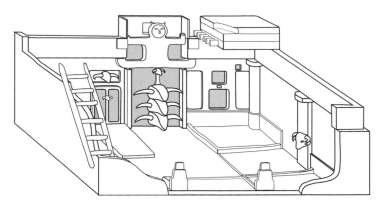

2-3. Composite reconstruction drawing of a shrine room at Chatal Huyuk, Turkey. c. 6500–5500 BCE

Many ancient Near Eastern cities still lie undiscovered. In most cases an archeological site in a region is signaled by a large mound—known locally as a *tell*, *tepe*, or *huyuk*—that represents the accumulated debris of generations of human habitation. When properly excavated, such mounds yield concrete evidence about the people who inhabited them. Valuable scientific information is lost when treasure hunters, who have no interest in the context in which they find things, loot sites for artifacts to sell on the international art market. To them, an object from an unknown context is just an object. Even scientific excavation destroys context, and subsequent investigators are forced to rely on the excavators' detailed records. This is especially true at Chatal Huyuk, which was reburied after it was excavated in the 1950s.

had bold geometric designs, painted animal scenes, actual animal skulls and horns, and three-dimensional shapes resembling breasts and horned animals. On some walls, women were shown giving birth to bulls. In one chamber, a leopard-headed woman—portrayed in a high-arched wall area above three large, projecting bulls' heads—braces herself as she gives birth to a ram (fig. 2-3). Although this dramatic image suggests worship of a fertility goddess, any such interpretation is risky because so little is known about the culture.

Like other early Near Eastern settlements, Chatal Huyuk seems to have been abandoned suddenly, for unknown reasons, and never reoccupied. The concentration of people and resources in such communities nevertheless represented a step toward the larger and more complex city-states that were to emerge in Mesopotamia and become usual in the ancient Near East.

SUMER First cities, then city-states, developed between about 3500 and 2800 BCE along the rivers of southern Mesopotamia, and the cities in this region are known collectively as Sumer. The inhabitants of this region had migrated from the north, but their origins are otherwise obscure.

The Sumerians have been credited with many "firsts": inventing the wagon wheel and the plow, casting objects in copper and bronze, and—perhaps the Sumerians' greatest contribution to later civilizations—inventing a system of writing between 3300 and 3000 BCE. This method used a **cuneiform** ("wedge-shaped") script impressed into clay tablets with a **stylus** (writing instrument) and was developed by wealthy temples to keep business records (see "Cuneiform Writing," page 66). Thousands of Sumerian tablets painstakingly translated by modern scholars document the gradual evolution of not only writing but also arithmetic, another tool necessary for commerce. They also show the emergence of an organized system of justice with written law codes and the world's first written literature (see "Sumerian Literature," page 67).

The Sumerians' most notable contribution to architecture was the **ziggurat**, a stepped pyramidal structure with a temple or shrine on top. The first such structures were the result of repeated rebuilding at a sacred site, with rubble from one structure serving as the foundation for the next. Elevating religious sites on platforms originally may have been a way to protect shrines from flooding. Whatever their origin, these sacred structures

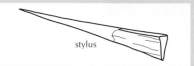

CUNEIFORM WRITING

The Sumerians developed the earliest known system of writing in the late third millennium BCE, apparently for the purpose of keeping agricultural records. The earliest preserved tablets date to around 3300 BCE and represent an accounting system for food and other products traded at Uruk. The symbols on these thin clay slabs are **pictographs**, simple pictures that represent a thing or a concept. The head of a bull, for example, represents "bull." These pictographs were incised in the moist clay with a pointed tool. Between 2900 and 2400 BCE, the symbols evolved from simple pictures into phonograms—representations of the sounds of syllables in the Sumerian language—thus becoming a true writing system. During the same centuries, scribes adopted a **stylus** with one triangular, wedge end and one pointed end that could be pressed rapidly and repeatedly into a wet clay tablet to create the symbols, or characters, now increasingly abstract. Early modern scholars termed the ancient writing of Mesopotamia **cuneiform**, from the Latin words for "wedge-shaped," after the wedge-shaped marks made by the stylus.

The illustration here shows several examples of the shift from pictograph to cuneiform writing. The drawing of a bowl, which means "bread" and "food" and dates from about 3100 BCE, had been reduced by about 2400 BCE to a four-stroke sign, and by about 700 BCE to a highly abstract vertical arrangement of strokes. Combined with the pictograph and, later, cuneiform sign for head, the composite sign came to mean "to eat."

Cuneiform writing was a difficult skill, and few people in ancient Mesopotamia mastered it. Selected children attended schools where they learned to read and write by copying their teachers' lessons. Clay exercise tablets have been excavated with a teacher's sample on one side and a student's efforts on the other. Only boys attended schools, but a small number of girls did learn to read and write, probably by being tutored at home. One of the fascinating things these ancient tablets reveal is that some 4,000 years ago there were textile businesses—concerned with both weaving and export—organized and operated by women entrepreneurs.

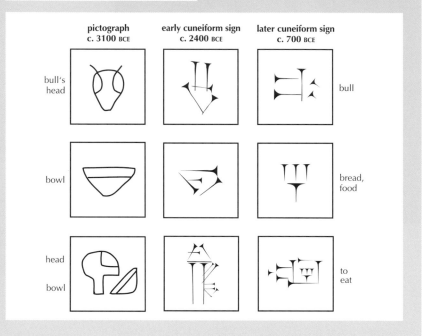

towering above the flat plain proclaimed the wealth, prestige, and stability of a city's rulers and glorified its protective gods. Ziggurats functioned symbolically, too, as lofty bridges between the earth and the heavens—a meeting place for humans and their gods. They were given names such as "House of the Mountain" and "Bond between Heaven and Earth," and temples were known as "waiting rooms" because the priests and priestesses waited there for the gods and goddesses to reveal themselves. Ziggurats were impressive not because of size alone but also because their exterior surfaces were decorated with elaborate patterns of colored clay mosaics and reliefs. The gods would have been pleased with all this handiwork, it was said, because they abhorred laziness in their people.

There were two large temple complexes at Uruk (modern Warka, Iraq), the first independent Sumerian city-state. One complex was dedicated to Inanna, the goddess of fertility, and the other probably to the sky god Anu, another major deity. The Anu Ziggurat was built up in stages over the centuries until it ultimately rose to a height of about 40 feet. Around 3100 BCE, a temple was erected on top that modern archeologists refer to as the White Temple because it was made of white-washed brick (fig. 2-4). This now-ruined structure was laid out as a simple rectangle oriented to the points of the compass. An off-center doorway on one of the long sides led into a large chamber containing a raised platform and altar; smaller spaces opened off this main chamber.

Many courtyards and interior walls in both the Inanna and the Anu compounds were decorated in a technique apparently invented at Uruk, the so-called **cone mosaic** (see "Cone Mosaic," page 68). Thousands of colored cones—shaped stone or baked clay—were pressed like thumbtacks into the wet plaster walls, their flat "heads" creating shimmering, multicolored designs. The technique was extremely labor intensive, but cone mosaics were exceptionally beautiful and durable.

About a thousand years after the completion of the White Temple, the people of Ur (modern Muqaiyir), a city along the Euphrates south of Uruk, built a ziggurat dedicated to the moon god Nanna, also called Sin, that illustrates the mature ziggurat form (fig. 2-5). Although

SUMERIAN LITERATURE Among the tens of thousands of cuneiform tablets excavated thus far in Sumer, only a small number—fewer than 6,000, containing about 30,000 lines of text—record religious myths, heroic tales, legendary histories, hymns, songs of mourning, and so-called wisdom texts, consisting of essays, debates, proverbs, and fables. These make up the world's oldest written literature, and they tell us much about Sumerian beliefs. Most are written as poetry, and some may have been performed with music.

One group of stories and hymns concerns the goddess Inanna. In one of these, Inanna, a young, untried upstart from Uruk, decides to go to Eridu, a city to the south of Uruk, to visit Enki, the god of wisdom.

> Enki and Inanna drank beer together.
> They drank more beer together.
> They drank more and more beer together.
> With their bronze vessels filled to overflowing,
> With the vessels of Urash,
> Mother of the Earth,
> They toasted each other; they challenged each other.
>
> Enki, swaying with drink, toasted Inanna:
> "In the name of my power!
> In the name of my holy shrine!
> To my daughter Inanna I shall give
> The high priesthood!
> Godship!
> The noble, enduring crown!
> The throne of kingship!"
>
> Inanna replied:
> "I take them!"

Enki toasts Inanna another thirteen times, each time bestowing upon her more of his special powers, and each time she accepts his gifts. Only after Inanna has gathered all eighty of his powers into her boat and sailed away does the drink-crazed old god realize what he has done. Desperate, he sends a series of supernatural forces after the retreating boat, but each time Inanna's servant fights them off. Inanna eventually enters Uruk's city gate amid much rejoicing and triumphantly presents her new divine powers, one by one, to her people. Enki and the city of Eridu are forced to acknowledge the glory of Inanna's Uruk, and all proceed to enjoy peace and prosperity. (Text and summary adapted from Wolkstein and Kramer, pages 12–27.)

The best-known literary work of ancient Mesopotamia is the *Epic of Gilgamesh*. Its origins are Sumerian, but only fragments of the Sumerian version survive. The fullest version, written in Akkadian, was found in the library of the Assyrian king Assurbanipal (ruled 669–c. 627 BCE) in Nineveh (modern Kuyunjik, Iraq). It recounts the adventures of Gilgamesh, a legendary Sumerian king of Uruk, and his companion Enkidu. When Enkidu dies, a despondent Gilgamesh sets out to find the secret of eternal life from Utnapishtim and his wife, the only survivors of a great flood sent by the gods to destroy the world, and the only people to whom the gods ever granted eternal life. Gilgamesh ultimately learns to accept his mortality.

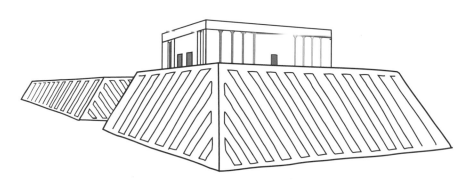

2-4. Reconstruction drawing of the Anu Ziggurat and White Temple, Uruk (modern Warka, Iraq). c. 3100 BCE

2-5. Nanna Ziggurat, Ur (modern Muqaiyir, Iraq). c. 2100–2050 BCE

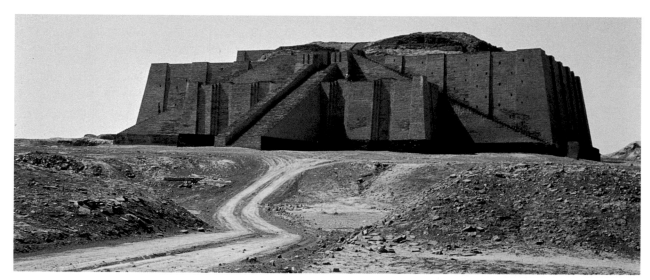

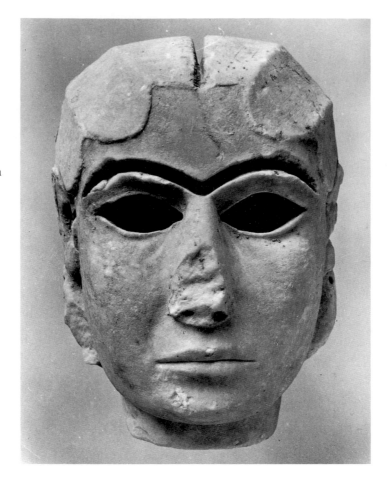

2-6. Face of a woman, from Uruk (modern Warka, Iraq). c. 3500–3000 BCE. Marble, height approx. 8" (20.3 cm). Iraq Museum, Baghdad

TECHNIQUE
CONE MOSAIC

To decorate wall surfaces and other architectural elements, Sumerians at Uruk devised the **cone mosaic**. The technique used small, cone-shaped cylinders of colored stone or baked clay that were pushed into a thick layer of wet plaster. The cones were closely spaced in rows to form bands of angular, decorative patterns such as zigzag, diamond, herringbone, and flame. Clay cones have been excavated in other sites throughout Mesopotamia, which suggests that other peoples adopted the Sumerian technique.

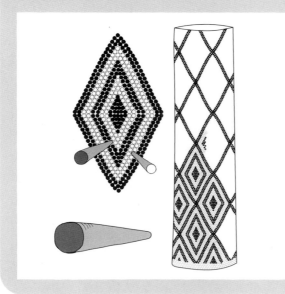

located on the site of an earlier temple, this imposing mud-brick structure was elevated by design, not as the result of successive rebuildings. Its base is a rectangle 190 by 130 feet with three sets of stairs converging at an imposing entrance gate atop the first platform. Each platform is angled outward from top to base, probably to prevent rainwater from forming puddles and eroding the mud-brick pavement. The first two levels of the ziggurat and their retaining walls have been reconstructed in recent times. Little remains of the upper level and the temple.

Sculpture of this period was associated with religion, and large statues were commonly placed in temples as objects of devotion. A striking marble face from Uruk may once have been part of such an image (fig. 2-6). Beardless, it may represent a goddess. With its compelling empty-eyed stare and sensitively rendered features, this lifesize face demonstrates the skill attained by Sumerian sculptors at roughly the time the White Temple was being built. The marble face would have been attached to a wooden head on a full-size wooden body. Now stripped of the plaited gold hair or flowing wig with which it was originally adorned, and lacking the **inlay**, that is, set-in decoration for the brows and eyes—probably shell for the whites and deep blue lapis lazuli for the pupils—and the paint on the lips and skin, the face is reduced to a stark, white mask.

A tall, carved, alabaster vase found near the ruins of a temple at Uruk almost certainly served some religious

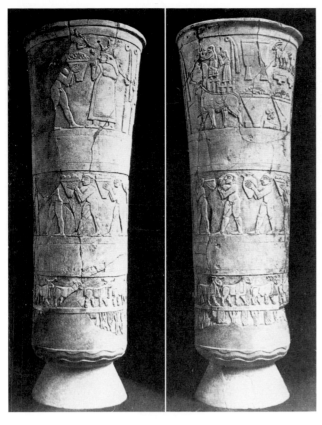

2-7. Carved vase (both sides), from Uruk (modern Warka, Iraq). c. 3500–3000 BCE. Alabaster, height 36" (91 cm). Iraq Museum, Baghdad

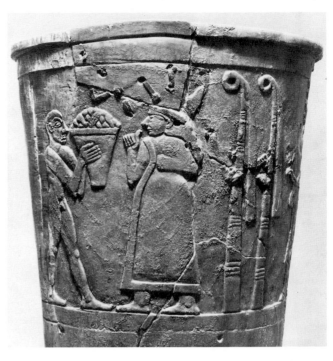

2-8. *Inanna Receiving an Offering*, detail of the upper register of the carved vase from Uruk (fig. 2-7)

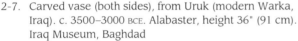

purpose (fig. 2-7). It is decorated with bands, or **registers**, in **low relief**, a technique in which figures are carved to project only slightly from a flat background. Its lower registers show the natural world, including plants and animals. In the lowest register, over a wavy line signifying water, barley and date palms grow; above them, on a solid **groundline**, rams and ewes alternate, facing right. In the middle register, facing in the opposite direction, a line of unclothed priests strides forward, carrying baskets heaped with food that may have been temple offerings or wedding gifts. Size was associated with importance in Mesopotamian art, and the sturdy priests are shown simultaneously in side or profile view (heads and legs) and in three-quarter view (torsos), which makes both shoulders visible and increases their breadth.

The repetition of figures found in the first two bands disappears in the top register, where the imagery is more complex. Inanna, in her role as fertility goddess, stands in front of her shrine, indicated by two reed door poles draped with curtains (fig. 2-8). She wears a long robe and the horned headdress of a deity. Her right hand is raised in a gesture of greeting or blessing, and she faces a naked priest, who presents a sort of cornucopia. Behind him are other offering bearers; the last one holds a tasseled belt for the figure ahead, who may be a ruler. Through the doorway to her shrine, her wealth is displayed: animals, containers of fruit, large vases like this one, and what appears to be a temple model with a man and woman inside. The scene is usually interpreted as the ritual mar-

riage between the divine female and a human male during the annual spring New Year's festival, which was meant to assure fertility for the city's crops, livestock, and people during the coming year.

The sculptors of the vase told their story with great economy and clarity through the use of symbolic detail. They organized the picture space into registers that show the symbolic ascent from plants and animals to the goddess and that mirror the physical ascent of a ziggurat from level to level. They also condensed and focused the narrative, much as modern comic-strip artists do. For the next 2,500 years this use of registers was the preferred Near Eastern method for relating events in visual terms.

Marble statues dated to about 2900–2600 BCE from ruins of a temple at Eshnunna (modern Tell Asmar, Iraq) reveal a somewhat humbler aspect of Mesopotamian religious art (fig. 2-9). These **votive figures**—statues made as an act of worship to the gods—depict individuals. They represent an early example of an ancient Near Eastern religious practice—the setting up of simple, small statues of individual worshipers in a shrine before the larger, more elaborate image of a god. The early figurines from Ain Ghazal may have served this function, and the face of a woman from Uruk may have been part of such a figure, although there is no proof of it. Apparently anyone who could afford to might commission a self-portrait and dedicate it to a shrine. A simple inscription might identify the figure just as "One who offers prayers." Longer inscriptions might recount in detail all

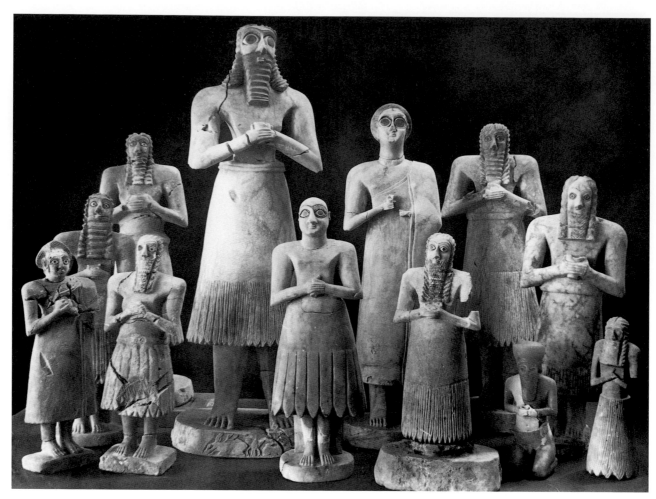

2-9. Votive statues, from the Square Temple, Eshnunna (modern Tell Asmar, Iraq). c. 2900–2600 BCE. Limestone, alabaster, and gypsum, height of largest figure approx. 30" (76.3 cm). The Oriental Institute of the University of Chicago; Iraq Museum, Baghdad

the things accomplished in the god's honor. Cuneiform texts reveal the importance of fixing on a god with an attentive gaze, hence the wide-open eyes. These stand-ins are at perpetual attention, making eye contact and chanting their donors' praises through eternity.

The sculptors of the Eshnunna statues reduced the face, hair, body, and clothing to simple geometric shapes. The figures stand solemnly, hands clasped in respect. Like the face of a woman from Uruk, arched brows inlaid with dark shell, stone, or bitumen once emphasized their huge, staring eyes. The male figures, bare-chested and dressed in sheepskin skirts, are stocky and muscular, with heavy legs and large feet, big shoulders, and cylindrical bodies. The two female figures (the tall, regal woman near the center and the smaller woman at the far left) have somewhat slighter figures but are just as square-shouldered as the men.

The earliest pottery in the Near East dates to about 7000 BCE. Decorated vessels excavated in large numbers from grave sites provide some sense of the development of pottery styles in various regions. One popular type of Sumerian painted ceramic was Scarlet Ware, produced from around 3000 to 2350 BCE (fig. 2-10). Designs on these vessels, predominantly in red with touches of black, were painted with colored mixtures of clay and water. Circles, herringbones, zigzags, diamonds, and other geometric patterns, as well as animal images, were common motifs. The vase pictured here is about a foot tall and includes human figures, which is unusual.

From about 3000 BCE on, Sumerian artisans worked in various metals, including the hard metal alloy bronze (hence the name "Bronze Age" for the period that followed the Neolithic). Many of their metal creations were decorated with—or were in the shape of—animals or composite animal-human-bird creatures. They did extraordinary work in precious metals, often combining them with other materials. A superb example of their skill is a lyre—a kind of harp—from the tomb of Queen Puabi of Ur (c. 2685 BCE), which combines wood, gold, lapis lazuli, and shell (fig. 2-11). From one end of the lyre, the three-dimensional head of a bearded bull glares. The head is intensely lifelike despite the fantastic, decoratively patterned blue beard and the simplified nose.

On the panel below the head, four horizontal regis-

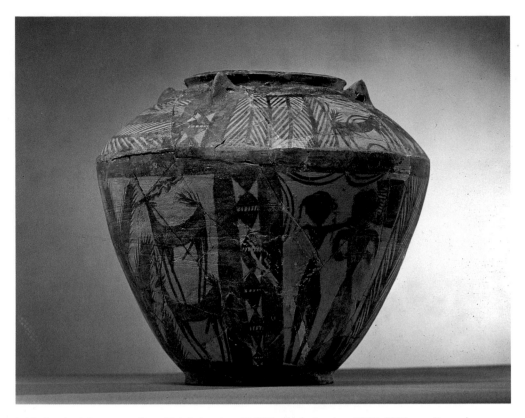

2-10. Scarlet Ware vase, from Tutub (modern Tell Khafajeh, Iraq). c. 3000–2350 BCE. Ceramic, height 11¾" (30 cm). Iraq Museum, Baghdad

The archeologist's best friend is the potsherd, or piece of broken pottery. Ceramic vessels are easily broken, yet the fragments are almost indestructible. Their earliest appearance at a site marks the time when people in the region began producing ceramics. Pottery styles, like automobile designs and fashions in clothing, change over time. Archeologists are able to determine the chronological order of such changes. By matching the potsherds excavated at a site with the types in this sequence, they can determine the relative date of the site (see "How Early Art Is Dated," page 49).

ters present scenes executed in inlaid shell (fig. 2-12). In the bottom register a man in scorpion dress holds what are probably ritual objects in his upraised hands. He is attended by a goat standing on its hind legs and holding out two tall cups, perhaps filled from the large container from which a ladle protrudes. The scene above this one depicts a pair of animal musicians. A seated donkey plucks the strings of a bull lyre—showing how such instruments were played—while a standing bear braces the instrument's frame and a seated jackal plays a small percussion instrument, perhaps a rattle. The next register shows animal attendants, also walking erect, bringing food and drink for a feast. On the left a wolf with a knife in its belt carries a table piled high with pork and mutton. A lion follows with a large wine jug and drinking bowl. In the top panel, facing forward, is an athletic man with long hair and a full beard, naked except for a wide belt. He is clasping two rearing human-headed bulls.

These scenes have puzzled scholars, but a new interpretation sheds light on their meaning. Because the lyre and others like it were found in graves and were used in funeral rites, their imagery probably depicts the fantastic realm of the dead. The animals are the traditional guardians at the gateway through which the newly dead must pass. Cuneiform tablets preserve songs of mourning from Sumer, which may have been chanted by priests to lyre music at funerals.

At roughly the same time written records first appeared, Sumerian temple staff and merchants developed stamps and seals for identifying documents and establishing property ownership. At first, Sumerians used simple clay stamps with designs **incised** (cut) into one surface to sign documents and to mark clay seals on container lids and storage-room doorways. Pressed against a damp clay surface, the seal left a mirror image of its distinctive design that could not be easily altered once dry. Around 3400 BCE, temple record keepers redesigned the stamp seal in the form of a cylinder. Sumerian **cylinder seals**, usually less than 2 inches high, were made of a hard stone, such as marble, so that the tiny but often elaborate scenes carved into them would not wear away. The scene on the fine example in figure 2-13 includes, on the right, a spoils-of-the-hunt depiction. The lone human

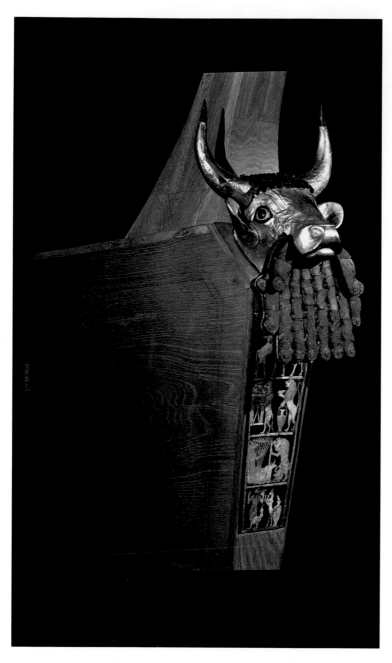

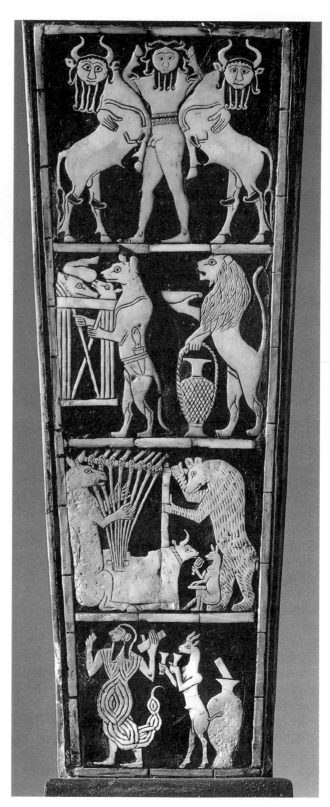

2-11. Bull lyre, from the tomb of Queen Puabi, Ur (modern Muqaiyir, Iraq). c. 2685 BCE. Wood with gold, lapis lazuli, and shell, reassembled in modern wood support. University Museum, University of Pennsylvania, Philadelphia

2-12. Mythological figures, detail of the sound box of the bull lyre from Ur (fig. 2-11). Wood with shell inlay, 12¼ x 4½" (31.1 x 11 cm)

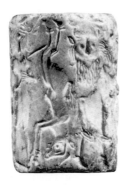

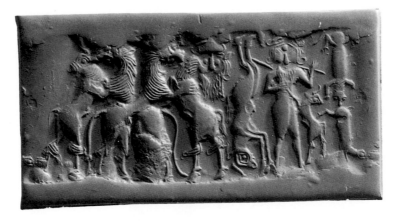

2-13. Cylinder seal from Sumer and its impression. c. 2500 BCE. Marble, height approx. 1³/₄" (4.5 cm). The Metro-politan Museum of Art, New York
Gift of Walter Hauser, 1955 (55.65.4)

The distinctive design on the stone cylinder seal on the left "belonged" to its owner, like a coat of arms in the European Middle Ages or a modern cattle-rancher's brand. When rolled across soft clay applied to the closure to be sealed—a jar lid, the knot securing a bundle, or the door to a room—the cylinder left a raised image, or band of repeated raised images, of the design. Sealing discouraged unauthorized people from secretly gaining access to goods or information.

is flanked by his kill, and he looks over his shoulder at the dead female deer hanging by its heels. On the left, two pairs of rearing, mane-draped beasts, one with a human face, appear to be sparring for dominance. As later Assyrian reliefs will show, it was an enduring tradition in Near Eastern art to depict leaders protecting their people from both human and animal enemies as well as exert-ing control over the natural world. Often the human enemies turned out to be warlike invaders, drawn by Sumer's natural resources and prosperity.

AKKAD

During the period of Sumerian power, the fertile Mesopotamian plain attracted a people known as the Akkadians, who settled the area near modern Baghdad to the north of Uruk and adopted Sumerian culture. Unlike the Sumerians, the Akkadians spoke a Semitic language (a language in the same fam-ily as Arabic and Hebrew). Under the powerful military and political figure Sargon I (ruled c. 2332–2279 BCE), they conquered the Sumerian cities and brought most of Mesopotamia under their control. For more than half a century, Sargon ruled this empire from his capital at Akkad, the actual site of which is yet to be discovered. As "King of the Four Quarters of the World," he assumed broad earthly powers. He also sought to elevate himself to the status of a god, setting a precedent followed by later Akkadian rulers.

Enheduanna, the daughter of Sargon I, was a major public figure who combined the roles of princess, priest-ess, politician, poet, and prophet and wielded excep-tional power. During her lifetime, she was considered the embodiment of the goddess Ningal, the wife of the moon god Nanna, and after her death she herself may have been elevated to the status of goddess. She was appar-ently the only person to hold the office of high priestess for both the ziggurat of Nanna, the moon god of Ur, and the ziggurat of Anu, the sky god of Uruk, Sumer's two most prestigious gods. She began the tradition of

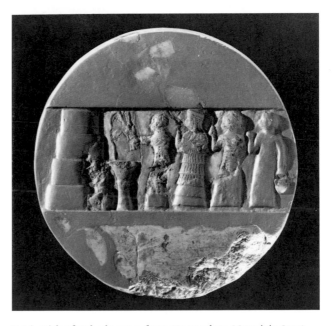

2-14. *Disk of Enheduanna*, from Ur (modern Muqaiyir, Iraq). c. 2300 BCE. Alabaster, diameter approx. 10" (25.4 cm). University Museum, University of Pennsylvania, Philadelphia

An inscription on the back of the disk reads: "Enhedu-anna, priestess of the moon god, [wife] of the moon god, child of Sargon the king of the universe, in Ishtar's temple of Ur she built [an altar] and named it . . . Offering Table of Heaven" (adapted from William W. Hallo, "Enheduanna," *Harvard Magazine*, May–June 1994, page 48).

princesses serving as high priestesses, and she comple-mented her father's political consolidation of his empire by uniting religious authority within it. Her hymns in praise of Sargon and Inanna are among the earliest liter-ary works whose author's name is known. She is memo-rialized on several cylinder seals, as well as on an inscribed alabaster disk that bears her picture (fig. 2-14).

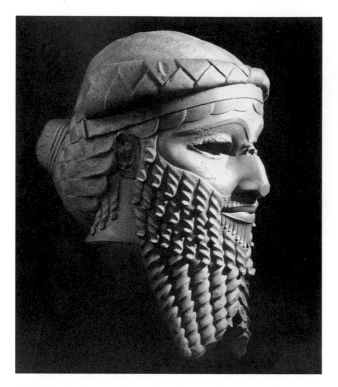

2-15. Head of a man, from Nineveh (modern Kuyunjik, Iraq). c. 2300–2200 BCE. Bronze, height 14³/8" (36.5 cm). Iraq Museum, Baghdad

The figures carved in **high relief** in a band across the middle of this disk are participating in a ritual at the base of a ziggurat, seen at the far left. A nude priest pours ceremonial liquid from a pitcher onto an offering stand. The tall figure behind him, wearing a flounced robe and priestess's headdress, is presumed to be Enheduanna. She and the two figures to her right, probably priests with shaven heads, raise one hand in a gesture of reverent greeting. The disk shape of this work is unique and may have to do with its dedication to the moon god.

Enheduanna's well-documented career is an exception to the otherwise sparse information available about the Akkadians. Few artifacts can be traced to the courts of Akkad, making a lifesize bronze head dating from about 2300–2200 BCE especially precious (fig. 2-15). Its facial features and hairstyle probably reflect a generalized male ideal rather than the appearance of a specific individual. Also, it is possible that the head was symbolically mutilated to destroy its power, for the ears appear to have been deliberately removed, as have the inlays that would have filled the eye sockets.

The concept of imperial authority was literally carved in stone in another Akkadian work, the *Stela of Naramsin* (fig. 2-16). This 6¹/2-foot-high **stela**, or upright stone slab, commemorates a military victory of Naramsin, Sargon's grandson and successor, and is an early example of a work of art created to celebrate the achievements of an individual ruler. In a sharp break with visual tradition, the sculptors replaced the horizontal registers with wavy ground lines. The images stand on their own, with no explanatory inscription. Watched over by three solar deities, symbolized by the rayed suns in the sky, Naramsin ascends a mountain

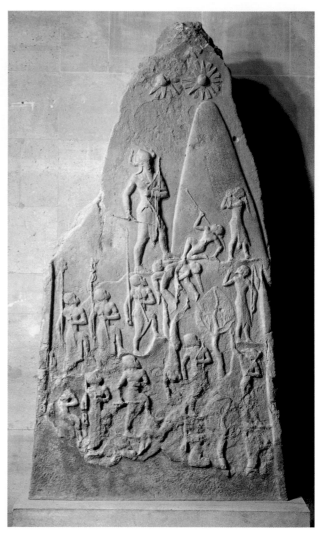

2-16. *Stela of Naramsin.* c. 2254–2218 BCE. Limestone, height 6'6" (1.98 m). Musée du Louvre, Paris

This stela probably came originally from Sippar, an Akkadian city on the Euphrates River, in what is now Iraq. It was not discovered at Sippar, however, but at the Elamite city of Susa (modern Shush, Iran), some 300 miles to the southeast. Raiders from Elam presumably took it there as booty in the twelfth century BCE.

wearing the horned crown used to identify gods. His soldiers follow at rhythmic intervals, passing conquered enemy forces sprawled in death or begging for mercy. Both the king and his warriors hold their weapons upright. The godlike king is immediately recognizable. He stands at the dramatic center of the scene, closest to the mountaintop, silhouetted against the sky. As in most art from the Near East, his greater size in relationship to his soldiers is an indication of his greater importance. Although this stela depicts Akkadians in triumph, they managed to dominate the region for only about another half century.

LAGASH In about 2180 BCE, the Akkadian Empire fell under attack by the Guti, a mountain people from the northeast. The Guti controlled most of the Mesopotamian plain for a brief time, then the Sumerians regained control of their own region and

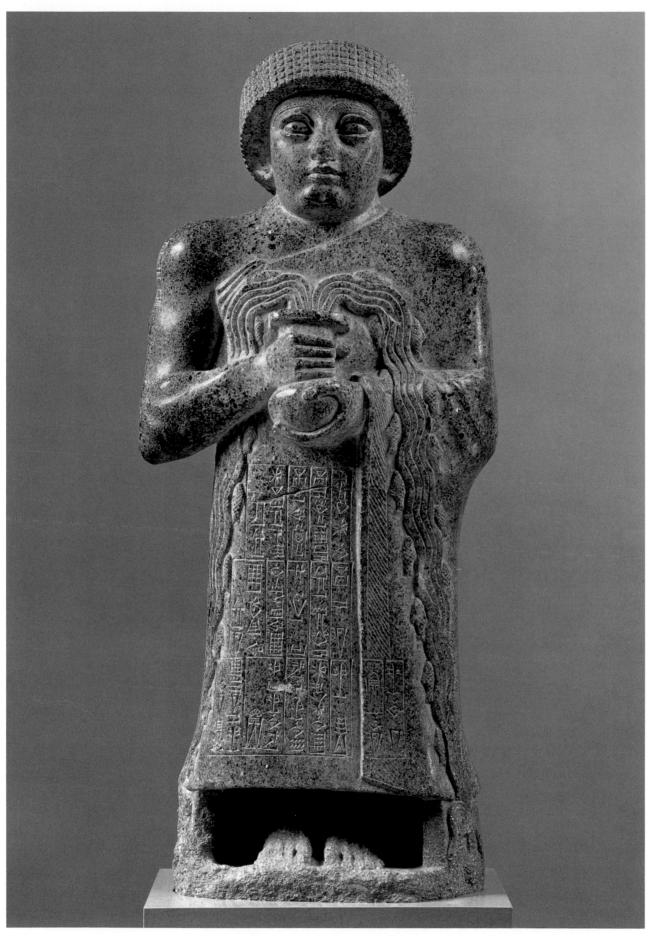

2-17. Votive statue of Gudea, from Lagash (modern Telloh, Iraq). c. 2120 BCE. Diorite, height 29" (73.7 cm).
Musée du Louvre, Paris

Akkad. One large Sumerian city-state remained independent during the period of Guti control. This was Lagash, on the Tigris River in the southeast, under the ruler Gudea. Gudea built and restored many temples, in which he placed votive statues representing both himself as governor and the ideal of good rule that he embodied. The statues are made of diorite, a very hard stone that was difficult to work, prompting the sculptors to use compact, simplified forms for the portraits that are unusually durable. Twenty of them survive, all looking much alike, making Gudea's face a familiar one in ancient Near Eastern art.

Whether the ruler was shown sitting or standing, the smooth fall of his robe provided ample space for long cuneiform inscriptions. The text of the one shown here (fig. 2-17) relates that Gudea dedicated himself, the sculpture, and the temple in which the sculpture resided to the goddess Geshtinanna, the divine poet and interpreter of dreams. Imposing and impressive, this statue seems **monumental**, although it is only 2½ feet tall. Here Gudea holds a vessel from which life-giving water flows in two streams filled with leaping fish. (At least one statue has been found of a goddess holding a vessel engineered to spout real water, which would have poured down her robe.) The full face below the cuffed sheepskin hat appears youthful and serene, and the smoothly muscled body is clothed in a long garment similar to that worn by the female votive figures from Eshnunna. The oversized, wide-open eyes—better to return the gaze of the deity—and broad, bunched-up shoulders express intense concentration. The sculptor's top-heavy treatment of the human body, as in other Mesopotamian figures, emphasizes its power centers: the eyes, head, chest, and arms. Images of Gudea present him as a strong, peaceful, pious ruler worthy of divine favor.

BABYLON AND MARI

For the next 300 years, periods of political turmoil alternated with periods of stable government in Mesopotamia. The Amorites, a Semitic-speaking people from the Arabian desert to the west, moved into the region and eventually reunited Sumer under Hammurabi (ruled 1792–1750 BCE). The capital city was Babylon, and the residents are called Babylonians. Among Hammurabi's achievements was a written legal code that listed the laws of his realm and the penalties for breaking them.

Hammurabi's code occupies most of the *Stela of Hammurabi*, a finely carved stone about 7 feet tall, but the relief sculpture at the top shows the king standing before the supreme judge, the sun god Shamash (fig. 2-18). The figures were executed in smooth, rounded forms with a minimum of linear surface detail. Shamash wears the four-tiered, horned headdress that marks him as a god and a robe that bares one shoulder and ends in a stiff, flounced skirt. Rays of the sun rise from behind his shoulders, and in his right hand he holds a measuring rod and a rope ring, symbols of justice and power. Hammurabi faces Shamash confidently, his hand raised in a gesture of greeting. Any suggestion of familiarity in the lack of

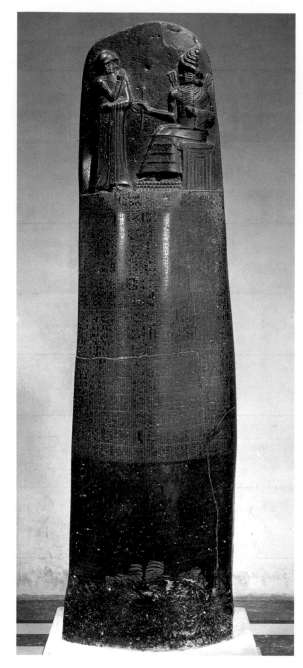

2-18. *Stela of Hammurabi*, from Susa (modern Shush, Iran). c. 1792–1750 BCE. Basalt, height of stela approx. 7' (2.13 m), height of relief 28" (71.1 cm). Musée du Louvre, Paris

In the introductory section of the stela's long cuneiform inscription, Hammurabi declared that with this code of law he intended "to cause justice to prevail in the land and to destroy the wicked and the evil, that the strong might not oppress the weak nor the weak the strong." Most of the 300 or so entries that follow deal with commercial and property matters. Only sixty-eight relate to domestic problems, and a mere twenty deal with physical assault. Punishments depended on the gender and social standing of the offender. Like the *Stela of Naramsin*, this stela was removed to Susa by Elamite invaders.

distance between the two is offset by the formality of his pose. The smaller, earthly law enforcer remains standing in the presence of the much larger divine judge, seated on his ziggurat throne. The Babylonian sculptor of this stela, like the Akkadian sculptor of the *Stela of Naramsin* (see fig. 2-16), indicated the relative importance of the

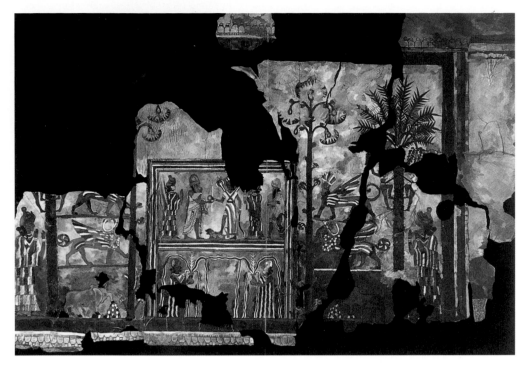

2-19. *Investiture of Zimrilim*, facsimile of a wall painting on mud plaster from the palace at Mari (modern Tell Hariri, Iraq), Court 106. c. 1750 BCE. Height 5'5" (1.7 m). Musée du Louvre, Paris

figures by size. The temple-form throne represented their mountain meeting site.

As kingship and empire became increasingly important, palace architecture overshadowed temple architecture. The great palace of another Amorite king, Hammurabi's contemporary Zimrilim (ruled 1779–1757 BCE), reflects this trend. Zimrilim's capital city of Mari was strategically located on the Euphrates River about 250 miles northwest of Babylon. It prospered from commercial traffic on the river and was notable for its well-built houses, sophisticated sanitation system, and bronze-working industry. The palace boasted an enormous courtyard paved in alabaster, several temples and shrines, hundreds of other rooms and courtyards, and a notable art collection. Zimrilim and Hammurabi had once been allies, but in 1757 BCE Hammurabi marched against Mari and destroyed Zimrilim's palace. A few murals from the palace have survived and provide rare examples of this fragile ancient Near Eastern art form.

The subjects of the murals range from geometric patterns in the royal family's quarters to military and religious scenes in the administrative areas. One, in the palace's main courtyard, shows Zimrilim receiving his authority from Ishtar, the Babylonian goddess of war, fertility, and love (fig. 2-19). The central panels, devoted to the investiture ceremony, are organized in the formal, symmetrical style familiar in earlier Sumerian art. In the framed upper register, the goddess, holding weapons and resting her foot on a lion—all emblems of power—extends to the king emblems of rule, the rod and the ring. Other deities look on, affirming the king's assumption of office. Below, a pair of goddesses face each other, holding tall plants in red vases. They are surrounded by streams of water that flow from the vases—a theme familiar from the Gudea statue (see fig. 2-17)—and merge in the center to form a canopy. Flanking these two

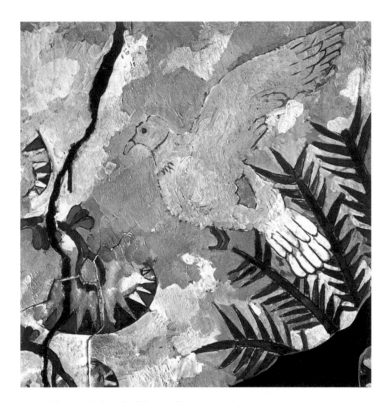

2-20. *Blue Bird*, detail of the wall painting from Mari (fig. 2-19)

panels are first a pair of towering aloelike plants with fan-shaped, **stylized** foliage. The **stylization** is especially evident in the patterned forms of the fronds, which exaggerate the spiny leaf shapes. Then there are three tiers of mythical animals—bulls, winged lions, and crowned, human-headed winged creatures—all facing inward. Beyond these are date palms being climbed by two fruit pickers. An enormous blue bird, of a species still found in the Mari region, spreads its wings in the right-hand tree (fig. 2-20). At the edges of the picture two

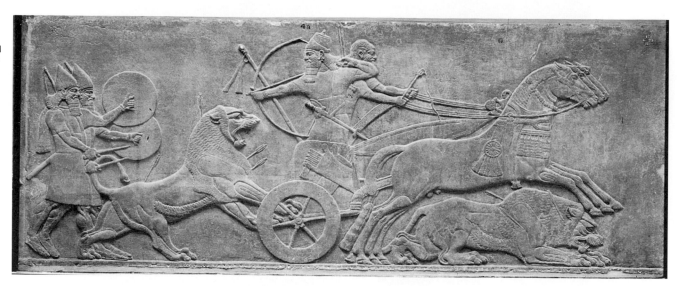

2-21. *Assurnasirpal II Killing Lions*, from the palace complex of Assurnasirpal II, Kalhu (modern Nimrud, Iraq). c. 850 BCE. Alabaster, height approx. 39" (99.1 cm). The British Museum, London

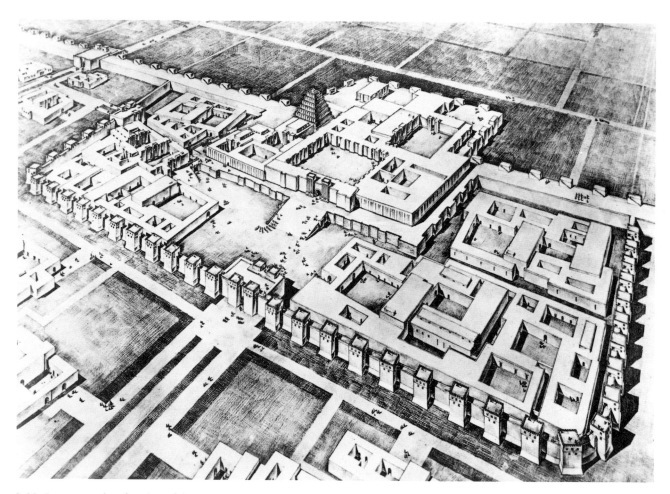

2-22. Reconstruction drawing of the citadel and palace complex of Sargon II, Dur Sharrukin (modern Khorsabad, Iraq). c. 721–706 BCE

gigantic goddesses, hands raised, bestow their approval. Eye-catching checked and striped patterning throughout the mural makes its surface sparkle. The colors have darkened considerably, but they probably included blue, orange, red, brown, and white. The way in which paint was used here reveals what Mesopotamian art looked like when it was new.

ASSYRIA

After the centuries of power struggles among Sumer, Akkad, Lagash, and Mari in southern Mesopotamia, a people called the Assyrians began to rise to dominance in northern Mesopotamia. They had become very powerful by about 1400 BCE, and after about 1000 BCE they began to conquer neighboring regions. By the end of the ninth century BCE, they controlled most of Mesopotamia, and by the early seventh century BCE they had extended their influence as far west as Egypt. Soon afterward they succumbed to internal weakness and external enemies, and by 600 BCE their empire had collapsed.

Various cities served at one time or another as the Assyrians' capital, and Assyrian architectural monuments include fine palaces set atop high platforms inside these fortified cities. The palaces were decorated with scenes of victorious battles, presentations of tribute to the king, combat between men and beasts, and religious imagery.

During his reign (883–859 BCE), Assurnasirpal II moved the capital to Kalhu (modern Nimrud) on the east bank of the Tigris River and undertook an ambitious building program. His architects fortified the city with mud-brick walls 5 miles long, 120 feet thick, and 42 feet high, and his engineers constructed a canal that irrigated fields and provided water for the expanded population of the city. According to an inscription commemorating the event, Assurnasirpal gave a party for 69,574 people to celebrate the dedication of the new capital in 879 BCE. Most of the buildings in Kalhu were made from mud bricks, but alabaster—a more impressive and durable material—was used for architectural decorations such as panels with scenes carved in low relief that depict the king participating in religious rituals, events from his war campaigns, and hunting expeditions.

In a vivid lion-hunting scene (fig. 2-21), Assurnasirpal II stands in a chariot pulled by galloping horses and draws his bow against an attacking lion that already has four arrows protruding from its body. Another beast, pierced by arrows, lies dead or dying on the ground. This was probably a ceremonial hunt, in which the king, protected by men with swords and shields, rode back and forth killing captured animals as they were released one by one into an enclosed area. The immediacy of this image marks a shift in Mesopotamian art away from a sense of timelessness and toward visual narrative. As in many earlier works, *Assurnasirpal II Killing Lions* shows a man confronting wild beasts. Unlike earlier works, however, the man is not part of nature, standing among animals as their equal, but has assumed dominion over nature. There is no question in this scene who will prevail.

Sargon II (ruled 721–705 BCE) built a new Assyrian capital at Dur Sharrukin (modern Khorsabad). An inscription says the grand project consumed the king day and night, but it was abandoned after his death. Excavations have enabled archeologists to reconstruct the city's appearance (fig. 2-22). A walled **citadel**, or fortress, containing 200 rooms and 30 courtyards lay at the northwest side of the city and straddled the city wall. The **palace complex**, centered at the back of the citadel on a raised, fortified platform about 52 feet high, is a monumental example of the use of art as propaganda to support political power. Guarded by two towers, it was accessible only by a wide ramp leading up from an open square, around which the residences of important government and religious officials were clustered. Beyond the ramp was the main courtyard, with service buildings on the right and

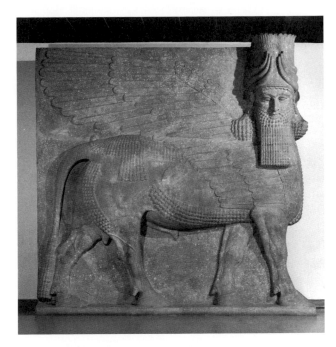

2-23. Guardian figure, from the entrance to the throne room, palace of Sargon II. c. 720 BCE. Limestone, height 16' (4.86 m). The Oriental Institute of the University of Chicago

Gates and doorways in Assyrian royal complexes were commonly protected by images of winged bulls with human heads. They were believed to guard against evil influences. As here, they were rendered with very realistic details—note the veins in the legs and the plumage of the wings—and their bodies were articulated in a lifelike way. At times, however, they were provided with a most unrealistic fifth leg, so that when viewed from the front they appeared to stand still, but when viewed from the side they seemed to be in motion.

temples on the left. The heart of the palace, protected by a reinforced wall with only two small, off-center doors, lay past the main courtyard. Within the inner compound was a second courtyard, lined with narrative relief panels showing tribute bearers, that functioned as an audience hall. Visitors would have entered the king's throne room from this courtyard through a stone gate sculpted in high relief with colossal guardian figures, such as the human-headed bull illustrated here (fig. 2-23). These hybrid creatures also flank the gates of the citadel. Ranging from 13 to 16 feet tall and weighing about 40 tons, they would have been formidable stone guardians for a royal audience.

The ziggurat at Dur Sharrukin was set off in an open space between the temple complex and the palace. It towered over the city, declaring the might of Assyria's kings and symbolizing their claim to empire. It probably had seven levels, each about 18 feet high and painted a different color. The four levels still remaining were once white, black, blue, and red. Instead of separate flights of stairs between the levels, a single, squared-off spiral ramp rose continuously from the base, becoming smaller in circumference as it went up.

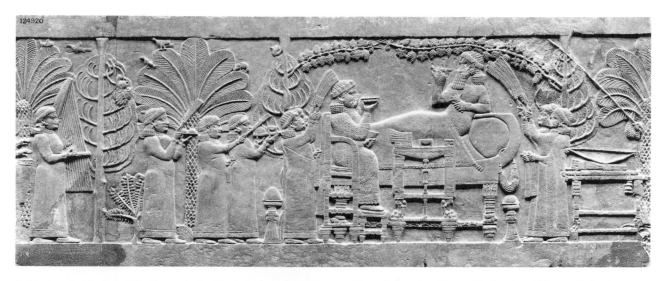

2-24. *Assurbanipal and His Queen in the Garden,* from the palace at Nineveh (modern Kuyunjik, Iraq). c. 647 BCE. Alabaster, height approx. 21" (53.3 cm). The British Museum, London

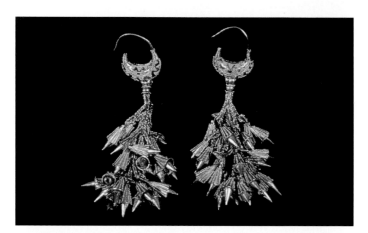

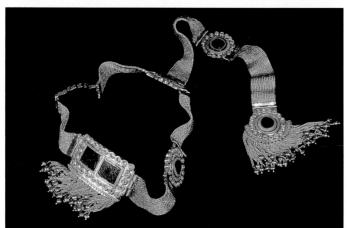

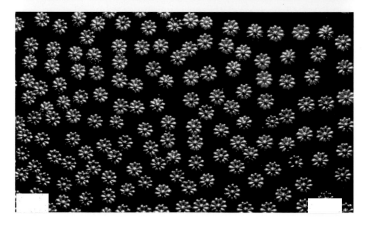

Assurbanipal (ruled 669–c. 627 BCE), king of the Assyrians three generations after Sargon II, had his capital at Nineveh (modern Kuyunjik). His palace was decorated with alabaster panels carved with pictorial narratives in low relief. Most show the king and his subjects in battle and hunting, but there are occasional scenes of palace life. One panel shows the king and queen in a pleasure garden (fig. 2-24). The king reclines on a couch, and the queen sits in a chair at his feet. Some servants arrive with trays of food, while others wave whisks to protect the royal couple from insects. A large, Egyptian-looking necklace hangs from the end of the couch at the right—perhaps the king has taken it off while he relaxes, or perhaps it is displayed here as a symbolic reference to Assurbanipal's conquest of Egypt in 663 BCE. This apparently tranquil domestic scene is actually a victory celebration. The king's weapons (sword, bow, and quiver of arrows) are on the table behind him, and the upside-down severed head of his vanquished enemy hangs from a tree at the far left. It was common during this period to display the heads and corpses of enemies as a form of psychological warfare, and Assurbanipal's generals would have sent him the head as a trophy.

Although much Assyrian art is relief carving, other arts were developing. One of the most spectacular archeological finds in the Near East was the discovery, beginning in 1988, of more than a thousand pieces of gold jewelry weighing more than 125 pounds in three Assyrian royal tombs at Kalhu dated from the ninth and eighth centuries BCE (fig. 2-25). The refinement and superb artistry of the crowns, necklaces, bracelets, armbands, ankle bracelets, and other ornaments recovered from these tombs—almost entirely Assyrian made—could never be discerned from depictions of jewelry in stone sculpture.

2-25. Earrings, crown, and rosettes, from the tomb of Queen Yabay, Kalhu (modern Nimrud, Iraq). Late 8th century BCE. Gold. Iraq Museum, Baghdad

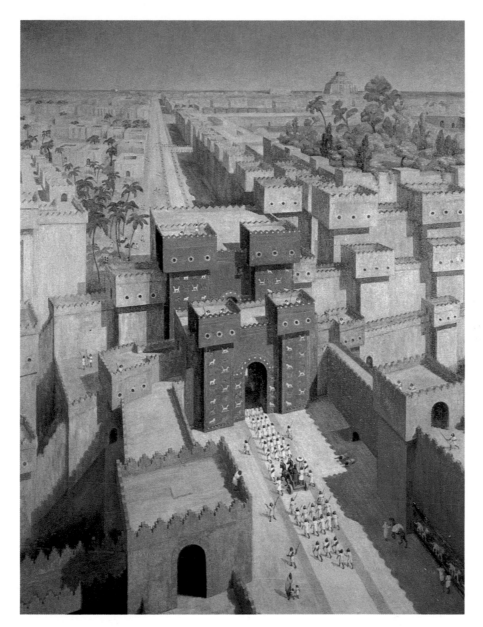

2-26. Reconstruction drawing of Babylon in the 6th century BCE. The Oriental Institute of the University of Chicago

In this view, the palace of Nebuchadnezzar II, with its famous Hanging Gardens, can be seen just behind and to the right of the Ishtar Gate, to the west of the Processional Way. The Marduk Ziggurat looms up in the far distance on the east bank of the Euphrates. This structure was at times believed to be the biblical Tower of Babel—Bab-il was an early form of the city's name.

NEO-BABYLONIA

At the end of the seventh century BCE, the Medes from western Iran and the Scythians from the frigid regions of modern Russia and Ukraine invaded the northern and eastern parts of Assyria. Meanwhile, under a new royal dynasty, the Babylonians reasserted themselves. This Neo-Babylonian kingdom began attacking Assyrian cities in 615 BCE and formed a treaty with the Medes. In 612 BCE, an allied army of Medes and Neo-Babylonians captured Nineveh. When the dust settled, Assyria was no more. The Medes controlled a swath of land below the Black and Caspian seas, and the Neo-Babylonians controlled a region that stretched from modern Turkey to northern Arabia and from Mesopotamia to the Mediterranean Sea.

The most famous Neo-Babylonian ruler was Nebuchadnezzar II (ruled 604–562 BCE). A great patron of architecture, he built temples dedicated to the Babylonian gods throughout his realm and transformed Babylon—the cultural, political, and economic hub of his empire—into one of the most splendid cities of its day. Babylon straddled the Euphrates River, its two sections joined by a bridge. The older eastern sector was traversed by a broad avenue named "May the Enemy Not Have Victory," also called the Processional Way because it was the route taken by religious processions honoring the city's patron god, Marduk (fig. 2-26). This street, laid with large stone slabs set in a bed of bitumen, was up to 66 feet wide at some points. It ran east from the Euphrates bridge past the temple district, then turned

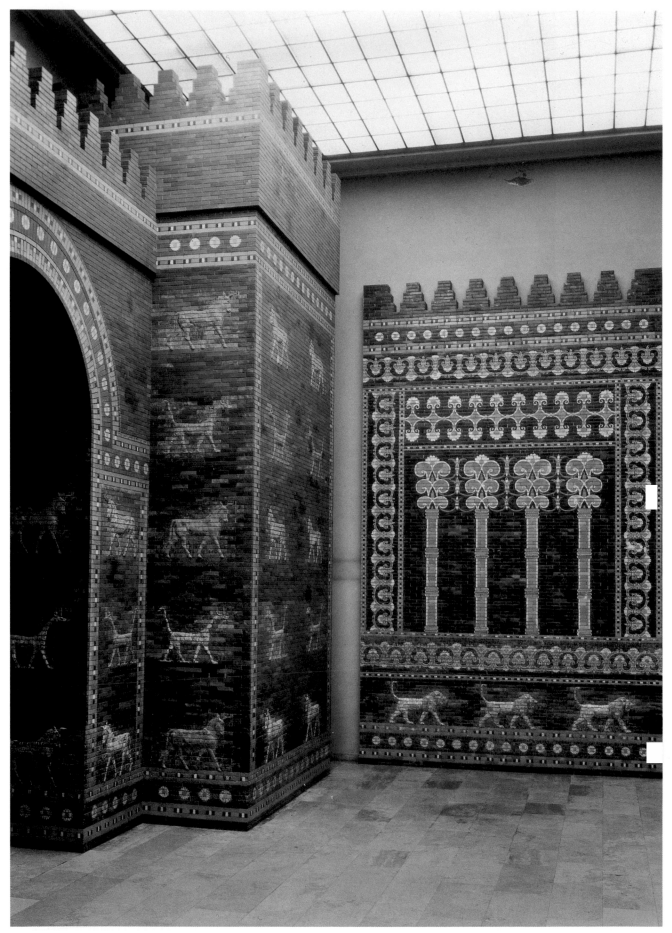

2-27. Ishtar Gate and throne room wall, from Babylon (Iraq). c. 575 BCE. Glazed brick. Staatliche Museen zu Berlin, Preussischer Kulturbesitz, Vorderasiatisches Museum

CE

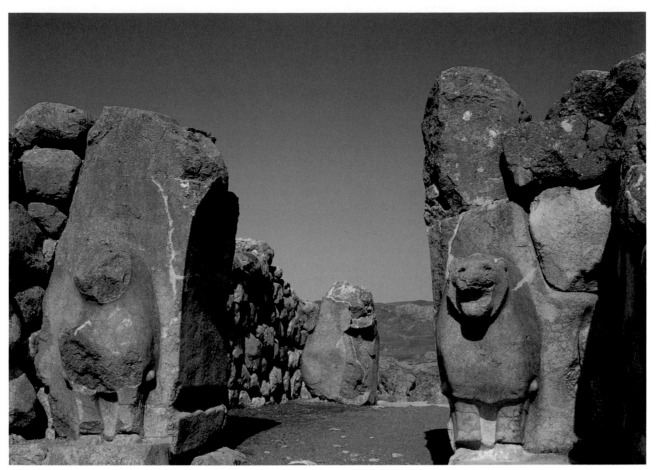

2-28. Lion Gate, Hattushash (near modern Boghazkeui, Turkey). c. 1400 BCE. Limestone

northward to end at the Ishtar Gate, one of the main entrances to the city. Along the way, the walls on both sides were faced with turquoise bricks that were **glazed** (painted and fired) and topped with notches, or **crenellation**. Among the brilliant turquoise bricks, specially molded, gold-colored bricks form images of lions striding along in honor of the goddess Ishtar.

The double-arched Ishtar Gate, a symbol of Babylonian power, was guarded by four crenellated towers. It is decorated with tiers of the dragons sacred to Marduk and the bulls with blue horns and tails associated with a number of other deities. Now reconstructed inside one of the Berlin State Museums, the Ishtar Gate is installed next to a panel from the outer wall of the throne room in Nebuchadnezzar's nearby palace (fig. 2-27). In this fragment, lions walk in a zone beneath stylized palm trees reminiscent of those in the mural from Mari (see fig. 2-19). Among Babylon's other marvels, none of which survive, were the city's walls, its fabled Hanging Gardens (see "The Seven Wonders of the World," page 102), and the Marduk Ziggurat. All that remains of this ziggurat, which ancient documents describe as painted white, black, crimson, blue, orange, silver, and gold, is the outline of its base and traces of the lower stairs.

Outside of Mesopotamia, other cultures—those of Anatolia, Elam, and Persia—were developing simultaneously and would have an impact on Mesopotamia before one of them, Persia, eventually overwhelmed it.

ANATOLIA

Anatolia, before the rise of the Assyrians, had been home to several independent cultures that resisted Mesopotamian domination. The most powerful was the Hittite civilization, whose founders had moved into the mountains and plateaus of central Anatolia from the east and established their capital at Hattushash (near modern Boghazkeui, Turkey) about 1600 BCE. Through trade and conquest, they created an empire that stretched along the coast of the Mediterranean Sea in the area of modern Syria and Lebanon, bringing them into conflict with the Egyptian Empire, which was expanding into the same region from the south (Chapter 3). The Hittites also made incursions into Mesopotamia. They were apparently the first people to work in iron, which they used for fittings for war chariots, weapons, sickles and plowshares for farmers, and chisels and hammers for sculptors and masons. They are noted for the artistry of their fine metalwork and for their imposing palace citadels with double walls and fortified gateways.

The foundations and base walls of the Hittite stronghold at Hattushash, which date to around 1400 BCE, were constructed with stone supplied from local quarries, but the upper walls, stairways, and walkways were finished in brick. The blocks of stone used to frame doorways were decorated in high relief with a variety of guardian figures, some 7-foot-tall, half-human–half-animal creatures, others naturalistically rendered animals like the lions shown here (fig. 2-28). These sculpted figures were

Some of the most bitter resentments spawned by war—whether in Mesopotamia in the twelfth century BCE or in our own time—have involved the "liberation" or "protection" of art objects and other artifacts of great value and meaning to the people from whom they were taken. Museums around the world have been enhanced, if not outright stocked, with paintings, sculpture, and other works either snatched by invading armies or acquired as a result of conquest, prolonged occupation, or economic domination. Two historically priceless objects unearthed in the excavations of Elamite Susa, for example—the Akkadian *Stela of Naramsin* (see fig. 2-16) and the Babylonian *Stela of Hammurabi* (see fig. 2-18)—were not Elamite at all, but Mesopotamian.

Both had been brought there as military trophies by an Elamite king, who added an inscription to the *Stela of Naramsin* explaining that he had merely "protected" it.

The same rationale has been used in modern times to justify the removal of countless works of art from their cultural contexts. The Rosetta Stone, the key to the modern decipherment of Egyptian hieroglyphics, was discovered in Egypt by French troops in 1799, fell into British hands when they forced the French from Egypt, and ultimately ended up in the British Museum in London. In the early nineteenth century, a British nobleman, Lord Elgin, removed many renowned Classical Greek reliefs from the Parthenon on the Acropolis in Athens with the blessing of the Ottoman authorities who governed Greece at the time. Although

his actions may indeed have protected the reliefs from neglect and the ravages of the Greek war of independence, they have remained installed, like the Rosetta Stone, in the British Museum, despite continuing protests from Greece. The Ishtar Gate from Babylon (see fig. 2-27) is now in a museum in Germany. Many works in German collections were similarly "protected" at the end of World War II and are surfacing now. In the United States, Native Americans are increasingly vocal in their demands that artifacts and human remains collected by anthropologists and archeologists and lodged in the country's museums be returned to them. "To the victor," it is said, "belong the spoils." It continues to be a matter of passionate debate whether or not this notion is appropriate in the case of revered cultural artifacts.

part of the architecture itself, not added to it separately. The boulders-becoming-creatures on the so-called Lion Gate harmonize with the colossal scale of this construction. Despite extreme weathering, the lions have endured over the millennia and still convey a sense of vigor and permanence.

ELAM

The strip of fertile plain known as Elam, between the Tigris River and the Zagros Mountains to the east (in present-day Iran), had become a flourishing farming region by 7000 BCE. About this time the city of Susa, later the capital of an Elamite kingdom, was established on the Shaur River. Elam had close cultural ties to Mesopotamia, but the two regions were often in conflict. In the twelfth century BCE, Elamite invaders looted art treasures from Mesopotamia and carried them back to Susa (see "Protection or Theft?," above).

In about 4000 BCE, Susa was a center of pottery production. Twentieth-century excavations there have uncovered nearly 8,000 finely formed and painted vessels (beakers, bowls, and jars), as well as coarse domestic **wares**. The fine wares have thin, fragile shells that suggest they were not meant for everyday use. Decorations painted in brown glaze on the pale yellow clay are sometimes purely geometric but are more often a graceful combination of geometric designs and stylized natural forms, mainly from the animal world, expertly balanced between repetition and variation of forms.

One handleless cup, or beaker, nearly a foot tall and weighing about 8 pounds, presents a pair of ibexes (only one of which is visible) that have been reduced to pure geometric form (fig. 2-29). On each side, the great sweep of the animals' horns encloses a small circular motif, or **roundel**, containing what might be a leaf pattern or a line of birds in flight. A narrow band above the ibexes shows

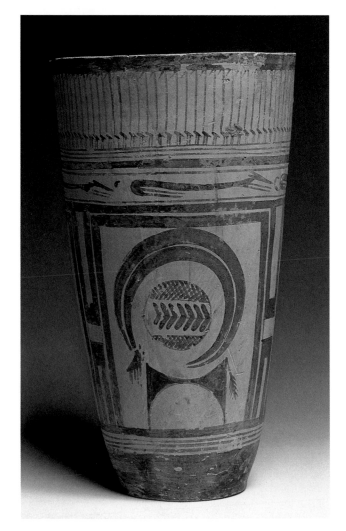

2-29. Beaker, from Susa (modern Shush, Iran). c. 4000 BCE. Ceramic, painted in brown glaze, height 11¼" (28.6 cm). Musée du Louvre, Paris

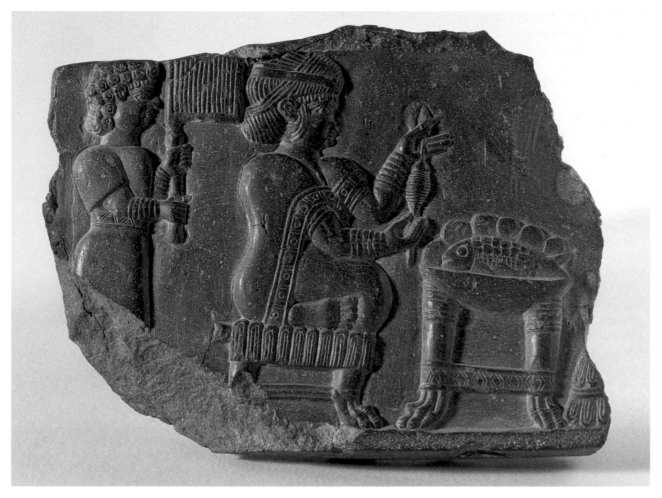

2-30. *Woman Spinning*, from Susa (modern Shush, Iran). c. 8th–7th century BCE. Bitumen compound, 3⁵/₈ x 5¹/₈" (9.2 x 13 cm). Musée du Louvre, Paris

short-haired, long-nosed dogs at rest. In the wide top band, stately wading birds stand motionless.

Susa's ingenious artisans produced a gray bitumen-based compound that could be molded while soft and carved when hard. From this compound, which still defies laboratory analysis, they made a variety of practical and decorative objects. An especially fine example, a 3⁵/₈-inch-high fragment from a larger relief, dates from the eighth to the seventh century BCE (fig. 2-30). It shows an important-looking woman adorned with many ornaments. Her hair is elegantly styled, and her garment has a patterned border. She sits barefoot and cross-legged on a lion-footed stool covered with sheepskin, spinning thread onto a large spindle. A fish lies on an offering stand in front of her, together with six round objects (perhaps fruit). A young servant, probably female, stands behind the woman, fanning her. At the lower right-hand corner of the fragment is what appears to be a portion of a long, flounced garment such as deities are frequently shown wearing, which might indicate the presence of a god or goddess to whom the offering is being made. Interpretation of this scene is difficult; it might be a banquet scene, perhaps in connection with a religious rite.

PERSIA

In the sixth century BCE, the Persians, a formerly nomadic, Indo-European-speaking people related to the Medes, began to seize power. From the region of Parsa, or Persis (modern Fars), southeast of Susa, they eventually overwhelmed Mesopotamia and the rest of the ancient Near East and established a vast empire. The rulers of this new empire traced their ancestry to a semilegendary Iranian king named Achaemenes and are known as the Achaemenids. Their dramatic expansion began in 559 BCE with the ascension of a remarkable leader, Cyrus II (called the Great, ruled 559–530 BCE). By the time of his death the Persian Empire included Babylonia; the land of the Medes, which stretched across northern Iran through Anatolia; and some of the Aegean islands far to the west. Cyrus's son Cambyses II (ruled 529–522 BCE) added Egypt and Cyprus. When Darius I (ruled 521–486 BCE), the son of a government official, took the throne, he proclaimed: "I am Darius, great King, King of Kings, King of countries, King of this earth." Darius and his successors went on to rule for nearly two centuries, expanding the Achaemenid Empire to both east and west.

Darius, like many powerful rulers, created monuments to serve as visible symbols of his authority. He made Susa his first capital and commissioned a 32-acre administrative compound to be built there. In about 518 BCE, he began construction of Parsa, a new capital in the Persian homeland in the Zagros highlands. Today this city, known as Persepolis, the name the Greeks gave it, is one of the best-preserved ancient sites in the Near East (fig. 2-31). Darius imported materials, workers, and artists from all over his empire for his building projects. He even ordered work to be executed in Egypt and transported to his capital. The result was a new style of art that combined many different cultural traditions, including Persian, Mede, Mesopotamian, Egyptian, and Greek. This artistic integration was simply a side effect of Darius's political strategy.

In Assyrian fashion, the imperial complex at Persepolis was set on a raised platform and laid out on a rectangular **grid,** or system of crossed lines. The platform was 40 feet high and measured 1,500 by 900 feet. It was accessible only from a single ramp made of wide, shallow steps to allow equestrians to ride up rather than dismount and climb on foot. Construction was spread out over nearly sixty years, and Darius lived to see the erection of only a treasury, the Apadana (audience hall), and a very small palace for himself. The Apadana, set above the rest of the complex on a second terrace (fig. 2-32),

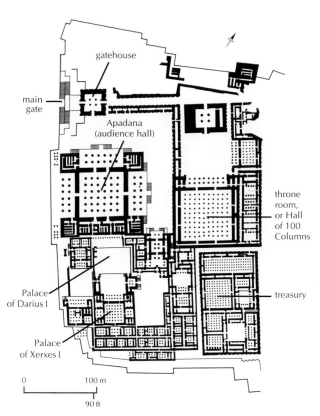

2-31. Plan of the ceremonial complex, Persepolis, Iran. 518–c. 460 BCE

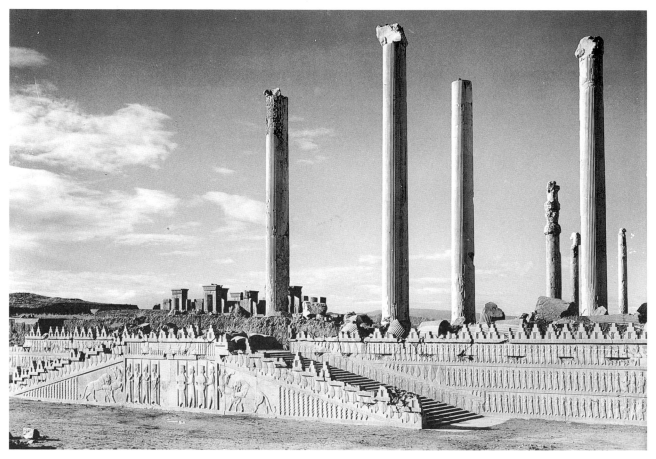

2-32. Apadana (audience hall) of Darius and Xerxes, ceremonial complex, Persepolis, Iran. 518–c. 460 BCE

The ancient historian Cleiarchus of Alexandria relates that Alexander the Great and his troops accidentally torched the royal compound at Persepolis during a wild banquet in celebration of their victory over the Persians. It is more probable that Alexander had it destroyed deliberately. The site was never rebuilt, and its ruins were never buried. Scholars have been measuring, mapping, and studying what remains of the complex for the past 200 years. Various pieces of architectural ornament have been stripped from Persepolis for display in museums around the world.

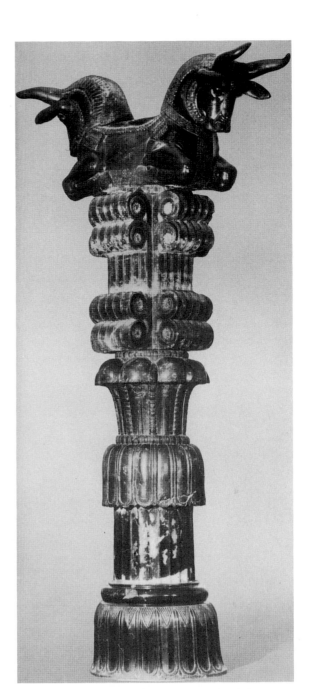
2-33. Partially reconstructed column with complete capital, from the ceremonial complex, Persepolis, Iran. Iranbastan Museum, Teheran

had open porches on three sides and a square hall large enough to hold several thousand people. Darius's son Xerxes I (ruled 485–465 BCE) added a sprawling palace complex for himself, enlarged the treasury building, and began a vast new public reception space, the Hall of 100 Columns, with its own guard gate. Most of the remaining work was done under Xerxes' heir, Artaxerxes I (ruled 464–425 BCE).

The multicultural composition of imperial Persia is evident in the varied appearance of the many hundreds of **columns** found in Persepolis (see "Elements of Architecture," page 101). Although they were all executed with a distinctly Persian flavor, the columns reflect design ideas from Mede, Egyptian, and possibly Greek sources. They stood atop bell-shaped **bases** (foundations) decorated with leaves. Their **shafts**, or vertical supports, were carved with evenly spaced vertical channels called **fluting**, which exaggerated their height and gave them a feeling of delicate refinement. The **capitals**, the top section of the columns on which ceiling beams rested, were lavishly decorated with a combination of palm fronds, papyrus flowers, other plant forms, double vertical scrolls, and the heads and forequarters of kneeling creatures placed back to back (fig. 2-33). Traces of pigment reveal that the Persepolis structures were originally richly painted in red, green, yellow, and blue. Large relief panels from Persepolis also show influences from Mesopotamian, Egyptian, and Greek cultures. In those panels, the garments that reveal the body beneath and have fine, knife-edged pleats especially reflect Greek sources and may indeed have been done by Greek sculptors.

Like some Assyrian palace reliefs, those at Persepolis were concerned with displays of allegiance and economic prosperity rather than with heroic exploits. In one relief Darius holds an audience while his son and heir, Xerxes, listens from behind the throne (fig. 2-34). Such

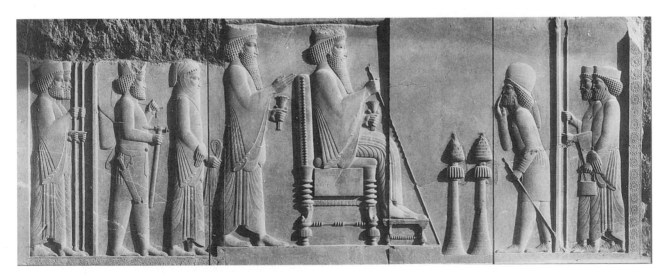

2-34. *Darius and Xerxes Receiving Tribute*, detail of a relief from the stairway leading to the Apadana, ceremonial complex, Persepolis, Iran. 491–486 BCE. Limestone, height 8'4" (2.54 m). Iranbastan Museum, Teheran

TECHNIQUE

PERSIAN METAL-WORKING

The intricate lion's-head **terminals** of the gold **torque** seen in figure 2-35 were probably made using the **lost-wax casting** process, a technique for fabricating fine metal objects developed at a very early date. A shape was carved out of wax exactly as the finished object was to look. This wax "sculpture" was then enclosed in a heat-resistant material such as clay or plaster. (If the piece was to be hollow, the wax was formed around a heat-resistant core.) Once the clay or plaster mold had dried, it was heated and the melted wax ran out through a vent. Molten metal was then poured into the mold. After the casting had cooled and the mold was removed, the metalsmith could decorate and finish the piece.

On this torque, tiny **inlays** made of lapis lazuli, turquoise, and mother-of-pearl are part of the design. First, the worker chiseled little wells in the surface of the face and lower part of the neck, then filled the holes with inlays of the same size and shape. Most of these inlays have been lost, but one piece can still be seen on the side of the head and two more at the top of the body. A different technique was used to create the intricate inlay work on the lion's neck. Here, pieces of fine gold wire, known as **filigree**, were arranged in a pattern on the neck and subjected to just enough heat to fuse them to it. Diamond-shaped inlays were then inserted into the spaces outlined by the filigree.

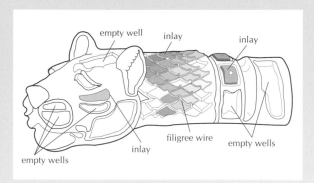

panels would have looked quite different when they were freshly painted in rich tones of deep blue, scarlet, green, purple, and turquoise, with metal objects such as Darius's crown and necklace covered in **gold leaf**, or sheets of hammered gold.

The Persians' decorative arts—including ornamented weapons, domestic wares, horse trappings, and jewelry—demonstrate high levels of technical and artistic sophistication. The imaginative use of animals in these arts can be seen in a late Achaemenid gold **torque**, or

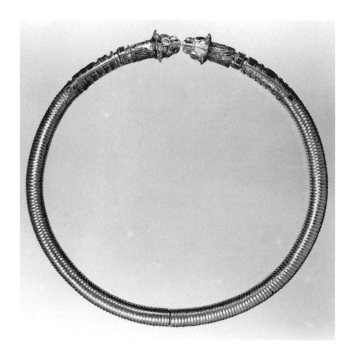

2-35. Torque with lion's-head terminals, from Susa (modern Shush, Iran). 4th century BCE. Gold with lapis lazuli, turquoise, and mother-of-pearl, diameter 8" (20.2 cm). Musée du Louvre, Paris

neckpiece, found in a Persian tomb at Susa and dated to the fourth century BCE (fig. 2-35). The tiny lion heads that form the ends, or **terminals**, of this piece are represented naturalistically, but the intricate inlays of lapis lazuli, turquoise, and mother-of-pearl transform them into pure ornament. In the Roman mosaic copy of a famous fourth-century BCE Greek painting (see fig. 5-70), Darius III of Persia (ruled 335–330 BCE) wears an identical torque.

The Persians learned to mint standard coinage from the Lydians of western Anatolia after Cyrus the Great defeated Lydia's fabulously wealthy King Croesus in 546 BCE (see "Coining Money," opposite). Croesus's wealth—the source of the lasting expression "rich as Croesus"—had made Lydia an attractive target for an aggressive empire builder like Cyrus. One type of Persian coin, the gold daric, named for Darius and first minted during his regime (fig. 2-36), is among the most valuable coins in the world today. Commonly called an "archer," it shows the well-armed emperor wearing his crown and carrying a lance in his right hand; he lunges forward as if he had just let fly an arrow from his bow.

At its height, the Persian Empire extended from Africa to India. Only mainland Greeks successfully resisted the armies of the Achaemenids, preventing them from advancing into Europe (Chapter 5). And it was a Greek who ultimately put an end to their empire. In 334 BCE, Alexander the Great of Macedonia crossed into Anatolia and swept through Mesopotamia, defeating Darius III and nearly laying waste the magnificent Persepolis in 331 BCE. Although the Persian Empire was at an end, the art style unified there during the Achaemenid period clearly shows its links with Greece as well as with Egypt, which may have been heavily influenced by Mesopotamian culture.

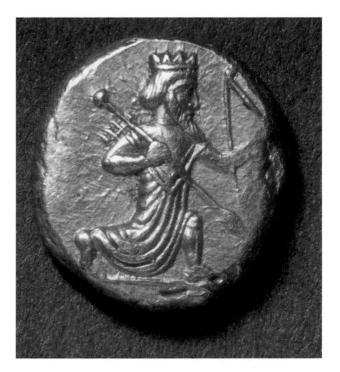

2-36. Daric, a coin first minted under Darius I of Persia. 4th century BCE. Gold. Heberden Coin Room, Ashmolean Museum, Oxford

TECHNIQUE

COINING MONEY

Long before the invention of coins, the people of the ancient world had used gold, silver, bronze, and copper in either raw lumps or bricks as a medium of exchange for trade. But each piece had to be weighed every time it was used to establish its exact value. The Lydians of western Anatolia began the practice of producing metal coins in standard weights in the seventh century BCE, adapting the concept of the seal—a Sumerian invention—to designate their value. Until about 525 BCE, coins bore an image on one side only. One of the most beautiful of these earliest coins is illustrated here, a coin first minted during the reign of the Lydian king Croesus (ruled 560–546 BCE). It is stamped with the heads and forelegs of a bull and lion, who face each other. The back side has only a squarish depression left by the punch used to force the metal into the mold.

To make two-faced coins, the ancients used a punch and anvil, each of which held a die, or mold, incised with the design to be impressed in the coin. A metal blank weighed out to the exact amount of the denomination was placed over the anvil die, the one containing the design for the obverse ("head") of the coin. The punch, with the die of the reverse ("tail") design, was then placed on top of the metal blank and struck with a mallet. After Cyrus the Great of Persia conquered Anatolia, he and his successors minted coins using the Lydian weight system. Beginning in the reign of Darius I, kings' portraits appear on coins, proclaiming the ruler's sovereignty and his control of the coin of the realm. This custom is still very much alive throughout the world. Because we often know at least approximately when a given ancient monarch ruled, the discovery in an archeological excavation of coins bearing that ruler's portrait helps to date the objects around them.

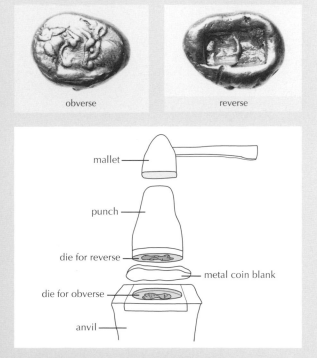

obverse   reverse

mallet

punch

die for reverse

metal coin blank

die for obverse

anvil

Front and back of a gold coin first minted under Croesus, king of Lydia. 560–546 BCE. Heberden Coin Room, Ashmolean Museum, Oxford

BCE 4000   3500   3000   2500

Hierakonpolis jar
c. 3500–3400

Palette of
Narmer
c. 3150–3125

Pyramids at Giz
c. 2601–2515

▲ PREDYNASTIC PRE-3150   ▲ EARLY DYNASTIC 3150–2700   ▲ OLD KINGDOM 2700–2190

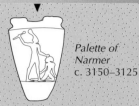
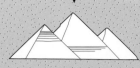

CHAPTER 3

Art of Ancient Egypt

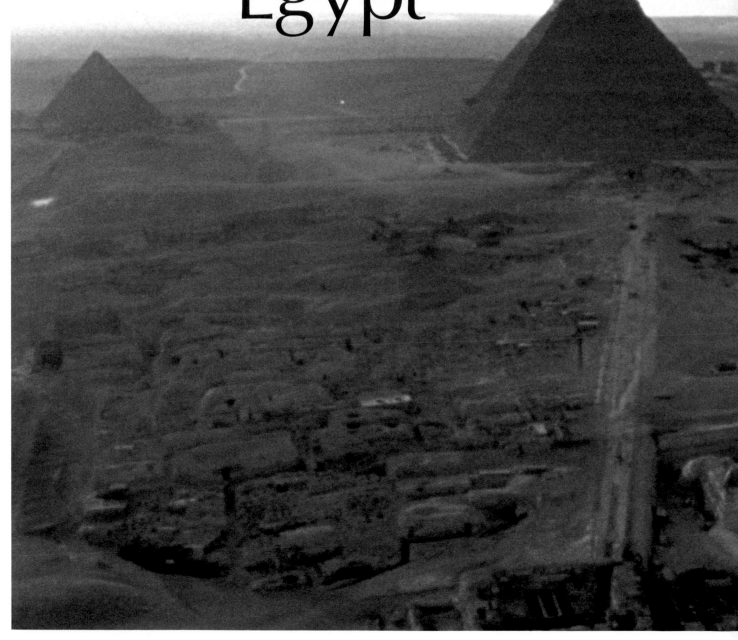

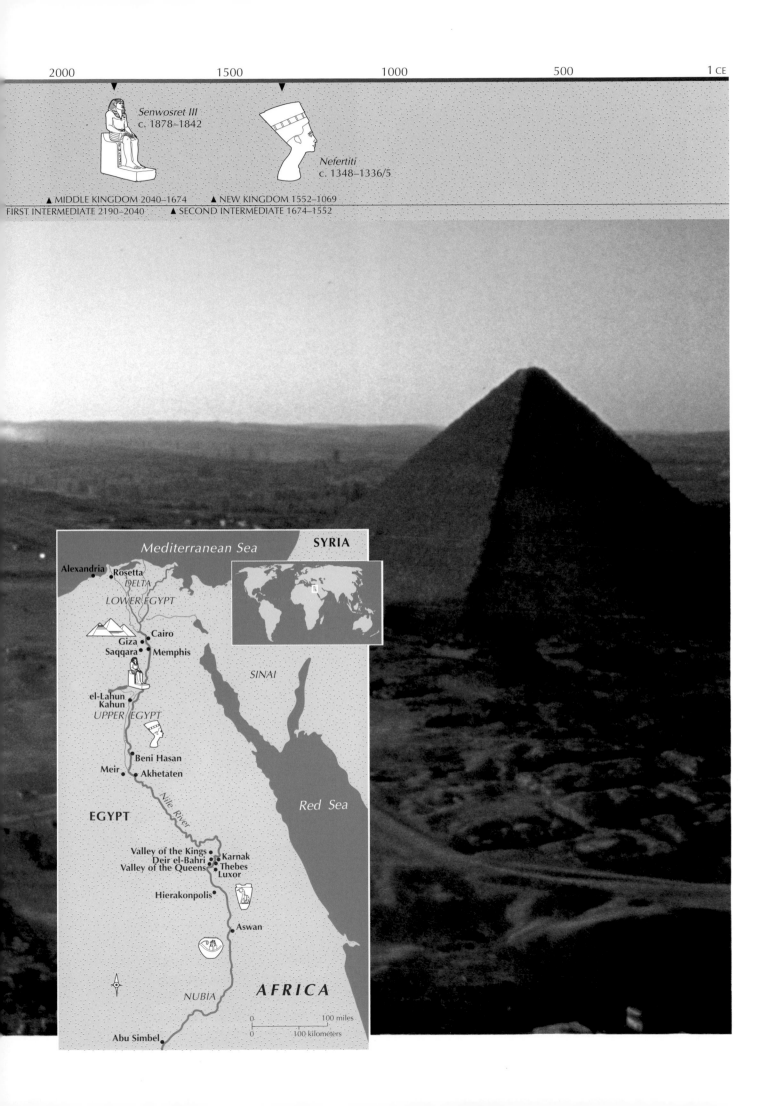

2000   1500   1000   500   1 CE

Senwosret III
c. 1878–1842

Nefertiti
c. 1348–1336/5

▲ MIDDLE KINGDOM 2040–1674   ▲ NEW KINGDOM 1552–1069
FIRST INTERMEDIATE 2190–2040   ▲ SECOND INTERMEDIATE 1674–1552

Mediterranean Sea

SYRIA

Alexandria • Rosetta
DELTA
LOWER EGYPT

Giza • Cairo
Saqqara • • Memphis

SINAI

el-Lahun
Kahun
UPPER EGYPT

Beni Hasan
Meir • • Akhetaten

Red Sea

Nile River

EGYPT

Valley of the Kings • • Karnak
Deir el-Bahri • • Thebes
Valley of the Queens • • Luxor

Hierakonpolis •

Aswan •

AFRICA

NUBIA

0   100 miles
0   100 kilometers

Abu Simbel •

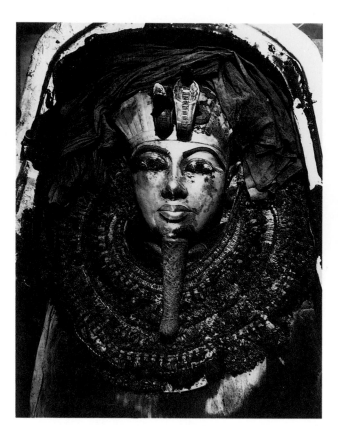
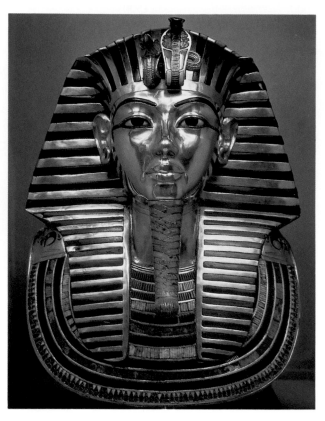

3-1. Funerary mask of Tutankhamun (ruled 1336/5–1327 BCE), from the tomb of Tutankhamun, Valley of the Kings, Deir el-Bahri, photographed the day it was discovered—October 28, 1925

A collar of dried flowers and beads covered the chest portion of the mask, and a linen scarf was draped around the head. The mask had been placed over the upper part of the young king's mummified body, which was enclosed in three coffins nested like a set of Russian dolls. These coffins were placed in a quartzite "box" that was itself encased within three gilt wooden shrines, each larger than the last. The innermost coffin, made of solid gold, is illustrated in figure 3-41. Tutankhamun's burial chamber was not the only royal tomb to survive unpillaged to the twentieth century, but it is by far the richest find.

3-2. Funerary mask of Tutankhamun. Gold inlaid with glass and semiprecious stones. Height 21¼" (54.5 cm). Egyptian Museum, Cairo

The first large-scale "archeological" expedition in history landed in Egypt with the armies of Napoleon in 1798. The French commander went there intending to take control of the region and to explore the possibility of digging a canal to connect the Mediterranean with the Red Sea. Clearly, he also sensed that Egypt sheltered great riches that might be won for France, for he took with him some 200 French scholars and charged them with mapping, excavating, and studying ancient sites. Napoleon's military adventure ended in failure, but the findings of his scholars, eventually published in thirty-six richly illustrated volumes, unleashed among his contemporaries a craze for all things Egyptian.

Popular fascination with this ancient African culture has not dimmed since Napoleon's time. As recently as May 1995, newspaper headlines around the world heralded a major discovery by archeologists working near Thebes, an ancient Egyptian capital some 300 miles south of Cairo. The huge, unusual burial complex they found in the Valley of the Kings has at least sixty-seven chambers, believed to hold the remains of many of Ramesses II's fifty-two sons. Because looters apparently have never penetrated the back chambers, the contents—including thousands of pieces of pottery, statue fragments, beads, and jewelry—provide extraordinary documentation of a period in the thirteenth-century BCE when Ramesses II was expanding the Egyptian empire and building some of the monumental architecture for which Egypt is known.

Looters, ancient and modern, have been attracted to tombs by simple greed, archeologists and historians by scholarly interest. Ironically, one reason that *this* burial complex had not been discovered by either group was that its entrance was obscured by debris from a nearby excavation in the 1920s: the remarkable tomb of Tutankhamun (King Tut). When the "Treasures of Tutankhamun" exhibit was mounted in the late 1970s, some 7 million visitors flocked to six of the world's major museums to marvel at a selection of artifacts placed in the tomb of an Egyptian ruler more than 3,000 years ago (figs. 3-1, 3-2, 3-41).

Much of what we know about life in ancient Egypt we owe to that culture's preoccupation with death. Many of Egypt's written records were lost in the accidental burning in Roman times of the great library at Alexandria—a fire that destroyed more than 700,000 ancient documents—and we must deduce what we can about Egypt from the decoration and outfitting of tombs like Tutankhamun's. The rulers of Egypt, even in earliest times, sought to immortalize themselves through the art and architecture they commissioned for their final resting places, and in a sense they succeeded richly. They are well remembered.

NEOLITHIC AND PREDYNASTIC EGYPT

The Greek traveler and historian Herodotus, writing in the fifth century BCE, remarked that "Egypt is the gift of the Nile." This great river—the longest in the world—has two major tributaries: the Blue Nile, which originates in the mountains of Ethiopia, and the White Nile, fed by a number of smaller rivers rising deep in equatorial Africa. The two tributary Niles merge at the city of Khartoum, in Sudan. From there, the Nile proper winds northward into Egypt, then flows through it in a relatively straight line to the Mediterranean, where it forms a broad delta before emptying into the sea. Before it was dammed in the twentieth century at Aswan, the lower river, swollen with the runoff of heavy seasonal rains in the south, overflowed its banks for several months each year. Every time the floodwaters receded, they left behind a new layer of rich silt, which made the valley and delta uncommonly fertile, an attractive habitat for prehistoric hunters and gatherers.

By about 8000 BCE, the valley's inhabitants had become relatively sedentary, living off its abundance of fish, game, and wild plants. It was not until about 5500 BCE that they adopted the agricultural, village way of life associated with Neolithic culture (Chapter 1). At that time the climate of North Africa was growing increasingly dry. To secure an adequate supply of water for their crops and their own domestic use, the early agriculturalists along the Nile—much as had those in Mesopotamia—cooperated to control the river's flow, constructing dams and irrigation canals. It was apparently this common need that led many smaller riverside settlements to form alliances with their neighbors. Over time, these primitive federations expanded further by conquering and absorbing weaker communities. By about 3500 BCE there were several larger states, or chiefdoms, in the lower Nile Valley.

The Predynastic period, roughly 4350 to 3150 BCE, was a time of social and political transition preceding the unification of Egypt under a single ruler and the formation of the dynasties, in which members of the same family inherited Egypt's throne. During this period, a new type of leadership emerged in which political control was bolstered by the rulers' claims to have divine powers. Their subjects, in turn, expected such leaders to protect them not only from outside aggression but also from natural catastrophes such as droughts and insect plagues. If a ruler failed to do this, he was removed from power and a more promising leader installed. A royal ritual practiced in the Dynastic period suggests that early rulers may even have been killed when their supposed supernatural powers failed to work. In this later ritual, called the *sed* festival, the king in the thirtieth year of his reign was symbolically buried and resurrected as a means of renewing his "divine" powers. Preceding this, he ran a race on a specially built track in order to prove his physical fitness.

The surviving art of the Predynastic period consists chiefly of ceramic figurines, decorated pottery, and reliefs carved on stone plaques and pieces of ivory. A few examples of Predynastic wall painting—lively scenes filled with small figures of people and animals—were found in

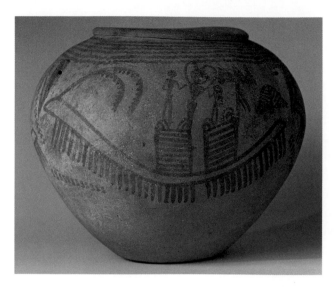

3-3. *Jar with River Scene*, from Hierakonpolis. Predynastic, c. 3500–3400 BCE. Painted clay, 7 x 8¼" (17.5 x 20.9 cm). The Brooklyn Museum

Excavations of H. deMorgan 1907–8 (09.889.400)

though the forms they represent are reduced to the barest means. Two figures of nearly equal size, a man and woman, stand on the roof of the cabin on the left. The woman arches her long arms over her head in a gesture that may be an expression of mourning, while the man beside her and a smaller figure atop the other cabin reach out toward her. These three people possess a quality of expressiveness: the power of what they *feel* is evident.

EARLY DYNASTIC EGYPT

About 3150 BCE Egypt became a consolidated state. According to Egyptian legend, the country had previously evolved into two major kingdoms—the Two Lands—Upper Egypt in the south and Lower Egypt in the north. Some powerful ruler from Upper Egypt, referred to in an ancient document as "Menes king–Menes god," finally conquered Lower Egypt and merged the Two Lands into a single kingdom. Modern Egyptologists, experts on the history and culture of ancient Egypt, suspect that the unification process was more gradual than the legend would have us believe.

In the third century BCE, an Egyptian priest and historian named Manetho compiled a chronological listing of Egypt's rulers since the most ancient times that was based on temple records and inscriptions on temple walls. He grouped them into dynasties, or families, and included the length of each king's reign. Although the list has been much modified since Manetho's time and scholars do not fully agree about many of its dates, this dynastic chronology is still the accepted guide to ancient Egypt's long history. Manetho listed thirty dynasties that ruled the country between about 3150 and 332 BCE, when it was conquered by the Greeks. Egyptologists have grouped these dynasties into larger periods reflecting broad historical developments. This chapter covers the Predynastic period through the New Kingdom (1069 BCE), and the dating system used throughout is based on the work of French Egyptologist Nicolas Grimal.

what was either a temple or a tomb at Hierakonpolis, in Upper Egypt. This Predynastic town of mud-brick houses distributed over about 100 acres was once home to as many as 10,000 people.

Among the artifacts found at Hierakonpolis is a pottery jar, dating from about 3500–3400 BCE. It is made of buff-colored clay and decorated with a river scene in a dark reddish brown (fig. 3-3). Zigzag lines around the mouth of the jar symbolize the waters of the Nile, upon which floats a boomerang-shaped boat. According to one interpretation, the boat is laden with coffins, and the scene symbolizes the human journey on the "river of Life and Death." Palm fronds affixed to a pole on the prow bend in the wind, indicating the direction of the vessel's movement. The boat has two cabins on its deck, and a row of vertical strokes along the bottom of its hull represents oars. These lines and strokes are a kind of **abstract** visual shorthand. We recognize what they stand for even

EGYPTIAN SYMBOLS

Symbolic of kingship, the crowned figure is everywhere in Egyptian art. The false beard of a dead king is long, braided, and ends in a knob. A living king is portrayed with a shorter, squared-off beard (see fig. 3-15). The cobra, "she who rears up," was equated with the sun, the king, and some deities.

The god Horus, king of the earth and a force for good, is represented most characteristically as a falcon. Horus's eyes (*wedjat*) were regarded as symbolic of the sun and moon. The *wedjat* here is the solar eye. The ankh is symbolic of everlasting life. The scarab was associated with the creator god Atum and the rising sun.

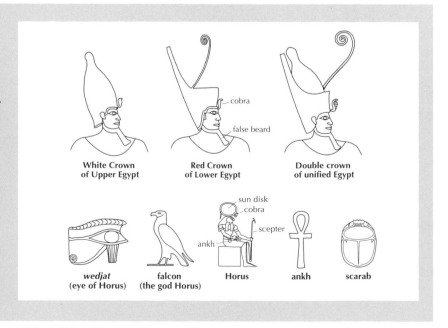

White Crown of Upper Egypt

Red Crown of Lower Egypt

cobra
false beard

Double crown of unified Egypt

wedjat (eye of Horus)

falcon (the god Horus)

sun disk
cobra
scepter
ankh

Horus

ankh

scarab

PARALLELS

Years	Period	Egypt	World
Before 3150 BCE	**Predynastic**	Painted clay pottery	**c. 3500–3000 BCE** Earliest pictographs (Sumer); pictographs evolve into ideograms and phonograms (China, India); Skara Brae settled (Scotland)
c. 3150–2700 BCE	**Early Dynastic (or Archaic)** Dynasties 1–2	Egypt united under "Menes"; *Palette of Narmer*; development of hieroglyphic writing; manufacture and export of papyrus scrolls	
c. 2700–2190 BCE	**Old Kingdom** Dynasties 3–6	Djoser's stepped pyramid; Great Pyramids at Giza	
c. 2190–2040 BCE	**First Intermediate** Dynasties 7–10		**c. 2000 BCE** *Gilgamesh* epic (Sumer); widespread use of bronze tools (Thailand, China, northern Europe); earliest Minoan palace at Knossos (Crete); first city-state in Anatolia
c. 2040–1674 BCE	**Middle Kingdom** Dynasties 11–14	Rock-cut tombs; faience *Hippopotamus*	
c. 1674–1552 BCE	**Second Intermediate** Dynasties 15–17	Hyksos, from eastern Mediterranean, occupy Nile Delta	**c. 1600–1500 BCE** Pacific islands colonized; Shang dynasty (China); citadel at Mycenae (Greece)
c. 1552–1069 BCE	**New Kingdom** Dynasties 18–20	Great Temple of Amun, Karnak; *Nefertiti*	**c. 1450–1200 BCE** Minoan palaces destroyed (Crete); spread of phonetic alphabet devised by Canaanites (eastern Mediterranean); Israelites led out of Egypt by Moses (Canaan); Olmec civilization (Mesoamerica)

Religious Beliefs

Herodotus thought the Egyptians the most religious people he had ever encountered. It is certainly true that religious beliefs permeate Egyptian art of all periods, and some knowledge of them is needed to understand the art.

At the time of the Early Dynastic period, Egypt's rulers were worshiped as gods after their deaths; thus, ordinary Egyptians considered their kings to be their link to the invisible gods of the universe. To please the gods and ensure their continuing goodwill toward the state, Egypt's kings built them splendid temples and provided for priests to maintain them. The priests were responsible for seeing to it that statues of the gods, placed deep in the innermost rooms of their temples, were never without fresh food and clothing. The many gods and goddesses were depicted in various forms, some as human beings, others as animals, and still others as creatures half human, half animal.

Osiris, for example, the god of the dead, regularly appears in human form, as does his wife, Isis. The sky god Horus, however, was most often depicted as having a human body but the head of a hawk. The sun god Ra appears at some times as a cobra, at other times as a scarab beetle (see "Egyptian Symbols," opposite).

Certain gods took on different forms over the course of time, and a given god might be worshiped in different parts of the country under different names. In the New Kingdom at Thebes, the great creation god Amun and the sun god Ra came to be venerated as the single deity Amun-Ra. Everywhere else in Egypt in this period the two continued to be thought of as separate gods. At the heart of Egyptian religion are stories that explain how the world, the gods, and human beings came into being (see "Egyptian Myths of Creation," page 96).

Egyptian religious beliefs reflect the sense of an ordered cosmos. The movements of the heavenly bodies,

EGYPTIAN MYTHS OF CREATION

Herodotus's contention that the Egyptians were the most obsessively religious people he knew is amply supported by the large number of gods encountered in ancient Egyptian documents. At one time even the Nile itself was revered as a god. Early Egyptian creation myths provide a convenient introduction to many of the earliest and most important deities in Egypt's confusing and sometimes contradictory pantheon. One myth, focusing on the origins of the gods themselves, relates that the sun god Ra—or Ra-Atum—formed himself out of the waters of chaos, or unformed matter, emerging from them seated atop a mound of sand hardened by his own rays. By spitting—or ejaculating—he then created the gods of wetness and dryness, Tefnut and Shu, who in turn begat the male Geb (earth) and the female Nut (sky). Geb and Nut produced two sons, Osiris and Seth—the gods of goodness and evil, respectively—and two daughters, Isis and Nephthys (Isis can be seen in figure 3-43).

Taking Isis as his wife, Osiris became king of Egypt. His envious brother Seth promptly killed Osiris and hacked his body to pieces, snatching the throne for himself. Isis and her sister, Nephthys, gathered up the scattered remains and, with the help of the god Anubis, patched Osiris back together. Despite her husband's mutilated condition, Isis somehow managed to conceive a son—Horus. Once Horus was on the scene (another power for good capable of guarding the interests of Egypt), he defeated Seth and became king of the earth, while Osiris retired to the underworld as overseer of the realm of the dead (see fig. 3-44).

As for the creation of human beings, it is said in one story that Ra once lost an eye. Unperturbed, he replaced it with a new one. When the old eye was found and brought back to him, it began to cry, angered that it was no longer of any use. Human beings were born from its tears. In a variation on this myth, the people of Memphis insisted that it was their local god Ptah who created humankind, having formed us on his potter's wheel.

Some rulers of Akkad in the ancient Near East were held to be gods, and by the time of the Early Dynastic period, Egypt's kings were revered as gods in human form. A New Kingdom practice helps to explain the Egyptian belief of that period regarding the origin of rulers. Each year as part of the *opet* festival, the celebration of the flooding of the Nile, the statue of the god Amun from the temple at Karnak was carried in rich procession, along with statues of his wife and son, Mut and Khonsu, to their alternate temple at Luxor, to the south. Inscriptions in the processional colonnade record that while at Luxor the all-powerful god miraculously conceives a future ruler of Egypt.

the workings of the gods, and the humblest of human activities were all thought to be part of a grand design of balance and harmony. Death was to be feared only by those who lived in such a way as to disrupt that harmony; upright souls could be confident that their spirits would live on eternally.

The *Palette of Narmer*

The legendary king-god Menes may have been an actual king named Narmer (Dynasty 1, ruled c. 3150–3125 BCE), known from a famous stone plaque, the *Palette of Narmer* (fig. 3-4), found at Hierakonpolis. The palette is a slate slab carved in low relief on both sides with scenes and identifying inscriptions. The ruler's name appears on both sides in **pictographs**, or picture writing, in a small square at the top: a horizontal fish *(nar)* above a vertical chisel *(mer)*. The cow heads on each side of his name symbolize the protective goddess Hathor.

Palettes, flat stones with a circular depression on one side, were common utensils of the time. They were used for mixing eye paint. Men and women both painted their eyelids to help prevent infections in the eyes and perhaps to reduce the glare of the sun, much as football players today blacken their cheekbones before a game. The *Palette of Narmer* has the same form as these common objects but is much larger. It and other large palettes decorated with animals, birds, and occasionally human figures probably had a ceremonial function.

King Narmer appears as the main character in the various scenes on the palette. They may commemorate a specific battle, or they may simply make use of established images of conquest to proclaim Narmer the great unifier, protector, and leader of the Egyptian people. As in the *Stela of Naramsin* (see fig. 2-16), the ruler is shown larger than the other human figures on the palette to indicate his divine status. Interestingly, the kneeling man that Narmer holds by the hair and prepares to strike with his heavy mace would be very close to the king's height if he were standing (fig. 3-4, left). His size suggests that he may represent Narmer's counterpart, the conquered ruler of Lower Egypt. Narmer himself wears the White Crown of Upper Egypt, and from his waistband hangs a ceremonial bull's tail signifying strength. He is barefoot, suggesting that this is not an illustration of an actual military encounter but rather a symbolic representation of a hero's preordained victory. An attendant standing behind Narmer holds his sandals. Above Narmer's kneeling foe, the god Horus, in the form of a hawk with a human hand, holds a rope tied around the neck of a man's head next to a few stylized stalks of **papyrus**, a plant that grew in profusion along the lower Nile. This combination of symbols again makes it clear that Lower Egypt has been tamed. In the bottom **register**, below Narmer's feet, two of his enemies appear to be running away, or perhaps they are sprawled on the ground just as they fell when they were killed.

On the other side of the palette (fig. 3-4, right), Narmer is shown in the top register wearing the Red Crown of Lower Egypt, making it clear that he now rules both lands. Here his name—the fish and chisel—appears not only in the rectangle at the top but also next to his

3200
4000 BCE   1 CE

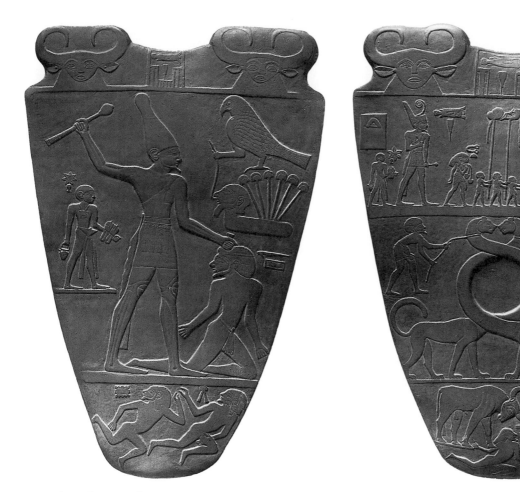

3-4. *Palette of Narmer*, from Hierakonpolis. Dynasty 1, c. 3150–3125 BCE. Slate, height 25" (63.5 cm). Egyptian Museum, Cairo

head. With his sandal bearer again in attendance, he marches behind his minister of state and four men carrying standards that may symbolize different regions of the country. Before them, under the watchful eye of the hawk Horus, is a gory depiction of the enemy dead. The decapitated bodies of Lower Egyptian warriors have been placed in two neat rows, their heads between their feet.

In the center register, the elongated necks of two monstrous creatures with feline heads, each held on a leash by an attendant, curve gracefully around the rim of the cup of the palette. The intertwining of their necks is possibly another reference to the union of the Two Lands. In the bottom register, a bull menaces a fallen foe outside the walls of a fortress. The bull, an animal known for its great strength and virility, is probably meant to symbolize the king.

The images carved on the palette are strong and direct, and although scholars disagree about some of their specific meanings, their overall message is simple and clear: a king named Narmer rules over the unified land of Egypt with a strong hand. Narmer's palette is particularly important because of the way it uses pictographs and symbols, showing much about the development of writing in Egypt. Moreover, it provides very early examples of the quite unusual way Egyptian artists solved the problem of depicting the human form in two-dimensional art such as relief sculpture or painting.

Representation of the Human Figure

Forceful and easy to comprehend, the images on the Narmer palette present a king's exploits as he wished them to be remembered. For the next several thousand years, much of Egyptian art was created to meet the demand of royal patrons for similarly graphic, indestructible testimonies to their glory.

Many of the figures on the palette are shown in poses that would be impossible to assume in real life. By Narmer's time, Egyptian artists, using the "memory image" (see Chapter 1), had arrived at a unique way of drawing the human figure. The Egyptians' aim was to represent each part of the body from the most characteristic angle. Heads are shown in profile, to best capture the subject's identifying features. Eyes, however, are most expressive when seen from the front, so artists rendered the eyes in these profile heads in frontal view. As for the rest of the body, they treated the shoulders as though from the front, but at the waist they twisted the figure drastically to be able to show hips, legs, and feet in profile. If both hands were required in front of a figure, artists routinely lengthened the arm reaching across the body rather than turn the body sideways. Unless the degree of action demanded otherwise, they placed one foot in front of the other on the **groundline**, showing both from the inside, with high-arched insteps and a single big toe. This artistic

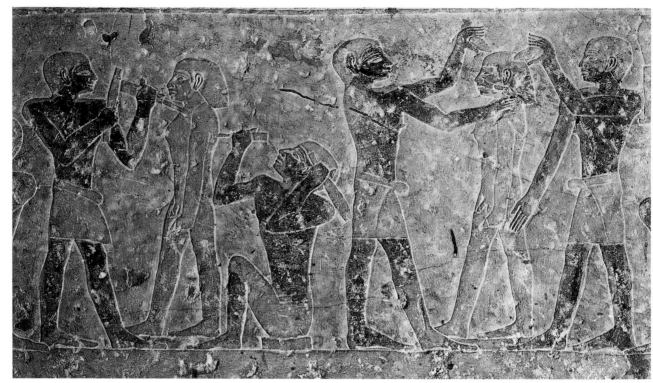

3-5. *Sculptors at Work*, relief from Saqqara. Dynasty 5, c. 2510–2460 BCE. Painted stone. Egyptian Museum, Cairo

tradition, or convention, was followed especially in the depiction of royalty and other dignitaries, and it was considered so successful that it persisted until the fourth century BCE. Persons of lesser social rank engaged in more active tasks tended to be represented more naturally (compare the figure of Narmer with those of his standard bearers in figure 3-4, right). Similarly, long-standing conventions governed the depiction of animals, insects, inanimate objects, landscape, and architecture. Flies, for example, are always shown from above, bees from the side.

In three-dimensional sculpture, figures could be constructed as they are in life. A painted relief from the funerary complex at Saqqara, created at least 600 years later than the *Palette of Narmer*, shows that artists working in two dimensions were perfectly capable of drawing "normal" figures as well (fig. 3-5). It shows a pair of sculptors putting the finishing touches on a statue. The "living" sculptors are portrayed in the conventional twisted pose, while the statue itself appears in full profile, as it would in reality.

Just as Egyptian artists adhered to artificial convention in the posing of figures, they also proportioned their figures in accordance with an ideal image of the human form, following an established **canon of proportions**. The ratios between a figure's height and all of its component parts were clearly prescribed. They were calculated as multiples of a specific unit of measure such as the width of the closed fist. It is likely that the ideal was in fact dictated to schools of artists by their royal patrons. Egypt's royalty in a given period may or may not have been of a different racial makeup than the general populace. In any case, they considered themselves a superior breed and

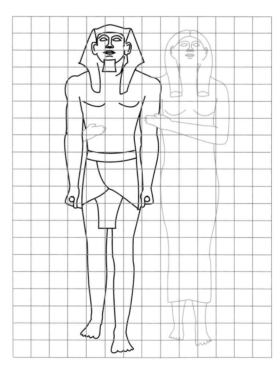

3-6. Diagram of a hypothetical grid for canon of proportions in use during the Old Kingdom

This canon set the height of the human body from heel to hairline at eighteen times the width of the fist. (There are eighteen squares between the heel of the king's left foot and the top of his headdress.) The hypothetical grid shown here is overlaid on a simple drawing of the statue of *Menkaure and His Wife, Queen Khamerernebty* (fig. 3-15). The proportions are for the figure on the left. Because the queen had to be smaller than the king, she was carved according to another, slightly smaller canon.

wished to have their own specific physical attributes held up to the masses as those befitting majesty.

The specific measure employed and the proportions derived from it varied slightly over time, but the underlying concept and the means by which it was implemented did not. Having determined the size of a desired figure, the artist first covered the area the figure was to occupy with a grid made up of a fixed number of squares (fig. 3-6). The figure could then be sketched quite mechanically. If the width of the fist was the canon's basic unit of measure, the artist saw to it that each hand was one square wide. Knowing that the knee should fall a prescribed number of squares above the groundline, the waist x number of squares above the knee, and so on made the process quite formulaic. The grid itself was either removed or covered up as the work progressed.

THE OLD KINGDOM

The Old Kingdom (2700–2190 BCE) was a time of social cohesion and political stability, despite changes in Egypt's climate that made droughts and plagues of insects increasingly common and the need of the country's rulers to mount occasional military excursions to defend its borders. The increasing wealth of the ruling families of the period is reflected in the size and complexity of the tomb structures they commissioned for themselves. Court sculptors were regularly called upon to create lifesize, even colossal royal portraits in stone. Kings were not the only patrons of the arts, however. Numerous government officials and administrators also could afford to have their tombs decorated with elaborate carvings.

Funerary Architecture

Central to ancient Egyptian religious belief was the notion that an essential part of every human personality was its life force, or spirit. This spirit, called the **ka**, lived on after the death of the body, forever engaged in the activities it had enjoyed in its former existence. The ka needed a body to live in, but in the absence of one of flesh and blood, a sculpted likeness of the deceased was adequate. It was especially important to provide a comfortable home for the ka of a departed king, so that even in the afterlife it would continue to ensure the well-being of the Egyptian state.

The need to fulfill the requirements of the ka led the Egyptians to develop elaborate funerary rites and structures. They preserved the bodies of the dead with care and placed them in burial chambers filled with all of the supplies and furnishings the ka might require throughout eternity (see "Preserving the Dead," page 121). The quantity and value of these grave goods were so great that tombs were routinely plundered by looters even in ancient times.

In the Early Dynastic period, the most common type of tomb structure in Egypt was the **mastaba**, a flat-topped, one-story building with slanted walls erected above an underground burial chamber (see "Elements of Architecture," page 103). Mastabas were customarily constructed of mud brick, but toward the end of Dynasty 3 more and more incorporated cut stone, at least as an exterior facing, or **veneer**. In its simplest form, the mastaba contained a **serdab**, a small, sealed room housing the ka statue of the deceased, and a chapel designed to receive mourning relatives with their offerings. A vertical shaft led from the top of the mastaba down to the actual burial chamber, where the remains of the deceased reposed in a **sarcophagus**, or stone coffin, surrounded by the appropriate grave goods. This chamber was sealed off once interment was completed. Mastaba burial remained the standard for Egyptian royalty for centuries. Many such structures were enlarged with numerous underground chambers to accommodate whole families.

The kings of Dynasties 3 and 4 were the first to devote huge sums to the design, construction, and decoration of more extensive aboveground funerary complexes. These structures tended to be grouped together in a **necropolis**—literally, a city of the dead—at the edge of the desert on the west bank of the Nile, for the land of the dead was held to be in the direction of the setting sun. Two of the most extensive of these early necropolises are those at Saqqara and Giza, just outside modern Cairo.

Djoser's Funerary Complex at Saqqara. For his tomb complex at Saqqara, King Djoser (Dynasty 3, ruled c. 2681–2662 BCE) commissioned the earliest known monumental architecture in Egypt (fig. 3-7). The designer of the complex was a man called Imhotep. His name appears inscribed on the pedestal of Djoser's ka statue in the serdab of the funerary temple to the north of the tomb. He is thus the first architect in history known by name. Born into a prominent family, Imhotep was highly educated and served as one of Djoser's chief advisers on affairs of state. It appears that he first planned Djoser's tomb as a single-story mastaba, then later decided to enlarge upon the concept. In the end, what he produced was a stepped pyramid (fig. 3-8) consisting of six mastabalike elements of decreasing size placed on top of each other (see "Elements of Architecture," page 103). Although his final structure resembles the **ziggurats** of Mesopotamia, it differs in both its planned concept and its purpose of protecting a tomb. Djoser's imposing structure was originally faced with a veneer of limestone. From its top a 92-foot shaft descended to a granite-lined burial vault.

The adjacent funerary temple, where priests performed their final rituals before placing the king's mummified body in its tomb, was also used for continuing worship of the dead king. In the form of his ka statue, Djoser was able to observe these devotions through two peepholes bored through the wall between the serdab and the funerary chapel. To the east of the pyramid were sham buildings—simple masonry shells filled with debris—representing chapels, palaces with courtyards, and other structures. They were provided so that the dead king could continue to observe the *sed* rituals that had ensured his long reign. His spirit could await the start of the ceremonies in a pavilion near the entrance to the

3-7. Plan of Djoser's funerary complex, Saqqara. c. 2681–
2662 BCE (Dynasty 3)

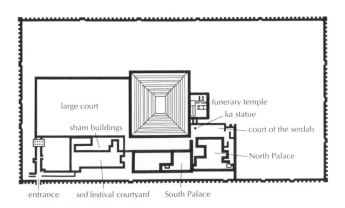

Situated on a level terrace, this huge commemorative
complex—some 1,800 feet long by 900 feet wide—
was designed as a sort of miniature replica of the king's
earthly realm. Its enclosing wall, fitted out with fourteen
gates, only one of which was actually functional, represented the realm's boundaries. Inside rose the tomb
structure proper, a funerary temple, and other buildings
and courtyards for the king's use in the hereafter.

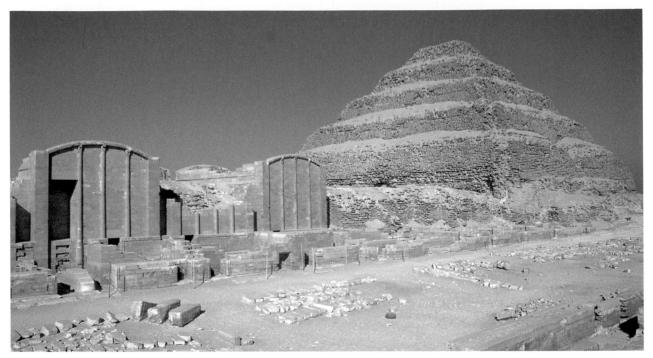

3-8.   Stepped pyramid of Djoser, Saqqara. Limestone, height 204' (62 m)

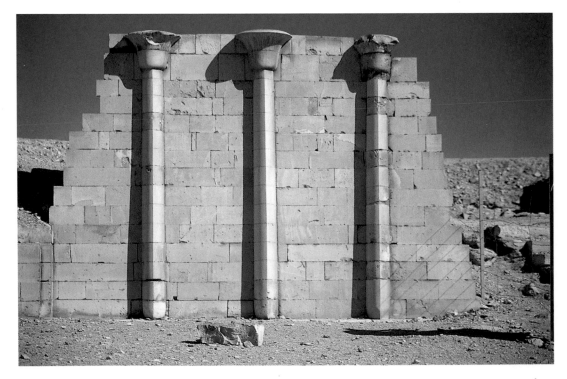

3-9.   Wall of the North Palace, with engaged columns in the form of papyrus blossoms. Funerary complex
of Djoser, Saqqara

ELEMENTS OF ARCHITECTURE
Column and Colonnade

A **column** is a cylindrical, upright **pillar** that has three sections: a **base**, a **shaft**, and a top, called a **capital**. Most columns are **freestanding** and are used to support weight, usually a roof. When used decoratively and attached to a wall, a column is referred to as an **engaged column** or **attached column** (see fig. 3-9).

A **colonnade** is a row of columns supporting a horizontal member. Egyptians used columns, with and without bases, in their **temple complexes**, in forms that are based on river plants. Persian columns use the same elements very differently.

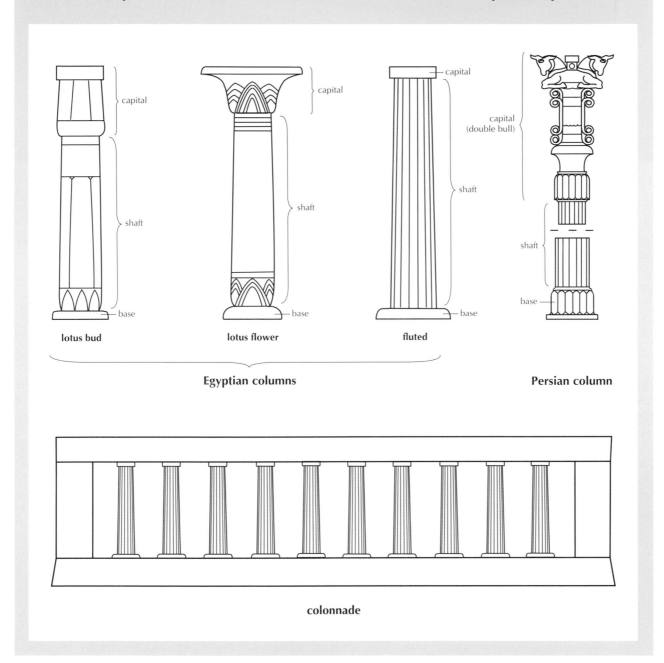

lotus bud   lotus flower   fluted

Egyptian columns   **Persian column**

colonnade

complex in its southeast corner. The running trials of the *sed* festival took place in a long outdoor courtyard within the complex. After proving himself, the king's spirit proceeded first to the South Palace then to the North Palace, to be symbolically crowned once again as king of Egypt's Two Lands.

Imhotep's architecture employs the most elemental structural techniques and the purest of geometric forms.

Although most of the stone wall surfaces were left plain, in some places he made effective use of **columns**. Some of these are plain except for fluting, others take the form of stylized plants. The **engaged columns** spaced along the exterior walls of the North Palace, for example (fig. 3-9), resemble stalks of papyrus. Stylized papyrus blossoms serve as their capitals. These columns may have been patterned after the bundled papyrus stalks early

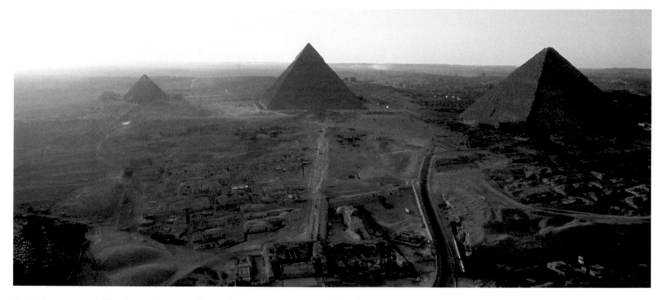

3-10. Great Pyramids, Giza. Dynasty 4, c. 2601–2515 BCE. Erected by (from left) Menkaure, Khafre, and Khufu. Granite and limestone, height of pyramid of Khufu 450' (137 m)

For many centuries it was not known that the pyramids were the tombs of early Egyptian rulers. One theory was that they were gigantic silos for storing grain during periods of drought and famine. This notion was fostered in part by the discovery that the pyramids' accessible interior spaces were empty. The designers of the pyramids tried to ensure that the king and the tomb "home" would never be disturbed. Khufu's builders placed his tomb chamber in the very heart of the mountain of masonry, at the end of a long, narrow, steeply rising passageway, sealed off after the king's burial by a 50-ton stone block. Three false passageways, either deliberately meant to mislead or the result of changes in plan as construction progressed, obscured the location of the tomb. Despite such precautions, early looters managed to penetrate to the tomb chamber and make off with Khufu's funeral treasure.

Egyptian builders used to reinforce mud walls and symbolized Lower Egypt. By contrast, the architectural decorations of the South Palace featured plants symbolic of Upper Egypt, the flowering sedge and the lotus (see "Elements of Architecture," page 101).

The Pyramids at Giza. The architectural form most closely identified with Egypt is the true pyramid with a square base and four sloping triangular faces. The first such structures were erected in Dynasty 4 (see "Elements of Architecture," opposite). The angled sides of the pyramids may have been meant to represent the slanting rays of the sun, for inscriptions on the walls of pyramid tombs built in Dynasties 5 and 6 tell of deceased kings climbing up the rays to join the sun god Ra.

Egypt's most famous funerary structures are the three great pyramid tombs at Giza (fig. 3-10). These were built by the Dynasty 4 kings Khufu (ruled c. 2601–2578 BCE), Khafre (ruled c. 2570–2544 BCE), and Menkaure (ruled c. 2533–2515 BCE). The Greeks were so impressed

THE SEVEN WONDERS OF THE WORLD Lists for travelers of marvelous sights not to miss are known from many ancient civilizations. Such lists—more or less consistent—make their appearance in the writings of various Greek authors as early as 200–100 BCE, their attractions heralded as the Seven Wonders of the World. Not surprisingly, the majority of the sites included were examples of the Greeks' own engineering and architectural skill. The oldest of these "wonders," and the only one still reasonably intact today, is the trio of pyramids at Giza (see fig. 3-10), built between 2601 and 2515 BCE. The next oldest, the so-called Hanging Gardens built for Nebuchadnezzar II in Babylon in the sixth century BCE (see fig. 2-26), had disappeared long before it made the list, although sections of what are believed to be its foundations have been excavated. The Greek entries, none of which survive, must be imagined from written descriptions, sculptural fragments, and archeological reconstructions. They include the temple of the goddess Artemis at Ephesos, from the sixth century BCE; the statue of the god Zeus at Olympia by Pheidias, about 430 BCE; the Mausoleum at Halikarnassos, fourth century BCE (figure 5-61 shows a conjectural reconstruction of it); the Colossus of Rhodes, a bronze statue of the sun god Helios the height of a ten-story building, completed in 282 BCE (our own word *colossal* comes from this Greek term for an outsize human statue); and the lighthouse that guarded the port at Alexandria, in Egypt, built about 290 BCE and more than four times as tall as the Colossus. It is intriguing that people at this point in history chose to list the world's wonders. It is particularly telling that all of these wonders were the work of human hands.

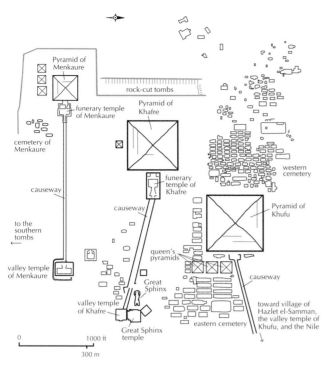

3-11. Plan of the funerary complex, Giza

by these huge, shining monuments—"pyramid" is a Greek term—that they numbered them among the world's architectural marvels (see "The Seven Wonders of the World," opposite). The early Egyptians referred to the Giza tombs as "Horizon of Khufu," "Great Is Khafre," and "Divine Is Menkaure," thus acknowledging the desire of these rulers to commemorate themselves as divine beings. The oldest and largest of the Giza pyramids is that of Khufu, which covers 13 acres at its base and rises to a height of about 450 feet in its deteriorated state. It was originally finished with a sheath of polished limestone that lifted its apex some 30 feet above the present summit, to roughly the height of a 48-story modern skyscraper. The pyramid of Khafre, the only one of the three that still has a remnant of its veneer at the top, is slightly smaller than Khufu's. Menkaure's is considerably smaller than the other two.

Next to each of the pyramids was a funerary temple connected by causeway, or elevated road, to a valley temple on the bank of the Nile (fig. 3-11). When a king died, his body was ferried across the Nile from the royal palace to his valley temple, where it was received with

ELEMENTS OF ARCHITECTURE
Mastaba to Pyramid

As the gateway to the afterlife for Egyptian kings and members of the royal court, the Egyptian burial structure began as a low rectangular **mastaba** with an internal serdab and chapel, then a mastaba with attached chapel and serdab (not shown). Later, mastaba forms of decreasing size were stacked over an underground burial chamber to form the stepped pyramid. The culmination of the Egyptian burial chamber is the pyramid, in which the actual burial site may be within the pyramid—not below ground—with false chambers, false doors, and confusing passageways to foil potential tomb robbers.

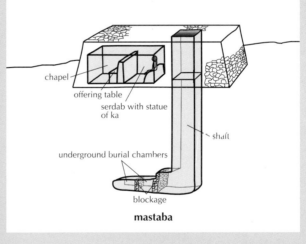

mastaba

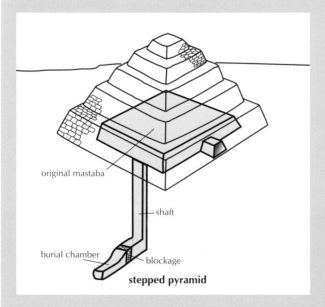

stepped pyramid

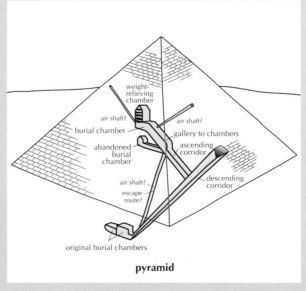

pyramid

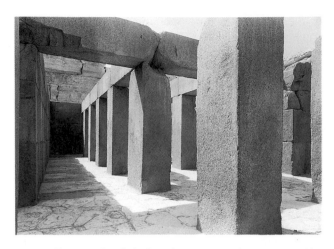

3-12. Valley temple of Khafre, Giza. Dynasty 4, c. 2570–2544 BCE. Granite posts and lintels, alabaster floor

elaborate ceremonies. It was then carried up the causeway to his funerary temple and placed in its chapel. There family members presented it with offerings of food and drink, and priests performed the rite known as the "opening of the mouth," in which the deceased's spirit consumed a meal. Then the body was entombed in a well-hidden vault inside the pyramid (see "Elements of Architecture," page 103). Khafre's funerary complex is the best preserved today. His valley temple was constructed of massive blocks of red granite. The corridor shown in figure 3-12 led to a chamber that once held a ka statue of the king (see fig. 3-13).

Constructing a pyramid was a formidable undertaking. A huge labor force had to be assembled, housed, and fed. Most of the cut stone blocks used in building the Giza complex—each weighing an average of two and a half tons—were quarried either on the site or nearby. Teams of workers transported them by sheer muscle power, at times employing small logs as rollers or pouring water on sand to create a slippery surface over which they could drag the blocks on sleds.

Scholars and engineers have advanced various theories about the method used in raising the pyramids. Some have been tested in computerized projections and a few in actual building attempts on a small but representative scale. The most efficient means of getting the stones into position might have been to build a temporary, gently sloping ramp around the body of the pyramid as it grew higher. The ramp might then be dismantled as the slabs of the stone veneer were laid from the top down. Clearly the architects who oversaw the building of such massive structures were capable of the most sophisticated mathematical calculations, for there was no room for trial and error. They had to make certain that the huge foundation layer was absolutely level and that the angle of each of the slanting sides remained constant so that the stones would meet precisely in the center at the top. They carefully oriented the pyramids to the points of the compass and may have incorporated other symbolic astronomical calculations as well. These im-

mense monuments reflect not only the desire of a trio of kings to attain immortality but also the strength of the Egyptians' belief that a deceased ruler continued to affect the well-being of the state and his people from beyond the grave.

Sculpture

As was the custom, Khafre commissioned various stone portraits of himself to perpetuate his memory for all time. In his roughly lifesize ka statue, discovered inside his valley temple, he was portrayed as an enthroned king (fig. 3-13). The Great Sphinx, a colossal monument some 65 feet tall standing just behind the valley temple, combines his head with the long body of a crouching lion (fig. 3-14). Both images have the same compactness, symmetry of form, and simple, blocklike shape. Carved from a large rock formation left intact after stone had been quarried around it, Khafre's Great Sphinx was not the first such portrayal of a king, and there are many later ones. But in size it has no equal.

In his ka statue, Khafre sits erect on a simple but elegant throne. Horus perches on the back of the throne, protectively enfolding the king's head with his wings. Lions—symbols of regal authority—form the throne's sides, and the intertwined lotus and papyrus plants beneath the seat symbolize the king's power over Upper and Lower Egypt. Khafre wears the traditional royal costume: a short kilt, a linen headdress with *uraeus*, the cobra symbol of Ra, and a false beard symbolic of royalty. Viewed from the front (fig. 3-13, left), the vertical lines of the legs, torso, and upper arms convey a strong sense of dignity, calm, and above all permanence. The statue was carved in diorite, a stone chosen for its great durability, and the figure's compactness—the arms pressed tight to the body, and the body firmly anchored in the block—ensured that the image would provide an alternative home for the king's ka for eternity.

When carving such a statue, Egyptian sculptors approached each face of the block as though they were simply carving a relief. In one the figure would be seen straight on from the front, in the others from the side or the back. Carving deeper and deeper, they finally ended up with a three-dimensional figure, and all that remained was to refine its forms and work up its surface details.

Dignity, calm, and permanence also characterize the double portrait of King Menkaure and Queen Khamerernebty, Khafre's son and daughter-in-law (fig. 3-15). But the sculptor's handling of the composition of this work, discovered in Menkaure's valley temple, makes it far less austere than Khafre's ka statue. The couple's separate figures, close in size, form a single unit, tied together by the stone out of which they emerge. They are further united by the queen's symbolic gesture of embrace. Her right hand emerges from behind to lie gently against his ribs, and her left hand rests on his upper arm. The king, depicted in accordance with the Egyptian ideal as an athletic, youthful figure nude to the waist, stands in a very Egyptian balanced pose with one foot in front of the other, his arms straight at his sides and his fists tightly

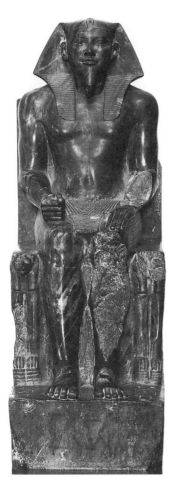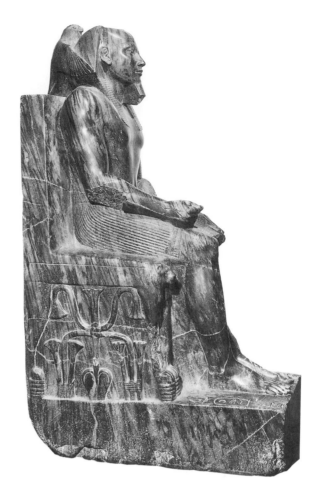

3-13. *Khafre*, from Giza. Dynasty 4, c. 2570–2544 BCE. Diorite, height 5'6¹/₈" (1.68 m). Egyptian Museum, Cairo

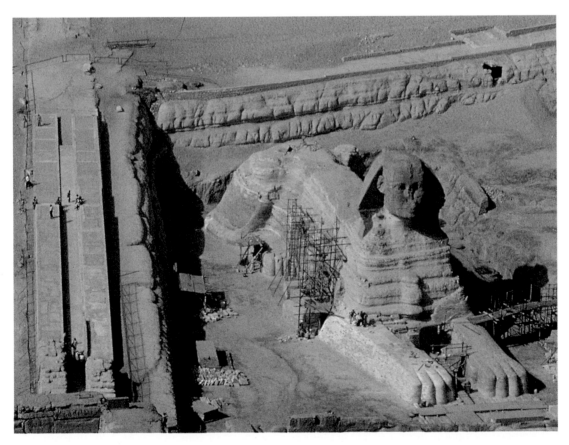

3-14. Great Sphinx, Giza. Dynasty 4, c. 2570–2544 BCE. Sandstone, height about 65' (19.8 m)

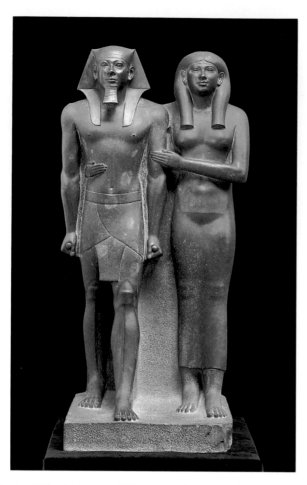

3-15. *Menkaure and His Wife, Queen Khamerernebty*, from Giza. Dynasty 4, c. 2515 BCE. Slate, height 54¹/₂" (142.3 cm). Museum of Fine Arts, Boston

Harvard University–MFA Expedition

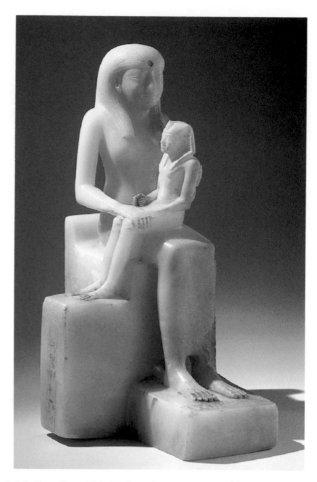

3-16. *Pepy II and His Mother, Queen Merye-ankhnes*. Dynasty 6, c. 2383–2289? BCE. Calcite, height 15¹/₄" (39.2 cm). The Brooklyn Museum

Charles Edwin Wilbour Fund (39.119)

clenched. His equally youthful queen mimics his striding pose but with a smaller step forward. The sculptor exercised remarkable skill in rendering her sheer, close-fitting garment, which clearly reveals the curves of her body. The time-consuming task of polishing this double statue was never completed, indicating that the work may have been undertaken only a few years before Menkaure's death in about 2515 BCE.

An example of a type of royal portraiture that made its appearance in Dynasty 6 (2460–2200 BCE) is presented in figure 3-16. In this statue the figure of Pepy II (ruled c. 2383–2289? BCE), wearing the royal kilt and headdress but reduced to the size of a child, is seated on his mother's lap. The work thus pays homage to Queen Merye-ankhnes, who wears a vulture-skin headdress linking her to the goddess Nekhbet and proclaiming her of royal blood. If Pepy II inherited the throne at the age of six, as Manetho claimed, then the queen may have acted as regent until he was old enough to rule alone. The sculptor placed the figure of the king at a right angle to that of his mother, thus providing two "frontal" views—the queen facing forward, the king to the side. In another break with convention, he freed the queen's arms and legs from the stone block of the throne, giving her figure greater independence.

Old Kingdom sculptors were commissioned to produce portraits not only of kings and nobles but also of many figures of lesser prominence. As can be seen from the *Seated Scribe* (fig. 3-17), a painted limestone statue from Dynasty 5, these works tend to be livelier and less formal than royal portraits. The scribe's sedentary occupation has taken its toll on his physique, leaving him soft and flabby. His face, however, reveals an alert intelligence. He sits holding a papyrus scroll partially unrolled on his lap, his right hand clasping a now-lost reed pen. The modern viewer is likely to think this portrait realistic, but in fact it is a quite conventional Old Kingdom depiction of a man of lower class—however respected his position. Many other such statues of the period exhibit the same round head and face, large wide-open eyes, genial expression, and cap of hair cut close to the skull.

Tomb Decoration

In order to provide the ka with the most pleasant possible living quarters for eternity, wealthy families often had the interior walls and ceilings of their tombs decorated with paintings and reliefs. Much of this decoration was symbolic or religious, especially in royal tombs, but it could also include a wide variety of everyday scenes

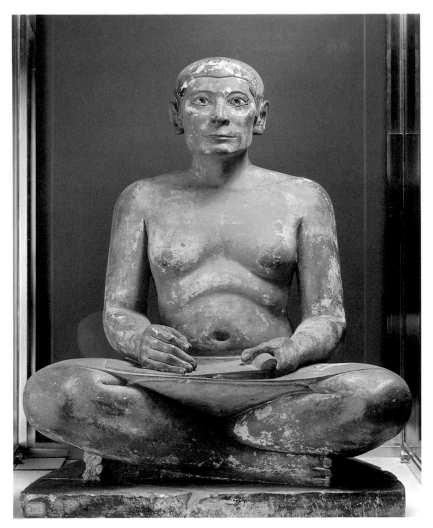

3-17. *Seated Scribe*. Dynasty 5, c. 2510–2460 BCE. Painted limestone, height 21" (53 cm). Musée du Louvre, Paris

Egyptian scribes began training in childhood. Theirs was a strenuously guarded profession, its skills generally passed down from father to son. Some girls learned to read and write, and although careers as scribes seem generally to have been closed to them, there is a Middle Kingdom word for female scribe. Would-be scribes were required to learn not only reading and writing but also arithmetic, algebra, religion, and law. The studies were demanding, but the rewards were great. An observation found in an exercise tablet, probably copied from a book of instruction, offers encouragement: "Become a scribe so that your limbs remain smooth and your hands soft, and you can wear white and walk like a man of standing whom [even] courtiers will greet" (cited in Strouhal, page 216). A high-ranking scribe with a reputation as a great scholar could hope to be appointed to one of several "houses of life," where lay and priestly scribes copied, compiled, studied, and repaired valuable sacred and scientific texts. Completed texts were placed in related institutions called "houses of books," some of the earliest known libraries.

recounting momentous events in the life of the deceased or showing them engaged in routine activities. Tombs therefore provide a wealth of information about ancient Egyptian culture.

A scene in the large mastaba of a Dynasty 5 government official named Ti—a commoner who had achieved great power at court and amassed sufficient wealth to build an elaborate home for his immortal spirit—shows him watching a hippopotamus hunt (fig. 3-18). The artists who created this painted limestone

relief employed a number of established conventions. They depicted the river as if seen from above, rendering it as a band of parallel wavy lines below the boats. The creatures in the river, however—fish, a crocodile, and hippopotamuses—are shown in profile for easy identification. The shallow boats carrying Ti and his men skim along the surface of the water unhampered by the papyrus stalks, shown as parallel vertical lines, that choke the marshy edges of the river. At the top of the panel, where Egyptian convention often placed background

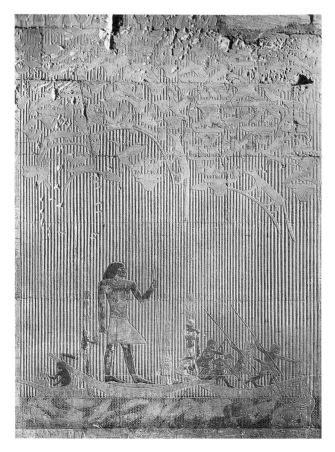

2400

4000 BCE   1 CE

3-18. *Ti Watching a Hippopotamus Hunt.* Tomb of Ti, Saqqara. Dynasty 5, c. 2510–2460 BCE. Painted limestone relief, height approx. 45" (114.3 cm)

This relief forms part of the decoration of a mastaba tomb discovered by the French archeologist Auguste Mariette in 1865. Among Mariette's many other famous finds was the ka statue of Khafre (see fig. 3-13). A pioneer Egyptologist, Mariette was a man of great heart, intellect, and diverse talents. It was he who provided the composer Giuseppe Verdi with the scenario for the opera *Aida*, set in ancient Egypt. He pressed the Egyptians to establish the National Antiquities Service to protect, preserve, and study the country's art monuments. In gratitude, they later placed a statue of him in the new Egyptian Museum in Cairo. At his death, his remains were brought back to his beloved Egypt for burial.

scenes, several animals are seen stalking birds among the papyrus leaves and flowers. The erect figure of Ti, rendered in the traditional twisted pose, looms over this teeming Nile environment. The actual hunters, being of lesser rank and engaged in more-strenuous activities, are rendered more realistically.

In Egyptian art, as in that of the ancient Near East, scenes showing a ruler hunting wild animals served to illustrate the power to maintain order and balance. By dynastic times, hunting had become primarily a showy pastime for the nobility. The hippopotamus hunt, however, was more than simple sport. Hippos tended to wander off into fields, inflicting untold damage on crops. Killing them was an official duty of members of the court. Furthermore, it was believed that the companions of

Seth, the god of darkness, disguised themselves as hippopotamuses. Tomb depictions of such hunts therefore illustrated not only the valor of the deceased but also the triumph of good over evil.

THE MIDDLE KINGDOM

The collapse of the Old Kingdom, with its long succession of kings ruling the whole of Egypt, was followed by roughly 150 years of political turmoil traditionally referred to as the First Intermediate period. In about 2040 BCE a prince Mentuhotep II, from Thebes, finally managed to reunite the country. He and his successors reasserted royal power, but beginning with the next dynasty, political authority became less centralized. Provincial governors claimed increasing powers for themselves, effectively limiting the king's responsibility to national concerns such as the defense of Egypt's frontiers. It was in the Middle Kingdom that Egypt's kings began maintaining standing armies to patrol the country's borders, especially its southern reaches in Lower Nubia, south of modern Aswan.

Another royal responsibility was the planning and construction of large-scale water management projects. Although farmers had long diverted the waters of the Nile to irrigate their crops, specific terms having to do with such projects—"canal" and "levee," for example—make their first appearance in Middle Kingdom documents and inscriptions. The first mention of ingenious methods of raising water from the level of the river to higher ground also dates from this period. Regional administrators and the farmers themselves were left to supervise irrigation locally. In this period Egypt's farmers enjoyed relatively liberal rights and freedoms, even though they were required to turn over most of what they produced to the nobles or priests who owned the land they worked. Those who failed to meet prescribed annual yields were subject to harsh punishments.

Architecture and Town Planning

The remains of Kahun, a town built by Senwosret II (Dynasty 12, ruled c. 1895–1878 BCE) near his pyramid tomb complex at el-Lahun, offer a unique view of the Middle Kingdom's social structure. Although the Egyptians used more-durable materials in the construction of tombs, they built their own dwellings with simple mud bricks. The bricks have either disintegrated over time or been carried away by farmers for their value as fertilizer, leaving only the foundations. From them, archeologists have developed a map of the site showing straight streets and avenues laid out in a mainly east-west orientation (fig. 3-19). The resulting rectangular blocks were divided into lots for homes and other buildings.

Kahun was built to provide housing for the king and the many officials, priests, and workers required in the service of his court. The town's design reflects three distinct economic and social levels. Appropriately, Senwosret's own semifortified residence occupied the highest ground and fronted on a large, open square. The district to the east of his palace, connected to the square by a

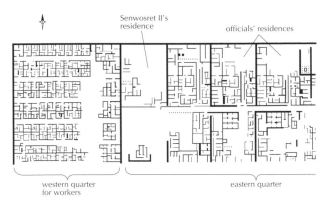

3-19. Plan of the northern section of Kahun, built during the reign of Senwosret II near modern el-Lahun. Dynasty 12, c. 1895–1878 BCE

wide avenue, was occupied by priests, court officials, and their families. Their houses were large and comfortable, with private living quarters and public rooms grouped around central courtyards. Some had as many as seventy rooms spread out over half an acre. The workers were housed in the western district, set off from the rest of the town by a solid wall. Their families made do with small, five-room row houses built back to back along straight, narrow streets.

Tomb Art and Tomb Construction

Tomb art reveals much about domestic life in the Middle Kingdom. Wall paintings, reliefs, and even small models of houses and farm buildings complete with figurines of workers and animals reproduce everyday scenes on the estates of the deceased. Many of these models survive because they were made of inexpensive materials of no interest to early grave robbers. One from Thebes, made of wood, plaster, and copper in about 2009–1997 BCE, reproduces a portion of a house (fig. 3-20). The flat-roofed structure opens into a walled garden through a **portico**, or columned porch, having papyrus columns with stylized lotus capitals. The garden has a central pool flanked by sycamore trees. Although water was precious and only the wealthy could afford their own backyard source, some pools, lined with masonry and stocked with water lilies and fish, were so large that a small boat might be kept at the edge for fishing.

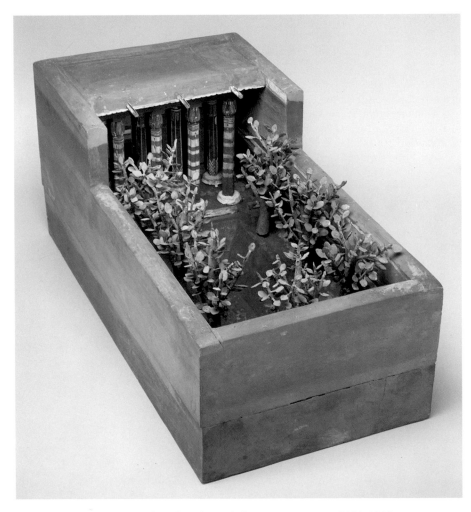

3-20. Model of a house and garden, from Thebes. Dynasty 11, c. 2009–1997 BCE. Painted and plastered wood and copper, length 33" (83.8 cm). The Metropolitan Museum of Art, New York

Purchase, Rogers Fund and Edward S. Harkness Gift, 1920 (20.3.13)

1600
4000 BCE   1 CE

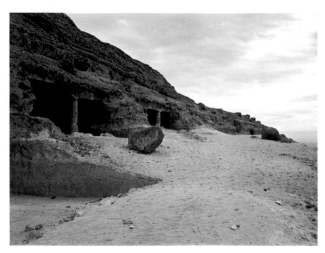

3-21. Rock-cut tombs, Beni Hasan. Dynasty 12, c. 1991–1785 BCE. At the left is the entrance to the tomb of the provincial governor and commander-in-chief Amen-emhet.

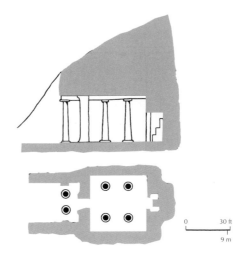

3-22. Plan and elevation of a typical rock-cut tomb at Beni Hasan

During Dynasties 11 and 12, members of the nobility and high-level officials frequently commissioned **rock-cut tombs**—burial places hollowed out of the faces of cliffs—such as those in the necropolis at Beni Hasan on the east bank of the Nile. The various chambers of such

tombs and their ornamental columns, lintels, false doors, and niches were all carved out of solid rock (fig. 3-21). Each one was therefore like a single, complex piece of sculpture, attesting to the great skill of their designers and carvers. A typical Beni Hasan tomb included an

TECHNIQUE

EGYPTIAN PAINTING AND RELIEF SCULPTURE

Painting relies for its effect on color and line. **Relief sculpture** usually depends on the play of light and shadow alone, but in Egypt, relief sculpture was also painted. The walls and closely spaced columns of Egyptian tombs and temples provided large surfaces for decoration, and in fact nearly every square inch of them was adorned with colorful figural scenes and hieroglyphic texts. Up until Dynasty 18 (New Kingdom), the only colors used were black, white, red, yellow, blue, and green. They were never mixed. **Modeling** might be indicated by overpainted lines in a contrasting color, but never by shading of the basic color pigment. In time, more colors were added to the palette, but the primacy of line was never challenged. In terms of composition, with comparatively few exceptions, figures, scenes, and texts were presented in bands, or registers. Usually the base line at the bottom of each register represented the ground. Determining the sequence in which a set of images is to be read can be problematic because it may run either horizontally or vertically.

The preliminary steps in the creation of paintings and relief carvings were virtually identical. Surfaces to be painted had to be smooth, so in some cases a coat of plaster was applied. The next step was to lay out the registers with painted lines and draw the appropriate grid (see fig. 3-6). In the remarkable photograph of a wall section in the unfinished Dynasty 19 tomb of Horemheb in the Valley of the Kings, the red base lines and horizontals of the grid are clearly visible. The general shapes of the hieroglyphs have also been sketched in red. The actual preparatory drawings from which the carver or

carvers were to work are in black. Egyptian artists worked in teams, each member of which had developed a particular skill. The sculptor who executed the carving on the right was following someone else's drawing. Had there been time to finish the tomb, other hands would have smoothed the surface of this limestone relief, and still others would have made fresh drawings to guide the artists assigned to paint it.

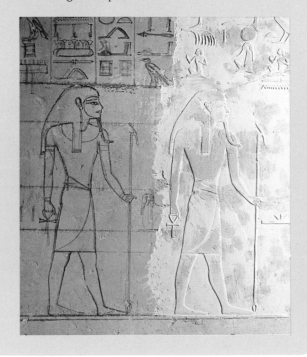

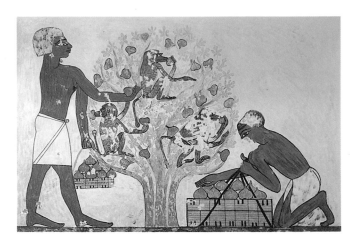

3-23. *Harvest Scene*, tempera facsimile by Nina de Garis Davies of a wall painting in the tomb of Khnumhotep, Beni Hasan. Dynasty 12, c. 1928–1895 BCE

entrance portico, a main hall, and a small burial chamber set back in its farthest recesses (fig. 3-22). The hall might be quite large, with slightly vaulted ceilings and rows of freestanding papyrus-style columns. Rock-cut tombs at other spots along the Nile exhibit variations on this simple plan, with different types of entrances and different interior layouts.

The walls of rock-cut tombs were commonly ornamented with painted scenes. Relief decorations were rare. Among the best-preserved paintings at Beni Hasan are those in the Dynasty 12 tomb of the local lord Khnumhotep, some of which present spirited depictions of life on his farms. In one scene, two men picking figs are forced to compete for the fruit with three friendly baboons seated in the trees (fig. 3-23). The baskets heaped high with neatly arranged figs indicate that the harvest is plentiful despite the animals' thievery. Like the hunters in the Old Kingdom painted relief of Ti on a hippopotamus hunt (see fig. 3-18), these active farmworkers are shown in almost full profile, not in the twisted pose prescribed for royalty.

Sculpture

Royal portraits from the Middle Kingdom do not always exhibit the idealized rigidity of earlier examples. Emulating a trend in nonofficial portrait sculpture, artists of the preceding First Intermediate period had already begun to move away from the conventional portrayal of kings as vigorous but placid young men. A number of Middle Kingdom sculptors continued in this direction, expressing a special awareness of the hardship and fragility of human existence. A statue of Senwosret III (Dynasty 12, ruled c. 1878–1842 BCE) serves as an example of this new sensibility (fig. 3-24). Senwosret was a dynamic king and successful general who led four military expeditions into Nubia, overhauled the central administration at home, and did much toward regaining control over the country's increasingly independent nobles. His portrait statue seems to reflect not only his achievements but also

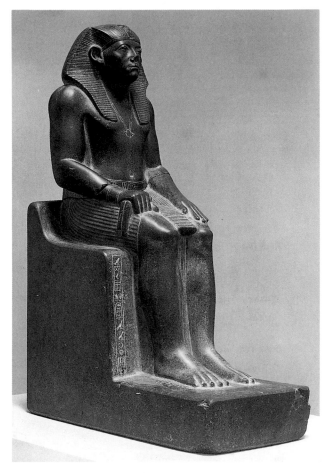

3-24. *Senwosret III*. Dynasty 12, c. 1878–1842 BCE. Black granite, height 21½" (54.8 cm). The Brooklyn Museum
Charles Edwin Wilbour Fund (52.1)

There is little indication of how ancient Egyptians viewed the artists who created portraits of kings and nobles and recorded so many details of contemporary life, but they must have been admired and respected. Some certainly had a high opinion of themselves, as we learn from an inscription on the tombstone of a Middle Kingdom sculptor: "I am an artist who excels in my art, a man above the common herd in knowledge. I know the proper attitude for a statue [of a man]; I know how a woman holds herself, [and how] a spearman lifts his arm. . . . There is no man famous for this knowledge other than I myself and my eldest son" (cited in Montet, page 159).

something of his personality and his inner thoughts. He appears to be a man wise in the ways of the world but lonely, saddened, and burdened by the weight of his responsibilities.

The statue shows the king in the conventional block-like pose, seated, immobile, frontal, and erect. Despite its size—it is less than 2 feet tall—it conveys the sense of monumentality already noted in the much larger ka statue of the Old Kingdom ruler Khafre (see fig. 3-13). There are nevertheless significant differences between the two. Khafre gazes into eternity confident and serene, whereas Senwosret III appears preoccupied and emotionally drained. Deep creases line his sagging cheeks, his eyes are sunken, his eyelids droop, and his jaw is sternly set.

Intended or not, his image betrays a pessimistic view of life, a degree of distrust similar to that reflected in the advice given by Amenemhet I, this Senwosret's great-great-grandfather and the founder of his dynasty, to his son Senwosret I (cited in Breasted, page 231):

> Fill not thy heart with a brother,
> Know not a friend,
> Nor make for thyself intimates, . . .
> When thou sleepest, guard for thyself thine
>   own heart;
> For a man has no people [supporters],
> In the day of evil.

Small Objects Found in Tombs

Middle Kingdom art of all kinds and in all mediums, from official portrait statues such as that of Senwosret III to the least-imposing symbolic objects and delicate bits of jewelry, exhibits the desire of the period's artists for well-observed, accurate detail. A hippopotamus figurine discovered in the Dynasty 12 tomb of a governor named Senbi, for example, has all the characteristics of the beast itself: the rotund body on stubby legs, the massive head with protruding eyes, the tiny ears and distinctive nostrils (fig. 3-25). The figurine is an example of Egyptian **faience**, with its distinctive lustrous glaze (see "Glassmaking and Egyptian Faience," below). The artist chose to make the hippo the watery blue of its river habitat, then painted lotus blossoms on its flanks, jaws, and head, giving the impression that the creature is standing in a tangle of aquatic plants. Such figures were often placed in tombs so that the deceased might engage in an eternal hippopotamus hunt, enjoying the sense of moral triumph that entailed (see the discussion of *Ti Watching a Hippopotamus Hunt*, fig. 3-18).

The simple beauty of this faience hippopotamus contrasts sharply with the intricate splendor of a pectoral, or chest ornament, found at el-Lahun (fig. 3-26). Executed in gold and inlaid with semiprecious stones, it was

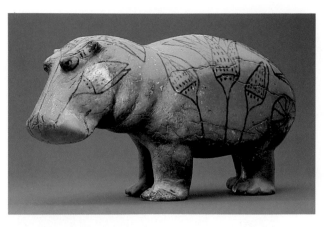

3-25. *Hippopotamus*, from the tomb of Senbi (Tomb B.3), Meir. Dynasty 12, c. 1962–1895 BCE. Faience, length 7⅞" (20 cm). The Metropolitan Museum of Art, New York
Gift of Edward S. Harkness, 1917 (17.9.1)

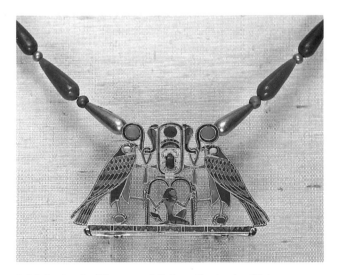

3-26. Pectoral of Senwosret II, from the tomb of Princess Sithathoryunet, el-Lahun. Dynasty 12, c. 1895–1878 BCE. Gold and semiprecious stones, length 3¼" (8.2 cm). The Metropolitan Museum of Art, New York
Purchase, Rogers Fund and Henry Walters Gift, 1916 (16.1.3)

TECHNIQUE

GLASSMAKING AND EGYPTIAN FAIENCE

Glass is produced by subjecting a mixture of sand, lime, and sodium carbonate or sodium sulphate to a very high temperature. It can be made to be transparent, translucent, or opaque and, with the addition of certain substances, can be created in a vast range of colors. No one knows precisely when or where the technique of glassmaking was first developed. By the Predynastic period, the Egyptians were already experimenting with a substance called glass paste, or Egyptian **faience**. When fired, this mixture produced a smooth and shiny opaque finish. At first it was used to form small objects, mainly beads, charms, and color **inlays**. It was later employed as an ornamental colored glaze for pottery wares and clay figurines (see fig. 3-25).

The first evidence of all-glass vessels and other hollow objects dates from the early New Kingdom. At that time glassmaking was restricted to royal workshops, and only the aristocracy and priestly class could commission work from them. The first objects to be made entirely of glass in Egypt were produced by the technique known as core glass. A lump of sandy clay molded into the desired shape of the finished vessel was wrapped in strips of cloth, then skewered on a fireproof rod. It was then briefly dipped into a pot of molten glass. Once the resulting coating of glass had cooled, the clay core was removed through the opening left by the skewer. To decorate the vessel thus created, glassmakers frequently heated thin rods of glass of different colors to the melting point and fused them to its surface in elegant wavy patterns, zigzags, and swirls (see fig. 3-39).

HIERO-GLYPHIC, HIERATIC, AND DEMOTIC WRITING

Ancient Egypt developed three types of writing, all of which are known today by the names the Greeks gave them. The earliest system employed a large number of symbols called **hieroglyphs** (from the Greek *hieros*, "sacred," and *glyphein*, "to carve"). As their name suggests, the Greeks believed they were filled with religious significance. Some of these symbols were simple pictures of creatures or objects, or **pictographs**, similar to those used by the Sumerians. Others were phonograms, or signs representing spoken sounds.

For record-keeping, correspondence, and manuscripts of all sorts, the earliest scribes must also have used this system of signs. In time, however, they evolved a kind of shorthand version of hieroglyphs—simplified forms that could be written more quickly in lines of script on papyrus scrolls. This type of writing is called **hieratic**, another term derived from the Greek word for "sacred." Even after this script was perfected, inscriptions in reliefs or paintings and on ceremonial objects continued to be written in hieroglyphics.

The third type of writing came into use only in the eighth century BCE, as written communication ceased to be restricted exclusively to priests and scribes. It was less formal and was easier to master, and the Greeks referred to it as **demotic** writing (from *demos*, "the people"). From this time on, all three systems were in use, each for its own specific purpose: religious documents were written in hieratic, inscriptions on monuments in hieroglyphics, and all other texts in demotic.

The Egyptian language gradually died out as the result of centuries of foreign rule, beginning with the arrival of the Greeks in 332 BCE. The last documents written in it date from the fourteenth century CE, by which time the great majority of Egypt's inhabitants spoke Arabic. Modern scholars were therefore faced with the task of deciphering these various types of writing in a long-forgotten language. The key appeared in the form of the Rosetta Stone, named after the Delta town

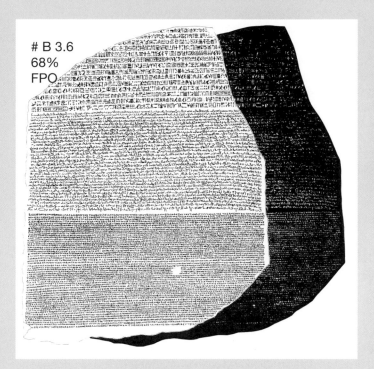

B 3.6
68%
FPO

The Rosetta Stone with its three tiers of writing, from top to bottom: hieroglyphic, demotic, and Greek. The stone itself is nearly black. It is shown here with the script reversed to appear black.

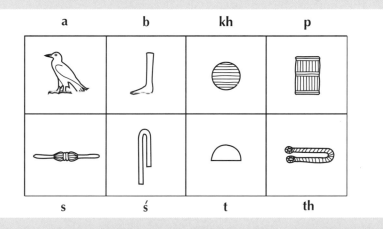

a	b	kh	p
s	ś	t	th

Eight hieroglyphs with the sounds they represent. Used in combinations, such phonogramic hieroglyphs were especially useful in rendering foreign names.

near the spot where one of Napoleon's officers discovered it in 1799. This irregular-shaped fragment of a stone stela dated from 196 BCE. On it, a decree issued by the priests at Memphis honoring the ruler Ptolemy V had been carved in hieroglyphics, hieratic, and demotic Greek. Even with the Greek translation, the two Egyptian texts proved to be incomprehensible until Thomas Young, an English physician interested in ancient Egypt, linked some of the hieroglyphs to specific names in the Greek ver-

sion in 1818. A short time later, the brilliant Frenchman Jean-François Champollion (1790–1832) located the names Ptolemy and Cleopatra in both of the Egyptian scripts. Having thereby determined the phonetic symbols for P, O, L, and T in demotic, he was able to slowly build up an "alphabet" of hieroglyphs, and by 1822 he had deciphered the two Egyptian texts. Thanks to him, today's Egyptologists are able to read each new inscription or document from ancient Egypt that comes to light.

discovered in the funerary complex of Senwosret II, in the tomb of the king's daughter Sithathoryunet. The pectoral's design incorporates the name of Senwosret II and a number of familiar symbols. Two Horus falcons perch on its base, and above their heads are a pair of coiled cobras, symbols of Ra, wearing the ankh, the symbol of life. Between the two cobras, a **cartouche**—an oval formed by a loop of rope—contains the **hieroglyphs** (symbols) of the king's name. The sun disk of Ra appears at the top, and a scarab beetle, another symbol of Ra suggestive of rebirth, at the bottom. Below the cartouche, a kneeling male figure helps the falcons support a double arch of notched palm ribs, a hieroglyphic symbol meaning "millions of years." Decoded, the pectoral's combination of images yields the message: "May the sun god give eternal life to Senwosret II."

THE NEW KINGDOM

During the Second Intermediate period—another turbulent interruption in the succession of dynasties ruling a unified country—an eastern Mediterranean people called the Hyksos invaded Egypt's northernmost regions. It was only under the early rulers of Dynasty 18 (established in 1552 BCE) that the country regained its political and economic strength. The first kings of what is known as the New Kingdom managed to regain control of the entire Nile region from Nubia in the south to the Mediterranean in the north. Roughly a century later, one of the same dynasty's most dynamic kings, Tuthmose III (ruled 1479–1425 BCE), even succeeded in extending Egypt's influence along the eastern Mediterranean coast as far as the region of modern Syria. His accomplishment was the result of some fifteen or more military campaigns and his own skill at diplomacy. Tuthmose III was the first ruler to refer to himself as "pharaoh," a term that simply meant "great house." Egyptians used it in the same way that people in the United States commonly speak of "the White House" when they really mean the current president. The successors of Tuthmose III continued to use the term, and it ultimately found its way into the Hebrew Bible—and modern usage—as the name for the kings of Egypt.

By the beginning of the fourteenth century BCE, the most powerful Near Eastern kings acknowledged the rulers of Egypt as their equals. Marriages contracted between Egypt's ruling families and Near Eastern royalty helped to forge a generally cooperative network of kingdoms in the region. Among the benefits of such cooperation were stimulated trade and the promise of mutual aid at times of natural disaster and outside threats to established borders. Over time, however, Egyptian influence beyond the Nile diminished, and the power of Egypt's kings began to wane even within the country itself.

Great Temple Complexes

At the height of the New Kingdom, rulers undertook extensive building programs along the entire length of the Nile. Their palaces, forts, and administrative centers

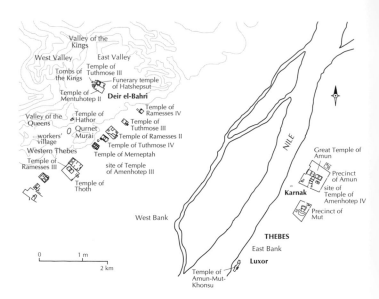

3-27. Map of the Thebes district

disappeared long ago, but remnants of temples and tombs of this great age have endured. Even in their ruined state, they grandly attest to the expanded powers and political triumphs of their builders. Early in this period the priests of the god Amun in Thebes, Egypt's capital city through most of the New Kingdom, had gained such dominance that worship of the Theban triad of deities—Amun, his wife Mut, and their son Khonsu—had spread throughout the country. Temples to these and other gods were a major focus of royal art patronage, as were tombs and temples erected to glorify the kings themselves.

Temples to the Gods at Karnak and Luxor. Two temple districts consecrated primarily to the worship of Amun, Mut, and Khonsu arose near Thebes, one at Karnak to the north and the other at Luxor to the south (fig. 3-27). Little of the earliest construction at Karnak survives, but the remains of New Kingdom additions to the Great Temple of Amun still dominate the landscape (fig. 3-28). Access to the heart of the temple, a sanctuary containing the statue of Amun, was through a principal courtyard, a **hypostyle hall**—a vast hall filled with columns—and a number of smaller halls and courts. Massive gateways, called **pylons**, set off each of these separate elements. The greater part of Pylons II through VI and the areas behind them were renovated or newly built and embellished with colorful wall reliefs between the reigns of Tuthmose I (Dynasty 18, ruled c. 1506–1493 BCE) and Ramesses II (Dynasty 19, ruled c. 1279–1212 BCE). A sacred lake to the south of the temple, where the king and priests might undergo ritual purification before entering the temple, was also added in this period. Behind the sanctuary of Amun, Tuthmose III erected a court and festival temple to his own glory. Amenhotep III (Dynasty 18, ruled 1390–1352 BCE) later placed a large stone statue of Khepri, the scarab beetle symbolic of the rising sun and everlasting life, next to the sacred lake.

Religious worship in ancient Egypt was not a matter of daily or weekly rituals performed in the presence of a congregation of laypeople. Only kings and priests were allowed to enter the sanctuary of Amun for the required devotions, including washing the god's statue every

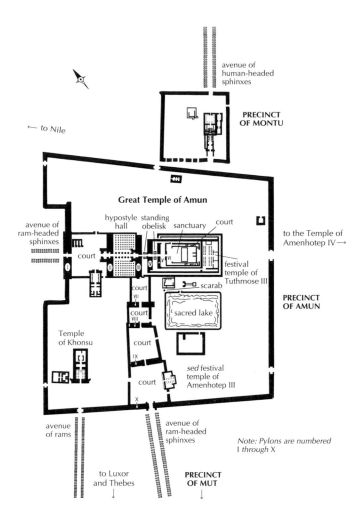

avenue of
human-headed
sphinxes

← to Nile

**PRECINCT
OF MONTU**

Great Temple of Amun

avenue of
ram-headed
sphinxes

hypostyle   standing
hall   obelisk   sanctuary   court

court

to the Temple of
Amenhotep IV→

festival
temple of
Tuthmose III

**PRECINCT
OF AMUN**

court
VII

court
VIII

scarab

sacred lake

Temple
of Khonsu

court
IX

court

sed festival
temple of
Amenhotep III

X

avenue
of rams

avenue of
ram-headed
sphinxes

*Note: Pylons are numbered
I through X*

to Luxor
and Thebes
↓

**PRECINCT
OF MUT**

3-28. Plan of the Great Temple of Amun, Karnak.
New Kingdom

The Karnak site had been an active religious center
for more than 2,000 years before these structures were
erected on it. Over the nearly 500 years of the New
Kingdom, successive kings busily renovated and expanded the Amun temple. Later rulers added pylons,
courtyards, hypostyle halls, statues, and temples or
shrines to other deities to the east, west, and south of
the main temple until the complex covered about 60
acres, an area as large as a dozen football fields. In this
ongoing process, it was common to demolish older
structures and use their materials in new construction.

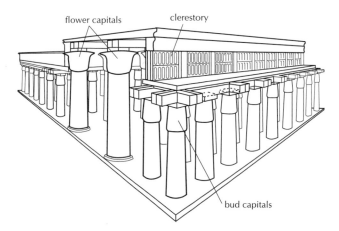

flower capitals   clerestory

bud capitals

3-29. Reconstruction drawing of the hypostyle hall, Great
Temple of Amun, Karnak. Dynasty 19, c. 1294–1212 BCE

1600
4000 BCE   1 CE

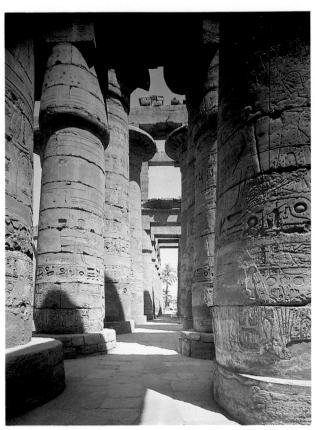

3-30. Hypostyle hall, Great Temple of Amun, Karnak

morning and clothing it in a new garment, as well as providing it with tempting meals twice a day. The god was
thought to derive nourishment from the spirit of the food,
which the priests then removed and ate themselves.
Ordinary people were rarely permitted beyond the fore-
courts of the hypostyle halls, where they found themselves surrounded by inscriptions and images of kings
and the god on columns and walls. During religious festivals, however, they lined the routes along which the
statues of the gods were carried in ceremonial boats. At
such times they were permitted to submit petitions to the
priests for requests and favors they wished the gods to
answer.

Between Pylons II and III at Karnak stands the enormous hypostyle hall erected in the reigns of the Dynasty
19 rulers Sety I (ruled 1294–1279 BCE) and his son
Ramesses II (ruled c. 1279–1212 BCE). Called the "Temple
of the Spirit of Sety, Beloved of Ptah in the House of
Amun," it was perhaps used for royal coronation ceremonies. Ramesses II referred to it in more mundane
terms as "the place where the common people extol the
name of his majesty." The hall was 340 feet wide and 170
feet long. Its 134 closely spaced columns supported a
stepped, flat stone roof, the center section of which rose
some 30 feet higher than the rest (figs. 3-29, 3-30). The
columns supporting this higher part of the roof are 66 feet
tall and 12 feet in diameter, with massive lotus flower
capitals. The smaller columns on each side have lotus
bud capitals that must have seemed to march off forever
into the darkness.

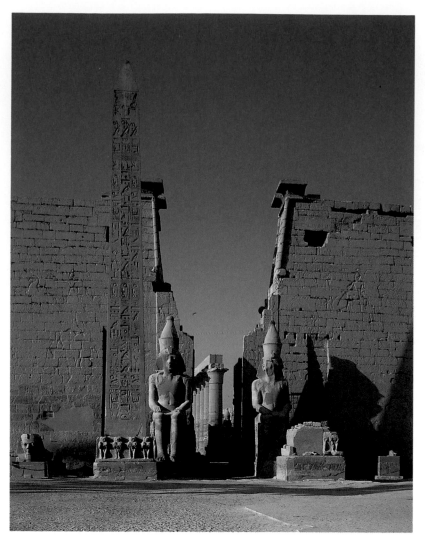

3-31. Pylon of Ramesses II with obelisk in the foreground, Temple of Amun, Mut, and Khonsu, Luxor. Dynasty 19, c. 1279–1212 BCE

In each of the side walls of the higher center section there was a long row of window openings, creating what is known as a **clerestory**. These openings were filled with stone grillwork, so they cannot have provided much light, but they did permit a cooling flow of air through the hall. Despite the dimness of the interior, artists were required to cover nearly every inch of the columns, walls, and cross-beams with reliefs.

The sacred district at Luxor was already the site of a splendid temple complex by the thirteenth century BCE. Ramesses II further enlarged the complex with the addition of a pylon and a **peristyle court**, or open courtyard ringed with columns and covered walkways (fig. 3-31). In front of his pylon stood two colossal statues of the king and a pair of **obelisks**—slender, slightly tapered square shafts of stone capped by a pyramidal shape called a **pyramidion**. The faces of the pylon are ornamented with reliefs detailing the king's military exploits. The walls of the courtyard present additional reliefs of Ramesses, shown together with various deities, his wife, seventeen of his sons, and other royal children, some hundred of whom he had by eight official wives and numerous concubines during his sixty-seven-year reign.

The Funerary Temple of Hatshepsut. The dynamic female ruler Hatshepsut (Dynasty 18, ruled c. 1478–1458 BCE) is a notable figure in a period otherwise dominated by male warrior-kings. Besides Hatshepsut, three other queens ruled Egypt—the little-known Sobekneferu and Twosret, and the notoriously famous Cleopatra, much later. The daughter of Tuthmose I, Hatshepsut married her half brother, who then reigned for fourteen years as Tuthmose II. When he died, she became regent for his underage son—Tuthmose III—born to one of his concubines. Hatshepsut had herself declared king by the priests of Amun, a maneuver that prevented Tuthmose III from assuming the throne for twenty years. In art she was represented in all the ways a male ruler would have been, even as a human-headed sphinx (fig. 3-32), and she was called "His Majesty." Sculpted portraits show her in the traditional royal trappings: kilt, linen headcloth, broad beaded collar, false beard, and bull's tail hanging from her waist.

Hatshepsut's closest adviser, a courtier named Senenmut, was instrumental in carrying out her ambitious building program. Her most innovative undertaking was her own funerary temple at Deir el-Bahri (fig. 3-33).

The structure was not intended to be her tomb; Hatshepsut was to be buried, like other New Kingdom rulers, in a necropolis known as the Valley of the Kings, about half a mile to the northwest (see fig. 3-27). Her funerary temple was magnificently positioned against high cliffs and oriented toward the Great Temple of Amun at Karnak, some miles away on the east bank of the Nile. The complex follows an **axial** plan—that is, all of its separate elements are symmetrically arranged along a dominant center line (fig. 3-34). An elevated causeway lined with sphinxes once ran from a valley temple on the Nile, since destroyed, to the first level of the complex, a huge open space before a long row of columns, or **colonnade** (see "Elements of Architecture," page 101). From there, the visitor ascended a long, straight ramp flanked by pools of water to the second level. At the ends of the columned porticos on this level were shrines to Anubis and Hathor.

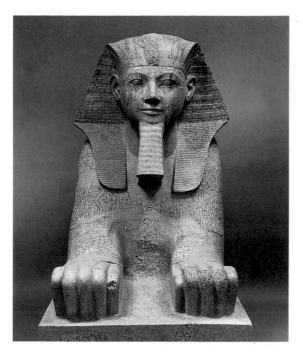

3-32. *Hatshepsut as Sphinx*, from Deir el-Bahri. Dynasty 18, c. 1478–1458 BCE. Red granite, height 5'4" (164 cm). The Metropolitan Museum of Art, New York

Rogers Fund, 1931 (31.3.166)

Of the Egyptian queens who went down in history as "living gods" themselves and not merely "wives of gods," Hatshepsut may well have been the most commanding. Among the reliefs in her funerary temple at Deir el-Bahri (see fig. 3-33), she placed—just as a male king might have—a depiction of her divine birth. There she is portrayed as the daughter of her earthly mother, Queen Ahmose, and the god Amun. She also honored her real father, Tuthmose I, by dedicating a chapel to him in her temple.

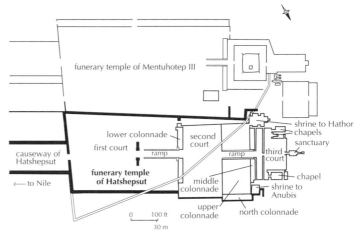

3-34. Plan of the funerary temple of Hatshepsut, Deir el-Bahri. Dynasty 18, c. 1478–1458 BCE

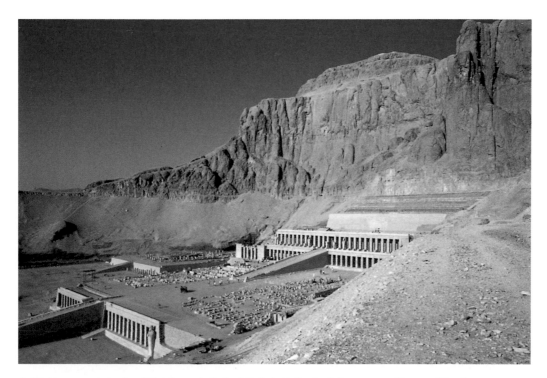

3-33. Funerary temple of Hatshepsut, Deir el-Bahri. At the far left, ramp and base of the funerary temple of Mentuhotep III. Dynasty 11, c. 2009–1997 BCE

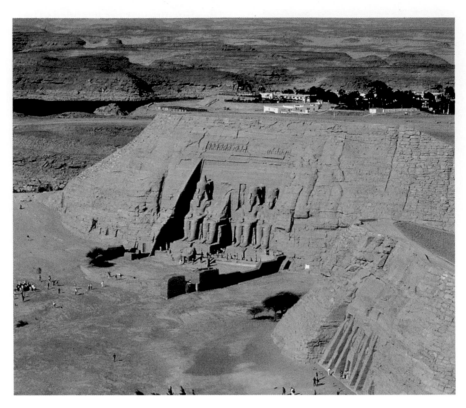

3-35. Temples of Ramesses II (left) and Nefertari (right), Abu Simbel, Nubia. Dynasty 19, c. 1279–1212 BCE

These two temples are no longer in their original location. That site was inundated as the result of the construction of the Aswan High Dam in the 1960s. An international campaign to salvage these monuments raised large sums of money, and astute engineers found a way to move the temples to a spot some 215 feet higher and 690 feet farther back from the river. The facade sculpture and the inner temple walls were cut into blocks and reassembled against artificial cliffs.

Relief scenes and inscriptions in the south portico relate that Hatshepsut sent a fleet of ships to Punt, an exotic, half-legendary kingdom probably located on the Red Sea or the Gulf of Aden, to bring back rare myrrh trees for the temple's terraces. The uppermost level consisted of another colonnade fronted by colossal royal statues, and behind this a large hypostyle hall with chapels to Hatshepsut, her father, and the gods Amun and Ra-Horakhty—the power of the sun at dawn and dusk. Centered in the hall's back wall was the entrance to the temple's innermost sanctuary. This small chamber was cut deep into the cliff in the manner of Middle Kingdom rock-cut tombs.

Hatshepsut's funerary temple, with its lively alternating of open spaces and grandiose architectural forms, projects an imposing image of authority. In its day, its remarkable union of nature and architecture, with many different levels and contrasting textures—water, stone columns, trees, and cliffs—made it far more impressive than the bleak expanse of stone ruins and sand that confronts the visitor today.

The Temple of Ramesses II at Abu Simbel. At the time of Ramesses II (ruled c. 1279–1212 BCE), whom some believe to be the "pharaoh" of the biblical story of Moses and the Exodus, Egypt was a mighty empire. Ramesses was a bold military commander and an effective political strategist. In about 1263 BCE he secured a peace agree-

ment with the Hittites, a rival power centered in Anatolia (Chapter 2) that had tried to expand its borders to the west and south at the Egyptians' expense. He reaffirmed that agreement a little over a decade later by marrying a Hittite princess.

In the course of his long and prosperous reign, Ramesses II initiated building projects on a scale rivaling the Old Kingdom pyramids at Giza. The most awe-inspiring of his many architectural monuments is found at Abu Simbel in Nubia, Egypt's southernmost region. There Ramesses ordered the construction of two temples, a large one to himself and a smaller one to his chief wife, Nefertari.

Like Hatshepsut's funerary temple at Deir el-Bahri, the monumental grandeur of the king's temple communicates to the viewer a sense of unlimited majesty. It was carved out of the face of a cliff in the manner of a rock-cut tomb but far surpasses earlier temples created in this way. Its dominant feature is a row of four colossal seated statues of the king, each more than 65 feet tall (fig. 3-35). Large figures of Nefertari and other family members stand next to his feet, but they seem mere dolls by comparison, since they do not even reach the height of the king's giant stone knees. The interior of the temple stretches back some 160 feet and was oriented in such a way that on the most important day of the Egyptian calendar the first rays of the rising sun shot through its entire depth to illuminate a row of four statues—the king

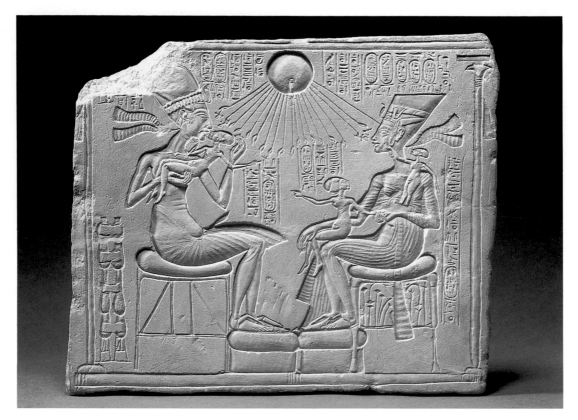

3-36. *Akhenaten and His Family*, from Akhetaten (modern Tell el-Amarna). Dynasty 18, 1348–1336/5 BCE. Painted limestone relief, 12¼ x 15¼" (31.1 x 38.7 cm). Staatliche Museen zu Berlin, Preussischer Kulturbesitz, Ägyptisches Museum

Egyptian relief sculptors often employed the technique seen here, called sunken relief. In ordinary reliefs, the background is carved away so that the figures project out from the finished surface. In this technique, the original flat surface of the stone is the background, and the outlines of the figures are deeply incised, permitting the development of three-dimensional forms within them. If an ordinary relief became badly worn, a sculptor might restore it by recarving it as a sunken relief.

and the gods Amun, Ptah, and Ra-Horakhty—placed against the back wall. The front of the smaller nearby temple to Nefertari is adorned with six statues 33 feet tall, two of the queen wearing the headdress of Hathor, and four of her husband.

Akhenaten and the Art of the Amarna Period

The most unusual ruler in the history of ancient Egypt was Amenhotep IV, who came to the throne in 1352 BCE (Dynasty 18). In his seventeen-year reign, he radically transformed the political, spiritual, and cultural life of the country. He founded a new religion honoring a single supreme god, the life-giving sun disk Aten, and accordingly changed his own name in 1348 BCE to Akhenaten ("One Who Is Effective on Behalf of Aten"). Abandoning Thebes, the capital of Egypt since the beginning of his dynasty and a city firmly in the grip of the priests of Amun, Akhenaten built a new capital much farther north, calling it Akhetaten ("Horizon of the Aten"). Borrowing from the modern name for this site, Tell el-Amarna, historians refer to his reign as the Amarna period.

The king saw himself as Aten's son, and at his new capital he presided over the worship of Aten as a divine priest. His chief queen, Nefertiti, served as a divine priest-

ess. Temples to Aten were open courtyards, where altars could be bathed in the direct rays of the sun. In art Aten is depicted as a round sun sending down long thin rays ending in human hands, some of which hold the ankh, or symbol of life.

Akhenaten stressed the philosophical principle of *maat*, or divine truth, and one of his kingly titles was "Living in Maat." Such concern for truth found expression in new artistic conventions. In portraits of the king artists emphasized his unusual physical characteristics—long, thin arms and legs, a protruding stomach, swelling thighs, a thin neck supporting an elongated skull. Unlike his predecessors, and in keeping with his penchant for candor, Akhenaten urged his artists to portray the royal family in informal situations. Even private houses in the capital city were adorned with reliefs of the king and his family, an indication that he managed to substitute veneration of the royal household for the traditional worship of families of gods, such as that of Amun, Mut, and Khonsu.

A painted relief of Akhenaten, Queen Nefertiti, and three of their daughters exemplifies the new openness and a new figural style (fig. 3-36). In this **sunken relief**—the outlines of the figures have been carved into the surface of the stone, making it unnecessary to cut away the background—the king and queen sit on cushioned thrones playing with their children. The base of the queen's

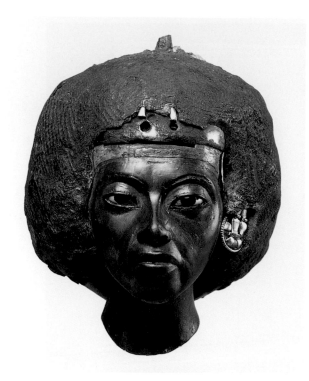

3-37. *Queen Tiy*, from Kom Medinet Ghurab (near el-Lahun). Dynasty 18, c. 1390–1352 BCE. Boxwood, ebony, glass, gold, lapis lazuli, cloth, clay, and wax, height 3¾" (9.4 cm). Staatliche Museen zu Berlin, Preussischer Kulturbesitz, Ägyptisches Museum

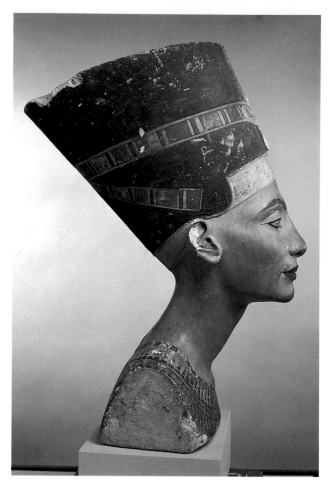

3-38. *Nefertiti*, from Akhetaten (modern Tell el-Amarna). Dynasty 18, c. 1348–1336/5 BCE. Limestone, height 20" (51 cm). Staatliche Museen zu Berlin, Preussischer Kulturbesitz, Ägyptisches Museum

This famous head was discovered along with various drawings and other items relating to commissions for the royal family in the studio of the sculptor Tuthmose at Akhetaten, the capital city during the Amarna period. Bust portraits, consisting solely of the head and shoulders, were rare in New Kingdom art. Scholars believe that Tuthmose may have made this one as a finished model to follow in sculpting or painting other images of his patron. From depictions of sculptors at work, we know that some statues were made in parts and then assembled, but there is no indication that this head was meant to be attached to a body.

throne is adorned with the stylized symbol of a unified Egypt, which has led some historians to conclude that Nefertiti acted as co-ruler with her husband. The royal couple is receiving the blessings of Aten, whose ray-hands penetrate the open pavilion and hold ankhs to their nostrils, giving them the "breath of life." Other ray-hands caress the hieroglyphic inscriptions in the center. The king holds one child and lovingly pats her head. The youngest of the three perches on Nefertiti's arm and tries to attract her attention by stroking her cheek. The oldest sits on the queen's lap, tugging at her mother's hand and pointing to her father. The children are nude, and the younger two have shaved heads, a custom of the time. The oldest wears the sidelock of youth, a patch of hair left to grow and hang at one side of the head in a braid. The artist has conveyed the engaging behavior of the children and the loving concern of their parents in a way not even hinted at in earlier royal portraiture in Egypt.

Akhenaten's goals were actively supported not only by Nefertiti but also by his mother, Queen Tiy. She had been the chief wife of the king's father, Amenhotep III (Dynasty 18, ruled 1390–1352 BCE), and played a significant role in affairs of state during his reign. Queen Tiy's personality emerges from a miniature portrait head that reveals the exquisite bone structure of her powerful face, with its arched brows, uptilted eyes, and expressive mouth (fig. 3-37). This portrait contrasts sharply with a head of Nefertiti, in which her comparatively expressionless face—the heavy-lidded eyes and half smile—divulges almost nothing about her personal qualities (fig. 3-38). Part of the beauty of this portrait head is the result of the

artist's dramatic use of color. The hues of the blue head-dress and its colorful band are repeated in the rich red, blue, green, and gold of the jewelry. The queen's brows, eyelids, cheeks, and lips are heightened with color, as they no doubt were with cosmetics in real life. Whether or not Nefertiti's beauty is exaggerated, phrases used by her subjects when referring to her—"Fair of Face," "Mistress of Happiness," "Great of Love," "Endowed with Favors"—tend to support the artist's rendering.

The art of glassmaking flourished in the Amarna period. The craft could only be practiced by artists working for the king, and Akhenaten's new capital had its own glassmaking workshops. A fish-shaped bottle produced there was meant to hold scented oil (fig. 3-39). It is an example of what is known as **core glass**, named to indi-

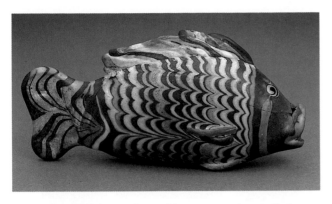

3-39. Fish-shaped vase, from Akhetaten (modern Tell el-Amarna). Dynasty 18, c. 1348–1336/5 BCE. Core glass, length 5¹⁄₈" (13 cm). The British Museum, London

cate the early technique used in its manufacture (see "Glassmaking and Egyptian Faience," page 112). Its body was created first from glass tinted with cobalt, a dark blue metallic oxide. The surface was then decorated with swags resembling fish scales by heating small rods of white and orange glass to the point that they fused to the body and could be manipulated with a pointed tool. The fish that lent its shape to the bottle has been identified as a *bolti*, a species that carried its eggs in its mouth and spit out its offspring when they hatched. It was therefore a common symbol for birth and regeneration, especially the sort of self-generation that Akhenaten attributed to the sun disk Aten.

Domestic objects routinely placed in tombs as grave goods often had similar symbolic significance. One such item is a hand mirror, less than 10 inches tall, discovered in a Dynasty 18 tomb (fig. 3-40). Its handle is formed by

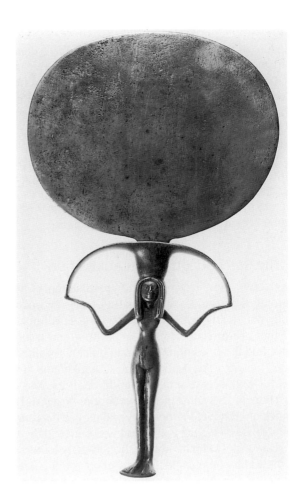

3-40. Hand mirror. Dynasty 18, c. 1552–1314/1295 BCE. Bronze, height 9³⁄₄" (24.6 cm). The Brooklyn Museum
Charles Edwin Wilbour Fund (37.365E)

PRESERVING THE DEAD The world's fascination with Egyptian mummies has a long history. In the Middle Ages and even up into the eighteenth century, Europeans prized pulverized mummy remains and swallowed them in various solutions, believing them to be of great medicinal value. One of the first concerns of the Egyptian National Antiquities Service after its founding in the second half of the nineteenth century was how to prevent people from stealing and destroying ancient human remains, as well as mummies of hundreds of thousands of cats and millions of ibises.

No actual ancient recipes for preserving the dead have been found, but the basic process seems clear enough from images found in tombs, the descriptions of later Greek writers such as Herodotus and Plutarch, scientific analysis of mummies, and modern experiments. By the time of the New Kingdom, the routine was

roughly as follows. The dead body was taken to a mortuary, a special structure used exclusively for embalming. Under the supervision of a priest, workers removed the brains, generally through the nose, and emptied the body cavity through an incision in the left side. They then placed the body, together with its major internal organs, in a vat of natron, a naturally occurring salt. It was left to steep in this solution for a period of a month or more. This caused the skin to blacken, so once the workers had retrieved a body from the vat and carefully dried it, they often dyed it to restore something of its color, using red ocher for a man, yellow ocher for a woman. They then packed the body cavity with clean linen, provided by the family of the deceased and soaked in various herbs and ointments. They wrapped the major organs in separate packets, either putting them in special containers to be placed in the tomb chamber or

stuffing them back into the body.

The tedious ritual of wrapping the body could now begin. They first wound the trunk and each of the limbs separately with cloth strips, then wrapped the whole body in a shroud. They then wound it in additional strips of cloth, layer after layer, to produce the familiar mummy shape. The linen winders often inserted good luck charms and other smaller objects among the wrappings. If the family happened to have furnished a Book of the Dead (see fig. 3-44), a selection of magic spells meant to help the deceased survive a "last judgment" and win everlasting life, it was tucked in between the mummy's legs.

Egyptians developed these techniques to ensure that the ka, or life force, could live on in the body in the afterlife. Whenever possible, a portrait statue was provided as an alternative home for the ka in the event that the mummy disintegrated.

the figure of a slender young woman, probably a dancer, balancing a giant lotus blossom on her head. Her arms reach out to support the flower's elongated sepals, forming with them a highly decorative shape. The mirror itself is a metal disk polished to a high gloss to create a reflecting surface. On one level, the young woman can be thought of as an attendant obediently holding the mirror for the person wishing to gaze in it. But she might also be interpreted as a fertility goddess supporting the sun disk. This elegant luxury item could have been placed in the tomb to symbolize the blessings of Aten and the hope that the deceased would live eternally in peace.

The Sarcophagus of Tutankhamun

Akhenaten's new religion and revolutionary ideas regarding the conduct appropriate for royalty outlived him by only a few years. His successors—it is not clear how they were related to him—had brief and troubled reigns, and the priesthood of Amun quickly regained its former power. The young king Tutankhaten (ruled 1336/35–1327 BCE) returned to traditional religious beliefs, changing his name to Tutankhamun. He also turned his back on Akhenaten's new city and moved his court to Memphis. He died quite young and was buried in the Valley of the Kings. Remarkably, although early looters did rob the tomb complex, his sealed inner tomb chamber was never plundered, and when it was opened in the 1920s its incredible riches were discovered just as they had been left. His body lay inside three nested coffins that identified him with Osiris, the god of the dead. The innermost coffin in the shape of a mummy is the richest of the three, for it is made of several hundred pounds of solid gold, with a "scrap value" of about $1.5 million (fig. 3-41). Its surface is decorated with colored enamelwork and semiprecious gemstones, as well as very finely incised linear designs and hieroglyphic inscriptions. The king holds a crook and a flail—an implement used in threshing grain. Both symbols were closely associated with Osiris and were a traditional part of the royal regalia at the time. The king's features as reproduced on the coffin are those of a very young man. Even though they may not reflect Tutankhamun's actual appearance, the unusually full lips and thin-bridged nose hint at the continued influence of the Amarna period style and its dedication to actual appearances.

Tomb Decoration

Living along the Nile was like living next to a major highway. Travel by boat was commonplace, an aspect of everyday life that is amply illustrated in tomb decorations. Paintings depict actual trips taken by the deceased, the ferrying upriver or down of their bodies in the course of funeral rites, and the symbolic journey into the afterlife, providing a great deal of information about Egyptian boats of this period. An especially beautiful, finely drawn example of such illustration dates from about 1348–1327 BCE (fig. 3-42). It comes from the tomb of the viceroy Amenhotep Huy at Qurnet Murai, across the Nile from

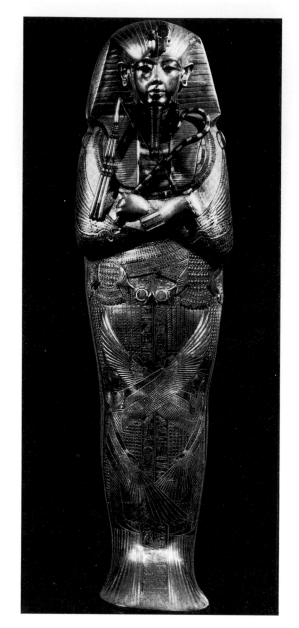

3-41. Inner coffin of Tutankhamun's sarcophagus, from the tomb of Tutankhamun, Valley of the Kings. Dynasty 18, 1336/5–1327 BCE. Gold inlaid with glass and semiprecious stones, height 6'7/8" (1.85 m). Egyptian Museum, Cairo

The English archeologist Howard Carter had worked in Egypt for more than twenty years before he undertook a last expedition, sponsored by the wealthy British amateur Egyptologist Lord Carnarvon, after World War I. In November 1922 Carter discovered the entrance to the tomb of King Tutankhamun, the only Dynasty 18 royal burial place still unidentified. By November his workers had cleared their way down to its antechamber, which was found to contain unbelievable treasures: jewelry, textiles, gold-covered furniture, a carved and inlaid throne, four gold chariots, and other precious objects. In February 1923, they pierced through the wall separating the anteroom from the actual burial chamber, and in early January of the following year—having taken great care to catalog all the intervening riches and prepare for their safe removal—they finally reached the king's astonishing sarcophagus. Figure 3-1 shows Tutankhamun's funerary mask as it was first seen in October 1925.

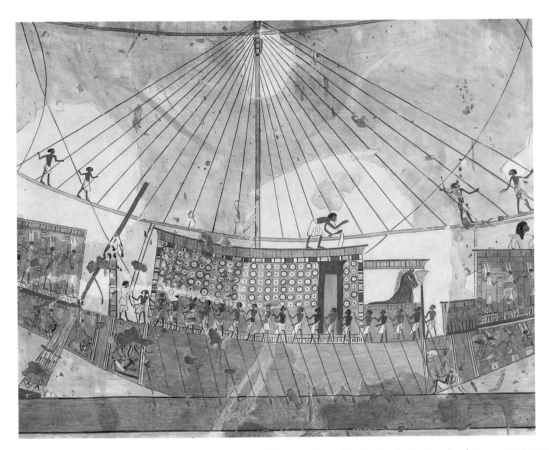

3-42. *State Ship*, detail of a tempera facsimile by Charles K. Wilkinson of a wall painting in the tomb of Governor Amenhotep Huy, Qurnet Murai. Dynasty 18, c. 1348–1327 BCE. The Metropolitan Museum of Art, New York
Rogers Fund, 1930 (30.4.19)

Thanks to the prevailing northerly winds, ships could easily sail southward up the Nile. When traveling downriver they were obliged to rely on oar power. Accordingly, the hieroglyph depicting a ship with a billowing sail came to mean "to travel south"—whether by water or on land—whereas the one showing a boat without a sail meant "to travel north." The earliest Egyptian boats were made of papyrus stalks tied tightly together to make them watertight. Wood was in short supply, and the materials required for building large wooden vessels such as the one shown here had to be imported. Because the banks of the Nile were often choked with reeds, Egyptian boats tended to have shallow hulls without a keel. They were steered by means of a rudder in the stern. A large vessel required a captain, a pilot, and a large crew to tend the oars and sails.

Thebes. Huy served as governor of Nubia, and here his official sailing ship is shown ready to set off in a southerly direction, perhaps to take him to Nubia. His horses are in their stalls, the rowers are in place, and the crew stands ready to trim the sails as soon as the navigator has tested the depth of the water and the captain has given the signal to depart.

The artists responsible for decorating the private tomb of Nefertari, the wife of Ramesses II, in the Valley of the Queens near Deir el-Bahri worked in a new style diverging very subtly but distinctively from earlier conventions. In one of the tomb's many beautiful, large-figured scenes, Nefertari offers jars of perfumed ointment to the goddess Isis (fig. 3-43). The queen wears the vulture-skin headdress of royalty, a royal collar, and a long, transparent white gown. Isis, seated on her throne behind a table heaped with offerings, holds a long scepter in her left hand, the ankh in her right. She too wears the vulture headdress, but hers is surmounted by the horns of Hathor framing a sun disk, clear indications of her divinity. The outline drawing and use of clear

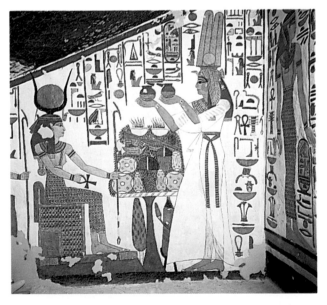

3-43. *Queen Nefertari Making an Offering to Isis*, wall painting in the tomb of Nefertari, Valley of the Queens, near Deir el-Bahri. Dynasty 19, c. 1279–1212 BCE

RESTORING THE TOMB OF NEFERTARI

The tomb of Queen Nefertari, wife of Ramesses II, was discovered in the Valley of the Queens, near Deir el-Bahri, in 1904. Although it had been looted of everything that could be carried away, it still contained splendid large-figure wall paintings of the deceased queen in the company of the gods (see fig. 3-43).

Thanks to Egypt's dry climate and the care with which most tombs were sealed, many such paintings remained in excellent condition for thousands of years. Strangely, the ones in Nefertari's tomb had begun to deteriorate soon after they were completed. Conservators have theorized that the walls were left quite damp when priests sealed the tomb, so that salts from the plaster leached to the surface. Over time, this tended to loosen the layer of pigment, causing it to flake. The dampness also allowed various funguses to attack the paint. The process of disintegration accelerated dramatically when the tomb was opened to the public. Its many visitors raised the humidity level and introduced dirt and bacteria from outside. The resulting damage was so great by 1940 that the tomb was closed to the public.

In 1968 the Egyptian National Antiquities Service and the Getty Conservation Institute in Santa Monica, California, undertook a multi-million-dollar conservation project to save the tomb's decorations. The painting restorers Paolo and Laura Mora were commissioned to supervise the work, which was carried out by a team of Italian and Egyptian conservators. Their first priority was to stop the paint from flaking and the plaster from crumbling any further. Over the course of a year, their crew applied over 10,000 "bandages" made of Japanese mulberry-pulp paper to the tomb's interior surfaces.

Once the paint and plaster had been stabilized, the restorers could begin their real work. Their goal was to salvage every flake of paint they could from these works created more than 3,000 years earlier. They carefully cleaned the paintings with cotton swabs dipped in distilled water. Using hypodermic needles and a special resin glue, they were able to reattach small spots of loose plaster or pigment. Larger detached areas were removed whole, cleaned, then glued back in place. In the past, it was common practice for conservators to re-create sections that had been wholly lost with conjectural painting of their own, but according to current thinking within the profession it is preferable to simply make such gaps less obvious by shading

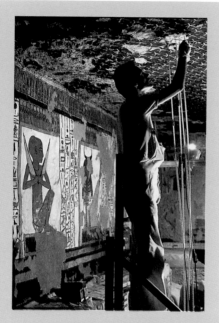

Getty Conservation Institute conservator S. Rickerby at work in Chamber K, Tomb of Nefertari, Valley of the Queens, near Deir el-Bahri

them in tones matched to adjacent work. This was the procedure in Nefertari's tomb.

Thanks to the extremely painstaking labor of professional restorers like these, many such ancient treasures have been rescued for the instruction and delight of future generations.

colors reflect traditional practices, but quite new is the slight modeling of the body forms by small changes of hue to increase their appearance of solidity. The skin color of these women is much darker than that conventionally used for females in earlier periods, and lightly brushed-in shading makes their eyes and lips stand out more than before (see "Restoring the Tomb of Nefertari," above). The tomb's artists used particular care in placing the hieroglyphic inscriptions around these figures, creating an unusually harmonious overall design.

Books of the Dead

By the time of the New Kingdom, the Egyptians had come to believe that only a person free from sin could enjoy an afterlife. The dead were thought to undergo a "last judgment" consisting of two tests presided over by Osiris and supervised by Anubis, the overseer of funerals and cemeteries, represented as a man with a jackal's head. The deceased were first questioned by a delegation of deities about their behavior in life. Then their hearts, which the

Egyptians believed to be the seat of the soul, were weighed on a scale against an ostrich feather, the symbol of Maat, goddess of truth.

These beliefs gave rise to one specific funerary practice especially popular among the nonroyal classes. Family members would commission papyrus scrolls containing magical texts or spells to help the dead survive the tests, and they had the embalmers place the scrolls among the wrappings of their loved ones' mummified bodies. Early collectors of Egyptian artifacts referred to such scrolls, often beautifully illustrated, as Books of the Dead. They varied considerably in content. A scene from a Dynasty 19 example, created for a man named Hunefer, shows him at three successive stages in his induction into the afterlife (fig. 3-44). At the left, Anubis leads him by the hand to the spot where he will weigh his heart, contained in a tiny jar, against the "feather of Truth." Maat herself appears atop the balancing arm of the scales wearing the feather as a headdress. A monster—part crocodile, part lion, and part hippopotamus—watches eagerly for a sign from the ibis-headed

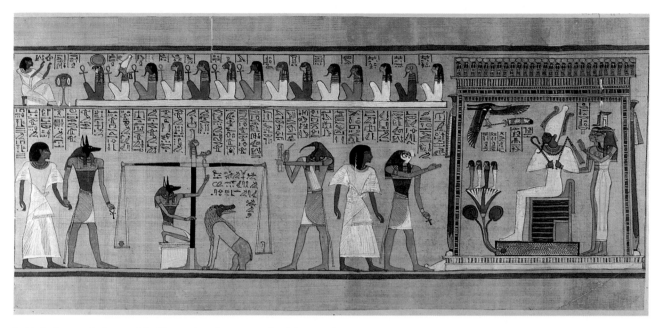

3-44. *Judgment before Osiris*, illustration from a Book of the Dead. Dynasty 19, c. 1285 BCE. Painted papyrus, height 15⅝" (39.8 cm). The British Museum, London

Osiris, the god of the underworld, appears on the right, enthroned in a richly ornamented pavilion, or chapel, in the "Hall of the Two Truths." Here the souls of the deceased were thought to be subjected to a "last judgment" to determine whether they were worthy of eternal life. Osiris was traditionally depicted as a mummified man wrapped in a white linen shroud. His other trappings are those of an Egyptian king. He wears the double crown, incorporating those of both Upper and Lower Egypt, a false beard, and a wide beaded collar, and he brandishes the symbolic crook and flail in front of his chest. The figure in the center combining a man's body with the head of an ibis, a wading bird related to the heron, is the god Thoth. He here functions as a sort of court stenographer—appropriately, for he was revered as the inventor of hieroglyphic writing.

god Thoth, who prepares to record the result of the weighing. This creature is Ammit, the dreaded "Eater of the Dead."

But the "Eater" is left to go hungry. Hunefer passes the test, and on the right Horus presents him to Osiris. The god of the underworld sits on a throne floating on a lake of natron, the substance used to preserve the flesh of the deceased from decay (see "Preserving the Dead," page 121). The four sons of Horus, each of whom was entrusted with the care of one of the deceased's vital organs, stand atop a huge lotus blossom rising up out of the lake. The goddesses Nephthys and Isis stand behind the throne, supporting the god's left arm with a tender gesture similar to the one seen in the Old Kingdom sculpture of Menkaure and his queen (see fig. 3-15). In the top register, Hunefer makes his appearance in the afterlife, kneeling before the nine gods of Heliopolis—the sacred city of the sun god Ra—and five personifications of life-sustaining principles.

Life was short in ancient times. Few people could expect to live beyond their twenties. All hoped to escape the "Eater" and live on eternally in the company of the gods. But they also doubtless heeded the advice given in "The Harper's Song," a poem inscribed on a wall in the tomb of the Dynasty 14 king Inyotef VII at Dra Abu el-Naga (cited in Strouhal, page 266):

None comes from there
To tell of their state
To calm our hearts
Until we go where they have gone.
Hence rejoice in your heart . . .
Make holiday, do not weary of it.

No one *has* come from there to tell us how the ancient Egyptians fared after death, but the art they produced has assured them of immortality. Their continuing creativity over many long centuries was acknowledged and admired by contemporary peoples—as it was by their eventual conquerors.

Cycladic figure
c. 2500–2200

▲ MINOAN 3000–1400
▲ CYCLADIC 3000–1600

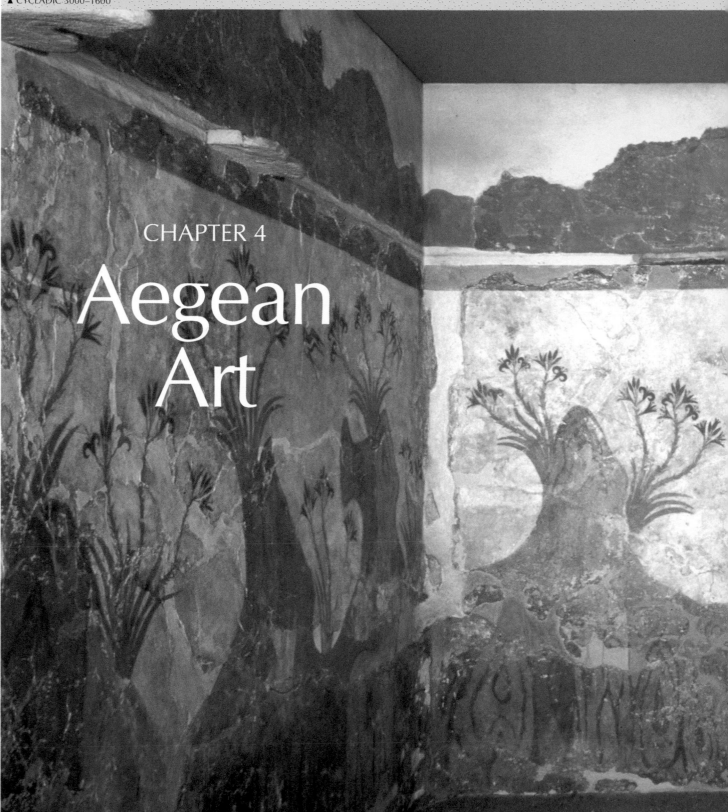

CHAPTER 4

Aegean Art

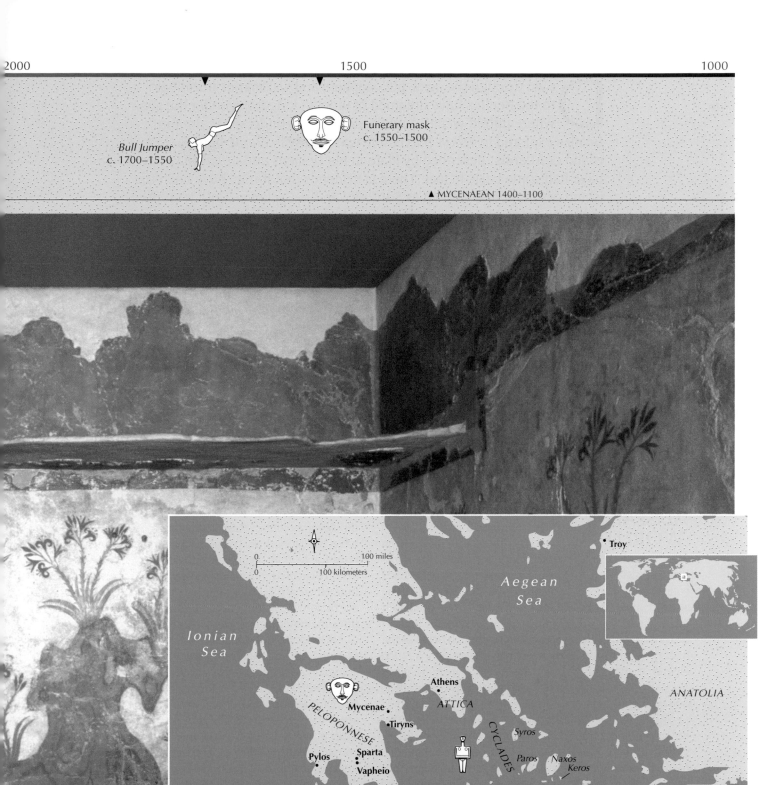

Bull Jumper
c. 1700–1550

Funerary mask
c. 1550–1500

▲ MYCENAEAN 1400–1100

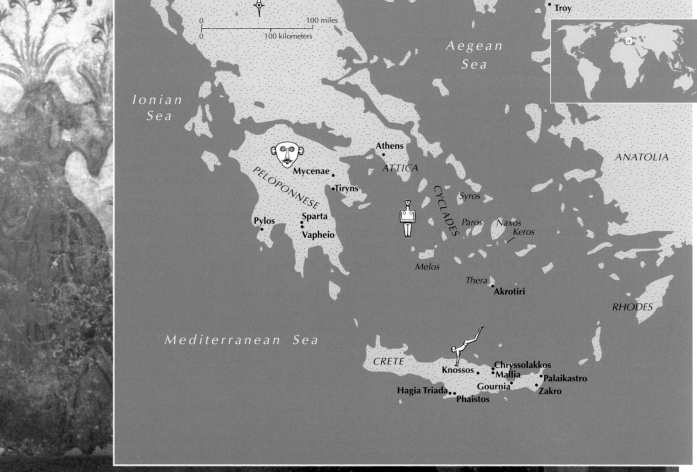

Down through the ages, philosophers and visionaries from Plato to the Beatles have dreamed of utopian kingdoms under the sea where untold wealth could be found. The undersea realm the Beatles explored in *Yellow Submarine* was clearly fictional, but the "lost island of Atlantis" described by Plato in his *Timaeus* and *Critias* may have had some basis in fact. There is evidence that it may have been the island of Thera, also known as Santorini, in the Cyclades. Until it erupted in the seventeenth century BCE, the nearly 5,000-foot-tall volcano that dominated the island must have looked much like Japan's Mount Fuji, a majestic presence whose lower slopes were home to many people. When the volcano came to life, people had time to escape with what they could carry, but then the entire peak blew apart and the greater part of the island, like the fabled Atlantis, disappeared into the sea. All that remained was a crescent of jagged cliffs, fragments of what had been the mountain's base, some 13 miles in diameter. Extensive excavations of the ancient site at Akrotiri, on Thera, have been carried out since 1967, and treasures have indeed been found. Under a layer of ash as much as 15 feet deep, well-preserved wall paintings and artifacts have been discovered that open a window on ancient Aegean culture during one of its richest periods.

THE AEGEAN WORLD

From about 5,000 to 3,000 years ago, the early European civilizations known as Aegean flourished on mainland Greece and on the islands offshore in the Aegean Sea, including the large southern island of Crete and a cluster of smaller ones called the Cyclades. Scholars of these cultures have long studied their ruined palaces, fortresses, and tombs. In recent years the collaboration of archeologists and art historians, working with researchers in such fields as the history of trade and climate change, is providing a much clearer picture of Aegean society in which to place Aegean architecture, sculpture, metalwork, ceramics, and wall paintings.

Although the Aegean peoples were primarily farmers and herders, their lives were greatly influenced by their proximity to the sea. The sea provided their dry, rocky homelands with a defense against invaders, but because they were skillful seafarers, it also provided them a convenient link between the mainland and the islands, as well as the world beyond. Their contacts with Egypt and the civilizations of the Near East were especially important.

From about 3000 to 1000 BCE, one of the hallmarks of Aegean society was the use of bronze, an alloy that was superior to pure copper for making weapons and tools. Using metal ores from Europe, Arabia, and Anatolia, Aegean peoples created metalwares that became prized exports. The sudden technological shift to bronze, presumably as a result of contact with other cultures, occurred at the end of the Aegean Neolithic period and spurred a new consolidation of political and economic power in the Aegean Bronze Age.

Beginning in the third millennium BCE, **palace complexes**, perhaps patterned after Near Eastern and Egyptian administrative centers, began to play a key role in the development of Aegean civilization. They appear to have functioned as religious, political, and economic hubs for Aegean society. A number of palace sites have been excavated, providing a wealth of art and information. However, a great many questions about that society remain unanswered, partly because only one of the three main Aegean writing systems has been deciphered.

What little is known about Aegean civilization from studying its art suggests that religion was probably epiphanic—meaning that during rituals gods and goddesses were believed to appear to their worshipers, often in the form of human stand-ins. The chief deities seem to have been goddesses who controlled various aspects of the natural world and therefore had much in common with goddesses in other early cultures. These Aegean deities may also have been the ancestors of the later Greek goddesses Demeter, Artemis, and Athena. Female images are the most common form of religious art found in Aegean graves, hilltop sacred sites, and palace shrines and may represent goddesses, priestesses, or female worshipers.

Probably the thorniest problem in Aegean archeology is that of dating (see "The Date Debate," opposite). Archeologists have developed a chronological system for the Aegean Bronze Age, but dating specific sites and objects continues to be difficult and controversial. You may therefore encounter dates different from those given here and should expect dating to change in the future.

Our study of Aegean art focuses on three cultures: early Cycladic (on the islands of the Cyclades), Minoan (on Crete), and Mycenaean (in mainland Greece). It begins about 3000 BCE and ends about 1100 BCE.

THE DATE DEBATE Considerable controversy has arisen over the dating of Aegean objects almost since they were first excavated. New evidence is challenging established ideas of *what* happened *when* in the Aegean. It is too soon to tell if the debate is truly over, but scholars using a combination of methods are very close to pinning down the key dates.

Because of the absence of written records, archeologists have used changes in pottery styles to construct a **relative chronology** for the Aegean Bronze Age. A relative chronology indicates how old objects are in relation to each other but cannot assign them absolute dates. Influenced by the division of Egyptian history into Old, Middle, and New Kingdoms, Sir Arthur Evans used ceramic finds from different excavation levels at Knossos to devise a similar chronological framework for Crete, dividing Minoan culture into three periods: Early Minoan, Middle Minoan, and Late Minoan. Later archeologists extended this system to the Cyclades and the mainland (the divisions of the Helladic period, Greece's Bronze Age, correspond more or less to those of the Minoan) and refined it over the years. Still, it remains inexact.

Fortunately, historical records have survived from the Near East and Egypt going back to the third millennium. By the careful cross-cultural referencing of lucky finds—datable foreign trade goods at undated Aegean sites or undated Aegean trade goods in datable foreign contexts—scholars are now beginning to be able to assign dates to the relative chronology's periods, with a view toward arriving at an **absolute chronology**. Radiocarbon, or carbon-14, dating is increasingly useful as a method for dating Aegean organic material, though some dates can only be determined within a span of two or three centuries.

After decades of painstaking work establishing relative and absolute chronologies for the Aegean, archeologists generally agreed that a huge volcanic explosion on the Cycladic island of Thera had thoroughly devastated Minoan civilization on Crete, only 60 miles to the south, about 1450 BCE.

New evidence—namely, stunted growth in tree rings from Ireland and California and traces of volcanic ash in ice cores from Greenland—puts the date of the Thera eruption in the 1620s. This finding leaves Minoan and Mycenaean dating in serious disarray, and the debate over how to realign the chronologies for Aegean civilizations and their trading partners, particularly Egypt, is just beginning.

How has this affected the dating of Minoan and Mycenaean artworks illustrated in this chapter? Specific dates cannot be assigned until the results of the debate are in. While experts ponder the evidence, the rest of us must fall back on the relative chronology system of dating established long ago for the Aegean region. Although this system also lost its chronological underpinnings when the date of the Thera eruption was called into question, many of the interrelationships and stylistic categories on which it is based must still be valid. For that reason, best-guess beginning and ending dates have here been assigned for the Middle and Late Minoan stylistic periods and for Helladic art, then the artworks have been placed within this framework in their familiar positions. Thus the dates given indicate only how old objects may be relative to each other between the more-or-less absolute cut-off dates of 2000 and 1100. Artworks from the island of Thera therefore have simply been dated "before 1630–1500 BCE."

3000 BCE   1000 BCE

THE CYCLADIC ISLANDS IN THE BRONZE AGE

A thriving late Neolithic and early Bronze Age culture existed on the Cycladic Islands, where people engaged in agriculture, herding, manufacturing, and trade. They used local stone to build fortified towns and hillside burial chambers. Because they left no written records and their origins remain obscure, their art is one of our main sources of information about them, as is the case with other Neolithic cultures. From about 6000 BCE on, Cycladic artists had used a coarse, poor-quality local clay to make a variety of objects. Some 3,000 years later, they continued to produce relatively crude but often engaging ceramic figurines of humans and animals, as well as domestic and ceremonial **wares**.

Among the more unusual products of Cycladic potters were vessels resembling large frying pans made of **terra-cotta**, an orange-brown, low-fired clay. They ornamented these "frying pans" with **stylized** designs, either painted or **incised** before firing. The vessels seem to have been used as display objects as well as containers. The elaborate decoration on one side of a pan from Syros, dated 2500–2200 BCE, indicates that it was never intended to be blackened by a cooking fire (fig. 4-1). A

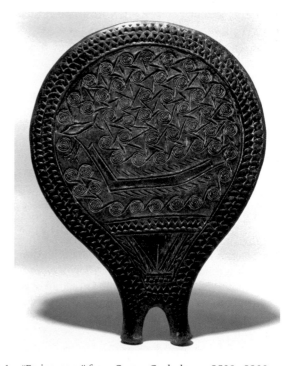

4-1. "Frying pan," from Syros, Cyclades. c. 2500– 2200 BCE. Terra-cotta, diameter 11" (28 cm), depth 2³/₈" (6 cm). National Archeological Museum, Athens

PARALLELS

Years	Culture	Aegean	World
c. 3000–1600 BCE	Cycladic	"Frying pans"; marble figures; landscape painting; destruction of Thera	c. 3000–2000 BCE Potter's wheel (China); Great Pyramids at Giza (Egypt); ziggurats (Sumer); Stonehenge (England)
c. 3000–1400 BCE	Minoan	Bronze tools and weapons; written scripts; Knossos and other palace complexes; *Woman or Goddess with Snakes*; *Bull Jumper*; gold jewelry; potter's wheel; Kamares Ware	c. 2000–1100 BCE *Gilgamesh* epic (Sumer); widespread use of bronze tools (Thailand, China, northern Europe); Shang dynasty (China); *Stela of Hammurabi* (Babylonia); Lion Gate (Turkey); Olmec civilization (Mesoamerica)
c. 1400–1100 BCE	Mycenaean	Citadel at Mycenae; beehive tombs; "Treasury of Atreus"; shaft-grave treasures; *Warrior Vase*	

wide, geometric border encircles a scene showing a boat on a sea of waves depicted as linked spirals. With its curved hull and long banks of oars, the boat resembles those seen in Neolithic Egyptian art from Hierakonpolis (see fig. 3-3). The large fish to the left is probably a carved prow ornament. In the small area set off in the "handle," the artist incised a triangular symbol for the female pubic area, perhaps an indication that these objects were symbolic representations of the uterus and female genitalia. The pans may therefore have had some magical association with pregnancy and childbirth, as well as death, for they are most often found at gravesites.

The Cyclades, especially the islands of Naxos and Paros, had ample supplies of a fine and durable white marble that became the medium of choice for sculptors. Out of it they created a unique type of nude figure ranging in size from a few inches to about 5 feet tall. To shape the stone, these sculptors used scrapers and chisels made of obsidian from the island of Melos and polishing stones of emery, or corundum, from Naxos. The introduction of metal tools may have made it possible for them to carve on a larger scale, but since the stone fractured easily, they continued to limit themselves to simplified sculptural forms.

A few male figurines have been found, including depictions of musicians and acrobats, but they are greatly outnumbered by representations of women. The earliest female figures had simple, violinlike shapes. From these, a more familiar type evolved that has become the best-known type of Cycladic art (fig. 4-2).

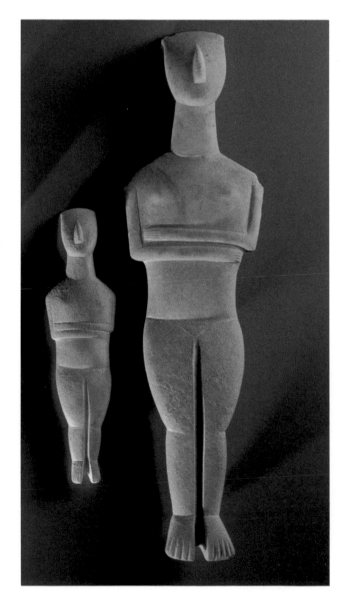

4-2. Two figures of women, from the Cyclades. c. 2500–2200 BCE. Marble, heights 13" (33 cm) and 25" (63.4 cm). Museum of Cycladic Art, Athens
Courtesy of the N. P. Goulandris Foundation

The smaller Cycladic figures have been mainly in and around graves. Although their specific use and meaning are unclear, one interpretation is that they were used by some of the population for worship in the home and then buried with their owners, often after being symbolically broken as part of the funeral ritual. According to this theory, the larger statues were not grave goods but were set up for communal worship, whether as representations of the supernatural or as **votive figures**. The contents of Aegean burial sites could point to a belief in an afterlife. From the evidence, however, it seems that Aegean culture, unlike that of Egypt, was primarily concerned with life in the present.

CRETE AND THE MINOAN CIVILIZATION

Around 3000 BCE, a distinctive culture now called Minoan came into being on the island of Crete. Its name comes from a much later legend that told of Minos, a king who ruled from the palace at Knossos (see "The Legend of the Minotaur," page 132). Crete is the largest of the Aegean islands, 150 miles long and 36 miles wide. It was economically self-sufficient, producing its own grains, olives and other fruits, and cattle and sheep. Because it lacked the ores necessary for bronze production, it was forced to look outward. Crete took advantage of its strategic location and many safe harbors to become a wealthy sea power, trading with mainland Greece, Egypt, the Near East, Anatolia, and perhaps beyond.

Minoan civilization reached its peak about 1600 BCE and remained powerful until about 1450 BCE. Although a number of written records from the period are preserved, very little is known about Minoan daily life. The two earliest forms of Cretan writing, called hieroglyphic and Linear A, continue to defy translation, and the surviving documents in a later script, Linear B—a very early form of Greek imported from the mainland—have proven to be only administrative records and temple inventories, offering no information about many aspects of Minoan culture.

The dominant architectural structures on Crete from roughly 1900 to 1300 BCE were great palace complexes, which were simultaneously administrative, commercial, and religious centers. Scattered across the island, these complexes were long thought to have been unfortified, but it is now known that they were safeguarded by formidable watchtowers and stone walls extending into the countryside. Little is known about the role kings might have played in palace society. Recent scholars have placed greater emphasis on the priestesses who seem to have overseen the all-important goddess worship in these centers. It has been speculated that the palace complexes, kingship, and priestess-run goddess cults are distinctively Minoan adaptations of Near Eastern or Egyptian institutions, but the evidence is contradictory. The Near Eastern palace of Zimrilim at Mari (see Chapter 2, especially fig. 2-19) provides an instructive comparison. It has many similarities to Cretan palaces, such as scale and layout and the depiction of goddesses or

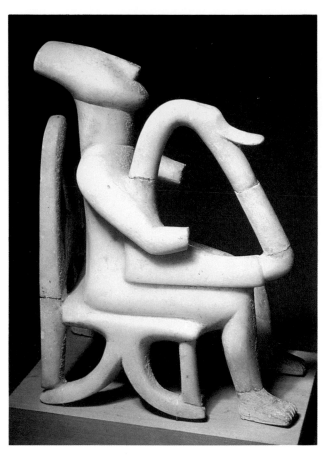

4-3. *Harp Player*, from Keros, Cyclades. c. 2500–2200 BCE. Marble, height 8¹/₂" (21.6 cm). National Archeological Museum, Athens

Compared with Egyptian statues from the same time (see fig. 3-13), Cycladic marbles from roughly 2500 BCE appear to many modern eyes like pared-down, elegant renderings of the figure's essence. With their simple contours, the female statuettes shown here seem not far removed from the marble slabs out of which they were carved. Their tilted-back heads, folded arms, and down-pointed toes indicate that the figures were intended to lie on their backs, as if asleep or dead. Anatomical detail has been kept to a minimum; the body's natural articulation lines at the hips, knees, and ankles are indicated, and the pubic area is marked with a lightly incised triangle. These statues are now paintless, but they originally had painted facial features, hair, and ornaments in black, red, and blue.

The *Harp Player* from Keros is fully developed **sculpture in the round** (fig. 4-3), yet its body shape is just as simplified as that of the female figurines. The sculptor gave equal attention to the negative, or empty, spaces and the solid forms, which balance each other. The figure has been reduced to its geometric essentials, yet with careful attention to those elements that best characterize an actual musician. The harpist sits on a high-backed chair with a splayed base, head tilted back as if singing, knees and feet apart for stability, and arms raised, bracing the instrument with one hand while plucking its strings with the other. So expressive is the pose that we can almost hear the song.

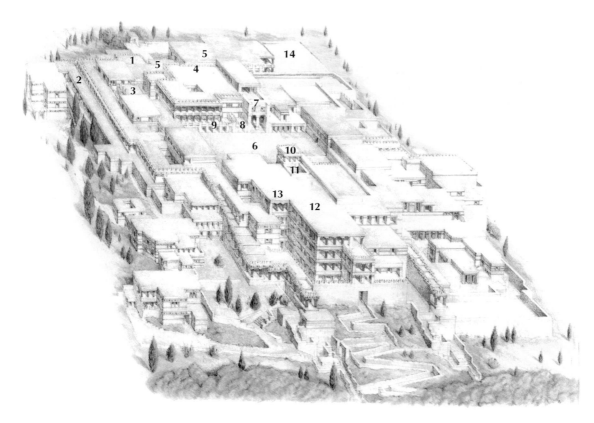

4-4. Bird's-eye reconstruction drawing of the palace complex, Knossos, Crete. c. 1700–1300 BCE

Key: 1. west porch; 2. main corridor; 3. main stairs; 4. north-south corridor; 5. warehouse storage; 6. central courtyard; 7. so-called Throne Room (actually a ritual space); 8. west staircase and stepped porch; 9. main shrine; 10. grand staircase; 11. light well; 12. Hall of the Double Axes (main reception hall); 13. so-called Queen's Quarters; 14. outdoor performance area

priestesses in wall paintings. However, Minoan architecture is less massive and more open, and its palace art does not celebrate kings.

The walls of early Minoan palaces were made of rubble and mud bricks faced with cut and finished limestone. This was the first use of **dressed stone** as a building material in the Aegean. Columns and other interior elements were made of wood. In both the palaces and their surrounding towns, timber appears to have been used for framing and bracing walls so that its strength and flexibility would minimize damage from earthquakes. Nevertheless, a major earthquake in about 1750 BCE damaged

---

THE LEGEND OF THE MINOTAUR According to Greek legend, the Minotaur was a monster, half man and half bull. He was the son of Pasiphae, the wife of King Minos of Crete, and a bull belonging to the sea god Poseidon. The monster lived in the so-called Labyrinth, a maze constructed by the king's court artist and architect, Daedalus. To satisfy the Minotaur's appetite for human flesh and to keep him tranquil, King Minos ordered the city of Athens, which he ruled, to pay him a yearly tribute tax of fourteen young men and women. Theseus, the son of King Aegeus of Athens, vowed to free his people from this grisly burden by slaying the monster.

He set out for Crete with the doomed young Athenians, promising his father that on his return voyage he would replace his ship's black sails with white ones as a signal of victory. In the manner of ancient heroes, Theseus won the heart of the Cretan princess Ariadne, who gave him a sword with which to kill the Minotaur and a spindle of thread to mark the path he took into the Labyrinth. Theseus defeated the Minotaur, followed his trail of thread back out of the maze, and sailed off to Athens with Ariadne and the relieved Athenians. Along the way, his ship put into port on the island of Naxos, where Theseus had a change of heart and left Ariadne behind as she lay sleeping. In his haste to return home, he "forgot" to raise the white sails.

When Aegeus saw the black-sailed ship approaching, he drowned himself in the sea that now bears his name. Theseus thus became king of Athens.

Such psychologically complex myths have long inspired European artists. In William Shakespeare's *A Midsummer Night's Dream*, the play-within-the-play celebrates the marriage of Theseus to the Amazon queen Hippolyta. The plight of Theseus's abandoned lover Ariadne—who finds comfort in the arms of the Greek god Dionysos—is the subplot of an opera by Richard Strauss. In our own time, Pablo Picasso used the Minotaur as a symbol of the Spanish dictator Francisco Franco and the horrors of the Spanish Civil War.

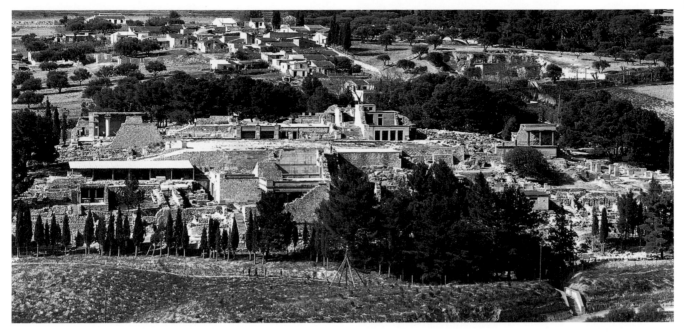

4-5. Palace complex, Knossos, Crete

The town at the foot of the palace had paved streets, comfortable houses, and an advanced water supply and drainage system. "Mansions" dotted the Cretan countryside outside such towns.

several palaces, including the best known of them at Knossos and Phaistos. The structures were then repaired and enlarged. The resulting "new palaces"—multistoried, flat-roofed, and with many columns—shared a number of features. They were designed to maximize light, air, and adaptability, as well as to define access and circulation patterns. Daylight and fresh air entered through staggered levels, open stairwells, and strategically placed air shafts and light wells.

The focus of the complex was inward, toward a spacious rectangular courtyard from which a maze of corridors and staircases led to other courtyards, private rooms and apartments, administrative and ritual areas, storerooms, and baths. Walls were generally coated with plaster, and some of them were painted with murals. Floors were either of plaster, plaster mixed with pebbles, stone, wood, or beaten earth. The palaces' residential quarters had many attractions: sunlit courtyards, richly colored murals, and extraordinarily sophisticated plumbing systems: at Knossos, a network of terra-cotta pipes was laid beneath the palace. Clusters of workshops in and around the complexes suggest that artistic production was officially controlled. Palaces were clearly commercial centers, for their storeroom walls were lined with enormous clay jars for oil and wine, and stone-lined pits in their floors were designed for the storage of grain. The huge scale of their centralized management of foodstuffs became apparent when excavators at Knossos found in a single storeroom enough ceramic jars to hold 20,000 gallons of olive oil.

The Palace Complex at Knossos

Minoan civilization remained very much a mystery until Sir Arthur Evans discovered the buried ruins of the extraordinary palace complex at Knossos, on Crete's north coast, in 1900 CE. Evans spent the rest of his life excavating and reconstructing the buildings he had found (see "Pioneers of Aegean Archeology," page 143). The site had been occupied in the Neolithic period, then built over with a succession of Bronze Age palaces. The last of these "old palaces," erected about 1900 BCE, formed the core of an elaborate new one built after an earthquake in about 1700 BCE. In its heyday, the palace complex covered six acres (figs. 4-4, 4-5). In later Greek legend the Knossos palace was called the Labyrinth, meaning the House of the Double Axes (Greek *labrys*, "double ax"), because double-ax motifs were used in it as architectural decoration (see fig. 4-12 for a three-dimensional example). Because the layout of the complex was so dauntingly complicated, the word *labyrinth* came to mean a maze.

In typical Cretan fashion, the religious, residential, manufacturing, and warehouse spaces of the new palace were organized around a large central courtyard. There were entrances at the four corners, but the main ceremonial approach seems to have been from the southwest. The route to the center of the complex from any of these entrances involved a number of turns. From the central courtyard, a few steps led down into the (misnamed) Throne Room to the west, and a grand staircase on the east side descended to the Hall of the Double

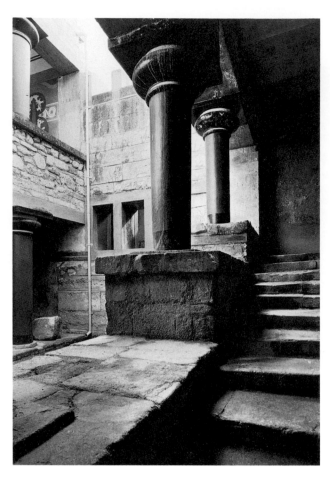

4-6. Court with staircase reconstructed by Sir Arthur Evans, leading to the southeast residential quarter, palace complex, Knossos, Crete

The hundreds of tapered, cushion-capitaled columns of the palace were made of wood, most painted a bright red, and only fragments of them survive. Sir Arthur Evans's restorers installed concrete replicas of columns, capitals, and lintels based on ceramic house models and paintings from the Minoan period. Today's archeologists might not attempt such wholesale reconstruction without absolutely authentic documentation, and they would make certain that reconstructed elements could never be mistaken for the originals.

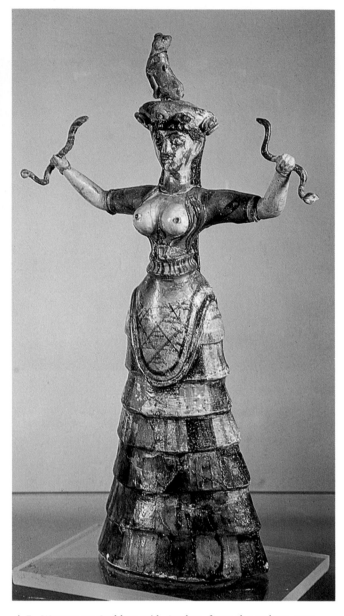

4-7. *Woman or Goddess with Snakes,* from the palace complex, Knossos, Crete. c. 1700–1550 BCE. Faience, height 11⅝" (29.5 cm). Archeological Museum, Iraklion, Crete

Axes, an unusually grand example of a Minoan hall. This hall and others were supported by the uniquely Minoan type of wood columns that became standard in Aegean palace architecture. The tree trunks from which they were made were inverted so that they tapered toward the bottom. Thus, the top, supporting massive roof beams, was wider than the bottom (fig. 4-6). There is some evidence to suggest that Minoan builders were eventually unable to replace columns damaged by earthquakes or burned by invaders because they had already stripped the island of large trees, and this deforestation may have been one of the reasons why the palace-complex structure was finally abandoned.

Sculpture

Surviving Minoan sculpture consists mainly of small, finely executed works, largely on religious subjects, in wood, ivory, precious metals, stone, and **faience**. The *Woman or Goddess with Snakes* from the palace at Knossos is intriguing both as a ritual object and as a work of art (fig. 4-7). Female figurines incorporating serpents were fashioned on Crete as far back as 6000 BCE and may have been associated—as they were elsewhere—with water, regenerative power, and protection of the home. Some early Minoan Bronze Age examples have tall, flaring headdresses with circles on the front and a writhing mass of intertwining snakes on the back.

The nearly foot-tall faience figurine from Knossos was found with other ceremonial objects in a pit in one of the palace's temple storerooms. Bare-breasted, arms extended, and brandishing a snake in each hand, the woman is a commanding presence. A wild cat is perched on her crown, which is ornamented with circles resembling those on the headdresses of earlier such statues. This shapely figure is dressed in a fitted, open bodice with

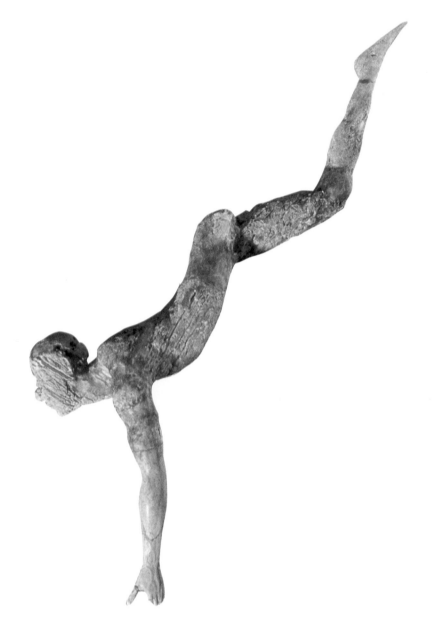

4-8. *Bull Jumper* (?), from the palace complex, Knossos, Crete. c. 1700–1550 BCE. Ivory with gilt bronze wire, length 11⅝" (29.5 cm). Archeological Museum, Iraklion, Crete

an apron over a typically Minoan long tiered skirt. A wide belt cinches the waist. The red, blue, and green geometric patterning on her clothing looks rather like snakeskin. In other pieces of this type, snakes sometimes wind around the woman's waist and arms.

Realistic elements and formal, stylized ones are so skillfully combined in this figure and others of its kind that they have both liveliness and power. In part because of this blending of elements, there is disagreement over whether these statues represent deities or their human attendants. These figures share certain stylistic and thematic features with Near Eastern sculpture, but both the style and the subject can be traced back to older Cretan examples as well.

A number of early cultures associated their gods and god-rulers with powerful animals, especially the lion and the bull. Depictions of bulls appear quite often in Minoan art, rendered with an intensity not seen since the prehis-

toric cave paintings at Altamira and Lascaux (Chapter 1), yet neither their images nor later myths offer any proof that the Minoans worshiped a bull god. According to later Greek legend, King Minos kept the bull-man called the Minotaur captive in his palace, but the creature was not an object of religious veneration (see "The Legend of the Minotaur," page 132). In addition to serving as livestock, bulls were apparently sacrificed by the Minoans on outdoor altars and figured in a rite called bull jumping. Paintings and sculpture show that both women and men, perhaps trained acrobats, took part in this dangerous contest, but its significance remains a mystery.

An ivory figurine of a nude leaping youth (fig. 4-8) was probably originally suspended above one of the ceramic bulls found with it in the palace at Knossos. Despite its deteriorated state, this lithe figure captures the energy of athleticism as it vaults through space. Later Greek culture glorified its athletes, and figures like this

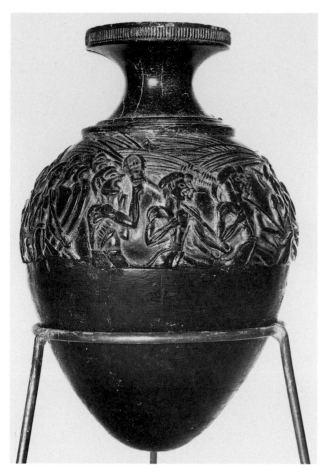

4-9. *Harvester Vase*, from Hagia Triada, Crete. c. 1650–1450 BCE. Steatite, diameter 4½" (11.3 cm). Archeological Museum, Iraklion, Crete

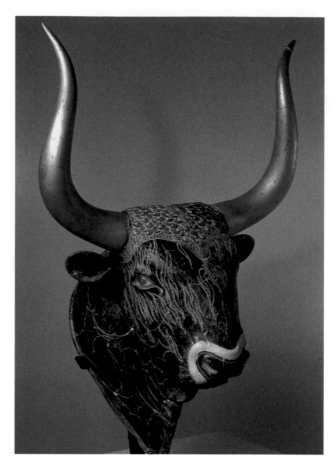

4-10. Bull's-head rhyton, from the palace complex, Knossos, Crete. c. 1550–1450 BCE. Steatite with shell, rock crystal, and red jasper, the gilt-wood horns restored, height 12" (30.5 cm). Archeological Museum, Iraklion, Crete

one may mark the beginning of the practice. The artistry of the ivory figurine is remarkable: its tiny fingernails, the raised veins on the backs of its hands, and its wavy hair are all painstakingly rendered—the latter with gilt, or gold-covered, wire.

Minoan sculptors also excelled in working in hard stone. One of the treasures of Cretan art is the *Harvester Vase*, an egg-shaped **rhyton**—a vessel used for pouring liquids during sacred ceremonies—barely 4½ inches in diameter (fig. 4-9). Made of steatite, or soapstone, it was probably originally covered with **gold leaf**, or sheets of hammered gold (see "Aegean Metalwork," opposite). A rowdy procession of twenty-seven men has been crowded onto its curving surface. The piece is exceptional for the freedom with which the figures occupy three-dimensional space, overlapping and jostling one another instead of marching in orderly single file across the surface in the manner of Near Eastern or Egyptian art. Also new is the exuberance of this scene, especially the emotions shown on the harvesters' faces. The merrymakers march and chant to the beat of a sistrum—a rattlelike percussion instrument—played by a man who sings at the top of his voice. The uneven arrangement of elements reinforces the boisterousness of the scene. The men have large, coarse features and sinewy bodies so thin that their ribs stick out. Perhaps they have suffered a lean time, which gives them all the more reason to celebrate a good harvest.

Rhytons were often given the form of a bull's head. The sculptor of one of this type found in a residence near the palace at Knossos used a block of greenish black steatite to create an image that approaches animal portraiture in its decorative detailing (fig. 4-10). Lightly engraved lines, filled with white powder to make them stand out, show the animal's coat: short, curly hair on top of the head, longer shaggy strands on the sides, and circular patterns to suggest its dappled coloring. White bands of shell outline the nostrils, and painted rock crystal and red jasper form the eyes. The horns, now restored, were made of wood covered with gold leaf. Bull's-head rhytons were used for pouring ritual fluids—water, wine, or perhaps even blood. They were not actual containers; liquid was poured into a hole in the neck and flowed out from the mouth.

Metalwork

By about 1700 BCE, Aegean metalworkers were producing decorative objects rivaling those of Near Eastern jewelers, whose techniques they seem to have borrowed. A necklace pendant in gold found at Chryssolakkos (fig. 4-11) employs several of these techniques (see "Aegean Metalwork," opposite). The artist arched a pair of bees or wasps around a honeycomb, providing their sleek bodies with a single pair of outspread wings—a visual "two in one." The pendant hangs from a spiderlike form, with

TECHNIQUE

AEGEAN METALWORK

Aegean artists imported gold to create exquisite luxury goods. Their techniques, some probably learned from Near Eastern metalsmiths, included **lost-wax casting**, **inlay**, **filigree**, **repoussé** (embossing), **granulation**, **niello**, and **gilding**. The *Vapheio Cup* (fig. 4-13) and the funerary mask (fig. 4-27) are examples of repoussé, in which the artist gently hammered out relief forms from the back of a thin sheet of gold. Experienced goldsmiths may have done simple designs freehand or used standard wood forms or punches. For more elaborate decorations they would first have sculpted the entire relief design in wood or clay and then used this form as a mold over which to shape the gold sheet.

Cretan jewelers were especially skilled at decorating their goldwork with minute granules, or balls, of gold fused to the surfaces, as seen on the bees/wasps pendant (fig. 4-11). The secret of this technique, called granulation, was only recently rediscovered after being lost for nearly a thousand years. The major mystery was how the granules were attached, since all modern solders—heated metal alloys used as adhesives—melted and overwhelmed the tiny, gold globules. The ancient smiths are now believed to have used a complex copper-based solder that fused strongly but nearly invisibly.

The artists who created the Mycenaean dagger blades (fig. 4-28) employed a special technique called niello, which has continued as a common method of metal decoration up to the present time. Powdered nigellum—a black alloy of lead, silver, and copper with sulfur—was rubbed into very fine engraved lines in the object being decorated, then fused to the surrounding metal with heat. Niello work was used for contrasting detail on both **relief** figures and backgrounds.

Gilding, the application of a gold finish to an object made of some other material, was a technically demanding process by which paper-thin sheets of hammered gold called **gold leaf** were meticulously affixed to the surface to be gilded. This was done with amazing delicacy for the individual bronze wire "hairs" of the Minoan ivory *Bull Jumper* (fig. 4-8) as well as for the now-bare stone surface of the *Harvester Vase* (fig. 4-9). The wooden horns of the bull's-head rhyton, too, were gilded (fig. 4-10).

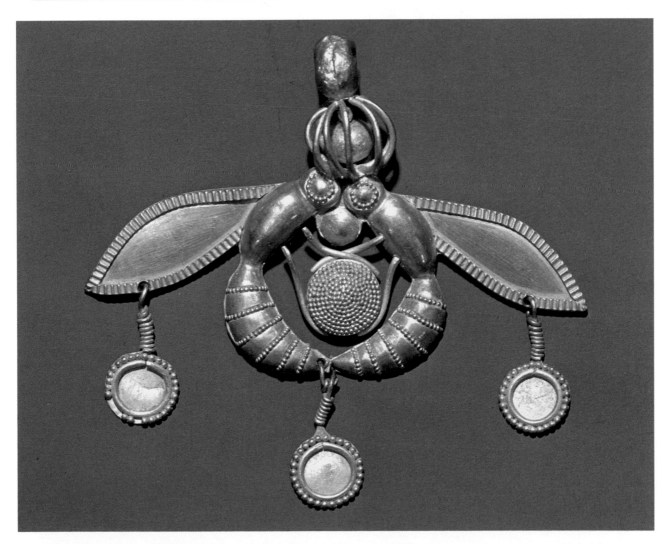

4-11. Pendant in the form of two bees or wasps, from Chryssolakkos, near Mallia, Crete. c. 1700–1550 BCE. Gold, height approx. 1¹³/₁₆" (4.6 cm). Archeological Museum, Iraklion, Crete

This pendant has been interpreted by some as two bees embracing a drop of honey, by others as two wasps fighting. Mallia's goldsmiths may have been influenced by Egyptian artists, who often depicted bees in this way.

what appear to be long legs encircling a tiny, gold ball. Small disks dangle from the ends of the wings and the point where the insects' bodies meet. The simplified geometric patterns and shapes manage to convey close observation of the insects' actual appearance.

Another object notable for its symmetry is the double ax, a motif familiar from the palace at Knossos. The double ax was both a tool and a prominent Minoan cult object associated with blood sacrifice. Since it some-

times appears painted above a bull's head on Minoan pottery, it would seem that bulls may have been sacrificed, and the Minotaur legend raises the possibility that human beings were as well. The double ax was associated with several deities, and its image appears in almost every Minoan art form, especially at religious sites. Both functional bronze axes and miniature gold replicas have been discovered. A large and richly decorated double ax made from a thick sheet of bronze was found in the central shrine treasury at Zakro, a palace complex on the eastern tip of Crete (fig. 4-12). The entire surface of its butterfly-shaped blades with perforated rims is incised with a design of lilylike flowers.

The skills of Minoan artists, particularly metalsmiths, made them highly sought after, especially in mainland Greece. Two magnificent gold cups found in a large tomb at Vapheio, on the mainland south of Sparta, were made about 1650–1450 BCE, either by Minoan artists or by local ones trained in Minoan style and techniques. One of them is shown here (fig. 4-13). Their relief designs were executed in **repoussé**—the technique of hammering from the inside. Their handles were attached with rivets, and they were then lined with sheet gold. In the scenes that circle the cups, men are depicted trying to capture bulls in various ways. On this one, a half-nude man has roped a bull's hind leg. The figures dominate the landscape, which literally bulges with a muscular vitality that belies the cups' small size—they are only 3½ inches tall. The indication of olive trees could mean that the scene is a sacred grove and that these might be illustrations of exploits in some long-lost heroic tale rather than commonplace hunting scenes.

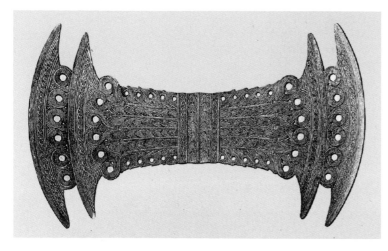

4-12. Drawing of a bronze double ax with double blades, from Zakro, Crete. c. 1650–1500 BCE

Double-bladed axes were associated with ritual use. This ax may have adorned the wooden column of a palace or been set atop a wooden pole, as double axes are shown to be on some sarcophagi.

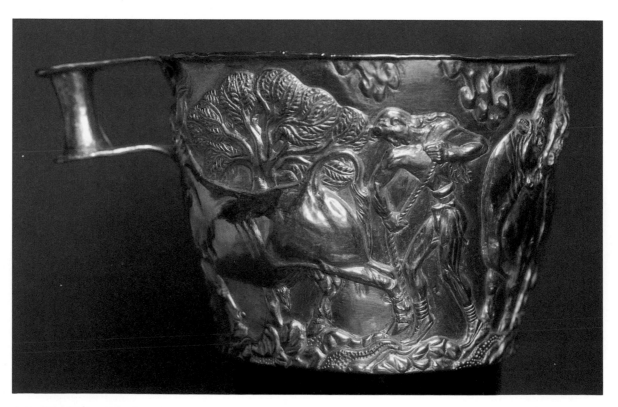

4-13. *Vapheio Cup*, found near Sparta, Greece. c. 1650–1450 BCE. Gold, height 3½" (8.9 cm). National Archeological Museum, Athens

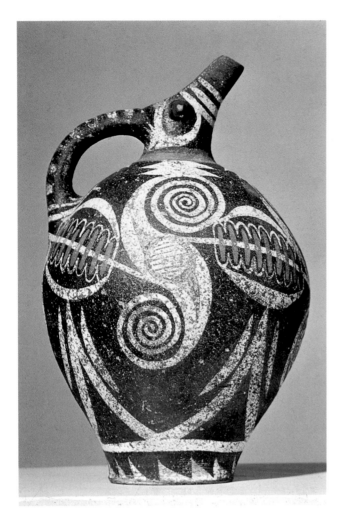

4-14. Kamares Ware jug, from Phaistos, Crete. c. 2000–1900 BCE. Ceramic, height 10⅝" (27 cm). Archeological Museum, Iraklion, Crete

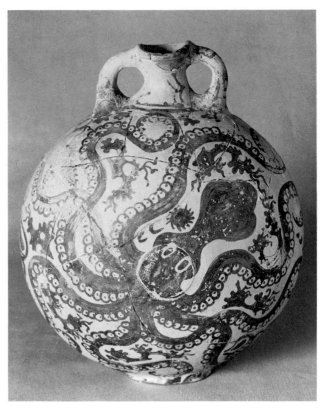

4-15. *Octopus Flask*, from Palaikastro, Crete. c. 1500–1450 BCE. Marine Style ceramic, height 11" (28 cm). Archeological Museum, Iraklion, Crete

Ceramics

The development of new types of clay wares was probably a result of the emergence of palace complexes in the early second millennium BCE, when the potter's wheel was introduced and large-scale production was centralized in palace workshops. One of these new types is called Kamares Ware, after the cave overlooking the palace complex at Phaistos, in southern Crete, where it was first discovered. The hallmarks of this select ware— exported as far away as Egypt and Syria—were its delicacy, its use of color, and its energetically stylized, painted decoration. An example from about 2000–1900 BCE has a globular body and a "beaked" pouring spout (fig. 4-14). Decorated with black, brown, red, and creamy white pigments, the jug's rounded contours are complemented by bold, curving forms derived from plants and animals.

Another striking vessel from the eastern site of Palaikastro, a stoppered bottle known as the *Octopus Flask*, was made about 1500–1450 BCE (fig. 4-15). This is one of a group of pieces decorated in the so-called Marine Style, which probably celebrates Cretan sea power, then at its height. Like microscopic life teeming in

a drop of pond water, sea creatures float across the sphere between an octopus's tangled tentacles. The decoration on the Kamares Ware jug reinforces the solidity of its surface, but here the pottery skin seems to dissolve. The painter captured the grace and energy of natural forms while presenting them as a stylized design in harmony with the vessel's shape.

Wall Painting

Minoan painters also worked on a larger scale, covering palace rooms with geometric borders, views of nature, and scenes of human activity. Murals can be painted either on a still-wet plaster surface or on a dry one. In the wet technique, pigments bind well to the wall, but the painter is forced to work very quickly. In the dry one, the painter does not need to hurry, but the pigments tend to flake off in time. There is some controversy over which technique was used by the artists at Knossos. They may have employed both techniques in different paintings, or even a combination of the two. Their standard colors were red, yellow, black, white, green, and blue. Like the Egyptian tomb painters, the Minoan palace artists filled in the outlines of their figures and objects with unshaded areas of pure color. Minoan wall painting, however, especially of landscapes, is quite different in feeling from Egyptian painting.

Almost all of the wall paintings in the Knossos palace complex date from the "new palace" period, after about 1700 BCE. By reconstructing them, archeologists

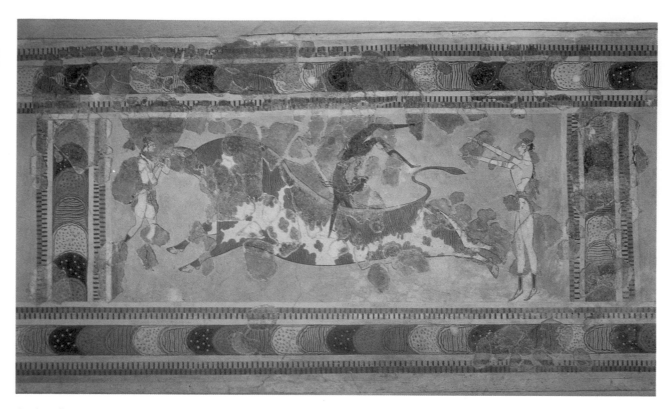

4-16. *Bull Jumping*, wall painting with areas of modern reconstruction, from the palace complex, Knossos, Crete. c. 1550–1450 BCE. Height approx. 24¹/₂" (62.3 cm). Archeological Museum, Iraklion, Crete

Careful sifting during excavation preserved many fragments of the paintings that once covered the palace walls. The pieces were painstakingly sorted and cleaned by restorers and reassembled into puzzle pictures that still had more pieces missing than found. The next step was to fill in the gaps with colors similar to the original ones, but lighter and grayer in tone. It is therefore obvious which are the restored portions, but the eye can still read and enjoy the image.

are learning more about the functions of some of the architectural spaces the paintings enhanced. For example, the small chamber in the west wing that Sir Arthur Evans called the Throne Room has now been identified as an epiphanic ritual space, in part on the basis of the imagery employed in its murals. Lilies, associated with goddess-priestess celebrations, are among their prominent motifs. Taken together, the wall paintings at Knossos may have referred to some seasonal festival or series of festivals in honor of a goddess.

One of the best-preserved scenes is *Bull Jumping*, part of a group of paintings with bulls as subjects from a

THE WRECK AT ULU BURUN

Shipwrecks can provide vast amounts of information about the material culture of societies whose contact with the rest of the world was by sea. The wreck of a trading vessel was discovered in the vicinity of Ulu Burun, off the south coast of modern Turkey between Rhodes and Cyprus. Thought to have sunk between 1400 and 1350 BCE, during the late Helladic period, the boat carried a cargo of metals, especially copper and tin ingots for making bronze, as well as a number of bronze weapons and tools. There was also a ton of terebinth on board, an aromatic resin used in making incense and perfume, as well as a variety of fruits, nuts, and spices. There were jewelry and beads, logs of African ebony for making fine furniture, ivory tusks for carving, ostrich eggs, and raw blocks of blue glass for use in faience and glassmaking workshops. Among the many gold objects was a scarab associated with Nefertiti, the wife of the Egyptian pharaoh Akhenaten (Chapter 3). The ship also carried more mundane items, including fishhooks, sinkers for fish lines and nets, sets of weights for use on scales, and ceramic wares made by potters from the Near East, mainland Greece, as well as Cyprus.

Its varied cargo suggests that this trading vessel cruised from port to port, loading and unloading goods as it went. Which direction it was headed when it sank and where its home port might have been are still unknown, but the boat had clearly made a large circuit encompassing the coasts of Egypt, the Middle East, the Near East, Anatolia, and mainland Greece. It may even have navigated in and out of the Black Sea and as far west as Sardinia. It is tempting to see this trading vessel as evidence of Aegean entrepreneurship—there were merchant-traders in the Near East by this time—but some scholars believe that Aegean foreign trade, like that in Egypt, was conducted exclusively as exchange between courts by palace administrators.

4-17. *Priestess* (?), detail of a wall painting from Akrotiri, Thera, Cyclades. Before 1630–1500 BCE. National Archeological Museum, Athens. (For an explanation of the date used here and for figure 4-18, see "The Date Debate," page 129.)

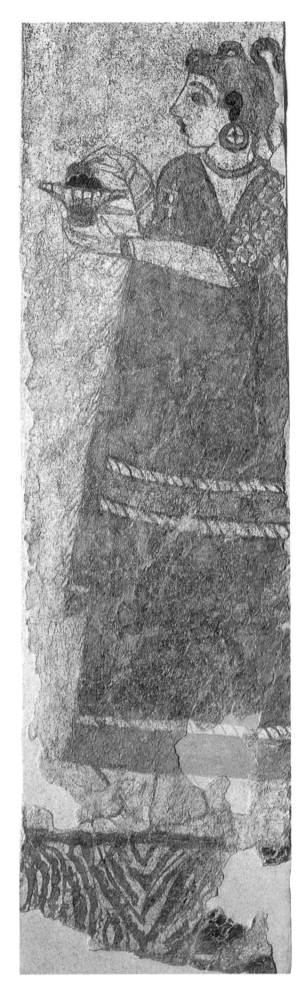

room in the palace's east wing (fig. 4-16). The work may represent an initiation or fertility ritual. Three scantily clad, youthful figures arc around a dappled, charging bull. The pale-skinned person at the right—probably a woman—is either beginning or finishing her vault, the dark-skinned man is in the midst of his, and the pale-skinned woman at the left grasps the bull by its horns. The bull's thundering power and sinuous grace are masterfully rendered. Variegated overlapping ovals set within striped bands frame the action.

The art of wall painting seems to have spread along with other Minoan cultural influences to both the Cyclades and mainland Greece. The Cycladic island Thera (today also called Santorini) was so heavily under Cretan influence at this time that it was virtually an outpost of Minoan culture. When the island literally blew apart in the 1620s BCE, vivid murals were preserved under layers of volcanic ash in residences at Akrotiri. These paintings provide clues about life on the island before the inhabitants fled. Some of the subjects also occur in Cretan art, but others are new. One fragment, for example, may show a young priestess of the snake goddess, a familiar Cretan subject, making a ceremonial offering (fig. 4-17). The beautifully drawn figure stands with her torso in three-quarter view and her head in profile. Her frontal eye suggests Egyptian conventions. Her features bear a striking resemblance to many modern Greek faces. The woman wears an elegant robe with patterned sleeves and ornamental bands, bracelets, a necklace, and large earrings. Such figures customarily have long, flowing hair, but this one appears to wear a fitted cap crowned by a snake. If the artists on Thera followed the Knossos practice of matching mural subject to room function, then this painting would have adorned a ritual space.

Another mural is an astonishing landscape unlike anything previously encountered in ancient art (fig. 4-18). A viewer standing in the center of the room is surrounded by orange-and-blue-striped rocky hillocks sprouting oversize deep red lilies. Swallows, represented by a few deft lines, swoop above and around the flowers. The artist's vision unifies the rhythmic flow of the undulating landscape, the stylized patterning imposed on the natural forms, and the decorative use of bright colors alternating with neutral tones, which were perhaps meant to represent areas of shadow. The impression is one of organic life and growth, a celebration of the natural world symbolized by the lilies.

For reasons not entirely clear, Minoan civilization declined after about 1500 BCE, and between about 1450 and 1375 BCE the Cretan palace complexes succumbed to conquest by mainland Greeks. Knossos was burned, but

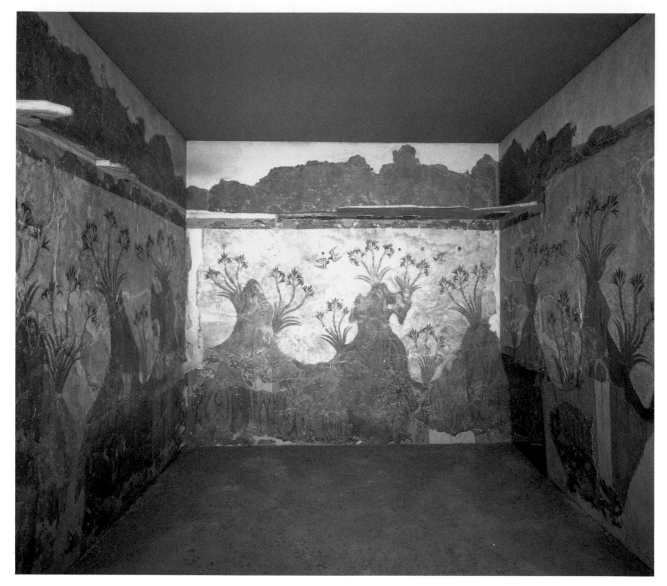

4-18. *Landscape*, wall painting with areas of modern reconstruction from Akrotiri, Thera, Cyclades. Before 1630–1500 BCE. National Archeological Museum, Athens

the invaders appear to have continued using the site for many years. By 1400 BCE the center of political and cultural power in the Aegean had shifted to mainland Greece, which at that time was home to wealthy warrior-kings.

MAINLAND GREECE AND THE MYCENAEAN CIVILIZATION

Archeologists have used the term *Helladic* (from *Hellas*, the Greek word for Greece) to designate the Bronze Age in Greece. The Helladic period extends from about 3000 to 1000 BCE, overlapping with the Minoan chronology of Crete. In the early part of this period, Greek-speaking peoples invaded the mainland. They brought advanced metalworking, ceramic, and architectural techniques and displaced the indigenous Neolithic culture. When Minoan culture declined after about 1500 BCE, a Late Helladic mainland culture known as Mycenaean, after the city of Mycenae, rose to dominance in the Aegean region.

Mycenaean culture was influenced by Minoan culture, but there was a marked difference in their social, political, and geographic circumstances. Life in Mycenaean strongholds such as Mycenae, Tiryns, and Pylos probably contrasted sharply with life in the open palace complexes on Crete 92 miles away. The communities centered around these strongholds were controlled by local princes or kings, and evidence from tombs dating to between 1600 and 1500 BCE suggests that at that time they were growing both increasingly wealthy and increasingly stratified.

The pioneering figure in the modern study of Aegean civilization was the German Heinrich Schliemann (1822–1890), who was inspired by Homer's epic tales, the *Iliad* and the *Odyssey*. The son of an impoverished minister, from whom he inherited a love of literature and languages, Schliemann was forced by economic circumstances to follow a "commercial" rather than a classical course of study and enter the business world. He worked hard, grew rich, and retired in 1863 to pursue his lifelong dream of becoming an archeologist. Between 1865 and 1868, he studied archeology and Greek in Paris, then in 1869–1870 he began conducting field work in Greece and Turkey.

Scholars of that time considered Homer's stories pure fiction, but by studying the descriptions of geography in the *Iliad*, Schliemann located the multilayered site at Hissarlik, in modern Turkey, the sixth level of which is generally accepted as being Homer's Troy. Although he had agreed to give the Turkish government half of all valuable finds in exchange for permission to dig, Schliemann kept for himself a copper pot containing objects in gold and silver that he discovered in May 1873. After having been sued by the Turks, he set up a fund to establish a national museum in Turkey, but he never returned the treasure, which was hidden for years. It came to light again only in the mid-1990s in Russia, where the Red Army had taken it, along with other art treasures, at the end of World War II.

After his success at Hissarlik, Schliemann pursued his hunch that the grave sites of Homer's Greek royal family would be found inside the citadel at Mycenae. He did indeed find opulent burials in shaft graves uncovered near the Lion(ess) Gate, but accumulated scientific data later proved the graves to be too early to contain the bodies of Atreus, Agamemnon, and their relatives—if these legendary figures ever existed. Today's scholars, however, do accept the possibility that some Homeric legends are based on actual events.

In 1887 Schliemann tried unsuccessfully to buy a site on the island of Crete, where he hoped to find the palace of the legendary King Minos. That discovery fell to a British archeologist, Sir Arthur Evans (1851–1941), who led the excavation of the palace at Knossos between 1900 and 1905. It was Evans who gave the name "Minoan"—after King Minos—to Cretan civilization from the Bronze Age. The chief focus in his study was on examples of early Minoan writing. He also made a first attempt to establish an absolute chronology for Minoan art, basing his conjectures on datable Egyptian artifacts found in the Cretan ruins and on Cretan finds in Egypt. Later scholars have revised and refined his datings.

Men were not the only energetic researchers in the field in those days. Sophia Schliemann contributed much to her husband's work, and an American woman, Harriet Boyd—assisted by Edith Hall—was responsible for the excavation of Gournia, which is one of the best-preserved Bronze Age towns in Crete. She published her findings in 1908.

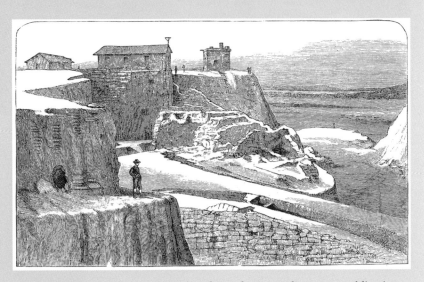

View of Schliemann's excavation site of Troy from a 19th-century publication

Architecture

The Citadel at Mycenae. Later Greek writers recalled Mycenae, located near the east coast of the Peloponnese in southern Greece, as the home of the conquerors of the great city of Troy (fig. 4-19). Even today, the monumental gateway to the **citadel** at Mycenae (fig. 4-20) is an impressive reminder of the city's warlike past. The gate itself dates from about 1300–1200 BCE, perhaps a century later than the first of the citadel's **ring walls**, or surrounding walls. Because of its size, proportions, and construction techniques, the gate conveys the same impression of military strength as does the Lion Gate of the ancient Hittite citadel near modern Boghazkeui,

Turkey (see fig. 2-28). Although formed of megaliths, this gate is very different in purpose and style from other megalithic structures of the time—Stonehenge, for example (Chapter 1). The basic architecture of this gate is **post-and-lintel construction** with a **relieving arch** above. The **corbel** arch "relieved" the lintel of the weight of the wall that rose above it to a height of about 50 feet. As in Near Eastern citadels, the gate was provided with guardian figures. The Mycenaean sculptors placed a pair of lions or lionesses nearly 9½ feet tall in the arch opening. Their missing heads were sculpted separately—of bronze or gold—then fastened into holes in the stone. The two animals, one on each side of a Minoan-style column, stand facing each other, their forepaws resting on

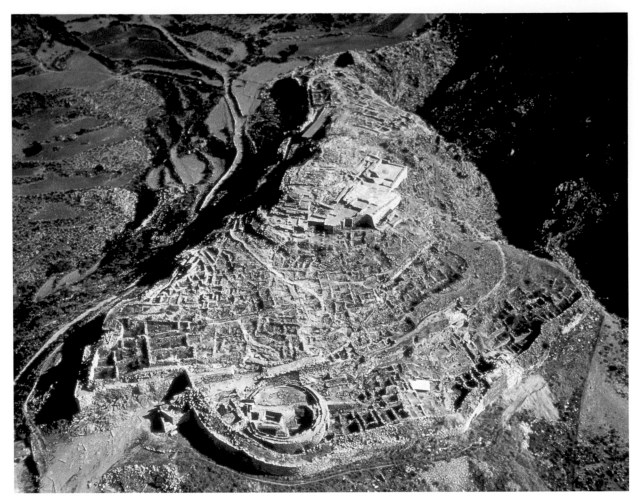

4-19. Mycenae, Greece. c. 1600–1200 BCE

The citadel's hilltop position and fortified ring wall are clearly visible. The Lioness Gate (fig. 4-20) is at the lower left, approached by a dirt path.

stone altars. From this gate, a long, stone passageway led into the citadel proper, at the center of which stood the king's palace.

Tombs assumed much greater prominence for Helladic period cultures of the mainland than for the Minoans, and ultimately they became the most architecturally sophisticated monuments of the entire Aegean period. By about 1600 BCE, the region's kings and princes had begun building large aboveground burial places commonly referred to as **beehive tombs** because of their rounded, conical shape. In their round plan, beehive tombs are somewhat similar to the prehistoric European megalithic tombs called **passage graves**, such as the one at Newgrange, Ireland (Chapter 1). In stone-lined pits off the center chambers of these structures, Helladic ruling families laid out their dead in opulent costumes and jewelry and surrounded them with ceremonial weapons, gold and silver wares, and other articles indicative of their high status, wealth, and power.

More than a hundred such tombs have been found on mainland Greece, nine of them in the vicinity of Mycenae. Possibly the most impressive is the so-called Treasury of Atreus (fig. 4-21), which dates from about 1300 to 1200 BCE. The structure is an example of **cyclopean construction**, so called because it was believed that only the

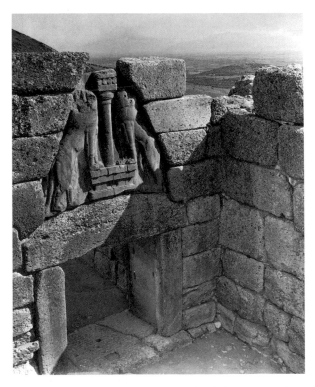

4-20. Lioness Gate, Mycenae. c. 1300–1200 BCE. Limestone relief, height of sculpture approx. 9'6" (2.9 m)

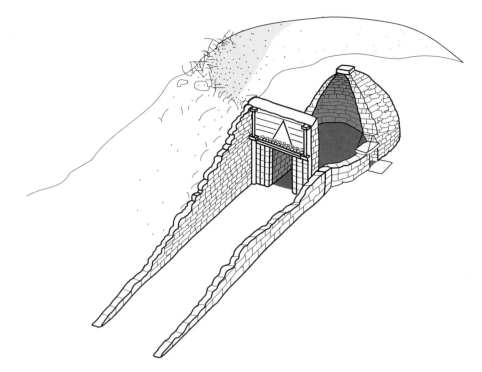

4-21. Cutaway drawing of the beehive tomb called the Treasury of Atreus, Mycenae, Greece. c. 1300–1200 BCE

race of giants known as the Cyclopes could have moved such massive stones. A walled passageway through the earthern mound covering the tomb, about 120 feet long and 20 feet wide and open to the sky, led to the tomb's entrance **facade**. The original entrance was 34 feet high and the door was 18 feet high, faced with bronze plaques and flanked by engaged, Minoan-type columns of green marble. The section above the lintel had smaller engaged columns on each side, and the relieving triangle was disguised behind a marble panel. The stone surfaces were incised with geometric bands and **chevrons**—inverted Vs—filled with **running spirals**, a favored Aegean motif seen in earlier Cycladic and Minoan art (see figs. 4-1, 4-12). The main tomb chamber (fig. 4-22) is a circular room 47 1/2 feet in diameter and 43 feet high. It is roofed with a **corbeled vault** built up in regular **courses**, or layers, of **ashlar**—squared stones—smoothly leaning inward and carefully calculated to meet in a single **capstone** at the peak, a remarkable engineering feat.

4-22. Corbeled vault, interior of the Treasury of Atreus. Stone, height of vault approx. 43' (13 m), diameter 47'6" (14.48 m)

This great beehive tomb, which remained half buried until it was excavated by Christos Stamatakis in 1878, is neither a storage space for treasures nor likely to be connected to Atreus, the father of King Menelaus and Agamemnon, who led the campaign against Troy in Homer's *Iliad*. For over a thousand years, this Mycenaean tomb remained the largest uninterrupted interior space built in Europe. The first European structure to exceed it in size was the Pantheon in Rome (Chapter 6), built in the first century BCE.

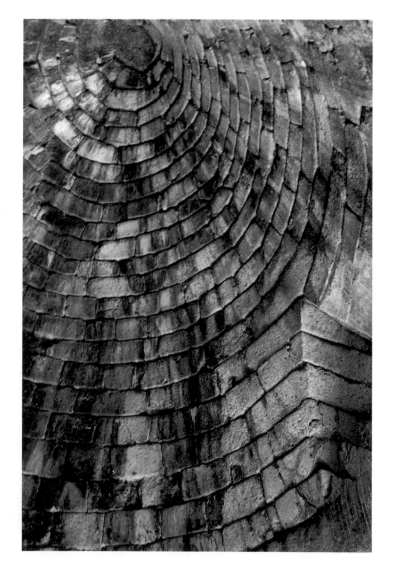

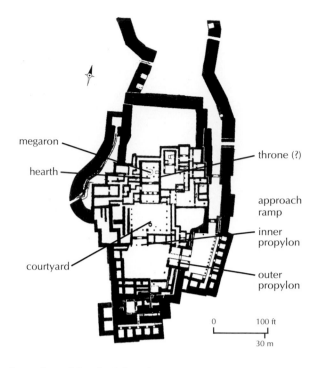

1500

3000 BCE 1000 BCE

megaron

hearth

courtyard

throne (?)

approach ramp

inner propylon

outer propylon

0   100 ft

30 m

4-23. Plan of the citadel at Tiryns, Greece. c. 1300–1200 BCE

The Citadel at Tiryns. The builders of the citadel at Tiryns (fig. 4-23), about ten miles from Mycenae, made up for the site's lack of natural defenses by drawing heavily on their knowledge of military strategy. Homer referred to the resulting fortress as "Tiryns of the Great Walls." Its ring wall was about 20 feet thick, and the inner palace walls were similarly massive. The main entrance gate was approached along a narrow ramp that rose clockwise along the ring wall, forcing attacking soldiers to climb with their right sides exposed to the defenders on top of the wall and awkwardly try to cover themselves with shields held on their left arms. If they were lucky enough to reach the entrance, they still had to fight their way through a series of inner fortified gates. Corbel-vaulted casemates, or enclosures within the thickness of the ring walls, provided spaces for storing armaments and emergency shelter for soldiers or even for townspeople seeking safety within the citadel (fig. 4-24). In the unlikely event that the citadel gate was breached, the people inside could escape through openings from which they could combat attackers without opening the main gate.

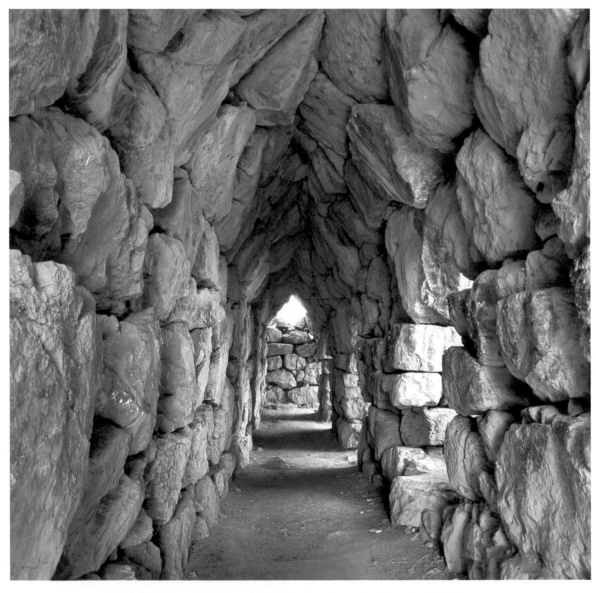

4-24. Corbel-vaulted casemate inside the ring wall of the citadel at Tiryns

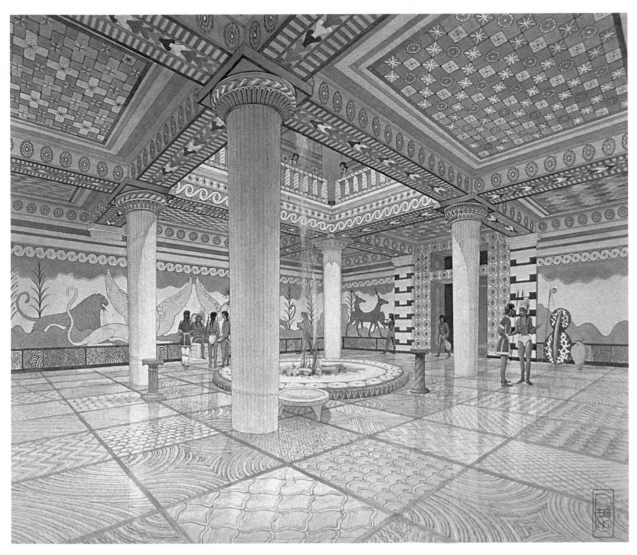

4-25. Reconstruction drawing of the megaron in the palace at Pylos, Greece. c. 1300–1200 BCE. Drawing in Antonopouleion Archeological Museum, Pylos

The palace area at Tiryns featured a large audience hall called a **megaron**, or "great room," accessible to the main courtyard through a porch and a vestibule—a much more direct approach than the winding path imposed on visitors in a Minoan palace. In the typical megaron plan, four large columns around a central hearth supported the ceiling. The roof section above the hearth was either raised or open to admit light and air and permit smoke to escape. Architectural historians surmise that the megaron eventually came to be specifically associated with royalty. The later Greeks therefore adapted its form when building temples, which they saw as earthly palaces for their gods.

The Palace at Pylos. Tiryns required heavy defense works because of its location. The people of Pylos, in the extreme southwest of the Peloponnese, perhaps felt that their more remote location made military attack there less likely. The palace at Pylos, built about 1300–1200 BCE, followed the megaron plan and was built on a raised site without walls. Set behind a porch and vestibule facing the courtyard, the Pylos megaron was a magnificent display of architectural and decorative prowess. The reconstructed view provided here (fig. 4-25) shows how the combined throne room and audience hall, with fluted Minoan-type columns supporting heavy ceiling beams, might have looked when new. Every inch was painted—the floors, ceilings, beams, and door frames with brightly colored abstract designs, and the walls with large mythical animals and highly stylized plant and landscape forms.

Linear B clay tablets found in the ruins of the palace include an inventory of the palace furnishings that indicates they were as elegant as the architecture. The listing on one tablet reads: "One ebony chair with golden back decorated with birds; and a footstool decorated with ivory pomegranates. One ebony chair with ivory back carved with a pair of finials and with a man's figure and heifers; one footstool, ebony inlaid with ivory and pomegranates." It may be that the people of Pylos should have taken greater care to protect themselves. Within a century of its construction, the palace was destroyed by fires, apparently set during the violent upheavals that brought about the collapse of Mycenaean Greek dominance.

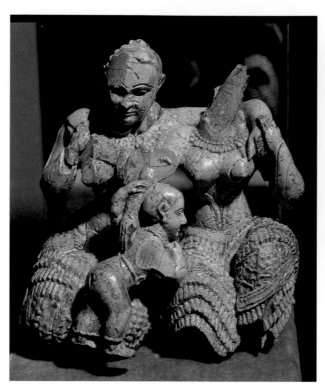

4-26. *Two Women with a Child*, found in the palace at Mycenae, Greece. c. 1400–1200 BCE. Ivory, height 2³⁄₄"
(7.5 cm). National Archeological Museum, Athens

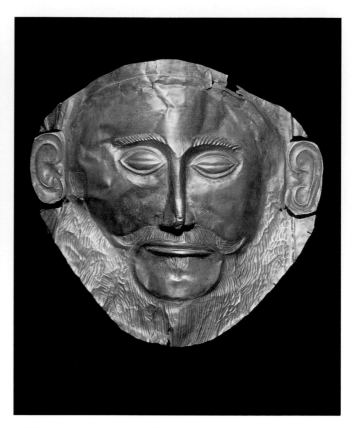

4-27. Funerary mask, from the royal tombs at Mycenae,
Greece. c. 1550–1500 BCE. Gold, height approx. 12"
(35 cm). National Archeological Museum, Athens

When Heinrich Schliemann excavated the royal shaft
graves just inside the Lion(ess) Gate at Mycenae in
1876, he believed that he had discovered the bodies of
the legendary family of Atreus, including his son
Agamemnon. Schliemann dubbed this gold mask from
one of the graves the "Mask of Agamemnon"—a
name it still carries in many books. Schliemann's discoveries at Mycenae and Troy have led scholars to
conclude that the Homeric tales may have been rooted
in historical fact, but Schliemann himself was unaware that the graves at Mycenae predate the possible
siege of Troy by about three centuries, so that the
funeral mask could not have been Agamemnon's, even
if he was an actual person.

Sculpture

Mainland artists were exposed to Minoan art through
trading and even perhaps by working side by side with
Minoan artists brought back by the Greek conquerors of
the island. A carved ivory group of two women and a
child (fig. 4-26), less than 3 inches high and found in the
palace shrine at Mycenae, appears to be a product of
Minoan-Mycenaean artistic exchange. Dating from
about 1400–1200 BCE, the miniature exhibits carefully
observed natural forms, an intricately interlocked composition, and finely detailed rendering. Because there are
no clues to the identity or the significance of the group,
we might easily interpret it as generational—with grandmother, mother, and child—but the figures could just as
well represent two nymphs or devotees attending a
child-god. In either case, the mood of affection and tenderness among the three is unmistakable, and, tiny as it
is, the sculpture counters the militaristic vein of so much
Mycenaean art.

Metalwork

The beehive tombs at Mycenae had been looted long
before Heinrich Schliemann arrived to search for Homeric Greece, but the contents of the **shaft graves** he
excavated in the 1870s reflect mainland culture at an
even earlier date (see "Pioneers of Aegean Archeology,"
page 143). Shaft graves were vertical pits 20 to 25 feet
deep, and those entombing rulers and their families were
enclosed in a circle of standing stone slabs. Magnificent
metal treasures in the form of swords, daggers, scepters,
jewelry, and drinking cups were often buried with members of the elite. As in the tombs of Egyptian royalty,
some of the men were found wearing masks of gold or a
silver-gold alloy called electrum, as if to preserve their
heroic features forever. The realistic features embossed
on the gold funerary mask often mistakenly called the
"Mask of Agamemnon" (fig. 4-27), dated about 1550–
1500 BCE, seem uncannily like those of a death mask cast
from the actual face of the deceased—broad cheekbones,
strong chin, thin, pointed nose, full beard and moustache, closed, bulging eyes, and narrow eyebrows.

Also found in one of the shaft graves at Mycenae
were three bronze dagger blades decorated with inlaid
scenes (fig. 4-28). The Mycenaean artist cut shapes out
of different-colored metals—copper, silver, and gold—
then set them into the bronze blades. Silver and gold
inlays had to be first backed with copper. The fine details

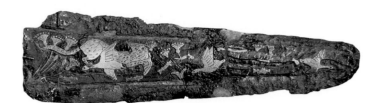

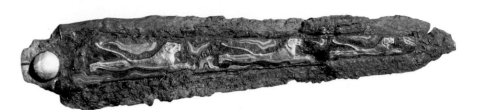

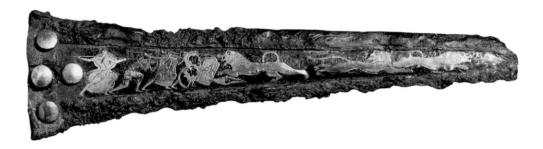

4-28. Dagger blades, from shaft graves at Mycenae, Greece. c. 1550–1500 BCE. Bronze inlaid with gold, silver, and copper, lengths 6³⁄₈" (16.3 cm), 8⁷⁄₁₆"(21.4 cm), and 9³⁄₈" (23.8 cm). National Archeological Museum, Athens

were added in **niello** (see "Aegean Metalwork," page 137). In the *Iliad*, Homer's epic poem about the Trojan War written before 700 BCE, Agamemnon's armor and Achilles's shield are described as having similar decorations. The decorations of the two larger blades—depicting men with shields battling three lions, and three lions racing across a rocky landscape—are typically Aegean in the animated and naturalistic treatment of the figures. Interestingly, the scene on the shortest blade, showing a leopard attacking ducks in a papyrus swamp, clearly reflects Egyptian influence.

Ceramics

In the final phase of the Helladic period, Mycenaean potters created highly refined ceramics in uniform sizes and shapes. Although their vessels were superior in terms of technique, the decorations applied to them were generally less innovative, more conventional than those of earlier wares. A narrative scene ornaments the Mycenaean *Warrior Vase*, dating from about 1300–1100 BCE (fig. 4-29). On the side shown here, a woman at the far left bids farewell to a group of helmeted men with beribboned lances and large shields marching off to the right. There is none of the vibrant energy of the *Harvester Vase* or the *Vapheio Cup* in this scene. The only indication of the woman's emotions is the symbolic gesture of an arm raised to her head, and the figures of the men are seemingly interchangeable parts in a rigidly disciplined war machine.

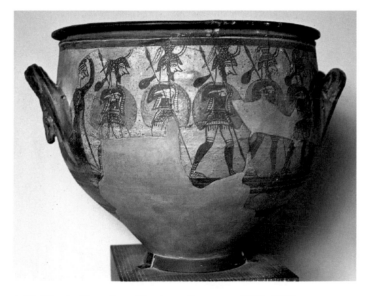

4-29. *Warrior Vase*, from Mycenae, Greece. c. 1300–1100 BCE. Ceramic, height 16" (41 cm). National Archeological Museum, Athens

Mycenaean civilization did not have a long history. By 1200 BCE, aggressive invaders were crossing into mainland Greece, and within a century they had taken control of the major cities and citadels. The period between about 1100 and 900 BCE was a kind of "dark age" in the Aegean, marked by political, economic, and artistic instability and upheaval. But a new culture was forming, one that looked back to the exploits of the Helladic warrior-princes as the glories of a heroic age and at the same time formed the basis of a new Greek civilization.

BCE 1000   800   600

Centaur
late 10th century

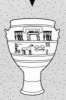

Dipylon
vase
c. 750

Corinthian
pitcher
c. 600

Kouros
c. 600

▲ PROTO-GEOMETRIC 1000–900 ▲ GEOMETRIC 900–700   ▲ ORIENTALIZING 700–600   ▲ ARCHAIC 600–480

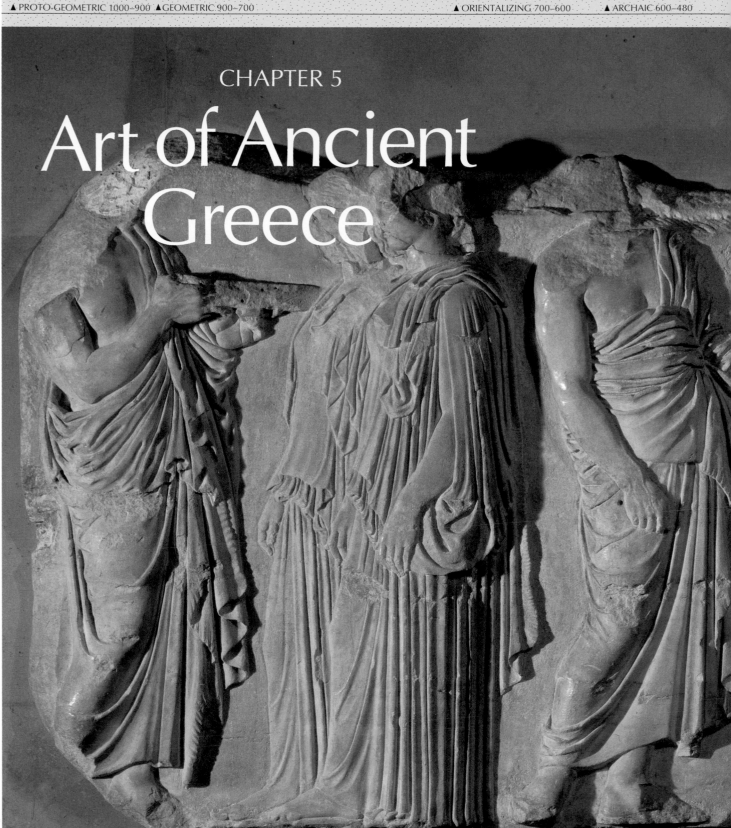

CHAPTER 5

Art of Ancient Greece

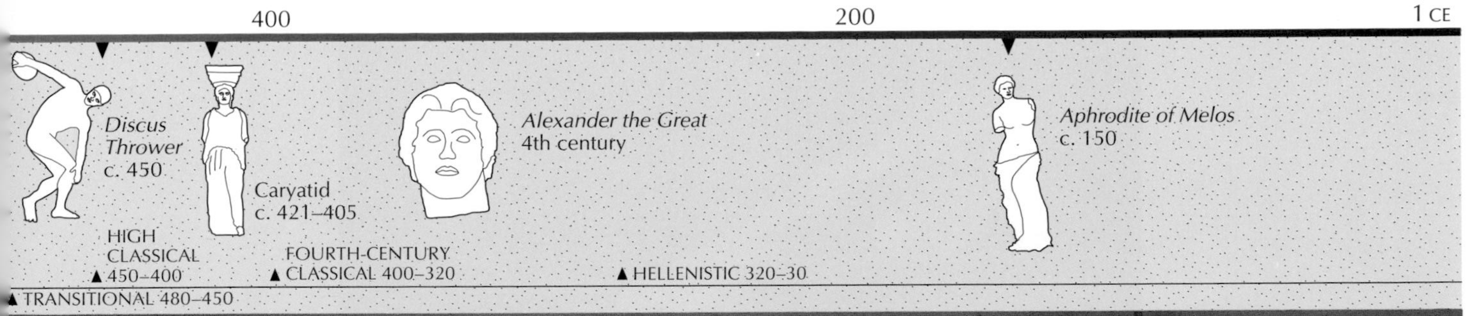

Discus
Thrower
c. 450

Caryatid
c. 421–405

Alexander the Great
4th century

Aphrodite of Melos
c. 150

HIGH
CLASSICAL
▲ 450–400

FOURTH-CENTURY
▲ CLASSICAL 400–320

▲ HELLENISTIC 320–30

▲ TRANSITIONAL 480–450

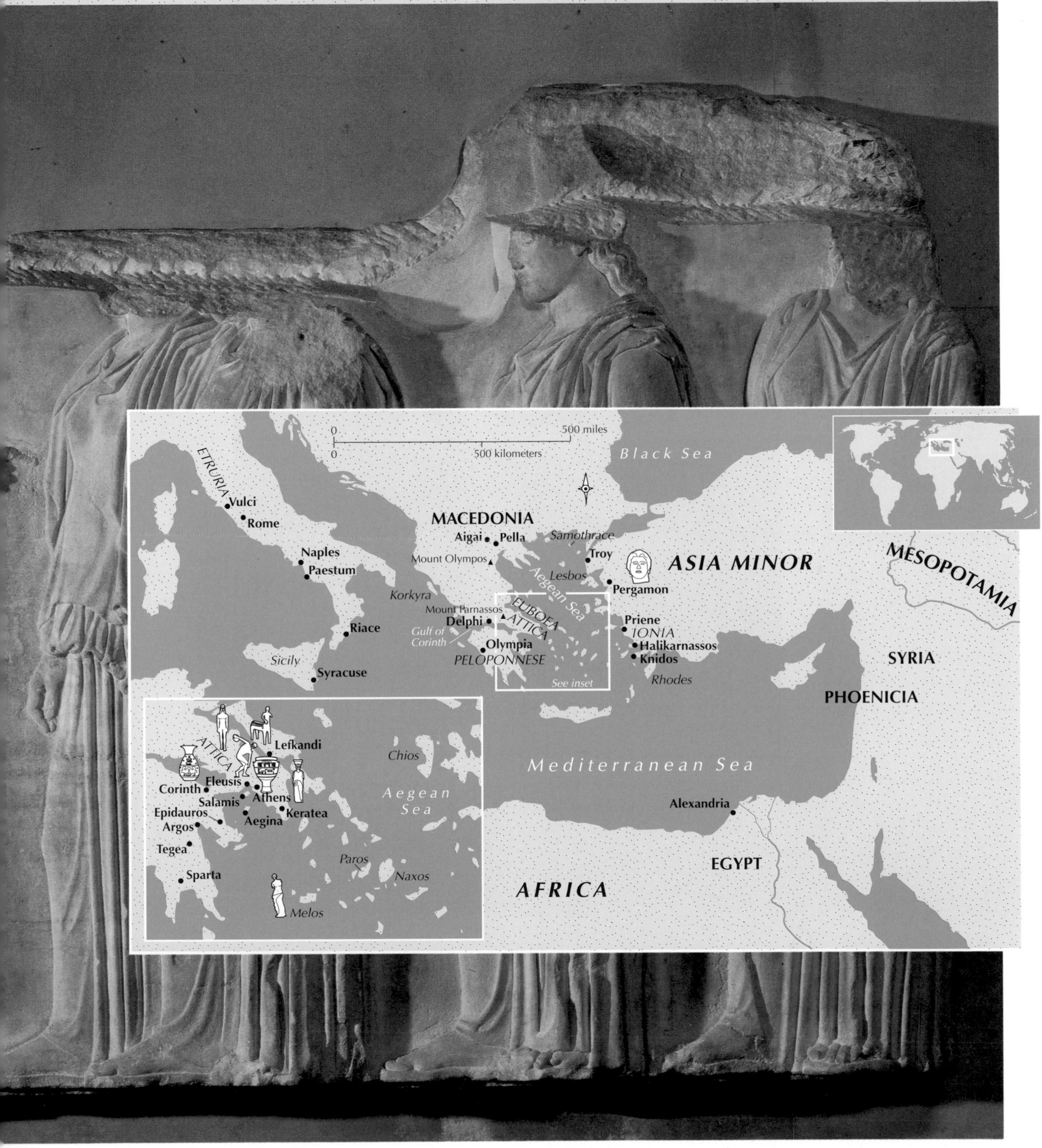

0   500 miles
0   500 kilometers

Black Sea

ETRURIA
Vulci
Rome

MACEDONIA
Aigai   Pella
Mount Olympos ▲

Samothrace

Troy

ASIA MINOR

MESOPOTAMIA

Naples
Paestum

Lesbos

Pergamon

Korkyra

Aegean Sea

EUBOEA

Mount Parnassos ▲   ATTICA

Priene

IONIA

Riace

Delphi
Gulf of
Corinth

Olympia

PELOPONNESE

See inset

Halikarnassos
Knidos

Rhodes

SYRIA

PHOENICIA

Sicily

Syracuse

Mediterranean Sea

Alexandria

ATTICA
Lefkandi

Chios

Corinth
Eleusis
Salamis   Athens
Epidauros   Keratea
Argos   Aegina
Tegea

Aegean
Sea

Sparta

Paros

Naxos

Melos

EGYPT

AFRICA

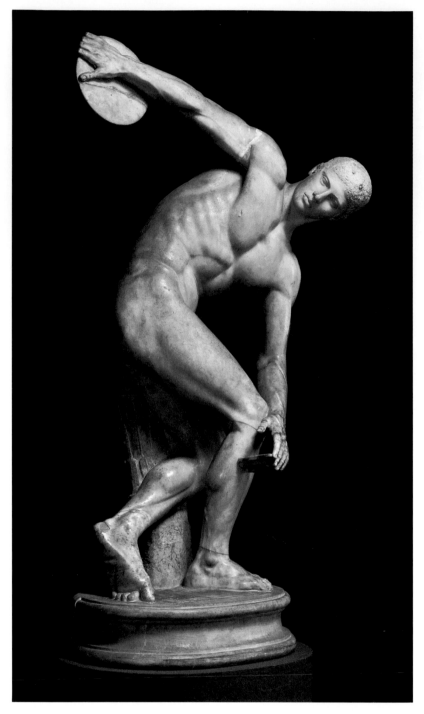

5-1. Myron. *Discus Thrower* (*Diskobolos*), Roman copy after the original bronze
of c. 450 BCE. Marble, height 5'1" (1.54 m). Museo Nazionale Romano,
Rome

A sense of awe fills the stadium when the athletes recognized as the
fastest runners in the world enter for the second day of competition. With the opening ceremonies behind them, each runner has
only one goal: to win—to earn recognition as the best, to receive the
award, the praise, and the financial rewards that accompany victory. The
runners have come from near and far, as will the wrestlers and riders,
the discus throwers and long jumpers, the boxers and javelin hurlers who
will compete within sight of the Olympic flame. The year is 776 BCE.

At first, the scene seems comfortably familiar. Every four years, then as now, the best athletes came together. Attention shifted from political confrontation to physical competition, to individual human beings who seemed able to surpass even their own abilities in the glory of an ideal. And indeed these are common elements. Yet at those first Olympian Games, the athletes gathered on sacred ground, the Sanctuary of Hera and Zeus, near Olympia, Greece, to pay tribute to the supreme god and his consort. The first day's ceremonies were sacrifices, and the awards given at the Temple of Hera were crowns of wild olives. The winners' deeds were celebrated by poets long after their victories, and the greatest of the athletes might well live the rest of their lives at public expense. They were idealized for centuries in extraordinary Greek sculpture, such as the *Discus Thrower* created in bronze by Myron in about 450 BCE (fig. 5-1). The Olympian Games were so significant that many Greeks date the beginning of their history as a nation to those first games. (The Roman emperor Theodosius banned the games in 394 CE, and they were not resumed until 1896.) In recognition of the original games, the modern Olympics begin with the lighting of a flame from a torch ignited by the sun at Olympia, Greece, and carried by relay to that year's site. For many people, this image is an appropriate symbol for the way the light of inspiration was carried from ancient Greece throughout the Western world.

THE EMERGENCE OF GREEK CIVILIZATION

More than 2,000 years have passed since the artists and architects of ancient Greece worked, yet their achievements continue to have a profound influence. The early Greeks' concepts of human beauty and of strength and dignity in architectural design no longer set the standards for Western art, but their genius and high aspirations are still awe-inspiring. Their legacy is especially remarkable given their relatively small numbers, the almost constant warfare that beset them, and the often harsh economic conditions of the time.

Greek artists sought a level of perfection that led them continually to improve upon their past accomplishments through changes in style and approach. For this reason, the history of Greek art contrasts dramatically with that of Egyptian art, where the desire for permanence and continuity induced artists to maintain many artistic conventions for nearly 3,000 years. In the relatively short span from around 900 BCE to about 100 BCE, Greek artists explored a succession of new ideas to produce a body of work in every medium—from pottery and painting to sculpture and architecture—that exhibits clear stylistic and technical progression. The periods into which ancient Greek art is traditionally divided reflect the definable stages in this stylistic progression rather than political developments. Nevertheless, knowledge of the politics, religion, and culture of ancient Greece is vital to understanding its art.

Following the collapse of Mycenaean dominance about 1100 BCE, the Aegean region experienced a period of disorganization during which most prior cultural developments, including writing, were destroyed or forgotten. The mainland, the Aegean islands, and the coastal areas of Asia Minor were left open to new waves of migrating peoples. Although nothing is known of their origins or the dates of their arrivals, some of these immigrants may have been responsible for bringing Iron Age technology to these regions.

No archeological evidence exists to support it, but later Greek legendary history claimed that people called Dorians had invaded the mainland from the north and displaced the earlier settlers, called Aeolians and Ionians, forcing their migration to the Aegean islands and western Asia Minor. The Spartans of Peloponnesos claimed to have descended from the god-hero Herakles through the Dorians, who established themselves in west central Greece. The Athenians claimed descent from the Ionians who had supposedly occupied the Attic peninsula (Athens and environs) in early times, and they maintained close political ties with the Ionian culture of western Asia Minor.

By about 900 BCE, the inhabitants of the Aegean region, living in self-sufficient, close-knit communities and all speaking some form of the same language, were again beginning to flourish. It was these people, a fusion of the new migrants and earlier inhabitants, who came to be called Greeks. The early Greeks developed a distinctive form of city-state in the ninth and eighth centuries BCE called the polis (plural poleis). These centers provided a

PARALLELS

Years	Period	Greece	World
c. 900–700 BCE	Geometric	Dipylon vase; Homer's *Iliad* and *Odyssey*; first Olympian Games; alphabet adopted	c. 900–700 BCE Upanishads (India); Olmec pyramids (Mesoamerica); Etruscans settle central Italy; legendary founding of Rome (Italy); fall of Zhou dynasty (China); first goldwork in South America
c. 700–600 BCE	Orientalizing	Black-figure and white-ground vase painting	c. 700–600 BCE Demotic script (Egypt); Assyrian empire falls; growth of permanent villages in North America
c. 600–480 BCE	Archaic	Doric and Ionic orders; Temple of Hera (Argos); Temple of Artemis (Korkyra); red-figure vase painting; *Calf Bearer*; *François Vase*; Temple of Hera I (Paestum, Italy); Sanctuary of Apollo, Siphnian Treasury (Delphi); Temple of Aphaia (Aegina); *Aesop's Fables*; *Kroisos*; Sappho	c. 600–400 BCE Hanging Gardens (Babylon); birth of Laozi, founder of Daoism, (China); Cyrus the Great (Persia) defeats Babylon; birth of Siddartha Gautama, founder of Buddhism (Nepal); Confucius (China); first fixed-value coins (Lydia); iron introduced in China; last Old Testament book written
c. 480–450 BCE	Transitional (Early Classical)	*Kritios Boy*; *Charioteer*; *Riace Warriors*; Myron's *Discus Thrower*; the Pan Painter's *Artemis Slaying Actaeon*; First Peloponnesian War; Sophocles; Aeschylus	
c. 450–400 BCE	High Classical	*The Canon* of Polykleitos; Polykleitos's *Spear Bearer*; *Little Girl with Birds*; Corinthian order; Perikles' rule; Kallikrates and Iktinos's Parthenon (Athens); Mnesikles' Propylaia and Erechtheion (Athens); Kallikrates' Temple of Athena Nike (Athens); Socrates; Herodotus; Euripides; Second Peloponnesian War	
c. 400–320 BCE	Fourth-Century (Late Classical)	Sanctuary of Athena Pronaia (Delphi); Mausoleum (Halikarnassos); Praxiteles' *Aphrodite of Knidos* and *Hermes and the Infant Dionysos*; Lysippos's *The Scraper*; rule of Alexander the Great; *Abduction of Persephone*; Plato; Aristotle	c. 400–30 BCE London founded (England); mound-building cultures (North America); lighthouse of Alexandria (Egypt); Rome subjugates Italy; Great Wall (China); Han dynasty (China); Rosetta Stone (Egypt); Great Stupa at Sanchi (India); Julius Caesar invades Gaul and Britain; sundial invented (China)
c. 320–30 BCE	Hellenistic	Theater at Epidauros; Cossutius's Temple of Olympian Zeus (Athens); Altar of Zeus (Pergamon); Colossos of Rhodes; Hagesandros, Polydoros, and Athanodoros's *Laocoön*; *Nike of Samothrace*; *Aphrodite of Melos*	

political identity for their residents, and they stimulated and nourished the emerging Greek civilization. Each was independent, deciding its own form of government, securing its own economic support, and managing its own domestic and foreign affairs.

The Greek mainland and the Aegean islands had little farmland, forcing the new communities, like their Bronze Age predecessors, to depend on trade with other regions to meet the needs of their growing populations. During the eighth century BCE, the Greeks, stimulated through such contacts, developed a new writing system, which was probably adopted from the Phoenicians, a Near Eastern people who dominated Mediterranean trade after the collapse of Mycenaean civilization. Many city-states developed sizable merchant fleets that ranged from the Black Sea to Africa, exchanging Aegean products—olive oil, pottery, and metal wares—for grain, textiles, precious metals, wood for shipbuilding, and other goods. To facilitate trade, the city-states established outlying colonies, some of which became wealthy, influential commercial centers in their own right while maintaining close cultural and economic ties to their cities of origin. Colonists from Corinth on mainland Greece, for example, founded the famed city of Syracuse on the eastern coast of Sicily.

The Greek city-states were at first ruled by aristocratic councils. Then, beginning about 700 BCE and extending into the sixth century BCE, self-appointed leaders called "tyrants" imposed a dictatorial form of rule, often with popular support, in many city-states. These tyrants were not always tyrannical in the modern sense, and many cities prospered and expanded under their rule. At their best, they fostered urban development at home and sought economic rather than military influence abroad. Among the emerging city-states, Corinth, located on major land and sea trade routes, was for a time the most powerful. By the sixth century BCE, Athens, located in Attica on the east coast of the mainland, began to assume both commercial and cultural preeminence.

Athens and the Concept of Democratic Rule

The Greeks contributed more to posterity than their art. Their customs, institutions, and ideas have also had an enduring influence in many parts of the world. Countries that highly esteem athletic prowess reflect an ancient Greek ideal. Systems of higher education in the United States and Europe also owe much to ancient Greek models. Perhaps most significant, representative governments throughout the world today owe a debt to ancient Greek experiments in democracy.

The idea that all citizens should share in the rights and responsibilities of government began to emerge in Athens in the sixth century BCE, although only a few privileged males were citizens. In 594 BCE the leaders of Athens, facing an economic crisis and popular discontent, appointed the poet-statesman Solon to institute reforms and revise the city's constitution, extending citizenship to males of many classes. In 560 BCE an aristo-

crat named Peisistratos seized control of Athens and ruled as tyrant until 527 BCE. A shrewd planner and visionary, Peisistratos generated considerable wealth for the city and enhanced it culturally by holding great festivals, building many temples and fountains, and having the official texts of Homer's works recorded. After Peisistratos's second son and successor was ousted in 510 BCE, the development of democratic institutions resumed. Following a period of factional sparring, a leader named Kleisthenes, with the support of the people, gained control of the city. Kleisthenes, often called the "father of democracy," instituted reforms that broadened the representative base of Athenian government, effectively reducing the dominance of the old aristocratic families. He made the deme, a territorial unit equivalent to a precinct, into the basic political unit that sent 50 representatives to a new 500-member council, called the boule. This council carried out routine administrative functions and prepared legislation for consideration by the assembly of all citizens. Although this form of government was democratic in principle, it was open only to adult male citizens. Women took no official part in government, nor did slaves or men born outside Athens.

Religious Beliefs and Sacred Places

The creation of the world, according to ancient Greek legend, involved a battle between the earth gods, called Titans or Giants, and the sky gods. The victors were the sky gods, whose home was believed to be atop Mount Olympos in the northeast corner of the Greek mainland. The Greeks saw their gods as immortal and endowed with supernatural powers, but, more than peoples of the ancient Near East and the Egyptians had, they visualized them in human form and attributed to them human weaknesses and emotions. Among the most important Olympian deities were the ruling gods Zeus and Hera; Apollo, god of the sun; Poseidon, god of the sea; Ares, god of war; Aphrodite, goddess of love; Artemis, goddess of hunting and the moon; and Athena, a powerful goddess who governed several important aspects of human life (see "Greek and Roman Deities and Heroes," page 156).

In addition to Mount Olympos, many sites throughout Greece, called **sanctuaries**, were sacred to one or more of the gods. The Greeks believed that the gods themselves selected these sites to show favor toward their human worshipers. Local people then enclosed the sanctuaries with walls and designated them as sacred ground. The earliest sanctuaries had one or more outdoor altars or shrines and a sacred natural element such as a tree, a rock, or a spring. As additional buildings were added over time, a sanctuary might become a palatial home for the gods, called a **temenos**, with one or more temples, several **treasuries** for storing valuable offerings, various monuments and statues, housing for priests and visitors, an outdoor dance floor or permanent theater for ritual performances and literary competitions, and a **stadium** for athletic events. The Sanctuary of Hera and Zeus near Olympia, in the western Peloponnese, housed an extensive athletic facility with training rooms and arenas

GREEK AND ROMAN DEITIES AND HEROES

The ancient Greeks had many deities, and myths about them varied over time. Many deities had several forms, or manifestations. Athena, for example, was revered as a goddess of wisdom, a warrior goddess, a goddess of victory, and a goddess of purity and maidenhood, among others. The Romans later adopted the Greek deities but sometimes attributed to them slightly different characteristics. What follows is a simplified list of the major Greek deities and heroes, with their Roman names in parentheses when they exist. The list includes some of the most important characteristics of each deity or hero, which often identify them in art.

According to the most widespread legend, twelve major sky gods and goddesses established themselves in palatial splendor on Mount Olympos in northeastern Greece after defeating the earth deities, called Giants or Titans, for control of the earth and sky. The first five deities are the children of Earth and Sky.

ZEUS (Jupiter), supreme deity. Mature, bearded man; holds scepter or lightning bolt; eagle and oak tree are sacred to him.

HERA (Juno), goddess of marriage. Sister/wife of Zeus. Mature; cow and peacock are sacred to her.

HESTIA (Vesta), goddess of the hearth. Sister of Zeus. Her sacred flame burned in communal hearths.

POSEIDON (Neptune), god of the sea. Holds a three-pronged spear; horse is sacred to him.

HADES (Pluto), god of the underworld, the dead, and wealth. His helmet makes the wearer invisible.

The remaining seven sky gods, the offspring of the first five, are:

ARES (Mars), god of war. Son of Zeus and Hera. Wears armor; vulture and dog are sacred to him.

HEPHAISTOS (Vulcan), god of the forge, fire, and metal handicrafts. Son of Hera (in some myths, also of Zeus); husband of Aphrodite. Lame, sometimes ugly; wears blacksmith's apron, carries hammer.

APOLLO (Phoebus), god of the sun, light, truth, music, archery, and healing. Sometimes identified with Helios (the Sun), who rides a chariot across the daytime sky. Son of Zeus and Leto (a descendant of Earth); brother of Artemis. Carries bow and arrows or sometimes lyre; dolphin and laurel are sacred to him.

ARTEMIS (Diana), goddess of the hunt, wild animals, and the moon. Sometimes identified with Selene (the Moon), who rides a chariot or oxcart across the night sky. Daughter of Zeus and Leto; sister of Apollo. Carries bow and arrows, is accompanied by hunting dogs; deer and cypress are sacred to her.

ATHENA (Minerva), goddess of wisdom, war, victory, the city, and civilization. Daughter of Zeus, sprang fully grown from his head. Wears helmet and carries shield and spear; owl and olive trees are sacred to her.

APHRODITE (Venus), goddess of love. Daughter of Zeus and Dione; alternatively, daughter of Poseidon, born of his sperm mixed with sea foam; wife of Hephaistos. Myrtle, dove, sparrow, and swan are sacred to her.

HERMES (Mercury), messenger of the gods, god of fertility and luck, guide of the dead to the underworld, and god of thieves, commerce, and the marketplace. Son of Zeus and Maia, the daughter of Atlas, a Giant who supports the sky on his shoulders. Wears winged sandals and hat; carries caduceus, a wand with two snakes entwined around it.

Other important deities include:

DEMETER (Ceres), goddess of grain and agriculture.

PERSEPHONE (Proserpina), goddess of fertility and queen of the underworld. Wife of Hades; daughter of Demeter.

DIONYSOS (Bacchus), god of wine, the grape harvest, and inspiration. Shown surrounded by grape vines and grape clusters; carries a wine cup. His female followers are called **maenads** (Bacchantes).

EROS (Cupid), god of love. In some myths, the son of Aphrodite.

Shown as an infant or young boy, sometimes winged; carries bow and arrows.

EOS (Aurora), goddess of dawn.

GE, goddess of the earth; mother of the Titans.

ASKLEPIOS (Aesculapius), god of healing.

AMPHITRITE, goddess of the sea. Wife of Poseidon.

PAN, protector of shepherds, god of the wilderness and of music. Half man, half goat, he carries panpipes.

NIKE, goddess of victory. Often shown winged and flying.

Some specifically Roman gods not worshiped by the Greeks include:

FORTUNA, goddess of fate (fortune).

PRIAPUS, god of fertility.

SATURN, god of harvests.

JANUS, god of beginnings and endings. Has two faces, enabling him to look forward and backward.

POMONA, goddess of gardens and orchards.

TERMINUS, god of boundaries.

Important human heroes include:

HERAKLES (Hercules). A man of great and diverse strengths; granted immortality for his achievements, including the Twelve Labors.

PERSEUS. Killed Medusa, the snake-haired monster.

THESEUS. Killed the Minotaur, a bull-monster that killed and ate young men and maidens in a labyrinth in the palace of King Minos of Crete (see "The Legend of the Minotaur," page 132).

Heroes of the Trojan War include:

ODYSSEUS (Ulysses), Achilles, Patroclus, and Ajax among the Greeks; Paris, Hector, Priam, Sarpedon, and Aeneas (progenitor of the Romans) among the Trojans.

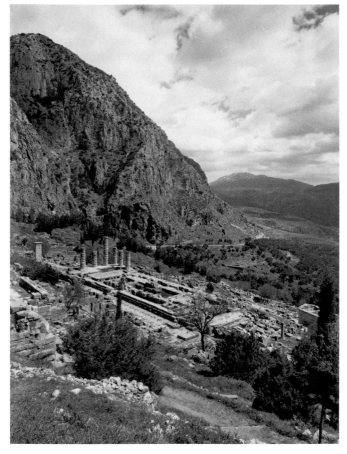

5-2. Sanctuary of Apollo, Delphi. 4th century BCE

A feature of this sacred home of the Greek god Apollo, built on the site of a sixth-century temple destroyed in an earthquake, was a natural site in the area believed to be an oracle, a place where the god communicated with humans. At this oracle, Apollo communicated through a woman medium called the Pythia. To prepare herself to receive his messages, she chewed sacred laurel leaves and drank water from the sacred Kassotis Spring, both of which are thought to have induced hallucinations. She then sat over the crevice on a three-legged stool, or tripod. When she had received the god's message, which might be a response to a petitioner's question, she conveyed it in often cryptic and ambiguous language. The Greeks attributed many twists of fate to misinterpretations of the Pythia's statements. King Croesus of Lydia in Asia Minor, for example, came to Delphi in the mid-sixth century BCE to consult Apollo about his military plans. The message he received was that he would cross a river and destroy a great kingdom. He took this to mean the Halys River, beyond which lay the Persian Empire, and he ordered his generals to launch an assault against the Persians. Ironically, the kingdom he destroyed was his own, when his troops crossed the Halys and were wiped out by the Persians.

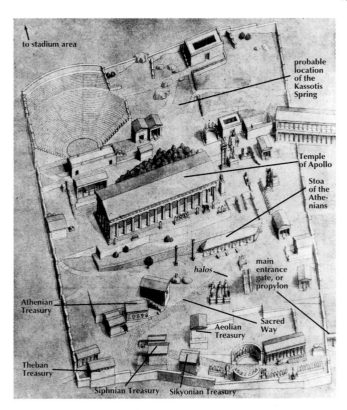

5-3. Reconstruction drawing of the Sanctuary of Apollo, Delphi. c. 400 BCE

the omphalos (navel) of the earth by an umbilical cord. Here too, it was said, Apollo fought and killed the Python, the serpent son of the earth goddess Ge, who stood guard over his mother's shrine in the gorge below the site. This myth has been interpreted as a metaphorical account of the conquest of the Early Bronze Age people of Greece, whose religion centered on female earth deities, by a wave of new settlers who believed in a supreme male sky god.

From very early times, the sanctuary at Delphi was renowned as an **oracle**, a place where a god was believed to communicate to humans by means of cryptic messages delivered to human intermediaries, or mediums. The Greeks and their leaders routinely sought advice at such places, relying on temple priests for help in interpreting the messages. Even foreign rulers sought help at Delphi, where the god Apollo spoke through a woman medium called the Pythia. Delphi was also the site of the Pythian Games, a festival that, like the Olympian Games, attracted participants from all over Greece. The principal events were not the athletic contests that took place, but rather the dance and poetry competitions in honor of Apollo. The sanctuary grounds were filled with hundreds of statues dedicated to the victors of the competitions, a kind of Pythian Games hall of fame (see fig. 5-37).

A reconstruction drawing of the Sanctuary of Apollo as it looked about 400 BCE (fig. 5-3) shows that the main temple, performance and athletic areas, and other

for track and field events. It was here, beginning in 776 BCE, that the ancient prototypes of today's Olympic Games were held.

The Sanctuary of Apollo at Delphi is located in a rugged landscape near the Gulf of Corinth on a high plateau in the shadow of Mount Parnassos (fig. 5-2). Here, according to Greek myth, the sky was attached to

buildings and monuments cleverly made full use of limited space while providing easy access. After visitors climbed the steep path up the lower slopes of Parnassos, they entered the sanctuary by a ceremonial gate in the southeast corner. From there they zigzagged up the Sacred Way, so named because it was the route of religious processions during festivals. Moving past the numerous treasuries and memorials built by Greece's various city-states (see fig. 5-16), they soon arrived at the long **colonnade** of the Temple of Apollo. This structure, built about 530 BCE on the ruins of an earlier temple, remained standing until it was destroyed by an earthquake in 373 BCE. Below the temple was a **stoa**, a columned pavilion open on three sides, built by the people of Athens. There visitors rested, talked, or watched ceremonial dancing on an outdoor pavement called a *halos.* At the back of the sanctuary on a higher level of the rocky plateau was a stadium area for athletic games.

Greek sanctuaries are quite different from the religious complexes of the ancient Egyptians (see, for example, the funerary complex of Hatshepsut, figs. 3-33, 3-34). Egyptian builders dramatized the power of gods or god-rulers by placing their temples at the ends of long, straight, processional ways. The Greeks, in contrast, treated each building and monument within a temenos as an independent element in an arrangement of structures to be integrated with the natural features of the site. It is tempting to draw a parallel between this manner of organizing space and the way Greeks organized themselves politically: every structure, like every Greek citizen, was a unique entity meant to be encountered separately within its own environment while being closely allied with other entities in a larger scheme of common purpose.

Historical Divisions of Greek Art

The names by which the major periods of Greek art are known have remained standard despite changing interpretations that have led some to question their appropriateness. The primary source of information about Greek art before the seventh century BCE is pottery, and the Geometric period owes its name to the geometric, or rectilinear, forms with which artists of the time decorated ceramic vessels. The Orientalizing period is named for the apparent influence of Egyptian and Near Eastern art on Greek pottery of that time, spread through trading contacts and also through the travels and migrations of artists themselves. The name of the third period, Archaic, meaning "old" or "old-fashioned," stresses a presumed contrast between the art of that time and the art of the following Classical period, which was thought to be the most admirable and highly developed—a view that no longer prevails among contemporary art historians.

The Classical period has been subdivided into three phases: the Transitional or Early Classical, from about 480 to 450 BCE; the High Classical, from about 450 to the end of the fifth century BCE; and the Late Classical, from about 400 to about 320 BCE. "Transitional" is particularly appropriate for the Early Classical period in sculpture because it bridges the change from the relatively stiff Archaic human figures to the more realistically active Classical figures, but it was also a time of change for architecture and painting. Art historians still use these subdivisions as convenient chronological markers, but they no longer see them as chapters in a story detailing the "rise and decline" of the Classical style. For this reason, the neutral term Fourth Century has largely replaced the term Late Classical, with its implication of decline.

The name of the final period of Greek art, Hellenistic, means "Greek-like." This period dates from the last decades of the fourth century, when Philip II of Macedon and his son Alexander conquered Greece and the Persian Empire. Hellenistic art was produced throughout this vast region as its non-Greek inhabitants gradually became imbued with Greek culture under Alexander and his successors. The history and art of ancient Greece end with the fall of Egypt, the last bastion of Hellenistic rule, to the Romans in 31–30 BCE.

THE GEOMETRIC PERIOD

The first appearance of a specifically Greek style of vase painting, as opposed to Minoan or Mycenaean, dates to about 1050 BCE. This style—known as Proto-geometric because it preceded and anticipated the Geometric style—was characterized by linear motifs, such as spirals, diamonds, and

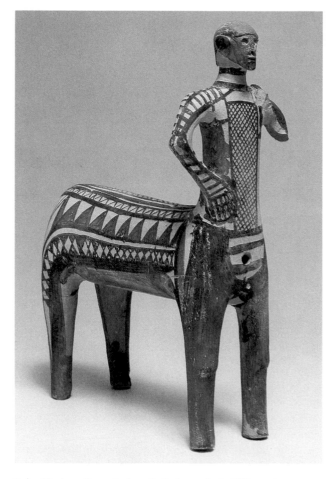

5-4. *Centaur,* from Lefkandi, Euboea. Late 10th century BCE. Terra-cotta, height 14⅛" (36 cm). Archeological Museum, Eretria

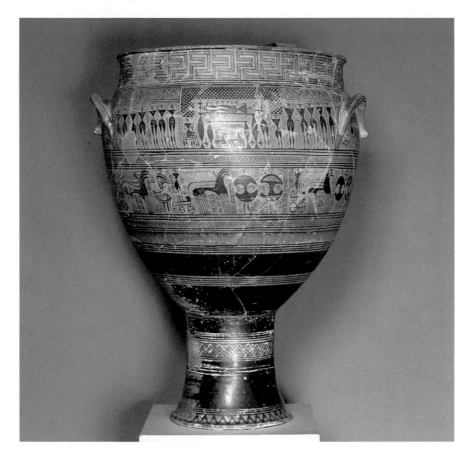

5-5. Vase, from the Dipylon Cemetery, Athens. c. 750 BCE. Terra-cotta, height 42⅝"
(108 cm). The Metropolitan Museum of Art, New York
Rogers Fund, 1914 (14.130.14)

crosshatching, rather than the stylized plants, birds, and
sea creatures characteristic of Minoan vase painting. The
Geometric style proper, an extremely complex form of
decoration, became widespread after about 900 BCE in all
types of art and endured until about 700 BCE.

Ceramic Decoration

A striking ceramic figure of a half-horse, half-human
creature called a centaur dates to the end of the tenth
century BCE (fig. 5-4). This figure exemplifies two aspects
of the Protogeometric style: the use of geometric forms
in painted decoration, and the reduction of human
and animal body parts in sculptural works to simple geometric solids such as cubes, pyramids, cylinders, and
spheres. It is unusual, however, because of its size (more
than a foot tall) and because its hollow body was formed
like a vase on a potter's wheel. The artist added solid
legs, arms, and a tail (now missing) to this body, and
when these were dry, painted on the bold, abstract
designs with a clay **slip**. The slip fired to dark brown,
standing out against the lighter color of the unslipped
portions of the figure. Centaurs, prominent in Greek
mythology, had both a good and a bad side and may have
symbolized the similar dual nature of humans. This centaur, discovered in a cemetery, had been deliberately broken into two pieces that were buried in adjacent graves.
Clearly, the object had special significance for the people
buried in the graves, their mourners, or both.

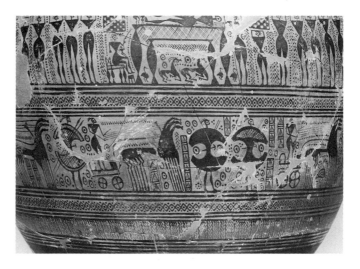

5-6. Detail of the Dipylon Cemetery vase (fig. 5-5)

Some vases discovered in the ancient cemetery of
Athens just outside the Dipylon Gate, once the main
western entrance into the city, exemplify the complex
decoration typical of the Geometric style proper. Here
human beings are depicted as part of a narrative, in a
sharp departure from vase painting of earlier periods.
The large funerary vase illustrated here, a grave marker
meant to hold offerings, dated to about 750 BCE, provides
a detailed record of the funerary rituals for an obviously
important person (figs. 5-5, 5-6). The body of the deceased is placed on its side on a high platform at the center of the top **register** of the vase. Male and female

figures stand on each side of the body, their arms raised and both hands placed on top of their heads in a gesture interpreted as expressing anguish—it suggests that the mourners are literally tearing their hair with grief. In the bottom register, horse-drawn chariots and foot soldiers, who look like walking shields with tiny antlike heads and muscular legs, form a well-ordered procession.

The **abstract** forms used to represent human figures on this vase—triangles for torsos, more triangles for the heads in profile, round dots for eyes, long, thin rectangles for arms, tiny waists, and long legs with bulging thigh and calf muscles—are typical of the Geometric style. Figures are shown in either full-frontal or full-profile views that emphasize flat patterns and outline shapes. No attempt has been made to create the illusion of three-dimensional forms occupying real space. The artist has nevertheless a deep sense of human loss by exploiting the rigidity, solemnity, and strong rhythmic accents of the carefully arranged elements.

Egyptian funerary art reflected the belief that the dead, in the afterworld, could continue to engage in activities they enjoyed while alive. Greek funerary art, in contrast, focused on the emotional reactions of the survivors, not the fate of the dead. The scene of human mourning and veneration on this vase contains no supernatural beings, nor any identifiable reference to an afterlife that might have provided solace for the bereaved. According to the Greeks, the deceased entered a place of mystery and obscurity that humans could not define precisely.

Metal Sculpture

Greek artists of the Geometric period produced many figurines of wood, ivory, clay, and especially cast bronze. These small statues of humans and animals are similar to those painted on the vases. A tiny bronze of this type, *Man and Centaur*, dates to about 750 BCE and is less than 4 1/2 inches tall (fig. 5-7). The sculptor reduced the body parts of the figures to simple geometric shapes, arranging them in a composition of solid forms and open, or **negative**, **spaces** that makes the piece pleasing from every view. Because the two figures confront each other in a seemingly peaceful way, they have been interpreted to be Achilles and Chiron, his teacher, but they could also be Herakles and the vengeful Nessos, who plotted his death, or an entirely different pair of mythical figures. Most such works have been found in sanctuaries, suggesting that they may have been votive offerings to the gods or perhaps trophies given to the winners of the various competitions regularly held at those sites.

The First Greek Temples

Few ancient Greek temples remain standing today. Their history has been pieced together largely from the debris of fallen columns, broken lintels, and fragments of sculptural decoration recovered from archeological excavations and somewhat from surviving ceramic models. The earliest remains of identifiably Greek temples date from

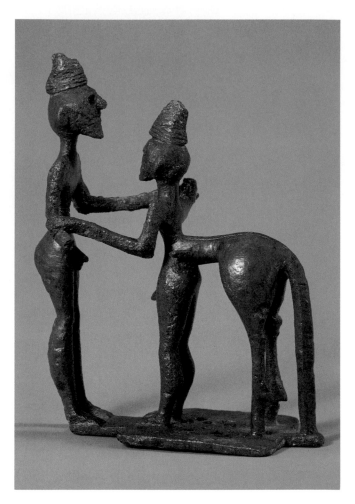

5-7. *Man and Centaur,* perhaps from Olympia. C. 750 BCE. Bronze, height 4⁵/₁₆" (11.1 cm). The Metropolitan Museum of Art, New York
Gift of J. Pierpont Morgan, 1917 (17.190.2072)

the Geometric period. They consist of stone foundations that define buildings laid out in a simple rectangle or in a rectangular form with one or both ends rounded, and they were built presumably to shelter a statue of the god to whom the temple was dedicated. Nothing is left of their walls and roofs, which were constructed of mud brick and wood.

Small ceramic models, such as one from the eighth century BCE found in the Sanctuary of Hera near Argos, give some idea how Geometric period temples might have looked (fig. 5-8). The rectangular structure has a door at one end sheltered by a projecting **porch** supported on two sturdy columns. The steeply pitched roof forms a triangular area, or **gable**, in the **facade**, or front wall, that is pierced by an opening directly above the door. The abstract designs painted on the roof and side walls are similar to those used on other Geometric period ceramics; whether they reflect the way temples were actually decorated is not known.

Temple interiors followed an enduring basic plan adapted from the Mycenaean palace **megaron** (compare fig. 4-23 with plan (a) in "Elements of Architecture," page 164). The large audience hall of the megaron became the

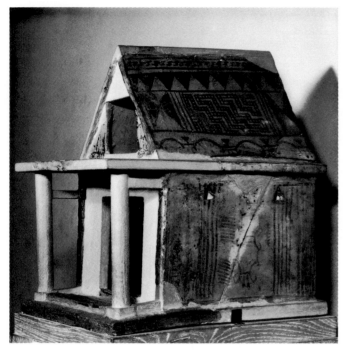

5-8. Model of a temple, found in the Sanctuary of Hera, Argos. Mid-8th century BCE. Terra-cotta, length 14½" (36.8 cm). National Archeological Museum, Athens

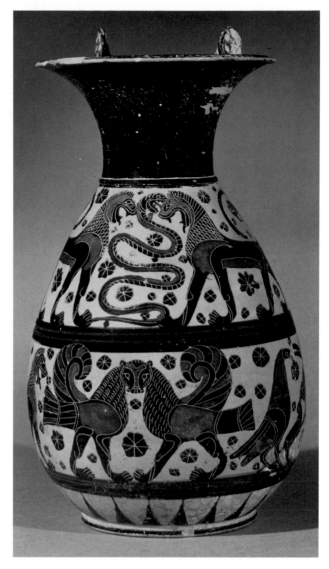

5-9. Pitcher (olpe), from Corinth. c. 600 BCE. Ceramic with black-figure decoration, height 11½" (30 cm). The British Museum, London

main room of the temple, called the **cella** or **naos**. In the center of this room, where the hearth would have been in the megaron, stood a statue of the god to whom the temple was dedicated. The small reception room that preceded the audience hall in the megaron became the temple's vestibule, called the **pronaos**.

THE ORIENTALIZING PERIOD

By the seventh century BCE, vase painters in major pottery centers in Greece had moved away from the dense decoration of the Geometric style to create more open compositions built around large motifs that included real and imaginary animals, abstract plant forms, and human figures. The source of these motifs can be traced to the arts of the Near East, Asia Minor, and Egypt. Greek painters did not simply copy the work of Eastern artists, however. Instead, they drew on work in a variety of mediums—including sculpture, metalwork, and textiles—to invent an entirely new approach to vase painting.

Among the first artists to make Orientalizing changes in pottery decoration were those of Corinth, a port city where luxury wares from eastern cultures were imported. A Corinthian **olpe**, or wide-mouthed pitcher, dating to about 600 BCE shows the Orientalizing style in the large mythical creatures silhouetted against a plain background dotted with stylized flower forms called **rosettes** (fig. 5-9). This vase also displays a new Corinthian technique for using background and foreground colors extending from black through browns and reds to pure white. The type shown here, called **black-figure**, features dark shapes silhouetted against a background of

very pale buff, the natural color of the Corinthian clay. Sometimes the background of a pot was painted as well, using a very fine, pure clay slip that turned almost white in the firing (see "Greek Painted Vases," page 162). The artist incised fine details inside the silhouetted shapes with a sharp tool and added touches of white and reddish purple **gloss**, or clay slip mixed with metallic color pigments, to enhance the design.

The new Corinthian techniques were soon picked up by rival centers of pottery production. An **oinochoe**, or wine pitcher, from the island of Rhodes, for example, which dates to about 650–625 BCE, was decorated with the black-figure and white-slip techniques (fig. 5-10). Against a plain background scattered with strong, simple geometric motifs, the artist arranged a two-register parade of ibexes, geese, songbirds, and a griffin, a mythical animal with a lion's body and an eagle's head and wings. The ibex was such a popular design element with the Rhodes painters that some art historians refer to their vase decoration as the "Wild Goat Style." The abstract

TECHNIQUE

GREEK PAINTED VASES

The three main types of Greek painted vase decoration are called **black-figure**, **red-figure**, and **white-ground**. The artists who produced them had to be both skilled painters and highly trained and experienced ceramic technicians. They did not simply paint designs on a finished clay vessel. To create their works they had to master a complex procedure involving the use of specially prepared **slips** (mixtures of clay and water), the application of the slips to different areas in varying thicknesses, and the careful manipulation of the firing process in a kiln, or closed oven, to control the amount of oxygen reaching the vessel. If all went as planned (and sometimes it didn't), the designs painted in slip, which could barely be seen on the clay pot before firing, emerged afterward in the desired range of colors.

The firing process for both black-figure and red-figure painting involved three stages. In the first, a large amount of oxygen was allowed into the kiln, which "fixed" the whole vase in one overall color that depended on the composition of the clay used. In the second, or "reduction," stage, the oxygen in the **kiln** was reduced to a minimum, turning the whole vessel black, and the temperature raised to the point at which the slip partially vitrified (became glasslike). In the third phase, oxygen was allowed back into the kiln, turning the unslipped areas red. The partially vitrified slipped areas, sealed against the oxygen, remained black.

In black-figure painting, artists painted designs—figures, objects, or abstract motifs—in silhouette on the clay vessel. Then, using a sharp tool called a **stylus**, they cut through the slip to the body of the vessel to incise linear details within the silhouettes. In red-figure painting, the approach was reversed, and the background around the designs was painted with the slip. The linear details inside the shapes were also painted with the same slip, instead of being incised. In both techniques, artists often enhanced their work with touches of white and reddish purple **gloss**, metallic pigments mixed with slip.

White-ground vases became very popular in the High Classical period, especially for funerary use. The white ground, used since Archaic times, was created by painting the vessel with a highly refined, purified clay slip that turned white during the firing. The design elements were added to the white ground with either the black- or red-figure technique. After firing, the artists frequently enhanced their compositions by painting on details and areas of bright and pastel hues using **tempera**, a paint made from egg yolks, water, and pigments. Because the tempera paints were fragile, these colors flaked off easily, and few perfect examples have survived.

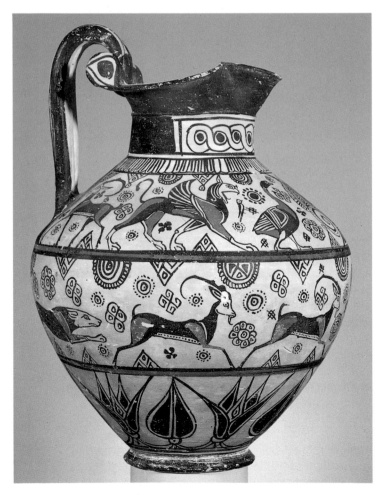

5-10. Wine pitcher (oinochoe), from Rhodes. c. 650–625 BCE. Ceramic with black-figure decoration on light ground, height 12¼" (31 cm). Museum of Fine Arts, Boston
Gift of Mrs. S. T. Morse

bud or leaf patterns in the bottom register are similar to the lotus-bud motifs found in Egyptian art.

THE ARCHAIC PERIOD

The Archaic period, from about 600 to 480 BCE, was one of cultural energy and achievement during which the Greek city-states on the mainland, on the Aegean islands, and in far-flung colonies grew and flourished. Athens, which had lagged behind the other city-states in population and economic development, began moving artistically, commercially, and politically to the forefront.

All Greek arts developed rapidly during the Archaic period. The poet Sappho on the island of Lesbos was writing poetry that would inspire the geographer Strabo, near the end of the millennium, to write: "Never within human memory has there been a woman to compare with her as a poet." On another island, the semilegendary slave Aesop was relating animal fables that became lasting elements in Western culture. Artists shared in the growing prosperity of the city-states by competing for lucrative commissions from city councils and wealthy individuals, who sponsored the creation of temples, shrines, government buildings, **monumental** sculpture, and fine ceramic wares. During this period, potters and vase painters first began to sign their works.

Temple Architecture

As Greek temples grew steadily in size and complexity over the centuries, stone and marble replaced the earlier mud-brick and wood construction. Temple builders evolved a number of standardized plans, ranging from simple one- and two-room structures with columned

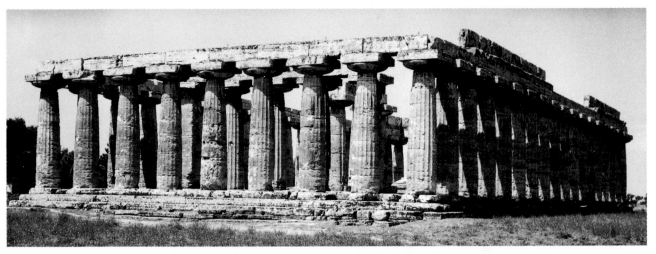

5-11. Temple of Hera I, Paestum, Italy. c. 550 BCE

600
1000 BCE   1 CE

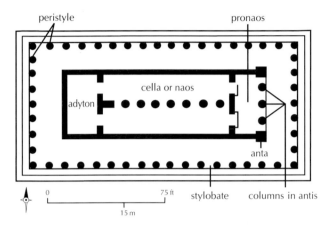

5-12. Plan of the Temple of Hera I, Paestum

peristyle

pronaos

cella or naos

adyton

anta

stylobate   columns in antis

0   75 ft
15 m

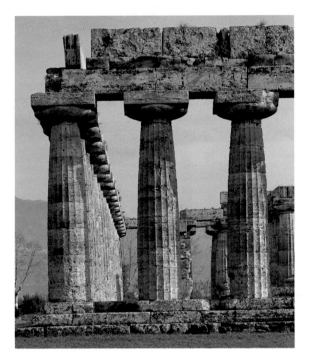

5-13. Corner view of the Temple of Hera I, Paestum

porches to multiroomed structures with double porches surrounded by columns (see "Elements of Architecture," page 164). They also experimented with the design of temple **elevations**—the arrangement, proportions, and appearance of the temple foundation, the columns, and the lintels. Two standardized elevation designs, the **Doric order** and the **Ionic order**, emerged during the Archaic period. The **Corinthian order**, a variant of the Ionic order, became so popular later that it too is treated today as a standard Greek order (see "Elements of Architecture," page 165).

The site of Paestum, a Greek colony established in the seventh century BCE about fifty miles south of the modern city of Naples, Italy, contains some rare examples of early Greek temples. Although these temples reflect contemporary architectural developments on mainland Greece, they also bear the stamp of their particular colonial setting and are not typical of all Archaic Greek temples. The earliest standing temple there, built about 550 BCE, was dedicated to Hera, the queen of the gods (fig. 5-11). It is known today as Hera I to distinguish it from a second temple to Hera built adjacent to it about a century later.

Hera I is a large, rectangular, stone **post-and-lintel** structure with a stepped foundation supporting a **peristyle**, a row of columns that surrounds all four sides (fig. 5-12). This single peristyle defines Hera I as a **peripteral** temple; a double peristyle (two rows of columns) defines

a **dipteral** temple. The columns stand on the top surface of the **stylobate**. The peristyle of Hera I originally supported a tall lintel area called the **entablature**. A peaked roof rested on the **cornice**, the slightly projecting topmost element of the entablature. At each end, the horizontal cornice of the entablature and the **raking** (slanted) **cornices** of the roof defined a triangular gable called the **pediment**.

The elevation design of Hera I was a local variation on the earliest major Greek order, the Doric. The standard form of the Doric order—incomplete on Hera I because of the damage it has suffered—includes fluted columns without bases resting directly on the stylobate; plain column capitals made up of two distinct parts, the round **echinus** and the square **abacus**; and a three-part entablature consisting of a plain, flat band, called the **architrave**, topped by a decorated band, called the **frieze**, and capped with a cornice of continuous carved stone bands called **moldings**. In the Doric frieze, flat

ELEMENTS OF ARCHITECTURE
Greek Temple Plans

The simplest early temples consist of a single room, the **cella** or **naos**, with side walls incorporating **pillars** projecting forward to frame two columns **in antis** (literally, "between the pillars") (a). In a **prostyle** temple (b) the columns form a **portico**, or walkway, only across the building's front. An **amphiprostyle** temple (c) has a row of columns (**colonnade**) at both the front and back ends of the structure, not on the sides. If the colonnade runs around all four sides of the building, forming a **peristyle**, the temple is **peripteral** (d); if the surrounding colonnade is two columns deep, the temple is **dipteral** (e).

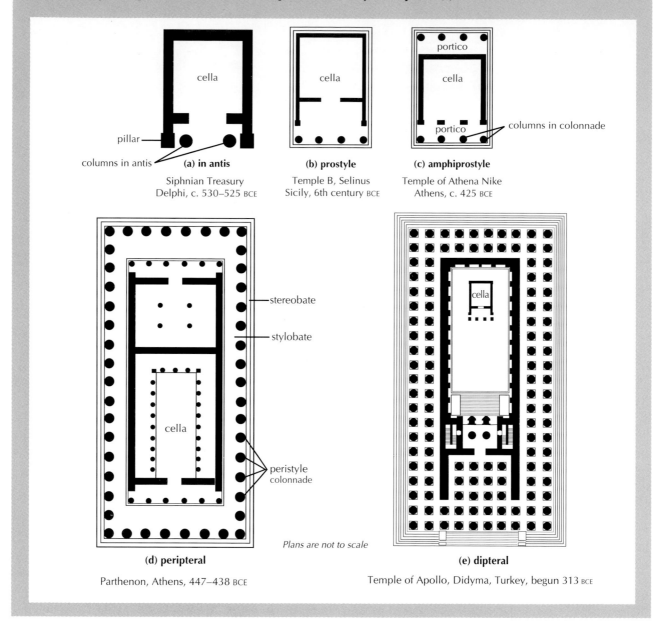

(a) in antis
Siphnian Treasury
Delphi, c. 530–525 BCE

(b) prostyle
Temple B, Selinus
Sicily, 6th century BCE

(c) amphiprostyle
Temple of Athena Nike
Athens, c. 425 BCE

Plans are not to scale

(d) peripteral
Parthenon, Athens, 447–438 BCE

(e) dipteral
Temple of Apollo, Didyma, Turkey, begun 313 BCE

areas called **metopes** alternate with **triglyphs**, projecting blocks with three vertical grooves. The metopes were usually decorated with figures, either painted on or sculpted in relief and then painted.

Fragments of terra-cotta tiles painted in bright colors have been found in the rubble of Hera I, suggesting that they adorned parts of the temple, possibly the metopes. No sculptural fragments have survived. The Hera I builders created an especially robust column, only about four times as high as its maximum diameter, topped with a widely flaring capital (fig. 5-13). This design creates an impression of great stability and permanence. As the column shafts rise, they swell in the middle and contract again toward the top, a common attribute of Greek columns known as **entasis**. This subtle adjustment gives a sense of energy and upward lift. In a local innovation not part of the standard Doric order, Hera I has an uneven number of columns—nine—across the short ends of the peristyle, placing a column instead of a space at the center of the ends. The entrance to the pronaos also has a central column, and a row of columns runs down the center of the wide cella to help support the ceiling. The statue of Hera may have been housed in the **adyton**, the small auxiliary space at the end of the cella proper. The unusual two-aisle arrangement suggests that the temple may have housed a second god statue, possibly of Zeus.

ELEMENTS OF ARCHITECTURE

The Greek Architectural Orders

The three classical Greek architectural orders are the Doric, the Ionic, and the Corinthian. The Doric and Ionic orders were well developed by about 600 BCE. The Doric order is the oldest and plainest of the three orders. The Ionic order is named after Ionia, a region occupied by Greeks on the west coast of Anatolia and the islands off the coast. The Corinthian order, a variation of the Ionic, began to appear around 450 BCE and was initially used by the Greeks in interiors. Later, the Romans appropriated the Corinthian order and elaborated it, as we shall see in Chapter 6.

The basic components of the Greek orders are the **column** and the **entablature**, which function as post and lintel. All types of columns have a **shaft** and a **capital**; some also have a **base**. Columns are formed of round sections, or **drums**, which are joined inside by metal pegs. In Greek temple architecture, columns stand on the **stylobate**, the "floor" of the temple; the levels below the stylobate form the **stereobate**.

The **Doric order** shaft rises directly from the stylobate, without a base. The shaft is **fluted** but not as deeply as in the other orders. At the top of the shaft is the **necking**, which provides a transition to the capital. The Doric capital itself has two parts, the rounded **echinus** and the tabletlike **abacus**. As in the other orders, the entablature includes the **architrave**, the **frieze**, and the **cornice**, the topmost, projecting horizontal element.

The **Ionic order** has more elegant proportions than the Doric, its height being about nine times the diameter of the column at its base, as opposed to the Doric column's five-and-a-half–to–one ratio. The flutes on the columns are deeper and closer together and are separated by flat surfaces, fillets. The hallmark of the Ionic capital, which has a thin, cushionlike abacus, is the distinctive scrolled **volute**.

The **Corinthian order** was originally developed by the Greeks for use in interiors but came to be used on temple exteriors as well. Its elaborate capitals are sheathed with stylized **acanthus** leaves, and sometimes **rosettes**, and they often have scrolled elements at the corners and a **boss**, or projecting ornament, at the top center of each "side."

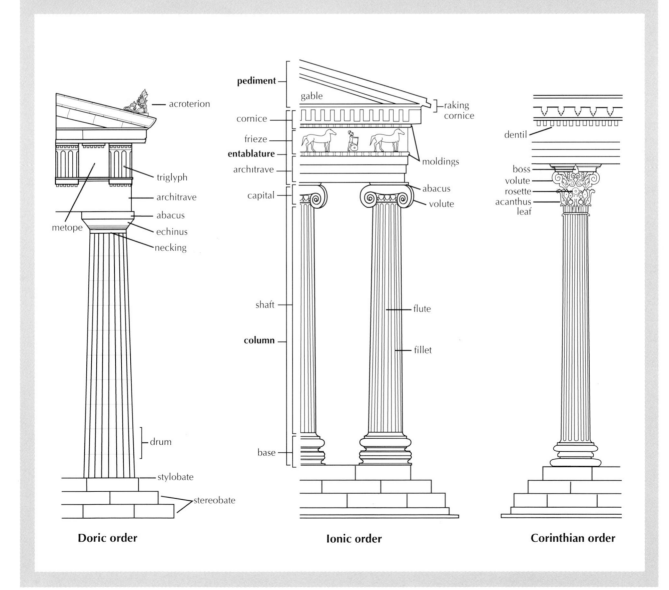

Doric order   **Ionic order**   **Corinthian order**

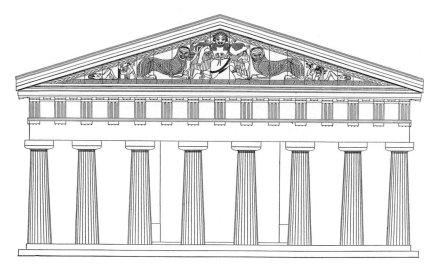

5-14. Reconstruction of the west pediment of the Temple of Artemis, Korkyra (Corfu),
after G. Rodenwaldt. c. 600–580 BCE

Architectural Sculpture

As Greek temples grew larger and more complex, sculptural decoration took on increased importance. The Greeks may have looked to the civilizations south and east of them for ideas on combining sculpture with architecture, but the results were far from Egyptian or Near Eastern in appearance.

Among the earliest surviving examples of Greek pedimental sculpture are fragments of the ruined Doric order Temple of Artemis on the island of Korkyra (Corfu) off the northwest coast of the mainland, which date to about 580 BCE (fig. 5-14). The figures in this sculpture were carved on separate slabs, then installed in the pediment space. They stand in such **high relief** from the background plane that they seem to burst out of their architectural frame, which was more than 9 feet tall at the peak. At the center is the rampaging snake-haired Medusa (fig. 5-15), one of three winged female monsters called Gorgons. Medusa had the power to turn humans to stone if they looked upon her face, and in this sculpture she fixes viewers with huge glaring eyes as if to work her dreadful magic on them. Flanking Medusa are the flying horse Pegasus on the left (only part of his rump and tail remain) and the giant Chrysaor on the right. These were Medusa's posthumous children, born from the blood that gushed from her neck after she was beheaded by the legendary hero Perseus. The crouching felines next to them literally bump their heads against the raking cornices of the roof. Dying human warriors lie on the ends of the pediment, their heads tucked into its corners and their knees rising with its sloping sides.

An especially noteworthy collaboration between builder and sculptor can still be imagined from the remains—housed today in the museum at Delphi—of the small but luxurious Siphnian Treasury, built in the Sanctuary of Apollo at Delphi between about 530 and 525 BCE. An old reconstruction of the facade of this building, now dismantled, shows a pronaos with two **caryatids**—

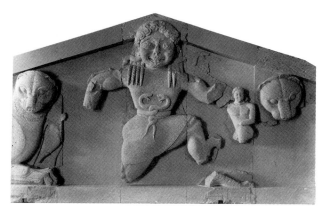

5-15. *Medusa*, fragment of sculpture from the west pediment of the Temple of Artemis, Korkyra. c. 580 BCE. Limestone, height of pediment at the center 9'2" (2.79 m). Archeological Museum, Korkyra

Ancient Greeks would have seen the image of Medusa at the center of this pediment as both menacing and protective. According to legend, countless people tried to kill this monster, only to die themselves merely because they looked at her face. The clever Greek hero Perseus succeeded because he beheaded her while looking only at her reflection in his polished shield. Thus the Medusa head became a popular decoration for Greek armor. See, for example, the shield of Ajax in figure 5-29.

columns carved in the form of draped women—set flush with the ends of the side walls, which were reinforced by square pillars, or **antae** (fig. 5-16). (This type of temple plan is called **in antis**, meaning "between the pillars"; see "Elements of Architecture," page 164.) The stately caryatids, with their finely pleated, flowing garments, are raised on **pedestals** and balance elaborately carved capitals on their heads. The capitals support a tall entablature conforming to the Ionic order, which features a plain, slightly extended architrave and a continuous

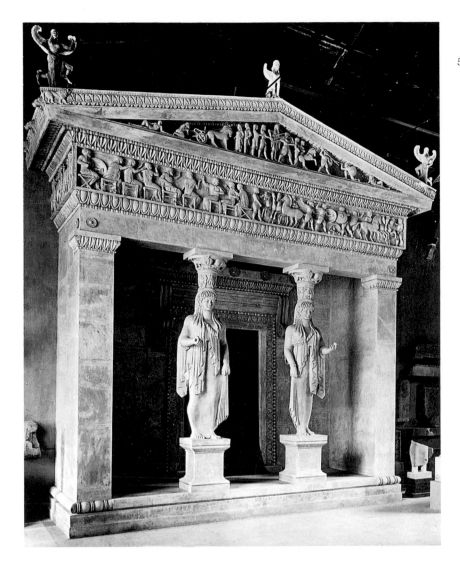

5-16. Reconstruction of the Siphnian Treasury, using fragments found in the Sanctuary of Apollo, Delphi. c. 530–525 BCE. Marble. Fragments: Archeological Museum, Delphi

This old reconstruction—probably from the east and west facades, using real sculptural remains filled out with reproductions—has been dismantled. The museum now exhibits separately the actual fragments of the treasury. The photograph is useful, however, in providing a general idea of how elegant and richly ornamented the eight small treasury buildings at Delphi were in their original state, perched near one another on the hillside. The figural sculpture and decorative moldings were probably once painted in strong colors, mainly dark blue, bright red, and white, with touches of yellow to resemble gold. The people who commissioned this treasury were from Siphnos, an island in the Aegean Sea just southwest of the Cyclades.

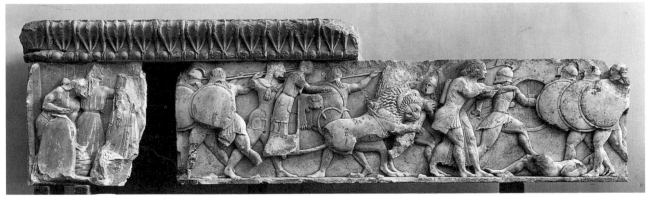

5-17. *Battle between the Gods and the Giants,* fragments of the north frieze of the Siphnian Treasury, from the Sanctuary of Apollo, Delphi. c. 530–525 BCE. Marble, height 26" (66 cm). Archeological Museum, Delphi

frieze, one uninterrupted by projecting elements. The frieze usually held a continuous band of figures carved in relief that was often set off by bands of richly carved moldings. The standard Ionic order column is slender and fluted, with a base of plain moldings and a distinctive **volute** capital, consisting of a square echinus with two opposing "rolled" sides topped by a thin abacus that may be decorated with carving (see "Elements of Architecture," page 165). As in this case, caryatids sometimes

substitute for the standard columns in the Ionic order.

Both the continuous frieze and the pediments of the Siphnian Treasury were originally filled with relief sculpture. A surviving section of the frieze from the building's north side, which shows a scene from the legendary battle between the sky gods and the earth gods, is one of the earliest known examples of a trend in Greek relief sculpture toward a more natural representation of space (fig. 5-17). To give a sense of three dimensions, the sculptor

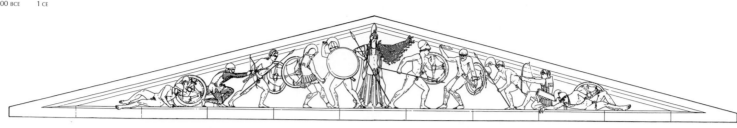

5-18. Reconstruction drawing of the east pediment of the Temple of Aphaia, Aegina. c. 480 BCE

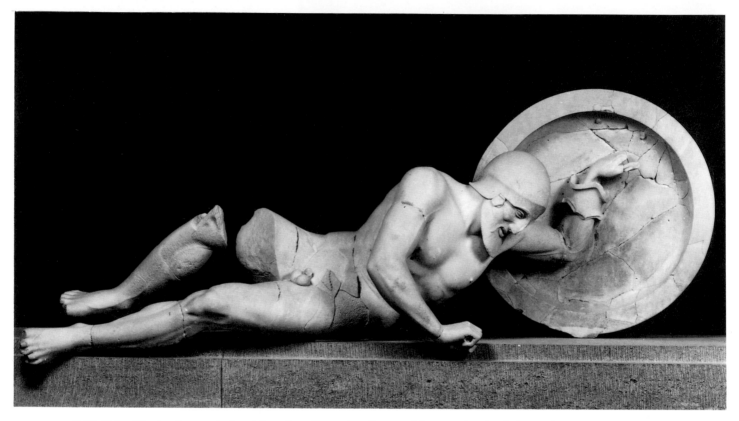

5-19. *Dying Warrior,* fragment of sculpture from the east pediment of the Temple of Aphaia, Aegina. c. 480 BCE. Marble, length 6' (1.83 m). Staatliche Antikensammlungen und Glyptothek, Munich

placed some figures behind others, overlapping as many as three of them and varying the depth of the relief from high on the foreground figures to lower and lowest on the figures behind. But countering any sense of deep recession, all the figures were made the same height with their feet on the same **groundline**.

The long pediments of Greek temples provided a perfect stage for storytelling, but the triangular pediment created a problem in composition. The sculptor of the east pediment of the Doric Temple of Aphaia at Aegina (fig. 5-18), dated to about 480 BCE, provided a creative solution that became a design standard, appearing with variations throughout the fifth century BCE. The subject of the Aphaia pediment, rendered in fully three-dimension-al figures, is most likely a Trojan War battle scene. Fallen warriors fill the angles at both ends of the pediment base, while others crouch, lunge, and reel, rising in height toward an image of Athena as warrior goddess under the peak of the roof. The erect goddess, larger than the other figures and flanked by two defenders facing approaching opponents, dominates the center of the scene and stabilizes the entire composition.

Among the best-preserved fragments from this pedimental scene is the *Dying Warrior* from the far left corner, a tragic but noble figure struggling to rise while dying (fig. 5-19). This figure originally would have been painted and fitted with authentic bronze accessories, heightening the sense of reality it conveys. Fully exploiting the difficult framework of the pediment corner, the sculptor portrayed the soldier's uptilted, twisted form turning in space, capturing his agony and vulnerability. The subtle modeling of the body conveys the softness of human flesh, which is contrasted with the hard, metallic geometry of the shield and helmet.

Freestanding Sculpture

In addition to decorating temple architecture, sculptors of the Archaic period created a new type of large, freestanding statue. A few surviving examples are made of wood or terra-cotta, but most are made of white marble, which is readily available in Greece, particularly on the islands of Paros and Naxos. Usually lifesize or larger, these male and female figures were depicted in reclining, seated, standing, and occasionally moving poses. They were painted in bright, lifelike colors and sometimes bore inscriptions indicating that they had been commissioned by individual men or women for some commemorative purpose. Many have been found marking graves, but the majority have been discovered in sanctuaries to the gods, where they were placed on pedestals lining the sacred way from the entrance to the main temple.

Traditionally, a female statue of this type is called a **kore** (plural korai), Greek for "young woman," and a male statue is called a **kouros** (plural kouroi), Greek for "young man." The Archaic korai were always clothed and are thought to have represented deities, priestesses, and nymphs, the young female immortals who served as attendants to the gods. The kouroi, nearly always nude, have been variously identified as gods, warriors, and victorious athletes. Because the Greeks associated young, athletic males with fertility and family continuity, the figures may have been symbolic ancestor figures. Pliny the Elder, a Roman naturalist and historian of the first century CE, believed that some of them portrayed famous athletes. He wrote:

> It was not customary to make effigies [portraits] of men unless, through some illustrious cause, they were worthy of having their memory perpetuated; the first example was a victory in the sacred contest, especially at Olympia, where it was the custom to dedicate statues of all who had been victorious; and in the case of those who had been winners there three times they moulded [sculpted] a likeness from the actual features of the person, which they call "icons" (*Naturalis Historia* 34.16-17, cited in Pollitt, page 30).

A kouros figure dating to about 600 BCE (fig. 5-20) is reminiscent of standing males in Egyptian sculpture, such as the statue of Menkaure with his queen (see fig. 3-15). Like Egyptian figures, this young Greek is shown

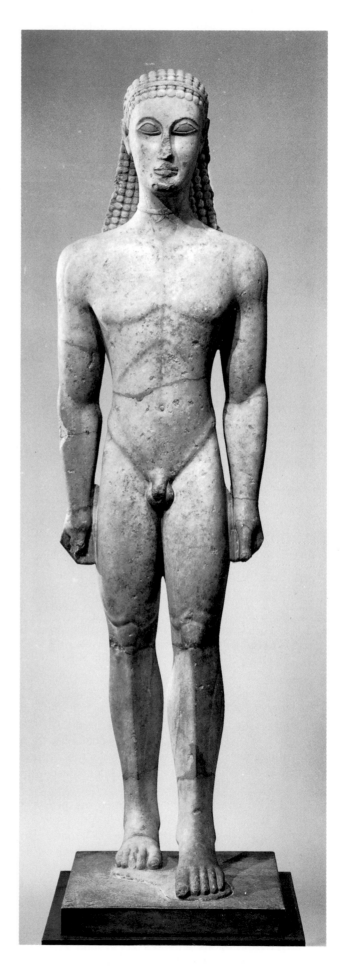

5-20. Kouros. c. 600 BCE. Marble, height 6'4" (1.93 m). The Metropolitan Museum of Art, New York Fletcher Fund, 1932 (32.11.1)

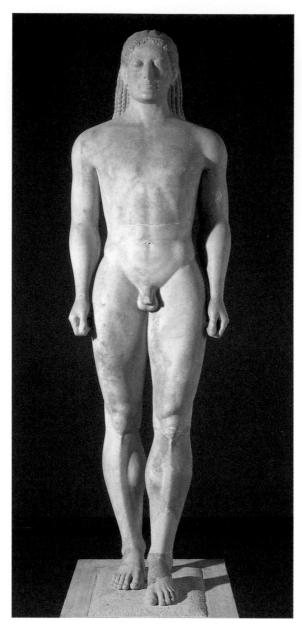

5-21. *Kroisos*(?), from a cemetery at Anavysos, near Athens.
c. 525 BCE. Marble with remnants of paint, height 6'4"
(1.93 m). National Archeological Museum, Athens

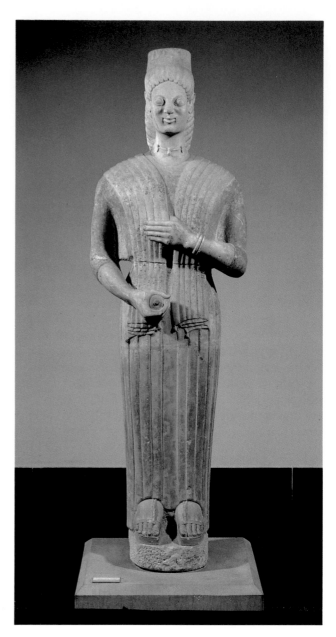

5-22. Kore, from a cemetery at Keratea, near Athens.
570–560 BCE. Marble with remnants of red paint,
height 6'3" (1.9 m). Staatliche Museen zu Berlin,
Preussischer Kulturbesitz, Antikensammlung

frontally, arms rigidly at his sides, fists clenched, and one leg slightly in front of the other. However, Greek artists of the Archaic period did not share the Egyptian obsession with permanence; they cut away all stone from around the body and introduced variations in appearance from figure to figure. Greek statues may be suggestive of the marble block from which they were carved, but they have a notable athletic quality quite unlike Egyptian statues. Here the artist delineated the figure's anatomy with ridges and grooves that form geometric patterns. The head is an ovoid shape with heavy features and schematized hair evenly knotted into tufts and tied back with a narrow ribbon. The eyes are relatively large and wide open, and the mouth forms a characteristic closed-lip smile known as the **Archaic smile**, apparently used to enliven the expressions of figures. In Egyptian sculpture, male figures were always at least partially clothed, wear-

ing articles associated with their status, such as the headdresses, beaded pectorals, and kilts that identified kings. The total nudity of the Greek kouroi, in contrast, removes them from a specific time, place, or social class.

A kouros dated about seventy-five years later than figure 5-20 clearly shows in its swelling, rounded body forms the increasing interest of artists and their patrons in a more lifelike rendering of the human figure (fig. 5-21). The pose, wiglike hair, and Archaic smile echo the earlier style of kouros, but the torso and limbs were rendered with greater anatomical accuracy and may have been done from a specific human model. The statue, a grave monument to a fallen war hero, often called *Kroisos*, may portray a particular individual of that name. The inscription reads: "Stop and grieve at the tomb of the dead Kroisos, slain by wild Ares [god of war] in the front rank of battle."

The first Archaic korai appear to date somewhat later than the earliest kouroi. An early kore found in a cemetery at Keratea, for example, dates to about 570–560 BCE (fig. 5-22). The erect, immobile pose, full-bodied figure, and 6-foot height—accentuated by a crown and thick-soled clogs—seem appropriate to a goddess, although the statue may represent a priestess or a nymph attendant. The thick robe falls in regularly spaced, parallel folds like the fluting on a Greek column, further emphasizing its stately appearance. Traces of pigment indicate that the robe was once red, a color often used as a base for the application of thin sheets of gold. The figure holds a pomegranate in her right hand, an **attribute** (identifying symbol) of Persephone, the goddess of the underworld and the harvest. A popular subject with artists was the myth in which young Persephone, the daughter of the earth goddess Demeter, was abducted by Hades, the god of the underworld. While she was mourning her separation from her mother, she became hungry and ate a pomegranate from Hades' garden, unaware that this act would destine her to become Hades' queen and live eternally in the underworld. Through her mother's intercession with Zeus, however, she was allowed to live aboveground for six months out of every year, from spring to autumn. Thus Persephone and the pomegranate—which has many seeds—symbolized fertility and the seasonal cycles of rebirth (spring and summer) and death (autumn and winter) associated with the cultivation of crops.

The *Peplos Kore* (fig. 5-23), which dates to about 530 BCE, was recovered from debris on the **Acropolis** of Athens, a flat topped hill that was the original site of the city and later served as a fortress and religious sanctuary (*acro* means "high" and *polis* means "city"). Many votive and commemorative statues like the *Peplos Kore* were placed in the sanctuary over the centuries, but few have survived. In 480 BCE the desperate Athenians, anticipating an attack by Persian forces, fled to the Acropolis and apparently used some of the statues there to build barricades. When the Persians later sacked the city, these works suffered further destruction, and they finally were used as fill in the reconstruction of the Acropolis after the Persian invasion.

The *Peplos Kore* is named for its distinctive garment, called a **peplos**—a draped rectangle of cloth, usually wool, folded over the top and belted to give a bloused effect. The *Peplos Kore* has the same motionless, vertical pose of the earlier kore but a more rounded, feminine figure. Its bare arms and head convey a greater sense of soft flesh covering a real bone structure, and its smile and hair are somewhat more individualized and less conventionalized. The figure once wore a metal crown and earrings and has traces of **encaustic** painting, a mixture of **pigments** and hot wax that left a shiny, hard surface when it congealed.

Another kore (fig. 5-24), dating to about 520 BCE, may have been made by a sculptor from Chios, an island off the coast of Asia Minor. Although the arms and legs of this figure have been lost and its face has been damaged, it is impressive for its sculpted costuming and the large

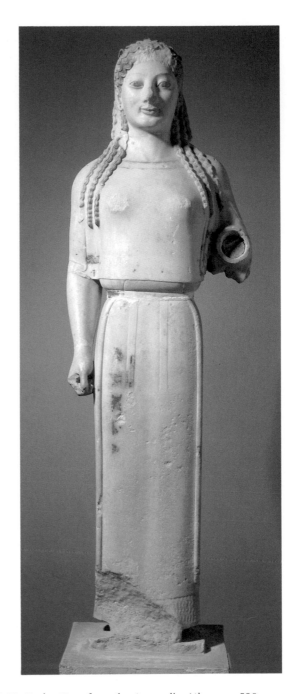

5-23. *Peplos Kore*, from the Acropolis, Athens. c. 530 BCE. Marble, height 48" (123 cm). Acropolis Museum, Athens

amount of paint that still adheres to it. Like the *Kroisos* (see fig. 5-21) and the *Peplos Kore,* it reflects a trend toward an increasingly lifelike depiction of anatomical forms that would peak in the fifth century BCE. The kore wears a garment called a **chiton**, a relatively lightweight, basic article of clothing that originated in Ionia on the coast of Asia Minor but became popular throughout Greece. Over it, a cloak called a **himation** is draped diagonally and fastened on one shoulder. The fine pleating and gathering of the chiton indicate that it was made of a lighter fabric than the peplos, probably linen. The elaborate hairstyle and abundance of jewelry add to the opulent effect. A close look at what remains of the figure's legs reveals a rounded thigh showing clearly through the thin fabric of the chiton.

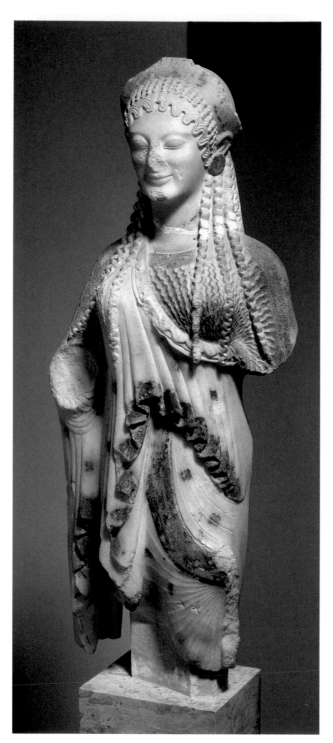

5-24. Kore, from Chios(?). c. 520 BCE. Marble, height 21⅞"
(56.6 cm). Acropolis Museum, Athens

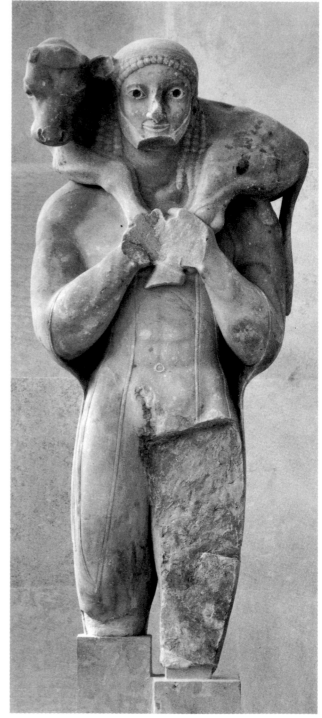

5-25. *Calf Bearer* (*Moschophoros*), from the Acropolis, Athens.
c. 560 BCE. Marble, height 5'5" (1.65 m). Acropolis
Museum, Athens

Not all Archaic statues followed the conventional kouros or kore models for standing figures. A different type is a large statue fragment called the *Calf Bearer* (*Moschophoros*) (fig. 5-25). This statue, dated about 560 BCE, was also found in the rubble of the Acropolis, in the Sanctuary of Athena. It probably represents a priest or worshiper carrying an animal intended for sacrifice on the altar of a deity. The figure's smile, tufted hairdo, and wide-open eyes with large irises and semicircular eyebrows all reflect the Archaic style. Its short-cropped

beard is similar to that of other statues of the period depicting men in active poses, but the gauze-thin robe is unusual. The sculptor has rendered the calf with acute detail, capturing its almost dazed look and the twisted position in which its captor holds its forelegs.

Vase Painting

Greek vases, no matter how richly decorated, were created in only a few forms, which combined beauty with

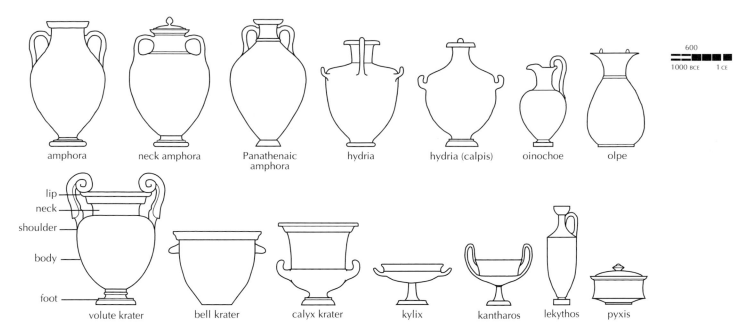

amphora   neck amphora   Panathenaic   hydria   hydria (calpis)   oinochoe   olpe
                           amphora

600
1000 BCE   1 CE

lip
neck
shoulder
body
foot

volute krater   bell krater   calyx krater   kylix   kantharos   lekythos   pyxis

5-26. Standard Greek vase shapes

specific utilitarian functions (fig. 5-26). The artists who painted them had to accommodate their work to these fixed shapes. During the Archaic period, Athens became the dominant center for pottery manufacture and trade in Greece. Athenian painters adopted many Corinthian techniques, especially black-figure painting, which became the principal mode of decoration throughout Greece in the sixth century BCE. Unlike the Corinthians, who painted large, mythical beasts against floral backgrounds, Athenian painters retained a format that was characteristic of the Geometric period, with narrow bands of decoration and relatively small figures. Compared with the Athenian Geometric period vases found in the Dipylon Cemetery (see fig. 5-5), there are fewer bands and the geometric patterning around the figures is reduced.

An important transitional work, the *François Vase*, illustrates these changes (fig. 5-27). This vase, which dates to about 570 BCE, is a **volute krater**. A **krater** is a large vessel used for mixing the traditional Greek drink of wine and water, and a volute krater is one with scroll-shaped, or volute, handles. The *François Vase* was discovered by an archeologist named François in an Etruscan cemetery; it had been brought to central Italy by a people especially fond of Greek vases. It is one of the earliest known vessels signed by both the potter who made it (Ergotimos) and the painter who decorated it (Kleitias). Kleitias's subjects were episodes from religious myth and legendary history, which he identified with inscriptions, providing an important pictorial record of the Greek pantheon. In all, the vase contains about 200 human and animal figures.

The main narrative scene, which occupies the third band down from the top and encircles the whole vase, is the marriage of Peleus and Thetis, the parents of Achilles. Thetis was a sea nymph and Peleus the king of Thessaly, and their wedding was attended by the Olympian gods. In the segment seen in figure 5-27, Peleus stands in front

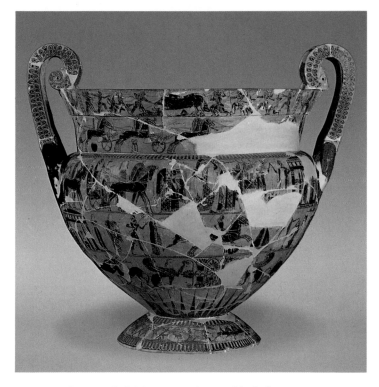

5-27. Ergotimos and Kleitias. *François Vase*, black-figure decoration on a volute krater. c. 570 BCE. Ceramic, height 26" (66 cm). Museo Archeològico Nazionale, Florence

This large mixing bowl was made and decorated by Athenian artists but discovered in modern times in an Etruscan tomb. The Etruscans, who were living in Etruria in central Italy at the time the early Roman civilization emerged, were great admirers and collectors of Greek pottery. Not only did they import vases, but they also brought in Greek artists to teach their techniques and styles to local artists. Because so much Greek and Greek-style pottery was discovered in Etruria, collectors in the nineteenth and early twentieth centuries called all ancient Greek vases "Etruscan."

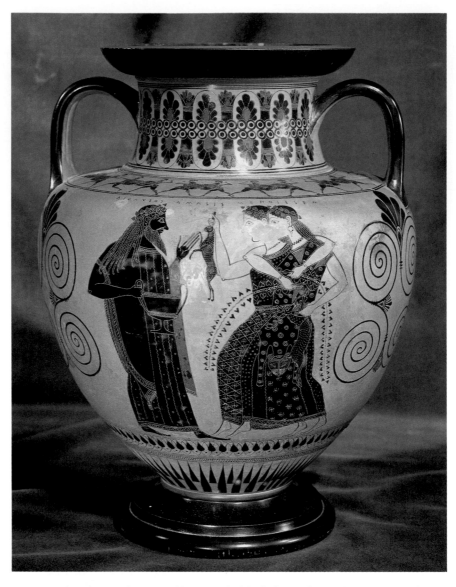

5-28. Amasis Painter. *Dionysos with Maenads,* black-figure decoration on an amphora.
c. 540 BCE. Ceramic, height of amphora 13" (33.3 cm). Bibliothèque Nationale, Paris

of his palace, on the right, greeting the deities, who are arriving in a grand procession of chariots. The scenes on the neck of the vessel show, from the top down: the hunt for the dangerous Kalydonian Boar, led by the hero Meleager, and the funeral games in honor of Patroclus, Achilles' close friend who died in the Trojan War. On the body of the krater, below Peleus and Thetis, is a depiction of the ambush of the Trojan prince Troilus by Achilles. The Orientalizing style (see figs. 5-9, 5-10) is still evident on this Archaic period vase in the next band down, decorated with deer, griffins, and plant forms. On the foot of the vessel, very small warriors do battle with long-necked cranes, illustrating a story dating back to Homer's day that became a popular theme with vase painters. There are only three bands of pure geometric design—one of elongated triangles radiating up from the foot of the vessel and two narrow bands of looped decoration on the foot.

Over time, Athenian vase painters continued to decrease the number of bands and increase the size of figures until a single scene, usually one per side, filled the whole body of a vessel. A mid-sixth-century BCE **amphora**—a large, all-purpose storage jar—illustrates this development (fig. 5-28). The decoration on this vessel, a depiction of the wine god Dionysos with **maenads**, his female worshipers, has been attributed to an anonymous artist called the Amasis Painter, because work of this distinctive style was first recognized on vessels signed by a prolific potter named Amasis. Most of the Amasis Painter's work is found on small vessels, but this handsome amphora is an exception.

In the scene shown here, two maenads, arms around each other's shoulders, skip forward to present their offerings—a long-eared rabbit and a small deer—to Dionysos. The maenad holding the deer wears the skin of a spotted panther (or leopard), its head still attached, draped over her shoulders and secured with a belt at her waist. The god, an imposing, richly dressed figure, clasps a large **kantharos** (wine cup). A band of grape leaves, an attribute of Dionysos, forms the groundline on which the

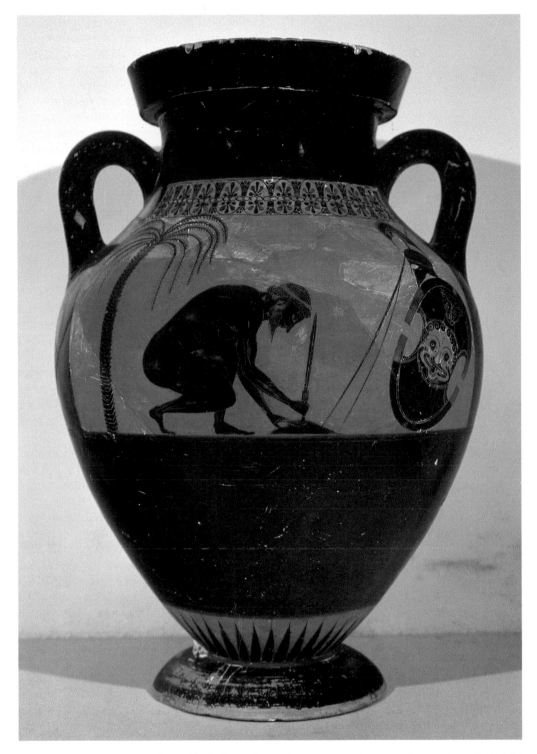

5-29. Exekias. *The Suicide of Ajax*, black-figure decoration on an amphora. c. 540 BCE. Ceramic, height of amphora 27" (69 cm). Château-Musée, Boulogne-sur-Mer, France

figures stand, and the maenads each carry a piece of grapevine. This encounter between humans and a god appears to be a joyful, celebratory occasion rather than one of reverence or fear. The Amasis Painter favored strong shapes and patterns, generally disregarding conventions for making figures appear to occupy real space, and emphasized fine details, such as the large, delicate petal and spiral designs below each handle, the figures' meticulously arranged hair, and the bold patterns on their clothing.

Another Athenian artist of the mid-sixth century BCE, Exekias, signed his vessels as both potter and painter. Exekias took his subjects from Greek legend, matching painted composition to vessel shape with great sensitivity. A scene on an amphora, *The Suicide of Ajax,* recounts an episode from the legends of the Trojan War (fig. 5-29). Ajax was a fearless Greek warrior, second only to Achilles in bravery. After the death of Achilles, however, the Greeks bestowed his magic armor on Odysseus rather than Ajax. Distraught by this humiliation—com-

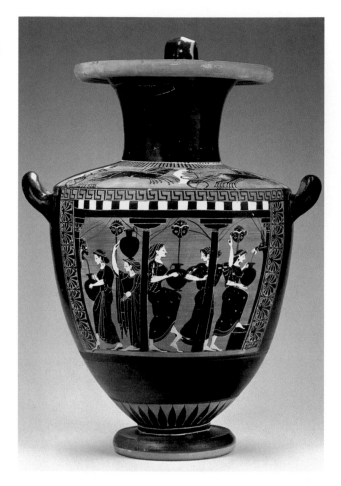

600

1000 BCE   1 CE

5-30. "A.D." Painter. *Women at a Fountain House*, black-figure decoration on a hydria. 520–510 BCE. Ceramic, height of hydria 20⅞" (53 cm). Museum of Fine Arts, Boston
William Francis Warden Fund

pounded by his family ties to Achilles, who was his cousin—Ajax killed himself. Other artists showed the great warrior either dying or already dead, but Exekias has captured the story's most poignant moment, showing Ajax preparing to die. He has set aside his helmet, shield, and spear and crouches beneath a tree, planting his sword upright in a mound of dirt so that he can fall upon it. The painting exemplifies the quiet beauty and perfect equilibrium for which Exekias's works are so admired today. Two upright elements—the tree on the left and the shield on the right—frame and balance the figure of Ajax, their in-curving lines echoing the swelling shape of the amphora and the rounding of the hero's powerful back as he bends forward. The whole composition focuses the viewer's attention on the head of Ajax and its dangerous proximity to the point of his sword.

Not all subjects used for vase painting involved gods and heroes. A handsome example of black-figure decoration, painted about 510 BCE on an Athenian **hydria**, or water jug, by an artist who signed the work with the initials "A.D.," gives an interesting insight into everyday Greek city life (fig. 5-30). The majority of women in ancient Greece were restricted to their homes and occupied with household tasks. Few houses had running

water, and the trip to the communal well, or fountain house, would have been an important daily event. The scene on the hydria shows five women gathered at such a place. In the shade of the columned porch, three of the women patiently fill hydrias like the one on which they are painted. A fourth balances her empty jug on her head as she waits, while a fifth woman, without a jug, appears to be waving in greeting to someone. The women's skin is painted white, a convention for female figures found also in Egyptian and Minoan art. Incising and touches of reddish purple paint were used to create fine details in the architecture and in the figures' clothing and hair.

The composition of this vase painting is a fine balance of vertical, horizontal, rectangular, and rounded elements. The columns, the decorative vertical borders, and even the streams of water flowing from the animal-head spigots echo the upright figures of the women. The wide black band forming the groundline, the architrave above the colonnade, and the left-to-right movement of the horse-drawn chariots across the shoulder area of the hydria emphasize the horizontal, friezelike arrangement of the women across the width of the vase. This geometric framework is softened by the rounded contours of the female bodies, the globular water vessels, the circular **palmettes** (fan-shaped petal designs) framing the main scene, and the arching bodies of the galloping horses on the shoulder.

In the last third of the sixth century BCE, while "A.D." and others were still creating handsome black-figure wares, some pottery painters turned away from this meticulous process to a variation called **red-figure** decoration (see "Greek Painted Vases," page 162). This new method, as its name suggests, resulted in vessels with red figures against a black background, the opposite of black-figure painting. In the earlier method, artists painted figures on a vessel in a slip that turned black in the firing process, leaving the unpainted body of the vessel as the reddish background. Linear details on the figures were incised through the slip. In red-figure wares, the same dark slip was painted on as background around the outlined figures, which were left unpainted. Linear details were applied on the figures with a fine brush dipped in the slip. The result was a lustrous dark vessel with light-colored figures with dark-painted details. The greater freedom and flexibility of this more direct approach led artists to adopt it widely in a relatively short time.

One of the best-known artists specializing in the red-figure technique was the Athenian Euphronios, who was praised especially for his study of human anatomy. His rendering of the *Death of Sarpedon,* which dates to about 515 BCE, is painted on a **calyx krater**, so called because its handles curve up like a flower calyx (fig. 5-31). According to Homer's *Iliad,* Sarpedon, a Trojan warrior, was killed by the Greek warrior Patroclus, who had borrowed the magic armor of his comrade Achilles. Euphronios shows the winged figures of Hypnos (Sleep) and Thanatos (Death) carrying the dead Trojan warrior from the battlefield. Watching over the scene is Hermes, the messenger of the gods, identified by his winged hat and

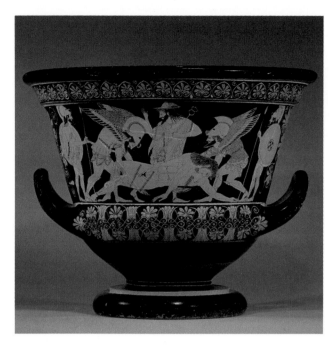

5-31. Euphronios. *Death of Sarpedon,* red-figure decoration on a calyx krater. c. 515 BCE. Ceramic, height of krater 18" (45.7 cm). The Metropolitan Museum of Art, New York

Puchase, Gift of Darius Ogden Mills, Gift of J. Pierpont Morgan, and Bequest of Joseph H. Durkee, by exchange, 1972 (1972.11.10)

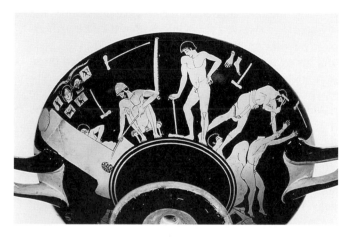

5-32. Foundry Painter. *A Bronze Foundry,* red-figure decoration on a kylix from Vulci, Italy. 490–480 BCE. Ceramic, diameter of kylix 12" (31 cm). Staatliche Museen zu Berlin, Preussischer Kulturbesitz, Antikensammlung

caduceus, a staff with coiled snakes. Hermes is there in another important role, as the guide who leads the dead to the netherworld.

Euphronios, like the painter "A.D.," created a perfectly balanced composition of verticals and horizontals that take the shape of the vessel into account. The bands of decoration above and below the scene echo the long horizontal of the dead fighter's body, which seems to levitate in the gentle grasp of its bearers, and the inward-curving lines of the handles mirror the arching backs of Hypnos and Thanatos. The upright figures of the lance bearers on each side and Hermes in the center counterbalance the horizontal elements of the composition. The

painter, while conveying a sense of the mass and energy of the subjects, also portrayed amazingly fine details of their clothing, musculature, and facial features with the fine tip of a brush. Euphronios created the impression of real space around the figures by **foreshortening** body forms and limbs—Sarpedon's left leg, for example—so that they appear to be coming toward or receding from the viewer.

A red-figure **kylix**, or drinking cup, from Vulci, Italy, provides another example of the adaptation of scenic composition to vessel shape (fig. 5-32). The artist used the entire circular underside of this piece, which dates to about 490–480 BCE, to illustrate the workings of a contemporary foundry for casting lifesize and monumental bronze figures. The artist, known as the Foundry Painter, successfully organized this continuous scene within the flaring space that extends upward from the foot of the vessel. The small circle that marks the attachment of the foot to the vessel serves as the groundline for all the figures. The wedges of background space between the figures are cleverly presented as the walls of the workshop, filled with hanging tools and other foundry paraphernalia: hammers, an ax and saw, molds of a human foot and hand, and several sketches. These sketches include one of a horse, some of human busts, and three of human figures, one in an active pose, one in a standing pose, and one seated.

On the section shown here, a worker wearing what looks like a modern-day construction helmet squats to tend the furnace on the left. The man in the center, perhaps the supervisor, leans on a staff, while a third worker, on the right, assembles the already-cast parts of a leaping figure that are braced against a molded support. The unattached head lies between his feet. The scene continues past the handles, where more workers are shown putting the finishing touches on a larger-than-lifesize striding warrior figure. This painting provides clear evidence that the Greeks were creating large **hollow-cast** bronze statues in active poses—in marked contrast to the static pose of the Archaic kouroi—as early as the first decades of the fifth century BCE. Unfortunately, no examples of these early bronze figures have yet been found.

THE TRANSITIONAL OR EARLY CLASSICAL PERIOD

In the early decades of the fifth century BCE, the Greek city-states, which for several centuries had developed relatively unimpeded by external powers, faced a formidable threat to their independence from the expanding Persian Empire. Cyrus the Great had incorporated the Greek cities of Ionia in Asia Minor into his empire in 546 BCE. After several failed invasions, in 480 BCE the Persians came with a large force and destroyed many Greek cities, including Athens. In a series of encounters—at Thermopylae and Plataea on land and in the straits of Salamis at sea—an alliance of Greek city-states led by Athens and Sparta, the dominant power on the Peloponnese, first blunted, then

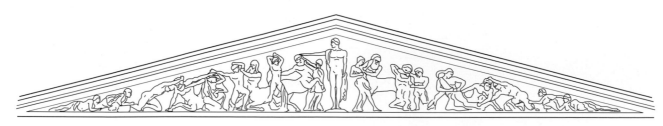

5-33. Reconstruction drawing of the west pediment of the Temple of Zeus, Olympia. c. 470–456 BCE

repulsed the invasion. By 479 BCE the stalwart armies and the small but formidable navies of the Greeks had triumphed over their enemies, and the victors turned to the task of rebuilding their devastated cities.

Some scholars have argued that the Greeks' success against the Persians imbued them with a self-confidence that accelerated the development of Greek art, inspiring artists to seek new and more effective ways to express their cities' accomplishments. In any case, the period that followed the Persian Wars, extending from about 480 to about 450 BCE, was a time of marked transition. Artists built on ideas that had emerged in earlier periods and at the same time initiated entirely new stylistic experiments. With the enthusiastic support of their patrons, they sought more **realistic** ways to portray the human figure in painting and sculpture and to place figures in more **naturalistic** settings (see "Realism and Naturalism," below).

Architectural Sculpture

Just a few years after the Persians had been routed, the citizens of Olympia began a new Doric temple to Zeus in the Sanctuary of Hera and Zeus. The temple was completed between 470 and 456 BCE. Today the massive temple base and columns, fallen capitals, and almost all the pediments remain, monumental even in ruins. Appropriately for its Olympian setting, the temple was decorated with works of sculpture celebrating legendary Greek victories, all of which are presented as due to the direct intervention of the gods Zeus, Apollo, and Athena.

The sculptural scene that once adorned the west pediment shows Apollo helping the Lapiths in their battle with the centaurs (fig. 5-33). This legendary battle erupted after the centaurs drank too much wine at the wedding feast of the Lapith king and tried to carry off some Lapith women. Apollo stands implacable at the center of the scene, quelling the disturbance supernaturally simply by raising his arm (fig. 5-34). Although some figures were restored later and may not exactly reflect their original appearance, the rising, falling, triangular composition attests to the skill of the artist. The contrast of angular forms with turning, twisting action poses dramatizes the physical struggle, which may have been symbolic of the triumph of reason over passion and civilization over barbarism.

The metope reliefs of the temple illustrated the mythological Twelve Labors imposed by King Eurystheus of Tiryns on Herakles. The hero, with the aid of the gods and his own phenomenal strength, accomplished these seemingly impossible tasks, thereby earning immortality. One of the labors was to steal gold apples from the garden of the Hesperides, the nymphs who guarded the trees that produced them. To do this, Herakles enlisted the aid of the giant Atlas, whose job was to hold up the heavens. Herakles offered to take on this job himself while Atlas fetched the apples for him. In the episode shown here (fig. 5-35), Herakles is at the center with the heavens on his shoulders. Atlas, on the right, holds out the gold apples to him. As we can see, and Atlas cannot, the human Herakles is backed, literally, by the goddess Athena, who effortlessly supports the sky with one hand.

REALISM AND NATURALISM Is it redundant to say that artists "sought more **realistic** ways to portray the human figure in painting and sculpture and to place figures in more **naturalistic** settings"? Are *realistic* and *naturalistic* interchangeable here, or is there a subtle difference in the way the two words are used?

Both realism and naturalism are defined as the attempt to depict observable things accurately and objectively, even imitatively. Thus, in the passage cited above, it may seem that the two words mean exactly the same thing and that the author was simply avoiding repetition. But as with many terms used in art historical writing, these words have a subtle shading that may not be apparent in their dictionary definitions.

In the visual arts, *realism* is most often used to describe the representation of people and other living creatures in an accurate, "warts and all" fashion. Detailed portraits of people, as well as pictures of animals or imaginary figures, are often described as "realistic." *Naturalism*, on the other hand, has a "softer" meaning, generally referring to the true-to-life depiction of the natural world, especially landscape and background elements. Although both terms involve realistic representation, they can carry a slightly different meaning depending on the context in which they are used—as demonstrated in the sentence above.

Many such words appear in the literature of art history. Those that are used in this book are explained in the text and are defined in the Glossary.

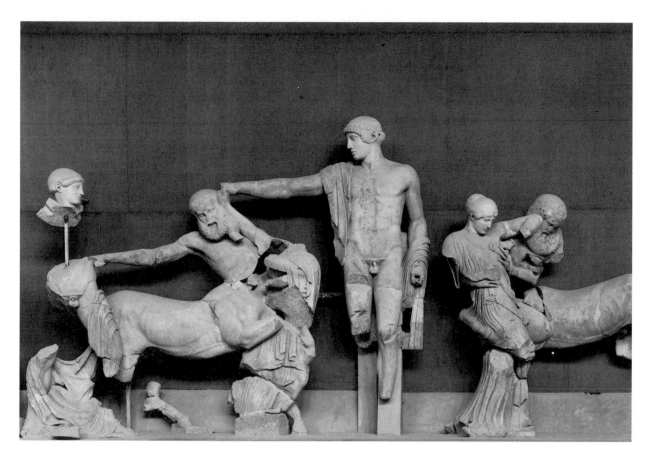

5-34. *Apollo with Battling Lapiths and Centaurs,* fragments of relief sculpture from the west pediment of the Temple of Zeus, Olympia. c. 470–456 BCE. Marble, height of *Apollo* 10'2" (3.1 m). Archeological Museum, Olympia

The artist has balanced the erect, frontal view of the heavily clothed Athena with profile views of the two nude male figures. Sculpted in high relief, the figures reflect a strong interest in realism. Even the rather severe columnlike figure of the goddess suggests the flesh of her body pressing through the graceful fall of heavy drapery.

Freestanding Sculpture

In the remarkably short time of only a few generations, Greek sculptors moved far from the rigid, frontal presentation of the human figure embodied in the Archaic

5-35. *Athena, Herakles, and Atlas,* metope relief from the frieze of the Temple of Zeus, Olympia. Marble, height 5'3" (1.59 m). Archeological Museum, Olympia

The Greeks believed Herakles was the founder of the Olympian Games, held every four years at Olympia beginning in 776 BCE. Supposedly, Herakles drew up the rules for the games and decided that the stadium should be 600 feet long. The contests had a strong religious aspect, and the victors were rewarded with olive branches from the Sacred Grove of the gods instead of gold, silver, or bronze medals. The Olympian Games came to be so highly regarded that the city-states suspended all political activities while the games were in progress. The games ended in 394 CE, when they were banned by the Christian emperor Theodosius. The discovery and excavation of the site of the sanctuary at Olympia in the late nineteenth century stimulated great interest in the games, inspiring the French baron Pierre de Coubertin to revive them on an international scale. The first modern Olympic Games were held in Athens in 1896.

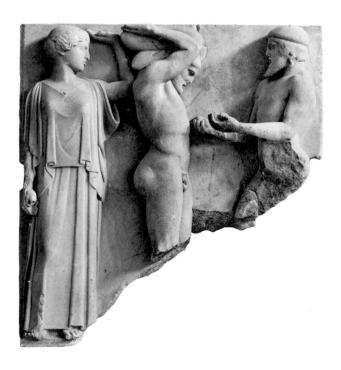

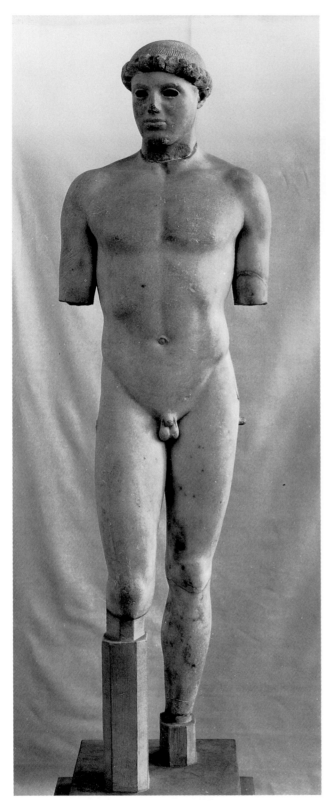

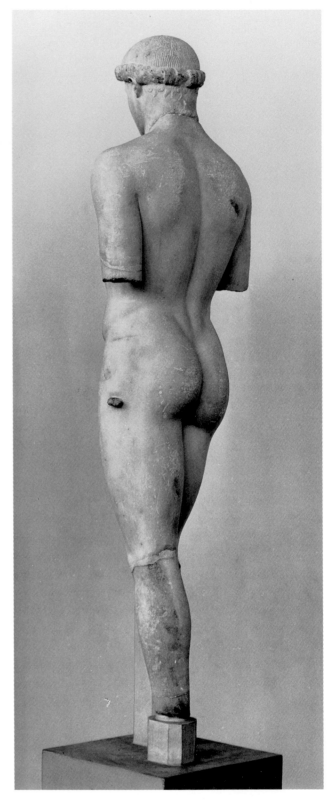

5-36. *Kritios Boy.* c. 480 BCE. Marble, height 46" (116 cm). Acropolis Museum, Athens

kouroi. One of the earliest and finest extant freestanding marble figures to exhibit more natural, lifelike qualities is the *Kritios Boy* of about 480 BCE (fig. 5-36). The damaged figure, excavated from the debris on the Athenian Acropolis, was thought by its finders to be by the Greek sculptor Kritios, whose work was known only from Roman copies. Unlike most Archaic kouroi, which represent young men and are usually large, the *Kritios Boy* appears adolescent, and the complete figure would have been only a little over 3 feet tall. Despite his age, the *Kritios Boy* looks like an accomplished athlete. The solid, rounded body forms, large facial features, and thoughtful expression—which lacks even a trace of the Archaic smile—give the figure an air of extraordinary solemnity. The easy pose contrasts markedly with the rigid, evenly balanced, straight-shouldered, forward-stepping pose of Archaic kouroi. The boy's weight rests on his left leg, making it the engaged leg, and his unengaged right leg bends slightly at the knee. A noticeable curve in his spine counters the slight shifting of his hips and a subtle drop of one of his shoulders.

A major problem for anyone trying to create a freestanding sculpture is to assure that it won't fall over. Solving this problem requires a familiarity with the statics of sculptural materials—their ability to maintain equilibrium under various conditions. At the end of the Archaic period a new technique for **hollow-casting** of bronze was developed. This technique created a far more flexible medium than solid marble or other stone and became the medium of choice for Greek sculptors. Although it is possible to create freestanding figures with outstretched arms and legs far apart in stone, hollow-cast bronze more easily permits vigorous and even off-balance action poses. After the introduction of the new technique, the figure in action became a popular subject among the ancient Greeks. Sculptors sought to find poses that seemed to capture a natural feeling of continuing movement rather than an arbitrary moment frozen in time.

Unfortunately, foundries began almost immediately to recycle metal from old statues into new works, so few original Greek bronzes have survived. A spectacular life-size bronze, the *Charioteer* (fig. 5-37), cast about 470 BCE, was saved from the metal scavengers only because it was buried during a major earthquake in 373 BCE. Archeologists found it in its original location in the Sanctuary of Apollo, along with fragments of a bronze chariot and horses. According to its inscription, it commemorates a victory by a driver sponsored by King Polyzalos of Gela (Sicily) in the Pythian Games of 478 or 474 BCE. The erect, flat-footed pose of the *Charioteer* and the long, columnar fluting of the robe are reminiscent of the Archaic style, but other characteristics place this work closer to the more lifelike *Kritios Boy*, recalling Pliny the Elder's claim that three-time winners in Greek competitions had their features memorialized in statues.

Unlike the Archaic *Kroisos*, for example (see fig. 5-21), the charioteer's head turns to one side, slightly away from the viewer. The rather intimidating expression is relieved by the use of glittering, colored-glass eyes and fine silver eyelashes. Although the smoothed-out facial features suggest an idealized conception of youthful male good looks, they are distinctive enough to be those of a particular individual. The feet, with their closely observed toes, toenails, and swelled veins over the instep, are so realistic that they seem to have been cast from molds made from the feet of a living person. The folds of the robe fall in a natural way, varying in width and depth, and the whole garment seems capable of swaying and rippling should the charioteer move slightly or encounter a sudden breeze.

In the early 1970s CE, divers recovered a pair of bigger-than-lifesize bronze figures from the seabed off the southern coast of Italy. Known as the *Riace Warriors,*

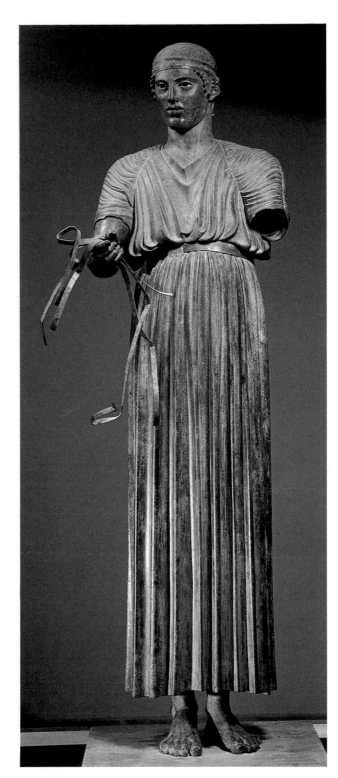

400
1000 BCE   1 CE

5-37. *Charioteer,* from the Sanctuary of Apollo, Delphi. c. 470 BCE. Bronze, height 5'11" (1.8 m). Archeological Museum, Delphi

The setting of a work of art affects the impression it makes. Today, this stunning figure is exhibited on a low base in the peaceful surroundings of a museum, isolated from other works and spotlighted for close examination. Its effect would have been very different in its original outdoor location, standing in a horse-drawn chariot atop a tall monument. Viewers in ancient times, exhausted from the steep climb to the sanctuary, possibly jostled by crowds of fellow pilgrims, could have absorbed only its overall effect, not the fine details of the face, robe, and body visible to today's viewers.

THE DISCOVERY AND CONSERVATION OF THE *RIACE WARRIORS* In 1972 a vacationer who was scuba diving in the Ionian Sea off the south coast of Italy near the beach resort of Riace found what appeared to be a human elbow and upper arm protruding from the sand in about 25 feet of water. Taking a closer look, he discovered that the arm was made of metal, not flesh, and when he pushed away the sand he realized that it was part of a large statue. Investigating further, he soon uncovered a second statue nearby. He marked the location with a diver's buoy and reported his discovery to the director of the local museum, who also happened to be the Superintendent of Antiquities for the region. An experienced team of underwater salvagers then raised the statues, which turned out to be bronze warriors more than 6 feet tall. They were complete in every respect, except for their swords, their shields, and one helmet.

Where did the *Warriors* come from? In ancient times, there had been a Greek colony at the tip of Italy. The statues had probably been on a ship bound from or to that colony. But there was no evidence of a shipwreck in the vicinity of the find, leading to the conclusion that they must have accidentally slipped off the deck in rough seas or been deliberately jettisoned. After centuries underwater, the *Warriors* were entirely corroded and covered with lime accretions on their exterior surfaces, as the illustration shows. The clay cores used in the casting process were still inside the statues, adding to the deterioration by absorbing lime and sea salts.

To restore the *Warriors,* conservators first removed all the exterior corrosion and lime encrustations using surgeon's scalpels, pneumatic drills with 3-millimeter heads, and high-technology equipment such as sonar (sound-wave) probes and micro-sanders. Then they painstakingly removed the clay core through existing holes in the heads and feet using hooks, scoops, jets of distilled water, and concentrated solutions of peroxide. Finally, they cleaned the figures thoroughly by soaking them in solvent solutions and sealed them with a fixative specially designed for use on metals (see fig. 5-38 left).

The *Warriors* were put on view in 1980. Since then, additional steps have been taken to assure their preservation for future generations. In 1993 conservators used a sonar probe mounted with two miniature video cameras to remove any remaining clay from inside the statues. With the cameras, they were able to find bits of clay, which they then blasted with sound waves from the probe. The statues were then flushed out with water.

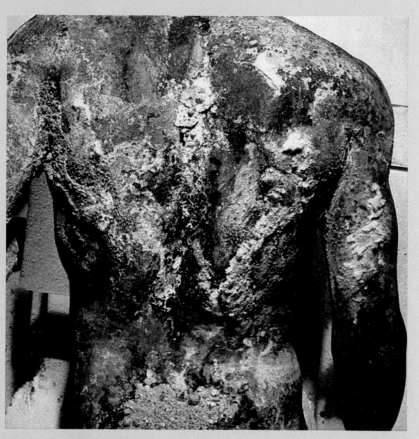

Back of the *Young Warrior* from Riace prior to conservation. Museo Archeològico Nazionale, Reggio Calabria, Italy

these original Greek statues date to about 460–450 BCE. Just what mishap sent them to the bottom is not known. They were not found with a wreck, so they may have fallen off a ship accidentally or perhaps been thrown from a ship in distress. The meticulous work of conservators has restored them to their original glory (see "The Discovery and Conservation of the *Riace Warriors,*" above). A look at one of them, the so-called *Young Warrior,* reveals a striking balance between idealized anatomical forms and naturalistic details (fig. 5-38). The supple athletic musculature suggests a youthfulness belied by the maturity of the almost haggard facial features. Sharp cheekbones protrude through the figure's thin flesh, deep lines run from the nose to the corners of the mouth, and unmistakable bags sag beneath the eyes. Other minutely detailed touches—the navel, the swelling veins in the backs of the hands, and the strand-by-strand rendering of the hair—are also in marked contrast to the idealized, youthful smoothness of the rest of the body. The sculptor heightened these lifelike effects by inserting eyeballs of bone and colored glass into the eye sockets, applying eyelashes and eyebrows of separately cast, fine strands

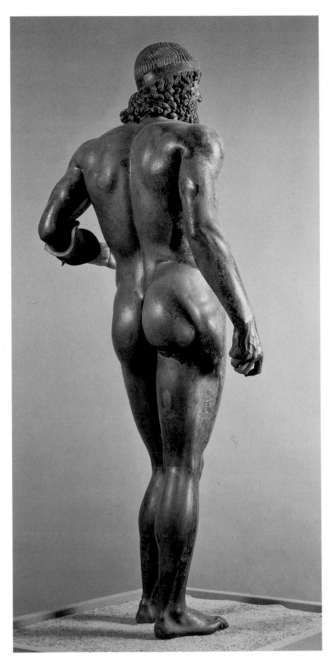

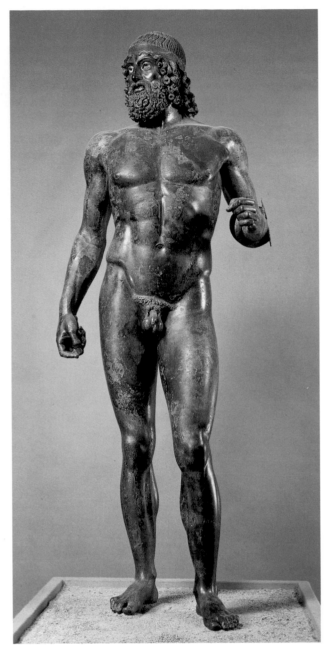

5-38. *Young Warrior*, found in the sea off Riace, Italy. c. 460–450 BCE. Bronze with bone and glass eyes, silver teeth, and copper lips and nipples, height 6'8" (2.03 m). Museo Archeològico Nazionale, Reggio Calabria, Italy

of bronze, insetting the lips and nipples with pinkish copper, and plating the teeth that show between the parted lips with silver.

The *Discus Thrower* (*Diskobolos*), reproduced at the beginning of this chapter, was created in bronze by the sculptor Myron probably about 450 BCE (see fig. 5-1). It is known today only from Roman copies in marble, but in its original form it must have been as lifelike in its details as the *Young Warrior* from Riace. Like a sports photographer, Myron caught the athlete at a critical moment, the breathless instant before the concentrated energy of his body will unwind to propel the discus into space. His muscular torso is coiled tightly into a forward arch, and his powerful throwing arm is poised at the top of his backswing. Myron earned the adulation of his contem-

poraries, and it is interesting that he was as warmly admired for a sculpture that has not survived—a bronze cow—as for the *Discus Thrower*.

Vase Painting

Vase painters continued to work with the red-figure technique throughout the fifth century BCE, refining their styles and experimenting with new compositions. Among the outstanding vase painters of the Transitional period was the prolific Pan Painter, who was inspired by the less-heroic myths of the gods to create an admirable body of red-figure works. The artist's name comes from a work involving the god Pan on one side of a bell-shaped krater that dates to about 470 BCE. The other side

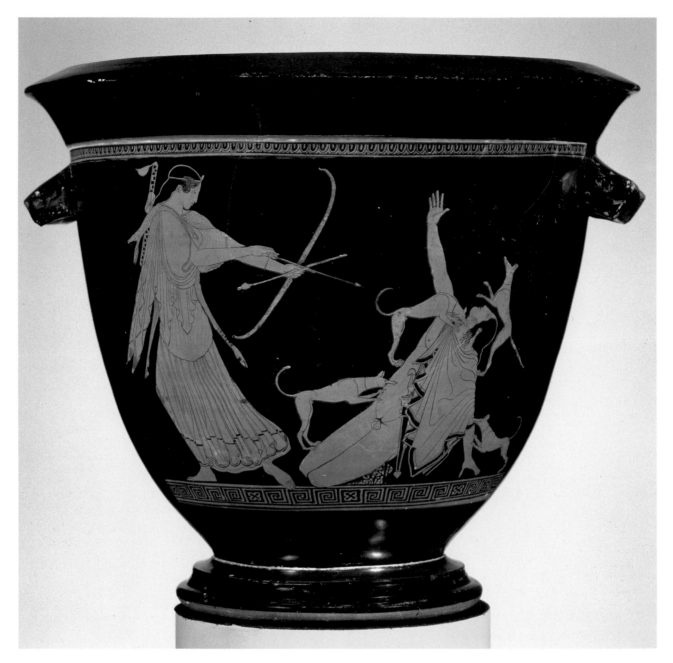

5-39. Pan Painter. *Artemis Slaying Actaeon,* red-figure decoration on a bell krater. c. 470 BCE. Ceramic, height of krater 14 5/8"
(37 cm). Museum of Fine Arts, Boston
James Fund and by Special Contribution

of this krater shows *Artemis Slaying Actaeon* (fig. 5-39). The most common version of this story is that Actaeon, while out hunting, happened upon Artemis, the goddess of the hunt, at her bath. The enraged goddess caused Actaeon's own dogs to mistake him for a stag, and they turned on him and killed him. The Pan Painter shows Artemis herself about to finish off the unlucky hunter with an arrow from her bow. The angry goddess and the fallen Actaeon each form roughly triangular shapes that conform to the flaring shape of the vessel. They are linked by the inverted triangular space between them. The scene is so dramatically rendered that one does not immediately notice the slender, graceful lines of the figures and the delicately detailed draperies that are the hallmarks of the Pan Painter's style.

THE HIGH CLASSICAL PERIOD

The High Classical period of Greek art, from about 450 to 400 BCE, corresponds roughly to an extended period of conflict between Sparta and Athens, which had emerged as the leading city-states in the Greek world in the wake of the Persian Wars. Sparta dominated the Peloponnese and much of the rest of mainland Greece. Athens dominated the Aegean and became the wealthy and influential center of a maritime empire. In a series of conflicts known as the First Peloponnesian War (461–445 BCE), the Athenians were ultimately foiled in their attempts to expand into mainland Greece. After a brief interlude of peace, war erupted once again. This new struggle, which was known as the Second Peloponnesian War (431–404 BCE), came

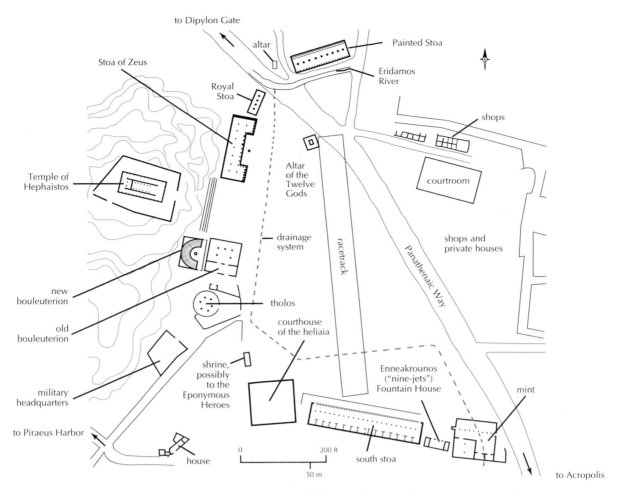

5-40. Plan of the Agora (marketplace), Athens, c. 400 BCE

to an end with the eventual defeat of Athens.

With the exception of a few brief interludes, a dynamic, charismatic leader named Perikles dominated Athenian politics and culture from 462 BCE until his death in 429 BCE. Although the comedy writers of the time sometimes mocked him, calling him "Zeus" and "the Olympian" because of his haughty, reserved personality, Athens achieved its greatest wealth and influence under his direction. He led Athens through the First Peloponnesian War and negotiated the peace that ended it. He instituted political reforms that greatly increased the scope of Athenian democracy. And he was a great patron of the arts, encouraging the use of Athenian wealth for the adornment of the city and utilizing the talents of the city's artists to promote a public image of peace, prosperity, and power. He brought new splendor to the sanctuaries of the gods who protected Athens and rebuilt much of the Acropolis, which had been laid waste by the Persians in 480 BCE. Perikles once said of his city and its accomplishments, "future generations will marvel at us, as the present age marvels at us now." It was a prophecy he himself helped fulfill.

Classical Greece is today strongly identified with Athens, and the study of Classical art has long focused on the abundance of architectural monuments that have graced that city. Athens originated as a Neolithic site on the Acropolis. As the city grew, the Acropolis was used primarily for religious rites and ceremonies, devoted mainly to the worship of the goddess Athena, the city's namesake and protector. The lower town, enclosed by a protective **ring wall**, became the residential and business center. In Athens, as in most cities of ancient Greece, commercial, civic, and social life revolved around the marketplace, or **agora**.

The Athens Agora

The Athens Agora, which has been extensively excavated and studied, was situated at the foot of the Acropolis (fig. 5-40). It began as an unadorned open square where farmers and artisans displayed their wares. Over time, various public and private structures were erected around and within its perimeter on both sides of the Panathenaic Way, a ceremonial road used during an important festival in honor of Athena. A stone drainage system was installed to prevent flooding, and a large fountain house was built to provide water for surrounding homes, administrative buildings, and shops. By 400 BCE, as figure 5-40 shows, the Agora contained several religious and administrative structures and even a small racetrack. Among the religious structures were a good-sized temple to Hephaistos, the god of the forge; an altar to the Twelve Gods (local deities not to be confused with the great gods of Mount Olympos); and a shrine that may have honored the Eponymous Heroes, the legendary ancestors of the Athenians. The Agora was home to the Athens city mint, its military headquarters, and two buildings devoted to court business. One of these was a large hall where the dikasts, who acted as both judges and jury, tried major cases. The other was a lesser court where the heliaia, a group of citizens selected by the drawing of lots, decided civil and criminal cases. Thanks to a reform by Perikles, the heliaia were paid for their services like modern jurors.

Several large stoas offered protection from the sun and rain, providing a place for strolling and talking business, politics, or philosophy. The stoa, a distinctively Greek structure found nearly everywhere people gathered, could range in appearance from a simple roof held up by columns to a substantial, sometimes architecturally impressive, building with two stories and shops along one side. The Painted Stoa, built on the north side of the Athens Agora about 460 BCE, was so called because it was decorated with paintings by the most famous artists of the time, including Polygnotos of Thasos (active c. 475–450 BCE). Nothing survives of Polygnotos's work, but his contemporaries praised him for his ability to create the illusion of spatial recession in landscapes, his ability to render female figures clothed in transparent draperies, and his skill at rendering facial expressions conveying the full range of human emotions.

While city business could be, and often was, conducted in the stoas, agora districts also came to include buildings with specific administrative functions. In the Athens Agora, the 500-member boule, or council, met in a building called the bouleuterion. This structure, built before 450 BCE, was laid out on a simple rectangular megaron plan with a vestibule and large meeting room. Near the end of the fifth century BCE, a new bouleuterion was constructed to the west of the old one. This too had a rectangular plan. The interior, however, may have had permanent tiered seating arranged in an ascending semicircle around a ground-level **podium**, or raised platform, as in the outdoor theaters of the time. Nearby was a small, round building with six columns supporting a conical roof, a type of structure known as a **tholos**. Built about 465 BCE, this tholos was the meeting place of the 50-member executive committee of the boule. The committee members dined there at the city's expense, and, rotating the responsibility among themselves, a few of them always spent the night there to be available for any pressing business that might arise.

Some private houses could also be found in the Agora at this time. Compared with the often grand public buildings, houses in Classical Athens were rarely more than simple rectangular structures of **stucco**-faced mud brick with wooden posts and lintels supporting roofs of terra-cotta tiles. Rooms were small and few, consisting mainly of a kitchen, a dayroom in which women could sew, weave, and do other chores, a dining room with couches for reclining around a small table, a bedroom or two, and occasionally an indoor bathroom. Where space was not at a premium, houses sometimes opened onto small courtyards or porches.

The Acropolis

After Persian troops destroyed the Acropolis in 480 BCE, the Athenians initially vowed to keep it in ruins as a memorial. Perikles convinced them otherwise and set about rebuilding it to a new magnificence. One reason for this project was to honor the gods, especially Athena, who had helped the Greeks defeat the Persians. But Perikles also hoped to create a visual expression of Athenian values and civic pride that would glorify his city and bolster its status as the capital of the empire he was instrumental in building. He placed his close friend Pheidias, a renowned sculptor, in charge of the rebuilding and assembled under him the most talented artists and artisans in Athens and its surrounding countryside.

The cost and labor involved in this undertaking were staggering. Quantities of gold, ivory, and exotic woods had to be imported. Some 22,000 tons of marble had to be transported 10 miles from mountain quarries to city workshops. Perikles was severely criticized by his political opponents for this extravagance, but it never cost him popular support. In fact, many working-class Athenians—laborers, carpenters, masons, sculptors, and the merchants and carters who kept them supplied and fed—benefited from his expenditures.

Work on the Acropolis continued after Perikles' death and was completed by the end of the fifth century BCE (fig. 5-41). Visitors to the Acropolis in 400 BCE would have climbed a steep ramp on the west side of the hill to the sanctuary entrance, perhaps pausing to admire the small, marble temple dedicated to Athena Nike (Athena as the goddess of victory in war), poised on a projection of rock above the ramp. Turning left, they would have passed through the center of an impressive porticoed gatehouse called the Propylaia. (The Greeks called the gate to a religious precinct a **propylon**, meaning "outer gateway"; for gateways and vestibules opening to large enclosed spaces, they used the plural, propylaia.) Upon emerging from the gatehouse, they would have confronted a huge bronze figure of Athena Promachos (the Defender). This statue, designed and executed by Pheidias between about 465 and 455 BCE, showed the goddess in a helmet and bearing a spear. So tall was it that sailors entering Athens's port of Piraeus, about 10 miles away, could see the sun reflected off the helmet and spear tip. Behind this statue was a walled precinct that enclosed the Erechtheion, a temple dedicated to several deities. Visitors would have been able to see the upper part of this temple above the precinct wall.

To the left they would have seen several other small religious structures. Immediately to their right was a large stoa with projecting wings dedicated to Artemis Brauronia (the protector of wild animals). Beyond this stoa on the right stood the largest building on the Acropolis, looming above the precinct wall that enclosed it. This was the Parthenon, a temple dedicated to Athena Parthenos (the Virgin Athena). Walking along the main path, visitors would have come to the propylon to the Parthenon precinct. Passing through, they would have viewed the temple from its northwest corner. Ahead of

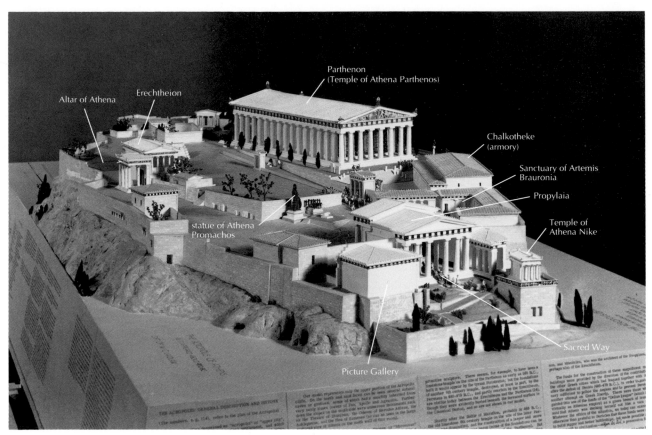

5-41. Model of the Acropolis, Athens, c. 400 BCE. Royal Ontario Museum, Toronto

them, to the right of the Parthenon, was the Chalkotheke, or armory. The cella of the Parthenon faced east. To reach it, the visitors would have had to walk along the north side of the temple past an outdoor altar to Athena, where priests and worshipers made offerings to the goddess. With permission from the priests, they would have climbed the east steps of the Parthenon to look into the cella and see a colossal gold and ivory statue of Athena, created by Pheidias and installed in the temple in 432 BCE.

Although a few small structures were added in the Hellenistic and Roman periods, the Acropolis changed little after 400 BCE. In the third century CE, it fell into disuse and disrepair. Later, the Erechtheion became first a Christian church, then a Turkish harem. The Parthenon, once the sacred home of Athena, also became a Christian church and later served as a mosque. In 1687 it was used by Ottoman soldiers to store gunpowder during a war between the Ottoman Empire and the Venetian Republic. A shell struck it and the gunpowder exploded, destroying the cella and the roof and toppling many columns. The Acropolis then lay in ruins until restoration projects were undertaken there in the nineteenth and twentieth centuries. Thanks to these restorations, modern visitors can again experience some of the splendor of the Athenian sanctuary to the gods and appreciate the great pride the people of ancient Athens took in it. Unfortunately, a dramatic rise in air pollution since the 1960s presents a new threat to the monuments and a new challenge to the conservators who are dedicated to preserving them.

The Parthenon. Sometime around 490 BCE the Athenians began work on a new temple to Athena Parthenos that was still unfinished when the Persians sacked the Acropolis a decade later. Kimon of Athens then hired the architect Kallikrates to begin rebuilding on the old site. Work was halted briefly and resumed by Perikles, who then commissioned the architect Iktinos to redesign a larger temple utilizing the existing foundation and stone elements already in place. No expense was spared on this elegant new palace for Athena. The finest white marble was used throughout, even on the roof, in place of the more usual terra-cotta tiles.

The planning and execution of the Parthenon required extraordinary mathematical and mechanical skills and would have been impossible without a large contingent of distinguished architects and builders, as well as talented sculptors and painters. The result is thus as much a testament to the administrative skills as to the artistic vision of Pheidias, who supervised the entire project. The building was completed in 438 BCE, and its sculptural decoration, designed by Pheidias and executed by himself and other sculptors in his workshop, was completed in 432 BCE (fig. 5-42).

The exterior form of the Parthenon is that of a typical Doric order peripteral temple on a three-step platform. The peristyle consists of forty-six columns, eight as viewed from each end and seventeen as viewed from the sides. The Parthenon's architects made many subtle adjustments in the lines of the structure and the placement of columns to refine the design and possibly to counter-

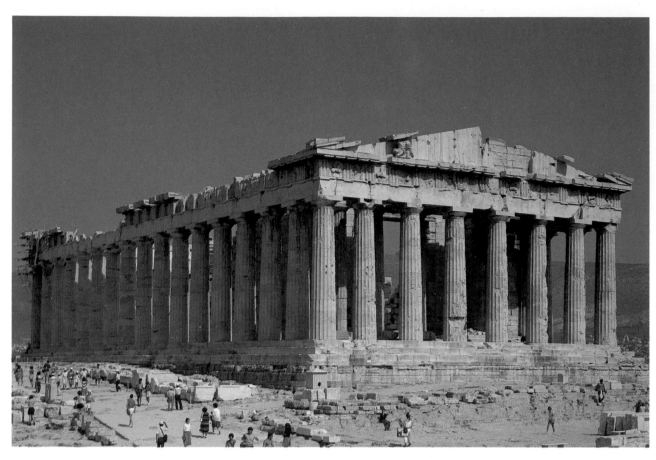

5-42. Kallikrates and Iktinos. Parthenon, Acropolis, Athens. 447–438 BCE. View from the northwest

act the effects of various optical illusions that would otherwise seem to distort its appearance when it was viewed from a distance. Long horizontal lines, for example, usually appear to sag in the center, but they do not here because the architects made both the base of the temple and the entablature curve upward slightly toward the center. In other refinements, the columns have a subtle swelling, or entasis, and tilt inward slightly from bottom to top, and the space between columns is less at the corners than elsewhere. These gentle curves and shifts in the arrangement of elements give the Parthenon a buoyant, organic appearance and prevent it from looking like a heavy, lifeless stone box. It is, in effect, a gigantic marble sculpture.

The extensive decoration of the Parthenon strongly reflects Pheidias's unifying vision despite being the product of many individuals. A coherent, stylistic whole, the sculptural decoration conveys a number of political and ideological themes: the triumph of the democratic Greek city-states over Persia's imperial forces, the preeminence of Athens thanks to the favor of Athena, and the triumph of an enlightened Greek civilization over despotism and barbarism.

Like the pediments of most temples, including the Temple of Aphaia at Aegina (see fig. 5-18), those of the Parthenon were filled with **sculpture in the round** set on the deep shelves of the cornice and secured to the wall with metal pins. Unfortunately, much of the Parthenon's pedimental sculpture has been damaged or lost over the

centuries. Using the locations of the pinholes, scholars nevertheless have been able to determine the placement of surviving statues and infer the poses of missing ones. The west pediment sculpture, facing the entrance to the Acropolis, illustrated the contest that Athena won over the sea god Poseidon for rule over the Athenians. The east pediment figures, above the entrance to the cella, illustrated the birth of Athena, fully grown and clad in armor, from the brow of her father, Zeus. The missing central element was probably Zeus seated on a throne with the just-born adult Athena standing at his side.

The statues from the east pediment are the best preserved of the two groups (fig. 5-43). Flanking the central figures were groups of three goddesses followed by single reclining male figures. In the left corner was the sun god Apollo in his chariot and in the right corner was the moon goddess Selene in hers. The reclining male nude on the left has been variously identified as Herakles, Ares, or Dionysos. His easy pose conforms to the slope of the pediment without a hint of awkwardness. The standing female figure just to the left of center is Iris, messenger of the gods, already spreading the news of Athena's birth. The three female figures on the right side (fig. 5-44), two sitting upright and one reclining, were once thought to be the Three Fates, whom the Greeks believed appeared at the birth of a child and determined its destiny. Most art historians now think that they are goddesses, perhaps Hestia (a sister of Zeus and the goddess of the hearth), Aphrodite, and her mother, Dione

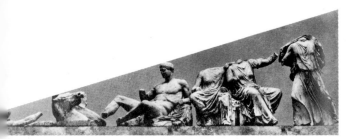

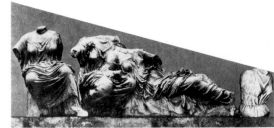

Apollo and horses   Dionysos   Persephone   Demeter   Iris
of his chariot team

Hestia (?)   Dione   Aphrodite   Selene and one horse
of her chariot team

5-43. Photographic mock-up of the east pediment of the Parthenon (using photographs of the extant marble sculpture c. 438–432 BCE). The missing sculpture in the center equals in amount what is seen here.

At the beginning of the nineteenth century, Thomas Bruce, the British earl of Elgin and ambassador to Constantinople, acquired much of the surviving sculpture from the Parthenon, which was being used for military purposes. He shipped it back to London in 1801 to decorate a lavish mansion for himself and his wife. By the time he returned to England a few years later, his wife had left him and the ancient treasures were at the center of a financial dispute. Finally, he sold the sculpture for a very low price. Referred to as the *Elgin Marbles,* most of the sculpture is now in the British Museum, including all the elements seen here except the torso of *Selene,* which is in the Acropolis Museum, Athens. The Greek government has tried unsuccessfully in recent times to have the *Elgin Marbles* returned.

(one of Zeus's many consorts). These monumental interlocked figures seem to be awakening from a deep sleep, slowly rousing from languor to mental alertness. The sculptor, whether Pheidias or someone working in the Pheidian style, expertly rendered the female form beneath the fall of draperies. The clinging fabric both covers and reveals, creating circular patterns rippling with a life of their own over torsos, breasts, and knees and uniting the three figures into a single mass.

The Doric frieze on the exterior of the Parthenon was decorated with ninety-two metope reliefs, fourteen on each end and thirty-two along each side. These reliefs, which took only six years to complete, depicted legendary battles, symbolized by combat between two representative figures: a Lapith against a centaur; a god against a Giant; a Greek against a Trojan; or a Greek against an Amazon, a member of the mythical tribe of female warriors sometimes said to be the daughters of the war god Ares.

Among the best-preserved metope reliefs are those from the south side, including several depicting the battle between the Lapiths and the centaurs. The small panel shown here (fig. 5-45)—with its choice of a perfect moment of pause within a fluid action, its reduction of forms to their most characteristic essentials, and its choice of a single, timeless image to stand for an entire historical episode—captures the essence of High Classical art. So dramatic is the **X**-shaped composition that we easily accept its visual contradictions. Like the *Discus Thrower* (see fig. 5-1), the Lapith is caught at an instant of total equilibrium. What should be a grueling tug-of-war between a man and a man-beast appears instead as an athletic ballet choreographed to show off the Lapith warrior's muscles and graceful movements against the implausible backdrop of his carefully draped cloak. As noted earlier (see fig. 5-34), the legend of the Lapiths and centaurs may have symbolized the triumph of reason over animal passion.

Enclosed within the Parthenon's Doric order peristyle, the body of the temple consists of a cella, opening to the east, and an unconnected auxiliary space opening

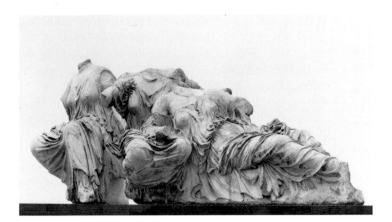

5-44. *Three Seated Goddesses* (possibly Hestia, Dione, and Aphrodite), from the east pediment of the Parthenon. Marble, over-lifesize. The British Museum, London

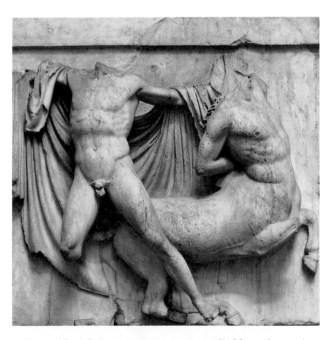

5-45. *Lapith Fighting a Centaur,* metope relief from the Doric frieze on the south side of the Parthenon. c. 440 BCE. Marble, height 56" (1.42 m). The British Museum, London

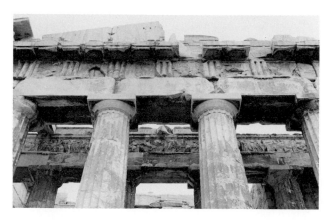

5-46. View of the outer Doric and inner Ionic friezes at the west end of the Parthenon

to the west. Short colonnades in front of each entrance support an entablature with an Ionic order frieze in relief that extends along both sides of the temples, for a total frieze length of 525 feet (fig. 5-46). The subject of this frieze is a procession almost certainly celebrating the festival of the Great Panathenaia, which took place in Athens every four years. In this ceremony, the women of the city carried a new wool peplos to the Acropolis sanctuary to clothe an ancient wooden cult statue of Athena housed there. Although the shrine housing the statue was partly ruined by the Persians in 480 BCE, the statue apparently remained there until it was moved to a new shrine to Athena in the Erechtheion about 405 BCE. The Panathenaic procession began just outside the city walls in the Kerameikos quarter, where the pottery-makers' workshops were located. People assembled there in a cemetery among the grave monuments of their ancestors. They then marched into the city through the Dipylon Gate, across the busy Agora along the Panathenaic Way, and up the ramp to the Acropolis. From the Propylaia, they moved onto the Sacred Way and completed their journey at Athena's altar.

The figures in Pheidias's portrayal of this major ceremony—skilled riders managing powerful steeds, for example (fig. 5-47), or graceful but physically sturdy young walkers (fig. 5-48)—seem to be representative types, ideal inhabitants of a successful city-state. The underlying message of the frieze as a whole is that the Athenians are a healthy, vigorous people, enjoying individual rights but united in a democratic civic body looked upon with favor by the gods. The people were inseparable from and symbolic of the city itself. Despite its patriotic intent, the frieze probably drew wrath from Athenians who felt that it was disrespectful of the gods to decorate a religious building with scenes of contemporary human activity rather than mythological figures. Pheidias was supposedly accused of even depicting himself and Perikles among the figures in the procession, but no one in modern times has been able to identify what might be their portraits.

As with the metope relief of the *Lapith Fighting a Centaur* (see fig. 5-45) viewers of the processional frieze easily accept its disproportions, spatial incongruities, and such implausible compositional features as all the animal and human figures standing on the same groundline, and upright men and women being as tall as rearing horses. Carefully planned rhythmic variations—changes in the speed of the participants in the procession as it winds around the walls—contribute to the effectiveness of the frieze: horses plunge ahead at full gallop; women proceed with a slow, stately step, parade marshals pause to look back at the progress of those behind them; and human-looking deities rest on conveniently placed benches as they await the arrival of the marchers. In executing the frieze, the sculptors took into account the spectators' low viewpoint and the dim lighting inside the peristyle. They carved the top of the frieze band in higher relief than the lower part, thus tilting the figures out to catch the reflected light from the pavement and permit a clearer reading of the action. The subtleties in the sculpture may not have been as evident to Athenians in the fifth century BCE as they are now, because the frieze, seen at the top of a high wall and between columns, was originally completely painted. The background was dark blue and the figures were in contrasting red and ocher, accented with glittering gold and real metal details such as bronze bridles and bits on the horses.

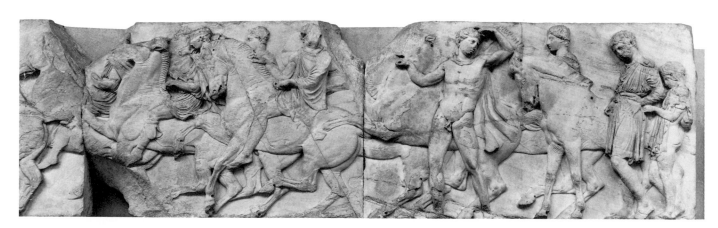

5-47. *Horsemen,* detail of the *Procession,* from the Ionic frieze on the north side of the Parthenon. c. 438–432 BCE. Marble, height 41¾" (106 cm). The British Museum, London

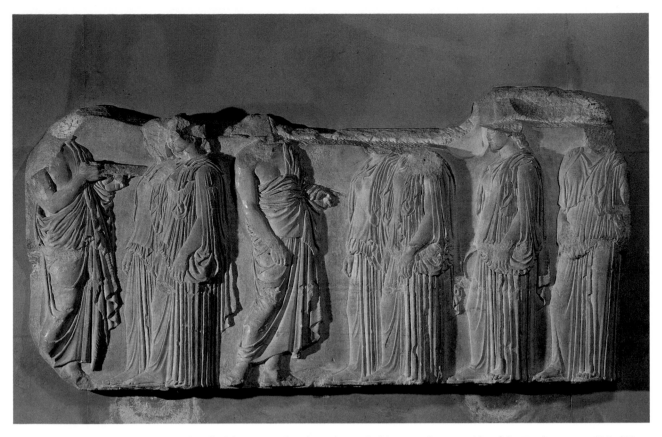

5-48. *Marshals and Young Women,* detail of the *Procession,* from the Ionic frieze on the east side of the Parthenon. c. 438–432 BCE. Marble, height 43" (109 cm). Musée du Louvre, Paris

The Propylaia and the Erechtheion. Upon completion of the Parthenon, Perikles commissioned an architect named Mnesikles to design the Propylaia (fig. 5-49). Work began on it in 437 and stopped in 432 BCE, with the structure still incomplete. Visitors approaching the gateway from either the city or the sanctuary side saw a Doric facade. Inside the central passageway, they walked along a ramp between rows of tall, slender, Ionic columns. These columns, which supported a raised roof, were placed far enough apart to allow wheeled vehicles to pass between them. The Propylaia had no sculptural decoration, but its north wing was the earliest known museum, a gallery built specifically to house a collection of paintings for public view. The unfinished right wing became a passageway to the Temple of Athena Nike.

The Erechtheion, also designed by Mnesikles, was the second-largest structure erected on the Acropolis under Perikles' building program (fig. 5-50). Work began on it in the 430s and ended in 405 BCE, just before the fall of Athens to Sparta. Its asymmetrical plan and several levels reflect its multiple functions in housing many different shrines, as well as the sharply sloping terrain on which it was located. The mythical contest between the sea god Poseidon and Athena for patronage over Athens was said to have occurred within the Erechtheion precinct. During this contest, Poseidon struck a rock with his trident (three-pronged harpoon), bringing forth a spout of water. This sacred rock, believed to bear the marks of the trident, was enclosed in the Erechtheion's

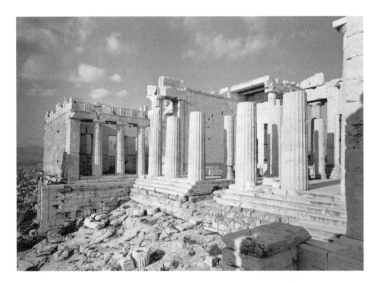

5-49. Mnesikles. Propylaia, Acropolis, Athens. 437–432 BCE. View from the southeast, facing the Picture Gallery

north porch. Another shrine housed a sacred spring dedicated to Erechtheus, a legendary king of Athens, during whose reign the goddess Demeter was said to have instructed the Athenians in the agricultural arts. The Erechtheion also contained a memorial to the legendary founder of Athens, Kekrops, half man and half serpent, who acted as the judge in the contest between Athena and Poseidon. And it housed a new shrine for the wooden cult statue of Athena that was the center of the Panathenaic festival.

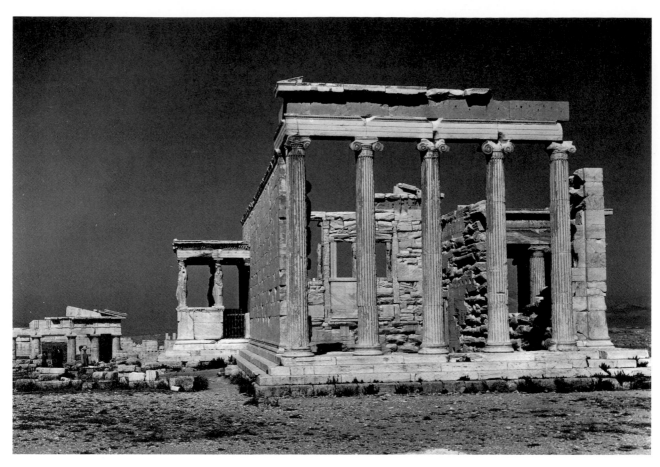

5-50. Mnesikles. Erechtheion, Acropolis, Athens. 430s–405 BCE. View from the east

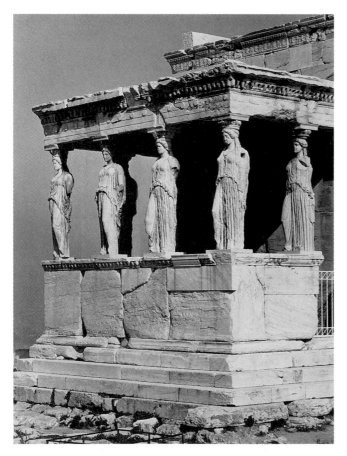

5-51. Porch of the Maidens (Caryatid Porch), Erechtheion, Acropolis, Athens. 421–405 BCE

The Erechtheion was entered from porches on the north, east, and south sides. The most famous of these is the Porch of the Maidens (fig. 5-51), on the south side facing the Parthenon. Raised on a high base, its six stately caryatids with simple Doric capitals support an Ionic entablature made up of bands of carved molding. In a pose characteristic of Classical figures, each caryatid's weight is supported on one engaged leg, while the free leg, bent at the knee, rests on the ball of the foot. Viewed from straight on, the three caryatids on the left have their right legs engaged, and the three on the right have their left legs engaged, creating a sense of symmetry and rhythm. The vertical fall of the drapery on the engaged side resembles the fluting of a column shaft and provides a sense of stability, whereas the bent leg gives an impression of relaxed grace and effortless support. The hair of each caryatid falls in a loose but massive knot around its neck, a device that strengthens the weakest point in the sculpture while appearing entirely natural.

The Temple of Athena Nike. The Temple of Athena Nike (Athena as the goddess of victory in war), located south of the Propylaia (fig. 5-52), was designed and built about 425 BCE, probably by Kallikrates. It is an Ionic order temple built on an **amphiprostyle** plan, that is, with a porch at each end (see "Elements of Architecture," page 164). The porch facing out over the city is **blind**, with no entrance to the cella. Reduced to rubble during the Turkish occupation of Greece in the seventeenth century, the

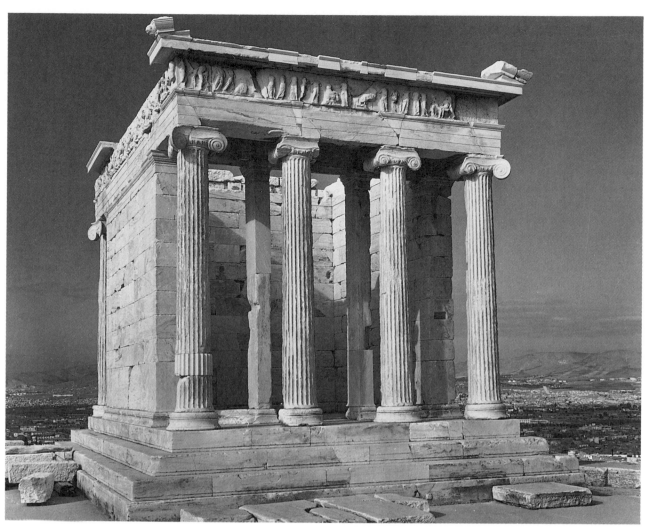

5-52. Kallikrates. Temple of Athena Nike, Acropolis, Athens. c. 425 BCE

temple has since been rebuilt. Its diminutive size, about 27 by 19 feet, and refined Ionic decoration are in marked contrast to the massive Doric Propylaia adjacent to it. Between 410 and 407 BCE, the temple was surrounded by a parapet, or low wall, faced with narrative relief panels depicting Athena presiding over her winged attendants, called Victories, as they prepared for a victory celebration. The parapet no longer exists, but some of the panels from it have survived. One of the most admired is of *Nike (Victory) Adjusting Her Sandal* (fig. 5-53). The figure bends forward gracefully, causing her ample chiton to slip off one shoulder. Her large wings, one open and one closed, effectively balance this unstable pose. Unlike the decorative swirls of heavy fabric covering the Parthenon goddesses or the weighty pleats of the robes of the Erechtheion caryatids, the textile covering this *Nike* appears delicate and light, clinging to her body like wet silk.

Sculpture and *The Canon* of Polykleitos

Just as Greek architects defined and followed a set of standards for ideal temple design, Greek sculptors sought an ideal of human beauty. Studying human appearances closely, the sculptors of the High Classical period selected those attributes they considered the most desirable, such as regular facial features, smooth skin, and particular body proportions, and combined them into a single ideal of physical perfection. This quest for the ideal can be seen also in the philosophy of Socrates (c. 470–399 BCE) and his disciple Plato (c. 429–347 BCE), both of whom argued that all objects in the physical world were reflections of ideal forms that could be discovered through reason.

The best-known art theorist of the Classical period was the sculptor Polykleitos of Argos. About 450 BCE he developed a set of rules for constructing the ideal human figure, which he set down in a treatise called *The Canon* (*kanon* is Greek for "measure," "rule," or "law"). To illustrate his theory, Polykleitos created a larger-than-lifesize bronze statue, the *Spear Bearer* (*Doryphoros*). Neither the treatise nor the original statue has survived, but both were widely discussed in the writings of his contemporaries, and later Roman artists made copies in stone of the *Spear Bearer*. By studying the most exact of these copies, or **replicas**, scholars have tried to determine the set of measurements that defined the ideal of human proportions in Polykleitos's canon, which must have

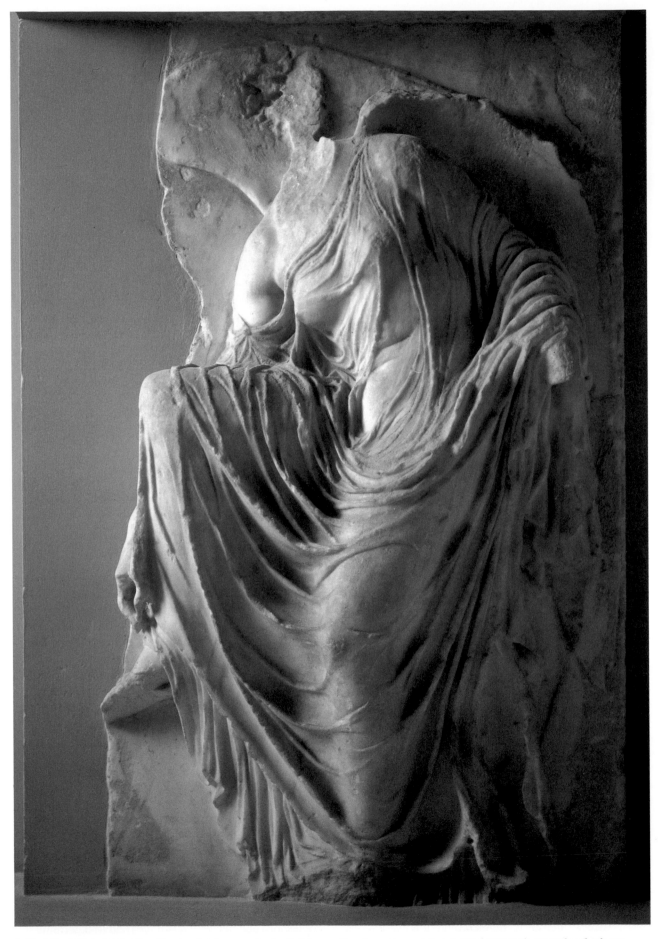

5-53. *Nike (Victory) Adjusting Her Sandal,* fragment of relief decoration from the parapet (now destroyed), Temple of Athena Nike, Acropolis, Athens. 410–407 BCE. Marble, height 42" (107 cm). Acropolis Museum, Athens

nition of the beautiful as it applied to the human figure, making it possible to replicate human perfection in the tangible form of sculpture.

The marble replica of the *Spear Bearer* illustrated here (fig. 5-54) shows a male athlete, perfectly balanced with the whole weight of the upper body supported over the straight (engaged) right leg. The left leg is bent at the knee, with the left foot poised on the ball with the heel raised high—an unnatural pose for anyone to try to maintain. The pattern of tension and relaxation is reversed in the arrangement of the arms, with the right relaxed on the engaged side and the left bent to support the weight of the (missing) spear. This dynamically balanced body pose—characteristic of High Classical standing figure sculpture—differs to some degree from that of the *Kritios Boy* (see fig. 5-36) of a generation earlier. The tilt of the hipline in the *Spear Bearer* is a little more pronounced to accommodate the raising of the left foot onto its ball, and the head is turned toward the same side as the engaged leg. A comparison of the *Spear Bearer* to the *Young Warrior* from Riace (see fig. 5-38) is also informative. The treatment of the torso and groin is quite similar in both, and their poses are nearly identical, except for the slightly different positions of the unengaged left legs and the fact that the heel of the *Spear Bearer* is raised. The *Young Warrior* seems to stand still in alert relaxation. The *Spear Bearer* appears to have paused for a moment in perfect equilibrium, ready to step forward instantly.

Stela Sculpture

Individual panels, or **stelae**, decorated in relief were extremely popular among the Greeks for memorials, votive offerings, and tomb monuments. Stela sculpture was affected by the same general trends as figural sculpture, but it also frequently showed more compositional variety and freedom. A relief panel depicting *Demeter, Persephone, and Triptolemos,* dating about 440 BCE, was found in the ruins of the Sanctuary of Demeter and Persephone at Eleusis, near Athens (fig. 5-55). The sanctuary was said to be located on the very spot where Persephone was picking flowers when Hades kidnapped her and took her to the underworld. The king of Eleusis extended his hospitality to Persephone's grieving mother, Demeter, the goddess of grain, as she searched for her lost daughter. In return for this kindness, Demeter gave his people the gift of grain and instructed them in farming.

The stela shows Demeter on the left and Persephone on the right. Triptolemos, the husky youth standing between them, is sometimes identified as Demeter's son but more often as a pupil chosen by the goddesses to help spread the knowledge of agriculture among the Greeks. The subject of the relief seems to be the initiation of the boy by Demeter, who holds up a sheaf of grain and presents him with what appears to be a bag of seeds while Persephone places her hand over his head in blessing. The robust, heavily draped bodies of the women bear a resemblance to the Pheidian treatment of women on the Parthenon, whereas their young initiate brings to mind the earlier *Kritios Boy* (see fig. 5-36). The sculptor

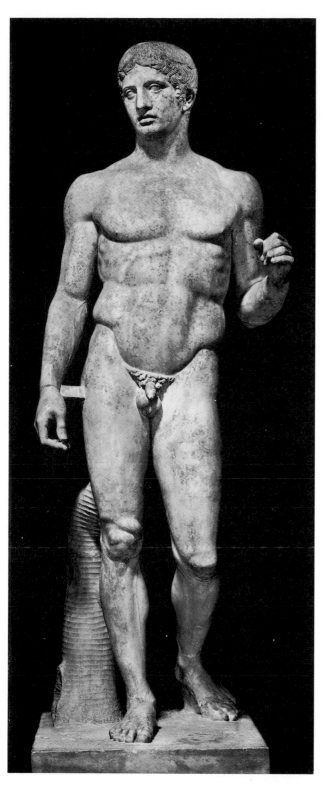

5-54. Polykleitos. *Spear Bearer* (*Doryphoros*), Roman copy after the original bronze of c. 450–440 BCE. Marble, height 6'6" (2 m); tree trunk and brace strut are Roman additions. Museo Archeològico Nazionale, Naples, Italy

been based on the ratios between some basic unit to the length of various body parts. Some studies suggest that his basic unit may have been the length of the figure's index finger or the width of its hand across the knuckles; others suggest that it was the height of the head from chin to hairline. To Polykleitos, the beautiful was synonymous with the good. He sought a mathematical defi-

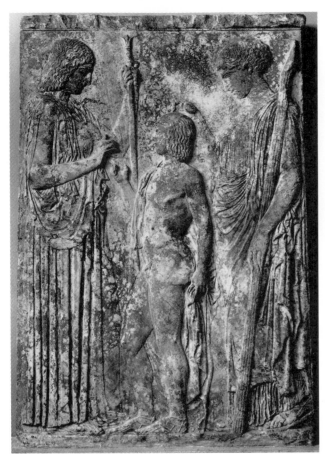

5-55. *Demeter, Persephone, and Triptolemos,* stela from Eleusis. c. 440 BCE. Marble, height 7'2³⁄₈" (2.19 m). National Archeological Museum, Athens

An extremely influential and mysterious cult developed around Demeter and Persephone, comparable to that of Isis and Osiris in Egypt. Unlike most sanctuaries, the Sanctuary of Demeter and Persephone at Eleusis was under the private control of two aristocratic families and closed to all but initiated worshipers. Cult members were forbidden on pain of death to describe what happened inside the walls, and any outsider found trying to enter illegally would have been killed. None of the cult's activities—the Mysteries of Eleusis—was ever revealed, but they probably involved a ritual reenactment of Persephone's abduction and descent into the underworld and her return to earth.

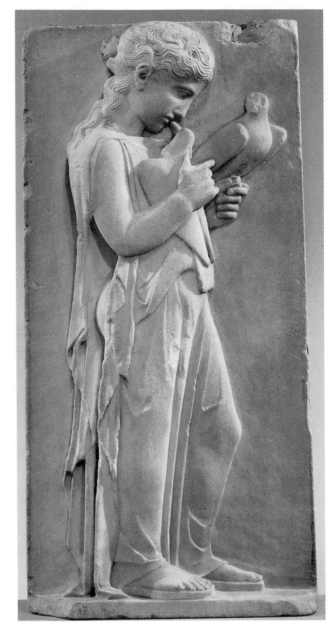

5-56. *Little Girl with Birds,* grave stela from Paros. c. 450–440 BCE. Marble, height 31½" (80 cm). The Metropolitan Museum of Art, New York
Fletcher Fund (1927.27.45)

has rendered the figures freely and naturally, rather than according to a strict canon, conveying not only the narrative elements of this symbolic event but also a sense of the warm maternal relationships among mother, daughter, and son-protégé.

The Greeks used stelae decorated with reliefs and inscriptions to mark graves, much as tombstones are used today. Although such markers were banned in Athenian cemeteries from about 510 to 430 BCE, no such restriction applied in other regions, where they remained popular. Children, as well as adults, were memorialized on these stones. Intimate, personalized scenes like that of the *Little Girl with Birds* were typical of High Classical grave stela decoration (fig. 5-56). Dating about 450–440 BCE, this stela was found on the Aegean island of Paros

and is made of fine white Parian marble. Its top is missing, but it probably once had a decorative **finial,** or crowning ornament.

The realistic treatment of the child's body and her idealized facial features suggest that the sculptor was familiar with stylistic developments in Athens, but the simple, dignified treatment of drapery, the stylized hairdo, and the subtle yet simple way in which the "story" or meaning of the relief is conveyed bring it closer in approach and feeling to the metope reliefs on the Temple of Zeus at Olympia (see fig. 5-35). The little girl is dressed as a miniature adult in the same type of peplos that her mother would have worn, and her hair is carefully arranged in waves and curls with a knot at the back of her head. Her chubby arms and the way she kisses one of her pet doves are purely childlike, however, and like a child, she seems unconcerned for her clothing. The peplos, a bit too long for her, pulls down at the center as though she were standing on its hem, and the claws of the doves have caught and pulled up the top. Traces of pigment indicate that the work was enhanced with some painted details.

Vase Painting

Although red-figure vase painting continued throughout the Classical period, a new style of **white-ground** decoration grew in popularity. White backgrounds had been applied on black-figure vases as early as the seventh century BCE (see fig. 5-9), but the white-ground techniques of the High Classical period were far more complex than those earlier efforts (see "Greek Painted Vases," page 162). Artists used either a black-figure or a red-figure technique to register basic design elements on a white background. They also began to enhance the fired vessel with a full range of colors using **tempera** paint, an opaque, water-based medium mixed with glue or egg white. This fragile decoration deteriorated easily but can still be seen on many vases. White-figure painting must have echoed the style of contemporary paintings on walls and panels, but no examples of those have survived for comparison.

White-ground vases were used in particular as devotional or commemorative pieces in the fifth century BCE. The tall, slender, one-handled **lekythos**, used to pour liquids during religious rituals, was the most common choice for these works. Funerary lekythoi have been found both in and on tombs. Some convey grief and loss with a scene of a departing figure bidding farewell, others with a picture of a grave stela draped with garlands. More common are scenes of the dead person in the prime of life, engaged in a seemingly everyday activity that on close scrutiny is imbued with signs of separation and loss.

A white-ground lekythos decorated about 450–440 BCE in the style of the Achilles Painter (an anonymous artist whose style is known from another vase depicting the hero Achilles) shows a young servant girl offering a small chest of valuables to a well-dressed woman of regal bearing, the dead person whom the vessel memorializes (fig. 5-57). The scene contains no overt signs of grief, but a quiet sadness pervades it. The two figures are separated by the white, central void of the vessel, and their glances just fail to meet. The woman does not actively reach to accept her jewels. Instead, she barely extends her arm, and the palm of her hand turns toward her body.

CLASSICAL ART OF THE FOURTH CENTURY

After the Spartans defeated Athens in 404 BCE, they set up a pro-Spartan government led by the tyrant Kritias. This government was so oppressive that within a year the Athenians rebelled against it, killed Kritias, and restored democracy. Athens recovered its independence and its economy

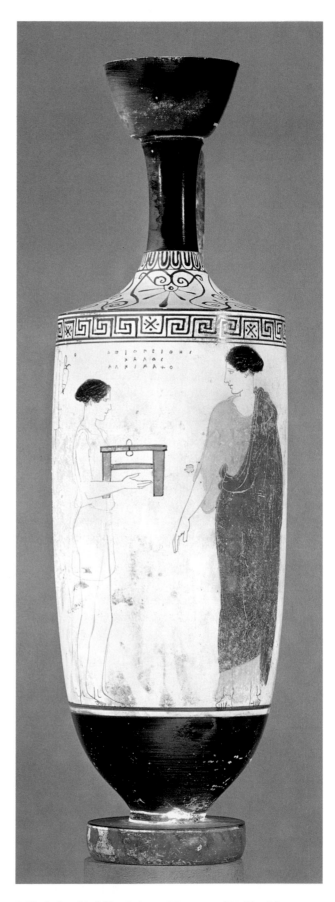

5-57. Style of Achilles Painter. *Woman and Maid*, white-ground and black-figure decoration on a lekythos, with additional painting in tempera. c. 450–440 BCE. Ceramic, height 15⅛" (38.4 cm). Museum of Fine Arts, Boston
Francis Bartlett Fund

revived, but it never regained its dominant political and military status. Sparta failed to establish a lasting pre-eminence over the rest of Greece, and the city-states again began to struggle among themselves. Although Athens had lost its empire, it retained its reputation as a center of artistic and intellectual accomplishment. In 387 BCE the great philosopher-teacher Plato founded a school just outside Athens, as did Plato's student Aristotle later.

Among Aristotle's students was young Alexander of Macedon, whose father, Philip II, established Macedonian dominance over the Greek city-states in 338 BCE. When Philip was assassinated two years later, his throne and empire passed to Alexander, known to history as Alexander the Great. This able young leader, just entering his twenties, quelled the still-rebellious Greek city-states, then rallied them behind him for a war of revenge and conquest that carried him to Egypt, where the priests of Amun greeted him as a god, and as far east as India, where his weary troops finally balked at further campaigning. His dreams of endless conquest frustrated, Alexander began retracing his path homeward but died of a fever in Babylon in 323 BCE, at the age of thirty-three. Art historians mark the end of the Classical period in Greek art with his death and the subsequent breakup of his vast new empire.

The work of Greek artists during the fourth century BCE exhibits a high level of creativity and technical accomplishment. Changing political conditions never seriously dampened the Greek creative spirit. Indeed, the artists of the second half of the century in particular experimented widely with new subjects and styles. Although they observed the basic Classical approach to composition and form, they no longer adhered rigidly to its conventions. Their innovations were supported by a sophisticated and diverse new group of patrons, including the Macedonian courts of Philip and Alexander, wealthy aristocrats in Asia Minor, and foreign rulers anxious to import Greek wares and sometimes Greek artists.

Architecture and Architectural Sculpture

Despite the instability of the fourth century BCE, Greek cities undertook innovative architectural projects. Architects developed variations on the Classical ideal in urban planning, temple design, and the design of two increasingly popular structures, the tholos and the monumental tomb. In contrast to the previous century, much of this activity took place outside of Athens and even in areas outside of mainland Greece, notably in Asia Minor.

The Orthogonal City Plan. In older Greek cities such as Athens, which grew up on the site of an ancient **citadel**, buildings and streets developed irregularly according to the needs of their inhabitants and the requirements of the terrain. As early as the eighth century BCE, however, builders in some western Greek settlements began to implement a rigid, mathematical concept of urban development based on the **orthogonal** (right-angled) **plan**. New cities or razed sections in old cities

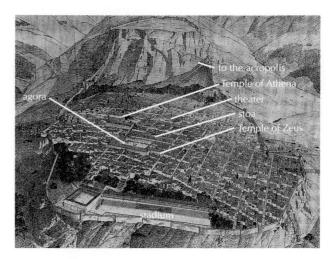

5-58. Plan and detail of the city of Priene, western Turkey. 4th century BCE

were laid out on straight, evenly spaced parallel streets that intersected at right angles to create rectangular blocks. These blocks, or plats, were then subdivided into identical building plots. The orthogonal plan probably originated in Egypt, where it was used early in the second millennium BCE at such sites as el-Lahun, a city built by Senwosret II in Upper Egypt about 1895–1878 BCE (see fig. 3-19).

During the High Classical period, Greek architects promoted the orthogonal system as an ideal for city planning. Hippodamos of Miletos, a major urban planner of the fifth century BCE, had views on the city philosophically akin to those of Socrates and aesthetically akin to those of Polykleitos; all three believed that humans could arrive at a model of perfection through reason. According to Hippodamos, who seems to have been more concerned with abstract principles of order than with the human individual, the ideal city should be divided into three zones—sacred, public, and private—and limited to 10,000 citizens divided into three classes—artists, farmers, and soldiers. The basic Hippodamian plat was a square 600 feet on each side, divided into quarters. Each quarter was subdivided into six rectangular building plots measuring 100 by 150 feet on a side, a scheme widely used in Western cities and suburbs today.

Many Greek cities with orthogonal plans were laid out on relatively flat land that posed few obstacles to regularity. Miletos, in Asia Minor, for example, was redesigned by Hippodamos after its partial destruction by the Persians. Later the orthogonal plan was applied on less-hospitable terrain, such as that of Priene, which lies across the plain from Miletos on a rugged hillside. Priene, which originated about 1000 BCE, was rebuilt on a variation of the Hippodamian plan in the mid-fourth century BCE (fig. 5-58). The terrain of the city sloped steeply toward a rocky acropolis. As a result, the broad avenues crossing the slope were on a fairly level grade, but the narrower intersecting streets had to be stepped like stairs in places to make them passable and maintain the orthogonal pattern. Public buildings lay near the

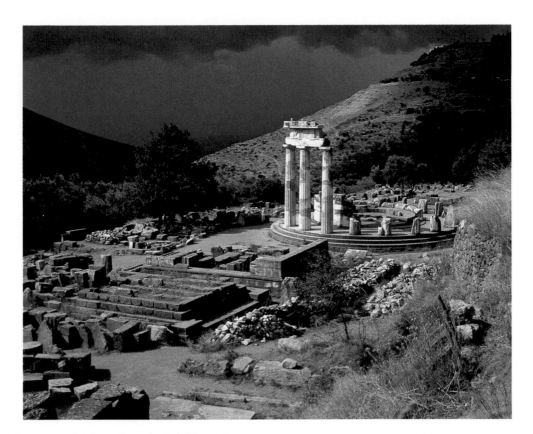

5-59. Tholos, Sanctuary of Athena Pronaia, Delphi. c. 400 BCE

> Often the term following the name "Athena" is an epithet, or title, identifying one of the goddess's many roles in ancient Greek belief. For example, as patron of craftspeople, she was referred to as Athena Ergane (Athena of the Worker). As guardian of the city-states, she was Athena Polias. The term "Pronaia" in this sanctuary name simply means "in front of the temples," referring to the sanctuary's location preceding several temples higher up along the mountain path.

intersection of the central axes, surrounded by private housing blocks measuring roughly 120 by 160 feet subdivided into building plots of about 30 by 80 feet. The agora, stadium, temple precincts, and other large structures occupied rectangular plots but interrupted the grid because of their size. The city's wall, unlike the city itself, followed the contours of the land, utilizing the defensive advantages offered by the site. The city's planners made no attempt to accommodate their grid to this irregular perimeter, leaving irregular plots wherever whole ones could not be imposed.

The Tholos. Buildings with a circular plan had a long history in Greece going back to Mycenaean beehive tombs (see fig. 4-21). In later times a variety of tholoi, or circular-plan buildings, were erected. Some were shrines or monuments and some, like the fifth-century BCE tholos in the Athens Agora (see fig. 5-40), were administrative buildings, but the function of many, such as a tholos built shortly after 400 BCE in the Sanctuary of Athena Pronaia at Delphi, is unknown (figs. 5-59, 5-60). Theodoros, the presumed architect, was from Phokaia in Asia Minor. The exterior was of the Doric order, as seen from

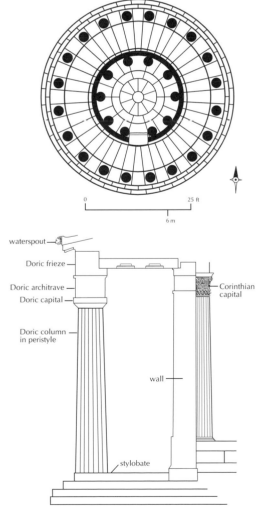

0   25 ft

6 m

waterspout

Doric frieze

Doric architrave

Doric capital

Corinthian capital

Doric column in peristyle

wall

stylobate

5-60. Plan and section of the tholos, Sanctuary of Athena Pronaia, Delphi

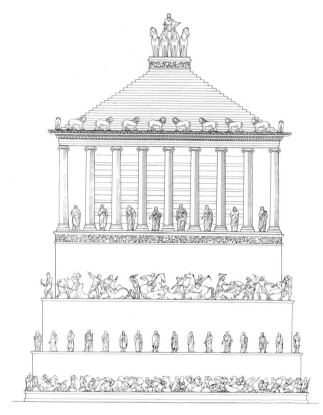

5-61. Reconstruction drawing of the Mausoleum (tomb of Mausolos), Halikarnassos (modern Bodrum, Turkey). c. 353 BCE

the three columns and a piece of the entablature that have been restored. Other remnants suggest that the interior featured a ring of columns with capitals carved to resemble the curling leaves of the acanthus plant. This type of capital came to be called "Corinthian" in Roman times (see "Elements of Architecture," page 165). It had been used on roof-supporting columns in temple interiors since the mid-fifth century BCE, but it was not used on building exteriors until the Hellenistic period.

The Monumental Tomb.   Monumental tombs were designed as large, showy memorials to their wealthy owners. One such tomb was built for Mausolos, prince of Karia, at Halikarnassos in Asia Minor, where Herodotus, the "father of history," had been born more than a century earlier. This monument (fig. 5-61) was so spectacular that later writers glorified it as one of the Seven Wonders of the World. Mausolos, whose name has given us the term **mausoleum** (a large burial structure), was the Persian governor of the region. He admired Greek culture and brought to his court Greek writers, entertainers, and artists, as well as the greatest sculptors to decorate his tomb. The structure was completed after his death in 353 BCE under the direction of his wife, Artemisia, who was rumored to have drunk her dead husband's ashes mixed with wine.

Except for traces of the foundation, a few scattered stones, and many fragments of sculpture and moldings that are now in various museums, Mausolos's tomb vanished in the Middle Ages. Although early descriptions are

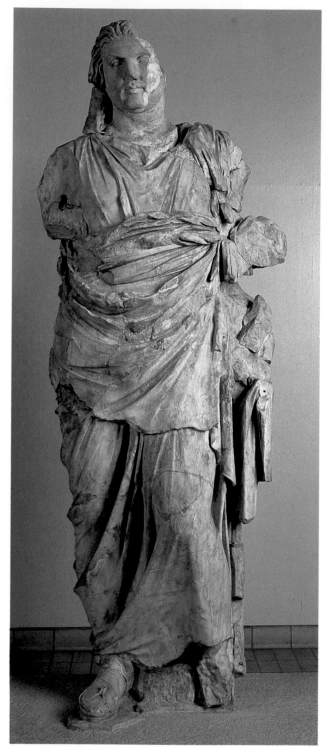

5-62. *Mausolos* (?), from the Mausoleum (tomb of Mausolos), Halikarnassos. Marble, height 9'10" (3 m). The British Museum, London

often ambiguous, the structure probably stood about 150 feet high and rose from a base measuring 126 by 105 feet. The elevation consisted of three main sections: a plain-surfaced podium, a colonnaded section in the Ionic order, and a stepped roof. The roof section measured about 24½ feet high and was topped with marble statues of a four-horse chariot and driver. The exterior decoration consisted of Ionic friezes and an estimated 250 freestanding statues, lifesize or larger, including more than 50 lions around the roofline. The friezes were sculpted in relief with battle scenes of Lapiths against centaurs and Greeks against Amazons. As reconstructed in figure 5-61, statues of Mausolos's relatives and ancestors stood between the columns in the colonnade; statues of hunters killing lions, boars, and deer encircled the next level down; below them was a circle of unidentified standing figures; and around the base was a battle between Greeks and Persians. Originally, all the sculptural elements of the tomb were painted.

A preserved male statue from the tomb was long believed to be of Mausolos himself (fig. 5-62). The man's broad face, long, thick hair, short beard and moustache, and stocky body could represent the features of a particular individual, but it is more likely that the statue represents a new heroic ideal—a glorification of experience, maturity, and intellect over youthful physical beauty and athletic vigor. The heavy swathing of drapery drawn into a thick mass around the waist reveals the underlying body forms while providing the necessary bulk to make the figure impressive to a viewer at the bottom of the monument.

Sculpture

Throughout the fifth century BCE, sculptors carefully maintained the equilibrium between simplicity and ornament that is fundamental to Greek Classical art. Standards established by Pheidias and Polykleitos in the mid-fifth century BCE for the ideal proportions and idealized forms of the human figure had generally been accepted by the next generation of artists. Fourth-century artists, on the other hand, challenged and modified those standards. The artists of mainland Greece, in particular, developed a new canon of proportions for male figures—some 8 or more "heads" tall rather than the 6½- or 7-head height of earlier works. The calm, noble detachment characteristic of earlier figures gave way to more sensitively rendered images of men and women with expressions of wistful introspection, dreaminess, or even fleeting anxiety. Patrons lost some of their interest in images of mighty Olympian gods and legendary heroes and acquired a taste for depictions of minor deities in lighthearted moments. This period also saw the earliest depictions of fully nude women in major works of art.

The fourth century BCE was dominated by three sculptors—Praxiteles, Skopas, and Lysippos. Praxiteles was active in Athens from about 370 to 335 BCE or later. According to the Greek traveler Pausanias, writing in the second century CE, one of Praxiteles' most popular works was a statue of the messenger god Hermes teasing the baby Dionysos with a bunch of grapes, which he finds irresistible. Just such a sculpture in marble, *Hermes and the Infant Dionysos,* was discovered in the ruins of the ancient Temple of Hera in the Sanctuary of Hera and Zeus at Olympia (fig. 5-63). It was accepted as an authentic work by Praxiteles until recent studies indicated that it is probably a very good Hellenistic or Roman copy of an original of about 300–250 BCE made by the followers of Praxiteles.

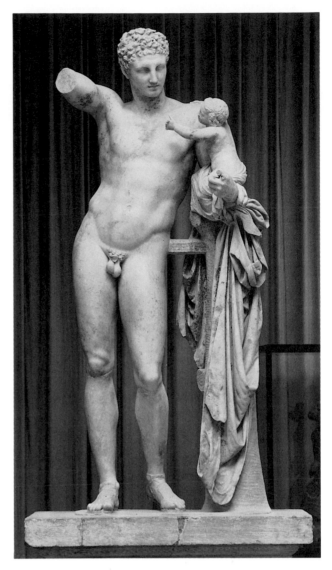

400

1000 BCE   1 CE

5-63. Followers of Praxiteles. *Hermes and the Infant Dionysos,* probably a Roman copy after an original of c. 300–250 BCE. Marble, with remnants of red paint on the lips and hair, height 7'1" (2.16 m). Archeological Museum, Olympia

Discovered in the rubble of the ruined Temple of Hera at Olympia in 1875, this statue is now widely accepted as a very good Roman copy. Support for this conclusion comes from certain elements typical of Roman sculpture: Hermes' sandals, which recent studies suggest are not accurate for a fourth-century BCE date; the supporting element of crumpled fabric covering a tree stump; and the use of a reinforcing strut, or brace, between Hermes' hip and the tree stump.

If it is a faithful copy, it reflects a number of differences between Praxiteles' style and that of the late fifth century. His Hermes has a smaller head and a more youthful body than Polykleitos's *Spear Bearer,* and its off-balance, **S**-curve pose contrasts clearly with that of the earlier work (see fig. 5-54). This sculptor also created a sensuous play of light over the figure's surface. The gleam of the smoothly finished flesh contrasts with the textured quality of the crumpled draperies and the rough locks of hair, even on the baby's head. Surely owed to Praxiteles is the humanized treatment of the subject—

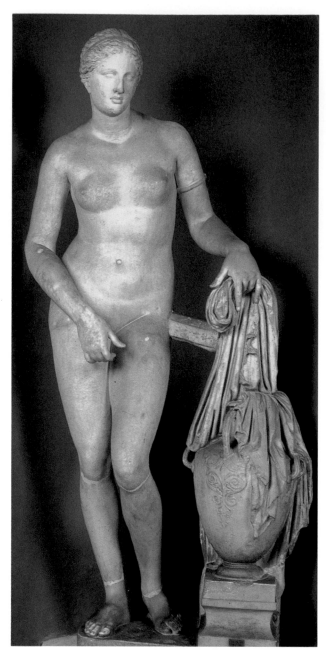

5-64. Praxiteles. *Aphrodite of Knidos,* composite of two similar Roman copies after the original marble of c. 350 BCE. Marble, height 6'8" (2.03 m). Musei Vaticani, Museo Pio Clementino, Gabinetto delle Maschere, Rome

In this composite of two Roman copies, the head is from one copy and the body from another. Seventeenth- and eighteenth-century restorers added the nose, the neck, the right forearm and hand, most of the left arm, and the feet and parts of the legs. This kind of restoration would rarely be undertaken today, but it was frequently done and considered quite acceptable in the past, when archeologists were trying to put together a body of work documenting the appearances of lost Greek statues. It was also done to create a piece suitable for sale to a private individual or for display in a museum.

two gods, one a loving adult and the other a playful child, caught in a moment of absorbed companionship. The interaction of the two across real space through gestures and glances creates an overall effect far different from that of the noble, austere deities of the fifth century BCE on the pediments and metopes of the Temple of Zeus (see figs. 5-34, 5-35), near where the work was found.

Around 350 BCE Praxiteles created a statue of Aphrodite that was purchased by the city of Knidos in Asia Minor. Although artists of the fifth century BCE had begun to hint boldly at the naked female body beneath tissue-thin drapery, as in *Nike Adjusting Her Sandal* (see fig. 5-53), and a few earlier works by lesser-known artists showed female nudity, this *Aphrodite* was apparently the first statue by a well-known Greek sculptor to depict a fully nude woman, and it set a new standard (fig. 5-64). Although nudity among athletic young men was admired in Greek society, among women it had been considered a sign of low character, which may explain the reticence to depict it. The eventual wide acceptance of female nudes in large statuary may be related to the gradual merging of the Greeks' concept of their goddess Aphrodite with some of the characteristics of the Phoenician goddess Astarte (the Babylonian Ishtar), who was nearly always shown nude in Near Eastern art.

In the version of the statue seen here, actually a composite of two Roman copies, the goddess is preparing to take a bath, with a water jug and her discarded clothing at her side. Her right arm and hand extend in what appears at first glance to be a gesture of modesty, which in fact seems only to emphasize her nakedness. The bracelet on her left arm has a similar effect. Her well-toned body, with its square shoulders, thick waist, and slim hips, conveys a sense of athletic strength. She leans forward slightly with one knee in front of the other in a seductive pose that emphasizes the swelling forms of her thighs and abdomen.

Writers of the time relate that Praxiteles' original statue was of such enchanting beauty that it served as a public model of high moral value. According to an old legend, the sculpture was so realistic that Aphrodite herself made a journey to Knidos to see it and cried out in shock, "Where did Praxiteles see me naked?" The Knidians were so proud of their *Aphrodite* that they placed it in an open shrine where people could view it from every side. Hellenistic and Roman copies probably numbered in the hundreds, and nearly fifty survive in various collections today.

Skopas, another artist who was greatly admired in ancient times, had a brilliant career as both sculptor and architect that took him around the Greek world. Unfortunately, little survives, either originals or copies, that can be reliably attributed to him, even though early writers credited him with one whole side of the sculptural decoration of Mausolos's tomb. If the literary accounts are accurate, Skopas introduced a new style of sculpture admired in its time and influential in the following Hellenistic period. In relief compositions, he favored very active, dramatic poses over balanced, harmonious ones, and he was especially noted for the expression of emo-

known today only from Roman copies, he chose a typical Classical subject, a nude male athlete, but treated it in an unusual way (fig. 5-66). Instead of a figure actively engaged in a sport or standing in the Classical shallow **S** curve, Lysippos depicted a young man methodically removing oil and dirt from his body with a scraping tool called a *strigil*. Judging from the athlete's expression, his thoughts are far from his mundane task. His deep-set eyes, dreamy stare, heavy forehead, and tousled hair may reflect the influence of Skopas.

The Scraper, tall and slender with a relatively small head, makes a telling comparison with Polykleitos's *Spear Bearer* (see fig. 5-54). Not only does it reflect a different canon of proportions, but the figure's weight is also more evenly distributed between the engaged leg and the free one, with the free foot almost flat on the ground. The legs are also in a wider stance to counterbalance the outstretched arms. The *Spear Bearer* is contained within fairly simple, compact contours and oriented to a frontal view. In contrast, the arms of *The Scraper* break free into the surrounding space, requiring the viewer to move around the statue to absorb its full aspect. Roman authors, who may have been describing the bronze original rather than a copy, remarked on the subtle modeling of *The Scraper*'s elongated body and the spatial extension of its pose.

Lysippos was widely known and admired for his monumental statues of Zeus, which may be why he was summoned to do a portrait of Alexander the Great. Lysippos portrayed Alexander as a full-length standing figure with an upraised arm holding a scepter, just as he is believed to have posed Zeus, though none of these statues still exists.

A head found at Pergamon that was once part of a standing figure is believed to be from one of several copies of Lysippos's original of Alexander (fig. 5-67). It depicts a ruggedly handsome, heavy-featured young man with a large Adam's apple and short, tousled hair. The treatment of the hair may be a visual reference to the mythical hero Herakles, who killed the Nemean Lion as his First Labor and is often portrayed wearing its head and pelt as a hooded cloak. Alexander would have felt great kinship with Herakles, whose acts of bravery and strength earned him immortality. The Pergamon head was not meant to be entirely true to life. The artist rendered certain features in an idealized manner to convey a specific message about the subject. The deep-set eyes are unfocused and meditative, and the low forehead is heavily lined, as though the figure were contemplating decisions of great consequence and waiting to receive divine advice.

According to the Roman-era historian Plutarch, Lysippos depicted Alexander in a characteristic meditative pose, "with his face turned upward toward the sky, just as Alexander himself was accustomed to gaze, turning his neck gently to one side" (cited in Pollitt, page 20). Because this description fits the marble head from Pergamon and others like it so well, the heads have been thought to be copies of the Alexander statue. On the other hand, the heads could also be viewed as

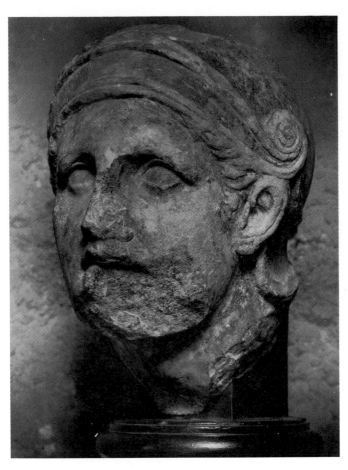

5-65. Skopas, or made in his workshop. Head from a pedimental figure, Temple of Athena Alea, Tegea. c. 340 BCE. Marble, height 11¾" (30 cm). National Archeological Museum, Athens

tion in the facial features and body gestures of his figures.

One of the most likely, though limited, sources of knowledge for his sculptural style is a group of fragments from the Temple of Athena Alea (Athena as goddess of good and bad fortune) at Tegea in southern Greece. Skopas supervised the construction of this temple, and if he did not actually create the statues, they must have been designed and executed according to his specifications, just as the sculptural decoration of the Parthenon was designed by Pheidias and executed by others under his close direction. Among the fragments is a head from a figure originally in one of the pediments (fig. 5-65). Even in its damaged condition, the head conveys intensity with its deep-set eyes, heavy brow, slightly parted lips, and a gaze that seems to look far into the future.

The sculptor Lysippos is unique in that many details of his life are known. He claimed to be entirely self-taught and asserted that "nature" was his only model, but he must have received training in the technical aspects of his profession in the vicinity of his home in Sikyon, near Corinth. Although he expressed great admiration for Polykleitos, his own figures reflect a different set of proportions than those of the fifth-century BCE master, with small heads and slender bodies like those of Praxiteles. For his famous work *The Scraper* (*Apoxyomenos*),

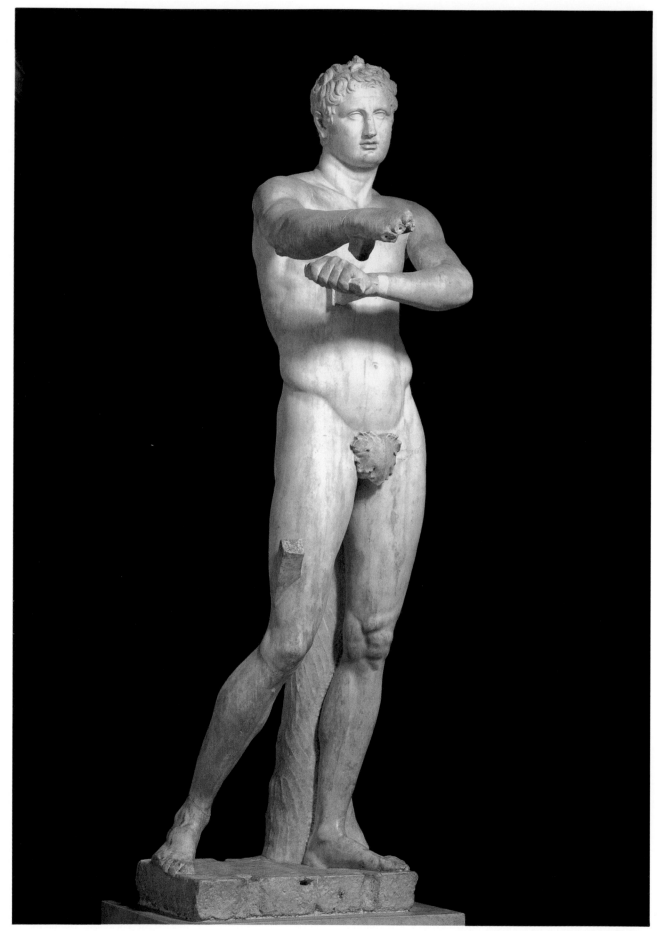

5-66. Lysippos. *The Scraper* (*Apoxyomenos*), Roman copy after the original bronze of c. 330 BCE. Marble, height 6'9" (2.06 m). Musei Vaticani, Museo Pio Clementino, Gabinetto dell'Apoxyomenos, Rome

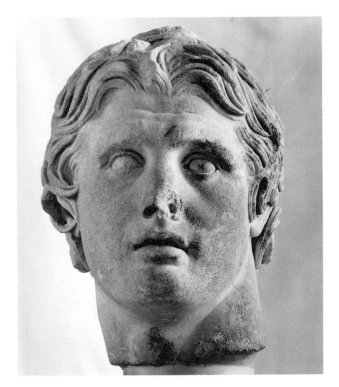

5-67. *Alexander the Great,* head from a Hellenistic copy (c. 200 BCE) of a statue, possibly after a 4th-century BCE original by Lysippos. Marble fragment, height 16⅛" (41 cm). Archeological Museum, Istanbul, Turkey

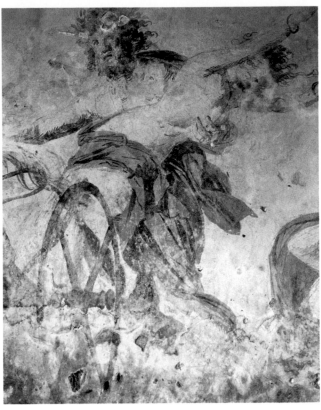

5-69. *Abduction of Persephone,* detail of a wall painting in Tomb I (Small Tomb), Vergina, Macedonia. c. 366 BCE. Height approx. 39½" (100.3 cm)

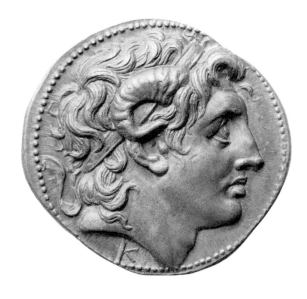

5-68. *Alexander the Great,* 4-drachma coin issued by Lysimachos of Thrace. 306–281 BCE. Silver, diameter 1⅛" (30 mm). The British Museum, London

conventional, idealized "types" rather than identifiable portraits of Alexander. A reasonably reliable image of Alexander is found on a coin issued by Lysimachos, king of Thrace, in the late fourth and early third centuries BCE (fig. 5-68). It shows Alexander in profile wearing the curled ram's-horn headdress that identifies him as the Greek-Egyptian god Zeus-Amun. It is interesting to compare the low forehead, high-bridged nose, large lips, and thick neck to the Pergamon head.

Wall Painting and Mosaics

Greek painting has so far been discussed only in terms of pottery decoration because little remains of paintings in other mediums. Some excavations in the 1970s have enriched our knowledge of fourth-century BCE painting. At Vergina, the ancient Macedonian capital of Aigai, two previously undiscovered tombs were found in a large mound called the Great Tumulus, in a cemetery complex. Dated from **potsherds** to around the middle of the fourth century BCE, both tombs were decorated with wall paintings. The larger of the tombs (Tomb II), which contained a rich casket, armor, and golden wreaths, may be that of Alexander's father, Philip II.

A mural in the smaller of the tombs (Tomb I) depicts the kidnapping of Persephone by Hades (fig. 5-69). Even in its deteriorated state, the *Abduction of Persephone* is clearly the work of an outstanding artist. This mural, with its vigorous drawing style, complex foreshortening, and dynamic brushwork, proves claims by early observers such as Pliny the Elder that Greek painters were skilled in capturing the appearance of the real world. It also contradicts the view often held before its discovery that dramatic, dynamic figural representation in Greek art was confined to Hellenistic sculpture of the third to first century BCE. Hades has just snatched Persephone and is carrying her off in his chariot. The convincing twists of the figures, the foreshortened view of the huge wheels on the chariot, and the swirl of draperies capture the story's

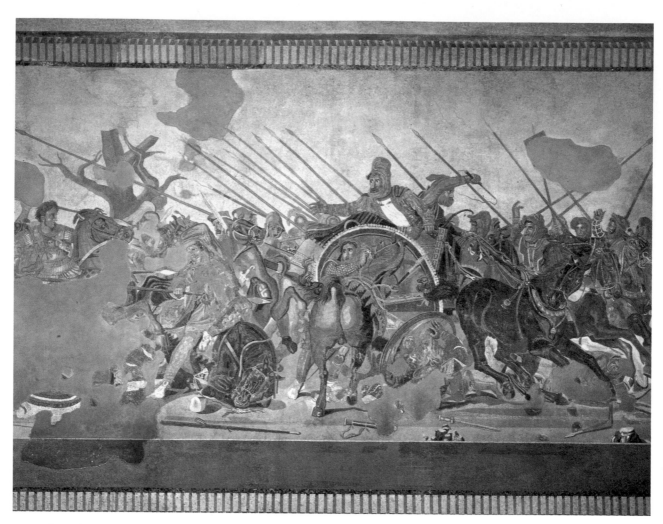

5-70. *Alexander the Great Confronts Darius III at the Battle of Issos,* Roman mosaic copy after a Greek painting of c. 310 BCE, perhaps by Philoxenos or Helen of Egypt. Museo Archeològico Nazionale, Naples

action, conveying the intensity of the struggle and the violent emotions it has provoked. Hades, with his determined expression, contrasts strikingly with the young Persephone, who evokes pity with her helpless gestures. The subject, certainly appropriate for a tomb painting, may be a metaphor for rebirth, the changing seasons, the cycle of life and death.

Later, Roman patrons greatly admired Greek murals and commissioned copies, as either wall paintings or mosaics, to decorate their homes. These copies provide another source of evidence about fourth-century BCE Greek painting. Together with evidence from red-figure vase painting, they indicate a growing taste for dramatic narrative subjects. A second-century BCE mosaic, *Alexander the Great Confronts Darius III at the Battle of Issos* (fig. 5-70), was based on an original wall painting of about 310 BCE. Pliny the Elder attributed the original to Philoxenos of Eretria; a recent theory claimed it was by a well-known woman painter, Helen of Egypt (see "Women Artists in Ancient Greece," opposite). Like the *Abduction*

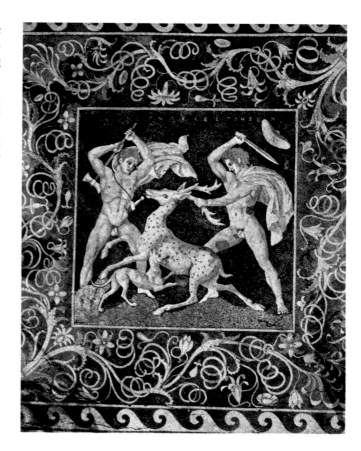

5-71. Gnosis. *Stag Hunt,* detail of mosaic floor decoration from Pella, Macedonia. 300 BCE. Pebbles, height 10'2" (3.1 m). Archeological Museum, Pella. Signed at top: "Gnosis made it"

WOMEN ARTISTS IN ANCIENT GREECE

Although their numbers must have been relatively few, women artists probably worked in many mediums in ancient Greece. Several of them are mentioned by ancient writers. Pliny the Elder, for example, listed Aristarete, Eirene, Iaia, Kalypso, Olympias, and Timarete. Helen, a painter from Egypt who had been trained by her father, is known to have worked in the fourth century BCE and may have been responsible for the original wall painting of Alexander the Great at the Battle of Issos (see fig. 5-70).

From pictorial evidence, we know that women worked in pottery-making workshops. The hydria illustrated here, dating from about 450 BCE, shows a woman artist in such a workshop, but it is somewhat ambiguous as to her status. The composition focuses on the male painters, who are being approached by Nikes bearing victory wreaths, symbolizing victory in an artistic competition. The woman, well-dressed, sits on a raised dais painting the largest vase in the workshop. She is isolated from the other artists and left out of the awards ceremony. Perhaps women were simply excluded from participating in public artistic competitions, as they were, for the most part, in athletics.

Another interpretation, however, is that the woman is the head of this workshop. Secure in her own status, perhaps she has encouraged her young assistants to enter contests so that they may further their own careers and bring glory to the workshop as a whole.

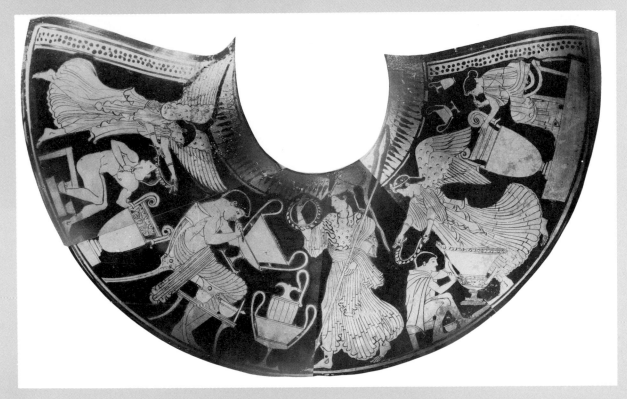

A Vase Painter and Assistants Crowned by Athena and Victories, composite photograph of the red-figure decoration on a hydria from Athens. c. 450 BCE. Private collection

of Persephone, this scene is one of violent action, gestures, and radical foreshortening, all devised to elicit the viewer's response to a dramatic situation. Astride a horse at the left, his hair blowing free and his neck bare, Alexander challenges the helmeted and armored Persian leader, who stretches out his arm in a gesture of defeat and apprehension as his charioteer whisks him back toward safety in the Persian ranks. Presumably in close imitation of the original painting, the mosaicist created the illusion of solid figures through modeling, mimicking the play of light on three-dimensional surfaces by touching protrusions with highlights and shading undercut areas and areas in shadow. The same techniques were used in the *Abduction of Persephone,* but its condition makes them difficult to see in a photographic reproduction.

The great interest of fourth-century BCE artists in creating a believable illusion of the real world was the subject of anecdotes repeated by later writers. One popular legend involved a floral designer named Glykera—widely praised for the artistry with which she wove blossoms and greenery into stunning wreaths, swags, and garlands for religious processions and festivals—and Pausias, the foremost painter of the day. Pausias challenged Glykera to a contest, claiming that he could paint a picture of one of her complex works that would appear as lifelike to the spectator as her real one. According to the legend, he succeeded. It is thus not surprising, although perhaps unfair, that the opulent floral borders so popular in later Greek painting and mosaics are described as "Pausanian" rather than "Glykeran."

A mosaic floor from a palace at Pella in Macedonia provides an example of a Pausanian design. Dated about 300 BCE, the floor features a series of framed hunting scenes, such as the *Stag Hunt* (fig. 5-71), prominently signed by an artist named Gnosis. Blossoms, leaves, spiraling tendrils, and twisting, undulating stems frame this scene, echoing the linear patterns formed by the hunters, the dog, and the struggling stag. The over-lifesize human and animal figures are accurately drawn and modeled in light and shade. The dog's front legs are expertly foreshortened to create the illusion that the animal is turning at a sharp angle into the picture. The work is all the more impressive because it was not made with uniformly cut marble in different colors but with a carefully selected assortment of natural pebbles. The background was formed of dark stones, and the figures and floral designs were made of light-colored stones. The smallest pebbles were used to "paint" in the delicate shading and to create subtle details.

The Art of the Goldsmith

The work of Greek goldsmiths, which gained international popularity in the Classical period, followed the same stylistic trends and achieved the same high standards of technique and execution found in the other art mediums. Goldsmiths' work was especially admired by the Scythians, a once-nomadic people from northern Asia who themselves had an ancient tradition of outstanding goldwork. An elaborate example of Greek artistry, a large, gold pectoral dating from the fourth century BCE, was found in a Scythian chief's tomb in the Caucasus Mountains (fig. 5-72). A series of four gold **torques** of increasing diameter separates each of the sections. The upper and lower bands have figures, and the center one contains a stylized floral design that strongly resembles the floral border on the Pella floor (see fig. 5-71). In the pectoral's top band, the artist re-created a typical scene of Scythian daily life. At the center, two men are making a cloth shirt, while at the right another man milks a goat. Around them are cows and horses with their nursing calves and foals, all portrayed with great naturalistic detail. In contrast, the bottom band is devoted to a Near Eastern theme of animal combat, with griffinlike beasts attacking a group of horses. Is there a lesson here—that the domestication of animals is justified because it offers them protection from the dangers of the wild?

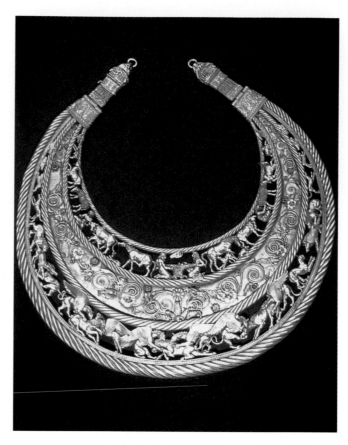

5-72. Pectoral, from the tomb of a Scythian at Ordzhonikidze, Russia. 4th century BCE. Gold, diameter 12" (30.6 cm). Historical Museum, Kiev

The jewelry designs popular with Greek women of the period were romantic ones. An embossed gold diadem dating from the late fourth century BCE, to be worn in the hair like a small crown (fig. 5-73), depicts a pair of mythological lovers, Ariadne—a Cretan princess abandoned by her lover, Theseus, on the island of Naxos—and the wine god Dionysos, who found and married her. The two recline back to back, listening to a concert played by women musicians seated between giant spiraling forms like those on both sides of the listening couple. The harpist at the near right in pose and instrument recalls

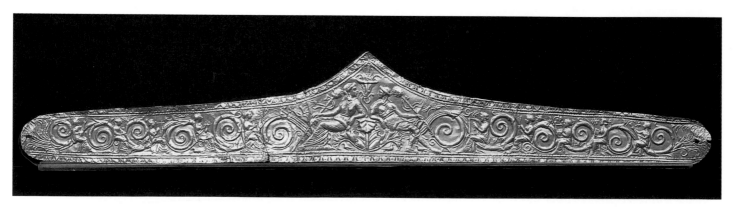

5-73. Diadem, reputed to have been found in a tomb near the Hellespont. Late 4th century BCE. Gold, 14½" (36.8 cm). The Metropolitan Musem of Art, New York
Rogers Fund, 1906 (06.1217.1)

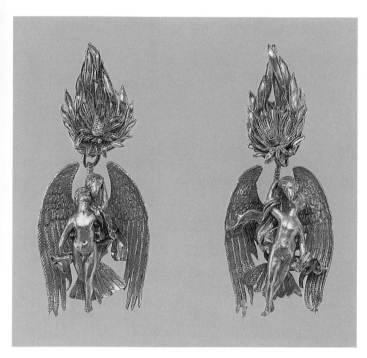

5-74. Earrings. c. 330–300 BCE. Hollow-cast gold, height
2³⁄₈" (6 cm). The Metropolitan Musem of Art, New York
Harris Brisbane Dick Fund, 1937 (37.11.9–10)

the Cycladic *Harp Player* (see fig. 4-3). The tumbling leafy spirals somewhat resemble the floral elements of the Scythian pectoral.

A specialty of Greek goldsmiths was the design of earrings in the form of tiny works of sculpture. These were often placed on the ears of marble statues of goddesses, but they adorned real ears as well. An earring designed as the youth Ganymede in the grasp of an eagle (Zeus) (fig. 5-74), dated about 330–300 BCE, is both a charming decoration and a technical tour de force. Slightly more than 2 inches high, it was hollow-cast using the **lost-wax** process, no doubt to make it light on the ear. Despite its small size, the earring conveys all the drama of its subject. Action subjects like this, with the depiction of swift movement through space, were to become a hallmark of Hellenistic art.

THE HELLENISTIC PERIOD

When Alexander died in 323 BCE, he left a vast empire with no administrative structure and no accepted successor. Almost at once his generals turned against one another, local leaders tried to regain their lost autonomy, and the empire began to break apart. The Greek city-states formed a new mutual-protection league but never again achieved significant power. Democracy survived in form but not substance in governments dominated by local rulers.

By the early third century BCE, three major powers had emerged out of the chaos, ruled by three of Alexander's generals and their heirs: Antigonus, Ptolemy, and Seleucus. The Antigonids controlled Macedonia and mainland Greece; the Ptolemies ruled Egypt; and the Seleucids controlled Asia Minor, Mesopotamia, and Persia. Over the course of the second and first centuries BCE these kingdoms succumbed to the growing empire centered in Rome. Ptolemaic Egypt endured the longest, almost two and one-half centuries. The death in 30 BCE of its last ruler, the remarkable Cleopatra, marks the end of the Hellenistic period.

Alexander's most lasting legacy was the spread of Greek culture far beyond its original borders. The Ptolemaic capital, Alexandria in Egypt, a prosperous seaport known for its lighthouse (another of the Seven Wonders of the World, according to ancient writers), emerged as a great Hellenistic center of learning and the arts. Its library, estimated to have contained 700,000 papyrus and parchment scrolls, was rivaled only by the library at Pergamon in Asia Minor.

Artists of the Hellenistic period had a vision noticeably different from that of their predecessors. Where earlier artists sought the ideal and the general, Hellenistic artists sought the individual and the specific. They turned increasingly away from the heroic and to the everyday, from gods to mortals, from aloof serenity to individual emotion, and from drama to melodramatic pathos. A trend introduced in the fourth century BCE—the appeal to the senses through lustrous or glittering surface treatments and to the emotions with dramatic subjects and poses—became more pronounced. Even the architecture of the Hellenistic period largely reflected the contemporary taste for high drama.

Theaters

In ancient Greece, the theater was more than mere entertainment; it was a vehicle for the communal expression of religious belief through music, poetry, and dance. In very early times, theater performances took place on the hard-packed dirt or stone-surfaced pavement of an outdoor threshing floor (*halos*)—the same type of floor later incorporated into religious sanctuaries. Whenever feasible, dramas were also presented facing a steep hill that served as a kind of natural theater. Eventually such sites were made into permanent open-air auditoriums. At first, tiers of seats were simply cut into the side of the hill. Later, builders improved them with stone.

During the fifth century BCE, the plays primarily were tragedies in verse based on popular myths and were performed at a festival dedicated to Dionysos. At this time, the three great Greek tragedians—Aeschylus, Sophocles, and Euripides—were creating the works that would define tragedy for centuries. Many theaters were built in the fourth century BCE, including those on the side of the Athenian Acropolis and in the sanctuary at Delphi, also for the performance of music and dance during the festival of Dionysos. Because theaters were used continuously and frequently modified over many centuries, no early theaters have survived in their original form.

The largely intact theater at Epidauros, however, which dates from the early third century BCE, presents good examples of the characteristics of early theaters

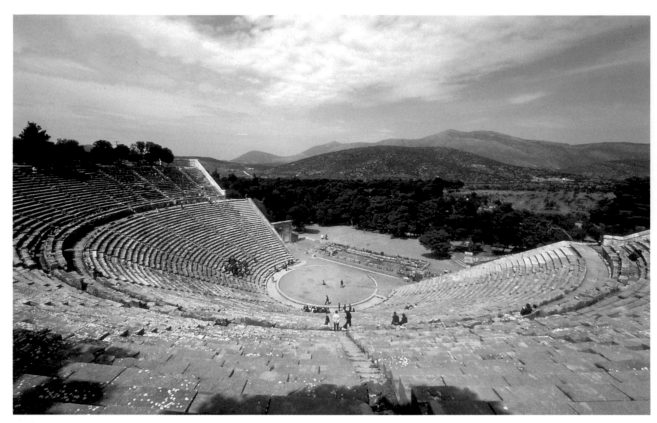

5-75. Theater, Epidauros. Early 3rd century BCE and later

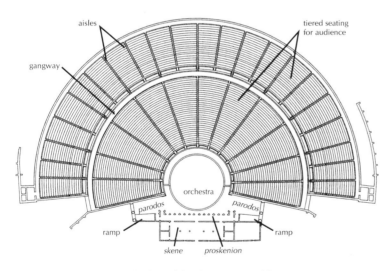

5-76. Plan of the theater at Epidauros

(figs. 5-75, 5-76). A semicircle of tiered seats built into the hillside overlooked the circular performance area, called the orchestra, at the center of which was an altar to Dionysos. Rising behind the orchestra was a two-tiered stage structure made up of the vertical *skene* (scene)—an architectural backdrop for performances and a screen for the backstage area—and the *proskenion* (**proscenium**), a raised platform in front of the *skene* that was increasingly used over time as an extension of the orchestra. Ramps connecting the *proskenion* with lateral passageways (*parodoi*; singular *parodos*) provided access to the stage for performers. Steps gave the audience access to the fifty-five rows of seats and divided the seating area into uni-

form wedge-shaped sections. The tiers of seats above the wide corridor, or gangway, were added at a much later date. This design provided uninterrupted sight lines and good acoustics and allowed for efficient crowd control of the 12,000 spectators. It has not been greatly improved upon since.

The Corinthian Order in Architecture

During the Hellenistic period there was increasing innovation in public architecture. A variant of the Ionic order featuring a tall, slender column with a Corinthian capital, for example, began to challenge the dominance of the Doric and Ionic orders on building exteriors. Invented in the late fifth century BCE, this highly decorative carved capital had previously been used only indoors, as in the tholos at Delphi (see fig. 5-60). Today, the Corinthian variant is routinely treated as a third Greek order (see "Elements of Architecture," page 165). In the Corinthian column the echinus becomes an unfluted extension of the column shaft set off by a collar molding called an **astragal**. From the astragal sprout curly acanthus leaves and coiled flower spikes reminiscent of the coiled volutes of the Ionic capital. The slightly flaring abacus has concave sides with a center relief element called a **boss**. The Corinthian entablature features a stepped-out architrave and bands of carved moldings, often including a line of vertical toothlike elements called **dentils**, just above the continuous frieze. The Corinthian design became a lasting symbol of elegance and refinement that is still used on banks, churches, and office buildings.

The Corinthian order Temple of the Olympian Zeus, located in the lower city of Athens at the foot of the Acropolis, was commissioned by the Seleucid ruler Antiochus IV and was designed by the Roman architect Cossutius in the second century BCE (fig. 5-77). The temple's unusually large foundation, measuring 135 by 354 feet, is that of an earlier temple dating to the mid-sixth century BCE. Work halted in 164 BCE and was not completed until three centuries later under Roman rule. The temple's great Corinthian columns may be the second-century BCE originals or Roman replicas of them. The peristyle soars 57 feet above the stylobate. Viewed through its columns the Parthenon seems modest in comparison. But for all its height and luxurious decoration, the design of the new temple followed long-established norms. It stood on a three-stepped base, it had an enclosed room or series of rooms enclosed within a screen of columns, and its proportions and details followed traditional standards. Quite simply, it is a Greek temple grown very large.

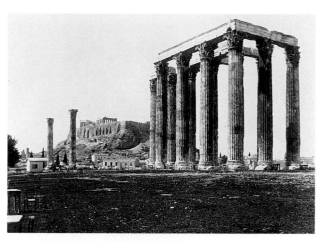

5-77. Temple of the Olympian Zeus, Athens. Building and rebuilding phases: foundation mid-6th century BCE; temple designed by Cossutius, begun 175 BCE, left unfinished 164 BCE, completed 132 CE using Cossutius's design

Sculpture

Hellenistic sculptors produced an enormous variety of work in a wide range of materials, techniques, and styles. The period was marked by two broad and conflicting trends. One (sometimes called anti-Classical) led away from Classical models and toward experimentation with new forms and subjects; the other led back to Classical models, with artists selecting aspects of certain favored works by fourth-century sculptors and incorporating them into new styles.

The Pergamene Style. The kingdom of Pergamon, a breakaway state within the Seleucid realm, established itself in the early third century BCE on the site of an ancient city in western Asia Minor. It quickly became a leading center of arts patronage and the hub of a new sculptural style that had far-reaching influence throughout the Hellenistic period. This new style is illustrated by a group of sculpture from a monument commemorating the victory in 230 BCE of Attalos I (ruled 241–197 BCE) over the Gauls, a Celtic people who invaded from the north. These figures, originally in bronze but known today only from Roman copies in marble, were mounted on a large pedestal. They depict the murder-suicide of the Gallic chieftain and his wife (fig. 5-78) and the slow demise of a wounded soldier-trumpeter (fig. 5-79), extolling their dignity and heroism in defeat. Their wiry, unkempt hair and the trumpeter's twisted neck ring, or torque (the only item of dress the Celts wore in battle), identify them as "barbarians." The artist has sought to arouse the viewer's admiration and pity for his subjects. The chieftain, for example, still supports his dead wife as he plunges the sword into his own breast. The trumpeter, fatally injured, struggles to stay up, but the slight bowing of his supporting right arm and his unseeing downcast gaze indicate that he is on the point of death. This kind of deliberate attempt to elicit a specific emotional response in the viewer is known as **expressionism**, and it was to become a characteristic of Hellenistic art.

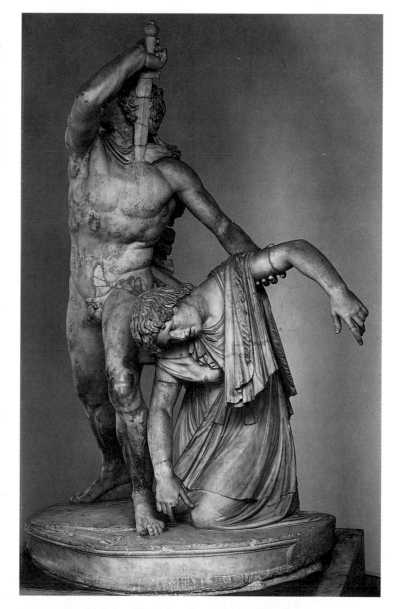

5-78. *Gallic Chieftain Killing His Wife and Himself*, Roman copy after the original bronze of c. 220 BCE. Marble, height 6'11" (2.1 m). Museo Nazionale Romano, Rome

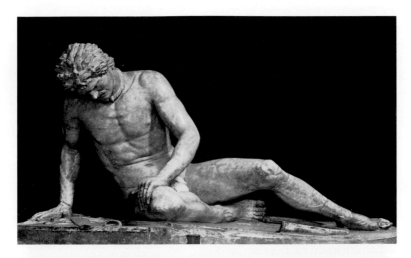

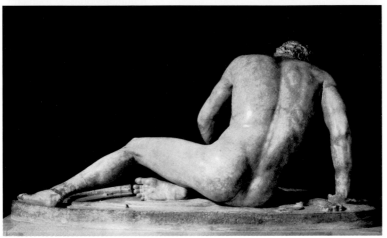

5-79. Epigonos(?). *Dying Gallic Trumpeter*, Roman copy after the original bronze of c. 220 BCE. Marble, lifesize. Museo Capitolino, Rome

The marble copies of these works are now separated, and no one knows exactly how the originals were positioned. Probably they formed part of an interlocked, multifigured pyramidal group that could have been viewed and appreciated from nearly every angle. Pliny the Elder described a work like the *Dying Gallic Trumpeter*, attributing it to an artist named Epigonos. Recent research indicates that Epigonos probably knew the early-fifth-century BCE sculpture of the Temple of Aphaia at Aegina, which included the *Dying Warrior* (see fig. 5-19), and could have had it in mind when he created his own works.

The style and approach of the works in the monument to the defeated Gauls became more pronounced and dramatic in later works, culminating in the decorative frieze on the base of the great altar at Pergamon (fig. 5-80). The wings and staircase to the entrance of the altar have been reconstructed inside a Berlin museum from fragments from the site. The original altar was a single-story structure with an Ionic colonnade raised on a high podium and entrances on each side. The main entrance, as shown here, was reached by a monumental staircase 68 feet wide and nearly 30 feet deep. The running frieze decoration, probably executed during the

reign of Eumenes II (197–159 BCE), depicts the battle between the Gods and the Giants, a mythical struggle that the Greeks are thought to have used as a metaphor for contemporary conflict—in this case, Pergamon's victory over the Gauls.

The panels are about 7½ feet high on the ends and taper to a few inches at the top of the steps. They show the Greek gods fighting not only human-looking Giants, but also grotesque hybrids emerging from the bowels of the earth. In a detail of the frieze (fig. 5-81), the goddess Athena at the left has grabbed the hair of a winged, serpent-tailed male monster and forced him to his knees. Inscriptions along the base of the sculpture identify him as Alkyoneos, a son of the earth goddess Ge, who rises from the ground on the right in maternal wrath as she reaches toward Athena. At the far right, a winged Nike rushes to Athena's assistance.

The figures in the Pergamon frieze not only fill up the sculptural space, they break out of their architectural boundaries and invade the space in front of it. They crawl out of the frieze onto the steps, where visitors had to pass them on their way up to the shrine. Many consider this theatrical and complex interaction of space and form to be a benchmark of the Hellenistic style, just as they con-

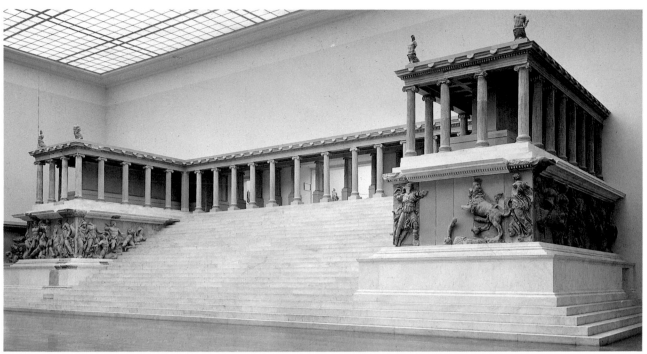

5-80. Reconstructed west front of the altar from Pergamon, Turkey. c. 166–156 BCE. Marble. Staatliche Museen zu Berlin, Preussischer Kulturbesitz, Pergamonmuseum

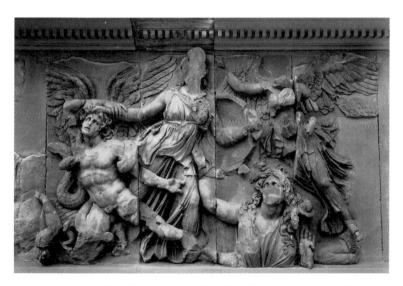

5-81. *Athena Attacking the Giants,* detail of the frieze from the east front of the altar from Pergamon. Marble, frieze height 7'6" (2.3 m). Staatliche Museen zu Berlin, Preussischer Kulturbesitz, Pergamon-museum

sider the balanced restraint of the Parthenon sculpture to be the benchmark of the High Classical style. Where fifth-century BCE artists sought horizontal and vertical equilibrium and control, the Pergamene artists sought to balance opposing forces in three-dimensional space along diagonal lines. The High Classical preference for smooth, sculpted surfaces reflecting a clear, even light has been replaced by a preference for dramatic contrasts of light and shade playing over complex forms sculpted in high relief with deep undercutting. The composure

and stability admired in the Classical style have given way to extreme expressions of pain, stress, wild anger, fear, and despair. In the High Classical style, figures stood remote in their own space. In the Fourth-Century style they reached out into their immediate environment. In the Hellenistic style, they impose themselves, often forcefully, on the spectator. Whereas the High Classical artist asked only for an intellectual commitment, the Hellenistic artist demanded that the viewer respond both physically and emotionally.

200
1000 BCE 1 CE

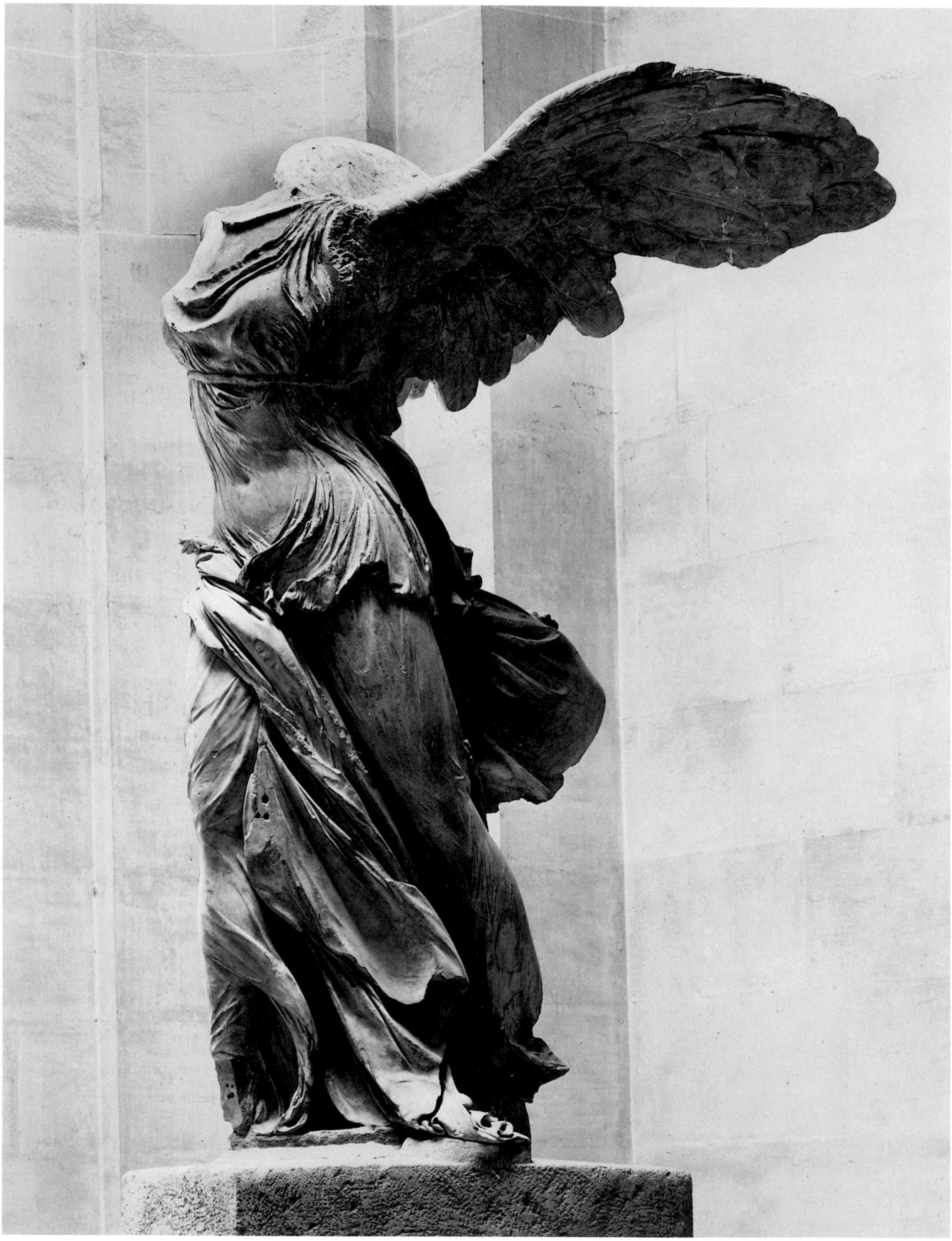

5-82. *Nike (Victory) of Samothrace,* from the Sanctuary of the Great Gods, Samothrace. c. 190 BCE (?). Marble, height 8' (2.44 m). Musée du Louvre, Paris

The wind-whipped costume and raised wings of this victory goddess indicate that she has just alighted on the prow of the stone ship that formed the original base of the statue. The work probably memorialized an important naval victory, perhaps the Rhodian triumph over the Seleucid king Antiochus III in 190 BCE. Lacking its head and arms, the Nike and a fragment of its ship base were discovered in the ruins of the Sanctuary of the Great Gods by a French explorer in 1863. Soon after, it entered the collection of the Louvre Museum in Paris. Poised high on the landing of the grand staircase, this famous Hellenistic sculpture continues to catch the eye and the imagination of thousands of museum visitors.

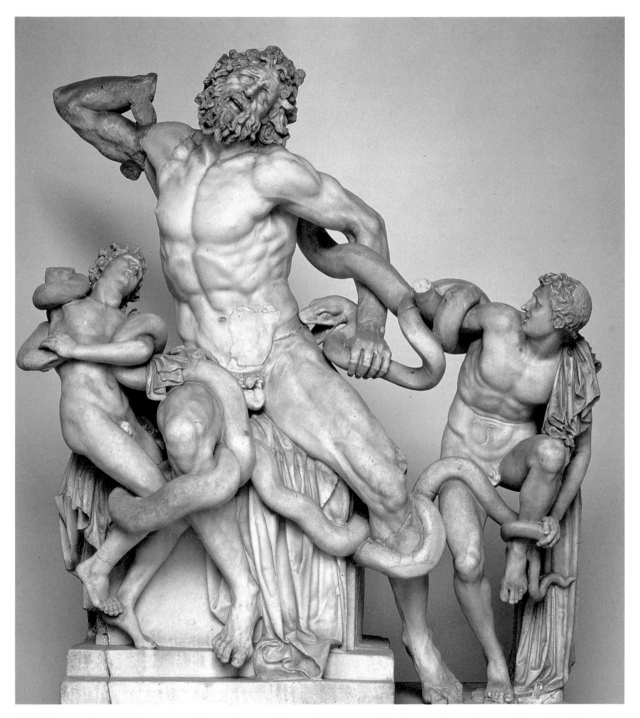

5-83. Hagesandros, Polydoros, and Athanadoros of Rhodes. *Laocoön and His Sons,* perhaps the original of the 2nd or 1st century BCE or a Roman copy of the 1st century CE. Marble, height 8' (2.44 m). Musei Vaticani, Museo Pio Clementino, Cortile Ottagono, Rome

The *Nike (Victory) of Samothrace* (fig. 5-82) is more theatrical still. In its original setting—in a hillside niche high above the city of Samothrace and perhaps drenched with spray from a fountain—this 8-foot-high goddess of victory must have reminded the Samothracians of the god-character in Greek plays who descends from heaven to determine the outcome of the drama. The fact that victory in real life does often seem miraculous makes this image of a goddess alighting suddenly on a ship breathtakingly appropriate for a war memorial. The forward momentum of the *Nike*'s heavy body is balanced by the powerful backward thrust of its enormous wings. The large, open movements of the figure, the strong contrasts of light and dark on the deeply sculpted forms, and the contrasting textures of feathers, fabric, and skin are reminiscent of the sculptures on the Altar of Zeus at Pergamon, though it is not known which work is earlier.

Pergamene artists very likely inspired the work of Hagesandros, Polydoros, and Athanadoros, three sculptors on the island of Rhodes named by Pliny the Elder as the creators of the famed *Laocoön and His Sons* (fig. 5-83). This work, in the collection of the Vatican since its

THE TROJAN WAR

The legend of the Trojan War and its aftermath held a central place in the imagination of the ancient Greeks, inspiring the great epics of Homer—the *Iliad* and the *Odyssey*—and providing the poets and artists of the Classical period and beyond with a rich source of subject matter. According to the legend, the cause of the war was a woman's infidelity. While on a visit to the city of Sparta in southern Greece, young Paris, the son of King Priam of Troy, fell in love with Helen, a human daughter of Zeus who was the wife of the Spartan king Menelaus. With the help of Aphrodite, the goddess of love, she and Paris fled to Troy, a rich city in northwestern Asia Minor. The angry Greeks dispatched ships and a huge army to bring Helen back. Led by Agamemnon, king of Mycenae and the brother of Menelaus, the Greek forces laid siege to Troy. The two sides were deadlocked for ten years, until a ruse devised by the warrior Odysseus allowed the Greeks to win: the Greeks pretended to give up the siege and built a huge wooden horse to leave behind as a parting gift to the goddess Athena, or so they led the Trojans to believe.

In fact, Greek warriors were hidden inside the wooden horse. After the Trojans pulled the horse inside the gates of Troy, the Greeks slipped out and opened the gates to their comrades, who slaughtered the Trojans and burned the city.

The source of this legend is thought to have been a real attack on a coastal city of Asia Minor by mainland Greeks during the Late Bronze Age. The assault more likely resulted from a struggle for control over trade in and out of the Black Sea than from the abduction of a Helladic ruler's wife. Tales of the conflict, modified over the centuries, endured in a tradition of oral poetry into the eighth or seventh century BCE, when the epics that are attributed to Homer were written down.

Homer's *Iliad* recounts an incident that took place during the long siege of Troy. Achilles, offended by Agamemnon, refuses to fight, and in his absence the Greeks suffer reverses. His friend Patroclus borrows his magical armor and kills many Trojans (including the warrior Sarpedon, see fig. 5-31) before he is killed by the Trojan hero Hector (another son of Priam). Achilles, to avenge his friend's death, returns to the battle and slays Hector. Homer's *Odyssey* recounts the trials and triumphs of Odysseus, who was doomed to years of wandering after the war before he could return to his faithful wife, Penelope. Among the many other stories of the Trojan War that found their way into art and literature were the death of Agamemnon, slain by his wife Clytemnestra when he arrived home, and the suicide of Ajax (see fig. 5-29).

The Romans, too, found inspiration in the legendary struggle at Troy.

Seeking heroic origins for themselves, they claimed descent from Aeneas, a Trojan warrior. As recounted in the *Aeneid,* an epic by the Roman poet Vergil (70–19 BCE), Aeneas and his followers escaped from Troy and found their way to Italy.

As early as the seventeenth century CE, adventurers began searching for Troy. In the early nineteenth century, the Englishman Charles MacLaren and the American Frank Calvert both concluded that the remains of the legendary city might be found at the Hissarlik Mound in northwestern Turkey. When this relatively small mound—less than 700 feet across—was excavated, first by the German archeologist Heinrich Schliemann from 1872 to 1890 (see "Pioneers of Aegean Archeology," page 143) and later by an American team under Carl Blegen in the 1930s, it was found to contain the remains of at least nine successive cities, the earliest of which dated to at least 3000 BCE. The seventh of these shows evidence of a terrible fire, which led early researchers to identify it as the Troy of legend. A more recent hypothesis, however, is that the so-called Troy 7 was destroyed by a fire of natural causes and that Homer's city is more likely to have been the earlier Troy 6. This city flourished for at least 500 years, between about 1800 and 1300 BCE. At its height, its fortifications were substantially reinforced, suggesting that it was threatened by a powerful enemy.

excavation in Rome in 1506, has been assumed by many art historians to be the original version, although others argue that it is a brilliant copy commissioned by an admiring Roman patron. The date of the original work is also uncertain—either second or first century BCE. The complex sculptural composition illustrates an episode from the Trojan War (see "The Trojan War," above). The Trojans' priest Laocoön warned them not to take the wooden horse (filled with Greeks) inside their walls. The gods who supported the Greeks in the war retaliated by sending serpents into Troy to destroy Laocoön and his sons. The struggling figures, anguished faces, intricate diagonal movements, and skillful unification of diverse forces in a complex composition all suggest a strong relationship between Rhodian and Pergamene sculptors. Unlike the monument to the conquered Gauls, the *Laocoön* was composed to be seen from the front,

within a short distance. As a result, although sculpted in the round, the three figures appear as very high relief and are more like the relief sculpture on the Altar of Zeus.

Small-Scale Statues. Although "huge," "enormous," and "larger-than-life" are terms correctly applied to much Hellenistic sculpture, artists of the time also created fine works on a small scale. The grace, dignity, and energy of the 8-foot-tall *Nike of Samothrace* can also be found in a bronze only 8½ inches tall (fig. 5-84). This figure of a heavily veiled and masked dancing woman twists sensually under the gauzy, layered fabric in a complex spiral movement. The dancer clearly represents an artful professional performer who would have been equally in demand for religious celebrations and secular court entertainments. Private patrons must have delighted in such intimate works, which were made in large

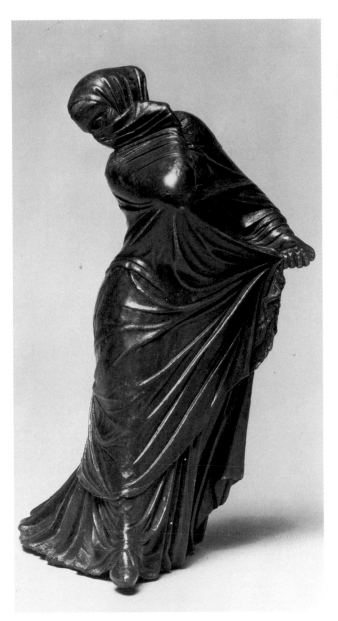

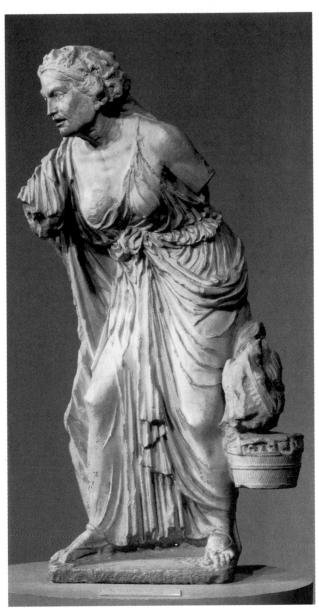

5-84. *Veiled and Masked Dancer.* Late 3rd or 2nd century BCE. Bronze, height 8⅛" (20.7 cm). The Metropolitan Museum of Art, New York
Bequest of Walter C. Baker, 1971 (1972.118.95)

5-85. *Market Woman.* 2nd century BCE. Marble, height 49½" (125.7 cm). The Metropolitan Museum of Art, New York
Rogers Fund, 1909 (09.39)

numbers and featured a wide variety of subjects and treatments. This bronze would have been costly, but many such graceful figurines were produced in inexpensive terra-cotta from preshaped molds and would have been accessible to a very broad market.

The appeal to the emotions in the sculpture at Pergamon signals a social change between the Classical and Hellenistic periods. In contrast to the Classical world, which was characterized by relative cultural unity and social homogeneity, the Hellenistic world was varied and multicultural. In this environment, artists turned from **idealism**, the quest for perfect form, to realism, the attempt to portray the world as it is. Portraiture, for example, became popular during the Hellenistic period, as did the representation of people from every level of

society. Patrons were fascinated by depictions of unusual physical types as well as of ordinary individuals.

A marble statue a little over 4 feet tall, which has long been called *Market Woman* (fig. 5-85), may represent a peasant woman on her way to the agora with three chickens and a basket of vegetables. Despite the bunched and untidy way the figure's dress hangs, it appears to be of an elegant design and made of fine fabric. The hair too bears some semblance of a once-careful arrangement. These characteristics, along with the woman's sagging lower jaw, unfocused stare, and lack of concern for her exposed breasts, have led some to speculate that she may represent an aging, dissolute follower of the wine god Dionysos on her way to make an offering. Whether an aging peasant or a Dionysian

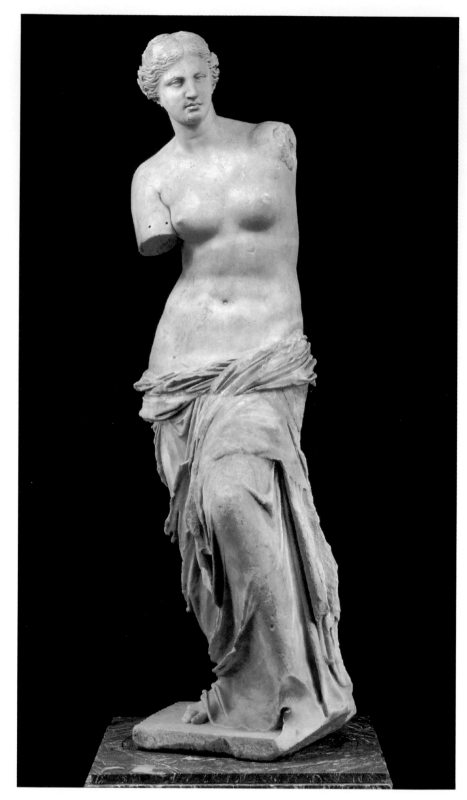

5-86. *Aphrodite of Melos* (also called *Venus de Milo*). c. 150 BCE. Marble, height 6'10" (2.1 m). Musée du Louvre, Paris

The original appearance of this famous statue's missing arms has been much debated. When it was dug up in a field in 1820, some broken pieces found with it (now lost) indicated that the figure was holding out an apple in its right hand. Many judged these fragments to be part of a later restoration, not part of the original statue. The image of Aphrodite admiring herself in the highly polished shield of the war god Ares was popular in the second century BCE, so this figure could have been holding a shield. If so, it would have been off to one side, tilted at an angle, and probably resting on the goddess's left thigh. This theoretical "restoration" seems to offer an explanation for the pronounced **S**-curve of the pose and the otherwise unnatural forward projection of the knee.

celebrant, the subject of this work is the antithesis of the *Nike of Samothrace*. Yet, in formal terms, both sculpted figures are **expressionistic**. Both stretch out assertively into the space around them, both demand an emotional response from the viewer, and both display technical virtuosity in the rendering of forms and textures. They are closer to each other stylistically than either is to the *Nike Adjusting Her Sandal* or the *Aphrodite of Knidos* (see figs. 5-53, 5-64).

The Classical Alternative. Not all Hellenistic artists followed the trend toward realism and expressionism that characterized the artists of Pergamon and Rhodes. Some turned to the past, creating an eclectic style by reexamining and borrowing elements from earlier Classical styles and combining them with new elements. Certain popular sculptors, no doubt encouraged by patrons nostalgic for the past, looked back especially to Praxiteles and Lysippos for their models. This renewed interest in the style of the fourth century BCE is exemplified by the *Aphrodite of Melos* (fig. 5-86), found on the island of Melos by French excavators in the early nineteenth century. The sculpture was intended by its maker to recall the *Aphrodite* of Praxiteles (see fig. 5-64), and indeed the head with its dreamy gaze is very Praxitelean. The figure has the heavier proportions of High Classical sculpture, but the twisting stance and the strong projection of the knee are typical of Hellenistic art of the third century BCE and later. The drapery around the lower part of the body also has the rich, three-dimensional quality associated with the Hellenistic sculpture of Rhodes and Pergamon. The sensuous juxtaposition of nude flesh with the texture of draperies, which seem about to slip off the figure, adds a strong, insistent note of erotic tension that can only be Hellenistic in concept and intent.

Also illustrative of this eclectic trend, but using other sources, is the larger-than-lifesize *Hellenistic Ruler* (fig. 5-87), which may reflect the heroic figure types favored for official and religious sculpture by Lysippos in the lost statues of Zeus and Alexander the Great. Certainly the elongated body proportions and small head recall Lysippos's *Scraper* (see fig. 5-66). Yet the impression of Hellenistic realism overrides the lingering suggestions of Classical heroism and idealism. Hellenistic rulers often fancied themselves divine, and the overdeveloped musculature of this figure, the individualized features of the jowly face, and the arrogant pose suggest the unbridled power of an earthly ruler elevated to the status of a demigod.

By the late first century BCE, the influence of Greek painting, sculpture, and architecture was paramount in the artistic communities of the emerging Roman civilization. Roman patrons and artists maintained their enthusiasm for Greek art into early Christian times. Indeed, so strong was the urge to emulate the great Greek artists

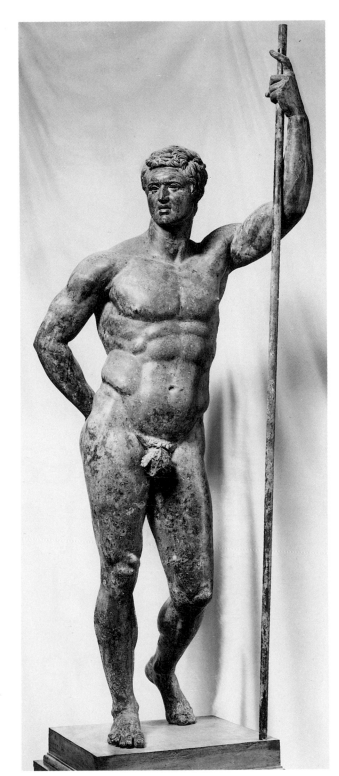

5-87. *Hellenistic Ruler.* c. 150–140 BCE. Bronze, height 7'9" (2.37 m). Museo Nazionale Romano, Rome

that, as we have seen throughout this chapter, much of our knowledge of Greek achievements comes primarily through Roman replicas of Greek artworks and descriptions of Greek art by Roman-era writers.

BCE 800   600   400

Apollo
from Veii
c. 500

She-Wolf
c. 500–480

▲ ETRUSCAN SUPREMACY 700–509   ▲ REPUBLICAN PERIOD 509–27

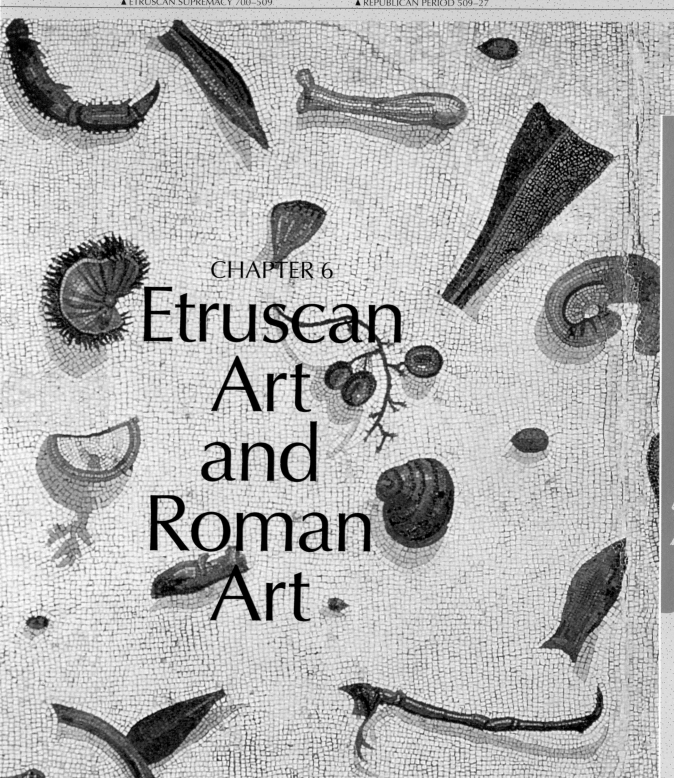

CHAPTER 6
Etruscan Art and Roman Art

ATLA
OC.

PORTUGAL

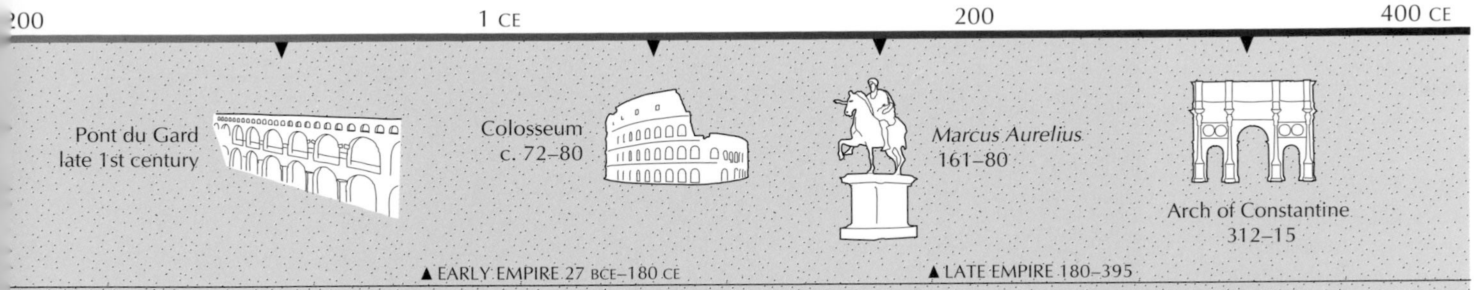
200
1 CE
200
400 CE
Pont du Gard
late 1st century
Colosseum
c. 72–80
Marcus Aurelius
161–80
Arch of Constantine
312–15
▲ EARLY EMPIRE 27 BCE–180 CE
▲ LATE EMPIRE 180–395

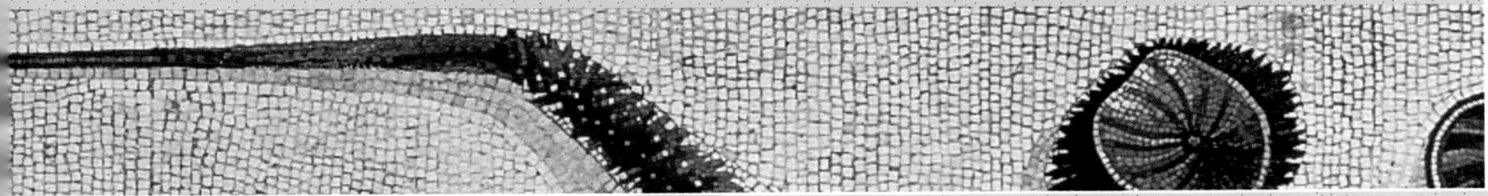

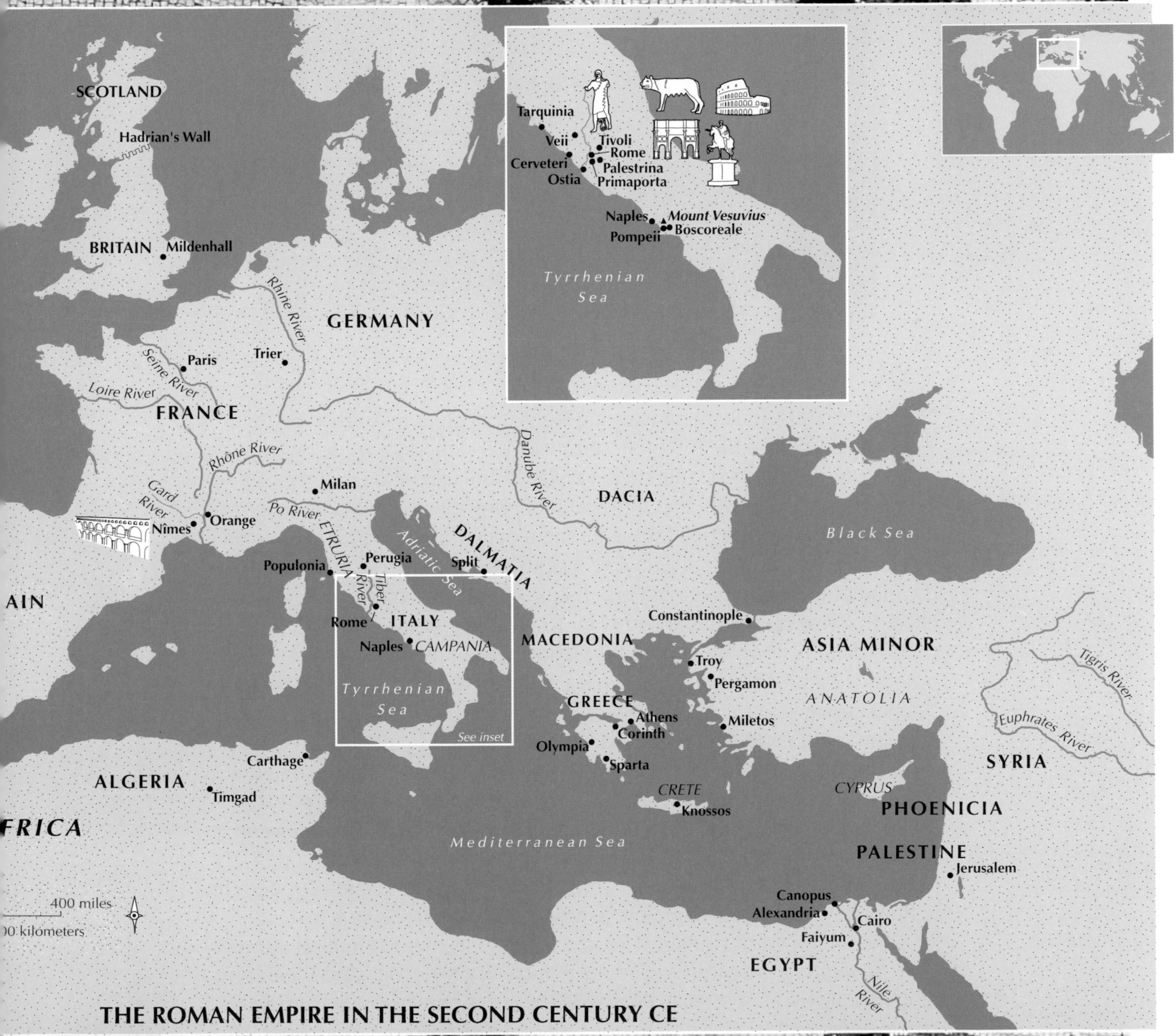
SCOTLAND
Hadrian's Wall
BRITAIN
Mildenhall
Rhine River
GERMANY
Trier
Paris
Seine River
Loire River
FRANCE
Rhône River
Gard River
Nîmes
Orange
Milan
Po River
ETRURIA
Populonia
Perugia
Tiber River
Rome
ITALY
Naples
CAMPANIA
Tyrrhenian Sea
See inset
Adriatic Sea
Split
DALMATIA
Danube River
DACIA
Black Sea
Constantinople
MACEDONIA
ASIA MINOR
Troy
Pergamon
ANATOLIA
Tigris River
Euphrates River
GREECE
Athens
Corinth
Olympia
Sparta
Miletos
SYRIA
CRETE
Knossos
CYPRUS
PHOENICIA
PALESTINE
Jerusalem
Mediterranean Sea
Carthage
ALGERIA
Timgad
AIN
FRICA
400 miles
00 kilometers
Canopus
Alexandria
Cairo
Faiyum
EGYPT
Nile River
Tarquinia
Veii
Tivoli
Rome
Cerveteri
Palestrina
Ostia
Primaporta
Naples
Mount Vesuvius
Pompeii
Boscoreale
Tyrrhenian Sea

THE ROMAN EMPIRE IN THE SECOND CENTURY CE

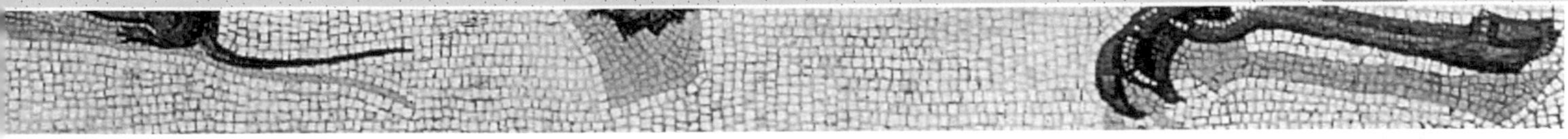

6-1. *Cityscape*, detail of a Second Style wall painting from a bedroom in the House of Publius Fannius Synistor, Boscoreale. Late 1st century CE. The Metropolitan Museum of Art, New York

Rogers Fund, 1903 (03.14.13)

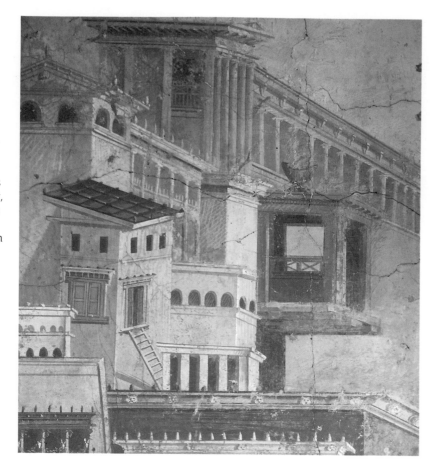

There must have been warning signs, that steamy August dawn in 79 CE, before the top of Mount Vesuvius exploded, spewing tiny fragments of volcanic rock, clouds of fine ash, and deadly gases over surrounding towns and farms and burying every trace of their existence. Those who fled took with them everything of value that could be carried. Those who stayed were quickly and completely entombed—the gladiator straining against his chains, the woman trying to shelter her child. In Pompeii, a popular resort for Roman patricians, some 2,000 people died. Among the eruption's victims was Pliny the Elder (23–79 CE), author of *Naturalis Historia* (*Natural History*), an encyclopedia of natural science, geography, and art. He was commander of the Roman fleet in the Tyrrhenian Sea and died from toxic gases while trying in vain to help those on shore. His nephew, Pliny the Younger, was also in the area but lived to describe the horror: "The sea appeared to have shrunk, . . . the shore had widened, and many sea creatures were beached on the sand. In the other direction loomed a horrible black cloud ripped by sudden bursts of fire, writhing snakelike and revealing sudden flashes larger than lightning. . . . And now came the ashes . . . " (*Letters to Tacitus* 6.16, 20).

Rain falling with the ashes created a "cement" that formed an airproof seal. Absolutely everything—people, plants, foods, houses and their contents, public buildings—was encased. The eruption was so powerful and the volcanic material so voluminous that the course of nearby rivers changed, and sea beaches were built up so much that the original site of Pompeii ended up farther from the sea, obscuring its original location for seventeen centuries. When the first excavators began to work, they found that even things that had disintegrated over time, such as flesh and wood, left perfect molds of their original shapes and textures in the solidified mass of volcanic material. Excavators devised methods for injecting plaster into such cavities and digging carefully around it to see what would be revealed—perhaps a man clutching his treasure, a hapless pet, or simply the root systems of garden plants and trees.

About three-fourths of Pompeii has now been excavated, and what has been revealed is a record of the material culture of first-century Roman civilization more detailed than any available for other early peoples. The fine examples of Republican buildings during a time of transition are especially remarkable. Most dramatic are the paintings on the walls of private dwellings. Some open "windows" onto bizarre urban landscapes that resemble stage sets (fig. 6-1), while others depict exotic rituals and dreamlike, sacred landscapes.

Pompeii's history—from its founding about 600 BCE by invaders who would later be overrun, to its becoming a Roman colony, to the disastrous moment it was frozen in time—mirrors that of the land from which it rose.

ETRUSCAN CIVILIZATION

The boot-shaped Italian peninsula, shielded to the north by the Alps, juts into the Mediterranean Sea, exposing its inhabitants in ancient times to the influence of Near Eastern, Egyptian, and Greek civilizations. Beginning about 750 BCE, Greek colonists dominated Italy's southern coastal regions. Between the seventh and sixth centuries BCE a people known as the Etruscans gained control of northern and much of central Italy. Central Italy was also home to a variety of peoples who spoke a closely related set of languages called Italic. Among these were the Latin-speaking inhabitants of Rome, a town on the Tiber River, who were, for a time, ruled by kings of Etruscan lineage. By the end of the first millennium BCE, the Romans had curtailed Etruscan power, unified Italy, and established an empire that encompassed the entire Mediterranean region.

Etruscan society emerged in the seventh century BCE in Etruria (modern Tuscany). No surviving examples of the Etruscans' literature have been found, but numerous inscriptions on tombs show that although their alphabet resembles the Greek alphabet, their language was apparently unrelated to any other European language. This linguistic distinctiveness for a long time made the Etruscans' origins a puzzle, but recent research suggests that they were the descendants of a people called the Villanovans, who had occupied the northern and western regions of Italy since the Bronze Age. Herodotus claimed that they had originally come from Lydia, in Asia Minor, in the twelfth century BCE.

Etruscan wealth was based on Etruria's fertile soil and abundance of metal ore. The Etruscans, who were noted as both metalworkers and sailors, exploited these resources in the close trading relations they maintained with the Greeks and with the Phoenicians, on the eastern coast of the Mediterranean Sea (in what is modern Lebanon). Organized into a loose federation of a dozen cities, including the major port of Populonia on the west coast of Italy, the Etruscans reached the height of their power in the sixth century BCE when they expanded into the Po River valley to the north and the Campania region to the south. Their power was in decline by the fifth century BCE, and by the third century BCE they had come within Rome's expanding dominion.

The Etruscans were deeply influenced by Greek culture except with respect to the role of women, who were better educated and more conspicuous in Etruscan than in Greek society, perhaps because of the prominence of female deities in Etruscan religion. Although Etruscan artists patronized Greek artists and drew inspiration from Greek and Near Eastern sources, they never slavishly copied what they admired. Instead, they assimilated these influences, combining them with their own traditions to create distinctive styles of architecture, sculpture, and wall painting. The Romans, too, borrowed heavily from the Greeks, and they also absorbed Etruscan culture, spreading Etruscan innovations in architecture and urban planning throughout their vast empire.

The Etruscan City

The Etruscan city was laid out on a grid plan around two main streets—one usually running north-south and the other east-west—that divided it into four sections, or quadrangles. The intersection of these streets was the town's business center, and residential areas spread out from it in all directions. Most cities were surrounded by walls with protective gates and towers. As a city's population grew, its boundaries expanded and building lots were added as needed, so that its overall plan was rarely

PARALLELS

Years	Period	Etruria/Rome	World
c. 800–700 BCE	Pre-Etruscan	Legendary founding of Rome; Greek colonies in southern Italy	**c. 800–700 BCE** Homer's *Iliad* and *Odyssey* (Greece); first Olympian Games (Greece); Greek alphabet adopted; Upanishads (India); fall of Zhou dynasty (China)
c. 700–509 BCE	Etruscan supremacy	Etruscan supremacy in central Italy; *Apollo* from Veii	**c. 700–500 BCE** Black-figure and red-figure vase painting (Greece); Byzantium founded; Sappho; Hanging Gardens (Babylon); birth of Laozi, founder of Daoism (China); Cyrus the Great (Persia) defeats Babylon; birth of Siddhartha Gautama, founder of Buddhism (Nepal); *Aesop's Fables* (Greece)
c. 509–27 BCE	Republican	Roman unification of Italy; Punic Wars (North Africa); invention of concrete; Sanctuary of Fortuna; Pont du Gard (Gaul); Cicero; Vergil	**c. 500–1 BCE** Greek orders; Confucius (China); Sophocles, Aeschylus, Euripides, Herodotus (Greece); last Old Testament book written; Polykleitos, Praxiteles, Lysippos (Greece); Parthenon (Greece); London founded (England); Alexander the Great (Greece) conquers Persia; Colossos of Rhodes; Han dynasty (China); unification of China; *Nike of Samothrace* (Greece); Great Wall (China); mound-building cultures (North America); *Ramayana* epic (India); *Aphrodite of Melos* (Greece)
c. 27 BCE–180 CE	Early Empire	Emperor Augustus; Ara Pacis; Horace; Julio-Claudian dynasties; Pliny the Elder; Colosseum; eruption of Vesuvius; Emperor Trajan; Emperor Hadrian; Pantheon; Tetrarchs; *Marcus Aurelius*; empire at greatest extent	**c. 1–400 CE** Crucifixion of Jesus (Jerusalem); Yayoi and Kofun eras (Japan); Maya civilization (Mesoamerica); first Gupta dynasty (India)
c. 180–395 CE	Late Empire	Severan emperors; Baths of Caracalla; Emperor Diocletian; Emperor Constantine; Constantinople established; Christianity becomes official religion of empire; empire permanently divided	

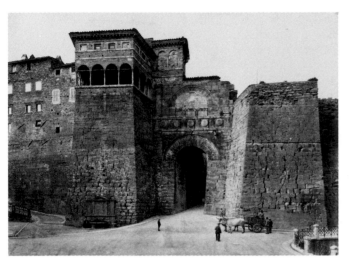

6-2. Porta Augusta, Perugia. 2nd century BCE

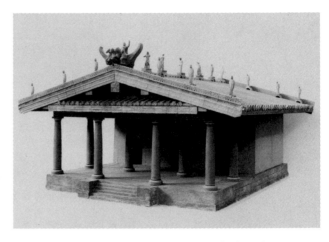

6-3. Reconstruction of an Etruscan temple, based on descriptions by Vitruvius. University of Rome, Istituto di Etruscologia e Antichità Italiche

the originally symmetrical walled quadrangles. Because the Etruscans created house-shaped funerary urns and decorated the interiors of tombs to resemble houses, we know that their houses were rectangular mud-brick structures built either around a central courtyard or around an **atrium**, a room with a shallow indoor pool for drinking, cooking, and bathing fed by rainwater through a large opening in the roof.

The second-century BCE city gate of Perugia, called the Porta Augusta, is one of the few surviving examples of Etruscan architecture (fig. 6-2). A tunnel-like passageway between two huge towers, this gate is significant for two features that anticipate developments in Roman architecture. One is the monumental **round arch**, which is extended into a semicircular ceiling, called a **barrel vault**, over the passageway. The other is the decorative **post-and-lintel** design superimposed on the plain face of the gate.

The round arch was not an Etruscan or Roman invention—ancient Near Eastern, Egyptian, and Greek builders had been familiar with it—but the Romans, apparently following Etruscan example, were the first to make widespread use of it (see "Elements of Architecture," page 226). Unlike the **corbeled** arch, formed when overhanging **courses** of masonry meet at the top, the round arch rises from **jambs**, or vertical stone supports, that border an opening. Precisely cut, wedge-shaped stone blocks called **voussoirs**, supported during construction by a temporary wooden frame, curve up and inward from the tops of the jambs and are locked into place by the insertion of the final voussoir, called the **keystone**, at the top center. The arch of the Porta Augusta, which consists of a double row of voussoirs, is set off by a square frame surmounted by a horizontal decorative element resembling an **entablature**. This is lined with a row of circular panels, or **roundels**, alternating with rectangular, columnlike uprights called **pilasters**. The effect is vaguely reminiscent of the **triglyphs** and **metopes** of a Greek Doric **frieze**. Above this entablaturelike element is a second, smaller arch opening, now filled in, that is flanked by tall pilasters.

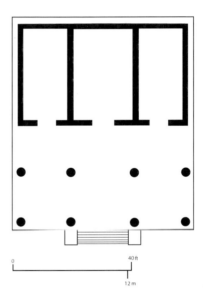

6-4. Plan of an Etruscan temple, based on descriptions by Vitruvius

Temples and Their Decoration

From early on, the Etruscans incorporated Greek deities and heroic figures into their pantheon. They also may have adapted from ancient Mesopotamia the practice of using divination to predict, and possibly alter, future events. Beyond this, little is known about their religious beliefs and practices. All that remains of Etruscan temples is a few foundations. Knowledge of their appearance comes from ceramic **votive** models and from the writings of the Roman architect Vitruvius, who sometime between 46 and 39 BCE compiled descriptions of the Etruscan and Roman architecture of his day. His account indicates that Etruscan temples (fig. 6-3) were generally similar to Greek **prostyle** temples (see "Elements of Architecture," page 164). They were raised on a platform called a **podium** and had a single flight of steps leading up to a front porch. Columns and an entablature supported the section of roof that projected over the porch. The ground plan (fig. 6-4) was almost square

ELEMENTS OF ARCHITECTURE

Arch, Vault, and Dome

The basic arch used in Western architecture is the round arch, and the most elemental type of vaulting is the extension of the round arch, called a barrel vault. The round arch and barrel vault were known and were put to limited use by Mesopotamians and Egyptians long before the Etruscans began their experiments with building elements. But it was the Romans who realized the potential strength and versatility of these architectural features and exploited them to the fullest degree.

The **round arch** displaces most of the weight, or downward thrust (see arrows on diagrams), of the masonry above it to its curving sides and transmits that weight to the supporting uprights (door or window **jambs**, **columns**, or **piers**), and from there to the ground. Arches may require added support, called **buttressing**, from adjacent masonry elements. Brick or cut-stone arches are formed by fitting together wedge-shaped pieces, called **voussoirs**, until they meet and are locked together at the top center by the final piece, called the **keystone**. Until the mortar dries, an arch is held in place by wooden scaffolding, called **centering**. The inside surface of the arch is called the **intrados**, the outside curve of the arch the **extrados**. The points from which the curves of the arch rise, called **springings**, are often reinforced by masonry **imposts**. The wall areas adjacent to the curves of the arch are **spandrels**. In a succession of arches, called an **arcade**, the space encompassed by each arch and its supports is called a **bay**.

The **barrel vault** is constructed in the same manner as the round arch. The outside pressure exerted by the curving sides of the barrel vault usually requires buttressing within or outside the supporting walls. When two barrel-vaulted spaces intersect each other on the perpendicular, the result is a **groin vault**, or **cross vault**. The Romans used the groin vault to construct some of their grandest interior spaces, and they made the round arch the basis for their great freestanding triumphal arches.

A third type of vaulted ceiling brought to technical perfection by the Romans is the hemispheric **dome**. The rim of the dome is supported on a circular wall, as in the Pantheon (figs. 6-55, 6-56). This wall is called a **drum** when it is raised on top of a main structure. Often a circular opening, called an **oculus**, is left at the top.

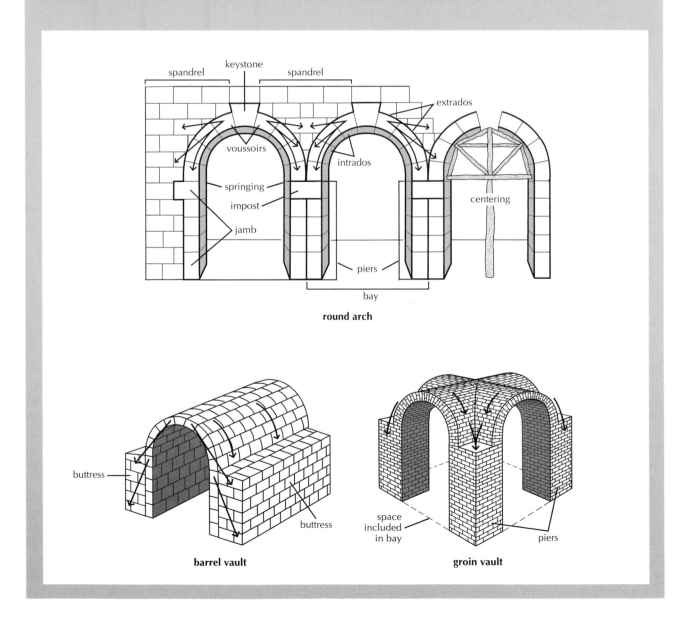

round arch

barrel vault

groin vault

and divided equally between porch and interior space. Often, as in figure 6-4, the interior space was divided into three rooms that probably housed cult statues. The building was entered directly from a courtyard or open city square.

The basic construction material of an Etruscan temple was mud brick. The columns and entablatures were made of wood or a quarried volcanic rock called tufa, which hardens upon exposure to the air. The bases, shafts (sometimes fluted), and capitals of the columns could resemble those of either the Greek Doric or the Greek Ionic orders, and the entablature had a frieze resembling that of the Doric order. Vitruvius used the term *Tuscan order* for the variation that resembled the Doric order, with an unfluted shaft and a simplified base, capital, and entablature (see "Elements of Architecture," below). Although Etruscan temples were stark and geometrically simple in form, they were embellished with

ELEMENTS OF ARCHITECTURE
Roman Architectural Orders

Both Greek and Roman orders—columns with their entablatures—are known as classical orders. Each order is made up of a system of interdependent parts whose proportions are based on mathematical ratios. In Greek and Roman architecture, no element of an order could be changed without producing a corresponding change in the other elements.

The Etruscans and Romans adapted Greek architectural orders to their own tastes and uses. For example, the Etruscans modified the Greek Doric order by adding a base to the column. The Romans created the **Composite order** by incorporating the **volute** motif of the Greek Ionic capital with other forms from the Greek Corinthian order. The sturdy, unfluted **Tuscan order**, also a Roman development, derived from the Greek Doric order by way of Etruscan models. In this diagram, the two Roman orders are shown on **pedestals**, which consist of a **plinth**, a **dado**, and a **cornice**.

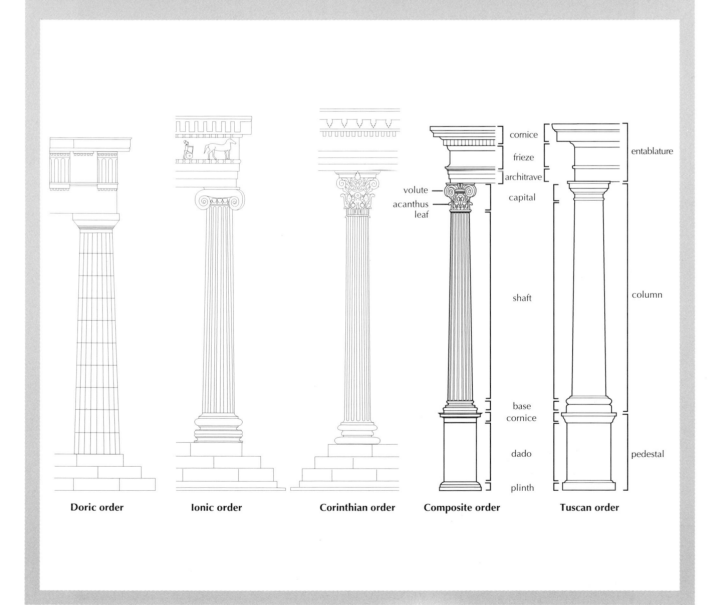

Doric order   Ionic order   Corinthian order   Composite order   Tuscan order

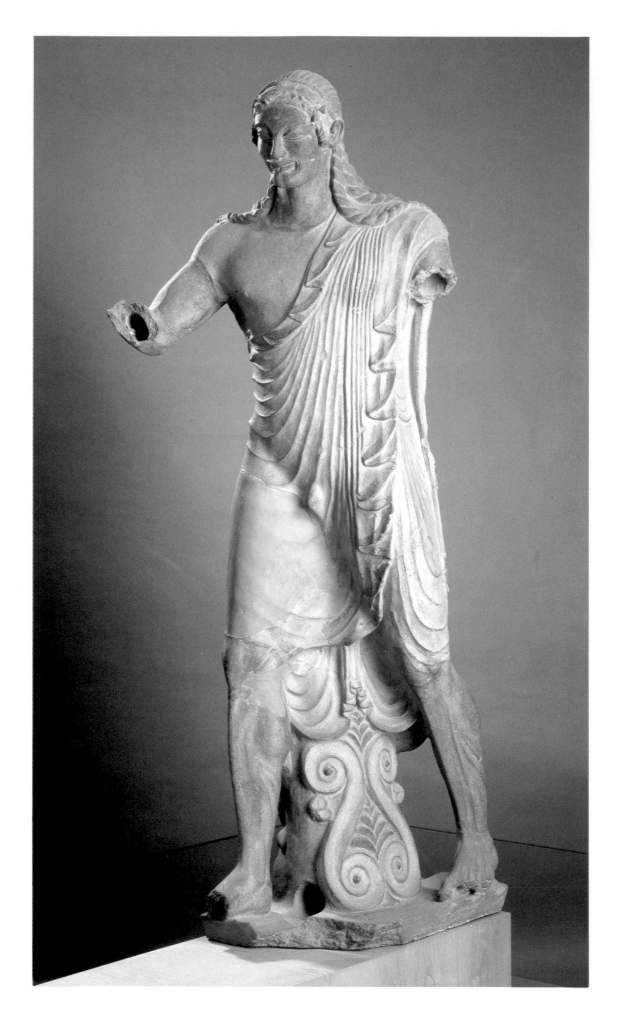

dazzling displays of terra-cotta sculpture. In an innovative feature, the temple roof served as a base for large statue groups.

Etruscan artists excelled at making monumental terra-cotta sculpture, a task of great technical and physical difficulty. A splendid example is a lifesize figure of Apollo. Dating from about 500 BCE and originally part of a four-figure scene depicting one of the labors of Hercules, the figure has survived from the temple at Veii (fig. 6-5). This scene showed Apollo and Hercules fighting for possession of a deer sacred to Diana while she and Mercury looked on (see "Roman Counterparts of Greek Gods," page 234). Apollo is shown in an active pose, looking as if he had just stepped over the decorative scrolled element that helps support the sculpture. This group of figures must have lent great vitality to the otherwise static appearance of the temple they graced.

The well-developed body form and the **Archaic smile** of the *Apollo* from Veii clearly demonstrate that Etruscan sculptors were familiar with the Greek Archaic period kouroi. A comparison of the *Apollo* and the nearly contemporary Greek *Kroisos* (see fig. 5-21) reveals differences as well as obvious similarities. Unlike the Greek figure, the body of the Etruscan *Apollo* is partially concealed by a robe with knife-edge pleats that cascades to his knees. The forward-moving pose of the Etruscan statue also has a vigor that is only implied in the balanced, tense stance of the Greek figure. This quality of energy expressed in purposeful movement is characteristic of Etruscan sculpture and, especially, tomb painting.

Tombs

Etruscan beliefs about the afterlife may have been somewhat similar to those of the Egyptians. Unlike the Egyptians, with their elaborate embalming techniques, the Etruscans favored cremation, but they nevertheless clearly thought of tombs as homes for the deceased. The Etruscan cemetery of La Banditaccia at Cerveteri (fig. 6-6) was laid out like a small town, with "streets" running between the grave mounds. The tomb chambers were partially or entirely excavated below the ground, and some were hewn out of bedrock. They were roofed over,

6-5. (opposite) *Apollo*, from Veii. c. 500 BCE. Painted terra-cotta, height 5'10" (1.8 m). Museo Nazionale di Villa Giulia, Rome

This lifesize figure is made of terra-cotta ("baked clay"), the same material used for pottery containers. Making and firing a large clay sculpture such as this one requires great technical skill. The artist must know how to construct the figures so that they do not collapse under their own weight while the clay is still wet and must know how to fire them, a process that requires precisely regulating the temperature in a large kiln for a long period of time. Etruscan terra-cotta artists must have been well known, for some of their names have come down to us, including that of a sculptor from Veii called Vulca, in whose workshop this *Apollo* may have been created.

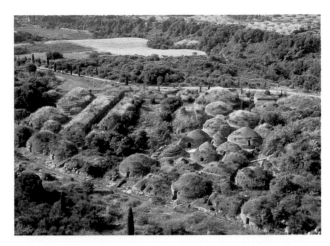

6-6. Etruscan cemetery of La Banditaccia, Cerveteri. 7th–4th century BCE

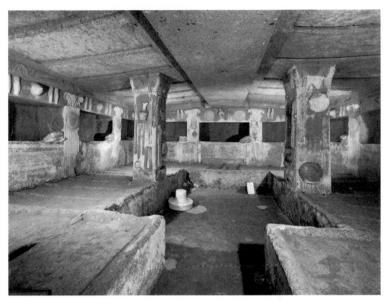

6-7. Burial chamber, Tomb of the Reliefs, Cerveteri. 3rd century BCE

sometimes with corbeled vaulting, and covered with dirt and stones.

Some tombs were carved out of the rock to resemble rooms in a house. The Tomb of the Reliefs, for example, has a flat ceiling supported by square, stone posts (fig. 6-7). Its walls were plastered and painted, and it was provided with a full range of furnishings, some real, others simulated in **stucco**, a slow-drying type of plaster that can be easily modeled or molded. Pots, jugs, robes, axes, and other items were carved into the posts to look like real objects hanging on hooks. Rendered in **low relief** at the bottom of the center post is the family dog. As these details suggest, the Etruscans made every effort to provide earthly comforts for their dead, but tomb decorations also sometimes included frightening creatures from Etruscan mythology. On the back wall of the Tomb of the Reliefs is another kind of dog—a beast with many heads—that probably represents Cerberus, the guardian of the gates of the underworld, an appropriate funerary image.

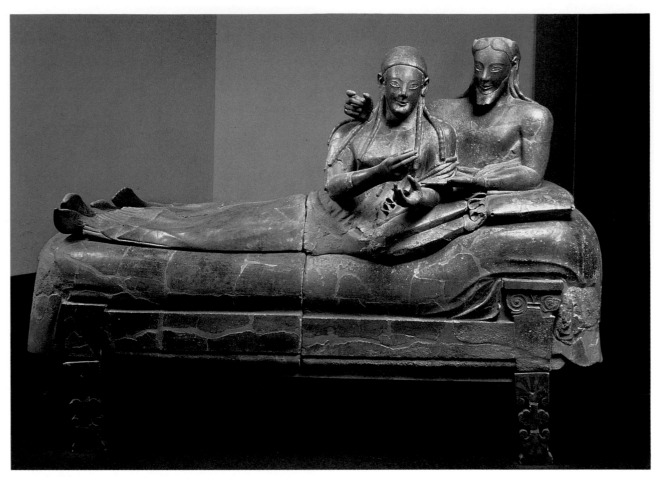

6-8. Sarcophagus, from Cerveteri. c. 520 BCE. Terra-cotta, length 6'7" (2.06 m). Museo Nazionale di Villa Giulia, Rome

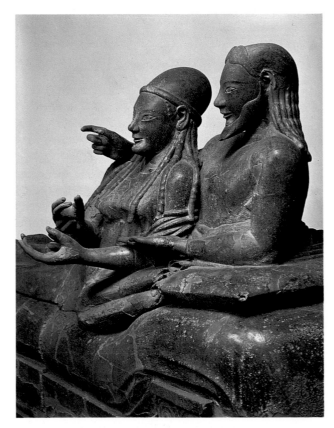

6-9. Detail of sarcophagus from Cerveteri

Sarcophagi, or coffins, also sometimes provided a domestic touch. In an example from Cerveteri of about 520 BCE, made entirely of terra-cotta (fig. 6-8), a husband and wife are shown reclining comfortably, as if they were on a couch. Rather than a cold, somber memorial to the dead, we see two lively, happy individuals rendered in sufficient detail to convey current hair and clothing styles (fig. 6-9). These genial hosts, with their smooth, conventionalized body forms and faces, their uptilted, almond-shaped eyes, and their benign smiles, make curious signs with their fingers, as if to communicate something important to the living viewer—perhaps an invitation to dine with them for eternity. Portrait coffins like this evolved from earlier terra-cotta cinerary jars with sculpted heads of the dead person whose ashes they held.

Brightly colored paintings of convivial scenes of feasting, dancing, musical performances, athletic contests, hunting, fishing, and other pleasures sometimes decorate tomb walls. Many of these murals are faded and flaking, but those on the tombs at Tarquinia are well preserved. In a detail of a painted frieze in the Tomb of the Lionesses, from about 480–470 BCE, a young man and woman engage in an energetic dance to the music of a double flute (fig. 6-10). These and other figures are grouped around the walls within a carefully arranged setting of stylized trees, birds, fish, animals, and architectural elements. Unlike in Greek tomb paintings,

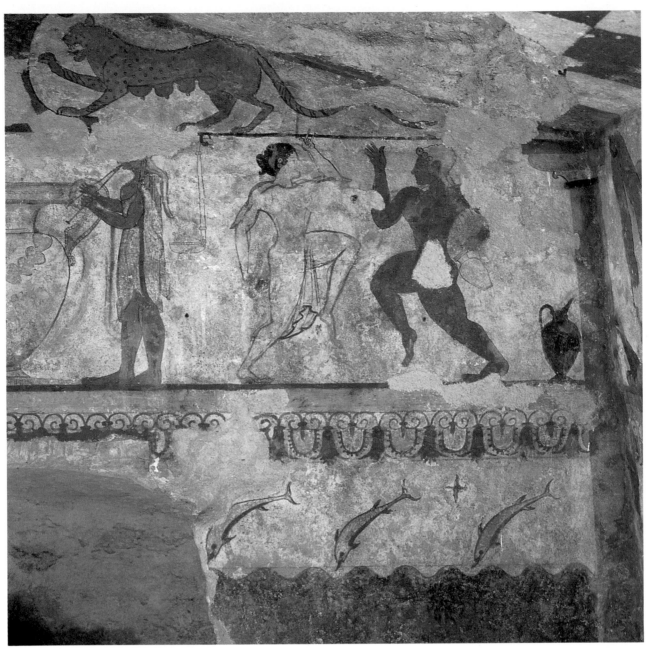

6-10. *Musicians and Dancers*, detail of a wall painting, Tomb of the Lionesses, Tarquinia. c. 480–470 BCE

The Etruscan method of painting decorations on walls has often been called fresco, but there are continuing doubts as to whether that designation is correct. Fresco is essentially painting with water-based pigments on a still-damp layer of fresh plaster applied in sections over a finished wall surface. The pigment soaks in and becomes an integral part of the plaster coating. Laboratory analyses to determine whether or not Etruscan wall paintings are true frescoes have been inconclusive. Some investigators think they are frescoes, while others claim that sections that appear to be fresco resulted from the artist accidentally painting on a wall before the plaster had dried.

women are active participants. The Etruscan painters had a remarkable ability to suggest that their subjects inhabit a bright, tangible world just beyond the tomb walls. The dancers and musicians seem to be here with us now, performing exuberantly, not enacting the formal rituals of a remote, long-dead civilization.

Bronze Work

The skill of Etruscan artists who worked in bronze was widely acknowledged in ancient times. Especially im-

pressive are the few examples of large-scale **sculpture in the round** that have survived the wholesale recycling of bronze objects over the centuries. One of these bronzes, which dates to about 500 BCE, portrays a she-wolf (fig. 6-11). This creature, with her open, snarling mouth, lean, tense body, thin flanks, protruding ribs, and heavy, milk-filled teats—evidence that she has recently given birth—appears at the same time ferocious and an object of sympathy. The naturalistic rendering of these details contrasts with the decorative, stylized rendering of the tightly curled ruff of fur around the animal's neck,

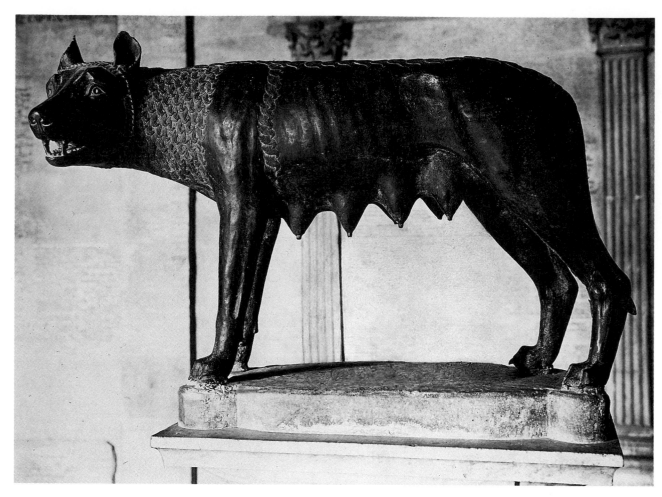

6-11. *She-Wolf.* c. 500–480 BCE. Bronze, height 33½" (85 cm). Museo Capitolino, Rome

Although this sculpture was almost certainly the work of an Etruscan artist, it has long been associated with Rome. According to an ancient Roman legend, twin infants named Romulus and Remus, who had been abandoned on the banks of the Tiber River by a wicked uncle and left there to die, were suckled by a she-wolf that had come to the river to drink. The twins were raised by a shepherd, and when they grew up, they decided to build a city near the spot where they had been rescued by the wolf. They quarreled, however, about its exact location. Romulus killed Remus and then established a small settlement that would become the great city of Rome, an event that, according to tradition, occurred in 753 BCE. Romulus ruled the city for forty years as its first king. Long after the Roman Empire had fallen, the people living in Rome, who remembered the legend, installed the *She-Wolf* on the Capitoline Hill. During the Renaissance, castings of Romulus and Remus as suckling infants were added to this original statue, which remains on the Capitoline Hill to this day in a museum—a symbol of the city's 2,000-year history. Sometimes it is referred to as the *Capitoline Wolf* or the *Wolf of Rome.*

which was incised with a sharp cutting tool. The eyes, made of glass paste, were inserted after the figure was cast and incised.

After Etruria had fallen within Rome's orbit, Etruscan artists continued in high regard and gained the support of Roman patrons. A head that was once part of a bronze statue of a man may be an example of an important Roman commission (fig. 6-12). Often alleged to be a portrait of Lucius Junius Brutus, the founder and first consul of the Roman Republic (in 509 BCE), the head traditionally has been dated about 300 BCE, long after Brutus's death. Although it may represent an unknown Roman dignitary of the third century BCE, it could also be an imaginary portrait of an ancient hero (perhaps Brutus), a type of sculpture that gained great popularity in the first century BCE. The rendering of the strong, broad face with

its heavy brows, firmly set lips, and wide-open eyes (made of painted ivory) is scrupulously detailed. The sculptor seems also to have sought to convey the psychological complexity of the subject, showing him as a somewhat world-weary man who nevertheless projects strong character and great strength of purpose. We saw a similar approach to portraiture in the statue of the Egyptian ruler Senwosret III (see fig. 3-24) made some fifteen centuries earlier.

Etruscan bronze workers also created small items for either funerary or domestic use, such as a bronze mirror that dates from about 350 BCE (fig. 6-13). The subject of the decoration engraved on the back is a winged man, identified by the inscription as the Greek priest Calchas, who accompanied the legendary army of Greek heroes under Agamemnon to Troy (see "The Trojan War," page

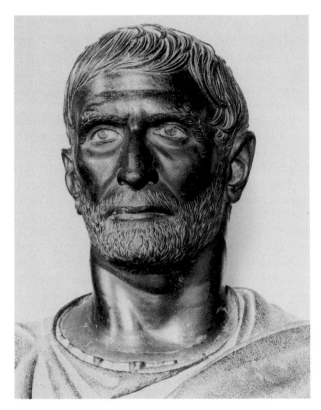

6-12. Head of a man. c. 300 BCE. Bronze, height 12½" (31.8 cm). Palazzo dei Conservatori, Rome

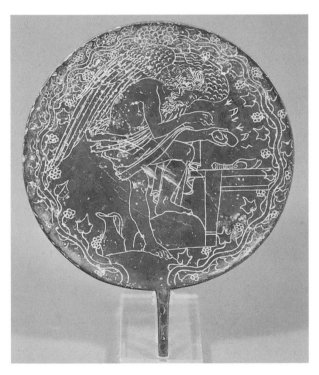

6-13. Mirror. c. 350 BCE. Engraved bronze, diameter 6" (15.3 cm). Musei Vaticani, Museo Gregoriano Etrusco, Rome

One of the methods the Etruscans used to attempt to predict the future involved interpreting the signs found in the entrails and organs, especially the liver, of sacrificial animals. That is the unusual subject engraved on the back of this sumptuous bronze mirror. Etruscan diviners (fortune tellers) would not only determine the meaning of what they saw in the animal entrails, they would also suggest a course of action to take according to whether the omens were good or bad.

216). According to Homer, the Greeks often consulted Calchas when they were uncertain about the gods' will or how to secure their favor in the war. Greeks, Etruscans, and Romans all believed the appearance of animal entrails could reveal the future. Here Calchas is shown bending over a table, intently studying the liver of a sacrificed animal, possibly a reference to an incident in the legend of the Trojan War in which Calchas, called upon to determine why the Greek fleet had been left becalmed on its way to Troy, told Agamemnon that he had to sacrifice his daughter Iphigenia. In another legend, Calchas retired after the war to his vineyards, where he died an ironic death, laughing at a prophecy that he would not live to drink his own wine. Perhaps alluding to this story, the artist has shown Calchas surrounded by grapevines and with a jug at his feet. The complex pose, the naturalistic suggestions of a rocky setting, and the pull and twist of drapery that emphasize the figure's three-dimensionality convey a sense of realism. About the time that this mirror was created, southern Etruria fell under the dominance of Rome, whose march to total control of the Italian peninsula was well under way.

ROMAN CIVILIZATION

At its greatest extent in the early second century CE, the Roman Empire reached from the Euphrates River to North Africa to Scotland. The vast territory ringed the Mediterranean Sea—*mare nostrum*, or "our sea," the Romans called it. As the Romans absorbed the peoples they conquered, they imposed on them a legal, administrative, and cultural structure that endured for some five centuries—in the eastern Mediterranean until the fifteenth century—leaving a lasting mark on the civilizations that emerged in Europe and elsewhere in their wake.

The people responsible for these accomplishments not surprisingly saw themselves in heroic terms and attributed heroic origins to themselves. According to one popular legend, rendered in epic verse by the poet Vergil (70–19 BCE) in his *Aeneid*, the Roman people were the offspring of a Trojan survivor of the Trojan War. This hero, Aeneas, was the mortal son of the goddess Venus. Thanks to his mother's intervention with Jupiter, the king of the gods, he and some compatriots escaped from the burning Troy and made their way to Italy. There they gave life to the race that, in fulfillment of a promise by Jupiter to Venus, was destined to rule the world. Another popular legend tells the story of Rome's founding by Romulus and Remus, the twin sons of Mars, the god of war, by a mortal princess from the central Italian city of Alba Longa (see caption, fig. 6-11).

Archeologists and historians have developed a more mundane picture of Rome's origins. In Neolithic times, groups of people who spoke a common language—Latin—and lived primarily by raising and tending sheep settled in permanent villages across the plains of Latium, south of the Tiber River, as well as on the seven hills that would eventually become Rome (the Palatine, Aventine, Caelian, Capitoline, Esquiline, Quirinal, and Viminal). These first settlements were little more than

REIGNS OF SIGNIFICANT ROMAN EMPERORS

	Augustus	27 BCE–14 CE
Julio-Claudian	Tiberius	14–37 CE
	Caligula	37–41
	Claudius	41–54
	Nero	54–68
Flavian	Vespasian	69–79
	Titus	79–81
	Domitian	81–96
	Nerva	96–98
	Trajan	98–117
	Hadrian	117–138
Antonine	Antoninus Pius	138–161
	Marcus Aurelius	161–180
	Commodus	180–192
Severan	Septimius Severus	193–211
	Caracalla	211–217
	Severus Alexander	222–235
	Diocletian	284–305
	Constantine I	306–337

ROMAN COUNTERPARTS OF GREEK GODS

Roman Name	Greek God
Jupiter	Zeus, king of the gods
Juno	Hera, Zeus's wife and sister, queen of the gods
Minerva	Athena, goddess of wisdom
Mars	Ares, god of war
Apollo, also Phoebus	Apollo, god of the sun and reason
Venus	Aphrodite, goddess of love
Diana	Artemis, goddess of the moon and hunting
Mercury	Hermes, messenger of the gods
Pluto	Hades, god of the underworld
Bacchus	Dionysos, god of wine
Vulcan	Hephaistos, god of fire
Vesta	Hestia, goddess of hearth and family
Ceres	Demeter, goddess of agriculture
Neptune	Poseidon, god of the sea
Cupid or Amor	Eros, god of love
Hercules	Herakles

Although sometimes worshiped as a god, strictly speaking Hercules is a hero known for his physical strength.

More information about Greek gods and their attributes appears on page 156, "Greek and Roman Deities and Heroes."

clusters of small, round huts, but by the sixth century BCE Rome, located at an important crossing of the Tiber, had developed into a major transportation hub and trading center. By the Republican period nearly a million people lived there.

Early Rome was governed by a series of kings and an advisory body of leading citizens called the Senate. The population was divided into two classes, a wealthy and powerful upper class, the patricians, and a lower class, the plebeians. The last kings of Rome were members of an Etruscan family, the Tarquins. Legend has it that the last ruler in this line, Tarquinius Superbus, was a despot whose behavior led to his overthrow in 509 BCE, marking the beginning of what is known as the Republican period. The Senate, dominated by patrician families, gained in prestige and authority, and the early history of the Republic was marked by a struggle by plebeians against patricians for political and economic equality.

During the fifth century BCE, by a process of alliance and conquest, Rome began to incorporate neighboring territories in Italy. By 275 BCE Rome controlled the entire Italian peninsula. This expansion led to a confrontation with the powerful empire of Carthage, the Phoenician city on the north coast of Africa, which controlled Spain, Sicily, and the western North African coast. In a series of conflicts known as the Punic Wars (264–146 BCE), the Romans ultimately subdued the Carthaginians, destroyed Carthage, and gained control of the western Mediterranean. By the mid-second century BCE they had subdued Macedonia and Greece, and by 44 BCE had conquered most of Gaul (modern France) and the eastern Mediterranean.

During this period of overseas expansion, Rome changed from an essentially agricultural society to a commercial and political power. The warfare and expansion strained Rome's political system, weakening the authority of the Senate and leading ultimately to a series of civil wars among powerful generals whose authority derived from the support of their troops. In 46 BCE Julius Caesar emerged victorious over his rivals, had himself declared dictator, assumed autocratic powers, and ruled Rome until his assassination in 44 BCE. The renewed fighting that followed Caesar's death ended with the unquestioned supremacy of his grandnephew and heir, Octavian, over Rome and all its possessions.

Although Octavian maintained the forms of Republican government, he retained real authority for himself, and his ascension marks the end of the Republic. In 27 BCE he was granted the religious title *Augustus*, which came to mean "supreme ruler," and he is known to history by that name as the first emperor of Rome (see "Reigns of Significant Roman Emperors," above). Assisted by his astute and pragmatic second wife, Livia, Augustus proved to be an incomparable administrator. He brought opposing factions under his control and established efficient rule throughout the empire. In 12 CE he was given the title *Pontifex Maximus*, or High Priest, and thus also became the empire's highest religious official. After his death in 14 CE, the Senate ordered him to be venerated as a state god. This powerful man laid the foundation for an extended period of stability, internal peace, and economic prosperity known as the *Pax Romana*—the Roman Peace—which lasted about 200 years.

Conquering and maintaining a vast empire required not only inspired leadership and tactics but also careful planning, massive logistical support, and great administrative skill. Some of Rome's most enduring contributions to Western civilization—its system of law, its governmental and administrative structures, and its enormous construction of civil architecture—reflect these qualities.

To facilitate the development and administration of the empire, as well as to make city life comfortable and attractive to its citizens, the Roman government undertook building programs of unprecedented scale and complexity, mandating the construction of central administrative centers (**basilicas**), racetracks (**circuses** and **stadiums**), theaters, public baths, roads, bridges, **aqueducts**, middle-class housing, and even whole new towns. To accomplish these tasks without sacrificing beauty, efficiency, and human well-being, Roman builders and architects developed rational planning, durable materials, and highly sophisticated engineering methods.

To move their armies about efficiently, speed communications between Rome and the farthest reaches of the empire, and promote commerce, the Romans built a vast and sophisticated network of roads. Many modern European highways still follow the lines laid down by Roman engineers, and Roman-era foundations underlie the streets of more than a few cities. Roman bridges are still in use, and remnants of Roman aqueducts need only repairs and connecting links to make them function once again to carry fresh water over long distances.

Despite their power, the Romans liked to portray themselves as simple country folk who had never lost their love of nature. Even though they were essentially city dwellers, the wealthy maintained country estates and the middle classes enjoyed their town-home gardens. Similar to United States presidents like George Washington and Thomas Jefferson, who returned regularly to their estates, many Roman emperors were attached to country villas, which served them both as functioning farms and as places of recreation. Wealthy Romans even brought nature indoors by commissioning artists to paint landscapes on the interior walls of their homes. As these wealthy Romans developed an ever more luxurious life, however, the cost of the expanding empire became an increasing burden on the less fortunate, which eventually led to the occurrence of intermittent internal conflict.

Like the Etruscans, the Romans greatly admired Greek and Hellenistic culture and borrowed heavily from it. Historians have even suggested that although Rome conquered the Hellenistic world, Greek culture conquered Roman culture. The Romans used Greek orders to decorate their architecture, imported Greek art, and employed Greek artists. In 146 BCE they stripped the Greek city of Corinth of its art treasures and shipped them back to Rome.

Ironically, this love of Greek art was not accompa-nied by universal admiration for artists. As Plutarch, a Greek commentator of the first century CE, wrote: "No gifted young man, upon seeing the Zeus of Pheidias at Olympia, ever wanted to be Pheidias nor, upon seeing the Hera at Argos, ever wanted to be Polykleitos. . . . For it does not necessarily follow that, if a work is delightful because of its gracefulness, the man who made it is worthy of our serious regard." Although there must have been significant exceptions, professional artists were generally considered little more than skilled laborers.

Again like the Etruscans, the Romans adopted the Greek gods and heroes as their own. (This chapter uses the Roman names of these figures; see "Roman Counterparts of Greek Gods," opposite.) The Romans assimilated Greek religious beliefs and practices into a form of state religion. When, after Augustus, the emperors were deified—in part to attract and focus the allegiance of the culturally diverse populations that had come under Roman rule—the state religion took on a highly political cast. Worship of ancient gods was mingled with homage to past rulers and oaths of allegiance to the living one, and the official religion became increasingly ritualized, perfunctory, and distant from the everyday life of the average person. As a result, many Romans adopted the more personal, mystical religious beliefs of the peoples they had conquered. The cult of Isis and Osiris was introduced from Egypt; from Anatolia came the cult of the Great Mother; and belief in the all-powerful God of Judaism and Christianity spread from Palestine. In the third century CE, an exclusively male cult of a Persian hero-god called Mithras also became popular, especially with the soldier-emperors and their troops. All these so-called mystery religions flourished alongside the state religion with its Olympian deities and deified emperors, despite occasional government efforts to suppress them.

ART OF THE REPUBLICAN PERIOD AND THE BEGINNING OF THE EMPIRE

During the Republic, the first great period of Roman architecture, sculpture, and painting initially reflected Etruscan influences. As the empire expanded, exposure to the art of Greece and of other cultures began to be reflected in increasingly eclectic styles. Although Roman architects built religious buildings, palaces, and tombs for the rich and powerful, they were also concerned with satisfying the needs of ordinary people in the large and varied population of their empire. To meet those needs as efficiently and inexpensively as possible, they created new building forms, discovered new structural principles, and developed new materials.

Architecture in Roman Italy

Roman architects relied heavily on the round arch and barrel vaulting. Beginning in the second century BCE, they also relied increasingly on a new building material, cast **concrete** (see "Elements of Architecture," page 236). In

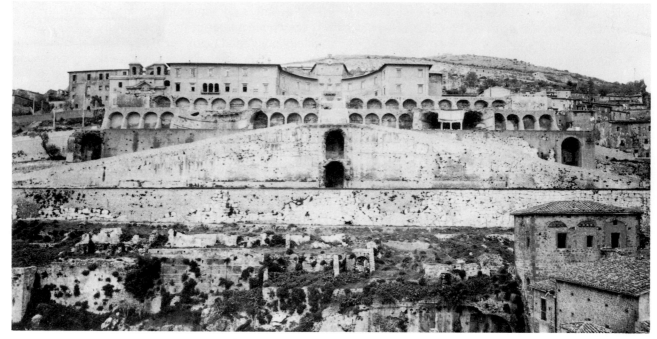

6-14. Sanctuary of Fortuna, Palestrina. Begun c. 100 BCE

ELEMENTS OF ARCHITECTURE

Roman Construction

The Romans were pragmatic, and their pragmatism extended from recognizing and exploiting undeveloped potential in construction methods and physical materials to organizing large-scale building works. Their exploitation of the arch and the vault is typical of their adapt-and-improve approach. Their "invention" and use of **concrete**, beginning in the first century BCE, was a technological breakthrough of the greatest importance.

In the earliest concrete wall construction, workers filled a framework of rough stones with concrete: stone rubble soaked in a binder made from volcanic sand and clay. This stone-wall construction method, called *opus incertum*, was followed by *opus reticulatum*, in which the framework is a diagonal web of smallish, pyramidal concrete bricks set in a cross pattern. By the first century CE, Roman builders were setting concrete bricks in level courses, pointed ends inward, in a technique called *opus testaceum*.

The composite-material bricks were homely and were generally covered, or **veneered**, with better-looking materials, such as marble, stone, mosaic, and tile. Thus, an essential difference between Greek and Roman architecture is that Greek buildings reveal the building material itself, whereas Roman buildings show only the applied surface.

Concrete-based construction freed the Romans from the limits of right-angle forms and comparatively short spans. With this freedom, Roman builders pushed the established limits of architecture, creating some very large and highly original spaces, many based on the curve.

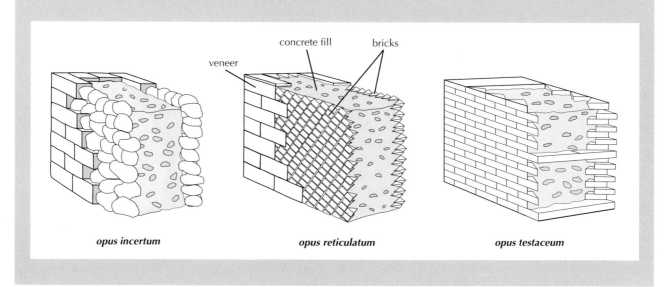

opus incertum   *opus reticulatum*   *opus testaceum*

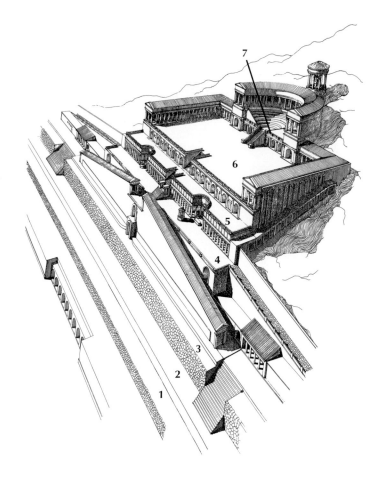

6-15. Axonometric reconstruction drawing of the Sanctuary of Fortuna, showing the seven terraces

contrast to stone—which was expensive, time-consuming to quarry, and difficult to transport, cut to size, and set in place—the components of concrete were cheap, light, and easily transported. Stone structures required skilled workers, whereas concrete structures could be built by a large, semiskilled work force directed by one or two trained and experienced supervisors.

Roman concrete consisted of powdered lime, sand (in particular a volcanic sand called pozzolana found in abundance near Pompeii), and various types of rubble, such as small rocks and broken pottery. These were mixed with water, causing a chemical reaction that hardened them into a strong, solid mass. At first concrete was used mainly for poured foundations, but with technical advances it became indispensable for the construction of walls, arches, and vaults for ever larger buildings. Its one weakness was that it absorbed moisture, so builders covered exposed concrete surfaces with a veneer of brick or cut stone; then they often added an overlay of plaster for good measure.

After World War II, teams clearing the rubble from bombings of Palestrina, about 16 miles southeast of Rome, discovered the remains of the Sanctuary of Fortuna, an example of Roman Republican architectural planning and concrete construction at its most creative (figs. 6-14, 6-15). The sanctuary, dedicated to the goddess of fate and chance, was begun about 100 BCE and was grander than any building in Rome in its time. Its design and size show the clear influence of Hellenistic architecture, such as the long colonnade and the co-

lossal scale of the great altar from Pergamon (see fig. 5-80). Built of concrete covered with a veneer of stucco and finely cut limestone, it consists of a series of open, partially open, and closed spaces on seven vaulted platforms or terraces that rise up a steep hillside. Worshipers ascended long ramps to the second level, then steep staircases to successively higher levels.

In a departure from Hellenistic style, the Romans incorporated several rounded elements that relieved the structure's strict regularity and created a new kind of architectural rhythm: symmetrically placed **exedrae** (half-circle niches) on the fourth level, rows of round-arch openings on the fifth and sixth levels, and finally, on the seventh level, a huge, theaterlike, semicircular colonnaded pavilion reached by a broad semicircular staircase from a large, open terrace. Behind this pavilion was a small **tholos** temple to Fortuna, hiding the ancient rock-cut cave where important acts of divination, predicting future events, had taken place from early times. The overall **axial** plan—the way it directs movement from the large, open terrace up the semicircular staircase, through the portico, to the tiny tholos temple, to the cave—brings to mind the great Egyptian temples, such as that of Hatshepsut at Deir el-Bahri (see fig. 3-33).

More typical of Roman religious architecture than isolated, walled sanctuaries like those favored by the Greeks were small urban temples built, in the Etruscan manner, in the midst of congested commercial centers. An early example in Rome, nearly contemporary with the Sanctuary of Fortuna, is a small, rectangular temple

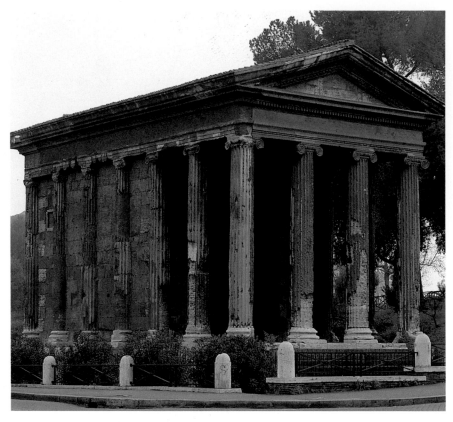

6-16. Temple perhaps dedicated to Portunus, Forum Boarium (cattle market), Rome. Late 2nd century BCE

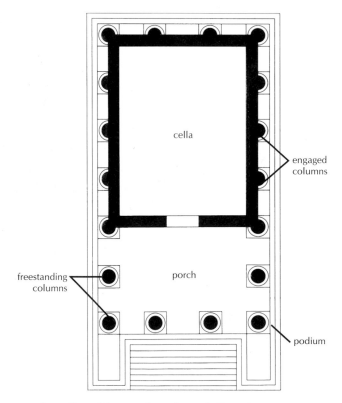

cella

engaged columns

freestanding columns

porch

podium

6-17. Plan of the temple perhaps dedicated to Portunus

perhaps dedicated to Portunus, the god of harbors and ports, that stands beside the Tiber River (figs. 6-16, 6-17). With a rectangular **cella** and a porch at one end reached by a single flight of steps, this temple, built in the late second century BCE, echoes the Greek prostyle plan. Almost like a piece of sculpture, it stands on a raised platform, or podium. The Ionic columns are freestanding on the porch and **engaged** around the cella. The entablature above the columns on the porch continues around the cella as a decorative frieze. The plan of this structure resembles that of a **peripteral** temple, but because the columns around the cella are engaged even though they appear to be freestanding, it is called **pseudo-peripteral**. This design, with variations in the orders used with it, was to become standard for Roman temples.

City Life and Domestic Architecture

Pompeii was a thriving center of about 20,000 inhabitants on the day Mount Vesuvius erupted. An ancient village that had grown and spread over many centuries, it lacked the gridlike regularity of newer Roman cities, but its layout was typical for its time. Temples and government buildings surrounded a main square, or **forum**; paved streets were lined with shops and houses; and enclosing all was a protective wall with fortified gates (fig. 6-18). The forum was the center of civic life in Roman towns and cities, as the **agora** was in Greek cities. Business was conducted in its basilicas and pavilions, religious duties performed in its temples, and

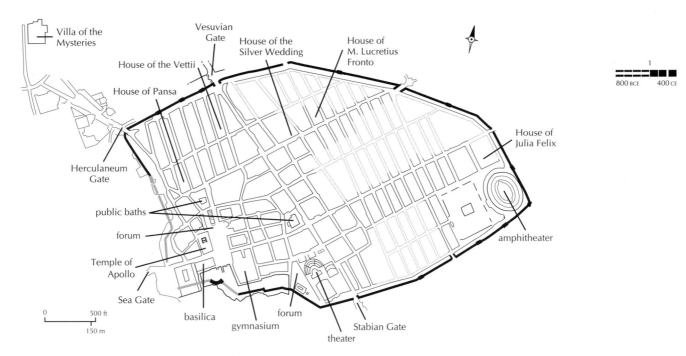

6-18. Plan of the city of Pompeii in 79 CE

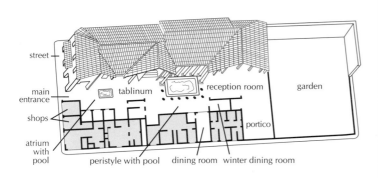

6-19. Reconstruction drawing and plan of the House of Pansa, Pompeii. 2nd century BCE

speeches presented in its open square. For recreation, people went to the nearby baths or the events in the amphitheater.

The people of Pompeii lived in houses behind or above a row of shops, or in two- or three-story apartment buildings, or in gracious private residences with one or more gardens. Even upper-class homes often had street-level shops. If there was no shop, the wall facing the street was usually solid except for the door, an indication of the emphasis on interior rather than exterior design. In a sense, the inner orientation of domestic architecture reflects the central and sacred place of hearth and home in Roman religion.

A Roman house usually consisted of small rooms laid out on a straight, generally symmetrical plan, as illustrated in the reconstruction drawing of the House of Pansa in Pompeii (fig. 6-19). From the entrance, a corridor led to the atrium, a large space with a shallow pool for catching rainwater through an opening in the roof. The organization of the front part of the house—the centrally located atrium surrounded by small rooms—originated with the Etruscans. Figure 6-20 shows the atrium

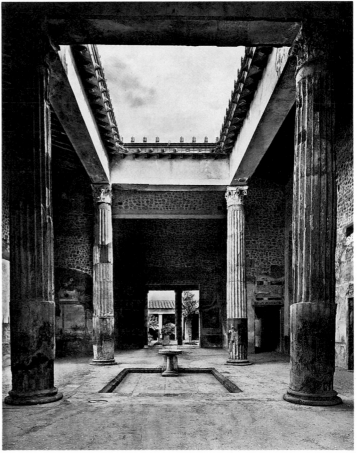

6-20. Atrium, House of the Silver Wedding, Pompeii. Early 1st century CE

Ancient Roman houses excavated at Pompeii and elsewhere are usually named after the families or individuals who once lived in them. In many cases, the owner is unknown. This house received its unusual name as a commemorative gesture. It was excavated in 1893, the year of the silver wedding anniversary of Italy's King Humbert and his wife, Margaret of Savoy, who had supported archeological fieldwork at Pompeii.

THE URBAN GARDEN

The remains of urban gardens preserved in the volcanic fallout at Pompeii have been the focus of a decades-long study by archeologist Wilhelmina Jashemski. Her work has revealed much about the layout of ancient Roman gardens and the plants cultivated in them. Early archeologists, searching for more tangible remains, usually destroyed evidence about gardens, but in 1973 Jashemski and her colleagues had the opportunity to work on the previously undisturbed **peristyle** garden—a planted interior court enclosed by columns—of the House of G. Polybius in Pompeii. Workers first removed layers of debris and volcanic material to expose the level of the soil as it was before the eruption in 79 CE. They then collected samples of pollen, seeds, and other organic material and carefully injected plaster into underground root cavities to make casts for later study. These materials enabled botanists to identify the types of plants and trees cultivated in the garden, to estimate their size, and to determine where they had been planted. Some houses had both peristyle gardens and separate vegetable gardens.

The evidence from this and other excavations indicates that most urban gardens served a practical function. They were planted with fruit- and nut-bearing trees and occasionally with olive trees. Only the great luxury gardens were rigidly landscaped. Most gardens were randomly planted or, at best, arranged in irregular rows.

The garden in the house of Polybius was surrounded on three sides by a portico, which protected a large cistern on one side that supplied the house and garden with water. Young lemon trees in pots lined the fourth side of the garden, and nail holes in the wall above the pots indicated that the trees had been espaliered—pruned and trained—a practice still in use today. Fig, cherry, and pear trees filled the garden space, and traces of a fruit-picking ladder, wide at the bottom and narrow at the top to fit among the branches, was found on the site. This evidence suggests that the garden was a densely planted orchard similar to the one painted on the dining-room walls of the villa of the empress Livia in Primaporta (see fig. 6-36).

An aqueduct built during the reign of the emperor Augustus gave Pompeii's residents access to a reliable and plentiful supply of water, replacing their dependence on wells and rainwater basins. This new source allowed them to add pools, fountains, and flowering plants that needed large amounts of water to their gardens. In contrast to the earlier, unordered plantings, formal gardens with low, clipped borders and plantings of ivy, ornamental box- wood, laurel, myrtle, acanthus, and rosemary—all mentioned by writers of the time—became fashionable. There is also evidence of topiary work, the clipping of shrubs and hedges into fanciful shapes. Sculpture and purely decorative fountains became popular. The peristyle garden of the House of the Vettii, for example, had more than a dozen fountain statues jetting water into marble basins (fig. 6-21). In the most elegant peristyles, mosaic decorations covered the floors, walls, and even the fountains. Some of the earliest wall mosaics, such as the one illustrated here, were created as backdrops for fountains.

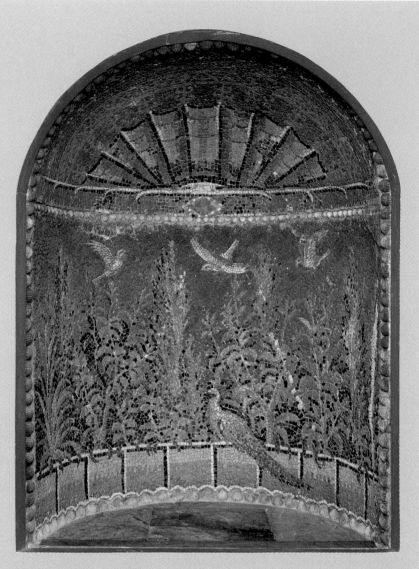

Wall niche, from a garden in Pompeii. Mid-1st century CE. Mosaic, 43¾ x 31½" (111 x 80 cm). Fitzwilliam Museum, University of Cambridge, England

in the well-preserved House of the Silver Wedding in Pompeii. Beyond the atrium, in a reception room called the tablinum, portrait busts of the family's ancestors might be displayed, and the head of the household conferred with clients. In later houses the tablinum often opened onto a central peristyle court, surrounded by a colonnaded walkway, or portico. The more private areas—such as the dining room, the family sitting room, bedrooms, the kitchen, and servants' quarters—usually were entered through the peristyle court.

Roman houses reflect architectural ideals seen also in monumental and public construction. The Romans, with their love of nature, softened the abstract regularity of their homes with beautifully planted gardens in the peristyle court (see "The Urban Garden," opposite). Larger residences also had a separate kitchen garden. In Pompeii, where the mild southern climate would have permitted gardens to flourish year-round, the peristyle court was often turned into an outdoor living room with wall murals, fountains, and sculpture on pedestals, as in the House of the Vettii (fig. 6-21), which dates from the mid-first century CE.

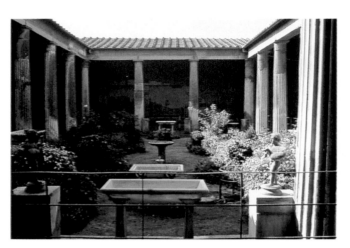

6-21. Peristyle garden, House of the Vettii, Pompeii. Mid-1st century CE

Architecture in the Provinces

In many areas of Europe and the Mediterranean, impressive examples of Roman engineering still stand, powerful reminders of Rome's rapid spread and enduring impact. The Pont du Gard near Nîmes in southern France has a 900-foot span and rises 180 feet above the Gard River (fig. 6-22). Still in use in the twentieth century as a bridge for pedestrians and carts, it was originally an aqueduct, part of a system that brought water to Nîmes from the springs of Uzès 30 miles to the north. This feat of hydraulic engineering, impressive even by modern standards, is thought to have been executed under the direction of Augustus's son-in-law Agrippa about 20 BCE. At the time it was built, the aqueduct could provide 100 gallons of water a day for every person in Nîmes.

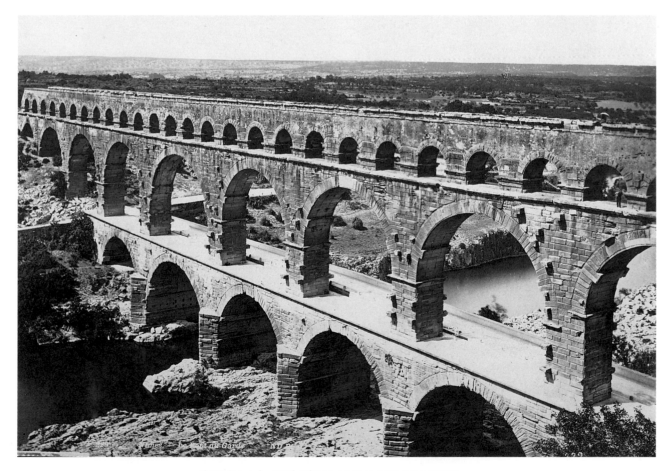

6-22. Pont du Gard, Nîmes, France. Late 1st century BCE

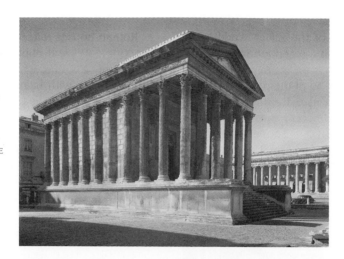

6-23. Maison
Carrée,
Nîmes,
France.
c. 20 BCE

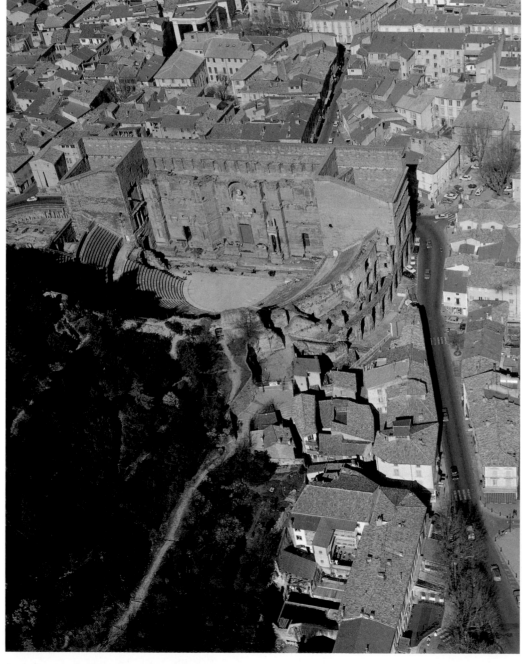

6-24. Roman theater, Orange, France. 1st century BCE

Because of renovations, plays can still be staged at this theater, one of the rare Roman theaters still being used for its original purpose.

ROMAN FUNERARY PRACTICES

Like the Etruscans, the early Romans generally cremated their dead and placed the ashes in special cinerary urns or vases. Unlike the Etruscans, however, they made no effort to provide an earthly domestic setting for the deceased. Instead, they frequently kept the ash containers, together with busts and casts from death masks of their ancestors and family documents, on view in their homes, often in a room called the tablinum at one end of the atrium.

In Rome related individuals or members of social clubs and other organizations established private group cemeteries. When a group's members had used up the ground-level space in their cemetery, they tunneled underground to create a **hypogeum**, or **catacomb**. The tunnels extended from one edge of the cemetery property to the other, descending to another level as space filled up. They were lined with niches for urns and busts of the dead and opened into small side chambers called **cubicula**.

The Romans memorialized their dead in elaborate funeral celebrations and left small offerings at their grave sites every February. They revered their ancestors and kept death masks as a way of remembering them. Pliny the Elder, writing in the first century CE, describes this practice: "Wax impressions of the face were set out on separate chests [at home], so that they might serve as the portraits which were carried in family funeral processions, and thus, when anyone died, the entire roll of his ancestors, all who ever existed, was present" (*Naturalis Historia* 35.6–7). The wax death masks were sometimes cast in plaster, and sculptors might be commissioned to create bust portraits of the dead. Sculptors might also be asked to create imaginary portraits of illustrious, long-dead ancestors to be displayed in the tablinum and carried in funeral processions.

An oration in honor of the deceased, delivered by the family's most eminent member, was an important part of a Roman funeral. For much of the Republican period, only men were honored by such orations, but in 102 BCE the consul Catulus set a new precedent by giving an oration for his mother, Popilia. One of Julius Caesar's famed speeches was an oration for his aunt Julia. In it he traced her lineage to Rome's kings on her mother's side and to the gods on her father's side.

The Pont du Gard was constructed of beautifully sized and precisely cut stones from a nearby quarry. It consists of three **arcades** (walls with a series of regularly spaced arched openings) stacked one on the other and exemplifies the simplest use of the arch as a structural element. The arches of the thick base arcade spring from huge stone piers (square or rectangular support posts) and support a roadbed approximately 20 feet wide. The arches of the second arcade span the same distance as those of the base, but it is much narrower than the first and set on one side of the roadbed. The third arcade, the narrowest and shortest of the three, supports the water trough. It has three arches for every one of the second arcade. A purely utilitarian structure, the aqueduct was left undecorated, and the projecting blocks inserted to support scaffolding during construction were left to provide easy access for repairs. It nevertheless conveys a sense of balance, proportion, rhythmic harmony, and integration into its natural setting.

The city of Nîmes is located in what was once one of the richest provinces of the empire and contains several other well-preserved Roman structures. One of these, a temple known as the Maison Carrée, or Square House, is similar to the temple dedicated to Portunus in Rome but is larger and much more richly decorated (fig. 6-23). Built in the forum at Nîmes about 20 BCE and later dedicated to Gaius and Lucius Caesar, the grandsons of Augustus, the Maison Carrée differs from its prototype only in its size and its use of the more opulent Corinthian order. Both the aqueduct and the temple seem to summarize Roman architecture: technologically advanced but conservative in design. It is perhaps these qualities that appealed to the American president and amateur architect Thomas Jefferson, who visited Nîmes and was said to have found inspiration in the Maison Carrée for his own designs.

The Romans carried on the Greek and Hellenistic tradition of building large outdoor theaters, using suitable hillsides for the purpose of creating freestanding structures on level terrain. A well-preserved example of the hillside type can be found at Orange, also in southern France but north of Nîmes, on the east side of the Rhône (fig. 6-24). As in Greek theaters, the seating is arranged in a semicircular cone shape. The orchestra, which in Greek theaters is circular and is part of the performance area, has here been reduced to a semicircle and made part of the seating area. A raised stage with an elaborate enclosing wall faces the audience. Built during the reign of Augustus in the first century BCE, the theater held as many as 7,000 spectators. In its heyday, the plain masonry of the wall, 335 feet long and 123 1/2 feet high, was disguised with columns and **pediments** and presided over by a statue of the emperor in a central niche. Unlike Greek-style theaters, in which the surrounding environment is part of the performance setting, this theater isolated audience and actors alike in an entirely architectural environment.

Republican Sculpture

Sculptors of the Republican period sought to create believable images based on careful observations of their surroundings. The convention of rendering accurate and faithful portraits of individuals, called **verism**, may be derived from Roman ancestor veneration and the practice of making death masks of deceased relatives (see "Roman Funerary Practices," above). In any case, patrons of the Republican period clearly admired veristic por-

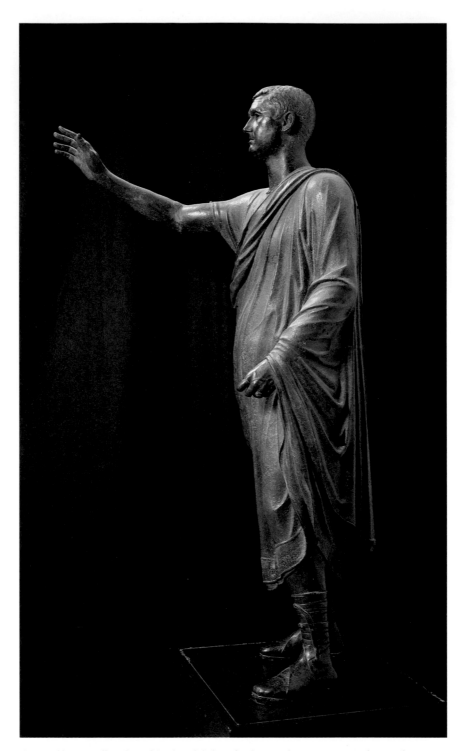

6-25. *Aulus Metellus*, found in the vicinity of Lake Trasimeno. Late 2nd or early
1st century BCE. Bronze, height 5'11" (1.8 m). Museo Archeològico Nazionale,
Florence

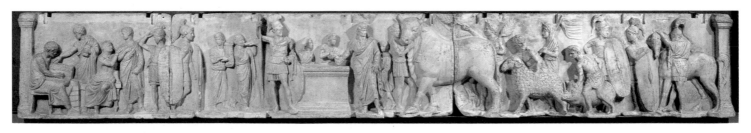

6-26. *Taking of the Roman Census*, frieze from a large base for statuary, possibly from the Temple of Neptune, Rome. c. 70 BCE.
Marble, height 32" (81.3 cm). Musée du Louvre, Paris

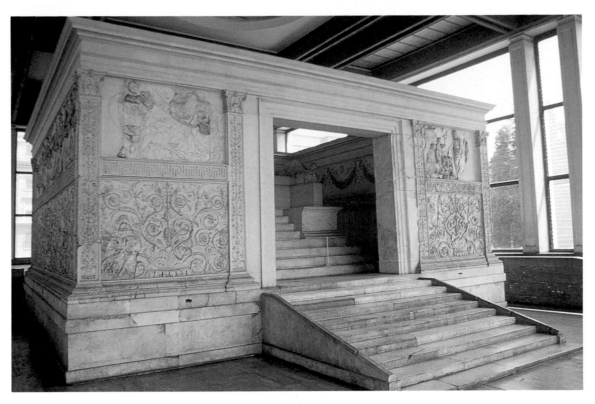

6-27. Ara Pacis. 13–9 BCE. Marble, approx. 34'5" (10.5 m) x 38' (11.6 m). Rome

The Ara Pacis—a war monument as famous in its day as the Vietnam Veterans' Memorial is in ours—has been reconstructed and is kept well preserved in a modern pavilion built at the time of the centennial of Italian unification in 1970. The pavilion is located beside the Tiber River near the tomb of Augustus, who commissioned the Ara Pacis as a memorial to his military conquests. The reign of Augustus marks the beginning of the *Pax Romana*, or Roman Peace, a period of stability in the empire that lasted nearly two centuries.

traits, and it is not surprising that they often turned to skilled Etruscan artists to execute them. The large bronze portrait statue of Aulus Metellus (fig. 6-25), the work of an Etruscan artist, dates to the late second or early first century BCE. The name of the subject, a Roman official, is inscribed on the hem of the toga in Etruscan letters. The statue, known from early times as "The Orator," depicts him addressing a gathering, his arm outstretched and slightly raised, a pose so expressive of authority and persuasiveness that it gained favor among later patrons. The orator wears sturdy laced leather boots and a folded and draped garment called a toga, both characteristic of a Roman official. According to Pliny the Elder, large statues like this were often placed atop columns as memorials to the individuals portrayed.

Historical events in ancient Rome were often preserved in the durable medium of relief sculpture. Perhaps the earliest historical reliefs discovered in Rome are two long marble panels dating from the early first century BCE, one of which depicts the *Taking of the Roman Census* (fig. 6-26). This panel and another now housed in a Munich museum may have been part of a base for a group of statues in one of Rome's temples, perhaps the Temple of Neptune. The left half of the panel shows the official registration of citizens; the right half shows a lustrum, a ritual that involved the sacrificial killing of animals, in this case a bull, a sheep, and a large pig being led in a procession to the altar at the center. The identity

of the censor (official census taker) commemorated in this panel is not certain, making it impossible to date precisely. Some scholars have suggested that he is Marcus Antonius, an orator who was elected censor of Rome in 97 BCE. The sculptor's desire to convey in detail specific contemporary events, which required depicting the subjects with complete clarity, overrode concerns for an artistically balanced composition.

Augustan Sculpture

Drawing inspiration from Etruscan and Greek art as well as Republican traditions, Roman artists of the imperial period made their own distinctive contribution to the history of sculpture. They enriched and developed the art of portraiture, creating both official images and representations of private individuals; they recorded contemporary historical events on commemorative arches, columns, and mausoleums erected in public places; and they contributed unabashedly to Roman imperial propaganda.

The Ara Pacis, the Altar of Augustan Peace, was erected in Rome by Augustus between 13 and 9 BCE to commemorate his triumphal return to the city following the end of civil war and the establishment of firm Roman rule in Spain and France (fig. 6-27). In form, the rectangular structure is a Roman adaptation of earlier Greek and Hellenistic altars. Its decoration is a thoughtful union of portraiture and allegory, religion and politics, the

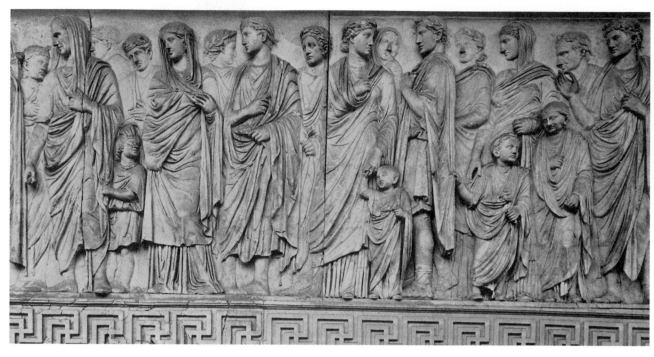

6-28. *Imperial Procession*, detail of a relief on the Ara Pacis. Height 5'2" (1.6 m)

> The middle-aged man with the shrouded head at the far left is Marcus Agrippa, who would have been Augustus's successor had he not died in 12 CE, the year after the Ara Pacis was dedicated. The bored but well-behaved youngster pulling at Agrippa's robe—and being restrained gently by the hand of the man behind him—is probably Agrippa's son, Gaius Caesar. The heavily swathed woman next to Agrippa on the right is probably Augustus's wife, Livia, followed by the elder of her two sons, Tiberius, who would become the next emperor. Behind Tiberius is Antonia, the niece of Augustus, looking back at her husband, Drusus, Livia's younger son. She grasps the hand of Germanicus, one of her younger children. Behind their uncle Drusus are Gnaeus and Domitia, children of Antonia's older sister, who can be seen standing quietly beside them. The depiction of children in an official relief was new to the Augustan period and reflects Augustus's desire to promote private family life.

private and the public. The interior re-creates in marble the temporary altar—surrounded by garlands of flowers suspended in **swags**, or loops, from bucrania (ox skulls)—that would have been set up for the triumphal celebration. The ox skulls symbolize sacrificial offerings, and the garlands, which include flowering plants from every season, signify continuous peace.

Roman realism reached a new level of specificity in the sculpted panels along the exterior of the north and south sides of the Ara Pacis, which depict long double lines of mostly senators and imperial family members. These people appear to be waiting, after a just-completed procession, for other ceremonies to begin. At the head of the line on the south side of the altar is the badly damaged figure of Augustus. Surrounded by priests and other officials, he is probably performing a religious ritual. A detail shows many members of his family waiting at some distance behind him (fig. 6-28). Unlike the Greek sculptors who created the procession on the frieze of the Parthenon (see fig. 5-48), the Roman sculptors of the Ara Pacis depicted actual individuals. They also attempted to suggest spatial depth by carving the closest elements in high relief and those farther back in increasingly lower relief. In a device reminiscent of the Altar of Zeus at Pergamon (see fig. 5-81), they have drawn us, as spectators, visually into the event by making the feet of the nearest figures project from the architectural **groundline** into our space. Like the Parthenon sculptors, the Roman sculp-

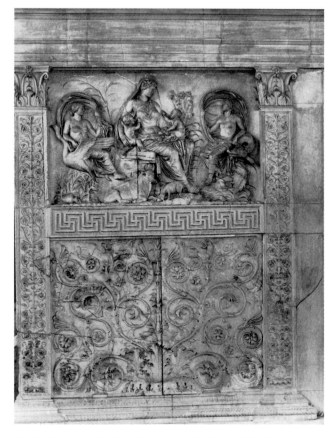

6-29. *Allegory*, relief on the Ara Pacis. Height 5'2" (1.6 m)

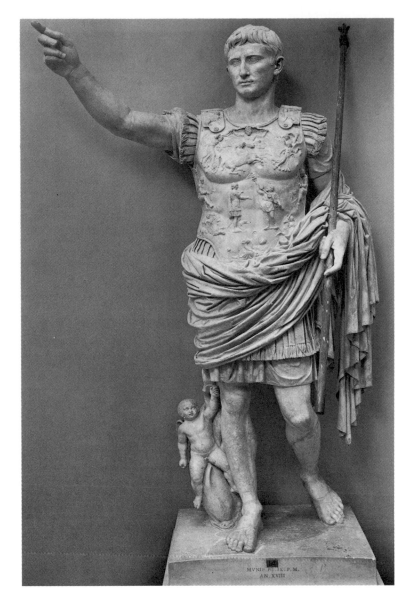

6-30. *Augustus of Primaporta*. Early 1st century CE (perhaps a copy of a bronze statue of c. 20 BCE). Marble, height 6'8" (2.03 m). Musei Vaticani, Braccio Nuovo, Rome

tors have provided no background setting for the figures.

Moving from this procession, with its immediacy and naturalness, to the east and west ends of the enclosure walls, we find panels of a quite different character. The best-preserved of these is a balanced and composed scene, an allegorical representation of the peace and prosperity that Augustus has presumably brought to the empire (fig. 6-29). Scholars disagree on the identity of the figures. The woman in the center may be Tellus Mater, or Mother Earth, symbolically nurturing the Roman people, represented by the two chubby babies in her arms. She may also be a maternal form of Venus, or Ceres, the goddess of grain, or simply a personification (symbol in human form) of peace. She is accompanied by two young women with billowing veils, one seated on the back of a flying swan, the other reclining on a sea monster or dragon. They are personifications of the sea wind and the land wind. The sea wind, symbolized by the sea dragon and waves, would have reminded Augustus's contemporaries of Rome's dominion over the Mediterranean; the land wind, symbolized by the swan, the jug of fresh water, and the wetlands vegetation, would have suggested the fertility of Roman lands. The underlying alle-gorical theme—the Abundant Earth—is reinforced by the flowers and foliage in the background and the domesticated animals in the foreground.

Although the inclusion in this panel of features of the natural world—sky, water, rocks, and foliage—represents something new in monumental sculpture, the idealized figures themselves are clearly drawn from Greek sources (see, for example, fig. 5-53). The artists have conveyed a sense of three-dimensionality and volume by turning the figures in space and wrapping them in revealing swaths of cloth. The scene is set into a frame of architectural elements carved in low relief. Corinthian order pilasters support a simple entablature. A wide **molding** with a Greek key pattern (**meander**) joins the pilasters and divides the wall into two horizontal segments. The lower panels are covered with stylized vine and flower forms. Similar forms, in a more rigid vertical pattern, overlay the pilasters, culminating in the **acanthus** capitals. The delicacy and minute detail with which these spiraling vegetal forms are rendered are characteristic of Roman architectural decoration.

The *Augustus of Primaporta* (fig. 6-30), so named because it was discovered in the country villa belonging

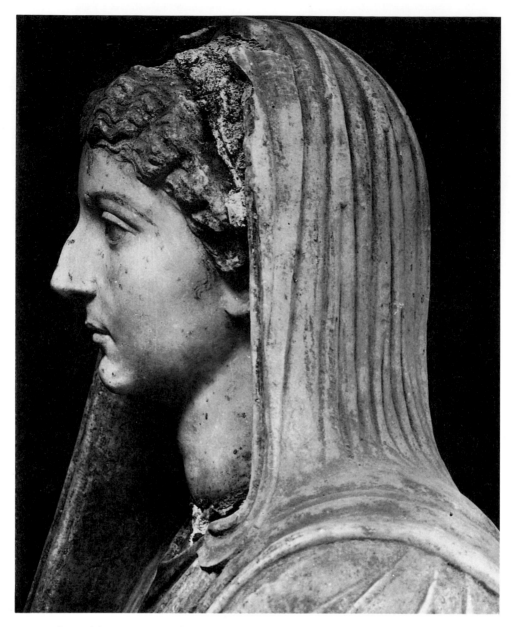

6-31. *Livia*. c. 20 BCE. Marble, height approx. 15" (38.5 cm). Antiquarium, Pompeii

to Augustus's wife, Livia, at Primaporta, demonstrates the creative assimilation of earlier sculptural traditions into a new context. It also illustrates the use of imperial portraiture for political propaganda, a practice among Romans that began with Augustus. The sculptor of this bigger-than-life marble statue eloquently adapted the orator's gesture of the *Aulus Metellus* (see fig. 6-25), combining it with the pose and body proportions prescribed by the Greek Polykleitos and exemplified in his *Spear Bearer* (see fig. 5-54). (Roman artists made many copies of this famous sculpture, and many Roman statues reflect its influence.) The god Cupid, son of the goddess Venus, rides a dolphin next to the emperor's right calf, probably a reference to the claim of the emperor's family, the Julians, to descent from the goddess Venus through her human son Aeneas. Although Augustus wears a cuirass (torso armor) and holds a commander's baton, his feet are bare, suggesting to some scholars that the work was made after his death and commemo-

rates his **apotheosis**, or elevation to divine status. Augustus was in his late seventies when he died, but the features of this statue are those of a vigorous, young ruler. If it is a posthumous work, it might have been copied from a now-lost bronze statue. Since the decorations on the cuirass allude to Augustus's victory over the Parthians in 20 BCE, the original statue may have commemorated that event.

Taken as a whole, this imposing statue creates a recognizable image of Augustus, but one that is far removed from the kind of intensely individualized portrait that was popular during the Republican period. Its purpose was to encourage the Roman people to identify the beneficence of the state with the emperor's person. Whether it is seen as a general praising his troops or a peacetime leader speaking words of encouragement to his people, it projects an image of the emperor as a benign ruler, touched by the gods, governing by reason and persuasion, not autocratic power.

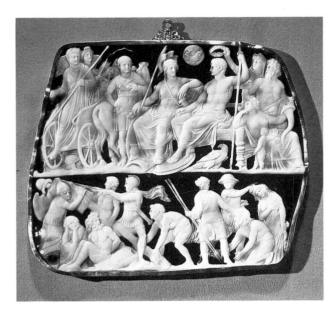

6-32. *Gemma Augustea*. Early 1st century CE. Onyx, 7½ x 9" (19 x 23 cm). Kunsthistorisches Museum, Vienna

rulers is the earthly one, where Roman soldiers are raising a **trophy**—a post or standard on which armor captured from the defeated enemy is displayed. Like prisoners who were paraded out during a celebration of Tiberius's victory over the Germans in 12 CE, the cowering, shackled barbarians on the bottom right wait to be tied to this trophy.

The sculptor of this exquisite low relief created it by carving the relief elements out of the white layer and leaving the lower layer of blue as a background. The execution was so skillful that it nearly overshadows the equally fine design and conception. The *Gemma Augustea* brilliantly combines idealized, heroic figures of a kind characteristic of Classical Greek art, the dramatic action of Hellenistic art, and a purely Roman approach to the depiction of historical events. Even though it is unusually large and its subject matter and treatment highly propagandistic, this cameo was probably commissioned by Augustus's widow for commemorative use.

Wall Painting

The study of the development of Roman wall painting after the second century BCE is greatly indebted to the recovery of many examples preserved relatively fresh and intact within the volcanic debris that descended over the communities surrounding Vesuvius during its eruption. The interior walls of Roman houses were plain, smooth plaster surfaces without any architectural features. On these invitingly flat, empty surfaces, artists painted decorations that varied greatly in appearance and subject matter. Their technique involved mixing pigment in a solution of lime and soap with a little wax added, applying the images, polishing with a special metal, glass, or stone burnisher, then buffing with a cloth. At Pompeii these decorations can be grouped into four types, or styles, that succeeded each other with some overlap. The first two began during the Republican period, and the last two are associated with the Roman Empire. Although the Pompeiian styles are no longer used to assign dates to architecture, they are a convenient way to examine wall painting in the Roman world.

In the First Style (c. 200–80 BCE), artists created the illusion that the walls were actually covered with thin slabs of colored marble set off by real architectural details such as molded plaster columns. In the Second Style (c. 80–15 BCE) they extended the space of a room visually with painted scenes of figures on a shallow "stage" or with a landscape or cityscape seen close up. Architectural details such as columns were painted rather than molded plaster. In the Third Style (c. 15 BCE–45 CE) they emphasized the wall surface again by painting it a solid color, decorated with slender, whimsical architectural details, within which small, delicate vignettes appear. The Fourth Style (beginning c. 45 CE) was a complex combination of the features found in the other three styles, bringing together the more realistic architectural details of the First and Second styles with even greater fantasy than in the Third Style. The Third and Fourth styles are treated beginning on page 256.

Augustus's wife, Livia, was a strong and resourceful woman who remained by his side for more than fifty years. For both, this was a second marriage. Augustus had married his first wife for political reasons and divorced her after the birth of what would be his only child, Julia. Livia had two children, Tiberius (the future second emperor of Rome) and Drusus, by her first husband, Tiberius Claudius Nero, who divorced her so that she could marry Augustus. A portrait bust of her, dated about 20 BCE, when she was in her mid-thirties, reveals a striking woman with strong features and a serene expression (fig. 6-31). Although her marriage to Augustus was childless, she was an influential promoter of social legislation aimed at increasing the Roman birth rate. She supported laws that favored marriage and family, provided increased legal protection to married women, and penalized bachelors, unmarried women, and childless wives or widows. These laws made family life not only a desirable state but a patriotic duty.

The apotheosis of Augustus after his death in 14 CE is apparently the subject of a large onyx **cameo** (a gemstone carved in low relief) known as the *Gemma Augustea* (fig. 6-32). The emperor, being crowned with a victor's wreath, sits at the center right of the top panel. He has assumed the identity of Jupiter, the king of the gods, and an eagle, sacred to Jupiter, stands at his feet. Sitting next to him may be Livia, portrayed as a goddess personification of Rome. The sea-goat in the roundel between them may represent Capricorn, one of the constellations in the zodiac, indicating the time of year. The shield that serves as Augustus-Jupiter's footstool refers to the alleged descent of the Julian family from the war god Mars through his human children Romulus and Remus. Tiberius, the adopted son of Augustus, is shown holding a lance and stepping out of a chariot at the left. Returning victorious from the German front, he is ready to assume the imperial throne as the designated heir of Augustus. Below the transcendent realm of the godly

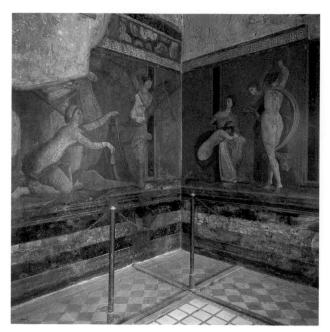

6-33. *Initiation Rites of the Cult of Bacchus* (?), detail of a Second Style wall painting in the Villa of the Mysteries, Pompeii. c. 50 BCE

One of the most famous painted rooms in Roman art is in the so-called Villa of the Mysteries at Pompeii (fig. 6-33). The room must have been a shrine or meeting place for a religious cult, probably that of Bacchus, the god of vegetation, fertility, wine, and the arts, who was one of the most important deities in Pompeii, along with Hercules and Venus. The Second Style murals depict what has been interpreted as the initiation rites of a new member of the cult, which was for a long time limited exclusively to women. The artists first painted an architectural setting consisting of a marble **dado**, a decoration on the lower part of a wall, and an elegant **frieze** supported by pilasters around the top of the wall. The action takes place along the top of the dado in a raised, shallow stage space with a backdrop painted a brilliant, deep red (now known as Pompeiian red) very popular with Roman painters. The stage runs around the entire room and the scenes on it depict a succession of events that culminate in the acceptance of the initiate into the cult.

The visual space of the paintings includes the viewer, who feels like a participant in the action. In the portion of the room seen in the illustration, a priestess (on the left) prepares to reveal draped cult objects, a

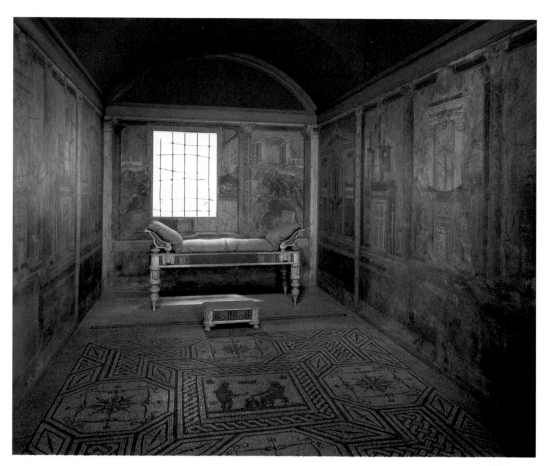

6-34. Reconstructed bedroom, from the House of Publius Fannius Synistor, Boscoreale, near Pompeii. Late 1st century CE, with some later furnishings. The Metropolitan Museum of Art, New York
Rogers Fund, 1903 (03.14.13)

Although the elements in the room are from a variety of places and dates, they give a sense of how the original furnished room might have looked. The floor mosaic, found near Rome, dates to the second century CE. At its center is an image of a priest offering a basket with a snake to a cult image of Isis. The couch and footstool, which are inlaid with bone and glass, date from the first century CE. The wall paintings, original to the Boscoreale villa, may have been inspired by theater scene painting.

winged figure whips a female initiate lying across the lap of another woman, and a devotee dances with cymbals, perhaps to drown out the cries from the whipping. According to another interpretation, the dancing figure is the initiate herself, who has risen to dance with joy at the conclusion of her trials. The whole may be showing a purification ritual meant to bring enlightenment and blissful union with the god.

The walls of a room from a villa at Boscoreale, a suburb of Pompeii, have been restored as a bedroom in the Metropolitan Museum of Art in New York and furnished with items roughly contemporary with the original villa. The Second Style paintings on the walls use the same type of shallow "stage" as the illusions in the Villa of the Mysteries, but in this case a fantastic urban panorama surrounds the room and provides a closed-off view of a Roman city (fig. 6-34). The wall surfaces dissolve into columns and cornices, swinging garlands, and niches. There is no sense of space beyond these forms into which the viewer might move. Were we able to walk through one of the painted doors we would find ourselves lost in an incomprehensible maze of floating forms. This scene is made for viewing only, like backdrops for a theatrical set, which may have been the inspiration for this type of home decoration. Other details in the room reinforce this theatrical association. On the rear wall, next to the window, for example, is a painting of a grotto with a fountain surmounted by a grape arbor, a visual reference to Bacchus, the traditional setting for a kind of drama known as a satyr play. On the side walls, theatrical masks hang from the center of each bay.

The splendid portal in the painting at the far left end of the left wall of the room is flanked by potted plants and a statue of a goddess. Beyond this portal is a complex jumble of buildings with balconies, windows, arcades, and roofs at different levels that end in a magnificent colonnade (fig. 6-35). The vine-wrapped column that seems to sit on the ledge painted at the bottom of the wall and to support an entablature near the top of it enhances the illusion that we are looking into space. The mask hanging in the center of this framing element is a reminder that the composition has more to do with

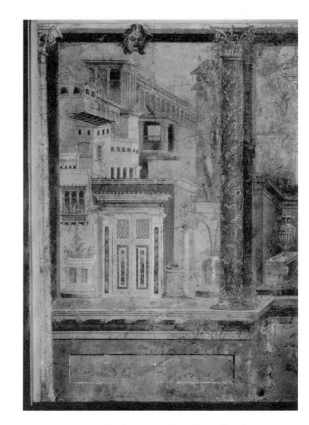

6-35. *Cityscape*, detail of a Second Style wall painting from a bedroom in the House of Publius Fannius Synistor, Boscoreale. Late 1st century CE. The Metropolitan Museum of Art, New York
Rogers Fund, 1903 (03.14.13)

theatrical design than with reality. Nevertheless, the artist has used **intuitive perspective** to create a general impression of real space. The architectural details follow diagonal lines that the eye interprets as parallel lines receding into the distance, and figures and objects that we are meant to understand as far away from the surface plane of the wall are shown smaller than those meant to appear near to it.

The Second Style decoration of the dining-room walls of the Villa of Livia at Primaporta exemplifies yet another approach to creating a sense of slightly expanded space (fig. 6-36). Instead of rendering a stage set or a

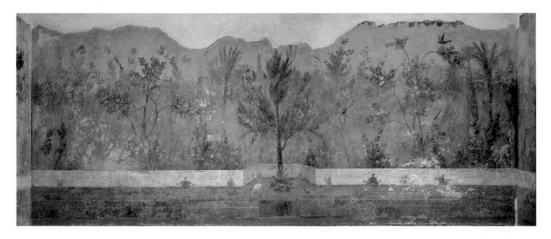

6-36. *Garden Scene*, detail of a Second Style wall painting from the Villa of Livia at Primaporta, near Rome. Late 1st century BCE. Museo Nazionale Romano, Rome

cityscape, the artist literally painted away the wall surfaces to create the illusion of being on a porch or pavilion looking out over a low, paneled wall toward an orchard of heavily laden fruit trees. These and the flowering shrubs are filled with a variety of wonderfully observed birds. When the Republican period drew to a close, the styles of painting, especially the Third Style, continued to dominate, but other art forms—most particularly architecture—would be put to new purposes.

THE EARLY EMPIRE: THE JULIO-CLAUDIAN AND FLAVIAN DYNASTIES

Augustus's successor was his stepson Tiberius, and in acknowledgment of the lineage of both, the dynasty—the succession of related rulers—that begins with Tiberius is known as the Julio-Claudian (14–69 CE). Although this dynasty produced some capable administrators, it was also marked by suspicion, intrigue, and terror in Rome. It ended with the reign of the despotic and capricious Nero. A brief period of civil war followed Nero's death in 68 CE, during which it became clear that the power to elevate emperors rested with the army and not with the Senate and other assemblies in Rome. Eventually, a powerful general, Vespasian, seized control of the government. The dynasty he founded, the Flavian, ruled from 69 to 96 CE. The emperors in this dynasty, Vespasian (ruled 69–79 CE), Titus (ruled 79–81 CE), and Domitian (ruled 81–96 CE), restored imperial finances and stabilized the empire's frontiers. Domitian's autocratic reign saw a return of intrigue and terror to the capital.

Architecture

The Colosseum, one of Rome's greatest monuments, was built during the reign of Vespasian (fig. 6-37). Construction on it began in 72 CE, and it was dedicated by Titus in 80 CE, after Vespasian's death. In this enormous entertainment center (it measures 615 by 510 feet and is 159 feet high) Roman audiences watched a variety of athletic events and spectacles, including animal hunts, fights to the death between gladiators or between gladiators and wild animals, performances of trained animals and acrobats, and even mock sea battles, for which the arena was flooded by a built-in mechanism. The Flavians erected it to bolster their popularity in Rome, and its name then was the Flavian Amphitheater. The name "Colosseum," by which it came to be known, derived from the Colossus, a bigger-than-life statue of Nero that had been left standing next to it. The opening performances in 80 CE lasted 100 days, during which time, it was claimed, 9,000 wild animals and 2,000 gladiators were killed.

The floor of the Colosseum was laid over a foundation of service rooms and tunnels that provided a backstage area for the athletes, performers, animals, and equipment. (This floor was covered in sand, or *arena* in Latin, hence the English term "arena.") Some 50,000 spectators could easily move through the seventy-six

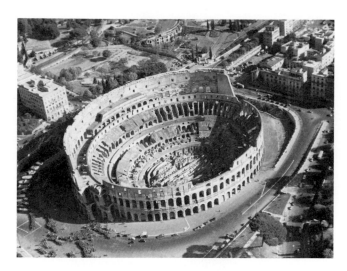

6-37. Colosseum, Rome. 72–80 CE

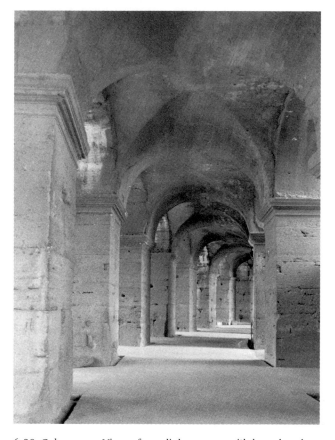

6-38. Colosseum. View of a radial passage with barrel and groin vaulting

entrance doors to the three sections of seats and the standing area at the top. Each had an uninterrupted view of the spectacle below. Like many stadiums today, the Colosseum was oval with a surrounding exterior wall and ascending tiers of seats laid over barrel-vaulted corridors that provided access to them (fig. 6-38). Entrance tunnels connected the ring corridors to the inside ramps and seats on each level. The intersection of the entrance tunnels and the ring corridors, both barrel-vaulted, created what is called a **groin vault** (see "Elements of Architecture," page 226). The walls on the top level of the

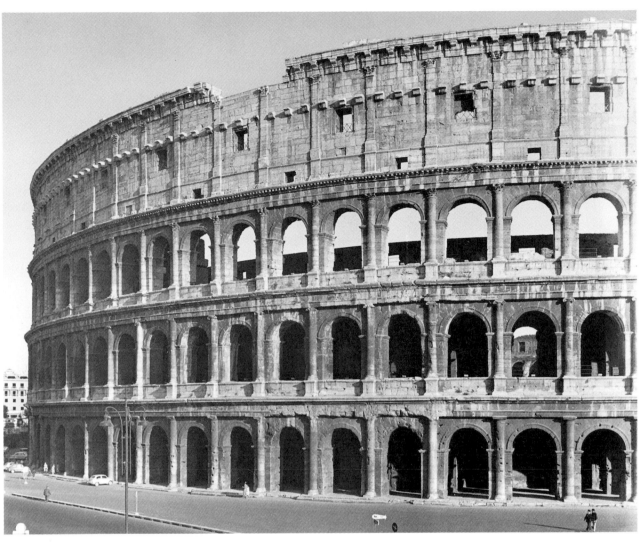

6-39. Colosseum

arena supported an awning system that could shade the seating areas. Former seamen who had experience in handling ropes, pulleys, and large expanses of canvas were employed to work the apparatus.

The curving, outer wall of the Colosseum consists of three levels of arcade surmounted by a wall-like **attic** (top) **story**. Each arch in the arcades is framed by engaged columns, which support entablaturelike bands marking the divisions between levels (fig. 6-39). Each level also uses a different architectural order: the plain Tuscan order on the ground level, the Ionic on the second level, the Corinthian on the third, and flat pilasters on the fourth. The attic story is broken only by small, square windows, which originally alternated with gilded-bronze shield-shaped ornaments called **cartouches**. These were supported on **corbels** (brackets) that are still in place and can be seen in the illustration. Engaged Corinthian pilasters above the Corinthian columns of the third level support another row of corbels beneath the projecting cornice. All of these elements are purely decorative and serve no structural function. As we saw with

the Porta Augusta (see fig. 6-2), the addition of post-and-lintel decoration to arched structures was an Etruscan innovation. The systematic use of the orders in a logical succession from sturdy Tuscan to lighter Ionic to decorative Corinthian follows a tradition inherited from Hellenistic architecture (see "Elements of Architecture," page 227). This orderly, dignified, and visually satisfying way of articulating (organizing) the facades of large buildings is still popular. Unfortunately, much of the facade and the rest of the Colosseum were dismantled as a source of marble, metal fittings, and materials for later buildings.

The Arch of Titus

When Domitian assumed the throne in 81 CE, he immediately commissioned a **triumphal arch** to honor his brother and deified predecessor, Titus (fig. 6-40). During a triumph—a formal victory celebration granted to a general or emperor on his return to Rome after a significant campaign—the victorious leader paraded with his

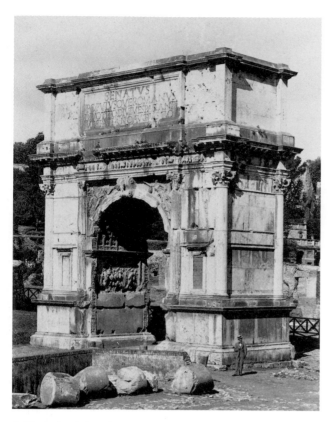

6-40. Arch of Titus, Rome. c. 81 CE. Concrete and white marble, height 50' (15 m)

The dedication inscribed across the tall attic story above the arch opening reads: "The Senate and the Roman People to the Deified Titus Flavius Vespasianus Augustus, son of the Deified Vespasian." The Romans typically recorded historic occasions and identified monuments with solemn prose and beautiful inscriptions in stone. The use by the sculptors of elegant Roman capital letters—perfectly sized and spaced to be read from a distance and cut with sharp terminals (serifs) to catch the light—established a standard that calligraphers and alphabet designers still follow.

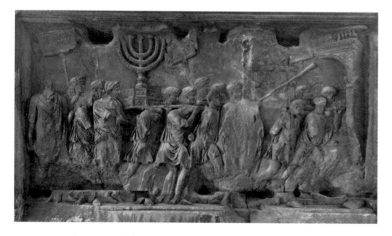

6-41. *Spoils from the Temple of Solomon, Jerusalem*, relief in the passageway of the Arch of Titus. Marble, height 6'8" (2.03 m)

troops, captives, and booty through the city. A triumphal arch was a freestanding stone arch erected to commemorate the occasion. The Arch of Titus memorializes his capture of Jerusalem in August 70 CE.

The arch, constructed of concrete and faced with marble, is essentially a freestanding gateway pierced by a passageway covered by a barrel vault. Originally the whole arch served as a giant base, 50 feet tall, for a statue of a four-horse chariot and driver, a typical triumphal symbol. Applied to the faces of the arch are columns in the **Composite order**—capitals are formed by superimposing Ionic **volutes** on a Corinthian capital—supporting an entablature. The inscription on the attic story declares that the Senate and the Roman people erected the monument to honor Titus.

Titus's capture of Jerusalem ended a fierce campaign to crush a revolt of the Jews in Palestine. His troops sacked and destroyed the Second Temple of Jerusalem and carted off its sacred treasures. These spoils were displayed in Rome during Titus's triumphal procession, impressing the Jewish eyewitness and historian Flavius Josephus (*The Jewish War*):

> The most interesting of all were the spoils seized from the Temple of Jerusalem: a gold table weighing many talents, and a lampstand, also made of gold, which was made in a form different from that which we usually employ. For there was a central shaft fastened to the base; then spandrels [branches] extended from this in an arrangement which rather resembled the shape of a trident, and on the end of each of these spandrels a lamp was forged. There were seven of these, emphasizing the honor accorded the number seven among the Jews. The law of the Jews [Ark of the Covenant] was borne along after these as the last of the spoils. . . . Vespasian drove along behind [it] . . . and Titus followed him; Domitian rode beside them, dressed in a dazzling fashion and riding a horse which was worth seeing.

The reliefs on the inside walls of the arch, capturing the drama of the occasion, depict Titus's soldiers flaunting this booty as they carry it through the streets of Rome (fig. 6-41). Viewing them, the observer can feel that boisterous, disorderly crowd and might expect at any moment to hear the shouts and chanting of the participants.

The mood of the procession depicted in these reliefs contrasts with the relaxed but formal solemnity of the procession depicted on the Ara Pacis (see fig. 6-28). Like the sculptors of the Ara Pacis, the sculptors of the Arch of Titus showed the spatial relationships among figures by rendering close elements in higher relief than those more distant. A **menorah**, or seven-branched candleholder, from the Temple of Jerusalem dominates the scene. Reflecting their concern for representing objects as well as people in a believable manner, the sculptors rendered this menorah as if seen from the low point of view of a spectator at the event, and they have positioned the arch on the right through which the procession is about to pass on a diagonal from the background. Using a technique also encountered on the Ara Pacis, the sculptors have **undercut** the foreground figures and have used low relief for the figures in the background. The panel on the other side of the arch interior shows Titus riding in his chariot as a participant in the ceremonies. On the vaulted ceiling, which shows his apotheosis, an eagle carries him to a heavenly meeting with the gods.

Plebeian Relief Sculpture

Like Rome's rulers, eminent individuals who could afford to do so also sought to memorialize themselves in art. Most of the private commissions by the plebeians were related to funerary situations. The most popular decorations of funerary reliefs were portraits of the deceased, garlands, and narrative themes, sometimes of mythological figures, sometimes of biographical scenes associated with the deceased. A fine example of such sculpture is a relief on the mausoleum of the plebeian Haterius family (fig. 6-42). The relief memorializes the construction of the mausoleum itself, an occurrence that has led some scholars to believe that it was perhaps created for the tomb of an architect or a builder. The sculptor of the relief, like the sculptor of the *Taking of the Roman Census* (see fig. 6-26), sacrificed clear organization and composition in order to convey as much information as possible—far more than can be readily absorbed. The viewer should approach the image as a "tourist," ready to wander about studying this and that area, and examining with fascination the giant, human-powered crane at the left being maneuvered into place over the still-unfinished mausoleum. For the student of architecture, the image of the mausoleum is an encyclopedia of decorative motifs—**egg-and-dart** moldings, garlands looped in swags, busts in shell-shaped niches, and vegetal reliefs that are symmetrical and upright. The robust Corinthian columns are heavily carved with spiraling garlands. Viewed as a whole, the jumbled structural elements and perspectives make the mausoleum look as if it is about to tumble to the ground.

Unlike the sculptors who worked on the Ara Pacis, the artists who created reliefs of the type found on the tomb of the Haterius family were relatively unfamiliar with the techniques and intentions of the Classical Greek sculptors. Their patrons were probably relatively unsophisticated, though quite clear about what they wanted. The sculptural style that emerged from such commissions was characterized by crowded compositions and deeply undercut forms, with stocky figures and a detailed but visually unrealistic way of presenting its subject matter or "story." This style, however, would become more and more prevalent, ultimately displacing the patrician style in both public and private art throughout the empire.

Portrait Sculpture

Two approaches to portrait sculpture were popular during the reign of the Flavians. A bust of a young woman, whose identity is not known, exemplifies one of

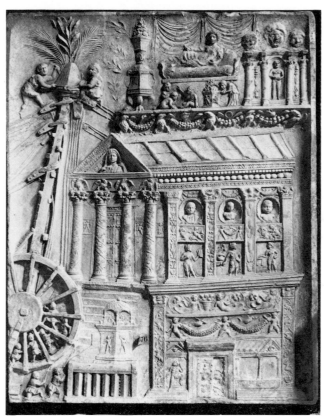

6-42. *Mausoleum under Construction*, relief from the tomb of the Haterius family, Via Labicana, Rome. Late 1st century CE. Marble, height 41" (104 cm). Musei Vaticani, Museo Gregoriano Profano, ex Lateranense, Rome

these (fig. 6-43). This bust is an idealized portrait in the manner of the *Augustus of Primaporta* (see fig. 6-30). It includes well-observed, recognizable features—a strong nose and jaw, heavy brows, deep-set eyes, and a long neck—but the smoothly rendered flesh and soft, full lips impart an idealized, youthful glow. The hair is piled high in a mass of ringlets in the latest court fashion. Executing it required skillful chiseling and **drillwork**. With a drill, a sculptor can rapidly cut deep grooves with straight sides that look like dark lines at a distance. In this case the drill created the holes in the center of the subject's curls. The overall effect, from a distance, is very lifelike. The play of natural light over the more subtly sculpted surfaces gives the illusion of being reflected off real skin and hair.

The second approach, exemplified by a bust of an older woman (fig. 6-44), reflects a revival of the verist style popular in the Republican period. The comic writers of the Flavian era liked to satirize older women who vainly sought to preserve their youthful looks, but the subject of this portrait, though she too wore her hair in the latest style, was apparently not at all proud about her looks. The work she commissioned shows her exactly as she appeared in her own mirror, with all the signs of her age—well earned and magnificent in their own way—recorded on her face for future generations to admire.

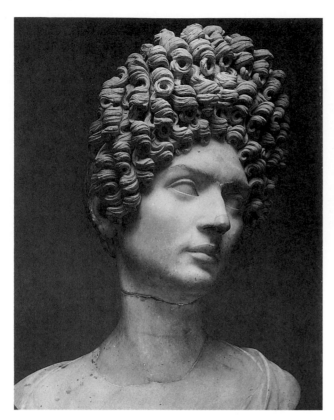

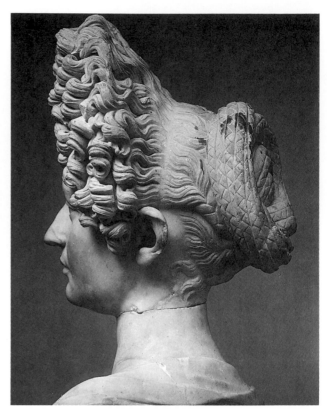

6-43. *Young Flavian Woman.* c. 90 CE. Marble, height 25" (65.5 cm). Museo Capitolino, Rome

The typical Flavian hairstyle seen on this woman and the older woman in figure 6-44 required a patient hairdresser handy with a curling iron and with a special knack for turning the back of the head into an intricate basketweave of braids. Male writers loved to scoff at the results. Martial described the style precisely as "a globe of hair." Statius spoke of "the glory of woman's lofty front, her storied hair." And Juvenal waxed comically poetic: "See her from the front; she is Andromache [an epic heroine]. From behind she looks half the size—a different woman you would think" (cited in Balsdon, page 256).

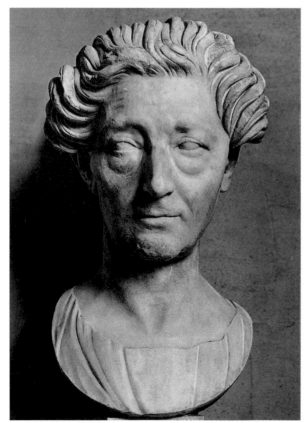

6-44. *Middle-Aged Flavian Woman.* Late 1st century CE.
Marble, height 9½" (24.1 cm). Musei Vaticani, Museo
Gregoriano Profano, ex Lateranense, Rome

Wall Painting

From the time of Augustus through about 45 CE, the third of the four styles identified at Pompeii predominated in Roman wall painting. In this Third Style, walls were treated mostly as solid, planar surfaces adorned with decorative details and "framed" paintings. The Third Style painting on a wall in the House of M. Lucretius Fronto in Pompeii dates to the mid-first century CE. As we see in a detail (fig. 6-45), the artist painted the wall in panels of black and red that emphasize its flatness. An echo of Second Style architecture can be seen in the borders between the panels and the suggestion of an upper level, but these elements show no logical layout and lack any significant illusion of depth. The rectangular pictures seem to be mounted on the black and red panels or placed in front of them, but they are actually painted on the wall. The scene with figures in the center is flanked by two small simulated window openings protected by grilles. The two pictures of country houses appear to be mounted on **filigree**.

The paintings that adorned Third and Fourth Style walls had every kind of subject, including historical and mythological scenes, landscapes and city views, portraits, and exquisitely rendered **still lifes**, or representations of inanimate objects. A still-life panel from a Fourth Style wall painting in the House of Julia Felix in Pompeii (fig. 6-46) depicts everyday domestic wares and the

800 BCE   400 CE

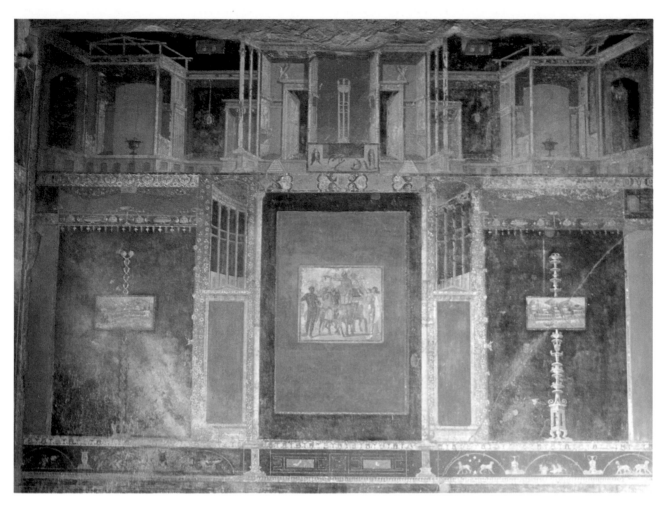

6-45. Detail of a Third Style wall painting in the House of M. Lucretius Fronto, Pompeii. Mid-1st century CE

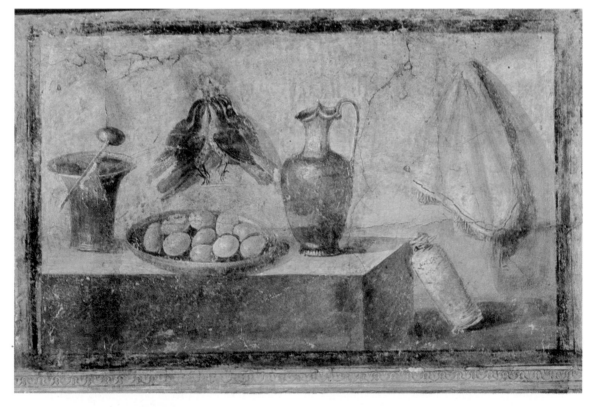

6-46. *Still Life*, detail of a wall painting from the House of Julia Felix, Pompeii. Late 1st century CE. Museo Archeològico Nazionale, Naples

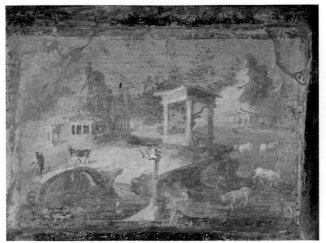

6-47. *Sacred Landscape*, detail of a wall painting, from Pompeii. 62–79 CE. Museo Archeològico Nazionale, Naples

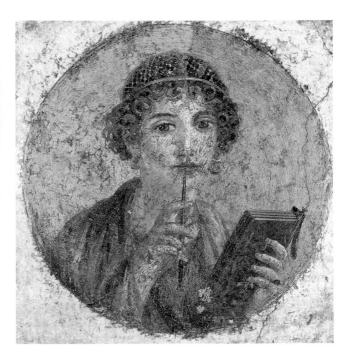

6-48. *Young Woman Writing*, detail of a wall painting, from Pompeii. Late 1st century CE. Diameter 14⅝" (37 cm). Museo Archeològico Nazionale, Naples

The fashionable young woman seems to be pondering what she will write about with her stylus on the beribboned writing tablet that she holds in her other hand. Romans used pointed styluses to engrave letters on thin, wax-coated ivory or wood tablets in much the way we might use a small chalkboard; errors could be easily smoothed over. When a text or letter was considered ready, it was copied onto expensive papyrus or parchment. Tablets like these were also used by schoolchildren for their homework.

makings of a meal—eggs and recently caught game birds. The items have been carefully grouped for clarity and balance in a near-symmetrical arrangement. The focus of the composition is the round plate filled with eggs and the household containers that flank it. The towel on a hook on the right of the painting and the subtle suggestion of triangularity in the bottle tilted against the end of the shelf echo the pyramidal shape of the brace of dead birds above the plate. A strong, clear light floods the picture from the left, casting shadows and enhancing the illusion of real objects in real space. Other paintings in this house show graphically the role of women at the time and how, so unlike their Greek contemporaries, they had an active life outside the home.

During the first century CE, landscape painting became especially accomplished in Pompeii. Its appeal was captured by Pliny the Elder, who described it in *Naturalis Historia* (35.116–117) as "that most delightful technique of painting walls with representations of villas, porticoes and landscape gardens, woods, groves, hills, pools, channels, rivers, coastlines—in fact, every sort of thing which one might want, and also various representations of people within them walking or sailing . . . and also fishing, fowling, or hunting or even harvesting the wine-grapes."

An example from Pompeii of a Third Style sacred landscape—a special type of landscape painting that usually includes shrines, statues, trees, water, rocks, figures, and animals—dates from the decade and a half between an earthquake in 62 CE and the final destruction of the city in 79 CE, the period in which Pliny wrote (fig. 6-47). In this scene, a brook runs through a meadow surrounded by rocky hills and trees. Altars and small temples are scattered about, and an open pavilion encloses a sacred tree. A shepherd crosses the bridge, followed by a goat. Watching over the scene is Terminus, the god of boundaries, in the form of a **herm** statue—a head and torso that merges at hip level into a plain plinth, or base. Two conventions

create the illusion of space: distant objects are rendered proportionally smaller than near objects, and the colors become slightly grayer near the horizon, an effect called **atmospheric perspective** that reproduces the tendency of distant objects to appear hazy.

Roman artists sought to capture a sense of peaceful, unspoiled nature in their landscapes, and the overall effect of this painting is one of wonder-invoking nature. It depicts the *locus amoenus*, the "lovely place" extolled by poets, where people lived effortlessly in union with the land. Such an idealized view of the world, rendered with free, fluid brushwork and delicate color, did not appear again in Western art until the latter part of the nineteenth century with the painting of the French Impressionists.

Portraits, perhaps imaginary ones, were popular for wall paintings. A late-first-century CE **tondo** (circular panel) from a house in Pompeii contains a portrait of a *Young Woman Writing* (fig. 6-48). The sitter has regular features and curly hair caught in a golden net. As in a modern studio portrait photograph, with its careful lighting and retouching, she is portrayed in an idealized fashion. In a convention popular among women patrons, she

ROMAN WOMEN AND THE ARTS If we were to judge from the conflicting accounts of Roman writers, Roman women were either shockingly wicked and willful, totally preoccupied with clothes, hairstyles, and social events, or well-educated, talented, and active members of family and society. In ancient Rome, as in the contemporary world, sin sold better than saintliness, and for that reason written attacks on women by their male contemporaries must be viewed with some reservation. In fact, careful study has shown that Roman women were far freer and more engaged in society than their Greek counterparts. Many women received a formal education, and a well-educated woman was admired as much as a well-educated man. The upper classes hired tutors for their daughters and less-affluent families sent both sons and daughters to school until they were twelve years old. In school, under a male teacher, boys and girls studied the same subjects. Although many middle-class women became physicians, shopkeepers, and even overseers in such male-dominated businesses as shipbuilding, education was valued not so much for any practical training it might provide as for the desirable status it imparted.

Ovid (43 BCE–c. 17 CE) advised all young women to read both the Greek classics and contemporary Roman literature, including his own, of course. Women conversant with political and cultural affairs and with a reputation for good conversation enjoyed the praise and admiration of some male writers. A few women even took up literature themselves. A woman named Julia Balbilla was well respected for her poetry. Another, Sulpicia, a writer of elegies, was accepted into male literary circles. Her works were recommended by the author Martial to men and women alike. The younger Agrippina, sister of the emperor Caligula and mother of Nero, wrote a history of her illustrious family.

Women were also encouraged to become accomplished singers, instrumentalists, and even dancers, so long as they did not perform publicly. During the imperial period, actors—both male and female—were considered among the most disreputable members of society, no matter how much their talents were admired, and men were forbidden by law to marry actresses. One courageous (and very wealthy) woman managed despite such restrictions to found and run her own dance company. Almost nothing appears in literature about women in the visual arts, no doubt because artists were not highly regarded. But the tomb relief illustrated here is clear proof that women did become professional painters. The tomb's occupant is shown in her studio with paint pots, palette, and brushes and a young nude model waiting for her to turn and begin work.

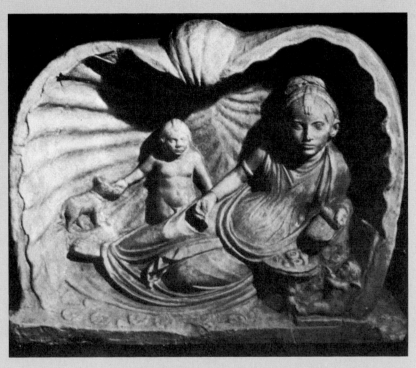

Painter in Her Studio, tomb relief. 2nd century CE. Villa Albani, Rome

is shown nibbling on the tip of a writing stylus. Her sweet mien and clear-eyed but unfocused and contemplative gaze suggest that she is composing a piece of writing. Perhaps, like many Roman women, she was a professional writer (see "Roman Women and the Arts," above) who wanted to be admired for her intellectual attainments. The paintings in Pompeii reveal much about the lives of women during this period. Some, like Julia Felix, were the owners of houses where paintings were found. Others were the subjects of the painters, and they are shown as rich and poor, young and old, employed as business managers and domestic workers. They participated in all aspects of daily life fully and apparently comparably to men.

THE EARLY EMPIRE: THE "GOOD EMPERORS" Five very competent rulers— Nerva (ruled 96–98 CE), Trajan (ruled 98–117 CE), Hadrian (ruled 117–138 CE), Antoninus Pius (ruled 138–161 CE), and Marcus Aurelius (ruled 161–180 CE)— succeeded the Flavians. Until Marcus Aurelius, none of them had natural sons, and they adopted able members of the Senate to be their successors. Known as the "Five Good Emperors," they oversaw a long period of stability and prosperity. Italy and the provinces flourished equally, and official and private patronage of the arts vastly increased. Under Trajan the empire reached its greatest extent. He annexed Dacia (roughly modern Romania) in

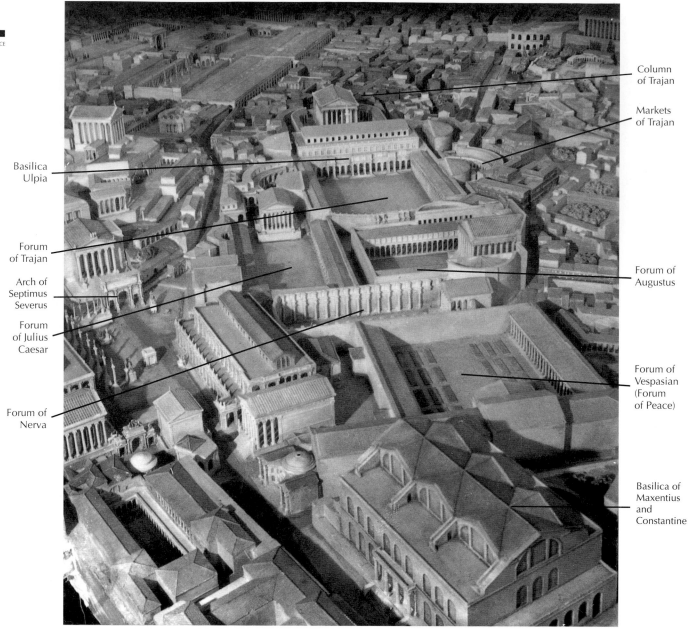

Column
of Trajan

Markets
of Trajan

Basilica
Ulpia

Forum
of Trajan

Arch of
Septimus
Severus

Forum
of Julius
Caesar

Forum of
Augustus

Forum of
Vespasian
(Forum
of Peace)

Forum of
Nerva

Basilica of
Maxentius
and
Constantine

6-49. Model of the Imperial Forums, Rome. c. 46 BCE–117 CE

106 CE and expanded the empire's boundaries in the Middle East. His successor, Hadrian, consolidated the empire's borders and imposed far-reaching social, administrative, and military reforms. Hadrian was well educated and widely traveled, and his admiration for Greek culture spurred new building programs throughout the empire. By the reign of Marcus Aurelius, the empire was facing increasing strains and external threats.

Architecture in Rome and Environs

The Romans believed that their rule extended to the ends of the Western world, but Rome remained the heart and nerve center of the empire. During his long and peaceful reign, Augustus paved the city's old Republican Forum, restoring its temples and basilicas, and built the first

Imperial Forum. These projects marked the beginning of a continuing effort to transform the capital itself into a magnificent monument to imperial rule. Modern Rome has almost obliterated the ancient city, so we can only imagine its appearance from drawings, plans, and models. These models show major monuments such as the Colosseum, the Arch of Titus, the Circus Maximus (a track for chariot races), the Imperial Forums, the round, domed temple called the Pantheon, and the aqueducts among the densely packed temples, monuments, baths, warehouses, and homes that choked the city center.

The largest and most elaborate of the Imperial Forums (fig. 6-49) was that of Trajan, which he had constructed on a large piece of property next to the earlier forums of Augustus and Julius Caesar. For this major undertaking, Trajan chose a Greek architect, Apollo-

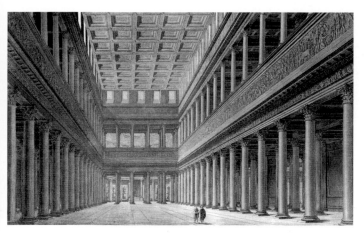

6-50. Reconstruction drawing of the central hall, Basilica Ulpia, Rome. 113 CE

dorus of Damascus, who designed the forum around a straight, central axis that leads from the Forum of Augustus through a triple-arched gate surmounted by a bronze chariot group into a large, colonnaded courtyard with a statue of Trajan on horseback at its center. Perpendicular to the courtyard and closing it off at the north end was the main building in the forum, the Basilica Ulpia, dedicated in 113 CE and named for the family to which Trajan belonged. A basilica was a large, rectangular building with a rounded extension, called an **apse**, at each end. A general-purpose administrative structure, it could be adapted to many uses. The Basilica Ulpia was a court of law. Others served as imperial audience chambers, army drill halls, and schools. An important feature of the basilica design was that it provided easy access in and out. Its capacious and adaptable interior later made it attractive to Christians, who appropriated it for their churches.

The Basilica Ulpia had several doors on the long sides. The interior space was partitioned into a large, central area bordered by two colonnaded aisles that were surmounted by open galleries (fig. 6-50). The central space was taller than the surrounding gallery, creating a **clerestory** with windows, as in the Egyptian **hypostyle hall** (see fig. 3-29), that brought light to the interior of the building. The apse spaces at each end of the building provided imposing settings for judges when the court was in session.

Just behind the Basilica Ulpia were twin libraries built to house the emperors' large collections of Latin and Greek manuscripts. These buildings flanked an open court in which Trajan erected a large column to commemorate his victory over the Dacians (fig. 6-51). The column was built between 106 and 113 CE and was both a monument to him and his tomb. The Temple of the Divine Trajan stands opposite the Basilica Ulpia, defining the fourth side of the court and closing off the end of the forum. It was built by the emperor Hadrian after his predecessor's death and apotheosis in 117.

The relief decoration on the Column of Trajan spirals upward in a band that would stretch about 656 feet if unfurled. Like a giant scroll, it contains a continuous pictorial narrative of the entire history of the Dacian

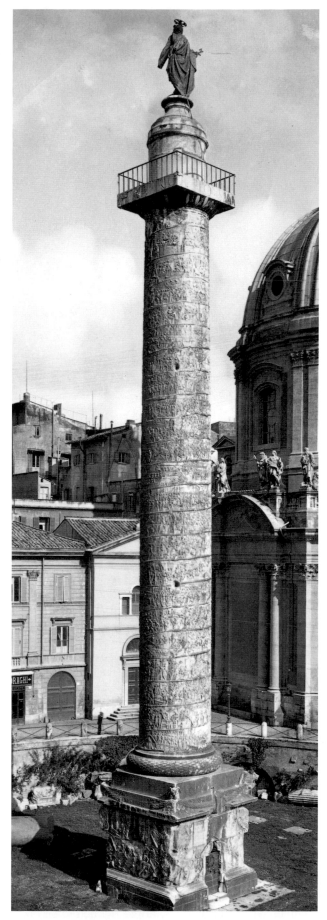

6-51. Column of Trajan, Rome. 106–13 CE. Marble, overall height with base 125' (38 m), column alone, 97'8" (29.77 m)

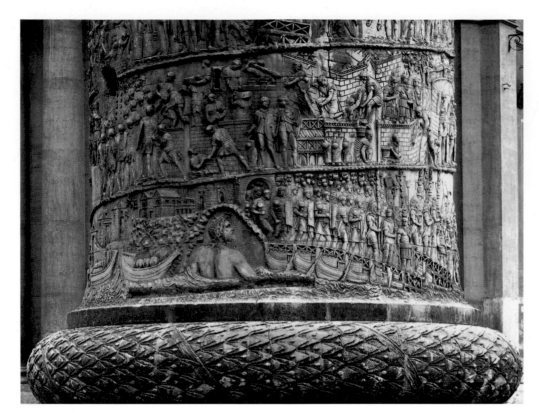

6-52. *Romans Crossing the Danube and Building a Fort*, detail of the lowest part of the Column of Trajan. Height of the spiral band approx. 36" (91 cm)

campaign. This remarkable sculptural feat involved creating more than 2,500 individual figures—including soldiers, animals, and hangers-on—linked by landscape, architecture, and the recurring figure of Trajan. The artist took care to make all of the scroll legible. The narrative band slowly expands from about 3 feet in height at the bottom, near the viewer, to 4 feet at the top, where it is far from the viewer, and the natural and architectural frames for the scenes have been kept small relative to the important figures in them.

The scene at the bottom of the column (fig. 6-52) shows the army crossing the Danube River on a pontoon (floating) bridge as the campaign gets under way. A giant river god, providing supernatural support, looks on. In the scene above, soldiers have begun constructing a battlefield headquarters in Dacia from which the men on the frontiers will receive orders, food, and weapons. Throughout the narrative, which is, after all, a spectacular piece of imperial propaganda, Trajan is portrayed as a strong, stable, and efficient commander of a well-run army, whereas his barbarian enemies are shown as pathetically disorganized and desperate. The hardships of war—death, destruction, and the suffering of innocent people—are ignored, and, of course, the Romans never lose a battle.

During the site preparation for the forum, much of the commercial district on the Quirinal Hill had to be razed and excavated. To make up for the loss, Trajan ordered the construction of a handsome public market in the shadow of the forum's wall (fig. 6-53). The complete ex-

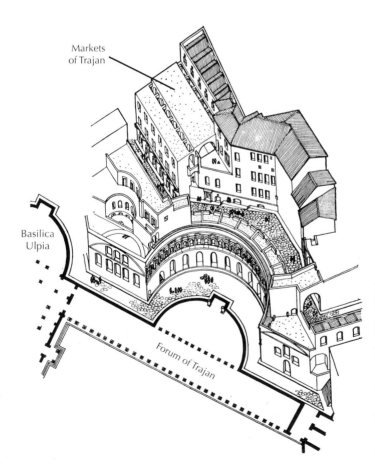

6-53. Axonometric drawing of the Markets of Trajan, Rome. 100–12 CE

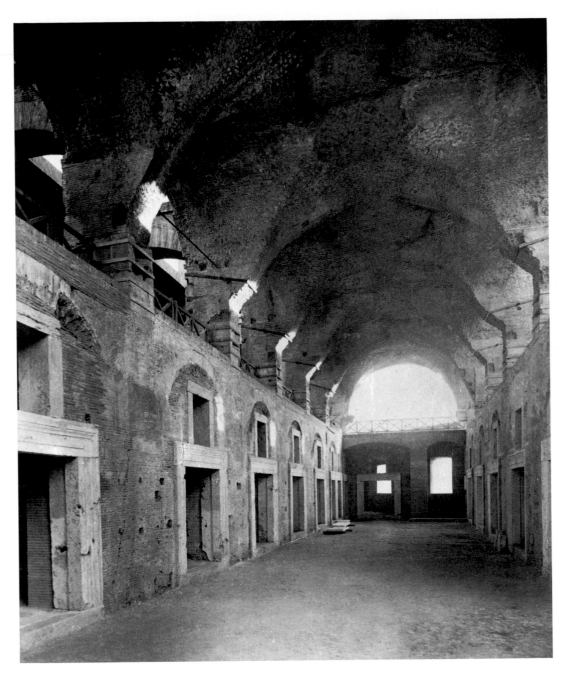

6-54. Main hall, Markets of Trajan

tent of this much-damaged structure, which would have compared favorably with any modern indoor shopping mall, is unknown. The remaining building is a semicircular structure that follows the shape of the huge exedra in the east wall of the Forum of Trajan. The market had more than 150 individual shop spaces on several levels and included a large groin-vaulted main hall (fig. 6-54). In compliance with a building code that was put into effect after a disastrous fire in 64 CE, it was made of brick-faced concrete, with only some detailing in stone and wood.

One of the most remarkable ancient buildings surviving in Rome is a temple to the Olympian gods called the Pantheon ("all the gods"). It was built under the patronage of Emperor Hadrian between 125 and 128 CE on the site of a temple erected by Agrippa in 27–25 BCE but

later destroyed. The approach to the temple gives little suggestion of what it must have looked like when it stood separate from any surrounding structures. Nor is there any hint of what lies beyond the entrance porch, which was raised originally on a podium (now covered by centuries of dirt and street construction) and made to resemble the facade of a typical Roman temple (fig. 6-55). Behind this porch is a giant **rotunda** (a circular building) with 20-foot-thick walls that rise nearly 75 feet. Supported on these is a huge, round, bowl-shaped dome, 143 feet in diameter and 143 feet from the floor at its summit (fig. 6-56). Standing at the center of this nearly spherical temple, the visitor feels isolated from the real world and intensely aware of the shape and tangibility of the space itself rather than the solid surfaces of the architecture

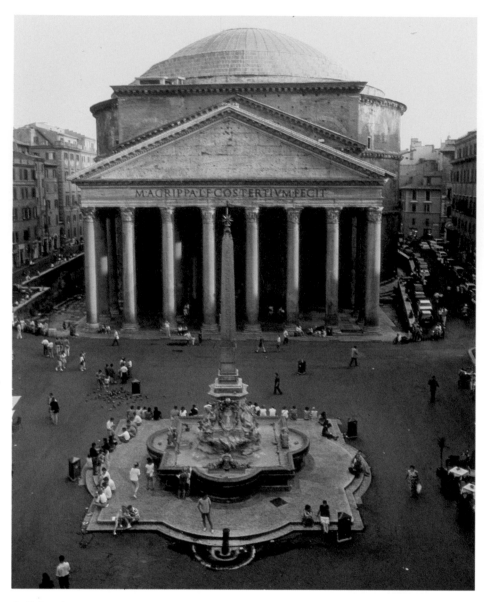

6-55. Pantheon, Rome. 125–28 CE

Although this magnificent monument was designed and constructed entirely during the reign of the emperor Hadrian, the long inscription on the architrave clearly states that it was built by "Marcus Agrippa, son of Lucius, who was consul three times." Agrippa, the son-in-law and valued adviser of Emperor Augustus, died in 12 BCE, but he was responsible for the building of a previous temple on this site in 27–25 BCE, which the Pantheon replaced. In essence Hadrian simply made a grand gesture to the memory of the illustrious Agrippa, rather than using the new building to memorialize himself.

enclosing it. The eye is drawn upward over the circle patterns made by the sunken panels, or **coffers**, in the dome's ceiling to the light entering the 29-foot-wide **oculus**, or central opening. Clouds can be seen through this opening on clear days; rain falls through it on wet ones, then drains off as planned by the original engineer; and occasionally a bird flies through it. But the empty, luminous space also imparts a sense of apotheosis, a feeling that one could rise buoyantly upward to escape the spherical hollow of the building and commune with the gods.

The simple shape of the Pantheon's dome belies its sophisticated design and engineering. Its surface of

marble veneer disguises the internal brick arches and concrete that support it. The walls, which form the structural **drum** that holds up and buttresses the dome, are disguised by a wealth of architectural detail—columns, exedrae, pilasters, and entablatures—in two tiers. Seven niches, rectangular alternating with semicircular, originally held statues of the gods. This simple repetition of square against circle, which was established on a large scale by the juxtaposition of the rectilinear portico against the rotunda, is found throughout the building. The square, boxlike coffers inside the dome, which help lighten the weight of the masonry, may once have contained gilded bronze **rosettes** or stars suggesting the heavens.

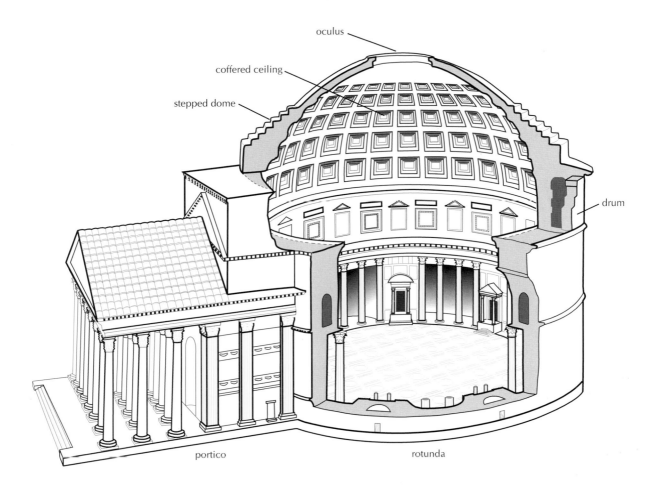

oculus

coffered ceiling

stepped dome

drum

portico

rotunda

6-56. Reconstruction drawing of the Pantheon

It is not clear what the early Romans themselves thought of this architectural monument, so well known to travelers and students today, because it was rarely mentioned by any contemporary writers. An exception was Ammianus Marcellinus, who described it in 357 CE with restrained praise as being "rounded like the boundary of the horizon, and vaulted with a beautiful loftiness." Although the Pantheon has inspired hundreds—perhaps thousands—of faithful copies, inventive variants, and eclectic borrowings over the centuries, only recently have the true complexity and the innovative engineering of its construction been fully understood.

Hadrian was a great builder whose undertakings extended beyond public architecture to private dwellings. For his splendid villa at Tivoli outside Rome (fig. 6-57), he instructed his architects to re-create his favorite places throughout the empire: the Grove of Academe outside Athens in which Plato had founded his academy; the Painted Stoa in the Agora of Athens; and various buildings in and near the Ptolemaic capital of Alexandria, Egypt. Hadrian's Villa was not a single building but an architectural complex of many buildings, lakes, and gardens spread over half a square mile. Each section had its own inner logic, and each took advantage of natural land formations and attractive views. The individual buildings were not large, but they were extremely complex, providing ingenious examples of Roman planning and engineering. The villa's architects exploited to the fullest the flexibility offered by concrete construction. They surfaced structures with veneers of marble and travertine and with exquisite mosaics resembling paintings (see fig. 6-69). And they landscaped with pools, fountains, and plants, turning the villa into a place of sensuous and sumptuous delight. An area with a long reflecting pool, called the Canopus after a site Hadrian had seen at that city on the Nile near Alexandria, was framed by a fanciful colonnade with alternating semicircular and straight entablatures (fig. 6-58). The spaces between the

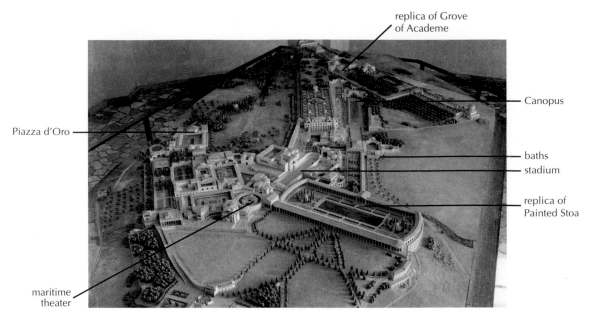

replica of Grove
of Academe

Canopus

baths

stadium

replica of
Painted Stoa

Piazza d'Oro

maritime
theater

6-57. Model of Hadrian's Villa, Tivoli. c. 135 CE

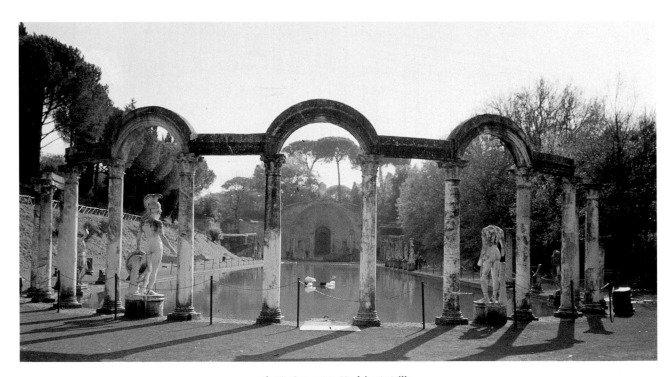

6-58. Canopus, Hadrian's Villa

columns were filled with copies of Greek statues. So great was Hadrian's love of Greek sculpture that he even had the **caryatids** of the Erechtheion (see fig. 5-51) replicated for his pleasure palace.

Architecture in the Provinces

During his reign, Trajan founded and built a new town at Timgad in the Algerian desert that was once home to 15,000 people (figs. 6-59, 6-60). This abandoned and ruined city has revealed almost as much about the culture of the empire as the cities buried by Vesuvius. The Roman architects who designed such new towns, cities,

and forts or who expanded and rebuilt existing ones were masters of urban planning. Adopting the grid plan of the Etruscan and later Greek cities, they divided towns into four quarters defined by intersecting north-south and east-west arteries, called, respectively, the *cardo* and the *decumanus* by modern archeologists. A town forum was usually located at this intersection. Terrain and climate had little effect on this simple, efficient plan, imposing in its symmetry, which remained much the same throughout the empire.

Timgad was a community where soldiers and their families, especially those who had served in the region, went when they retired. As such, it reflects the depen-

6-59. Plan of Timgad, Algeria. Begun c. 100 CE

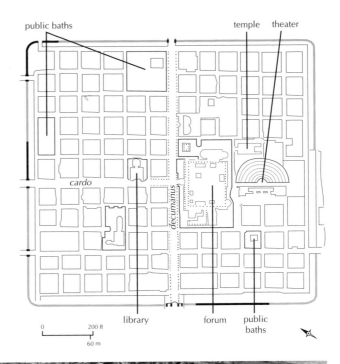

dence of emperors on the support of their troops, for retiring soldiers received a pension in money or land. As land became scarce in Italy, the emperors established provincial communities like Timgad. As initially laid out, it was a square of about 30 acres with four equal districts set off by the main streets. The forum and a theater straddled the *cardo* just south of the intersection with the *decumanus* at the town center. Other amenities included a library and several public baths. Elaborate triumphal arches marked the main entrances to the town, and its streets, paved with precisely cut and fitted ashlar blocks, were once colonnaded (fig. 6-61).

Another of Trajan's projects was a grand market on the south side of Miletos in Asia Minor. Markets were an essential part of city life, and improving them, often with

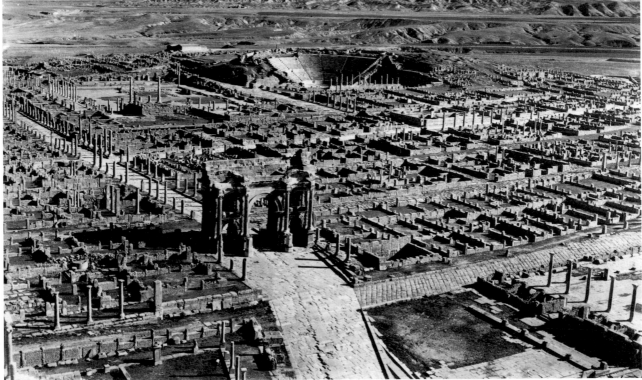

6-60. Ruins of Timgad

6-61. *Decumanus* (main east-west thoroughfare), Timgad

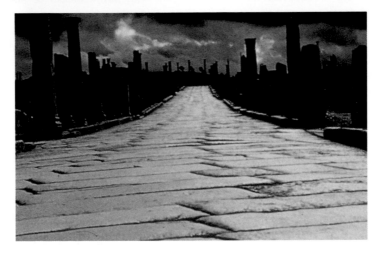

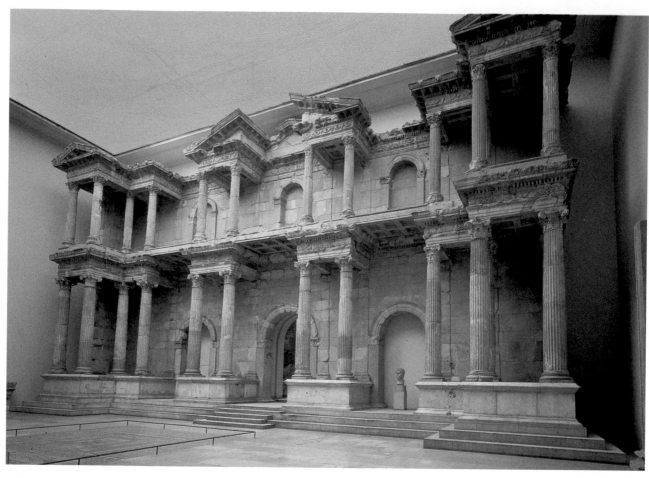

6-62. Market Gate, from Miletos (Turkey). C. 120 CE. Staatliche Museen zu Berlin, Preussischer Kulturbesitz, Antikensammlung

splendid architectural settings, was a way for wealthy families as well as emperors to curry popular favor. Only the core of Trajan's market buildings survives. The gate added in 120 CE, however, exemplifies the grandeur of some of these provincial projects (fig. 6-62). The two-story structure, now inside a museum in Berlin, is about 54 feet wide and resembles somewhat the backdrop of a Roman theater. It also brings to mind the fanciful illusionistic architecture seen in Pompeiian wall paintings. In its original setting, it functioned as a porchlike entrance to the market square. The facade, with its projecting ends, has three arched openings, and the whole is screened by a series of paired columns. The columns on the lower level are of the Composite order. These support short sections of entablature with carved friezes that in turn support the cornice of the second level. The shorter Corinthian columns and entablatures on the second level repeat the design of the lower level, except that the two center pairings support a **broken pediment**, which consists of the ends of a typical triangular pediment without a middle. The overall effect of structures like the gate at Miletos, with their design and structural innovations, was to evoke a sense of awe in the everyday passerby.

Hadrian's Wall, in northern Britain, was at the opposite end of the empire (fig. 6-63). Unlike the market gate, with its commercial, civilian setting, the wall and the forts that protected it were strictly military structures. This stone barrier snakes from coast to coast across a narrow (80-mile-wide) part of Britain. Some 4 to 5 feet thick and originally 15 feet high, it created a symbolic as well as a physical boundary between Roman territory and that of the barbarian Picts and Scots to the north. Towers were located at every mile mark. Seventeen larger camps, located at regular intervals, housed auxiliary forces ready to respond to any trouble the sentries might spot. These camps—like towns modeled on them—were laid out in a grid, with main streets dividing them into blocks (fig. 6-64). In the center were the praetorium (the commander's house and administrative headquarters), granaries, and the hospital, and surrounding these were barracks. These facilities and the wall itself are impressive reminders of the Roman occupation of northern Europe.

Relief Sculpture

The port of Ostia near Rome had grown so busy by the early empire that it was expanded with a new artificial harbor a short distance from the sea and connected to it by a canal. This harbor came to be known as Trajan's Harbor after he expanded it further. A relief panel created about 200 CE and discovered near the harbor marvelously combines a depiction of bustling seaport life

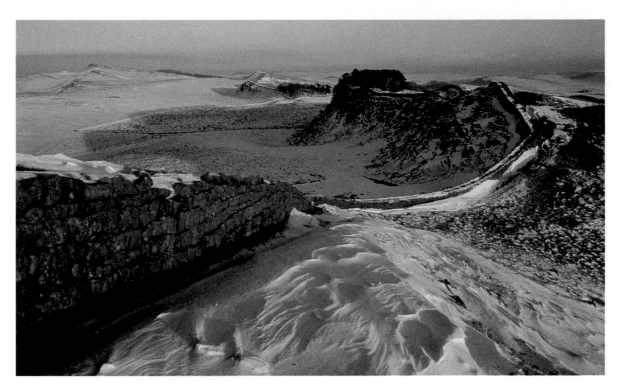

6-63. Hadrian's Wall, seen near Housesteads, England. 2nd century CE

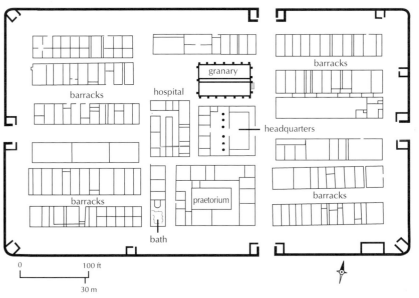

6-64. Plan of the former Roman fort near Housesteads, England. 2nd century CE

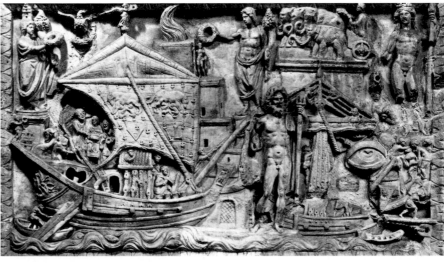

6-65. *Allegorical Harbor Scene*, relief found near Trajan's Harbor, Ostia. c. 200 CE. Marble. Museo Torlonia, Rome

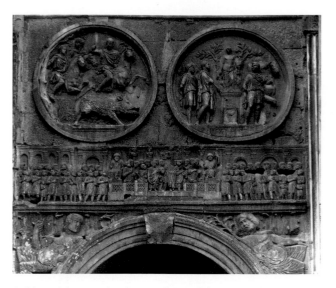

6-66. *Hadrian Hunting Boar and Sacrificing to Apollo*, roundels made for a monument to Hadrian and reused on the Arch of Constantine. 130–38 CE. Marble, roundel diameter 40" (102 cm)

with an allegorical representation of Rome's maritime power (fig. 6-65). Like earlier plebeian sculpture, this panel conveys a great deal of specific information. Minutely detailed figures of sailors, dockworkers, and harbor supervisors are shown hard at work, ship passengers settle themselves under sails, and large figures of the gods in Classical Greek poses overlook the activities. At the top right is Bacchus, leaning on his staff and pouring wine from a jug into the sea. At the center stands the sea god Neptune holding his trident. The well-outfitted ship that appears to be entering the harbor bears the symbol of Rome on its sail—a she-wolf nursing the twins Romulus and Remus. Flying above the ship is an eagle, and on each side of it are two figures—a personification of the Senate on the right and of the Roman people on the left—extending wreaths of triumph. In the background is the harbor's lighthouse with its perpetual flame, and on the right, behind the ship with furled sails, can be seen the attic story of a triumphal arch, atop which is a statue of a rider and a chariot pulled by four elephants.

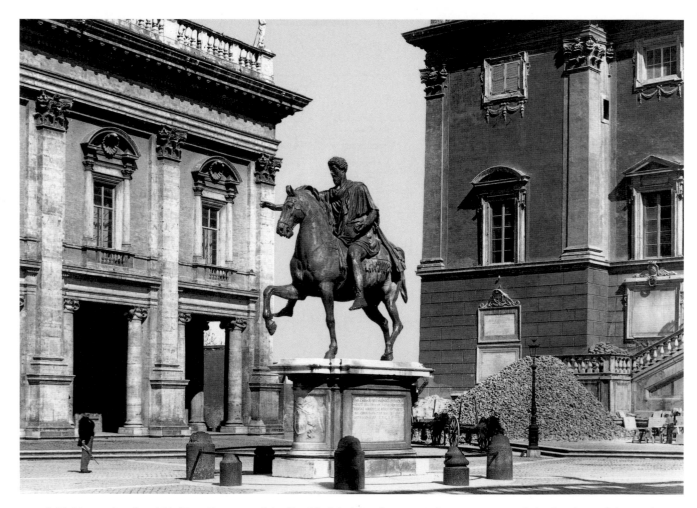

6-67. *Marcus Aurelius*. 161–80 CE. Bronze, originally gilded; height of statue 11'6" (3.5 m). Formerly in the Piazza del Campidoglio, Rome

This statue stood for centuries in the piazza fronting on the palace and church of Saint John Lateran in Rome. In January 1538 Pope Paul III had it moved to the Capitoline Hill, where it became the focus of a renovation and building program that created the Piazza del Campidoglio as it looks today. The statue is shown here in its original location, in the center of the piazza with the Palazzo Senatorio behind it and the Palazzo Nuovo (New Palace, today the Capitoline Museum) at the left. After being removed from its base for cleaning and restoration work some years ago, it was taken inside the Capitoline Museum to preserve it from the continued effects of Rome's polluted air.

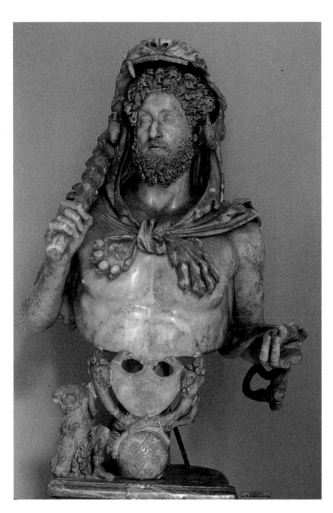

6-68. *Commodus as Hercules.* c. 190 CE. Marble, height 46½"
(118 cm). Palazzo dei Conservatori, Rome

The emperor Commodus, son of Marcus Aurelius, was
not just decadent, he was probably insane. He claimed
at various times to be the reincarnation of Hercules
and the incarnation of the god Jupiter, and he even
appeared in public as a gladiator. He ordered the
months of the Roman year to be renamed after him
and changed the name of Rome to Colonia Commo-
diana. When he proposed to assume the consulship
dressed and armed as a gladiator, his associates,
including his mistress, arranged to have him strangled
in his bath by a wrestling partner. In this portrait,
the emperor is shown in the guise of Hercules, adorned
with references to the hero's legendary labors: his
club, the skin and head of the Nemean Lion, and the
golden apples from the garden of the Hesperides.

An example of official imperial sculpture offers an
enlightening contrast to the *Allegorical Harbor Scene.*
Like his predecessors, Hadrian used monumental sculpture to promote himself and his accomplishments. Several large, circular reliefs or roundels—originally part of
a monument that no longer exists—contain images
designed to affirm his imperial stature and right to rule
(fig. 6-66). In the scene on the left, he demonstrates his
courage and physical prowess in a boar hunt. Other
roundels, not included here, show him confronting a
bear and a lion. At the right, in a show of piety and appreciation to the gods for their support of his endeavors,
Hadrian makes a sacrificial offering to Apollo at an outdoor altar. As did the sculptor of the Column of Trajan,

the sculptor of these roundels has included elements of
a natural landscape setting but kept them relatively
small, using them to frame the proportionally larger
figures. The idealized heads, form-enhancing drapery,
and graceful yet energetic movement of the figures owe
a distant debt to the works of Praxiteles and Lysippos
(Chapter 5), but the well-observed details of the features
and the bits of landscape are characteristically Roman.
Much of the sculpture of the mid-second century CE
shows the influence of Hadrian's love of Greek art, and
for a time Roman artists achieved a level of idealized
figural depiction close to that of Classical Greece. In the
fourth century CE, Emperor Constantine had the roundels
from the Hadrian monument placed on his own triumphal arch (see fig. 6-84) and had Hadrian's head in
each scene recarved with his own features or those of his
father, Constantius Chlorus.

Portrait Sculpture

Marcus Aurelius, like Hadrian, was a successful military
commander, but he was equally proud of his intellectual
attainments. In a lucky error—or twist of fortune—a
once-gilded bronze equestrian statue of the emperor
(fig. 6-67) came early but mistakenly to be revered as a
statue of Constantine, the first Christian emperor, and
escaped the fate of being melted down, which befell all
other bronze equestrian statues from antiquity. The
emperor is dressed in the tunic and short, heavy cloak of
a commander. The raised foreleg of his horse is poised to
trample a figure of a crouching barbarian (lost). His head,
with its thick, curly hair and full beard (a style that was
begun by Hadrian to enhance his image and then
became popular among Roman men), resembles the traditional "philosopher" portraits of the Republican period.
The emperor wears no armor and carries no weapons;
like the Egyptian kings, he conquers effortlessly by the
will of the gods. And like his illustrious predecessor
Augustus, he reaches out to the people in a persuasive,
beneficent gesture.

It is difficult to balance the composition of an equestrian portrait so that the rider stands out as the dominant
figure without making the horse look too small. The
sculptor of this equestrian statue of Marcus Aurelius
found a balance acceptable to viewers of the time and, in
doing so, created a model for later artists. The horse's
high-arched neck, massive head, and short body suggest
that it is from a Spanish breed of strong, compact, agile,
and relatively small animals prized as war steeds.

Marcus Aurelius was succeeded by his son Commodus, a man without political skill, administrative
competence, or intellectual distinction. During his unfortunate reign (180–192 CE) he devoted himself to luxury
and frivolous pursuits. He did, however, attract some of
the finest artists of the day for his commissions. A marble bust of Commodus dressed as Hercules reflects his
character (fig. 6-68). The sculptor's sensitive modeling
and expert drillwork exploit the play of light and shadow
on the figure and bring out the textures of the hair, beard,
facial features, and drapery. The portrait conveys the

TECHNIQUE
ROMAN MOSAICS

Mosaics were used widely in Hellenistic times and became enormously popular for decorating homes in the Roman period. **Mosaic** designs are created with pebbles or with small, regularly shaped pieces of hard stone, marble, or manufactured colored glass, called **tesserae**. Today the stones are usually glued onto a firm backing, but in ancient times they were pressed into a kind of soft cement called grout. When the stones were firmly set, the spaces between them were also filled with cement. After the surface dried, it was cleaned and polished. At first, mosaics were used mainly as durable, water-resistant coverings on floors and pavements. They were done in a narrow range of colors depending on the natural color of the stone—often earth tones or simply black or some other dark color on a light background. When they began to appear on walls at outdoor fountains, a wide range of colors was used (see "The

Urban Garden," page 240). So accomplished were some mosaicists that they could create works that looked like paintings. In fact, at the request of patrons, they often copied well-known paintings employing a technique in which very small tesserae, in all the needed colors, were laid down in irregular, curving lines that very effectively mimicked painted brushstrokes.

Mosaic production was made more efficient by the development of emblemata (the plural of **emblema**, "central design"). These small, mosaic compositions were created in the artist's workshop in square or rectangular trays of marble or terra-cotta. They could be made in advance, carried to a work site, and inserted into a floor or wall otherwise decorated with a simple background mosaic in a plain or geometric pattern. Emblemata were often salvaged from older floors and reused in new ones much later.

illusion of life and movement, but it also captures its subject's foolishness. The weakness of the man comes through the grand pretensions of his costume.

Mosaics

Pictorial mosaics covered the floors of fine houses, villas, and public buildings throughout the empire. Working

with very small tesserae (pieces of glass or stone) and a wide range of colors, mosaicists achieved remarkable illusionistic effects (see "Roman Mosaics," above). A floor mosaic from Hadrian's Villa at Tivoli illustrates extraordinary artistry (fig. 6-69). It may be a copy of a work by the Greek artist Zeuxis, of the late fifth century BCE, who was said to have done a much-admired painting of a fight between centaurs and wild animals. In a

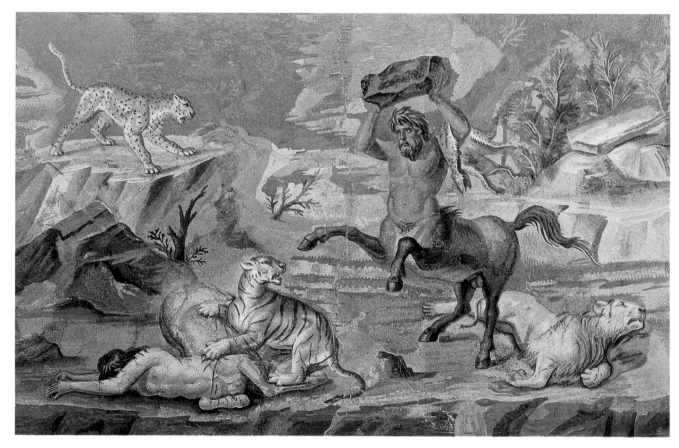

6-69. *Battle of Centaurs and Wild Beasts,* from Hadrian's Villa, Tivoli. c. 118–28 CE. Mosaic, 23 x 36" (58.4 x 91.4 cm). Staatliche Museen zu Berlin, Preussischer Kulturbesitz, Antikensammlung

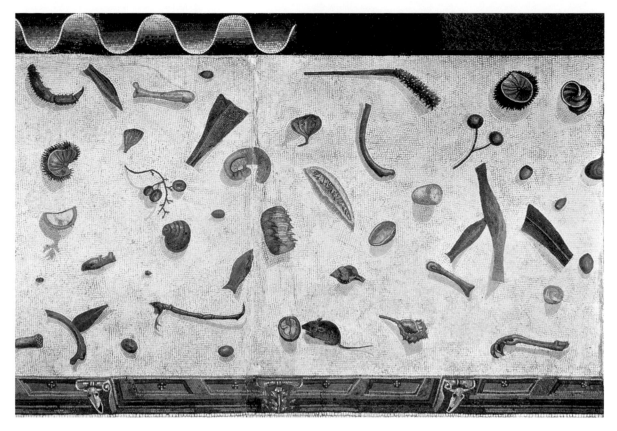

6-70. Heracleitus. *The Unswept Floor*, mosaic variant of a 2nd-century BCE painting by Sosos of Pergamon. 2nd century CE. Musei Vaticani, Museo Gregoriano Profano, ex Lateranense, Rome

rocky landscape with only a few bits of green, an enraged male centaur raises a large boulder over his head to crush a tiger that has attacked and severely wounded another centaur. Two other felines apparently took part in the attack—the white leopard on the rocks to the left and the dead lion at the feet of the male centaur. The mosaicist rendered the figures with three-dimensional shading, **foreshortening**, and a great sensitivity to a range of figure types, including human torsos and powerful animals, living and dead, in a variety of poses.

The skill of Hellenistic painters like Pausias (Chapter 5) in creating images of flowers and fruit that fooled the beholder into thinking they were real seems to have inspired a long-lasting tradition of realistic still-life illustration. These works fascinated and amused both artists and patrons of the Roman period. In the second century BCE, in Pergamon, an artist named Sosos created a large painting that included a **trompe l'oeil** ("fool the eye") representation of a floor littered with refuse. Three centuries later, the Roman mosaicist Heracleitus adapted this design in a work called *The Unswept Floor* (fig. 6-70). It shows a mouse among table scraps—meat bones, shellfish, fruit, and nuts—seemingly tossed aside for the family pets. The objects are all intensely observed and re-created in meticulous detail, even to the shadows they cast on the floor, which seem to be the result of a single light source—perhaps an open door—raking across from the right.

THE LATE EMPIRE: FROM THE SEVERAN DYNASTY TO THE TETRARCHS

The reign of Commodus marked the beginning of a period of political and economic decline. Barbarian groups pressed on Rome's frontiers, and many settled within them, disrupting provincial government. As strains spread throughout the empire, imperial rule became increasingly military. Soon the army controlled the government, and the Imperial Guards set up and deposed rulers almost at will, often selecting candidates from among poorly educated, power-hungry provincial leaders in their own ranks.

Under the Severan emperors (193–235 CE) who succeeded Commodus, the arts continued to flourish. Septimius Severus (ruled 193–211 CE) and his Syrian wife, Julia Domna, restored public buildings, commissioned official portraits, and made some splendid additions to the old Republican Forum, including the transformation of the House of the Vestal Virgins, who served the Temple of Vesta, into a large, luxurious residence. Septimius's sons, Caracalla and Geta, succeeded him as co-emperors in 211 CE, but in 212 CE, Caracalla murdered Geta and ruled alone until he in turn was murdered by his successor in 217 CE.

The death of Severus Alexander (ruled 222–235 CE), the last in the Severan line, began a half-century of

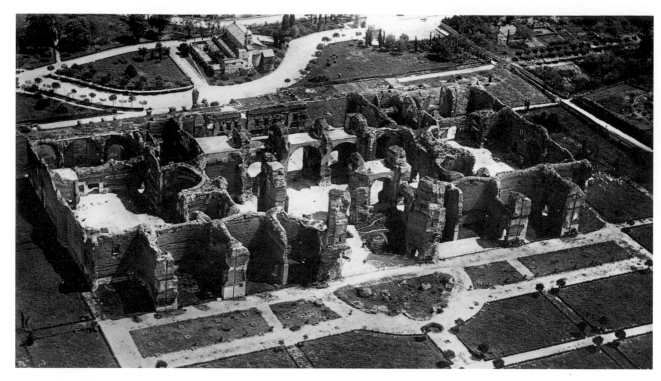

6-71. Baths of Caracalla, Rome. c. 211–17 CE

Although the well-to-do usually had private baths in their homes, women and men enjoyed the pleasures of socializing at the public baths. They did not do so together, however. In some cities, women and men had separate bathhouses, but it was also common for them to share one facility at different times of the day. Everyone—from nobles to working people—was allowed to use the public baths, no matter how grand. Men had access to the full range of facilities, including hot, tepid, and cold baths, moist- and dry-heat chambers (like saunas), pools for swimming, and outdoor areas for sunbathing or exercising in the nude. Women generally refrained from using very hot baths, dry-heat chambers, and the outdoor areas.

anarchy that ended with the rise to power of Emperor Diocletian (ruled 284–305 CE). This brilliant politician and general reversed the empire's declining fortunes, but he also initiated an increasingly autocratic form of rule, and toward the end of his reign he unleashed the persecution of Christians. He and his successors imposed ever more burdensome taxes on their subjects, and under them the social structure of the empire became increasingly rigid.

To distribute the task of defending and administering the empire and to assure an orderly succession, Diocletian devised a form of government called the Tetrarchy, or rule by four. Diocletian divided the empire in two; with the title of Augustus he would rule in the East, while another Augustus, Maximian, would rule in the West. Each Augustus designated a subordinate and heir, who held the title of Caesar. Each of the two regions was thus administered by one of these two co-rulers and his second-in-command. Although Diocletian intended that on the death or retirement of an Augustus, his Caesar would replace him and name a new Caesar, the plan failed when Diocletian tried to implement it.

Architecture

The year before his death in 211, Septimius Severus began a popular public-works project, the construction of magnificent new public baths on the southeast side of Rome (fig. 6-71). The baths were inaugurated in 216–217 CE by his son and successor, Caracalla. For the Romans,

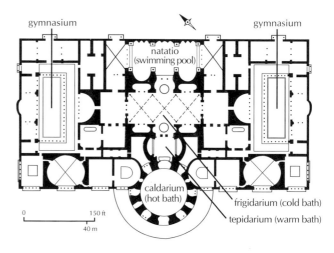

6-72. Plan of the Baths of Caracalla

baths were recreational and educational centers, not simply places to clean themselves, and the emperors built large bathing complexes to gain public favor. The marble, brick, and concrete Baths of Caracalla, as they are now called, were laid out on a strictly symmetrical plan. The bathing facilities were located together in the center of the main building to make efficient use of the below-ground furnaces that heated them and to allow bathers to move comfortably from hot to cold pools and finish with a swim (fig. 6-72). Many other facilities—exercise rooms, shops, latrines, and dressing rooms—were housed on each side of the bathing block. The baths alone covered 5 acres. The entire complex, which included gardens, a

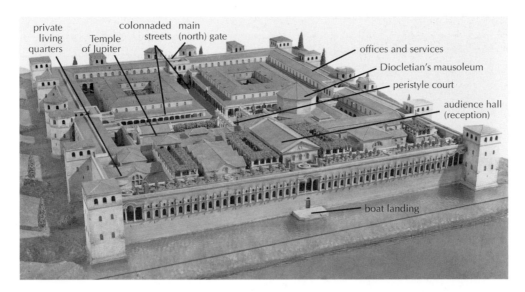

labels on figure 6-73:
private living quarters
Temple of Jupiter
colonnaded main streets
(north) gate
offices and services
Diocletian's mausoleum
peristyle court
audience hall (reception)
boat landing

200 CE
800 BCE   400 CE

6-73. Model of Palace of Diocletian, Split, Serbian Croatia. C. 300 CE. Museo della Civiltà Romana, Rome

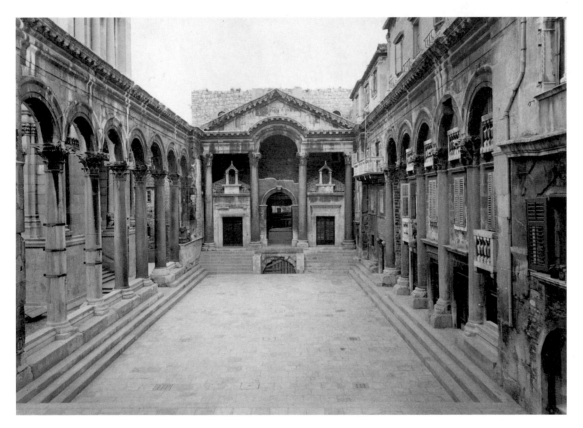

6-74. Peristyle court, Palace of Diocletian

stadium, libraries, a painting gallery, auditoriums, and huge water reservoirs, covered an area of 50 acres.

The great palaces such as Hadrian's Villa were often as extensive and semipublic as the Minoan palace at Knossos. Diocletian broke this tradition by building a huge and well-fortified imperial residence at Split, on the Dalmatian coast, after he retired from active rule (fig. 6-73). Revolutionary in design, the building recalls the compact, regular plan of a Roman army camp rather than the irregular, sprawling design of Hadrian's Villa. The palace was surrounded by a wall, a reflection of the unstable conditions of the time. It consisted of a rectangu-

lar enclosure 650 by 550 feet crossed by two colonnaded streets that divided it into quarters, each with a specific function. The emperor's residential complex, which included the reception hall on the main, north-south axis of the palace, faced the sea. Ships bearing supplies or providing transport for the emperor tied up at the narrow landing stage. The support staff lived and worked in buildings near the main gate. A colonnaded avenue extended from this entrance, leading to a peristyle court that ended in a grand facade with an enormous arched doorway through which the emperor made his ceremonial appearances (fig. 6-74). Like the Canopus at

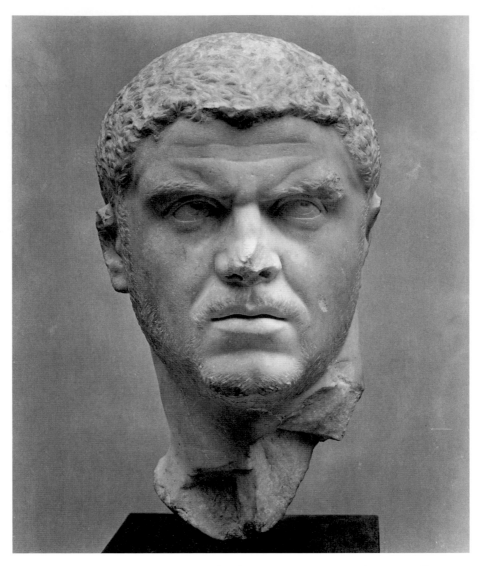

6-75. *Caracalla*. Early 3rd century CE. Marble, height 14½" (36.2 cm). The Metropolitan Museum of Art, New York

Samuel D. Lee Fund, 1940 (40.11.1A)

The emperor Caracalla (ruled 211–217 CE) was consistently represented with a malignant, scowling expression, a convention meant to convey a particular message to the viewer: the emperor was not a god, not an effete intellectual, not a soft patrician, but a hard-as-nails, battle-toughened military man, a lethal opponent ready to defend himself and his empire.

Hadrian's Villa, the columns of the peristyle court supported arches rather than entablatures (see fig. 6-58). On one side of the court, the arcade opened onto Diocletian's mausoleum; on the other side, it opened onto the Temple of Jupiter.

Portrait Sculpture

Emperor Caracalla emerges from his portraits as a man of chilling and calculating ruthlessness. In the example shown here (fig. 6-75) the sculptor has enhanced the intensity of the emperor's expression by producing strong contrasts of light and dark with sensitive drill and chisel work. Even the marble eyes have been drilled and engraved to catch the light in a way that makes them glit-

ter. It is hard to believe that Caracalla could have favored a portrait that showed him in such unflattering terms, yet he clearly did. Unable to charm his subjects, he apparently preferred to terrify them. The contrast between this style and that of the portraits of Augustus is a telling reflection of the changing character of imperial rule. Augustus presented himself as the first among equals, ruling by persuasion; Caracalla presented himself as a no-nonsense ruler of iron-fisted determination.

The successors of the Severan emperors—the more than two dozen so-called soldier-emperors who attempted to rule the empire before the rise of Diocletian—continued to favor the style of Caracalla's portraits. A bust of Philip the Arab (ruled 244–249 CE), however, does not convey the same malevolence as

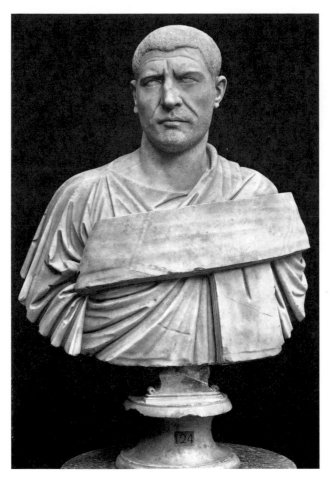

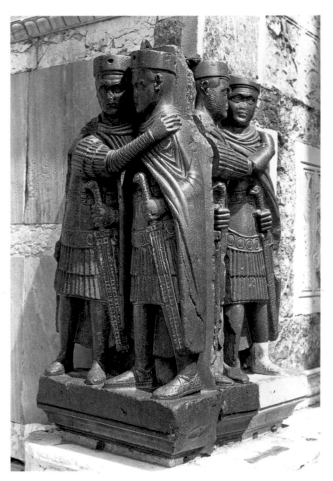

6-76. *Philip the Arab*. 244–49 CE. Marble, height 26" (71.1 cm). Musei Vaticani, Braccia Nuovo, Rome

6-77. *The Tetrarchs*. c. 305 CE. Porphyry, height of figures 51" (129 cm). Installed in the Middle Ages at the corner of the facade of the Church of San Marco, Venice

Caracalla's portraits (fig. 6-76). Philip's expression is more tense and worried, suggesting a troubled man in troubled times. Philip had been the head of the Imperial Guard but had plotted to murder and replace his predecessor, Emperor Gordian III (ruled 238–244 CE), whom he was pledged to defend. Philip's own short reign also ended in assassination.

Philip is shown wearing a new style of toga that is typical of late imperial dress. Made of heavy material, it hangs in a few stiff folds and drapes across the chest in a broad, flat band. The sculptor first modeled the broad structure of the emperor's head, then used both chisel and drill to deepen shadows and heighten the effects of light in the furrows of his face and in his drapery. Unlike the portraits of Marcus Aurelius and Commodus, in which hair and beard were carved to show individual locks, in this portrait tiny flicks of the chisel suggest the texture of hair. Around the mouth, these small scratches sometimes give the impression of tension as they catch the light playing over the surface. The overall impact of the work depends on the effects of light and the imagination of the spectator as much as on the carved stone itself. What comes through from Philip's twisted brow, sidelong upward glance, quizzical lips, and tightened jaw muscles is a sense of guile, deceit, and fear.

During the turmoil of the third century, Roman artists lost interest in representing the natural world, emphasizing instead the symbolic or general qualities of their subjects and expressing them in increasingly simplified, geometric forms. By the mid-third century, portraits had begun to convey the anxious state of mind of the emperors and the people they ruled. A further turn toward abstraction and symbolic representation can be seen in *The Tetrarchs*, a depiction of Diocletian and his three co-rulers from the early fourth century CE (fig. 6-77). Hardly a realistic portrait of Diocletian, his co-ruler Maximian, and their Caesars, it reads instead like a symbolic representation of four-man rule. The four figures—two with beards, probably the senior Augusti, and two clean shaven, probably the Caesars, their adopted sons—are nearly identical. Dressed in military garb and clasping swords at their sides, they embrace each other in a show of imperial unity, proclaiming a kind of peace through concerted strength and vigilance. As a piece of propaganda and a summary of the state of affairs at the time, it is unsurpassed. The sculpture is made of porphyry, a purple stone from Egypt reserved for imperial use. The hardness of the stone, which makes it difficult to carve, and perhaps the sculptor's familiarity with Egyptian artistic conventions, may have contributed to the extremely

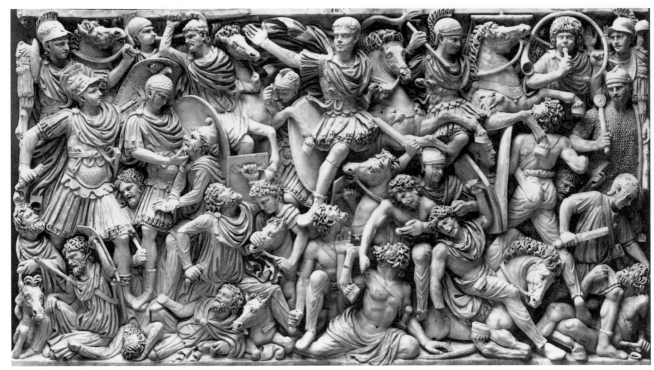

6-78. *Battle between the Romans and the Barbarians*, detail of the *Ludovisi Battle Sarcophagus*, found near Rome. c. 250 CE. Marble, height approx. 5' (1.52 m). Museo Nazionale Romano, Rome

abstract style of the work. The most striking features of *The Tetrarchs*—the simplification of natural forms to geometric shapes, the disregard for normal human proportions, and the emphasis on a message or idea—can nevertheless be seen in most Roman art by the end of the third century.

Sarcophagus Reliefs

Although portraits and narrative reliefs were the major forms of public sculpture during the second and third centuries CE, changing funerary practices—a shift from cremation to burial—led to a growing demand for funerary sculpture. A wealthy Roman might commission an elegant stone or marble sarcophagus to be placed in a mausoleum. Workshops throughout the empire produced thousands of these sarcophagi, which were carved with reliefs that ranged in complexity from simple geometric or floral ornaments to scenes involving large numbers of figures. The subjects of the more elaborate reliefs varied widely. Some included events from the life of the deceased and some showed dramatic scenes from Greek mythology and drama, such as the tragedies of Agamemnon's family, the events of the Trojan War, or the Labors of Hercules. Scenes of Bacchus and his followers were extremely popular, no doubt because this cult offered its worshipers an afterlife of perpetual ecstasy in union with the god.

A famous carved stone coffin known as the *Ludovisi Battle Sarcophagus* (after a seventeenth-century owner) dates to about 250 CE (fig. 6-78). It shows a battle be-

tween Romans and barbarians in a style that has roots in the sculptural traditions of Hellenistic Pergamon. The Romans at the top of the panel are efficiently dispatching the barbarians—clearly identifiable by their heavy, twisted locks and scraggly beards—who lie fallen, dying, or beaten at the bottom of the panel. The artist has made no attempt to create a realistic spatial environment. The bare-headed young Roman commander, addressing his troops with an outstretched arm from the back of his valiant steed, is shown in the midst of the battle in a formal equestrian pose like that of the equestrian statue of Marcus Aurelius (see fig. 6-67).

Painting

A portrait of the family of Septimius Severus provides a remarkable insight into the history of the Severan dynasty in addition to revealing something about early-third-century CE painting (fig. 6-79). The work is in the highly formal style of a region in northwestern Egypt called Faiyum, and it is probably a souvenir of an imperial visit to Egypt. The emperor, clearly identified by his distinctive divided beard and curled moustache, wears an enormous crown. Next to him is his wife, Julia Domna, portrayed with similarly recognizable features—full face, large nose, and masses of waving hair. She looks out at the viewer in a defiant manner. Their two sons, Geta and Caracalla, stand in front of them, but Geta's features have been defaced. Perhaps because we know that he grew up to be a ruthless dictator, little Caracalla looks in this portrait like a disagreeable child. Soon

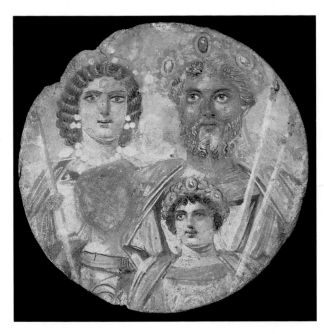

6-79. *Septimius Severus, Julia Domna, and Their Children, Caracalla and Geta*, from Faiyum, Egypt. c. 200 CE. Painted wood, diameter 14" (35.6 cm). Staatliche Museen zu Berlin, Preussischer Kulturbesitz, Antikensammlung

after Septimius's death, Caracalla murdered Geta, perhaps with Julia Domna's help, and in a decree called *damnatio memoriae* declared that Geta's memory be abolished. Clearly the owners of this painting complied with the decree. The work emphasizes the trappings of imperial wealth and power—crowns, jewels, and direct, forceful expressions—rather than attempting a deep, psychological study. The rather hard drawing style, with its broadly brushed-in draperies, contrasts markedly with that of earlier portraits, such as the *Young Woman Writing* (see fig. 6-48).

Despite the trend toward abstraction, the earlier tradition of slightly idealized but realistic portraiture was slow to die out, probably because it showed patrons as they wanted to be remembered. In the *Family of Vunnerius Keramus* (fig. 6-80), the subjects are rendered as individuals, although the artist has emphasized their great almond-shaped eyes. The work seems to reflect the advice of Philostratus, who, writing in the late third century CE, commented: "The person who would properly master this art [of painting] must also be a keen observer of human nature and must be capable of discerning the signs of people's characters even though they are silent; he should be able to discern what is revealed in the expression of the eyes, what is found in the character of

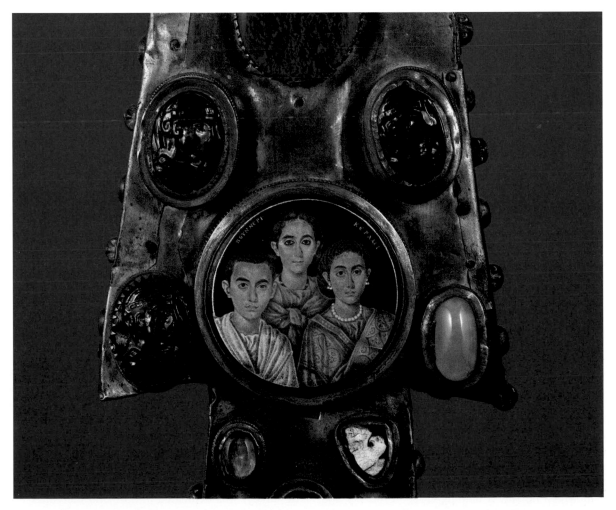

6-80. *Family of Vunnerius Keramus*. c. 250 CE. Gold leaf sealed between glass, diameter 2⅜" (6 cm). Museo Civico dell'Età Cristiana, Brescia

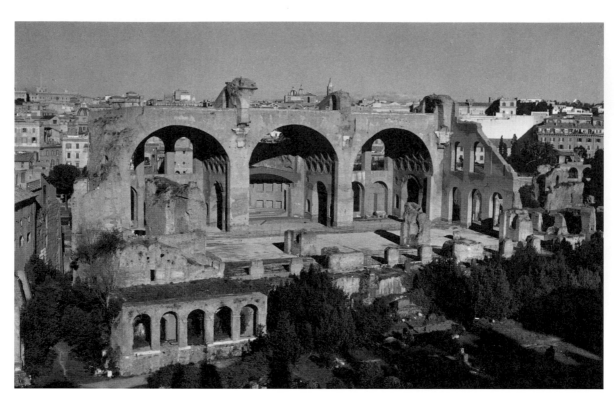

6-81. Basilica of Maxentius and Constantine, Rome. 306–13 CE

the brows, and, to state the point briefly, whatever indicates the condition of the mind."

The *Family of Vunnerius Keramus* was engraved and painted on sheets of **gold leaf**, then cut out and sealed between two layers of glass. This fragile, delicate medium, most often used for the bottoms of glass bowls or cups—many of which survive—seems appropriate for an age of material insecurity and emotional intensity. Curiously, this particular piece was inserted by a later Christian owner as the central jewel in a decorated seventh-century cross.

THE LATE EMPIRE: CONSTANTINE THE GREAT AND HIS LEGACY

In 305 CE Diocletian abdicated and forced his fellow Augustus, Maximian, to do likewise. The orderly succession he had hoped for failed to occur, and Augusti and Caesars began almost immediately to jockey with each other for position and advantage. Two main contenders emerged in the western part of the empire: Maximian's son Maxentius (ruled 306–312 CE), and Constantine I, known as The Great (ruled 306–337 CE), son of the Augustus Constantius. Constantine emerged victorious in 312 after defeating Maxentius at the Battle of the Milvian Bridge, at the entrance to Rome. According to a legend popular for centuries, Constantine had a vision the night before the battle in which he saw a flaming cross in the sky and heard these words: "In this sign you shall conquer." The next morning he ordered that his army's shields and standards be inscribed with the monogram ✗ (formed of the Greek letters *chi* and *rho*, standing for *Christos*). The legend says that the victorious Constantine then showed his gratitude by ending persecution of Christians and recognizing Christianity as a lawful religion. (In fact *chi* and *rho* used together had long been an abbreviation of the Greek word *chrestos*, meaning "auspicious," and this was probably the reason Constantine used the monogram.) Whatever the impulse, in 313 CE, together with Licinius, who was Augustus in the East, Constantine issued the Edict of Milan, a model of religious toleration: "With sound and most upright reasoning. . . we resolved that authority be refused to no one to follow and choose the observance or form of worship that Christians use, and that authority be granted to each one to give his mind to that form of worship which he deems suitable to himself, to the intent that the Divinity . . . may in all things afford us his wonted care and generosity" (Eusebius, *Ecclesiastical History* 10.5.5). The Edict of Milan granted freedom to all religious groups, not just Christians. Constantine remained the *Pontifex Maximus*, or High Priest, of Rome's state religion and also reaffirmed his devotion during his reign to the military's favorite god, Mithras, and to the Invincible Sun, *Sol Invictus*, a manifestation of Helios Apollo, the sun god.

In 324 Constantine defeated Licinius, his last rival, and would rule as sole emperor until his death in 337. He made the port city of Byzantium his new capital, renaming it Constantinople. This new capital (modern Istanbul, in Turkey) was dedicated in 330, and thereafter Rome, which had already ceased to be the seat of government in the West, declined in importance.

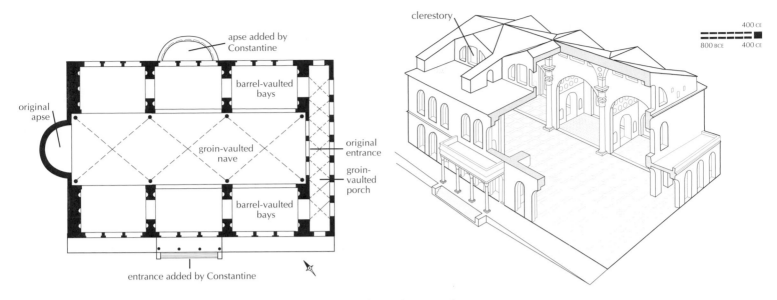

6-82. Plan and isometric reconstruction of the Basilica of Maxentius and Constantine

The original plan for the basilica called for a single entrance on the southeast side, facing a single apse on the northwest. After building had begun, Constantine's architects added another entrance on the southwest, probably to accommodate crowds, and another apse across the hall. The effect was to dilute the focus on the original apse, with its gigantic statue of the emperor (see fig. 6-86).

Architecture

Maxentius, who controlled Rome throughout his short reign, ordered the repair of many buildings there and had others built. His most impressive undertaking was a huge new basilica just southeast of the Imperial Forums called the Basilica Nova, or New Basilica (fig. 6-81). Now known as the Basilica of Maxentius and Constantine, this was the last important imperial government building erected in Rome itself. It functioned, like all basilicas, as an administrative center and provided a magnificent setting for the emperor when he appeared as supreme judge. Earlier basilicas, such as Trajan's Basilica Ulpia (see fig. 6-50), had been columnar halls, but Maxentius ordered his engineers to create the kind of large, unbroken, vaulted space found in public baths. The central hall was covered with groined vaults, and the side aisles were covered with lower barrel vaults that acted as **buttresses**, or projecting supports, for the central groin vault and allowed generous window openings in the clerestory areas over the side walls. Three of these brick-and-concrete barrel vaults still loom beside the streets of modern Rome. The basilica originally measured 300 by 215 feet and the vaults of the central **nave** rose to a height of 114 feet. A groin-vaulted porch extended across the short side (on the southeast) and sheltered a triple entrance to the central hall. At the opposite end of the long axis of the hall was an apse of the same width, which acted as a focal point for the building (fig. 6-82).

Constantine undertook a building campaign that became empirewide by the later years of his reign (Chapter 7). Among his achievements was a new palace and a basilica, built about 310 CE, at Trier, the capital of the northern Germanic territories. The exterior of this build-

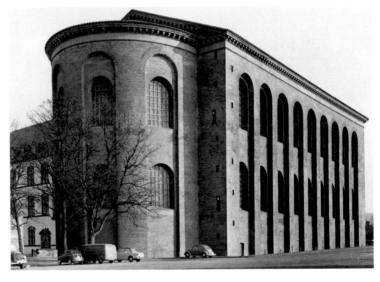

6-83. Basilica, Trier, Germany. Early 4th century CE

ing still looks much as it did in the early fourth century, with a few exceptions (fig. 6-83). Over the centuries, the ground level has risen and covered a high podium beneath the structure, and decorative exterior elements on walls and around windows have disappeared. Unlike the Basilica Ulpia, the building is entered through one end and has a single apse opposite the entrance, on which all attention is focused. Inside, it carries further the preference for large, unbroken spaces seen in the Basilica of Maxentius and Constantine. It has no side aisles, has a flat wooden-truss ceiling, and is lit by two rows of windows in the long walls and around the apse. The directional focus along a central axis from entrance to apse was adopted by Christians for use in churches.

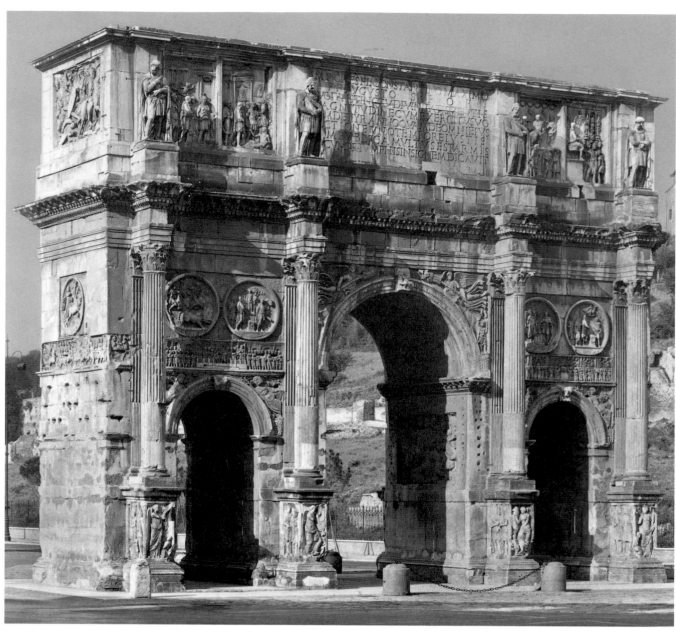

400 CE
800 BCE   400 CE

6-84. Arch of Constantine, Rome. 312–15 CE (dedicated July 25, 315)

This massive, triple-arched monument to Emperor Constantine's victory over Maxentius in 312 CE is a wonder of recycled sculpture. On the attic story, flanking the inscription over the central arch, are relief panels taken from a monument celebrating the victory of Marcus Aurelius over the Germans in 174 CE. On the attached piers framing these panels are large statues of prisoners made to celebrate Trajan's victory over the Dacians in the early second century CE. On the inner walls of the central arch (not seen here) are reliefs also commemorating Trajan's conquest of Dacia. Over each of the side arches are pairs of giant roundels taken from a monument to Hadrian (see fig. 6-66). The rest of the decoration is contemporary with the arch.

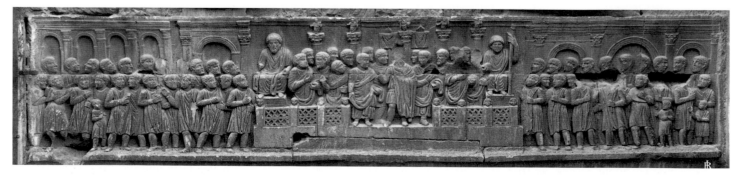

6-85. *Constantine Speaking to the People*, relief panel from the Arch of Constantine. Marble

The Arch of Constantine

In Rome, next to the Colosseum, the Senate erected a memorial to Constantine's victory over Maxentius (fig. 6-84), a huge, triple arch that dwarfs the nearby Arch of Titus (see fig. 6-40). Its three barrel-vaulted passageways are flanked by columns on high pedestals and surmounted by a large attic story with elaborate sculptural decoration and a traditional laudatory inscription: "To the Emperor Constantine from the Senate and the Roman People. Since through divine inspiration and great wisdom he has delivered the state from the tyrant and his party by his army and noble arms, [we] dedicate this arch, decorated with triumphal insignia." The "triumphal insignia" were in part looted from earlier monuments made for Constantine's illustrious predecessors, the "good emperors" Trajan, Hadrian, and Marcus Aurelius. The reused items in effect transferred the old Roman virtues of strength, courage, and piety associated with these earlier emperors to Constantine. New reliefs made for the arch recount the story of his victory and symbolize his power and generosity. A panel in one of the **lintels**, for example, depicts Constantine, in the center, making his first public speech after the triumph over Maxentius (fig. 6-85). The emperor (his head is missing) is seated in the Republican Forum on a temporary speaker's platform in front of a monument to the Tetrarchs (the columns with the statues on top of them) and flanked by images of Marcus Aurelius and Hadrian. The Basilica Julia and the Arch of Tiberius are to the left and the Arch of Septimius Severus is to the right.

Although these new reliefs reflect the long-standing Roman affection for depicting important events with realistic detail, they nevertheless represent a significant change in style, approach, and subject matter that distinguishes them from the reused elements in the arch. The stocky, mostly frontal, look-alike figures—reminiscent of figures in plebeian-style works—are compressed by the miniature buildings of the forum into the foreground plane. The arrangement and appearance of the uniform and undifferentiated participants below the enthroned Constantine clearly isolate the new Augustus and connect him visually with the illustrious predecessors on each side of him. This two-dimensional, hierarchical approach and stiff style is far removed from the realism of earlier imperial reliefs. With its emphasis on authority, ritual, and symbolic meaning rather than outward form, this style was adopted by the emerging Christian Church. Constantinian art is thus a bridge between the art of the imperial past and the art of the European Middle Ages (roughly 476 to 1453 CE).

Portrait Sculpture

Constantine, seeking to impress the people of Rome with visible symbols of his authority, put his own stamp on projects Maxentius had started. To the Basilica Nova he added an imposing new entrance in the center of the long side and a giant apse facing it across the three aisles. After he had begun to construct his new capital in

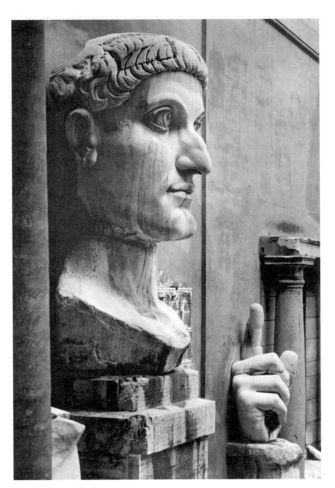

6-86. *Constantine the Great*, from the Basilica of Maxentius and Constantine, Rome. 325–26 CE. Marble, height of head 8'6" (2.6 m). Palazzo dei Conservatori, Rome

This fragment came from a statue of the seated emperor. The original sculpture combined marble, wood, and bricks. Only a few marble fragments survive—the head, a hand, a knee, an elbow, and a foot. The body might have been made of colored stone or of wood and bricks sheathed in bronze. This statue, although made of less-expensive materials, must have been as awe-inspiring as the gigantic ivory and gold-clad statues of Zeus at Olympia and Athena on the Acropolis in Athens, made in the fifth century BCE by Pheidias, the favorite sculptor of Perikles. Constantine was a master at the use of portrait statues to spread imperial propaganda. Heads like this, made according to official specifications, were shipped throughout the provinces to be attached to bodies that were locally sculpted.

the East, he commissioned a colossal, 30-foot portrait statue of himself and had it placed in the original apse (fig. 6-86). This statue was, in effect, a permanent stand-in for the emperor in Rome, representing him whenever the conduct of business legally required his presence. The sculpture combines features of traditional Roman portraiture with the abstract qualities evident in *The Tetrarchs* (see fig. 6-77). The defining characteristics of Constantine's face—his heavy jaw, hooked nose, and jutting chin—have been incorporated into a rigid, symmetrical pattern in which other features, such as his eyes, eyebrows, and hair, have been simplified into repeated

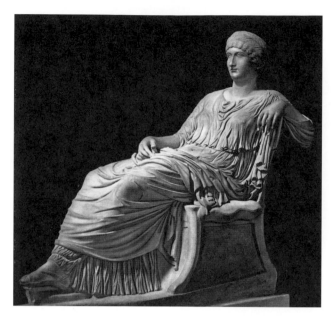

6-87. *Helen, Mother of Constantine*. c. 320 CE. Marble. Museo Capitolino, Rome

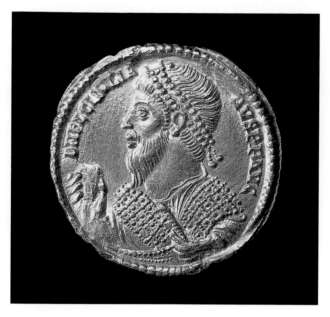

6-88. *Julian the Apostate*, coin issued 361–63 CE. Gold. The British Museum, London

geometric arcs. The result is a work that projects imperial power and dignity with no hint of human frailty or imperfection.

Constantine's mother, Helen, a devout Christian, played an important part in her son's career. Credited by legend with the discovery of Christ's cross, she was later made a saint and represented in Christian art. In one monumental portrait (fig. 6-87), she was depicted in the manner of a Classical Greek reclining goddess.

THE LATE EMPIRE: ROMAN TRADITIONALISM IN ART AFTER CONSTANTINE

Constantine was baptized formally into the Christian religion on his deathbed in 337 CE. After his death there was a period of civil war, the reuniting of the empire under his son, Constantius II, then the brief reign (361–363 CE) of Julian, bringing with it religious tumult. Julian the Apostate, as Christian writers called him (apostate means "religious defector"), rejected Christianity and sought to reinstate the worship of Rome's ancestral gods. Himself a follower of Mithras, Julian officially forbade Christian scholars from teaching pre-Christian Greek and Roman literature and wrote treatises attacking the ideas of contemporary Christian writers. He did not ban Christianity but tried to undermine it by adapting some of its liturgical devices and charitable practices for the worship of the traditional gods. He had himself portrayed on coins as a bearded scholar-philosopher (fig. 6-88), an ancient portrait convention also favored by his illustrious predecessor Marcus Aurelius.

Julian died in battle and was succeeded by a series of Christian emperors. By the end of the fourth century, Christianity had become the official religion of the empire, and non-Christians had become the targets of persecution. Many people resisted this shift and tried to revive classical culture. Among them were the Roman patricians Quintus Aurelius Symmachus, a strong opponent of Christianity, and Virius Nicomachus Flavianus, a champion of paganism. A famous ivory **diptych**—a pair of panels attached with hinges—attests to the close relationship between their families. One family's name is inscribed at the top of each joined panel of the diptych, which may commemorate a marriage between the families. On the panel inscribed "*Symmachorum*" (fig. 6-89), a stately, elegantly attired priestess makes a ritual offering, apparently to Bacchus, at a beautifully decorated altar. She is assisted by a small child, and the event takes place out of doors under the oak tree sacred to Jupiter. The Roman ivory carvers of the fourth century were extremely skillful, and their wares were widely admired and commissioned by pagans and Christians alike. For conservative patrons like the Nichomachus and Symmachus families, they were able to imitate Augustan style effortlessly. The exquisite rendering of the drapery and foliage is reminiscent of the reliefs on the Ara Pacis (see fig. 6-28).

Classical subject matter remained attractive to artists and patrons, and imperial repression could not immediately extinguish it. Even such great Christian thinkers as bishop and saint Gregory of Nazianzus spoke out in support of the right of the people to appreciate and enjoy their classical heritage, so long as they were not seduced by it to return to pagan practices. As a result, stories of the ancient gods and heroes entered the secular realm as lively, visually delightful, and even erotic decorative elements. As a large silver platter dating from the mid-fourth century CE shows, themes involving Bacchus, the god of grapevines and fertility, continued to

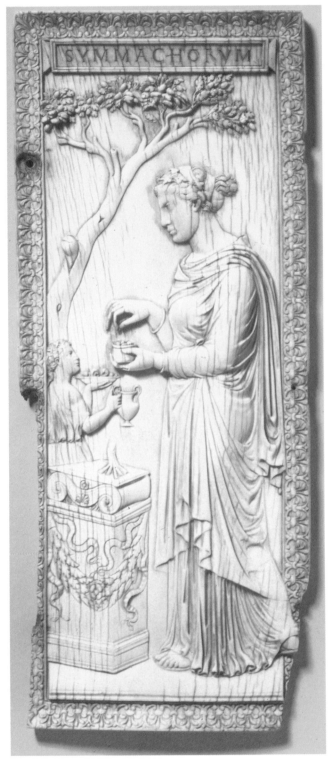

6-89. *Priestess of Bacchus* (?), right panel of a diptych.
c. 390–401 CE. Ivory, 11³/₄ x 5¹/₂" (29.9 x 14 cm).
Victoria and Albert Museum, London

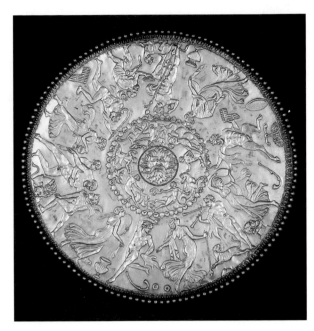

6-90. Dish, from Mildenhall, England. Mid-4th century CE.
Silver, diameter approx. 24" (61 cm). The British
Museum, London

provide artists with the opportunity to create elaborate
figural compositions displaying the nude or lightly
draped human body in complex, dynamic poses (fig.
6-90). The Bacchic revelers whirl, leap, and sway in a
dance to the piping of satyrs (half men, half goats)
around a circular central design. In the center, the head
of the sea god Oceanus is ringed by nude females frolicking in the waves with fantastic sea creatures. In the
outer circle, Bacchus is the one stable element. Wine jug
on his shoulder and one foot on the haunches of his panther, he listens to a male follower begging for another
drink. Only a few figures away, the pitifully drunken hero
Hercules has lost his lion-skin mantle and collapsed in a
stupor into the supporting arms of two satyrs. The detail,
clarity, and liveliness of this platter reflect the work of a
skillful artist. Deeply engraved lines emphasize the contours of the subtly modeled bodies, echoing the technique of undercutting used to add depth to figures in
stone and marble reliefs and suggesting a connection
between silver working and relief sculpture.

Found in a cache of both pagan and Christian treasures near Mildenhall, England, the platter may have
been made elsewhere and imported into Britain. It suggests the wealth to be found in the outlying provinces of
the Roman Empire. Such opulent items were often hidden away or buried to protect them from theft and looting, a sign of the breakdown of the long Roman peace.
The plate's style and subject matter reflect a society in
transition. Even as Roman authority gave way to local
rule by powerful barbarian tribes in much of the West,
many people continued to appreciate classical learning
and to treasure Greek and Roman art. In the East, classical traditions and styles endured to become an important
element of Byzantine art.

100 CE   300   500   700

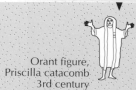

Orant figure,
Priscilla catacomb
3rd century

Old Saint Peter's
c. 320–27

Mausoleum of Galla
Placidia c. 425–26

Hagia Sophia
532–37

▲ EARLY CHRISTIAN c. 100–6TH CENTURY   ▲ IMPERIAL CHRISTIAN 313–c. 6TH CENTURY   ▲ EARLY BYZANTINE 527–867

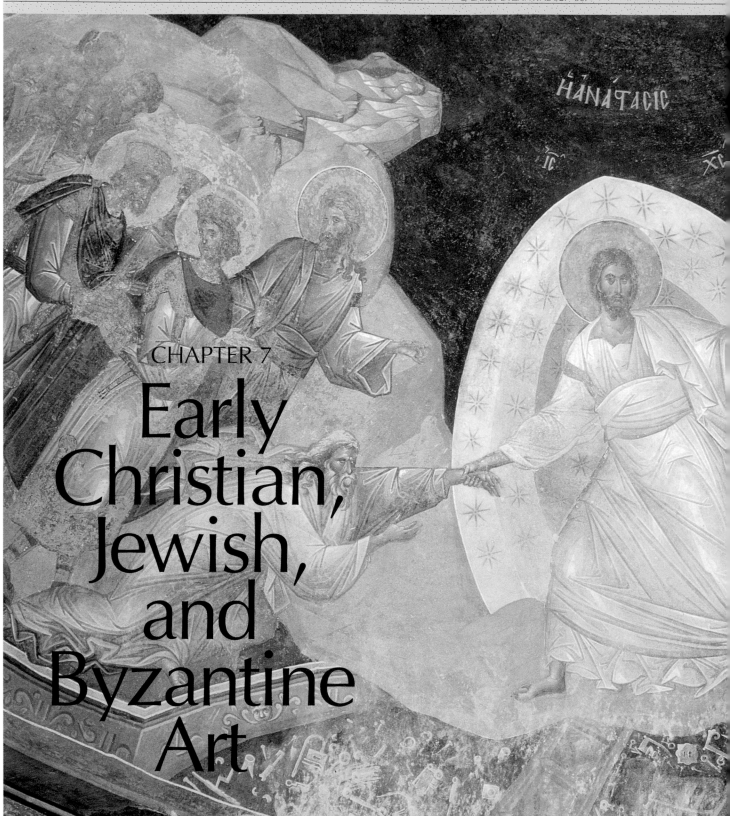

CHAPTER 7

Early Christian, Jewish, and Byzantine Art

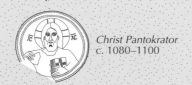

Christi Pantokrator
c. 1080–1100

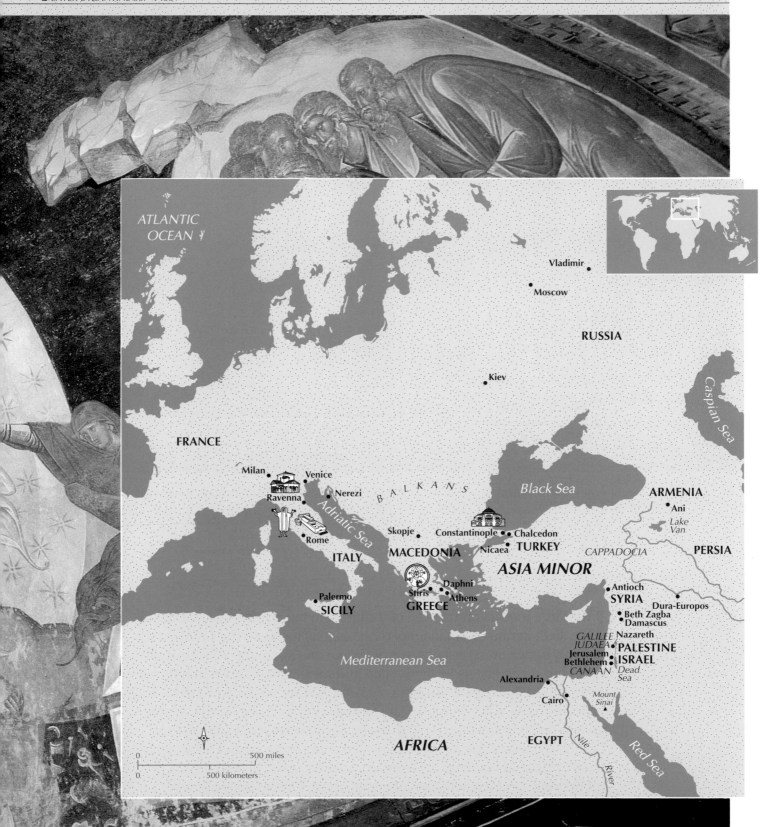

ATLANTIC OCEAN

Vladimir

Moscow

RUSSIA

Kiev

FRANCE

Milan
Venice
Ravenna
Nerezi
B A L K A N S
Adriatic Sea
Skopje
Constantinople
Chalcedon
Rome
ITALY
MACEDONIA
Nicaea
TURKEY
Stiris
Daphni
Palermo
Athens
SICILY
GREECE

Black Sea

Caspian Sea

ARMENIA
Ani
Lake Van

CAPPADOCIA
PERSIA

ASIA MINOR

Antioch
SYRIA
Dura-Europos
Beth Zagba
Damascus

GALILEE Nazareth
JUDAEA
Jerusalem PALESTINE
Bethlehem ISRAEL
CANAAN *Dead Sea*

Alexandria

Mediterranean Sea

Cairo
Mount Sinai ▲

AFRICA
EGYPT
Nile River
Red Sea

0   500 miles
0   500 kilometers

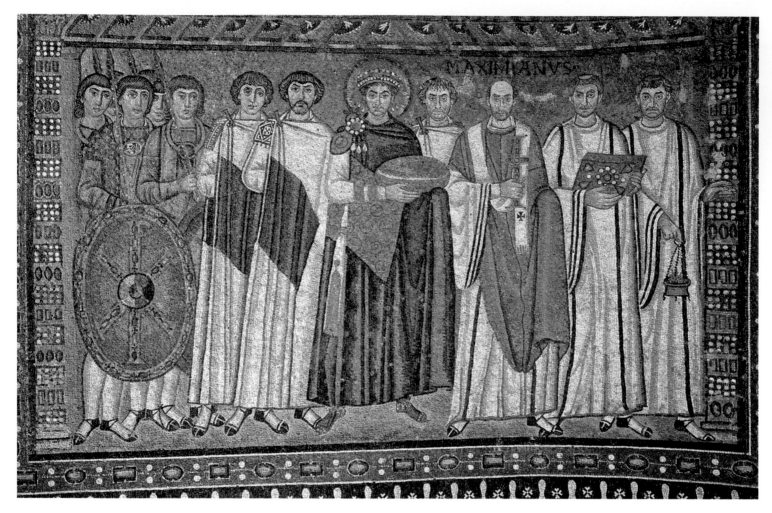

7-1. *Emperor Justinian and His Attendants*, mosaic on north wall of the apse, Church of San Vitale, Ravenna, Italy. c. 547. 8'8" x 12' (2.64 x 3.65 m)

In a large mosaic on the wall of a church on the northeast coast of Italy, the sixth-century Roman emperor known as Justinian the Great stands firmly between representatives of church and state (fig. 7-1). He dominates the scene just as he dominated his times, which are often referred to as the Golden Age of Justinian. As head of state, Justinian wears a huge jeweled crown and a purple cloak; as head of church, he carries a large golden paten to hold the Host, the symbolic body of Jesus Christ. The Church officials at his left hold a jeweled cross and a gospel book symbolizing Christ and his church. Justinian's soldiers stand behind the chi rho monogram, Greek letters, the initials of Christ. On the opposite wall Empress Theodora, also dressed in royal purple, offers a golden chalice, for the liturgical wine (see fig. 7-32).

Ironically, neither Justinian nor Theodora probably ever set foot in the Church of San Vitale in Ravenna, whose dedication these mosaics commemorate. Nevertheless, the mosaics are shimmering examples of a major art form of the time that dramatically illustrate the close relationship between secular and religious power in Justinian's world.

JEWS AND CHRISTIANS IN THE ROMAN EMPIRE

Three religions that arose in the Near East dominate the spiritual life of the Western world: Judaism, Christianity, and Islam. All three religions are monotheistic; followers hold that only one god created and rules the universe. Traditional Jews believe that God made a covenant, or pact, with their ancestors, the Hebrews, and that they are God's chosen people. They await the coming of a savior, the Messiah, "the anointed one." Traditional Christians believe that Jesus of Nazareth was that Messiah (the title *Christ* is derived from the Greek term meaning "Messiah"). They believe that God took human form, preached among men and women and suffered execution, then rose from the dead and ascended to heaven after establishing the Christian Church under the leadership of the apostles (his closest disciples). Muslims, while accepting the Hebrew prophets and Jesus as divinely inspired, believe Muhammad to be God's (Allah's) last and greatest prophet, the Messenger of God through whom Islam was revealed some six centuries after Jesus' lifetime. All three are "religions of the book" that have written records of their God's will and words: the Hebrew Scriptures of the Jews; the Christian Bible, which includes the Hebrew Scriptures as its Old Testament as well as the Christian New Testament; and the Muslim Koran, believed to be the Word of God revealed in Arabic directly to Muhammad through the angel Gabriel. Jewish and Early Christian art and Byzantine art, including some of the later art of the Eastern Orthodox Church, are considered in this chapter. Islamic art is discussed in Chapter 8, and Christian art of the European Middle Ages in Chapters 14, 15, and 16.

Early Judaism

The Jewish people trace their origin to the patriarchs Abraham, Isaac, and Jacob. According to the Hebrew Scriptures, Jacob's twelve sons founded the twelve tribes of Israel, who migrated to Egypt, where they lived for several hundred years until harshly oppressed by one of the pharaohs. In the thirteenth century BCE the prophet Moses led them out of slavery in Egypt and back to the promised land of Canaan between the Mediterranean Sea and the Jordan River in what was later called Palestine. The Hebrew Scriptures relate how, on their journey, God (YHWH, or Yahweh) reaffirmed his special relationship with the Israelites and gave Moses the Ten Commandments, the Tablets of the Law, on Mount Sinai.

The Tablets of the Law were housed in the profoundly sacred Ark of the Covenant, a gold-covered wooden box whose construction was prescribed in the Hebrew Scriptures (Exodus 25:10–21), topped by two **cherubim**, or attendant angels. The Israelites carried the ark with them on their desert wanderings until they finally conquered Canaan and built a permanent temple in Jerusalem in the tenth century BCE under King Solomon. The Babylonians destroyed the First Temple in 586 BCE, and about seventy years later, a second, smaller temple was built. Herod the Great, king of the region (ruled 37 BCE–4 CE), began the rebuilding and enlarging of the Second Temple. It was the rebuilt Second Temple of Jerusalem whose destruction and looting by the Romans in 70 CE were so vividly described by the Jewish chronicler Josephus (Chapter 6). The sacred treasures carried off to Rome in triumph included ritual articles and the great golden **menorah**, the seven-arm lamp illustrated on the Arch of Titus (see fig. 6–41).

The Jews had the Temple in Jerusalem, but they also had buildings where they gathered, later known as synagogues. Specialized architecture was less central in Judaism than in many religions, and a synagogue could be any large room. Synagogues' role as places of study expanded, and they began to serve as places for prayer for the dispersed community following the destruction of Jerusalem. They were also the sites where Torah scrolls, containing the Pentateuch, the first five books of the Hebrew Scriptures (Genesis, Exodus, Leviticus, Numbers, and Deuteronomy), were read publicly and kept in curtained shrines. Judaism's rich ceremonial affirmation of Jewish history and belief inspired the creation of scrolls, books, and ritual objects. Important rituals included commemorative meals, among them the Passover seder marking the Israelites' perilous journey out of Egypt. Early Jewish spiritual life emphasized religious learning and an individual's direct relationship with God. After the destruction of the Second Temple, there no longer was an organized priesthood.

Early Christianity

Christians believe in one God manifest in three Persons: the Trinity of Father (God), Son (Jesus Christ), and Holy Spirit. According to Christian belief, Jesus was the son of God by a human mother, the Virgin Mary (the Incarnation). His ministry on earth ended when he was executed by being nailed to a cross (the Crucifixion). He rose from the dead (the Resurrection) and ascended into heaven (the Ascension). Christian belief, especially about the divinity of Jesus, was formalized at the first all-Church Council, called by Constantine I at Nicaea (modern Iznik, Turkey) in 325.

The life and teachings of Jesus of Nazareth, who was born sometime between 8 and 4 BCE and was crucified at the age of thirty-three, were recorded between about 70 and 100 CE in the New Testament as books attributed to the Four Evangelists, Matthew, Mark, Luke, and John. These books are known as the Gospels (from an Old English translation of a Latin word derived from the Greek *euangelion,* "good news"). In addition to the Gospels, the New Testament includes an account of the Acts of the Apostles (one book) and the Epistles, twenty-one letters of advice and encouragement to Christian communities in cities and towns in Greece, Asia Minor, and other parts of the Roman Empire. Thirteen of these letters are attributed to a Jewish convert, Saul, who took the Christian name of Paul. The twenty-seventh and final book is the Revelation (the Apocalypse), a series of enigmatic visions and prophecies concerning the eventual triumph of

ROME, CONSTANTINOPLE, AND CHRISTIANITY

The relationship of church and state in the Roman-Byzantine world between the fourth and twelfth centuries was complex. This is a simplified account of the intertwined histories of the Roman and Byzantine Empires and the Eastern and Western Churches.

At its height in the second century CE, the Roman Empire extended from the Euphrates River to Scotland, an immense territory that was nearly impossible to defend and administer. Emperor Diocletian (ruled 284–305 CE) attempted a solution by dividing rule among four imperial tetrarchs (including himself) to oversee the Eastern and Western holdings of the empire in 286. Diocletian's experiment failed, leaving political chaos in its wake (Chapter 6). After Constantine I (ruled 306–337) defeated his rivals and became sole emperor in 324, he instituted numerous reforms. These included moving the empire's capital in 330 from Rome to Byzantium, located at the intersection of Europe and Asia. The site offered great advantages in military defense and trade, as well as escape from deteriorating conditions in Rome. The new capital, renamed Constantinople, was the sole seat of the Roman Empire until 395, when the empire split permanently in two, becoming the Western (Roman) Empire and the Eastern (Byzantine) Empire. What remained of the greatly weakened Roman Empire in the West collapsed in 476.

Constantinople inherited Rome's role as the center of power and culture. At its greatest extent, in the sixth century, the Eastern Empire included most of the area around the Mediterranean, including northern Africa, the Levant, Anatolia, and all of Greece, much of Italy, and a small part of Spain. The Byzantines always called themselves Romans and their empire the Eastern Roman Empire, despite the cultural division that had existed between the two parts of the Roman Empire: the Latin-speaking West, where urban society was the product of comparatively recent imperial conquest, and the Greek-speaking East, heir to much older civilizations. The Byzantine Empire lasted until 1453, when Constantinople became an Islamic capital under the Ottoman Turks.

When the empire divided in the late fourth century, the Christian Church developed two branches, Eastern and Western; although in disagreement for centuries over doctrine and jurisdiction, the Church did not officially split until 1054. Since then, there has been the Western, or Catholic, Church and the Eastern, or Orthodox, Church. Through all this, Rome has continued as the seat of the Western Church, led by the pope. The patriarch of Constantinople has headed the Eastern Church, which, over time, has developed along regional lines, with several national patriarchs as semiautonomous leaders.

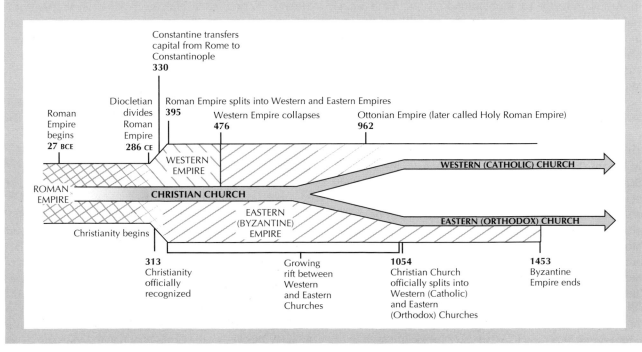

God at the end of the world, written about 95 CE.

Jesus was born during the reign of Emperor Augustus (ruled 27 BCE–14 CE), when Herod the Great ruled as a Roman protectorate the Jewish kingdom of Judaea and much of the rest of Palestine, as well as parts of what are now Lebanon, Syria, and Jordan. Following Herod's death in 4 BCE, Judaea came under direct Roman rule, leading to widespread political and social unrest. Among the movements opposing Roman oppression were Jewish religious cults centered on prophetic figures such as Jesus. This religious dissent was documented in the famous Dead Sea Scrolls found in caves near the Dead Sea in the 1940s and 1950s. Tiberius (ruled 14–37 CE) was emperor during the three-year period in which Jesus is thought to have preached. Jesus' arrest and crucifixion probably occurred not long after Pontius Pilate was appointed administrator of Judaea in 26 CE.

The Gospels' sometimes conflicting accounts relate that Jesus was a descendant of the Jewish royal house of King David and that he was born in Bethlehem in Judaea, where his mother, Mary, and her husband, Joseph, had gone to be registered in the Roman census. He grew up in Nazareth in Galilee (in what is now northern Israel), where Joseph was a carpenter. At the age of thirty, Jesus gathered about him a group of disciples, male and female, preaching love and charity, a personal relationship with God, the forgiveness of sins, and the promise of life after death.

Jesus limited his ministry primarily to Jews; Paul and the apostles, as well as later followers, took Jesus' teachings to non-Jews. Despite sporadic persecutions, Christianity persisted and spread throughout the Roman Empire. The faith had great appeal for the poor and powerless. Yet many early converts were women and people from the privileged classes. As more well-educated, upper-class Romans joined the Church during its first century of rapid growth, they gradually instituted a more elaborate organizational structure coupled with increasingly sophisticated doctrine, both of which evolved over the next centuries. The New Testament underwent significant editing, and the early Church tended to merge biblical stories, changes reflected in later Christian ritual and art. Saint Augustine (354–430) and Saint Gregory of Nazianzus (c. 330–c. 389) incorporated elements of Greek and Roman philosophy into the texts.

Christian communities were organized by geographical units, along the lines of Roman provincial governments. Senior Church officials called bishops served as governors of dioceses made up of smaller units, parishes, headed by priests. Bishops' headquarters—known as sees, or seats—were often in former provincial capitals. (A bishop's church is a cathedral, a word derived from the Latin word *cathedra*, which meant "chair," but took on the meaning "bishop's throne.") More powerful bishops came to be called archbishops, among whom the archbishops of Jerusalem, Rome, Constantinople, Alexandria, and Antioch (in southern Turkey) were the most important. The bishop of Rome eventually became head of the Western Church, holding the titles patriarch and pope. The patriarch of Constantinople became the head of the

Eastern Church. In spite of tensions between East and West, the Church remained united until 1054, when the Western pope and Eastern patriarch declared one another to be in error, and the Church split in two. Since this schism, the pope has been the supreme authority in the Western, Catholic Church, and the patriarch with his metropolitans (equivalent to archbishops) has governed the Eastern, Orthodox Church. (See "Rome, Constantinople, and Christianity," opposite.)

JEWISH ART AND EARLY CHRISTIAN ART

Jews were forbidden to make images that might be worshiped as idols, but this prohibition against representational art was applied primarily to sculpture in the round in early Judaism. Jewish art during the Roman Empire combined both Near Eastern and classical Greek and Roman elements to depict Jewish subject matter, both symbolic and narrative. Since Christianity claimed to have arisen out of Judaism, its art incorporated many symbols and narrative representations from the Hebrew Scriptures and other Jewish sources. Christian rites prompted the development of special buildings—churches and baptistries—as well as specialized equipment, and Christians began to use the visual arts to instruct the laity as well as to glorify God. Almost no examples of specifically Christian art exist before the early third century, and even then it drew its styles and imagery from Jewish and classical traditions. In this process, known as **syncretism**, artists assimilate images from other traditions, giving them new meanings; such borrowings can be unconscious or quite deliberate. **Orant** figures—worshipers with arms outstretched—for example, can be pagan, Jewish, or Christian, depending on the context in which they occur.

Perhaps the most important of these syncretic images is the **Good Shepherd**. In pagan art, he was Hermes the shepherd or Orpheus among the animals, but Jews and Christians saw him as the Good Shepherd of the Twenty-third Psalm: "The Lord is my shepherd; there is nothing I lack" (Psalms 23:1).

Painting and Sculpture

A late-second- or early-third-century mural in the Catacomb of Priscilla, one of the underground burial chambers outside Rome (see "Roman Funerary Practices," page 243), shows a group of men and women dressed in white and arranged around a semicircular table with platters and a large drinking cup (fig. 7-2). This *Banquet Scene,* painted in the crescent-shaped upper part of the wall called a **lunette**, may depict a Passover seder. Alternatively, it could represent either a pagan or a Christian banquet, because the pictorial theme is common to all three religions.

Although the subject of the *Banquet Scene* is difficult to be sure of, Jewish catacombs usually display certain symbolic objects specific to Judaism. A lunette mural in a Jewish catacomb in the Villa Torlonia in Rome, for

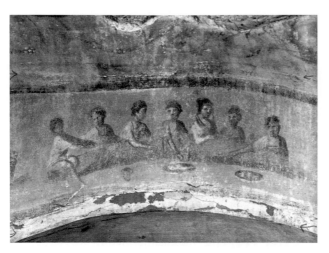

7-2. *Banquet Scene*, wall painting in the Catacomb of Priscilla, Rome. Late 2nd or early 3rd century

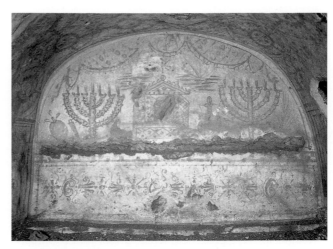

7-3. *Menorahs and Ark of the Covenant*, wall painting in a Jewish catacomb, Villa Torlonia, Rome. 3rd century. 3'11" x 5'9" (1.19 x 1.8 m)

example (fig. 7-3), shows the Ark of the Covenant flanked by two seven-branch menorahs that resemble the one carved on the Arch of Titus (see fig. 6-41). The original menorah had been constructed to light the portable sanctuary, or tabernacle, which had housed the ark during the early years of the Israelite kingdom (Exodus 25:31–40). After the First Temple had been built in Jerusalem, the menorah and ark were placed in it. The menorah form was probably derived from the ancient Near Eastern Tree of Life, symbolizing both the end of exile and the paradise to come. The painting includes two symbols of the Jewish autumn harvest festival of Sukkoth, which also commemorates the Israelites' period of wandering in the desert: a palm branch on the right and an etrog (citron fruit) on the left.

Christians used catacombs for burials and funeral services before their religion was granted official recognition. In the Christian Catacomb of the Jordani, dating from the third century, long rectangular niches in the walls, called **loculi**, each held two or three bodies (fig. 7-4). More affluent families created small rooms, or **cubicula**, off the main passages to house **sarcophagi**. The cubicula were hewn out of the soft tufa, a volcanic rock, then plastered and painted with imagery related to their owners' religious beliefs. The painters used the rapid brushwork, brilliant colors, and shaded forms of contemporary Roman painting. The finest Early Christian catacomb paintings imitated murals in houses such as those preserved at Pompeii and Primaporta (see figs. 6-33, 6-36). Each scene was composed simply and clearly to convey its religious message.

Communal Christian worship focused on the central "mystery," or miracle, of the Incarnation and the promise of salvation. At its core was the ritual consumption of bread and wine, identified as the body and blood of Christ, which Jesus had instructed his followers to eat and drink in remembrance of him. Around these acts an elaborate religious ceremony, or liturgy, called the Eucharist (also known as Holy Communion or Mass) developed. The grapevine and grape cluster of the

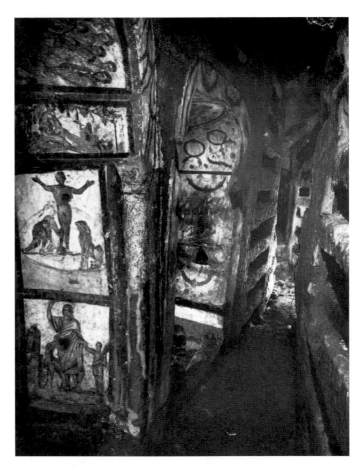

7-4. Catacomb of the Jordani, Rome. 3rd century

The narrow underground passage is lined with rectangular burial niches, once sealed with tile or stone slabs. On the left, arched doorways lead to small burial chambers that held sarcophagi and more wall niches. Typical subjects for Christian tomb paintings are Old Testament redemption stories, symbolizing God's power to save his people from death. At the center of the upper square panel on the left is Daniel in a den of lions that, miraculously, did not eat him (Daniel 6:16–23). The panel below shows Abraham, whom God tested by commanding him to sacrifice his son Isaac (Genesis 22:1–14).

PARALLELS

Years	Period	Roman/Byzantine Empires	World
c. 100–6th century CE	Early Christian	New Testament completed; catacomb paintings; persecution of Christians; Constantinople established; Christians granted freedom to worship in empire	**c. 100–300** Yayoi and Kofun eras (Japan); Maya civilization (Mesoamerica); Goths invade Asia Minor; Three Kingdoms period (China); Buddhism spreads in China
313–c. 6th century	Imperial Christian	Old Saint Peter's; Santa Costanza; Christianity is official religion of empire; empire permanently divided; Vulgate Bible; Mausoleum of Galla Placidia; Italy falls to Ostrogoths	**c. 300–500** First Gupta dynasty (India); Arabic script developed; library at Alexandria burns (Egypt); Attila the Hun; earliest surviving Hindu temples (India)
527–867	Early Byzantine	Hagia Sophia; San Vitale; Sant'Apollinare; Emperor Justinian reconquers Italy; Second Council of Nicaea refutes Iconoclasm	**c. 500–900** Birth of Muhammad, founder of Islam (Arabia); Buddhism in Japan; plague kills half the population of Europe; Koran; Muslim conquests; first block-printed text (China); first permanent Japanese capital at Nara; Charlemagne is made emperor of the West; bronze casting in South America; *Diamond Sutra* (China)
867–1453	Later Byzantine	Hosios Loukas; separation of Eastern and Western Christian Churches; San Marco; Crusaders sack Constantinople; Dante's *Divine Comedy*; Boccaccio's *Decameron*; beginning of the Renaissance in Europe; Muslim Turks conquer Constantinople	**c. 900–1450** First Viking colony in Greenland; Lady Murasaki's *Tale of Genji* (Japan); the Crusades; Jenghiz Khan rules Mongols; Magna Carta (England); Hundred Years' War (England, France); Black Death in Europe; Chaucer's *Canterbury Tales* (England); Joan of Arc (France)

Roman god Bacchus were borrowed to symbolize the wine of the Eucharist and the blood of Christ (see "Christian Symbols," page 294). Feast scenes such as that in the Catacomb of Priscilla (see fig. 7-2) were appropriated to represent the Last Supper, in which Jesus inaugurated the Eucharist at a Passover meal with his disciples.

In a lunette painting in another cubiculum of the Catacomb of Priscilla, a veiled female orant—hands raised in prayer—dominates the room (fig. 7-5). The woman is flanked by images of a teacher-philosopher with pupils on the left and a woman holding a child on her lap on the right. Although its context indicates that this is a Christian site, its imagery derives from traditional classical

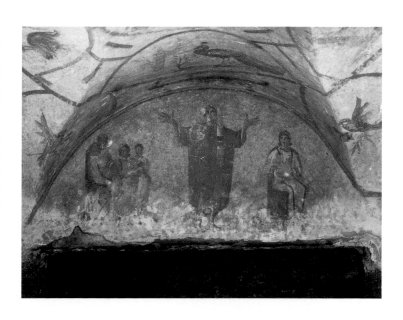

7-5. *Teacher and Pupils, Orant, and Woman and Child*, wall painting in a lunette, Crypt of the Veiled Lady, Catacomb of Priscilla, Rome. 3rd century

CHRISTIAN SYMBOLS

Symbols have always played an important part in Christian art. Some were devised just for Christianity, but most were borrowed from pagan and Jewish traditions and adapted for Christian use.

Dove

The Old Testament dove is a symbol of purity, representing peace when it is shown bearing an olive branch. In Christian art a white dove is the symbolic embodiment of the Holy Spirit and is often shown descending from heaven, sometimes haloed and radiating celestial light.

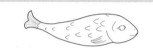

Fish

The fish was one of the earliest symbols for Jesus Christ. Because of its association with baptism in water, it came to stand for all Christians. Fish are sometimes depicted with bread and wine to represent the Eucharist.

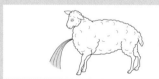

Lamb (Sheep)

The lamb, an ancient sacrificial animal, symbolizes Jesus' sacrifice on the cross as the Lamb of God, its pouring blood redeeming the sins of the world. The Lamb of God (*Agnus Dei* in Latin) may appear holding a cross-shaped scepter and/or a victory banner with a cross (signifying Christ's resurrection). The lamb sometimes stands on a cosmic rainbow or a mountaintop. A flock of sheep represents the apostles—or all Christians—cared for by their Good Shepherd; Jesus Christ. John the Baptist points to the Lamb of God, that is, Christ.

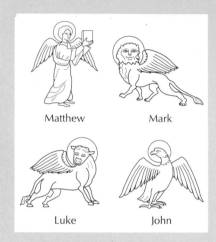

Four Evangelists

The evangelists who wrote the New Testament Gospels are traditionally associated with the following creatures: Saint Matthew, a man (or angel); Saint Mark, a lion; Saint Luke, an ox; and Saint John, an eagle. These emblems derive from visionary biblical texts and may be depicted either as the saints' **attributes** (identifying accessories) or their embodiments (stand-ins for the saints themselves).

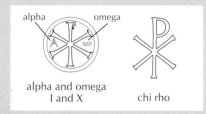

Monograms

Alpha (the first letter of the Greek alphabet) and omega (the last) signify God as the beginning and end of all things. This symbolic device was popular from Early Christian times through the Middle Ages. Alpha and omega often flank the abbreviation *IX* or *XP*. The initials *I* and *X* are the first letters of *Jesus* and *Christ* in Greek. The initials *XP*, known as the chi rho, were the first two letters of the word *Christos*. These emblems are sometimes enclosed by a circle.

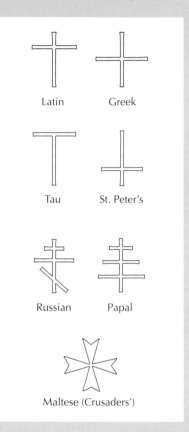

Cross

The primary Christian emblem, the cross, symbolizes the suffering and triumph of Jesus' crucifixion and resurrection as Christ. It also stands for Jesus Christ himself, as well as the Christian religion as a whole. Crosses have taken various forms at different times and places, the two most common in Christian art being the Latin and Greek.

themes: philosopher, mother and child, and praying supplicant. In a Christian interpretation, the philosopher can be seen as Jesus teaching and the woman as the Virgin Mary with the Christ Child, both important in later Christian art.

A fourth-century Roman catacomb contained bones, or relics, of Saints Pietro and Marcellino. Pietro and Marcellino were two third-century Roman stalwarts executed—martyred—for their Christian faith. Catacombs with niches for the bones of martyrs and saints were sought-after burial places. Here the domed ceiling of a cubiculum is partitioned by five medallions linked by the arms of a cross (fig. 7-6). At the center is a Good Shepherd, whose pose has roots in Greek sculpture. In its new context, the image was a reminder of Jesus' promise: "I am the good shepherd. A good shepherd lays down his

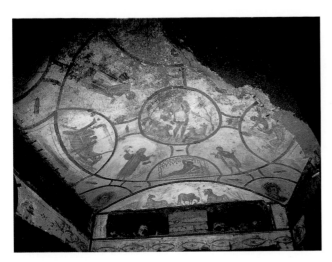

7-6. *Good Shepherd, Orants, and Story of Jonah*, painted ceiling of the Catacomb of Pietro and Marcellino, Rome. 4th century

catacombs. On the left, Jonah is thrown from the boat; on the right, the monster spews him up; and at the center, Jonah reclines in the shade of a gourd vine, a symbol of paradise. Orants praying for the souls of the departed stand between the medallions.

Sculpture that is clearly Christian is even rarer than painting from before the time of Constantine I. What there is consists mainly of small statues and reliefs, many of them Good Shepherd images. A remarkable set of marble figurines, probably made in the third century in Asia Minor, also depicts the Jonah story (fig. 7-7); their function is unknown. Carved of a fine alabasterlike marble, they illustrate the biblical story with the same literalness and enthusiasm as the paintings on the catacomb ceiling.

life for the sheep" (John 10:11). The semicircular compartments at the ends of the arms of the cross tell the Old Testament story of Jonah and the sea monster (Jonah 1–2), in which God caused Jonah to be thrown overboard in a storm, swallowed by a monster, and released, repentant and unscathed, three days later. This story was reinterpreted by Christians as a parable of Christ's death and resurrection—and hence of the everlasting life awaiting true believers—and was a popular subject in Christian

Dura-Europos

The variety of religious buildings found in modern Syria at the abandoned Roman outpost of Dura-Europos, a Hellenistic fortress taken over by the Romans in 165 CE, illustrates the cosmopolitan character of frontier Roman society in the second and third centuries. Although Dura-Europos was destroyed in 256 CE by Persian forces, important parts of the stronghold have been excavated, including a Jewish **house-synagogue**, a Christian **house-church**, shrines to the Persian gods Mithras and Zoroaster, and temples to Roman ancestral gods. The Jewish and Christian structures were preserved because they had been built against the inside wall of the southwest rampart. When the desperate citizens attempted to

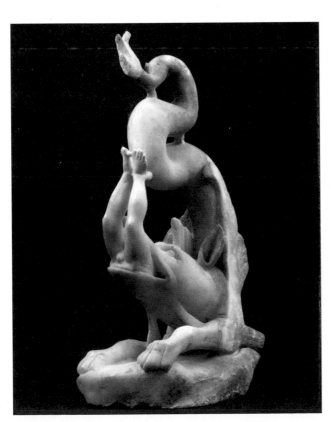

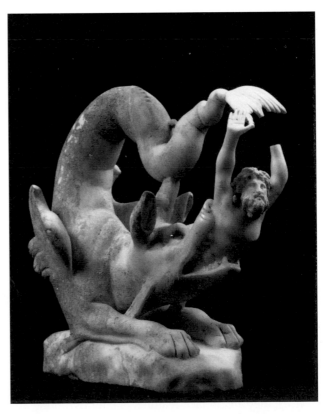

7-7. *Jonah Swallowed* and *Jonah Cast Up*, two statuettes of a group from the eastern Mediterranean, probably Asia Minor. 3rd century. Marble, heights 20 5/16" (51.6 cm) and 16" (40.6 cm). The Cleveland Museum of Art
John L. Severance Fund, 65.237, 65.238

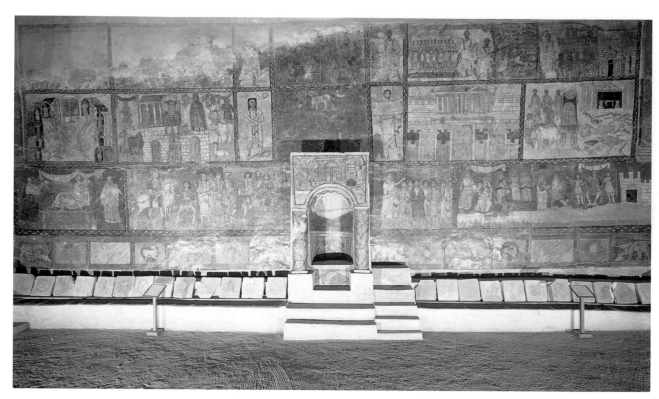

7-8. Wall with Torah niche, from a house-synagogue, Dura-Europos, Syria. 244–45. Tempera on plaster, section approx. 40' long. Reconstructed in the National Museum, Damascus, Syria

strengthen this fortification in futile preparation for the final attack, they buried these buildings. The entire site was abandoned and rediscovered only in 1920 by a French army officer.

In the house-synagogue, the congregational area was sealed off from the rest of the building. Its main room had only two special architectural features, a bench along its walls and a niche for the Torah scrolls (fig. 7-8). Women were seated in an alcove, separated from men.

Jewish representational art flourished in the third century, as seen in the murals that covered this synagogue's interior. Narrative and symbolic scenes depicting events from Jewish history unfold in three registers of framed panels. The work of more than one artist, they are done in a style in which statically posed, almost two-dimensional figures float against a neutral background. In *Finding of the Baby Moses* (fig. 7-9), Moses' mother sets him afloat in a reed basket in the shallows of the Nile in an attempt to save him from the pharaoh's decree that all Jewish male infants be put to death (Exodus 1:8–2:10). He is found by the pharaoh's daughter, who acknowledges him as her own child. The painting shows these events unfolding in a continuous narrative set in a narrow foreground space. At the right, the princess sees the child hidden in the bulrushes; at the center, she wades nude into the water to save him; and at the left, she hands him to a nurse (actually his own mother). The frontal poses, strong outlines, and flat colors are distinctive pictorial devices; they are, in fact, features of later Byzantine art, perhaps derived from works such as this.

The Christian house-church, which was about 300 yards from the house-synagogue, had been a Roman-

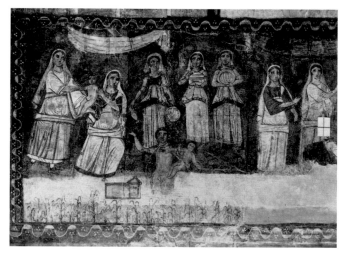

7-9. *Finding of the Baby Moses*, detail of a wall painting from a house-synagogue, Dura-Europos, Syria. Second half of 3rd century. Copy in tempera on plaster. Yale University Art Gallery, New Haven, Connecticut
Dura-Europus Collection

style dwelling built around a peristyle court. A red cross painted above the main entrance designated it as a gathering place for Christians. The congregation seems to have grown so much that by about 231 the space devoted to the church included a large meeting or dining hall, a room with a raised platform at one end for the leaders, and a small chamber that served perhaps for teaching initiates or as a place for storing liturgical equipment. Opening off this large hall was a **baptistry**, or place for

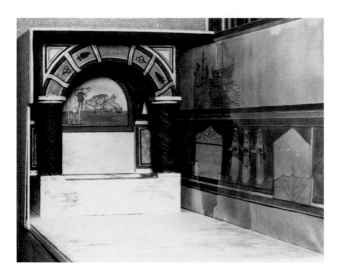

7-10. Small-scale model of walls and baptismal font, from the baptistry of a Christian house-church, Dura-Europos, Syria. c. 240. Yale University Art Gallery, New Haven, Connecticut

Dura-Europos Collection

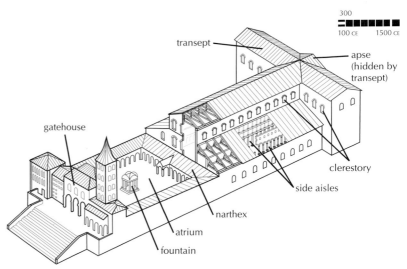

7-11. Reconstruction drawing of Old Saint Peter's basilica, Rome. c. 320–27; atrium added in later 4th century

baptism, built into a niche and equipped with a water basin, above which were images of the Good Shepherd and of Adam and Eve (fig. 7-10). These murals reminded new Christians that humanity had been deprived of immortality by Original Sin, when the first man and woman disobeyed God and ate fruit from the forbidden tree of the knowledge of good and bad offered them by an evil serpent. But the Good Shepherd (Jesus Christ) came to earth to carry his sheep (Christians) to salvation and eternal life. Baptism washed away sin, leaving the initiate reborn as a member of the community of the faithful.

IMPERIAL CHRISTIAN ARCHITECTURE AND ART

In 313 the Edict of Milan granted all people in the Roman Empire freedom to worship whatever god they wished. This religious toleration, combined with Constantine's active support of Christianity, allowed Christianity to enter a new phase, developing a sophisticated philosophical and ethical system that incorporated many ideas from Greek and Roman philosophy. Church scholars edited and commented on the Bible, and Saint Jerome (c. 347–c. 420), the papal secretary, undertook a new translation from Hebrew, Greek, and Latin versions into Latin, the language of the Western Church. Completed about 400, this so-called Vulgate became the official version of the Bible. (The term *Vulgate* derives from the same Latin word as *vulgar*, meaning "common" or "popular.") Christians also gained political influence in this period. The Christian writer Lactantius (c. 240–320), for example, tutored Constantine I's son Crispus; and Eusebius (c. 260–c. 339), bishop of Caesarea, was a trusted imperial adviser from about 315 to 339. These transformations in the philosophical and political arenas coincided with a dramatic increase in imperial architecture.

Architecture and Its Decoration

As soon as he had consolidated imperial power, around 324, Constantine I began a vast building program that included many religious structures (Chapter 6). Among these was a grand palace complex for the city's bishop, the highest-ranking Church official in the Roman Empire. The emperor ordered a monumental **basilica** constructed at the place where Christians believed Saint Peter to be buried. Also, after Constantine's mother, Helena, visited Palestine about 325, she convinced him to build a number of churches and shrines in Jerusalem; shrines were constructed as personal acts of devotion, sometimes commemorating a person or event in the patron's life.

Basilica-Plan Churches. In the early second century Christians in Rome had placed a monument over what they believed to be the burial place of the apostle Peter. According to tradition, Saint Peter (died c. 64 CE), the first bishop of Rome, was crucified upside down at his own request so that his martyrdom would be seen as lesser than Jesus' crucifixion. Perhaps as early as 320, Constantine decided to construct a grand new basilica on the site of Peter's tomb to protect it and make it accessible to the faithful, glorifying the memory of the martyred apostle. As the pope's church, it came to signify as well the superior power of the bishop of Rome over all other bishops in Christendom.

Our knowledge of Old Saint Peter's (so called because it was completely replaced by a new building in the sixteenth century) is based on written descriptions, drawings made before and while it was being dismantled, the study of other churches inspired by it, and modern archeological excavations at the site (fig. 7-11). Its builders leveled the hillside cemetery on which it was to be located, destroying many tombs; then atop a large, concrete foundation they erected a building complex arranged on

ELEMENTS OF ARCHITECTURE

Basilica-Plan and Central-Plan Churches

The forms of early Christian buildings were based on two classical prototypes: rectangular Roman basilicas (see figs. 6-49, 6-50) and round-domed structures—rotundas—such as the Pantheon (see figs. 6-55, 6-56). As in Old Saint Peter's in Rome (fig. 7-11), **basilica-plan** churches are characterized by a forecourt, the **atrium**, leading to a porch, the **narthex**, spanning one of the building's short ends. Doorways—known collectively as the church's **portal**—lead from the narthex into a long central area called a **nave**. The high-ceiling nave is separated from aisles on either side by rows of columns. The nave is lit by windows along its upper story—called a **clerestory**—that rises above the side aisles' roofs. At the opposite end of the nave from the narthex is a semicircular projection, the **apse**. The apse functions as the building's symbolic core where the altar, raised on a platform, is located. Sometimes there is also a **transept**, a horizontal wing that crosses the nave in front of the apse, making the building **T**-shaped; this is known as a Tau plan. When additional space (a choir) separates the transept and the apse, the plan is called a **Latin cross**.

Central-plan structures were first used by Christians as tombs, baptism centers (**baptistries**), and shrines to martyrs (**martyria**). (The **Greek-cross plan**, in which two similarly sized "arms" intersect at their centers, is a type of central plan.) Instead of the longitudinal axis of basilican churches, which draws worshipers forward toward the apse, central-plan churches such as Ravenna's San Vitale (see figs. 7-29, 7-30) have a more vertical axis. This makes the **dome**, a symbolic "vault of heaven," a natural focus over the main worship area. Like basilicas, central-plan churches generally have an atrium, a narthex, and an apse. The **naos** is the space containing the central dome, sanctuary, and apse.

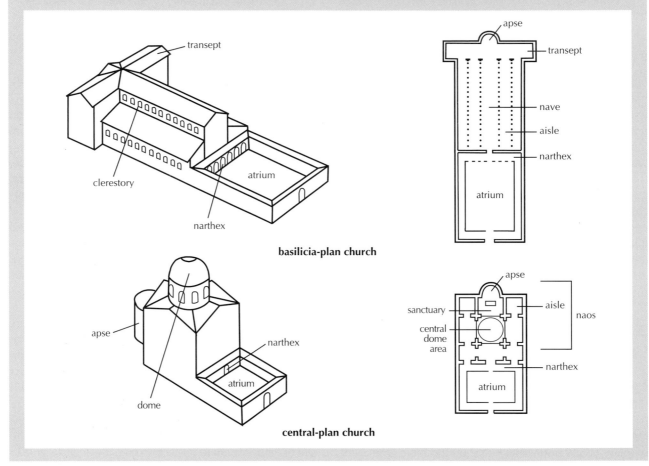

basilicia-plan church

central-plan church

a central axis similar to the old Forum of Trajan (see fig. 6-49). Worshipers climbed a flight of steps to a large gatehouse and crossed a colonnaded atrium with a central fountain to reach the church's entrance.

Old Saint Peter's included architectural elements arranged in a way that has characterized Christian basilica-plan churches ever since (see "Elements of Architecture," above). A narthex, or porch, across the width of the building protected five doorways—a large, central portal into the nave and two portals on each side opening directly to double side aisles. The nave rose one story higher than these aisles to provide for an upper-level clerestory, the windows of which lit the interior. Nave and aisles had open, timberwork ceilings. The nave was lined with columns supporting an entablature, whereas the columns of the side aisles supported a series of round arches. At the end of the nave and aisles was a transept, which crossed them at right angles and projected at each end, a **T** form that anticipated the later Latin-cross church plan. This area served as common ground for rituals in which both congregation and clergy participated.

Saint Peter's bones supposedly lie below, marked in the nave by a permanent, pavilionlike structure supported on four columns called a **ciborium**. Catacombs lay

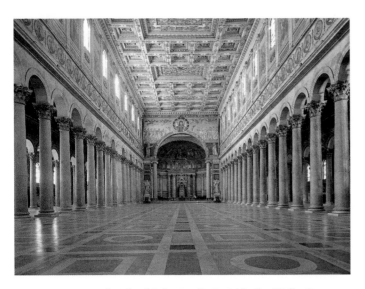

7-12. Nave, Church of Saint Paul's Outside the Walls, Rome. Begun 385; rebuilt after a fire in 1823

proportions, simple geometric forms, and a dramatic contrast between exterior simplicity and interior luxury. A view of the nave of the Church of Saint Paul's Outside the Walls, begun in 385, gives some sense of what the interior of Old Saint Peter's might have been like (fig. 7-12). The long nave ends, like Old Saint Peter's, in a triumphal arch that springs from columns topped with short sections of entablature. Unlike Saint Peter's, arcades of tall Corinthian columns supporting arches define both nave and side aisles. After a fire in the early nineteenth century, the original open-rafter ceiling was replaced by a **coffered** one with recessed panels.

The combination of architectural grandeur, adaptability, and practicality in fourth-century basilica-plan churches proved so valuable that Roman architects almost a century later looked to them for inspiration when designing the Church of Santa Maria Maggiore (Saint Mary the Great, fig. 7-13). As in Old Saint Peter's, columns supporting an entablature line the two-story nave, which ends in a triumphal arch leading to the sanctuary, where the altar is located. Santa Maria Maggiore was the first church in Rome dedicated to the Virgin Mary after the Church Council of Ephesus (431) declared her to be Theotokos, bearer of God. In the mosaics of this church, the humble earthly mother of Jesus was first given the regal appearance often seen in Western art. (The Virgin remains a humble mother in Eastern representations.) On the triumphal arch's left **spandrel**—the surface between the exterior curves of adjoining arches or walls—she is shown enthroned, flanked by attending angels and crowned as an empress.

beneath the church, and over time a large **crypt**, or underground vault, was used for the burial of popes. Sarcophagi and tomb monuments eventually also lined the side aisles. Old Saint Peter's thus served a variety of functions. It was a congregational church, a pilgrimage shrine commemorating a place of martyrdom and containing the relics of a holy person, and a funeral hall–burial place. Old Saint Peter's could hold at least 14,000 worshipers, and it remained the largest of all Christian churches until the eleventh century.

Like many later churches, Old Saint Peter's depended for its aesthetic effect on sheer size, harmonious

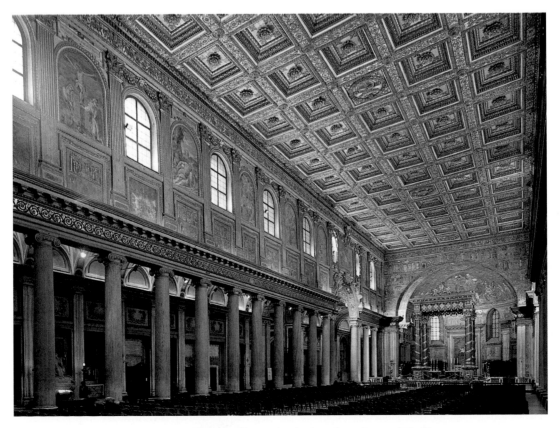

7-13. Nave, Church of Santa Maria Maggiore, Rome. 432–40

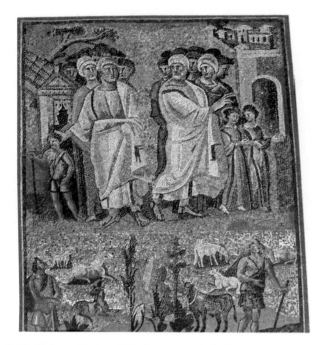

The mosaics of the Church of Santa Maria Maggiore reflect a renewed interest in the earlier classicizing style of Roman art that arose during the reign of Pope Sixtus III (432–440). The mosaics along the nave walls, in framed panels high above the worshipers, illustrate Old Testament stories of the Jewish patriarchs and heroes—Abraham, Jacob, Moses, and Joshua—whom Christians believe foretold the coming of Christ and his activities on earth. Twenty-seven of the original forty-two **triforium** mosaics remain. These panels were not only didactic—that is, they were not simply intended to instruct the congregation. Instead, like most of the decorations in great Christian churches from this time forward, they were meant to praise God through their splendor, to make churches symbolic embodiments of the Heavenly Jerusalem that awaited believers, and to tell a history.

Some of the most effective compositions are those in which a few large figures dominate the foreground space, as in the *Parting of Lot and Abraham* (fig. 7-14), a story told in the first book of the Hebrew Scriptures (Genesis 13:1–12). The people of Abraham and his nephew Lot, dwelling together, had grown too numerous, so the two agreed to separate and lead their followers in different directions. On the right, Lot and his daughters turn toward the land of Jordan, while Abraham and his wife stay in the land of Canaan. This parting is highly significant to both Jews and Christians since Abraham was the founder of the Israelite nation from which Jesus descended.

In the mosaic, the toga-clad men share a parting look as they gather their robes about them and turn decisively away from each other. The space between them in the center of the composition emphasizes their irreversible decision to part. Clusters of heads in the background represent Abraham's and Lot's followers, a contemporary artistic convention used effectively here. References to the earlier Roman **illusionistic** style can be seen in the solid three-dimensional rendering of foreground figures, the hint of perspective in the building, and the landscape setting, with its bit of foliage and touches of blue sky. The mosaic was created with thousands of marble and glass **tesserae** set closely together. The use of graduated colors creates shading from light to dark, producing three-dimensional effects that are offset by strong outlines. These outlines, coupled with the sheen of the gold tesserae, tend to flatten the forms.

Central-Plan Churches. A second type of ancient building—the **tholos**, or tomb with central plan and vertical axis—also served Christian builders for tombs, martyrs' churches, and baptistries (see "Elements of Architecture," page 298). One of the earliest surviving central-plan Christian buildings is the **mausoleum** of Constantina, the daughter of Constantine, which was built outside the walls of Rome just before 350 (fig. 7-15). The mausoleum was consecrated as a church in 1256 and is now dedicated to Santa Costanza (the Italian form of the Christian princess's name). The building consists of a tall rotunda with an encircling **barrel-vaulted** passageway called an **ambulatory** (fig. 7-16). A double ring of paired columns with Composite capitals and richly

7-14. *Parting of Lot and Abraham*, mosaic in the nave arcade, Church of Santa Maria Maggiore. Panel approx. 4'11" x 6'8" (1.2 x 2 m)

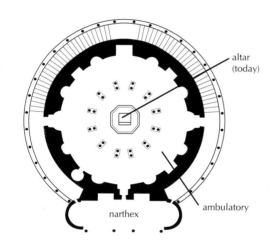

altar (today)

narthex

ambulatory

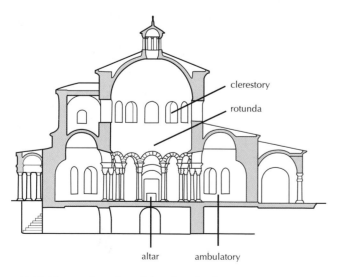

clerestory

rotunda

altar   ambulatory

7-15. Plan and section of the Church of Santa Costanza, Rome. c. 338–50

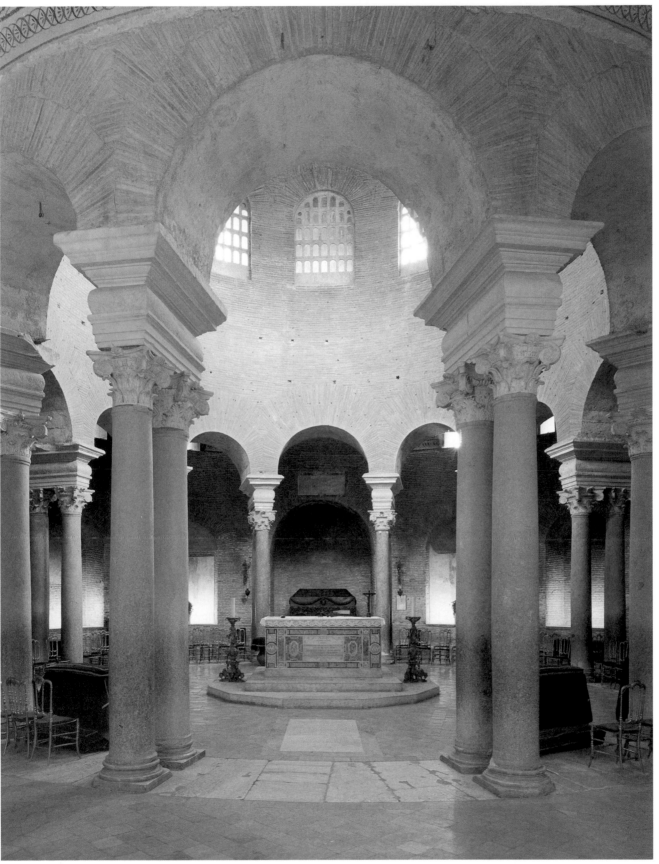

7-16. Church of Santa Costanza. View through ambulatory into central space

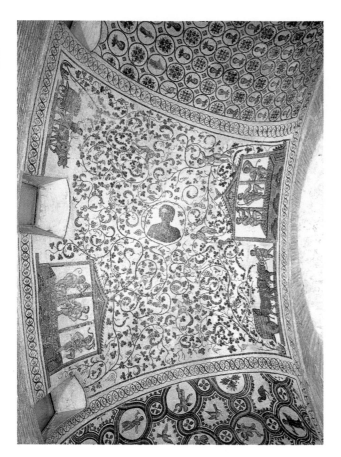

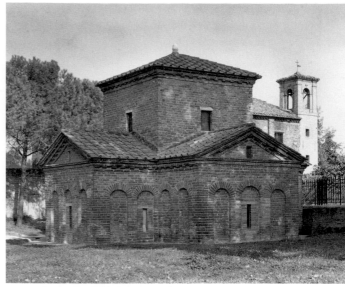

7-17. *Harvesting of Grapes*, mosaic in the the ambulatory vault, Church of Santa Costanza

7-18. Mausoleum of Galla Placidia, Ravenna, Italy. c. 425–26

molded entablature blocks supports the arcade and dome. The building's interior was entirely sheathed in mosaics and fine marble.

Mosaics in the ambulatory vault recall the catacombs' syncretic images. One section, for example, is covered with a tangle of grapevines filled with **putti**—naked male child-angels, or cherubs, derived from classical art—who vie with the birds to harvest the grapes (fig. 7-17). Along the bottom edges on each side, putti drive wagonloads of grapes toward pavilions covering large vats in which more putti trample the grapes into juice. The technique, subject, and style are Roman, but the meaning has been altered. The scene would have been familiar to the pagan followers of Bacchus, but in a Christian context the wine could suggest the wine of the Eucharist. For Constantina the scene probably evoked only one, Christian, interpretation; her pagan husband, however, may have recognized the double allusion.

As Rome lost its political importance, major buildings were erected in the new Italian capitals of Milan and Ravenna, to the north. In 395 Emperor Theodosius I split the Roman Empire into Eastern and Western divisions, each ruled by one of his sons. Arcadius (ruled 383–408), who had already ruled the Eastern part of the empire from Constantinople jointly with his father, assumed complete control of the Eastern Empire. The younger Honorius (ruled 395–423) established himself first at the new Western Roman Empire capital of Milan in northern Italy. When Germanic settlers laid siege to Milan in 402,

Honorius moved his capital to the east coast of Italy at Ravenna, whose naval base, Classis, had been important since the early days of the empire. In addition to military security, Ravenna offered direct access by sea to Constantinople. Ravenna flourished under Roman rule, and when Italy fell to the Ostrogoths in 476, the city became one of their headquarters. It still contains a remarkable group of well-preserved fifth- and sixth-century monuments.

One of the earliest surviving Christian structures in Ravenna is a funerary chapel attached to the church of the imperial palace (now Santa Croce, meaning "Holy Cross"). Built about 425–426, the chapel was constructed when Honorius's half sister, Galla Placidia, was acting as regent (ruled 425–c. 440) in the West for her son. The chapel came to be called the Mausoleum of Galla Placidia because she and her family were once believed to be buried there (fig. 7-18). This small building is **cruciform**, or cross-shaped; each of its arms is covered with a barrel vault, and the space at the intersection of the arms is covered with a **pendentive dome,** a dome continuous with its **pendentives**. The plain exterior is decorated with **blind arcading**—a series of ornamental arches applied to a solid wall—tall slit windows, and a simple **cornice** that surrounds and unifies the four arms. The vaults covering the arms of the cross have been hidden from view on the outside by sloping, tile-covered roofs.

The interior of the chapel contrasts remarkably with the exterior, a transition designed to simulate the passage from the real world into a supernatural one (fig. 7-19). The worshiper looking from the western entrance across to the eastern bay of the chapel sees a brilliant, abstract pattern of mosaic filling the barrel vault, suggesting a starry sky. Panels of veined marble sheath the walls below. Bands of luxuriant foliage and floral designs derived from funerary garlands cover the four central arches, and the walls above them are filled with the figures of standing apostles gesturing like orators. Birds

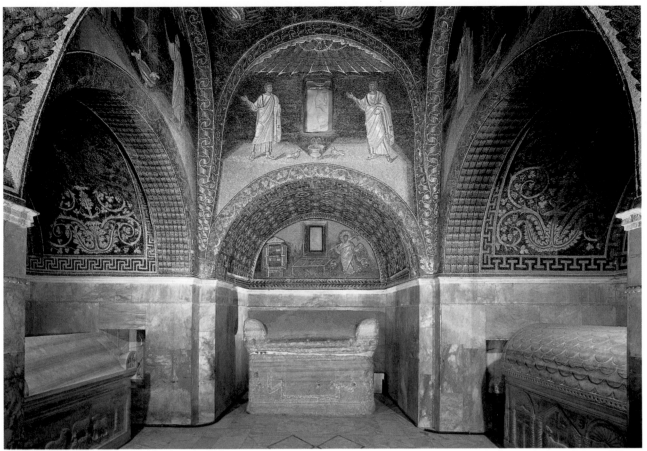

7-19. Mausoleum of Galla Placidia, eastern bays with sarcophagus niches in the arms and lunette mosaic of the *Martyrdom of Saint Lawrence*

flanking a small fountain between the apostles symbolize eternal life in heaven. In the lunette, a mosaic symbolically depicts the third-century martyrdom of Saint Lawrence, to whom the building was probably dedicated. The saint holds a cross and gestures under the window toward the metal gridiron, or grill, on which he was literally roasted. At the left stands a tall cabinet containing the Gospels, signifying the faith for which he died.

Opposite Saint Lawrence, in a lunette over the entrance portal, is the *Good Shepherd* (fig. 7-20). A comparison of this version with a fourth-century depiction of the same subject (see fig. 7-6) reveals significant changes in content and design. The Ravenna mosaic contains many familiar classical elements, such as illusionistic shading and shadows to suggest a single light source acting on solid forms, a suggestion of landscape, and traditional animal poses. The image of Jesus, however, has changed. In the fourth-century painting he was a simple shepherd boy carrying an animal on his shoulders; in the mosaic he is a young adult wearing imperial robes of gold and purple and holding a long, golden staff that ends in a cross instead of a shepherd's crook. There is a large, golden halo behind his head, a device artists used to distinguish rulers from ordinary people. (Later, halos were reserved for holy personages—God, Jesus Christ, the Virgin Mary, angels, or saints.) The stylized elements of a natural landscape are there but are arranged more rigidly than before. Individual plants have been placed at regular intervals to fill the spaces between animals, and the

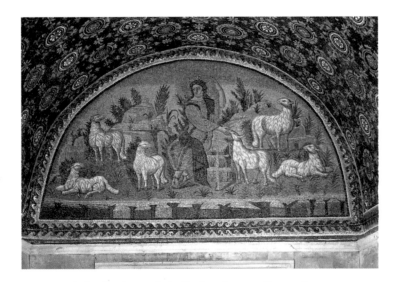

7-20. *Good Shepherd*, mosaic in the lunette over the west entrance, Mausoleum of Galla Placidia

rocks are stepped back into a shallow space that rises from the foreground plane and ends in foliage fronds. The rocky band at the bottom of the lunette scene, resembling a cliff face riddled with clefts, separates the divine image from worshipers.

Just as the political role of Ravenna changed in the fourth and fifth centuries, so did the religious belief of its leaders. The early Christian Church faced many

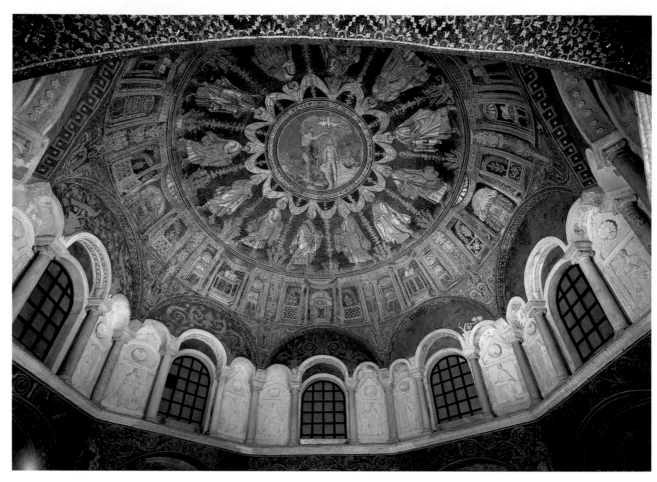

7-21. Clerestory and dome, Baptistry of the Orthodox, Ravenna, Italy. Early 5th century; dome remodeled c. 450–60

philosophical and doctrinal controversies, some of which resulted in serious splits, called schisms, within the Church. When this happened, its leaders gathered in church councils to decide on the orthodox, or official, position and denounce others as heretical. Two early forms of Christianity that were rejected were Arianism and Monophysitism.

Arianism was named after Arius (c. 250–336), a leader in the church of Alexandria. He and his followers believed that Jesus was coeternal with God but not fully divine, having been made by God. The first Church Council, called by Constantine at Nicaea in 325, declared the doctrine of the Trinity to be orthodox and denounced Arianism as heretical.

Monophysites took the opposite viewpoint from Arians. They believed that Jesus was an entirely divine being even while on earth. Attempting to address this belief, the Council of Chalcedon, near Constantinople, in 451 declared Jesus to be of two natures—human and divine—united in one. This declaration did not put an end to Monophysitism, which remained strong in Egypt, Syria, Palestine, and Armenia in Asia Minor.

In Ravenna two baptistries still stand as witness to these disputes: the Baptistry of the Orthodox and the Baptistry of the Arians. The Baptistry of the Orthodox was constructed next to the Cathedral of Ravenna in the early fourth century. Bishop Neon had it renovated and refurbished between 450 and 460, replacing the wooden ceiling with a dome and adding splendid interior decoration in marble, stucco, and mosaic (fig. 7-21). On the clerestory level, an arcade springing from columns with large **impost** blocks repeats blind arcading below. Each main arch contains three arches framing a window. Flanking the windows are figures of Old Testament prophets in relief surmounted by pediments containing shell motifs. The pediment above the figure to the left of each window is round, whereas that on the right is pointed. The main arcading acts visually to turn the domed ceiling into a huge canopy tethered to the imposts of the columns.

In the dome itself, concentric rings of decoration draw the eye upward to a central image that reflects the structure's function: the baptism of Jesus by Saint John the Baptist, Jesus' older cousin, a desert hermit whom Christians regard as the last of the Old Testament prophets and the first of the New Testament saints, the forerunner of Jesus. The lowest ring consists of **trompe l'oeil**—a French term applied to highly illusionistic painting that "fools the eye." Among these deceptive "architectural elements" are eight circular niches, four of them containing altars holding gospel books. The four niches alternating with them hold empty thrones under ciboria. The empty thrones symbolize the throne that awaits Christ's Second Coming (Matthew 25:31–36), when he will return to earth and prepare his people for Judgment Day. In the next ring, toga-clad apostles stand holding

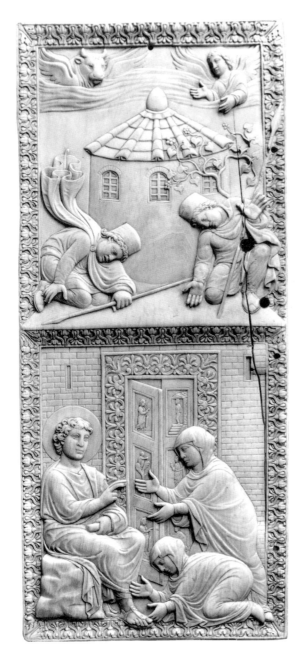

7-22. *Resurrection and Angel with Two Marys at the Tomb*, panel of a diptych, found in Rome. c. 400. Ivory, 14½ x 5⅜" (37 x 13.5 cm). Castello Sforzesco, Milan

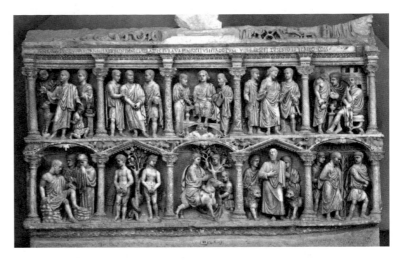

7-23. *Sarcophagus of Junius Bassus*. c. 359. Marble, 4' x 8' (1.2 x 2.4 m). Grottoes of Saint Peter, Vatican, Rome.

Sculpture

In sculpture, as in architecture, Christians adapted Roman forms for their own needs. Commemorative ivory **diptychs**—two carved panels hinged together—originated with Roman politicians elected to the post of consul, who sent to friends and colleagues notices of that event, and, later, other events, inscribed in wax on the inner sides of a pair of carved ivory panels (see fig. 6-89). Christians adapted the practice for religious use at least by the fifth century, inscribing a diptych with the names of people to be remembered with prayers during Mass. An ivory panel found in Rome and dating to about 400 may have been an early example of this practice (fig. 7-22). The top register shows the moment of Christ's resurrection in both symbolic and narrative terms. While the soldiers guarding his tomb sleep, the evangelists Luke (represented by the ox in the upper left) and Matthew (represented by the man in the upper right) acknowledge the event from the clouds. The bottom register shows the moment when Mary mother of James and Mary Magdalen learn from a young man whose "appearance was like lightning and . . . clothing was white as snow" (Matthew 28:1–6) that the tomb is empty. The top panels of the carved doors of the tomb show the Raising of Lazarus, the Gospel story in which Jesus brings a man back to life to prove his divine power. In the top right door panel the shrouded Lazarus emerges from his tomb, symbolizing the Christian promise of life after death. The varied natural poses of the figures, the solid modeling of the bodies beneath their drapery, the architectural details of the tomb, and the decorative framing patterns all indicate the classical roots of this work, which in its theme is completely Christian.

Monumental stone sculpture can be studied in sarcophagi, such as the elaborately carved *Sarcophagus of Junius Bassus* (fig. 7-23). Bassus was a Roman official who, as an inscription here tells us, died on August 25,

their crowns of martyrdom, stylized golden plant forms dividing the deep blue ground between them. Although the figures cast dark shadows on the pale green grass, their cloudlike robes, shot through with golden rays, give them an otherworldly presence. The landscape setting of the Baptism of Jesus in the central **tondo**—a circular image—exhibits classical roots, and the representation of the Jordan River in human form recalls pagan imagery. The background, however, is not the blue of the earthly sky but the gold of paradise. Already in the mid-fifth century, artists working for the Christian Church had begun to reinterpret and transform Roman naturalism into an abstract style better suited to the spiritual goals of their patrons.

ICONOGRAPHY OF THE LIFE OF JESUS

Iconography is the study of subject matter in art. It involves identifying both what a work of art represents—its literal meaning—and the deeper significance of what is represented—its symbolic meaning. Stories about the life of Jesus, grouped in "cycles," form the basis of Christian iconography. What follows is an outline of those cycles and the main events of each.

THE INCARNATION CYCLE AND THE CHILDHOOD OF JESUS

This cycle contains events surrounding the conception and birth of Jesus.

The Annunciation: The archangel Gabriel informs the Virgin Mary that God has chosen her to bear his son. A dove represents the Incarnation, her miraculous conception of Jesus through the Holy Spirit.

The Visitation: Mary visits her older cousin Elizabeth, pregnant with the future Saint John the Baptist. Elizabeth is the first to acknowledge the divinity of the child Mary is carrying. The two women rejoice.

The Nativity: Jesus is born to Mary in Bethlehem. The Holy Family—Jesus, Mary, and her husband, Joseph—is shown in a house, a stable, or, in Byzantine art, in a cave.

The Annunciation to the Shepherds and **The Adoration of the Shepherds**: An angel announces Jesus' birth to humble shepherds. They hasten to Bethlehem to honor him.

The Adoration of the Magi: The Magi—wise men from the East—follow a bright star to Bethlehem to honor Jesus as King of the Jews, presenting him with precious gifts: gold (symbolizing kingship), frankincense (divinity), and myrrh (death). In the European Middle Ages the Magi were identified as three kings.

The Massacre of the Innocents and **The Flight into Egypt**: An angel warns Joseph that King Herod—to eliminate the threat of a newborn rival king—plans to murder all the babies in Bethlehem. The Holy Family flees to Egypt.

The Presentation in the Temple: Mary and Joseph bring the infant Jesus to the Temple in Jerusalem, where he is presented to the high priest. It is prophesied that Jesus will redeem humankind but that Mary will suffer great sorrow.

Jesus among the Doctors: In Jerusalem for the celebration of Passover, Joseph and Mary find the twelve-year-old Jesus in serious discussion with Temple scholars. This is seen as a sign of his coming ministry.

THE PUBLIC MINISTRY CYCLE

In this cycle Jesus preaches his message.

The Baptism: At age thirty Jesus is baptized by John the Baptist in the Jordan River. He sees the Holy Spirit and hears a heavenly voice proclaiming him God's son. This marks the beginning of his ministry.

The Calling of Matthew: Passing by the customhouse, Jesus sees Matthew, a tax collector, to whom he says, "Follow me." Matthew complies, becoming one of the apostles.

Jesus and the Samaritan Woman at the Well: On his way from Judaea to Galilee, Jesus rests by a spring called Jacob's Well. Contrary to Jewish custom, he asks a local Samaritan woman drawing water for a drink. The apostles are surprised to find them conversing.

Jesus Walking on the Water: The apostles, in a storm-tossed boat, see Jesus walking toward them on the water. Peter tries to go out to meet Jesus, but begins to sink, and Jesus saves him. When Jesus reaches the boat, the storm stops.

The Raising of Lazarus: Jesus brings his friend Lazarus back to life four days after he has died. Lazarus emerges from the tomb wrapped in his shroud.

The Delivery of the Keys to Peter: Jesus designates Peter as his successor, symbolically turning over to him the keys to the kingdom of heaven.

The Transfiguration: Jesus is transformed into a dazzling vision on Mount Tabor in Galilee as his closest disciples—Peter, James, and John the Evangelist—look on. A cloud overshadows them, and a heavenly voice proclaims Jesus to be God's son.

The Cleansing of the Temple: Jesus, in anger, drives money changers and animal traders from the Temple.

THE PASSION CYCLE

This cycle contains events surrounding Jesus' death and resurrection. (*Passio* is Latin for "suffering.")

The Entry into Jerusalem: Jesus, riding a donkey, and his disciples enter Jerusalem in triumph. Crowds honor them, spreading clothes and palm fronds in their path.

The Last Supper: During the Passover seder, Jesus reveals his impending death to his disciples. Instructing them to drink wine (his blood) and eat bread (his body) in remembrance of him, he lays the foundation for the Christian Eucharist (Mass).

Jesus Washing the Apostles' Feet: After the Last Supper, Jesus humbly washes the apostles' feet to set an example of humility. Peter, embarrassed, protests.

The Agony in the Garden: In the Garden of Gethsemane on the Mount of Olives, Jesus struggles between his

---

359, at the age of forty-two. The front panel has two registers divided by columns into shallow stage spaces of equal width. On the top level, the columns are surmounted by an entablature incised with the inscription in Roman capital letters. On the bottom register, they support alternating triangular and arched roof gables resembling little houses. Each stage, with the exception of one in the lower register containing the nude figures of Adam and Eve, is filled by toga-clad figures with short legs, long bodies, and large heads. Fragments of architecture, various types of seating, and occasional trees suggest the material setting for each scene.

human fear of pain and death and his divine strength to overcome them (*agon* is Greek for "contest"). An angelic messenger bolsters his courage. The apostles sleep nearby, oblivious.

The Betrayal (The Arrest): Judas Iscariot, one of the apostles, accepts a bribe to point Jesus out to his enemies. Judas brings an armed crowd to Gethsemane. He kisses Jesus, a prearranged signal. Peter makes a futile attempt to defend Jesus from the Roman soldiers who seize him.

The Denial of Peter: Jesus is brought to the palace of the Jewish high priest, Caiaphas, to be interrogated for claiming to be the Messiah. Peter follows, and there he three times denies knowing Jesus, as Jesus predicted he would.

Jesus before Pilate: Jesus is taken to Pontius Pilate, the Roman governor of Judaea, and charged with treason for calling himself King of the Jews. He is sent to Herod Antipas, ruler of Galilee, who scorns him. Pilate proposes freeing Jesus but is shouted down by the mob, which demands that he be crucified. Pilate washes his hands before the crowd to signify that Jesus' blood is on its hands, not his.

The Flagellation (The Scourging): Jesus is whipped by his Roman captors.

Jesus Crowned with Thorns (The Mocking of Jesus): Pilate's soldiers torment Jesus. They dress him in royal robes, crown him with thorns, and kneel before him, hailing him as King of the Jews.

The Bearing of the Cross (The Road to Calvary): Jesus bears the cross from Pilate's house to Golgotha, where he is executed. Medieval artists depicted this event and its accompanying incidents in fourteen images known as the Stations of the Cross: (1) Jesus is condemned to death; (2) Jesus picks up the cross; (3) Jesus falls for the first time; (4) Jesus meets his grieving mother; (5) Simon of Cyrene is forced to help Jesus carry the cross; (6) Veronica wipes Jesus' face with her veil; (7) Jesus falls again; (8) Jesus admonishes the women of Jerusalem; (9) Jesus falls a third time; (10) Jesus is stripped; (11) Jesus is nailed to the cross; (12) Jesus dies on the cross; (13) Jesus is taken down from the cross; (14) Jesus is entombed.

The Crucifixion: The earliest representations of the Crucifixion are abstract, showing either a cross alone or a cross and a lamb. Later depictions include some or all of the following narrative details: two criminals (one penitent, the other not) are crucified on either side of Jesus; the Virgin Mary, John the Evangelist, Mary Magdalen, and other followers mourn at the foot of the cross; Roman soldiers torment Jesus—one extends a sponge on a pole with vinegar instead of water for him to drink, another stabs him in the side with a spear, and others gamble for his clothes; a skull identifies the execution ground as Golgotha, "the place of the skull," where Adam was buried. The association symbolizes the promise of redemption: the blood flowing from Jesus' wounds will wash away Adam's Original Sin.

The Descent from the Cross (The Deposition): Jesus' followers take his body down from the cross. Joseph of Arimathea and Nicodemus wrap it in linen with myrrh and aloe. Also present are the grief-stricken Virgin, John the Evangelist, and sometimes Mary Magdalen, other disciples, and angels.

The Lamentation (Pietà or *Vesperbild*): Jesus' sorrowful followers gather around his body. An image of the Virgin mourning alone with Jesus across her lap is known as a pietà (from the Latin *pietas*, "pity") or, in German, a *Vesperbild*.

The Entombment: Jesus' mother and friends place his body in a nearby sarcophagus, or rock tomb. This is done hastily because of the approaching Jewish Sabbath.

The Descent into Limbo (The Harrowing of Hell): No longer in mortal form, Jesus, now called Christ, descends into limbo, or hell, to free deserving souls, among them Adam, Eve, and Moses.

The Resurrection (The Anastasis): Three days after his death, Christ leaves his tomb while the soldiers guarding it sleep.

The Marys at the Tomb (The Holy Women at the Sepulchre): Christ's female followers—usually including Mary Magdalen and the mother of the apostle James, also named Mary—discover his empty tomb. An angel announces Christ's resurrection. The soldiers guarding the tomb sleep.

***Noli Me Tangere* ("Do Not Touch Me"), The Supper at Emmaus**, and **The Incredulity of Thomas**: Christ makes a series of appearances to his followers in the forty days between his resurrection and his ascension. He first appears to Mary Magdalen, who thinks he is a gardener. She reaches out to him, but he warns her not to touch him. In the Supper at Emmaus, he shares a meal with his apostles. In the Incredulity of Thomas, Christ invites the doubting apostle to touch the wound in his side to convince Thomas of his resurrection.

The Ascension: Christ ascends to heaven from the Mount of Olives, disappearing in a cloud. His disciples, often accompanied by the Virgin, watch.

The scenes illustrate events in both the Old and New Testaments arranged in symbolic rather than narrative order. On the top left, Abraham, the first Hebrew patriarch, learns that he has passed the test of faith and need not sacrifice his son Isaac. Christians saw in this story a prophetic sign of Christ's sacrifice on the cross. In the next frame to the right, the apostle Peter has just been arrested for preaching after the death of Jesus. Jesus himself appears in the center frame as a teacher-philosopher flanked by Saints Peter and Paul. In a reference to the pagan past, Christ in this scene rests his feet on the head of Aeolus, the god of the winds in classical mythology,

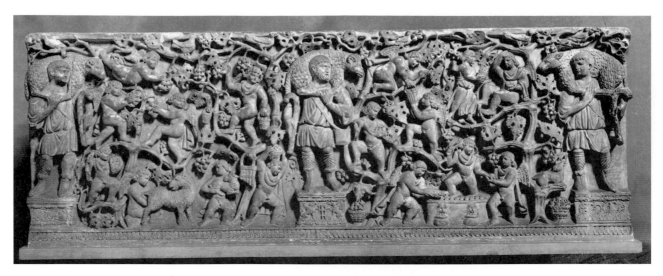

7-24. *Good Shepherd Sarcophagus*, from the Catacomb of Praetextatus, Rome. Late 4th century. Marble. Monumenti, Musei e Gallerie Pontificie, Vatican, Rome

shown with a veil billowing behind him. To Christians he personified the skies, so that Christ is meant to be seen as seated above, in heaven, where he is giving the Christian Law to his disciples, imitating the Hebrew Scriptures' account of God dispensing the Law to Moses. Next are two scenes from Christ's Passion (see "Iconography of the Life of Jesus," page 307), his arrest (second from right) and his appearance before Pontius Pilate (far right). The frame on the bottom left shows the Old Testament story of Job, whose trials provided a model for the sufferings of Christian martyrs. Next on the right is the Fall of Adam and Eve. Lured by the serpent, they have eaten the forbidden fruit and, becoming conscious of their nakedness, are trying to hide their genitals with leaves. At the bottom center, Jesus makes his triumphal entry into Jerusalem. The next frame to the right shows Daniel in the lions' den, and the frame on the bottom right shows Saint Paul being led to his martyrdom. These exemplars of Old and New Testament faith and acceptance of divine will merge here with the theme of salvation through Jesus Christ.

Another sarcophagus found in Rome, known as the *Good Shepherd Sarcophagus*, dates to the end of the fourth century (fig. 7-24). It combines an image of the Good Shepherd with a pattern of putti harvesting grapes like that found on the ceiling of the Church of Santa Costanza (see fig. 7-17). The sculptors clearly intended the shepherds to be seen as statues raised on bases, and the large sheep arching over their shoulders set off their heads like halos. The busy putti climb through the vines to pluck grapes, which they trample in the winepress between the statue bases on the right. On the left, one milks a ewe while his companion holds the lamb that would otherwise be nursing from its mother. The shallow relief was made to seem higher through deep undercutting around the figures and the use of **drillwork**. The imagery of the catacomb paintings here finds enduring three-dimensional form.

EARLY BYZANTINE ART

During the fifth and sixth centuries, while people living in the Italian peninsula experienced invasions and religious controversy, the Eastern Empire flourished. Its capital, Constantinople, remained secure behind massive walls defended by the imperial army and navy. Its control of land and sea routes between Europe and Asia made many of its people wealthy. Their patronage, as well as that of the imperial family, made the city an artistic center, and Greek scholarship and philosophy continued to be taught in its schools. Influences from the regions under the empire's control—Syria, Palestine, Egypt, Persia, and Greece—gradually combined to create a distinctive Byzantine culture.

In the sixth century, Byzantine political power, wealth, and culture reached its height under Emperor Justinian I (ruled 527–565), ably seconded by Empress Theodora (c. 500–548). With the leadership of General Belisarius, imperial forces recovered northern Africa, Sicily, much of Italy, and part of Spain. Ravenna became the administrative capital of Byzantine Italy. The pope, although officially subject to Ravenna, remained head of the Western Church. However, the Byzantine policy of caesaropapism, whereby the emperor was head of both church and state, became a growing source of friction between the two halves of Christendom (see "Rome, Constantinople, and Christianity," page 290). As Slavs and Bulgars moved into the Balkan peninsula in southeastern Europe, they, too, came under the sway of the empire. Only on the frontier with the Persian Empire to the east did Byzantine armies falter, and there Justinian bought peace with tribute. To centralize his government and impose a uniform legal system, Justinian began a thorough compilation of Roman law known as the Justinian Code. Written in Latin, this code was later to serve as the foundation for the legal systems of Europe.

The Church and Its Decoration

Constantinople. Justinian focused his building and renovation campaign on the capital of the Eastern Empire, Constantinople, but little remains of his architectural projects or of the old imperial city itself. A magnificent exception is the Church of Hagia Sophia (Holy Wisdom, fig. 7-25). This church replaced a fourth-century building erected during the reign of Constantine's son and successor in the East, Constantius II, after the old church was destroyed during riots in 532. Spurred by Justinian's religious and political foes, the excitable crowds at a racetrack close to the imperial palace took to the streets. They set fire to the church, and soon half the city was destroyed. The empress Theodora, a brilliant, politically shrewd woman, is said to have spurred Justinian to resist the rioters, saying, "Purple makes a fine shroud"—meaning that she would rather die an empress (purple was the royal color) than flee for her life. Taking up her words as a battle cry, imperial forces under Belisarius crushed the rebels. As soon as order was restored, Justinian and Theodora embarked on a building campaign that overshadowed any in the city since the reign of Constantine two centuries earlier.

Justinian chose two scholar-theoreticians, Anthemius of Tralles and Isidorus of Miletus, to rebuild Hagia Sophia as an embodiment of imperial power and Christian glory. Anthemius was a specialist in geometry and optics, and Isidorus a specialist in physics who had also studied vaulting. They developed a daring and magnificent design. The dome of the church provided a vast, golden, light-filled canopy high above a processional space for the many priests and members of the imperial court who assembled there to celebrate the Eucharist.

The new Hagia Sophia was not constructed by the miraculous intervention of angels, as was rumored, but by mortal builders in only five years (532–537). The architects, engineers, and masons who built it benefited from the accumulated experience of a long tradition of great architecture. Procopius of Caesarea, who chronicled Justinian's reign, claimed poetically that Hagia Sophia's gigantic dome seemed to hang suspended on a "golden chain from Heaven." Legend has it that Justinian himself, aware that architecture can be a potent symbol of earthly power, compared his accomplishment with that of the legendary builder of the First Temple in Jerusalem, saying, "Solomon, I have outdone you."

Hagia Sophia was based on a central plan with a dome inscribed in a square (fig. 7-26). To form a longitudinal nave, **conches**—semidomes—expand outward from the central dome to connect with the narthex on one end and the conch of the sanctuary apse on the other. This central core, called the **naos** in Byzantine architecture, is flanked by side aisles; **galleries**, or stories open to and overlooking the naos, are located above the aisles.

The main dome of Hagia Sophia is supported on pendentives, triangular curving wall sections built between the four huge arches that spring from piers at the corners of the dome's square base (see "Elements of Architec-

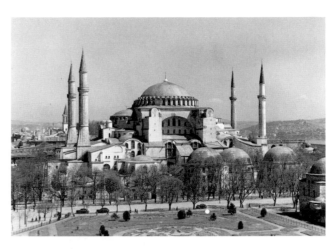

7-25. Anthemius of Tralles and Isidorus of Miletus. Church of Hagia Sophia, Istanbul, Turkey. 532–37. View from the southwest

The body of the original church is now surrounded by later additions, including the minarets built after 1453 under the Ottoman Turks.

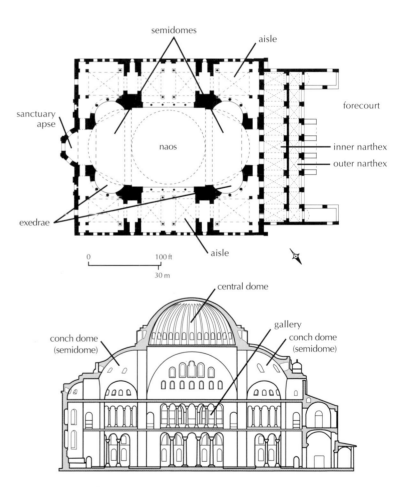

7-26. Plan and section of the Church of Hagia Sophia

ture," page 310). The origin of the dome on pendentives, which became the preferred method for supporting domes in Byzantine architecture, is obscure, but Hagia Sophia represents its earliest use in a major building. Here two semidomes flanking the main dome rise above **exedrae** with their own conch domes at the four corners

ELEMENTS OF ARCHITECTURE
Pendentives and Squinches

Pendentives and squinches are two methods of supporting a round dome or its drum over a square or rectangular space. Pendentives are structural elements between arches that form a circular opening on which the dome sits. Squinches are bracketlike constructions or **corbels**, fitted into the walls' upper corners beneath the dome. Because squinches create an octagon, which is close in shape to a circle, they provide a solid base on which a dome may rest. Byzantine builders experimented with both pendentives (as at Hagia Sophia, fig. 7-27) and squinches. Elaborate squinch-supported domes became a hallmark of Islamic interiors (as at Córdoba's Great Mosque, see fig. 8-7).

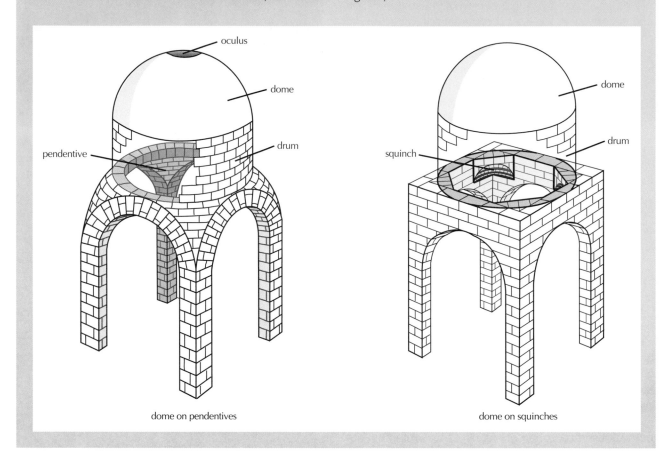

dome on pendentives   dome on squinches

of the nave. Unlike the Pantheon's dome, which is solid with an **oculus** at the top (see fig. 6-56), Hagia Sophia's dome has a band of forty windows around its base. This daring concept challenged architectural logic by weakening the integrity of the masonry but created the all-important circle of light that makes the dome appear to float (fig. 7-27). In fact, when the first dome fell in 558, it did so because a pier and pendentive shifted and the dome was too shallow, not because of the windows. Confident of their revised technical methods and undeterred, the architects designed a steeper dome that put the summit 20 feet higher above the floor. Exterior **buttressing** was added, and although repairs had to be made in 869, 989, and 1346, the church has since withstood the shock of earthquakes.

As in a basilica-plan church, worshipers entered Hagia Sophia through a forecourt and outer and inner narthexes on a central axis. Once through the portals, though, their gaze was drawn upward into the dome and then forward by the succession of domed spaces to the distant sanctuary. With this inspired design Anthemius and Isidorus had reconciled an inherent conflict in church architecture between the desire for a symbolically soaring space and the need to focus attention on the altar and the liturgy. The domed design came to be favored by the Eastern Church.

The liturgy used in Hagia Sophia in the sixth century has been lost, but it presumably resembled the later rites of the Eastern Orthodox Church. Assuming that was the case, the celebration of the Mass took place behind a screen—at Hagia Sophia an embroidered curtain, in later churches an **iconostasis**, or wall hung with devotional paintings called **icons** ("images" in Greek). The emperor was the only layperson permitted to enter the sanctuary. Others stood in the aisles (men) or galleries (women). Processions of clergy moved in a circular path from the sanctuary into the nave and back five or six times during the ritual. The focus of the congregation was on the screen of images and up into the dome rather than ahead to the altar and apse. The upward focus reflects the interest of Byzantine philosophers in Neoplatonic theories that viewed meditation as a way to rise from the material world into a spiritual state. Worshipers standing on the church floor must have felt such a spiritual uplift as

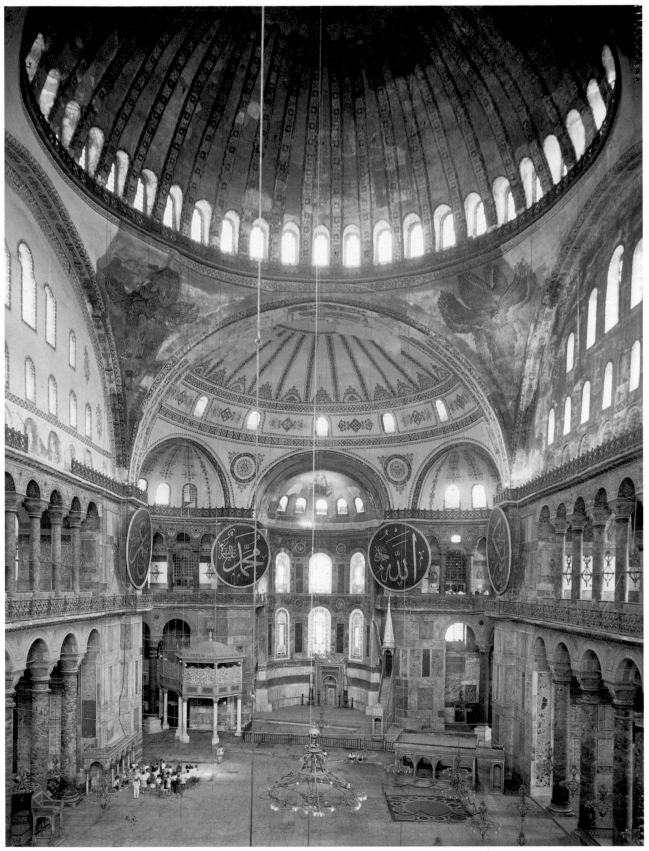

7-27. Church of Hagia Sophia

Hypatius of Ephesus, writing in the mid-sixth century, justified decorating churches in a luxurious manner as a means to inspire piety in the congregation. He wrote: "We, too, permit material adornment in the sanctuaries, not because God considers gold and silver, silken vestments and vessels encrusted with gems to be precious and holy, but because we allow every order of the faithful to be guided in a suitable manner and to be led up to the Godhead, inasmuch as some men are guided even by such things towards the intelligible beauty, and from the abundant light of the sanctuaries to the intelligible and immaterial light" (cited in Mango, page 117).

EARLY CHRISTIAN, JEWISH, AND BYZANTINE ART　　311

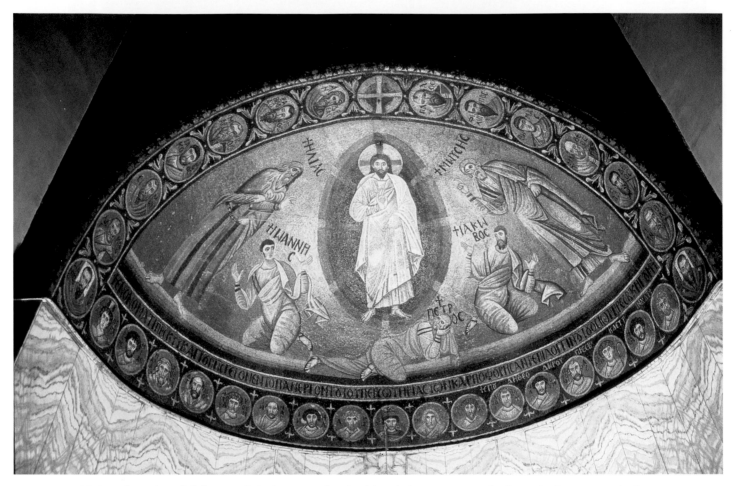

7-28. *Transfiguration of Christ*, mosaic in the apse, Church of the Virgin, Monastery of Saint Catherine, Mount Sinai, Egypt. c. 548–65

they gazed at the mosaics of saints, angels, and, in the golden central dome, heaven itself.

The churches of Constantinople were once filled with the products of imperial patronage: mosaics, rich furniture, and objects of gold, silver, and silk. Mosaics now in the Monastery of Saint Catherine on Mount Sinai in Egypt were one such donation. The apse mosaic of the monastery's church depicts the Transfiguration on Mount Tabor (see "Iconography of the Life of Jesus," page 306) in a simple, direct manner (fig. 7-28). Dated between 548 and 565, this imposing work shows the transfigured Christ in a triple blue **mandorla**, an almond-shaped halo that surrounds Christ's whole figure, against a golden sky that fills the apse conch. The visionary figure of Christ emits rays of light, and the standing Old Testament prophets Moses and Elijah descend to affirm his divinity. The astonished apostles on the ground are identified as

Saint Peter below, Saint John at the left, and Saint James at the right. A supernatural wind seems to catch the ends of their robes, whipping them into curiously jagged shapes. The apostles fall to the ground in fear and amazement, while Christ stands calmly in the relaxed pose of a Greek-Roman athlete or orator. Mount Tabor is suggested only by a narrow strip at the bottom, half green and half reflecting the golden light. This abstract rendering contrasts with the continuing classical influence seen in the figures' substantial bodies, revealed by their tightly wrapped drapery.

The formal character of the *Transfiguration of Christ* mosaic reflects an evolving approach to representation that began several centuries earlier. As was discussed in Chapter 6, the character of imperial rule began to change in the fourth century in ways that were reflected in works of art like *The Tetrarchs* (see fig. 6-77) and the relief pan-

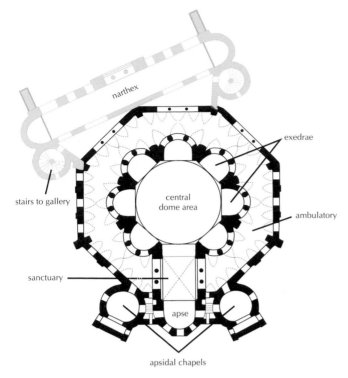

narthex

exedrae

stairs to gallery

central
dome area

ambulatory

sanctuary

apse

apsidal chapels

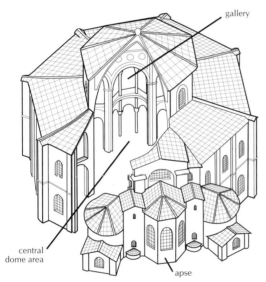

gallery

central
dome area

apse

abstraction of figures, use of reverse perspective, and standardized conventions to portray individuals and events.

Ravenna. Ravenna was conquered by the Byzantine Empire from the Ostrogoths in 540 and served as a base for the further conquest of Italy, completed by Justinian I in 553. Much of our knowledge of the art of this turbulent period—from the time of Honorius (emperor of the Western Roman Empire) through Arian Ostrogothic control to the triumphant victory of the Byzantine Empire—comes from the well-preserved monuments at Ravenna.

In 526 Ecclesius, bishop of Ravenna from 521 to 532, commissioned two new churches, one for the city and one for its port, Classis. With funding from a wealthy local banker, construction began on a central-plan church in Ravenna dedicated to the fourth-century Roman martyr Saint Vitalis and a basilica-plan church in the port dedicated to Saint Apollinaris, the first bishop of Ravenna. Neither was completed until after Justinian had conquered Ravenna and established it as the Byzantine administrative capital of Italy. The Church of San Vitale was dedicated in 547, followed by the Church of Sant' Apollinare in Classe two years later.

The design of San Vitale is basically an octagon extended by exedralike semicircular bays, ambulatory, and gallery that are covered by a round dome (fig. 7-29). The strict symmetry of the design is broken by the extension of one bay into a rectangular sanctuary and apse that projects through one of the octagonal sides of the shell. Circular chapels with rectangular altar spaces flank this apse projection. A separate but long-gone narthex in the form of a long, oval vestibule set off-axis led to a palace complex. Triangular bays led to cylindrical stair towers that gave access to the second-floor gallery. This sophisticated design has distant roots in Roman buildings such as Santa Costanza (see fig. 7-15).

The floor plan of San Vitale only begins to convey the effect of the complex, interpenetrating interior spaces of the church, an effect that was enhanced by the offset narthex with its double sets of doors leading into the nave. People entering from the right saw only arched openings, whereas those entering from the left approached on axis with the sanctuary, which they saw straight ahead of them. The round dome, hidden on the exterior by an octagonal shell and a tile-covered roof, is a light, strong structure ingeniously created out of interlocking ceramic tubes and mortar. The whole rests on eight large piers that frame the exedrae and the sanctuary. These two-story exedrae open through arches into the outer aisles on the ground floor and into galleries on the second floor. They expand the circular central space physically and also create an airy, floating sensation, reinforced by the liberal use of gold tesserae in the surface decoration.

els on the Arch of Constantine (see fig. 6-85). The emperor became an increasingly remote figure surrounded by pomp and ceremony; orators often used terms like *Sacred, Majestic,* or *Eternalness* to address him. In the official art of the period, a conventionalized style somewhat similar to that seen in Egyptian and Near Eastern works displaced the naturalism of Greek and Roman classicism. In Christian art, especially, an early interest in capturing the visual appearance of the material world gave way to a new **hieratic**—formally abstract or priestly—style that sought to express essential religious meaning rather than exact external appearance. Attempting to create tangible images that would stand for intangible Christian concepts, artists rejected the space, light, color, and physicality of the real world in favor of a timeless supernatural world. The new style was characterized by geometric simplification of forms, an expressionistic

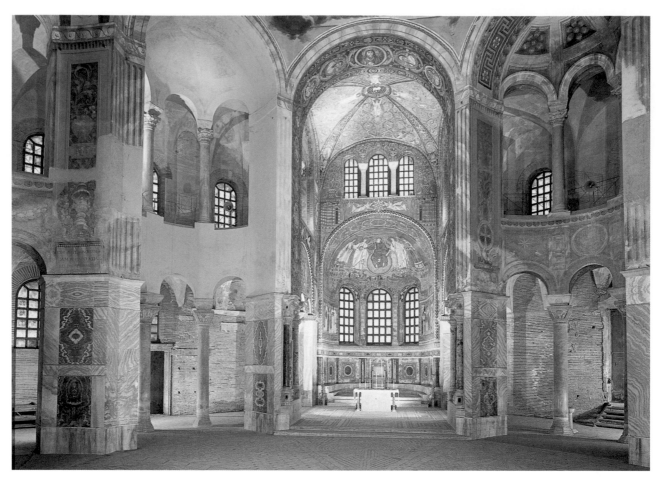

7-30. Church of San Vitale. View across the central space toward the sanctuary apse with mosaic showing Christ enthroned and flanked by Saint Vitalis and Bishop Ecclesius

In the conch of the sanctuary apse, an image of Christ enthroned is flanked by Saint Vitalis and Bishop Ecclesius, who presents a model of the church to Christ (fig. 7-30). The other sanctuary images relate to its use for the celebration of the Eucharist. Pairs of lambs flanking a cross decorate impost blocks above the intricately interlaced carving of the marble column capitals. The lunette on the south wall shows an altar table set with a chalice for wine and two patens, liturgical plates, to which the high priest Melchizedek on the right brings an offering of bread, and Abel, on the left, carries a sacrificial lamb (fig. 7-31). Their identities are known from the inscriptions above their heads.

The prophets Isaiah (right) and Moses (left) appear in the spandrels. Moses, while tending his sheep, heard the voice of an angel of God coming from a bush that was burning with a fire that did not destroy it. Moses is shown reaching down to remove his shoes, a symbolic gesture of respect in the presence of God or on holy ground. In the gallery zone of the sanctuary the Four Evangelists are depicted, two on each wall, and in the vault the Lamb of God supported by four angels appears in a field of vine scrolls.

Justinian and Theodora did not attend the dedication ceremonies for the Church of San Vitale conducted by Archbishop Maximianus in 547—they may never have set foot in Ravenna—but two large mosaic panels that face each other across its apse make their presence known. Justinian (see fig. 7-1), on the north wall, carries a large golden paten for the Host and stands next to Maximianus, who holds a golden, jewel-encrusted cross. The priestly celebrants at the right carry the Gospels, encased in a gold-and-jewel book cover, symbolizing the coming of the Word, and a censer containing burning incense to purify the altar prior to the Mass.

Theodora, singled out by a gold halolike disk and a fluted shell canopy, carries a huge golden chalice studded with jewels (fig. 7-32). She presents this both as an offering for the Mass and as a gift of great value for Christ. With it she emulates the Magi (see "Iconography of the Life of Jesus," page 306), depicted at the bottom of her purple robe, who brought valuable gifts of gold, frankincense (fragrant wood), and myrrh (expensive, perfumed oil) to the infant Jesus. A courtyard fountain stands to the left of the panel and patterned draperies adorn the openings at left and right. The huge jeweled and pearl-hung crown nearly dwarfs her delicate features, yet the empress dominates these worldly trappings by the intensity of her gaze.

The mosaic decoration in the Church of San Vitale presents a unique mixture of imperial ritual, Old Testament narrative, and Christian liturgical symbolism that dissolves its architecture into shimmering light and color. The setting around Theodora—the conch, the

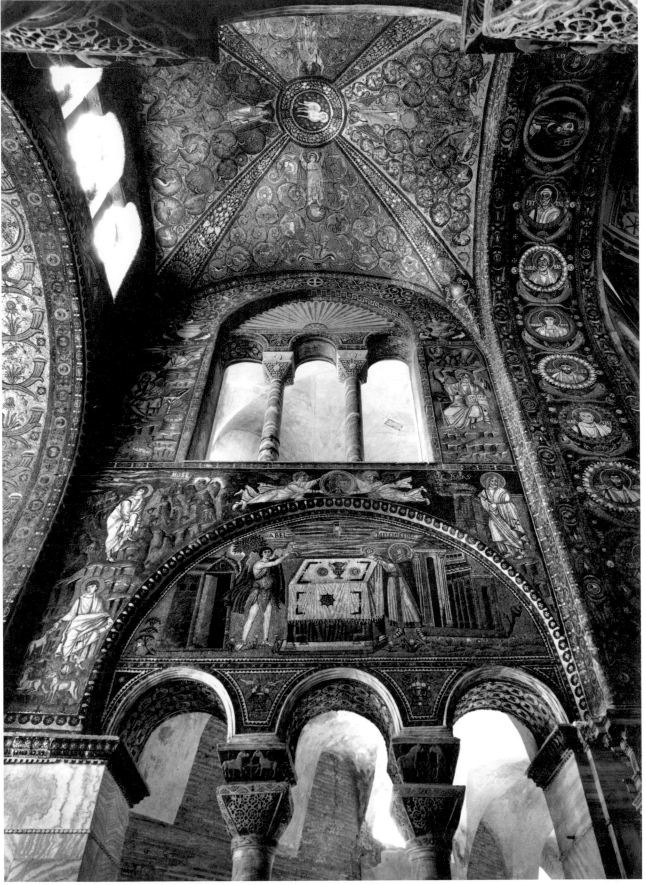

7-31. Church of San Vitale, south wall of the sanctuary, with Abel and Melchizedek in the lunette, Moses and Isaiah in the spandrels, portraits of the evangelists in the gallery zone, and the Lamb of God in the vault

500
100 CE   1500 CE

7-32. *Empress Theodora and Her Attendants,* mosaic on south wall of the apse, Church of San Vitale. c. 547. 8'8" x 12' (2.64 x 3.65 m)

Just like royalty today, Theodora was the subject of much comment and conjecture in her time. Described in a "secret history" by a contemporary, the historian Procopius, as a small-boned woman with sparkling eyes and a will of iron, she was said to have been an actress, considered a risqué profession. Her father was an animal trainer for the circus, where the young heir to the imperial throne, Justinian, met her. Although Theodora's background was unacceptable in high circles, Justinian remained devoted to her. He named a new province, Theodorias, for her and treated her almost as if she were co-emperor. Theodora died in 548, not long after this mosaic portrait was completed.

fluted pedestal, the open door, and the swagged draperies—are classical illusionistic devices, yet the mosaicists deliberately avoid making them space-creating elements. Byzantine artists accepted the idea that objects exist in space, but they no longer conceived pictorial space the way Roman artists had, as a view of the natural world seen through a "window," the picture plane, and extending back from it toward a distant horizon. In Byzantine aesthetic theory, eye and image were joined by invisible rays of sight so that pictorial space extended forward from the picture plane to the eye of the beholder and included the real space between them. Parallel lines appear to diverge as they get farther away and objects seem to tip up in a representational system known as **reverse perspective**.

Bishop Maximianus consecrated the Church of Sant'Apollinare in Classe in 549 (fig. 7-33). The atrium has disappeared, but the simple geometry of the brick exterior clearly reflects the basilica's interior spaces. A narthex entrance spans the full width of the ground floor; a long, tall nave with a clerestory ends in a semicircular apse; and side aisles flank the nave.

On the interior, nothing interferes visually with the movement forward from the entrance to the raised sanctuary (fig. 7-34), which extends directly from a triumphal-arch opening into the semicircular apse. The conch mosaic depicts an array of human and animal figures in

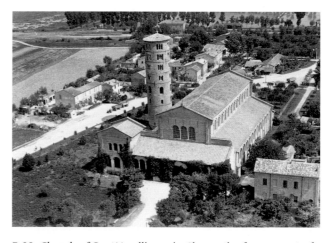

7-33. Church of Sant'Apollinare in Classe, the former port of Ravenna (Classis), Italy. 533–49

a stylized landscape and has many levels of meaning. A jeweled cross with the face of Christ at its center symbolizes the Transfiguration—Jesus' revelation of his divinity. The Hand of God reaches down from glowing clouds. The Old Testament figures Moses and Elijah emerge from clouds at each side, symbolically legitimizing the newer religion and attesting to the divine event. The apostles Peter, James, and John—represented here by the three sheep with raised heads—likewise witness

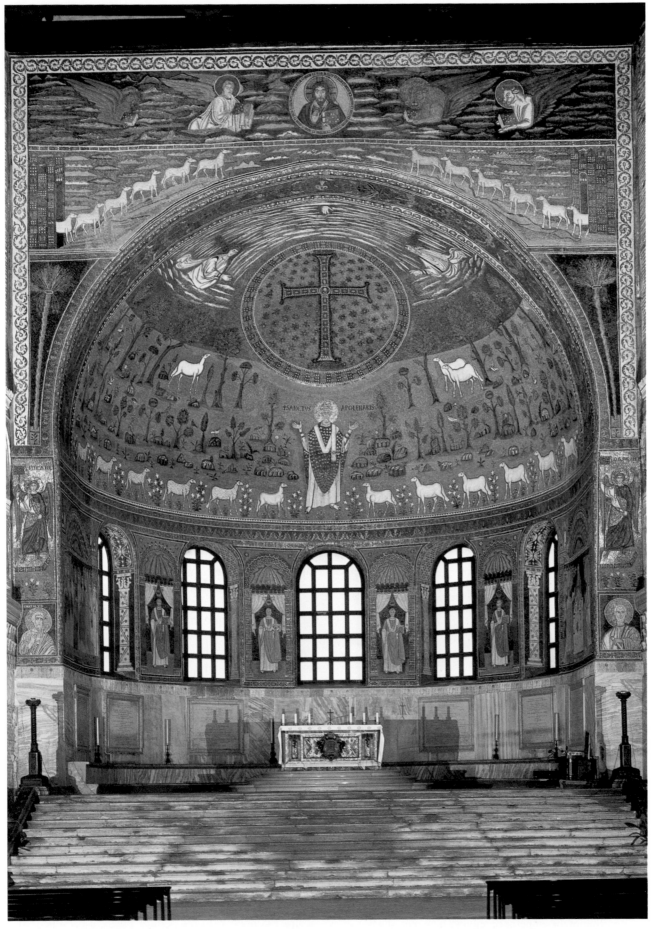

7-34. *The Transfiguration of Christ with Saint Apollinaris, First Bishop of Ravenna*, mosaic in the apse, Church of Sant'Apollinare in Classe

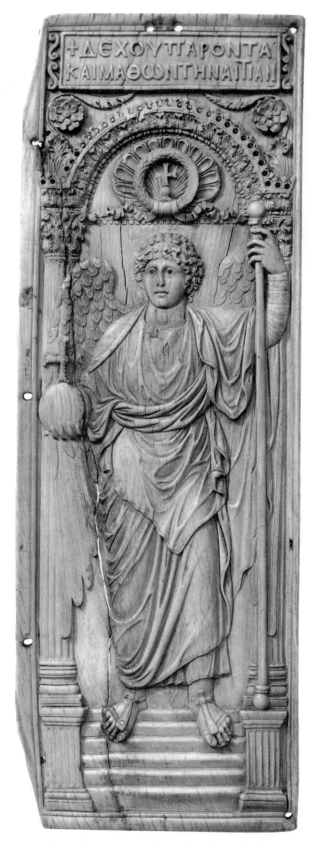

7-35. *Archangel Michael,* panel of a diptych, probably from the court workshop at Constantinople. Early 6th century. Ivory, 17 x 5½" (43.3 x 14 cm). The British Museum, London

The other half of this devotional piece, now lost, would have completed the Greek inscription across the top, which begins: "Receive these gifts, and having learned the cause. . . ." Perhaps the other panel contained the portrait of the emperor or another high official who was presenting the panels as a gift to an important colleague, acquaintance, or family member.

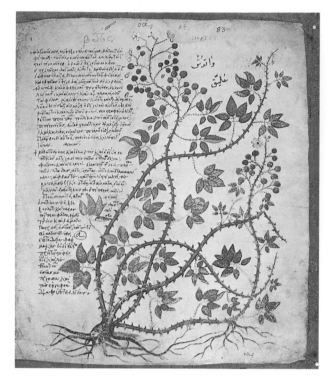

7-36. Page with *Wild Blackberry,* from *De Materia Medica,* by Pedanius Dioscorides (1st century), copy made and illustrated in Constantinople for Princess Anicia Juliana. c. 512. Tempera on vellum, 15 x 13" (38.1 x 33 cm). Österreichische Nationalbibliothek, Vienna

the event. At the center below the cross, Saint Apollinaris, in bishop's robes, is shown as an orant. The twelve lambs flanking him represent the apostles. Stalks of blooming lilies, along with tiny trees and other plants, birds, and oddly shaped rocks, fill the green mountain landscape. Unlike the landscape in the *Good Shepherd* lunette of the Mausoleum of Galla Placidia (see fig. 7-20), these highly stylized forms bear little resemblance to nature. The artists eliminated any suggestion of spatial recession by making the trees and lambs at the top of the golden sky larger than those at the bottom. The pictorial abstraction of the gigantic cross bearing the face of Christ dominates the conch.

In the mosaics on the wall above the apse, which were added in the seventh and ninth centuries, Christ, now portrayed with a cross inscribed in his halo and flanked by symbols representing the evangelists, blesses and holds the Gospels. Sheep (the apostles) emerge from triumphal gateways and climb golden rocks toward their leader and teacher.

Ivories, Manuscripts, and Panel Paintings. Ivory reliefs were a popular product of the court workshops of Constantinople in the early sixth century. A treasured example of this form is a panel depicting an archangel, a high-ranking angel, probably Michael (fig. 7-35). The artist has rendered the figure in a classical style but has otherwise created an image meant entirely to convey certain abstract concepts. In his beauty, physical presence, and elegant setting, the archangel is comparable to the priestess of Bacchus in the Symmachus panel (see fig. 6-89). His

EARLY FORMS OF THE BOOK Since people began to write some 5,000 years ago, they have kept records on a variety of materials, including clay or wax tablets, pieces of broken pottery, papyrus, animal skins, and finally paper. The extended works that we call books have taken two forms: **rotulus** and **codex**. A rotulus is a continuous rolled strip, or scroll. A codex (plural codices), like the modern book, is made up of sheets bound together on one side. Egyptian scribes made scrolls from sheets of papyrus glued together. Scrolls were also made from thin sheets of cleaned, scraped, and trimmed sheep- or calfskin, a material known as **parchment** or, when softer and lighter, **vellum**. Scrolls were written to be read either horizontally or vertically. Each end was attached to a rod; the reader slowly unfurled the scroll from one rod to the other.

At the end of the first century CE, the codex replaced the scroll as the predominant book form in the West. A basic unit of the early codex was the eight-leaf quire, made by folding a large sheet of parchment three times, cutting it, and then sewing it on one side, or by folding two sheets and sewing the two stacked sheets together.

Until the invention of printing, all books were **manuscripts**, that is, written by hand. From early on, manuscripts often included illustrations, but techniques for combining pictures and text varied. The simplest solution was to place illustrations above or below the text, but they might also be placed within the text or set off with frames. Illustrations in books came to be called **miniatures**, from *minium*, the Latin word for a reddish lead pigment. Manuscripts decorated with gold and colors were said to be **illuminated**. Manuscript illumination became increasingly specialized during the European Middle Ages, with some experts doing only borders, others decorating initials, others painting pictures, and still others applying gold leaf.

Heavy covers in the form of wooden boards covered with leather functioned as a press to keep the sheets of a codex flat. Very rich manuscripts sometimes had covers decorated with precious metals, jewels, ivory, and enamels. The thickness and weight of parchment and vellum made it impractical to produce a very large manuscript, such as an entire Bible, in a single volume. As a result, individual sections were made into separate books. The Gospels, the Psalms, and the first five books of the Old Testament (the Pentateuch), for example, were often bound individually. These weighty tomes were stored flat on shelves in cabinets like the one holding the Gospels shown here and visible in the mosaic of Saint Lawrence in the Mausoleum of Galla Placidia.

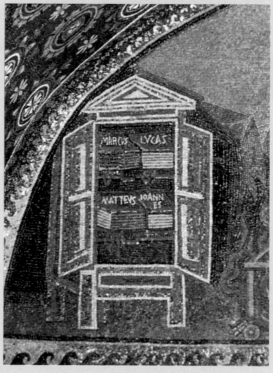

Bookstand with Gospels codices, detail of a mosaic in the eastern lunette, Mausoleum of Galla Placidia, Ravenna, Italy. c. 425–26 (see fig. 7-19)

spatial relation to the architectural frame around him, however, is not realistic. His heels rest on the top step of a stair that clearly lies behind the columns and pedestals, but the rest of his body projects in front of them in a way that would cause a human to teeter and fall forward. The image suggests both the joyful promise of life in the hereafter and its sobering counterpart, the torments of hell for those found wanting in the eyes of God. The angel is shown here as a divine messenger, holding a staff of authority in his left hand and a sphere symbolizing worldly power in his right, a message reinforced by repetition: within the arch is a cross-topped orb, framed by a wreath, against the background of a scalloped-shell canopy.

Manuscripts, or handwritten books, were also commissioned by the Byzantine court. Among these was a botanical encyclopedia known by its Latin title, *De Materia Medica*, listing the appearance, properties, and medicinal uses of plants. The encyclopedia was compiled in the first century CE by a Greek physician named Pedanius Dioscorides (c. 40–c. 90), who probably traveled as a physician with the Roman army. His work was the first systematic treatment of such material and, in its time, was a highly regarded scientific treatise. Generations of scribes—professional document writers—copied it. The earliest known surviving copy, from Constantinople and dated to about 512, was given to Princess Anicia Juliana, whose father had been emperor in the West for a few months in 472. It is in codex form, consisting of individual sheets bound together on one side (see "Early Forms of the Book," above). The illustrators transformed what was a practical reference book in Greek into an exquisitely illustrated work suitable for the imperial library (fig. 7-36).

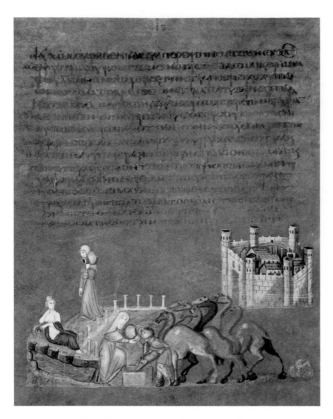

7-37. Page with *Rebecca at the Well*, from *Book of Genesis*, probably made in Syria or Palestine. Early 6th century. Tempera, gold, and silver paint on purple-dyed vellum, 13¼ x 9⅞" (33.7 x 25 cm). Österreichische National-bibliothek, Vienna

Although Dioscorides' work is secular and pagan, Christians found religious as well as medical significance in the plants it catalogs. For example, the wild blackberry bramble illustrated here came by tradition to represent the burning bush of Moses and the purity of the Virgin Mary.

Byzantine manuscripts often used very costly materials. Although plain sheets of **vellum** (a fine writing surface made from calfskin) and natural pigments were used in this copy of *De Materia Medica*, purple-dyed vellum and inks of gold and silver were used in a *Book of Genesis* (fig. 7-37). The book was probably made in Syria or Palestine, and the purple vellum indicates that it may have been for an imperial patron (costly purple dye, made from the shells of murex mollusks, often was restricted to imperial use). The Genesis book, like the *De Materia Medica*, is in codex form and written in Greek. Illustrations appear below the text at the bottom of the pages. The illustration of the story of Rebecca at the Well (Genesis 24) shown here appears to be a single scene, but it actually mimics the continuous narrative of a scroll. Events that take place at different times in the story follow in succession. Rebecca, the heroine of the story, appears at the left walking away from the walled city of Nahor with a large jug on her shoulder to fetch water. She walks along a miniature colonnaded road toward a spring personified by a reclining pagan water nymph with a flowing jar. In the foreground, Rebecca, her jug now full, encounters a thirsty camel driver and offers him

water to drink. Unknown to her, he is Abraham's servant Eliezer in search of a bride for Abraham's son Isaac. Her generosity leads to marriage with Isaac. Although the realistic poses and rounded, full-bodied figures in this painting reflect an earlier Roman painting tradition, the unnatural purple of the background and the glittering silver ink of the text act to remove the scene from the mundane world.

An illustrated Gospels, signed by a monk named Rabbula and completed in February 586 at the Monastery of Saint John the Evangelist in Beth Zagba, Syria, provides a near-contemporary example of a quite different approach to religious manuscript decoration. Its illustrations may have been inspired by church paintings and mosaics. They are intended not only to depict biblical events but also to present the Christian story through a complex, multileveled symbolism. Besides full-page illustrations like those of the Crucifixion and the Ascension shown here, there are also lively smaller scenes, or **vignettes**, in the margins.

The Crucifixion in the *Rabbula Gospels* presents a detailed picture of Christ's death and resurrection (fig. 7-38). He appears twice, on the cross in the center of the upper register and with the two Marys—the mother of James and Mary Magdalen—at the right in the lower register. The Byzantine Christ is a living king who triumphs over death. He is shown as a mature, bearded figure, not the youthful shepherd depicted in the catacombs. Even on the cross he is dressed in a long, purple robe, called a colobium, that signifies his royal status. (In many Byzantine images he also wears a jeweled crown.) At his sides are the repentant and unrepentant criminals who were supposedly crucified with him. Beside the thief at the left stand the Virgin and Saint John the Evangelist; beside the thief at the right are the holy women. Soldiers beneath the cross throw dice for Jesus' clothes. A centurion stands on either side of the cross. One of them, Longinus, pierces Jesus' side with a lance; the other, Stephaton, gives him vinegar instead of water to drink from a sponge. The small disks in the heavens represent the sun and moon. In the lower register, directly under Jesus on the cross, stands the tomb, with its open door and stunned or sleeping guards. This scene represents the Resurrection. The angel reassures the holy women at the left, and Christ himself appears to them at the right. All these events (described in Matthew 28) take place in an otherworldly setting indicated by the glowing bands of color in the sky. The austere mountains behind the crosses give way to the lush foliage of the garden around the tomb. This very complete representation of the orthodox view of the Crucifixion may have been intended to counter the claim of the Monophysites that Christ was entirely divine.

The ascension of Christ into heaven (fig. 7-39) is described in the New Testament: "[A]s they [his apostles] were looking on, he was lifted up, and a cloud took him from their sight" (Acts of the Apostles 1:9). The cloud has been transformed into a **mandorla** supported by two angels. Two other angels follow, holding victory crowns in fringed cloths. The image directly under the mandorla

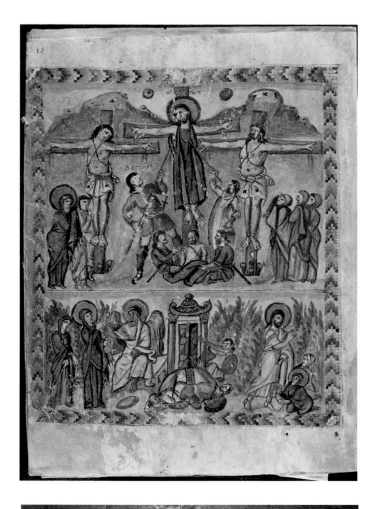

7-38. Page with *The Crucifixion,*
from the *Rabbula Gospels,*
from Beth Zagba, Syria. 586.
13¼ x 10½"(33.7 x 26.7 cm).
Biblioteca Medicea Lauren-
ziana, Florence

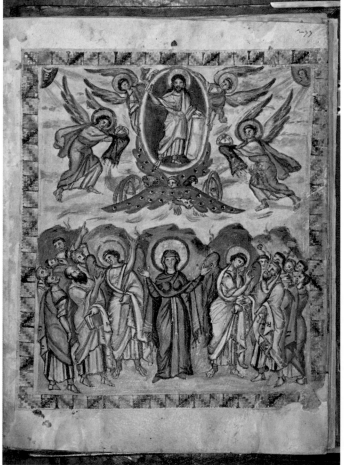

7-39. Page with *The Ascension,*
from the *Rabbula Gospels*

ICONOCLASM Christianity, like Judaism and Islam, has always been uneasy with the power of religious images. The early Church feared that the faithful would worship the works of art themselves instead of what they represented. This discomfort grew into a major controversy in the Eastern Church as images increasingly replaced holy relics as objects of devotion from the late sixth century on. Many **icons** were believed to have been created miraculously, and all were thought to have magical protective and healing powers. Prayer rituals came to include prostration before images surrounded by candles, practices that seemed to some dangerously close to idol worship.

In 726 Emperor Leo III launched a campaign of **iconoclasm** ("image breaking"), decreeing that all religious images were idols and should be destroyed. In the decades that followed, Iconoclasts undertook widespread destruction of devotional pictures of Jesus Christ, the Virgin Mary, and the saints. Those who defended devotional images (Iconodules) were persecuted. The veneration of images was briefly restored under Empress Irene following the Second Council of Nicaea in 787, but the Iconoclasts regained power in 814. In 843 Empress Theodora, widow of Theophilus, the last of the iconoclastic emperors, reversed her husband's policy.

While the Iconoclasts held power, they enhanced imperial authority at the expense of the Church by undermining the untaxed wealth and prestige of monasteries, whose great collections of devotional art drew thousands of worshipers. They also increased tensions between the Eastern Church and the papacy, which defended the veneration of images and refused to acknowledge the emperor's authority to ban it. The Iconoclasts claimed that representations of Jesus Christ, because they portrayed him as human, promoted heresy by separating his divine from his human nature or by misrepresenting the two natures as one. Iconodules countered that upon assuming human form as Jesus, God took on all human characteristics, including visibility. According to this view, images of Christ, testifying to that visibility, demonstrate faith in his dual nature and not, as the Iconoclasts claimed, denial of it: "How, indeed, can the Son of God be acknowledged to have been a man like us . . . if he cannot, like us, be depicted?" (Saint Theodore the Studite, cited in Snyder, page 128).

Those who defended images made a distinction between veneration—a respect for icons as representations of sacred personages—and worship of icons as embodiments of divinity, or idols. Moreover, they saw image making not only as an effective teaching tool but also as a humble parallel to the divine act of creation, when "God created man in his image" (Genesis 1:27).

---

combines fiery wheels and the four beasts of the Hebrew prophet Ezekiel's vision (Ezekiel 1). The four beasts also appear in the New Testament's Revelation and are associated with the Four Evangelists: Matthew, an angel; Mark, a lion; Luke, an ox; and John, an eagle. Christians interpreted this vision as a precursor of the vision of Judgment Day described in Revelation.

Below the vision, the Virgin Mary stands calmly in the pose of an orant, while angels at her side confront the astonished apostles. One angel gestures at the departing Christ and the other appears to be offering an explanation of the event to attentive listeners (Acts of the Apostles 1:10–11). The prominence accorded Mary here can be interpreted as a result of her status of Theotokos, or God-bearer. She may also represent the Christian community on earth, that is, the Church. As we noted earlier, the Christian world at this time was filled with debate over the exact natures of Christ, the Trinity, and the Virgin Mary. Taken as a whole, the *Rabbula Gospels* would provide evidence of the owner's adherence to orthodoxy.

Eastern Christians prayed to Christ, Mary, and the saints while looking at images of them on icons. The first such image was believed to have been a portrait of Jesus that appeared miraculously on the scarf with which Saint Veronica wiped his face along the road to the execution ground. Church doctrine toward the veneration of icons was ambivalent. Key figures of the Eastern Church, such as Saint Basil the Great of Cappadocia (c. 329–379) and Saint John of Damascus (c. 675–749), distinguished between idolatry—the worship of images—and the veneration of an idea or holy person depicted in a work of art. The Eastern Church thus prohibited the worship of icons but accepted them as aids to meditation and prayer. The images were thought to act as intermediaries between worshipers and the holy personages they depicted.

Most early icons were destroyed in the eighth century in a reaction to the veneration of images known as iconoclasm (see "Iconoclasm," above), making those that have survived especially precious. A few very beautiful examples were preserved in the Monastery of Saint Catherine on Mount Sinai, among them the *Virgin and Child with Saints and Angels* (fig. 7-40). As Theotokos, Mary was viewed as the powerful, ever-forgiving intercessor, or go-between, appealing to her Divine Son for mercy on behalf of repentant worshipers. She was also called the Seat of Wisdom, and many images of the Virgin and Child, like this one, show her holding Jesus on her lap in a way that suggests that she represents the throne of Solomon. The Christian warrior-saints Theodore (left) and George (right)—both legendary figures said to have slain dragons, representing the triumph of the Church over the "evil serpent" of paganism—stand at each side, while angels behind them look heavenward. The artist who painted the Christ Child, the Virgin, and the angels worked in a Roman-derived, illusionistic technique and created almost realistic figures. The male saints are much more stylized; this artist barely hints at real bodies beneath the richly patterned textiles of their cloaks.

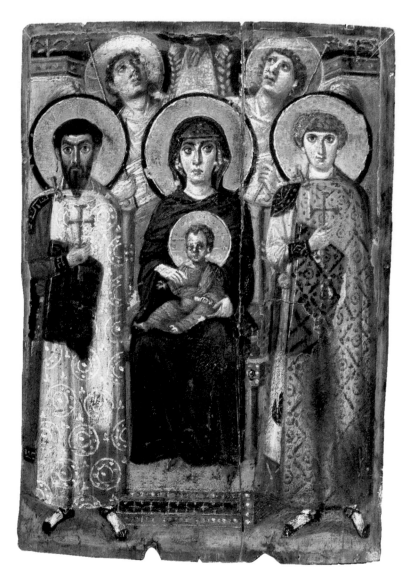

7-40. *Virgin and Child with Saints and Angels*, icon, Monastery of Saint Catherine, Mount Sinai, Egypt. Second half of 6th century. Encaustic on wood, 27 x 18⁷/₈" (69 x 48 cm)

LATER BYZANTINE ART

Byzantine Christian art enjoyed three major productive phases. The first golden age began with the reign of Justinian I in the sixth century and centered on Constantinople, ending in the eighth century, when the Iconoclasts rose to power in the Eastern Church. A second golden age began in 867 under the Macedonian dynasty and lasted until Christian Crusaders from the West occupied Constantinople in 1204 (Chapter 15). Byzantine culture flourished again in the fourteenth and early fifteenth centuries until Constantinople was conquered by Muslim Ottoman Turks in 1453. Because Byzantine art was the art of the Eastern Orthodox Church, it spread with Christianity through eastern Europe and became the source for national styles that still exist today. The Byzantine artistic tradition was, in the words of one scholar, "monumental, kaleidoscopic, constantly open to fashion, energizing and far-reaching" (Beckwith, page 344).

Architecture and Its Decoration

When Constantinople became a Muslim city in 1453, many of its churches were destroyed or extensively rebuilt, but enough remain to give us an idea of what the city's Christian architecture looked like during the preceding centuries. Many central-plan domed churches, so favored by Byzantine architects, also survived in outlying regions. These structures exhibit the builders' taste for a multiplicity of geometric forms, verticality, and rich, decorative effects both inside and out. Some of the earliest surviving examples, abandoned and partially ruined today, are in ancient Armenia, a land fought over for much of its history by the various empires surrounding it. Christianity arrived very early in this region and became so entrenched that foreign traders traveling the east-west Silk Road in the seventh century called its capital, Ani, the "city of a thousand and one churches." The Armenian Orthodox Church was separate from the Eastern Orthodox

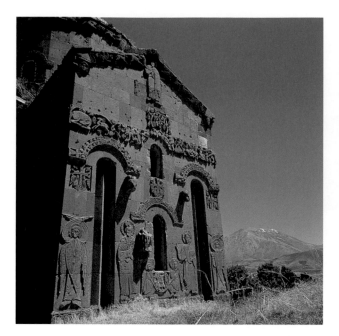

7-41. Church of the Holy Cross, Isle of Aght'amar, Lake Van, Armenia (modern Turkey). 915–21

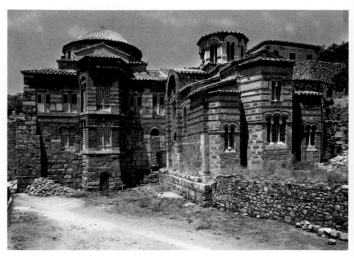

7-42. Churches of the Monastery of Hosios Loukas, near Stiris, Greece. Katholikon (left), early 11th century; Church of the Virgin Theotokos (right), 10th century

Church, and the two architectural styles, while sharing certain features, sometimes diverged markedly.

One of the most exceptional Armenian central-plan domed churches is the Church of the Holy Cross, built between 915 and 921 on the Isle of Aght'amar in Lake Van in eastern Asia Minor (fig. 7-41). Originally part of a luxurious royal complex, the church was the product of the unusual and sophisticated taste of King Gagik of Vaspurakan (ruled 900/904–937). To build it, the king brought artisans "who came from every land" (cited in Thierry, page 173). A profusion of exterior stone sculpture is carved directly into the building blocks. Included are stylized figures in low, almost flat, relief; frieze bands in higher relief with deep undercutting; and fully three-dimensional projecting animal heads. King Gagik is shown at the bottom, to the left of the center window, holding a nearly three-dimensional model of the church. Interestingly, Gagik is taller and more impressive in his wreathlike halo and patterned robes than Christ on the right. Various saints and archangels surround the bottom of the building, and two frieze bands, one above the arched openings and the other running under the eaves, show animals amid grapevines, a reminder of the heavenly paradise.

The two Churches of the Monastery of Hosios Loukas, built a few miles from the village of Stiris, Greece, in the tenth and eleventh centuries, provide excellent examples of the architecture of the second Byzantine golden age (figs. 7-42, 7-43). The Church of the Virgin Theotokos, on the right in the illustration, is joined to the Katholikon, on the left. Both churches are essentially compact, central-plan structures. Their exterior decoration is striking—light-colored stone and red brick arranged in decorative patterns. This style of decoration is known as cloisonné because the courses of brick outline the stone blocks and set them off like the fine-line

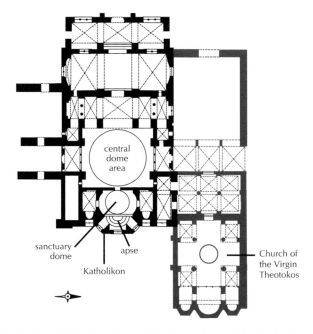

7-43. Plan of the Churches of the Monastery of Hosios Loukas

partitions (cloisons) in enamelwork. The dome of the Theotokos rises on pendentives over a square core; that of the Katholikon rises on squinches and an octagonal core. (Squinches, like pendentives, are devices for supporting a dome on a square base; see "Elements of Architecture," page 310.) The domes are enriched by high vaults covering interior bays. Narthexes and tall sanctuary apses with flanking rooms further complicate the space.

The high central space in the interior of the Katholikon carries the eye of the worshiper upward into the main dome, which soars above a ring of tall arched windows (fig. 7-44). Unlike Hagia Sophia, with its clear, sweeping geometric forms, the two churches of Hosios Loukas have a complex variety of forms, including domes, groin vaults, barrel vaults, pendentives, and

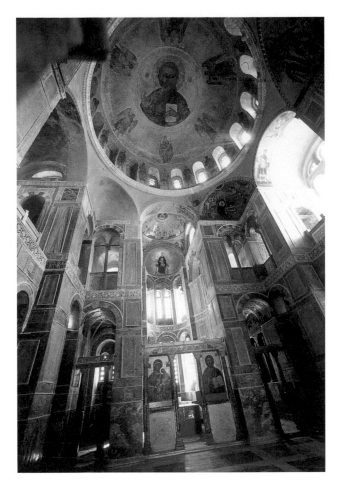

7-44. Central dome and apse, Katholikon, Monastery of Hosios Loukas. Early 11th century and later

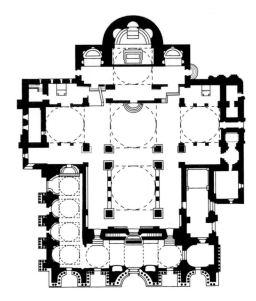

7-45. Plan of the Cathedral of San Marco, Venice. Begun 1063

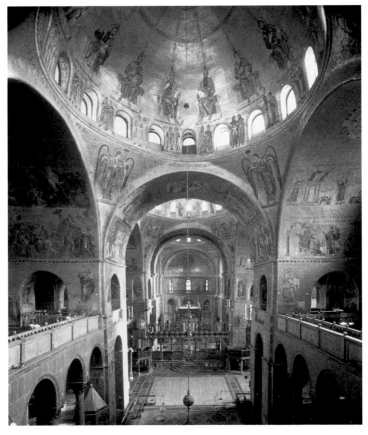

7-46. Cathedral of San Marco. View looking toward apse

The church is the third one built on the site. It is both the palace chapel and the martyrium where the bones of the patron of Venice, Saint Mark, are preserved. This great multidomed structure, consecrated as the Venice Cathedral in 1807, has been reworked continually, right to the present day.

squinches. (The squinches in the Katholikon are the small, fan-shaped niches above the corners of the lower walls.) Single, double, and triple windows create intricate and unusual patterns of light, illuminating a painting (originally a mosaic) of Christ Pantokrator, Ruler of the Universe, in the center of the main dome. The secondary, sanctuary dome of the Katholikon is decorated with a mosaic of the Lamb of God surrounded by the Twelve Apostles, and the apse conch has a mosaic of the Virgin and Child. Scenes from the Old and New Testaments and figures of saints fill the interior with brilliant color and dramatic images.

At the end of the tenth century, Constantinople granted the northeastern Italian city of Venice, already a dominant sea power in the Adriatic, a special trade status that allowed its merchants to control much of the commercial interchange between the East and the West. Venetian architects looked to the Byzantine domed church for inspiration when the city's ruler, the doge, commissioned a much larger church to replace the palace chapel in 1063. This chapel had served since the ninth century as a **martyrium**, holding the relics of the martyr Saint Mark the Apostle, which were brought to Venice from Alexandria in the ninth century. The Cathedral of San Marco has a Greek-cross plan, each square unit of which is covered by a dome (fig. 7-45). There are five great domes in all, separated by barrel vaults and

supported by pendentives. Unlike Hagia Sophia, with its flow of space from the narthex through the nave to the apse (see fig. 7-27), San Marco's domed compartments—covered with golden mosaics—produce a complex space with five vertical axes (fig. 7-46).

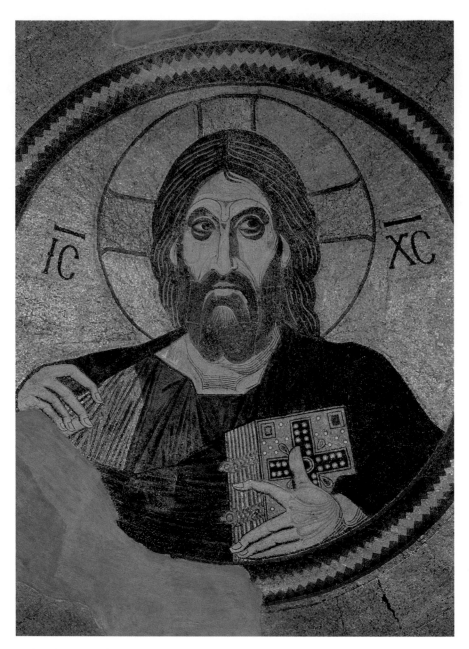

7-47. *Christ Pantokrator*, mosaic in the central dome, Church of the Dormition, Daphni, Greece. Central dome, c. 1080–1100

Eleventh-century mosaicists looked with renewed interest at models from the past, studying both classical art and the art of the Justinian era. They conceived their compositions in terms of an intellectual rather than a physical ideal. While representing the human figure and narrative subjects, some artists eliminated all unnecessary details, focusing on the essential elements of a scene to convey its mood and message. Other artists seemed absorbed in depicting anecdotal details, so that well-proportioned figures clothed in form-defining garments might also have draperies with patterns of geometric folds and jagged, flying ends bearing no relation to gravity. Instead of modeling forms with subtle tonal gradations, artists often relied on strong juxtapositions of light and dark areas.

The decoration of the Church of the Dormition at Daphni, Greece, provides an excellent eleventh-century example of these developments. (The term *dormition*—which comes from the Latin word for "sleep," which, in turn, derives from the Greek word for "sleep"—refers to the ascension to heaven of the Virgin Mary at the moment of her death.) The *Christ Pantokrator*, a bust-length mosaic portrayal, fills the central dome of the church (fig. 7-47). This awe-inspiring image, hovering in golden glory, is more than a picture of the Christian Savior; it is a powerful evocation of his promised judgment, with its reward for the faithful and punishment for sinners.

On a wall in the north arm of the church is an image of Christ crucified (fig. 7-48). Jesus is shown with bowed head and sagging body, his eyes closed in death. Gone is the royal robe; a nearly nude figure hangs on the cross. Unlike the Crucifixion scene in the sixth-century *Rabbula Gospels*, which depicts many people, some anguished

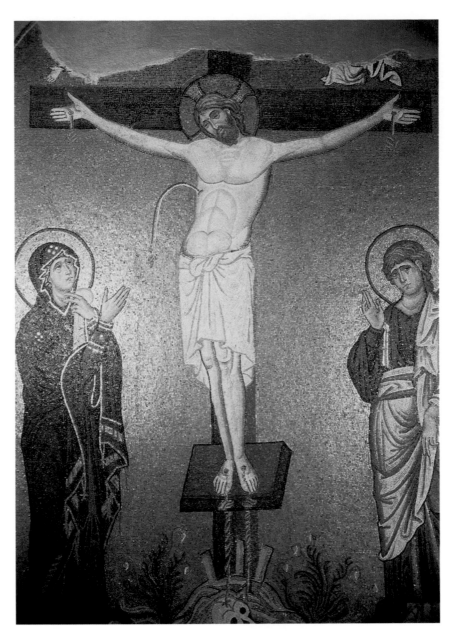

7-48. *Crucifixion*, mosaic in the north arm of the east wall, Church of the Dormition

and others indifferent or hostile (see fig. 7-38), the artist of this image shows just two other figures, Mary and the young apostle John, to whom Jesus had entrusted the care of his mother after his death. John cannot hide his grief, but Mary, gesturing toward Christ, seems briefly to have overcome hers. The arc of blood and water springing from Jesus' side refers to the Eucharist. The simplification of contours and reduction of forms to essentials give the image great emotional power. It conveys a sense of timelessness and otherworldly space, a golden universe anchored to the material world by a few flowers, which suggest the promise of new life. The mound of rocks and the skull at the bottom of the cross represent Golgotha, the "place of the skull," a hill outside ancient Jerusalem where Adam was thought to be buried and the Crucifixion was said to have taken place. To the faithful, Jesus Christ was the new Adam sent by God to save

humanity through his own sacrifice. As Paul wrote in his First Letter to the Corinthians: "For just as in Adam all die, so too in Christ shall all be brought to life" (I Corinthians 15:22). The timelessness and simplicity of the image aid the Christian worshiper seeking to achieve a mystical union with the divine through prayer and meditation.

Other notable mosaics were created on the island of Sicily, a crossroads of Byzantine, Muslim, and European influence. Sicily was ruled by Muslims from 827 to the end of the eleventh century, when it fell to the Normans, descendants of the Viking settlers of northern France. The Norman Roger II (ruled 1105–1154) was crowned king in Palermo in 1130, and the pope, who assumed ecclesiastical jurisdiction over Sicily for "God and Saint Peter," endorsed Norman rule. In the first half of the twelfth century, Sicily became one of the richest and most enlightened kingdoms in Europe. Roger II extended

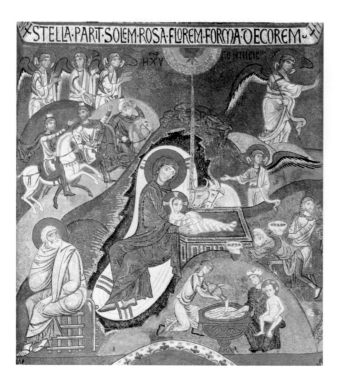

7-49. Nativity, wall mosaic in the Palatine Chapel, Palermo, Sicily. c. 1140–89

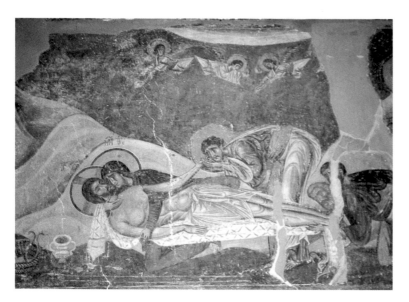

7-50. Lamentation, fresco in the Church of Saint Panteleimon, Nerezi, near Skopje, Republic of Macedonia. c. 1164

religious toleration to the kingdom's diverse population, which included Latins, Greeks, Arabs, and Jews. He involved all factions in his government, permitted everyone to participate equally in the kingdom's economy, and issued official documents in Latin, Greek, and Arabic.

Roger's court in his capital city of Palermo was a brilliant and exotic mixture of Norman, Muslim, and Byzantine cultures. The Palatine (palace) Chapel there reflects this diversity. The Western-style basilica-plan church has a Byzantine dome on squinches over the crossing.

An Islamic-style timber ceiling, inlaid marble floor and lower walls, and mosaic upper walls dramatically combine classical, Islamic, and Byzantine elements into an exotic whole.

Of special interest are the mosaic decorations completed between about 1140 and 1189 using the Byzantine style and technique but showing a Western preference for narrative over iconic images (fig. 7-49). In a wall mosaic, the Nativity story's events have been transformed into an exciting multipart drama, with each scene isolated by the rhythmic contours of hillocks and caves. At the center is the cave that, in the Eastern tradition, was the birthplace of Jesus. Mary lies on a mattress and supports the newborn Jesus on a solid, altarlike manger, where he is adored by the ox and the ass, symbols for Jews and Christians. At the lower right, the two midwives who had assisted at the birth are preparing a basin of water to bathe the baby. At the upper left, three angels seem to urge the Magi forward while pointing at the Star of Bethlehem, from which a single ray descends to the infant Jesus. The angel at the upper right has just announced the birth to three shepherds who appear in an extension of the mosaic on a neighboring wall, not shown here, at a right angle to this one. Two of the Magi appear a second time at the right presenting their gifts (the third is on the wall with the shepherds). Only Joseph at the lower left sits alone, lost in quiet contemplation of the miraculous events.

When money was no object, mosaic was the medium of choice for Byzantine wall decorations, but the less expensive and less durable medium of wall painting was also used effectively in many places. Paintings cover the walls of the small domed church dedicated to Saint Panteleimon on a mountainside near the Macedonian city of Skopje. Built in about 1164 under a distant relative of Emperor Alexios I, the church may have been decorated by painters from a major center working with local artists. Among the finest paintings is the *Lamentation*, a scene showing the body of the crucified Jesus mourned by his mother, John, Peter, and perhaps Joseph of Arimathea, the wealthy man who offered his nearby mausoleum to house the body (fig. 7-50). The tension and quietude of this scene, which evoke the repressed feelings of the mourners for the untimely loss of a son, a friend, and a leader, contrast with the joyful bustle surrounding the Palermo *Nativity*. The horizontal composition emphasizes the prostrate form of the dead Jesus, and the repetition of rounded backs and rounded hills seems to make visible the waves of emotion sweeping over the living participants. The tender gestures of Mary pressing her cheek to her dead son's and John kissing his limp hand also convey the intensity of the moment. Because it evokes a powerful emotional rather than an intellectual response, the work is said to be **expressionistic**.

The third golden age of Byzantine art began after Western Crusaders, who had occupied Constantinople in 1204, were expelled from the city in 1261. The patronage of emperors, wealthy courtiers, and the Church stimulated renewed church building. In this new work, the physical requirements of the clergy and the liturgy took

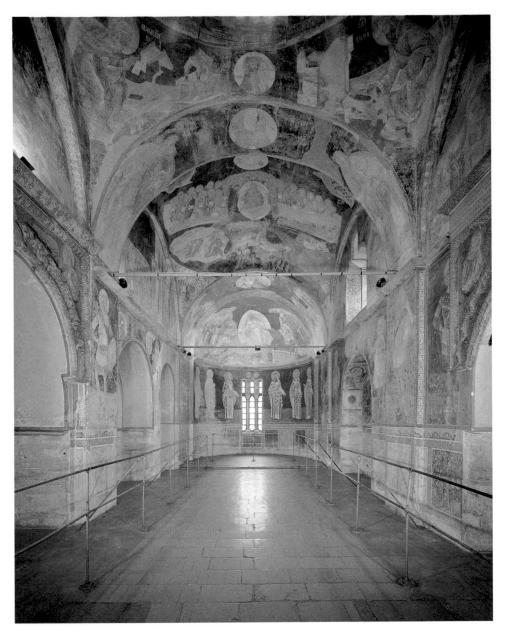

7-51. Funerary chapel, Church of the Monastery of Christ in Chora (now Kariye djami), Istanbul, Turkey. c. 1315–21

precedence over costly interior decorations. The buildings, nevertheless, often reflect excellent construction skills and elegant and refined design.

New ambulatory aisles, narthexes, and side chapels were added to many small, existing churches. Among these is the former Church of the Monastery of Christ in Chora, Constantinople, now a mosque known as Kariye djami. The expansion of this church was one of several projects that Theodore Metochites, the administrator of the Imperial Treasury at Constantinople, sponsored between 1315 and 1321. A humanist, poet, and scientist, Metochites became a monk in this monastery sometime after 1330. He added a two-story annex to its church on the north side, two narthexes on the west side, and a funerary chapel on the south side. These structures contain the most impressive interior decorations remaining in Constantinople from the late Byzantine period.

The funerary chapel is entirely painted (fig. 7-51). The resurrection of Christ, depicted in the apse conch, and the Last Judgment, painted on the ceiling vault, are themes appropriate to a funerary chapel. Large figures of the church fathers (a group of especially revered early Christian writers of the history and teachings of the Church), saints, and martyrs line the walls below. Sarcophagi, surmounted by portraits of the deceased, once stood in the side niches. Trompe l'oeil ("fool the eye") painting imitates marble panels in the surrounding **dado**. The painters bound their pigments with oil or egg and applied them directly over fresh wet plaster. This frescolike technique allowed rapid work and produced rich colors.

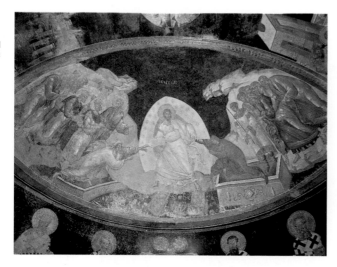

7-52. *Anastasis*, painting in the apse of the funerary chapel, Church of the Monastery of Christ in Chora

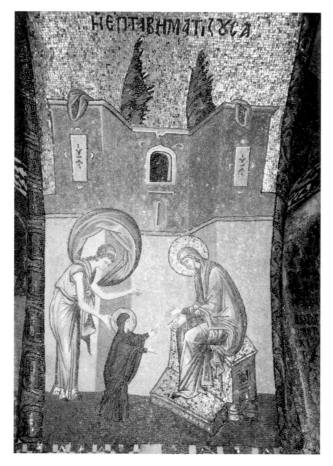

7-53. *The First Steps of Mary*, mosaic in the inner narthex, Church of the Monastery of Christ in Chora

A painting of the Resurrection known as the *Anastasis* fills the funerary chapel's apse vault (fig. 7-52). Artists in the West usually depicted the Resurrection as the Triumphant Christ (*Christus Triumphans*) emerging from his tomb in glory. The *Anastasis*, instead, depicts Christ's Harrowing of Hell to rescue Adam and Eve and other devout people from Satan. Christ appears as a savior in white,

moving with such force that even his star-studded mandorla has been set awry. He has trampled down the doors of hell; tied Satan into a helpless bundle; and shattered locks, chains, and bolts, which lie scattered over the ground. He drags the elderly Adam and Eve from their open sarcophagi with such force that their bodies seem airborne. Behind him are Old Testament prophets and kings, as well as his cousin John the Baptist.

In the inner narthex of the church, mosaics depicting scenes from the life of the Virgin Mary, a popular medieval cycle that included many subjects taken from popular tradition rather than from the Bible, fill the upper walls and vaults. Among them is a touching portrayal of Mary as an infant just learning to walk (fig. 7-53). The child, who appears as a tiny adult swathed in the dark draperies she will be shown wearing in later life, totters away from her nurse toward the encouraging arms of her mother, Anna (Saint Anne). The gestures and movement of the figures, although drawn with the exaggerated, elongated proportions and angular drapery of the late Byzantine style, create a mood of amused tenderness. The swinging draperies reinforce the curving arcs of the women's bodies, which along with the architectural elements form a protective, enfolding screen around the insecure toddler.

Constantinople had close ties with Russia, and Christianity was introduced there in the late tenth century. Orthodox churches in Russia followed the traditional Byzantine plan of a dome over a Greek cross. Over the centuries the Russian preference for complexity and height led to a spectacular architectural style epitomized by the Cathedral of Saint Basil the Blessed in Moscow (fig. 7-54). Originally dedicated to the Intercession of the Virgin Mary, it was rededicated to Saint Basil the Blessed. The first Russian czar, Ivan IV, known as the Terrible (1530–1584), commissioned the church, and the architects Barma and Postnik designed it. Construction took place between 1555 and 1561. One of its most striking features is its combination of a Byzantine domed church with the steeply pitched Russian tent roof form called a **shater**, which kept dangerously large accumulations of snow from forming. The large, central *shater* seems to have spawned a brood of lesser domes of varying sizes. The multiplication of shapes and sizes and the layering of the surfaces with geometric relief elements all work to distract us from the underlying central plan—a central building surrounded by four arms ending in domed octagons and four domed cubical areas (fig. 7-55). Such an arrangement, a square with four corner units plus a center unit, is called a **quincunx**. Each of the exterior units has its own tall drum and a dome that seems to grow budlike from a tall, slender stalk. This spectacular church shows the evolution of Byzantine art into a distinctly national style found in later Russian Orthodox churches elsewhere, including the United States.

Ivories and Metalwork

During the second Byzantine golden age, from 867 to the Crusaders' occupation of Constantinople in 1204, artists

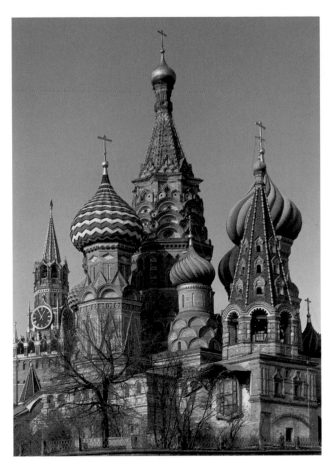

7-54. Barma and Postnik. Cathedral of Saint Basil the Blessed, Moscow. 1555–61

Like most mid-sixteenth-century Russian churches, the entire exterior of Saint Basil's was originally painted white, and the domes were gilded. The bright colors we see today were added by later generations. The name of the church has also changed. It was originally dedicated to the Intercession of the Virgin Mary, a reflection of the veneration of Mary in the Eastern Church.

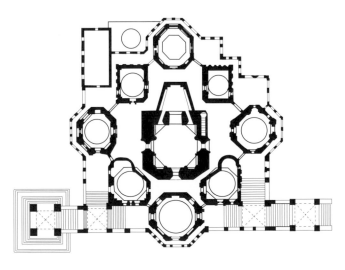

7-55. Plan of the Cathedral of Saint Basil the Blessed

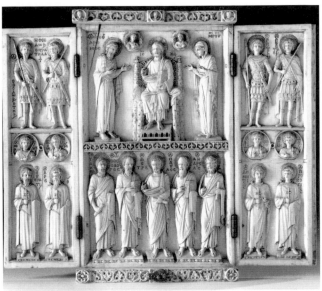

7-56. *Harbaville Triptych*. Late 10th century. Ivory, 11 x 9½" closed (28 x 24.1 cm). Musée du Louvre, Paris

of impeccable ability and high aesthetic sensibility produced small luxury items of a personal nature for members of the court as well as for the Church. Many of these items were commissioned by rulers and high secular and church functionaries as official gifts for one another. As such they had to be portable, sturdy, and exquisitely refined. In style these works tended to combine classical elements with iconic compositions, successfully joining simple beauty and religious meaning. Such a piece is the *Harbaville Triptych*, dating from the late tenth century (fig. 7-56). This small ivory devotional piece represents Christ flanked by Mary and Saint John the Baptist, a group known as **Deesis**. The saints act as intercessors on behalf of worshipers. The figures exist in a neutral space given definition only by the small bases under the feet of the saints and by Christ's throne. Although conceived as essentially frontal and rigid, the figures have rounded shoulders, thighs, and knees that suggest physical substance beneath a linear, decorative drapery.

The refined taste and skillful work that characterize the arts of the eleventh and twelfth centuries were also expressed in precious materials such as silver and gold. One of the prizes the Crusaders took back to Venice in 1204, after their sack of Constantinople, was a silver-gilt and enamel icon of the archangel Michael. The icon was presumably made in the tenth century in a court workshop (fig. 7-57). The angel's head and hands, executed in relief, are surrounded by intricate relief and enamel decoration. Halo, wings, and liturgical garments are in delicate **cloisonné** and the framing borders are inset with enamel **roundels** (see "Byzantine Metalworking," page 333). The colorful brilliance of the patterned setting removes the image from the physical world, although the archangel appears here in essentially the same frontal pose and with the same idealized and timeless youthfulness with which he was portrayed in a sixth-century ivory panel (see fig. 7-35). The sheer artistry of this icon

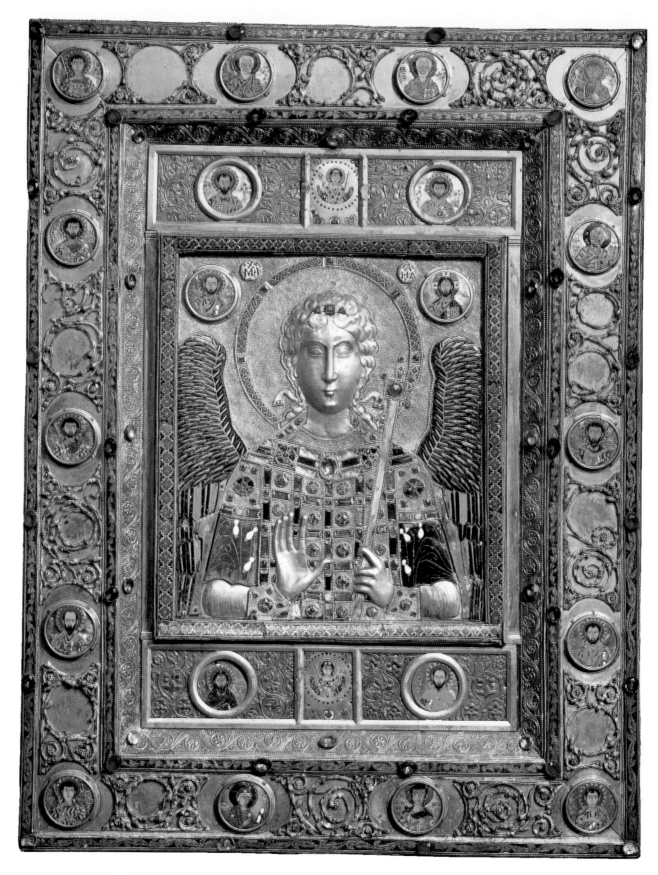

7-57. *Archangel Michael*, icon. 10th century. Silver gilt and enamel, 19 x 14" (48 x 36 cm). Treasury of the Cathedral of San Marco, Venice

TECHNIQUE

BYZANTINE METAL-WORKING

Byzantine metalworkers and enamelers had an international reputation for their high-quality work. They were particularly skilled in the use of **cloisonné** enamel, which is produced by soldering a network of fine copper, gold, or silver wires in a desired pattern to a panel made of similar metal and then filling up the cells (**cloisons**) with powdered colored glass. When the object is heated, the glass powder melts and fuses onto the surface of the metal to create small, jewellike sections.

The icon of Archangel Michael (fig. 7-57) is an especially elaborate example of Byzantine metalwork. Using the **repoussé** technique, the artists pounded out the central image of the archangel from the back of a thin plate of silver. The silver was then gilded. Colorful cloisonné creates the effect of silk garments with jewels, and small cloisonné portrait medallions decorate the border. Such medallions are often found detached from their original context and incorporated into new works.

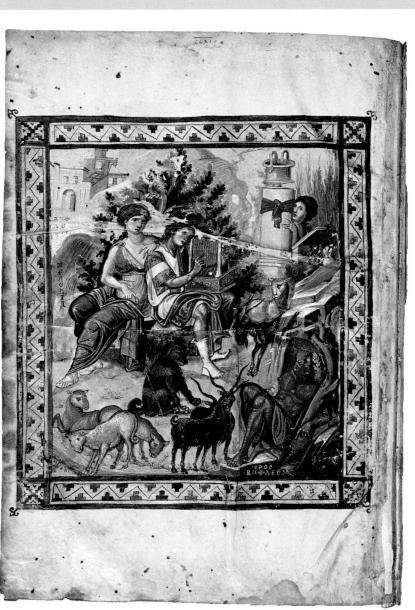

7-58. Page with *David the Psalmist*, from the *Paris Psalter*. Mid-10th century. Paint on vellum, sheet size 14 x 10¼" (35.6 x 26 cm). Bibliothèque Nationale, Paris

About a third of the Old Testament was written in poetry, and among its most famous poems are those in the Book of Psalms. According to ancient tradition, the author of the Psalms was King David himself, the young shepherd and musician who killed the Philistine giant Goliath and later became king of Israel. In Christian times, the Psalms were also copied into a book called a Psalter, used for private reading and meditation. *Psalm* and *Psalter* come from a word meaning the sound or action of playing a stringed instrument (the psaltery).

seems to lift the image to a lofty plane where light and color supplant form and material substance becomes pure spirit, an effect valued by the Neoplatonic Church philosophers of the time.

Manuscripts

Several luxuriously illustrated manuscripts have survived from the second golden age. As was true of the artists who decorated church interiors, the illustrators of these manuscripts combined intense religious expression, aristocratic elegance, and a heightened appreciation for rich decorative forms. The *Paris Psalter* from the mid-tenth century is one example (fig. 7-58). Like the earlier *Rabbula Gospels* (see figs. 7-38, 7-39), the Psalter (a version of the Psalms) includes scenes set off in frames on pages without text. Fourteen full-page paintings illustrate the *Paris Psalter*, the first of which is devoted to

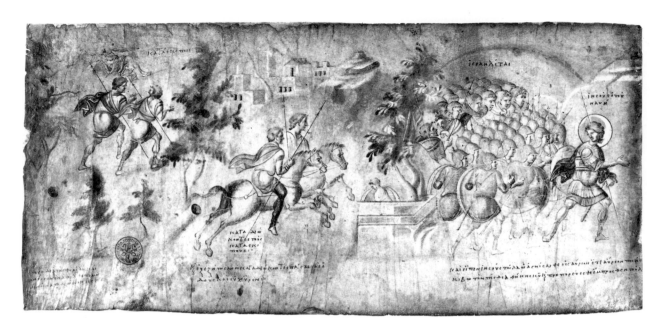

7-59. Page with *Joshua Leading the Israelites,* from the *Joshua Roll,* made in Constantinople. 10th century. Vellum rotulus with brown ink and colored washes, height of scroll 12¾" (32.4 cm). Biblioteca Apostolica Vaticana, Rome

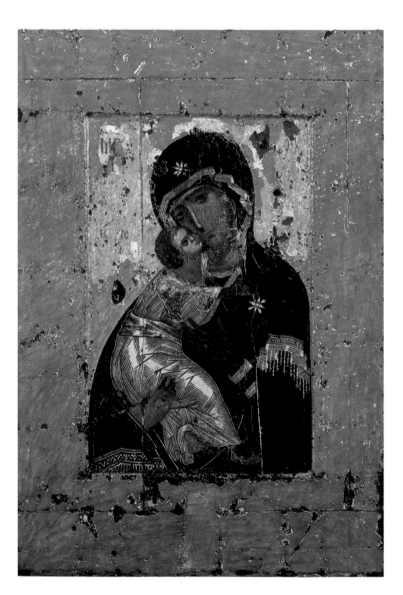

David, the Israelite king, traditionally the author of the Old Testament's Book of Psalms. The illuminators turned to earlier classical illustrations as source material. The idealized, massive, three-dimensional figures reside in a receding space with lush foliage and a meandering stream that seem directly transported from a Roman "sacred landscape" (see fig. 6-47). The architecture of the city and the ribbon-tied memorial column also derive from conventions in Greek and Roman funerary art, and in the ancient manner, the illustrator has personified abstract ideas and landscape features, an artistic technique known as **allegory**. Melody, a female figure, leans casually on David's shoulder, while another woman, perhaps the wood nymph Echo, peeks out from behind the column. The reclining youth in the lower foreground is a personification of Mount Bethlehem, as we learn from his inscription. The dog watching over the sheep and goats while his master strums the harp suggests the classical subject of Orpheus's charming the wild animals with music. The subtle modeling of forms, the integration of the figures into a three-dimensional space, and the use of **atmospheric perspective** all enhance the classical flavor of the painting.

The *Joshua Roll* (fig. 7-59), a tenth-century manuscript in scroll form also believed to have been created in a Constantinople **scriptorium** (writing room for scribes), reflects an approach different from that of the *Paris Psalter.* The illustrators worked on plain vellum, using ink and colored washes to convey the exploits of Moses' suc-

7-60. *Virgin of Vladimir,* icon, probably from Constantinople. Faces only, 12th century; the rest has been retouched. Tempera on panel, height approx. 31" (78 cm). Tretyakov Gallery, Moscow

cessor, Joshua, the Old Testament hero of the Battle of Jericho (Joshua 6:1–20), who conquered the promised land and whom Christians considered a precursor of Christ. In the section shown here, the events described in the text are depicted in a continuous landscape that recedes from the large foreground figures to distant cities and landforms. Strategically placed labels within the pictures identify the figures. The main character, Joshua, is at the far right. Crowned with a halo, unhelmeted but wearing upper-body armor, he leads his soldiers toward the Jordan River. Despite its stylization, this painting, too, serves as a reminder of the classical roots of Byzantine culture.

Painted Icons

The distinction drawn in Church doctrine between the worship of images, which was forbidden as idolatry, and the veneration of the idea or person they represented was frequently lost on the laity, many of whom attributed miraculous powers to icons. A new way of portraying the Virgin and Child in Byzantine art that emerged in the eleventh and twelfth centuries reflects a growing desire for a more immediate and personal religion. (A similar trend was seen in the art of western Europe about the same time.) Paintings of this type, known as the Virgin of Compassion, show Mary and the Christ Child pressing their cheeks together and gazing tenderly at each other. The source for this humanized portrayal was widely thought to be a portrait painted by the evangelist Luke following a vision he had of the Nativity. An icon of this type known as the *Virgin of Vladimir* remains to this day perhaps the most revered holy image in Russia (fig. 7-60). Some worshipers believed it to be the very painting done by Luke. Almost from its creation (probably in Constantinople) the panel was thought to protect the people of the city where it resided. It arrived in Kiev sometime between 1131 and 1136 and was moved to the city of Suzdal and then to Vladimir in 1155. In 1480 it was moved permanently to Moscow, where it graced the Cathedral of the Dormition in the Kremlin.

Another remarkable icon, this one from the third period in Byzantine art, is *The Old Testament Trinity (Three Angels Visiting Abraham)*, a large panel created between 1410 and 1420 by the famed artist-monk Andrey Rublyov (fig. 7-61). It was commissioned in honor of the abbot Sergius of the Trinity-Sergius Monastery, near Moscow. This icon clearly illustrates how late Byzantine artists relied on time-honored mathematical conventions to create ideal figures, as did the ancient Greeks, thus giving their work remarkable consistency. Unlike the Greeks, who based their formulas on close observation of nature, Byzantine artists invented an ideal geometry and depicted human forms and features according to it. Here the circle forms the underlying geometric figure, emphasized by

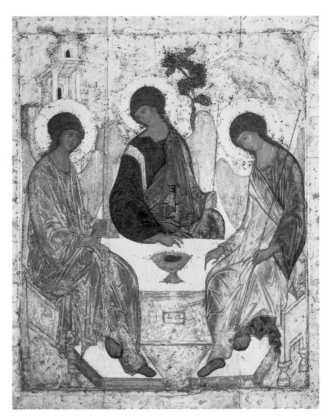

7-61. Andrey Rublyov. *The Old Testament Trinity (Three Angels Visiting Abraham)*, icon. c. 1410–20. Tempera on panel, 55½ x 44½" (141 x 113 cm). Tretyakov Gallery, Moscow

Representing the dogma of the Trinity—one God in three Persons—was a great challenge to artists. One solution, used here and in other late-medieval work, was to show God as three identical individuals and to use an event in the Old Testament, the story of the Hebrew patriarch Abraham and his wife, Sarah, who entertained three strangers who were in fact divine beings.

the form of the haloed heads. Although this formulaic approach imposed a basic uniformity, talented artists like Rublyov managed, nevertheless, to create a personal style of expression within it. To capture the sense of the spiritual in his work, Rublyov relied on typical conventions—simple contours, elongation of the body, and a focus on a limited number of characters—such as those in the mosaics at Daphni (see figs. 7-47, 7-48). Yet a sweet, poetic ambience distinguishes Rublyov's work.

In this artist's hands, the Byzantine style took on new life just as western European artists were beginning a classically inspired revivalist movement called the Renaissance. During the same period in the East, Constantinople was overrun by the forces of the Ottoman sultan Muhammad II, and the Eastern Empire became part of the Islamic world, with its own very rich aesthetic heritage.

Dome of the Rock
c. 687–91

Great Mosque
at Córdoba
785–86

▲ EARLY CALIPHS 633–61   UMAYYAD
                          ▲ DYNASTY 661–750   ▲ ABBASID DYNASTY 750–1258

▲ SPANISH UMAYYAD DYNASTY (756–1031)   ▲ ANATOLIAN SELJUK
                                                                   DYNASTY (1037–1194)

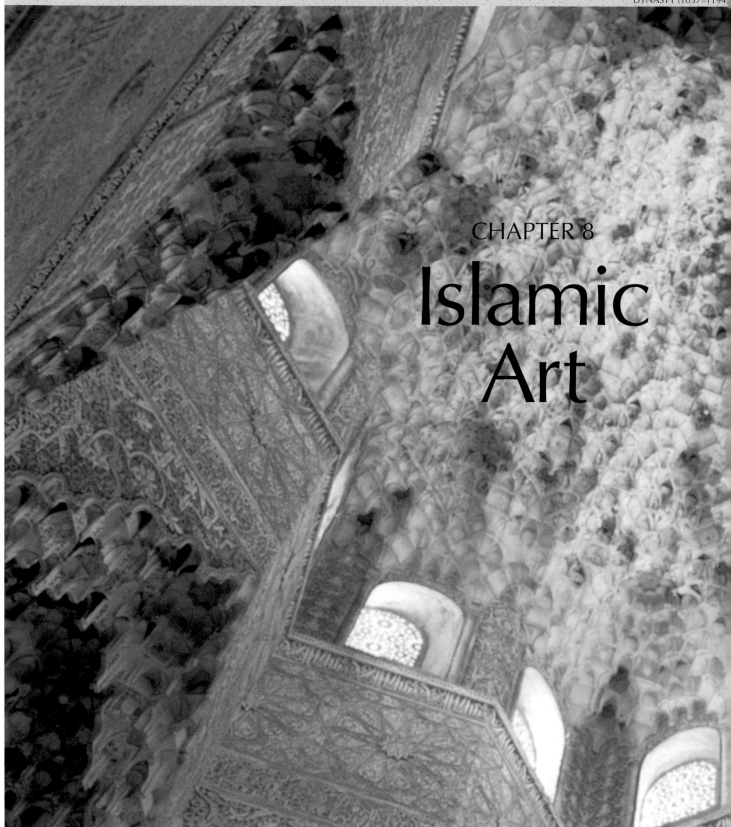

CHAPTER 8

Islamic Art

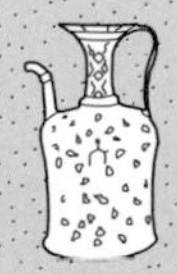

Seljuk pitcher
early 13th century

Tugra
c. 1555–60

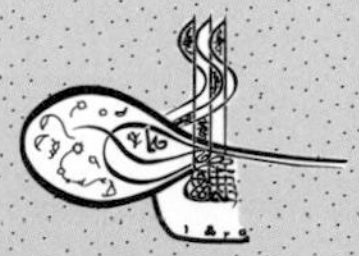

▲ OTTOMAN EMPIRE 1290–1918
▲ EGYPTIAN MAMLUK DYNASTY (1252–1517)
▲ SPANISH NASRID DYNASTY (1232–1492)   ▲ TURKIC TIMURID DYNASTY (1370–1507)

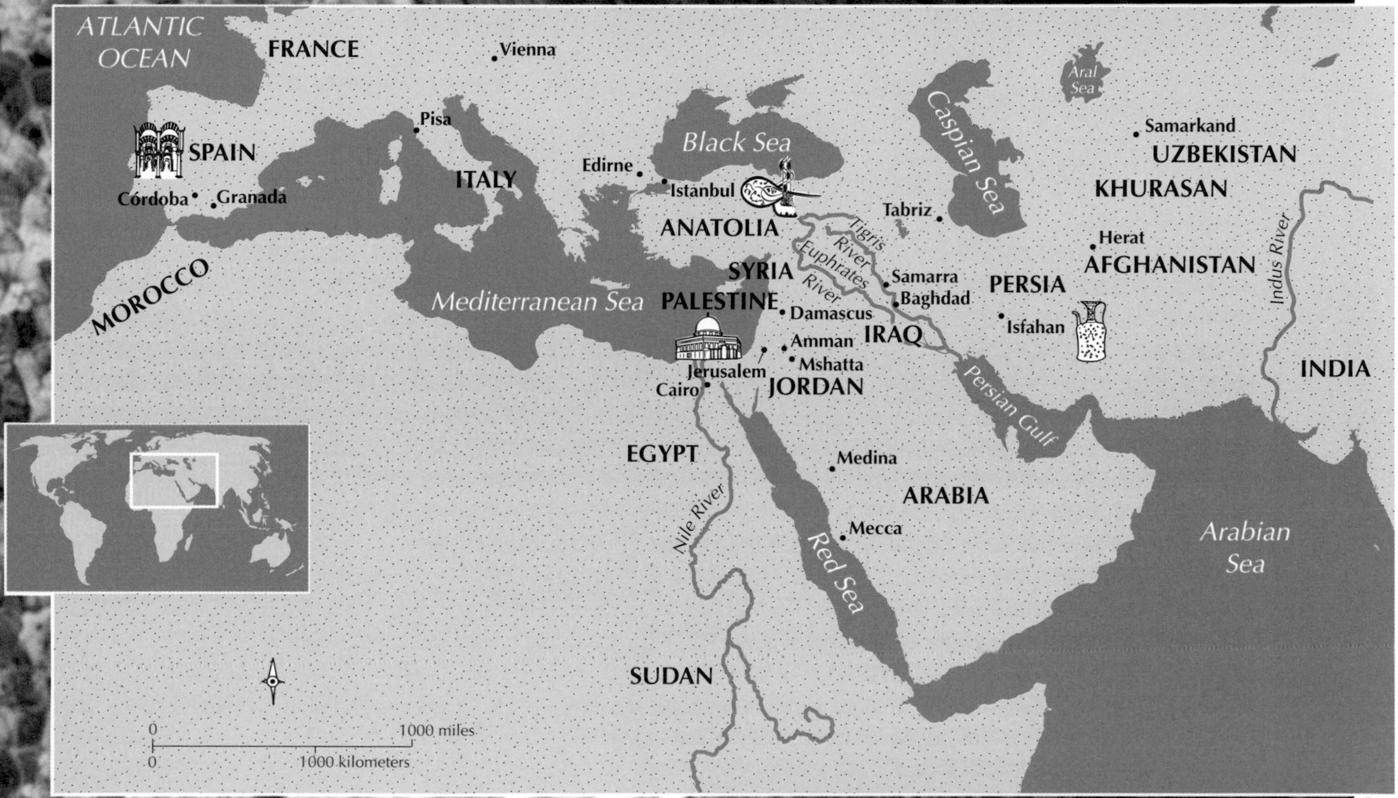

ATLANTIC OCEAN

FRANCE

Vienna

SPAIN

Pisa

Córdoba • • Granada

ITALY

Edirne

Black Sea

Caspian Sea

Aral Sea

Samarkand

UZBEKISTAN

KHURASAN

Istanbul

ANATOLIA

Tabriz

MOROCCO

Mediterranean Sea

SYRIA

PALESTINE

Tigris River

Euphrates River

Herat

AFGHANISTAN

Indus River

Damascus

Samarra

Baghdad

PERSIA

Jerusalem

Amman

Mshatta

IRAQ

Isfahan

Cairo

JORDAN

INDIA

EGYPT

Medina

ARABIA

Persian Gulf

Nile River

Mecca

Red Sea

Arabian Sea

SUDAN

0   1000 miles
0   1000 kilometers

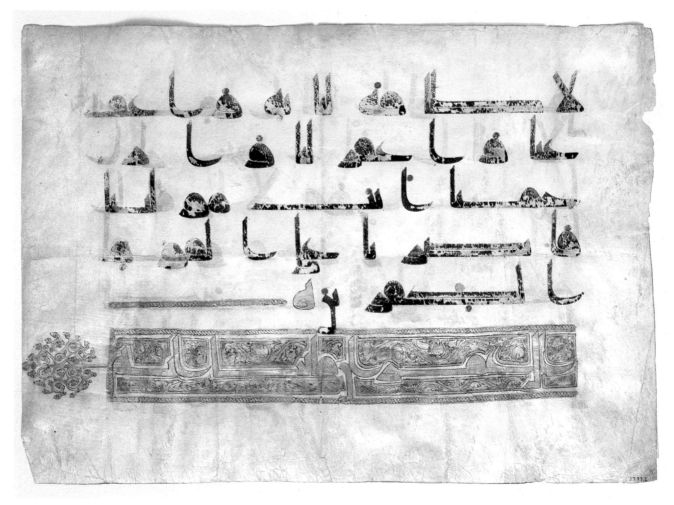

8-1. Page from Koran (surah 47:36) in kufic script, from Syria. 9th century. Ink, pigments, and gold on vellum, 9³⁄₈ x 13¹⁄₈"
(23.8 x 33.3 cm). The Metropolitan Museum of Art, New York
Rogers Fund, 1937 (37.99.2)

During the holy month of Ramadan in 610 CE, a merchant named al-Amin ("the Trusted One") sought solitude in a cave on Mount Hira, a few miles north of Mecca, in Arabia. On that night, "The Night of Power and Excellence," the angel Gabriel is believed to have appeared to him and commanded him to recite revelations from God. In that moment this merchant became Muhammad, the Messenger of God. The revelations dictated by Gabriel at Mecca formed the basis of a religion called Islam ("submission to God's will"), whose adherents are referred to as Muslims ("those who have submitted to God"). Today, nearly a billion Muslims turn five times a day toward Mecca to pray.

The Word of God was recorded in a book known as the Koran ("recitation"), which is a compilation of Muhammad's revelations. To transcribe these revelations, Arabic was adopted as the uniform script wherever Islam spread, and the very act of transcribing the Koran became sacred.

To accomplish this holy task, which is summarized in the ancient Arabic expression "Purity of writing is purity of the soul," scribes developed **calligraphy**, the art of writing, to an extraordinary degree (fig. 8-1). A prohibition against depicting representational images in religious art, as well as the naturally decorative nature of Arabic script, led to the use of calligraphic decoration on religious architecture, carpets, and handwritten documents. Perhaps the foremost characteristic of Islamic religious art, wherever it is found in the world and among every race, is the presence of Koranic Arabic, used for reading and prayer, and for decoration.

ISLAM AND EARLY ISLAMIC SOCIETY

Islam spread rapidly after its founding, encompassing much of Africa, Europe, and Asia. The art of this vast region draws its distinctive character both from Islam itself and from the diverse cultural traditions of the world's Muslims. Because Islam discouraged the use of figurative images, particularly in religious contexts—unlike Christian art of the same period—Islamic artists developed a rich vocabulary of **aniconic**, or nonfigural, ornament that is a hallmark of Islamic work. This vocabulary includes complex geometric patterns and the scrolling vines known outside the Islamic world as arabesques. Figural representation, to the extent it was permitted (which varied from time to time and place to place), first developed most prominently in regions with strong pre-Islamic figural traditions, such as those that had been under the control of the Byzantine and Roman empires. Stylized forms for representing animals and plants developed in the regions that had been under the control of the Sassanian dynasty of Persia (modern Iran), the heirs of the artistic traditions of the ancient Near East, who ruled from 226 to 641. Because the Arabian birthplace of Islam was not noted for its art, these Persian and Roman-Byzantine influences shaped Islamic art in its formative centuries.

Much of Islamic art can be seen as an interplay between pure abstraction and organic form. For Muslims, abstraction helps free the mind from the contemplation of material form, opening it to the enormity of the divine presence. Islamic artists excelled in surface decoration, using repeated and expanding patterns to suggest timelessness and infinite extension. Shimmering surfaces created by dense, highly controlled patterning are characteristic of much later Islamic art, including architecture, carpet making, calligraphy, and book illustration.

Muslims date the beginning of their history to the flight of the Prophet Muhammad from Mecca to Medina—an exodus called in Arabic the *hijra*—in 622 (see "The Life of the Prophet Muhammad," pages 340, 341). Over the next decade Muhammad succeeded in uniting the warring clans of Arabia under the banner of Islam.

Following the Prophet's death in 632, four of his closest associates assumed the title of caliph, or successor: Abu Bakr (ruled 633–634), Umar (ruled 634–644), Uthman (ruled 644–656), and finally Ali (ruled 656–661). According to tradition, during the time of Uthman, the Koran assumed its final form.

The accession of Ali provoked a power struggle that led to his assassination. Muawiya (ruled 661–680), Ali's rival and a close relative of Uthman, then became caliph, founding the Umayyad dynasty (661–750). This struggle resulted in enduring divisions within Islam. Followers of Ali, known as Shiites, regard him as the Prophet's rightful successor and the first three caliphs as illegitimate. Sunni Muslims, in contrast, recognize all of the first four caliphs as "rightly guided." Today about 10 percent of the world's Muslims are Shiites and about 85 percent Sunni.

Beginning in the seventh century, Islam expanded dramatically. In just two decades, seemingly unstoppable Muslim armies conquered the Sassanian Persian Empire, Egypt, and the Byzantine provinces of Syria and Palestine. By the early eighth century, under the Umayyads, they had reached India, conquered all of North Africa and Spain, and penetrated France to within 100 miles of Paris before being turned back. The circumstances in Islamic lands of Christians and Jews who did not convert to Islam was neither uniform nor consistent. In general, as "People of the Book"—non-Muslim followers of a monotheistic religion based on a revealed scripture—they enjoyed a protected status. However, they were also subject to a special tax and restrictions on dress and employment.

Islam has proven a remarkably adaptable faith. Part of that adaptability is due to its emphasis on the believer's direct, personal relationship with God through prayer and a corresponding lack of ceremonial paraphernalia. Every Muslim must observe the Five Pillars, or duties, of faith. The most important of these is the statement of faith: "There is no god but God and Muhammad is his messenger." Next come ritual prayer five times a day, charity to the poor, fasting during the month of Ramadan, and a pilgrimage to Mecca—Muhammad's birthplace and the site of the Kaaba, Islam's holiest structure—once in a lifetime for those able to undertake it.

THE LIFE OF THE PROPHET MUHAMMAD

Muhammad, the prophet of Islam, was born about 570 in Mecca, a major pilgrimage center in west-central Arabia, to a prominent family that traced its ancestry to Ishmael, son of the biblical patriarch Abraham. Orphaned as a small child, Muhammad spent his early years among the Beduin, desert nomads. When he returned to Mecca, he became a trader's agent, accompanying caravans across the desert. At the age of twenty-five he married his employer, Khadija, a well-to-do, forty-year-old widow, and they had six children.

After Muhammad received the revelations from God in 610, the first to accept him as Prophet was his wife. Other early converts included members of his clan and a few friends, among them the first four successors, or caliphs, who led the faithful after Muhammad's death. As the number of converts grew, Muhammad encountered increasing opposition from Mecca's ruling clans, including some leaders of his own clan. They objected to both his religious teachings and the threat they posed to the trade that accompanied Mecca's status as a pilgrimage site. In 622 Muhammad and his companions fled Mecca and settled in the oasis town of Yathrib, which the Muslims renamed Medina, the Prophet's City. It is to this event, called the *hijra* ("emigration"), that Muslims date the beginning of their history. After years of fighting, Muhammad and his follow-

ers won control of Mecca in 630 with an army of 10,000, and its inhabitants converted to Islam. The Kaaba—a cube-shaped stone structure draped with black cloth that had once been the focus of idol worship—became the sacred center of Islam, toward which Muslims around the globe still turn to pray. Shortly thereafter, Islam spread throughout Arabia.

Muhammad married eleven times. (Muslim law allows men four coequal wives at once, although the Prophet was permitted more.) Some of these marriages were political and others were to provide for women in need—a social duty in a society in which clan feuds killed many men. Within the framework of Islam, women gained rights where there had been none before. Their degree of freedom depended greatly on the time and the place, but some became monarchs of countries such as Yemen and Indonesia, and many were significant sponsors of architecture programs.

Muhammad is reputed to have been a vigorous, good-looking man for whom the world was a fragrant paradise. One of his wives, Aisha, provided much of the information available about his personal life. "People used to ask [Aisha] how the Prophet lived at home. Like an ordinary man, she answered. He would sweep the house, stitch his own clothes, mend his own sandals, water the camels, milk the goats, help the servants at their work, and eat his meals with them; and he

would go fetch a thing we needed from the market" (cited in Glassé, page 281).

After making a farewell pilgrimage to Mecca, Muhammad died in Medina in 632. According to his wishes, he was buried in his house, in Aisha's room, where he breathed his last. His tomb is a major pilgrimage site. A generation after his death his revelations, which he continued to receive throughout his life, were assembled in 114 chapters, called surahs, organized from longest to shortest, each surah divided into verses. This is the sacred scripture of Islam, called the Koran ("recitation"), which is the core of the faith. Another body of work, the Hadith ("account"), compiled over the centuries, contains sayings of the Prophet, anecdotes about him, and additional revelations. The Koran and the Hadith are the foundation of Islamic law, guiding the lives of nearly a billion Muslims around the world.

Muslims consider Muhammad to be the last in a succession of prophets, or messengers of God, that includes Adam, Abraham, Ishmael, Moses, and Jesus. Like Judaism and Christianity but unlike the other religions prevalent in Arabia at the time, Islam is monotheistic, recognizing only a single, all-powerful deity. Muhammad's teaching emphasized the all-pervading immateriality of God and banned idol worship.

This painting shows Muhammad traveling by camel to a desert market fair to seek the support of his

---

Muslims are expected to participate in congregational worship at a **mosque** (*masjid* in Arabic) on Friday. When not at a mosque, the faithful simply kneel wherever they are to pray, facing the Kaaba in Mecca. The Prophet Muhammad himself lived simply and advised his companions not to waste their resources on elaborate architecture. Instead, he instructed and led them in prayer in a mud-brick structure, now known as the Mosque of the Prophet, adjacent to his home in Medina. This was a square enclosure with verandas supported by palm-tree trunks that framed a large courtyard. Muhammad spoke from a low platform on the south veranda. This simple arrangement—a walled courtyard with a separate space on one side housing a **minbar** (pulpit) for the imam (prayer leader)—became the model for the design of later mosques.

ART DURING THE EARLY CALIPHATES

The caliphs of the aggressively expansionist Umayyad dynasty ruled from their capital at Damascus (in modern Syria). They were essentially desert chieftains who had scant interest in fostering the arts except for poetry, which had been held in high esteem among Arabs since pre-Islamic times, and architecture. The building of shrines and mosques throughout the empire in this period represented both the authority of the new rulers and the growing acceptance of Islam. The caliphs of the Abbasid dynasty, who replaced the Umayyads in 750 and ruled until 1258, governed in the grand manner of ancient Persian emperors from their capitals at Baghdad and Samarra (in modern Iraq). Their long and cosmopolitan reign saw achievements in med-

powerful uncle for his religious movement as well as to make converts among the fairgoers. He is accompanied by two close associates, the merchant Abu Bakr and the young warrior Ali. Abu Bakr, the first caliph, was the father of Muhammad's wife Aisha. Ali, husband of Muhammad's daughter Fatima, was the fourth caliph. The power struggle that ended in his death led to the rise of the Shiite sect. Although the faces of Abu Bakr and Ali are shown, that of Muhammad, in keeping with the Islamic injunction against idolatry and the making of idols, is not. The degree of representation permitted in Islamic art varied from place to place and from period to period depending in part on the strictness with which the injunction against idol making was interpreted and the purpose a work of art was to serve. This example suggests what was acceptable for an illustration of its type at the Ottoman court at the end of the sixteenth century.

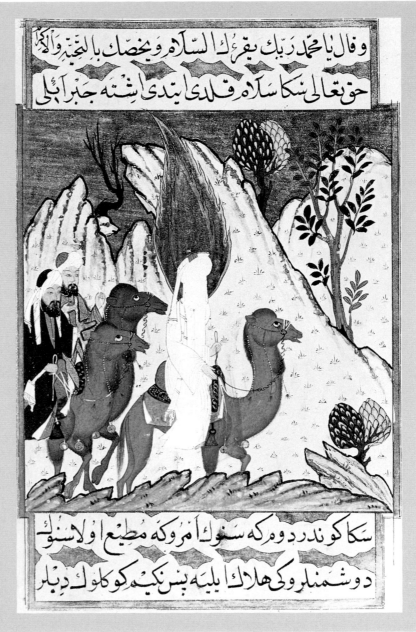

The Prophet Muhammad and His Companions Traveling to the Fair, from a later copy of the *Siyar-i Nabi* (Life of the Prophet) of al-Zarir (14th century), Istanbul, Turkey. 1594. Pigments and gold on paper, 10⅝ x 15″ (27 x 38 cm). New York Public Library, New York. Spencer Collection

icine, mathematics, the natural sciences, philosophy, literature, music, and art. They were generally tolerant of the ethnically diverse populations in the territories they subjugated and admired the cultural traditions of Byzantium, Persia, India, and China. (The early art of India is discussed in Chapter 9 and that of China in Chapter 10.)

Architecture

As Islam spread, architects adapted freely from Roman, Christian, and Persian models, which include the basilica, the martyrium, the peristyle house, and the palace audience hall. The Dome of the Rock in Jerusalem, built about 687–691, is the oldest surviving Islamic sanctuary and is today the holiest site in Islam after Mecca and Medina (fig. 8-2). It stands on the summit of the Temple

Mount (Mount Moriah) and encloses a rock outcropping (fig. 8-3) that has long been sacred to the Jews, who identify it as the site on which Abraham prepared to sacrifice his son Isaac. Jews, Christians, and Muslims associate the site with the creation of Adam and the Temple of Solomon. Muslims also identify it as the site from which Muhammad, led by the angel Gabriel, ascended to heaven in the Night Journey, passing through the spheres of heaven to the presence of God.

The Dome of the Rock was built by Syrian artisans trained in the Byzantine tradition, and its centralized plan—octagons within octagons—derived from both Byzantine and early Christian architecture. Unlike its Byzantine models, however, with their plain exteriors, the Dome of the Rock, crowned with a golden dome that dominates the Jerusalem skyline, is opulently decorated

PARALLELS

Years	Period	Early Islam	World
633–661	Early caliphs	Conquest of Arabia, Sassanian Persia, Egypt, Syria, Palestine	**c. 600–800** *Beowulf* (England); first Japanese capital at Nara; first block-print text (China)
661–750	Umayyad dynasty	Conquest of India, North Africa, southern France; capital at Damascus; Dome of the Rock; Mshatta palace	
750–1258	Abbasid dynasty	Umayyad dynasty in Spain; Great Mosque at Córdoba; capital at Baghdad, then Samarra (836); Great Mosque at Samarra; Samarkand ware; Seljuk dynasty in Anatolia; Masjid-i Jami at Isfahan; Mamluk dynasty in Egypt	**c. 800–1000** Charlemagne is made emperor of the West; bronze casting in South America; *Diamond Sutra* (China); first Viking colony in Greenland **c. 1000–1200** Lady Murasaki's *Tale of Genji* (Japan); separation of Eastern and Western Christian Churches; William the Conqueror (England); the Crusades **c. 1200–1500** Jenghiz Khan rules Mongols; Magna Carta (England); Kublai Khan rules Mongols; Dante's *Divine Comedy* (Italy); beginning of Renaissance in Europe; Hundred Years' War (England/France); Black Death in Europe; Great Schism of Roman Church; Chaucer's *Canterbury Tales* (England); Joan of Arc (France); Gutenberg first prints Bible (Germany); Columbus's voyages (Spain); Spanish Inquisition
1290–1918	Ottoman Empire	Alhambra at Granada; Ottomans take Constantinople; Selimiye Cami (Edirne)	

both outside and inside. The central space is covered by a dome on a tall **drum** supported by an arcade. Concentric aisles enclose the rock. As at San Vitale in Ravenna (see fig. 7-30), interior surfaces were originally decorated with marble **dadoes** at ground level and glass mosaics above. Remains of the mosaics show Byzantine-style foliage combined in a new style with jewel-like Sassanian Persian insignia. This imagery consists of a double-winged motif often associated with Sassanian royalty. The more than 700 feet of Arabic inscriptions on the structure are a distinctly Islamic feature. Written in one script on the interior and another on the exterior, these inscriptions include the references to Jesus Christ in the Koran. Later Islamic architects built similar domed octagonal sanctuaries and saints' tombs from Morocco to China.

The Umayyad caliphs, disregarding the Prophet's advice about architectural austerity, built for themselves palatial hunting retreats on the edge of the desert. With profuse interior decoration depicting exotic human and animal subjects in stucco, mosaic, and paint, some had swimming pools, baths, and domed, private rooms. One of the later desert palaces was begun in the 740s at Mshatta (near present-day Amman, Jordan). Although never completed, this square, stone-walled complex is nevertheless impressively monumental (fig. 8-4). It measured about 470 feet on each side, and its outer walls and gates were guarded by towers and bastions reminiscent of a Roman fort. The space was divided roughly into thirds, with the center section containing a huge courtyard. The main spaces were a mosque and a domed, basilica-plan audience hall that was flanked by four

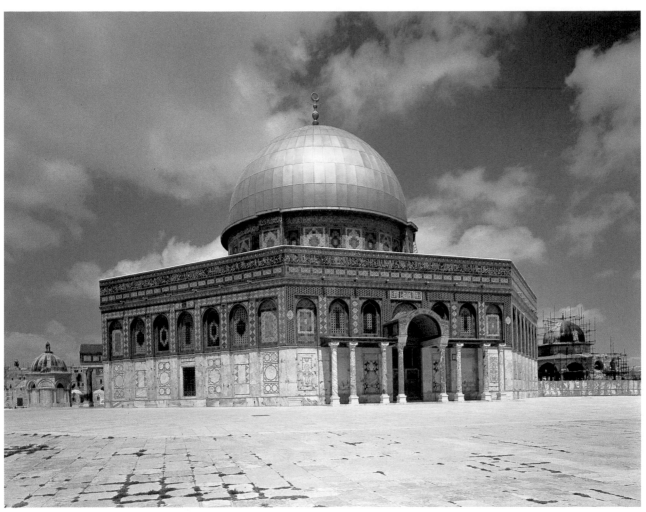

8-2. Dome of the Rock, Jerusalem, Israel. c. 687–91

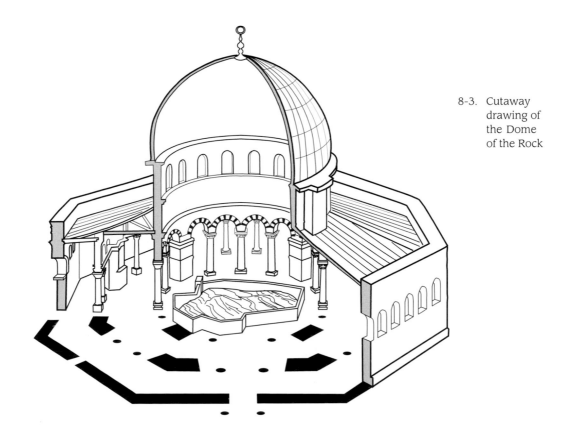

8-3. Cutaway drawing of the Dome of the Rock

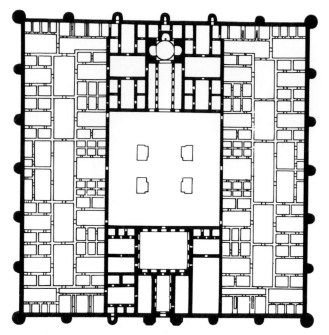

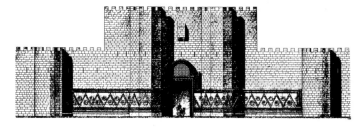

8-4. Plan and facade of the palace, Mshatta, Jordan. c. 750

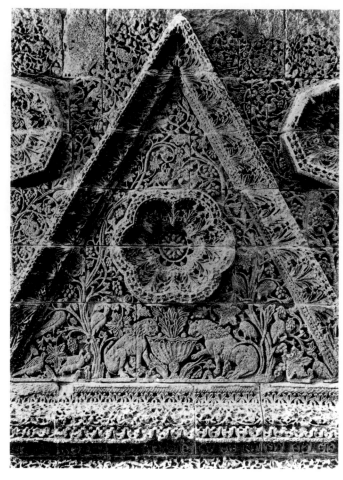

8-5. Frieze, detail of facade, palace, Mshatta. Stone. Staatliche Museen zu Berlin, Preussischer Kulturbesitz, Museum für Islamische Kunst

private apartments, or *bayts*. *Bayts* grouped around small courtyards, for the use of the caliph's relatives and guests, occupied the remainder of the building.

Unique among the surviving palaces, Mshatta was decorated with a **frieze** that extended in a band about 16 feet high across the base of its facade. This frieze was divided by a zigzag molding into triangular compartments, each punctuated by a large **rosette** carved in high relief (fig. 8-5). The compartments were filled with intricate carvings in low relief that included interlacing scrolls inhabited by birds and other animals (there were no animals on the mosque side of the building), urns, and candlesticks. Similar designs in both sculpture and mosaic adorned the interiors of Roman and Byzantine buildings but were never on exterior surfaces, and the designs were not so densely interwoven. Beneath one of the rosettes, two facing lions drink from an urn from which grows the Tree of Life, an ancient Persian motif.

With the development of mosque architecture during the early Umayyad period, the characteristic elements of this place of communal worship began to emerge (see "Elements of Architecture," opposite). There were facilities for ritual cleansing before entering the consecrated space, a *sahn*, or courtyard, and a large covered space to accommodate Friday prayers. Worshipers prayed facing the **qibla** wall, which was oriented toward Mecca. A niche called a **mihrab** differentiated the qibla wall from the others. The imam delivered a sermon from the minbar, near the qibla wall. Some mosques included an enclosure called a *maqsura* near the mihrab for dignitaries. Muezzins, or criers, called the faithful to prayer from one or more towers, or **minarets** (literally "lighthouses"), on the exterior. Some early mosques were housed in modified pre-Islamic buildings.

When the Abbasids overthrew the Umayyads in 750, a survivor of the Umayyad dynasty, Abd ar-Rahman I (ruled 756–788), fled across North Africa into southern Spain (known as "al-Andalus" in Arabic), where, with the support of Syrian Muslim settlers, he established himself as the provincial ruler, or amir. The Umayyads continued to rule in Spain from their capital in Córdoba for the next three centuries (756–1031) and were noted patrons of the arts. Thus one of the finest surviving examples of Umayyad architecture, the Great Mosque of Córdoba, is in Spain.

This sprawling structure was begun on the site of a church in 785. Repeatedly enlarged until the fifteenth century, when it returned to Christian use, it combines

ELEMENTS OF ARCHITECTURE

Mosque Plans

The earliest mosques were pillared **hypostyle halls** such as the Great Mosque at Córdoba (see fig. 8-6). Approached through an open courtyard, the *sahn*, their interiors are divided by rows of columns leading, at the far end, to the mihrab niche of a qibla wall, which is oriented toward Mecca.

A second type, the **four-iwan mosque**, was originally associated with **madrasas** (schools for advanced study). The iwans—monumental barrel-vaulted halls with wide-open, arched entrances—faced each other across a central *sahn*; related structures spread out behind and around the iwans. Four-iwan mosques were most developed in Persia, in buildings like Isfahan's Masjid-i Jami (see fig. 8-13).

Central-plan mosques, such as the Selimiye Cami at Edirne (see fig. 8-17), were derived from Istanbul's Hagia Sophia (see fig. 7-27) and are typical of Ottoman Turkish architecture. Central-plan interiors are dominated by a large domed space uninterrupted by structural supports. Worship is directed, as in other mosques, toward a qibla wall and its mihrab opposite the entrance.

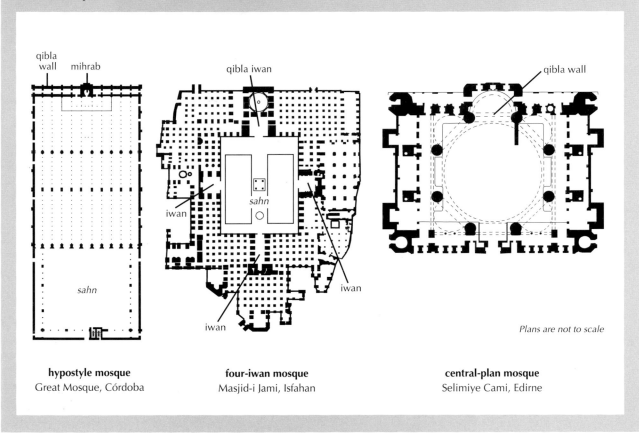

hypostyle mosque
Great Mosque, Córdoba

four-iwan mosque
Masjid-i Jami, Isfahan

Plans are not to scale

central-plan mosque
Selimiye Cami, Edirne

Umayyad, Abbasid, and pre-Islamic influences into a distinctive Western Islamic style. The marble columns and capitals in the **hypostyle** prayer hall were recycled from the ruins of classical buildings in the region, which had been a wealthy Roman province (fig. 8-6). Two tiers of arches, one over the other, surmount these columns; the upper tier springs from rectangular posts that rise from the columns. This double-tiered design, which was widely imitated, effectively increases the height of the interior space and provides ample light and air within it. The distinctively shaped **horseshoe arches**—a form known from Roman times and favored by the Visigoths, Spain's pre-Islamic rulers—came to be closely associated with Islamic architecture in the West (see "Elements of Architecture," page 347). Another distinctive feature of these arches, also adopted from Roman and Byzantine precedents, is the alternation of pale stone and red brick **voussoirs** forming the curved arch. In the view of one art historian, the overall effect of these features transforms the hall into "a wild three-dimensional maze, a hall of mirrors in which the constant echo of arches and the unruly staccato of colors confuse the viewer, presenting a challenge to unravel the [mosque's] complexities" (Dodds, pages 12–13).

In the final century of Umayyad rule, Córdoba emerged as a major commercial and intellectual hub and a flourishing center for the arts. It surpassed Christian Europe economically and in science, literature, and philosophy. Beginning with Abd ar-Rahman III (ruled 912–961), the Umayyads boldly claimed the title of caliph. Al-Hakam II (ruled 961–976) made the Great Mosque a focus of royal patronage, commissioning costly and luxurious renovations that disturbed many of his subjects. The caliph attempted to answer their objections to paying for such ostentation with an inscription giving thanks to God, who "helped him in the building of this eternal place, with the goal of making this mosque more spacious for his subjects, something which both he and they greatly wanted" (cited in Dodds, page 23). Among al-Hakam's renovations was a new mihrab with three bays

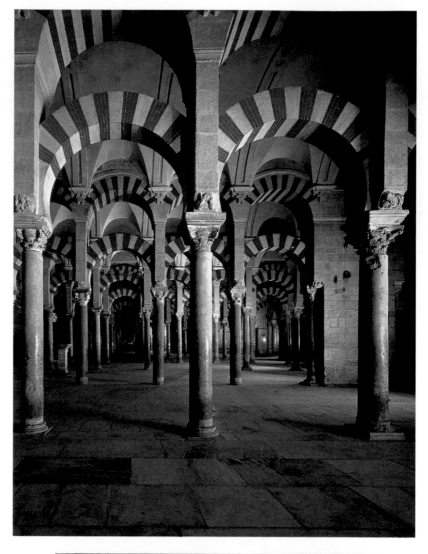

8-6. Prayer hall, Great Mosque, Córdoba, Spain. Begun 785–86

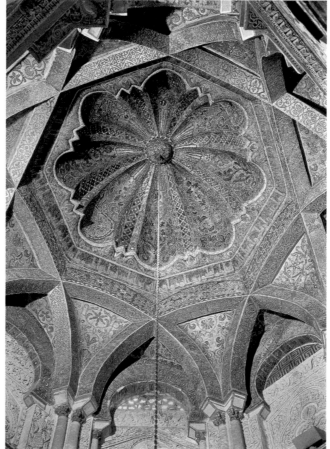

8-7. Dome in front of the mihrab, Great Mosque. 965

ELEMENTS OF ARCHITECTURE

Arches and Muqarnas

Islamic builders used a number of innovative structural devices. Among these were two arch forms, the **horseshoe arch** (see fig. 8-6) and the **ogival**, or pointed, **arch** (see fig. 8-14). There are many variations of each, some of which disguise their structural function beneath complex decoration.

Technically, a **muqarnas** is a **corbeled squinch** (see "Elements of Architecture," page 310). *Muqarnas* may be used singly or in multiples (see fig. 8-12). Originally they served a structural purpose as interlocking, load-bearing, niche-shaped vaulting units. Over time they became increasingly ornamental, intricately faceted surfaces. They are frequently used to line mihrabs and, on a larger scale, to support domes.

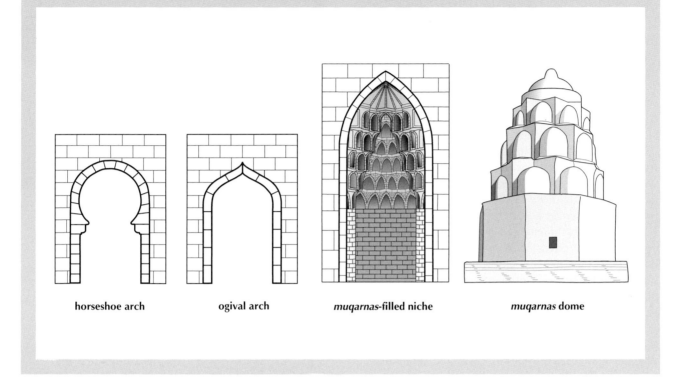

| horseshoe arch | ogival arch | *muqarnas*-filled niche | *muqarnas* dome |

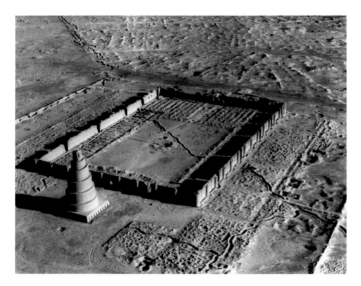

8-8. Great Mosque of al-Mutawakkil, Samarra, Iraq. 847–52

Minarets, the most readily identifiable feature of Islamic religious architecture, began as rectangular, stepped towers. They were first erected in western Asia, probably as commemorative victory monuments. Visible from many miles away, they may also have functioned as signposts on desert caravan routes. The classic tall, cylindrical minaret evolved in Persia in roughly the mid-tenth century.

in front of it. The melon-shaped, ribbed dome seems to float over a web of intersecting arches that emerge from their supporting piers (fig. 8-7). Lushly patterned mosaics with inscriptions, geometric motifs, and stylized vegetation clothe the domes in brilliant color and gold.

In the eastern Islamic world, the caliphs of the Abbasid dynasty ruled from Baghdad for more than a century after they seized power from the Umayyads. In 836, however, Caliph al-Mutasim (ruled 833–842) established a heavily fortified new capital at Samarra, about 60 miles north of Baghdad. In the mid-ninth century, Caliph al-Mutawakkil (ruled 847–861) began construction of the Great Mosque of Samarra (fig. 8-8). In ruins today, it was for a long time the largest mosque in the Islamic world. It featured a hypostyle prayer hall 525 feet wide at the qibla wall and 25 perpendicular aisles. The fortresslike wall enclosing the complex was more than 8 feet thick and about 33 feet high, with curved buttressing and round corner towers. The facade may originally have had mosaic decoration. An unusual spiral-ramp minaret, perhaps inspired by the **ziggurats** of the ancient Near East, rises more than 160 feet next to the mosque wall.

Calligraphy

The Arabic language and script have held a unique position in Islamic society and art from the beginning. As the language of the Koran and Muslim liturgy, Arabic has been a powerful unifying force within Islam. Reverence for the Koran as the word of God extended by association to the act of writing, and generations of extraordinary scribes made Arabic calligraphy one of the glories of Islam. Arabic script is written from right to left, and each of its letters takes one of three forms depending on its position in a word. With its rhythmic interplay between verticals and horizontals, this system lends itself to myriad variations.

Writing pervaded Islamic art. In addition to manuscripts, it featured prominently in architecture and on smaller-scale objects made of metal, glass, cloth, ceramic, and wood. The earliest scripts, called kufic (from the city of Kufa in modern Iraq), were angular and evolved from inscriptions on stone monuments. Kufic scripts were especially suitable for carved or woven inscriptions, as well as those on coins and other metalware; they are still used for Koran chapter headings. Most early Korans had only three to five lines per page and customarily had large letters because two readers shared one book (although they would have known the text by heart). A page from a ninth-century Syrian Koran exemplifies a style common from the eighth to the tenth century (see fig. 8-1). Red diacritical marks (pronunciation guides) accent the dark brown ink. Horizontals are elongated and fat-bodied letters are also emphasized. The chapter heading is set against an ornate gold band that contrasts with the simplicity of the letters.

Because calligraphy was a holy occupation, calligraphers enjoyed the highest status of all artists in Islamic society. Included in their numbers were a few princes and women. Their training was long and arduous, and their work usually anonymous. Not until the later Islamic centuries did it become common for calligraphers to sign their work, and even then only the most accomplished were allowed this privilege. Apprentice scribes had to learn secret formulas for inks and paints, become skilled in the proper ways to sit, breathe, and manipulate their tools, and develop their individual specialties. They also had to absorb the complex literary traditions and numerical symbolism that had developed around Arabic letters over the centuries.

The Koran was usually written on **vellum**, which, like parchment, was made from animal skin. Paper, a Chinese invention, was first imported into the Islamic realm in the mid-eighth century. Muslims subsequently learned how to make high-quality, rag-based paper and established their own paper mills. By about 1000, paper had largely replaced vellum and parchment, encouraging the proliferation of increasingly elaborate and decorative cursive scripts, which generally superseded kufic by the thirteenth century. Among the most influential calligraphers in this process was a woman named Shuhda. By the tenth century, more than twenty cursive scripts had come into use. They were standardized by Ibn Muqla

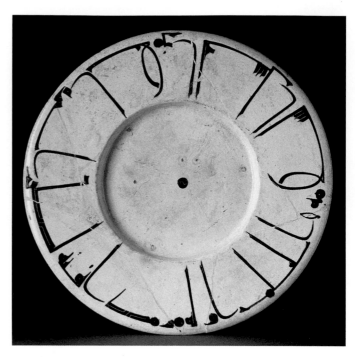

8-9. Bowl with kufic border, Samarkand, Uzbekistan. 9th–10th century. Earthenware with slip, pigment, and glaze, diameter 14½" (37 cm). Musée du Louvre, Paris

The white ground of this piece imitated prized Chinese porcelains made of fine white kaolin clay. Both Samarkand and Khurasan were connected to the Silk Road (Chapter 10), the great caravan route to China, and were influenced by Chinese culture.

(d. 940), an Abbasid minister, who fixed the proportions of the letters in each and devised a method for teaching calligraphy that is still in use. The great calligrapher Yaqut al-Mustasim (d. 1299), the Turkish secretary of the last Abbasid caliph, codified six basic calligraphic styles, including thuluth (see fig. 8-20), naskhi (see the illustration in "The Life of the Prophet Muhammad," page 341), and *muhaqqaq* (see fig. 8-14). Al-Mustasim reputedly made more than 1,000 copies of the Koran.

Ceramic and Textile Arts

Kufic-style letters were used effectively as the only decoration on a type of white pottery made in the ninth and tenth centuries in and around Nishapur (a region also known as Khurasan, in modern northeastern Iran) and Samarkand (in modern Uzbekistan in Central Asia). Now known as Samarkand ware, it was the ancestor of a ware produced until fairly recently by Central Asian peasants. In the example here, a bowl of medium quality, clear lead glaze was applied over a black inscription on a white slip-painted ground (fig. 8-9). The letters have been elongated to fill the bowl's rim, stressing their vertical elements. The inscription translates: "Knowledge, the beginning of it is bitter to taste, but the end is sweeter than honey," an apt choice for tableware. Inscriptions on Samarkand ware provide a storehouse of such popular sayings.

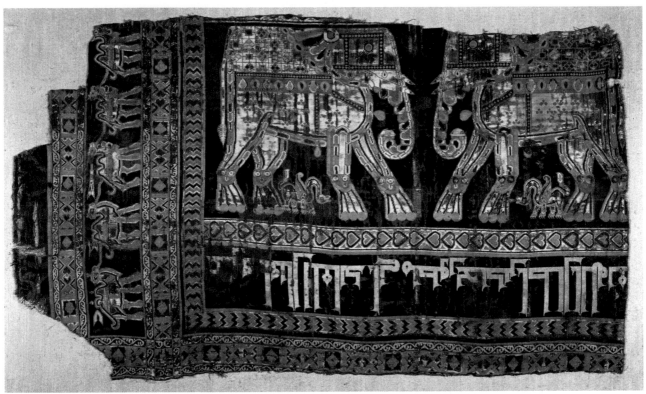

8-10. Textile with elephants and camels, from Khurasan, Persia (Iran). c. 960. Dyed silk, compound weave, largest fragment 37 x 20½" (94 x 52 cm). Musée du Louvre, Paris

Silk textiles were both sought-after luxury items and a medium of economic exchange. Government-controlled factories, known as *tiraz*, produced cloth for the court as well as for official gifts and payments. A number of fine Islamic fabrics have been preserved in the treasuries of medieval European churches, where they were used for priests' ceremonial robes, altar cloths, and covers for Christian saints' relics.

A different kufic inscription appears on a roughly contemporary fragment of silk from Khurasan (fig. 8-10): "Glory and happiness to the Commander Abu Mansur Bukhtakin, may God prolong his prosperity." Such formulaic inscriptions were extremely common in Islamic art, appearing as generic blessings on ordinary goods sold in the marketplace or, as here, personalized on "special orders." They can sometimes help determine where and when a work was made, but they can also be frustratingly uninformative when not much is known about the patron named in an object's inscription. Stylistic comparisons—in this case with other textiles, with the way similar subjects appear in other mediums, and with other kufic inscriptions—can reveal more about it than the inscription alone.

This fragment shows two elephants with rich ornamental coverings facing each other on a dark red ground, each with a mythical griffin between its hooves. A caravan of two-humped, Bactrian camels linked with rope moves up the left side, part of the elaborately patterned borders. The inscription at the bottom is upside-down, suggesting that the missing portion of the textile was the mirror image of the surviving fragment, with another pair of elephants joined back-to-back to this pair. The piece was created using an enormously complicated and expensive-to-operate drawloom weaving system that was best suited for this kind of repetitive pattern. The technique and design derive from the sumptuous pattern-woven silks of Sassanian Persia. The Persian weavers had, in turn, adapted Chinese silk technology to the Sassanian taste for paired heraldic beasts and other Near Eastern imagery. This tradition, with modifications—the depiction of animals, for example, became less naturalistic—continued after the Islamic conquest of Persia.

LATER ISLAMIC ART The Abbasid caliphate began to disintegrate in the ninth century, and thereafter power in the Islamic world became fragmented among the more or less independent regional rulers. The eleventh century saw the rise of the Seljuks, a Turkic people who had served as soldiers for the Abbasid caliphs and converted to Islam in the tenth century. Seljuk rulers united Persia and most of Mesopotamia, establishing a dynasty that endured from 1037 to 1194. A branch of the dynasty ruled much of Anatolia (Turkey) from the late eleventh to the beginning of the fourteenth century. Among the Seljuks of Anatolia, a number of queens and princesses were avid patrons of the arts and sponsored the building of mosques, mausoleums, schools, and baths. In the early thirteenth century, the Mongols—non-Muslims led by Jenghiz Khan (ruled 1206–1227) and his successors—swept out of Central Asia, encountering weak resistance as far as Egypt, where the young Mamluk dynasty (1252–1517), founded by descendants of slave soldiers (*mamluk* means "slave"), held them off. In the West,

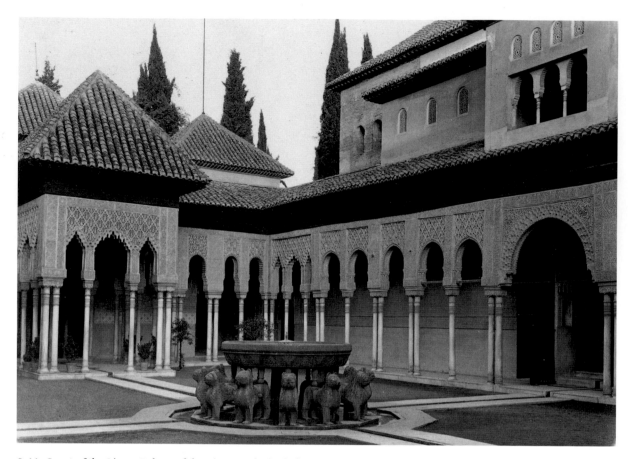

8-11. Court of the Lions, Palace of the Lions (Palacio de los Leones), Alhambra, Granada, Spain. Completed c. 1380

Granada, with its ample water supply, had long been known as a city of gardens. The twelve stone lions in the fountain in the center of this court were salvaged from the ruins of an earlier palatial complex on the Alhambra hill. The earlier structure was begun in the late eleventh century by a high Granadan official of Jewish heritage named Samuel ibn Naghralla and completed by his son Yusuf in the early twelfth century. Commentators of the time praised this complex, with its pools, fountains, and gardens. No doubt it was a source of inspiration for the builders of the later palaces.

Islamic control of Spain gradually succumbed to expanding Christian forces, ending altogether in 1492.

With the breakdown of Seljuk power in Anatolia in the early fourteenth century, another group of Muslim Turks seized power in the northwestern part of that region, having migrated there from their homeland in Central Asia. Known as the Ottomans, after an early leader named Osman, they pushed their territorial boundaries westward and, in spite of setbacks inflicted by the Mongols, ultimately created an empire that extended over Anatolia, western Persia, Iraq, Syria, Palestine, western Arabia (including Mecca and Medina), India, Southeast Asia, North Africa (including Egypt and the Sudan), and much of eastern Europe. In 1453 they captured Constantinople (renaming it Istanbul) and brought the Byzantine Empire to an end. The Ottoman Empire lasted until the end of World War I in 1918. Another dynasty, the Safavids, established a Shiite state in Persia in the early years of the sixteenth century.

Although Islam remained a dominant and unifying force throughout these developments, the later history of Islamic society and art is a largely regional phenomenon. The following discussion focuses on architecture, portable arts, manuscript illumination, and calligraphy from Spain, North Africa, and western Asia.

Architecture

The best-preserved later Islamic monument left standing after the Christian reconquest of Spain in 1492 is the Alhambra. This fortified hilltop palace complex was the seat of the Nasrids (1232–1492), the last Spanish Muslim dynasty, whose territory had shrunk to the region around Granada in southeastern Spain. The Alhambra remained fairly intact in part because it represented the defeat of Islam to the victorious Christian monarchs, who restored, maintained, and occupied it as much for its commemorative value as for its beauty.

The Alhambra, which emerged from the distinctive local traditions established by the Córdoba Umayyads, exemplifies the growing regionalism in Islamic art. The complex was begun in 1238 on the site of a pre-Islamic fortress by the founder of the Nasrid dynasty. Successive rulers expanded it, and it took its present form in the fourteenth century. Literally a small town extending for about half a mile along the crest of a high hill overlook-

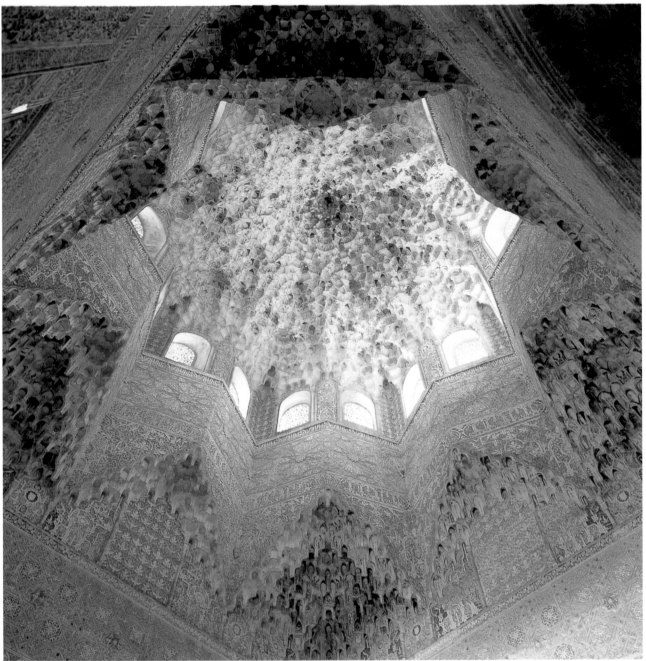

8-12. *Muqarnas* dome, Hall of the Abencerrajes, Palace of the Lions

ing Granada, it included government buildings, royal residences, gates, mosques, baths, servants' quarters, barracks, stables, a mint, workshops, and gardens.

Although it offered views to the landscape below, the architectural focus of the Alhambra was largely inward toward its lush courtyard gardens. They embodied the Muslim vision of paradise as a well-watered, walled garden (the English word *paradise* comes from the Persian term for an enclosed park, *faradis*). The so-called Palace of the Lions was a private retreat built by Muhammad V (ruled 1362–1391) in the late fourteenth century. At its heart is the Court of the Lions, a rectangular courtyard named for a marble fountain surrounded by stone lions (fig. 8-11). Although sanded today, the Court of the Lions was originally a garden, probably planted with aromatic

shrubs, flowers, and small citrus trees between the water channels that radiate from the fountain. Second-floor balconies overlook the courtyard. On the outside wall of a pavilion on the north side of the court (not visible in the illustration), a second-floor **mirador**—a projection with windows on three sides—looked out onto a large, lower garden and the plain below.

Four pavilions used for dining and performances of music, poetry, and dance open onto the Court of the Lions. One of these, the two-storied Hall of the Abencerrajes on the south side, may have been used year-round as a music room. Like the other pavilions (all of which had good acoustics), it is covered by a domed ceiling (fig. 8-12). The star-shaped dome rests on clustered **squinches** called *muqarnas* (see "Elements of Architecture,"

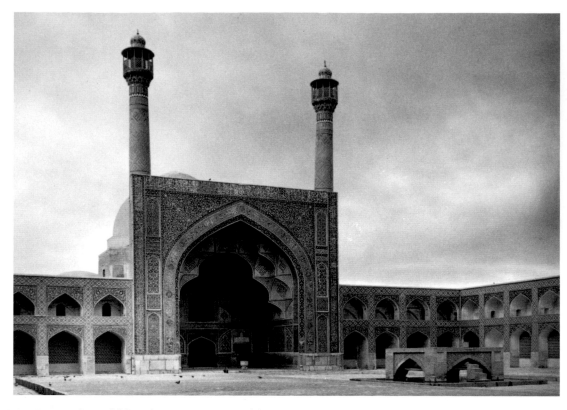

8-13. Courtyard, Masjid-i Jami (Great Mosque), Isfahan, Persia (Iran). 11th–18th century. View from the northeast

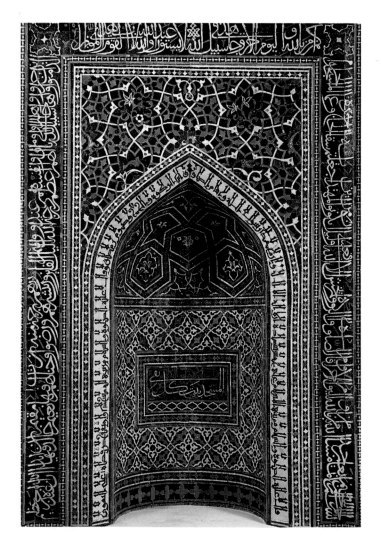

page 347). A honeycomb of *muqarnas* likewise covers the apex of the dome. The effect is of architectural lace, material form made immaterial.

The Alhambra was a sophisticated pleasure palace, an attempt to create paradise on earth. Imagining it as it once was—glittering with carved and painted stucco ornament, stained glass, glazed tiles, and lush carpets, its pavilions and gardens filled with courtiers dressed in glowing silks, jewelry, and cloth-of-gold—one can understand why it was legendary in its own time.

In the eastern Islamic world, the Seljuk rulers proved themselves enlightened patrons of the arts. One far-reaching development during their reign was the introduction of the four-iwan mosque. In this plan, **iwans**, which are large, rectangular, barrel-vaulted halls with monumental arched openings, face each other across a courtyard. Reflecting the influence of Sufism, a literary and philosophical movement that arose in the late tenth and early eleventh centuries, iwans may represent symbolic gateways between outside and inside, open and closed, the material and the spiritual.

Iwans first appeared in **madrasas**, schools for advanced study that were the precursors of the modern uni-

8-14. Mosaic mihrab, from the Madrasa Imami, Isfahan, Persia (Iran). c. 1354 (restored). Glazed and painted ceramic on plaster, 11'3" x 7'6" (3.43 x 2.89 m). The Metropolitan Museum of Art, New York
Harris Brisbane Dick Fund (39.20)

One of the three Koranic inscriptions on this mihrab dates it to approximately 1354. Note the combination of decorated kufic and cursive *muhaqqaq* scripts.

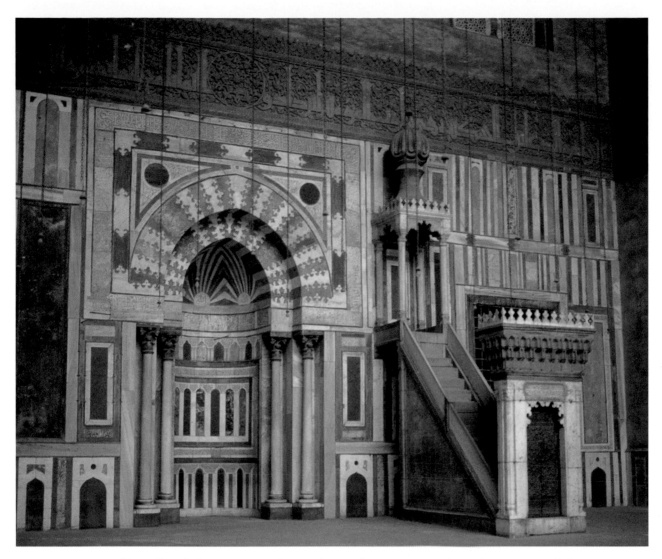

8-15. Qibla wall, main iwan (mosque), in a madrasa, Sultan Hasan complex, Cairo, Egypt. 1356–63

versity. Beginning in the eleventh century, hundreds of these institutions were founded and many are still in existence. Rulers and wealthy individuals endowed them as a form of pious charity. The four-iwan mosque may have evolved from the need to provide separate quarters for four schools of thought within madrasas.

The Masjid-i Jami (Great Mosque) in the center of the Seljuk capital of Isfahan (in modern Iran) was originally a hypostyle mosque. In the late eleventh century it was refurbished with two great brick domes, and in the twelfth century with four iwans and a monumental gate flanked by paired minarets (fig. 8-13). Construction continued sporadically on this mosque into the eighteenth century, but it retained its basic four-iwan layout, which became standard in Persia. The massive qibla iwan, on the south, is a twelfth-century structure with fourteenth-century *muqarnas* and seventeenth-century exterior tilework and minarets. The brick masonry on the interior of the iwans is unadorned; the facades, however, are sheathed in brilliant blue architectural tilework—an Islamic trademark for which this monument is justly famous.

A fourteenth-century mosaic mihrab originally from a madrasa in Isfahan but now in the Metropolitan Museum of Art in New York is one of the finest examples of early architectural ceramic decoration in Islamic art (fig. 8-14). More than 11 feet tall, it was made with a painstaking process that involved cutting each piece of tile individually, including the pieces making up the letters on the curving surface of the niche. The color scheme—white against turquoise and cobalt blue with accents of dark yellow and green—was typical of this type of decoration, as was the harmonious but contrasting use of dense organic and geometric patterns.

A madrasa-mausoleum-mosque complex built in the mid-fourteenth century by the Mamluk sultan Hasan in Cairo, Egypt, shows Seljuk influence (fig. 8-15). The iwans in this structure functioned as classrooms, and students were housed in neighboring rooms. Hasan's domed tomb lies beyond the qibla wall of the largest of the four iwans, which served as the mosque for the entire complex. The walls and vaulting inside this main iwan are undecorated except for a wide stucco frieze band. Originally painted, this band combines calligraphy and

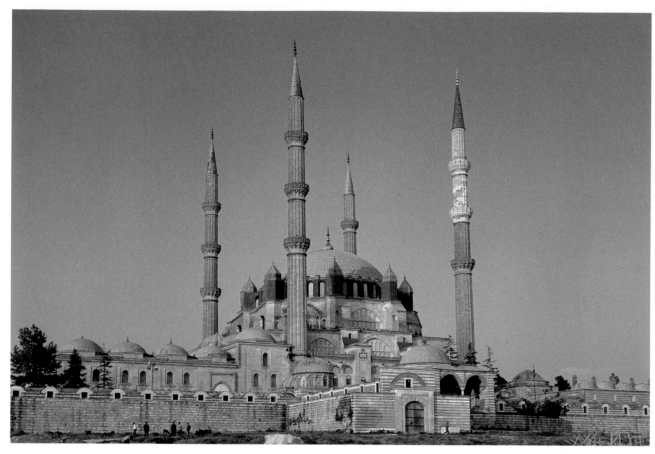

8-16. Sinan. Selimiye Cami (Mosque of Selim), Edirne, Turkey. 1570–74

The minarets that pierce the sky around the prayer hall of this mosque, their sleek, fluted walls and needle-nosed spires soaring to more than 295 feet, are only 12½ feet in diameter at the base, an impressive feat of engineering. Only royal mosques were permitted multiple minarets, and more than two was highly unusual.

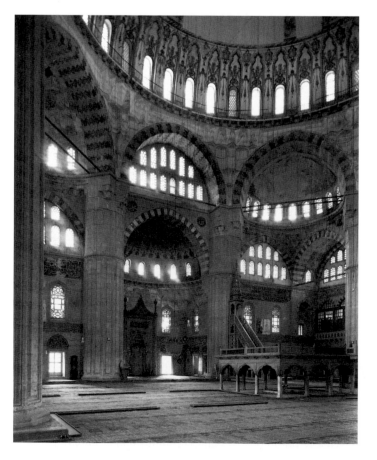

intricate carved scrollwork. The mihrab features marble panels, a double recess, and slender columns supporting **ogival arches**, a pointed form characteristic of Seljuk architecture (see "Elements of Architecture," page 347). Marble inlays create blue, red, and white stripes on the voussoirs, echoing the brick and stone bands of Umayyad architecture (see figs. 8-4, 8-6). Except for its elaborately carved door, the thronelike minbar at the right is made of carved stone instead of the usual wood.

After conquering Constantinople, the rulers of the Ottoman Empire converted the church of Hagia Sophia into a mosque, framing it with graceful Turkish-style minarets and adding calligraphic decorations to the interior (see figs. 7-25, 7-27). Inspired by this great Byzantine structure, Ottoman architects developed a domed, **central-plan** mosque. The finest example of this new form was the work of the architect Sinan (c. 1490–1588). Sinan began his career in the army and was chief engineer during the Ottoman siege of Vienna (1526–1529). He rose through the ranks to become chief architect for Suleyman (known as "the Lawgiver" and "the Magnificent"), the tenth Ottoman sultan (ruled 1520–1566). Suleyman, whose reign marked the height of Ottoman power, sponsored a building program on a scale not seen since the glory days of the Roman Empire. Sinan is credited with

8-17. Selimiye Cami

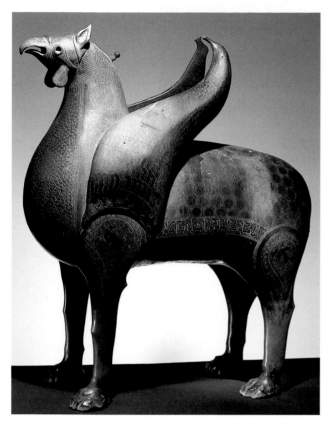

8-18. Griffin, from the Islamic Mediterranean. 11th century. Bronze, height 42⅛" (107 cm). Museo dell'Opera del Duomo, Pisa

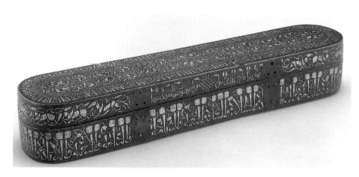

8-19. Shazi. Pen box, from Persia (Iran) or Afghanistan. 1210–11. Brass with silver and copper; height 2", length 12⅝", width 2½" (5 x 31.4 x 6.4 cm). Freer Gallery of Art, Smithsonian Institution, Washington, D.C. (36.7)

The inscriptions on this box include some twenty honorific phrases extolling its owner, al-Mulk. The inscription in naskhi script on the lid calls him the "luminous star of Islam." The largest inscription, written in animated naskhi (an animated script is one with human or animal forms in it), asked twenty-four blessings for him from God. Shazi, the designer of the box, signed and dated it in animated kufic on the side of the lid, making it one of the earliest examples of a signed work in Islamic art. Al-Mulk enjoyed his box for only ten years; he was killed in the Mongol sack of Merv in 1221.

more than 300 imperial commissions, including palaces, madrasas and Koran schools, burial chapels, public kitchens and hospitals, caravansaries—way stations for caravans—treasure houses, baths, bridges, viaducts, and 124 large and small mosques.

Sinan's crowning accomplishment, completed when he was at least eighty, was a mosque he designed at the provincial capital of Edirne for Suleyman's son, Selim II (ruled 1566–1574), in the third quarter of the sixteenth century (fig. 8-16). The gigantic spherical dome that tops this structure is more than 102 feet in diameter, larger than the dome of Hagia Sophia. It covers a building of great geometric complexity on the exterior and complete coherence on the interior, a space at once soaring and serene. In addition to the mosque, the complex housed a madrasa and other educational buildings, a burial ground, a hospital, and charity kitchens, as well as an income-producing covered market and baths. Framed by the vertical lines of four minarets, the mosque shifts from square to octagon to circle as it moves upward and inward. Raised on a base at the city's edge, it dominates the skyline.

The interior seems superficially very much like Hagia Sophia's: an open expanse under a vast dome floating on a ring of light (fig. 8-17). The mosque, however, is a true central-plan structure and lacks Hagia Sophia's longitudinal pull from entrance to sanctuary. A small fountain covered by a muezzin platform emphasizes this centralization. The arches supporting the dome spring from eight enormous piers topped with *muqarnas*. Smaller half-domes between the piers define the corners of a square. Windows at every level flood the interior's cream-colored stone, restrained tile decoration, and softly glowing carpets with light.

Portable Arts

Islamic society was cosmopolitan, fostering the circulation of goods and the movement of people through trade and pilgrimage. In this context, portable objects such as textiles and books assumed greater cultural importance than buildings, and decorative objects were valued as much for the status they bestowed as for their usefulness.

Metal. Islamic metalworkers inherited the techniques of their Roman, Byzantine, and Sassanian predecessors, applying them to new forms, such as incense burners and water pitchers in the shape of fanciful animals and birds. One example of their work, an unusually large and stylized griffin, may originally have been a fountain spout (fig. 8-18). Its place of origin is unknown—suggestions range from Persia to Spain—but it found its way somehow, through trade or pillage, to Italy, where it was displayed atop the cathedral in Pisa from about 1100 to 1828. Made of cast bronze, it is decorated with incised feathers, scales, and silk trappings. The trappings on the creature's thighs include animals in medallions; the bands of cloth across its chest and back are decorated with kufic lettering and scale and circle patterns.

The Islamic world was administered by educated leaders who often commissioned personalized containers—emblems of their class—for their pens, ink, and blotting sand. One such container, an inlaid brass box, was the possession of Majd al-Mulk al-Muzaffar, the grand vizier, or chief minister, of Khurasan in the early thirteenth century (fig. 8-19). The work of an artist

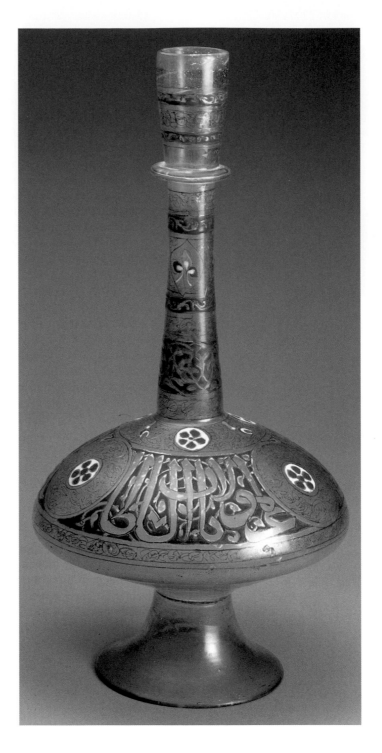

8-20. Bottle, from Syria. Mid-14th century. Blown glass with enamels and gilding, 19½ x 9¾" (49.7 x 24.8 cm). Freer Gallery of Art, Smithsonian Institution, Washington, D.C. (34.20)

named Shazi, it was cast, engraved, embossed, and inlaid with consummate skill. Scrolls, interlacing designs, and human and animal figures enliven its calligraphic inscriptions. All these elements, animate as well as inanimate, seem to be engaged in lively conversation. That a work of such quality was made of brass rather than a costlier metal may seem odd. A severe silver shortage in the mid-twelfth century had prompted the development of inlaid brass pieces like this one that used the more precious metal sparingly. Humbler brassware would have been available in the marketplace to those of more modest means than the vizier.

Glass. Glass, according to the twelfth-century poet al-Hariri, is "congealed of air, condensed of sunbeam

motes, molded of the light of the open plain, or peeled from a white pearl" (cited in Jenkins, page 3). Made with the most ordinary of ingredients—sand and ash—glass is the most ethereal of materials. It first appeared roughly 4,000 years ago, and the tools and techniques for making it have changed little in the past 2,000 years. Like their counterparts working in metal, Islamic glassmakers generally adapted earlier practices to new forms. They were particularly innovative in the application of enameled decoration in gold and various colors. A tall, elegant enameled bottle from the mid-fourteenth century exemplifies their skill (fig. 8-20). One of several objects either given by Mamluk rulers to the Rasulid rulers of Yemen (southern Arabia) or ordered by the Rasulids from Mamluk workshops in Syria, it bears a large inscription nam-

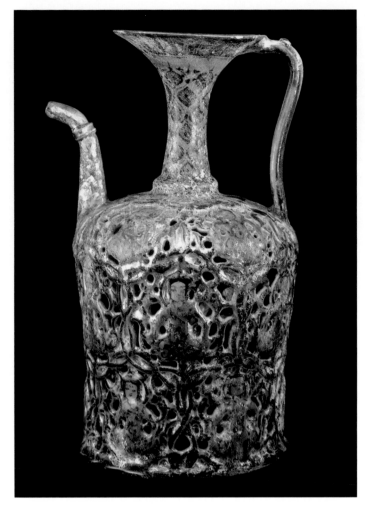

8-21. Pitcher, from Kashan, Persia (Iran). Early 13th century. Glazed and painted fritware, height 11¹³/₁₆" (30 cm). The al-Sabah Collection, Kuwait

Fritware was used to make beads in ancient Egypt and may have been rediscovered there by Islamic potters searching for a substitute for Chinese porcelain. Composed of one part white clay, ten parts quartz, and one part quartz fused with soda, it produced a brittle, white ware when fired. The colors on this double-walled pitcher and others like it were produced by applying mineral glazes over black painted detailing. The deep blue comes from cobalt and the turquoise from copper. Lusterware, a thin, transparent glaze with a metallic sheen, was applied over the colored glazes. Lusterware was to become a trademark of later Islamic ceramics.

ing and honoring a Rasulid sultan in thuluth—a popular Mamluk cursive script—and the Rasulid insignia, a five-petaled red rosette.

Ceramics. Seljuk potters produced tableware in a range of styles and techniques. Unusual among them was a double-walled form found on a group of early-thirteenth-century pitchers that may have derived from a similar form used by Roman glassmakers. The Seljuk pitchers, with their carved openwork shells and solid inner bodies, were difficult to execute. The form was probably intended more to be decorative than to serve a practical function like insulation. The shell of one of them (fig. 8-21) is a forest of twining vines in which perch cross-legged figures. Textilelike patterning covers its

neck and an inscription encircles its rim. The pitchers are made of **fritware**—a mixture of white clay, quartz, and soda that fires into a brittle, white material—and are coated with a thin, transparent glaze that is known as **lusterware**.

Textiles. The tradition of silk weaving that passed from Sassanian Persia to Islamic artisans in the early Islamic period (see fig. 8-10) was kept alive in Muslim Spain, where it was both economically and culturally important. Spanish designs, with their emphasis on architecture-like forms beginning in the thirteenth century, reflect a different aesthetic than those found in the earlier works. The pattern in the central section of a magnificent silk and gold banner (fig. 8-22) resembles the plan of a

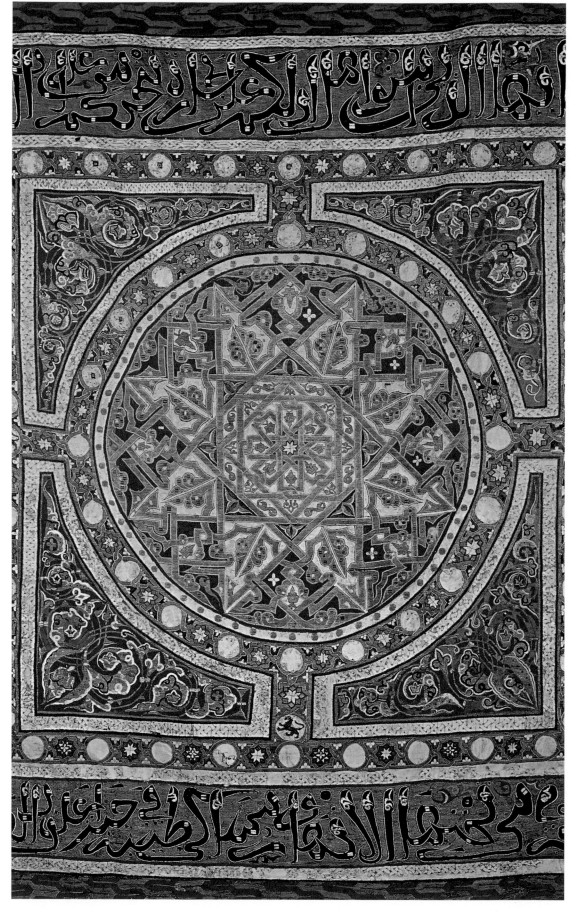

8-22. Banner of Las Navas de Tolosa, from southern Spain. First half of 13th century. Silk tapestry-weave with gilt parchment, 10'9⅞" x 7'2⅝" (3.3 x 2.2 m). Museo de Telas Medievales, Monasterio de Santa Maria la Real de Las Huelgas, Burgos, Spain. Patrimonio Nacional

TECHNIQUE

CARPET MAKING

Because textiles, especially floor coverings, are destroyed through use, very few rugs from before the sixteenth century have survived. There are two basic types of carpets: flat-weaves and pile, or knotted. Both can be made on either vertical or horizontal frames. The best-known flat-weaves today are Turkish kilims, which are typically woven in wool with bold, geometric patterns and sometimes with embroidered details. Kilim weaving is done in the **tapestry** technique, which allows free placement of each area of color (a).

Knotted carpets are an ancient invention. The oldest known example, excavated in Siberia and dating to the fourth or fifth century BCE, has designs evocative of Achaemenid Persian art, suggesting that the technique may have originated in ancient Persia. In knotted rugs the pile—the plush, thickly tufted surface—is made by tying colored strands of yarn, usually wool but occasion-

square inch, each one tied separately by hand.

Although royal workshops produced the most luxurious carpets (see fig. 8-23), most knotted rugs have traditionally been made in tents and homes (see fig. 8-24). Carpets were woven by either women or men, depending on local custom. The photograph in this box shows two women, sisters in Ganakkale province in Turkey, weaving a large carpet in a typical Turkish pattern. The woman in the foreground pushes a row of knots tightly against the row below it with a wood comb called a beater. The other woman pulls a dark red weft yarn against the warp threads before tying a knot. Working between September and May, these women may weave five carpets, tying up to 5,000 knots a day. Generally, an older woman works with a young girl, who learns the art of carpet weaving at the loom and eventually passes it on to the next generation.

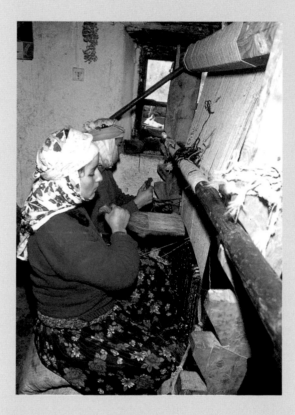

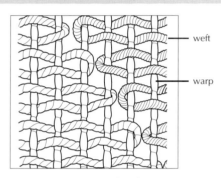

a. Kilim weaving pattern used in flat-weaving

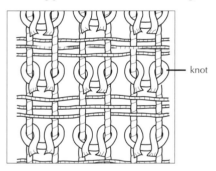

b. Turkish knots, used typically in Anatolia (Turkey) to make pile, or knotted, carpets

ally silk for deluxe carpets, onto the vertical elements (**warp**) of a yarn grid (b or c). These knotted loops are later sheared, cut, and trimmed to form the plush surface of the carpet. Rows of knots alternate with flat-woven rows (**weft**) that hold the carpet together. The weft is usually in undyed yarn and is eventually hidden by the colored knots. Two common tying techniques are the symmetrical "Turkish" knot, which works well for straight-line designs (b), and the asymmetrical "Persian" knot, used for rendering curvilinear patterns (c). The greater the number of knots, the denser and more durable the pile. The finest carpets have a hundred knots per

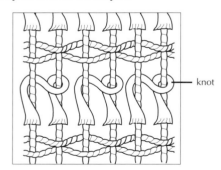

c. Persian knots, favored by Persian carpet makers

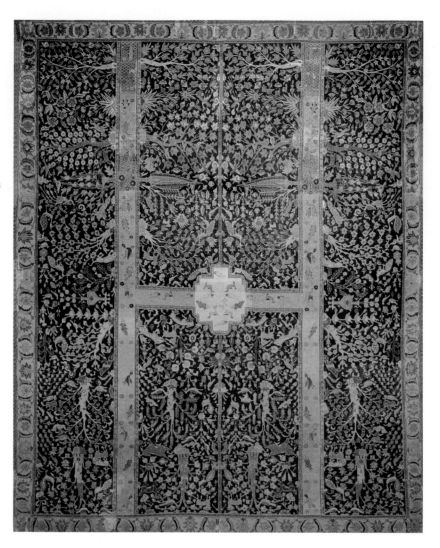

8-23. Garden carpet, from central Persia (Iran). Second half of 17th century. Woolen pile, cotton warps, cotton and wool wefts, 17'5" x 14'2" (5.31 x 4.32 m). The Burrell Collection, Glasgow Museums, Scotland

Spanish courtyard garden (see fig. 8-11), and the Koranic inscriptions that surround it include a reference to the Garden of Eden as a refuge from earthly suffering. The banner was captured in battle by Christian forces not long after it was made.

Since the late Middle Ages, the Islamic art form best known in the non-Islamic West has probably been the carpet. Knotted rugs (see "Carpet Making," page 359) from Persia and Turkey were so highly prized among Westerners that they were often displayed on tables rather than floors. Persian taste favored intricate, elegant designs that evoked the gardens of paradise. Written accounts indicate that such designs appeared on Persian carpets as early as the seventh century. In one fabled royal carpet, garden paths were rendered in real gold, leaves were modeled with emeralds, and highlights on flowers, fruits, and birds were created from pearls and other jewels.

A special kind of garden carpet, possibly derived from drawings by town planners and mapmakers, shows a bird's-eye view of an enclosed park. One such carpet from the second half of the seventeenth century depicts a walled hunting preserve irrigated by an **H**-shaped system of channels. In the middle is a basin filled with floating plants, fish, and birds (fig. 8-23). All kinds of animals and birds, some resting and others hunting, inhabit the

dense forests of leafy trees and blooming shrubs in the rectangular sections. The very finest carpets, like this, woven of cotton and wool or silk and wool in royal workshops, were as much status symbols *within* the Islamic world as they were *beyond* it.

Rugs and mats have long been used for Muslim prayer, which involves repeated kneeling and touching of the forehead to the floor. Prayer rugs came to be distinguished, particularly in Turkey, by mihrab-shaped frames or arches. The worshiper oriented the arch toward Mecca and stood within it. Portable, individual-size carpets could be unrolled as needed for the five daily prayers, either at a mosque or elsewhere. (This is still done today.) Like garden carpets, these were emblems of social prestige and were considered lucky, even magical. Many mosques were literally "carpeted" with wool pile rugs received as pious donations; wealthy patrons gave large, multiple-arched prayer rugs (note, for example, the rugs on the floor of the Selimiye Cami in figure 8-17).

An eighteenth-century carpet from western or central Turkey contains a representation of the Kaaba surrounded by its barricade and framed by a calligraphylike enclosure wall in the shape of a mihrab arch (fig. 8-24). Minarets in the enclosure wall flank the Kaaba barricade, and a minbar, banner flying, stands in front of it flanked by more minarets. Medallions dot the lower portion of

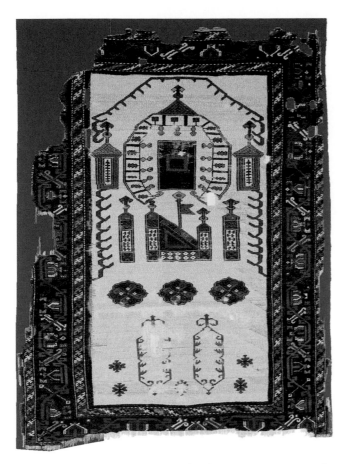

8-24. Prayer carpet with the Kaaba, from western or central Turkey. 18th century. Wool, 57½ x 43¾" (146 x 111 cm). Museum of Turkish and Islamic Arts, Istanbul

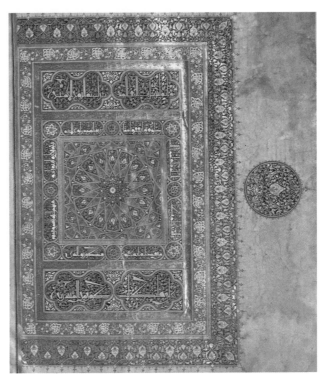

8-25. Koran frontispiece (right half of two-page spread), Cairo, Egypt. c. 1368. Ink, pigments, and gold on paper, 24 x 18" (61 x 45.7 cm). National Library, Cairo. Ms. 7

The Koran to which this page belonged was donated in 1369 by Sultan Shaban to the madrasa established by his mother. Throughout the manuscript, as here, there is evidence of close collaboration between illuminator and scribe.

the carpet. The elongated six-sided shapes at the bottom may be foot marks.

Manuscript Illumination and Calligraphy

The art of book production flourished in the later Islamic centuries. Muslim societies enjoyed a high level of literacy among both women and men thanks to Islam's emphasis on the study of the Koran. Books on a wide range of secular as well as religious subjects were available, although even modest books copied on paper were fairly costly. Libraries, often associated with madrasas, were endowed by members of the educated elite. Books made for royal patrons had luxurious bindings and highly embellished pages, the result of workshop collaboration between noted calligraphers and illustrators. New scripts were developed for new literary forms.

The **illuminators**, or manuscript illustrators, of Mamluk Egypt executed superlative nonfigural designs for Korans. Geometric and botanical ornamentation reached unprecedented heights of sumptuousness and mathematical complexity in their work. As in contemporary architectural decoration, strict underlying geometric organization was combined with luxurious allover patterning. In an impressive frontispiece page originally paired with its mirror image on the facing left page, energy radi-

ates from a sixteen-pointed starburst, filling the central square (fig. 8-25). The surrounding ovals and medallions are filled with interlacing foliage and stylized flowers that provide a backdrop for Koranic quotations. The page's resemblance to court carpets was not coincidental: designers worked in more than one medium, leaving the execution of their efforts to specialized artisans.

In addition to religious works, scribes also copied and recopied famous secular texts, especially scientific treatises, manuals of all kinds, fiction, and poetry. Painters supplied illustrations for these books and created individual small-scale paintings—**miniatures**—that were collected by the wealthy and placed in albums. Miniature painting was highly regarded because of its connection with books, whereas mural painting (associated with the far less exalted craft of architecture) was not. One of the great royal centers of miniature painting was at Herat in Khurasan (in modern Iran). An academy of painting and calligraphy was founded there in the early fifteenth century under the cultured patronage of the Turkic Timurid dynasty (1370–1507).

The most famous artist of this school was Kamal al-Din Bihzad (c. 1440–1514). He headed the academy from about 1469 until the Safavids supplanted the Timurids and established their capital at Tabriz (in northwestern Persia) in 1506. Following this upheaval, Bihzad moved

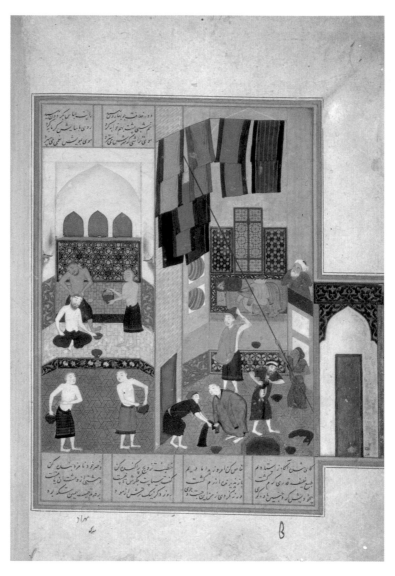

8-26. Kamal al-Din Bihzad. *The Caliph Harun al-Rashid Visits the Turkish Bath*, from a later copy of the *Khamsa* (Five Poems) of Nizami (12th century), Herat, Khurasan (Iran). c. 1494. Ink and pigments on paper, approx. 7 x 6" (17.8 x 15.3 cm). The British Library, London.

Oriental and India Office Collections (Ms. Or. 6810, fol. 27v)

Despite early warnings against it as a place for the dangerous indulgence of the pleasures of the flesh, the bathhouse *(hammam)*, adapted from Roman and Hellenistic predecessors, became an important social center in much of the Islamic world. The remains of an eighth-century *hammam* are still standing in Jordan, and a twelfth-century *hammam* is still in use in Damascus. *Hammams* had a small entrance to keep in the heat, which was supplied by ducts running under the floors. The main room had pipes in the wall with steam vents. Unlike the Romans, who bathed and swam in pools of water, Muslims preferred to splash themselves from basins, and floors were slanted for drainage. A *hammam* was frequently located near a mosque, part of the commercial complex provided by the patron to generate income for the mosque's upkeep.

to Tabriz and briefly resumed his career there. The Herat academy, and Bihzad himself, executed commissions for both royal and nonroyal patrons. Under his leadership, top painters for the first time were permitted to sign their work. Unsigned miniatures by the more talented of his numerous students are often confused with his. Bihzad is remembered for having injected a vivid new naturalism and an interest in the psychological drama of everyday subjects into the super-refined, glittering dreamworld of the academy style. His influence on the next generations of painters was enormous.

Among Bihzad's authentic works are paintings done around 1494 to illustrate the *Khamsa* (Five Poems) by the twelfth-century mystic poet Nizami. These paintings

demonstrate Bihzad's ability to render human activity convincingly. He set his scenes within complex, stagelike architectural spaces that are stylized according to Timurid conventions, creating a visual balance between activity and architecture. In *The Caliph Harun al-Rashid Visits the Turkish Bath* (fig. 8-26), the bathhouse, its tiled entrance leading to a high-ceilinged dressing room with brick walls, provides the structuring element. Attendants wash long, decorative towels and hang them to dry on overhead clotheslines. A worker reaches for one of the towels with a long pole, and a client prepares to wrap himself discreetly in a towel before removing his outer garments. The blue door on the left leads to a room where the caliph is being groomed by his barber while

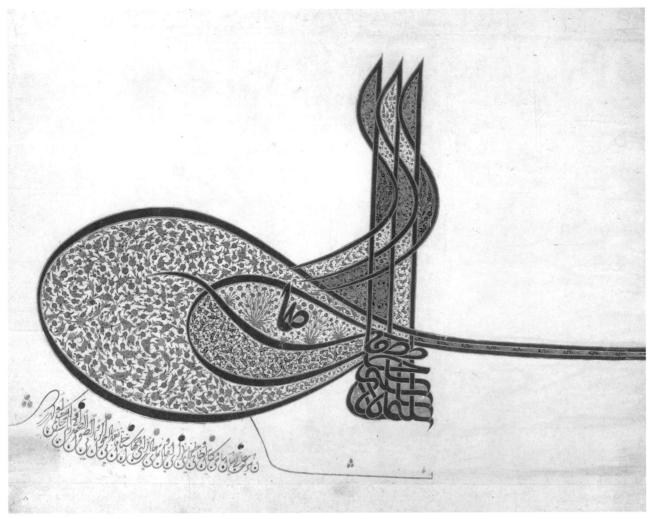

8-27. Illuminated *tugra* of Sultan Suleyman, from Istanbul, Turkey. c. 1555–60. Ink, paint, and gold on paper, removed from a firman and trimmed to 20½ x 25⅜" (52 x 64.5 cm). The Metropolitan Museum of Art, New York

Rogers Fund, 1938 (38.149.1)

attendants bring buckets of water for his bath. The balanced placement of colors and architectural ornaments within each section ties the scene together in a unified whole.

A half century later at the Ottoman court of Sultan Suleyman in Constantinople, the imperial workshops also produced remarkable illuminated manuscripts. In addition, following a practice begun by the Seljuks and Mamluks, the Ottomans put calligraphy to another, political use, developing the design of imperial emblems—***tugras***—into a specialized art form. Ottoman *tugras* combined the ruler's name with the title khan ("lord"), his father's name, and the motto "Eternally Victorious" into an unvarying monogram. *Tugras* symbolized the authority of the sultan and of those select officials who were also granted an emblem. They appeared on seals, coins, and buildings, as well as on official documents called firmans, imperial edicts supplementing Muslim law, or sharia.

Suleyman issued hundreds of firmans. A high court official was entrusted with the important responsibility of affixing Suleyman's *tugra* at the top of official scrolls. For documents like imperial grants to charitable projects that required particularly fancy *tugras*, specialist calligraphers and illuminators were employed. The *tugra* shown here

(fig. 8-27) is from a document endowing an institution in Jerusalem that had been established by Suleyman's wife, Sultana Hurrem.

Tugras on paper were always outlined in black or blue with three long, vertical strokes (*tug* means "horse-tail") to the right of two horizontal teardrops, one inside the other. Early *tugras* were purely calligraphic, but decorative fill patterns became fashionable in the sixteenth century. This fill decoration had become more naturalistic by the 1550s and in later centuries spilled outside the emblems' boundary lines.

Figure 8-27 shows a rare, oversized *tugra* that required more than the usual skill to execute. The sweeping, fluid line had to be drawn with perfect control according to set proportions, and a mistake meant starting over. The color scheme of the delicate floral interlace enclosed in the body of the *tugra* was inspired by Chinese blue-and-white ceramics; similar designs appear on Ottoman ceramics and textiles.

The Ottoman *tugra* is a sophisticated merging of abstraction with naturalism, boldness with delicacy, political power with informed patronage, and function—both utilitarian and symbolic—with adornment. As such, it is a fitting conclusion for this brief survey of Islamic art.

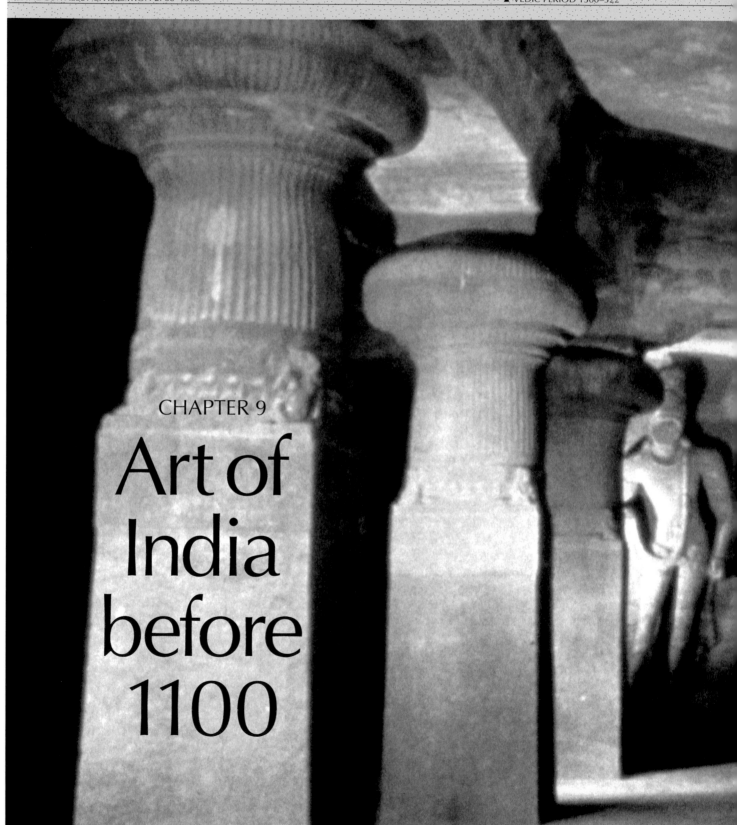

CHAPTER 9

Art of India before 1100

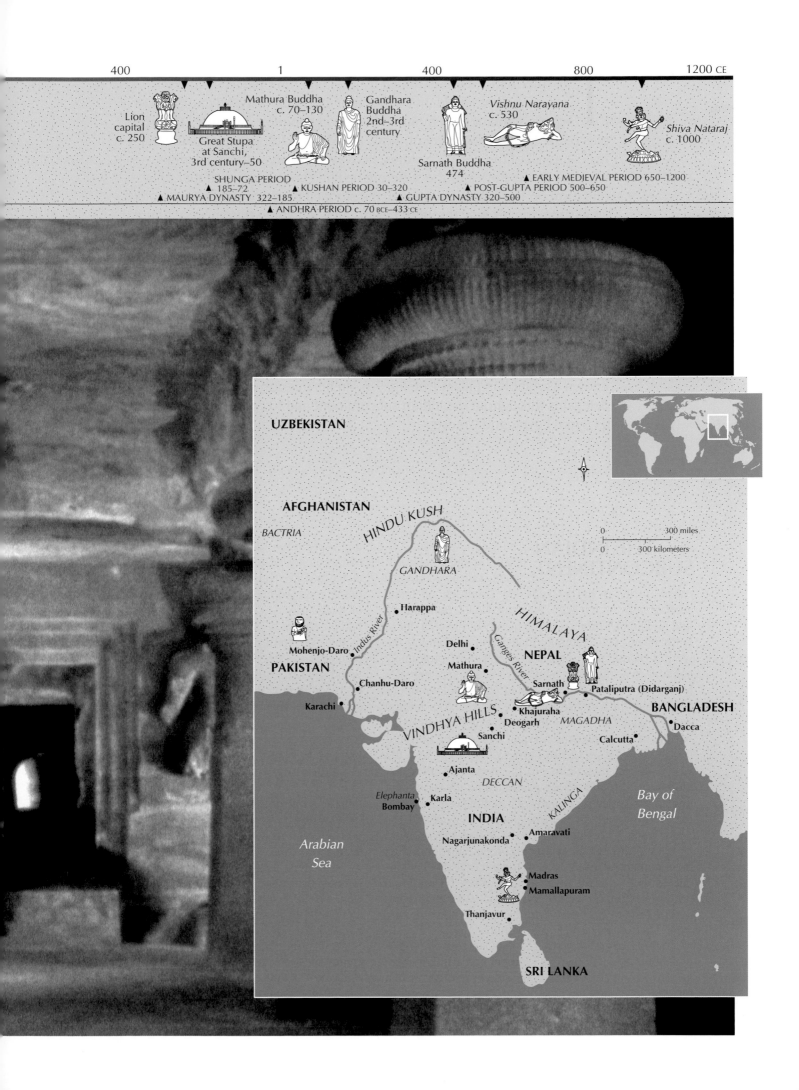

400   1   400   800   1200 CE

Lion capital c. 250

Mathura Buddha c. 70–130

Gandhara Buddha 2nd–3rd century

Great Stupa at Sanchi, 3rd century–50

Vishnu Narayana c. 530

Sarnath Buddha 474

Shiva Nataraj c. 1000

SHUNGA PERIOD ▲ 185–72

▲ KUSHAN PERIOD 30–320

▲ EARLY MEDIEVAL PERIOD 650–1200

▲ POST-GUPTA PERIOD 500–650

▲ MAURYA DYNASTY 322–185

▲ GUPTA DYNASTY 320–500

▲ ANDHRA PERIOD c. 70 BCE–433 CE

UZBEKISTAN

AFGHANISTAN

BACTRIA

HINDU KUSH

GANDHARA

Harappa

Indus River

Mohenjo-Daro

PAKISTAN

Chanhu-Daro

Karachi

Delhi

Mathura

HIMALAYA

Ganges River

NEPAL

Sarnath

Pataliputra (Didarganj)

BANGLADESH

Dacca

VINDHYA HILLS

Khajuraha

Deogarh

MAGADHA

Sanchi

Calcutta

Ajanta

DECCAN

Elephanta   Karla

Bombay

KALINGA

Bay of Bengal

INDIA

Nagarjunakonda   Amaravati

Arabian Sea

Madras

Mamallapuram

Thanjavur

SRI LANKA

0   300 miles
0   300 kilometers

The ruler Ashoka was stunned by grief and remorse as he looked across the battlefield. In the tradition of his dynasty, he had gone to war, expanding his empire until he had conquered many of the peoples of the Indian subcontinent. Now, in 261 BCE, after the final battle in his conquest of the northern states, he was suddenly—unexpectedly—shocked by the horror of the suffering he had caused. It is said that only one form on the battlefield moved, the stooped figure of a Buddhist monk slowly making his way through the carnage. Watching this spectral figure, Ashoka abruptly turned the moment of triumph into one of renunciation. Decrying violence and warfare, he gave his royal support to Buddhism to help establish it as a major official religion of his realm. From that moment on, he set a noble example by living his belief in nonviolence and kindness to all beings.

In his impassioned propagation of Buddhism, Ashoka stimulated an intensely rich period of art. He erected monuments to the Buddha throughout his empire—shrines, monasteries, sculpture, and the columns known as Ashokan pillars (see fig. 9-6). In his missionary ardor, he sent delegates throughout the Indian subcontinent and to countries as distant as Syria, Egypt, and Greece.

THE INDIAN SUBCONTINENT

The South Asian subcontinent, or Indian subcontinent, as it is commonly called, includes the present-day countries of India, southeastern Afghanistan, Pakistan, Nepal, Bangladesh, and Sri Lanka. Throughout the history of the area, these lands have been culturally linked and are among the world's oldest, most productive, and most profoundly spiritual civilizations. Present-day India is approximately one-third the size of the United States. A low mountain range, the Vindhya Hills, acts as a kind of natural division that demarcates North India and South India, which are of approximately equal size. On the northern border rises the protective barrier of the Himalaya, the world's tallest mountains. To the northwest are other mountains through whose passes came invasions and immigrations that profoundly affected the civilization of the subcontinent. Over these passes, too, wound the major trade routes that linked the Indian subcontinent by land to the rest of Asia and Europe. Surrounded on the remaining sides by oceans, India has also been connected to the world since ancient times by maritime trade, and during much of the period under discussion here it formed part of a coastal trading network that extended from eastern Africa to China.

Differences in language, climate, and terrain within India have fostered distinct regional and cultural characteristics and artistic traditions. However, despite such regional diversity, several overarching traits tend to unite Indian art. Most immediately evident is a distinctive sense of beauty. Indian artists delight in full forms and a profusion of ornament, texture, and color. This extraordinary visual generosity is considered auspicious, and it reflects a belief in the abundance and favor of the gods. Another characteristic is the pervasive role of symbolism, which imbues Indian art with intellectual and emotional depths far beyond its immediate appeal to the eye. Third, and perhaps most important, is an emphasis on capturing the vibrant, pulsating quality of a world seen as infused with the dynamics of the divine. Gods and humans, ideas and abstractions come forth clothed in tactile, sensuous forms, radiant with inner spirit.

INDUS VALLEY CIVILIZATION

The earliest civilization of South Asia was nurtured in the lower reaches of the Indus River (in present-day Pakistan and in northwestern India). Known as the Indus Valley or Harappan civilization (after Harappa, the first-discovered site), it flourished from approximately 2700 to 1500 BCE, or during roughly the same time as the Old Kingdom period of Egypt, the Minoan civilization of the Aegean, and the dynasties of Ur and Babylon in Mesopotamia. Indeed, it is considered along with Egypt and Mesopotamia as one of the world's earliest urban, river-valley civilizations.

It was the chance discovery in the late nineteenth century of some small seals like those in figure 9-1 that provided the first clue that an ancient civilization had existed in this region. The seals appeared to be related to, but not the same as, seals known from ancient Mesopotamia (see fig. 2-13). Excavations begun in the 1920s

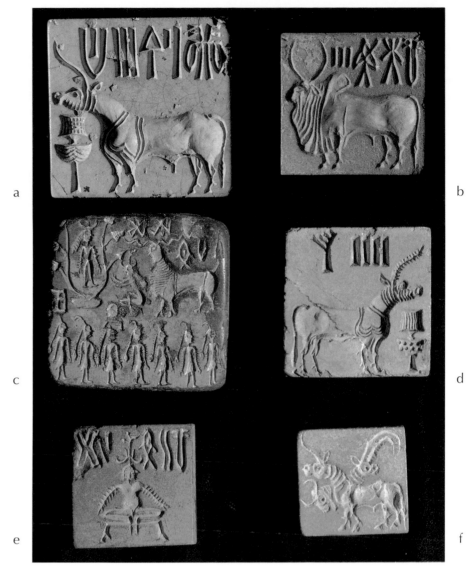

a

b

c

d

e

f

9-1. Seal impressions, from the Indus Valley civilization: a., d. horned animal; b. buffalo; c. sacrificial rite to a goddess (?); e. yogi; f. three-headed animal. c. 2500–1500 BCE. Seals: steatite, each approx. 1¼ x 1¼" (3.2 x 3.2 cm)

More than 2,000 small seals and impressions have been found, offering an intriguing window on the Indus Valley civilization. Usually carved from steatite stone, the seals were coated with alkali and then fired to produce a lustrous, white surface. A perforated knob on the back of each may have been for suspending them. The most popular subjects are animals, the most common being a one-horned bovine standing before an altarlike object (a, c). Animals on Indus Valley seals are often portrayed with remarkable naturalism, their taut, well-modeled surfaces implying their underlying skeletal structures. The function of the seals, beyond sealing packets, remains enigmatic, and the pictographic script that appears so prominently in the impressions has yet to be deciphered.

and continuing into the present have subsequently uncovered a number of major urban areas at points along the lower Indus River, including Harappa, Mohenjo-Daro, and Chanhu-Daro.

The ancient cities of the Indus Valley resemble each other in design and construction, suggesting a unified and coherent culture. At Mohenjo-Daro, the best preserved of the sites, archeologists discovered an elevated **"citadel"** area, presumably containing important government structures, surrounded by a wall about 50 feet high. Among these buildings is the so-called Great Bath, a large, watertight pool that may have been used for ritual purposes. Stretching out below this elevated area was the city, arranged in a gridlike plan with wide avenues and narrower side streets. Its houses, often two stories high, were generally built around a central courtyard. Like other Indus Valley cities, Mohenjo-Daro was constructed of fired brick, in contrast to the less-durable sun-dried brick used in other cultures of the time. The city included a network of covered drainage systems that

■■■■■ ■
2800 BCE   1200 CE

Years	Dynasty/Period	Indian Subcontinent	World
c. 2700–1500 BCE	**Indus Valley civilization**	Mohenjo-Daro "citadel"; seals; Harappa torso	**c. 2700–1500 BCE** Great Pyramids at Giza (Egypt); Stonehenge (England); Minoan culture (Crete); citadel at Mycenae (Greece)
c. 1500–322 BCE	**Vedic period**	Aryan invasions; Veda; Upanishads; birth of Siddhartha Gautama, founder of Buddhism; birth of Mahavira, founder of Jainism; *Mahabharata*; *Ramayana*	**c. 1500–1000 BCE** *Stela of Hammurabi* (Babylonia); Israelites led out of Egypt by Moses (Canaan); Olmec civilization (Mesoamerica) **c. 1000–500 BCE** Legendary founding of Rome (Italy); first Olympian Games (Greece); black-figure and red-figure vase painting (Greece); Hanging Gardens (Babylon); Sappho (Greece); birth of Laozi, founder of Daoism (China); Cyrus the Great (Persia) defeats Babylon; *Aesop's Fables* (Greece)
c. 322–185 BCE	**Maurya dynasty**	"Conversion" of Ashoka; Ashokan pillars	**c. 500 BCE–100 CE** Confucius (China); Sophocles, Aeschylus, Euripides, Herodotus (Greece); *The Canon* of Polykleitos (Greece); Parthenon (Greece); Alexander the Great (Greece) conquers Persia; Colossos of Rhodes; Han dynasty (China); *Nike of Samothrace*, *Aphrodite of Melos* (Greece); crucifixion of Jesus (Jerusalem); Emperor Augustus (Italy); Colosseum (Italy)
c. 185 BCE–30 CE	**Shunga/early Andhra period**	Shunga dynasty (central India); Andhra dynasty (southern India); Great Stupa at Sanchi; rock-cut halls	
c. 30–433 CE	**Kushan/later Andhra period**	Kushan dynasty (northern India and Central Asia); Andhra dynasty (southern India); rule of Kanishka; first images of the Buddha; Gandhara, Mathura, and Amaravati schools	**c. 100–500 CE** Pantheon (Italy); Yayoi and Kofun eras (Japan); Buddhism in China; Maya civilization (Mesoamerica); Emperor Constantine (Italy)
c. 320–500 CE	**Gupta dynasty**	Mathura and Sarnath Gupta schools	
c. 500–650 CE	**Post-Gupta period**	Pallava dynasty (southern India); rise of Hinduism; Dharmaraja Ratha (temple)	**c. 500–800 CE** Hagia Sophia (Turkey); Buddhism in Japan; birth of Muhammad, founder of Islam (Arabia); plague kills half of European population; Tang dynasty (China); Koran (Arabia); Muslim conquests of Arabia, Persia, Syria, Iraq, Egypt, Carthage; Charlemagne is made emperor of the West
c. 650–1100 CE	**Early Medieval period**	Pallava dynasty (southern India); Chola dynasty (southern India); Pala dynasty (northeastern India); Chandella dynasty (northern India); *Dancing Shiva*; conquest by Islam	**c. 800–1100 CE** First Viking colony in Greenland; Lady Murasaki's *Tale of Genji* (Japan); separation of Eastern and Western Christian Churches; the Crusades

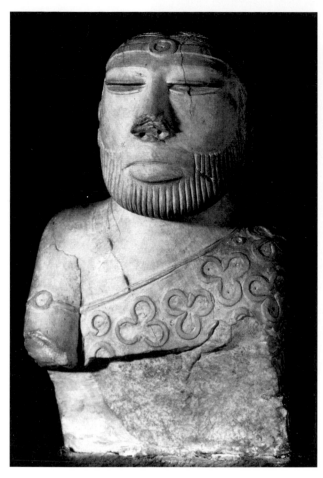

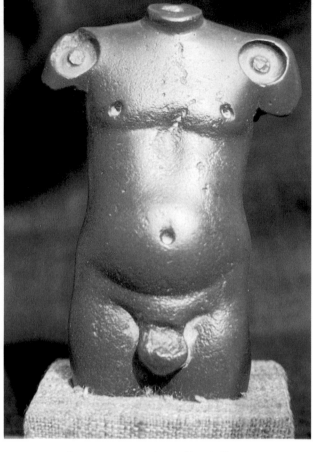

9-2. Bust of a man, from Mohenjo-Daro, Indus Valley civilization. c. 2000 BCE. Limestone, height 6⅞" (17.5 cm). National Museum of Pakistan, Karachi

9-3. Torso, from Harappa, Indus Valley civilization. c. 2000 BCE. Red sandstone, height 3¾" (9.5 cm). National Museum, New Delhi

channeled away waste and rainwater. Clearly the technical and engineering skills of this civilization were highly advanced. At its peak, about 2500 to 2000 BCE, Mohenjo-Daro was approximately 6 to 7 square miles in size and had a population of about 20,000 to 50,000.

Although little is known about the Indus Valley civilization, a majority of motifs on the seals as well as the few artworks that have been discovered strongly suggest continuities with later South Asian culture. Seal (f) in figure 9-1, for example, depicts a man in the meditative posture associated in Indian culture with a yogi, one who seeks mental and physical purification and self-control, usually for spiritual purposes. In seal (d), persons with elaborate headgear in a row or procession observe a figure standing in a tree—possibly a goddess—and a kneeling worshiper. This scene may offer some insight into the religious or ritual customs of Indus Valley peoples, whose deities may have been ancient prototypes of later Indian gods and goddesses.

Numerous **terra-cotta** figurines and a few small stone and bronze statuettes have been found. They reveal an astonishing maturity of artistic conception and technique. Two main styles appear: one is related to Mesopotamian art in its motifs and rather abstract rendering, while the other foreshadows the later Indian artistic tradition in its sensuous naturalism.

The bust of a man in figure 9-2 is an example of the Mesopotamian style. The man's garment is patterned with a **trefoil**, or three-lobed, motif found in Mesopotamian art as well. Although the striated beard and the smooth, planar surfaces of the face reflect Mesopotamian treatment of the head, distinctive physical traits emerge, including a narrow forehead, a broad nose, thick lips, and large, wide eyes. These traits may well record something of the appearance of the Indus Valley peoples. The depressions of the trefoil pattern were originally filled with red paste and the eyes **inlaid** with shell. The narrow band encircling the head falls in back into two long strands and may be an indication of rank. Certainly with its formal pose and simplified, geometric form the statue conveys a human presence of great dignity.

A nude male torso found at Harappa is an example of the contrasting naturalistic style (fig. 9-3). Less than 4 inches tall, it is one of the most extraordinary portrayals of the human form to survive from any early civilization. In contrast to the more athletic male ideal developed in ancient Greece, this sculpture emphasizes the soft texture of the human body and the subtle nuances of muscular form. The abdomen is relaxed in the manner of a yogi able to control his breath. With these characteristics the Harappa torso forecasts the essential aesthetic attributes of later Indian sculpture.

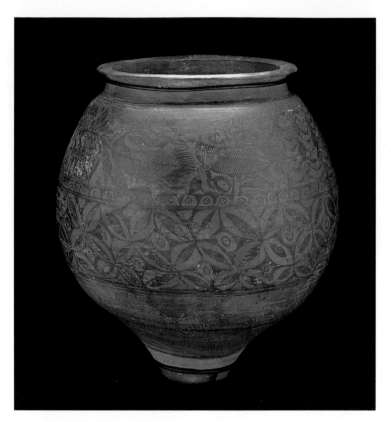

9-4. *Large Painted Jar with Border Containing Birds*, from Chanhu-Daro, Indus Valley civilization. c. 2400–2000 BCE. Reddish buff clay, height 9⅞" (25 cm). Museum of Fine Arts, Boston

Joint Expedition of the American School of Indic and Iranian Studies and the Museum of Fine Arts, Boston

No paintings from the Indus Valley civilization have yet been found, but there are remains of handsome painted ceramic vessels (fig. 9-4). Formed on a potter's wheel and fired at high temperatures, the vessels are quite large and generally have a rounded bottom. They are typically decorated with several zones of bold, linear designs painted in black **slip**. Flower, leaf, bird, and fish motifs predominate. The elegant vessel here, for example, is decorated with peacocks poised gracefully among leafy branches in the upper zone and rows of leaves formed by a series of intersecting circles in the lower zone. Such geometric patterning is typical of Indus Valley decoration.

The reasons for the demise of this flourishing civilization are not yet understood. All we know is that apparently around 1500 BCE—possibly because of climate changes, a series of natural disasters, or invasions—the cities of the Indus Valley civilization declined, and over the next thousand years predominantly rural societies evolved.

THE VEDIC PERIOD

The centuries between the demise of the Indus Valley civilization and the rise of the first unified empire in the late fourth century BCE are generally referred to as the Vedic period. Named for the Vedas, a body of sacred writings that took shape over these centuries, the Vedic peri-od witnessed profound changes in social structure and the formation of three of the four major enduring religions of India—Hinduism, Buddhism, and Jainism.

The period is marked by the dominance of Indo-European Aryans, a pastoral, seminomadic warrior people believed to have entered India sometime around 1500 BCE from the northwest. Gradually they supplanted the indigenous populations that had created the Indus Valley urban centers. The Aryans brought a language called Sanskrit, a hierarchical social order, and religious practices that centered on the propitiation of gods through fire sacrifice. The oldest layers of the Vedas, dating from the first centuries of Aryan presence, consist of hymns to such Aryan gods as the divine king Indra—the Vedic counterpart of the later Greek god Zeus. The importance of the fire sacrifice and the concept of religiously sanctioned social classes persisted through the Vedic period. At some point, the class structure became hereditary, with lasting consequences for Indian society.

During the latter part of this period, from about 800 BCE, the Upanishads were composed. These metaphysical texts examine the meanings of the earlier, more cryptic Vedic hymns. They focus on the relationship between the individual soul, or atman, and the universal soul, or Brahman, as well as on other concepts central to subsequent Indian philosophy. One is the assertion that the material world is illusory and that only Brahman is real

HINDUISM Hinduism is not one integral religion but many related sects, each taking its particular deity as supreme. In Vaishnavism the supreme deity is Vishnu, in Shaivism it is Shiva, and in Shaktism it is the Goddess, Devi—a deity worshiped under many different names and in various forms. Each deity is revealed and depicted in multiple ways. Vishnu, for example, has ten major incarnations in which he manifests himself in the world. Shiva has numerous, complex "aspects" that reveal his nature, which is full of apparent contradictions and extremes. Devi has forms indicative of beauty, wealth, and auspiciousness, but also forms of wrath, pestilence, and power. Indeed, she can be more powerful than the male gods.

Though these three major Hindu sects differ from one another, they all draw upon the texts of the Vedas, which are believed to be sacred revelation. Of critical importance to all Hindu practice is ritual sacrifice, which harks back to ancient times—possibly as early as the Indus Valley period—when offerings were placed into fire in the belief that it would carry prayers to the gods. Purity is essential if the sacrifice is to be effective. If any element of the sacrificial rite becomes polluted, Hindus believe that the deity will be displeased and the sacrifice rejected. As Brahmins, a social category dating back to Vedic times, priests are highly trained ritual specialists and are considered more pure than others. They perform ceremonies on behalf of other Hindus.

Hindu sacrifice is performed for a purpose, which is generally to obtain the favor of a deity in the hope that this will lead to moksha, or liberation from samsara, the endless cycle of birth, death, and rebirth. Hindu belief also holds that all action is performed for a purpose and that every action has its consequences. Desire for the fruits of our actions keeps us trapped in samsara. But there is hope. If we can consider our actions as sacrificial offerings to god, then we will no longer be attached to their fruits, for these now properly belong also to the deity. With this in mind, we will act for the god's sake, not out of desire for ourselves. Pleased with our devotion, he or she will grant us moksha, an eternal state of *sat*, *cit*, and *ananda*—pure being, pure consciousness, and pure bliss. The most compelling and influential expression of these beliefs occurs in the *Bhagavad Gita*, a section of the *Mahabharata*, where Krishna, an incarnation of Vishnu, reveals them as truths to the warrior Arjuna on the battlefield.

Philosophically, Hindu deities are believed to arise from a state of being called Brahman or Formless One—a state of pure *sat*, *cit*, and *ananda*—into a Subtle Body stage. From the Subtle Body emanates our world of space-time and all that it contains. Into this world the deity then manifests itself in Gross Body form in order to help living beings. These three stages of a deity's emanation from One to the Many— Formless One, Subtle Body, and Gross Body—underlie much Hindu art and architecture.

and eternal. Another holds that our existence is cyclical and that beings are caught in samsara, a relentless cycle of birth, life, death, and rebirth. The goal of religious life is to attain liberation from samsara and to unite our individual atman with the eternal universal Brahman.

The latter portion of the Vedic period also saw the flowering of India's epic literature, written in the melodious and complex Sanskrit language. By around 400 BCE, the eighteen-volume *Mahabharata*, the longest epic in world literature, and the *Ramayana*, the most popular and enduring religious epic in India and Southeast Asia, were taking shape. These texts, the cornerstones of Indian literature, relate histories of gods and humans that bring the philosophical ideas of the Vedas to a more accessible and popular level.

In this stimulating religious, philosophical, and literary climate numerous religious communities arose. The most influential teachers of these times were Shakyamuni Buddha and Mahavira. The Buddha, or "enlightened one," lived and taught in India around 500 BCE; his teachings form the basis of the Buddhist religion (see "Buddhism"). Mahavira (599–527 BCE), regarded as the last of twenty-four highly purified super-beings called "pathfinders" *(tirthankaras)*, was the founder of the Jain religion. Both Shakyamuni Buddha and Mahavira espoused some basic Upanishadic tenets, such as the cyclical nature of existence and the need for liberation from the material world. However, they rejected the authority of the Vedas, and with it the legitimacy of the fire sacrifice and the hereditary class structure of Vedic society, with its powerful, exclusive priesthood. In contrast, Buddhism and Jainism were open to all, regardless of social position.

Buddhism became a vigorous force in South Asia and provided the impetus for much of the major art created between the third century BCE and the fifth century CE. The Vedic tradition, meanwhile, continued to evolve, emerging later as Hinduism, a loose term that encompasses the many religious forms that resulted from the mingling of Vedic culture with indigenous, local beliefs (see "Hinduism").

THE MAURYA PERIOD After about 700 BCE, cities again began to appear on the subcontinent, especially in the north, where numerous kingdoms arose. For most of its subsequent history, India remained a constantly shifting mosaic of regional dynastic kingdoms. From time to time, however, a particularly powerful dynasty formed an empire. The first of these was the Maurya dynasty (c. 322–185 BCE), which extended its rule over all but the southernmost portion of the subcontinent.

The art of the Maurya period reflects an age of heroes and the rise to prominence of Buddhism, which became

BUDDHISM The Buddhist religion developed from the teachings of Shakyamuni Buddha, who lived from about 563 to 483 BCE in the present-day regions of Nepal and central India. He was born Prince Siddhartha Gautama, the child of the ruler of the small kingdom of the Shakya clan. At his birth, it is believed, it was foretold that he would become either a chakravartin—a "world-conquering" ruler—or a buddha—a "fully enlightened" being. Hoping for a ruler rather than a holy man, Siddhartha's father tried to surround his son with pleasure and shield him from pain. Yet the prince was eventually exposed to the sufferings of old age, sickness, and death—the inevitable fate of all mortal beings. Deeply troubled by what he perceived to be the desperate human condition, Siddhartha left the palace, his family, and his inheritance to live as an ascetic in the wilderness. He was twenty-nine years old. After six years of meditation, he attained complete enlightenment while sitting under a pipal tree at Bodh Gaya.

Following his enlightenment, Shakyamuni, meaning "sage of the Shakyas," gave his first teaching in the Deer Park at Sarnath. Here he expounded the Four Noble Truths, which are the foundation of Buddhism: (1) life is suffering; (2) this suffering has a cause, which is ignorance; (3) this ignorance can be overcome and extinguished; (4) the way to overcome this ignorance is by fol-lowing the eightfold path of right view, right resolve, right speech, right action, right livelihood, right effort, right mindfulness, and right concentration. The Buddha continued to teach until his death at the age of eighty. After he died, his many disciples developed his teachings and established the world's oldest monastic institutions.

A buddha is not a god but rather one who sees the ultimate nature of the world and is therefore no longer subject to samsara, the cycle of birth, death, and rebirth that otherwise holds us in its grip, no matter whether we are born into the worlds of the various gods, humans, animals, tortured spirits, or hell beings.

The early form of Buddhism, known as Theravada or Hinayana, stresses self-cultivation for the purpose of attaining nirvana, which is the extinction of samsara for oneself. Around the turn of the millennium, however, major developments took place in Buddhism that greatly enlarged its scope. Its philosophical basis was clarified and its literature expanded. The goal was no longer nirvana for oneself, but buddhahood for every being throughout the universe. Compassion for all beings became the primary motivating force. The attainment of buddhahood, viewed as a higher state than nirvana, was the ultimate means by which one could fulfill the compassionate vow of saving all beings. This form of Buddhism, known as Mahayana, became popular mainly in northern India and eventually also took root and flourished in China, Korea, and Japan. Theravada Buddhism, in contrast, continued mainly in southern India, Sri Lanka, and Southeast Asia.

Mahayana Buddhism recognizes not only Shakyamuni Buddha but also numerous other buddhas from the past, present, and future. Some of these buddhas became as popular as Shakyamuni. One such is Maitreya, the next buddha to appear on earth. Another is Amitabha Buddha, the Buddha of Infinite Light and Infinite Life (that is, incorporating all space and time), who dwells in a paradise known as the Western Pure Land. Amitabha Buddha became particularly popular in East Asia. Mahayana Buddhism also developed the category of **bodhisattvas**, meaning "those whose essence is wisdom." Bodhisattvas are saintly, great beings who are on the brink of achieving buddhahood but have vowed to help others achieve buddhahood before crossing over themselves.

In art, bodhisattvas and buddhas are most clearly distinguished by their clothing and adornments: bodhisattvas wear the princely garb of India, while buddhas wear a monk's robe. In Hinduism a deity may dwell in its image, but in Buddhism portrayals of buddhas and bodhisattvas are recognized as purely symbolic, and no spirit is believed to reside within.

the official state religion under the greatest king of the dynasty, Ashoka (ruled c. 273–232 BCE). The belief of the time fostered the ideal of upholding dharma, the divinely ordained moral law believed to keep the universe from falling into chaos. The authority of dharma seems fully embodied in a lifesize statue found at Didarganj, near the Maurya capital of Pataliputra (fig. 9-5). The statue probably represents a **yakshi**, a spirit associated in popular belief with the productive forces of nature. With its large breasts and pelvis, the figure embodies the Indian association of female beauty with procreative abundance, bounty, and auspiciousness—qualities that in turn reflect the generosity of the gods and the workings of dharma in the world.

Sculpted from fine-grained sandstone, the statue conveys the yakshi's authority through the frontal rigor of her pose, the massive volumes of her form, and the strong, linear patterning of her ornaments and dress. Alleviating and counterbalancing this hierarchical formality are her soft, youthful face, the precise definition of prominent features such as the stomach muscles, and the polished sheen of her exposed flesh. This lustrous polish, the technique of which is a lost secret, is a special feature of Mauryan sculpture.

In addition to depictions of popular deities like the yakshis and their male counterparts, **yakshas**, the Maurya period is known for art associated with the imperial sponsorship of Buddhism. Emperor Ashoka, grandson of the dynasty's founder, is considered one of India's greatest rulers. After viewing the carnage on the bloody battlefield described at the beginning of this chapter, he vowed to become a chakravartin, or "world-conquering" ruler, not through the force of arms but through spreading the teachings of the Buddha. Among the monuments

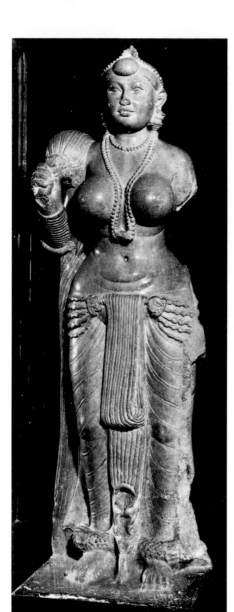

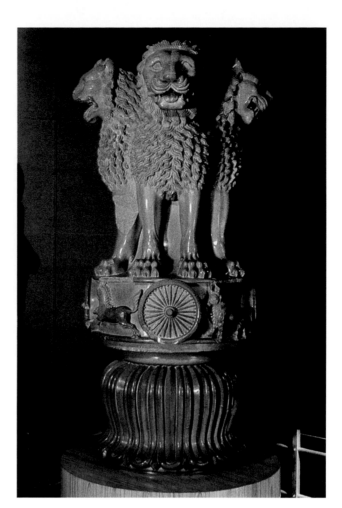

9-6. Lion capital, from an Ashokan pillar at Sarnath, Uttar Pradesh, India. Maurya period, c. 250 BCE. Polished sandstone, height 7' (2.13 m). Archaeological Museum, Sarnath

9-5. *Yakshi Holding a Fly Whisk*, from Didarganj, Patna, Bihar, India. Maurya period, c. 250 BCE. Polished sandstone, height 5'4¼" (1.63 m). Patna Museum, Patna

Discovered near the ancient Maurya capital of Pataliputra, this sculpture has become one of the most famous works of Indian art. Holding a fly whisk in her raised right hand, the yakshi wears only a long shawl and a skirtlike cloth. The cloth rests low on her hips, held in place by a girdle. Subtly sculpted parallel creases indicate that it is gathered closely about her legs. The ends, drawn back up over the girdle, cascade down to her feet in a broad, central loop of flowing folds ending in a zigzag of hems. Draped low over her back, the shawl passes through the crook of her arm and then flows to the ground. (The missing left side of the shawl probably mirrored this motion.) The yakshi's jewelry is prominent. A double strand of pearls hangs between her breasts, its shape echoing and emphasizing the voluptuous curves of her body. Another strand of pearls encircles her neck. She wears a simple tiara, plug earrings, and rows of bangles. The nubbled tubes about her ankles probably represent anklets made of beaten gold. Her hair is bound in a large bun in back, and a small bun sits on her forehead. This hairstyle appears again in Indian sculptures of the later Kushan period (c. second century CE).

he erected to Buddhism throughout his empire were monolithic **pillars** set up primarily at sites related to events in the Buddha's life.

Pillars had been used as flag-bearing standards in India since earliest times. The creators of the Ashokan pillars seem to have adapted this already-ancient form to the symbolism of Indian creation myths and the new religion of Buddhism. The fully developed Ashokan pillar, a slightly tapered sandstone **shaft**, usually rested on a stone foundation slab sunk more than 10 feet into the ground and rose to a height of around 50 feet. On it were carved inscriptions referring to Buddhist teachings or exhorting the Buddhist community to unity. At the top, carved from a separate block of sandstone, an elaborate **capital** bore animal sculpture. Both shaft and capital were given the characteristic Maurya polish. Scholars believe that the pillars symbolized the *axis mundi*, or "axis of the world," joining earth with the cosmos. It represented the vital link between the human and celestial realms, and through it the cosmic order was impressed onto the terrestrial world.

The capital in figure 9-6 originally crowned the pillar erected at Sarnath in northeast India, the site of the

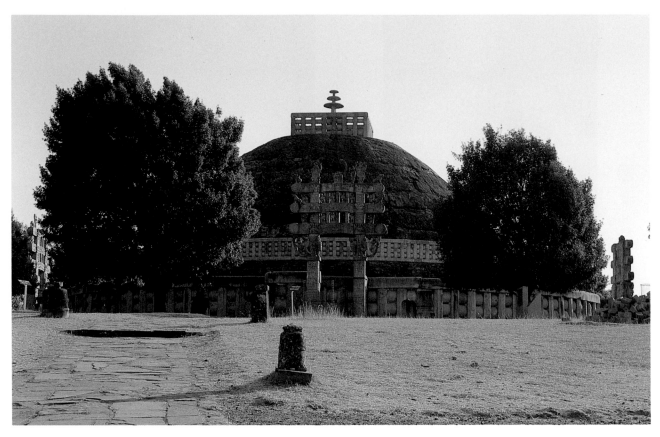

9-7. Great Stupa, Sanchi, Madhya Pradesh, India. Founded 3rd century BCE, enlarged c. 150–50 BCE

Buddha's first teaching. The lowest portion represents the down-turned petals of a lotus blossom. Because the lotus flower emerges from murky waters without any mud sticking to its petals, it symbolizes the presence of divine purity in the imperfect world. Above the lotus is an **"abacus"** embellished with **low-relief** carvings of wheels, called chakras, alternating with four different animals: lion, horse, bull, and elephant. The animals may symbolize the four great rivers of the world, which are spoken of in the same Indian creation myth that express-es the important *axis mundi* concept. Standing on this abacus are four back-to-back lions. Facing the four cardinal directions, the lions may be emblematic of the universal nature of Buddhism. Their roar might be com-pared to the speech of the Buddha that spreads far and wide. The lions may also refer to the Buddha himself, who is known as "the lion of the Shakya clan" (the clan into which the Buddha was born as crown prince). The lions originally supported a great copper wheel, now lost. A universal Buddhist symbol, the wheel refers to Buddhist teaching, for with his sermon at Sarnath the Buddha "set the wheel of the doctrine in motion."

Their formal, heraldic pose imbues the lions with something of the monumental quality evident in the stat-ue of the yakshi earlier. We also find the same delight in the strong patterning of realistic elements: veins and ten-dons stand out on the legs; the claws are large and pow-erful; the mane is richly textured; and the jaws have a loose and fluttering edge.

THE PERIOD OF THE SHUNGAS AND EARLY ANDHRAS

With the demise of the Maurya Empire, India returned to local rule by regional dynasties. Be-tween the second century BCE and the early first century CE, the most important of these dynasties were the Shungas in central India and the early Andhras in South India. Dur-ing this period, Buddhism continued as the main inspira-tion for art, and some of the most important and magnificent early Buddhist structures were created.

Stupas

Probably no early Buddhist structure is more famous than the Great Stupa at Sanchi in central India (fig. 9-7). Originally built by King Ashoka in the Maurya period, the Great Stupa was part of a large monastery complex crowning the top of a hill. During the mid-second centu-ry BCE the stupa was enlarged to its present size, and the surrounding stone railing was constructed. About 100 years later, elaborately carved stone gateways were added to the railing.

Stupas are fundamentally important in the Buddhist world (see "Elements of Architecture," opposite). The first Buddhist stupas were constructed to house the Bud-dha's relics—the remains after his cremation. At that time (c. 483 BCE) the relics were divided into eight por-tions and placed in eight **reliquaries**. Each reliquary was

ELEMENTS OF ARCHITECTURE

Stupas and Temples

Buddhist architecture in South Asia consists mainly of stupas and temples, often at monastic complexes containing **viharas** (monks' cells and common areas). All of these may be either structural—built up from the ground—or rock-cut—hewn out of a mountainside. **Stupas** derive from burial mounds and contain relics beneath a solid, dome-shaped core. A major stupa is surrounded by a railing that creates a sacred path for ritual circumambulation at ground level. This railing is punctuated by gateways called **toranas**, aligned with the cardinal points; access is through the eastern torana. The stupa sits on a round or square **plinth**; stairs lead to an upper circumambulatory path around the platform's edge. On top of the stupa's dome a railing defines a square, from the center of which rises a mast supporting tiers of disk-shaped "umbrellas."

Hindu architecture in South Asia consists mainly of temples, either structural or rock-cut, executed in a num-ber of styles and dedicated to a vast range of deities. The two general Hindu temple types are the northern and southern styles—corresponding to North India and South India, respectively. Within these broad categories there is great stylistic diversity. Hindu temples are raised on plinths and are dominated by their superstructures, tow-ers called **shikharas** in the North and **vimanas** in the South. Shikharas are crowned by **amalakas**, vimanas by large **capstones**. On the interior, a series of **mandapas** (halls) leads to an inner sanctuary, the *garbhagriha*, which contains a sacred image. An *axis mundi* runs verti-cally up from the cosmic waters below the earth, through the *garbhagriha*'s image, and out through the top of the tower. Unlike a Buddhist stupa's *axis mundi*, however, that of a Hindu temple is implied rather than actual.

Jain architecture consists mainly of structural and rock-cut monasteries and temples. Jain halls and temples have much in common with their Buddhist and Hindu counterparts. Buddhist, Hindu, and Jain temples may share a site.

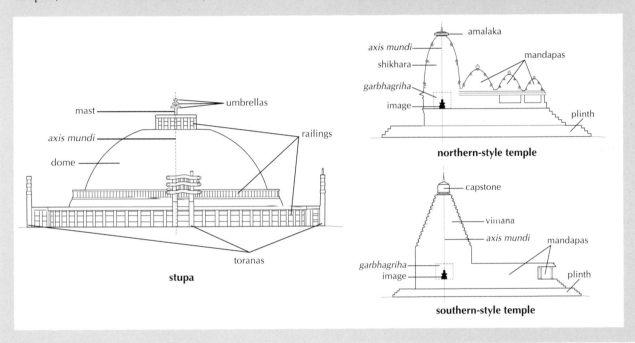

then encased in its own burial mound, called a stupa. In the mid-third century BCE King Ashoka opened these original eight stupas and divided their relics among many more stupas, probably including the one at Sanchi. Since the early stupas held actual remains of the Buddha, they were venerated as his body and, by extension, his enlightenment and attainment of nirvana—liberation from rebirth. The method of veneration was, and still is, to circumambulate, or walk around, the stupa in a clock-wise direction, following the sun's path across the sky. Anyone was free to venerate the stupa, for in the Bud-dhist tradition a monastery and its stupa are open to all.

A stupa may be small and plain or large and elabo-rate. Its form may vary from region to region, but its symbolic meaning remains virtually the same. The Great Stupa at Sanchi is a representative of the early central Indian type. Its solid, hemispherical **dome** was built up from rubble and dirt, faced with **dressed stone**, then covered with a shining white plaster made from lime and powdered seashells. The dome—echoing the arc of the sky—sits on a raised base. Around its perimeter is an upper circumambulatory walkway enclosed by a railing and approached by a pair of staircases. As is often true in religious architecture, the railing provides a physical and symbolic boundary between an inner, sacred area and the outer, profane world. On top of the dome, another stone railing, square in shape, defines the abode of the gods atop the cosmic mountain. It encloses the top of a mast bearing three stone disks, or "umbrellas," of decreasing size. These disks have been interpreted in various ways. They may refer to the Buddhist concept of the three realms of existence—desire, form, and form-lessness. The mast itself is an *axis mundi*, connecting the cosmic waters below the earth with the celestial realm above it and anchoring everything in its proper place. The stupa's plan is a carefully calculated **mandala**, or

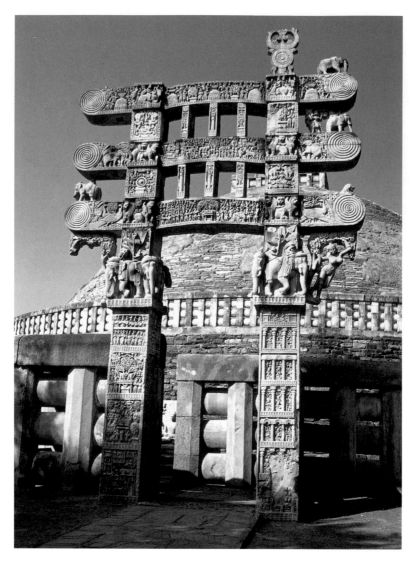

9-8.   North torana of the Great Stupa at Sanchi. Early Andhra period, mid-1st century BCE. Stone, height 35' (10.66 m)

cosmic diagram, in the form of an ancient solar symbol called a svastika.

An 11-foot-tall stone railing rings the entire stupa, enclosing another, wider, circumambulatory path at ground level. Carved with octagonal uprights and lens-shaped crossbars, it probably simulates the wooden railings of the time. This design became a pervasive motif in early Indian art, appearing time and again both in relief sculpture and as architectural ornament. Four stone gateways, or **toranas**, punctuate the railing (fig. 9-8). Set at the four cardinal directions, the toranas symbolize the Buddhist cosmos. According to an inscription, they were sculpted by ivory carvers from the nearby town of Vidisha. The only elements of the Great Stupa at Sanchi to be ornamented with sculpture, the toranas rise to a height of 35 feet. Their square posts are carved with symbols and scenes drawn mostly from the Buddha's life and his past lives. Vines, lotuses, geese, and mythical animals decorate the sides, while guardians sculpted on the lowest panel of each inner side protect the entrance. The "capitals" above consist of four back-to-back elephants

on the north and east gates, dwarfs on the south gate, and lions on the west gate. The capitals in turn support a three-tiered superstructure whose posts and crossbars are elaborately carved with still more symbols and scenes and studded with freestanding sculpture depicting such subjects as yakshis and yakshas, riders on real and mythical animals, and the Buddhist wheel. As in all known early Buddhist art, the Buddha himself is not shown in human form. Instead, he is represented by symbols such as his footprints, an empty "enlightenment" seat, or a stupa.

Forming a bracket between each capital and the lowest crossbar is a sculpture of a yakshi (fig. 9-9). These yakshis are some of the finest female figures in Indian art, and they make an instructive comparison with the yakshi of the Maurya period (see fig. 9-5). The earlier figure was distinguished by a formal, somewhat rigid pose, an emphasis on realistic details, and a clear distinction between clothed and nude parts of the body. In contrast, the Sanchi yakshi leans daringly into space with casual abandon, supported by one leg as the other charmingly crosses

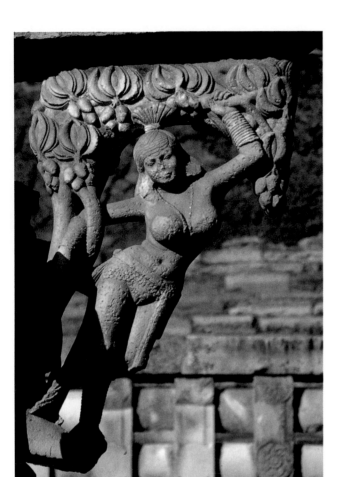

9-9. Yakshi bracket figure, on the east torana of the Great Stupa at Sanchi. Stone, height approx. 60" (152.4 cm)

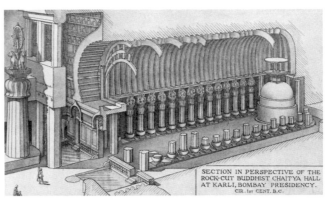

9-10. Section of the chaitya hall at Karla, Maharashtra, India. Early Andhra period, second half of 1st century BCE

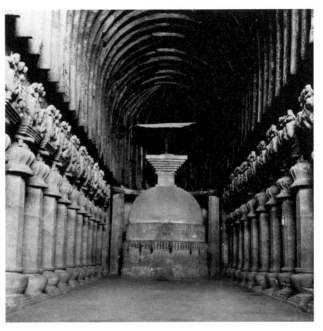

9-11. Chaitya hall at Karla

behind. Her thin, diaphanous garment is noticeable only by its hems, and so she appears almost nude, which emphasizes the unity of her form. The band pulling gently at her abdomen accentuates the suppleness of her flesh. The swelling forms of her body with their lovely arching curves seem to bring this deity's procreative and bountiful essence to life. As anthropomorphic symbol of the waters, she is the source of life. Here she personifies the sap of the tree, which flowers at her touch.

The profusion of designs, symbols, scenes, and figures carved on all sides of the gateways to the Great Stupa not only relate the history and lore of Buddhism but also represent the teeming life of the world and the gods. Arrayed as protectors of the stupa, these forms, by their auspicious presence, indicate the wondrous nature of the site and augur the happiness of those who come to it.

Buddhist Rock-Cut Halls

From ancient times caves have been considered hallowed places in India, for they were frequently the abode of holy ones and ascetics. Around the second century BCE, Buddhist monks began to hew caves for their own use out of the stone plateaus in the western region of India known as the Deccan. The exteriors and interiors were carved from top to bottom like great pieces of sculpture, with all details completely finished in stone.

To enter one of these remarkable halls is to feel immediately removed to an otherworldly, sacred space. The energy of the living rock, the mysterious atmosphere created by the dark recess, the echo that magnifies the smallest sound—all combine to promote a state of intensely heightened awareness.

The monastic community made two types of rock-cut halls. One was the **vihara**, used for the living quarters of the monks, and the other was the **chaitya**, meaning "sacred," which usually enshrined a stupa. A chaitya hall at Karla, dating from around the latter half of the first century BCE, is the largest and most fully developed example of these early Buddhist works (figs. 9-10, 9-11). At the entrance, a series of columns once supported a balcony, in front of which a pair of Ashokan-type pillars stood. The walls of the vestibule area are carved in relief with rows of small balcony railings and arched windows, simulating the facade of a great multistoried palace. At the base of the side walls, enormous statues of elephants seem to be supporting the entire structure on their backs. Filling almost the entire upper portion of the main facade is a large horseshoe-shaped opening called a "sun window" or "chaitya window," which provides the main source of light for the hall's interior. The window was originally fitted with a carved wood screen, some of which still remains, that softened and filtered the light within.

Three entrances in the main facade lead to the interior. The two side entrances are each approached through a shallow pool of water, which symbolically purifies visitors as it washes their dusty feet. Flanking the entrances are sculpted panels of **mithuna** couples, amorous male and female figures that evoke the harmony and fertility of life. The interior hall, 123 feet long, has a 46-foot-high ceiling carved in the form of a **barrel vault** ornamented with arching wooden ribs. A wide central aisle and two narrower side aisles lead to the stupa situated in the rounded **apse** at the far end.

The closely spaced columns that separate the side aisles from the main aisle are unlike any known in the West, and they are important examples in the long and complex evolution of the many Indian styles. The base resembles a large pot set on a stepped pyramid of planks. From this potlike form rises a massive octagonal shaft. Crowning the shaft, a bell-shaped lotus capital supports an inverted pyramid of planks, which serves in turn as a platform for sculpture. The statues facing the main aisle depict pairs of kneeling elephants, each bearing a *mithuna* couple; those facing the side aisles depict pairs of horses also bearing couples. These figures, the only sculpture within this austere hall, represent the nobility coming to pay homage at the temple. The pillars around the apse are plain, and the stupa is simply portrayed. A railing motif ornaments the base; the dome was once crowned with wooden "umbrella" disks, only one of which remains. The symbolism of this stupa is the same as that of the stupa at Sanchi, although it, like nearly everything in the cave, is carved from the living rock. Both exterior and interior were once brightly painted.

THE KUSHAN AND LATER ANDHRA PERIOD

Around the first century CE the regions of present-day Afghanistan, Pakistan, and North India came under the control of the Kushans, a nomadic people from Central Asia. The impact of the Kushan dynasty on Indian culture was significant, but their history is clouded by lack of clear dates. The beginning of the long reign of their most illustrious king, Kanishka, is variously dated from 78 to 143 CE. A patron of Buddhism, Kanishka caused many stupas and monasteries to be built, thus giving a renewed impetus to the religion.

Buddhism during this period was undergoing the profound developments that resulted in the form known as Mahayana, or Great Vehicle (see "Buddhism," page 371). This vital new movement, which was to sweep most of northern India and eastern Asia, probably inspired the first depictions of the Buddha himself in art. (Previously, as in the Great Stupa at Sanchi, the Buddha had been indicated solely by symbols.) It is not known where the first Buddha image appeared. However, the

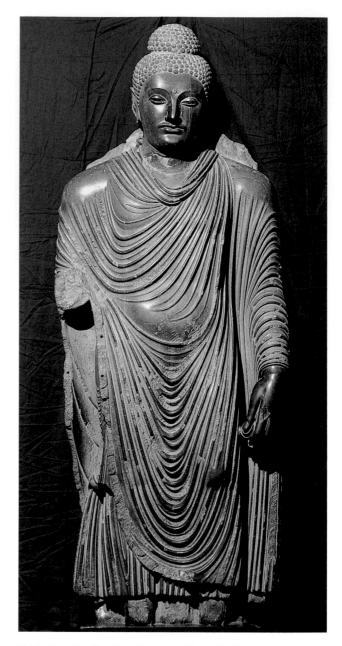

9-12. *Standing Buddha*, from Gandhara (Pakistan). Kushan period, c. 2nd–3rd century CE. Schist, height 7'6" (2.28 m). Lahore Museum, Lahore

two earliest schools of representation arose in the Gandhara region in the northwest (present-day Pakistan and Afghanistan) and in the famous religious center of Mathura in central India. Both of these areas were ruled by the Kushans. Slightly later, a third school, known as the Amaravati school after its most famous site, developed to the south in the region ruled by the Andhras.

While all three schools cultivated distinct styles, they shared a basic **iconography** in which the Buddha is readily recognized by certain characteristics. He wears a monk's robe called a **sanghati**, a long length of cloth draped over the left shoulder and around the body. The Buddha is said to have had thirty-two major distinguishing marks, called **lakshana**, some of which also passed into the iconography of his image (see "Buddhist Symbols," page 427). These include a golden-colored body,

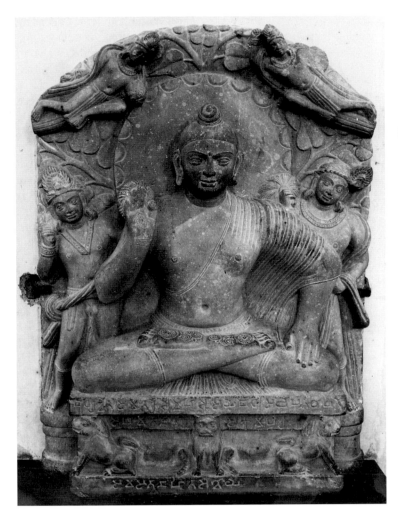

9-13. *Buddha and Attendants*, from Katra Keshavdev, Mathura, Madhya Pradesh, India. Kushan period, c. late 1st–early 2nd century CE. Red sandstone, height 27¼" (69.2 cm). Government Museum, Mathura

long arms that reached to his knees, the impression of a wheel (chakra) on the palms of his hands and the soles of his feet, and the *urna*—a tuft of white hair between his eyebrows. Because he had been a prince in his youth and had worn the customary heavy earrings, his earlobes are usually shown elongated. The top of his head is said to have had a protuberance called an *ushnisha*, which in images often resembles a bun or topknot and is symbolic of his enlightenment.

The Gandhara School

A typical image from the Gandhara school portrays the Buddha as a superhuman figure, more powerful and heroic than an ordinary human (fig. 9-12). This over-lifesize Buddha dates to the fully developed stage of the Gandhara style around the third century CE. It is carved from schist, a fine-grained dark stone. The Buddha's body, revealed through the folds of the garment, is broad and massive, with heavy shoulders and limbs and a well-defined torso. His left knee bends gently, suggesting a slightly relaxed posture.

The treatment of the *sanghati* is especially characteristic of the Gandhara manner. Tight, riblike folds alternate with delicate creases, setting up a clear, rhythmic pattern of heavy and shallow lines. On the upper part of the figure the folds break asymmetrically along the left

arm; on the lower part they drape in a symmetric U shape. The strong tension of the folds suggests life and power within the image. This complex fold pattern resembles the treatment of togas on certain Roman statues (see fig. 6-25), and it exerted a strong influence on portrayals of the Buddha in Central and East Asia. The Gandhara region's history of relations with the Hellenistic world may have prepared the ground for this strongly Western style in its art. Pockets of Hellenistic culture had thrived in neighboring Bactria (present-day northern Afghanistan and southern Uzbekistan) since the fourth century BCE, when the Greeks under Alexander the Great reached the borders of India. Also, Gandhara's position near the East-West trade routes appears to have stimulated contact with Roman culture in the Near East during the early centuries of the first millennium CE.

The Mathura School

The second major school of Buddhist art in the Kushan period, that at Mathura, was not allied with the Hellenistic-Roman tradition. Instead, its style evolved from representations of yakshas, the indigenous male nature deities. Images produced at Mathura during the early days of the school may well be the first representations of the Buddha to appear in art.

The **stela** in figure 9-13 is one of the finest of the

MUDRAS

Mudras (meaning "signs" in Sanskrit) are ancient symbolic hand gestures seen primarily in Buddhist art, where they function iconographically. Mudras are regarded as physical expressions of different states of being and are used during meditation to release these energies. Following are the most common mudras in Asian art.

Dharmachakra mudra

The gesture of teaching, setting the chakra (wheel) of the dharma (law, or doctrine) in motion. Hands are at chest level.

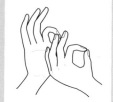

Dhyana mudra

A gesture of meditation and balance, symbolizing the path toward enlightenment. Hands are in the lap, the lower representing maya, the physical world of illusion, the upper representing nirvana, enlightenment and release from the world.

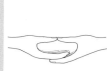

Vitarka mudra

This variant of *dharmachakra* mudra stands for intellectual debate. The right hand is at shoulder level, pointing downward, while the left is at hip level pointing upward.

Abhaya mudra

The gesture of reassurance, blessing, and protection, this mudra means "do not fear." The right hand is at shoulder level, palm outward.

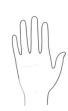

Bhumisparsha mudra

This gesture calls the earth to witness Shakyamuni Buddha's enlightenment at Bodh Gaya. A seated figure's right hand reaches toward the ground, palm inward.

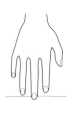

Varada mudra

The gesture of charity, symbolizing the fulfillment of all wishes. Alone, this mudra is made with the right hand; when combined with *abhaya* mudra in standing buddha figures, the left hand is shown in *varada* mudra.

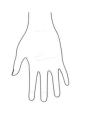

early Mathura images. Carved in **high relief** from a block of red sandstone, it depicts a seated Buddha with two attendants. The Buddha sits in a yogic posture on a pedestal supported by lions. His right hand is raised in a symbolic gesture meaning "have no fear." Images of the Buddha rely on a repertoire of such symbolic gestures, called **mudras**, to communicate certain ideas, such as teaching, meditation, or the attaining of enlightenment (see "Mudras"). The Buddha's *urna*, his *ushnisha*, and the impressions of wheels on the palms and soles of his feet are all clearly visible in this figure. Behind his head is a large, circular halo; the scallop points of its border represent radiating light. Behind the halo are branches of the pipal tree, the tree under which the Buddha was seated when he achieved enlightenment. Two celestial beings hover above.

As in the Gandhara school, a powerful impression of the Buddha is emphasized. Yet the Mathura Buddha's riveting outward gaze and alert posture impart a more intense, concentrated energy to the image. The robe is pulled tightly over the body, allowing the fleshy form to be seen as almost nude. Where the pleats of the *sanghati* appear, such as over the left arm and fanning out between the legs, they are depicted abstractly through compact parallel formations of ridges with an **incised** line in the center of each ridge. This characteristic Mathura tendency to abstraction also appears in the face, whose features take on geometric shapes, as in the rounded forms of the widely opened eyes. Nevertheless, the heavy torso with its subtle and soft modeling is strongly naturalistic.

The Amaravati School

Events from the Buddha's life were popular subjects in the reliefs decorating Buddhist stupas and temples. One example from Nagarjunakonda, a site of the third major school of this period, the southern or Amaravati school, depicts a scene from the Buddha's life when he was a prince called Siddhartha, before his renunciation and subsequent quest for enlightenment (fig. 9-14). Carved in low relief, the panel reveals a scene of pleasure around a pool of water. Gathered around Siddhartha, the largest figure and the only male, are some of the palace women. One holds his foot, entreating him to come into the water; another sits with legs drawn up on the nearby rock; others lean over his shoulder or fix their hair; one comes into the scene with a box of jewels on her head. The panel is framed by decorated columns, crouching lions, and amorous *mithuna* couples. (One of these couples is visible at the right of the illustration.) The scene is skillfully orchestrated to revolve around the prince as the main focus of all eyes. Typical of the southern school, the figures are slighter than those of the Gandhara and Mathura schools. They are sinuous and mobile, even while at rest. The rhythmic nuances of the limbs and varied postures not only create interest in the activity of each individual but also engender a light and joyous effect.

During the first to third century CE, each of these three major schools of Buddhist art developed its own distinct

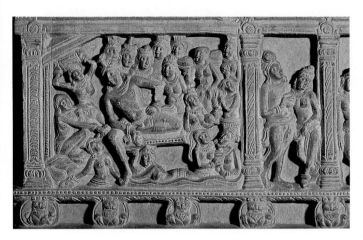

9-14. *Siddhartha in the Palace*, detail of a relief from Nagarjunakonda, Andhra Pradesh, India. Later Andhra period, c. 3rd century CE. Limestone. National Museum, New Delhi

In his *Buddhacharita*, a long poem about the life of the Buddha, the great Indian poet Ashvagosha (c. 100 CE) describes Prince Siddhartha's life in the palace: "The monarch [Siddhartha's father], reflecting that the prince must see nothing untoward that might agitate his mind, assigned him a dwelling in the upper storeys of the palace and did not allow him access to the ground. Then in the pavilions, white as the clouds of autumn, with apartments suited to each season and resembling heavenly mansions come down to earth, he passed the time with the noble music of singing-women." Later, during an outing, a series of unexpected encounters confront Siddhartha with the nature of mortality. Deeply shaken, he cannot bring himself to respond to the perfumed entreaties of the women who greet him on his return: "For what rational being would stand or sit or lie at ease, still less laugh, when he knows of old age, disease and death?" In this relief, the prince, though surrounded by women in the pleasure garden, seems already to bear the sobering demeanor of these thoughts, which were to change his life profoundly and affect the world.

,(Translated by E. H. Johnston)

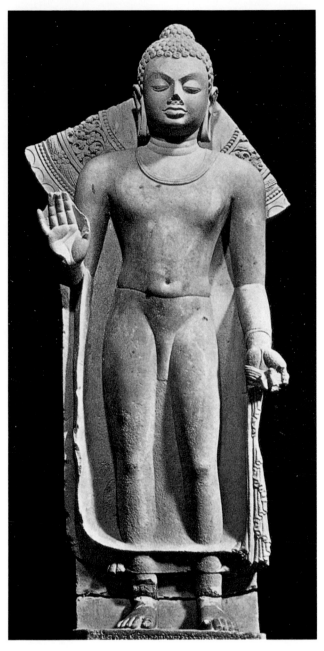

9-15. *Standing Buddha*, from Sarnath, Uttar Pradesh, India. Gupta period, 474 CE. Chunar sandstone, height 6'4" (1.93 m). Archaeological Museum, Sarnath

idiom for expressing the complex imagery of Buddhism and depicting the image of the Buddha. The Gandhara and Amaravati schools declined over the ensuing centuries, mainly due to the demise of the major dynasties that had supported their Buddhist establishments. However, the schools of central India, including the school of Mathura, continued to develop, and from them came the next major development in Indian Buddhist art.

THE GUPTA PERIOD

The Guptas, the founders of a dynasty in the eastern region of central India known as Magadha, expanded their territories during the course of the fourth century to form an empire that encompassed northern and much of southern India. Though the peak of Gupta power lasted only about 130 years (c. 320–450 CE), the influence of Gupta culture was felt for centuries.

The Gupta period, extending from around 320 to 500 CE, is renowned for its high artistic and literary culture. Buddhism reached its greatest influence, and Hinduism, sponsored by Gupta monarchs, began the ascendancy that led to its eventual domination of Indian religious life. Art flourished, and the Gupta legacy includes some of India's most widely admired masterpieces of sculpture and painting.

Buddhist Sculpture

Two schools of Buddhist sculpture dominated in northern India: the Mathura, one of the major schools of the earlier Kushan period, and the school at Sarnath. Both reached their artistic peak during the second half of the fifth century.

The standing Buddha in figure 9-15 embodies the fully developed Sarnath Gupta style. Carved from fine-grained sandstone, the figure stands in a mildly relaxed

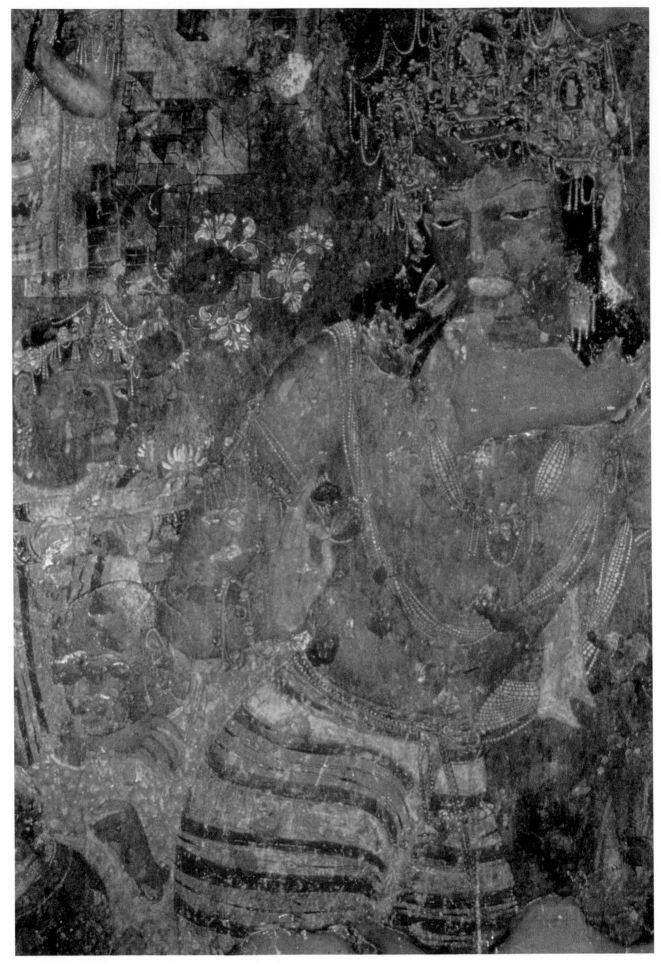

9-16. *Bodhisattva*, detail of a wall painting in Cave I, Ajanta, Maharashtra, India. Gupta period, c. 475 CE

pose, the body clearly visible through a clinging robe. This plain *sanghati*, portrayed with none of the creases and folds so prominent in the Kushan period images, is distinctive of the Sarnath school. Its effect is to concentrate attention on the perfected form of the body, which emerges in high relief. The body is graceful and slight, with broad shoulders and a well-proportioned torso. Only a few lines of the garment at the neck, waist, and hems interrupt the purity of its subtly shaped surfaces. Even the face, smooth and ovoid, shows this refined elegance. The downcast eyes suggest otherworldly introspection, yet the gentle, open posture maintains a human link. Behind the head are the remains of a large, circular halo. Carved in concentric circles of pearls and foliage, it would have contrasted dramatically with the plain surfaces of the figure.

The Sarnath Gupta style reveals the Buddha in perfection and equilibrium. He is not interpreted as a powerful, superhuman presence but as a being whose spiritual purity is evidenced by, and in some way fused with, his physical purity. The nature of the fully enlightened seems completely synonymous with the nature of the fully human—an expression fitting the true nature of a buddha.

Painting

The Gupta aesthetic also found expression in painting. Some of the finest surviving works are murals from the Buddhist rock-cut halls of Ajanta in the Deccan area of western India. Under a local dynasty, many caves were carved around 475 CE, including Cave I, a large vihara hall with monks' chambers around the sides and a Buddha shrine chamber in the back. The walls of the central court were covered with murals painted in **fresco** technique with mineral pigments on a prepared plaster surface. Some of these paintings depict episodes from the Buddha's past lives. Flanking the entrance to the shrine are two large bodhisattvas, one of which is seen in figure 9-16.

Bodhisattvas are beings who are in the process of becoming buddhas and have reached a high level of spiritual attainment already. They are distinguished from buddhas in art by their princely garments (like those worn by Shakyamuni as a prince) rather than the monk's *sanghati*. The bodhisattva here is lavishly adorned with delicate ornaments. He wears a complicated crown with many tiny pearl festoons, large earrings, long necklaces of twisted pearl strands, armbands, and bracelets. A striped cloth covers his lower body. The graceful bending posture imparts his sympathetic attitude as he gazes serenely outward toward the viewer. His spiritual power is suggested by his large size in comparison with the surrounding figures.

The naturalism of the style balances outline and softly graded color tones. The outline drawing, always a major ingredient of Indian painting, creates clearly defined shapes; the tonal gradations impart the illusion of three-dimensional form, with lighter tones used for protruding parts such as the nose, brows, shoulders, and chest muscles. Together with the details of the jewels,

these highlighted areas resonate against the subdued tonality of the figure and the somber, flower-strewn background. Interest in sophisticated, realistic detail is balanced, in typical Gupta fashion, by the magnetic beauty of the languorous human form. In no other known examples of Indian painting do bodhisattvas appear so magnanimous and graciously divine yet at the same time so palpably human. This particular synthesis, evident also in the Sarnath statue, is the glory of Gupta artistic achievement.

THE POST-GUPTA PERIOD

As Buddhism flourished in India during the fifth century, Hinduism, supported by the Gupta monarchs, began to rise in popularity. Hindu temples and sculptures of the Hindu gods, though known earlier, appeared with increasing frequency during the Gupta period and its aftermath in the post-Gupta era of the sixth to mid-seventh century.

The Early Northern Temple

The Hindu temple developed many different forms throughout India, but it can be classified broadly into two types, northern and southern. The northern type is chiefly distinguished by a superstructure called a **shikhara** (see "Elements of Architecture," page 375). The shikhara rises as a solid mass above the flat stone ceiling and windowless walls of the sanctum, or **garbhagriha**, which houses an image of the temple's deity. As it rises, it curves inward in a mathematically determined ratio. (In mathematical terms, the shikhara is a paraboloid.) Crowning the top is a circular, cushionlike element called an **amalaka**, which means "sunburst." From the amalaka a **finial** takes the eye to a point where the earthly world is thought to join the cosmic world. An imaginary *axis mundi* penetrates the entire temple, running from the point of the finial, through the exact center of the amalaka and shikhara, down through the center of the *garbhagriha* and its image, finally passing through the base of the temple and into the earth below. In this way the temple becomes a conduit between the celestial realms and the earth. This theme, familiar from Ashokan pillars and Buddhist stupas, is carried out with elaborate exactitude in Hindu temples, and it is one of the most important elements in the rationale behind their form and function (see "Meaning and Ritual in Hindu Temples and Images," page 385).

One of the earliest northern-style temples is the temple of Vishnu at Deogarh in central India, which dates from around 530 CE (fig. 9-17). Much of the shikhara has crumbled away, and so we cannot determine its original shape with precision. Nevertheless, it was clearly a massive, solid structure built of large cut stones. It would have given the impression of a mountain, which is one of several metaphoric meanings of a Hindu temple. This early temple has only one chamber, the *garbhagriha*, which corresponds to the center of a sacred diagram called a mandala on which the entire temple site is patterned. As the deity's residence, the *garbhagriha* is likened to a sacred cavern within the "cosmic mountain" of the temple.

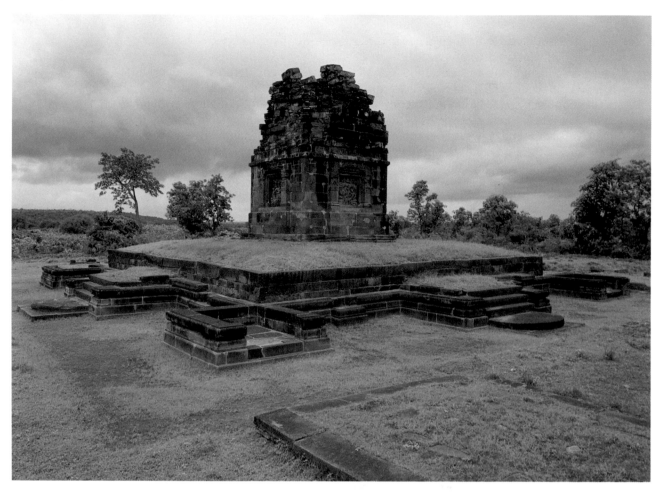

9-17. Vishnu Temple at Deogarh, Uttar Pradesh, India. c. 530 CE

The entrance to a Hindu temple is elaborate and meaningful. The doorway at Deogarh is well preserved and an excellent example (fig. 9-18). Because the entrance takes a worshiper from the mundane world into the sacred, stepping over a threshold is considered a purifying act. Two river goddesses, one on each upper corner of the **lintel**, symbolize the purifying waters flowing down over the entrance. These imaginary waters also provide symbolic nourishment for the vines and flowers decorating some of the vertical **jambs**. The innermost vines sprout from the navel of a dwarf, one of the popular motifs in Indian art. *Mithuna* couples and small replicas of the temple line other jambs. At the bottom, male and female guardians flank the doorway. Above the door, in the center, is a small image of the god Vishnu, to whom the temple is dedicated.

Large panels sculpted in relief with images of Vishnu appear as "windows" on the temple's exterior. These elaborately framed panels are not windows in the ordinary sense. They do not function literally to let light *into* the temple; they function symbolically to let the light of the deity *out* of the temple so it may be seen by those outside. The panels thus symbolize the third phase of Vishnu's threefold emanation from Brahman, the Formless One, into our physical world. (For a discussion of the emanation of Hindu deities, see "Hinduism," page 372.)

One panel depicts Vishnu lying on the Cosmic Waters at the beginning of creation (fig. 9-19). This vision

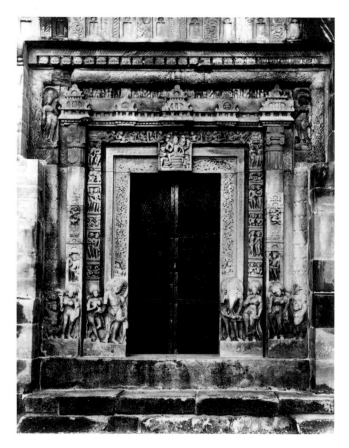

9-18. Doorway of the Vishnu Temple at Deogarh

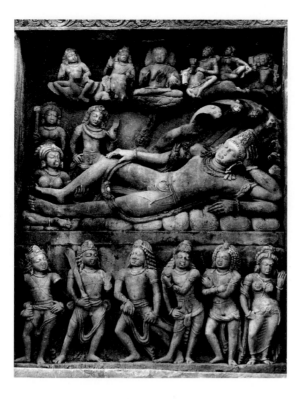

9-19. *Vishnu Narayana on the Cosmic Waters*, relief panel in the Vishnu Temple at Deogarh. Stone

MEANING AND RITUAL IN HINDU TEMPLES AND IMAGES

The Hindu temple is one of the most complex and meaningful architectural forms in Asian art. Age-old symbols and ritual functions are embedded not only in a structure's many parts but also in the process of construction itself. Patron, priest, and architect worked as a team to ensure the sacred nature of the structure from start to finish. No artist or artisan was more highly revered in Indian society than the architect, who could oversee the construction of an abode in which a deity would dwell.

For a god to take up residence, however, everything had to be done properly. By the sixth century CE, the necessary procedures and explanations had been recorded in exacting detail in a group of texts called the *Silpa Shastra*. First, a site was chosen that was auspicious—promised to bode well. A site near water was especially favored, for water makes the earth fruitful. Next, the ground was prepared, an elaborate process that took several years. Various spirits who were already inhabiting the site were "invited" to leave so that the temple might be raised on pure ground. The ground was then plowed and planted, and the resulting crop was harvested through two seasons. After that, cows—sacred beasts since the Indus Valley civilization—were pastured there. Through their stomping, breathing, and feeding on the site, they lent it their potency. When construction began, each phase was accompanied by ritual to ensure its purity and sanctity.

All Hindu temples are built on a mystical plan known as a **mandala**, a schematic design of a sacred realm or space. Specifically, Hindu temples are based on the Vastupurusha mandala, the mandala of the Cosmic Man, the primordial progenitor of the human species. His body, fallen on earth, is imagined as superimposed on the mandala design; together, they form the base on which the temple rises.

Although the Vastupurusha mandala can be drawn in any number of different ways, it always takes the form of a square subdivided into a number of equal squares (usually sixty-four) surrounding a central square. The central square represents Brahman, the primordial, unmanifest Formless One. This square corresponds to the temple's sanctum, the windowless *garbhagriha*, or "womb chamber." The nature of Brahman is clear, pure light; that we perceive the *garbhagriha* as dark is a testament to our deluded nature. The surrounding squares belong to lesser deities, while the outermost compartments hold protector gods. These compartments are usually represented by the enclosing wall of a temple compound.

The *garbhagriha* houses the temple's main image—most commonly one of the forms of Vishnu, Shiva, or Devi. Usually this image is a sculpture made of stone, bronze, or wood. The image is made with the understanding that the god will inhabit it. To ensure perfection, its proportions follow a set canon, and rituals surround its making. When the image is completed, a priest recites mantras, or mystic syllables, that bring the deity into the image. The belief that a deity is literally present is not taken lightly. Even in India today, any image "under worship"—whether it be in a temple or a field, an ancient work or a modern piece—will be respected and not taken from the people who worship it.

A Hindu temple is a place for individual devotion, not congregational worship. It is the place where a devotee can make offerings to one or more deities and be in the presence of the god who is embodied in the image in the *garbhagriha*. Worship generally consists of prayers and offerings such as food and flowers or water and oil for the image, but it can also be much more elaborate, including dancing and ritual sacrifices.

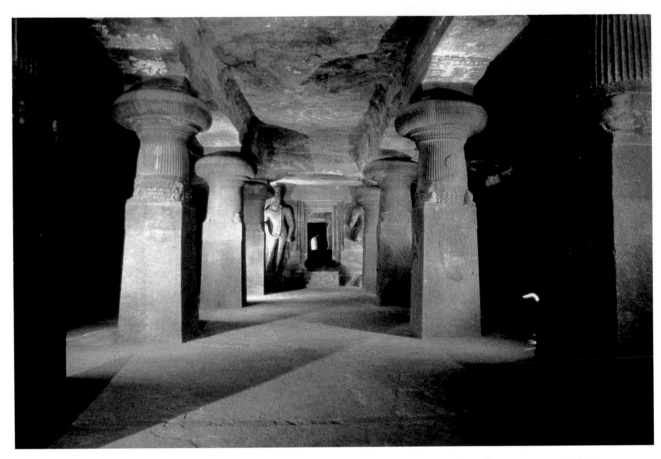

9-20. Cave-Temple of Shiva at Elephanta, Maharashtra, India. Mid-6th century CE. View along the east-west axis to the lingam shrine

represents the Subtle Body, or second, stage of the deity's emanation. Vishnu sleeps on the serpent of infinity, Ananta, whose body coils endlessly into space. Stirred by his female aspect (shakti, or female energy), personified here by the goddess Lakshmi, seen holding his foot, Vishnu dreams the universe into existence. From his navel springs a lotus (shown in this relief behind Vishnu), and the unfolding of space-time begins. The first being to be created is Brahma (not to be confused with Brahman), who appears here as the central, four-headed figure in the row of gods portrayed above the reclining Vishnu. Brahma turns himself into the universe of space and time by thinking, "May I become Many."

The sculptor has depicted Vishnu as a large, resplendent figure with four arms. His size and his many arms connote his omniscient powers. He is lightly garbed but richly ornamented. The ideal of the Gupta style persists in the smooth, perfected shape of the body and in the delight in details of jewelry, including Vishnu's characteristic cylindrical crown. The four rightmost figures in the frieze below personify Vishnu's powers. They stand ready to fight the appearance of evil, represented at the left of the frieze by two demons who threaten to kill Brahma and jeopardize all creation.

The birth of the universe and the appearance of evil are thus portrayed here in three clearly organized **registers**. Typical of Indian religious and artistic expression,

these momentous events are set before our eyes not in terms of abstract symbols but as a drama acted out by gods in superhuman form. The birth of the universe is imagined not as a "big bang" of infinitesimal particles from a supercondensed black hole but as a lotus unfolding from the navel of Vishnu.

Monumental Narrative Reliefs

Another major Hindu god, Shiva, was known in Vedic times as Rudra, "the howler." He was "the wild red hunter" who protected beasts and inhabited the forests. As Shiva, which means "benign," this god exhibits a wide range of aspects or forms, both gentle and wild: he is the Great Yogi who dwells for vast periods of time in meditation in the Himalaya; he is also the Husband par excellence who makes love to the goddess Parvati for eons at a time; he is the Slayer of Demons; and he is the Cosmic Dancer who dances the destruction and re-creation of the world. Shiva takes such seemingly contradictory natures purposefully, in order to make us question reality.

Many of these forms of Shiva appear in the monumental relief panels adorning the Cave-Temple of Shiva carved in the mid-sixth century on the island of Elephanta off the coast of Bombay in western India. The cave-temple is complex in layout and conception, perhaps to reflect the nature of Shiva. While most temples

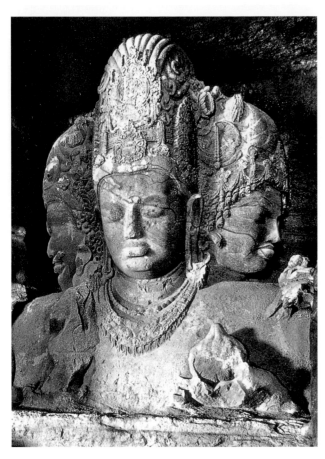

9-21. *Eternal Shiva*, rock-cut relief in the Cave-Temple of Shiva at Elephanta. Mid-6th century CE. Height approx. 11' (3.4 m)

center of the illustration. Each of its four entrances is flanked by a pair of colossal standing guardian figures. In the center of the shrine is the lingam, the phallic symbol of Shiva. The lingam represents the presence of Shiva as the unmanifest Formless One, or Brahman. It symbolizes both his erotic nature and his aspect as the Great Yogi who controls his seed. The lingam is synonymous with Shiva and is seen in nearly every Shiva temple and shrine.

The main focus of the north-south axis, in contrast, is a relief on the south wall depicting Shiva in his Subtle Body, the second stage of the threefold emanation. A huge bust of the deity represents his Sadashiva, or Eternal Shiva, aspect (fig. 9-21). Three heads are shown resting upon the broad shoulders of the upper body, but five heads are implied: the fourth in back and the fifth, never depicted, on top. The heads summarize Shiva's fivefold nature as creator (back), protector (left shoulder), destroyer (right shoulder), obscurer (front), and releaser (top). The head in the front depicts Shiva deep in introspection. The massiveness of the broad head, the large eyes barely delineated, and the mouth with its heavy lower lip suggest the serious depths of the god. Lordly and majestic, he easily supports his huge crown, intricately carved with designs and jewels, and the matted, piled-up hair of a yogi. On his left shoulder, his protector nature is depicted as female, with curled hair and a pearl-festooned crown. On his right shoulder, his wrathful, destroyer nature wears a fierce expression, and snakes encircle his neck.

Like the relief panels at the temple to Vishnu in Deogarh (see fig. 9-19), the reliefs at Elephanta are early examples of the Hindu monumental narrative tradition. Measuring 11 feet in height, they are set in recessed niches, one on either side of each of the three entrances and three on the south wall. The panels portray the range of Shiva's powers and some of his different aspects, presented in the context of narratives that help devotees understand his nature. Taken as a whole, the reliefs represent the third stage of emanation, the Gross Body manifestation of Shiva in our world. Indian artists often convey the many aspects or essential nature of a deity through multiple heads or arms. Their gift is to portray these additions with such convincing naturalism that we readily accept their visions. Here, for example, the artist has united three heads onto a single body so skillfully that we still relate to the statue as an essentially human presence.

The third great Hindu deity is Devi, a designation covering many deities who embody the feminine. In general, Devi represents the brilliant power of shakti, a divine energy understood as feminine. Shakti is needed to overcome the demons of our afflictions, such as ignorance and pride. Among the most widely worshiped goddesses are Lakshmi, goddess of wealth and beauty, and Durga, the warrior goddess.

Durga is the essence of the splendid conquering powers of the gods. A large relief at Mamallapuram, near Madras, in southeastern India, depicts Durga in her popular form as the slayer of Mahishasura, the buffalo

have one entrance, this temple offers three—one facing north, one east, and one west. The interior, impressive in its size and grandeur, is designed along two main axes, one running north-south, the other east-west. The three entrances provide the only source of light, and the resulting cross- and back-lighting effects add to the sense of the cave as a place of mysterious, almost confusing complexity. A worshiper seems to be in a world where the usual expectations are absent and is thrown off-balance—fit preparation for a meeting with Shiva, the most unpredictable of the Hindu gods.

Along the east-west axis, large pillars cut from the living rock appear to support the low ceiling and its beams although, as with all architectural elements in a cave-temple, they are not structural (fig. 9-20). The pillars form orderly rows, but the rows are hard to discern within the framework of the cave shape, which is neither square nor longitudinal, but a combination of overlapping mandalas that create a symmetric yet irregular space. The pillars are an important aesthetic component of the cave. An unadorned, square base rises to nearly half the total height. Above is a circular column, which has a pleasingly curved contour and a billowing "cushion" capital. Both column and capital are delicately **fluted**, adding a surprising refinement to these otherwise sturdy forms. The main focus of the east-west axis is a square **lingam shrine**, shown here at the

9-22. *Durga Mahishasura-mardini (Durga as Slayer of the Buffalo Demon)*, rock-cut relief, Mamallapuram, Tamil Nadu, India. Pallava period, c. mid-7th century CE. Granite, height approx. 9' (2.7 m)

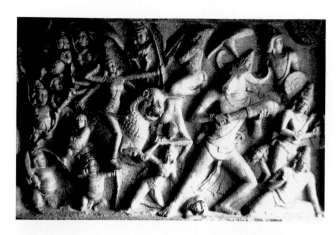

demon (fig. 9-22). Triumphantly riding her lion, a symbol of her shakti, the eight-armed Durga battles the demon. His huge figure with its human body and buffalo head is shown lunging to the right, fleeing from her onslaught. His warriors are falling to the ground. Accompanied by energetic, dwarfish warriors, victorious Durga, though smaller in size, sits erect and alert, flashing her weapons. Thus the moods of victory and defeat are clearly distinguished between the left and right sides of the panel. The artist clarifies the drama by focusing our attention on the two principal actors. Surrounding figures play secondary roles that support the main action, adding visual interest and variety.

Stylistically, this and other panels at Mamallapuram represent the final flowering of the Indian monumental relief tradition. Here, as elsewhere, the reliefs portray stories of the gods and goddesses, whose heroic deeds unfold before our eyes. Executed under the dynasty of the Pallavas, which flourished in southern India from the seventh to ninth century CE, this panel also illustrates the gentle, simplified figure style characteristic of Pallava sculpture. Figures tend to be slim and elegant with little ornament, and the rhythms of line and form have a graceful, unifying, and humanizing charm.

9-23. Dharmaraja Ratha, Mamallapuram, Tamil Nadu, India. Pallava period, c. mid-7th century CE

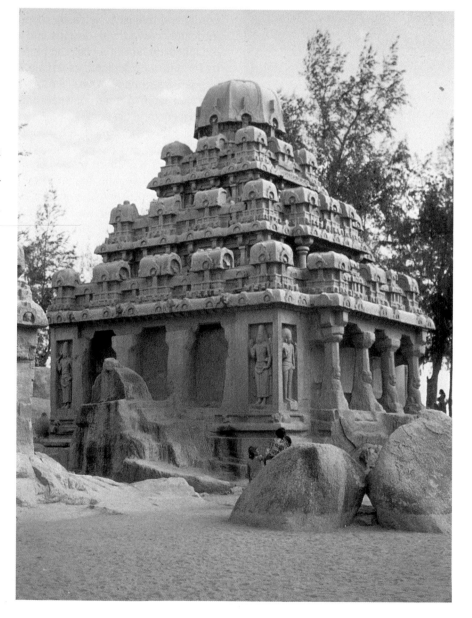

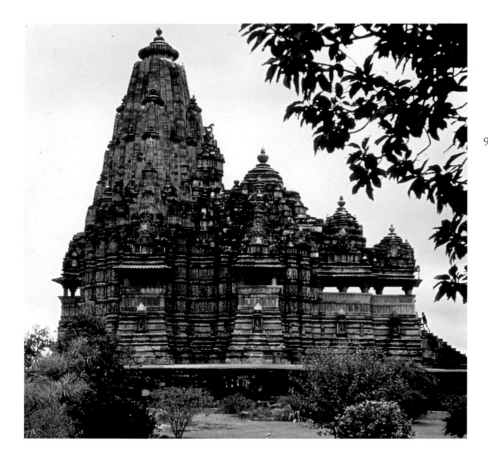

1200 CE

2800 BCE   1200 CE

9-24. Kandariya Mahadeva temple, Khajuraho, Madhya Pradesh, India. Chandella dynasty, Early Medieval period, c. 1000 CE

The Early Southern Temple

The coastal city of Mamallapuram was also a major temple site under the Pallavas. Along the shore are many large granite boulders and cliffs, and from these the Pallava stone cutters carved reliefs, halls, and temples. Among the most interesting Pallava creations is a group of temples known as the Five Rathas, which preserve a sequence of early architectural styles. As with other rock-cut temples, the Five Rathas were probably carved in the style of contemporary wood or brick structures that have long since disappeared.

One of this group, the Dharmaraja Ratha, epitomizes the early southern-style temple (fig. 9-23). Though strikingly different in appearance from the northern style, it uses the same symbolism and it, too, is based on a mandala. The temple, square in plan, remains unfinished, and the *garbhagriha* usually found inside was never hollowed out. On the lower portion, only the columns and exterior niches have been carved. The use of a single deity in each niche forecasts the main trend in temple sculpture in the centuries ahead. As the tradition of narrative reliefs began dying out, the stories they told became concentrated in statues of individual deities, which alone suffice to conjure up entire mythological episodes through characteristic poses and a few symbolic objects.

Southern and northern temples are most clearly distinguished by their respective superstructures. The Dharmaraja Ratha does not culminate in the paraboloid of the northern shikhara but in a pyramidal tower called a **vimana**. Each story of the vimana is articulated by a **cornice** and carries a row of miniature shrines. Both shrines and cornices are decorated with a window motif from

which faces peer. The shrines not only serve to demarcate each story but also provide a measure of the loftiness of this palace for a god. Crowning the vimana is a dome-shaped octagonal **capstone** quite different from the amalaka of the northern style.

During the centuries that followed, both northern- and southern-style temples developed into complex, monumental forms, but their basic structure and symbolism remained the same as those we have seen in these simple, early examples at Deogarh and Mamallapuram.

THE EARLY MEDIEVAL PERIOD

During the Early Medieval period, which extends roughly from the mid-seventh to the eleventh century, many small kingdoms and dynasties flourished. Some were relatively long-lived, such as the Pallavas and Cholas in the south and the Palas in the northeast. Though Buddhism remained strong in a few areas—notably under the Palas—it generally declined. On the other hand, the Hindu gods Vishnu, Shiva, and the Goddess (mainly Durga) grew increasingly popular. Local kings rivaled each other in the building of temples to their favored deity, and many complicated and subtle variations of the Hindu temple emerged with astounding rapidity in different regions. By around 1000 CE the Hindu temple had reached unparalleled heights of grandeur and engineering.

The Monumental Northern Temple

The Kandariya Mahadeva, a temple dedicated to Shiva at Khajuraho in central India, was probably built by a ruler of the Chandella dynasty in the late tenth or early

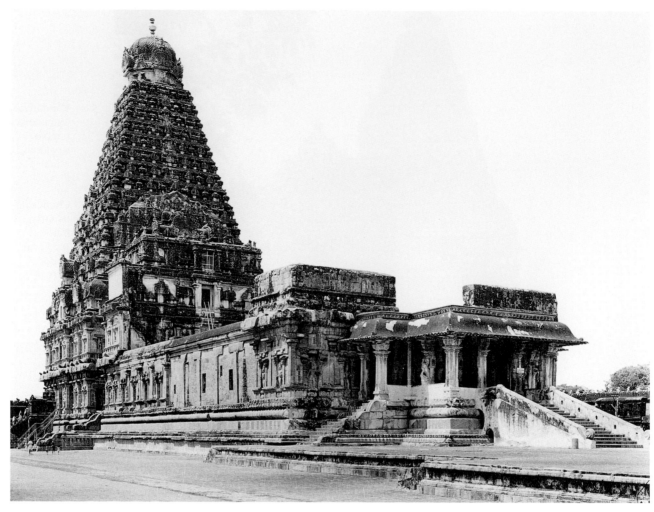

9-25. Rajarajeshvara Temple to Shiva, Thanjavur, Tamil Nadu, India. Chola dynasty, Early Medieval period, 1003–1010 CE

eleven century (fig. 9-24). Khajuraho was the capital and main temple site for the Chandellas, who constructed more than eighty temples there, about twenty-five of which are well preserved. The Kandariya Mahadeva temple is in the northern style, with a shikhara rising over its *garbhagriha*. Larger, more extensively ornamented, and expanded through the addition of halls on the front and porches to the sides and back, the temple seems at first glance to have little in common with its precursor at Deogarh (see fig. 9-17). Actually, however, the basic elements and their symbolism remain unchanged.

As at Deogarh, the temple rests on a stone terrace that sets off a sacred space from the mundane world. A steep flight of stairs at the front (to the right in the illustration) leads to a series of three halls (distinguished on the outside by three pyramidal roofs) preceding the *garbhagriha*. Called **mandapas**, the halls symbolically represent the Subtle Body stage of the threefold emanation. They serve as spaces for ritual, such as dances performed for the deity, and for the presentation of offerings. The temple is built of stone blocks using only **post-and-lintel construction**. The vault and arch are not used, and thus the interior spaces are not large.

The exterior has a strong sculptural presence, and

the total effect is of a massive mountain (again, the "cosmic mountain") composed of ornately carved stone. Rising over the *garbhagriha*, the shikhara is the tallest element of the temple, reaching to a little over 100 feet. The top is crowned by an amalaka, which is rather small on this particular temple.

The shikhara is bolstered by the addition of many smaller shikhara motifs bundled around it. This decorative scheme adds a complex richness to the surface, but it also somewhat obscures the shape of the main shikhara. As a whole the shikhara is rather slender and its upward movement quite swift and impetuous. The roofs of the mandapas contribute to the impression of rapid ascent by growing progressively taller as they near the shikhara.

Despite its apparent complexity, the temple has a clear structure and forms a unified composition. The towers of the superstructure are separated from the lower portion by strong horizontal **moldings** and by the open spaces over the mandapas and porches. The moldings and rows of sculpture adorning the lower part of the temple create a horizontal emphasis that stabilizes the vertical thrust of the superstructure. Three rows of sculpture—some 600 figures—are integrated into the exterior walls. Approximately 3 feet tall and carved in high relief, the sculptures depict gods and goddesses, some in erotic postures. They are thought to express Shiva's divine bliss, the manifestation of his presence within, and the transformation of one to many.

In addition to its horizontal emphasis, the lower portion of the temple is characterized by vertical convex/concave movements created by protruding and receding elements. These impart an impression similar to **engaged columns** and **buttressing** segments, and they account for much of the rich texture of the exterior. The porches, two on each side and one in the back, contribute to the impression of complexity by adding outward expansions to the ground plan, yet their curved bases also reinforce the sweeping vertical movements that unify the entire structure.

The Monumental Southern Temple

The Cholas, who superseded the Pallavas in the mid-ninth century, founded a dynasty that governed most of the far south well into the late thirteenth century. The Chola dynasty reached its peak during the reign of Rajaraja I (ruled 985–1014 CE). As an expression of gratitude for his many victories in battle, Rajaraja built the Rajarajeshvara Temple to Shiva in his capital, Thanjavur (Tanjore). Known alternatively as the Brihadeshvara, this temple is the supreme achievement of the southern style of Hindu architecture (fig. 9-25). The temple stands within a huge, walled compound near the banks of the Kaveri River. Though some smaller shrines dot the compound, the Rajarajeshvara dominates the area.

Clarity of structure combined with a formal balance of parts and refined decor create a majestically powerful structure in the Rajarajeshvara. Rising to an astonishing height of 216 feet, this temple was probably the tallest structure in India in its time. Like the Kandariya Mahadeva temple at Khajuraho, the Rajarajeshvara has a longitudinal axis and greatly expanded dimensions, especially with regard to its superstructure. Typical of the southern style, the mandapa halls at the front of the Rajarajeshvara have flat roofs, as opposed to the pyramidal roofs of the northern style.

The base of the vimana, which houses the *garbhagriha*, rises for two stories, with each story emphatically articulated by a large cornice. The exterior walls are ornamented with niches, each of which holds a single statue, usually depicting a form of Shiva. The clear, regular, and wide spacing of the niches imparts a calm balance and formality to the lower portion of the temple, in marked contrast to the irregular, sloping, concave-convex rhythms of the northern style.

The vimana of the Rajarajeshvara is a towering, four-sided, hollow pyramid that rises for thirteen stories. Each story is decorated with miniature shrines, window motifs, and robust dwarf figures who seem to be holding up the next story. Because these sculptural elements are not large in the overall scale of the vimana, they appear well integrated into the surface and do not obscure the powerful shape. This is quite different from the effect of the

smaller shikhara motifs on the shikhara of the Kandariya Mahadeva temple. Notice also that in the earlier southern style as embodied in the Dharmaraja Ratha (see fig. 9-23), the shrines on the vimana were much larger in proportion to the whole and thus appeared individually nearly as prominent as the vimana's overall shape.

Because the Rajarajeshvara vimana is not obscured by its decorative motifs, its skyward ascent becomes more forceful and aggressive. At the top is an octagonal dome-shaped capstone similar to the one that crowned the earlier southern-style temple. This huge capstone is exactly above, and the same size as, the *garbhagriha* housed thirteen stories below. It thus evokes the presence of the shrine a final time before the point separating the worldly from the cosmic sphere above.

The Bhakti Movement in Art

Throughout the Early Medieval period two major religious movements were taking place that affected Hindu practice and its art: the tantric, or esoteric, and the bhakti, or devotional. Although both movements evolved throughout India, the influence of tantric sects appeared during this period primarily in the art of the north, while the bhakti movements found artistic expression mostly in the south.

The bhakti devotional movement was based on ideas expressed in ancient texts, especially the *Bhagavad Gita*. Bhakti revolves around the ideal relationship between humans and deities. According to bhakti, it is the gods who create maya, or illusion, in which we are all trapped. They also reveal truth to those who truly love them and whose minds are open to them. Rather than focusing on ritual and the performance of dharma according to the Vedas, bhakti stresses an intimate, personal, and loving relation with god, and the complete devotion and giving up of oneself to god. Inspired and influenced by bhakti, southern artists produced some of India's greatest and most humanistic works, as revealed in the few remaining paintings and in the famous bronze works of sculpture.

Rajaraja's building of the Rajarajeshvara was in part a reflection of the fervent movement of Shiva bhakti that had already reached its peak by that time. The corridors of the circumambulatory passages around its *garbhagriha* were originally adorned with frescoes. Overpainted in later times, they were only recently rediscovered. One painting apparently depicts the ruler Rajaraja himself, not as a warrior or majestic king on his throne, but as a simple mendicant humbly standing behind his religious teacher (fig. 9-26). With his white beard and dark skin, the aged teacher contrasts with the youthful, bronze-skinned king. The position of the two suggests that the saintly teacher, who in the devotee's or bhakta's view is equated with god, is both closely and yet respectfully treated by the king. Both figures openly allude to their devotion to Shiva by holding a small flower as an offering, and both emulate Shiva in their appearance by wearing their hair in the "ascetic locks" of Shiva in his Great Yogi aspect.

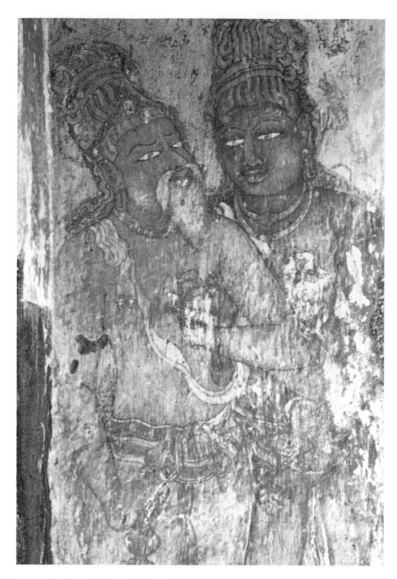

9-26. *Rajaraja I and His Teacher*, detail of a wall painting in the Rajarajeshvara Temple to Shiva. Chola dynasty, Early Medieval period,
c. 1010 CE

The portrayal does not represent individuals so much as a contrast of types: the old and the youthful, the teacher and the devotee, the saint and the king—the highest religious and worldly models, respectively—united as followers of Shiva. Line is the essence of the painting. With strength and grace, the even, skillfully executed line defines the boldly simple forms and features. There is no excessive detail, very little shading, and no high-lighting such as we saw in the Gupta paintings at Ajanta (see fig. 9-16). A cool, sedate calm infuses the monumental figures, but the power of line also invigorates them with a sense of strength and inner life.

Perhaps no sculpture is more representative of Chola bronzes than the famous statue of Shiva Nataraja, or Dancing Shiva (fig. 9-27). The dance of Shiva is a dance of cosmic proportions, signifying the cycle of death and rebirth of the universe; it is also a dance for each individual, signifying the liberation of the believer through

Shiva's compassion. In the iconography of the Nataraja, perfected over the centuries, this sculpture shows Shiva with four arms dancing on the prostrate body of Apas-maru, a dwarf figure who symbolizes "becoming" and whom Shiva controls. Shiva's extended left hand holds a ball of fire; a circle of fire, now lost, formerly ringed the god as well. The fire is emblematic of the destruction of samsara and the physical universe as well as the destruc-tion of maya and our ego-centered concepts. Shiva's back right hand holds a drum; its beat represents the irrevocable rhythms of creation and destruction, birth and death. His front right arm gestures the "have no fear" mudra (see "Mudras," page 380). The front left arm, gracefully stretched across his body with the hand point-ing to his raised foot, signifies the promise of liberation.

The artist has rendered the complex pose with great clarity. The central axis of the figure, which aligns with the nose, navel, and insole of the weight-bearing foot,

9-27. *Nataraja: Shiva as King of Dance.* South India, Chola dynasty, 11th century. Bronze, H. 43⁷/₈" (111.5 cm). The Cleveland Museum of Art
© The Cleveland Museum of Art, 1998, Purchase from the J. H. Wade Fund, 1930.331

The fervent religious devotion of the bhakti movement was fueled in no small part by the sublime writings of a series of poet-saints who lived in the south of India. One of these poet-saints, Appar, who lived from the late sixth to mid-seventh century, wrote this tender, personal vision of the Shiva Nataraja. The ash the poem refers to is one of many symbols associated with the deity. In penance for having lopped off one of the five heads of Brahma, the first created being, Shiva smeared his body with ashes and went about as a beggar.

> If you could see
> the arch of his brow,
> the budding smile
> on lips red as the kovvai fruit,
> cool matted hair,
> the milk-white ash on coral skin,
> and the sweet golden foot
> raised up in dance,
> then even human birth on this wide earth
> would become a thing worth having.

> (Translated by Indira Vishvanathan Peterson)

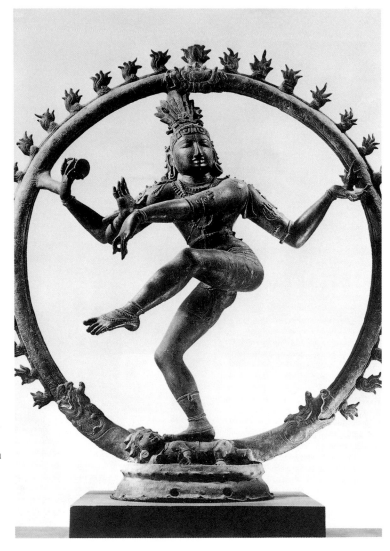

maintains the center of balance and equilibrium while the remaining limbs extend asymmetrically far to each side. Shiva wears a short loincloth, a ribbon tied above his waist, and delicately tooled ornaments. The scant clothing reveals the beauty of his perfected form with its broad shoulders tapering to a supple waist. The jewelry is restrained and the detail does not detract from the unity of the body.

The deity does not appear self-absorbed and introspective as he did in the Eternal Shiva relief at Elephanta (see fig. 9-21). Instead, he turns to face the viewer while openly extending his body to the sides. He appears lordly and aloof, yet fully aware of his benevolent role as he generously displays himself for the devotee. Like the Sarnath Gupta Buddha (see fig. 9-15), the Chola Nataraja presents a characteristically Indian synthesis of the godly and the human, this time expressing the bhakti belief in the importance of an intimate and personal rela-

tionship with a lordly god through whose compassion one is saved. The earlier Hindu emphasis on ritual and the depiction of the heroic feats of the gods, though not denied, is subsumed into the all-encompassing, humanizing factor of grace.

The bhakti movement spread during the ensuing Late Medieval period into North India. This period, however, also witnessed the incursion of a new religious culture into the subcontinent, Islam. From the tenth century on, the passes at the northwest again brought invaders, this time in the form of various Turkic, Persian, and Afghan Islamic factions. Islam brought with it a rich artistic tradition of its own. Yet just as new religious forms eventually evolved from Islam's long and complex interaction with the peoples of the subcontinent, so too did uniquely Indian forms of Islamic art arise, adding yet another dimension to India's artistic heritage.

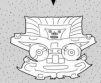

Deity image from a *cong*
before 3000 BCE

▲ NEOLITHIC c. 5000–2000 BCE

CHAPTER 10

Chinese Art before 1280

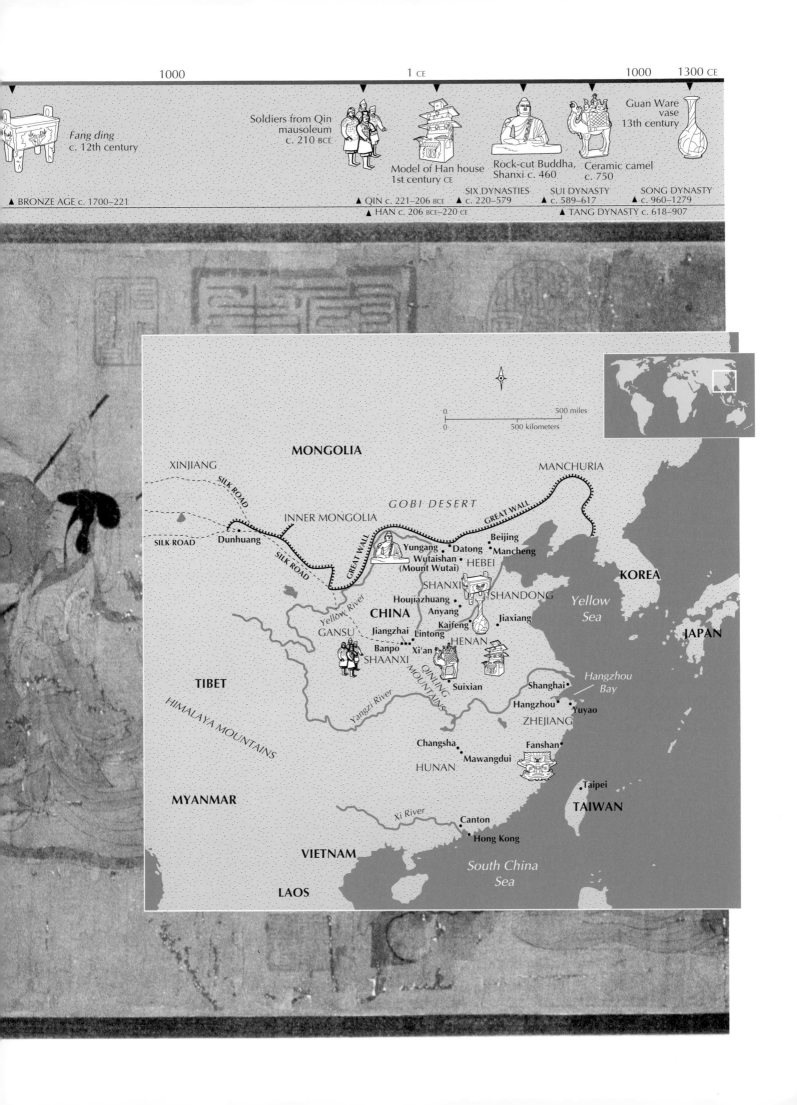

Fang ding
c. 12th century

Soldiers from Qin
mausoleum
c. 210 BCE

Model of Han house
1st century CE

Rock-cut Buddha,
Shanxi c. 460

Ceramic camel
c. 750

Guan Ware
vase
13th century

▲ BRONZE AGE c. 1700–221

▲ QIN c. 221–206 BCE

SIX DYNASTIES
▲ c. 220–579

SUI DYNASTY
▲ c. 589–617

SONG DYNASTY
▲ c. 960–1279

▲ HAN c. 206 BCE–220 CE

▲ TANG DYNASTY c. 618–907

MONGOLIA

XINJIANG

MANCHURIA

SILK ROAD

GOBI DESERT

GREAT WALL

INNER MONGOLIA

GREAT WALL

SILK ROAD

SILK ROAD   Dunhuang

Beijing

Yungang   Datong
Wutaishan   Mancheng
(Mount Wutai)

HEBEI

KOREA

GREAT WALL

Yellow River

SHANXI   SHANDONG

*Yellow
Sea*

CHINA

Houjiazhuang
Anyang

JAPAN

GANSU

Jiangzhai
Lintong

Kaifeng

Jiaxiang

TIBET

Banpo   Xi'an

HENAN

SHAANXI

QINLING
MOUNTAINS

Suixian

Shanghai

*Hangzhou
Bay*

Yangzi River

Hangzhou
Yuyao

ZHEJIANG

HIMALAYA MOUNTAINS

Changsha

Fanshan

MYANMAR

Mawangdui

HUNAN

Taipei

TAIWAN

Xi River

Canton

Hong Kong

VIETNAM

*South China
Sea*

LAOS

0   500 miles
0   500 kilometers

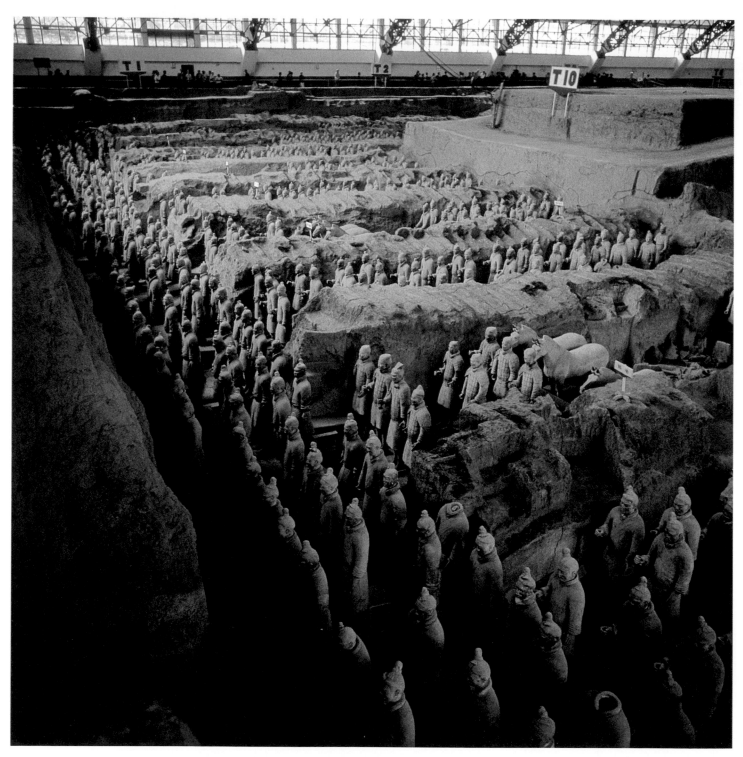

10-1.   Soldiers, from the mausoleum of the first emperor of Qin, Lintong, Shaanxi. Qin dynasty, c. 210 BCE. Earthenware, lifesize

As long as anyone could remember, the huge mound in China's Shaanxi province had been part of the landscape. No one dreamed that an astonishing treasure lay beneath the surface until one day in 1974 when peasants digging a well accidentally brought to light the first hint of the riches. When archeologists began to excavate the mound, they were stunned by what they found: a vast underground army of more than 7,000 lifesize clay soldiers and horses standing in military formation, facing east, ready for battle (fig. 10-1). Originally painted in vivid colors, they emerged from the earth a ghostly gray. For more than 2,000 years, while the tumultuous history of China unfolded overhead, they had guarded the tomb of Emperor Shihuangdi, the ruthless ruler who first united the states of China into an empire.

In 1990 a road-building crew in central China accidentally uncovered an even richer vault, containing perhaps tens of thousands of terra-cotta figures. Although excavations there are barely under way, the artifacts so far uncovered are exceptional both in artistic quality and in what they tell us about life—and death—during the Han dynasty, about 100 years later than the Qin find.

Archeology is a relatively young discipline in China. Only since the 1920s have scholars methodically dug into the layers of history that lie buried at thousands of sites across the country. Yet in that short period so much has been unearthed that ancient Chinese history has been rewritten many times.

THE MIDDLE KINGDOM

Among the cultures of the world, China is distinguished by its long, uninterrupted development, now traced back some 8,000 years. From Qin, pronounced "chin," comes our name for the country the Chinese call the Middle Kingdom, the country in the center of the world. Modern China occupies a large landmass in the center of Asia, covering an area slightly larger than the continental United States. Within its borders lives one-fifth of the human race.

The historical and cultural heart of China—sometimes called Inner China—is the land watered by its three great rivers, the Yellow, the Yangzi, and the Xi. The Qinling Mountains divide Inner China into north and south, regions with strikingly different climates, cultures, and historical fates. In the south the Yangzi River flows through lush green hills to the fertile plains of the delta. Along the southern coastline, rich with natural harbors, arose China's port cities, the focus of a vast maritime trading network. The Yellow River, nicknamed "China's Sorrow" because of its disastrous floods, winds through the north. The north country is a dry land of steppe and desert, hot in the summer and lashed by cold winds in the winter. Over its vast and vulnerable frontier have come the nomadic invaders that are a recurring theme in Chinese history, as well as caravans and emissaries from Central Asia, India, Persia, and, eventually, Europe.

NEOLITHIC CULTURES

Early archeological evidence led scholars to believe that agriculture, the cornerstone technology of the Neolithic period, made its way to China from the ancient Near East. More recent findings, however, have shown that agriculture based on rice and millet arose independently in East Asia before 5000 BCE and that knowledge of Near Eastern grains followed some 2,000 years later. One of the clearest signs of Neolithic culture in China is the vigorous emergence of towns and cities. At Jiangzhai, near modern Xi'an, for example, the foundations of more than 100 dwellings have been discovered surrounding the remains of a community center, a cemetery, and a kiln. Dated to about 4000 BCE, the ruins point to the existence of a highly developed early society. Elsewhere, the foundations of the earliest known palace have been uncovered and dated to about 2000 BCE.

PARALLELS

Years	Period	China	World
c. 5000–2000 BCE	Neolithic	Beginning of agriculture; Painted Pottery cultures	c. 5000–2000 BCE Beginning of agriculture in North Africa; potter's wheel (Egypt); Great Pyramids at Giza (Egypt); Indus Valley civilization (India)
			c. 2000–1000 BCE Minoan and Mycenaean cultures (Aegean); *Stela of Hammurabi* (Babylonia); development of metallurgy (Near East); Olmec civilization (Mesoamerica)
c. 1700–221 BCE	Bronze Age	Legendary (?) Xia dynasty; Shang dynasty; development of writing; bronze casting; Zhou dynasty; birth of Confucius, Laozi, Mozi; iron tools and weapons	
c. 221–206 BCE	Qin dynasty	Unification of China; centralized bureaucracy; standardized coinage; standardized written language; clay figures; Great Wall	c. 1000 BCE–500 CE First Olympian Games (Greece); black-figure and red-figure vase painting (Greece); birth of Siddhartha Gautama, founder of Buddhism (Nepal); Parthenon (Greece); Great Stupa at Sanchi (India); crucifixion of Jesus (Jerusalem); Colosseum (Italy); first Gupta dynasty (India); first Hindu temples (India)
c. 206 BCE–220 CE	Han dynasty	Silk Road; Daoism; Confucianism made state philosophy; Buddhism introduced	
c. 220–579 CE	Six Dynasties	Nomad invasions; growth of Buddhism; rock-cut caves; monumental buddhas	c. 500–1300 CE Birth of Muhammad, founder of Islam (Arabia); Muslim conquests; Hagia Sophia (Turkey); separation of Eastern and Western Christian Churches; the Crusades; Spanish Inquisition
c. 589–617 CE	Sui dynasty	Reunification of China; Pure Land Buddhism grows; Daoism ascendant	
c. 618–907 CE	Tang dynasty	Repression of Buddhism; figure painting; Nanchan Temple	
c. 960–1279 CE	Song dynasty	Neo-Confucianism; landscape painting; Guan Ware; invasion by Kublai Khan's Mongols	

Painted Pottery

In China as elsewhere distinctive forms of Neolithic pottery identify different cultures. One of the most interesting objects thus far recovered is a shallow red bowl with a turned-out rim (fig. 10-2). Found in the village of Banpo near present-day Xi'an, it was crafted sometime between 5000 and 3000 BCE. The bowl is an artifact of the Yangshao culture, one of the most important of the so-called Painted Pottery cultures of Neolithic China. Although the potter's wheel had not yet been developed, the bowl is perfectly round and its surfaces are highly polished, bearing witness to a distinctly advanced technology. The decorations are especially intriguing. The marks on the rim may be among the earliest evidence of the beginnings of writing in China, which had been fully developed by the time the first definitive examples appeared in the later Bronze Age.

Inside the bowl, a pair of stylized fish suggest that fishing and hunting were important activities for the villagers. The image between the fish represents a human face with four more fish, one on each side. Although there is no certain interpretation of the image, it probably served some magical purpose. Perhaps it is a depic-

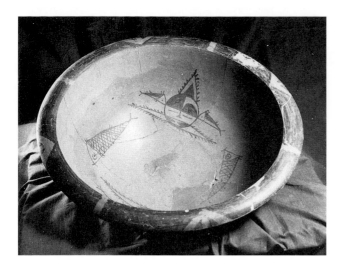

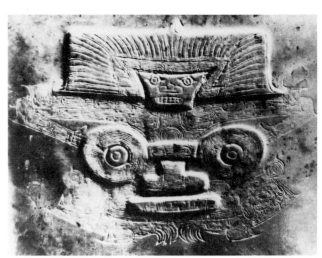

10-2. Bowl, from Banpo, near Xi'an, Shaanxi. Neolithic period, Yangshao culture, 5000–3000 BCE. Painted pottery, height 7" (17.8 cm). Banpo Museum

tion of an ancestral figure who could assure an abundant catch, for worship of ancestors and nature spirits was a fundamental element of later Chinese beliefs.

Beyond the Yellow River Valley

Banpo lies near the great bend in the Yellow River, in the area traditionally regarded as the cradle of Chinese civilization—though archeological finds have revealed that Neolithic cultures arose over a far broader area. Recent excavations in sites near the Hangzhou Bay, in the southeastern coastal region, have turned up half-human, half-animal images more than 5,000 years old (fig. 10-3). Large, round eyes linked by a bar like the frames of eyeglasses, a flat nose, and a rectangular mouth protrude slightly from the background pattern of wirelike lines. Above the forehead, a second, smaller face grimaces from under a huge headdress. The image is one of eight carved in **low relief** on the outside of a large jade *cong*, an object resembling a cylindrical tube encased in a rectangular block. This *cong* must have been an object of great importance, for it was found near the head of a person buried in a large tomb at the top of a mound that served as an altar. Hundreds of jade objects have been recovered from this mound, which measures about 66 feet square and rises in three levels.

The intricacy of the carving shows the technical sophistication of this jade-working culture, named the Liangzhu, which seems to have emerged around 4000 BCE. Jade, cherished by the Chinese throughout their history, is extremely hard and is difficult to carve. Liangzhu artists must have used sand as an abrasive to slowly grind the stone down, but we can only wonder at how they produced such fine work.

The meaning of the masklike image is open to interpretation. Its combination of human and animal features seems to show how the ancient Chinese imagined supernatural beings, either deities or dead ancestors. Strikingly similar masks later formed the primary deco-

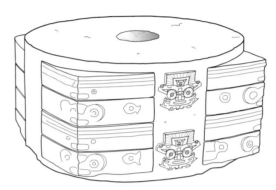

Schematic drawing of a *cong*

10-3. Image of a deity, detail from a *cong* recovered from Tomb 12, Fanshan, Yuyao, Zhejiang. Neolithic period, Liangzhu culture, before 3000 BCE. Jade, 3 1/2 x 6 7/8" (8.8 x 17.5 cm). Zhejiang Provincial Museum, Hangzhou

The *cong* is one of the most prevalent and mysterious of early Chinese jade shapes. Originating in the Neolithic era, it continued to play a prominent role in burials through the Shang and Zhou dynasties. Many scholars believe that the *cong* was connected with shamanism, the practice of contacting the spirit world. They suggest that the circle symbolized heaven; the square, earth; and the hollow, the axis connecting these two realms. The animals found carved on many *cong* may have portrayed the shaman's helpers or alter egos.

rative motif of Bronze Age ritual objects. Still later, Chinese historians began referring to the ancient motif as **taotie**, but its original meaning had already been lost. The jade carving here seems to be a forerunner of this most central and mysterious image. It suggests that eventually the various Neolithic cultures of China merged to form a single culture despite their separate origins thousands of miles apart.

BRONZE AGE CHINA

China entered its Bronze Age in the second millennium BCE. As with agriculture, scholars at first theorized that the technology had been imported from the Near East. It is now clear, however, that bronze

TECHNIQUE

PIECE-MOLD CASTING

The early **piece-mold technique** for bronze casting is more complex than the **lost-wax** process developed in the ancient Mediterranean and Near East. Although we do not know the exact steps ancient Chinese artists followed, we can deduce the general procedure for casting a simple vessel.

First, a model of the bronze-to-be was made of clay and dried. To create the mold, damp clay was pressed onto the model; after the clay dried, it was cut away in pieces, which were keyed for later reassembly and then fired. The model itself was shaved down to serve as the core for the mold. The pieces of the mold were reassem-

bled around the core and held in place by bronze spacers, which locked the core in position and ensured an even casting space. The reassembled mold was then covered with another layer of clay, and a spue, or pouring duct, was cut into the clay to receive the molten metal. A riser duct may also have been cut to allow the hot gases to escape. Molten bronze was then poured into the mold. When the metal had cooled, the mold was broken apart with a hammer. Finally, the vessel could be burnished—a long process that involved scouring the surface with increasingly fine abrasives.

casting using the **piece-mold casting** technique arose independently in China, where it was brought to an unparalleled level of excellence.

Shang Dynasty

Traditional Chinese histories tell of three Bronze Age dynasties: the Xia, the Shang, and the Zhou. Modern scholars had tended to dismiss the Xia and Shang as legendary, but recent archeological discoveries have now fully established the historical existence of the Shang (c. 1700–1100 BCE) and point strongly to the historical existence of the Xia as well.

Shang kings ruled from a succession of capitals in the Yellow River Valley, where archeologists have found walled cities, palaces, and vast royal tombs. Their state was surrounded by numerous other states—some rivals, others clients—and their culture spread widely. Society

seems to have been highly stratified, with a ruling group that had the bronze technology needed to make weapons. They maintained their authority in part by claiming power as shamans, intermediaries between the supernatural and human realms. The chief Shang deity, Shangdi, may have been a sort of Great Ancestor. Nature and fertility spirits were also honored, and regular sacrifices were believed necessary to keep the spirits of dead ancestors alive so that they might help the living.

Shang shamans communicated with the supernatural world through **oracle** bones. An animal bone or piece of tortoiseshell was inscribed with a question and heated until it cracked. Then a shaman interpreted the crack as an answer. Oracle bones, many of which have been recovered and deciphered, contain the earliest known form of Chinese writing, a script fully recognizable as the ancestor of the system still in use today (see "Chinese Characters," below).

CHINESE CHARACTERS

Each word in Chinese is represented by its own unique picture, called a character or **calligraph**. Some characters originated as **pictographs**, images that mean what they depict. Writing reforms over the centuries have often disguised the resemblance, but if we place modern characters next to their oracle-bone ancestors, the picture comes back into focus:

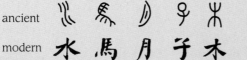

water horse moon child tree mountain

ancient

modern

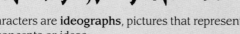

Other characters are **ideographs**, pictures that represent abstract concepts or ideas:

sun   +   moon   =   bright

日   月   明

woman + child = good

女   子   好

Most characters were formed by combining a radical, which gives the field of meaning, with a phonetic, which

originally hinted at pronunciation. For example, words that have to do with water have the character for "water" 水 abbreviated to three strokes 氵 as their radical. Thus "to bathe" 沐, pronounced *mu*, consists of the water radical and the phonetic 木, which by itself means "tree" and is also pronounced *mu*. Here are other "water" characters. Notice that the connection to water is not always literal.

river sea weep pure, clear extinguish, destroy

河 海 泣 清   滅

These phonetic borrowings took place centuries ago. Many words have shifted in pronunciation, and for this and other reasons there is no way to tell how a character is pronounced or what it means just by looking at it. While at first this may seem like a disadvantage, in the case of Chinese it is actually a strength. Spoken Chinese has many dialects. Some are so far apart in sound as to be virtually different languages. But while speakers of different dialects cannot understand each other, they can still communicate through writing, for no matter how they say a word, they write it with the same character. Writing has thus played an important role in maintaining the unity of Chinese civilization through the centuries.

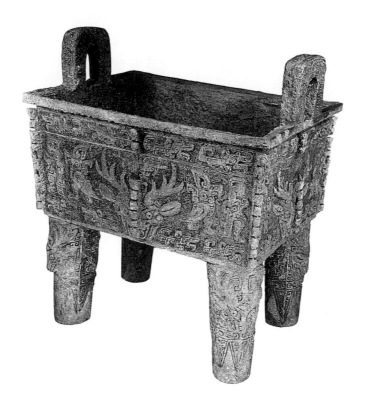

10-4. *Fang ding*, from Tomb 1004, Houjiazhuang, Anyang, Henan. Shang dynasty, Anyang period, c. 12th century BCE. Bronze, height 24¹/₂" (62.2 cm). Academia Sinica, Taipei, Taiwan

Ritual Bronzes. Shang tombs reveal a warrior culture of great splendor and violence. Many humans and animals were sacrificed to accompany the deceased. In one tomb, for example, chariots were found with the skeletons of their horses and drivers; in another, dozens of human skeletons lined the approaches to the central burial chamber. Above all, the tombs contain thousands of jade, ivory, and lacquer objects, gold and silver ornaments, and bronze vessels. The enormous scale of Shang burials illustrates the great wealth of the civilization and the power of a ruling class able to consign such great quantities of treasure to the earth, as well as reverence for the dead in this culture.

Bronze vessels are the most admired and studied of Shang artifacts. Like oracle bones and jade objects, they were connected with shamanistic practices, serving as containers for ritual offerings of food and wine. A basic repertoire of about thirty shapes evolved. Some shapes clearly derive from earlier pottery forms, others seem to reproduce wooden containers, while still others are purely sculptural and take the form of fantastic composite animals.

The illustrated bronze *fang ding*, a square vessel with four legs, is one of hundreds of vessels recovered from the royal tombs near the last of the Shang capitals, Yin, present-day Anyang (fig. 10-4). Weighing more than 240 pounds, it is one of the largest Shang bronzes ever recovered. In typical Shang style its surface is decorated with a complex array of images based on animal forms. The taotie, usually so prominent, does not appear. Instead, a large deer's head adorns the center of each side, and images of deer are repeated on all four legs. The rest of the surface is filled with images resembling birds, dragons, and other fantastic creatures. Such images seem to be related to the hunting life of the Shang,

but their deeper significance is unknown. Sometimes strange, sometimes fearsome, Shang creatures seem always to have a sense of mystery, evoking the Shang attitude toward the supernatural world.

Zhou Dynasty

Around 1100 BCE, the Shang were conquered by the Zhou, from western China. During the Zhou dynasty (1100–221 BCE), a feudal society developed, with nobles related to the king ruling over numerous small states. (Zhou nobility are customarily ranked in English by such titles as duke and marquis.) The supreme deity became known as Tian, or Heaven, and the king ruled as the Son of Heaven. Heaven remained the personal cult of China's sovereigns until the end of imperial rule in the early twentieth century.

The first 300 years of this longest Chinese dynasty were generally stable and peaceful. In 771 BCE, however, the Zhou suffered defeat at the hands of a nomadic tribe in the west. Although they quickly established a new capital to the east, their authority had been crippled, and the later Eastern Zhou period was a troubled one. States grew increasingly independent, giving the Zhou kings merely nominal allegiance. Smaller states were swallowed up by their larger neighbors. During the time historians call the Spring and Autumn period (770–476 BCE), ten or twelve states, later reduced to seven, emerged as powers. During the ensuing Warring States period (402–221 BCE), intrigue, treachery, and increasingly ruthless warfare became routine.

Against this background of constant social unrest, China's great philosophers arose, such thinkers as Confucius, Laozi, and Mozi. Traditional histories speak of China's "one hundred schools" of philosophy, indicating a shift of focus from the supernatural to the human

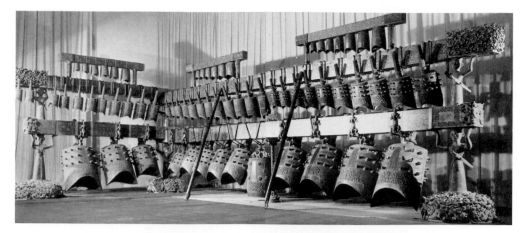

10-5. Set of sixty-five bells, from the tomb of Marquis Yi of Zeng, Suixian, Hubei. Zhou dynasty, 433 BCE. Bronze, with bronze and timber frame; frame height 9' (2.74 m), length 25' (7.62 m). Hubei Provincial Museum, Wuhan

world. Nevertheless, elaborate burials on an even larger scale reflected the continuation of traditional beliefs.

Ritual bronze objects continued to play an important role during the Zhou dynasty, and new forms developed. One of the most spectacular recent discoveries is a carillon of sixty-five bronze bells arranged in a formation 25 feet long (fig. 10-5), found in the tomb of Marquis Yi of the state of Zeng. Each bell is precisely calibrated to sound two tones—one when struck at the center, another when struck nearer the rim. The bells are arranged in scale patterns in a variety of registers, and several musicians would have moved around the carillon, striking the bells in the appointed order.

Music may well have played a part in rituals for communicating with the supernatural, for the taotie typically appears on the front and back of each bell. The image is now much more intricate and stylized, partly in response to the refinement available with the lost-wax process, which had replaced the older piece-mold technique. On the coffin of the marquis are painted guardian warriors with half-human, half-animal attributes. The marquis, who died in 433 BCE, must have been a great lover of music, for among the more than 15,000 objects recovered from his tomb were many musical instruments. Zeng was one of the smallest and shortest-lived states of the Eastern Zhou, but the contents of this tomb, in quantity and quality, attest to the high level of its culture.

THE CHINESE EMPIRE: QIN DYNASTY

Toward the middle of the third century BCE, the state of Qin launched military campaigns that led to its triumph over the other states by 221 BCE. For the first time in its history, China was united under a single ruler. This first emperor of Qin, Shihuangdi, a man of exceptional ability, power, and ruthlessness, was fearful of both assassination and rebellion. Throughout his life, he sought ways to attain immortality. Even before uniting China, he began his own **mausoleum** at Lintong, in Shaanxi province. This project continued throughout his life and after his death, until rebellion abruptly ended the dynasty in 206 BCE. Since that time, the mound over the mausoleum has always

been visible, but not until its accidental discovery in 1974 was the army of clay soldiers and horses even imagined (see fig. 10-1). Modeled from clay and then fired, the figures claim a prominent place in the great tradition of Chinese ceramic art. Individualized faces and meticulously rendered uniforms and armor demonstrate the sculptors' skill. Literary sources suggest that the tomb itself, which has not yet been opened, reproduces the world as it was known to the Qin, with stars overhead and rivers and mountains below. Thus did the tomb's architects try literally to ensure that the underworld—the world of souls and spirits—would be as good as the human world.

Qin rule was harsh and repressive. Laws were based on a totalitarian philosophy called legalism, and all other philosophies were banned, their scholars executed, and their books burned. Yet the Qin also established the mechanisms of centralized bureaucracy that molded China both politically and culturally into a single entity. Under the Qin, the country was divided into provinces and prefectures, the writing system and coinage were standardized, highways were built to link different parts of the country with the capital, and battlements on the northern frontier were connected to form the Great Wall. China's rulers to the present day have followed the administrative framework first laid down by the Qin.

HAN DYNASTY

The commander who overthrew the Qin became the next emperor and founded the Han dynasty (206 BCE– 220 CE). During this period the Chinese enjoyed a peaceful, prosperous, and stable life. Borders were extended and secured, and Chinese control over strategic stretches of Central Asia led to the opening of the Silk Road, a land route that linked China by trade all the way to Rome (see "The Silk Road," opposite).

The early Han dynasty marks the twilight of China's so-called mythocentric age, when people believed in a close relationship between the human and supernatural worlds, reflected in all the art we have looked at so far. From this time comes one of the most valuable works in Chinese art, a T-shaped silk banner that summarizes this early worldview (fig. 10-6). Found in the tomb of a noblewoman on the outskirts of present-day Changsha, the

THE SILK ROAD At its height, in the second century CE, the Silk Road was the longest road in the world, a 5,000-mile network of caravan routes from the Han capital of Luoyang on the Yellow River to Rome. The Western market for Chinese luxury goods such as silk and lacquer seemed limitless. For these goods, Westerners paid in gold and silver, for the West produced nothing that China desired in trade.

The journey began at the Jade Gate (Yumen), at the westernmost end of the Great Wall, where Chinese merchants turned their goods over to Central Asian traders. Goods would change hands many more times before reaching the Mediterranean. Caravans headed first for the desert oasis of Dunhuang. Here northern and southern routes diverged to skirt the vast Taklamakan Desert. At Khotan, travelers on the southern route could turn off toward a mountain pass into Kashmir, in northern India. Or they could continue on, meeting up with the northern route at Kashgar, on the western border of the Taklamakan, before proceeding over the Pamir Mountains into present-day Afghanistan. There, travelers could turn off into the Kushan Empire that stretched down into India, or they could continue on west through present-day Uzbekistan, Iran, and Iraq, arriving finally at Antioch, in Syria, on the coast of the Mediterranean. From there, land and sea routes led on to Rome.

Sections of the Silk Road were used throughout history by traders, travelers, conquerors, emissaries, pilgrims, missionaries, explorers, and adventurers. But only twice was the entire length of it open, with relatively safe passage likely from end to end. The first time was during the days of the Han dynasty and the Roman Empire. The second was during the thirteenth and fourteenth centuries, when the route lay within the borders of the vast Mongol Empire.

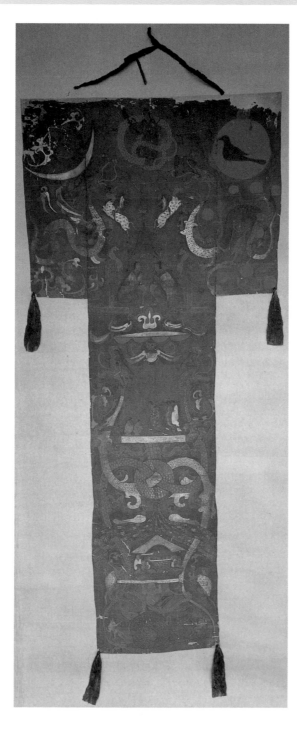

10-6. Painted banner, from the tomb of the wife of the Marquis of Dai, Mawangdui, Changsha, Hunan. Han dynasty, c. 160 BCE. Colors on silk, height 6'8½" (2.05 m). Hunan Provincial Museum, Changsha

DAOISM

Daoism is a kind of nature mysticism that brings together many ancient Chinese ideas regarding humankind and the universe. One of its first philosophers is said to have been a contemporary of Confucius (551–479 BCE) named Laozi, who is credited with writing a slim volume called the *Daodejing*, or *The Way and Its Power*. Later, a philosopher name Zhuangzi (369–286 BCE) took up many of the same ideas in a book that is known simply by his name, *Zhuangzi*. Together the two texts formed a body of ideas that crystallized into a school of thought during the Han period.

A *dao* is a way or path. The *Dao* is the Ultimate Way, the Way of the universe. The Way cannot be named or described, but it can be hinted at. It is like water. Nothing is more flexible and yielding, yet water can wear down the hardest stone. Water flows downward, seeking the lowest ground. Similarly, a Daoist sage seeks a quiet life, humble and hidden, unconcerned with worldly success. The Way is great precisely because it is small. In fact, it is nothing, yet nothing turns out to be essential (cited in Cleary, page 14):

When the potter's wheel makes a pot
the use of the pot
is precisely where there is nothing.

To recover the Way, we must unlearn. We must return to a state of nature. To follow the Way, we must practice *wu wei*, or nondoing. "Strive for non-striving," advises the *Daodejing*.

All our attempts at asserting our egos, at making things happen, are like swimming against a current and thus ultimately futile, even harmful. If we let the current carry us, however, we will travel far. Similarly, a life that follows the Way will be a life of pure effectiveness, accomplishing much with little effort.

It is often said that the Chinese are Confucians in public and Daoists in private, and the two approaches do seem to balance each other. Confucianism is a rational political philosophy that emphasizes morality, conformity, duty, and self-discipline. Daoism is an intuitive philosophy that emphasizes individualism, nonconformity, and a return to nature. If a Confucian education molded scholars outwardly into responsible, ethical officials, Daoism provided some breathing room for the artist and poet inside.

---

banner dates from the second century BCE and is painted with scenes representing the three levels of the universe: heaven, earth, and the underworld.

The heavenly realm is shown at the top, in the crossbar of the **T**. In the upper right corner is the sun, inhabited by a mythical crow; in the upper left, a mythical toad stands on a crescent moon. Between them is a primordial deity shown as a man with a long serpent's tail—a Han imagining of the Great Ancestor. Dragons and other celestial creatures swarm below.

A gate, indicated by two upside-down **T**s and guarded by two seated figures, stands where the horizontal of heaven meets the banner's long, vertical stem. Two intertwined dragons loop through a circular jade piece known as a *bi*, itself usually a symbol of heaven, dividing this vertical segment into two areas. The portion above the *bi* represents the earthly realm. Here, the deceased woman and her three attendants stand on a platform while two kneeling figures offer gifts. The lower portion represents the underworld. Silk draperies and a stone chime hanging from the *bi* form a canopy for the platform below. Like the bronze bells we saw earlier, stone chimes were ceremonial instruments dating from Zhou times. On the platform, ritual bronze vessels contain food and wine for the deceased, just as they did in Shang tombs. The squat, muscular man holding up the platform stands in turn on a pair of fish whose bodies form another *bi*. The fish and the other strange creatures in this section are inhabitants of the underworld.

Daoism and Confucianism

The Han dynasty marked not only the end of the mythocentric age but also the beginning of a new age. During this dynasty, Daoism and Confucianism, two of the many philosophies formulated during the troubled times of the Eastern Zhou, became central in Chinese thought.

Their influence since then has been continuous and fundamental.

Daoism emphasizes the close relationship between humans and nature. It is concerned with bringing the individual life into harmony with the *Dao*, or Way, of the universe (see "Daoism," above). For some a secular, philosophical path, Daoism on a popular level developed into an organized religion, absorbing many traditional folk practices such as shamanism and the search for immortality.

Immortality was as intriguing to Han rulers as it had been to the first emperor of Qin. Daoist adepts experimented endlessly with diet, physical exercise, and other techniques in the belief that immortal life could be achieved on earth. A popular Daoist legend told of the Isles of the Immortals in the Eastern Sea, depicted on a bronze incense burner from the tomb of Prince Liu Sheng, who died in 113 BCE (fig. 10-7). Around the bowl, gold **inlay** outlines the stylized waves of the sea. Above them rises the mountainous island, busy with birds, animals, and people who had discovered the secret of immortality. Technically, this exquisite piece represents the ultimate development of the long tradition of bronze casting in China.

Confucianism and the State

In contrast to the metaphysical focus of Daoism, Confucianism is concerned with the human world, and its goal is the attainment of peace. To this end, it proposes an ethical system based on correct relationships among people. Beginning with self-discipline in the individual, Confucianism goes on to achieve correct relationships with the family, including ancestors, then, in ever-widening circles, with friends and others all the way up to the emperor (see "Confucius and Confucianism," opposite).

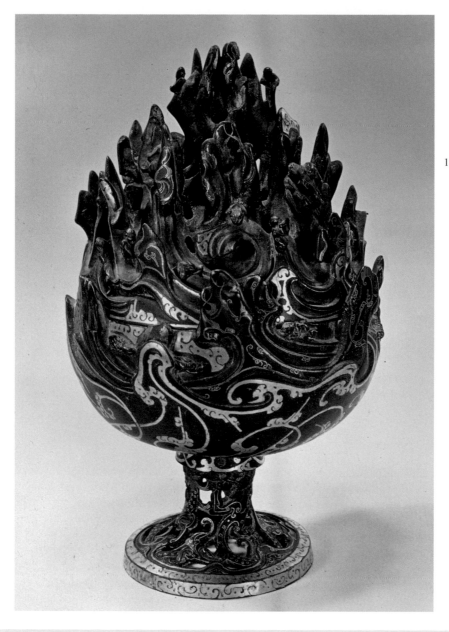

10-7. Incense burner, from the tomb of Prince Liu Sheng, Mancheng, Hebei. Han dynasty, 113 BCE. Bronze with gold inlay, height 10¼" (26 cm). Hebei Provincial Museum, Shijiazhuang

CONFUCIUS AND CONFUCIANISM

Confucius was born in 551 BCE in the state of Lu, roughly present-day Shandong province, into a declining aristocratic family. While still in his teens he set his heart on becoming a scholar; by his early twenties he had begun to teach.

By Confucius's lifetime, warfare for supremacy among the various states of China had begun, and the traditional social fabric seemed to be breaking down. Looking back to the early Zhou dynasty as a sort of golden age, Confucius thought about how a just and harmonious society could again emerge. For many years he sought a ruler who would put his ideas into effect, but to no avail. Frustrated, he spent his final years teaching. After his death in 479 BCE, his sayings were collected by his disciples and their followers into a book known in English as the *Analects*, which is the only record of his words.

At the heart of Confucian thought is the concept of *ren*, or human-heartedness. *Ren* emphasizes morality and empathy as the basic standards for all human interaction. The virtue of *ren* is most fully realized in the Confucian ideal of the *junzi*, or gentleman. Originally indicating noble birth, the term was redirected to mean one who through education and self-cultivation had become a superior person, right-thinking and right-acting in all situations. A *junzi* is the opposite of a petty or small-minded person. His characteristics include moderation, inner integrity, self-control, loyalty, reciprocity, and altruism. His primary concern is justice.

Together with human-heartedness and justice, Confucius emphasized *li*, or etiquette. *Li* includes scrupulous everyday manners as well as ritual, ceremony, protocol—all of the formalities of social interaction. Such forms, Confucius felt, choreographed life so that an entire society moved in harmony. *Ren* and *li* operate in the realm of the Five Constant Relationships that define Confucian society: parent and child, husband and wife, elder sibling and younger sibling, elder friend and younger friend, ruler and subject. Deference to age is clearly built into this view, as is the deference to authority that made Confucianism popular with emperors. Yet responsibilities flow the other way as well: the duty of a ruler is to earn the loyalty of subjects, of a husband to earn the respect of his wife, of age to guide youth wisely.

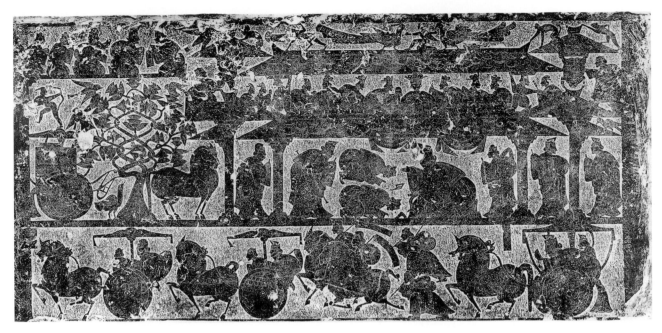

10-8. Detail from a rubbing of a relief in the Wu family shrine (Wuliangci), Jiaxiang, Shandong. Han dynasty, 151 CE. Stone, 27½ x 66½" (70 x 169 cm)

Emphasis on social order and respect for authority made Confucianism especially attractive to Han rulers, who were eager to distance themselves from the disastrous legalism of the Qin. The Han emperor Wu (ruled 141–87 BCE) made Confucianism the official imperial philosophy, and it remained the state ideology of China for more than 2,000 years, until the end of imperial rule in the twentieth century. Once institutionalized, Confucianism took on so many rituals that it too eventually assumed the form and force of a religion. Han philosophers contributed to this process by infusing Confucianism with traditional Chinese cosmology. They emphasized the Zhou idea, taken up by Confucius, that the emperor ruled by the mandate of heaven. Heaven itself was reconceived more abstractly as the moral force underlying the universe. Thus the moral system of Confucian society became a reflection of the universal order.

Confucian subjects turn up frequently in Han art. Among the most famous examples are the reliefs from the Wu family shrines built in 151 CE in Jiaxiang. Carved and engraved in low relief on stone slabs, the scenes were meant to teach such basic Confucian themes as respect for the emperor, filial piety, and wifely devotion. Daoist motifs also appear, as do figures from traditional myths and legends. Such mixed **iconography** is characteristic of Han art.

One relief shows a two-story building, with women in the upper floor and men in the lower (fig. 10-8). The central figures in both floors are receiving visitors, some of whom bear gifts. The scene seems to depict homage to the first emperor of the Han dynasty, indicated by his larger size. The birds and small figures on the roof may represent mythical creatures and immortals, while to the

left the legendary archer Yi shoots at one of the sun-crows. (Myths tell how Yi shot all but one of the ten crows of the ten suns so that the earth would not dry out.) Across the lower register, a procession brings more dignitaries to the reception.

When compared to the Han dynasty banner (see fig. 10-6), this late Han relief clearly shows the change that has taken place in the Chinese worldview. The banner places equal emphasis on heaven, earth, and the underworld; human beings are dwarfed by a great swarming of supernatural creatures and divine beings. In the Wu shrine, the focus is clearly on the human realm. The composition conveys the importance of the emperor as the holder of the mandate of heaven and illustrates the fundamental Confucian themes of social order and decorum.

Architecture

Contemporary literary sources are eloquent on the wonders of the Han capital. Unfortunately, nothing of Han architecture remains except ceramic models. One model of a house found in a tomb, where it was provided for the dead to use in the afterlife, represents a typical Han dwelling (fig. 10-9). Its four stories are crowned with a watchtower and face a small walled courtyard. Pigs and oxen probably occupied the ground floor, while the family lived in the upper stories.

Aside from the multilevel construction, the most interesting feature of the house is the bracketing system supporting the rather broad eaves of its tiled roofs. **Bracketing** became a standard element of East Asian architecture, not only in private homes but more typically in palaces and temples. Another interesting aspect of

creators and custodians of China's high culture—turned to Daoism, which contained a strong escapist element. Educated to serve the government, they increasingly withdrew from public life. They wandered the landscape, drank, wrote poems, practiced calligraphy, and expressed their disdain for the world through willfully eccentric behavior.

The rarefied intellectual escape route of Daoism was available only to the educated elite. Far more people sought answers in the magic and superstitions of Daoism in its religious form. Though weak and disorganized, the southern courts continued to patronize traditional Chinese culture, and Confucianism remained the official doctrine. Yet ultimately it was a new influence, Buddhism, that brought the greatest comfort to the troubled China of the Six Dynasties.

Painting

Although few paintings survive from the Six Dynasties, abundant descriptions in literary sources make it clear that the period was an important one. Landscape, later a major theme of Chinese art, first appeared as a subject during this era. For Daoists, wandering through China's countryside was a source of spiritual refreshment. Painters and scholars of the Six Dynasties found that wandering in the mind's eye through a painted landscape could serve the same purpose. This new emphasis on the spiritual value of painting contrasted with the Confucian view, which had emphasized art's moral and didactic uses.

Reflections on the tradition of painting also inspired the first works on theory and aesthetics. One of the earliest and most succinct formulations of the ideals of Chinese painting are the six principles set out by the scholar Xie He (c. 500–c. 535 CE). The first two principles in particular offer valuable insight to anyone seeking to understand the spirit in which China's painters worked.

The first principle announces that "spirit consonance" imbues a painting with "life's movement." This "spirit" is the Daoist *qi*, the breath that animates all creation, the energy that flows through all things. When a painting has *qi*, it will be alive with inner essence, not merely outward resemblance. Artists must cultivate their own spirit so that this universal energy flows through them and infuses their work. The second principle recognizes that brushstrokes are the "bones" of a picture, its primary structural element. The Chinese judge a painting above all by the quality of its brushwork. Each brushstroke is a vehicle of expression; it is through the vitality of a painter's brushwork that "spirit consonance" makes itself felt. We can sense this attitude already in the rapid, confident brushstrokes that outline the figures of the Han banner and again in the more controlled, rhythmical lines of one of the most important of the very few works surviving from this period, a painted scroll known as *Admonitions of the Imperial Instructress to Court Ladies*. Attributed to the painter Gu Kaizhi (c. 344–406 CE), it alternates illustrations and text to relate seven Confucian stories of wifely virtue from Chinese history.

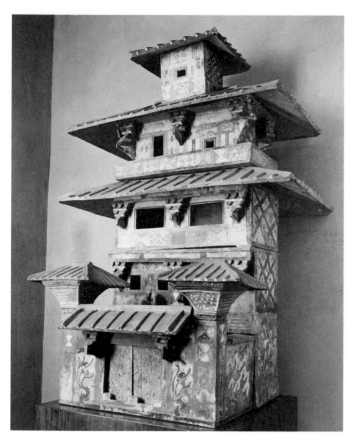

10-9.   Tomb model of a house. Eastern Han dynasty, 1st century CE. Painted earthenware, 52 x 33½ x 27" (132.1 x 85.1 x 68.6 cm). The Nelson-Atkins Museum of Art, Kansas City, Missouri
Purchase, Nelson Trust (33–521)

the model is the elaborate painting on the exterior walls. Much of the painting is purely decorative, though some of it illustrates structural features such as posts and lintels. Still other images evoke the world outdoors: notice the trees flanking the gateway with crows perched in their branches. Literary sources describe the walls of Han palaces as decorated with paint and lacquer but also inlaid with precious metals and stones.

SIX DYNASTIES   With the fall of the Han dynasty in 220 CE, China splintered into three warring kingdoms. In 280 CE the empire was briefly reunited, but invasions by nomadic peoples from Central Asia, a source of trouble throughout Chinese history, soon forced the court to flee south. For the next 250 years, northern and southern China developed separately. In the north, sixteen kingdoms carved out by invaders rose and fell before giving way to a succession of largely foreign dynasties. Warfare was commonplace. Tens of thousands of Chinese fled south, where six short-lived Dynasties succeeded each other in a period of almost constant turmoil broadly known as Six Dynasties or Southern and Northern Dynasties (220–579 CE).

In such chaos, the Confucian system lost much influence. In the south especially, many intellectuals—the

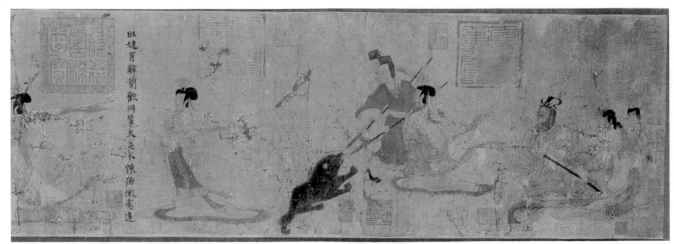

10-10. Attributed to Gu Kaizhi. Detail of *Admonitions of the Imperial Instructress to Court Ladies*. Six Dynasties period, c. 344–406 CE. Handscroll, ink and colors on silk, 9³/₄" x 11'6" (24.8 cm x 3.5 m). The British Museum, London

The first illustration depicts the courage of Lady Feng (fig. 10-10). An escaped circus bear rushes toward her husband, a Han emperor, who is filled with fear. Behind his throne, two female servants have turned to run away. Before him, two male attendants, themselves on the verge of panic, try to fend off the bear with spears. Only Lady Feng is calm as she rushes forward to place herself between the beast and the emperor.

The style of the painting is typical of the fourth century. The figures are drawn with a brush in a thin, even-width line, and a few outlined areas are filled with color. Facial features, especially those of the men, are quite well depicted. Movement and emotion are shown through conventions such as the bands flowing from Lady Feng's dress, indicating that she is rushing forward, and the upturned strings on both sides of the emperor's head, suggesting his fear. There is no hint of a setting; instead, the artist relies on careful placement of the figures to create a sense of depth.

The painting is on silk, a Chinese material with origins in the remote past. Silk was typically woven in bands about 12 inches wide and up to 20 or 30 feet long. Early Chinese painters thus developed the format used here, the handscroll—a long, narrow, horizontal composition, compact enough to be held in the hands when rolled up. **Handscrolls** are intimate works, meant to be viewed by only two or three people at a time. They were not displayed completely unrolled as we commonly see them today in museums. Rather, viewers would open a scroll and savor it slowly from right to left, displaying only a foot or two at a time.

Calligraphy

The emphasis on the expressive quality and structural importance of brushstrokes finds its purest embodiment in **calligraphy**. The same brushes are used for both painting and calligraphy, and a relationship between them was recognized as early as Han times. In his teachings Confucius had extolled the importance of the pursuit of knowl-

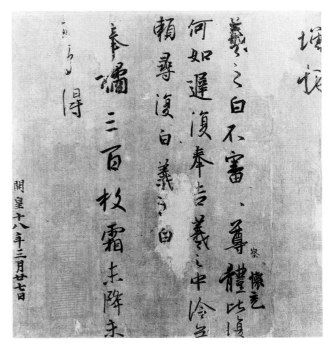

10-11. Wang Xizhi. Portion of a letter from the *Feng Ju* album. Six Dynasties period, mid-4th century CE. Ink on paper, 9³/₄ x 18¹/₂" (24.7 x 46.8 cm). National Palace Museum, Taipei, Taiwan

The stamped calligraphs that appear on Chinese artworks are seals—personal emblems. The use of seals dates from the Zhou dynasty, and to this day seals traditionally employ the archaic characters, known appropriately as "seal script," of the Zhou or Qin. Cut in stone, a seal may state a formal, given name, or it may state any of the numerous personal names that China's painters and writers adopted throughout their lives. A treasured work of art often bears not only the seal of its maker but also those of collectors and admirers through the centuries. In the Chinese view, these do not disfigure the work but add another layer of interest. This sample of Wang Xizhi's calligraphy, for example, bears the seals of two Song dynasty emperors, a Song official, a famous collector of the sixteenth century, and two emperors of the Qing dynasty of the eighteenth and nineteenth centuries.

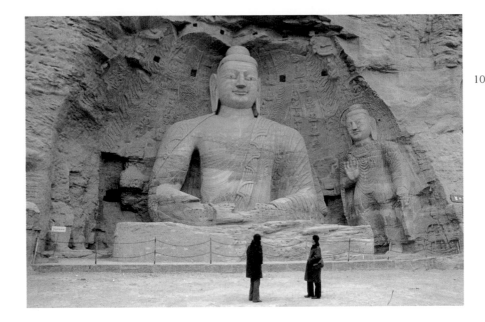

10-12. Seated Buddha, Cave 20, Yungang, Datong, Shanxi. Northern Wei dynasty, c. 460 CE. Stone, height 45' (13.7 m)

edge and the arts. Among the visual arts, painting was felt to reflect moral concerns, while calligraphy was believed to reveal the style and character of the writer.

Calligraphy is regarded as one of the highest forms of expression in China. For more than 2,000 years, China's literati ("educated"), all of them Confucian scholars, have enjoyed being connoisseurs and practitioners of this abstract art. During the fourth century, calligraphy came to full maturity. The most important practitioner of the day was Wang Xizhi (c. 303–361 CE), whose works have served as models of excellence for all subsequent generations. The example here comes from a letter, now somewhat damaged and mounted as part of an album, known as *Feng Ju* (fig. 10-11).

Feng Ju is an example of "walking" style, which is neither too formal nor too free but is done in a relaxed, easy-going manner. Brushstrokes vary in width and length, creating rhythmic vitality. Individual characters remain distinct, yet within each character the strokes are run together and simplified as the brush moves from one to the other without lifting off the page. The effect is fluid and graceful, yet still strong and dynamic. It was Wang Xizhi who first made this an officially accepted style, to be learned along with other styles.

Buddhism

Buddhism originated in India during the fifth century BCE (Chapter 9), then gradually spread north into Central Asia. With the opening of the Silk Road during the Han dynasty, its influence reached China. To the Chinese of the Six Dynasties, beset by constant warfare and social devastation, Buddhism offered consolation in life and the promise of salvation after death. The faith spread throughout the country to all social levels, first in the north, where many of the invaders promoted it as the official religion, then slightly later in the south, where it found its first great patron in the emperor Liang Wudi (ruled 502–549 CE). Thousands of temples and monasteries were built, and many people became monks and nuns.

Almost nothing remains in China of the Buddhist architecture of the Six Dynasties, but we can see what it must have looked like in the Japanese temple Horyu-ji (see fig. 11-5), which was based on Chinese models of this period. The slender forms and linear grace of Horyu-ji have much in common with the figures in Gu Kaizhi's handscroll, and they indicate the delicate, almost weightless style cultivated in southern China.

The most impressive works of Buddhist art surviving from the Six Dynasties are the hundreds of northern rock-cut caves that line the Silk Road between Xinjiang in Central Asia and the Yellow River Valley. Both the caves and the sculpture that fill them were carved from the solid rock of the cliffs. Small caves high above the ground were retreats for monks and pilgrims, while larger caves at the base of the cliffs were wayside shrines and temples.

The caves at Yungang, in Shanxi province, contain many examples of the earliest phase of Buddhist sculpture in China, including the monumental seated Buddha in Cave 20 (fig. 10-12). The figure was carved in the latter part of the fifth century by imperial decree of a ruler of the Northern Wei dynasty (386–535 CE), the longest-lived and most stable of the northern kingdoms. Most Wei rulers were avid patrons of Buddhism, and under their rule the religion made its greatest advances in the north.

The front part of the cave has crumbled away, and the 45-foot statue is now exposed to the open air, clearly visible from a distance. The elongated ears, protuberance on the head (*ushnisha*), and monk's robe (*sanghati*) are traditional attributes of the Buddha. The masklike face, full torso, massive shoulders, and shallow, stylized drapery indicate strong Central Asian influence. The overall effect is remote and even slightly severe, a far cry from the more sensuous expression of the early traditions in India. The image of Buddha became increasingly formal and unearthly as it traveled east from its origins, reflecting a fundamental difference in the way the Chinese and the Indians visualize their deities.

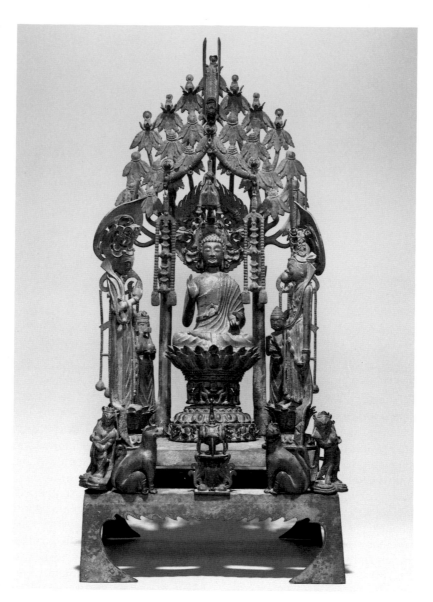

10-13. Altar to Amitabha Buddha. Sui dynasty, 593 CE. Bronze, height 30⅛"
(76.5 cm). Museum of Fine Arts, Boston

Gift of Mrs. W. Scott Fitz (22.407) and Gift of Edward Holmes Jackson in memory of
his mother, Mrs. W. Scott Fitz (47.1407–1412)

SUI AND TANG DYNASTIES

In 589 CE a general from the last of the northern dynasties replaced a child emperor and established a dynasty of his own, the Sui. Defeating all opposition, he molded China into a centralized empire as it had been in Han times. The new emperor was a devout Buddhist, and his reunification of China coincided with a fusion of the several styles of Buddhist sculpture that had developed. This new style is seen in a bronze altar to Amitabha Buddha (fig. 10-13), one of the many buddhas espoused by Mahayana Buddhism. Amitabha dwelled in the Western Pure Land, a paradise into which his faithful followers were promised rebirth. With its comparatively simple message of salvation, the Pure Land sect eventually became the most popular form of Buddhism in China.

The altar depicts Amitabha in his paradise, seated on a lotus throne beneath a canopy of trees. Each leaf cluster is set with jewels. Seven celestial nymphs sit on the topmost clusters, and ropes of pearls hang from the tree trunks. Behind Amitabha's head is a halo of flames. To his left, the **bodhisattva** Guanyin holds a pomegranate; to his right, another bodhisattva clasps his hands in prayer. Behind are four disciples who first preached the teachings of the Buddha. On the lower level, an incense burner is flanked by seated dogs and two smaller bodhisattvas. Focusing on Amitabha's benign expression and filled with objects symbolizing his power, the altar combines the sensuality of Indian styles, the schematic abstraction of Central Asian art, and the Chinese emphasis on linear grace and rhythm into a harmonious new style.

The short-lived Sui dynasty fell in 617 CE, but in reunifying the empire it paved the way for one of the greatest dynasties in Chinese history, the Tang (618–907 CE). Even today many Chinese living abroad still call themselves "Tang people." To them, Tang implies that part of

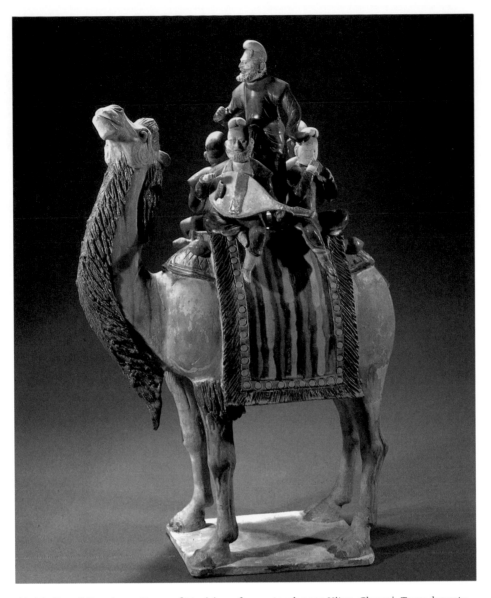

10-14. *Camel Carrying a Group of Musicians*, from a tomb near Xi'an, Shanxi. Tang dynasty, c. mid-8th century CE. Earthenware with three-color glaze, height 26 1/8" (66.5 cm). Museum of Chinese History, Beijing

the Chinese character that is strong and vigorous (especially in military power), noble and idealistic, but also realistic and pragmatic.

Under a series of ambitious and forceful emperors, Chinese control again reached over Central Asia. As in Han times, goods, ideas, and influence flowed across the Silk Road. In the South China Sea, Arab and Persian ships carried on a lively trade with coastal cities. Chinese cultural influence in East Asia was so important that Japan and Korea sent thousands of students to study Chinese civilization.

Cosmopolitan and tolerant, Tang China was confident in itself and curious about the world. Many foreigners came to the splendid new capital, Chang'an (present-day Xi'an), and they are often depicted in the art of the period. A ceramic statue of a camel carrying a troupe of musicians reflects the Tang fascination with the "exotic" Turkic cultures of Central Asia (fig. 10-14). The

three bearded musicians (one with his back to us) are Central Asian, while the two smooth-shaven ones are Han Chinese. Two-humped Bactrian camels, themselves exotic Central Asian "visitors," were beasts of burden in the caravans that crisscrossed the Silk Road. The motif of musicians on camelback seems to have been popular in the Tang dynasty, for it also appears in some paintings.

Stylistically, the statue reveals a new interest in **naturalism**, an important trend in both painting and sculpture. Compared to the rigid, staring ceramic soldiers of the first emperor of Qin, the Tang group is alive with gesture and expression. The majestic camel throws its head back; the musicians are vividly captured in mid-performance. Ceramic figurines such as this, produced by the thousands for Tang tombs, offer a glimpse into the gorgeous variety of Tang life. The statue's three-color **glaze** technique was a specialty of Tang ceramicists. The glazes—usually chosen from a restricted palette of

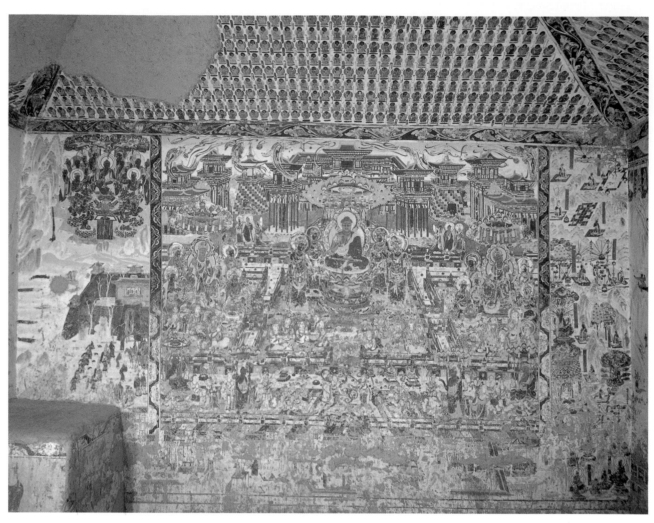

10-15. *The Western Paradise of Amitabha Buddha*, detail of a wall painting in Cave 217, Dunhuang, Gansu. Tang dynasty, c. 750 CE. 10'2" x 16' (3.1 x 4.86 m)

amber, yellow, green, and white—were splashed freely and allowed to run over the surface during firing to convey a feeling of spontaneity. The technique seems symbolic of Tang culture itself in its robust, colorful, and cosmopolitan expressiveness.

Buddhist Art and Architecture

Buddhism reached its greatest development in China during the Tang dynasty. From emperors and empresses to common peasants, virtually the entire country adopted the Buddhist faith. A Tang vision of the most popular sect, Pure Land, was expressed in a wall painting from a cave in Dunhuang (fig. 10-15). A major stop along the Silk Road, Dunhuang has some 500 caves carved out of its sandy cliffs, all filled with painted clay sculpture and decorated with wall paintings from floor to ceiling. The site was worked on continuously from the fifth to the fourteenth century, a period of almost a thousand years. Rarely in art's history do we have the opportunity to study such an extended period of stylistic and iconographic evolution in one place. Amitabha Buddha is seated in the center, surrounded by four bodhisattvas who serve as his messengers to the world. Two other groups of bodhisattvas are clus-

tered at the right and left. In the foreground, musicians and dancers create a heavenly atmosphere. In the background, great halls and towers rise: the artist has imagined the Western Paradise in terms of the grandeur of Tang palaces. Indeed, the lavish entertainment could just as easily be taking place at the imperial court. This worldly vision of paradise contrasts tellingly with the simple portrayal in the earlier Sui altarpiece (see fig. 10-13), and it gives us our best visualization of the splendor of Tang civilization at a time when Chang'an was probably the greatest city in the world.

The early Tang emperors proclaimed a policy of religious tolerance, but during the ninth century a conservative reaction set in. Confucianism was reasserted and Buddhism was briefly persecuted as a "foreign" religion. Thousands of temples, shrines, and monasteries were destroyed and innumerable bronze statues melted down. Nevertheless, several Buddhist structures survive from the Tang dynasty, one of which, the Nanchan Temple, is the first important example of Chinese architecture.

Nanchan Temple. Of the few structures earlier than 1400 to have survived, the Nanchan Temple is the most significant, for it shows characteristics of both temples

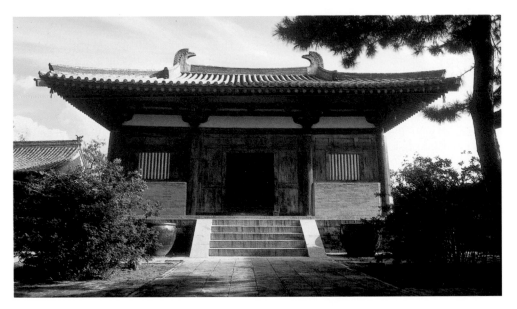

10-16. Nanchan Temple, Wutaishan, Shanxi. Tang dynasty, 782 CE

and palaces of the Tang dynasty (fig. 10-16). Located on Mount Wutai in the eastern part of Shanxi province, this small hall was constructed in 782 CE. The tiled roof, first seen in the Han tomb model (see fig. 10-9), has taken on a curved silhouette. Quite subtle here, this curve became increasingly pronounced in later centuries. The very broad overhanging eaves are supported by a correspondingly elaborate bracketing system.

Also typical is the **bay** system of construction, in which a cubic unit of space, a bay, is formed by four posts and their lintels. The bay functioned in Chinese architecture as a sort of module, a basic unit of construction. To create larger structures, an architect multiplied the number of bays. Thus the Nanchan Temple—modest in scope with three bays—gives an idea of the vast, multistoried palaces of the Tang depicted in such paintings as the one from Dunhuang.

Great Wild Goose Pagoda. Another important monument of Tang architecture is the Great Wild Goose Pagoda at the Ci'en Temple in Xi'an, the Tang capital (fig. 10-17). The temple was constructed in 645 CE for the famous monk Xuanzang on his return from a sixteen-year pilgrimage to India. At Ci'en Temple, Xuanzang taught and translated the materials he had brought back with him.

The **pagoda**, a typical East Asian Buddhist structure, originated in the Indian Buddhist **stupa**, the elaborated burial mound that housed relics of the Buddha (see "Elements of Architecture," page 414). In India the stupa had developed a multistoried form in the Gandharan region under the Kushan dynasty (c. 50–250 CE). In China this idea blended with a traditional Han watchtower to produce the pagoda. Built entirely in masonry, the Great Wild Goose Pagoda nevertheless imitates the wooden architecture of the time. The walls are decorated in low relief to resemble bays, and bracket systems are reproduced

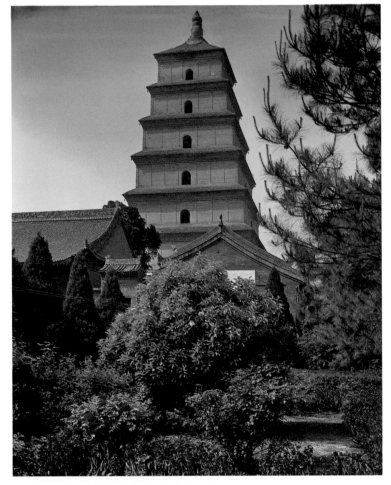

10-17. Great Wild Goose Pagoda at Ci'en Temple, Xi'an, Shanxi. Tang dynasty, first erected 645 CE; rebuilt mid-8th century CE

under the projecting roofs of each story. Although modified and repaired in later times (its seven stories were originally five), the pagoda still preserves the essence of Tang architecture in its simplicity, symmetry, proportions, and grace.

ELEMENTS OF ARCHITECTURE
Pagodas

Pagodas are the most characteristic of East Asian architectural forms. Originally associated with Buddhism, pagodas developed from Indian stupas as Buddhism spread northeastward along the Silk Road. Stupas merged with the watchtowers of Han dynasty China in multistoried stone structures with projecting tiled roofs. This transformation culminated in wooden pagodas with upward-curving roofs supported by elaborate bracketing in China, Korea, and Japan. Buddhist pagodas retain the *axis mundi* masts of stupas. Like their South Asian prototypes, early East Asian pagodas were solid, with small devotional spaces hollowed out; later examples often provided access to the ground floor and sometimes to upper levels. The layout and construction of pagodas, as well as the number and curve of their roofs, vary depending on the time and place.

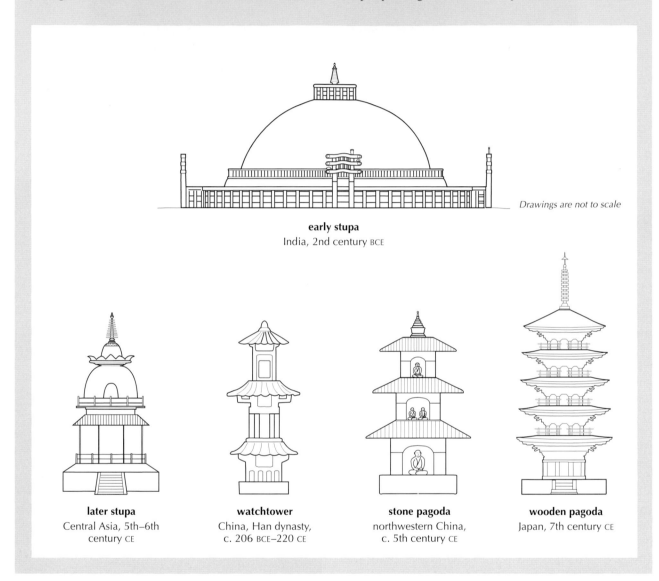

Drawings are not to scale

early stupa
India, 2nd century BCE

later stupa
Central Asia, 5th–6th century CE

watchtower
China, Han dynasty, c. 206 BCE–220 CE

stone pagoda
northwestern China, c. 5th century CE

wooden pagoda
Japan, 7th century CE

Figure Painting

Later artists looking back on their heritage recognized the Tang dynasty as China's great age of figure painting. Unfortunately, very few scroll paintings that can be definitely identified as Tang still exist. We can get some idea of the character of Tang figure painting from the wall paintings of Dunhuang (see fig. 10-15). Another way to savor the particular flavor of Tang painting is to look at copies made by later Song dynasty artists, which are far better preserved. An outstanding example of this practice is *Ladies Preparing Newly Woven Silk*, attributed to Huizong (ruled 1101–1125 CE), the last emperor of the Northern Song dynasty (fig. 10-18). A long handscroll in several sections, it depicts the activities of court women as they weave and iron silk. An inscription on the scroll informs us that the painting is a copy of a famous work by Zhang Xuan, an eighth-century painter known for his depictions of women at the Tang court. The original no longer exists, so we cannot know how faithful the copy is. Still, its refined lines and bright colors seem to share not only the grace and simplicity of Tang sculpture and architecture but also the quiet beauty characteristic of Tang painting.

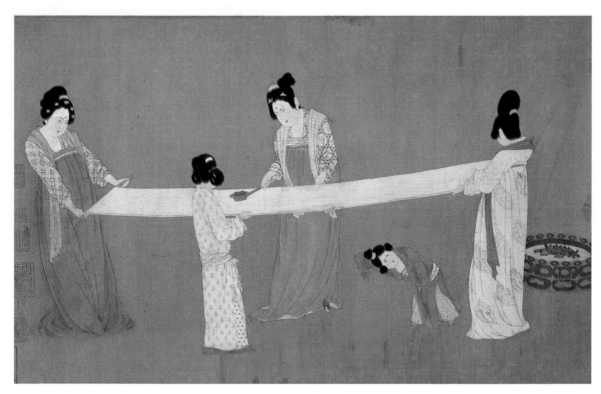

10-18. Attributed to Emperor Huizong. Detail of *Ladies Preparing Newly Woven Silk,* copy after a lost painting by Zhang Xuan. Northern Song dynasty, early 12th century. Handscroll, ink and colors on silk, 14½ x 57¼" (36.8 x 145.5 cm). Museum of Fine Arts, Boston

Chinese and Japanese Special Fund

Confucius said of himself, "I merely transmit, I do not create; I love and revere the ancients." In this spirit, Chinese painters regularly copied paintings of earlier masters. Painters made copies both to absorb the lessons of their great predecessors and to perpetuate the achievements of the past. In later centuries, painters took up the practice of regularly executing a work "in the manner of" some particularly revered ancient master. This was at once an act of homage, a declaration of artistic allegiance, and a way of reinforcing a personal connection with the past.

SONG DYNASTY

A brief period of disintegration followed the fall of the Tang dynasty before China was again united, this time under the Song dynasty (960–1279 CE), which established a new capital at Bienjing (present-day Kaifeng), near the Yellow River. In contrast to the outgoing confidence of the Tang, the mood during the Song was more introspective, a reflection of China's weakened military situation. In 1126 the Jurchen tribes of Manchuria invaded China, sacked the capital, and took possession of much of the northern part of the country. Song forces withdrew south and established a new capital at Hangzhou. From this point on, the dynasty is known as Southern Song (1127–1279), with the first portion in retrospect called Northern Song (960–1126).

Although China's territory had diminished, its wealth had increased because of advances in agriculture, commerce, and technology begun under the Tang. Patronage was plentiful, and the arts flourished. Song culture is noted for its highly refined taste and intellectual grandeur. Where the Tang had reveled in exoticism, eagerly absorbing influences from Persia, India, and Central Asia, Song culture was more self-consciously Chinese. Philosophy experienced its most creative era since the "one hundred schools" of the Zhou. Song scholarship was brilliant, especially in history, and its poetry is noted

for its depth. But the finest expressions of the Song are in art, especially painting and ceramics.

Neo-Confucianism

Song philosophers continued the process, begun during the Tang, of restoring Confucianism to dominance. In strengthening Confucian thought, philosophers drew on Daoism and especially Buddhism, even as they openly rejected Buddhism itself as foreign. These innovations provided Confucianism with a metaphysical aspect it had previously lacked, allowing it to propose a more satisfying, all-embracing explanation of the universe. This new synthesis of China's three main paths of thought is called Neo-Confucianism.

Neo-Confucianism teaches that the universe consists of two interacting forces known as *li* (principle or idea) and *qi* (matter). All pine trees, for example, consist of an underlying *li* we might call "Pine Tree Idea" brought into the material world through *qi*. All the *li* of the universe, including humans, are but aspects of an eternal first principle known as the Great Ultimate, which is completely present in every object. Our task as human beings is to rid our *qi* of impurities through education and self-cultivation so that our *li* may realize its oneness with the Great Ultimate. This lifelong process resembles the striving to attain buddhahood, and if we persist in our attempts, one day we will be enlightened—the term itself comes directly from Buddhism.

Landscape Painting

The Neo-Confucian ideas found visual expression in art, especially in landscape, which became the most highly esteemed subject for painting. Northern Song artists studied nature closely to master its many appearances—the way each species of tree grew, the distinctive character of each rock formation, the changes of the seasons, the myriad birds, blossoms, and insects. This passion for realistic detail was the artist's form of self-cultivation: mastering outward forms showed an understanding of the principles behind them.

Yet despite the convincing accumulation of detail, the paintings do not record a specific site. The artist's goal was to paint the eternal essence of mountain-ness, for example, not to reproduce the appearance of a particular mountain. Painting a landscape required an artist to orchestrate his cumulative understanding of *li* in all its aspects—mountains and rocks, streams and waterfalls, trees and grasses, clouds and mist. A landscape painting thus expressed the desire for the spiritual communion with nature that was the key to enlightenment. As the tradition progressed, landscape also became a vehicle for conveying human emotions, even for speaking indirectly of one's own deepest feelings.

In the earliest times, art reflected the mythocentric worldview of the ancient Chinese. During the period when the three religions dominated people's lives, there was a major shift in which religious images and human actions became the most important subjects. The choice of landscape as the chief means of expression, reflecting the general Chinese desire to avoid direct depiction of the human condition and to show things instead in a symbolic manner, was the second great shift in the focus of Chinese art. The major form of Chinese artistic expression thus moved from the mythical, through the religious and ethical, and finally to the philosophical and aesthetic.

One of the first great masters of Song landscape was the eleventh-century painter Fan Kuan (active c. 990–1030), whose surviving major work, *Travelers among Mountains and Streams*, is generally regarded as one of the greatest monuments in the history of Chinese art (fig. 10-19). The work is physically large—almost 7 feet high—but the sense of monumentality also radiates from the composition itself, which makes its impression even when much reduced.

The composition unfolds in three stages, comparable to the three acts of a drama. At the bottom a large, low-lying group of rocks, taking up about one-eighth of the picture surface, establishes the extreme foreground. The rest of the landscape pushes back from this point. In anticipating the shape and substance of the mountains to come, the rocks introduce the main theme of the work, much as the first act of a drama introduces the principal characters. In the middle ground, travelers and their

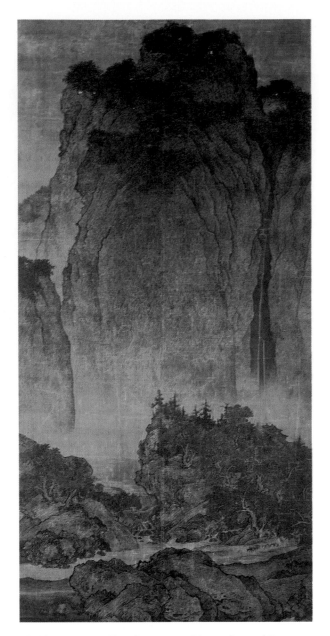

10-19. Fan Kuan. *Travelers among Mountains and Streams*. Northern Song dynasty, early 11th century. Hanging scroll, ink and colors on silk, height 6'9 1/4" (2.06 m). National Palace Museum, Taipei, Taiwan

mules are coming from the right. They are somewhat shocking, for we suddenly realize our human scale—how small we are, how vast nature is! This middle ground takes up twice as much picture surface as the foreground, and, like the second act of a play, shows variation and development. Instead of a solid mass, the rocks here are separated into two groups by a waterfall spanned by a bridge. In the hills to the right, the rooftops of a temple stand out above the trees.

Mist veils the transition to the background, with the result that the mountain looms suddenly. This background area, almost twice as large as the foreground and middle ground combined, is the climactic third act of the drama. As our eyes begin their ascent, the mountain solidifies. Its ponderous weight increases as it billows upward, finally bursting into the sprays of energetic brushstrokes that describe the scrubby growth on top. To

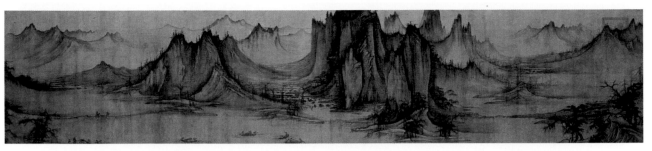

10-20. Xu Daoning. Detail of *Fishing in a Mountain Stream*. Northern Song dynasty, mid-11th century. Handscroll, ink on silk, 19" x 6'10" (48.9 cm x 2.09 m). The Nelson-Atkins Museum of Art, Kansas City, Missouri
Purchase, Nelson Trust (33–1559)

the right, a slender waterfall plummets, not to balance the powerful upward thrust of the mountain but simply to enhance it by contrast. The whole painting, then, conveys the feeling of climbing a high mountain, leaving the human world behind to come face to face with the Great Ultimate in a spiritual communion.

All the elements are depicted with precise detail and in proper scale. Jagged brushstrokes describe the contours of rocks and trees and express their rugged character. Layers of short, staccato strokes (called "raindrop texture" in Chinese) accurately mimic the texture of the rock surface. Spatial recession from foreground through middle ground to background is logically and convincingly handled, if not yet quite continuous.

Although it contains realistic details, the landscape represents no specific place. In its forms, the artist expresses the ideal forms behind appearances; in the rational, ordered composition, he expresses the intelligence of the universe. The arrangement of the mountains, with the central peak flanked by lesser peaks on each side, seems to reflect both the ancient Confucian notion of social hierarchy, with the emperor flanked by his ministers, and the Buddhist motif of the Buddha with bodhisattvas at his side. The landscape, a view of nature uncorrupted by human habitation, expresses a kind of Daoist ideal. Thus we find the three strains of Chinese thought united, much as they are in Neo-Confucianism itself.

The ability of Chinese landscape painters to take us out of ourselves and to let us wander freely through their sites is closely linked to the avoidance of **perspective** as it is understood in the West. Fifteenth-century European painters, searching for fidelity to appearances, developed a "scientific" system for recording exactly the view that could be seen from a single, fixed vantage point. The goal of Chinese painting is precisely to get away from such limits and show a totality beyond what we are normally given to see. If we can imagine the ideal for centuries of Western painters as a photograph, which shows only what can be seen from a fixed viewpoint, we can imagine the ideal for Chinese artists as a film camera aloft in a balloon: distant, all-seeing, and mobile.

The sense of shifting perspective is clearest in the handscroll, where our vantage point changes constantly as we move through the painting. One of the finest handscrolls to survive from the Northern Song is *Fishing in a Mountain Stream* (fig. 10-20), a 7-foot-long painting

executed in the middle of the eleventh century by Xu Daoning (c. 970–c. 1052). Starting from a thatched hut in the right foreground, we follow a path that leads to a broad, open view of a deep vista dissolving into distant mists and mountain peaks. (Remember that viewers observed only a small section of the scroll at a time. To mimic the effect, use two pieces of paper to frame a small viewing area, then move them slowly leftward.) Crossing over a small footbridge, we are brought back to the foreground with the beginning of a central group of high mountains that show extraordinary shapes. Again our path winds back along the bank, and we have a spectacular view of the highest peaks from another small footbridge the artist has placed for us. At the far side of the bridge, we find ourselves looking up into a deep valley, where a stream lures our eyes far into the distance. We can imagine ourselves resting for a moment in the small pavilion the artist offers us halfway up the valley on the right. Or perhaps we may spend some time with the fishers in their boats as the valley gives way to a second, smaller group of mountains, serving both as an echo of the spectacular central group and as a transition to the painting's finale, a broad, open vista. As we cross the bridge here, we meet travelers coming toward us, who will have our experience in reverse. Gazing out into the distance and reflecting on our journey, we again feel that sense of communion with nature that is the goal of Chinese artistic expression.

Such handscrolls have no counterpart in the Western visual arts and are often compared instead to the tradition of Western music, especially symphonic compositions. Both are generated from opening motifs that are developed and varied, both are revealed over time, and in both our sense of the overall structure relies on memory, for we do not see the scroll or hear the composition all at once.

The Northern Song fascination with exactitude extended beyond landscape. The emperor Huizong, whose copy of *Ladies Preparing Newly Woven Silk* was seen in figure 10-18, gathered around himself a group of court painters who shared his passion for quiet, exquisitely detailed, delicately colored paintings of birds and flowers. Other painters specialized in domestic and wild animals, still others in palaces and buildings. One of the most spectacular products of this passion for observation is *Spring Festival on the River*, a long handscroll painted in the first quarter of the twelfth century by Zhang

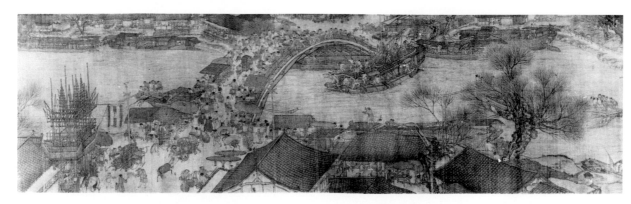

10-21. Zhang Zeduan. Detail of *Spring Festival on the River*. Northern Song dynasty, early 12th century. Handscroll, ink and colors on silk, 9³⁄₄" x 7'4" (24.8 cm x 2.28 m). The Palace Museum, Beijing

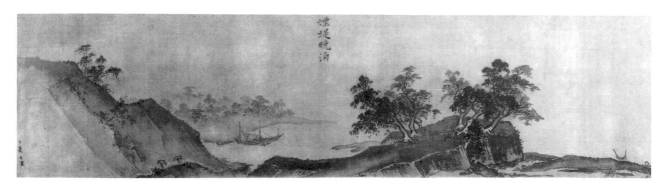

10-22. Xia Gui. Detail of *Twelve Views from a Thatched Hut*. Southern Song dynasty, early 13th century. Handscroll, ink on silk, height 11" (28 cm), length of extant portion 7'7¹⁄₄" (2.31 m). The Nelson-Atkins Museum of Art, Kansas City, Missouri Purchase, Nelson Trust (32-159/2)

Zeduan, an artist connected to the court (fig. 10-21). Beyond its considerable visual delights, the painting is also an invaluable record of daily life in the Song capital.

The painting is set on the day of a festival, when local inhabitants and visitors from the countryside thronged the streets. One high point is the scene reproduced here, which takes place at the Rainbow Bridge. The large boat to the right is probably bringing goods from the southern part of China up the Grand Canal that ran through the city at that time. The sailors are preparing to pass beneath the bridge by lowering the sail and taking down the mast. Excited figures on ship and shore gesture wildly, shouting orders and advice, while a noisy crowd gathers at the bridge railing to watch. Stalls on the bridge are selling food and other merchandise; wine shops and eating places line the banks of the canal. Everyone is on the move. Some people are busy carrying goods, some are shopping, some are simply enjoying themselves. Each figure is splendidly animated and full of purpose; the buildings and boats are perfect in every detail—the artist's knowledge of this bustling world was indeed encyclopedic.

Little is known about the painter Zhang Zeduan other than that he was a member of the scholar-official class, the highly educated elite of imperial China. Interestingly, some of Zhang Zeduan's peers were already beginning to cultivate quite a different attitude toward painting as a form of artistic expression, one that placed overt skill at the lowest end of the scale of values. This emerging scholarly aesthetic later came to dominate Chi-

nese thinking about art, with the result that only in the twentieth century has *Spring Festival* again found an audience willing to hold it in the highest esteem.

Southern Song

Landscape painting took a very different course after the fall of the north and the removal of the court to its new capital in the south, Hangzhou. This new sensibility is reflected in the extant portion of *Twelve Views from a Thatched Hut* (fig. 10-22) by Xia Gui (c. 1180–1230), a member of the newly established Academy of Painters. In general, academy members continued to favor such subjects as birds and flowers in the highly refined, elegantly colored court style patronized by Huizong. Xia Gui, however, was interested in landscape and cultivated his own style. Only the last four of the twelve views that originally made up this long handscroll have survived, but they are enough to illustrate the unique quality of his approach.

In sharp contrast to the majestic, austere landscapes of the Northern Song painters, Xia Gui presents an intimate and lyrical view of nature. Subtly modulated, perfectly controlled ink washes evoke a landscape veiled in mist, while a few deft brushstrokes suffice to indicate the details showing through—the grasses growing by the bank, the fishers at their work, the trees laden with moisture, the two bent-backed figures carrying their heavy load along the path that skirts the hill. Simplified forms, stark contrasts of light and dark, asymmetrical composition, and great expanses of blank space suggest a fleeting world that can be captured only in glimpses. The intangible is somehow more real than the tangible. By limiting himself to a few essential details, the painter evokes a far deeper feeling for what lies beyond.

This development in Song painting from the rational and intellectual to the emotional and intuitive, from the tangible to the intangible, had a parallel in philosophy. During the late twelfth century a new school of Neo-Confucianism called "School of the Mind" insisted that self-cultivation could be achieved through contemplation, which might lead to sudden enlightenment. The idea of

osity and freely intuitive insights of Xia Gui's landscape.

In 1279 the Southern Song dynasty fell to the conquering forces of the Mongol leader Kublai Khan. China was subsumed into the vast Mongol empire, the largest empire the world has ever seen. Mongol rulers founded the Yuan dynasty (1279–1368), setting up their capital in the northeast, in what is now Beijing. Yet the cultural center of China remained in the south, in the cities that rose to prominence during the Song. This separation of political and cultural centers, coupled with a lasting resentment of "barbarian" rule, created the climate for later developments in the arts.

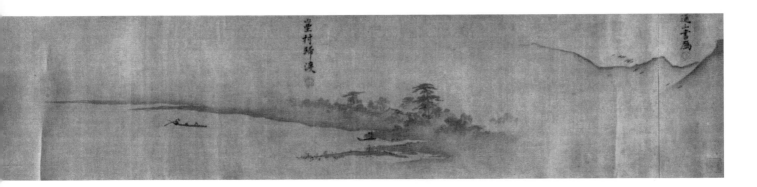

sudden enlightenment may have come from Chan Buddhism, better known in the West by its Japanese name, Zen. Chan Buddhists rejected such formal paths to enlightenment as scripture, knowledge, and ritual in favor of meditation and techniques designed to "short-circuit" the rational mind. Xia Gui's painting seems also to follow this intuitive approach.

The subtle and sophisticated paintings of the Song were created for a highly cultivated audience equally discerning in other arts such as ceramics. Building on the considerable accomplishments of the Tang, Song potters achieved a technical and aesthetic perfection that has made their wares models of excellence throughout the world. Like their painter contemporaries, Song potters turned away from the exuberance of Tang styles to create more quietly beautiful pieces.

The most highly prized of the many types of Song ceramics is Guan Ware, made mainly for imperial use (fig. 10-23). The everted lip, high neck, and rounded body of this simple vase show a strong sense of harmony. Aided by a lustrous white glaze, the form flows without break from base to lip. The piece has an introspective quality as eloquent as the blank spaces in Xia Gui's painting. The aesthetic of the Song is most evident in the crackle pattern that spreads over the surface. The crackle technique was probably discovered accidentally, but it came to be used deliberately in some of the finest Song wares. In the play of irregular, spontaneous crackles over a perfectly regular, perfectly planned form we can sense the same spirit that hovers behind the self-effacing virtu-

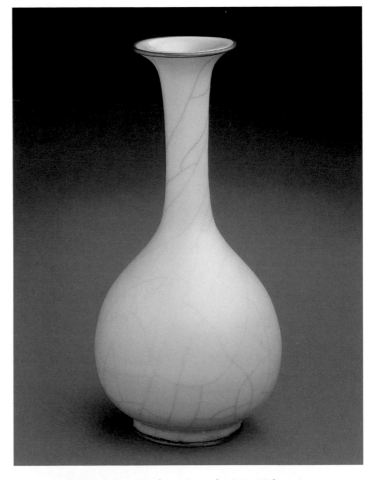

10-23. Guan Ware vase. Southern Song dynasty, 13th century. Porcelaneous stoneware with crackled glaze, height 6⁵/₈" (16.8 cm). Percival David Foundation of Chinese Art, London

Jomon figure
c. 2000 BCE

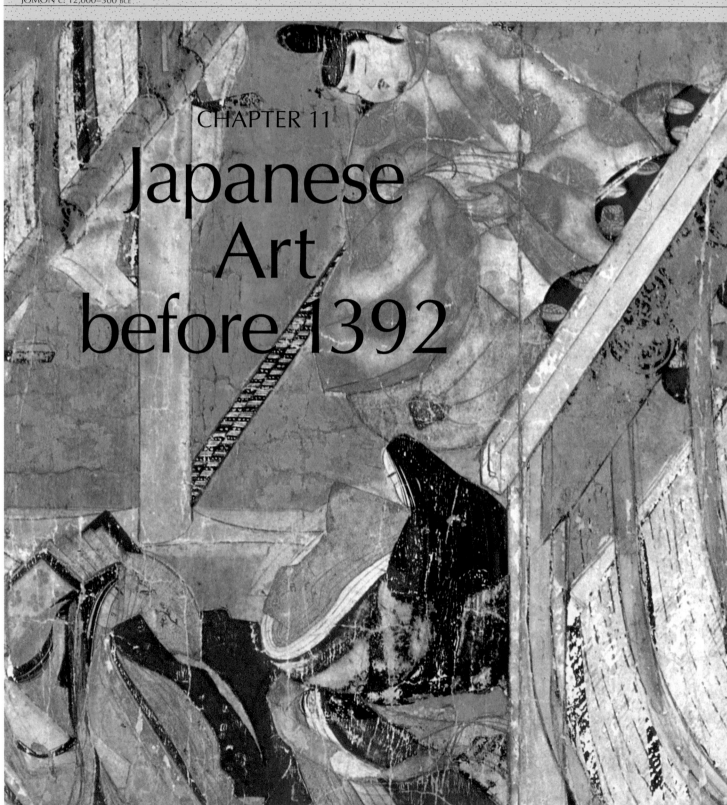

CHAPTER 11

Japanese Art before 1392

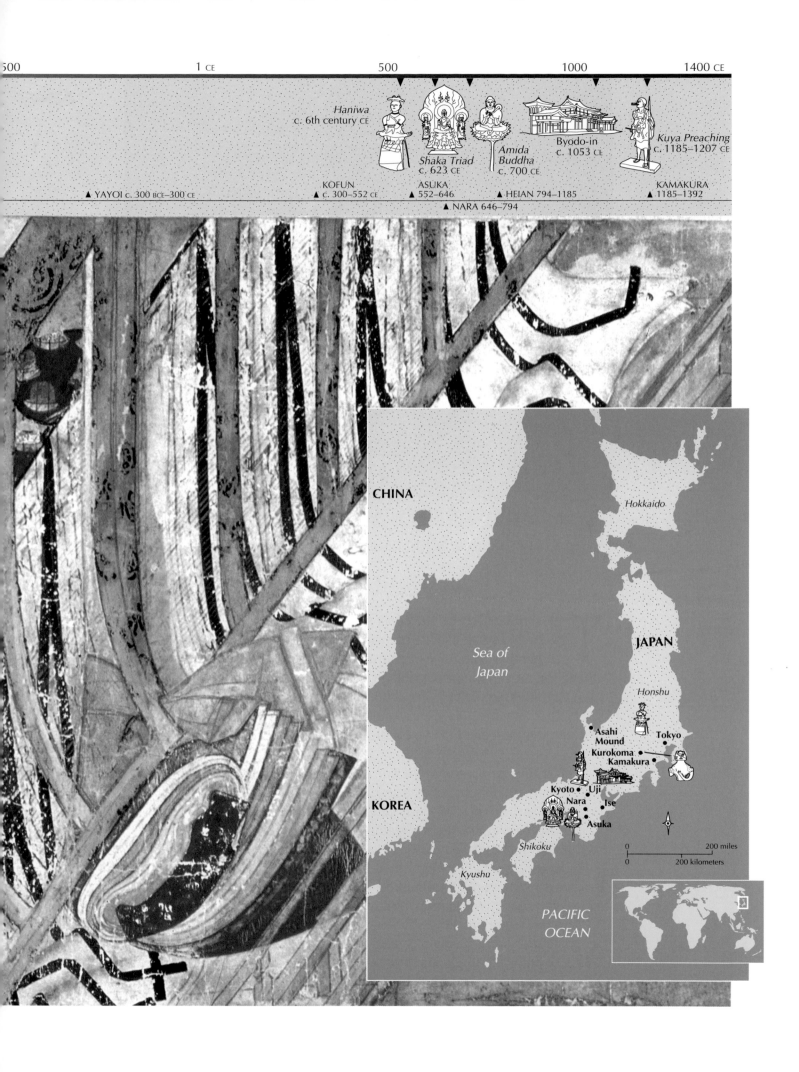

Haniwa
c. 6th century CE

Shaka Triad
c. 623 CE

*Amida
Buddha*
c. 700 CE

Byodo-in
c. 1053 CE

Kuya Preaching
c. 1185–1207 CE

KOFUN
c. 300–552 CE

ASUKA
552–646

▲ HEIAN 794–1185

KAMAKURA
1185–1392

▲ YAYOI c. 300 BCE–300 CE

▲ NARA 646–794

CHINA

Hokkaido

JAPAN

*Sea of
Japan*

Honshu

• Asahi
Mound

Kurokoma

Tokyo

Kamakura

KOREA

Kyoto •

• Uji

• Nara

• Ise

• Asuka

Shikoku

0   200 miles

0   200 kilometers

Kyushu

*PACIFIC
OCEAN*

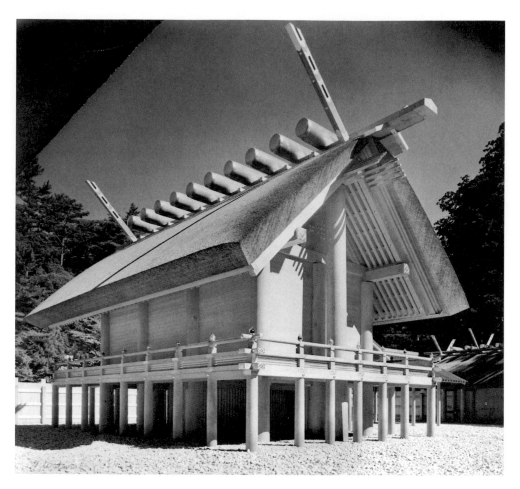

11-1.   Inner shrine, Ise, Mie Prefecture. Early 1st century CE; rebuilt 1993

The shrine at Ise, on the coast southwest of Tokyo, is rebuilt every twenty years in exactly the same ancient Japanese style by expert carpenters who have been trained in this task since childhood. One of the most popular pilgrimage sites in Japan, visited by millions each year, this exquisitely proportioned shrine has been ritually rebuilt at intervals for nearly 2,000 years, most recently in 1993 (fig. 11-1). In this way, the temple—like Japanese culture itself—is both ancient and endlessly new.

The shrine, dedicated to the sun goddess, the legendary progenitor of Japan's imperial family, reflects several of the recurring features in Japanese art. Over a period of many centuries and in works of art in many mediums, these characteristic features appear, seem to vanish, then reappear in different guises in different epochs. The first of these characteristics is a respect for and delight in natural materials. Wooden architecture, for example, is often left unpainted—as is the bare cypress wood at Ise—and ceramics frequently display all or some of their clay bodies.

Another feature is a taste for asymmetry. Instead of the evenly balanced compositions frequently seen in Chinese and European art, the Japanese enjoy paintings and prints that seem off-balance but are actually adroitly composed. This affection for asymmetry is also evident in Japanese poetry, typically three or five lines long rather than the even number of lines in the verse of most other cultures.

Japanese art is also marked by a sense of humor and playfulness that can appear in the most unexpected contexts, including religious art of great power and depth. In many Japanese works of art, strong contrasts create a sense of drama that heightens this spirit of fun.

Finally, the Japanese have been able over the centuries to tolerate, even welcome, paradoxes and illogic in their lives and art. They have produced at the same time works that are simple and profound as well as works that are ornate and decorative. They have strongly preserved their own cultural heritage while welcoming and creatively transforming foreign influences—first from China and Korea and more recently from the West. As the shrine at Ise so eloquently illustrates, they also have maintained a sense of history while always being up-to-date.

PREHISTORIC JAPAN

The earliest traces of human habitation in Japan are at least 30,000 years old. At that time the islands were still linked to the East Asian landmass, forming a ring from Siberia to Korea around the present-day Sea of Japan, which was then a lake. With the end of the last Ice Age there, some 15,000 years ago, melting glaciers caused the sea level to rise, gradually submerging the lowland links and creating the islands as we know them today. Sometime after, Paleolithic peoples gave way to Neolithic hunter-gatherers, who crafted stone tools and gradually developed the ability to make and use ceramics. Recent scientific dating methods have shown some works of Japanese pottery to date earlier than 10,000 BCE, making them the oldest now known.

Jomon Period

The Jomon period (c. 12,000–300 BCE) is named for the cord-marked patterns found on much of the pottery produced during this time. Jomon people were able to develop an unusually sophisticated hunting-gathering culture in part because they were protected from large-scale invasions by their island setting and also because of their abundant food supply. Around 5000 BCE, agriculture emerged with the planting and harvesting of beans and gourds. Some 4,000 years later rice began to be cultivated, but still the Jomon remained primarily a hunting-gathering society using stone tools and weapons. Its people lived in small communities; in the early Jomon period there were seldom more than ten or twelve dwellings together. All in all, the Jomon people seem to have enjoyed a peaceful life, giving them the opportunity to develop their artistry for even such practical endeavors as ceramics.

Jomon ceramics may have begun in imitation of reed baskets, as many early examples suggest. Other early Jomon pots have pointed bottoms. Judging from the burn marks along the sides, they must have been planted firmly into soft earth or sand, then used for cooking. Applying fire to the sides rather than the bottom allowed the vessels to heat more fully and evenly. Still other early

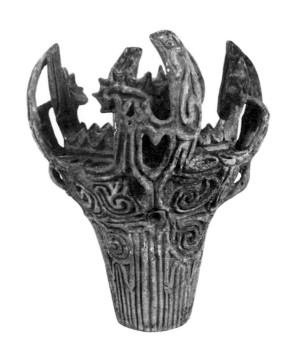

11-2. Vessel, from the Asahi Mound, Toyama Prefecture. Jomon period, c. 2000 BCE. Low-fired ceramic, height 14¾" (37.4 cm). Collection of Tokyo University

vessels were crafted with straight sides and flat bottoms, a shape that was useful for storage as well as cooking and eventually became the norm. Often the vessels were decorated with patterns made by pressing cord onto the damp clay (*jomon* means "cord markings"). Jomon usually crafted their vessels by building them up with coils of clay, then firing them in bonfires at relatively low temperatures. It is thought that Jomon pottery was made by women, as was the practice in most early societies, especially before the use of the potter's wheel.

During the middle Jomon period (2500–1500 BCE), pottery reached a high degree of creativity. By this time communities were somewhat larger, and each family may have wanted its ceramic vessels to have a unique design. The basic form remained the straight-sided cooking or storage jar, but the rim now took on spectacular, flamboyant shapes, as seen in one example from the Asahi Mound (fig. 11-2). Middle Jomon potters made full

PARALLELS

Years	Period	Japan	World
c. 12,000–300 BCE	Jomon	Hunting and gathering; beginning of agriculture; decorated ceramic vessels; *dogu* figures	c. 12,000–300 BCE End of Ice Age in Europe; plants and animals domesticated (Near East, Southeast Asia, the Americas); development of metallurgy (Near East); development of writing (China, India); Great Pyramids at Giza (Egypt); Shang dynasty (China); Olmec civilization (Mesoamerica); birth of Siddhartha Gautama, founder of Buddhism (Nepal); Parthenon (Greece); Alexander the Great (Greece) conquers Persia
c. 300 BCE–300 CE	Yayoi	Class structure; bronze tools and weapons; ironworking	c. 300 BCE–300 CE Roman unification of Italy; Han dynasty (China); Great Wall (China); crucifixion of Jesus (Jerusalem); Emperor Augustus (Italy); Buddhism in China; *Ramayana* epic (India); Maya civilization (Mesoamerica)
c. 300–552 CE	Kofun	Centralization of government; *haniwa* figures; Shintoism	c. 300–800 CE First Gupta dynasty (India); Christianity becomes official religion of Roman Empire; Attila the Hun (Mongolia); first Hindu temples (India); birth of Muhammad, founder of Islam (Arabia); Hagia Sophia (Turkey); Muslim conquests; Tang dynasty (China); Koran (Arabia); *Beowulf* (England); first block-print text (China); Charlemagne made emperor of the West
c. 552–646 CE	Asuka	Buddhism; influx of writing and other culture from China and Korea; Horyu-ji	
c. 646–794 CE	Nara	First permanent capital at Nara; Todai-ji; first histories and poetry collections; golden age of Buddhist painting; capital moved to Kyoto	
c. 794–1185 CE	Heian	Lady Murasaki's *Tale of Genji*; Esoteric Buddhism and Pure Land Buddhism arise; Byodo-in; development of Japanese writing system	c. 800–1400 CE Bronze casting in South America; *Diamond Sutra* (China); first Viking colony in Greenland; the Crusades; Jenghiz Khan rules Mongols; Renaissance begins in Europe; Black Death in Europe; Chaucer's *Canterbury Tales* (England)
c. 1185–1392 CE	Kamakura	Rise of Minamoto and Taira clans; Pure Land Buddhism dominates; *raigo*; Zen Buddhism arises	

use of the tactile quality of clay, bending and twisting it as well as **incising** and applying designs. They favored asymmetrical shapes, although certain elements in the geometric patterns are repeated. Some designs may have had specific meanings, but the lavishly creative vessels also display a playful artistic spirit. Rather than working toward practical goals (such as better firing techniques or more useful shapes), the Jomon potters seem to have been simply enjoying to the full their imaginative vision.

The people of the middle and late Jomon period also used clay to fashion small human figures. These figures were never fully realistic but rather were distorted into fascinating shapes. Called *dogu*, they tend to have large faces, small arms and hands, and compact bodies. Some of the later *dogu* seem to be wearing round goggles over their eyes. Others have heart-shaped faces. One of the finest, from Kurokoma, has a face remarkably like a cat's (fig. 11-3). The slit eyes and mouth have a haunting quality, as does the gesture of one hand touching the chest. The marks on the face, neck, and shoulders suggest tattooing and were probably incised with a bamboo stick. The raised area behind the face may indicate a Jomon hairstyle.

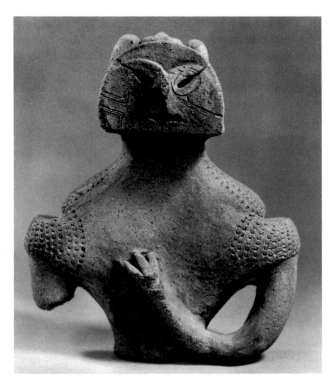

11-3. *Dogu*, from Kurokoma, Yamanashi Prefecture. Jomon period, c. 2000 BCE. Low-fired earthenware, height 10" (25.2 cm). Tokyo National Museum

The purpose of Jomon *dogu* remains unknown, but most scholars believe that they were effigies, figures representing the owner or someone else, and that they manifested a kind of sympathetic magic. Jomon people may have believed, for example, that they could transfer an illness or other unhappy experience to a *dogu*, then break it to destroy the misfortune. So many of these figures were deliberately broken and discarded that this theory has gained acceptance, but *dogu* may have had different functions at different times. Regardless of their purpose, the images still retain a powerful sense of magic thousands of years after they were created.

Yayoi and Kofun Periods

During the Yayoi (300 BCE–300 CE) and Kofun (300–552 CE) eras, several features of Japanese culture became firmly established. Most important of these was the transformation of Japan into an agricultural nation, with rice cultivation becoming widespread. This momentous change was stimulated by the arrival of immigrants from Korea, who brought with them more complex forms of society and government.

As it did elsewhere in the world, the shift from hunting and gathering to agriculture brought profound social changes, including larger permanent settlements, the division of labor into agricultural and nonagricultural tasks, more hierarchical forms of social organization, and a more centralized government. The emergence of a class structure can be dated to the Yayoi period, as can the development of metal technology. Bronze was used to create weapons as well as ceremonial objects such as

bells. Iron knives were developed later in this period, eventually replacing stone tools in everyday life.

Yayoi people lived in thatched houses with sunken floors and stored their food in raised granaries. The granary architecture, with its use of natural wood and thatched roofs, reveals the Japanese appreciation of natural materials, and the style of these raised granaries persisted in the architectural designs of shrines in later centuries (see fig. 11-1).

The trend toward centralization of government became more pronounced during the ensuing Kofun, or "old tombs," period, named for the large royal tombs that were built then. With the emergence of a more complex social order, the veneration of leaders grew into the beginnings of an imperial system. Still in existence today in Japan, this system eventually equated the emperor (or, very rarely, empress) with deities such as the sun goddess. When an emperor died, chamber tombs were constructed following Korean examples. Various grave goods were placed inside the tomb chambers, including large amounts of pottery, presumably to pacify the spirits of the dead and to serve them in their next life. Many Korean potters came to Japan in the fifth century, bringing their knowledge of finishing techniques and improved kilns. Their new form of gray-green pottery was first used for ceremonial purposes in Japan and later entered daily life.

The Japanese government has never allowed the major sacred tombs to be excavated, but much is known about the mortuary practices of Kofun era Japan. Some of the huge tombs of the fifth and sixth centuries were constructed in a shape resembling a large keyhole and surrounded by **moats** dug to preserve the sacred land from commoners. Tomb sites might extend over more than 400 acres, with artificial hills built over the tombs themselves. On the top of the hills ceramic sculptures called **haniwa** were placed.

The first *haniwa* were simple cylinders that may have held jars with ceremonial offerings. Gradually these cylinders came to be made in the shapes of ceremonial objects, houses, and boats. Still later, living creatures were added to the repertoire of *haniwa* subjects, including birds, deer, dogs, monkeys, cows, and horses. Finally, *haniwa* in human shapes were crafted, including males and females of all types, professions, and classes (fig. 11-4).

Haniwa illustrate several enduring characteristics of Japanese aesthetic taste. Unlike Chinese tomb ceramics, which were often beautifully glazed, *haniwa* were left unglazed to reveal their clay bodies. *Haniwa* do not show the interest in technical skill seen in Chinese ceramics. Instead, their makers explored the expressive potentials of simple and bold form. *Haniwa* shapes are never perfectly symmetrical; the slightly off-center placement of the eye slits, the irregular cylindrical bodies, and the unequal arms give them great life and individuality. No one knows what purpose *haniwa* served. The popular theory that they were intended as tomb guardians is weakened by their origin as cylinders and by the mundane subjects they portray. Indeed, they seem to

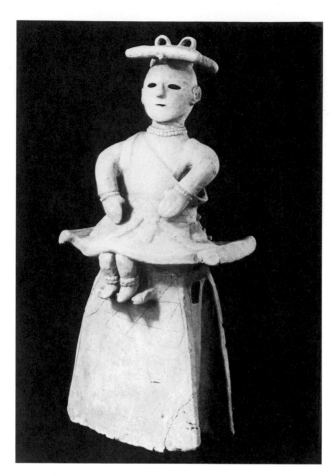

400 CE

2600 BCE   1400 CE

11-4. *Haniwa,* from Kyoto. Kofun period, 6th century CE. Earthenware, height 27" (68.5 cm). Tokyo National Museum

There have been many theories as to the function of *haniwa.* The figures seem to have served as some kind of link between the world of the dead, over which they were placed, and the world of the living, from which they could be viewed. This figure has been identified as a seated female shaman, wearing a robe, belt, and necklace and carrying a mirror at her waist. In early Japan, shamans acted as agents between the natural and the supernatural worlds, just as *haniwa* figures were links between the living and the dead.

represent every aspect of Kofun period society. They may also reflect some of the beliefs of Shinto.

Shinto is often described as the indigenous religion of Japan, but whether it was originally a religion in the usual sense of the word is debatable. Perhaps Shinto is most accurately characterized as a loose confederation of beliefs in deities (kami). These kami were thought to inhabit many different aspects of nature, including particularly hoary and magnificent trees, rocks, waterfalls, and living creatures such as deer. Shinto also represents the ancient beliefs of the Japanese in purification through ritual use of water. Later, in response to the arrival of Buddhism in the sixth century CE, Shinto became somewhat more systematized, with shrines, a hierarchy of deities, and more strictly regulated ceremonies. Nevertheless, even today in many parts of Japan a **torii**, or wooden gateway, is the only sign that a place is sacred. Nature itself, not the gateway, is venerated.

One of the great Shinto monuments is the shrine at Ise (see fig. 11-1). Features typical of Shinto architecture include wooden piles raising the building off the ground, a thatched roof held in place by horizontal logs, the use of unpainted cypress wood, and the overall feeling of natural simplicity rather than overwhelming size or elaborate decoration. Only members of the imperial family and a few Shinto priests are allowed inside the fourfold enclosure housing the sacred shrine. The shrine in turn houses the three sacred symbols of Shinto—a sword, a mirror, and a jewel. This structure, which still preserves some features of Yayoi era granaries, is the one rebuilt every twenty years.

ASUKA PERIOD

Japan has experienced several periods of intense cultural transformation. Perhaps the greatest time of change was the beginning of the Asuka period (552–646 CE). During a single century, new forms of philosophy, medicine, music, foods, clothing, agricultural methods, city planning, and arts and architecture were introduced into Japan from Korea and China. The three most significant introductions, however, were Buddhism, a centralized governmental structure, and a system of writing. Each was adopted and gradually modified to suit Japanese conditions, and each has been an enduring heritage.

Buddhism reached Japan in Mahayana form, with its many buddhas and **bodhisattvas** (see "Buddhism," page 371). After being accepted by the imperial family, it was soon adopted as a state religion. Buddhism represented not only different gods but an entirely new concept of religion itself. Where Shinto had found deities in beautiful and imposing natural areas, Buddhist worship was focused in temples. At first this change must have seemed strange, for the Chinese-influenced architecture and elaborate **iconography** introduced by Buddhism (see "Buddhist Symbols," opposite) contrasted sharply with the simple and natural aesthetics of earlier Japan. Yet Buddhism offered a rich cosmology with profound teachings of meditation and enlightenment. Moreover, the new religion was accompanied by many highly developed aspects of continental culture, including new methods of painting and sculpture.

The most significant surviving early Japanese temple is Horyu-ji, located on Japan's central plains not far from Nara. The temple was founded in 607 CE by Prince Shotoku (574–622 CE), who ruled Japan as a regent and became the most influential early proponent of Buddhism. Rebuilt after a fire in 670, Horyu-ji is the oldest wooden temple in the world. It is so famous that visitors are often surprised at its modest size. Yet its just proportions and human scale, together with the artistic treasures it contains, make Horyu-ji an enduringly beautiful monument to the early Buddhist faith of Japan.

The main compound of Horyu-ji consists of a rectangular courtyard surrounded by covered corridors, one of which contains a gateway. Within the compound are only two buildings, the *kondo*, or golden hall, and a five-story **pagoda**. The simple layout of the compound is

BUDDHIST SYMBOLS A few of the most important Buddhist symbols, which have myriad variations, are described here in their most generalized forms.

Lotus flower

Usually shown as a white water lily, the lotus (Sanskrit, *padma*) symbolizes spiritual purity, the wholeness of creation, and cosmic harmony. The flower's stem is an *axis mundi*.

Lotus throne

Buddhas are frequently shown seated on an open lotus, either single or double, a representation of nirvana.

Chakra

An ancient sun symbol, the wheel (chakra) symbolizes both the various states of existence (the Wheel of Life) and the Buddhist doctrine (the Wheel of the Law). A chakra's exact meaning depends on how many spokes it has.

Marks of a buddha

A buddha is distinguished by thirty-two physical attributes (*lakshanas*). Among them are a bulge on top of the head (*ushnisha*), a tuft of hair between the eyebrows (*urna*), elongated earlobes, and thousand-spoked chakras on the soles of the feet.

Mandala

Mandalas are diagrams of cosmic realms, representing order and meaning within the spiritual universe. They may be simple or complex, three- or two-dimensional—as in an Indian stupa (see fig. 9-7) or a hanging scroll—and they assume a wide array of forms. The Womb World mandala, an early Japanese type used for meditation, depicts and symbolizes different aspects of "buddha nature." One is shown in figure 11-9

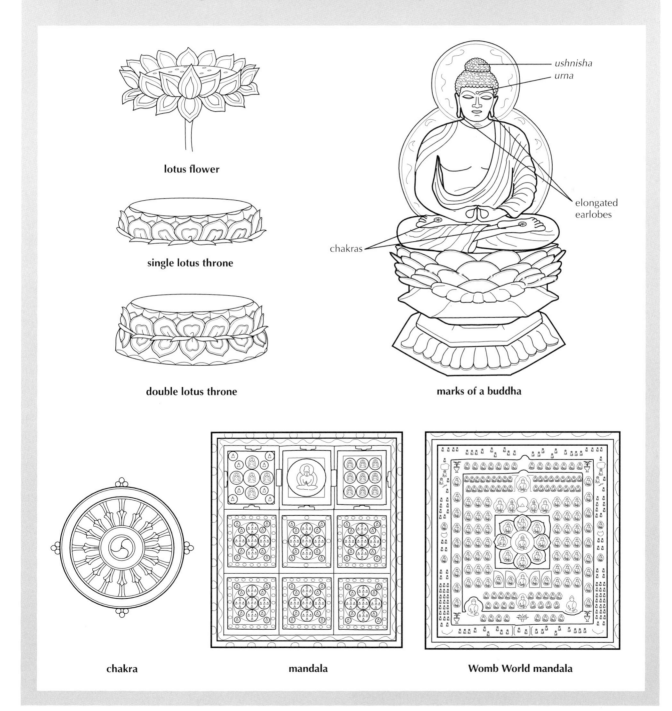

lotus flower

single lotus throne

double lotus throne

ushnisha
urna
elongated earlobes
chakras

marks of a buddha

chakra

mandala

Womb World mandala

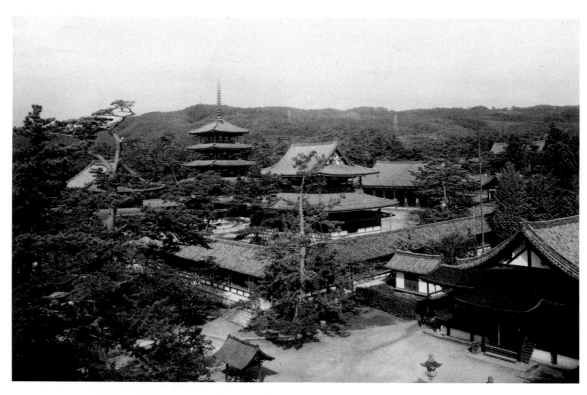

11-5. Main compound, Horyu-ji, Nara Prefecture. Asuka period, 7th century CE

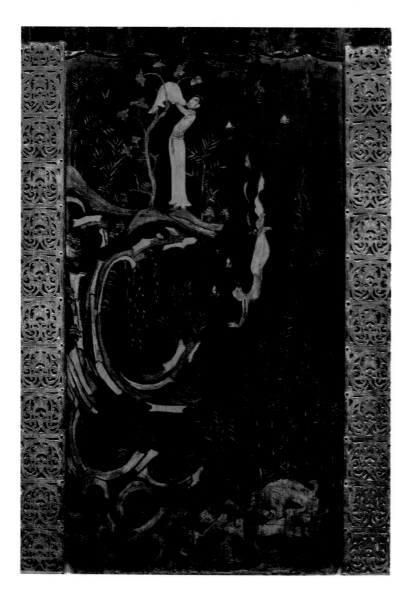

asymmetrical, yet the large *kondo* is perfectly balanced by the tall, slender pagoda (fig. 11-5). The *kondo* is filled with Buddhist images and is used for worship and ceremonies. The pagoda serves as a reliquary and is not entered. Other monastery buildings lie outside the main compound, including an outer gate, a lecture hall, a repository for sacred texts, a belfry, and dormitories for monks.

Among the many treasures still preserved in Horyu-ji is a miniature shrine decorated with paintings in lacquer. It is known as the Tamamushi Shrine after the tamamushi beetle, whose iridescent wings were originally affixed to the shrine to make it glitter, much like mother-of-pearl. There has been some debate whether the·shrine was made in Korea, in Japan, or perhaps by Korean artisans in Japan. The question of whether it is, in fact, a "Japanese" work of art misses the point that Buddhism was so international at that time that matters of nationality were irrelevant.

The Tamamushi Shrine is a replica of an even more ancient palace-form building, and its architectural details preserve a tradition predating Horyu-ji itself. Its paintings are among the few two-dimensional works of art to survive from the Asuka period. Most celebrated among them are two that illustrate jataka tales, stories about former lives of the Buddha. One depicts the future Buddha nobly sacrificing his life in order to feed his body ·to a starving tigress and her cubs (fig. 11-6). The tigers are at first too weak to eat him, so he must jump off a cliff to break open his flesh. The anonymous artist has

11-6. *Hungry Tigress Jataka*, panel of the Tamamushi Shrine, Horyu-ji. Asuka period, c. 650 CE. Lacquer on wood, height of shrine 7'7¾" (2.33 m). Horyu-ji Treasure House

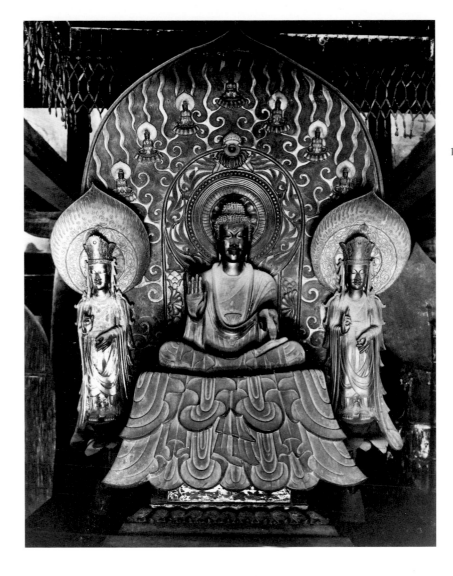

11-7. Tori Busshi. *Shaka Triad*, in the *kondo*, Horyu-ji. Asuka period, c. 623 CE. Gilt bronze, height of seated figure 34½" (87.5 cm)

created a full narrative within a single frame. The graceful form of the Buddha appears three times, harmonized by the curves of the rocky cliff and tall sprigs of bamboo. First, he hangs his shirt on a tree, then he dives downward onto the rocks, and finally he is devoured by the starving animals. The elegantly slender renditions of the figure and the somewhat abstract treatment of the cliff, trees, and bamboo represent an international Buddhist style largely shared during this time by China, Korea, and Japan. These illustrations for the jataka tales helped spread Buddhism in Japan.

Another example of the international style of early Buddhist art at Horyu-ji is the sculpture called the *Shaka Triad*, by Tori Busshi (fig. 11-7). (Shaka is the Japanese name for Shakyamuni, the historical Buddha.) Tori Busshi was a third-generation Japanese, whose grandfather had emigrated to Japan from China as part of an influx of craftspeople and artists. The *Shaka Triad* reflects the strong influence of Chinese art of the Northern Wei dynasty (see fig. 10-12). The frontal pose, the outsized face and hands, and the linear treatment of the drapery all suggest that Tori Busshi was well aware of earlier continental models, while the fine bronze casting of the figures shows his advanced technical skill. The *Shaka Triad* and the Tamamushi Shrine reveal how

quickly Buddhist art became an important feature of Japanese culture. During an age when Japan was being unified under an imperial system, Buddhism introduced a form of compassionate idealism that is clearly expressed in its art.

NARA PERIOD The Nara period (646–794) is named for Japan's first permanent imperial capital. Previously, when an emperor died, his capital was considered tainted, and for reasons of purification (and perhaps also of politics) his successor usually selected a new site. With the emergence of a complex, Chinese-style government, however, this custom was no longer practical. By establishing a permanent capital in Nara, the Japanese were able to enter a new era of growth and consolidation. Nara swelled to a population of perhaps 200,000 people. During this period the imperial system finally established an effective government that could no longer be threatened by the powerful aristocratic families that had traditionally dominated the political world.

One positive result of strong central authority was the construction in Nara of magnificent Buddhist temples and monasteries that dwarfed those built previously. Even today a large area of Nara is a park where numerous temples preserve magnificent Nara period art and architecture. The grandest of these temples, Todai-ji, is so large that the area surrounding only one of its pagodas could accommodate the entire main compound of Horyu-ji. When it was built, and for a thousand years thereafter, Todai-ji was the largest wooden structure in the world. The park area of Nara also contains a number of other splendid temples, but not all the monuments of Nara are Buddhist. There are several Shinto shrines, and deer wander freely, reflecting Japan's Shinto heritage.

Buddhism and Shinto have coexisted quite comfortably in Japan over the ages. One seeks enlightenment, the other purification, and since these ideals did not clash, neither did the two forms of religion. Although there were occasional attempts to promote one over the other, more often they were seen as complementary, and to this day most Japanese see nothing inconsistent about having Shinto weddings and Buddhist funerals.

While Shinto became more formalized during the Nara period, Buddhism advanced to become the single most significant element in Japanese culture. One important method for transmitting Buddhism in Japan was through the copying of Buddhist sacred texts, the sutras. They were believed to be so beneficial and magical that occasionally a single word would be cut out from a sutra and worn as an amulet. Someone with hearing problems, for example, might use the word for "ear."

Copying the words of the Buddha was considered an effective act of worship by the nobility; it also enabled Japanese courtiers as well as clerics to become familiar with the Chinese system of writing—with both secular and religious results. During this period, the first histories of Japan were written, strongly modeled upon Chinese precedents, and the first collection of Japanese poetry, the *Manyoshu*, was compiled. The *Manyoshu* includes Buddhist verse, but the majority of the poems are secular, including many love songs in the five-line tanka form such as this example by the late-seventh-century courtier Hitomaro (all translations from Japanese are by Stephen Addiss unless otherwise noted):

> Did those
> who lived in past ages
> lie sleepless
> as I do tonight
> longing for my beloved?

Unlike the poetry, most other art of the Nara period is sacred, with a robust splendor that testifies to the fervent belief and great energy of early Japanese Buddhists. Some of the finest Buddhist paintings of the late seventh century were preserved in Japan on the walls of the golden hall of Horyu-ji until a fire in 1949 defaced and partially destroyed them. Fortunately, they had been thoroughly documented before the fire in a series of color photographs. These murals represent what many scholars believe to be the golden age of Buddhist painting, an era that embraces the Tang dynasty in China (618–907 CE), the United Silla period in Korea (668–935 CE), and the Nara period in Japan.

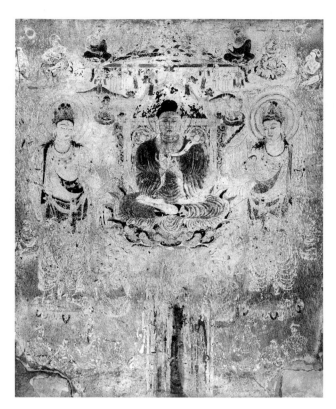

11-8. *Amida Buddha*, fresco in the *kondo*, Horyu-ji. Nara period, c. 700 CE. Ink and colors (now severely damaged), 10'3" x 8'6" (3.13 x 2.6 m)

One of the finest of the Horyu-ji murals is thought to represent Amida (Amitabha in Chinese and Sanskrit), the Buddha of the Western Paradise (fig. 11-8). Delineated in the thin, even brushstrokes known as iron-wire lines, Amida's body is rounded, his face is fully fleshed and serene, and his hands form the "revealing the Buddhist law" **mudra** (see "Mudras," page 380). Instead of the somewhat abstract style of the Asuka period, there is now a greater emphasis on realistic detail and body weight in the figure. The parallel folds of drapery show the enduring influence of the Gandharan style current in India 500 years earlier (see fig. 9-12), but the face is fully East Asian in contour and spirit.

The Nara period was an age of great belief, and Buddhism permeated the upper levels of society. Indeed, one of the few empresses in Japanese history wanted to cede her throne to a Buddhist monk. Her advisers and other influential courtiers became extremely worried, and they finally decided to move the capital away from Nara, where they felt Buddhist influence had become overpowering. The move of the capital to Kyoto marked the end of the Nara period.

HEIAN PERIOD

The influences from China and Korea were fully absorbed and transformed by the Japanese during the Heian period (794–1185). Generally peaceful conditions contributed to a new air of self-reliance on the part of the Japanese. Ties to China were severed in the mid-ninth century, and the imperial government was sustained by support from aristocratic families. An efficient method of writing the Japanese language was developed, and the rise of vernacular literature generated such masterpieces as the

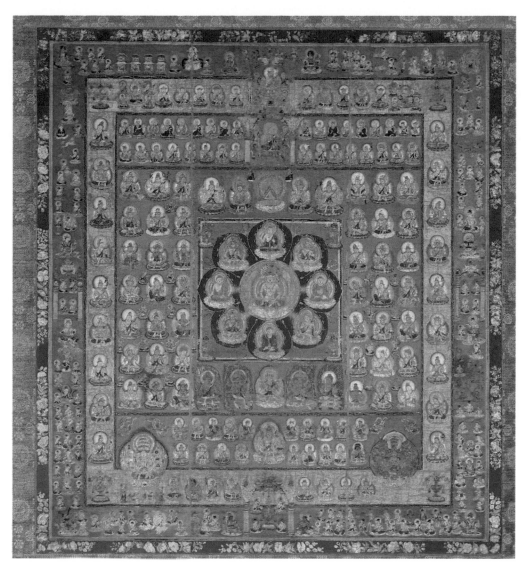

11-9. Womb World mandala, To-ji, Kyoto. Heian period, late 9th century CE. Hanging scroll, colors on silk, 6' x 5'1½" (1.83 x 1.54 m)

Mandalas are used not only in teaching but also as vehicles for practice. A monk, initiated into secret teachings, may gradually work out from the center, meditating upon and assuming the gestures of each deity in turn so that he absorbs some of the deity's powers. The monk may also recite magical phrases called mantras as an aid to meditation. The goal is to achieve enlightenment through the powers of the different forms of the Buddha. Mandalas are created in sculptural and architectural forms as well as in paintings. Their integration of the two most basic shapes, the circle and the square, is an expression of the principles of ancient geomancy (divining by means of lines and figures) as well as Buddhist cosmology.

world's first novel, Lady Murasaki's *Tale of Genji*. During these four centuries of splendor and refinement, two major forms of religion emerged: first Esoteric, tantric Buddhism and later Pure Land Buddhism.

Esoteric Buddhism

With the removal of the capital to Kyoto, the older Nara temples lost their influence. Soon two new Esoteric sects of Buddhism, named Tendai and Shingon, grew to dominate Japanese religious life. Strongly influenced by polytheistic religions such as Hinduism, Esoteric Buddhism included a daunting number of deities, each with magical powers. The historical Buddha was no longer very

important. Instead, the universal Buddha (called Dainichi, "Great Sun," in Japanese) was believed to preside over the universe. He was accompanied by buddhas and bodhisattvas, as well as guardian deities who formed fierce counterparts to the more benign gods.

Esoteric Buddhism is hierarchical, and its deities have complex relationships to each other. Learning all the different gods and their interrelationships was assisted greatly by works of art, especially **mandalas**, cosmic diagrams of the universe that portray the deities in schematic order. The Womb World mandala from To-ji, for example, is entirely filled with depictions of gods. Dainichi is at the center, surrounded by buddhas of the four directions (fig. 11-9). Other deities, including some

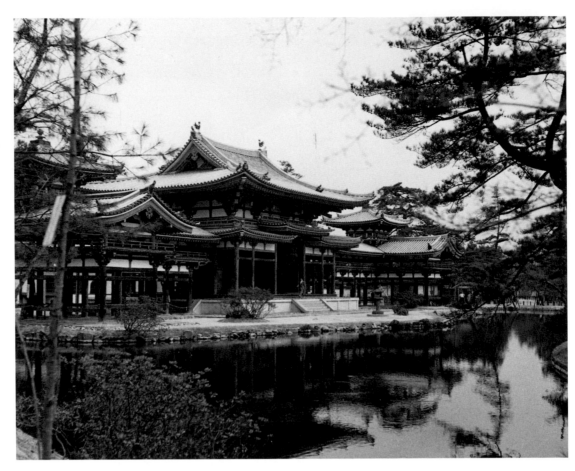

11-10. Byodo-in, Uji, Kyoto Prefecture. Heian period, c. 1053

with multiple heads and limbs, branch out in diagrammatical order, each with a specific symbol of power. To believers the mandala represents an ultimate reality beyond their visible world.

Perhaps the most striking attribute of many Esoteric Buddhist images is their sense of spiritual force and potency, especially in depictions of the wrathful deities, which are often surrounded by flames. Esoteric Buddhism, with its intricate theology and complex doctrines, was a religion for the educated aristocracy, not for the masses. Its network of deities, hierarchy, and ritual found a parallel in the elaborate social divisions of the Heian court.

Pure Land Buddhism

During the latter half of the Heian period, a rising military class threatened the peace and tranquillity of court life. The beginning of the eleventh century was also the time for which the decline of Buddhism had been prophesied. In these uncertain years, many Japanese were ready for another form of Buddhism that would offer a more direct means of salvation than the elaborate rituals of the Esoteric sects.

Pure Land Buddhism, although it had existed in Japan earlier, now came to prominence. It taught that the Western Paradise (the Pure Land) of the Amida Buddha could be reached through nothing more than faith. In its ultimate form, Pure Land Buddhism held that the mere chanting of a mantra—the phrase *Namu Amida Butsu* ("Hail to Amida Buddha")—would lead to rebirth in Amida's paradise. This doctrine soon swept throughout Japan. Spread by traveling monks who took the chant to all parts of the country, it appealed to people of all levels of education and sophistication. Pure Land Buddhism has remained the most popular form of Buddhism in Japan ever since.

One of the most beautiful temples of Pure Land Buddhism is the Byodo-in, located in the Uji Mountains not far from Kyoto (fig. 11-10). The temple itself was originally a secular palace created to suggest the palace of Amida in the Western Paradise. It was built for a member of the powerful Fujiwara family who served as the leading counselor to the emperor. After the counselor's death in the year 1052 the palace was converted into a temple. The Byodo-in is often called Phoenix Hall, not only for the pair of phoenix images on its roof but also because the shape of the building itself suggests the mythical bird. The lightness of its thin columns gives the Byodo-in a sense of airiness, as though the entire temple could easily rise up through the sky to the Western Paradise of Amida. The hall rests gently in front of an artificial pond created in the shape of the Sanskrit letter *A*, the sacred symbol for Amida.

The Byodo-in's central image of Amida, carved by the master sculptor Jocho (d. 1057), exemplifies the

trayals of buddhas and bodhisattvas for the many temples constructed and dedicated to the Pure Land faith. It also reaffirmed the Japanese love of wood, which during the Heian period became the major medium for sculpture.

Surrounding the Amida on the walls of the Byodo-in are smaller wooden figures of bodhisattvas and angels, some playing musical instruments. Everything about the Byodo-in was designed to suggest the paradise that awaits the fervent believer after death. Its remarkable state of preservation after more than 900 years allows visitors to experience the late Heian period religious ideal at its most splendid.

Poetry and Calligraphy

While Buddhism pervaded the Heian era, a refined secular culture also arose at court that has never been equaled in Japan. Gradually over the course of four centuries, the influence from China waned. Although court nobles continued to write many poems in Chinese, both men and women wrote in the new kana script of their native language (see "Writing, Language, and Culture," page 434). With its simple, flowing symbols interspersed with more complex Chinese characters, the new writing system allowed Japanese poets to create an asymmetrical **calligraphy** quite unlike that of China.

Refinement was greatly valued among the Heian period aristocracy. A woman would be admired merely for the way she arranged the twelve layers of her robes by color, or a man for knowing which kind of incense was being burned. Much of court culture was centered upon the sophisticated expression of human love through the five-line tanka. A courtier leaving his beloved at dawn would send her a poem wrapped around a single flower still wet with dew. If his words or his calligraphy were less than stylish, however, he would not be welcome to visit her again. In turn, if she could not reply with equal elegance, he might not wish to repeat their amorous interlude. Society was ruled by taste, and pity any man or woman at court who was not accomplished in several forms of art.

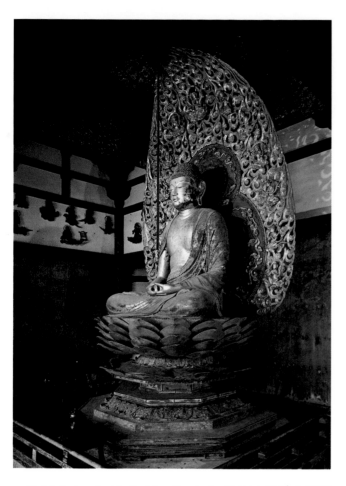

11-11. Jocho. *Amida Buddha*, Byodo-in. Heian period, c. 1053. Gold leaf and lacquer on wood, height 9'8" (2.95 m)

serenity and compassion of the Buddha who welcomes the souls of all believers to his paradise (fig. 11-11). When reflected in the water of the pond before it, the Amida image seems to shimmer in its private mountain retreat. The figure was not carved from a single block of wood like earlier sculpture but from several blocks in Jocho's new **joined-wood** method of construction. This technique allowed sculptors to create larger but lighter por-

---

TECHNIQUE

JOINED-WOOD SCULPTURE

Wood is a temperamental medium, as sculptors who work with it quickly learn. Cut from a living, sap-filled tree, it takes many years to dry thoroughly. The outside dries first, then the inside gradually yields its moisture. As the core dries, however, the resulting shifts in tension can open up gaping cracks. A large statue carved from a single solid block thus runs the risk of splitting as it ages—especially if it has been painted or lacquered, which interferes with the wood's natural "breathing."

One strategy adopted by Japanese sculptors to prevent cracking was to split a completed statue into several pieces, hollow them out, then fit them back together.

A more effective method was the **joined-wood** technique. Here the design for a statue was divided into sections, each of which was carved from a separate block. These sections were then hollowed out and assembled. By using multiple blocks, sculptors could produce larger images than they could from any single block. Moreover, statue sections could be created by teams of carvers, some of whom became specialists in certain parts, such as hands or crossed legs or lotus thrones. Through this cooperative approach, large statues could be produced with great efficiency to meet a growing demand.

WRITING, LANGUAGE, AND CULTURE

Chinese culture enjoyed great prestige in East Asia. Written Chinese served as an international language of scholarship and cultivation, much as Latin did in medieval Europe. Educated Koreans, for example, wrote almost exclusively in Chinese until the fifteenth century. In Japan, Chinese continued to be used for certain kinds of writing, such as philosophical and legal texts, into the nineteenth century.

When it came to writing their own language, the Japanese initially borrowed Chinese characters, or kanji. Differences between the Chinese and Japanese languages made this system extremely unwieldy, so during the ninth century two syllabaries, or kana, were developed from simplified Chinese characters. (A syllabary is a system in which each symbol stands for a syllable.) Katakana, now generally used for foreign words, consists of mostly angular symbols, while the more frequently used hiragana has graceful, cursive symbols.

Japanese written in kana was known as "women's hand," possibly because prestigious scholarly writing still emphasized Chinese, which women were rarely taught. Yet despite the respect for Chinese, Japan had an ancient and highly valued poetic tradition of its own, and women as well as men were praised as poets from earliest times. So while women rarely became scholars, they were often authors. During the Heian period kana were used to create a large body of literature, written either by women or sometimes for women by men.

A charming poem originated in Heian times to teach the new writing system. In two stanzas of four lines each, it uses almost all of the syllable sounds of spoken Japanese and thus almost every kana symbol. It was memorized as we would recite our ABCs. The first stanza translates as:

Although flowers glow with color
They are quickly fallen,
And who in this world of ours
Is free from change?

(Translation by Earl Miner)

Like Chinese, Japanese is written in columns from top to bottom and across the page from right to left. (Following this logic, Chinese and Japanese narrative paintings also read from right to left.) Below is the stanza written three ways. At the right, it appears in katakana glossed with the original phonetic value of each symbol. (Modern pronunciation has shifted slightly.) In the center, the stanza appears in flowing hiragana. To the left is the mixture of kanji and kana that eventually became standard. This alternating rhythm of simple kana symbols and more complex Chinese characters gives a special flavor to Japanese calligraphy.

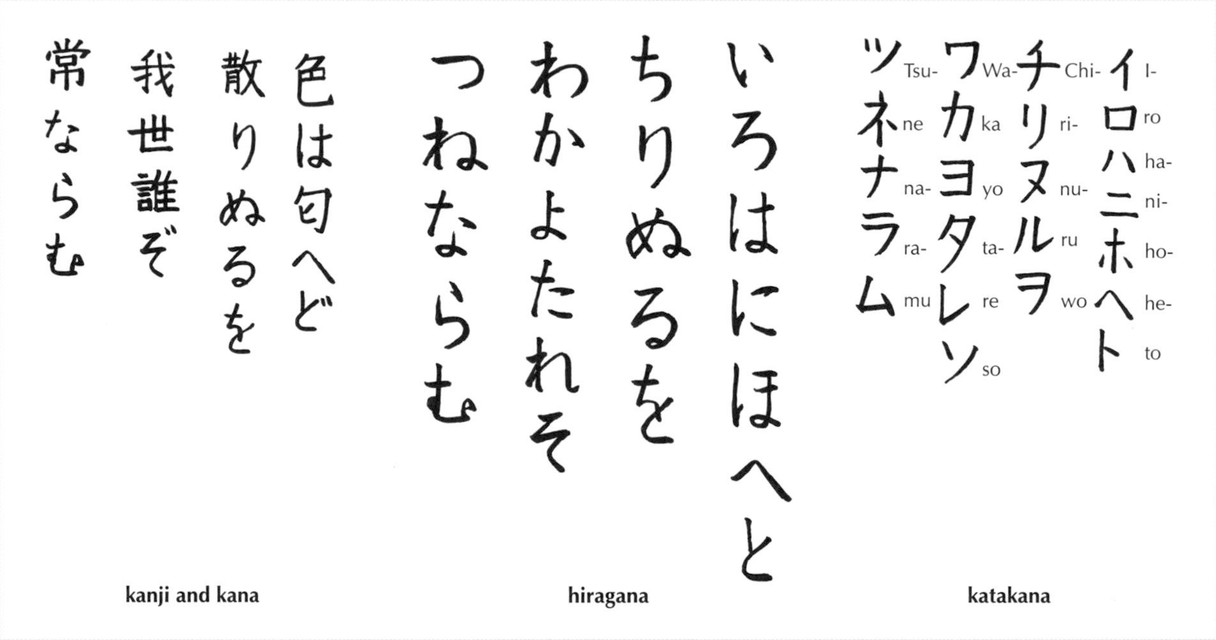

常ならむ　我世誰ぞ　散りぬるを　色は匂へど　つねならむ　わかよたれそ　ちりぬるを　いろはにほへと

イ I-ro ハ ニ ホ ヘ ト ／ チ Chi-ri-nu-ru-wo リ ヌ ル ヲ ／ ワ Wa-ka-yo-ta-re-so カ ヨ タ レ ソ ／ ツ Tsu-ne-na-ra-mu ネ ナ ラ ム

kanji and kana　　**hiragana**　　**katakana**

During the later Heian period, the finest tanka were gathered in anthologies. The poems in one famous early anthology, the *Thirty-Six Immortal Poets*, are still known to educated Japanese today. This anthology was produced in sets of albums called the *Ishiyama-gire*. These albums consist of tanka written elegantly on high-quality papers decorated with painting, **block printing**, scattered gold and silver, and sometimes paper **collage**. The page shown here reproduces two tanka by the courtier Ki no Tsurayuki (fig. 11-12). Both poems express sadness for the loss of a lover, the first lamenting:

Until yesterday
I could meet her,
But today she is gone—
Like clouds over the mountain
She has been wafted away.

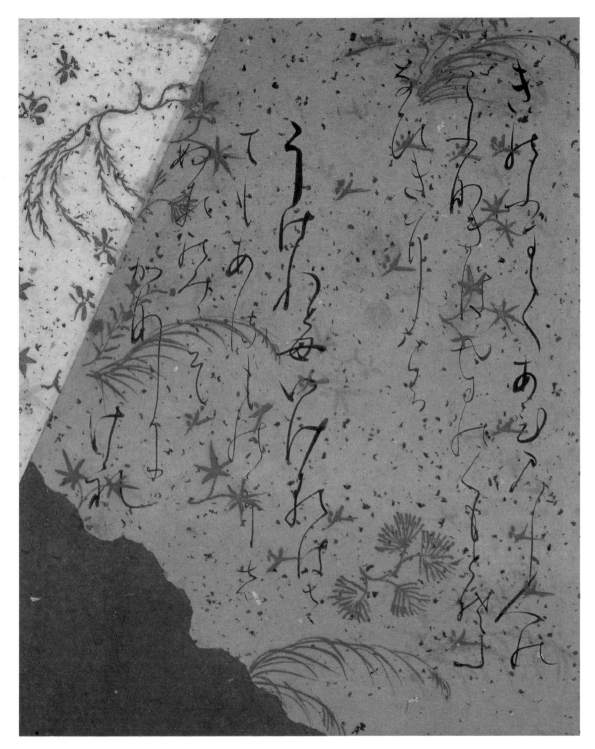

11-12. Album leaf from the *Ishiyama-gire*. Heian period, early 12th century. Ink with gold and silver on decorated and collaged paper, 8 x 6³/₈" (20.3 x 16.1 cm). Freer Gallery of Art, Smithsonian Institution, Washington, D.C.

The spiky, flowing calligraphy and the patterning of the papers, the rich use of gold, and the suggestions of natural imagery match the elegance of the poetry, epitomizing courtly Japanese taste.

Although writing in Japanese, such as in the *Ishiyama-gire*, was considered "women's hand," it is not known how much of the calligraphy of the time was actually written by women. It is sure, however, that women were a vital force in Heian society. Although the place of women in Japanese society was to decline in later periods, they contributed greatly to the art at the Heian court.

Secular Painting

Women were noted for both their poetry and their prose, including diaries, mythical tales, and courtly romances. *The Tale of Genji*, transposing the life-style of the Heian court into fiction in the first known novel, was written at

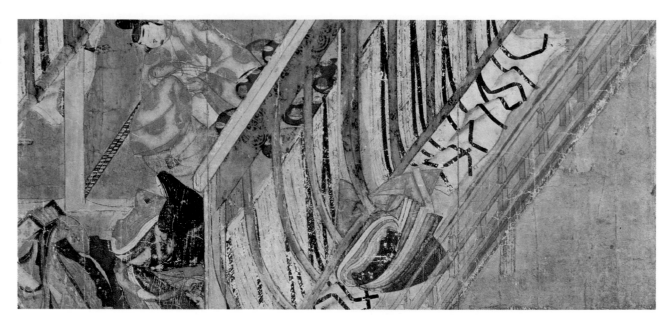

11-13. Scene from *The Tale of Genji*. Heian period, 12th century. Handscroll, ink and colors on paper, 8⅝ x 18⅞"
(21.9 x 47.9 cm). Tokugawa Art Museum, Nagoya

Twenty chapters from *The Tale of Genji* have come down to us in illustrated scrolls such as this one. Scholars assume, however, that the entire novel of fifty-four chapters must have been written out and illustrated—a truly monumental project. Each scroll seems to have been produced by a team of artists. One was the calligrapher, most likely a member of the nobility. Another was the master painter, who outlined two or three illustrations per chapter in fine brushstrokes and indicated the color scheme. Next, colorists went to work, applying layer after layer of color to build up patterns and textures. After they had finished, the master painter returned to reinforce outlines and apply the finishing touches, among them the details of the faces.

the beginning of the eleventh century by Lady Murasaki. It was written in Japanese at a time when men still wrote prose primarily in Chinese, and it remains one of Japan's—and the world's—great novels. Underlying the story of the love affairs of Prince Genji and his companions is the Japanese conception of fleeting pleasures and ultimate sadness in life, an echo of the Buddhist view of the vanity of earthly pleasures.

One of the earliest extant secular paintings from Japan is a series of scenes from *The Tale of Genji*, painted in the twelfth century by unknown artists in "women's hand" painting style. This style was characterized by delicate lines, strong if sometimes muted colors, and asymmetrical compositions usually viewed from above through invisible, "blown-away" roofs. The Genji paintings have a refined, subtle emotional impact. They generally show court figures in architectural settings with the frequent addition of natural elements, such as sections of gardens, that help to represent the mood of the scene. Thus a blossoming cherry tree appears in a scene of happiness, while unkempt weeds appear in a depiction of loneliness. Such correspondence between nature and human emotion is an enduring feature of Japanese poetry and art.

The figures in *The Tale of Genji* paintings do not show their emotions directly on their faces, which are simply rendered with the fewest possible lines. Instead, their feelings are conveyed by colors, poses, and the total composition of the scenes. One evocative scene portrays a seemingly happy Prince Genji holding a baby boy borne by his wife, Nyosan (fig. 11-13). In fact, the baby was fathered by another court noble. Since Genji himself has not been faithful to Nyosan, who appears in profile below him, he cannot complain; meanwhile the true father of the child has died, unable to acknowledge his only son. The irony is even greater because Genji himself is the illegitimate son of an emperor. Thus what should be a joyful scene has undercurrents that lend it a sense of irony and sorrow.

One might expect a painting of such an emotional scene to focus on the people involved. Instead, they are rendered in rather small size, and the scene is dominated by a screen that effectively squeezes Genji and his wife into a corner. This composition deliberately represents how their positions in courtly society have forced them into this unfortunate situation. In typical Heian style Genji expresses his emotion by murmuring a poem:

> How will he respond,
> The pine growing on the mountain peak,
> When he is asked who planted the seed?

The Tale of Genji scroll represents courtly life as interpreted through refined sensibilities and the "women's hand" style of painting. Heian painters also cultivated a contrasting "men's hand" style. Characterized by strong ink play and lively brushwork, it most often depicts subjects outside the court. One of the masterpieces of this style is *Frolicking Animals*, a set of scrolls satirizing the life of many different levels of society. Painted entirely in ink, the scrolls are attributed to Toba Sojo, the abbot of a

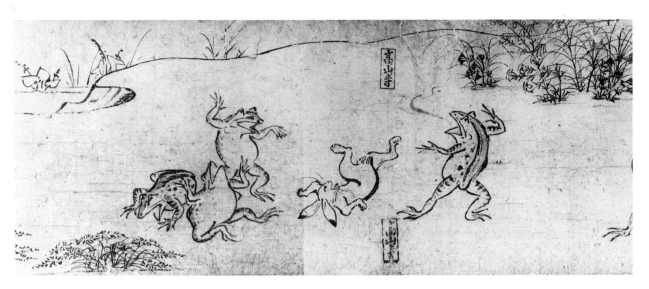

11-14. Attributed to Toba Sojo. Detail of *Frolicking Animals*. Heian period, 12th century. Handscroll, ink on paper, height 12" (30.5 cm). Kozan-ji, Kyoto

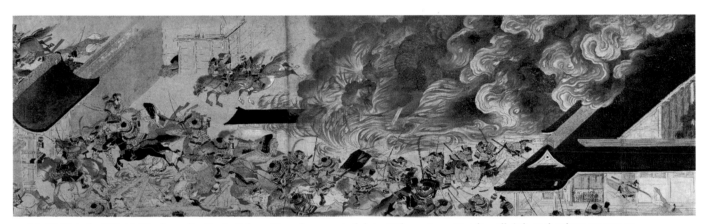

11-15. Detail of *Night Attack on the Sanjo Palace*. Kamakura period, late 13th century. Handscroll, ink and colors on paper, height 16¼" (41.3 cm). Museum of Fine Arts, Boston

Fenollosa-Weld Collection

The battles between the Minamoto and Taira clans were fought primarily by mounted and armored warriors, who used both bows and arrows and the finest swords. In the year 1060, some 500 rebels opposed to the retired emperor Go-Shirakawa carried out a daring raid on the Sanjo Palace. In a surprise attack in the middle of the night, they abducted the emperor. The scene was one of great carnage, much of it caused by the burning of the wooden palace. Despite the drama of the scene, this was not the decisive moment in the war. The Minamoto rebels would eventually lose more important battles to their Taira enemies. In turn the Taira clan would eventually be destroyed in 1185 by the victorious Minamoto forces, heirs to those who carried out this raid.

Buddhist temple, and they represent the humor of Japanese art to the full.

In one scene, a frog is seated as a buddha upon an altar while a monkey dressed as a monk prays proudly to him; in other scenes frogs, donkeys, foxes, and rabbits are shown playing, swimming, and wrestling, with one frog boasting of his prowess when he flings a rabbit to the ground (fig. 11-14). Playful and irreverent though it may be, the quality of the painting is remarkable. Each line is brisk and lively, and there are no strokes of the brush other than those needed to depict each scene. Unlike the Genji scroll, there is no text to *Frolicking Animals*, and we must make our own interpretations of the people and events being satirized. Nevertheless, the visual humor is so lively and succinct that we can recognize not only the Japanese of the twelfth century, but perhaps also ourselves.

KAMAKURA PERIOD

The courtiers of the Heian era became so engrossed in their own refinement that they neglected their responsibilities for governing the country. Clans of warriors—samurai—from outside the capital grew increasingly strong. Drawn into the factional conflicts of the imperial court, these samurai leaders soon became the real powers in Japan.

The two most powerful warrior clans were the Minamoto and the Taira, whose battles for domination became famous not only in medieval Japanese history but also in literature and art. One of the great painted handscrolls depicting these battles is *Night Attack on the Sanjo Palace* (fig. 11-15). Painted perhaps a hundred years after the actual event, the scroll conveys a sense of eyewitness reporting even though the anonymous artist

ARMS AND ARMOR

Battles such as the one depicted in *Night Attack on the Sanjo Palace* (see fig. 11-15) were fought largely by archers on horseback. Samurai archers charged the enemy at full gallop and loosed their arrows just before they wheeled away. The scroll clearly shows their distinctive bow, with its asymmetrically placed handgrip. The lower portion of the bow is shorter than the upper so it can clear the horse's neck. The samurai wear a long, curved sword at the waist.

By the tenth century, Japanese swordsmiths had perfected techniques for crafting their legendarily sharp swords. Sword makers face a fundamental difficulty: steel hard enough to hold a razor-sharp edge is brittle and breaks easily, but steel tough enough to withstand rough use is too soft to hold a keen edge. The Japanese ingeniously forged a blade from up to four strengths of steel, cradling a hard cutting edge in a softer, tougher support.

Samurai armor, illustrated here, was made of overlapping iron and lacquered leather scales, punched with holes and laced together with leather thongs and brightly colored silk braids. The principal piece wrapped around the chest, left side, and back. Padded shoulder straps hooked it back to front. A separate piece of armor was tied to the body to protect the right side. The upper legs

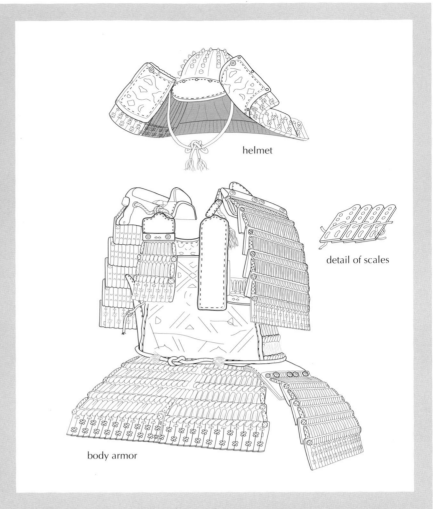

helmet

detail of scales

body armor

were protected by a skirt of four panels attached to the body armor, while two large rectangular panels tied on with cords guarded the arms. The helmet was made of iron plates riveted together. From it hung a neckguard flared sharply outward to protect the face from arrows shot at close range as the samurai wheeled away from an attack.

---

had to imagine the scene from verbal (and at best semifactual) descriptions. The style of the painting includes some of the brisk and lively linework of *Frolicking Animals* and also traces of the more refined brushwork, use of color, and bird's-eye viewpoint of *The Tale of Genji* scroll. The main element, however, is the savage depiction of warfare (see "Arms and Armor," above). Unlike the Genji scroll, *Night Attack* is full of action: flames sweep the palace, horses charge, warriors behead their enemies, court ladies try to hide, and a sense of energy and violence is conveyed with great sweep and power. The era of poetic refinement was now over in Japan, and the new world of the samurai began to dominate the secular arts.

The Kamakura era (1185–1392) began when Minamoto Yoritomo (1147–1199) defeated his Taira rivals and assumed power as shogun (general-in-chief). In order to resist the softening effects of courtly life in Kyoto, he established his military capital in Kamakura. While

paying respects to the emperor, Yoritomo kept both military and political power for himself. He thus began a tradition of rule by shogun that lasted in various forms until 1868.

Pure Land Buddhist Art

During the early Kamakura period, Pure Land Buddhism remained the most influential form of religion. As noted earlier, it had been spread throughout the country by traveling monks who taught the chant *Namu Amida Butsu*. One of these monks, Kuya (903–972), encouraged people to chant by going through the countryside and singing such simple ditties as:

> I've heard it said that
> Paradise is very far,
> But anyone who tries
> Can surely get there.

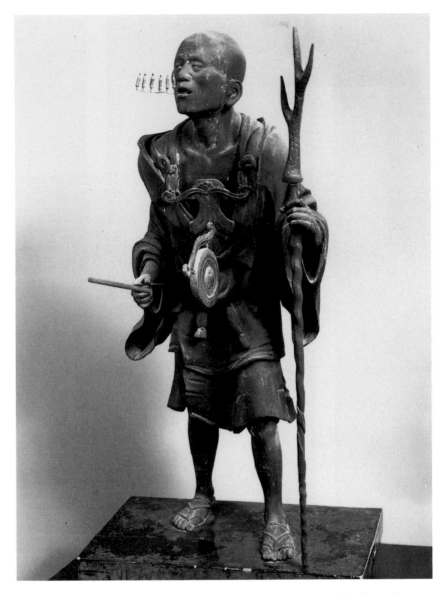

11-16. Kosho. *Kuya Preaching.* Kamakura period, before 1207. Painted wood,
height 46¼" (117.5 cm). Rokuhara Mitsu-ji, Kyoto

Even by chanting
The name of Amida only once,
A person cannot fail
To reach the Lotus Land.

Kuya was depicted in sculpture by Kosho in the early thirteenth century. A son of the more famous sculptor Unkei, Kosho was a master in the new **naturalistic** style that evolved at this time. Just as the *Night Attack* revealed the political turbulence of the period through its vivid colors and forceful style, Kamakura era portraiture also saw a new emphasis on **realism**, including the use of crystal eyes in sculpture for the first time. Perhaps the warriors had a taste for realism, for many sculptors and painters of the Kamakura period became expert in depicting faces, forms, and drapery with great attention to naturalistic detail. Kosho took on the more difficult task of representing in three dimensions not only the person of the famous monk Kuya but also his chant.

Kosho's solution to putting words into sculptural form was simple but brilliant (fig. 11-16). He carved six small buddhas emerging from Kuya's mouth, one for each of the six syllables *Na-mu-A-mi-da-Buts(u)* (the final *u* is not articulated). Believers would have understood that these six small buddhas embodied the Pure Land chant. The traveling clothes, the small gong, the staff topped by deer horns, and especially the sweetly intense expression of Kuya give this sculpture a radiant sense of faith.

Pure Land Buddhism taught that even one sincere invocation of the sacred chant could lead the most wicked sinner to the Western Paradise. Paintings called *raigo* (literally "welcoming approach") were created depicting the Amida Buddha, accompanied by bodhisattvas, coming down to earth to welcome the soul of the dying believer. Golden cords were often attached to these paintings, which were taken to the homes of the dying. A person near death held onto these cords, hoping that Amida would escort the soul directly to paradise.

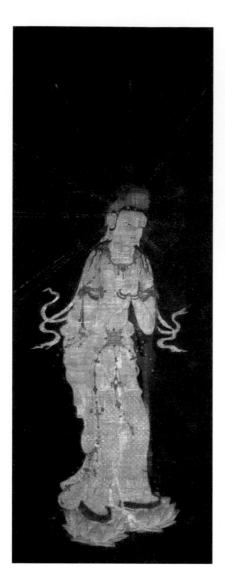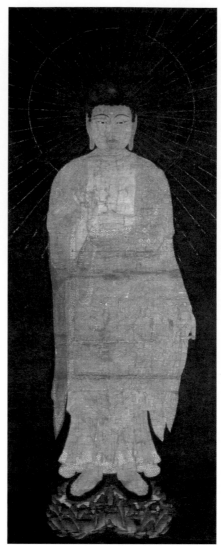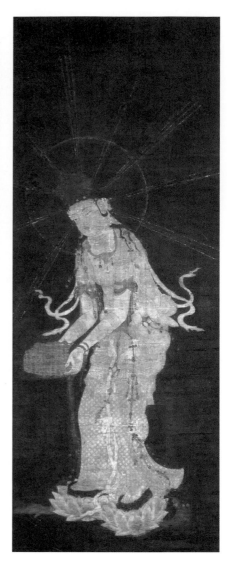

11-17. *Descent of the Amida Trinity, raigo* triptych. Kamakura period, late 13th century. Ink and colors with cut gold on silk; each scroll 54 x 19³/₄" (137.2 x 50.2 cm). The Art Institute of Chicago
Kate S. Buckingham Collection, 1929.855–1929.857

Raigo paintings are quite different in style from the complex mandalas and fierce guardian deities of Esoteric Buddhism. Like Jocho's sculpture of Amida at the Byodo-in, they radiate warmth and compassion. One magnificent *raigo*, a set of three paintings, portrays Amida Buddha descending to earth with two bodhisattvas to welcome the soul of a dying believer (fig. 11-17). They have been portrayed not only with gold paint but also with slivers of **gold leaf** cut in elaborate patterning to suggest the radiance of their draperies. The sparkle of the gold over the figures is heightened by the darkening of the silk behind them, so that the deities seem to come forth from the surface of the painting. In the flickering light of oil lamps and torches, *raigo* paintings would have glistened and gleamed in magical splendor in a temple or a dying person's home.

In every form of Buddhism paintings and sculpture became vitally important elements in religious teaching and belief. In their own time they were not considered works of art but rather visible manifestations of belief.

The Introduction of Zen

Toward the latter part of the Kamakura period still another type of Buddhism appeared, the last major form to reach Japan. This was Zen. In some ways, Zen resembles the original teachings of the historical Buddha in stressing that individuals must reach their own enlightenment through meditation, without the help of deities or magical chants. It was very different from both Esoteric and Pure Land Buddhism, and the time was ripe in Japan for a new approach to age-old Buddhist truths.

Zen had already been highly developed in China for some time, but it had been slow to reach Japan because of the severing of relations between the two countries during the Heian period. During the Kamakura era, however, relations with China were reestablished. Zen was brought to Japan by both visiting Chinese and returning Japanese monks. It appealed to the self-disciplined spirit of the warriors, who were not satisfied with the older forms of Buddhism connected with the Japanese court.

Zen temples were usually built in the mountains rather than in larger cities. An abbot named Kao at an early Zen temple was a pioneer in the kind of rough and simple ink painting that so directly expresses the Zen spirit. We can see this style in a remarkable ink portrait of a monk sewing his robe (fig. 11-18). Bearing the seals of Kao, it has the blunt style, strong sense of focus, and visual intensity of the finest Zen paintings. The almost humorous compression of the monk's face, coupled with the position of the darker robe, focuses our attention on his eyes, which then lead us out to his hand pulling the needle. We are drawn into the activity of the painting rather than merely sitting back and enjoying it as a work of art. This sense of intense activity within daily life, involving the viewer directly with the painter and the subject, is a feature of the best Zen figure paintings.

Buddhist prelates of other sects undoubtedly had assistants to take care of such mundane tasks as repairing a robe, but in Zen Buddhism each monk, no matter how advanced, is expected to do all tasks for himself. This principle extends to the entire monastery. There is no need to depend on contributions from the court or from wealthy believers. Zen monks grow and cook their own food, clean their temples, and are held as responsible for their lives as for their enlightenment. This spirit of self-reliance appealed especially to samurai. As a result, toward the end of the fourteenth century Zen began to dominate many aspects of Japanese culture.

EMPERORS AND WARRIORS

Japan is famous for its imperial system, but for most of its history emperors were under the political control of regents, powerful ministers, or shoguns. It could be argued that the imperial system survived because of this division of power. While the emperors always maintained their social and cultural authority, the fact that they did not rule politically allowed them to remain personally sacrosanct. Occasionally, however, an emperor decided to attempt to hold true power himself. One of these ambitious sovereigns was Go-Daigo (1288–1339), who managed to overthrow the Kamakura shogunate in 1333 and assume full power. His loyalist movement could not control events, however, and by 1392 power had reverted to the shogun. Control of government by the military was reaffirmed, and it was to last in various forms for 500 more years. As the Kamakura era ended, the seeds of the future were planted: warrior control and Zen aesthetics had become established as the leading forces in Japanese life and art.

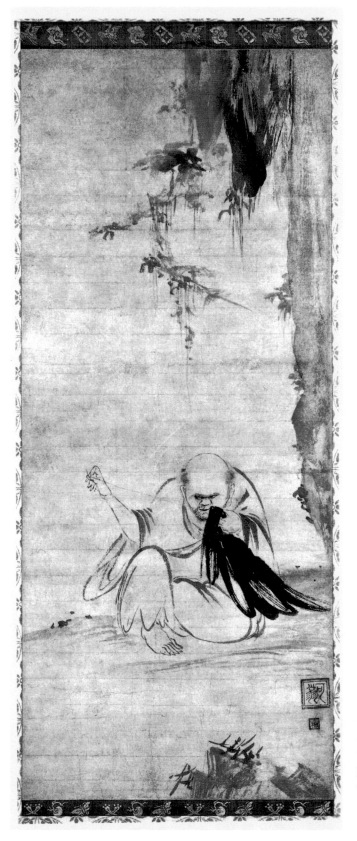

11-18. Attributed to Kao. *Monk Sewing*. Kamakura period, early 14th century. Ink on paper, 32⅞ x13¾" (83.5 x 35.4 cm). The Cleveland Museum of Art
John L. Severance Fund, 62.163

1500 BCE   1100   700   300

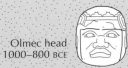

Olmec head
1000–800 BCE

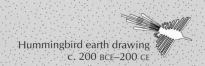

Hummingbird earth drawing
c. 200 BCE–200 CE

▲ FORMATIVE/PRECLASSIC PERIOD c. 1500 BCE–250 CE

     ▲ OLMEC c. 1200–400 BCE   ▲ CHAVÍN DE HUÁNTAR c. 800–200 BCE   ▲ PARACAS c. 300 BCE–200 CE

                                  ▲ ADENA c. 600 BCE–200 CE   ▲ HOPEWELL c. 200 BCE–200 CE

                                                             ▲ MOGOLLONE c. 200 BCE–1250

                                                             ▲ HOHOKAM c. 200 BCE–1200

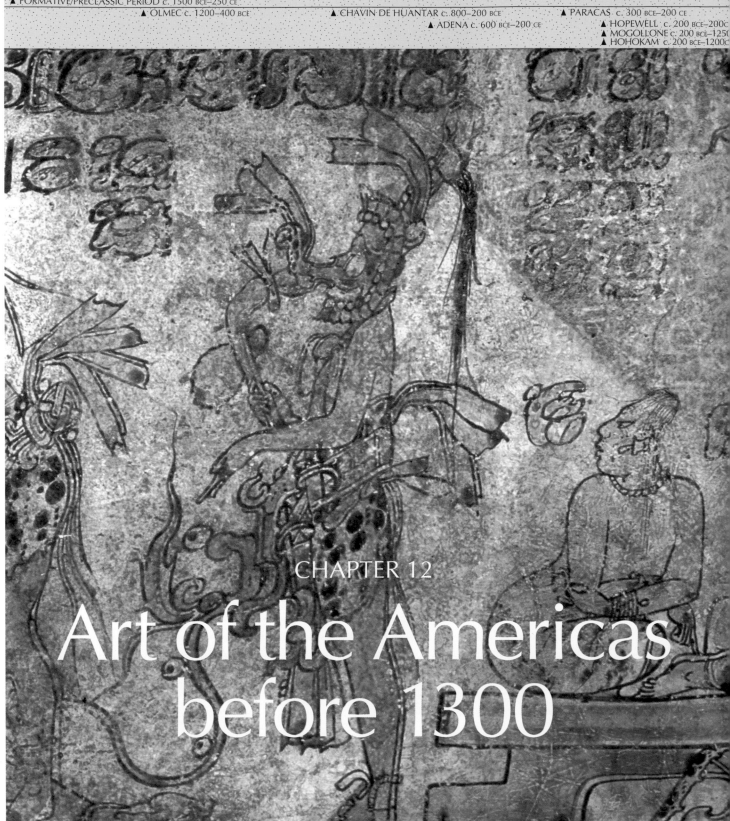

CHAPTER 12

Art of the Americas
before 1300

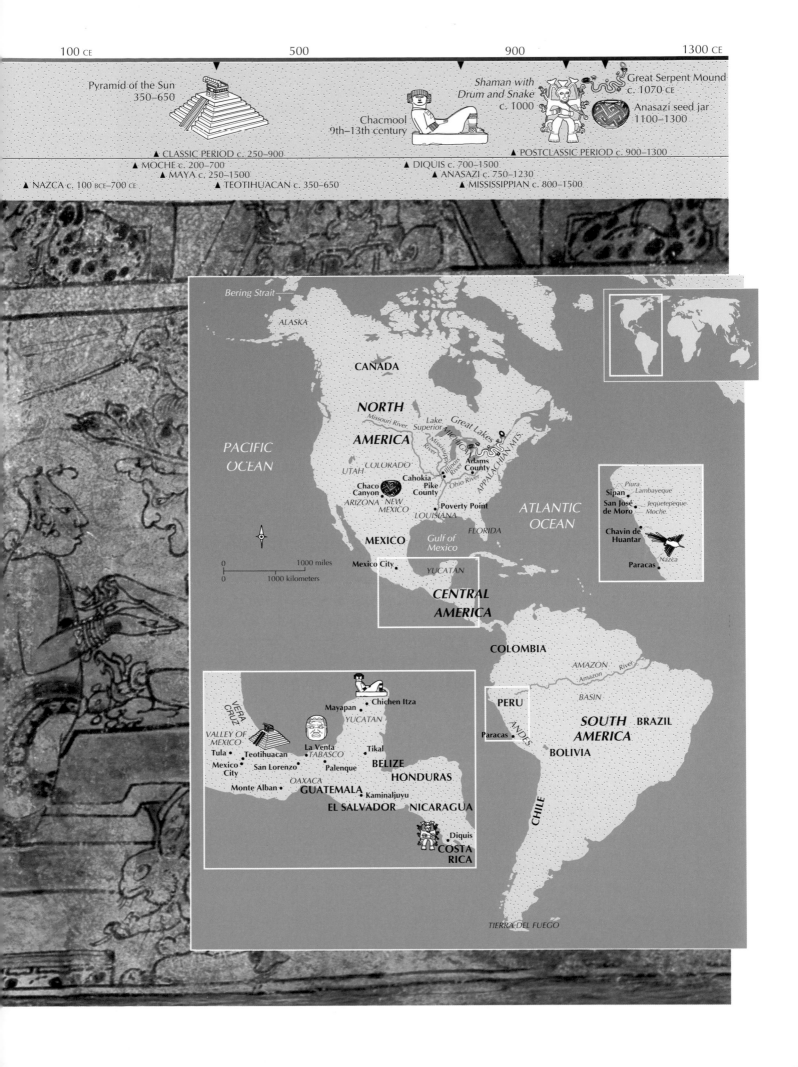

100 CE   500   900   1300 CE

Pyramid of the Sun
350–650

Shaman with
Drum and Snake
c. 1000

Great Serpent Mound
c. 1070 CE

Chacmool
9th–13th century

Anasazi seed jar
1100–1300

▲ CLASSIC PERIOD c. 250–900   ▲ POSTCLASSIC PERIOD c. 900–1300
▲ MOCHE c. 200–700   ▲ DIQUIS c. 700–1500
▲ MAYA c. 250–1500   ▲ ANASAZI c. 750–1230
▲ NAZCA c. 100 BCE–700 CE   ▲ TEOTIHUACAN c. 350–650   ▲ MISSISSIPPIAN c. 800–1500

Bering Strait

ALASKA

CANADA

NORTH
AMERICA

PACIFIC
OCEAN

Missouri River
Lake Superior
Great Lakes
LAKE MICHIGAN
Mississippi River
Illinois River
Ohio River
APPALACHIAN MTS.

Adams County

COLORADO
UTAH
Chaco Canyon   Cahokia
Pike County
ARIZONA   NEW MEXICO
Poverty Point
LOUISIANA

ATLANTIC
OCEAN

FLORIDA

MEXICO

Gulf of
Mexico

Mexico City

YUCATAN

CENTRAL
AMERICA

0   1000 miles
0   1000 kilometers

Piura
Lambayeque
Sipan
San José   Jequetepeque
de Moro   Moche
Chavin de
Huantar
Nazca
Paracas

COLOMBIA

AMAZON   River
Amazon
BASIN

PERU

SOUTH
AMERICA   BRAZIL

Paracas   ANDES

BOLIVIA

CHILE

VERA CRUZ
VALLEY OF MEXICO
Tula   Teotihuacan
Mexico City   San Lorenzo
Monte Alban   OAXACA

Mayapan   Chichen Itza
YUCATAN
La Venta
TABASCO   Tikal
Palenque   BELIZE
HONDURAS
GUATEMALA   Kaminaljuyu
EL SALVADOR   NICARAGUA
Diquis
COSTA
RICA

TIERRA DEL FUEGO

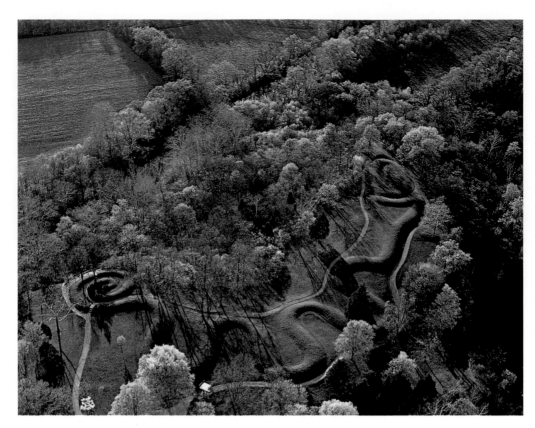

12-1. Great Serpent Mound, Adams County, Ohio. c. 1070 CE. Length approx. 1,400' (426.7 m)

When the boldest of the white settlers in North America pushed beyond the Appalachian Mountains, they literally walked into a mystery. They found themselves facing, and in some cases climbing over, strange mounds of earth, large and small, that clearly had been created by human hands—a great many hands. The mounds took various forms. Some were shaped like birds and other animals. One, in present-day Ohio, a writhing earthen snake 1,254 feet long and 20 feet wide, meandered along the crest of a ridge overlooking a stream, with its head at the highest point of the ridge (fig. 12-1). The mounds were most concentrated near the Mississippi and Ohio rivers, but at least a few were found throughout the very wide area from the Great Lakes to the Gulf Coast.

The eighteenth-century settlers began to dig around in the mounds—sometimes to sate curiosity, sometimes to seek treasure, sometimes simply to plant their crops. What they found further puzzled them. Some mounds covered piles of refuse from permanent agricultural villages where none had been known to exist. Others were burial sites where human skeletons had been interred with carved artifacts unlike any seen before, sometimes made from materials not native to the area. Theories abounded about the creators of these mounds—including speculations that they had been survivors from the lost island of Atlantis or one of the lost tribes of Israel. Before he became president, Thomas Jefferson had excavated a burial mound in Virginia and had come close to the truth: that these monumental earthworks, in fact, were 800-year-old creations of the earliest peoples to settle the New World.

THE NEW WORLD

During the last Ice Age, which began about 2.5 million years ago, glaciers periodically trapped enough of the world's water to lower the level of the oceans and expose land between Asia and North America. At its greatest extent, this land bridge was a vast, rolling plain a thousand miles wide, where grasses, sagebrush, sedge, and groves of scrub willow provided food and shelter for animals and birds.

Although most areas of present-day Alaska and Canada were covered by glaciers during the Ice Age, a narrow, ice-free corridor provided access to the south. Sometime before about 12,000 years ago, perhaps as early as 20,000 to 30,000 years ago, Paleolithic hunter-gatherers emerged through this corridor and began to spread out into two vast, uninhabited continents. Between 10,000 and 12,000 years ago, bands of hunters whose tool kits included sophisticated fluted-stone spearheads traveled across most of North America. The earliest uncontested evidence puts humans at the southern end of South America by 11,000 years ago. Although contact between Siberia and Alaska continued after the ice had retreated and rising oceans had flooded the Bering Strait, the peoples of the Western Hemisphere were essentially cut off from the peoples of Africa and Eurasia until they were overrun by European conquerors beginning in the late fifteenth century CE.

In this isolation New World peoples experienced many of the same transformations that followed the end of the Paleolithic era elsewhere. In many regions they developed an agricultural way of life, based on the cultivation of corn, beans, and squash. Other plants first domesticated in the New World included potatoes, tobacco, cacao (chocolate), tomatoes, and avocados. New World peoples also domesticated many animals: turkeys, guinea pigs, llamas (and their cousins, the alpacas, guanacos, and vicuñas), and, as did the peoples of the Old World, dogs.

As elsewhere, the shift to agriculture in the Americas was accompanied by population growth and, in some places, the rise of hierarchical societies, the appearance of ceremonial centers and towns with monumental architecture, and the development of elaborate artistic traditions. New World cities such as Teotihuacan in the Valley of Mexico rivaled those of the Old World in size and splendor. New World civilizations produced sophisticated ceramic wares, although they did not develop the potter's wheel or the wheel in general, perhaps because they lacked beasts of burden like horses and oxen for exploiting its potential. The peoples of Mesoamerica—the region that extends from central Mexico to northern Central America—developed writing, a complex and accurate calendar, and a sophisticated system of mathematics. Central and South American peoples developed an advanced metallurgy and produced exquisite gold, silver, and copper jewelry. The smiths of the Andes began to produce metal weapons and agricultural implements in the first millennium CE, but Native Americans in general made tools and weapons from such other materials as bone, ivory, stone, wood, and, where it was available, obsidian, a volcanic glass capable of holding a cutting edge as fine as surgical steel. Native Americans were skilled in basketry, and in the Andes, beginning about 2000 BCE, they developed an enduring tradition of weaving that produced some of the world's finest textiles (see "Andean Textiles," page 458).

Later civilizations such as the Aztec, Inca, and Pueblo of the North American Southwest are perhaps more familiar today, but before 1300 CE extraordinary artistic traditions already flourished in many regions in the Americas. This chapter explores the accomplishments of some of the cultures in five of those regions—Mesoamerica, Central America, the central Andes of South America, the southeastern woodlands and great river valleys of North America, and the North American Southwest.

MESO-AMERICA

Ancient Mesoamerica encompasses the area from north of the Valley of Mexico (the location of Mexico City) to modern Belize, Honduras, and western Nicaragua in Central America. The region is one of great contrasts, ranging from tropical rain forest to semiarid mountains. Reflecting this physical diversity, the civilizations that arose in Mesoamerica varied, but they were linked by trade and displayed an overall cultural unity. Among their common features are a complex calendrical system based on interlocking 260-day and 365-day cycles, a

---

THE COSMIC BALL GAME

The ritual ball game was one of the defining characteristics of Mesoamerican society. Played in some version throughout the region at the time of the Spanish conquest, this game had its origins deep in antiquity, dating at least to Olmec times. The ball game was generally played on a long, rectangular court with a large, solid, heavy rubber ball. Using their elbows, knees, or hips—but not their hands—heavily padded players directed the ball toward a goal or marker. The rules, the size and shape of the court, the number of players on a team, and the nature of the goal varied. The largest surviving ball court, at Chichen Itza, was about the size of a modern football field. The goals of the Chichen Itza court were large stone rings set in the walls of the court about 25 feet above the field.

The game had profound religious and political significance and was a common subject of Meso-american art. Players, complete with equipment, appear as figurines and on stone votive sculpture; the game and its attendant rituals were represented in relief sculpture. The movement of the ball represented celestial bodies—the sun, moon, or stars—held aloft and directed by the skill of the players. The ball game was also associated with warfare. Captive warriors might have been made to play the game, and players were often sacrificed.

PARALLELS

Years	Period/Culture Peak	Americas	World
Before 10,000 BCE		Paleolithic hunter-gatherers migrate to New World	**Before 10,000 BCE** Ice Age in Europe
c. 1500 BCE–250 CE	**Formative/Preclassic period in Mesoamerica**		**c. 1500 BCE–250 CE** Development of metallurgy (Near East); Great Pyramids at Giza (Egypt); development of writing (China, India); Minoan, Mycenaean cultures (Greece); black-figure and red-figure vase painting (Greece); birth of Siddhartha Gautama, founder of Buddhism (Nepal); Parthenon (Greece); Great Stupa at Sanchi (India); crucifixion of Jesus (Jerusalem); Pantheon (Italy)
	Olmec (Mesoamerica; c. 1200–400 BCE)	San Lorenzo; La Venta; ritual ball games; colossal heads; earliest writing and calendars; early Maya	
	Chavin de Huantar (Andes; Early Horizon period, c. 800–200 BCE)	Innovation in ceramics, metallurgy, textiles	
	Adena (Ohio; c. 600 BCE–200 CE)	Mound building	
	Paracas (Peru; c. 300 BCE–200 CE)	Weaving; embroidery	
	Hokokam (Arizona; c. 200 BCE–1200 CE)	Canals	
	Hopewell (Illinois, Ohio; c. 200 BCE–200 CE)	Mound building; carved jewelry; stone pipes	
	Mogollon (New Mexico, Arizona; c. 200 BCE–1250 CE)	Pit houses	
c. 250–900 CE	**Classic period in Mesoamerica**		**c. 250–900 CE** *Haniwa* figures (Japan); earliest surviving Hindu temples (India); Hagia Sophia (Turkey); birth of Muhammad, founder of Islam (Arabia); Muslim conquests of Arabia, Persia, Egypt, Syria, Palestine, India, North Africa; first block-print text (China)
	Nazca (Peru; c. 100 BCE–700 CE)	Weaving; polychrome pottery; colossal geoglyphs	
	Moche (Peru; c. 200–700 CE)	Sipan; Moche; Pyramid of the Sun	
	Maya (Mesoamerica; c. 250–900 CE)	Tikal; Palenque; hieroglyphic writing; calendar; codex-style painting	
	Teotihuacan (Mesoamerica; c. 350–650 CE)	Temple of the Feathered Serpent; Pyramids of the Sun and the Moon	
c. 900–1500 CE	**Postclassic period in Mesoamerica**	Maya center at Chichen Itza; Castillo	**c. 900–1500 CE** First Viking colony in Greenland; Lady Murasaki's *Tale of Genji* (Japan); the Crusades (Europe); Jenghiz Khan rules Mongols (Central Asia)
	Diquis (Costa Rica; c. 700–1500 CE)	Lost-wax casting; goldwork	
	Anasazi (Four Corners, American southwest; c. 750–1230 CE)	Multistory "apartments"; Pueblo Bonita	
	Mississippian (Illinois; c. 800–1500 CE)	Earthenwork palaces; temples	

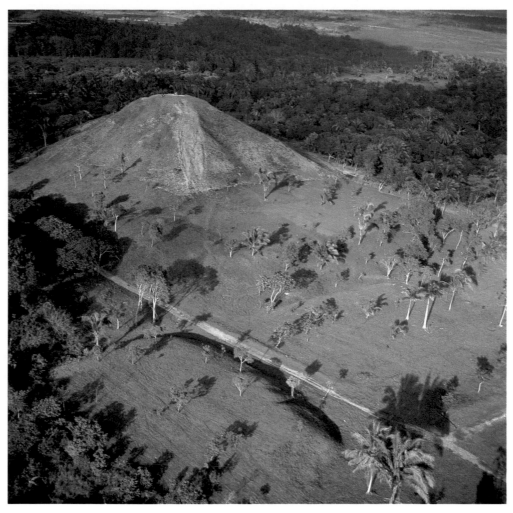

12-2.   Great Pyramid and ball court, La Venta, Mexico. Olmec culture, c. 900–600 BCE. Pyramid height approx. 100' (30 m)

ritual ball game (see "The Cosmic Ball Game," page 445), and aspects of the construction of monumental ceremonial centers. Mesoamerican society was sharply divided into elite and commoner classes.

The transition to farming began in Mesoamerica between 7000 and 6000 BCE, and by 3000 to 2000 BCE settled villages were widespread. Archeologists traditionally have divided the region's subsequent history into three broad periods: Formative or Preclassic (1500 BCE–250 CE), Classic (250–900 CE), and Postclassic (900–1500 CE). This chronology derives primarily from the archeology of the Maya—the people of Guatemala and the Yucatan peninsula. The Classic period brackets the time during which the Maya erected dated stone monuments. The term reflects the view of early Mayanists that it was a kind of golden age, the equivalent of the Classical period in ancient Greece. Although this view is no longer current and the periods are only roughly applicable to other parts of Mesoamerica, the terminology has endured.

The Olmec

The first major Mesoamerican civilization, the Olmec, emerged during the Formative period along the Gulf of Mexico, in the swampy coastal jungles of the modern Mexican states of Veracruz and Tabasco. In dense vegetation along slow, meandering rivers, the Olmec cleared farmland, drained fields, and raised earth mounds on which they constructed religious and political centers. These centers probably housed an elite group of ruler-priests supported by a larger population of farmers who lived in villages of pole-and-thatch houses. The presence at Olmec sites of goods like obsidian, iron ore, and jade that are not found in the Gulf region but come from throughout Mesoamerica indicates that the Olmec participated in extensive long-distance trade.

The earliest Olmec center, at San Lorenzo, flourished from about 1200 to 900 BCE and was abandoned by 400 BCE. The archeological findings here include a possible ball court, an architectural feature of other major Olmec sites. Another center, at La Venta, rose to prominence after San Lorenzo declined, thriving from about 900 to 400 BCE. La Venta was built on high ground between rivers. Its most prominent feature, an earth mound known as the Great Pyramid, still rises to a height of about 100 feet (fig. 12-2). This scalloped mound may have been intended to resemble a volcanic mountain, but its present form may simply be the result of erosion after thousands of years of the region's heavy rains. The Great Pyramid stands at the south end of a large, open court, possibly used as a playing field, arranged on a north-south axis and defined by long, low mounds. An elaborate drainage system of stone troughs may have been used as part of a ritual honoring a water deity. Many of the physical features of La Venta—including the symmetrical arrangement of earth mounds, platforms, and central open spaces along an axis that was probably determined by astronomical observations—are characteristic of later monumental and ceremonial architecture throughout Mesoamerica. Found buried within the site were carved jade, serpentine stone, and granite artifacts.

Among Olmec carvings, the most pervasive images are jaguars and so-called were-jaguars, creatures that combine human and feline features. These images suggest that Olmec religion may have involved a belief in jaguar deities that could assume human form, as well as shaman figures who could assume animal (jaguar) form and mediate between humans and the spirit world. There is also sculpture showing a woman and a jaguar in close association, suggesting an origin myth involving the union of a human with a feline deity.

In addition to the smaller works in jade and serpentine, the Olmec produced an abundance of monumental basalt sculpture, including colossal heads, altars, and seated figures. The huge basalt blocks for the large works of sculpture were quarried at distant sites and transported to San Lorenzo, La Venta, and other centers. The colossal heads, ranging in height from 5 to 12 feet and weighing from 5 to more than 20 tons, are probably the best-known Olmec sculpture today (fig. 12-3). The heads represent adult males wearing close-fitting caps with chin straps and large, round earplugs. The fleshy faces have almond-shaped eyes, flat broad noses, thick protruding lips, a slight frown, and down-turned mouths. Each face is different, suggesting that they may represent specific individuals. Most scholars now consider them to be portraits of rulers. Nine heads were found at San Lorenzo; all had been mutilated and buried about 900 BCE, about the time the site went into decline. Seventy-seven basalt monuments were found at La Venta, including four heads, which faced each other across the ceremonial core of the site.

The colossal heads and the subjects depicted on other monumental sculpture suggest that the Olmec elite, like their counterparts in later Mesoamerican civilizations, particularly the Maya, were preoccupied with the commemoration of rulers and historic events. This preoccupation was probably an important factor in the development of writing and calendrical systems, which first appeared around 600 to 500 BCE in areas with strong Olmec influence. By 200 CE forests and swamps were reclaiming Olmec sites, but Olmec civilization had spread widely throughout Mesoamerica and was to have an enduring influence on its successors. As the Olmec centers of the Gulf Coast faded, the great Classic period centers at Teotihuacan in the Valley of Mexico, at Monte Alban in the Valley of Oaxaca, and in the Maya region were beginning their ascendancy.

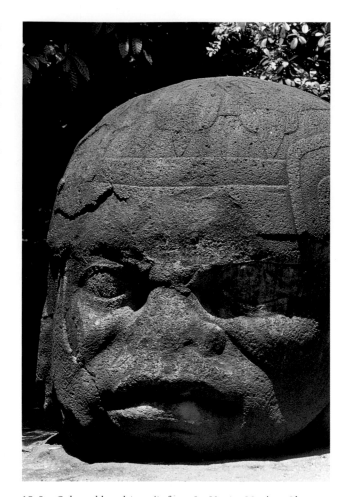

12-3. Colossal head (no. 4), from La Venta, Mexico. Olmec culture, c. 900–500 BCE. Basalt, height 7'5" (2.26 m). La Venta Park, Villahermosa, Tabasco, Mexico

The naturalistic colossal heads found at La Venta and San Lorenzo are sculpture in the round that measure about 8 feet in diameter. They are carved from basalt boulders that were transported to the Gulf Coast from the Tuxtla Mountains, more than 60 miles inland.

Teotihuacan

Teotihuacan is located some 30 miles northeast of present-day Mexico City. Early in the first millennium CE it began a period of rapid growth, and by 200 it had emerged as a significant center of commerce and manufacturing, the first large city-state in the Americas. One reason for its wealth was its control of a source of high-quality obsidian. Goods made at Teotihuacan, including obsidian tools and pottery, were distributed widely throughout Mesoamerica in exchange for luxury items such as the brilliant green feathers of the quetzal bird, used for priestly headdresses, and the spotted fur of the jaguar, used for ceremonial garments. The city's farmers terraced hillsides and drained swamps, and on fertile, reclaimed land they grew the common Mesoamerican staple foods, including corn, squash, and beans. From the fruit of the spiky-leafed maguey plant they fermented pulque, a mildly alcoholic brew still consumed today.

At its height, between 350 and 650 CE, Teotihuacan covered nearly 9 square miles and had a population of some 200,000, making it the largest city in the Americas

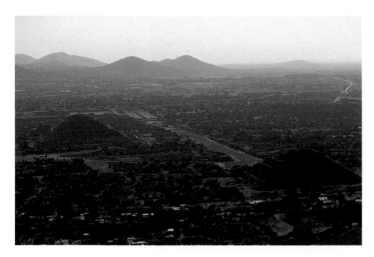

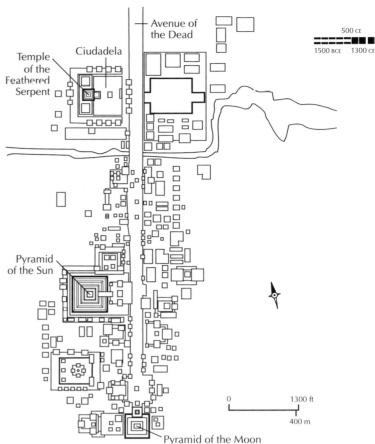

12-4. Ceremonial center of the city of Teotihuacan, Mexico. Teotihuacan culture, 350–650 CE

The Pyramid of the Moon is at the lower right, the Pyramid of the Sun at the middle left, and the Ciudadela and the Temple of the Feathered Serpent at the upper left.

12-5. Plan of the ceremonial center of Teotihuacan

and one of the largest in the world at that time (figs. 12-4, 12-5). Whether through conquest or trade—archeologists are not certain which—it exerted far-reaching influence. The site of Kaminaljuyu in the highlands of Guatemala, for example, shows evidence of close contact with Teotihuacan. The people of Teotihuacan worshiped many gods that were recognizably antecedent to gods worshiped by later Mesoamerican people, including the Aztec, who dominated central Mexico at the time of the Spanish conquest. Among these are the Rain God (possibly also the god of war and sacrifice), known to the Aztec as Tlaloc, and the Feathered Serpent, known to the Maya as Kukulcan and to the Aztec as Quetzalcoatl.

Sometime in the middle of the eighth century disaster struck Teotihuacan: the ceremonial center burned, and the city went into a permanent decline. Nevertheless, its influence continued as other centers throughout northern Mesoamerica borrowed and transformed its art and imagery over the next several centuries. The site was never entirely abandoned, however, because it remained a legendary pilgrimage center until the time of the Spanish conquest in the early sixteenth century. The Aztec revered the site, believing it to be the place where the gods created the sun and the moon. Its name, Teotihuacan, is an Aztec word meaning "The City (gathering place) of the Gods." Its principal monuments include the Pyramid of the Sun and the Pyramid of the Moon.

The so-called Avenue of the Dead, the heart of the city, is a broad thoroughfare laid out on a north-south axis and extending for more than 3 miles. Another major thoroughfare intersects it at right angles, establishing a grid to which the rest of the city strictly conforms. Much of the ceremonial center, in a pattern typical of Mesoamerica, is characterized by the symmetrical arrangement of structures around open courts or plazas. The Pyramid of the Sun flanks the Avenue of the Dead to the east. It is built over a four-chambered cave with a spring

that may have been the original focus of worship at the site and the source of its prestige. The largest of Teotihuacan's architectural monuments, the Pyramid of the Sun is more than 210 feet high and measures about 720 feet on each side at its base. It rises in a series of sloping steps to a flat platform, where a two-room temple once stood. A monumental stone stairway led from level to level up the side of the pyramid to the temple platform. The exterior was faced with stone and **stucco** and painted. The Pyramid of the Moon, not quite as large as the Pyramid of the Sun, stands at the north end of the Avenue of the Dead, facing a large plaza flanked by smaller, symmetrically placed platforms.

In the heart of the city, at the intersection of the Avenue of the Dead and the main east-west thoroughfare, is the Ciudadela, a vast sunken plaza surrounded by temple platforms. One of the city's principal religious and political centers, the Ciudadela could accommodate an assembly of more than 60,000 people. Its focal point was the Temple of the Feathered Serpent, or Quetzalcoatl. This structure exhibits the ***talud-tablero*** construction that is a hallmark of the Teotihuacan architectural style. The sloping base, or *talud*, of each platform supports a vertical *tablero*, or **entablature**, which is surrounded by a frame and often filled with sculptural decoration. The Temple of the Feathered Serpent was enlarged several times, and typical of Mesoamerican practice, each enlargement completely enclosed the previous structure, like the concentric layers of an onion.

12-6. Temple of the Feathered Serpent, the Ciudadela, Teotihuacan, Mexico. Teotihuacan culture, c. 350 CE (?)

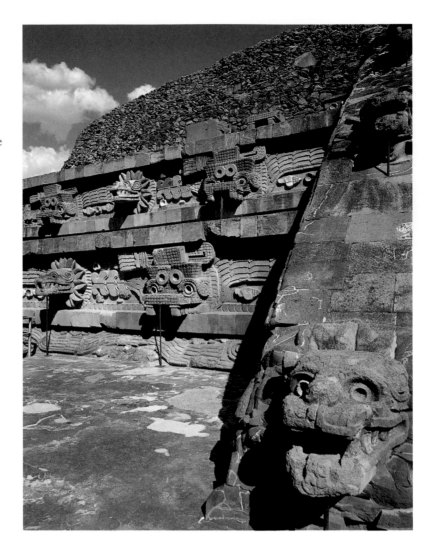

Archeological excavations of earlier-phase *tableros* and a stairway balustrade have revealed painted reliefs of the Feathered Serpent, the goggle-eyed Rain God (or Fire God, according to some), and aquatic shells and snails (fig. 12-6). Their flat, angular, abstract style is typical of Teotihuacan art and is a marked contrast to the three-dimensional, curvilinear style of Olmec art. The Rain God has a squarish, stylized head with protruding lips, huge round eyes originally inlaid with obsidian and surrounded by colored circles, and large, circular earspools. The fanged serpent heads, perhaps composites of snakes and other creatures, emerge from an aureole of stylized feathers. It is tempting to read cosmic imagery into the sculpture. The Rain God and the Feathered Serpent may represent alternating wet and dry seasons, may be symbols of regeneration and cyclical renewal, or may have some other meaning that has been lost.

The residential sections of Teotihuacan adhered to the grid established in the city's center. The large palaces of the elite, with as many as forty-five rooms and seven patios, stood nearest the ceremonial center. Artisans, foreign traders, and peasants lived farther away, in less luxurious compounds. The palaces and more humble homes alike were rectangular, one-story structures with high walls, thatched roofs, and suites of rooms arranged symmetrically around open courts. Walls were plastered and, in the homes of the elite, covered with paintings.

Teotihuacan's artists worked in a true **fresco** technique, applying pigments directly on damp lime plaster. Their flat, abstract-style drawing is assured, and their use of color is subtle—one work may include five shades of red with touches of ocher, green, and blue. A detached fragment of a wall painting, now in The Cleveland Museum of Art, depicts a bloodletting ritual in which an elaborately dressed man enriches and revitalizes the earth with his own blood (fig. 12-7). The man's Feathered Serpent headdress, decorated with precious quetzal feathers, indicates his high rank. He stands between rectangular plots of earth planted with bloody maguey spines and scatters seeds or drops of blood from his right hand, as indicated by the panel with conventionalized symbols for blood, seeds, and flowers. The **speech scroll** emerging from his open mouth symbolizes his ritual chant. The visual weight accorded the headdress and speech scroll suggests that the man's priestly office and chanted words are essential elements of the ceremony. Above the figure is a two-headed, spotted serpent holding two birds in its angular coils. Such bloodletting rituals were not limited to Teotihuacan but were widespread in Mesoamerica.

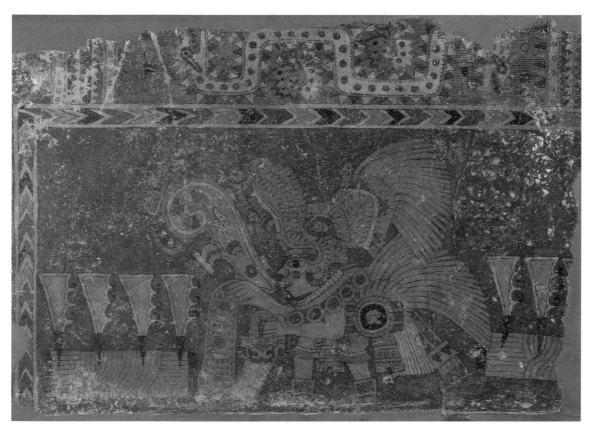

12-7. *Maguey Bloodletting Ritual*, fragment of a fresco from Teotihuacan, Mexico. Teotihuacan culture, 600–750 CE. Pigment on lime plaster, 32¼ x 45¼" (82 x 116.1 cm). The Cleveland Museum of Art
Purchase from the J. H. Wade Fund (63.252)

The maguey plant supplied the people of Teotihuacan with food; fiber for making clothing, rope, and paper; and the sacramental drink pulque. As this painting indicates, priestly officials used it in rituals of self-sacrifice to draw their own blood.

The Maya

The Maya homeland in southern Mesoamerica includes Guatemala, the Yucatan peninsula, Belize, and the eastern part of Honduras and El Salvador. The remarkable civilization created there endured to the time of the Spanish conquest and is still reflected in the culture of the Maya's present-day descendants. The ancient Maya are noted for a number of achievements. They developed ways to produce high agricultural yields in the seemingly inhospitable tropical rain forest of the Yucatan. In densely populated cities they built imposing pyramids, temples, palaces, and administrative structures. They developed the most advanced hieroglyphic writing in Mesoamerica and the most sophisticated version of the Mesoamerican calendrical system (see "Maya Record Keeping," page 452). With these tools they documented the accomplishments of their rulers in monumental commemorative **stelae**, in books, on ceramic vessels, and on wall paintings. (Scholars have determined the relationship between the Maya calendar and the European calendar, making it possible to date Maya artifacts with a precision unknown elsewhere in the Americas.) They studied astronomy and the natural cycles of plants and animals and developed the mathematical concepts of zero and place value before they were known in Europe.

An increasingly detailed picture of the Maya has been emerging from recent archeological research and advances in deciphering their writing. That picture shows a society divided into competing centers, each with a hereditary ruler and an elite class of nobles and priests supported by a far larger class of farmer-commoners. Rulers established their legitimacy, maintained links with their divine ancestors, and sustained the gods through elaborate rituals, including ball games, bloodletting ceremonies, and human sacrifice. These rituals occurred in the pyramids, temples, and plazas that dominated Maya cities. Rulers commemorated such events and their military exploits on carved stelae. A complex pantheon of deities, many with several manifestations, presided over the Maya universe.

Olmec influence was widespread in the Maya area during the middle Preclassic period (1000–300 BCE). The earliest distinctively Maya centers emerged during the late Preclassic period (300 BCE–250 CE), and Maya civilization reached its peak in the southern lowlands of the Yucatan peninsula during the Classic period (250–900 CE). Probably due to increased warfare and growing pressure on agricultural resources, the sites in the southern lowlands were abandoned at the end of the Classic period. The focus of Maya civilization then shifted to the northern Yucatan during the Postclassic period (900–1500 CE).

MAYA RECORD KEEPING Since the rediscovery of the Classic period Maya sites in the nineteenth century, scholars have puzzled over the meaning of the hieroglyphic writing that abounds in Maya artwork. They soon realized that many of the glyphs were numeric notations in a complex calendrical system. By the early twentieth century the calendrical system had been interpreted and approximately correlated with the European calendar. The Maya calendar counts time from a starting date some 5,000 years ago, now securely established as August 13, 3114 BCE. This system, known as the long count, incorporates the short-count system, based on interlocking 260-day and 365-day cycles, of other Mesoamerican societies. The long count is unique to the Classic period Maya.

The meaning of the noncalendric inscriptions remained obscure until the late 1950s. Before that time many prominent Mayanists argued that the inscriptions dealt with astronomical and astrological observations, not historical events. This interpretation was in accord with the prevailing view that the Classic period Maya were a peaceful people ruled by a theocracy of learned priests. Since the late 1950s scholars have made enormous progress in deciphering Maya writing. The results of their work, combined with the results of archeological research, have overturned the earlier view of Maya society and Maya writing. The inscriptions on Maya architecture and the many stone stelae erected at Maya sites are, it turns out, almost entirely devoted to historic events in the lives of Maya rulers and the Maya elite. They record the dates of royal marriages, births of heirs, alliances between cities, and great military victories, tying them to astronomical events and propitious periods in the Maya calendar.

Maya writing, like the Maya calendar, is the most advanced in ancient Mesoamerica. About 800 glyphs have been identified, equivalent to the number in ancient Egyptian writing at some periods. The system combines logographs—symbols representing entire words—and symbols representing syllables in the Maya language.

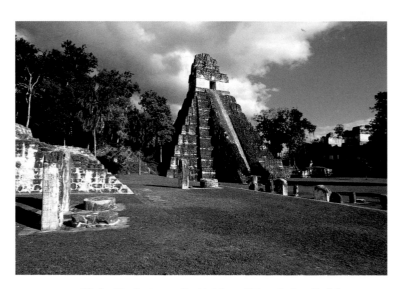

12-8. North Acropolis (right) and Temple I, called the Temple of the Giant Jaguar (tomb of Au Cacau), Tikal, Guatemala. Maya culture. North Acropolis, 5th century CE; Temple I, c. 700 CE

Tikal has been the focus of an extended program of research directed by archeologists from the University of Pennsylvania in cooperation with the Guatemalan government. This research is part of an explosive growth in Maya studies that has enormously enriched our understanding of Maya culture and history.

Classic Period Architecture at Tikal and Palenque.

The monumental buildings of Maya cities were masterful examples of the use of architecture for public display and propaganda. Seen from outside and afar, they would have impressed the common people with the power and authority of the elite and the gods they served.

Tikal, in what is now northern Guatemala, was the largest Classic period Maya city, with a population of as many as 70,000 at its height. Like other Maya cities—and unlike Teotihuacan, with its rigid grid—Tikal conformed to the uneven terrain of the rain forest. Plazas, pyramid-temples, ball courts, and other structures stood on high ground connected by elevated roads, or causeways. One major causeway, 80 feet wide, led from the center of the city to outlying residential areas.

Figure 12-8 shows part of the ceremonial core of Tikal. The structure on the right, known as the North Acropolis, follows a north-south axis and dates to the early Classic period. It contained many royal tombs and covers earlier structures that date to the origin of the city, about 500 BCE. The tall pyramid in the center is known as Temple I or the Temple of the Giant Jaguar. It covers the tomb of Au Cacau (Lord Chocolate, 682–c. 727), who began an ambitious expansion of Tikal after a period in the sixth and early seventh century CE when there was little new construction at this or other major Maya sites. Under Au Cacau and his successors, Tikal's influence grew, with evidence of contacts that extended from highland Mexico to Costa Rica.

Temple I faces a companion pyramid, Temple II, across a large plaza. These two structures changed the orientation of the ceremonial center from north-south to east-west. The new plaza provided a monumental entrance to the North Acropolis, and the two new pyramids framed the ancestral core of the city, visually linking old and new.

From Au Cacau's tomb in the limestone bedrock, Temple I rises above the forest canopy to a height of more than 140 feet. It has nine layers, probably reflecting the belief, current among the Aztec and the Maya at the time of the Spanish conquest, that the underworld had nine levels. Priests climbed the steep stone staircase on the exterior to the temple on top, which consists of two long, parallel rooms covered with a steep roof supported by **corbeled vaults**. It is typical of Maya enclosed stone structures, which resemble the kind of pole-and-thatch

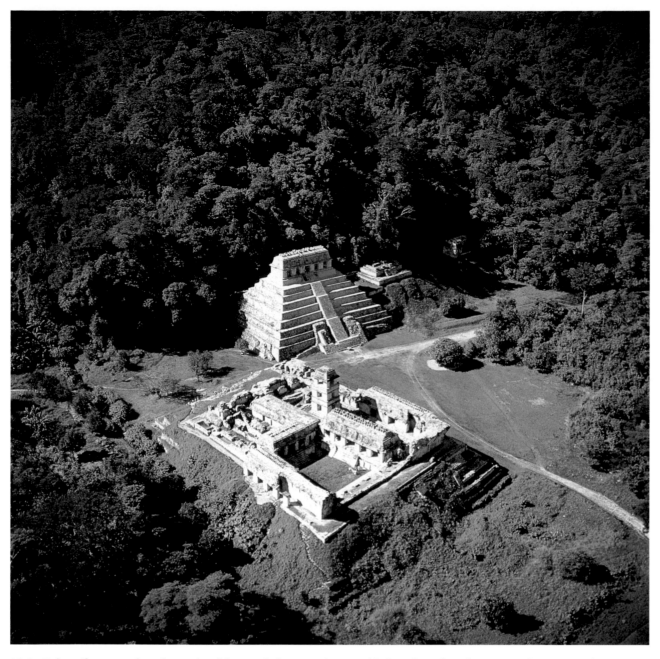

12-9.   Palace (foreground) and Temple of the Inscriptions (tomb-pyramid of Lord Pacal), Palenque, Mexico. Maya culture, 7th century CE

houses the Maya still build in parts of the Yucatan today. The only entrance to the temple was on the long side, facing the plaza and the commemorative stelae erected there. The crest that rises over the roof of the temple, known as a **roof comb**, was originally covered with brightly painted sculpture.

Palenque, located in the Mexican state of Chiapas, rose to prominence in the late Classic period. Hieroglyphic inscriptions record the beginning of its royal dynasty in 431 CE, but the city had only limited regional importance until the ascension of a powerful ruler, Lord Pacal (Maya for "shield"), who ruled from 615 to 683 CE. He and the son who succeeded him commissioned most of the structures visible at Palenque today. As at Tikal, major buildings are grouped on high ground. A northern complex has five temples, two nearby adjacent temples,

and a ball court. A central group includes the so-called Palace, the Temple of the Inscriptions, and two other temples (fig. 12-9). A third group of temples lies to the southeast.

The palace in the central group—a series of buildings on two levels around three open courts, all on a raised terrace—may have been an administrative rather than a residential complex. The Temple of the Inscriptions next to it is a pyramid that rises to a height of about 75 feet. Like Temple I at Tikal, it has nine levels. The shrine on the summit consisted of a portico with five entrances and a three-part, vaulted inner chamber surmounted by a tall roof comb. Its facade still retains much of its stucco sculpture. The inscriptions that give the building its name were carved on the back wall of the portico and the central inner chamber.

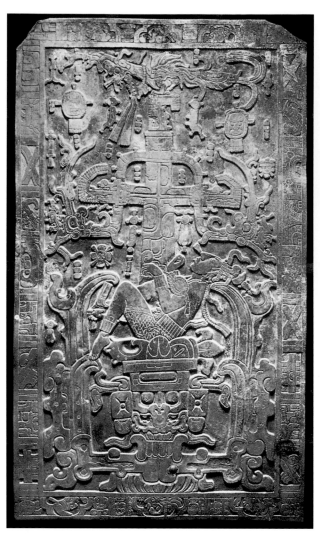

12-10. Sarcophagus lid, in the tomb of Lord Pacal, Temple of the Inscriptions, Palenque, Mexico. Maya culture. c. 683 CE. Limestone, approx. 12'6" x 7' (3.8 x 2.14 m)

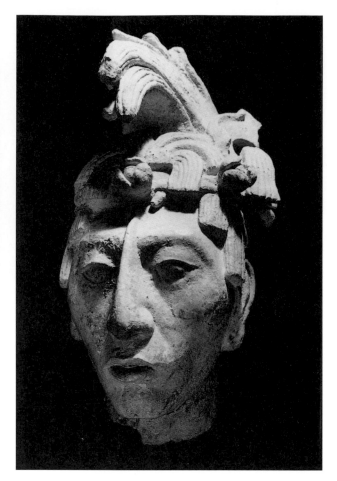

12-11. Portrait of Lord Pacal, from his tomb, Temple of the Inscriptions. Mid-7th century CE. Stucco, height 16⅞" (43 cm). Museo Nacional de Antropología, Mexico City

This portrait of the youthful Lord Pacal may have been placed in his tomb as an offering. Possibly it formed part of the original exterior decoration of the Temple of the Inscriptions.

In 1952 an archeologist studying the structure of the Temple of the Inscriptions discovered a corbel-vaulted stairway beneath the summit shrine. This stairway descended almost 80 feet to a small subterranean chamber that contained the undisturbed tomb of Lord Pacal himself, and in it were some remarkable examples of Classic sculpture.

Classic Period Sculpture. Lord Pacal lay in a monolithic sarcophagus with a lid carved in low relief that showed him balanced between the spirit world and the earth (fig. 12-10). With knees bent, feet twisted, and face, hands, and torso upraised, he lies on the head of a creature that represents the setting sun. Together they are falling into the jaws of the underworld. The image above him, which ends in the profile head of a god and a fantastic bird, represents the sacred tree of the Maya. Its roots are in the earth, its trunk is in the world, and its branches support the celestial bird in the heavens. The message is one of death and rebirth. Lord Pacal, like the setting sun, will rise again to join the gods after falling into the underworld. Lord Pacal's ancestors, carved on the side of his sarcophagus, witness his death and **apotheosis**. They wear elaborate headdresses and are shown only from the waist up, as though emerging from the earth. Among them are Lord Pacal's parents, Lady White Quetzal and Lord Yellow Jaguar-Parrot, supporting the contention of some scholars that both maternal and paternal lines transmitted royal power among the Maya.

Elite men and women, rather than gods, were the usual subjects of Maya sculpture, and most show rulers dressed as warriors performing religious rituals in elaborate costumes and headdresses. The Maya favored low-relief carving with sharp outlines on flat stone surfaces, but they also excelled at three-dimensional clay and stucco sculpture. A stucco portrait of Lord Pacal found with his sarcophagus shows him as a young man wearing a diadem of jade and flowers (fig. 12-11). His features—sloping forehead and elongated skull (babies had their heads bound to produce this shape), large curved nose (enhanced by an ornamental bridge, perhaps of latex), full lips, and open mouth—are characteristic of the Maya ideal of beauty. Traces of pigment indicate that this portrait, like much Maya sculpture, was colorfully painted.

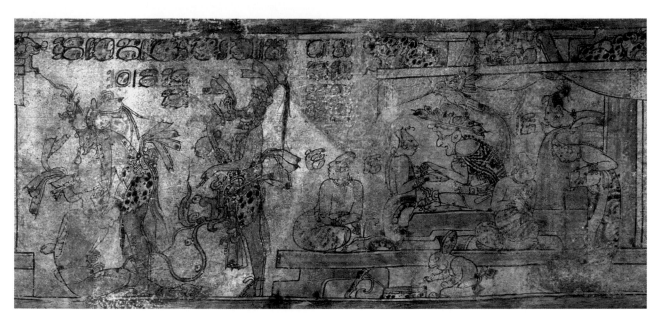

12-12. Cylindrical vessel (composite photograph in the form of a roll-out). Maya culture, 600–900 CE. Painted ceramic; diameter 6½" (16.6 cm); height 8³⁄₈" (21.5 cm). The Art Museum, Princeton University, New Jersey

The clay vessel was first covered by a creamy white slip and then painted in light brown washes and dark brown or black lines. The painter may have used turkey feathers to apply the pigments.

Classic Period Painting. Maya painting survives on ceramics and a few large murals. Most illustrated books have perished except for a few postconquest examples with astronomical and divinatory information. Scribes and vase painters were often members of the ruling elite and perhaps included members of the royal family not in the direct line of succession. Vases painted in the so-called **codex style**, referring to books of folded paper made from the maguey plant, often show a fluid line and elegance similar to that of the manuscripts.

A late Classic cylindrical vase in the codex style (fig. 12-12) may illustrate an episode from a legend recounted in the Book of Popol Vuh, a compendium of Maya myths written in Spanish in the sixteenth century by a Maya noble. The protagonists of this legend, the mythical Hero Twins, defeat the Lords of Xibalba, the Maya underworld, and overcome death. The vessel shows one of the Lords of Xibalba, an aged-looking being known to archeologists as God L, sitting inside a temple on a raised platform. Five female deities attend him. The god ties a wrist cuff on the attendant kneeling to his left. Another attendant, seated outside the temple, looks over her shoulder at a scene in which two men sacrifice a bound victim. A rabbit in the foreground writes in a manuscript, reminding us of the Maya obsession with historical records, as well as of the many books now lost. The two men may be the Hero Twins and the bound victim a bystander they sacrificed and then brought back to life in order to gain the confidence of the Xibalban lords. The inscriptions on the vessel have not been entirely translated. They include a calendar reference to the Death God and to Venus, the evening star, which the Maya associated with war and sacrifice.

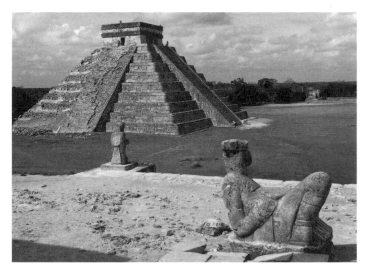

12-13. Castillo, with Chacmool in foreground, Chichen Itza, Yucatan, Mexico. Maya culture, 9th–13th century

Postclassic Art. A northern Maya group called the Itza rose to prominence when the focus of Maya civilization shifted northward in the Postclassic period. Their principal center, Chichen Itza, which means "at the mouth of the well of the Itza," grew from a village located near a sacred well. The city flourished from the ninth to the thirteenth century CE, eventually covering about 6 square miles. It shares many features with the site of Tula in central Mexico, but archeologists are uncertain what relationship the two centers had to each other.

One of Chichen Itza's most conspicuous structures is a massive pyramid in the center of a large plaza (fig. 12-13). Embellished with figures of the Feathered Serpent, this structure is known today as the Castillo (Spanish for "castle"). A stairway on each side leads to a square, blocky temple on its summit. At the spring and fall equinoxes, the rising sun casts an undulating, serpentlike shadow on the stairway balustrades. Like earlier Maya pyramids, the Castillo has nine levels, but many other features of Chichen Itza are markedly different from earlier sites. The Castillo, for example, is lower and broader than the stepped pyramids of Tikal and Palenque, and Chichen Itza's buildings have wider rooms. Another prominent feature not found at earlier sites is the use of pillars and columns. Chichen Itza has broad, open galleries surrounding courtyards and inventive columns in the form of inverted, descending serpents. Brilliantly colored relief sculpture covered the buildings of Chichen Itza, and paintings of feathered serpents, jaguars, coyotes, eagles, and composite mythological creatures adorned its interior rooms. The surviving works show narrative scenes that emphasize the prowess of warriors and the skill of ritual ball players.

Sculpture at Chichen Itza, including the serpent columns and the half-reclining figures known as **Chacmools** (see fig. 12-13), has the sturdy forms, proportions, and angularity of architecture. It lacks the curving forms and subtlety of Classic Maya sculpture. The Chacmools probably represent fallen warriors and were used to receive sacrificial offerings. They once typified pre-Columbian sculpture for many Westerners.

After Chichen Itza's decline, Mayapan, on the north coast of the Yucatan, became the principal Maya center. But by the time the Spanish arrived, Mayapan, too, had declined. The Maya people and much of their culture would survive the conquest despite the imposition of Hispanic customs and beliefs. They continue to speak their own languages, to venerate traditional sacred places, and to follow traditional ways.

CENTRAL AMERICA

Unlike their neighbors in Mesoamerica, who lived in complex hierarchical societies, the people of Central America generally lived in extended family groups led by chiefs. A notable example of these small chiefdoms was the Diquis culture, which developed in present-day Costa Rica from about 700 CE to about 1500.

The Diquis occupied fortified villages without monumental architecture or sculpture and seem to have engaged in constant warfare with one another. They nevertheless produced fine featherwork, ceramics, textiles, and gold objects. (The name Costa Rica, which means "rich coast" in Spanish, probably reflects the value the Spaniards placed on the gold.)

Metallurgy and the use of gold and copper-gold alloys were widespread in Central America. The technique of **lost-wax casting** probably first appeared in present-day Colombia between 500 and 300 BCE. From there it spread north to the Diquis. The small, exquisite pendant shown in figure 12-14 illustrates the sophisticated design and technical facility of Diquis goldwork. The pendant depicts a male figure wearing bracelets, anklets, and a belt with a snake-headed penis sheath. He plays a drum while holding the tail of a snake in his teeth and its head in his left hand. The wavy forms with ser-

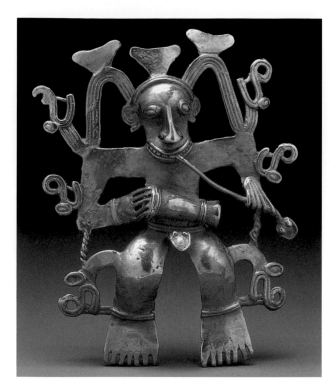

12-14. *Shaman with Drum and Snake*, from Costa Rica. Diquis culture, c. 1000 CE. Gold, 4¼ x 3¼"(10.8 x 8.2 cm). Museos del Banco Central de Costa Rica, San José, Costa Rica

pent heads emerging from his scalp suggest an elaborate headdress, and the creatures emerging from his legs suggest some kind of reptile costume. The inverted triangles on the headdress probably represent birds' tails.

In Diquis mythology serpents and crocodiles inhabited a lower world, humans and birds a higher one. Their art depicts animals and insects as fierce and dangerous. Perhaps the man in the pendant is a shaman transforming himself into a composite serpent-bird or performing a ritual snake dance surrounded by serpents or crocodiles. The scrolls on the sides of his head may represent the shaman's power to hear and understand the speech of animals. Whatever its specific meaning, the pendant evokes a ritual of mediation between earthly and cosmic powers involving music, dance, and costume.

Whether gold figures of this kind were protective amulets or signs of high status, they were certainly more than personal adornment. Shamans and warriors wore gold to inspire fear, perhaps because gold was thought to capture the energy and power of the sun. This energy was also thought to allow shamans to leave their bodies and travel into cosmic realms.

SOUTH AMERICA: THE CENTRAL ANDES

Like Mesoamerica, the central Andes of South America—primarily present-day Peru and Bolivia—saw the development of complex hierarchical societies with rich and varied artistic traditions. The area is one of dramatic contrasts. The narrow coastal plain, bordered by the Pacific Ocean on the west and the abruptly soaring Andes on the east, is one of the driest deserts in the world. Life here depends on the rich marine

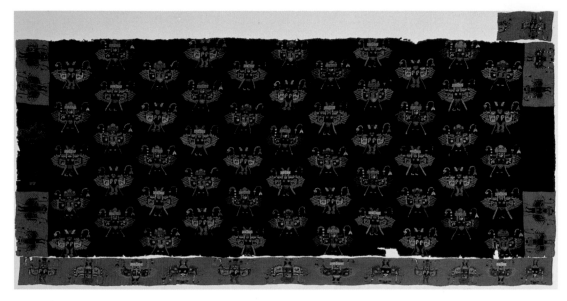

12-15. Mantle with bird impersonators, from the Paracas peninsula south coast, Peru. Paracas culture, c. 50–100 CE. Plain weave with stem-stitch embroidery, approx. 40" x 7'11" (101 cm x 2.41 m). Museum of Fine Arts, Boston
Denman Waldo Ross Collection

The stylized figures display the remarkable Paracas sense of color and pattern. The all-directional pattern is also characteristic of Paracas art.

resources of the Pacific and the rivers that descend from the Andes, forming a series of valley oases from south to north. The Andes themselves are a region of lofty snow-capped peaks, high grasslands, steep slopes, and deep, fertile river valleys. The high grasslands are home to the Andean camelids—llamas, alpacas, vicuñas, and guanacos—that have served for thousands of years as beasts of burden and a source of wool and meat. The lush eastern slopes of the Andes descend to the tropical rain forest of the Amazon basin.

The earliest evidence of monumental architecture in Peru dates to the third millennium BCE, contemporary with the earliest pyramids in Egypt. On the coast, sites with ceremonial mounds and plazas were located near the sea. The inhabitants of these centers depended on marine and agricultural resources, farming the floodplains of nearby coastal rivers. Their chief crops were cotton, used to make fishing nets, and gourds, used for floats. Early centers in the highlands consisted of multi-roomed stone-walled structures with sunken central fire pits that served to burn ritual offerings.

In the second millennium BCE, herding and agriculture became prevalent in the highlands. On the coast, people became increasingly dependent on agriculture. They began to build canal irrigation systems, greatly expanding their food supply. Settlements were moved inland, and large, U-shaped ceremonial complexes with circular sunken plazas were built. These complexes were oriented toward the mountains, the direction of the rising sun and the source of the water that nourished their crops. The shift to irrigation agriculture also corresponded to the spread of pottery and ceramic technology in Peru.

Between about 800 and 200 BCE an art style associated with the northern highland site of Chavin de Huantar spread through much of the Andes. In Andean chronology, this era is known as the Early Horizon, the first of three so-called Horizon periods marked by the widespread influence of a single style.

The Chavin site was located on a major trade route between the coast and the Amazon basin, and Chavin art features images of many tropical forest animals. The political and social forces behind the spread of the Chavin style are not known. Many archeologists suspect that they involved an influential religious cult. In any event, the period was one of artistic and technical innovation in ceramics, metallurgy, and textiles. These innovations found continued expression in the textiles of the Paracas culture on the south coast of Peru, the art of the subsequent Nazca culture there, and the ceramics and metalwork of the Moche culture on the north coast.

The Paracas and Nazca Cultures

The Paracas culture of the south coast flourished from about 300 BCE to 200 CE, overlapping with the Chavin period. It is best known for its stunning textiles, which were found in cemeteries wrapped in many layers around the dead. Some bodies were wrapped in as many as fifty pieces of cloth.

Weaving is of great antiquity in the central Andes and continues to be among the most prized arts in the region (see "Andean Textiles," page 458). Fine textiles were a source of prestige and wealth, and the production of textiles was an important factor in the domestication of both cotton and llamas. Andean peoples developed a simple, portable **backstrap loom** in which the **warp** (lengthwise thread) was looped and stretched between two poles. One pole was tied to a stationary object and the other to a strap circling the waist of the weaver. The weaver controlled the tension of the warp threads by leaning back and forth while threading a **bobbin**, or shuttle, through the warp to create the **weft** (crosswise thread).

The designs on Paracas textiles include repeated **embroidered** (needlework) figures of warriors, dancers, and composite creatures such as bird-people (fig. 12-15). Embroiderers used tiny overlapping stitches to create

ANDEAN TEXTILES The creation of ancient Andean textiles, among the most technically complex cloths ever made, consumed a major portion of their societies' resources. Dyers, weavers, and **embroiderers** used nearly every textile technique known, some of them unique inventions of these cultures, and the production of a single textile might involve a dozen processes requiring highly skilled workers. A tunic would have taken approximately 500 hours of work. Some of the most elaborate textiles were woven, unwoven, and rewoven to achieve special effects that were prized for their labor-intensiveness and difficulty of manufacture as well as their beauty. The most finely woven pieces contain a staggering 500 threads per square inch. Because of their complexity, deciphering how these textiles were made can be a challenge, and scholars rely on contemporary Andean weavers—inheritors of this tradition—for guidance. Then, as now, textile production was primarily in the hands of women.

Cotton was grown in Peru by 3000 BCE and was the most widely used plant fiber. The earliest Peruvian textiles were made without looms, and twining, knotting, wrapping, braiding, and looping continued to be used even after looms were invented in the early second millennium BCE. **Tapestry**-weaving (see below) was the main cloth-making technique for the next thousand or so years, followed by the introduction of embroidery on camelid fibers (llama, alpaca, or vicuña hair), the Andean equivalent of wool. (Embroidery on camelid fiber is seen in the Paracas mantle in figure 12-15.) From about 400 BCE on, animal fibers—superior in warmth and dye absorption—largely replaced cotton in the mountains, where cotton was hard to cultivate.

In tapestry, a technique especially suited to representational textiles, an undyed cotton **warp** was frequently combined with a vividly colored camelid-fiber **weft** that completely covered it. Each colored section was woven as an independent unit (see illustration). Since the shuttle was not passed across the entire width of the fabric in one motion, as in other kinds of weaving, tapestry allowed greater pictorial freedom but was quite time-consuming.

Fabrics were colored with dyes made from plants and a few animals. The deep blue of the Paracas mantle, for instance, was probably derived from the indigo plant. Dyeing technology, too, was an advanced art form in the ancient Andes, with some textiles containing dozens of colors.

Textiles were of enormous importance in Andean life, serving significant functions in both private and public events. Specialized fabrics were developed for everything from ritual burial shrouds and shamans' costumes to rope bridges and knotted record-keeping devices. Clothing indicated ethnic group and social status and was customized for certain functions, the most rarefied being royal ceremonial garments made for specific occasions and worn only once.

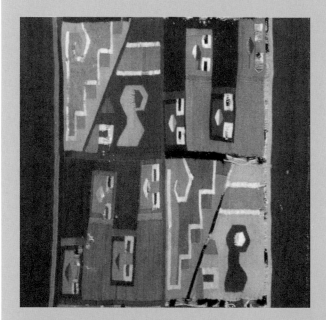

Detail of tapestry-weave mantle, from Peru. c. 700–1100 CE. Wool and cotton. The Cleveland Museum of Art
Gift of William R. Carlisle, 56.84

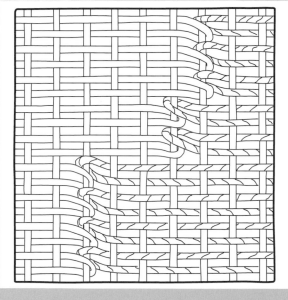

Diagram of toothed tapestry-weaving technique, one of many sophisticated methods used in Andean textiles

colorful, curvilinear patterns, sometimes using as many as twenty-two different colors within a single figure. The effect of the clashing and contrasting colors and tumbling figures is dazzling.

The Nazca culture, which dominated the south coast of Peru from about 100 BCE to 700 CE, overlapped the Paracas culture. Nazca artisans continued to weave fine fabrics, but they also produced multicolored pottery with painted and modeled images reminiscent of those on Paracas textiles.

The Nazca are probably best known for their colossal earthworks, or **geoglyphs**, which dwarf even the most ambitious twentieth-century environmental sculpture. On great stretches of desert they literally drew in the earth. By removing a layer of dark gravel, they exposed the lighter underlying soil, then edged the resulting lines

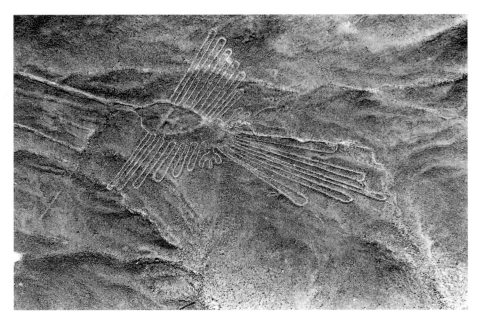

12-16. Earth drawing of a hummingbird, Nazca Plain, southwest Peru. Nazca culture, c. 200 BCE–200 CE. Length approx. 450' (138 m); wingspan approx. 200' (60.5 m)

with stones. In this way they created gigantic images—including a hummingbird, a killer whale, a monkey, a spider, a duck, and other birds—similar to those with which they decorated their pottery. They also made abstract patterns and groups of straight, parallel lines that extend for up to 12 miles. The beak of the hummingbird in figure 12-16 consists of two parallel lines, each 120 feet long. The purpose of these geoglyphs is not known.

The Moche Culture

The Moche culture dominated the north coast of Peru from the Piura Valley to the Huarmey Valley—a distance of some 370 miles—between about 200 and 700 CE. Moche lords ruled each valley in this region from a ceremonial-administrative center. The largest of these, in the Moche Valley (from which the culture takes its name), contained the so-called Pyramids of the Sun and the Moon. Both pyramids were built entirely of **adobe** bricks. The Pyramid of the Sun, the largest ancient structure in South America, was originally a cross-shaped structure 1,122 feet long by 522 feet wide that rose in a series of terraces to a height of 59 feet. This site had been thought to be the capital of the entire Moche realm, but evidence is accumulating that the Moche were not so centralized.

The Moche were exceptional potters and metalsmiths. They developed ceramic molds, which allowed them to mass-produce some forms. Vessels were made in the shape of naturalistically modeled human beings, animals, and architectural structures. They also created realistic portrait vessels and recorded mythological narratives and ritual scenes in intricate fine-line painting. Similar scenes were painted on the walls of temples and administrative buildings. Moche smiths, the most sophisticated in the central Andes, developed several innovative alloys.

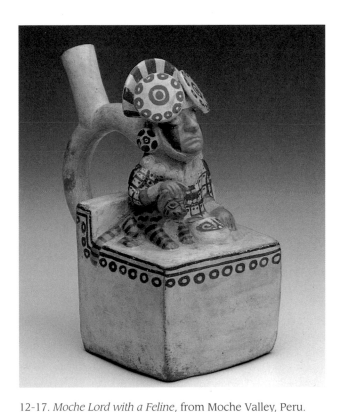

12-17. *Moche Lord with a Feline*, from Moche Valley, Peru. Moche culture, c. 100 BCE–500 CE. Painted ceramic, height 7½" (19 cm). Art Institute of Chicago
Buckingham Fund, 1955–2281
Behind the figure is the distinctive stirrup-shaped handle and spout. Vessels of this kind, used in Moche rituals, were also treasured as special luxury items and were buried in large quantities with individuals of high status.

The ceramic vessel in figure 12-17 shows a Moche lord sitting in a structure associated with high office. He wears an elaborate headdress and large earspools and strokes a cat or perhaps a jaguar cub. The so-called

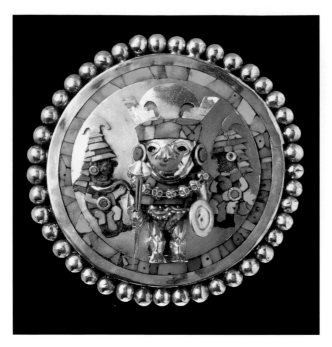

12-18. Earspool, from Sipan, Peru. Moche culture, c. 300 CE. Gold, turquoise, quartz, and shell, diameter approx. 5" (12.7 cm). Bruning Archeological Museum, Lambayeque, Peru

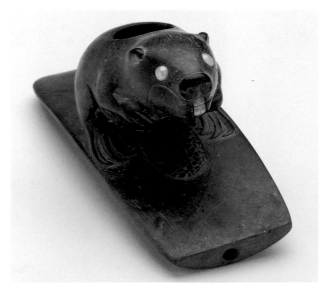

12-19. Beaver effigy platform pipe, from Bedford Mound, Pike County, Illinois. Hopewell culture, c. 100–200 CE. Pipestone, pearl, and bone, length 4¹/₂" (11.4 cm). Gilcrease Museum, Tulsa, Oklahoma

Pipes made by the Hopewell culture may have been used for smoking hallucinatory plants, perhaps during rituals involving the animal carved on the pipe bowl.

stirrup, or **U**-shaped, spout appears on many high-quality Moche vessels. Paintings indicate that vessels of this type were used in Moche rituals.

A central theme in Moche iconography is the sacrifice ceremony, in which prisoners captured in battle are sacrificed and several elaborately dressed figures drink their blood. Archeologists have labeled the principal figure in the ceremony as the Warrior Priest and other important figures as the Bird Priest and the Priestess. The recent discovery of a number of spectacularly rich Moche tombs indicates that the sacrifice ceremony was an actual Moche ritual and that Moche lords assumed the roles of the principal figures. The occupant of a tomb at the site of Sipan in the Lambayeque Valley was buried with the regalia of the Warrior Priest. In a tomb at the site of San José de Moro in the Jequetepeque Valley, an occupant was buried with the regalia of the Priestess.

Among the riches accompanying the Warrior Priest at Sipan was a pair of exquisite gold-and-turquoise earspools, each of which depicts three Moche warriors (fig. 12-18). The central figure is made of beaten gold and turquoise. He and his companions are adorned with tiny gold-and-turquoise earspools. They wear spectacular gold-and-turquoise headdresses topped with delicate sheets of gold that resemble the crescent-shaped knives used in sacrifices. The crests, like feathered fans of gold, would have swayed in the breeze as the wearer moved. The central figure has a crescent-shaped nose ornament and carries a gold club and shield. A necklace of owl's-head beads strung with gold thread hangs around his shoulders. Many of his anatomical features have been rendered in painstaking detail.

NORTH AMERICA

Compared to the densely inhabited agricultural regions of Mesoamerica and South America, most of North America remained sparsely populated until the arrival of European conquerors in the fifteenth century. People lived primarily by hunting, fishing, and gathering edible plants. In the Southeast, in the lands drained by the Mississippi and Missouri river system, a more settled way of life began to emerge, and by around 1000 BCE—in Louisiana as early as 2800 BCE, according to some anthropologists—nomadic hunting and gathering had given way to more settled communities. People cultivated squash, sunflowers, and other plants to supplement their diet of game, fish, and berries. People in the American Southwest began to adopt a sedentary, agricultural life toward the end of the first millennium BCE.

The Mound Builders

Sometime before 1000 BCE, people living in the Mississippi River Valley began building monumental earthworks and burying their leaders with valuable grave goods. The earliest of these earthworks, at Poverty Point in Louisiana, dates to about 1300 BCE. One of the most impressive is the Great Serpent Mound in present-day Adams County, Ohio (see fig. 12-1). Its date is unknown, but it is located near a burial mound of the Adena culture (600 BCE–200 CE). There have been many interpretations of the writhing snake form, especially the "head" at the highest point, which some see as opening its jaws to swallow a huge egg formed by a heap of stones.

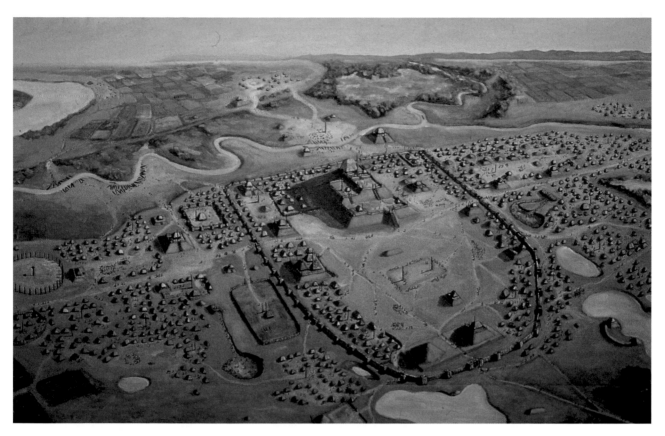

12-20. Reconstruction of central Cahokia, East St. Louis, Illinois. Mississippian culture, c. 1150 CE. Earth mounds and wooden structures; east-west length approx. 3 miles (4.5 km), north-south length approx. 2¼ miles (3.6 km); base of great mound, 1,037 x 790' (316 x 241 m), height approx. 100' (30 m). Painting by William R. Iseminger

The people of the Mississippi and Ohio valleys traded widely with other regions. For example, burials of the Adena culture and another mound-building culture, the Hopewell (centered in the Illinois and Ohio valleys, 200 BCE–200 CE), contained jewelry made with copper from Michigan's upper peninsula and silhouettes cut in sheets of mica from the Appalachian Mountains. The Hopewell people also made pipes of fine-grain pipestone carved with realistic representations of forest animals and birds, sometimes with inlaid eyes and teeth of freshwater pearls and bone. The Hopewell exchanged this pipestone and a flintlike stone used for tool-making for turtle shells and sharks' teeth from Florida. Hopewell pipes and pipestone have been found from Lake Superior to the Gulf of Mexico.

In a combination of realism and aesthetic simplification that is exceptionally sophisticated, a beaver crouching on a platform forms the bowl of a pipe found in Illinois (fig. 12-19). As in a modern pipe, the bowl—a hole in the beaver's back—could be filled with dried leaves (the Hopewell may not have grown tobacco), the leaves lighted, and smoke drawn through the hole in the stem. A second way that these pipes were used was to blow smoke inhaled from another vessel through the pipe to envelop the animal carved on it.

The people of the Mississippian culture (800–1500 CE) continued the mound-building tradition of the earlier southeastern cultures. Cahokia, 16 miles northeast of St. Louis near the juncture of the Illinois, Missouri, and Mis-

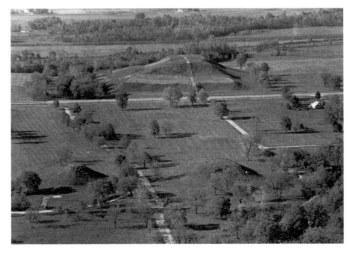

12-21. Cahokia

sissippi rivers (now East St. Louis, Illinois), was an urban center that at its height had a population of between 10,000 and 20,000 people, with another 10,000 in the surrounding countryside (figs. 12-20, 12-21). The site's most prominent feature is an enormous earth mound covering 15 acres. The location of the mound and the axis of the ceremonial center it dominated were established during the early part of the city's occupation (c. 900–1050 CE), but most construction occurred later, between about 1050 and 1250. A **stockade**, or fence, of upright wooden posts—a sign of increasing warfare—surrounded the

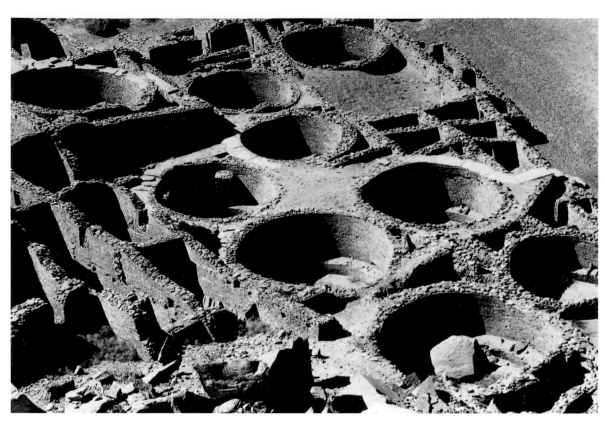

12-22. Pueblo Bonito, Chaco Canyon, New Mexico. Anasazi culture, c. 900–1250 CE

250-acre core. Within this barrier the principal mound rose in four stages to a height of about 100 feet. On its summit was a small, conical platform that supported a wood fence and a rectangular temple or house. Smaller rectangular and conical mounds in front of the principal mound surrounded a large, roughly rectangular plaza. In all, the walled enclosure contained more than 500 mounds, platforms, wooden enclosures, and houses. The various earthworks functioned as tombs and as bases for palaces and temples. A conical burial mound, for example, was located next to a platform that may have been used for sacrifices.

Postholes indicate that wooden **henges** were a feature of Cahokia. The largest, with a diameter of about 420 feet, had forty-eight posts and was oriented to the cardinal points. Sight lines between a forty-ninth post set east of the center of the enclosure and points on the perimeter enabled native astronomers to determine solstices and equinoxes.

The American Southwest

Three farming cultures emerged in the arid southwestern region of what is now the United States beginning around 200 BCE. The Mogollon culture, located in the mountains of west-central New Mexico and east-central Arizona, flourished from circa 200 BCE to about 1250 CE. The Hohokam culture, centered in central and southern Arizona, emerged around 200 BCE and endured until after about 1200 CE. The Hohokam built large-scale irrigation systems with canals that were deep and narrow to reduce evaporation and lined with clay to reduce seepage. The Hohokam shared a number of customs with their Mesoamerican neighbors to the south, including the ritual ball game.

The third southwestern culture, the Anasazi (Navajo word meaning "the ancient ones"), emerged in the Four Corners region, where Colorado, Utah, Arizona, and New Mexico meet. The Anasazi, who adopted the irrigation technology of the Hohokam, turned to an agricultural, village way of life somewhat later than the other two groups. Around 750 CE they began building elaborate, multistoried, apartmentlike structures with many rooms for specialized purposes, including communal food storage. The Spaniards called these communities pueblos, or "towns." The descendants of the Anasazi, including the Hopi and Zuni, still occupy similar communities in the Four Corners area.

The largest known ancient Anasazi center is Pueblo Bonito in Chaco Canyon, which was built in stages between the tenth and mid-thirteenth centuries CE (fig. 12-22). In its final form this remarkable, **D**-shaped structure had hundreds of rooms and rose four stories high. Its outer perimeter wall was 1,300 feet long. The sandstone masonry walls on the ground floor were 4 feet thick, and trunks of ponderosa pines were used for roof beams. As new rooms were added over time, older rooms lost access to natural light. Amazingly, all aspects

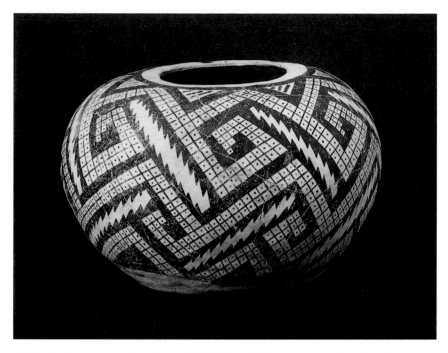

12-23. Seed jar. Anasazi culture, 1100–1300 CE. Earthenware and black and white pigment, diameter 14½" (36.9 cm). The St. Louis Art Museum, St. Louis, Missouri

Purchase: Funds given by the Children's Art Festival 175:1981

of construction—including quarrying, timber cutting, and transport—were done without draft animals, wheeled vehicles, or metal tools.

Securing a steady food supply in the arid Southwest must have been a constant concern for the people of Chaco Canyon. At Pueblo Bonito the number of rooms far exceeds the evidence of human habitation, and many rooms were almost certainly devoted to food storage. Pueblo Bonito also has more than thirty **kivas**, which were centers of community ritual among pueblo dwellers. The presence of so many of them at Pueblo Bonito—including two that are more than 60 feet in diameter—attests to the importance of ritual at this site. The top of these circular, underground rooms became part of the floor of the communal plaza. Interlocking pine logs formed a shallow, domelike roof with a hole in the center through which only men would have entered. A pit in the floor directly under the entrance hole symbolized the place where the Anasazi ancestors had emerged from the earth in the mythic "first times." Here men performed important rituals and instructed youths in their adult ritual and social responsibilities.

Pueblo Bonito stood at the center of a network of wide, straight roads, in some places with curbs and paving. Almost invisible today, the roads were discovered and studied through aerial photography. The major roads run north and south in perfectly straight lines. The builders made no effort to avoid topographic obstacles;

when they encountered cliffs, they ran stairs up them. These characteristics suggest that the roads served as processional ways rather than practical thoroughfares.

Probably as a result of a climate change that made the Southwest increasingly arid, the population of Chaco Canyon declined during the twelfth century, and building at Pueblo Bonito ceased around 1230.

Women were the potters in Anasazi society. In the eleventh century they perfected a functional, aesthetically pleasing, coil-built earthenware, or low-fired ceramic. This ceramic tradition continues today among the Pueblo peoples of the Southwest. One type of vessel, a widemouthed seed jar with a globular body and holes near the rim (fig. 12-23), would have been suspended from roof poles, by thongs attached to the holes, out of reach of voracious rodents. The example shown here is decorated with black-and-white checkerboard and zigzag patterns. The patterns conform to the body of the jar, and in spite of their angularity, they enhance its curved shape. The intricate play of dark and light, positive and negative, suggests lightning flashing over a grid of irrigated fields.

Throughout the Americas for the next several hundred years, artistic traditions would continue to emerge, develop, and be transformed as the indigenous peoples of various regions interacted. The sudden incursions of Europeans, beginning in the late fifteenth century, would have dramatic and lasting impact on these civilizations and their art.

2500 BCE   1800   1200   600

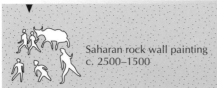

Saharan rock wall painting
c. 2500–1500

Nok head
c. 500 BCE–200 CE

▲ SAHARAN ROCK ART c. 8000–500

NOK
▲ c. 500 BCE–200 C

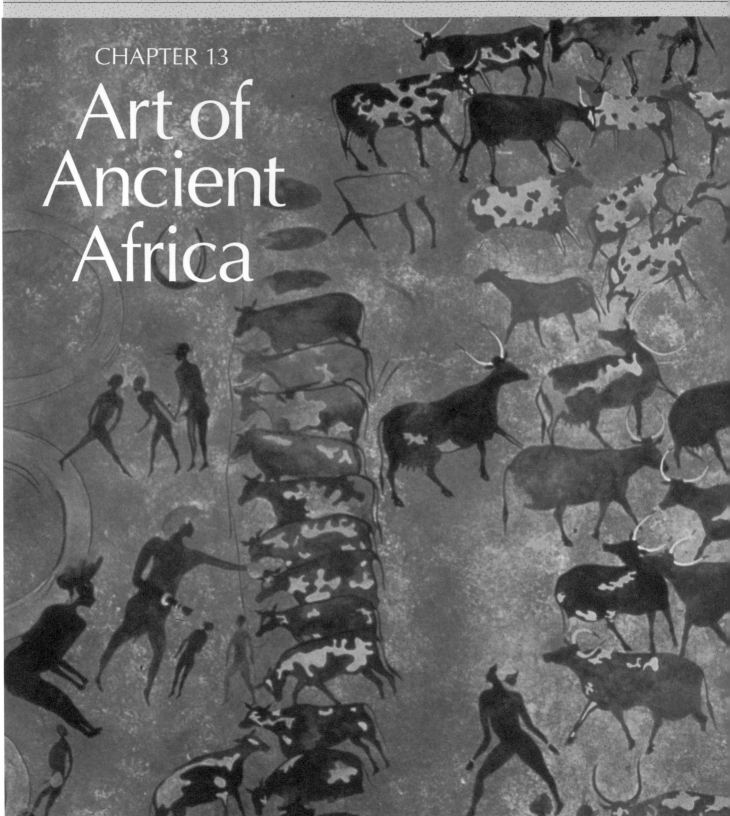

CHAPTER 13

Art of Ancient Africa

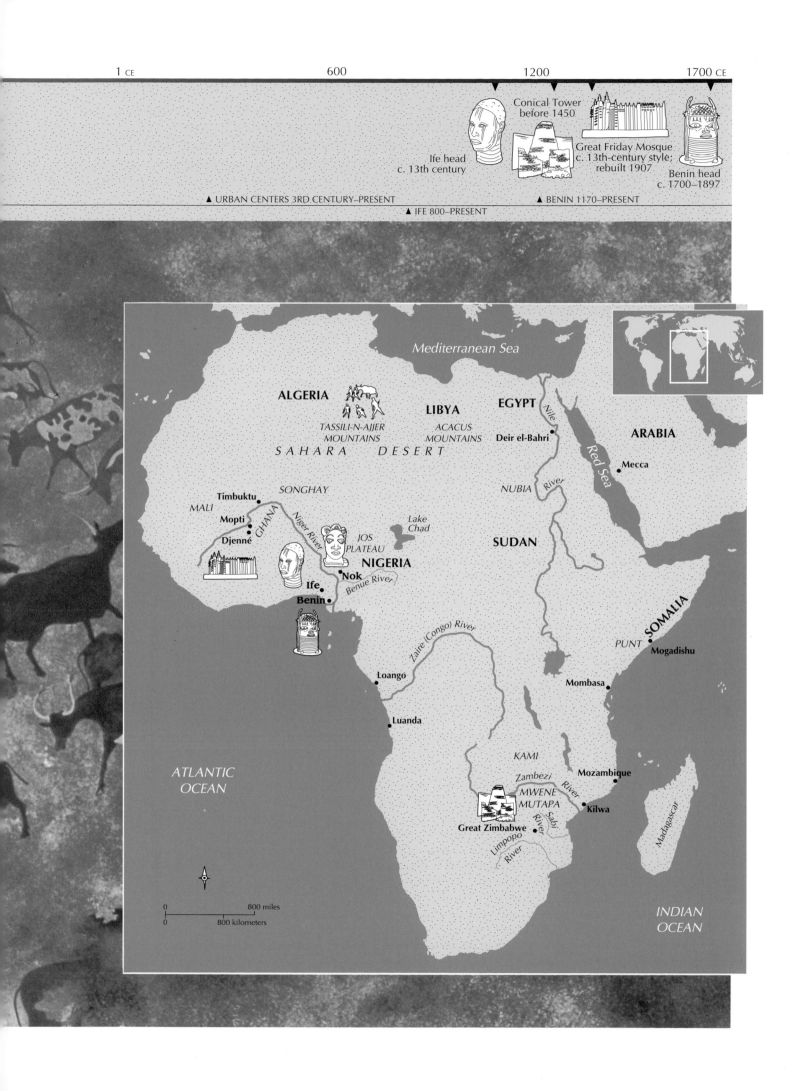

Conical Tower
before 1450

Ife head
c. 13th century

Great Friday Mosque
c. 13th-century style;
rebuilt 1907

Benin head
c. 1700–1897

▲ URBAN CENTERS 3RD CENTURY–PRESENT   ▲ BENIN 1170–PRESENT

▲ IFE 800–PRESENT

Mediterranean Sea

ALGERIA

LIBYA

EGYPT

ARABIA

TASSILI-N-AJJER
MOUNTAINS

ACACUS
MOUNTAINS

Deir el-Bahri

Nile

Red Sea

Mecca

S A H A R A   D E S E R T

NUBIA

River

SONGHAY

Timbuktu

MALI

Mopti

GHANA

Djenné

Niger River

Lake
Chad

JOS
PLATEAU

NIGERIA

Nok

SUDAN

Benue River

Ife

Benin

Zaire (Congo) River

SOMALIA

PUNT

Mogadishu

Loango

Mombasa

ATLANTIC
OCEAN

Luanda

KAMI

Mozambique

Zambezi

River

MWENE
MUTAPA

Kilwa

Great Zimbabwe

Sabi

River

Madagascar

Limpopo

River

INDIAN
OCEAN

0   800 miles

0   800 kilometers

descended [the Nile] with three hundred asses laden with incense, ebony, grain, panthers, ivory, and every good product." Thus the Egyptian envoy Harkhuf described his return from Nubia, the Black African land to the south of Egypt, in 2300 BCE. Some eight centuries after Harkhuf's journey, the Egyptian queen Hatshepsut, drawn by such treasures, ordered an expedition to the land of Punt, an African kingdom on the northern coast of present-day Somalia. So important was this kind of contact that portraits of the king and queen of Punt appear in Hatshepsut's funerary temple at Deir el-Bahri.

THE LURE OF ANCIENT AFRICA

The riches of Africa attracted merchants and envoys in ancient times, and through trade the continent was in contact with the rest of the world. Egyptian relations, such as Hatshepsut's with African kingdoms to the south, continued through the Hellenistic era and beyond. To the west, dozens of settlements were founded along the Mediterranean coast of North Africa between 1000 and 300 BCE by Phoenicians and Greeks so that they could extend trade routes across the Sahara to the peoples of Lake Chad and the bend of the Niger River. When the Romans took control of North Africa, they continued this lucrative trans-Saharan trade. In the seventh and eighth centuries CE, the expanding empire of Islam swept across North Africa, and thereafter Islamic merchants were regular visitors to Bilad al-Sudan, the Land of the Blacks. Islamic scholars chronicled the great West African empires of Ghana, Mali, and Songhay, and West African gold financed the flowering of Islamic culture.

East Africa, meanwhile, had been drawn since at least the beginning of the Common Era into the maritime trade that ringed the Indian Ocean and extended east to Indonesia and the South China Sea. Arab, Indian, and Persian ships plied the coastline. A new language, Swahili, evolved from centuries of contact between Arabic-speaking merchants and Bantu-speaking Africans, and great port cities such as Mozambique, Kilwa, Mombasa, and Mogadishu arose.

In the fifteenth century, European ships ventured into the Atlantic Ocean and down the coast of Africa. After being cut off for centuries because of hostile relations with Islam, Europeans were only then rediscovering the continent at first hand. What they found often astonished them. "Dear King My Brother," wrote a fifteenth-century Portuguese king to his new trading partner, the king of Benin in West Africa. The Portuguese king's respect was well founded—Benin was vastly more powerful and more wealthy than the small European country that had just stumbled upon it.

European presence, benign and respectful at first, became over the centuries increasingly aggressive and territorial, culminating with the imposition of colonial rule over the entire continent during the late nineteenth century. European colonization was a watershed for Africa, dividing its long history of relatively independent development and forcing its entry into a world not of its own making.

As we saw in Chapter 3, Africa was home to one of the world's earliest great civilizations, that of ancient Egypt, and as we saw in Chapter 8, Egypt and the rest of North Africa contributed prominently to the development of Islamic art and culture. This chapter examines the artistic legacy of the rest of ancient Africa, beginning with the early peoples of the Sahara, then turning to other early civilizations.

SAHARAN ROCK ART

Like the Paleolithic inhabitants of Europe, early Africans painted and inscribed an abundance of images on the walls of the caves and rock shelters in which they sought refuge. Rock art has been found all over Africa, in sites ranging from small, isolated shelters to great, cavernous formations. The mountains of the central Sahara—principally the Tassili-n-Ajjer range in the south of present-day Algeria and the Acacus Mountains in present-day Libya—have especially fascinating examples of rock art. The images there span a period of thousands of years, recording not only the artistic and cultural development of the peoples who lived in the region, but also the transformation of the Sahara from the fertile grassland it once was to the vast desert we know today.

The earliest images of Saharan rock art are thought to date from at least 8000 BCE, during the transition into a geological period known as the Makalian Wet Phase. At that time the Sahara was a great grassy plain, perhaps much like the game-park areas of modern East Africa. Vivid images of hippopotamus, elephant, giraffe, antelope, and other animals incised into rock surfaces testify to the abundant wildlife that roamed the region. Like the cave paintings in Altamira and Lascaux (Chapter 1), these images may have been intended as magic to ensure plentiful game or a successful hunt, or they may have been symbolic of other life-enhancing activities, such as healing or rainmaking.

By 4000 BCE the climate had become more arid, and hunting had given way to herding as the primary life-sustaining activity of the Sahara's inhabitants. Among the most beautiful and complex examples of Saharan rock art created in this period are scenes of sheep, goats, and cattle and of the daily lives of the people who tended them. One such scene, *The Herders' Village*, was found at Tassili-n-Ajjer and probably dates from late in the herding period, about 2500–1500 BCE (fig. 13-1). Men and women are gathered in front of their round, thatched houses, the men tending the cattle, the

PARALLELS

Years	Center	Africa	World
c. 8000–500 BCE	Sahara	Rock art; herding; settled agriculture; Great Pyramids at Giza; Sahara becoming desert; horse introduced; camel introduced; ironworking	**c. 8000–500 BCE** Bronze Age in Europe; plants and animals domesticated (Near East, Southeast Asia, the Americas); development of metallurgy (Near East); development of writing (Near East, China, India); Olmec civilization (Mesoamerica); birth of Laozi, founder of Daoism (China); birth of Siddhartha Gautama, founder of Buddhism (Nepal); Confucius (China)
c. 500 BCE–200 CE	Nok	First known sculpture; terracotta figures	**c. 500 BCE–1000 CE** Parthenon (Greece); crucifixion of Jesus (Jerusalem); Colosseum (Italy); Pantheon (Italy); first Gupta dynasty (India); earliest surviving Hindu temples (India); Hagia Sophia (Turkey); birth of Muhammad, founder of Islam (Arabia); Muslim conquests
c. 200–present	Djenné	Great Friday Mosque	
c. 800 CE–present	Ife	Terra-cotta sculpture; bronze sculpture	
c. 1000 CE–1500 CE	Great Zimbabwe	Stone structures; carvings	**c. 1000–1700 CE** Separation of Eastern and Western Christian Churches; the Crusades; Spanish Inquisition; beginning of Renaissance in Europe; Aztec civilization (Mexico); end of Byzantine Empire; Columbus's voyages; the Reformation; first English colony in North America
c. 1170 CE–present	Benin	Memorial sculpture; trade with Portuguese; Early, Middle, Late periods	

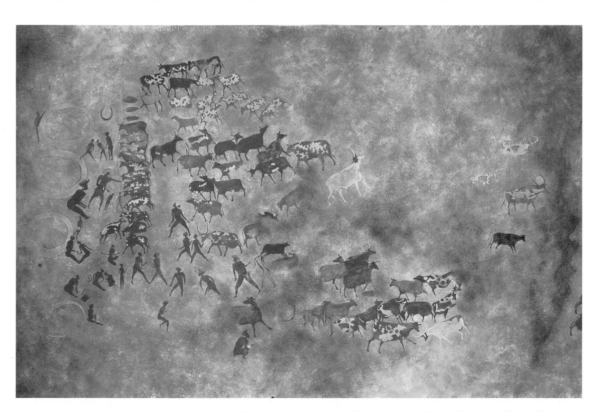

13-1. *Cattle Gathered next to a Group of Huts*, detail of *The Herders' Village*, rock-wall painting, Tassili-n-Ajjer, Algeria. c. 2500–1500 BCE. Watercolor facsimile painted by students of Henri Lhote. Musée de l'Homme, Paris

THE MYTH OF "PRIMITIVE" ART

The word *primitive* has often been used by Western art historians to lump together the art of Africa, the Pacific islands, and North, South, and Central America before the arrival of Columbus. The label implies, among other things, that all these areas are in some way similar cultures that produced similar art for similar reasons.

The term itself means "early," and its very use implies that these civilizations are frozen at an early stage of development, rather than that their cultures have developed along different paths than those of Europe. In the past, the criteria used for assigning the label *primitive* to a people included so-called Stone Age technology, absence of written histories, and failure to build "great" cities. Yet the accomplishments of the peoples of Africa, to take just one example, strongly belie this categorization: Africans south of the Sahara have smelted and forged iron since at least 500 BCE, as the evidence of the Nok culture in northern Nigeria makes quite clear, and Africans in many areas have long smelted high-quality steel for weapons and tools. Many African peoples have recorded their histories in Arabic since at least the tenth century. And the first European visitors to western Africa expressed their admiration for the political, economic, and social sophistication of such urban centers as Benin, Luanda, and Mbanza Kongo.

Why, then, have labels like *primitive* persisted? Many historical attitudes were formed by Christian missionaries, who long described the people among whom they worked as "heathen," "barbaric," "ignorant," "tribal," "primitive," and other terms rooted in racism and colonialism. As these usages were perpetuated, they were extended to the creations of the cultures, and *primitive art* became the dominant label for the cultural products of these peoples. If the illogical notion that technological development equals quality of art were in fact valid, then the art of twentieth-century Japan, for example, would be considered greater than the art of fifteenth-century Italy.

women preparing a meal and caring for children. A large herd of cattle, many of them tethered to a long rope, has been driven in from pasture. The cattle shown are quite varied. Some are mottled, others are white, red, or black. Some have short, thick horns, while others have graceful, lyre-shaped horns. The overlapping forms and the confident placement of near figures low and distant figures high in the picture create a sense of depth and distance.

By 2500–2000 BCE the Sahara had dried considerably and the great game had gone, but other animals were introduced that appear in the rock art. The horse was brought from Egypt by about 1500 BCE and is seen regularly in rock art over the ensuing millennia. The fifth-century BCE Greek historian Herodotus described a chariot-driving people called the Garamante, whose kingdom corresponded roughly to present-day Libya, and rock-art images of horse-drawn chariots bear out his account. Around 600 BCE the camel was introduced into the region from the east, and images of camels have been painted on and incised into the rock from then to now.

The desiccation of the Sahara coincides with the rise of Egyptian civilization along the Nile Valley to the east. Similarities have been noted between Egyptian and Saharan motifs, among them images of rams with what appear to be disks between their horns. These similarities have been viewed as evidence of Egyptian influence on the less-developed regions of the Sahara. Yet in light of the great age of Saharan rock art, it seems just as plausible that influence flowed the other way, carried by people who had migrated into the Nile Valley in search of arable land and pasture when the grasslands of the Sahara dried up. This migration, by greatly expanding the population of the valley, may also have contributed to the tensions that resulted in the emergence of complex forms of social organization there.

SUB-SAHARAN CIVILIZATIONS

Saharan peoples presumably migrated southward as well, into the Sudan, the broad belt of grassland that stretches across Africa south of the Sahara desert, bringing with them knowledge of settled agriculture and animal husbandry. The earliest evidence for settled agriculture in the Sudan dates from about 3000 BCE. Toward the middle of the first millennium BCE, at the same time that iron technology was being developed elsewhere in Africa, knowledge of ironworking spread across the Sudan, enabling its inhabitants to create more efficient weapons and farming tools. In the wake of these developments, larger and more complex societies emerged, especially in the fertile basins of Lake Chad in the central Sudan and the Niger and Senegal rivers to the west.

Nok Culture

Some of the earliest evidence of iron technology in sub-Saharan Africa comes from the so-called Nok culture, which arose in the western Sudan, in present-day Nigeria, as early as 500 BCE. The Nok people were farmers who grew grain and oil-bearing seeds, but they were also smelters with the technology for refining ore. Slag and the remains of furnaces have been discovered, along with clay nozzles from the bellows used to fan the fires. The Nok people created the earliest known sculpture of sub-Saharan Africa, producing accomplished **terra-cotta** figures of human and animal subjects between about 500 BCE and 200 CE.

Nok sculpture was discovered in modern times by tin miners digging in the alluvial deposits on the Jos plateau north of the confluence of the Niger and Benue rivers. Presumably, floods from centuries past had removed the

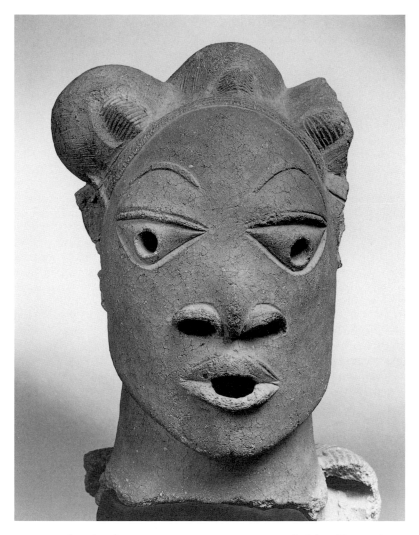

13-2. Head. Nok culture, c. 500 BCE–200 CE. Terra-cotta, height 14³/₁₆" (36 cm). National Museum, Lagos, Nigeria

figures from their original contexts, dragged and rolled them along, then redeposited them. This rough treatment had scratched and broken many, often leaving only the heads from what must have been complete human figures. Following archeological convention, scholars gave the name of a nearby village, Nok, to the culture that created these works. Nok-style sculpture has since been found in numerous sites over a wide area.

The Nok head shown here (fig. 13-2), slightly larger than lifesize, originally formed part of a complete figure. The triangular or **D**-shaped eyes are characteristic of Nok style and appear also on sculpture of animals. Holes in the pupils, nostrils, and mouth allowed air to pass freely as the figure was fired. Each of the large buns of its elaborate hairstyle is pierced with a hole that may have held ornamental feathers. Other Nok figures boast large quantities of beads and other prestige ornaments. Nok sculpture may represent ordinary people dressed up for a special occasion, or it may portray people of high status, providing evidence of social stratification in this early farming culture. At the very least, the sculpture provides evidence of considerable technical accomplishment. The skill and artistry it reflects have led many

scholars to speculate that Nok culture was built on the achievements of an earlier culture still to be discovered.

Ife

Following the disappearance of the Nok culture, the region of present-day Nigeria remained a vigorous cultural and artistic center. The **naturalistic** sculpture created by the artists of the city of Ife, which arose in the southern, forested part of that region by about 800 CE, are among the most remarkable in art history (see "Who Made African Art?," page 470).

Ife was, and remains, the sacred city of the Yoruba people. Yoruba myth tells how at Ife the gods descended from heaven on iron chains to create the world. A tradition of naturalistic sculpture began there about 1050 CE and flourished for some four centuries. Although the line of Ife kings, or *onis*, continues unbroken from that time to the present, the knowledge of how these works were used has been lost. When archeologists showed the sculpture to members of the contemporary *oni*'s court, however, they identified symbols of kingship on sculpture that had been worn within living memory, indicating that the figures represent rulers.

WHO MADE AFRICAN ART?

Today many art museums boast extensive collections of African art. Yet on label after label, a standard piece of information is missing. Where are the artists' names? Who made this art?

Until quite recently, the role of the artist in many African societies was greatly misunderstood, and the answer would have been, "It doesn't matter—the question is irrelevant." Artists working in Africa used to be commonly portrayed as obedient craftsworkers. Bound to the style and iconography dictated to them by village elders, they carved by rote the same images again and again; their work was said to be anonymous and interchangeable.

Over the past several decades, however, these misconceptions have begun to crumble. One of the first non-Africans to understand that African art, as much as European art, was the work of identifiable artists was the Belgian art historian Frans Olbrechts. During the 1930s, while assembling a group of objects from present-day Zaire for an exhibition, Olbrechts noticed that as many as ten figures had been carved in a very distinctive style. A look at the labels revealed that two of the statues had been collected in the same town, Buli, in eastern Zaire. As a scholar of Western art history, Olbrechts was familiar with the practice of identifying individual styles and, when names were not available, assigning the artist an identity such as the Master of Frankfurt or the Master of the Saint Catherine Legend. Accordingly, he named the unknown African artist the Master of Buli.

In the years since Olbrechts's exhibition, eleven more works have been identified as coming either directly from the hand of the Master of Buli or from his workshop. Interestingly, although the town of Buli is in an area populated predominantly by the Luba people, the style of the objects is closer to that of the Hemba people, who live just to the east. It may be that the Master of Buli was a Hemba artist working for Luba clients or for a large clientele spread across southeastern Zaire.

In the late 1970s, an object in the style of the Master of Buli was discovered in the Hemba area. Its owners identified the artist as Ngongo ya Chintu, of Kateba village, a short distance away. Kateba villagers in turn remembered Ngongo ya Chintu as an artist of great skill. His reputation had spread throughout southeastern Zaire, and he had attracted clients from a large area. Clearly, then, African artists did not work anonymously. So why have their names not been preserved?

One reason has to do with some African systems of patronage. As was the case in many lands, artists in many African countries created their works in response to specific commissions rather than to express a personal message. Art might be commissioned by an individual, a family, an organization, or an entire community, and negotiations between patrons and artists over the details of a commission were often protracted. Once the work had been created, however, the name of the artist was not necessarily made public. Instead, the work was generally associated with the names of its owners or commissioners.

Another reason is that early collectors simply failed to ask. During the late nineteenth and early twentieth centuries, when many Western collections of African art were being formed, Westerners generally did not believe that Africans shared their sense of the uniqueness and importance of the individual. Thus the explorers, colonial officers, and missionaries who filled the storerooms of European museums rarely asked who had made or owned the objects they were acquiring. Nor did they always distinguish carefully what part of Africa a work came from. In European eyes Africa was a single country .

As the story of Ngongo ya Chintu indicates, however, Africans are fully aware of the names of their artists. Inspired by Olbrechts's example, art historians and anthropologists have since identified numerous African artists and compiled catalogs of their work. In the case of the Yoruba people of present-day Nigeria, for example, we now know of such artists as Agbonbiofe of the Adeshina family of Efon-Alaye (d. 1945), Obembe Alaye of Efon-Alaye (1869–1939), Maku of Erin (d. 1928), and many others.

Certainly we will never know the names of the vast majority of African artists of the past, just as we do not know the names of the sculptors responsible for the sculpture portraits of late Rome or the monumental reliefs of the Hindu temples of South Asia. As elsewhere, the greatest artists in Africa were famous and sought after, while the others labored honorably at their art.

A lifesize brass head (fig. 13-3) shows the extraordinary artistry of ancient Ife. The modeling of the flesh is supremely sensitive, especially the subtle transitions around the nose and mouth. The lips are full and delicate, and the eyes are strikingly similar in shape to those of some modern Yoruba. The face is covered with thin, parallel **scarification** patterns (decorations made by scarring) in a style that was still occasionally seen on Nigerians until recently.

Holes along the scalp apparently permitted hair or perhaps a beaded veil to be attached. Large holes around the base of the neck may have allowed the head itself to be attached to a wooden mannequin for display during memorial services for a deceased *oni*. The mannequin was probably dressed in the *oni*'s robes and his crown was probably attached to the head by means of the holes along the hairline.

The artists of ancient Ife also worked in terra-cotta. Unlike their brass counterparts, terra-cotta heads are not fitted for attachments. They were probably placed in shrines devoted to the memory of each dead king. Two of the most famous Ife sculptures were not found by archeologists but had been preserved through the centuries in the *oni*'s palace. One, a terra-cotta head, is said to represent Lajuwa, a court retainer who usurped the throne by intrigue and impersonation (fig. 13-4). The other, a lifesize copper mask, is said to represent Obalufon, the ruler who introduced bronze casting.

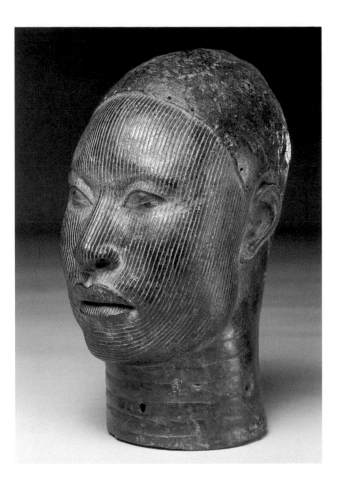

13-3. Head of a king, from Ife. c. 13th century CE. Brass, height 11⁷⁄₁₆" (29 cm). Museum of Ife Antiquities, Ife, Nigeria

The naturalism of Ife sculpture contradicted everything Europeans thought they knew about African art. The German scholar who "discovered" Ife sculpture in 1910 suggested that it had been created not by Africans but by survivors from the legendary lost island of Atlantis. Later scholars speculated that influence from ancient Greece or Renaissance Europe must have reached Ife. Scientific dating methods, however, finally put such misleading comparisons and prejudices to rest. When naturalism flowered in Ife, the ancient Mediterranean world was long gone and the European Renaissance still to come. In addition, the proportions of the few known full figures are characteristically African, with the head comprising as much as one quarter of the total height. These proportions probably reflect a belief in the head's importance as the abode of the spirit and the focus of individual identity.

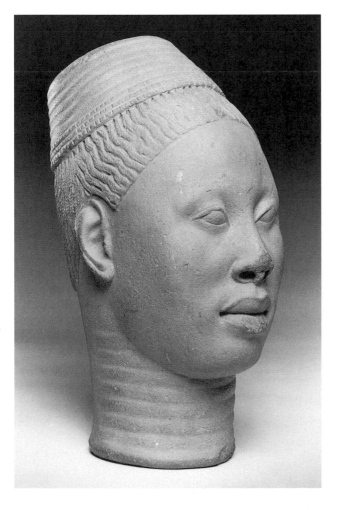

Scholars continue to debate whether the Ife heads are true portraits. Their striking anatomical individuality strongly suggests that they are. The heads, however, all seem to represent men of the same age and seem to embody a similar concept of physical perfection, suggesting that they are **idealized** images. In the recent past, Africans have not produced naturalistic portraits, fearing that they could house malevolent spirits that would harm the soul of the subject. If the Ife heads are portraits, then perhaps the institution of kingship and the need to revere royal ancestors were strong enough to overcome such concerns.

Benin

Ife was probably the artistic parent of the great city-state of Benin, which arose some 150 miles to the southeast. According to oral histories, the earliest kings of Benin belonged to the Ogiso, or Skyking, dynasty. After a long period of misrule, however, the people of Benin asked the *oni* of Ife for a new ruler. The *oni* sent Prince Oranmiyan, who founded a new dynasty in 1170 CE. Some two centuries later, the fourth king, or *oba,* of Benin decided to start a tradition of memorial sculpture like that of Ife, and he sent to Ife for a master metal caster named

13-4. Head said to represent the Usurper Lajuwa, from Ife. c. 1200–1300 CE. Terra-cotta, height 12¹⁵⁄₁₆" (32.8 cm). Museum of Ife Antiquities, Ife, Nigeria

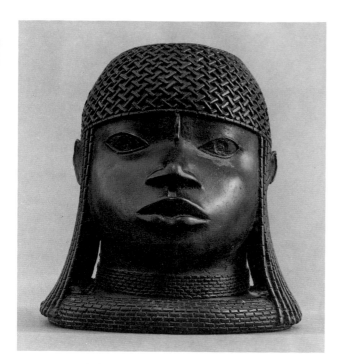

13-5.   Memorial head, from Benin. c. 1400–1550 CE (Early
Period). Brass, height 9⅜" (23.4 cm). The Metropolitan Museum of Art, New York

The Michael C. Rockefeller Memorial Collection, Bequest of
Nelson A. Rockefeller, 1979 (1979.206.86)

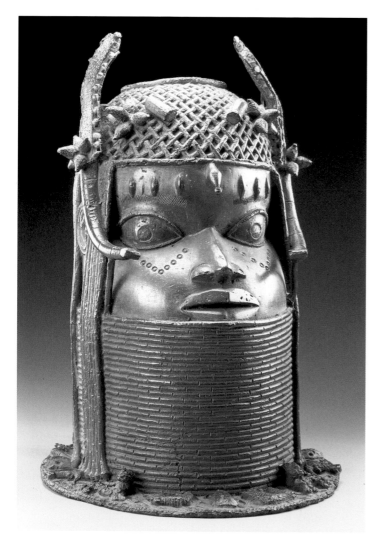

Iguegha. The tradition of casting memorial heads for the
shrines of royal ancestors endures among the successors
of Oranmiyan to this day.

Benin came into contact with Portugal in the late fifteenth century. The two kingdoms established cordial
relations and carried on an active trade, at first in ivory
and other forest products but eventually in slaves. Benin
flourished until 1897, when, in reprisal for the massacre
of a party of trade negotiators, British troops sacked
and burned the royal palace, sending the *oba* into an exile from which he did not return until 1914. The palace
was later rebuilt, and the present-day *oba* continues the
dynasty started by Oranmiyan.

The British invaders discovered shrines to deceased
obas filled with brass heads, bells, and figures. They also
found wooden rattles and enormous ivory tusks carved
with images of kings, court attendants, and sixteenth-
century Portuguese soldiers. The British appropriated the
treasure as war booty, making no effort to note which
head came from which shrine. As a result, they destroyed
evidence that would have helped establish the relative
age of the heads and determine a chronology for the evolution of Benin style. Nevertheless, scholars have managed to piece together a chronology from other evidence.

Benin brass heads range from small, thinly cast,
and naturalistic to large, thickly cast, and highly stylized.
The heads that were being made at the time of the
British invasion are of the latter variety, as are those
still being cast today. Many scholars have concluded that
the smallest, most naturalistic heads were created
during a so-called Early Period (1400–1550 CE), when
Benin artists were still heavily influenced by Ife (fig.
13-5). Heads grew increasingly stylized during the Middle
Period (1550–1700 CE). Heads from the ensuing Late
Period (1700–1897 CE) are very large and heavy, with angular, stylized features and an elaborate beaded crown (fig.
13-6). A similar crown is still worn by the present-day *oba*.

All of the heads include representations of coral-bead
necklaces, which have formed part of the royal costume
from earliest times to the present day. Small and few in
number on Early Period heads, they increase in number
until they conceal the chin during the Middle Period. During the Late Period, the necklaces form a tall, cylindrical
mass that greatly increases the weight of the sculpture.
Broad, horizontal flanges, or projecting edges, bearing
small images cast in low relief ring the base of the Late
Period statues, adding still more weight. The increase in
size and weight of Benin memorial heads over time may
reflect the growing power and wealth flowing to the *oba*
from Benin's expanding trade with Europe.

The art of Benin is a royal art, for only the *oba* could
commission works in brass. Artisans who served the
court lived in a separate quarter of the city and were
organized into guilds. Among the most remarkable visual records of court life are the hundreds of brass
plaques, each about 2 feet square, that once decorated

13-6.   Head of an *oba* (king), from Benin. c. 1700–1897 CE
(Late Period). Brass, height 17¼" (45 cm). Museum
für Völkerkunde, Vienna/Musée Dapper, Paris

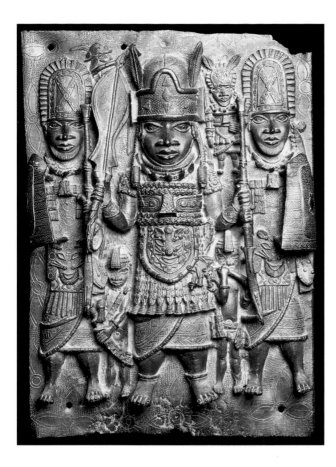

13-7. *General and Officers,* from Benin. c. 1550–1650 CE (Middle Period). Brass, height 21" (53.5 cm). National Museum, Lagos, Nigeria

The general wears an elaborate, appliqué apron depicting the head of a leopard, and the flanking officers wear leopard pelts. Leopards were symbols of royalty in Benin. Live leopards were kept at the royal palace, where they were looked after by a special keeper. Water pitchers in the form of leopards were cast in bronze and placed on altars dedicated to ancestors. An engraving from a European travel book of the sixteenth century depicts a procession of courtiers in Benin led by a pair of magnificent leopards.

the walls and columns of the royal palace. Produced during the Middle Period, the plaques are modeled in relief, sometimes in such high relief that the figures are almost freestanding. An exceptionally detailed plaque (fig. 13-7) shows a general in elaborate military dress holding a spear in one hand and a ceremonial sword in the other. Flanking the general, two officers, whose helmets indicate their rank, brandish spears and shields. Smaller figures appear between the three principal figures, one carrying a sword, another sounding a horn. Above the tip of the general's sword is a small figure of a Portuguese soldier.

Obas also commissioned important works in ivory. One example is a beautiful ornamental mask (fig. 13-8)

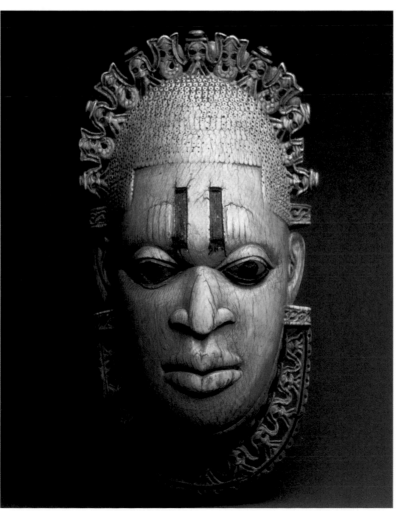

13-8. Mask representing an *iyoba,* from Benin. c. 1550 CE. Ivory, iron, and copper, height 9³⁄₈" (23.4 cm). The Metropolitan Museum of Art, New York

The Michael C. Rockefeller Memorial Collection, Gift of Nelson A. Rockefeller, 1972 (1978.412.323)

that represents an *iyoba,* or queen mother. The woman who had borne the previous *oba's* first male child (and thus the mother of the current *oba*), the *iyoba* ranked as the senior female member of the court. This mask may represent Idia, the first and best-known *iyoba.* Idia was the mother of Esigie, who ruled as *oba* from 1504 to 1550 CE. She is particularly remembered for raising an army and using her magical powers to help her son defeat his enemies.

The mask was carved as a belt or hip ornament and was probably worn at the *oba's* waist. Its pupils were originally inlaid with iron, as were the scarification patterns on the forehead. The necklace represents heads of Portuguese soldiers with beards and flowing hair. Like Idia, the Portuguese helped Esigie expand his kingdom. In the crown, more Portuguese heads alternate with figures of mudfish, which in Benin iconography symbolized Olokun, the Lord of the Great Waters. Mudfish live on the riverbank, mediating between water and land, just as the *oba,* who is viewed as semidivine, mediates between the human world and the supernatural world of Olokun.

URBAN CENTERS

Ife and Benin were but two of the many cities that arose in ancient Africa. The first European visitors to the West African coast at the end of the fifteenth century were impressed not only by Benin, but also by the cities of Loango and Luanda near the mouth of the Zaire River. Exploring the East African coastline, European ships happened on cosmopolitan cities that had been busily carrying on long-distance trade across the Indian Ocean and as far away as China and Indonesia for hundreds of years.

Important centers also arose in the interior, especially across the central and western Sudan. There cities and the states that developed around them grew wealthy from the trans-Saharan trade that had linked West Africa to the Mediterranean from at least the first millennium BCE. Indeed, the routes across the desert were probably as old as the desert itself. Among the most significant goods exchanged in this trade were salt from the north and gold from West Africa. Such fabled cities as Mopti, Timbuktu, and Djenné were great centers of commerce, where merchants from all over West Africa met caravans arriving from the Mediterranean.

Djenné

In 1655, the Islamic writer al-Sadi wrote this description of Djenné:

> This city is large, flourishing, and prosperous; it is rich, blessed, and favoured by the Almighty. . . . Jenne [Djenné] is one of the great markets of the Muslim world. There one meets the salt merchants from the mines of Teghaza and merchants carrying gold from the mines of Bitou. . . . Because of this blessed city, caravans flock to Timbuktu from all points of the horizon. . . . The area around Jenne is fertile and well populated; with numerous markets held there on all the days of the week. It is certain that it contains 7,077 villages very near to one another.

> (Translated by Graham Connah in Connah, page 97)

By the time al-Sadi wrote his account, Djenné, in present-day Mali, already had a long history. Archeologists have determined that the city was established by the third century CE and that by the middle of the ninth century it had become a major urban center. By the ninth century also, Islam was becoming an economic and religious force in West Africa, having incorporated North Africa and the northern terminals of the trans-Saharan trade routes into the Islamic empire. Much of what we know about African history from this time on is based on the accounts of Islamic scholars, geographers, and travelers.

When Koi Konboro, the twenty-sixth king of Djenné, converted to Islam in the thirteenth century, he transformed his palace into the first of three successive **mosques** in the city. Like the two that followed, the first mosque was built of **adobe** brick, a sun-dried mixture of clay and straw. With its great surrounding wall and tall towers, it was said to have been more beautiful and more lavishly decorated than the Kaaba, the central shrine of Islam, at Mecca. The mosque eventually attracted the attention of austere Muslim rulers, who objected to its sumptuous furnishings. Among these was the early-nineteenth-century ruler Sekou Amadou, who had it razed and a far more humble structure erected on a new site. This second mosque was in turn replaced by the current grand mosque, constructed between 1906 and 1907 on the ancient site and in the style of the original. The reconstruction was supervised by the architect Ismaila Traoré, the head of the Djenné guild of masons.

The mosque's eastern, or "marketplace," facade boasts three tall towers (fig. 13-9). The finials, or crowning ornaments, at the top of each tower bear ostrich eggs, symbols of fertility and purity. The facade and sides of the mosque are distinguished by tall, narrow, engaged columns, which act as buttresses. These columns are characteristic of West African mosque architecture, and their cumulative rhythmic effect is one of great verticality and grandeur. The most unusual feature of West African mosques are the *torons*, wooden beams projecting from the walls. *Torons* provide permanent supports for the scaffolding erected each year so that the exterior of the mosque can be replastered.

Great Zimbabwe

Several thousand miles from Djenné, in southeastern Africa, an extensive trade network developed along the Zambezi, Limpopo, and Sabi rivers. Its purpose was to funnel gold, ivory, and exotic skins to the coastal trading towns that had been built by Arabs and Swahili-speaking Africans. There, the gold and ivory were exchanged for prestige goods, including porcelain, beads, and other manufactured items. Between 1000 and 1500 CE, this trade was largely controlled from a site that was called Great Zimbabwe.

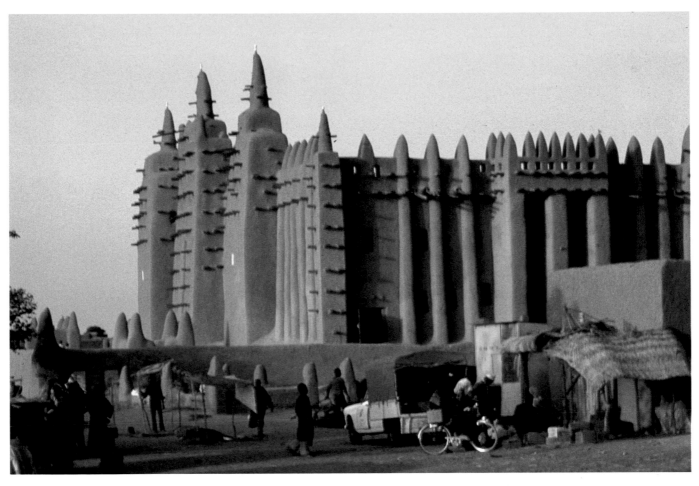

13-9. Great Friday Mosque, Djenné, Mali, showing the eastern and northern facades. Rebuilding of 1907, in the style of 13th-century original

The plan of the mosque is quite irregular. Instead of a rectangle, the building forms a parallelogram. Inside, nine long rows of heavy adobe columns some 33 feet tall run along the north-south axis, supporting a flat ceiling of palm logs. A pointed arch links each column to the next in its row, thereby forming nine east-west archways facing the mihrab, the niche that indicates the direction of Mecca. The mosque is augmented by an open courtyard for prayer on the west side, which is enclosed by a great double wall only slightly lower than the walls of the mosque itself.

The word *zimbabwe* derives from the Shona term for "venerated houses" or "houses of stone." Scholars agree that the stone buildings at Great Zimbabwe were constructed by ancestors of the present-day Shona people, who still live in the region. The earliest construction at the site took advantage of the enormous boulders abundant in the vicinity. Masons incorporated the boulders and used the uniform granite blocks that split naturally from them to build a series of tall enclosing walls high on a hilltop. Each enclosure defined a family's living or ritual space and housed dwellings made of adobe with conical, thatched roofs.

The largest building complex at Great Zimbabwe is located in a broad valley below the hilltop enclosures.

Known as Imba Huru, the Big House, the complex is ringed by a masonry wall more than 800 feet long, 32 feet tall, and 17 feet thick at the base. The buildings at Great Zimbabwe were built without mortar; for stability the walls are **battered**, or built so that they slope inward toward the top. Inside the great outer wall are numerous smaller stone enclosures and adobe foundations.

The complex seems to have evolved with very little planning. Additions and extensions were begun as labor and materials were available and need dictated. Over the centuries, the builders grew more skillful, and the later additions are distinguished by **dressed stones**, or smoothly finished stones, laid in fine, even, level courses. One of these later additions is a fascinating structure

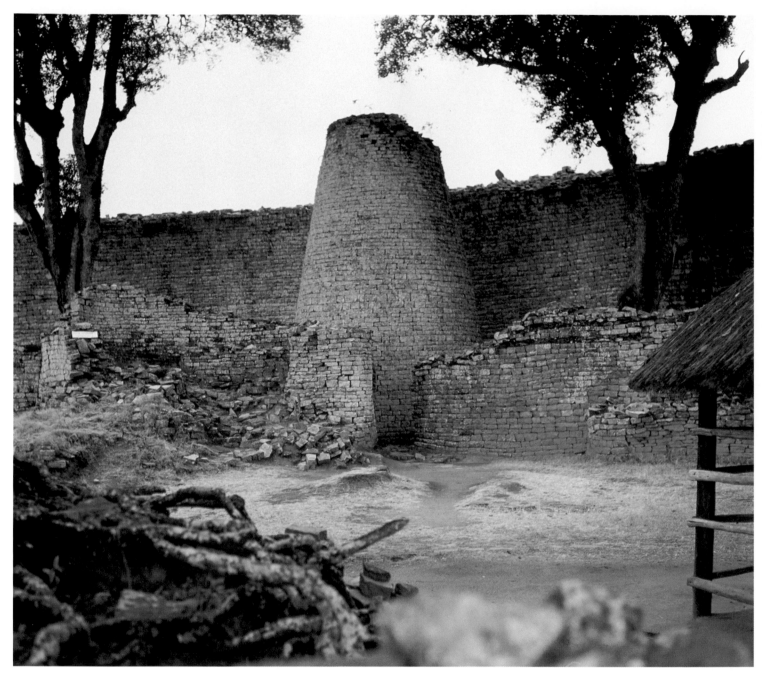

13-10. Conical Tower, Great Zimbabwe. Before 1450 CE

known simply as the Conical Tower (fig. 13-10). Some 18 feet in diameter and 30 feet tall, the tower was originally capped with three courses of ornamental stonework. It may have represented the good harvest and prosperity believed to result from allegiance to the ruler of Great Zimbabwe, for it resembles a present-day Shona granary built large.

Among the many interesting finds at Great Zimbabwe are a series of carved soapstone birds (fig. 13-11). The carvings, which originally crowned tall **monoliths**, seem to depict birds of prey, perhaps eagles. They may, however, represent mythical creatures, for the species cannot be identified. Traditional Shona beliefs include an eagle called *shiri ye denga,* or "bird of heaven," who brings

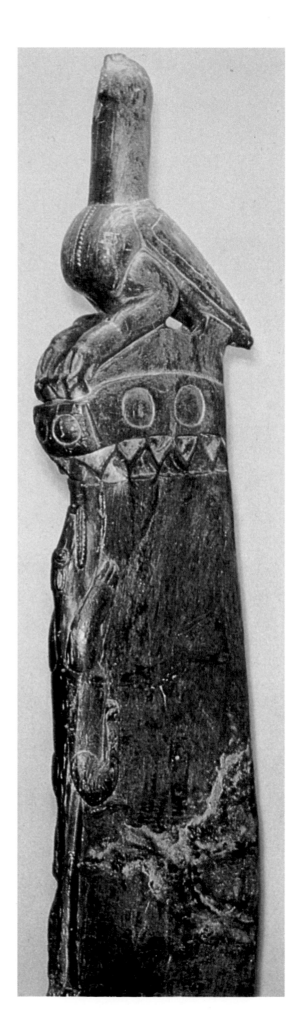

13-11. Bird, top part of a monolith, from Great Zimbabwe. c. 1200–1400 CE. Soapstone, height 14½" (36.8 cm). Great Zimbabwe Site Museum, Zimbabwe

lightning, a metaphor for communication between the heavens and earth. These soapstone birds may have represented such messengers from the spirit world, or they may have served as symbols of royalty, expressing the king's power to mediate between his subjects and the supernatural world of spirits.

Although some of the enclosures at Great Zimbabwe were built on hilltops, there is no evidence that they were constructed as fortresses. There are neither openings for weapons to be thrust through nor battlements for warriors to stand on. Instead, the walls and structures seem intended to reflect the wealth and power of the city's rulers. The Big House was probably a royal residence, or palace complex, and other structures housed members of the ruler's family and court. The complex formed the nucleus of a city that radiated for almost a mile in all directions. It is estimated that at the height of its power in the fourteenth century, Great Zimbabwe and its surrounding city housed a population of more than 10,000 people. A large cache of goods containing items of such far-flung origin as Portuguese medallions, Persian pottery, and Chinese porcelain testify to the extent of its trade. Yet beginning in the mid-fifteenth century Great Zimbabwe was gradually abandoned. Its power and control of the lucrative southeast African trade network passed to the Mwene Mutapa and Kami empires only a short distance away.

During the twentieth century, the sculpture of traditional African societies—wood carvings of astonishing formal inventiveness and power—have found admirers the world over, becoming virtually synonymous with "African art." Admiration for these art forms was evident in earlier periods as well. In the mid-seventeenth century, for example, a German merchant named Christopher Weickman collected a Yoruba divination board, textiles from the Kongo, and swords with nubbly ray-skin sheaths from the Akan, all of which are now housed in a museum in Ulm, Germany. Wood decays rapidly, however, and little of African wood sculpture remains from before the nineteenth century. As a result, much of ancient Africa's artistic heritage has probably been as irretrievably lost as have, for example, the great monuments of wooden architecture of dynastic China. Yet the beauty of ancient African creations in such durable materials as terracotta, stone, and bronze bears eloquent witness to the skill of ancient African artists and the splendor of the civilizations in which they worked.

500 CE   600   700

South Cross
Ahenny
8th century

▲ CAROLINGIAN
PERIOD 750–900

▲ CHRISTIAN SPAIN 500–
▲ BRITAIN/IRELAND 500–

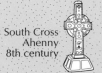

CHAPTER 14

Early Medieval Art in Europe

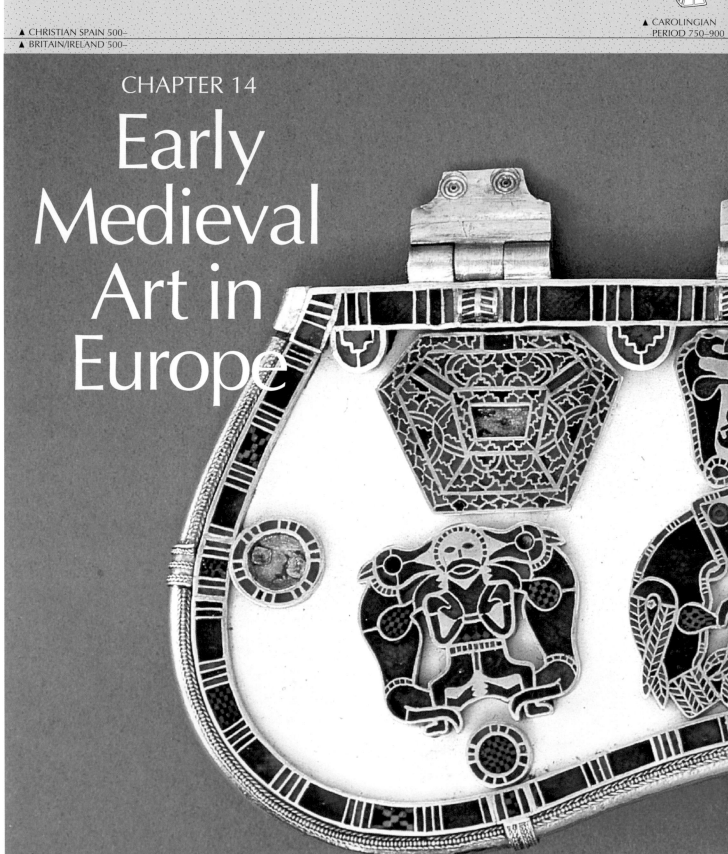

Palace Chapel
of Charlemagne
792–805

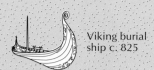

Viking burial
ship c. 825

Bird and Serpent,
from a Spanish
manuscript 975

Adam and Eve,
from the Hildesheim
doors 1015

▲ OTTONIAN PERIOD 900–1000

▲ SCANDINAVIAN VIKING 800–1100

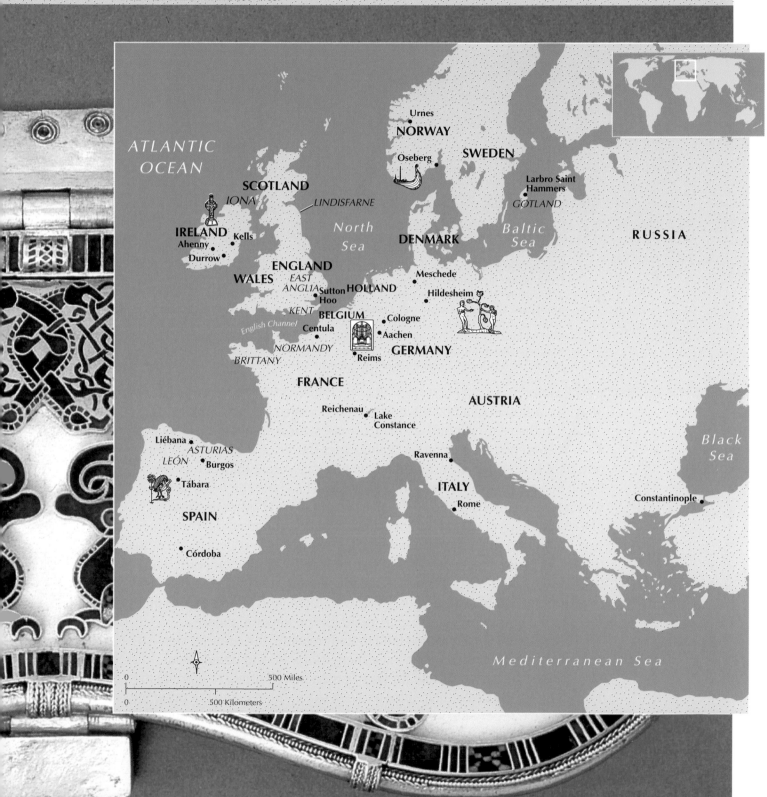

ATLANTIC
OCEAN

Urnes

NORWAY

SWEDEN

Oseberg

Larbro Saint
Hammers

GOTLAND

SCOTLAND

IONA

LINDISFARNE

North
Sea

Baltic
Sea

RUSSIA

IRELAND   Kells

DENMARK

Ahenny

Durrow

ENGLAND

Meschede

WALES   *EAST
ANGLIA* Sutton HOLLAND
Hoo

Hildesheim

KENT BELGIUM
Cologne
English Channel   Centula
Aachen

NORMANDY Reims   GERMANY

BRITTANY

FRANCE

AUSTRIA

Reichenau
Lake
Constance

Liébana

ASTURIAS

LEÓN   Burgos

Ravenna

Black
Sea

Tábara

ITALY
Rome

Constantinople

SPAIN

Córdoba

Mediterranean Sea

0   500 Miles
0   500 Kilometers

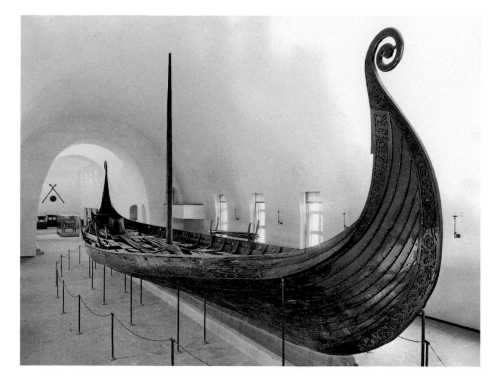

14-1. Burial ship, from Oseberg, Norway. c. 800. Wood, length 75'6" (23 m). Viking-skiphuset, Universitets Oldsaksamling, Oslo, Norway

This vessel, propelled by both sail and oars, was designed not for ocean voyages but for travel in the relatively calm waters of fjords, narrow coastal inlets. The shelter at the center of this ship was used as the burial chamber for two women. A cart and four sleds, all made of wood with beautifully carved decorations, were stored on board. Fourteen horses, an ox, and three dogs had been sacrificed to accompany the women into the grave. It is also quite possible that one of the women was a willing sacrificial victim for the other, since Viking society believed that a courageous and honorable death was a guarantee of reward in the afterlife.

As a flotilla of 2,000 Viking ships approached Constantinople early in the tenth century, so the story goes, the intimidated Byzantines stretched an enormous chain across the strait to stop them. The remarkable mariners from Scandinavia had sailed eastward across the Baltic Sea and down rivers to the Black Sea. The chain they encountered was no more an obstacle to them than waterfalls and other impassable places on the rivers they had navigated, and they got around it the same way: they lifted their ships from the water, put them on rollers made of tree trunks, and rolled them around the barrier. The Byzantine emperor was so cowed by their ingenuity and aggressiveness that he paid the Vikings a huge tribute, established a trade treaty with them, and hired some of these "ax-bearing barbarians" as an elite guard for the imperial palace.

These Viking ships crossed land to find treasure, but another ship—a 75-foot-long vessel discovered in Oseberg, Norway, and dated about 800—served as the burial site for two women on a journey to eternity (fig. 14-1). The Vikings saw their ships as sleek sea serpents, and the prow and stern of the Oseberg ship rise and coil like a serpent's tail. These suggestive spirals may have been meant to terrify enemies and to protect against evil forces. Although the burial chamber was long ago looted of jewelry and precious objects, the ship itself and the remaining artifacts attest to the wealth and prominence of the ship's owner and have provided insight into the culture of Scandinavia in the Early Middle Ages.

THE MIDDLE AGES

The roughly 1,000 years of European history between the collapse of the Western Roman Empire in the fifth century and the Renaissance in the fifteenth are known as the Middle Ages, or the medieval period. These terms reflect the view of early historians that this was a dark "middle" age of ignorance, decline, and barbarism between two golden ages. Although this view no longer prevails—the Middle Ages are now known to have been a period of great richness, complexity, and innovation that gave birth to modern Europe—the terms have endured. Art historians commonly divide the Middle Ages into three periods: Early medieval (ending in the tenth century), Romanesque (eleventh and twelfth centuries), and Gothic (extending from the mid-twelfth century into the fifteenth). The terms *Romanesque* and *Gothic* refer to distinctive artistic styles that were prevalent during the periods that bear their names. Chapters 7 ("Early Christian, Jewish, and Byzantine Art") and 8 ("Islamic Art") have already touched on some aspects of early medieval art. This chapter covers the art of the Early Middle Ages in western and northern Europe—Scandinavia, Britain, Ireland, Christian Spain, France, and Germany—from the sixth century to the eleventh century. Chapter 15 covers Romanesque art, and Chapter 16 discusses Gothic art.

As Roman authority crumbled at the outset of the Middle Ages, it was replaced by strong local leaders—including the leaders of the various Germanic and other barbarian groups that had invaded or been drawn into the empire over the centuries—and by the Church, which was centered in Rome and retained the hierarchical administrative structure of the empire. The breakdown of central power, the fusion of Germanic and Roman culture, and the unifying influence of Christianity produced distinctive new political, social, and cultural forms. In a process that led ultimately to a type of social organization known as feudalism, relationships of patronage and dependence between the powerful—nobles and church officials—and the less powerful became increasingly important. A pattern of mutual support developed between secular leaders and the Church, with secular leaders defending the claims of the Church and the Church validating their rule. The Church emerged as a repository of learning, and church officials and the nobility became the principal patrons of the arts. The focus of their patronage was the Church itself, its buildings and liturgical equipment, including altars, altar vessels, crosses, candlesticks, **reliquaries** (containers for holy relics), vestments, portrayals of Christian figures and stories, and copies of sacred texts.

As Christianity continued to spread north beyond the borders of the empire, northern artistic traditions similarly worked their way south. Out of a tangled web of themes and styles from north and south, east and west, pagan and Christian, urban and rural, brilliant new artistic styles were born.

SCANDINAVIA

Scandinavia, which encompasses the modern countries of Denmark, Norway, and Sweden, was never part of the Roman Empire. In the fifth century CE it was a land of small kingdoms and independent agricultural communities. Most of its inhabitants spoke variants of a language called Norse and shared a rich mythology with other Germanic peoples. Among other deities, they worshiped Odin, chief of the gods, who protected the courageous in battle and rewarded the fallen by allowing them entrance into Valhalla, the great hall where heroic souls were received.

Sometime in the late eighth century seafaring bands of Scandinavians known as Vikings (*Viken* originally meant "people from the coves" but eventually came to be synonymous with "raiders" or "pirates") began descending on the rest of Europe. Setting off in flotillas of as many as 350 ships, they explored, plundered, traded, and colonized over a vast area. Intermittently looting and destroying coastal and inland river communities, they were an unsettling presence in Europe for nearly 300 years. Frequently, their targets were isolated, but wealthy, Christian monasteries. Among the earliest recorded Viking attacks were two devastating raids: one in 793, on the religious community on Lindisfarne, an island off the northeast coast of Britain, and another, in 794, at Iona, off the west coast. Vikings explored the north Atlantic, settling in Iceland about 870 and Greenland by 1000. They established a short-lived outpost in North America after 1000. They also raided and settled in Ireland, England, Scotland, and France. In the early tenth century, the rulers of France bought off Scandinavian raiders (the Normans, or North men) with a large grant of land that became the duchy of Normandy. Some Viking groups also sailed down rivers to the Black Sea and Constantinople, while others established settlements around Novgorod, which ultimately became the northern state of Rusland, or Russia.

The Danish king Harold Bluetooth brought Christianity to Scandinavia in the middle of the tenth century. In Norway, Olaf Haraldsson, later canonized Saint Olaf (died 1030), is credited with converting his people. Olaf accepted Christianity in Rouen, France while on a Viking expedition. During the eleventh century the new religion spread through the rest of the Scandinavian peninsula. By the beginning of the twelfth century, kings supported by Christian bishops had broken the power of regional rulers. With these developments and the rise of powerful monarchies in England and France, Viking raids and the Viking era came to an end.

During the first millennium BCE, trade, warfare, and migration brought a variety of jewelry, coins, textiles, and other portable objects into northern Europe. Scandinavian artists, who had exhibited a fondness for abstract patterning from early prehistoric times, incorporated the solar disks, spirals, and stylized animals on these objects into their already rich artistic vocabulary (see fig. 1-27). Beginning about 300 CE, Roman influences were noticeable in Scandinavia. By the fifth century CE, the so-called animal style displayed an impressive array of serpents and four-legged beasts, and squat human forms. Certain underlying principles govern works in this complex style: they are generally symmetrically composed, and they

PARALLELS

Years	European Cultural Centers	Europe	World
c. 800–1100	Scandinavian Viking	Viking expeditions in northern Europe; colonies in Russia, Iceland, Greenland, North America; Christianization	**500–1000** Rise of Hinduism (India); Hagia Sophia (Turkey); birth of Muhammad, founder of Islam (Arabia); Muslim conquests of Arabia, Persia, Egypt, Syria, Palestine; Buddhism in Japan; a plague kills half of European population; Tang dynasty (China); Koran (Arabia); first block-print text (China); bronze casting in South America; *Diamond Sutra* (China)
c. 500–present	Britain/Ireland	Celtic culture; Anglo-Saxon culture; *Beowulf*; Hiberno-Saxon Style; *Book of Kells*	
c. 500–present	Christian Spain	Visigoth presence; monumental architecture; Islam conquests; Mozarabic style; *Commentary on the Apocalypse*	
c. 750–900	Carolingian period	Rule of Charlemagne; strengthening of Roman Empire; Caroline minuscule script; *Utrecht Psalter*	
c. 900–1000	Ottonian period	Otto I creates Holy Roman Empire; *Liuthar Gospels*	

depict animals in their entirety from a variety of perspectives—in profile, from above, and sometimes with their ribs and spinal columns exposed as if they had been X-rayed.

The Gummersmark brooch (fig. 14-2), a large silver-gilt pin, probably one of a pair, was used to fasten a cloak around the wearer's shoulders. It is worked in an intricate animal style design. Dating from the sixth century CE and made in Denmark, this elegant ornament consists of a large, rectangular headplate and a medallionlike, open-work footplate connected by an arched central element which acts as a spring to help hold the pin on the garment. Its abstract, geometric motifs include spirals, narrow bands, bird heads, human figures, dogs, and dragons. The artist created a glittering surface by faceting in a technique called chip carving. Earlier, Romans had developed chip carving as a cheap, fast way of decorating molded hardware for military uniforms. The northern artists who adopted the technique carefully crafted each item by hand, turning a process intended for fast production into an art form of great refinement.

The Vikings erected large memorial stones both at home and abroad. Those covered mostly with inscriptions are called **rune stones**; those with figural decoration are called **picture stones**. Runes are letters of an early Germanic alphabet that was probably derived from ancient italic (Italian) alphabets. Traces of pigments suggest that these memorial stones were originally painted in bright colors. Picture stones from Gotland, an island off the east coast of Sweden, share a common design

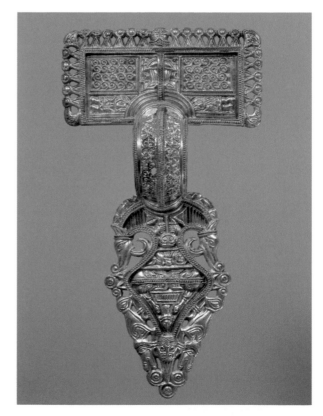

14-2. Gummersmark brooch, Denmark. 6th century. Silver gilt, height 5¾" (14.6 cm). Nationalmuseet, Copenhagen

The faceted surface of this pin seems to seethe with abstract human, animal, and grotesque forms such as the eye-and-beak motif that frames the headplate, the man compressed between dragons just below the bridge element, and the pair of crouching dogs with spiraling tongues that forms the tip of the footplate.

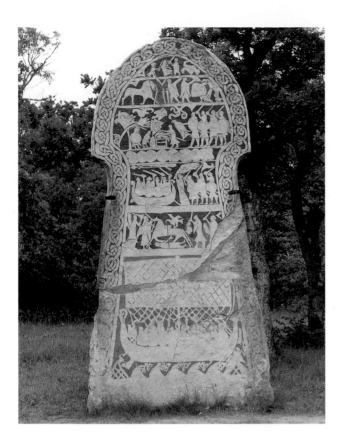

14-3. Memorial stone, Larbro Saint Hammers, Gotland, Sweden. 8th century

Much of what we know about Viking beliefs comes from later writings, especially the *Prose Edda,* compiled in the early thirteenth century by a wealthy Icelandic farmer-poet, Snorri Sturluson (1178–1241), as a guide to Norse religion and a manual for writing poetry. Among the stories he recounts is that of Gudrun and her brothers, Gunnar and Hogni, which may be the subject of the scene in the register just above the large ship on this stone. According to this legend, Gudrun was engaged to King Atli, who was interested in her only for the treasures her brothers had hidden. The scene on the stone—which shows men with raised swords on each side of a horse trampling a fallen victim and a woman with a sword boldly confronting the horse—may illustrate Gudrun and her brothers in battle against Atli. The brothers were captured in this battle and horribly murdered. Gudrun then made peace with Atli and married him, but she later avenged her family's honor by serving him the hearts and blood of their children at a feast, following which she and a nephew killed Atli and burned his castle.

and a common theme—heroic death in battle and the journey of the dead warriors to Valhalla. An eighth-century stone from Larbro Saint Hammers on Gotland has a characteristic "mushroom" shape (fig. 14-3). The scenes are organized into horizontal registers and surrounded by a band of **ribbon interlace**, a complex pattern of woven and knotted lines that may derive from similar border ornamentation in ancient Greek and Roman mosaics. In northern art such popular patterns probably were not merely decorative but carried some symbolic significance. The bottom panel shows a large Viking ship with a broad sail, intricate rigging, and a full

crew sailing over foamy waves. In Viking iconography, ships symbolize the dead warrior's passage to Valhalla. Viking chiefs were sometimes cremated in a ship in the belief that this hastened their ascent to Valhalla.

The other registers show scenes of battle and scenes from Norse mythology, including rituals associated with the cult of Odin. The third register down, just above a horizontal band of interlace, depicts the ritual hanging of a willing victim in sacrifice to Odin, who among many other titles was known as "the god to the hanged." Directly in front of the hanged man is a burial mound, called the hall of Odin, and above it are symbols of Odin, the eagle and the triple knot.

In the Viking-era burial ship discovered in Oseberg (see fig. 14-1), two women, one young and one old, were laid out in the cabin on separate beds with comforters, blankets, and pillows. The cabin also contained empty chests that no doubt once held precious goods, as well as two looms, perhaps an indication of the craft of one or both women. The cabin walls had been covered with tapestries, fragments of which survived. Among the ship's artifacts are some of the few surviving examples of Scandinavian wood carving, a craft known to have been practiced with skill and imagination throughout the region. The bands of carved low relief running along the ship's bow and stern feature a type of design called **animal interlace**, in which the bodies of animals and birds are elongated into interwoven serpentine ribbons.

Images of strange beasts adorned all sorts of Viking belongings—jewelry, houses, tent poles, beds, wagons, sleds—and later even churches. Found in the cabin of the Oseberg ship were several wooden animal-head posts about 3 feet long with handles, the purpose of which is unknown (fig. 14-4). Although each is unique in style and design, all represent similar long-necked, grotesque, dog- or catlike creatures with bulging eyes, short muzzles, snarling mouths, and large teeth. These ferocious creatures are encrusted with a writhing mass of delicately carved beasts that clutch at each other with small, claw-like hands (fig. 14-5). This type of animal interlace, known as "gripping beasts," is a hallmark of Viking ornament. The beasts are organized into roughly circular, interlocking groups surrounded by decorated bands. The faceted cutting emphasizes the flicker of light over the densely carved surfaces.

The penchant for carved relief decorations seen on the Oseberg ship endured in the decoration of Scandinavia's earliest churches. The facades of these structures often teem with intricate animal interlace. A church at Urnes, Norway, entirely rebuilt in the twelfth century, still has some remnants of the original eleventh-century carving (fig. 14-6). Although it did not originate with this church, the style of these carvings is known as "Urnes." The animal interlace in the Urnes style is composed of serpentine creatures snapping at each other, a transformation of the vicious little gripping beasts of the Oseberg headpost and the interlace pattern of the Oseberg ship's bow and stern. The satin-smooth carving of rounded surfaces, the contrast of thick and very thin elements, and the organization of the interlace into harmoniously balanced figure-8 patterns are characteristic of the Urnes

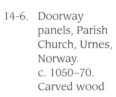

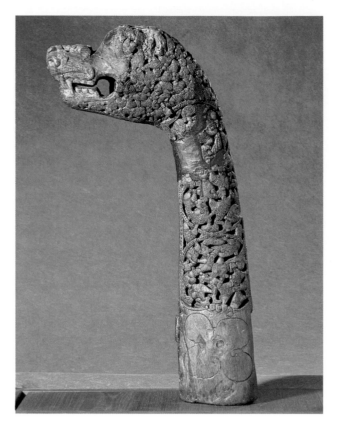

14-4. Post, from the Oseberg burial ship (fig. 14-1). c. 825.
Wood, length approx. 36" (92.3 cm). Vikingskiphuset,
Universitets Oldsaksamling, Oslo, Norway

style. The effect is one of aesthetic and technical control
rather than wild disarray. Works such as the Urnes doorway panels suggest the persistence of Scandinavia's
mythological tradition into the Early Christian period and
demonstrate its enriching influence on the vocabulary of
Christian art.

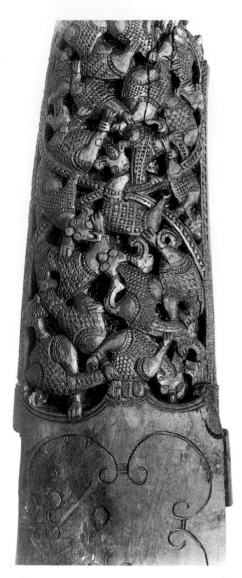

14-5. Detail of the Oseberg burial-ship post (fig. 14-4)

14-6. Doorway
panels, Parish
Church, Urnes,
Norway.
c. 1050–70.
Carved wood

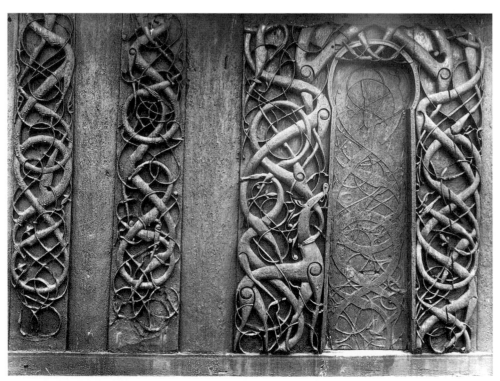

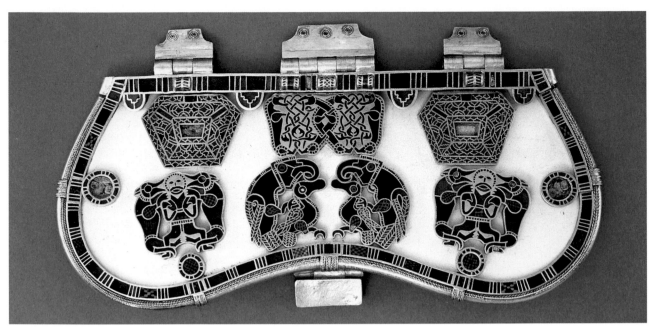

14-7. Purse cover, from the Sutton Hoo burial ship, Suffolk, England. c. 615–30. Cloisonné plaques of gold, garnet and checked millefiore enamel, length 8" (20.3 cm). The British Museum, London.

Only the decorations on this purse cover are original. The lid itself, of a light tan ivory or bone, deteriorated and disappeared centuries ago, and the white backing is a modern replacement. The purse was designed to hang at the waist. A leather pouch held thirty-seven coins, struck in France, the latest dated in the early 630s.

BRITAIN AND IRELAND

When Roman armies first ventured into Britain in 55–54 BCE, it was a well-populated, thriving agricultural land of numerous small communities with close trading links to nearby regions of the European continent. Like the inhabitants of Ireland and much of Roman Gaul (modern France), the Britons were Celtic. (Welsh, Breton—the language of Brittany, in France—and the variants of Gaelic spoken in Ireland and Scotland are all Celtic languages.) Following the Roman subjugation of the island in 43 CE, its fortunes rose and fell with those of the empire. Roman Britain experienced a final period of wealth and productivity from about 296 to about 370. Christianity flourished during this period and spread to Ireland, which was never under Roman control.

The Roman army abandoned Britain in 406 to help defend Gaul against various Germanic peoples pushing into the empire across the Rhine, leaving behind a power vacuum. The historical record for the subsequent period is sketchy, but it appears that civil disturbances erupted, the economy faltered, and large towns lost their commercial function and declined. Powerful Romanized British leaders took control of different areas, vying for dominance with the help of mercenary soldiers from the continent. These mercenaries—Angles, Saxons, and Jutes—soon began to operate independently, settling largely in the southeast part of Britain and gradually extending their control northwest across the island. Over the next 200 years the people under their control adopted Germanic speech and customs, and this fusion of Romanized British and Germanic cultures produced a new Anglo-Saxon culture. By the beginning of the seventh century, several large kingdoms had emerged in Britain, and the arts, which had suffered a serious decline, made a brilliant recovery. Celtic, Roman, and Germanic influences all contributed to vigorous new styles and techniques, especially in metalworking.

Anglo-Saxon literature is filled with references to splendid and costly jewelry and military equipment decorated with gold and silver. Leaders apparently gave such objects to their followers and friends, but few examples survive. The Anglo-Saxon epic *Beowulf*, composed perhaps as early as the seventh century, describes its hero's burial with a hoard of treasure in a mound grave near the sea. Such a grave, located near the North Sea coast in East Anglia at a site called Sutton Hoo (*hoo* means "hill"), was discovered in 1938. As at Oseberg, the grave's occupant had been buried in a ship. His body had disintegrated and no inscriptions record his name.

The treasures buried with him confirm that he was, in any case, a wealthy and powerful man. His burial ship was 86 feet long and shaped much like the Oseberg vessel. In it were weapons, armor, other equipment for the afterlife, and many luxury items, including a large purse filled with coins. Although the leather of the pouch and the bone or ivory of the lid have disintergrated, the gold and garnet fittings and decorations survive (fig. 14-4). The gold frame is set with cloisonne garnets and blue checkered millefiore enamels. The ornaments, in the same materials, consist of truncated pyramids in purely geometrical patterns. Between them four animals with interlacing legs and jaws reinforce the essential symmetry of the design. Below, large, curved-beaked birds attack ducks. Flanking the birds are images of men

THE MEDIEVAL SCRIPTORIUM

Today books are made with the aid of computer software that can lay out pages, set type, and insert and prepare illustrations. Modern presses can produce hundreds of thousands of identical copies in full color. In Europe in the Middle Ages, however, before the invention there of printing from movable type in the mid-1400s, books were made by hand, one at a time, with ink, pen, brush, and paint. Each one was an important, time-consuming, and expensive undertaking.

Medieval books were usually made by monks and nuns in a workshop called a **scriptorium** (plural scriptoria), which was usually within a monastery or a convent. As the demand for books increased, lay professionals joined the work, and great

rulers set up palace workshops supervised by well-known scholars. Books were written on animal skin—either **vellum**, which was fine and soft, or **parchment**, which was heavier and shinier. (Paper did not come into common use in Europe until the early 1400s.) The *Book of Kells* (see fig. 14-9) required the skins of more than 150 calves, a great treasure considering the value of livestock at the time. The skins were cleaned, stripped of hair, and scraped to create a smooth surface that would absorb metallic inks and water-based paints, which themselves required time and experience to prepare. Many pigments—particularly blues and greens—had to be imported and were as costly as semiprecious stones. In early manuscripts, bright yellow was used to suggest gold, but later manu-

scripts were decorated with real **gold leaf** or gold paint.

Sometimes work on a book was divided between a scribe, who copied the text, and one or more artists, who did the illustrations, large initials, and other decorations. More often in the Early Middle Ages, scribe and artist were one. Although most books were produced anonymously, scribes and illustrators began to sign their work and provide a little background information on a page called the **colophon** (see fig. 14-13). One scribe even took the opportunity to warn the reader: "O reader, turn the leaves gently, and keep your fingers away from the letters, for, as the hailstorm ruins the harvest of the land, so does the injurious reader destroy the book and the writing" (cited in Dodwell, page 247).

spread-eagled between two standing beasts. The theme of a human attacked by or controlling a pair of animals is widespread in ancient Near Eastern art and in the Roman world, but this variation of the theme is a Swedish design. The rich blend of motifs in this work heralds the complex Hiberno-Saxon style that flourished in England and Ireland during the seventh and eighth centuries (Hibernia was the Roman name for Ireland).

Although the Anglo-Saxons who settled in Britain were pagans, Christianity endured through the fifth and sixth centuries in southwestern England and in Wales, Scotland, and Ireland. Monasteries began to appear in these regions in the late fifth century. Some were located in inaccessible places, isolating the monks in them from the outside world. In many others, however, monks interacted with local Christian communities. The priests in the Christian communities spoke Celtic languages and had some familiarity with Latin. Cut off from Rome, they developed their own liturgical practices, church calendar, and distinctive artistic traditions. Before the Roman Church reestablished contact with Britain at the end of the sixth century, Irish Christians had founded influential missions in Scotland and northern England. In 597 Pope Gregory the Great (590–604), beginning a vigorous campaign of conversion in England, dispatched a mission from Rome to King Ethelbert of Kent, who had a Frankish Christian wife. The head of this mission, the monk Augustine (d. 604), became the archbishop of Canterbury in 601 and soon established several other bishoprics. The Roman Christian authorities and the Irish monasteries, although allied in the effort to Christianize England, came into conflict over their divergent practices. The Roman Church wanted to bring British Christianity under its authority and eventually triumphed in liturgical and calendrical matters. Local traditions, however, continued to dominate both secular and religious art.

Rich and impressive copies of biblical scripture, especially the Gospels, were among the most prominent expressions of artistic creativity throughout Europe in the Early Middle Ages. Gospel books rested on the altar of every church and quickly became venerated objects as well as the source of liturgical readings. They were produced in local workshops called scriptoria (see "The Medieval Scriptorium," above). Scriptoria became major centers of learning and played a critical role in the diffusion of artistic styles and themes.

Irish monks produced many large, elaborately decorated Gospels, among them the *Gospel Book of Durrow*, dating to about 675. This manuscript is named for Durrow, in Ireland, where it was kept in the late medieval period, but no one knows exactly where it was made. A likely possibility is the monastery founded on the island of Iona off the northwest coast of Scotland by the Irish abbot Columba in the sixth century. The format and text of the book reflect a knowledge of Roman Christian prototypes, but its decoration is practically an encyclopedia of local design motifs, many of them adopted from metalwork. Each of the four books of the Gospel is preceded by a page of pure ornament, followed by a page with the symbol of the Evangelist and then with a decorated letter to begin the text. In the Book of Durrow, the lion, normally the symbol of Saint Mark, introduces the Gospel of Saint John (fig. 14-8). Following an early Christian tradition, the artist applied a very old convention and reversed the lion and eagle, using the lion for John and the eagle for Mark. The lion is a ferocious beast with sharp claws, jagged teeth, curling tail, and wild eye (fig. 14-8). The stylization of the body is based on Pictish (Scottish) stone carving, rather then on a flesh and blood creature. Its eye, tail, and paws and the stylized muscles around hip and shoulder joints are painted yellow to suggest gold. Its head is decorated with a uniform stippled

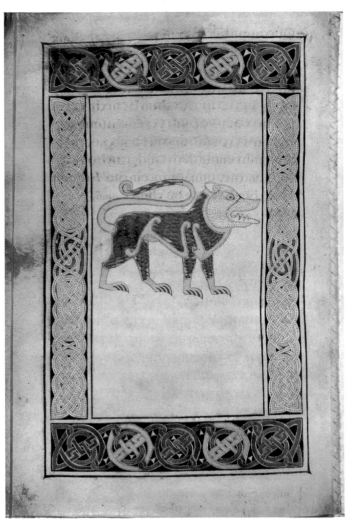

14-8. Page with *Lion,* Book of John, *Gospel Book of Durrow,* probably made at Iona, Scotland. c. 675. Ink and tempera on parchment, 9⁵/₈ x 5¹¹/₁₆" (24.5 x 14.5 cm). The Board of Trinity College, Dublin, MS 57 (A.4.5), fol. 191v

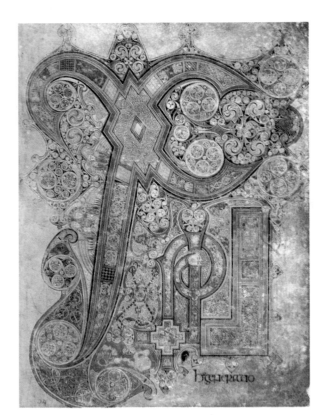

14-9. *Chi Rho Iota* page, Book of Matthew, *Book of Kells,* probably made at Iona, Scotland. Late 8th or early 9th century. Tempera on vellum, 13 x 9¹/₂" (33 x 25 cm). The Board of Trinity College, Dublin, MS 58 (A.1.6.), fol. 34v

The Greek letters *chi rho iota* (*XPI,* or *chri*) form the abbreviation for *Christi,* the first word in the Latin sentence *Christi autem generatio,* meaning: "Now this is how the birth of Jesus Christ came about" (Matthew 1.18). The word *autem* appears as another Latin abbreviation resembling an *h,* which is followed by *generatio* written out. The text continues on the next page. Medieval scribes had to learn a long list of standard abbreviations for Latin words, which were used like modern shorthand to save time and space in transcribing long documents or copying texts. Scribes in the courts of popes and secular rulers were even given the official title of "abbreviator."

pattern, and the surface of its body is covered with diamond patterns similar to those found in enamelwork. The two types of ribbon interlace on the wide border—a dotted pattern on the vertical bands and shifting bright green, red, and yellow on the horizontal bands—also suggest metallic decoration.

The *Book of Kells,* which an eleventh-century observer described as "the chief relic [religious object] of the Western world," is one of the most beautiful, original, and inventive of the surviving Hiberno-Saxon gospel books. It was probably made at the monastery on Iona in the late eighth century and brought to the monastery at Kells, in Ireland, in the late ninth century.

In the twelfth century a priest named Gerald of Wales, describing a Hiberno-Saxon gospel book very much like the *Book of Kells,* wrote: "Fine craftsmanship is all about you, but you might not notice it. Look more keenly at it,

and you will penetrate to the very shrine of art. You will make out intricacies, so delicate and subtle, so exact and compact, so full of knots and links, with colors so fresh and vivid, that you might say that all this was the work of an angel, and not of a man" (cited in Henderson, page 195). A close look at perhaps the most celebrated page in the *Book of Kells*—the one from the Book of Matthew (1:18–25) that begins the account of Jesus' birth—reveals what he means (fig. 14-9). The Greek letters *chi, rho,* and *iota,* the abbreviation for *Christi,* dominate the page. They are set within an irregularly shaped form that resembles a metal brooch. At first glance, the page seems completely abstract. The lines rippling out from the arms of the *chi* may suggest water, perhaps a reference to the mystery of Christ's conception and birth or to the four rivers that were thought to flow from heaven, bringing health to the Church. For those who would "look keenly,"

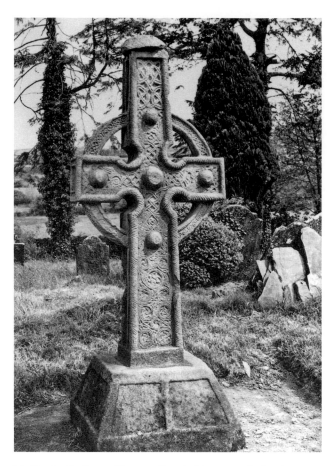

14-10. South Cross, Ahenny, County Tipperary, Ireland. 8th century

however, there is more. Hidden in the dense thicket of spirals and interlaces are human and animal forms. The curve of the *rho* in the center of the page, for example, ends in the head of a youth with red hair, perhaps representing Christ, the heart of the world, from whom flow the "rivers" of health. Three angels, perhaps representing heaven or air, hold the left edge of the *chi*. Below them, just to the right of the long stroke of the *chi* is a pair of crouching cats defending the Christian wafer (the host, or body, of Christ) from evil mice. Nearby an otter catches a salmon. Such images are not just ornamental, but form a subtle commentary on the text. Even the monastery cats join in the fight against the devil.

Like manuscript **illumination**, the monumental stone crosses erected in Ireland in the eighth century also reflect the influence of metalwork designs and motifs. The origin of these crosses is obscure, but they began to appear throughout the British Isles at roughly the same time. In the Irish "high crosses," so called because of their size, a circle encloses the arms of the cross. The South Cross of Ahenny, County Tipperary, is an especially well-preserved example of this type (fig. 14-10). It seems to have been deliberately modeled on metal ceremonial or **reliquary** crosses, that is, containers of holy relics in the form of a cross. It is outlined with **gadrooning** (notched, convex molding) and covered with spirals and interlace. The large **bosses** (buttonlike projections), which form a cross within the cross, resemble the jewels that were similarly placed on metal crosses.

CHRISTIAN SPAIN

As Roman control of western Europe deteriorated in the fourth and fifth centuries, a Germanic group known as the Visigoths, converts to Arian Christianity (Chapter 7), migrated across Gaul and into Spain. By the sixth century the Visigoths had established themselves as an aristocratic elite over the indigenous Spanish-Roman population, which probably outnumbered them by about 40 to 1. Although the Visigoths adopted Latin for writing and had switched to orthodox Christianity by the seventh century, they were never fully assimilated into Spanish society. Visigothic metalworkers, following the same late-Roman–Germanic tradition they shared with their counterparts in the north, created magnificent cloisonné jewelry similar in style and technique to the Sutton Hoo purse lid (see fig. 14-7).

The few sixth- and seventh-century churches surviving in Spain are among the best-preserved examples of monumental architecture in western Europe from this period. Santa Maria de Quintanilla de las Viñas, located about 150 miles north of Toledo, was built in the late seventh century. This **basilica-plan** church (modeled on the Roman basilica; see "Elements of Architecture," page 298) originally had a nave and two aisles, which no longer exist. The aisles opened through narrow doorways into the **choir**, the area reserved for the clergy, which extended the full width of the church. The narrow doorways suggest that the choir acted more as a barrier than as a connection between the congregation and the priests celebrating the Eucharist in the square sanctuary apse. This marked partitioning of the nave from the choir and sanctuary, found in other Spanish churches of the same period, may reflect a change in liturgical practice in which the congregation was barred from approaching the altar to receive Communion.

A **horseshoe arch** frames the entrance to the apse at Santa Maria at Quintanilla de las Viñas (fig. 14-11), refuting the popular belief that Islamic architects introduced this form in the eighth century (see the discussion of the Great Mosque of Córdoba in Chapter 8 and figure 8-6). The base of the arch juts inward slightly into the apse entrance, and the freestanding columns and large **impost blocks** likewise restrict it. The themes of the crisp bands of carving on the arch and impost blocks are found frequently in Early Christian art. On the impost blocks is Christ Triumphant between Angels. On the arch is a scrolling vine, the loops of which encircle birds and bunches of grapes, symbolic of the Eucharist (fig. 14-12). Like the carved decoration on the roughly contemporary South Cross at Ahenny, the style of these low-relief decorations is reminiscent of metalwork. A grooved border like the setting of a brooch contains the images on the arch, and the little lines that punctuate the border and scrollwork suggest fine threads of metal banding.

The Islamic conquest of Spain in 711 ended Visigothic rule. With some exceptions, Christians and Jews who did not convert to Islam but acknowledged the authority of the new rulers and paid the taxes required of non-Muslims were left free to follow their own religious practices. Christians in the Arab territories were called Mozarabs

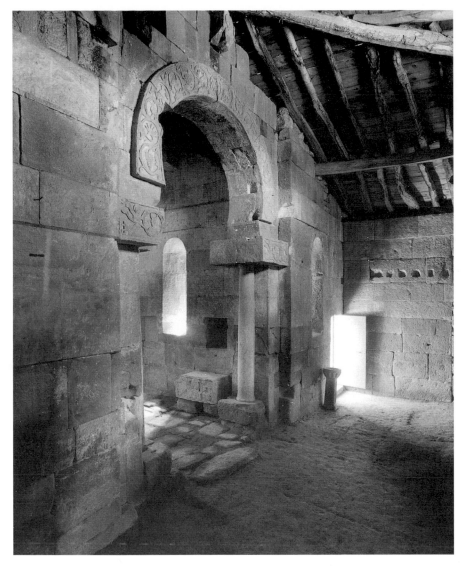

14-11. Church of Santa Maria, Quintanilla de las Viñas, Burgos, Spain. Late 7th century. View from the choir into the apse

(from the Arabic *mustarib,* meaning "would-be Arab"). The conquest resulted in a rich exchange of artistic influences between the Islamic and Christian communities. Christian artists adapted many features of Islamic style to their traditional themes, creating a unique, colorful new style known as Mozarabic. When Mozarabic artists migrated to the monasteries of northern Spain, which reverted to Christian rule not long after the initial Islamic invasion, they took this style with them, and it is known there as transported Mozarabic.

In northern Spain, the antagonisms among Muslims, orthodox Christians, and the followers of various heretical Christian cults provided fertile material for religious

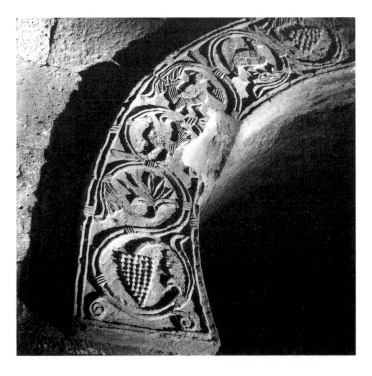

14-12. *Grapes, Vines, and Birds,* carving on the triumphal arch, Church of Santa Maria, Quintanilla de las Viñas

commentaries. One of the most influential of these was the *Commentary on the Apocalypse* compiled in the eighth century by Beatus, abbot of the Monastery of San Martín at Liébana, in the north Spanish kingdom of Asturias. The commentary is an analysis of the visions set down in the Apocalypse (also called the Book of Revelation), which is filled with vivid descriptions of the final, fiery triumph of Christ. Beatus's work is an impassioned justification of orthodox beliefs. It thus had enduring appeal for northern Christians in their long struggle against the Muslim rulers of the rest of Spain, and it was widely read, copied, and illustrated. Two copies from the late tenth century, illustrated in the Mozarabic style, were produced under the direction of the scribe-painter Emeterius, a monk in the workshop of the Monastery of San Salvador at Tábara in the kingdom of León.

The first of these commentaries was completed in 970 by Emeterius and a scribe-painter named Senior, who identified themselves in the manuscript. Artists were beginning to emerge from anonymity throughout Europe at this time. Mozarabic scribes often signed their work, sometimes showed themselves occupied with pen and brush, and occasionally offered the reader spontaneous comments and opinions (see "The Medieval Scriptorium," page 486). On the **colophon**, the page of a manuscript or book that identifies its producers, is a picture of the five-story tower of the Tábara Monastery and the two-story scriptorium attached to it, the earliest known depiction of a medieval scriptorium (fig. 14-13). The tower, with horseshoe-arched windows, and the workshop have been rendered in a two-dimensional cross section that reveals many details of the interior and exterior simultaneously. In the scriptorium, Emeterius on the right and Senior on the left, identified by inscriptions over their heads, are at work at the same small table. A helper in the next room cuts sheets of **parchment** or **vellum** for book pages. A monk standing inside (or perhaps outside) the ground floor of the tower pulls the ropes to the bell in the turret on the right. Three other men climb ladders between the floors, apparently on their way to the balconies on the top level. Brightly glazed tiles in geometric patterns, a common feature of Islamic architecture, cover what could be the tower's interior or exterior wall.

The other Beatus Commentary was produced five years later for a named patron, Abbot Dominicus. The colophon identifies Senior as the scribe for this project. Emeterius and a woman named Ende, who signed herself "painter and servant of God," shared the task of illustration. A full-page painting from this book shows an eaglelike bird with a luxurious tail grasping a glittering snake in its beak (fig. 14-14). With abstract shapes and cloisons of bright color recalling Visigothic metalwork, the image illustrates a metaphorical description in Beatus of the triumph of Christ over Satan. A bird with a powerful beak and beautiful plumage (Christ) covers itself with mud to trick the snake (Satan). Just when the snake decides the bird is harmless, the creature swiftly attacks and kills it. "So Christ in his Incarnation clothed himself in the impurity of our [human] flesh that through

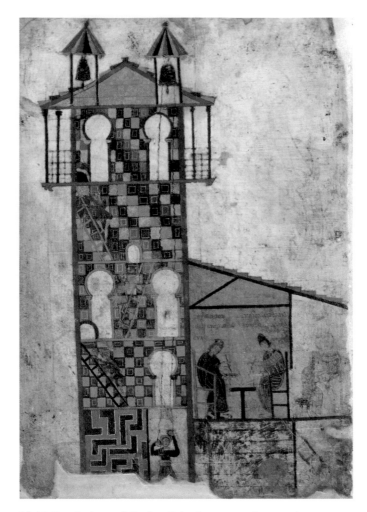

14-13. Emeterius and Senior. Colophon page, *Commentary on the Apocalypse* by Beatus and *Commentary on Daniel* by Jerome, made for the Monastery of San Salvador at Tábara, León, Spain. Completed July 27, 970. Tempera on parchment, 14¼ x 10⅛" (36.2 x 25.8 cm). Archivo Histórico Nacional, Madrid, MS 1079B (formerly 1240)

In medieval manuscripts the colophon was used to provide specific information about the production of a book. In addition to identifying himself and Senior on this colophon, Emeterius also praised his teacher, "Magius, priest and monk, the worthy master painter," who had begun the manuscript prior to his death in 968. Emeterius also took the opportunity to comment on the profession of bookmaking: "Thou lofty tower of Tábara made of stone! There, over thy first roof, Emeterius sat for three months bowed down and racked in every limb by the copying. He finished the book on July 27th in the year 1008 [970, by modern dating] at the eighth hour" (cited in Dodwell, page 247).

a pious trick he might fool the evil deceiver. . . . [W]ith the word of his mouth [he] slew the venomous killer, the devil" (from the Beatus Commentary, cited in Williams, page 95). Symbolic stories, or **allegories**, such as this were popular among artists, writers, and theologians in the Middle Ages. Because allegories translate abstract ideas into concrete events and images, their implications are accessible to almost anyone of any level of education.

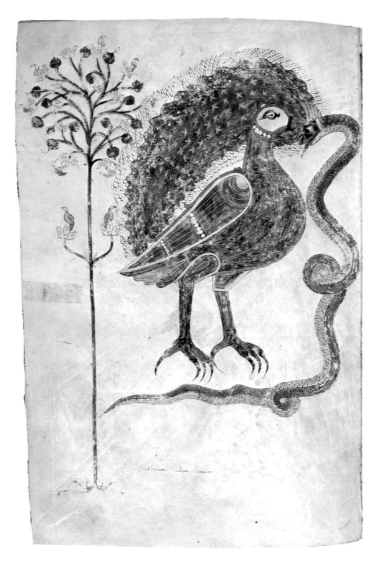

14-14. Emeterius and Ende, with the scribe Senior. Page with *Battle of the Bird and the Serpent, Commentary on the Apocalypse* by Beatus and *Commentary on Daniel* by Jerome, made for Abbot Dominicus, probably at the Monastery of San Salvador at Tábara, León, Spain. Completed July 6, 975. Tempera on parchment, 15¾ x 10¼" (40 x 26 cm). Cathedral Library, Gerona, Spain, MS 7[11], fol. 18v

THE CAROLINGIAN PERIOD

A new empire emerged in continental Europe during the second half of the eighth century that was forged by a dynasty known as Carolingian, after its greatest member, Charlemagne, or Charles the Great (*Carolus* is Latin for "Charles"). The Carolingians were Franks, a Germanic people who had settled in northern Gaul by the end of the fifth century. Under Charlemagne (ruled 768–814) the Carolingian realm reached its greatest extent, encompassing western Germany, France, a bit of Spain, and the Low Countries (modern Belgium and Holland). Charlemagne imposed Christianity, sometimes brutally, throughout this territory and promoted church reform. In 800 Pope Leo III (795–816), in a ceremony in the Church of Saint Peter in Rome, granted Charlemagne the title of emperor, declaring him to be the rightful successor to the first Christian Roman emperor, Constantine. This event reinforced Charlemagne's authority over his diverse realm and strengthened the bonds between the papacy and secular government in the West.

Charlemagne sought to restore the Roman Empire as a Christian state and to revive the arts. He placed great emphasis on education, gathering around him the finest scholars of the time, and his court became the leading intellectual center of western Europe. His architects, painters, and sculptors turned to Rome and Ravenna for inspiration, but what they created was not a simple copy of the Imperial Christian style.

Architecture

Charlemagne's biographer, Einhard, reported that the ruler, "beyond all sacred and venerable places . . . loved

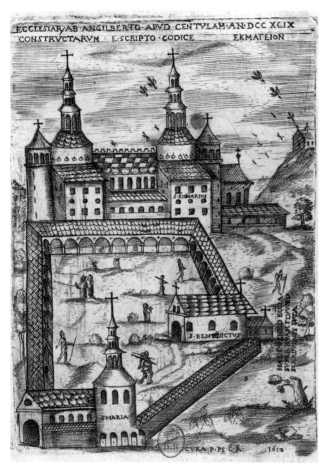

ECCLESIAR AB ANGILBERTO APVD CENTVLAM AN DCC XCIX
CONSTRVCTARVM E SCRIPTO CODICE EKMATEION

14-15. Abbey Church of Saint Riquier, Monastery of Centula, France, dedicated 799. Engraving dated 1612, after an 11th-century drawing. Bibliothèque Nationale, Paris

the church of the holy apostle Peter at Rome." Not surprisingly, Charlemagne's architects turned to Saint Peter's, a basilica-plan church with a long nave and side aisles ending in a projecting apse (see fig. 7-11), as a model for his own churches. These churches, however, included purely northern features and were not simply imitations of Roman Christian structures. Among these northern features was a multistory **narthex**, or vestibule, flanked by attached stair towers. Because church entrances traditionally faced west, this type of narthex is called a **westwork**.

The Abbey Church of Saint Riquier at the Monastery of Centula in northern France was an example of the Carolingian reworking of the Roman basilica-plan church. Built when Angilbert, a Frankish scholar at Charlemagne's court, was abbot at Centula, it was completed about 799. No longer standing, it is known today from archeological evidence and an engraved copy after a lost eleventh-century drawing of the abbey (fig. 14-15). A triangular enclosure linking the church and two independent chapels may have served as a **cloister** for the abbey's more than 300 monks. Cloisters are porticoed courtyards, sometimes with gardens linking the church with the buildings for the monastic community. The small, barnlike building at the right in the drawing was a

chapel dedicated to Saint Benedict. The more elaborate structure at the lower left, a basilica with a rotunda ringed with chapels was dedicated to the Virgin and the twelve Apostles. The interior would have had an altar of the Virgin in the center, an **ambulatory** passageway around it, and altars for each of the apostles against the perimeter walls.

The Church of Saint Riquier followed a basic basilica plan, but it also included two features that gave equal weight to both ends of the nave: a multistory westwork with flanking stair towers to the left and, to the right, a similar structure over the **transept**, the part of the church that crosses the nave at the sanctuary end. A square choir space beyond the **crossing**, the intersection of the nave and transept, lengthened the sanctuary space. The towers, soaring from cylindrical bases through three arcaded levels to cross-topped spires, would have been the most striking feature of the building. They were apparently made of timber, which posed fewer problems for tall construction than masonry. This vertical emphasis was a northern contribution to Christian architecture.

Charlemagne, who enjoyed hunting and swimming, was drawn to the forests and natural hot springs of Aachen (Aix-la-Chapelle in French), in the northern part of his empire. He built a palace complex there and installed his court in it about 794, making it his capital. The complex included administrative offices and royal workshops for making books and luxury items. Directly across from the royal audience hall on the north-south axis of the complex stood the Palace Chapel (fig. 14-16). This structure functioned as Charlemagne's private chapel, the church of his imperial court, a **martyrium** for certain precious relics of saints, and, after the emperor's death, the imperial **mausoleum**. To satisfy all these needs, the emperor's architects created a large, central-plan building similar to that of the Church of San Vitale in Ravenna (see fig. 7-29), adding a square projecting entrance facade with a tall, cylindrical tower on each side. The chapel originally had a very large, walled forecourt where crowds could assemble. Spiral stairs in the twin towers led to a throne room on the second level that opened onto the chapel **rotunda**, allowing the emperor to participate in the Mass. Relics were housed above the throne room on the third level.

The central core of the chapel is an octagon that rises to a **clerestory** above the **gallery** level (fig. 14-17). An ambulatory aisle surrounds this central core to form a sixteen-sided outer wall. The gallery also opens on the central space through arched openings supported by two tiers of Corinthian columns. Compared to San Vitale, where the central space seems to flow outward from the dome into semidomes and the exedra, the Aachen chapel has a clarity created by flat walls and geometric forms. The columns and grilles on the gallery level lie flush with the opening overlooking the central area, screening it from the space beyond. The effect is to create a powerful vertical visual pull from the floor of the central area to the top of the vault. Unlike San Vitale, which is covered by a smooth, round dome, the vault over the Palace Chapel rises from its octagonal base in eight curving masonry

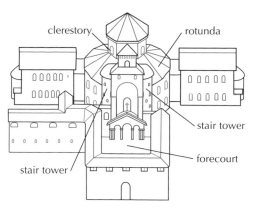

14-16. Reconstruction drawing of the Palace Chapel of Charlemagne, Aachen (Aix-la-Chapelle), Germany. 792–805

14-17. Palace Chapel of Charlemagne

Although this sturdily constructed chapel retains its original design and appearance, much of its decoration either has been restored or dates from later periods. The Gothic-style chapel seen through the center arches on the ground floor replaced the eighth-century sanctuary apse. The enormous "crown of light" suspended over the central space was presented to the church by Emperor Frederick Barbarossa in 1168. Extensive renovations took place both in the nineteenth century, when the chapel was reconsecrated as the Cathedral of Aachen, and in the twentieth century, after it was damaged in World War II.

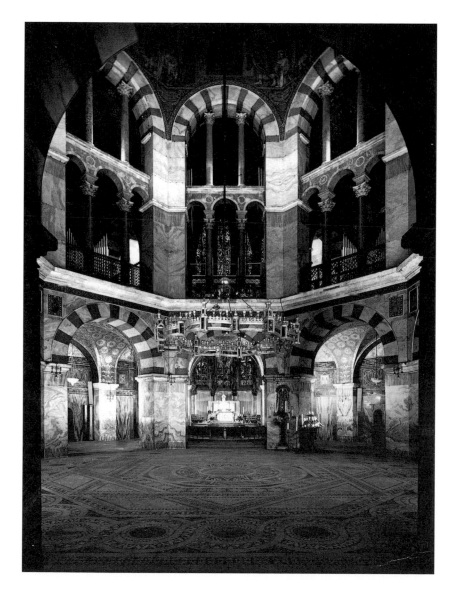

over the Palace Chapel rises from its octagonal base in eight curving masonry segments. The clear division of the structure into parts and the vertical emphasis are both hallmarks of the new style that developed under Charlemagne.

Monastic communities had grown numerous by the Early Middle Ages and had spread across Europe. In the early sixth century, Benedict of Nursia (c. 480–543) wrote his *Rule for Monasteries,* a set of guidelines for monastic life. Benedictine monasticism quickly became dominant, displacing earlier forms, including the Irish monasticism that had developed in the British Isles. In the early ninth century, Abbot Haito of Reichenau developed a general plan for the construction of monasteries for his colleague Abbot Gozbert of the Benedictine Abbey of Saint Gall near Lake Constance (in modern Switzerland). The Saint Gall

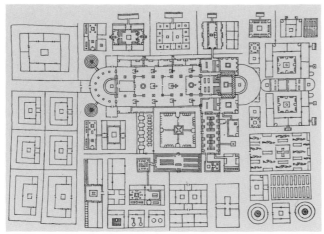

14-18. Plan of the Abbey of Saint Gall (redrawn). c. 817. Original in red ink on parchment, 28 x 44⅛" (71.1 x 112.1 cm). Stiftsbibliothek, St. Gallen, Switzerland, Cod. Sang. 1092

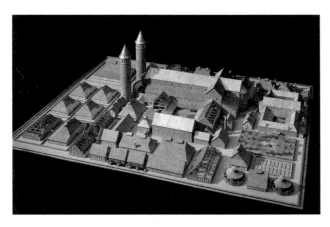

14-19. Model after the Saint Gall monastery plan (fig. 14-18), constructed by Walter Horn and Ernst Born, 1965

plan (fig. 14-18), originally drawn on five pieces of parchment sewn together, combines Benedictine guidelines with later ideas developed at Church councils. Figure 14-19 shows a model based on the original plan.

This extremely functional plan was widely adopted and can still be seen in many Benedictine monasteries. It reserved a central place for a basilica-plan church with apses at both ends and a transept crossing the nave at the eastern end. These apses would have housed separate chapels and displays of relics. Together with the adjacent cloister and **refectory** (dining hall), the church was the heart of the monastery's communal life. Monks entered it from the cloister or by stairs directly from their quarters. Members of the lay community that inevitably developed outside the walls of a large monastery used the main entryway. In the surrounding buildings, monks pursued their individual tasks. Scribes and painters, for example, spent much of their day in the scriptorium studying and copying books, and teachers staffed the monastery's schools and library. Benedictine monasteries generally had two schools, one inside the monastery proper for young monks and novices (those hoping to take vows and become brothers), and another outside for educating the sons of the local nobility.

Benedict insisted that monks extend hospitality to all visitors, and the large building in the upper left of the plan may be a hostel, or inn, for housing them. A porter would have looked after visitors, supplying them from the food produced by the monks. The plan also included a hospice for the poor and an infirmary. A monastery of this size had most of the features of a small town and would have indirectly or directly affected many hundreds of people. Essentially self-supporting, it would have had livestock, barns, agricultural equipment, a bakery and brewery, kitchen gardens (farm fields lay outside the walls), and even a cemetery. It would also have drawn on the support of extensive and widely scattered estates elsewhere.

Books

Books played a central role in the efforts of Carolingian rulers to promote learning, propagate Christianity, and standardize Church law and practice. As a result, much of the artistic energy of the period found an outlet in the empire's great northern scriptoria. One of the main tasks of these centers was to produce authoritative copies of key religious texts, free of the errors that tired, distracted, or confused scribes had introduced over the generations. The scrupulously edited versions of ancient texts that emerged are among the lasting achievements of the Carolingian period. The Anglo-Saxon scholar Alcuin of York, whom Charlemagne called to his court, spent the last eight years of his life producing a corrected copy of the Latin Vulgate Bible. His revision served as the standard text of the Bible for the rest of the Carolingian and subsequent medieval periods.

Carolingian scribes also developed a new, legible script to replace the confusing and hard-to-read scripts used since Roman times. Known as **Caroline minuscule**, it featured consistent separation of words and large capital letters for the opening of important sections. It is similar to many modern printed alphabets and is quite legible to modern readers.

One of the first surviving manuscripts in the new script, produced at Charlemagne's court between 781 and 783, was a collection of readings from the Gospels compiled by the Frankish scribe Godescalc and known as the *Godescalc Gospel Lectionary* or *Godescalc Evangelistary*. This richly illustrated and sumptuously made book (it has gold and silver letters and purple-dyed vellum pages) has a full-page portrait of the evangelist at the beginning of each Gospel section. The style of these illustrations suggests that Charlemagne's artists were familiar with the illusionistic painting style of imperial Rome as it had been preserved in Byzantine manuscripts.

In his portrait Mark is in the act of writing at a lectern tilted up to display his work (fig. 14-20). He appears to be attending closely to the small haloed lion in the upper left corner, the source of his inspiration and the iconographic symbol by which he is known. The artist has modeled the form of his arms, hips, and knees beneath his garment and rendered the bench and lectern to give a hint of three-dimensional space despite the otherwise flat background. Mark's round-shouldered posture and

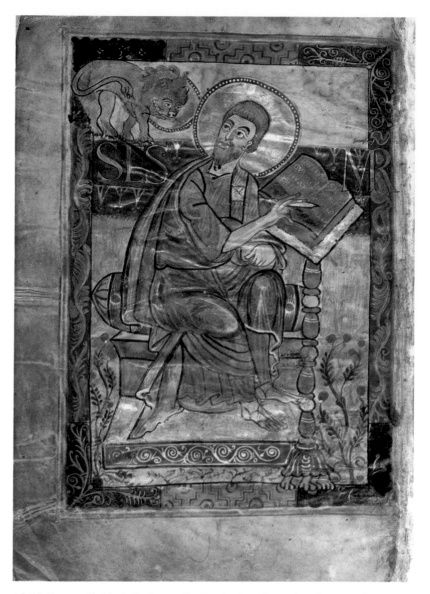

14-20. Page with *Mark the Evangelist*, Book of Mark, *Godescalc Evangelistary*. 781–83. Ink and colors on vellum. Bibliothèque Nationale, Paris, MS lat. 1203, fol. 16

sandaled feet, solidly planted on a platform decorated with a classical spiraling-vine motif, contribute an additional naturalistic touch. Stylized plants set the scene out of doors, a convention seen also in an Early Christian mosaic (see fig. 7-14). Probably commissioned to commemorate the baptism of two of Charlemagne's sons in Rome, the *Godescalc Evangelistary* remained at the court for several decades, providing a model for a later series of famous, luxuriously decorated gospel books.

Louis the Pious, Charlemagne's son and only successor, appointed his childhood friend Ebbo as archbishop of Reims, and Ebbo established that northeastern French town as another brilliant center of bookmaking. A portrait of Matthew from a gospel book made for Ebbo, begun after 816 at the Abbey of Hautevillers near Reims, illustrates the unique style that emerged there (fig. 14-21). Although there are some similarities between this painting and the evangelist portraits in books produced at Charlemagne's court (fig. 14-20), the differences

are striking. The figure of Matthew vibrates with intensity, and the landscape in the background threatens to run off the page, contained only by the painted border. Even the acanthus-leaf trim in the frame seems blown by a violent wind. The rapid, calligraphic style focuses attention less on the physical appearance of the evangelist than on his inner, spiritual excitement as he hastens to transcribe the Word of God coming to him from the distant angel (Matthew's symbol) in the upper right corner. His head and neck jut awkwardly out of hunched shoulders, and his left hand clumsily grasps the book and inkhorn. His twisted brow and prominent eyebrows, represented by long, diagonal slashes, lend his gaze an intense, theatrical quality. As if to echo the saint's turbulent emotions, the desk, bench, and footstool tilt every which way and the top of the desk seems about to detach itself from the pedestal.

The most famous of all Carolingian manuscripts, the *Utrecht Psalter*, dating probably between 825 and 850,

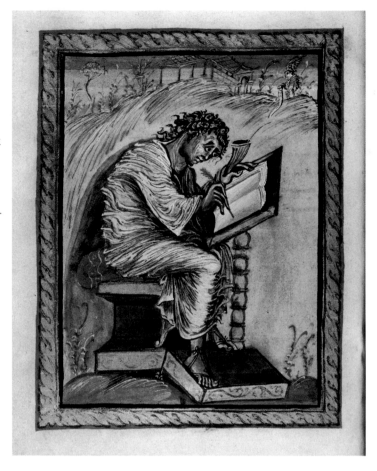

14-21. Page with *Matthew the Evangelist*, Book of Matthew, *Ebbo Gospels*. c. 816–40. Ink and colors on vellum, 10¼ x 8¾" (26 x 22.2 cm). Bibliothèque Municipale, Epernay, France, MS 1, fol.18v

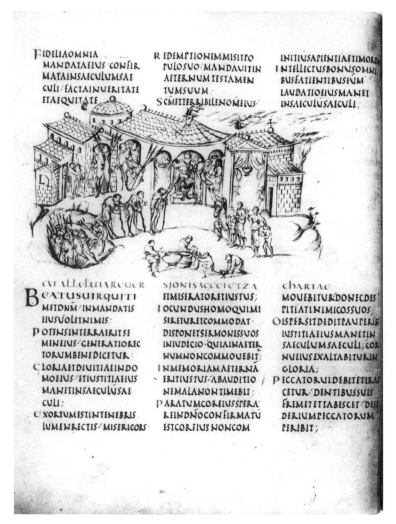

was also a product of the Reims workshop (fig. 14-22). This volume contains the Old Testament Book of Psalms illustrated with ink drawings that reflect the same linear vitality as the paintings in the Ebbo gospel book. The Psalms are difficult to represent because they do not tell a straightforward story. The *Utrecht Psalter* solves this problem by combining images derived from the core ideas of each Psalm into a single scene. The drawing in figure 14-22 illustrates Psalm 112.

1 Happy are those who fear the Lord,
    who greatly delight in God's commands.
2 Their descendants shall be mighty in the land,
    a generation upright and blessed.
3 Wealth and riches shall be in their homes;
    their prosperity shall endure forever.
4 They shine through the darkness, a light for the
    upright; they are gracious, merciful, and just.
5 All goes well for those gracious in lending,
    who conduct their affairs with justice.
6 They shall never be shaken;
    the just shall be remembered forever.
7 They shall not fear an ill report;
    their hearts are steadfast, trusting the Lord.
8 Their hearts are tranquil, without fear,
    till at last they look down on their foes.

14-22. Page with the end of Psalm 111 and Psalm 112, with an illustration for Psalm 112 (CXI in the Vulgate Bible), *Utrecht Psalter*. c. 825–50. Ink on vellum or parchment, 13 x 9⅞" (33 x 25 cm). Bibliotheek der Rijksuniversiteit, Utrecht, the Netherlands, MS script. ecol. 484, fol. 73v

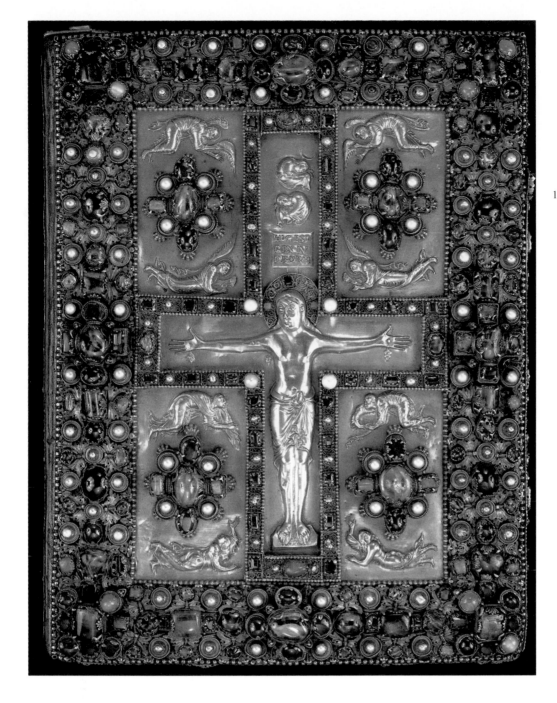

14-23. *Crucifixion with Angels and Mourning Figures,* outer cover, *Lindau Gospels.* c. 870–80. Gold, pearls, and gems, 13³/₄ x 10³/₈" (36.9 x 26.7 cm). The Pierpont Morgan Library, New York, MS 1

⁹ Lavishly they give to the poor;
    their prosperity shall endure forever;
    their horn shall be exalted in honor.
¹⁰ The wicked shall be angry to see this;
    they will gnash their teeth and waste away;
    the desires of the wicked come to nothing.

The hand of God is shown emerging from the clouds above the church on the right to bless "those who fear the Lord" (verse 1). The substantial stone buildings with tiled roofs represent their enduring prosperity (verse 3). The numerous hanging lamps in the buildings represent the "light for the upright" shining "through the darkness" (verse 4). A couple dispenses alms to the poor in the doorway of the central building, a deer's head with antlers ("their horn," verse 9, a symbol of vitality and honor) mounted on the roof above them. The people in the foreground, engaged in business, are "gracious in

lending" and "conduct their affairs with justice" (verse 5). Such high moral conduct naturally draws "foes," represented here by armed soldiers in the buildings on the left (verse 8). But the wicked, rounded up and tossed into a pit by the devil, "gnash their teeth and waste away" (verse 10). Illustrations like this convey the characteristically close association between text and image in Carolingian art.

The magnificent illustrated manuscripts of the medieval period represented an enormous investment in time, talent, and materials, so it is not surprising that they were often protected with equally magnificent covers. But because these covers were themselves made of valuable materials—ivory, enamelwork, precious metals, and jewels—they were frequently reused or broken up. The elaborate book cover of gold and jewels shown in figure 14-23 was probably made between 870 and 880 at one of the workshops of Charles the Bald (ruled 840–877),

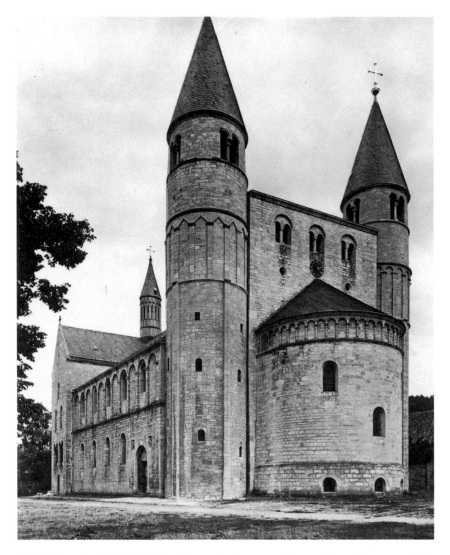

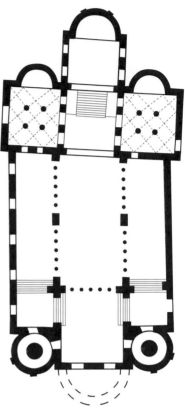

14-24. Church of Saint Cyriakus, Gernrode, Germany. Begun 961 and consecrated 973. The apse seen here replaced the original westwork entrance in the late 12th century.

14-25. Plan of the Church of Saint Cyriakus (after Broadley)

who inherited the portion of Charlemagne's empire that corresponds roughly to modern France after the death of his father, Louis the Pious. It is not known what book it was made for, but sometime before the sixteenth century it became the cover of a Carolingian manuscript known as the *Lindau Gospels*, which was prepared at the Monastery of Saint Gall in the late ninth century.

The cross and the Crucifixion were common themes for medieval book covers. The Crucifixion scene on the front cover of the *Lindau Gospels* is made of gold with figures in **repoussé** relief surrounded by heavily jeweled frames. Angels hover above the arms of the cross. Over Jesus' head, hiding their faces, are figures representing the sun and moon. The graceful, expressive poses of the mourners who float below the arms of the cross reflect the style of the *Utrecht Psalter* illustrations. Jesus has been modeled in a rounded, naturalistic style suggesting classical influence, but his stiff posture and stylized drapery counter the emotional expressiveness of the other figures. He stands straight and wide-eyed with outstretched arms, announcing his triumph over death and welcoming believers into the faith.

THE OTTONIAN PERIOD

The Carolingian Empire broke up when it was divided among the heirs of Louis the Pious. In the tenth century, control of the eastern portion of the empire, which corresponded roughly to modern Germany and Austria, passed to a dynasty of Saxon rulers known as the Ottonians, after its three principal figures, Otto I (ruled 936–973), Otto II (ruled 973–983), and Otto III (ruled 983–1002). Otto I, who took control of Italy in 951, was crowned emperor by the pope in 962, and thereafter he and his successors dominated the papacy and appointments to other high Church offices. This union of Germany and Italy under a German ruler came to be known as the Holy Roman Empire. Modern geographical names are used for convenience. No such country as Germany or Italy existed before the nineteenth century.

Architecture

The Ottonian rulers, in keeping with their imperial status, sought to replicate the splendors of Christian Roman architecture within their realm. The German court in

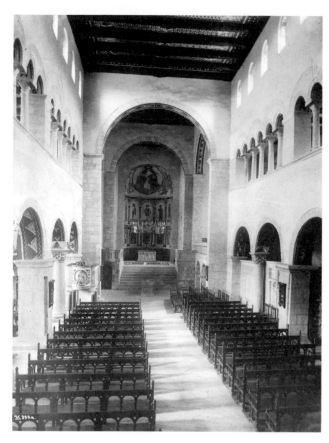

14-26. Nave, Church of Saint Cyriakus

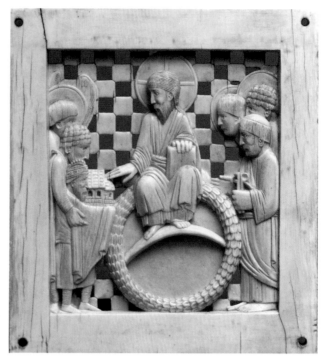

14-27. *Otto I Presenting Magdeburg Cathedral to Christ,*
one of a series of nineteen ivory plaques, known as
the *Magdeburg Ivories*. German or North Italian.
c. 962–973. Ivory plaque, 5 x 4¹/₂" (12.7 x 11.4 cm).
The Metropolitan Museum of Art, New York
Bequest of George Blumenthal, 1941 (41.100.157)

During the reign of Otto I, Magdeburg was on the
edge of a buffer zone between the Ottonian Empire
and the pagan Slavs. In the 960s, Otto established
a religious center there from which the Slavs could
be converted. One of the important saints of Magdeburg was Maurice, a Roman Christian commander
of African troops who is said to have suffered martyrdom in the third century for refusing to worship in
pagan rites. In later times, he was often represented
as a dark-skinned African (see fig. 16-58). The warrior
saint appears here presenting both Otto and Magdeburg Cathedral to Christ.

Rome gave northern architects access to Roman designs,
which they reinterpreted in light of their own local materials and time-tested techniques to create a new Ottonian style. Some of their finest churches were also
strongly inspired by Carolingian structures like the Abbey
Church of Saint Riquier (see fig. 14-15).

One of the best-preserved Ottonian buildings is the
Church of Saint Cyriakus at Gernrode (fig. 14-24). A German
noble named Gero founded the convent of Saint Cyriakus
and commissioned the church in 961. Following the Ottonian policy of appointing relatives and close associates to
important church offices, he made his widowed daughter-
in-law the convent's first abbess. A basilica-plan structure,
Saint Cyriakus originally had a westwork, which was
replaced by a second apse in the twelfth century (fig. 14-25).
The elevated floor of the choir and sanctuary apse at the
east end covers a vaulted space known as a **crypt**. Two
entrances on the south provided access between the
church and the convent's cloister and dormitories. The towers and other vertical features that dominate the east and
west ends of the church are reminiscent of similar features
at Saint Riquier's, although not so dramatic as the towers
that soared over that church. Windows, arcades, and
blind arcades break the severity of the church's exterior.

The interior of Saint Cyriakus (fig. 14-26) has three
levels: an arcade separating the nave from the side aisles,
a gallery with groups of three arched openings, and a
clerestory. A **triumphal arch** opening defines the end of
the nave, and the flat ceiling is made of wood. Most of
these features were also characteristic of Constantinian
basilica-plan churches (see fig. 7-12). The alternation of
columns and rectangular piers in Saint Cyriakus, how-

ever, creates a different rhythmic effect than the uniform
arcading of such earlier churches, which pulled the
viewer's gaze forward. Saint Cyriakus is likewise marked
by vertical shifts in visual rhythm, with two pairs of arches between piers on the nave level surmounted by three
pairs of arches on the gallery level, surmounted in turn by
three windows in the clerestory. This seemingly simple
architectural aesthetic, with its rhythmic alternation of
heavy and light supports and its balancing of rectangular
and round forms and horizontal and vertical movement,
was to inspire architects for the next 300 years, finding full
expression in the Romanesque period.

Sculpture

Carved ivory panels for book covers and diptychs were
among the products of both Carolingian and Ottonian
bookmaking workshops. An Ottonian plaque that shows
Otto I presenting a model of the Magdeburg Cathedral to
Christ may once have been part of the decoration of an
altar or pulpit in the cathedral, which was dedicated in
968 (fig. 14-27). Otto is the diminutive figure holding the

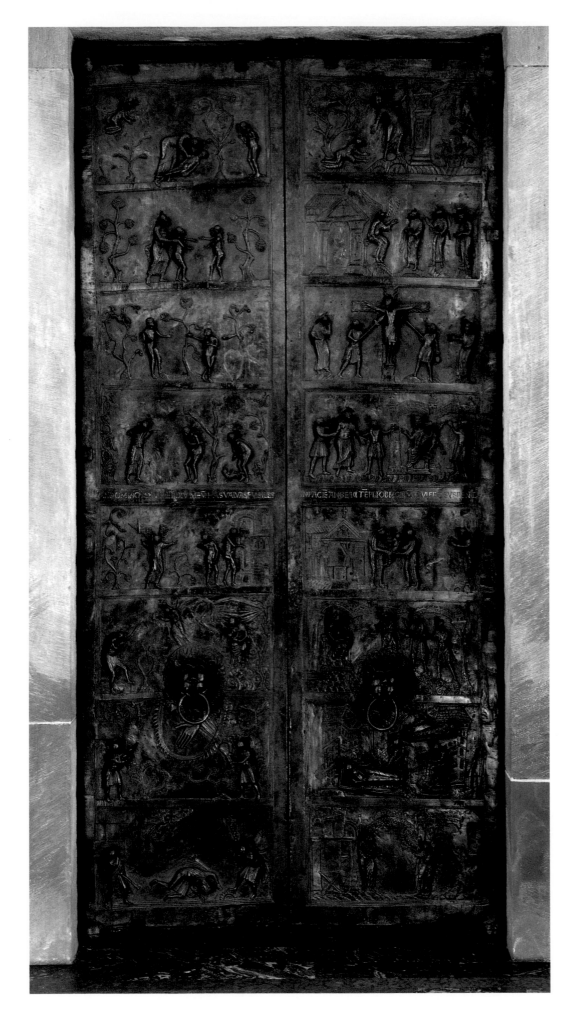

14.28. (opposite) Doors of Bishop Bernward, Cathedral (Abbey Church of Saint Michael), Hildesheim, Germany. 1015. Bronze, height 16'6" (5 m)

    The design of these magnificent doors anticipated by nearly a century the great sculptural programs that would decorate the exteriors of European churches in the Romanesque period. Bishop Bernward, who was both a scholar and a talented artist, is thought to have been intimately involved in planning the iconography of the scenes.

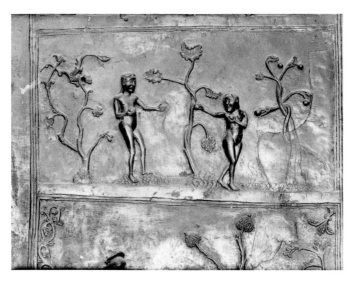 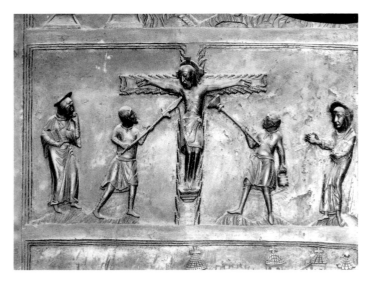

14-29. *The Temptation* (left) and *The Crucifixion* (right), detail of the Doors of Bishop Bernward

cathedral on the left. Christ is seated on a wreath, which may represent the heavens, and his feet rest on an arc that may represent the earth. Christ and Otto are surrounded by a crowd of witnesses. Saint Peter, patron of churches, faces Otto, and Saint Maurice, an important saint in Magdeburg, wraps his arm protectively around him. The action takes place on a very shallow stage. The heavy dignity and intense concentration of the figures are characteristic of the Ottonian court style.

    In the eleventh century, Ottonian artists in northern Europe, drawing on Roman, Byzantine, and Carolingian models, created a new tradition of large sculpture in wood and bronze that would have a significant influence on later medieval art. An important patron of these sculptural works was Bishop Bernward of Hildesheim, who was himself an artist. His biographer, the monk Thangmar, described Bernward as a skillful goldsmith who closely supervised the artisans working for him. A pair of bronze doors made under his direction for his Abbey Church of Saint Michael represented the most ambitious and complex bronze-casting project since antiquity (fig. 14-28). The bishop had lived for a while in Rome as tutor for Otto III and may have been inspired by the carved wooden doors of the fifth-century Church of Santa Sabina located near Otto's palace there.

    The inscription in the band running across the center of the doors states: "In the year of our lord 1015 Bishop Bernward installed the doors." They stand more than 16 feet tall and are decorated with Old Testament scenes on the left and New Testament scenes on the right. The Old Testament history begins in the upper left-hand panel with the Creation and continues downward to Adam and Eve's expulsion from Paradise, depicting their difficult and sorrowful life on earth, and ends with the terrible sin of brother murdering brother, the story of Cain and Abel. The New Testament follows, beginning with the Annunciation, at the lower right, and reading upward through the early life of Christ and his mother, Mary, through the Crucifixion to the Resurrection, symbolized by the Marys at the tomb and the meeting of Christ and Mary Magdalene in the garden. The Old Testament prefigured the New, and the scenes are paired across the doors to make the relationship clear. For example, the third panel down shows on the left the temptation of Adam and Eve in the Garden of Eden, believed to be the source of human sin, suffering, and death (fig. 14-29). This is paired on the right with the crucifixion of Jesus, whose sacrifice and suffering redeemed humankind, atoned for Adam and Eve's Original Sin, and brought the promise of eternal life.

    The doors' rectangular panels recall the framed miniatures in Carolingian gospel books, and the style of the scenes within them is reminiscent of illustrations in works like the *Utrecht Psalter*. Small, extremely active figures populate nearly empty backgrounds. Architectural elements and features of the landscape are depicted in very low relief, forming little more than a shadowy stage for the actors in each scene. The figures stand out prominently, sculpted in varying degrees of relief, with their heads fully modeled in three dimensions. The result is lively and visually stimulating.

    Another treasure of Ottonian sculpture is the *Gero Crucifix*, one of the few large works of carved wood to

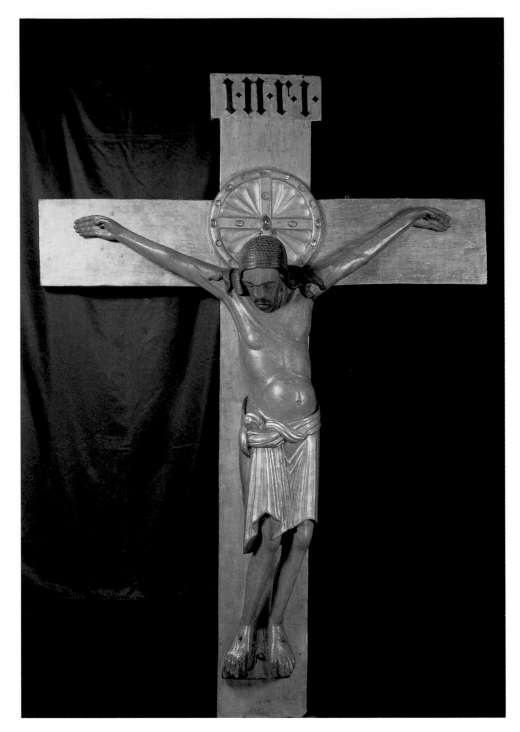

14-30. *Gero Crucifix*, Cologne Cathedral, Germany. c. 970. Painted and gilded wood, height of figure 6'2" (1.87 m)

This lifesize sculpture is both a crucifix to be suspended over an altar and a special kind of reliquary. A cavity in the back of the head was made to hold a piece of the host, or communion bread, already consecrated by the priest. Consequently, the figure not only represents the body of the dying Jesus but also contains within it the "body of Christ" obtained through the Eucharist.

survive from that period (fig. 14-30). It was commissioned by Gero, archbishop of Cologne (969–976), in northwest Germany, and was presented about 970 to his cathedral. (This is a different Gero from the patron of Saint Cyriakus at Gernrode.) The body of Jesus is more than 6 feet tall and made of painted and gilded oak. The focus here, following Byzantine models, is on Jesus' suffering. He is shown as a tortured martyr, not, as on the cover of the *Lindau Gospels* (see fig. 14-23), a triumphant hero. The intent is to inspire pity and awe in the viewer. Jesus' broken body, near death, sags on the cross and his head falls forward, eyes closed. The fall of his golden drapery heightens the impact of his drawn face, emaciated arms and legs, sagging torso, and limp, bloodied hands. In this image of

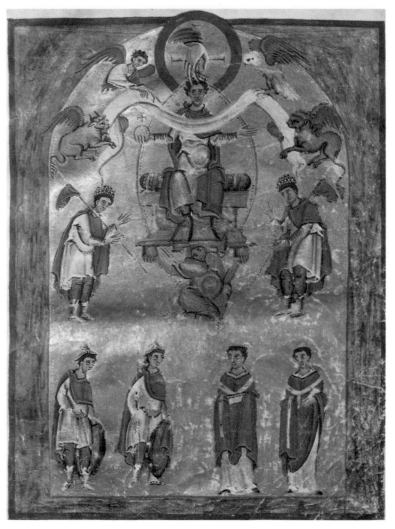

14-31. Page with *Otto III Enthroned, Liuthar Gospels (Aachen Gospels)*.
c. 1000. Ink and colors on vellum, 10⁷/₈ x 8¹/₂" (27.9 x 21.8 cm).
Cathedral Treasury, Aachen

distilled anguish, the miracle and triumph of Resurrection seem distant indeed.

Books

Great variation in style and approach is characteristic of book illustration in the Ottonian period. Artists worked for different patrons in widely scattered centers, using different models or sources of inspiration. The *Liuthar* (or *Aachen*) *Gospels*, made for Otto III around 1000, is the work of the so-called Liuthar School, named for the scribe or patron responsible for the book. The center of this school was probably a monastic scriptorium in the vicinity of Reichenau or Trier. The dedication page of the *Liuthar Gospels* (fig. 14-31) is as much a work of imperial propaganda as the ancient Roman *Gemma Augustea* (see fig. 6-32). It establishes the divine underpinnings of Otto's authority and depicts him as a near-divine being himself. He is shown enthroned in heaven, surrounded by a **mandorla** and symbols representing the evangelists. The hand of God descends from above to place a

crown on his head. Otto's arms are extended in an all-embracing gesture, and he holds the orb of the world surmounted by a cross in his right hand. His throne, in a symbol of his worldly dominion, rests on the crouching Tellus, the personification of earth. In what may be a reference to the dedication on the facing page—"With this book, Otto Augustus, may God invest thy heart"—the evangelists represented by their symbols hold a white banner across the emperor's breast, dividing body, below, from soul (heart and head) above.

On each side of Otto is an emperor bowing his crowned head toward him. These may represent his Ottonian predecessors or subordinate rulers acknowledging his sovereignty. The bannered lances they hold may allude to the Ottonians' most precious relic, the Holy Lance, believed to be the one with which the Roman soldier Longinus pierced Jesus' side. In the lower register, two warriors face two bishops, symbolizing the union of secular and religious power under the emperor.

A second Gospels made for Otto III by the Liuthar School at about the same time as the *Liuthar Gospels*

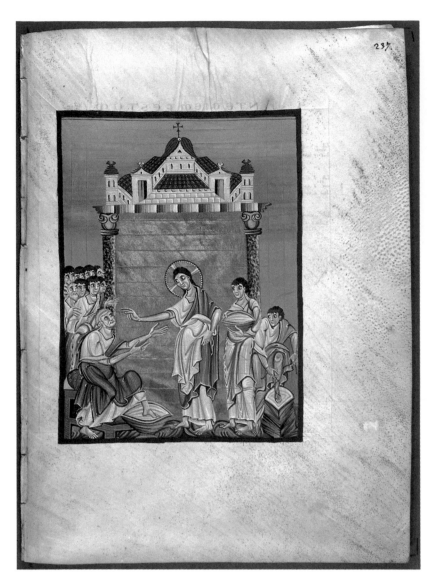

14-32. Page with *Christ Washing the Feet of His Disciples, Gospels of Otto III.* c. 1000. Staatsbibliothek, Munich

The washing of the disciples' feet, as told in John 13, was both a human gesture of hospitality, love, and humility and a symbolic transfer of spiritual power from Jesus to his "vicars," who would remain on earth after his departure to continue his work. At the time this manuscript was made, both the Byzantine emperor and the Roman pope practiced the ritual of foot-washing once a year following the model provided by Jesus: "If I, therefore, the master and teacher, have washed your feet, you ought to wash one another's feet" (13:14). The pope still carries out this ritual, washing the feet of twelve priests on every Maundy Thursday, the day before Good Friday.

contains a full-page illustration of an episode recounted in Chapter 13 of the Gospel according to John (fig. 14-32). Jesus, in one of his acts on the night before his crucifixion, gathered his disciples together to wash their feet. Peter, feeling unworthy, at first protests. The painting shows Jesus in the center, larger than the other figures, extending an elongated arm and hand in blessing toward the elderly apostle. Peter, his foot in a basin of water, reaches toward Jesus with similarly elongated arms. A disciple on the far right unbinds his sandals, and another, next to him, carries a basin of water. Eight other dis-

ciples look on from the left. The story is one of humility and mutual service, but the artist has transformed it into a symbolic representation of the all-powerful Christ of the Resurrection. The scene takes place outdoors in front of a gold curtain hung between green marble columns. Behind this barrier is a church, emphasizing an inherent message of the scene, the conferral of Jesus' blessing and authority on the apostles, his vicars on earth after his death.

The illustration on the presentation page of a Gospels made for Hitda (d. 1041), the abbess of the convent

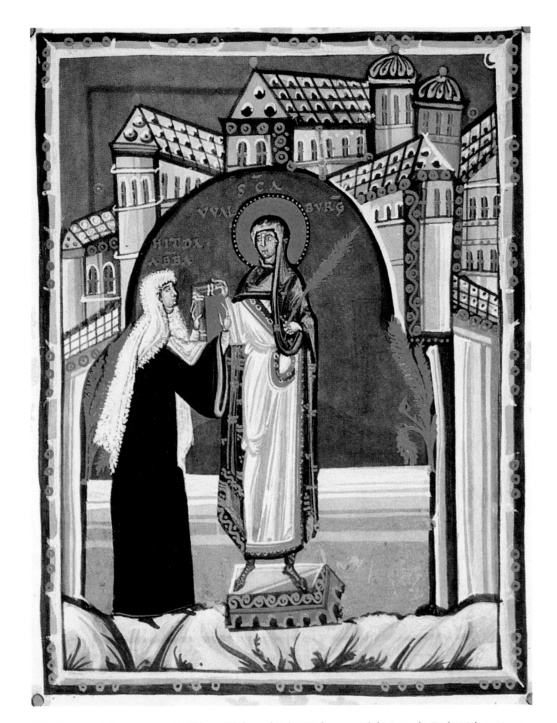

14-33. Presentation page with Abbess Hitda and Saint Walpurga, *Hitda Gospels*. Early 11th century. Ink and colors on vellum, 11³⁄₈ x 5⁵⁄₈" (29 x 14.2 cm). Hessische Landes- und Hochschul-Bibliothek, Darmstadt, Germany

at Meschede, near Cologne, also in the early eleventh century, shows the abbess offering her book to Walpurga, her convent's patron saint (fig. 14-33). The simple contours of the stately figures give them a monumental quality. The artist has arranged the architectural lines of the convent in the background to frame the figures and draw attention to their transaction. The size of the convent underscores the abbess's position of authority. The foreground setting—a rocky, uneven strip of landscape—is meant to be understood as holy ground, separated from the rest of the world by the huge arch-shaped aura

that silhouettes Saint Walpurga. The calm atmosphere conveys a sense of spirituality and contained but deeply felt emotion.

These final manuscript paintings in a sense summarize the high intellectual and artistic qualities of Ottonian art as well as its great variety. Ottonian artists, drawing inspiration from the past—as reflected in the art of Christian Rome—created a monumental style for a Christian, German-Roman empire, the Holy Roman Empire. From such groundwork during the early medieval period emerged the arts of European Romanesque culture.

1050 CE · 1080 · 1110

Speyer
Cathedral
c. 1030–
early 1100s

Cathedral
complex Pisa
begun 1063

Bayeux Tapestry
c. 1066–77

Sainte–Foy
late 10th–11th century

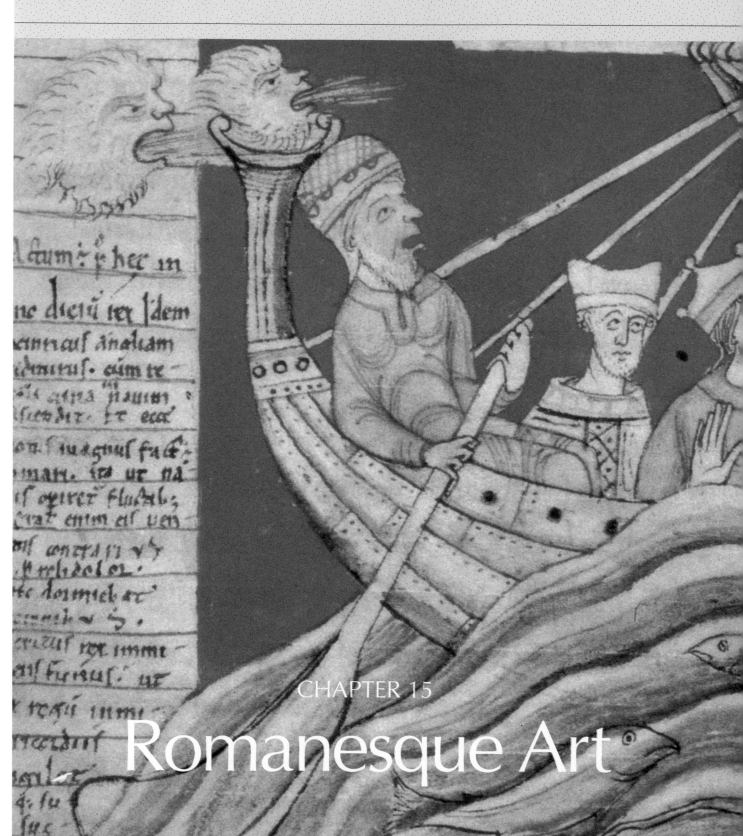

CHAPTER 15

Romanesque Art

Griffin
aquamanile
c. 1130

Battló Crucifix
mid–12th century

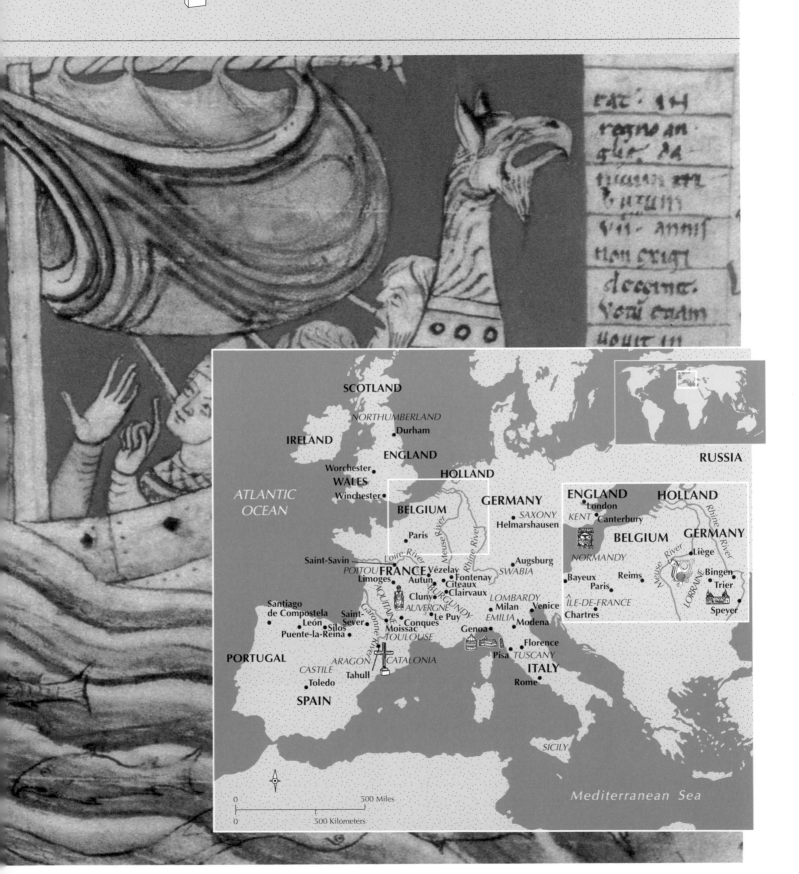

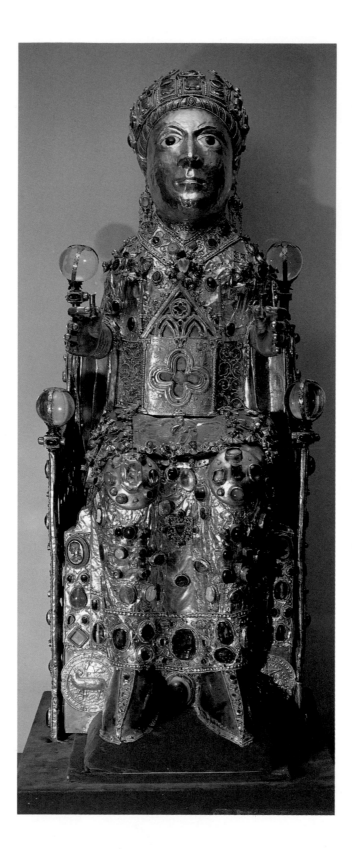

15-1. Reliquary statue of Saint Foy, made in the Auvergne region, France, for the Abbey Church of Sainte-Foy, Conques, Rouergue, France. Late 10th–11th century. Gold repoussé and gemstones over wood core (incorporating a Roman helmet and Roman cameos; later additions 12th–19th centuries), height 33½" (85 cm). Cathedral Treasury, Conques, France

According to legend, Saint Foy was a child martyr, burned to death in 303 for refusing to make sacrifices to pagan gods. The symbolic as well as visual focus of the reliquary, which contains the saint's cranium behind a Roman helmet, is its oversized crowned head. The statue originally stood on an altar in the sanctuary of the church, separated from pilgrims in the ambulatory by a screen. The reliquary and other treasures were discovered inside a wall of the church during restoration in the 1860s. The monks had hidden them there for safekeeping, probably shortly before the abbey was burned by Protestants in 1568. This accident of survival helps us to imagine the original splendor of Romanesque churches.

D uring the late Middle Ages, people in western Europe once again began to travel in large numbers as traders, soldiers, and Christians on pilgrimages. Pilgrims throughout history have journeyed to holy sites—the ancient Greeks to Delphi, early Christians to Jerusalem and to Rome, Muslims to Mecca—but in the eleventh century, pilgrimages to the holy places of Christendom dramatically increased, despite the great financial and physical hardships they entailed (see "The Pilgrim's Journey," page 513).

As difficult and dangerous as these journeys were, there were also rewards along the route even before the pilgrims reached their destination. They were often entertained by itinerant minstrels singing poems of epic heroes, perhaps to attract travelers to the sites where legendary figures were supposed to have been buried. One of the most celebrated epics to have come down through the centuries is *La Chanson de Roland (The Song of Roland)*, composed about 1100 and telling of the heroic death of one of Charlemagne's knights, Roland, who perished defending the Franks from the Moors. The climax of the story is set in the Pyrenees mountains in northwest Spain on the very road taken by pilgrims to the tomb of the apostle Saint James (Santiago) in Santiago de Compostela.

Crowds of pilgrims traveling to the major shrines stopped along the way to venerate relics of local saints. Remains of bodies and items said to have come in contact with a holy person were encased in richly decorated containers called **reliquaries**. The pilgrams left donations and offerings with the churches and monasteries that housed the relics. These relics were widely believed to have miraculous powers, and the demand for them was so great that as early as the seventh century the bodies of saints were divided up and moved from place to place. As a result of the attraction of prestigious relics, monasteries sometimes competed for them. The Benedictine Abbey Church of Sainte-Foy at Conques in south-central France, for instance, drew pilgrims from far and wide to view the skull of the child saint in its famous jewel-encrusted golden reliquary (fig. 15-1). A monk from Conques had stolen her bones from another abbey in the ninth century, and by 883 Saint Foy was the patron of Conques.

To accommodate the faithful and instruct them in Church doctrine, many monasteries on the major pilgrimage routes built large new churches and filled them with sumptuous altars, crosses, and reliquaries. Sculpture and paintings on the walls illustrated important religious stories and doctrines and served to instruct as well as fascinate the faithful. These awe-inspiring works of art and architecture, like most of what has come down to us from the Romanesque period, had a Christian purpose. One monk wrote that by decorating the church "well and gracefully" the artist showed "the beholders something of the likeness of the paradise of God" (Theophilus, page 79).

ROMANESQUE CULTURE

Romanesque means "in the Roman manner," and the term applies specifically to a medieval European style. The word was coined in the early nineteenth century to describe European church architecture of the eleventh and twelfth centuries, which displayed the solid masonry walls, rounded arches, and masonry vaults characteristic of Roman imperial buildings. Soon the term was applied to all the arts of the period from roughly the mid-eleventh to the late-twelfth century, even though the art reflects influences from many sources, including Byzantine, Islamic, and early medieval Europe, as well as Roman art.

During the eleventh and twelfth centuries western Europe was divided into many small territories. The nations we know today did not exist. At the beginning of the eleventh century, Europe was still divided into many small political and economic units ruled by powerful families. The southern part of the region had closer linguistic and cultural ties to northern Spain, and the king of France truly ruled only a small area around Paris. The duke of Normandy (a former Viking region on the northwest coast) and the duke of Burgundy paid the king only token homage. By the end of the twelfth century, however, the French monarchy centered in the Île-de-France around Paris was beginning to emerge as the core of a national state. After the Norman conquest of Anglo-Saxon Britain in 1066, England, too, became a nation. In

Germany and northern Italy, in contrast, the power of local rulers and towns ultimately prevailed against the attempts of the monarchs of the Holy Roman Empire to impose a central authority, and these regions remained politically fragmented until the nineteenth century. Sicily and southern Italy, previously in the hands of Byzantine and Islamic rulers, fell under the control of the Norman adventurers. This political fragmentation led to the many distinctive regional styles that characterize Romanesque art.

An increase in trade during the eleventh and twelfth centuries, promoted the growth of towns, cities, and an urban class of merchants and artisans. Europe remained, however, a predominately agricultural society, with land being the primary source of wealth and power. In many regions the feudal system that had developed in the Early Middle Ages governed social and political relations. In this system, a lord, a landowning aristocrat, granted some of his property to a vassal, offering the vassal protection and receiving in return the vassal's allegiance and promise of military service as an armed knight. Vassals, in turn, could become lords, granting part of their holdings to their own vassals.

The economic foundation for this political structure was the manor, an agricultural estate in which peasants worked in exchange for a place to live, food, military protection, and other services from the lord. Feudal estates, community-based and almost entirely self-sufficient, became hereditary over time. Economic and political power thus came to be distributed through a network of largely inherited but constantly shifting allegiances and obligations that defined relations among lords, vassals, and peasants. Women generally had a subordinate position in this hierarchical, military social system. When necessary, however, aristocratic women took responsibility for managing estates in their male relatives' frequent absences on military missions or pilgrimages. They could also achieve positions of authority and influence as the heads of religious communities. Among peasants and artisans, women and men often worked side by side.

In the Early Middle Ages the Church and state had forged an often fruitful alliance. Christian rulers helped assure the spread of Christianity throughout Europe and supported monastic communities and Church leaders, who were often their relatives, with grants of land. The Church, in return, provided rulers with crucial social and spiritual support, and it supplied them with educated officials. As a result secular and religious authority became tightly intertwined. In the eleventh century the papacy sought to make the Church independent of lay authority, and so sparked a conflict with secular rulers known as the Investiture Controversy over the right to "invest" Church officials with the symbols of office.

In the eleventh and twelfth centuries, Christian Europe, previously on the defense against the expanding forces of Islam, became the aggressor. In Spain the armies of the Christian north were increasingly successful against the Islamic south. In 1095 Pope Urban II, responding to a request for help from the Byzantine

emperor, called for a Crusade to retake Jerusalem and the Holy Land. This First Crusade succeeded in establishing a short-lived Christian state in Palestine. Although subsequent Crusades were, for the most part, military failures, the crusading movement as a whole had far-reaching cultural and economic consequences. The West's direct encounters with the more sophisticated material culture of the Islamic world and the Byzantine Empire created a demand for goods from the East. This in turn helped stimulate trade, and with it the rise of an increasingly urban society.

Western scholars rediscovered many classical Greek and Roman texts that had been preserved for centuries in Islamic Spain and the eastern Mediterranean. The combination of intellectual ferment and increased financial resources enabled the arts to flourish. The first universities were established at Bologna (eleventh century) and Paris, Oxford, and Cambridge (twelfth century). This renewed intellectual and artistic activity has been called the twelfth-century "renaissance," a cultural "rebirth." Monastic communities continued to be powerful and influential in Romanesque Europe, as they had been in the Early Middle Ages. Some monks and nuns were highly regarded for their religious devotion, for their learning, as well as for the valuable services they provided, including taking care of the sick and destitute, housing travelers, and educating the laity in monastic schools. Because monasteries were major landholders, they were part of the feudal power structure. The children of aristocratic families who joined religious orders also helped forge links between monastic communities and the ruling elite. As life in Benedictine communities grew increasingly comfortable, reform movements arose within the order itself. The first of these reform movements originated in the abbey of Cluny, founded in 910 in present-day east-central France.

FRANCE AND NORTHERN SPAIN For most of the Romanesque period, power in France was divided among the nobility, the Church, and the kings of the Capetian dynasty, the successors to the Carolingians. Royal power was negligible in the eleventh century, but Burgundy was stronger than the Île-de-France, the region around Paris. Beginning in the twelfth century, the Capetians began to consolidate their authority in the Île-de-France.

The Iberian peninsula (present-day Spain and Portugal) remained divided between Muslim rulers in the south and Christian rulers in the north. The power of the Christian rulers was growing, however. Their long struggle with the Muslims had heightened their religious fervor, and they joined forces to extend their territory gradually to the south throughout the eleventh and twelfth centuries. The Christians in 1085 reconquered the Muslim capital and stronghold Toledo, a center of Islamic and Jewish culture in Castile. Toledo had been an oasis of concord between Christians, Muslims, and Jews until the early twelfth century; its scholars played an important role in the transmission of classical writings to the rest of Europe, contributing to the cultural renaissance of the twelfth century.

Architecture

The eleventh and twelfth centuries were a period of great building activity in Europe. Castles, churches, and monasteries arose everywhere. As one eleventh-century monk noted, "Each people of Christendom rivaled with the other, to see which should worship in the finest buildings. The world shook herself, clothed everywhere in a white garment of churches" (Radulphus Glaber, cited in Holt, *A Documentary History of Art*, I, page 18). That labor and funds should have been committed on such a scale to monumental stone architecture at the same time as the Crusades and in a period of frequent domestic warfare seems extraordinary today. The buildings that still stand, despite the ravages of weather, vandalism, neglect, and war, testify to the power of religious faith and local pride.

In one sense, Romanesque churches were the result of master builders solving the problems associated with each individual project: its site, its purpose, the building materials and work force available, the builders' own knowledge and experience, and the wishes of the patrons providing the funding. The process was slow, often requiring several different masters and teams of masons over the years. The churches nevertheless exhibit an overall unity and coherence, in which each element is part of a geometrically organized, harmonious whole.

Like the Carolingian churches, the basic form of the Romanesque church derives from earlier churches inspired by Early Christian basilicas. Romanesque builders made several key structural advances and changes in this form. Stone masonry vaulting replaced wooden roofs, increasing the protection from fire and improving the acoustics for music. The addition of ribs—curved and usually projecting stone members—as structual elements to both barrel vaults and **groin vaults** permitted builders more flexibility in laying out interior space (see "Elements of Architecture," page 552). Masonry **buttresses** reinforced walls at critical points. The introduction of an **ambulatory** (walkway) around the apse allowed worshipers to reach additional, radiating chapels and to view relics displayed there. Builders of Romanesque churchs emphasized the symbolic importance of towers, especially over the crossing and the west facade (the entrance to the church and, by extension the gateway to paradise). This new form arose along the pilgrimage

1050 CE   1200 CE

PARALLELS

Europe	1050–1125	1125–1200
France/northern Spain	Strong aristocracy, divided political power; Capetian dynasty; illuminations of Beatus *Commentary*; Church of Santiago de Compostela; Christians capture Toledo from Muslims; Cluny III; Cistercian order founded; *La Chanson de Roland*; Church of Saint-Savin-sur-Gartempe; Church of Saint-Pierre, Moissac; elaborate sculptured portals, the San Clemente Master	Increasingly strong monarchy; University of Paris founded; Virgin Mary as Throne of Wisdom images
Britain and Normandy	Norman Conquest of England; William the Conqueror crowned; Durham Cathedral; *Bayeux Tapestry*; *Domesday Book*; Oxford University founded	*Winchester Psalter*; *Worcester Chronicle*
Germany/Meuse Valley	Salian dynasty; Investiture Controversy; Speyer Cathedral; Saxon metalwork	Aquamaniles introduced from East; Hildegard of Bingen's *Liber Scivias*
Italy	Baptistry of San Giovanni; Pisa Cathedral; Normans control Sicily and southern Italy the Cluniac; Gregory VII elected pope; Rome sacked by Normans; first narrative portal sculpture; Church of San Clemente rebuilt	Church of San Marco, Venice
World	Separation of Eastern and Western Christian Churches; Seljuk Turks capture Baghdad; Christian Crusaders take Jerusalem; Song dynasty (China); Great Zimbabwe civilization (Africa); mound-building cultures (North America)	Omar Khayyam's *Rubaiyat* (Persia); Muslim conquests in India; Kamakura period (Japan); Jenghiz Khan rules Mongols; Benin civilization (Africa)

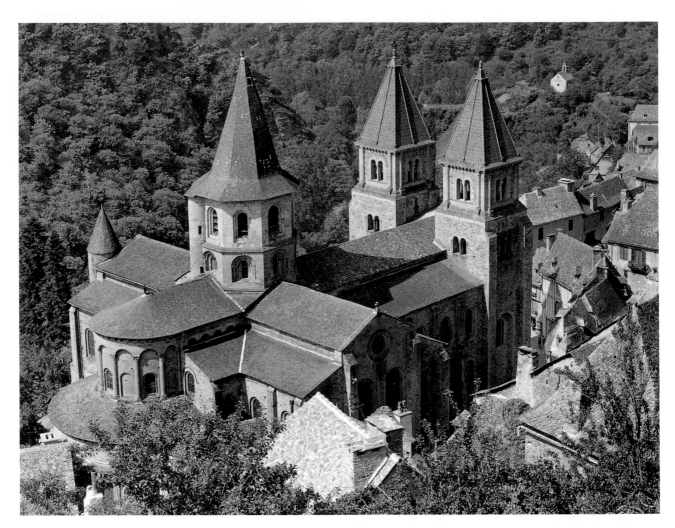

15-2. Abbey Church of Sainte-Foy, Conques, Rouergue, France. Mid-11th–12th century. Western towers rebuilt in the 19th century; crossing tower rib-vaulted in the 14th century, restored in the 19th century. View from the northeast

The contrast of nave and transepts, as well as the apse and lower ambulatory, are clearly seen in this exterior view, which supports a French scholar's characterization of Romanesque architecture as "additive."

routes to Santiago de Compostela. One surviving example of such a pilgrimage church, the Benedictine Abbey Church of Sainte-Foy, perches on a remote hillside at Conques in south-central France (fig. 15-2). As already noted, the church was renowned for its golden reliquary with the remains of a child saint (see fig. 15-1).

Construction of a new, larger church at Conques to accommodate the influx of pilgrims began in the mid-eleventh century and continued into the next century. The original **cruciform** (cross-shaped) plan with a wide, projecting transept was typical of Romanesque pilgrimage churches (fig. 15-3). At the west a **portal**—large doorway—opens directly into the broad nave. The facades of the largest churches have three doors, the central leading into the nave and the flanking doors into the side aisles. The elongated **sanctuary** encompasses the **choir** and the **apse**, with its surrounding **ambulatory** and ring of chapels.

The building is made of local sandstone that has weathered to a golden color (fig. 15-4). Light enters indirectly through windows in the outer walls of the aisles and upper-level **galleries**. The galleries replace the

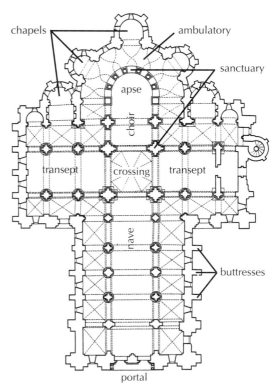

15-3. Plan of Abbey Church of Sainte-Foy

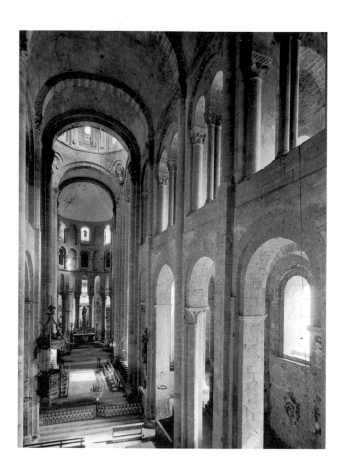

clerestory along the side aisles and overlook the nave. Ribbed barrel vaults cover the nave, groin vaulting spans the side aisles, and half-barrel vaulting called **quadrant vaulting**, the arc of which is one quarter of a circle, covers the galleries. The vaults over the galleries help strengthen the building by carrying the outward thrust of the nave vaults to the outer walls and buttresses.

The solid masonry piers that support the nave arcade have attached half columns on all four sides. This type of support, known as a **compound pier**, gives sculptural form to the interior and was a major contribution of Romanesque builders to architectural structure and aesthetics. Compound piers helped organize the architectural space by marking off the individual square, vaulted bays. Conques' square crossing is lit by an open, octagonal **lantern** tower resting on **squinches**. Light streaming in from the lantern and apse windows acted as a beacon, directing the worshipers' attention forward. During the Middle Ages the laity stood in the nave, separated from the priests and monks who celebrated the Mass in the choir.

Pilgrims arrived at Conques weary after many long days of difficult, perilous travel through dense woods and

THE PILGRIM'S JOURNEY

The eleventh and twelfth centuries in Western Europe saw an explosive growth in the popularity of religious pilgrimages. The rough roads that led to the most popular destinations—the Constantinian churches of Rome and the Cathedral of Santiago de Compostela (Saint James at Compostela) in the northwest corner of Spain—were often crowded with travelers, who had to contend at times with bandits, and dishonest innkeepers and merchants. Pilgrims also set out for the Church of the Holy Sepulchre in Jerusalem. Journeys could last a year or more.

The stars of the Milky Way, it was said, marked the way to Santiago de Compostela (see fig. 17). Still, a guidebook helped, and in the twelfth century the priest Aymery Picaud wrote one for pilgrims on their way to the great shrine through what is now France. In Picaud's time, four main pilgrimage routes crossed France, merging into a single road in Spain at Puente-la-Reina and leading on from there through Burgos and León to Compostela. Conveniently spaced monasteries and churches offered food and lodging. Roads and bridges were maintained by a guild of bridge builders and guarded by the Knights of Santiago.

Picaud described the best-traveled routes and most important shrines to visit. Chartres, for example, housed the tunic that the Virgin was said to have worn when she gave birth to Jesus. At Vézelay were the bones of Saint Mary Magdalen, and at Conques, those of Saint Foy, an early local martyr (see fig. 15-1). Churches associated with miraculous cures—Autun, for example, which claimed to house the bones of Saint Lazarus, raised by Jesus from the dead—were filled with the sick and injured praying to be healed. Like travel guides today, Picaud's book also provided shopping tips, advice on local customs, comments on food and the safety of drinking water, and pocket dictionaries of useful words in the languages the pilgrim would encounter en route. His warnings about the people who prey on travelers seem all too relevant today.

"Das ist der Rom Weg," late map of pilgrimage routes to Rome from Denmark. c. 1500. Woodcut, 15³⁄₄ x 11¹⁄₄" (40 x 28.5 cm). The British Library, London

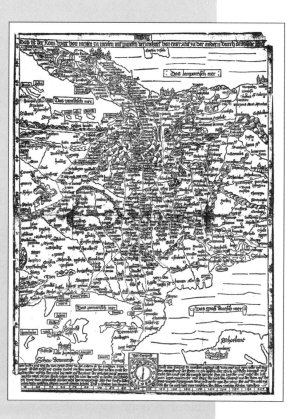

mountains, probably thankful that they had been protected by the saint against bandits on the way. They no doubt paused in front of the west entrance to study its portal sculpture, a notable feature of Romanesque pilgrimage churches. Portal sculpture communicated the core doctrines of the Church to those who came to read its messages. At Conques, the Last Judgment in the **tympanum** (the **lunette** over the doorway) marked the passage from the secular world into the sacred world within the church. Inside, the walls resounded with the music of the plainchant, also called Gregorian chant after Pope Gregory I (590–604). The Benedictines spent eight-and-a-half to ten hours a day in religious services. Today they still spend two-and-a-half to three hours.

A different Romanesque architecture could be found at the Benedictine Abbey Church of Cluny in Burgundy, founded in 910 as a reformed monastery. Cluny had a special independent status, its abbot answering directly to the pope in Rome rather than to the local bishop and feudal lord. This unique freedom, jealously safeguarded by a series of long-lived and astute abbots, enabled Cluny to become influential and prosperous in the eleventh and early twelfth centuries. Cluniac reform spread to other monasteries within Burgundy and beyond, to the rest of France, Italy, and Germany. Cluny attracted the patronage of successive rulers, as well as the favor of the pope in Rome. By the second half of the eleventh century there were some 300 monks in the abbey at Cluny alone. Cluny founded more than 200 priories (religious houses) in other locations—many along pilgrimage routes—and many more houses were loosely affiliated with it. At the height of its power 1,450 houses answered to the strong central administration of the abbot of Cluny.

Cluniac monks and nuns dedicated themselves to the scholarly and artistic interests of their order. Most important was the celebration of the eight Hours of the Divine Office, including prayers, scripture readings, psalms and hymns, and the Mass, the symbolic rite of the Last Supper, celebrated after the third hour (terce). They depended for support on the labor of laymen and laywomen who had not taken vows. Cluny's extensive land holdings, coupled with gifts of money and treasure, made it wealthy. Cluny and its affiliates were among the major patrons of art in Western Europe.

The great Hugh de Semur, abbot of Cluny for sixty years (1049–1109), began a new church at Cluny in 1088 with the help of financing from King Alfonso VI of León and Castile in northern Spain (ruled 1065–1109). Known to art historians as Cluny III (because it was the third building at the site), it was the largest and most spectacular church in all Europe when it was completed in 1130. Used as a stone quarry in the early 1800s after the French Revolution, the monastery is known today through the work of archeologists (fig. 15-5). Richly carved, painted, and furnished, it was described by a contemporary observer as fit for angels. Music and art were densely interwoven in Cluniac life, shaped by the Cluniac conception of the house of God. The proportions of Cluny III were based on harmonic relationships discussed in ancient Greek musical theory and mathematics. The

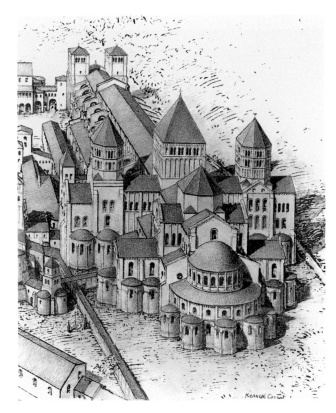

15-5. Reconstruction drawing of the Abbey Church (Cluny III), Cluny, Burgundy, France. 1088–1130. View from the east (after Conant)

The magnificence of this church and the Cluniac power it represented made it a particular target of anti-Church violence. It was nearly destroyed after the French Revolution when the owner sold its stones as building material. Only the southeast transept and its tower survive.

towering barrel-vaulted ceiling—more than 100 feet high in a space more than 500 feet long from end to end—enhanced the sound of the monks' chants. Sculpture, too, picked up the musical theme: carvings on two surviving column capitals depict personifications of the eight modes of the plainchant. The hallmarks of Cluniac churches were functional design, skillful masonry technique, and the assimilation of elements from Roman and early medieval architecture and sculpture. Individual Cluniac monasteries, however, were free to follow regional traditions and styles; consequently Cluny III was widely influential, though not copied exactly.

Several new religious orders devoted to an austere spirituality arose in the late eleventh and early twelfth centuries. Among these were the Cistercians, another reform group within the Benedictine order. The Cistercians turned away from Cluny's elaborate liturgical practices and emphasis on the arts to a simpler monastic life. The order was founded in the late eleventh century at Cîteaux (*Cistercium* in Latin, hence the order's name), also in Burgundy. Led by the commanding figure of Abbot Bernard of Clairvaux (abbacy, 1115–1154), the Cistercians thrived on strict mental and physical discipline. These virtues enabled them to settle and reclaim vast tracts of wilderness. In time, their enterprises stretched from present-day Russia to Ireland, and by the end of the

Middle Ages there were approximately 1,500 Cistercian abbeys, half of which were for women. Although their very success eventually undermined their austerity, they were able for a long time to sustain a way of life devoted to prayer and intellectual pursuits combined with shared manual labor. Like the Cluniacs, however, they depended on the assistance of laypersons.

Early Cistercian architecture reflects the ideals of the order. The Abbey Church of Notre-Dame at Fontenay, begun in 1139, is the oldest surviving Cistercian structure in Burgundy. The abbey has a simple geometric plan (fig. 15-6). The church has a long nave with rectangular chapels in the square-ended transept arms, and a shallow choir with a straight end wall. Lay brothers entered through the west doorway, monks from the attached cloister or upstairs dormitory. Situated far from the distractions of the secular world, the building made few concessions to the popular taste for architectural adornment, either outside or in. In other ways, however, Fontenay and other Cistercian monasteries fully reflect the architectural developments of their time in their masonry, vaulting, and proportions.

The Cistercians relied on harmonious proportions and fine stonework, not elaborate surface decoration, to achieve beauty in their architecture (fig. 15-7). A feature of Fontenay often found in Cistercian architecture is the

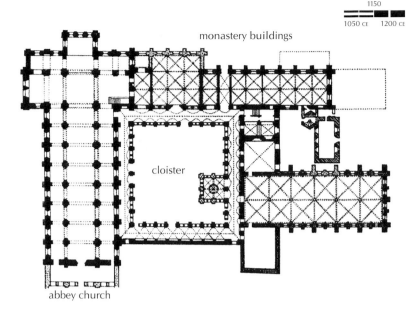

15-6. Plan of the Abbey of Notre-Dame, Fontenay, Burgundy, France. 1139–47

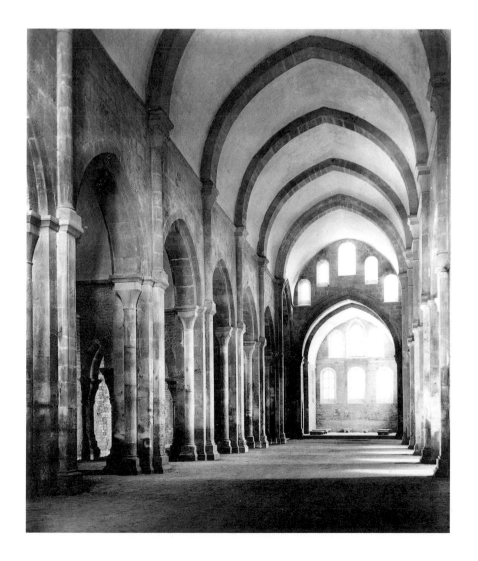

15-7. Nave, Abbey Church of Notre-Dame, Fontenay. 1139–47

The pointed arch began to be used in northwestern Europe in the Romanesque period. Its origin may have been in Islamic building in southern Europe. Pointed arches are structurally more stable than round ones, directing more weight down into the floor instead of outward to the walls, and they can span greater distances at greater heights without collapsing. Visually, pointed arches draw the eye inward and upward, an effect that directs thoughts toward heaven.

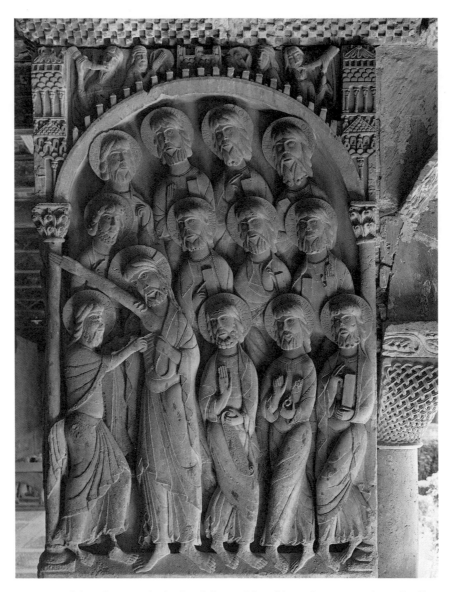

15-8. *Doubting Thomas*, pier in the cloister of the Abbey of Santo Domingo de Silos, Castile, Spain. c. 1100

use of pointed ribbed vaults over the nave and pointed arches in the nave arcade and side-aisle bays. Furnishings included little else than altars and candles. The large windows in the end wall, rather than a clerestory, provided light. The triple windows reminded the monks of the Trinity.

This simple architecture spread from the Cistercian homeland in Burgundy to become an international style. From Scotland and Germany to Spain and Italy, Cistercian designs and building techniques varied only slightly. The masonry vaults and harmonious proportions were to be influential in the development of the Gothic style later in the Middle Ages.

Architectural Sculpture

Like Cluny and unlike the severe churches of the Cistercians, many Romanesque churches have a remarkable variety of painting and sculpture. Christ Enthroned in Majesty in heaven may be illustrated, as well as stories of

Jesus among the people, or images of the lives and the miracles of the saints. The Virgin Mary gains importance in the paintings, and the prophets, kings, and queens of the Old Testament prefigure (symbolically foretell) events in the New Testament. Contemporary bishops, abbots, other noble patrons, and even ordinary folk are represented. A profusion of monsters, animals, plants, geometric ornament, allegorical figures such as Lust and Greed, and depictions of real and imagined buildings surround the major works of sculpture. The Elect rejoice in heaven with the angels; the Damned suffer in hell, tormented by demons. Biblical and historical tales come alive, along with scenes of everyday life. All these events seem to take place in a contemporary medieval setting.

Superb reliefs embellish the corner piers in the cloister of the Abbey of Santo Domingo de Silos in the kingdom of Castile. One of these illustrates the story, recounted in the Gospel of John (Chapter 20), in which Christ, appearing to his apostles after the Crucifixion, permits Thomas to touch his wounds to convince the

ELEMENTS OF ARCHITECTURE

The Romanesque Church Portal

The doorways of major Romanesque churches are often grand sculpted **portals**. Wood or metal doors are surrounded by elaborate stone sculpture arranged in zones to fit the architectural elements. The most important imagery is in the semicircular **tympanum** directly over the door lintel.

Archivolts—curved moldings formed by the **voussoirs** of which the arch is constructed—frame the tympanum. **Spandrels** are the flat areas at the outside upper corners of the tympanum area. On both sides of the doors are **jambs** carved in the form of jamb columns, typically decorated with figures, called jamb figures. **Pedestals** sometimes form the bases of jamb columns. The receding jambs form a shallow porch leading into the church.

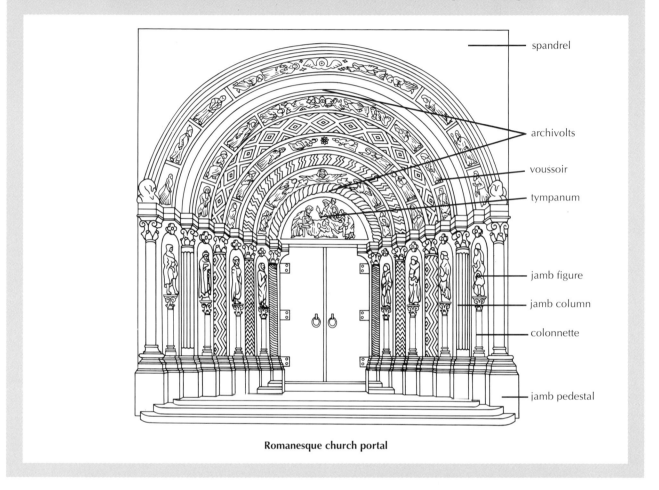

spandrel

archivolts

voussoir

tympanum

jamb figure

jamb column

colonnette

jamb pedestal

Romanesque church portal

doubting apostle of his Resurrection (fig. 15-8). The organization of the composition is expert. Christ is shown larger than his disciples and placed off-center in the left foreground. His outstretched right arm forms a strong diagonal that bisects the space between his haloed head and that of Thomas in the lower left. Thomas's outstretched arm, reaching toward Christ's side, forms an opposing diagonal parallel to the slope between their heads, leading the eye back to Christ's face. The massed presence of the other apostles, bearing witness to the miracle, gives visual weight to the scene through the rhythmic repetition of form. The effect parallels the way the repetition of the nave bays in a Romanesque church culminates in the apse, its symbolic core.

Miniature buildings and musicians crown the arch that forms a canopy over the apostles' heads in the Silos pier relief. The sculptors used these lively images from medieval life to frame the biblical story, just as medieval preachers used elements of daily life in their sermons to provide a context for biblical messages. The art and literature of the period frequently combined "official" and "popular" themes in this way.

Carved portals are among the most significant innovations of Romanesque art. These complex works, which combine biblical narrative, legends, folklore, history, and Christian symbolism, represent the first attempt at large-scale architectural sculpture since the end of the Roman Empire. By the early twelfth century, sculpture depicting Christ in Majesty (the Second Coming), the Last Judgment, and the final triumph of good over evil at the Apocalypse could be seen on the portals of churches in northern Spain, southern France, and Burgundy. The churches of Conques and Cluny had carved portals; so did the Churches of Saint-Pierre in Moissac in southern France, the Cathedral of Saint-Lazare at Autun, the Churches of Sainte-Madeleine at Vézelay in Burgundy, and Sainte-Foy at Conques. (We will look at Moissac and Autun as typical examples.)

The Cluniac priory of Saint-Pierre at Moissac was a major pilgrimage stop on the route to Santiago de

15-9. South
portal
and porch,
Priory
Church
of Saint-
Pierre,
Moissac,
Toulouse,
France.
c. 1115–30

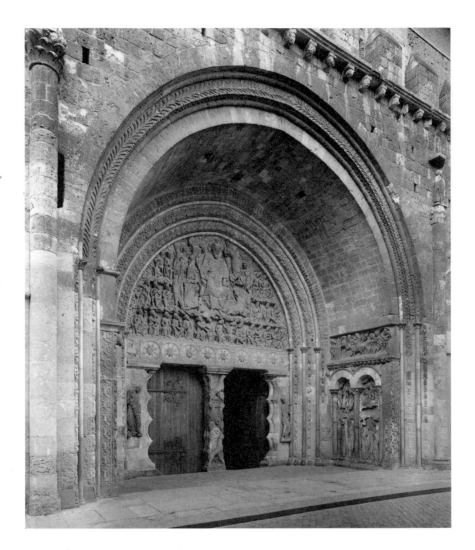

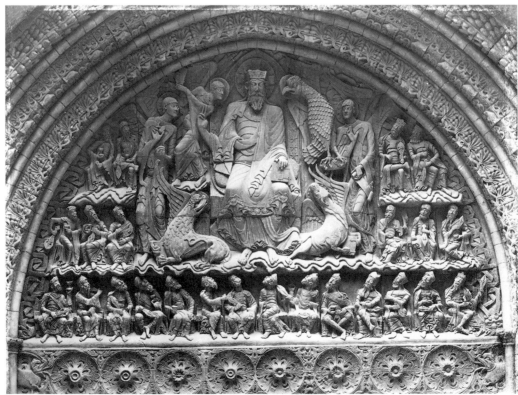

15-10. *Christ in Majesty*, tympanum of the south portal, Priory Church of Saint-Pierre. Width approx. 18' 6" (5.68 m)

Compostela. The original shrine at the site was reputed to have existed in the Carolingian period. After joining the congregation of Cluny in 1047, the monastery prospered from the donations of pilgrims and the local nobility, as well as from its control of shipping on the nearby Garonne River.

Moissac's monks launched an ambitious building campaign, and much of the sculpture from the cloister (c. 1100) and the church (1115–1130) has survived. The church was completed during the tenure of Abbot Roger (1115–1131), who commissioned the sculpture on the south portal and porch (fig. 15-9). This sculpture represented a genuine departure from earlier works in both the quantity and quality of the carving. The sculpture covers the **tympanum** (the **lunette** over the doorway), the **archivolts** (the curved rows of **voussoirs** outlining the tympanum), and the lintel, doorposts, and porch walls (see "Elements of Architecture," page 517). The stones still bear traces of the original paint.

The sculpture of Christ in Majesty dominates the huge tympanum (fig. 15-10). The scene combines images from the description of the Second Coming of Christ in Chapters 4 and 5 of the Apocalypse with others derived from Old Testament prophecies, all filtered through the early twelfth century's view of Scripture. A gigantic Christ, like an awe-inspiring Byzantine Pantokrator (see fig. 7-47), stares down at the viewer as he blesses and points to the book "sealed with seven seals" (Revelation 5:1). He is enclosed by a **mandorla**, and a cruciform halo rings his head. Four winged creatures symbolizing the evangelists—Matthew the Man (upper left), Mark the Lion (lower left), Luke the Ox (lower right), and John the Eagle (upper right)—frame Christ on either side, each holding a scroll or book representing his Gospel. Two elongated seraphim (angels who view God) stand one on either side of the central group, each holding a scroll. A band beneath Christ's feet and another passing behind his throne represent the waves of the "sea of glass like crystal" (Revelation 4:6). These define three registers in which sit twenty-four elders with "gold crowns on their heads" in varied poses, each holding either a harp or a gold bowl of incense (Revelation 4:4 and 5:8). According to the medieval view, the elders were the kings and prophets of the Old Testament and, by extension, the ancestors and precursors of Christ.

The figures in the tympanum relief reflect a hierarchy of scale and location. Christ, the largest figure, sits at the top center, the spiritual heart of the scene, surrounded by smaller figures of the evangelists and angels. The elders, farthest from Christ, are roughly one-third his size. Despite this formality and the limitations forced on them by the tympanum's shape, the sculptors created a sense of action by turning and twisting the gesturing figures, shifting their poses off-center, and avoiding rigid symmetry or mirror images. Nonfigural motifs above and below Christ, too, skirt the central vertical axis, contributing to the dynamic play across the tympanum's surface. The sculptors carved the tympanum from twenty-eight stone blocks of different sizes. The elders were carved one or two per block, whereas the figures of the central group

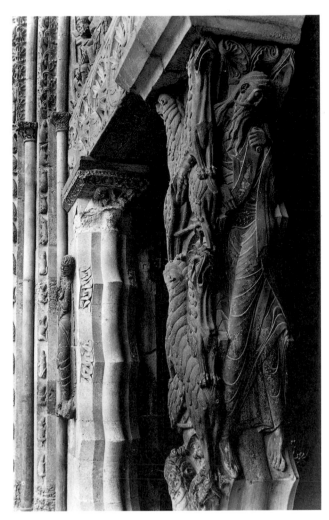

15-11. *Lions and Prophet Jeremiah (?)*, trumeau of the south portal, Priory Church of Saint-Pierre

In a letter to fellow cleric William of Saint Thierry, Bernard of Clairvaux, leader of the Cistercian order, objected to what he felt was excessive architectural decoration of Cluniac churches and cloisters. "So many and so marvellous are the varieties of diverse shapes on every hand," he wrote, "that we are more tempted to read in the marble than in our books, and to spend the whole day in wondering at these things rather than in meditating the law of God. For God's sake, if men are not ashamed of these follies, why at least do they not shrink from the expense?" (cited in Davis-Weyer, page 170).

covered one or more blocks as needed. Paint would originally have disguised the join lines. The crowns and incense bowls—described as made of gold in Revelation—may have been gilded. Foliate and geometric ornament covers every surface. Monstrous heads in the lower corners of the tympanum spew ribbon scrolls that run up its periphery. Similar creatures, akin to the beasts seen in the Scandinavian **animal style** of the Early Middle Ages (see fig. 14-5), appear at each end of the lintel, their tongues growing into ropes encircling a line of eight acanthus **rosettes.** A similar combination of animals, interlace, and rosettes can be found in Islamic art. Heraldic beasts and rosettes appeared together on Byzantine and Islamic textiles. Processions of naturalistically

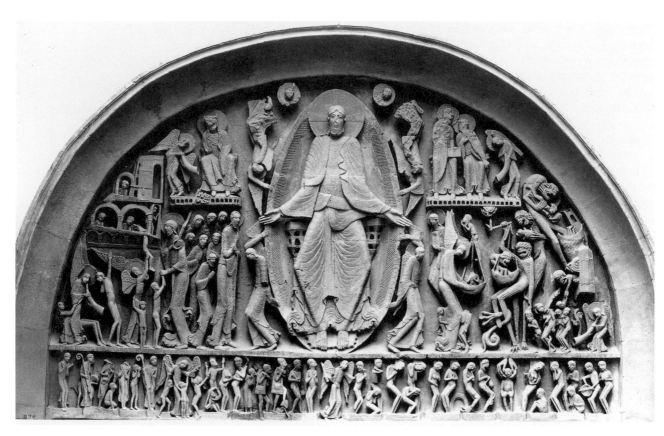

15-12. Gislebertus. *Last Judgment*, tympanum of the west portal, Cathedral of Saint-Lazare, Autun, Burgundy, France. c. 1120–35

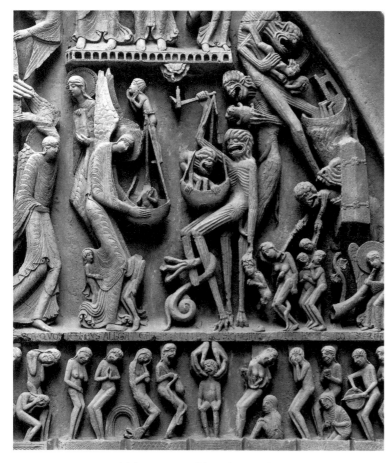

15-13. Gislebertus. *Weighing of Souls*, detail of *Last Judgment*

depicted rats and rabbits climb the piers on either side of the doors (fig. 15-11). Halos, crowns, and Christ's throne in the tympanum are adorned with stylized foliage.

Two side **jambs** and a central pier—known as a **trumeau**—support the weight of the lintel and tympanum. Moissac's jambs and trumeau have scalloped profiles (see fig. 15-9). Saint Peter (holding his attribute, the key to the gates of heaven) is carved in high relief on the left jamb, the Old Testament prophet Isaiah on the right jamb. Saint Paul is carved on the left side of the trumeau, and another Old Testament prophet, usually identified as Jeremiah, is on the right. On the front face of the trumeau are pairs of lions crossing each other in **X** patterns. The tall, thin prophet in figure 15-11 twists toward the viewer with his legs crossed. The sculptors placed him skillfully within the constraints of the scalloped trumeau, his head, pelvis, knees and feet falling on the pointed cusps of the curved forms. On the front of the trumeau the lions' bodies also fit the cusps of the scalloped frame. Between each pair of lions are more rosettes. Such decorative scalloping resembles Islamic art. The sculpture at Moissac was created shortly after the First Crusade and Europe's resulting encounter with the Islamic art and architecture of the Holy Land. The lord of the Moissac region was a leader of the Crusade, and his followers presumably brought Eastern art objects and ideas home with them.

A very different pictorial style is seen in Burgundy. On the west portal of the Cathedral of Saint-Lazare at Autun

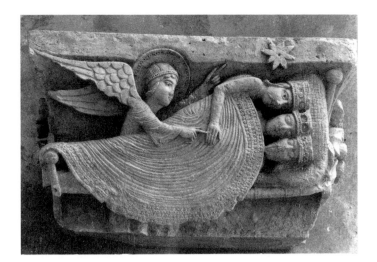

15-14. *The Magi Asleep*, capital from the nave, Cathedral of Saint-Lazare. c. 1120–32. Musée Lapidaire, Autun

(fig. 15-12), Christ has returned to judge the cowering, naked human souls at his feet. The Damned writhe in torment at his right, while the saved enjoy serene bliss at the left (the right hand of Christ). Christ dominates the composition as he did at Moissac. The surrounding figures are thinner and taller than those at Moissac and are arranged in less regular compartmentalized tiers. The overall effect is less consciously balanced than the pattern-filled composition at Moissac. The stylized figures, stretched out and bent at sharp angles, are powerfully expressive, successfully conveying the terrifying urgency of the moment as they swarm around the magisterially detached Christ figure. Delicate weblike engraving on the robes may have derived from metalwork or manuscript illumination.

Angels trumpet the call to the Day of Judgment at the far left and right of the middle register. Angels also help the departed souls to rise from their tombs and line up to await judgment. In the bottom register two men at the left carry walking staffs and satchels bearing the cross and a scallop-shell badge, attributes identifying them as pilgrims to Jerusalem and Santiago de Compostela. A pair of giant, pincerlike hands descends at the far right to scoop up a soul (fig. 15-13). Above and to the left of these hands, in a scene reminiscent of Egyptian Books of the Dead (see fig. 3-44), the archangel Michael oversees the weighing of souls on the scale of good and evil. In the early decades of the twelfth century, Church doctrine came increasingly to stress the role of the Virgin Mary and the saints as intercessors who could plead for mercy on behalf of repentant sinners. The tympanum at Autun shows angels also acting as intercessors. The archangel Michael shelters some souls in the folds of his robe and may be jiggling the scales a bit. Another angel boosts a saved soul into heaven, bypassing the gate and Saint Peter. By far the most riveting players in the drama are the grotesquely decomposed, screaming demons grabbing at terrified souls and trying to cheat by pushing down souls and yanking the scales to favor evil.

A lengthy inscription in the band beneath Christ's feet identifies the Autun tympanum as the work of Gisle-bertus. This same sculptor may also have been responsible for a representation of the Magi asleep (fig. 15-14), one of the many capitals that illustrate the Bible and the lives of the saints in the nave at Autun. The ingenious compression of instructive narrative scenes into the geometric confines of column capitals was an important Romanesque contribution to architectural decoration. The underlying form was usually that of the flaring **Corinthian** capital. Sculptors used **undercutting**, a technique known since ancient times, to sharpen contours and convey depth.

The Magi Asleep is one of a series of capitals depicting events surrounding the birth of Jesus. Medieval tradition identified the three Magi, or wise men—whom the Gospels say brought gold, frankincense, and myrrh to the newborn Jesus—as the kings Caspar, Melchior, and Balthasar. Caspar, the oldest, is shown bearded here; Melchior has a moustache; and Balthasar, the youngest, is clean shaven. Later, he is often shown as a black African. The Magi, following heavenly signs, traveled from afar to acknowledge Jesus as King of the Jews. The position of the capital in the nave of the church suggests that it was meant to remind worshipers that they were embarking on a metaphorically parallel journey to find Christ. The slumbering Magi, wearing their identifying crowns, share a bed and blanket. An angel has arrived to hurry them on their way, awakening Balthasar and pointing to the Star of Bethlehem that will guide them. The sculptor's use of two vantage points simultaneously—the Magi and the head of their bed viewed from above, the angel and the foot of the bed seen from the side—communicates the key elements of the story with wonderful economy and clarity.

Independent Sculpture

Reliquaries, altar frontals, crucifixes, devotional images, and other sculpture once filled medieval churches. One form of devotional image that became increasingly popular during the later Romanesque period was that of the

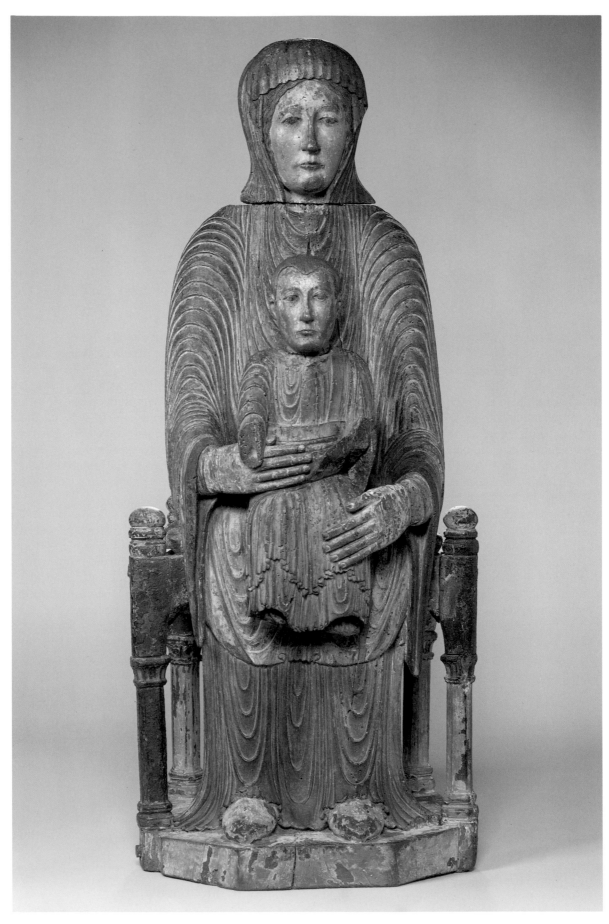

15-15. *Virgin and Child*, from the Auvergne region, France. c. 1150–1200. Oak with polychromy, height 31" (78.7 cm).
The Metropolitan Museum of Art, New York
Gift of J. Pierpont Morgan, 1916 (16.32.194)

Virgin Mary holding the Christ Child on her lap, a type known as the Throne of Wisdom. A well-preserved example in painted wood dates from the second half of the twelfth century (fig. 15-15). Such images were a specialty of the Auvergne region of France, but are found throughout Europe. Mother and Child are frontally erect, as rigid as they are regal. Mary is seated on a thronelike bench symbolizing the lion throne of the Old Testament king and symbol of wisdom, Solomon. She supports Jesus with both hands. The small but adult Jesus holds a book—the Word of God—in his left hand and raises his (now missing) right hand in blessing. To the medieval believer, Christ represented the priesthood; Mary, the Church; Christ, humankind and God; Mary, his throne. Mary as earthly mother and God-bearer (Theotokos) gives Jesus his human nature and forms a throne on which he sits in majesty. In Christ, the Wisdom of God has become human; in the medieval scholar's language, he is the Logo Incarnate. As a fourteenth-century churchman wrote, "The throne of the true Solomon is the Most Blessed Virgin Mary, in which sat Jesus Christ, the true Wisdom." (trans: Forsyth, p. 27.)

Earlier in the Middle Ages, small, individual works of art were generally made of costly materials for royal or aristocratic patrons. In the twelfth century, however, when abbeys and local parish churches of more limited means began commissioning hundreds of statues, painted wood became an increasingly common medium. These lightweight devotional images were frequently carried in processions from place to place both inside and outside the churches. A statue of the Virgin and Child, like the one shown here, could also have played an important role in the liturgical drama performed at the Feast of the Epiphany, which in the Western Church celebrates the arrival of the Magi to pay homage to the baby Jesus. Participants representing the Magi would act out their journey by searching through the church until they came to the statue. (Some scholars see this as perhaps the earliest western European drama.)

The Crucifixion continued to be a primary devotional theme in the Romanesque period. The image of Jesus in the mid-twelfth-century *Batlló Crucifix* from Catalonia (fig. 15-16) derives from Byzantine sources and is quite different from the nearly nude, tortured Jesus of the Ottonian-period *Gero Crucifix* (see fig. 14-30). Jesus' bowed head, downturned mouth, and heavy-lidded eyes convey a sense of deep sadness or contemplation; however, he still wears royal robes that emphasize his kingship (see *Rabbula Gospels*, pages 320, 321). He wears a long, medallion-patterned tunic with **pseudo-kufic** inscriptions—designs meant to resemble Arabic script—on the hem. The garment reflects how valuable silk brocades from Islamic Spain were in Europe at this time. They were widely used as **cloths of honor** to designate royal and sacred places, appearing, for example, behind rulers' thrones, or as altar coverings and backdrops. Many wooden crucifixes have survived from the Romanesque period. They were displayed over church altars and, like other devotional statues, were carried in processions.

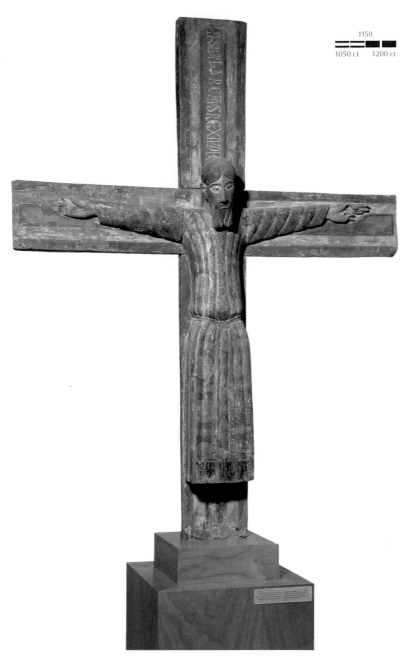

15-16. *Batlló Crucifix*, from the Olot region, Catalonia, Spain. Mid-12th century. Wood with polychromy, height approx. 36" (91 cm). Museu Nacional d'Art de Catalunya, Barcelona

This crucifix was modeled on a famous medieval sculpture called the *Volto Santo* (Holy Face) that had supposedly been brought from Palestine to Italy in the eighth century. Legend had it that this image had been made by Nicodemus, who helped Joseph of Arimathea bury Jesus. Many replicas of the *Volto Santo* still exist.

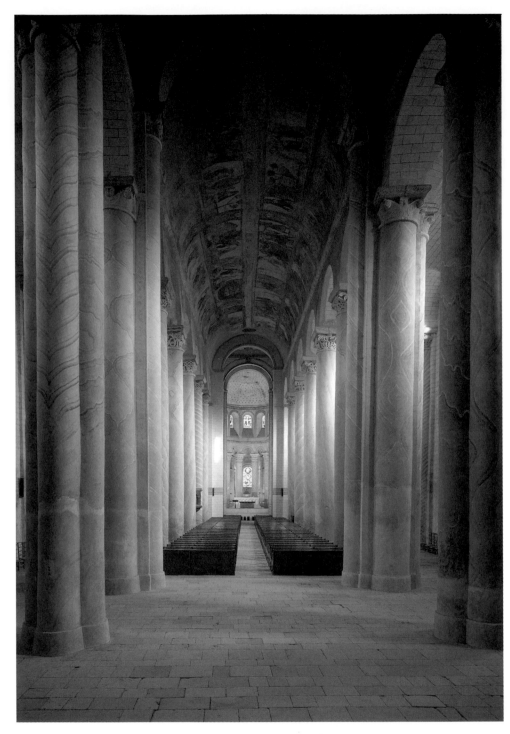

15-17. Nave, Abbey Church of Saint-Savin-sur-Gartempe, Poitou, France. c. 1100

The columns of Saint-Savin, painted to resemble veined marble, support an arcade and barrel vault without intermediate galleries or clerestory windows.

Wall Painting

Throughout Europe paintings on church walls glowed in flickering candlelight amid clouds of incense. Wall painting was subject to the same influences as the other visual arts: The painters were inspired by models available to them locally. Some must have seen examples of Byzantine art. Others had Carolingian or even Early Christian models. During the Romanesque period, painted decoration largely replaced mosaics on the walls of churches. This change occurred, at least partly, because growing demand, due to more churches, led to the use of less expensive materials and techniques.

One of the most extensive programs of Romanesque wall painting is at the Benedictine abbey church of Saint-Savin-sur-Gartempe in the Poitou region of western France. The tunnel-like barrel vault running the length of the nave and choir provides a surface ideally suited to

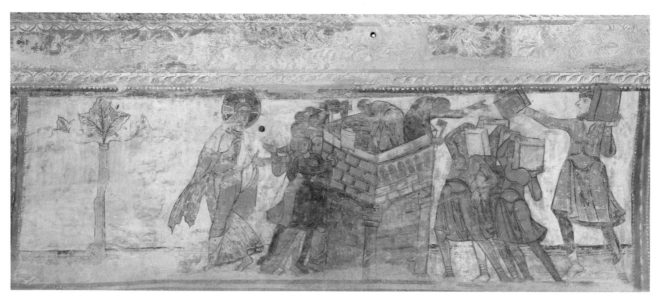

15-18. *Tower of Babel*, detail of painted nave vaulting, Abbey Church of Saint-Savin-sur-Gartempe

painted decoration (fig. 15-17). The narthex, **crypt**, and chapels were also painted. Old Testament scenes can be seen in the nave; New Testament scenes and scenes from the lives of two local saints, Savin and Cyprian, appear in the transept, ambulatory, and chapels. The paintings were all done about 1100. The painters may have used manuscripts as their primary inspiration. They did not use the wet-plaster **fresco** technique favored in Italy for its long-lasting colors, but they did moisten the walls before painting, which allowed some absorption of pigments into the plaster, making them more permanent than paint applied to a dry surface. Consequently, the colors of the vault have a soft, powdery effect in contrast to the richer, more brilliant colors of Byzantine-inspired painting. Several artists or teams of artists worked in different parts of Saint-Savin. While the vault suggests the energy of Carolingian artists, like those working for Archbishop Ebbo, and the narrative drama of the Ottonian Hildesheim doors, the lives of the saints were painted by artists working under Byzantine inspiration.

The painters of the nave vault seem to have immediately followed the masons and used the same scaffolding. Perhaps this intimate involvement with the building process accounts for the vividness with which they portrayed the biblical story of the Tower of Babel (fig. 15-18). According to the account in Genesis (11:1–9), God punished the prideful people who tried to build a tower to heaven by scattering them and making their languages mutually unintelligible. The tower in the painting is a medieval-looking structure, reflecting the practice of depicting legendary events in contemporary settings. Workers haul heavy stone blocks to the tower, lifting them to masons on the top with a hoist. The giant Nimrod, on the far right, simply hands the blocks up. God confronts the people on the far left. He is shown in a twisting pose like that of the prophet on the trumeau at Moissac (see fig. 15-11). The scene's dramatic action,

large figures, strong outlines, broad areas of color, and simplified modeling all help make it intelligible to a viewer looking up at it in dim light from far below.

Many Romanesque wall paintings survived in churches in the isolated mountain valleys of the Catalonian Pyrenees in northern Spain. The paintings have been detached from the walls and placed in museums for security. Among these are the paintings from the Church of San Clemente in Tahull. A magnificently expressive Christ in Majesty fills the curve of the semidome of the apse (fig. 15-19). Christ's powerful presence recalls the contemporary sculpture at Moissac and Autun (see figs. 15-9, 15-12, 15-13) and the tympanum sculptors may have been inspired by monumental paintings. The San Clemente Christ illustrates a Romanesque transformation of the Byzantine depiction of Christ Pantokrator, ruler and judge of the world. The iconography is traditional. Christ sits within a mandoria; the symbols alpha and omega are on each side of his head. He holds the open Gospel inscribed *"ego sum lux mundi"* (I am the light of the world. John 8:12). Four angels, each grasping an evangelist symbol, float at his sides. At Christ's feet are six apostles, of whom Bartholomew and John are visible here, and the Virgin Mary holding a bowl. Flanking them are columns with stylized capitals and wavy lines indicating marble shafts. The mosaiclike intensity of the colors was created by building up many thin coats of paint, a technique called **glazing**.

The San Clemente Master as the otherwise anonymous Tahul painter is known, was one of the finest Spanish painters of the Romasque period. The elongated oval faces, large staring eyes, and long noses, as well as the placement of figures against flat colored bands and the use of heavy outlining, reflect Mozarabic influence (Chapter 14). The Western artists, however, have adapted the Byzantine style to their own taste for geometric simplicity of form. Faces and figures are strictly

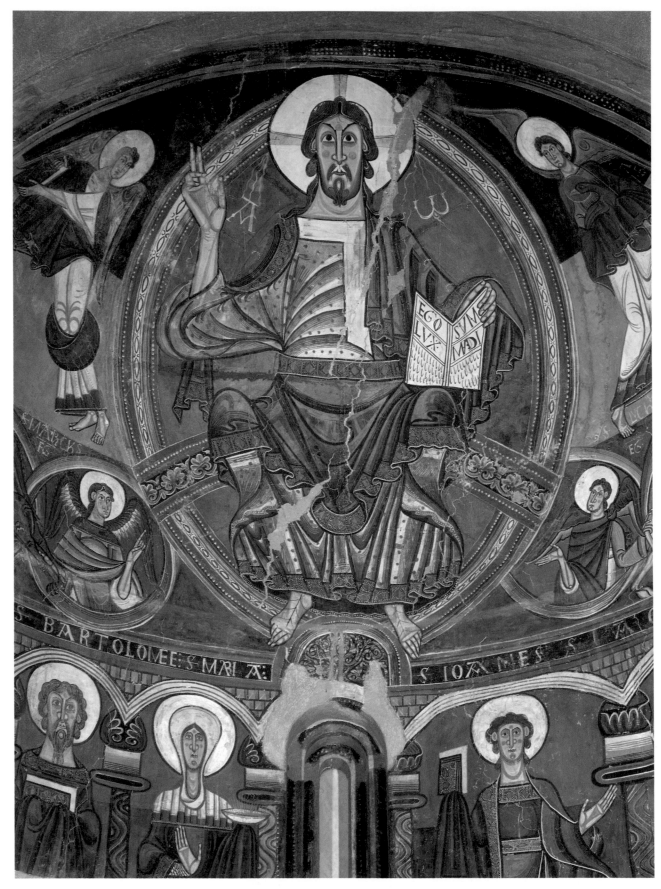

15-19. *Christ in Majesty*, detail of apse painting from the Church of San Clemente, Tahull, Lérida, Spain. c. 1123. Museu
Nacional d'Art de Catalunya, Barcelona

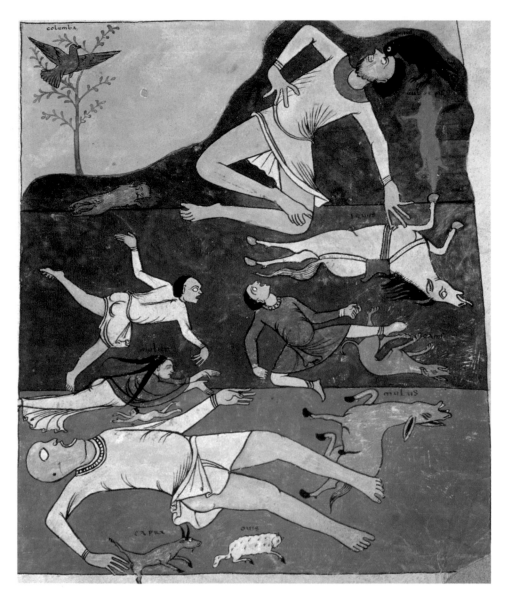

15-20. Stephanus Garsia. Page with *Flood, Commentary on the Apocalypse*, by Beatus of
Liébana, made for the Abbey of Saint-Sever, Gascony, France. 1028–72. Ink and tem-
pera on vellum, 14¹/₂ x 11" (36.5 x 28 cm). Bibliothèque Nationale, Paris,
MS lat. 8678, fol. 85r

frontal and symmetrical. Modeling from light to dark is
accomplished through repeated colored lines of varying
width in three shades—dark, medium, and light. Details
of faces, hair, hands, and muscles are turned into elegant patterns.

Books

As today, illustrated books played a key role in the transmission of artistic styles and other cultural information
from one region to another. Like other arts, the output of
books increased dramatically in the eleventh and twelfth
centuries, despite the labor and materials required to
make them. Monastic **scriptoria** continued to be the centers of production, where monks copied books in the
monastic libraries (see "The Medieval Scriptorium," page

486). These monastic scriptoria, sometimes also employed lay artisans who might be itinerant, moving from
place to place. Most books had religious subject matter,
including scholarly commentaries, lives of saints, collections of letters, and even histories. Liturgical works were
often large and lavish; other works were more modest,
their embellishment confined to the initial letter of each
section of text.

During the Romanesque period, scribes in northern
Spain and France continued to copy and illustrate
the *Commentary on the Apocalypse* written by Beatus of
Liébana in the eighth century. They evoke the dramatic
terror of the Apocalypse in a stark, two-dimensional,
intensely colored, and emotional style that was introduced by Mozarabic monks in the tenth century (see fig.
14-13). The page shown here (fig. 15-20) is from a copy

15-21. Page with *Pentecost*, *Cluny Lectionary*. Early 12th century. Ink and tempera on vellum, 9 x 5" (23 x 12.5 cm). Bibliothèque Nationale, Paris, MS lat. 2246, fol. 79v

of the *Commentary* illuminated by a monk named Stephanus Garsia in the middle of the eleventh century for the Abbey of Saint-Sever in Gascony (southern France). It illustrates the ravages of the final flood. Corpses are scattered helter-skelter, broken and awry. A black bird pecks at an eyeball of the man lying on the upper right, compounding the horror. Intense colors— yellow, purple, red, and green—resonate with anguished force across the boldly banded field. The preoccupation with the Apocalypse may reflect the ongoing struggle between Christians and Muslims for control of Spain. In any case, Beatus manuscripts remained a regional phenomenon, although they were influential far beyond the Pyrenees.

An illuminated **lectionary** (fig. 15-21) made for the wealthy monastery of Cluny in the early 1100s seems calm and dignified compared to the Saint-Sever Apocalypse. Lectionaries contained biblical excerpts arranged according to the Church calendar for reading during Mass. This page contains the beginning of the eighth reading (*lectio octava*). The framed scene illustrates the beginning of the second chapter of the Acts of the Apostles, which recounts how "tongues as of fire" from the Holy Spirit descended on each of the apostles while they were assembled for Pentecost, and they began to speak "in tongues." Christ appears at the top of the picture, and glowing red rays—tongues of fire—stream from the gold banner draped over him to the heads of the Twelve Apostles below. Just under the picture is a beautifully interlaced *A*, the first letter of the word *audivimus* ("we have been hearing"). The subject—an unusual one for medieval art—may have been chosen as a symbolic reminder of Cluny's direct tie to the papacy. The picture may suggest that just as the apostles received miraculous powers from Christ, so Cluny derived its power directly from the pope, the heir to the apostle Peter. The image of Christ, like the Tahull *Christ in Majesty* (see fig. 15-19), is a reinterpretation of the Byzantine Pantokrator type. The faces of the figures have been delicately rendered with green and red highlighting. The drapery seems to fall over fleshy limbs. The illuminator deliberately de-emphasized the drama of the supernatural event described in the text, conveying instead the psychological bond among the figures.

Despite their ascetic teachings and austere architecture, the Cistercians produced many elaborately illustrated books. A symbolic image known as the Tree of Jesse appears on a page from a copy of *Saint Jerome's Commentary on Isaiah* made in the scriptorium of the Cistercian mother house at Cîteaux about 1125 (fig. 15-22). Jesse was the father of King David, who was an ancestor of Mary and, through her, of Jesus. The Cistercians were particularly devoted to the Virgin and are credited with popularizing the Tree of Jesse as a device for showing her position as the last link in the genealogy connecting Jesus Christ to the house of David. In the manuscript illustration, *The Tree of Jesse* depicts Jesse asleep, a small tree trunk growing from his body. A monumental Mary, standing on the forking branches of the tree, dwarfs the sleeping patriarch. The Christ Child sits on her right arm, which is swathed in her veil. Following late Byzantine and Romanesque convention, he is portrayed as a miniature adult with his right hand raised in blessing. His cheek presses against Mary's, a display of affection similar to that shown in Byzantine icons like the *Virgin of Vladimir* (see fig. 7-60). Mary holds a flowering sprig from the tree, a symbol for Christ. The building held by the angel on the left refers to Mary as the Christian Church, and the crown held by the angel on the right refers to her as Queen of Heaven. The dove above her halo represents the Holy Spirit. The linear depiction of drapery in **V**-shaped folds and the jeweled hems of Mary's robes reflect Byzantine influence and her elevated status. The subdued colors are in keeping with Cistercian restraint.

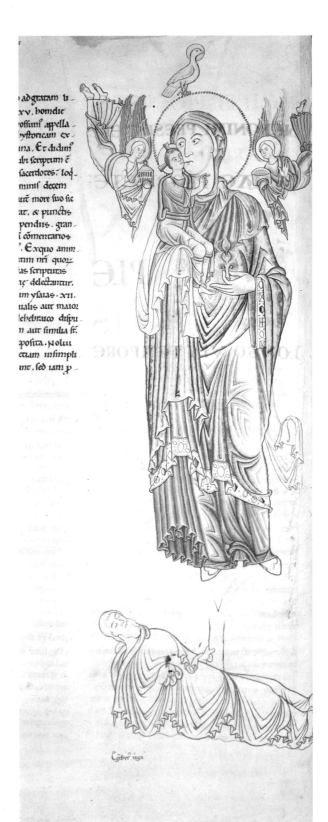

15-22. Page with *The Tree of Jesse, Explanatio in Isaiam* (*Saint Jerome's Commentary on Isaiah*), from the Abbey, Cîteaux, Burgundy, France. c. 1125. Ink and tempera on vellum, 15 x 4¾" (38 x 12 cm). Bibliothèque Municipale, Dijon, France, MS 129, fol. 4v

The Tree of Jesse, a pictorial representation of the genealogy of Jesus, was used to illustrate the Church's doctrine that Christ was both human and divine. The growing importance of devotion to Mary as the mother of God led to an emphasis on her place in this illustrious royal line.

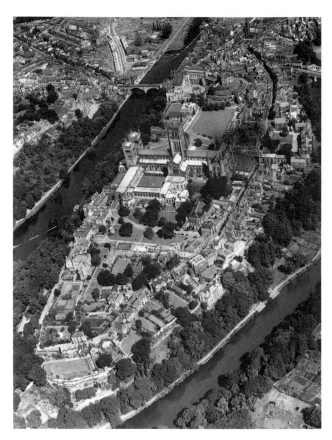

15-23. Castle-monastery-cathedral complex, Durham, Northumberland, England. c. 1075–1100s, plus later alterations and additions

Since 1837, the castle has housed the University of Durham (now joined with the University of Newcastle). The castle was added to and rebuilt over the centuries. The Norman portion extends to the left of the keep. The castle and cathedral share a parklike green. South of the cathedral (lower in the photograph), the cloister with chapterhouse, dormitory (now a library), and kitchens are clearly visible. Houses of the old city cluster around the buildings as they would have in earlier days. Trees, however, would
not have been allowed to grow near the approaches to this fortified outpost against the Scots.

BRITAIN AND NORMANDY

In the early tenth century a band of Norse raiders seized a peninsula in northwest France that came to be known as Normandy. In 911 their leader, Rollo, gained recognition as duke of the region from the weak Carolingian king. Within little more than a century, Rollo's successors had transformed Normandy into one of Europe's most powerful feudal domains. The Norman dukes were astute and skillful administrators. They formed a close alliance with the Church, supporting it with grants of land and gaining in return the allegiance of abbots and bishops, many of whom also served as vassals of the duke. In 1066 Duke William II of Normandy (1035–1087) invaded England and, as William I ("the Conqueror"), became that country's new king. Norman nobles replaced the Anglo-Saxon nobility, and England became politically and culturally allied to northern France.

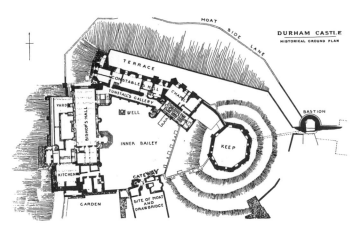

15-24. Plan of Durham Castle

In Norman times, the bishops of Durham lived in a three-story residence. An exterior staircase led from the courtyard (inner bailey) to a single undivided, multipurpose room on the middle floor occupied by the bishop and his principal servants (Constable's Hall and the Tunstall's Gallery in the plan). Other people occupied humbler wood structures within the castle complex or outside its walls in the village that served it. The structures at the left date from Gothic times.

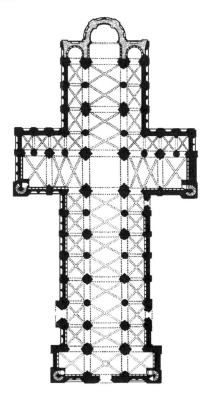

15-25. Plan of Durham Cathedral. 1093–1133

Architecture

Strategically located on England's northern frontier with Scotland, Durham grew after the Norman Conquest into a great fortified complex with a castle, a monastery, and a cathedral (fig. 15-23). (Durham had the relics of Saint Cuthbert, the revered seventh-century bishop of Lindisfarne.) The Norman bishops of Durham also held secular titles, powers, and responsibilities as vassals of the king.

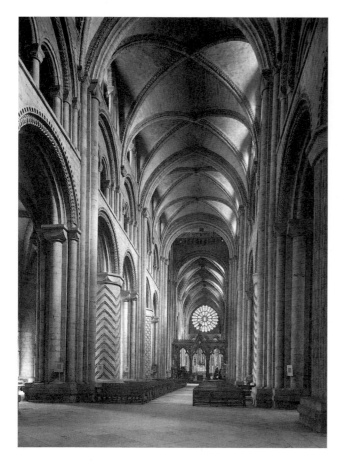

15-26. Nave of Durham Cathedral. 1087–1133. Original apses replaced by a Gothic choir, 1242–c. 1280. View from the west

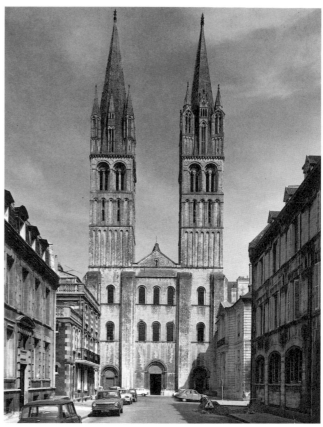

15-27. Church of Saint-Étienne, Caen, Normandy, France. Begun 1064; facade late 11th century; spires 13th century

Durham Castle is an excellent example of a Norman fortress (fig. 15-24). The only way in and out was over a drawbridge, which was controlled from a gatehouse. Beyond the gatehouse was the **bailey**, or courtyard. In times of danger, the castle's defenders took refuge in the **keep** (*donjon* in French), the massive tower to the east of the bailey. The keep stood atop a steep mound. Other buildings, including the great hall in which the bishops conducted their business, extended along the northern rampart overlooking a sheer cliff. The Norman chapel, located between the great hall and the keep, was built about 1075 and may have been the first stone structure in the compound. Medieval fortresses were often surrounded by a defensive water-filled ditch known as a **moat**. At Durham, the Wear River acted as a natural moat, looping around the high, rocky outcrop on which the complex was built.

Durham Cathedral (figs. 15-23 and 15-25) and its adjoining monastery were built to the south of the castle. The cathedral, begun in 1087 and vaulted beginning in 1093, is one of the most impressive medieval churches. Like most buildings that have been in continuous use, it has been altered several times. The visible parts of the towers, for example, are Gothic with eighteenth-century modifications. The cathedral's decor is as ambitious as its scale (fig. 15-26). Enormous compound piers alternating with robust columns support the nave arcade. The columns are carved with **chevrons**, spiral fluting, and dia-

mond patterns, and some have scalloped, cushion-shaped capitals. The arcades have round moldings and chevron ornaments. All this ornamentation was originally painted.

Above the cathedral's massive walls rise ribbed vaults. While most builders were still using timber roofs, the masons at Durham developed a new system of vaulting. The typical Romanesque ribbed groin vault (best seen in Milan, fig. 15-42) used round arches that produced separate domed-up spatial units. To create a more unified interior space, the Durham builders divided each bay with two pairs of crisscrossing ribs and so kept the crown of the vault at almost the same height as the keystone of the transverse arches. In the transept they also experimented with rectangular rather than square bays. Between 1093 and 1133, when the project was essentially complete, they developed a system of vaulting that was carried to the Norman homeland in France, was perfected in churches such as Saint-Étienne at Caen, then was adopted by French masons in the Gothic period (see "Elements of Architecture," page 552).

Saint-Étienne at Caen (fig. 15-27) was begun nearly a generation before Durham Cathedral, but work continued there through the century (the timber roof was not replaced by a stone vault until 1120). William the Conqueror had founded the monastery and had begun construction of its church by the time of his conquest of England. William's queen, Matilda, had already established an abbey for women in Caen. In spite of the

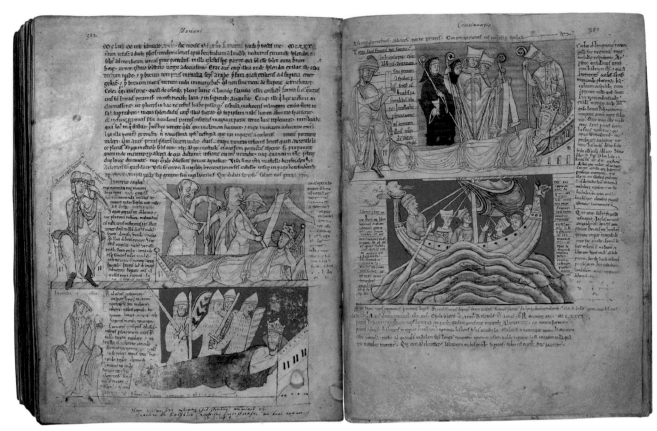

15-28. John of Worcester. Page with *Dream of Henry I*, *Worcester Chronicle*, Worcester, England, c.1140. Ink and tempera on vellum, each page 12³/₄ x 9³/₈" (32.5 x 23.7 cm). Corpus Christi College, Oxford

One of the most significant achievements of Henry's father, William the Conqueror, was a comprehensive census of English property owners, the *Domesday Book*. Compiled into two huge volumes, this document was used to assess taxes and settle property disputes. After Henry, too, increased taxes and encountered protests, a series of visions and a life-threatening storm at sea made him promise a seven-year delay in implementing higher taxes.

devastation of Normandy in World War II, the two churches survived, their western towers still dominating the skyline. Soaring height was a Norman architectural goal, continuing the tradition of towers and verticality begun by Carolingian builders (see fig. 14-24). The west facade of Saint-Étienne was constructed at the end of the eleventh century, probably about 1096–1100. Wall buttresses divide the facade into three vertical sections, and small **stringcourses**, unbroken cornicelike moldings, at each window level suggest the three stories of the building's interior. Consequently, the design of the facade reflects the plan and elevation of the church itself, an idea that would be adopted by Gothic builders. Norman builders, with their brilliant technical innovations and sophisticated designs, in fact prepared the way for the architectural feats seen in Gothic cathedrals of the twelfth and thirteenth centuries.

Books

The great Anglo-Saxon tradition of book illumination, which declined for a time in the wake of the Norman Conquest, revived after about 1130. The *Worcester Chronicle* is the earliest known illustrated English history. This record of contemporary events by a monk named John was an addition to a work called *The Chronicle of England*, written by Florence, another monk. The pages shown here concern King Henry I (ruled 1100–1135), the second of William the Conqueror's sons to sit on the English throne (fig. 15-28). The text relates a series of dreams the king had on consecutive nights in 1130 in which his subjects demanded tax relief. The illustrations depict the dreams with energetic directness. On the first night, angry farmers confront the sleeping king; on the second, armed knights; and on the third, monks, abbots, and bishops. In the fourth illustration, the king is in a storm at sea and saves himself by promising God to lower taxes for a period of seven years. The *Worcester Chronicle* assured its readers that this story came from a reliable source, the royal physician Grimbald, who appears in the margins next to most scenes.

More characteristic of Romanesque illumination are illustrated psalters. The so-called *Hellmouth* page from a psalter written in Latin and Norman French is one of the masterpieces of English Romanesque art (fig. 15-29). The psalter was produced at a renowned Anglo-Saxon monastic scriptorium in Winchester. The vigorous narrative style for which the scriptorium was famous had its roots in the style of the ninth-century workshop at Reims that produced the *Utrecht Psalter* (see fig. 14-22). The page depicts the gaping jaws of hell, a traditional Anglo-Saxon

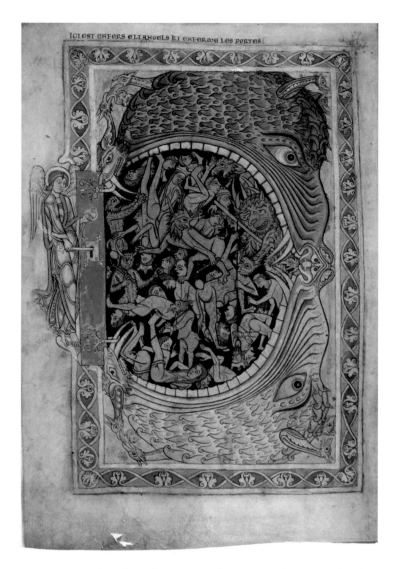

15-29. Page with *Hellmouth*, *Winchester Psalter*, Winchester, England. c. 1150. Ink and tempera on vellum, 12¾ x 9⅛" (32.5 x 23 cm). The British Library, London

There are fascinating parallels between Hellmouth images and the liturgical dramas—known in England as mystery plays— that were performed throughout Europe from the tenth through the sixteenth century. Depictions of the Hellmouth in Romanesque English art were based on the large and expensive stage props used for the hell scenes in mystery plays. Carpenters made the infernal beast's head out of wood, papier-mâché, fabric, and glitter and placed it over a trapdoor on stage. The wide jaws of the most ambitious Hellmouths, operated by winches and cables, opened and closed on the actors. Smoke, flames, foul smells, and loud noises came from within, to the delight of the audience. Hell scenes, with their often scatological humor, were by far the most popular parts of the plays. Performances are still given today.

subject, one that inspired poetry and drama as well as the vivid descriptions of the terrors and torments of hell with which the clergy enlivened their sermons.

The inscription at the top of the page reads: "Here is hell and the angels who are locking the doors." The ornamental frame that fills the page represents the door to hell. An angel on the left turns the key to the door in the keyhole of the big red doorplate. The frenzy of the Last Judgment, as depicted on the tympanum at Autun (see fig. 15-12), has subsided. Inside the door the last of the damned are crammed into the mouth of hell, the wide-open jaw of a grotesque double-headed monster. Sharp-beaked birds and fire-breathing dragons sprout from the monster's mane. Hairy, horned demons torment the lost souls, who tumble around in a dark void. Among them are kings and queens with golden crowns and monks with shaved heads, a daring reminder to the clergy of the vulnerability of their own souls.

The *Bayeux Tapestry*

The best-known work of Norman art is undoubtedly the *Bayeux Tapestry* (fig. 15-30). This narrative wall hanging, 230 feet long and 20 inches high, documents events surrounding the Norman Conquest of England in 1066. Despite its name, the work is **embroidery**, not tapestry. It was embroidered in eight colors of wool on eight lengths of undyed linen that were then stitched together (see "Embroidery Techniques," below). It was made for William the Conqueror's half brother Odo, who was bishop of Bayeux in Normandy and earl of Kent in southern England. Odo commissioned it for his Bayeux Cathedral, and it may have been completed in 1077, in time for the cathedral's consecration. According to an inventory made in 1476, it was "hung round the nave of the church on the Feast of relics" (Rud, page 9). Scholars disagree as to where it was made. Some argue for the famous embroidery workshops of Canterbury, in Kent, and others for Bayeux itself. A Norman probably directed the telling of the story and either an illuminator from a scriptorium or a specialist from an embroidery workshop provided drawings. Recent research suggests that the embroiderers were women.

The *Bayeux Tapestry* is a major political document, celebrating William's victory, validating his claim to the English throne, and promoting Odo's interests as a powerful leader himself. Today it is also a treasury of information about Norman and Anglo-Saxon society and technology, with depictions of everything from farming

TECHNIQUE

EMBROIDERY TECHNIQUES

The embroiderers of the *Bayeux Tapestry* probably followed drawings provided by a Norman, perhaps even an eyewitness to some of the events. The style of the embroidery, however, is Anglo-Saxon, and the embroiderers were probably women. They worked in tightly twisted wool, dyed in eight colors with dyes made from plants and minerals. Only two stitches were used. The quick, overlapping, linear stem stitch produced a slightly jagged outline. The more time-consuming laid-and-couched work used to form blocks of color required three steps. The embroiderer first "laid" a series of long, parallel covering stitches, anchored them with a second layer of regularly spaced crosswise stitches, and finally tacked everything down with tiny "couching" stitches. Some of the tapestry's laid-and-couched work was done in contrasting colors for particular effects. Skin and other light-toned areas were represented by the bare linen ground.

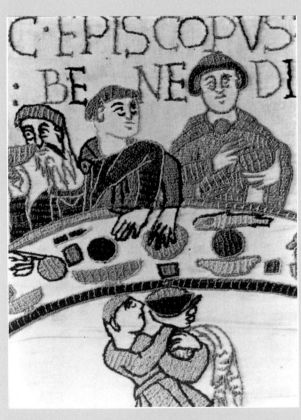

Laid-and-couched work and stem-stitch techniques are clearly visible in this detail of figure 15-30. Stem stitching outlines all the solid areas, is used to draw the facial features, and forms the letters of the inscription.

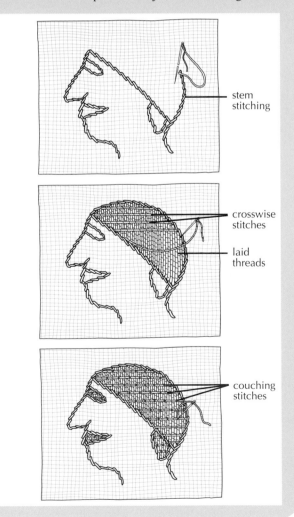

stem stitching

crosswise stitches

laid threads

couching stitches

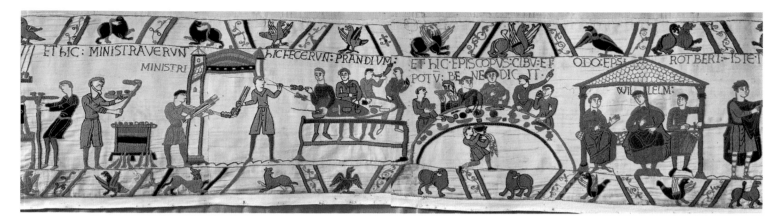

15-30. *Bishop Odo Blessing the Feast*, section 47–48 of the *Bayeux Tapestry*, Norman–Anglo-Saxon embroidery from Canterbury, Kent, England, or Bayeux, Normandy, France. c. 1066–82. Linen with wool, height 20″ (50.8 cm). Centre Guillaume le Conquérant, Bayeux, France

The top and bottom registers of the *Bayeux Tapestry* contain a variety of subjects separated by diagonal bars. These include heraldic beasts, stylized plants, and figures spilling over from the action in the central register, as well as a knight killing a tethered bear, a pair of naked lovers, and a farmer plowing. Such peripheral imagery was an English specialty throughout the Middle Ages. The sheer number of images in the *Bayeux Tapestry* is staggering: there are some 50 surviving scenes containing 623 human figures, 202 horses, 55 dogs, 505 other creatures, 37 buildings, 41 ships and boats, 49 trees, and nearly 2,000 inch-high letters.

implements to table manners to warfare. The *Bayeux Tapestry* shows broadly gesturing actors on a narrow stage with the clarity and directness of English manuscript illustration. It is laid out in three registers. In the middle register, the central narrative, explained by Latin inscriptions, unfolds in a continuous scroll from left to right. Secondary subjects and decorative motifs adorn the top and bottom registers.

The section illustrated here shows Odo and William, feasting on the eve of battle. Attendants provide roasted birds on skewers, placing them on a makeshift table of the knights' shields laid over trestles. The diners, summoned by the blowing of a horn, gather at a curved table laden with food and drink. Bishop Odo—seated at the center, head and shoulders above William to his right—blesses the meal while others eat. The kneeling servant in the middle proffers a basin and towel so that the diners may wash their hands. The man on Odo's left points impatiently to the next event, a council of war between William (now the central and tallest figure), Odo, and a third man labeled "Rotbert," probably Robert of Mortain, another of William's half brothers. These men held power after the conquest.

GERMANY AND THE MEUSE VALLEY

In the early eleventh century a new dynasty, the Salians, replaced the Ottonians on the throne of the Holy Roman Empire. The third Salian emperor, Henry IV (ruled 1056–1106), became embroiled in the dramatic conflict with the papacy known as the Investiture Controversy. This dispute involved the right of lay rulers to "invest" high-ranking clergy with the sym-bols of their spiritual offices. In 1075 Pope Gregory VII (papacy, 1073–1085) declared that only the pope and his bishops could appoint bishops, abbots, and other important clergy. The clergy now depended on the pope, not the emperor. Many German nobles sided with the pope; some nobles, with the emperor. The conflict unleashed by the Investiture Controversy divided Germany into many small competing states. The efforts of Holy Roman emperors of the late twelfth and early thirteenth centuries to reimpose imperial authority failed, and Germany remained divided until the late nineteenth century.

Religious and political problems sapped energy and wasted financial resources. Nevertheless, building and the other arts continued. Carolingian and Ottonian cultural traditions persisted in the German lands during the eleventh and twelfth centuries. Ties with the northern Italian region of Lombardy also remained strong and provided another source of artistic influence.

Architecture

The imperial cathedral at Speyer in the Rhine region of southwest Germany was a colossal structure that rivaled Cluny in size and magnificence. The Romanesque cathedral building was constructed on the foundations of an Ottonian imperial church between 1082 and 1106, during the reign of Henry IV. The emperor was fresh from recent successes against the papacy and a German rival, King Rudolf of Swabia, and the monumental rebuilding project was a testament to his power.

A seventeenth-century drawing shows the Romanesque cathedral, which more-recent construction has

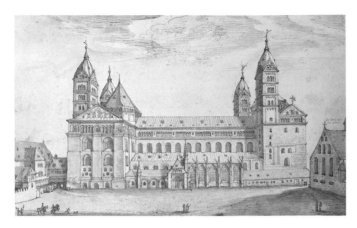

15-31. Imperial cathedral (Speyer II), Speyer, Germany. 1030–early 1100s. Ink drawing by Wenzel Hollar, c. 1620. Graphische Sammlung Albertina, Vienna

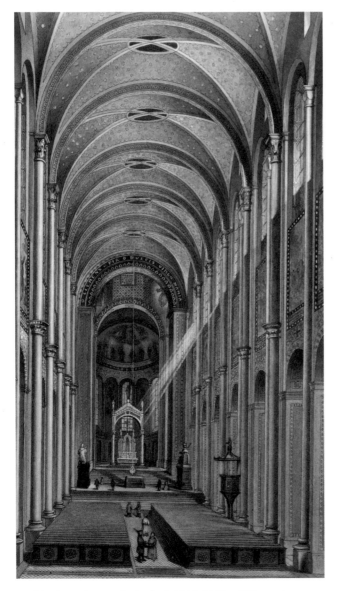

15-32. Nave, Speyer Cathedral. 1082–1100s; 19th-century alterations. Colored engraving by Carl Mayer, after a painting by J. M. Bayrer, 1855

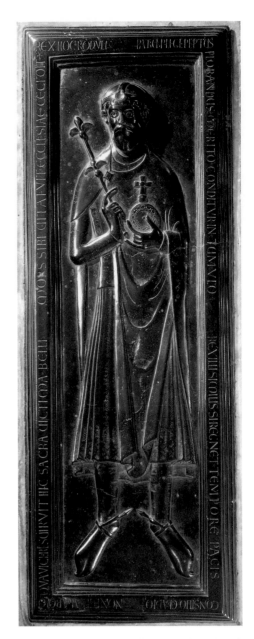

15-33. Tomb cover with effigy of Rudolf of Swabia; from Saxony, Germany. After 1080. Bronze with niello, approx. 6'5½" x 2'2½" (1.97 x .68 m). Cathedral, Merseburg, Germany

obscured (fig. 15-31). The east and west ends of the church, like its Ottonian predecessor, had nearly equal visual weight, emphasized by clusters of vertical elements. Tall stair towers rose at each side of the narthex and the apse, and octagonal lantern domes marked the crossing and the center narthex bay. Speyer's unusually wide nave, about 45 feet, is balanced by the great height of the groin-vaulted bays, which soar more than 100 feet overhead (fig. 15-32). Massive compound piers mark each nave bay and support the transverse ribs of the high vault. Lighter, simpler piers mark the aisle bays where two smaller bays cover the distance. This rhythmic alternation of heavy and light piers, first suggested for aesthetic reasons in Ottonian architecture, such as in Saint Cyriakus at Gernrode (see fig. 14-24), is regularized in Speyer and became an important design element in

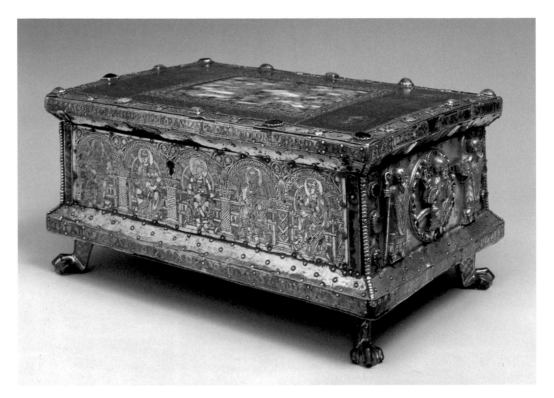

15-34. Roger of Helmarshausen. Portable altar of Saints Kilian and Liborius, from the Abbey, Helmarshausen, Saxony, Germany. c. 1100, with later additions. Silver with niello and gemstones,
6½ x 13⅝ x 8⅜" (16.5 x 34.5 x 21 cm). Erzbischöfliches Diözesanmuseum und Domschatz-
kammer, Paderborn, Germany

Roger, a monk, was also paid for a gold cross and another altar. Some scholars identify him with
"Theophilus," the pseudonym used by a monk who wrote an artist's handbook, *On Diverse Arts*,
about 1100. The book gives detailed instructions for painting, glassmaking, and goldsmithing.
In contrast to Abbot Bernard of Clairvaux, "Theophilus" assured artists that "God delights in em-
bellishments" and that artists worked "under the direction and authority of the Holy Spirit." He
wrote, "most beloved son, you should not doubt but should believe in full faith that the Spirit of
God has filled your heart when you have embellished His house with such great beauty and
variety of workmanship. . . . Set a limit with pious consideration on what the work is to be, and
for whom, as well as on the time, the amount, and the quality of work, and, lest the vice of greed
or cupidity should steal in, on the amount of the recompense (Theophilus, page 43). The last
admonishment is a worldly reminder about fair pricing.

Romanesque architecture. The ribbed groin vaults also
relieve the stress on the side walls of the building so that
windows can be larger. The result is both a physical and
a psychological lightening of the building.

Metalwork

For centuries, three centers in western Germany supplied
much of the best metalwork for aristocratic and ecclesiastical patrons throughout Europe: Saxony, the Meuse
valley region (in modern Belgium), and the lower Rhine
valley. The metalworkers in these areas drew on a variety
of stylistic sources, including the work of contemporary
Byzantine and Italian artists, as well as classical precedents as reinterpreted by their Carolingian forebears.

In the late eleventh century, Saxon metalworkers,
already known for their large-scale bronze casting,
began making bronze **tomb effigies**, or portraits of the
deceased. Thus began a tradition of funerary art that
spread throughout Europe and persisted for hundreds

of years. The oldest known bronze tomb effigy is that of
King Rudolf of Swabia (fig. 15-33), who sided with the
pope against Henry IV during the Investiture Controversy. The effigy, made soon after Rudolf's death in battle in 1080, is the work of an artist originally from the
Rhine region. Nearly lifesize, it has fine linear detailing in
niello, an incised design filled with a black alloy. The
king's head has been modeled in higher relief than his
body. The spurs on his oversized feet identify him as a
heroic warrior. In his hands he holds the scepter and orb,
emblems of kingship.

Most work of the time is anonymous, but according
to the account books of the Abbey of Helmarshausen in
Saxony, an artist named Roger was paid on August 15,
1100, for a portable altar dedicated to Saints Kilian and
Liborius. Preserved in the treasury of the cathedral there,
the foot-long, chestlike altar (one of two extant examples
attributed to this artist) was made of silver with gemstones and niello (fig. 15-34). It rests on three-dimen-
sionally modeled animal feet. On one end, in high relief,

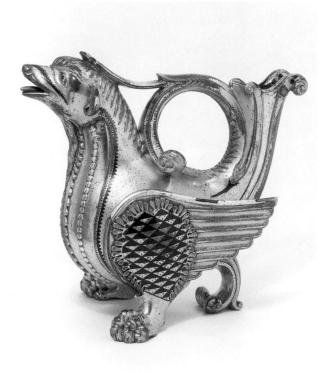

15-35. Griffin aquamanile, from Mosan, near Liège,
Belgium. c. 1130. Gilt bronze, silver, and niello,
height 7¼" (18.5 cm). Victoria and Albert
Museum, London

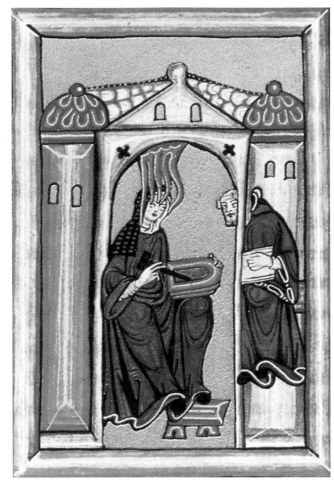

15-36. Page of facsimile with *Hildegard's Vision, Liber Scivias*.
c. 1150–1200. Original manuscript lost during World
War II

The text that accompanies this picture of Hildegard of
Bingen reads: "In the year 1141 of the incarnation of
Jesus Christ the Son of God, when I was forty-two
years and seven months of age, a fiery light, flashing
intensely, came from the open vault of heaven and
poured through my whole brain. . . . And suddenly I
could understand what such books as the psalter, the
gospel and the other catholic volumes of the Old and
New Testament actually set forth" (*Scivias*, I, 1).

are two standing saints flanking Christ in Majesty, enthroned on the arc of the heavens. On the front are five
apostles, each posed somewhat differently, executed in
two-dimensional engraving and niello. Saint Peter sits in
the center, holding his key, with two other apostles on
each side of him. Roger adapted Byzantine figural conventions to his personal style, and he gave his subjects a
sense of life despite their formal setting. He was clearly
familiar with classical art, but his geometric treatment of
natural forms, his use of decorative surface patterning,
and the linear clarity of his composition are departures
from the classical aesthetic.

Metalworkers in the Meuse Valley excelled in a very
different style, perhaps the most distinctive of all Romanesque regional styles. They were well known for
sumptuous small pieces, such as the gilt bronze **aquamanile** shown here, which was made about 1130 (fig.
15-35). Aquamaniles (from the Latin *aqua*, "water," and
manus, "hand") were introduced into western Europe
from the Islamic East, probably by returning Crusaders.
In their homelands, Muslims used aquamaniles for
rinsing their hands at meals. In the West, they found
their way to church altars, where priests purified themselves by pouring water over their hands. This griffin
aquamanile recalls its Islamic prototypes (see fig. 8-18).
In its liturgical context, however, the hybrid beast known
as a griffin symbolized the dual nature of Christ: divine
(half eagle) and human (half lion). Black niello sets off the
gleaming gold and silver, and the circular handle echoes
the curved forms of the rest of the vessel.

Books

The great Carolingian and Ottoman manuscript tradition
continued in the Romanesque period. A painting on an
opening page from the earliest illustrated copy of the
Liber Scivias by Hildegard of Bingen (1098–1179) is as
notable for the text it illustrates as for its artistic merit
(fig. 15-36). Born into an aristocratic German family,
Hildegard transcended the barriers that limited most
medieval women, and she became one of the towering
figures of her age. Like many women of her class, she
entered a convent as a child. Developing into a scholar
and a capable administrator, Hildegard began serving
as leader of the convent in 1136. In about 1147 she
founded a new convent near Bingen. Since childhood
she had been subject to what she interpreted as divine
visions, and in her forties, with the assistance of the

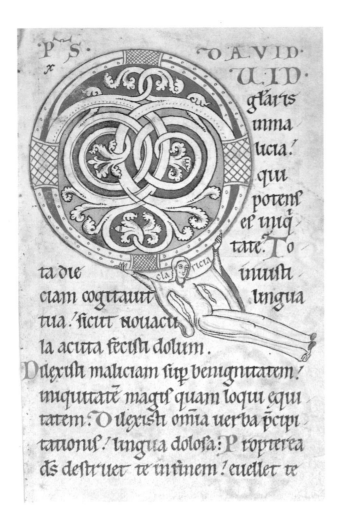

15-37. Page with initial *Q*, in a psalter from a nunnery in Augsburg(?), Swabia, Germany. Late 12th century. Tempera on vellum. Walters Art Gallery, Baltimore, W. 26, fol. 64

monk Volmar, she began to record them. Her book, *Scivias* (from the Latin *scite vias lucis*, "know the ways of the light"), records her visions. In addition to *Scivias*, Hildegard wrote treatises on a variety of subjects, including medicine and natural science. Emerging as a major figure in the intellectual life of her time, she corresponded with emperors, popes, and the Cistercian Abbot Bernard of Clairvaux.

The opening page of this copy of *Scivias* shows Hildegard receiving a flash of divine insight, represented by the tongues of flame encircling her head. She records the vision on a tablet while Volmar, her scribe, waits in the wings. Stylistic affinities suggest to some art historians that this copy of *Scivias* was made at the scriptorium of the monastery of Saint Matthias in Trier, whose abbot was a friend of Hildegard. Others suggest it was made at Bingen under the direction of Hildegard herself.

In the Romanesque period, as earlier in the Middle Ages, women were involved in the production of books as authors, scribes, painters, and patrons (see fig. 14-14). A woman named Claricia may have worked on the decoration of a late-twelfth-century psalter probably from Augsburg, the Swabian capital. On a page from this psalter, a blithely swinging woman forms the tail of the initial *Q* (fig. 15-37). Her uncovered, flying braids and fashionably long-sleeved dress suggest that she was a young, unmarried layperson. A nun or married woman would be dressed modestly, with her head covered. Written on each side of her head is the name Claricia, suggesting that this may be a self-portrait. Recently scholars have questioned this interpretation and have suggested that Clarissa personifies the gossip described in the text.

ITALY

The eleventh and twelfth centuries were a period of significant change on the Italian peninsula. The north, deeply embroiled in the conflict between the papacy and the German emperors, experienced both economic growth and increasing political fragmentation. Toward the end of the eleventh century, towns such as Pisa and Genoa became self-governing municipal corporations known as communes, and by the middle of the twelfth century the major cities and towns of northern and central Italy were independent civic entities, feuding with one another incessantly in a pattern that continued for the next several hundred years. Port cities like Pisa, Genoa, and Venice maintained a thriving Mediterranean trade and also profited from their role in transporting Crusaders and pilgrims to the Holy Land. The great bishops of these urban centers played a leading role as patrons of the arts in the building and furnishing of their cathedrals. In Sicily and southern Italy in the late eleventh century, as Norman adventurers took control and displaced Islamic and Byzantine rulers, a distinctively northern influence appeared. Throughout Italy, moreover, artists looked to the still-standing ruins of imperial Rome. All these influences shaped the character of the Italian Romanesque.

Architecture

Pisa, on the west coast of Tuscany, was a great maritime power from the ninth through the thirteenth century. An expansionist republic, it competed with Muslim centers for control of trade in the western Mediterranean. In 1063 Pisa won a decisive victory over Muslim forces, and the jubilant city soon began constructing an imposing new cathedral dedicated to the Virgin Mary (fig. 15-38). The cathedral complex eventually included the cathedral itself; a **campanile**, or freestanding bell tower, a feature of Italian church architecture since the sixth century (now known for obvious reasons as the Leaning Tower); a baptistry; and the Campo Santo, a walled burial ground. The cathedral, designed by the master builder Busketos, was not completed until the late thirteenth century. Its plan is an adaptation on a grand scale of the cruciform basilica. It has a long nave with double side aisles crossed by a projecting transept each with aisles and an apse like the nave and main sanctuary. Three portals open on the nave and side aisles, and a clerestory rises above the side aisles and second-story galleries. A dome covers the crossing. Pilasters, blind arcades, and narrow galleries adorn the five-story, pale-marble facade. An Islamic bronze griffin sat atop the building from about 1100 until 1828 (see fig. 8-18).

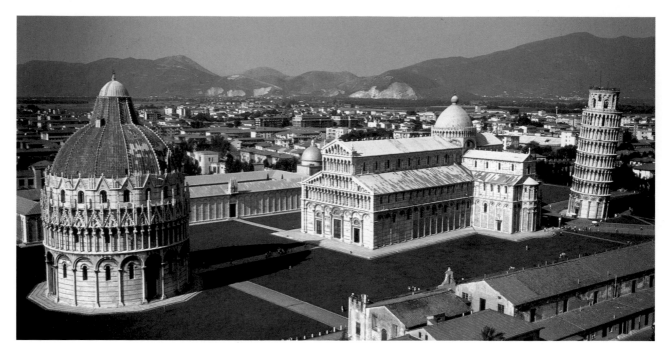

15-38. Cathedral complex, Pisa, Tuscany, Italy. Cathedral begun 1063; baptistry begun 1153; campanile begun 1174; Campo Santo dates from 13th century

When finished in 1350, the "Leaning Tower of Pisa" stood 179 feet high. It had begun to tilt while it was still under construction, and today it leans about 13 feet off the perpendicular. In the latest effort to keep it from toppling, engineers filled the base with tons of lead.

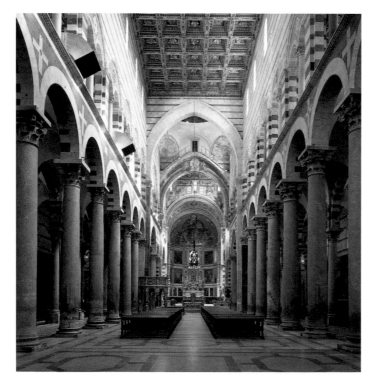

15-39. Nave, Pisa Cathedral. 1063–1100s

The nave arcade on the interior of the cathedral (fig. 15-39), has evenly spaced Corinthian-style columns and a flat, coffered timber ceiling reminiscent of Early Christian basilical churches. The rhythmically progressing arches, a stringcourse, and the plain walls of the clerestory reinforce the horizontal movement. In the gallery arcade, intermediate columns between piers support two-part openings. Contrasting bands of dark green marble decorate the arches and piers.

The tradition of erecting separate bell towers and round or octagonal baptistries continued in Italy. The Pisa Baptistry was begun in 1153. The arcading and galleries on the lower levels of its exterior match those on the cathedral. The ornate upper levels are in a later, Gothic style. The present exterior dome is also later. The campanile was begun in 1174 by the master Bonanno Pisano. Built on inadequate foundations, it began to lean almost immediately. The cylindrical tower is encased in tier upon tier of marble arcades. This creative reuse of an ancient, classical theme is characteristic of Italian Romanesque art; artists and architects seem always to have been conscious of their Roman past, whether in the marble columns of Pisa or the monumental brickwork of Lombardy in northern Italy.

In Lombardy, the city of Milan had been the capital of the Western Roman Empire for a brief period in the fourth century, and the city's first bishop, Ambrose (d. 397), was one of the "fathers" of the Christian Church. In 1080, construction began on a new Church of Sant'Ambrogio (Saint Ambrose), replacing an often-renovated ninth-century church (figs. 15-40, 15-41). The builders reused much of the earlier structure, including the freestanding tenth-century "monks' tower" (shown at the right in figure 15-40). Lombard Romanesque architecture depended for its austere dignity on harmonious proportions and the restrained use of exterior motifs derived from architectural forms. The exterior of Sant'Ambrogio is decorated

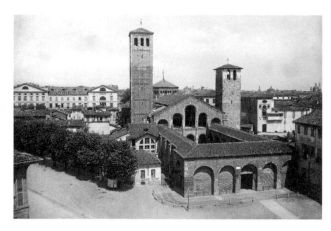

15-40. Church of Sant'Ambrogio, Milan, Lombardy, Italy.
c. 1080–early 12th century. Restored after World War II

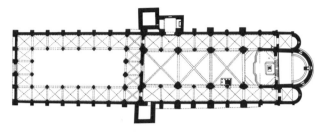

15-41. Plan of Church of Sant'Ambrogio

vertically with strip buttresses and horizontally with arched **corbel tables** (appearing as a scallop motif at a distance). The elements can be seen most clearly on the twelfth-century north tower (at the left in figure 15-40). The atrium, narthex, and semi-independent towers reflect the influence of Early Christian architecture still standing in Milan. Five huge arches, which correspond to the nave and side aisles, follow the roofline of the gabled, or pitch-roofed, second-story gallery and give it a dramatic appearance. Many churches in northern Italy adopted this type of gabled facade. The simple architectural decoration of strip buttresses and arched corbel tables was carried to Germany, Normandy, and elsewhere by Lombard clerics and masons.

Following an earthquake in 1117, masons rebuilt the church using a technically advanced system of four-part rib vaulting (fig. 15-42). Compound piers support three domed-up ribbed groin vaults over the nave, and smaller intermediate piers support the ribbed groin vaulting over the side-aisle bays. In addition to the vaulting system, the builders took other steps to assure the stability of the church. Sant'Ambrogio has a nave that was wider than that of Cluny III (with which it was roughly contemporary), but, at 60 feet, only a little more than half as high. Vaulted galleries buttress the nave, and there are windows only in the outer walls.

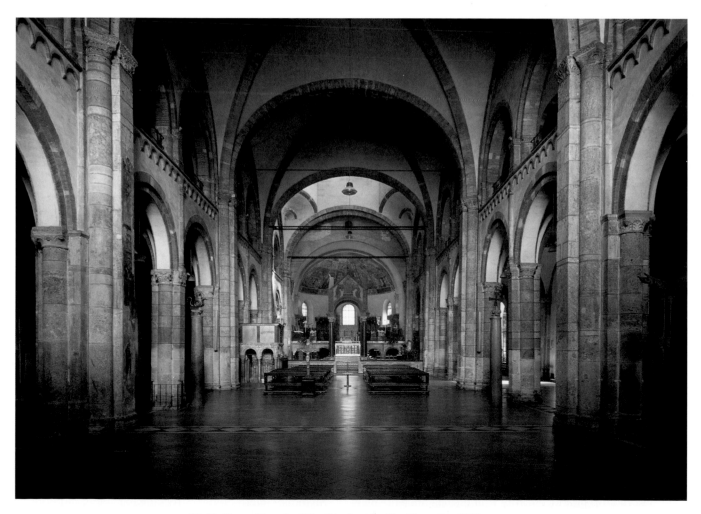

15-42. Nave, Church of Sant'Ambrogio. Vaulting after 1117

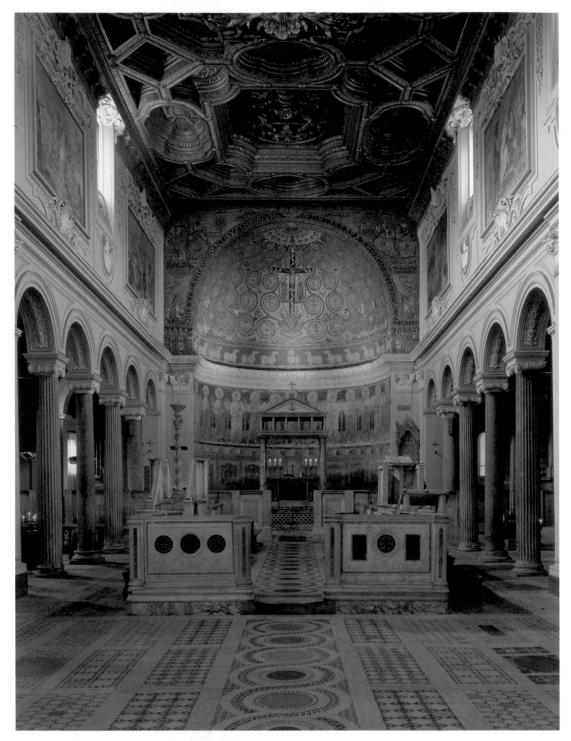

15-43. Nave, Church of San Clemente, Rome c. 1120–30

Ninth-century choir screens were reused from the earlier church. Upper wall and ceiling decoration are eighteenth century. San Clemente contains one of the earliest surviving collections of church furniture: choir stalls, pulpit, lectern, candlestick, and also the twelfth-century inlaid floor pavement.

During the Investiture Controversy, Pope Gregory VII called on the Norman rulers of southern Italy for help when the forces of Emperor Henry IV threatened Rome in 1084. These erstwhile allies, however, looted and burned the city. Among the architectural victims was the eleventh-century Church of San Clemente. The Benedictines rebuilt the church between 1120 and 1130 as part of a program to restore Rome to its ancient splendor. The new church, built on top of the remains of both a fourth-century basilica and the eleventh-century church, reflects a conscious effort to reclaim the artistic and spiritual legacy of the early Church (fig. 15-43). However, a number of features mark it as a Romanesque structure. A characteristic of early basilica churches, for example, was a strong horizontal movement down the nave to the sanctuary. In the new San Clemente, the rhythmic alternation of rectangular piers and Ionic columns interrupts this horizontal flow. In a configura-

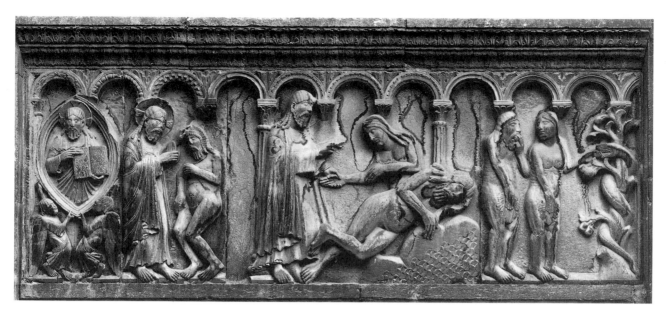

1150
1050 CE   1200 CE

15-44. Wiligelmus. *Creation and Fall*, on the west facade, Modena Cathedral, Emilia, Italy. 1106–20. Height approx. 3' (92 cm)

tion that came to be called the Benedictine plan, the nave and the side aisles each end in a semicircular apse. The different sizes of the apses, caused by the difference in the widths of the nave and the narrower side aisles, creates a stepped outline. The apse of the church followed the outline of the apse of the older structure beneath and was too small to accommodate all the participants in the liturgy of the time. As a result, the choir, defined by the low barrier in the foreground of figure 15-43, was extended into the nave.

Mosaic was a rarely used medium in twelfth-century Europe because it required expensive materials and specialized artisans. The apse of San Clemente, however, is richly decorated with colored marble inlay and a gold mosaic apse semidome, another reflection of its builders' desire to recapture the past. The subject matter—a crucified Jesus, with his mother and Saint John placed against a vine scroll, and sheep representing the apostles and the Lamb of God—and style of the mosaics are likewise archaic. As in other Italian churches of the period, inlaid geometric patterns in marble embellish the floors of San Clemente. They are known as Cosmati work, from the family who perfected it. Ninth-century panels with relief sculptures, saved from the earlier church, formed the wall separating the choir from the nave. A **baldachin** (baldacchino), or canopy of honor symbolizing the Holy Sepulchre, covers the main altar in the apse.

Architectural Sculpture

The spirit of ancient Rome also seems to pervade the sculpture of Romanesque Italy. Horizontal bands of relief on the west facade of the Modena Cathedral, in north-central Italy, are among the earliest narrative portal sculpture in Italy (c. 1106–1120). Wiligelmus, the sculptor, must have seen the sculpture of ancient sarcophagi

and may also have looked at Ottonian carving. He took his subjects from the Old Testament Book of Genesis and included events from the Creation to the Flood. The panel in figure 15-44 shows the Creation and the Fall of Adam and Eve. On the far left is a half-length Christ framed by a mandorla supported by two angels. The scene to the right shows God bringing Adam to life. Next, he brings forth Eve from Adam's side. On the right, Adam and Eve cover their genitals in shame as they greedily eat the fruit of the forbidden tree, around which the serpent twists.

Wiligelmus's deft carving and undercutting give these low-relief figures a strong three-dimensionality. While most Romanesque sculpture seems controlled by a strong frame or architectural setting, Wiligelmus used the arcade to establish a stagelike setting. Rocks and a tree add to the impression that figures interact with stage props. Wiligelmus's figures, although not particularly graceful, have a sense of life and personality and effectively convey the emotional depth of the narrative. Bright paint, now almost all lost, must have increased the impact of the sculpture.

An inscription on one of the panels reads: "Among sculptors, your work shines forth, Wiligelmo [Wiligelmus]." This self-confidence turned out to be justified. Wiligelmus's influence can be traced throughout Italy and as far away as the cathedral of Lincoln in England. Wiligelmus, Roger, Gislebertus, and many anonymous women and men of the eleventh and twelfth centuries created a new art that—although based on the Bible and the lives of the saints—focused on human beings, their stories, and their beliefs. The artists worked on a monumental scale in painting, sculpture, and even embroidery, and their art moved from the cloister to the public walls of churches. While they emphasized the spiritual and intellectual concerns of the Christian Church, they also began to observe and record what they saw around them. In so doing they laid the groundwork for the art of the Gothic period.

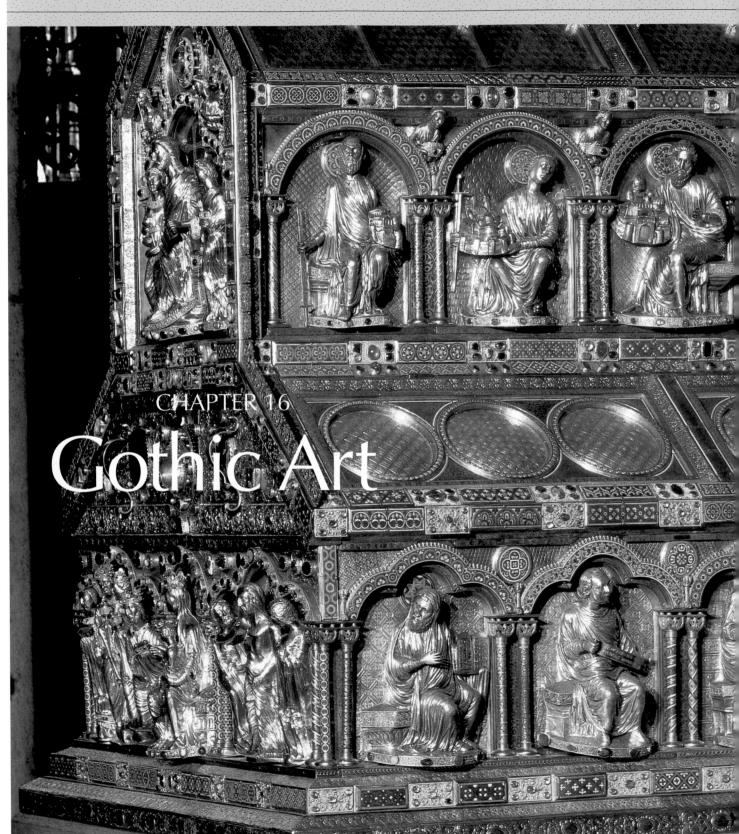

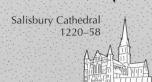
Cathedral of Notre-Dame,
Chartres c. 1134–1220

Salisbury Cathedral
1220–58

Palma Cathedral
begun 1306

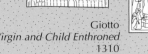
Giotto
Virgin and Child Enthroned
1310

CHAPTER 16
Gothic Art

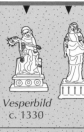
Vesperbild
c. 1330

Virgin and Child,
Paris c. 1339

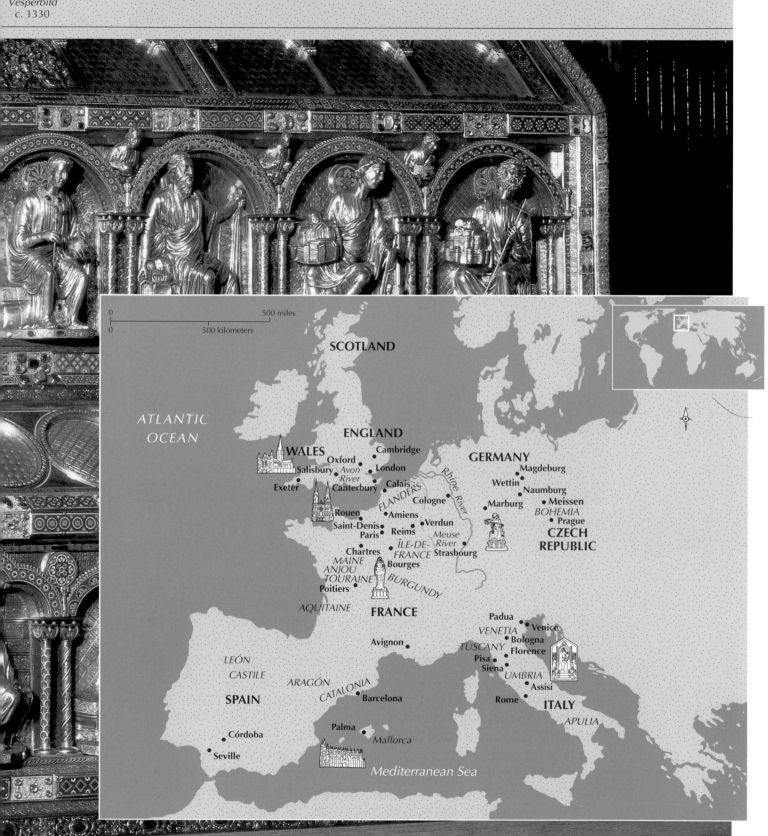

SCOTLAND

ATLANTIC
OCEAN

ENGLAND

GERMANY

WALES

Cambridge

Oxford London   Magdeburg

Salisbury   Avon   Wettin

River   Calais   Naumburg

Exeter   Canterbury   Marburg   Meissen

FLANDERS   Cologne   BOHEMIA

Rouen   Amiens   Prague

Saint-Denis   Verdun

Paris   Reims   Meuse   CZECH

ÎLE-DE-   River   REPUBLIC

Chartres   FRANCE   Strasbourg

MAINE   Bourges

ANJOU

TOURAINE   BURGUNDY

Poitiers

AQUITAINE   FRANCE

Padua

VENETIA   Venice

Avignon   TUSCANY   Bologna

Pisa   Florence

LEÓN   Siena

CASTILE   ARAGÓN   UMBRIA

CATALONIA   Assisi

SPAIN   Barcelona   Rome   ITALY

APULIA

Córdoba   Palma

Seville   Mallorca

Mediterranean Sea

Rhine River

0   500 miles

0   500 kilometers

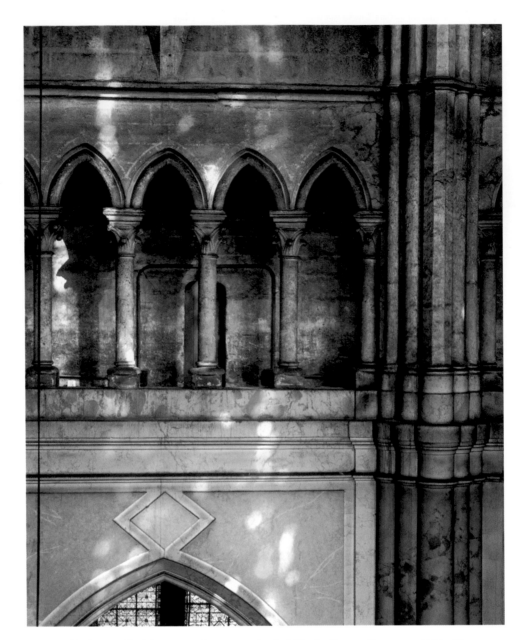

16-1.   Triforium wall of the nave, Chartres Cathedral, Île-de-France, France. c. 1200–60

T he twelfth-century Abbot Suger of Saint-Denis was, according to
his biographer Willelmus, "small of body and family, constrained
by twofold smallness, [but] he refused, in his smallness, to be a
small man" (cited in Panofsky, page 33). He was educated at the monastery of Saint-Denis, near Paris, and rose from modest origins to become a
powerful adviser to kings—even regent when the king was on crusade.
And he built what many consider the first Gothic structure in Europe.

   After Suger was elected abbot of Saint-Denis, he was determined to
rebuild its church, where the relics of the patron saint were housed
and the kings of the Franks had been buried since the seventh century.
Suger saw Saint-Denis as the preeminent church in France, a church that
embodied the history of the royal dynasty, and he waged a successful
campaign to gain both royal and popular support for his rebuilding plans.
The current building, he pointed out, had become inadequate. With a

touch of exaggeration, he claimed that the crowds of worshipers had become so great that women were being crushed and monks sometimes had to flee with their relics by jumping through windows.

In carrying out his duties, the abbot had traveled widely—in France, the Rhineland, and Italy, including four trips to Rome. As he began his plans for the church, he was familiar with the latest architecture and sculpture of Romanesque Europe. He also turned for inspiration to the authority of Church writings, including treatises erroneously attributed to a first-century follower of Saint Paul named Dionysius, who identified radiant light with divinity. Through the centuries Dionysius had become confused with Saint Denis, so Suger not unreasonably adapted his concept of divine luminosity into the redesign of the church dedicated to Saint Denis. Accordingly, when Suger began work on the choir after completing a magnificent Norman-inspired facade and narthex, he created "a circular string of chapels" so that the whole church "would shine with the wonderful and uninterrupted light of most luminous windows, pervading the interior beauty" (cited in Panofsky, page 101). Although Abbot Suger died before he was able to finish rebuilding Saint-Denis, his presence remained: this cleric of modest origins had himself portrayed in a sculpture at Christ's feet in the central portal, in a mosaic in the chapel, and in a stained-glass window in the apse. Suger is remembered not for these representations, however, but for his inspired departure from traditional architecture in order to achieve radiant light. It was this innovation that introduced the concept of large stained-glass windows, such as those that bathe the inside walls of Chartres Cathedral with sublime washes of color (fig. 16-1).

THE GOTHIC STYLE

In the middle of the twelfth century, when builders throughout Europe worked in the Romanesque style, a distinctive new architecture known today as Gothic emerged in the Île-de-France, the domain of French kings around Paris. The appearance of the new style and building technique there coincided with the emergence of the monarchy as a powerful centralizing force in France. The Gothic style prevailed in western European art from about 1150 to 1400, though it lingered for another century in some regions—the spire of the north tower of Chartres Cathedral, for example, was finished between 1507 and 1513, a period during which Michelangelo was creating Renaissance masterpieces in Florence and Rome. The term *Gothic* was introduced in the sixteenth century by the Italian artist and historian Giorgio Vasari. Vasari, who esteemed Michelangelo above all others, disparagingly attributed the style to the Goths, Germanic northerners who had destroyed the classical civilization of the Roman Empire that he and his contemporaries so admired. In its own day the Gothic style was simply called modern style or the French style. As it spread from the Île-de-France, it gradually displaced Romanesque forms but took on regional characteristics inspired by those forms. England developed a distinctive national style, which also influenced architectural design in continental Europe. The Gothic style was slow to take hold in Germany but ultimately endured there well into the sixteenth century. Italy proved more resistant to French Gothic elements, and by 1400, Italian artists and builders there sought a return to classical traditions. In the late fourteenth century, the various regional styles of Europe coalesced into what is known as the International Gothic style.

Gothic architecture's elegant, soaring interiors, the light, colors, and sense of transparency produced by great expanses of stained glass, and its linear qualities became more pronounced over time. The style was adapted to all types of structures—including town halls, meeting houses, market buildings, residences, and Jewish synagogues, as well as churches and palaces—and its influence extended beyond architecture and architectural sculpture to other mediums.

The people of western Europe experienced both great achievements and great turmoil during the Gothic period. In the twelfth and thirteenth centuries Europe was enjoying a period of vigor and growth. Town life stimulated intellectual life, and urban universities and cathedral schools supplanted rural monastic schools as centers of learning. The first European university, at Bologna, Italy, was founded in the eleventh century, and

Europe	1140–1275	1275–1400
France	Saint-Denis; Gothic style emerges; Louis VII; Eleanor of Aquitaine; Notre-Dame de Paris designed; Chartres Cathedral; troubadour songs; University of Paris founded; Amiens Cathedral; Reims Cathedral; Thomas Aquinas; Villard d'Honnecourt's sketchbook; the Sainte-Chapelle; book arts flourish	Papacy in Avignon; Duke Philip the Bold of Burgundy; King Charles V; courtly love themes in literature and art
England	Henry II and Eleanor of Aquitaine found Plantagenet dynasty; Canterbury Cathedral; Cambridge and Oxford universities founded; King John signs Magna Carta; Salisbury Cathedral; Decorated style; Henry III and barons feud	*Windmill Psalter*; opus anglicanum; Hundred Years' War with France begins; first English translation of the Bible; Chaucer's *Canterbury Tales*
Spain	King Alfonso X; Christian reconquest of Muslim Spain continues	Palma Cathedral (Mallorca)
Germany	Nicholas of Verdun; hall churches develop; Holy Roman Emperor Frederick II	Gothic synagogue built in Prague (Bohemia); *Andachtsbilder*
Italy	Pisa Campanile; Saint Francis; Franciscan order founded; Padua University founded; Nicola Pisano; Giovanni Pisano; Cimabue's *Crucifix*	Giotto's frescoes; Duccio's *Maestà*; Dante's *Divine Comedy*; Boccaccio's *Decameron*; Florence Cathedral; "Great Schism" in Western Christian Church; Renaissance style emerges
World	Second to Ninth Crusades; Benin civilization (Africa); Muslim conquest of India; Kamakura period (Japan); Aztec conquer Toltec (South America); Mississippian pottery (North America); Marco Polo in China; Jenghiz Khan invades China; Kublai Khan rules Mongols	Wu Chen's landscapes (China); Black Death ravages Europe; Ming dynasty (China); Tamerlane's conquests in Asia; Golden Pavilion (Japan)

important universities in Paris, Cambridge, and Oxford soon followed. The Gothic period also saw the flowering of distinctive art forms among the nobility—poetry and music in particular—centered on the concept of courtly love (see "Courtly Love," opposite).

Although Europe remained overwhelmingly rural during the Gothic period, towns gained increasing prominence. Nearly all the major cities in western Europe today were sizable urban centers by the late twelfth century. As towns grew, they became increasingly important centers of artistic patronage. The production and sale of goods in many towns was controlled by guilds. Artisans of all types, from bakers to painters, and merchants formed these associations to advance their professional interests. Medieval guilds also played an important social role, safeguarding members' political interests, organizing religious celebrations, and looking after members and their families in times of trouble.

A town's walls enclosed streets, wells, market squares, shops, churches, and schools. Homes ranged from humble wood-and-thatch structures to imposing stone town houses. Although wooden dwellings crowded together made fire an ever-present danger and hygiene was rudimentary at best, towns fostered an energetic civic life and a strong communal identity, reinforced by public projects and ceremonies. An idealized portrait of the town of Siena in the mid-fourteenth century conveys some of the richness and energy of late-medieval civic life (fig. 16-2).

Urban cathedrals, the seats of the ruling bishops, superseded rural monasteries as centers of religious patronage throughout western Europe during the Gothic period. So many of these monumental testaments to the power of the Church were erected between 1150 and 1400 that this period is also known as the great age of cathedral building. Cathedral precincts functioned almost as towns within towns. The great churches dominated their surroundings and were central fixtures of urban life. Their grandeur inspired love and admiration; their great expense and the intrusive power of their bishops inspired resentment and fear. The twelfth century witnessed a growth of intense religiosity among the laity,

COURTLY LOVE

The ideal of courtly love arose in southern France in the early twelfth century during the cultural renaissance that followed the First Crusade. It involved the passionate devotion of lover and loved one. The relationship was almost always illicit—the woman the wife of another, often a lord or patron—and its consummation was usually impossible. This movement transformed the social habits of western Europe's courts and has had an enduring influence on modern ideas of love. Images of gallant knights serving refined ladies, who bestowed tokens of affection on their chosen suitors or cruelly withheld their love on a whim, captured the popular imagination.

The literature of courtly love was initially spread by the musician-poets known as troubadours, some of them professionals, some of them amateur nobles, and at least twenty of them women. They sang of love's joys and heartbreaks in daringly personalized terms, extolling the ennobling effects of the lovers' selfless devotion. From this tradition came the famous romance of Tristam and Ysolt (Tristan and Isolde), so well known that it was the decorative motif on a hair comb from the fifteenth century, seen at the right.

Chrétien de Troyes, a French poet writing in the late twelfth century, tells of the love of the knight Lancelot for Guinevere, the wife of King Arthur. The literature of courtly love marked a major shift from the usually negative way in which women had previously been portrayed as sinful daughters of Eve. The following example, a stylized lovers' debate (the woman speaks first), is an example of courtly love poetry of southern France.

> Friend, because of you I'm filled
> with grievous sorrow and despair,
> but I doubt you feel a trace
> of my affliction.
> Why did you become a lover,
> since you leave the suffering to me?
> Why don't we split it evenly?
>
> Lady, such is love's nature
> when it links two friends together,
> that whatever grief or joy they have
> each feels according to his way.
> The way I see it, and I don't
> exaggerate, all the worst pain's
> been on my end of the game.
>
> Friend, I know well enough how skilled
> you are in amorous affairs,
> and I find you rather changed
> from the chivalrous knight you used to be.
> I might as well be clear,
> for your mind seems quite distracted:
> do you still find me attractive?
>
> Lady, may sparrow-hawk not ride my wrist,
> nor siren fly beside
> me on the chase, if ever
> since you gave me perfect joy
> I possessed another woman;
> I don't lie: out of envy
> evil men insult my name.
>
> (Attributed to the Countess
> of Dia and Raimbaut
> d'Orange, late twelfth
> century; cited in Bogin,
> pages 147, 149)

The tradition of courtly love had a lasting influence on the development of Western literature. In Italy the Florentine poet Dante Alighieri (1265–1321) incorporated the form into his great work, *La Divina Commedia (The Divine Comedy,* c. 1310–1320), in which his idealized woman, Beatrice, guides him through paradise.

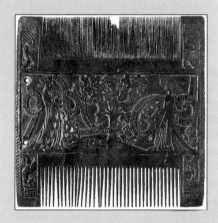

Comb, carved with *The Meeting of Tristam and Ysolt*, from eastern France or Switzerland. Early 15th century. Wood coated with gesso and paint, height 7³/₄ x 7⁵/₈" (19.7 x 19.5 cm). Museum of Fine Arts, Boston
H. E. Bolles Fund

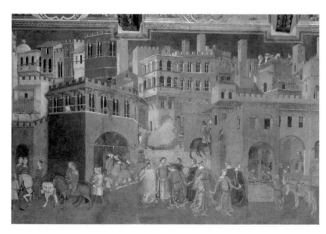

16-2. Ambrogio Lorenzetti. Detail of fresco *Allegory of Good Government in the City*, in the Sala della Pace, Palazzo Pubblico, Siena. 1338–39

particularly in Italy and France. The same devotional intensity gave rise in the early thirteenth century to two new religious orders, the Franciscans and the Dominicans, both of which went out into the world to preach and minister to those in need, rather than confining themselves in monasteries.

The Crusades continued throughout the thirteenth century. In 1204, soldiers of the Fourth Crusade who had set out to conquer Egypt from the Muslims instead seized Constantinople—capital of the Byzantine Empire and the center of the Eastern Christian Church—and the city remained under Western control until 1261. The Crusades and the trade that followed from them brought western Europeans into contact with the Byzantine and Islamic worlds, and through them many literary works of classical antiquity, particularly those of Aristotle. These works posed a problem for medieval scholars because they promoted rational inquiry rather than faith as the path to truth, and their conclusions did not always fit comfortably with Church doctrine. In the thirteenth century, Thomas Aquinas finally brought together faith and reason—the old belief and the new logic—in Scholastic philosophy, which has endured as a basis of Catholic thought to this day.

The all-embracing intellectual systems of the Scholastic thinkers had a profound influence on the arts. The sculptural programs in many cathedrals are as encyclopedic as the *Speculum Maius* (Greater Mirror) of Vincent de Beauvais, a thirteenth-century Parisian Dominican. He organized his eighty-volume encyclopedia to include categories of the Natural World, Doctrine, History, and Morality. Gothic master builders, like the Scholastics, saw divine order in geometric relationships and expressed these relationships in sculpture and architecture. Unlike their Romanesque predecessors, who used stylization and distortion to achieve emotional impact, thirteenth-century sculptors created more naturalistic forms that reflect the idealism and reasoned analysis of Scholastic thought. Gothic religious imagery became all-encompassing, and like Romanesque imagery its purpose was to instruct and convince the viewer. Its effects, however, are more varied and subtle. In the Gothic cathedral it incorporates a wide range of subjects drawn from the natural world. Scholastic logic intermingles with the mysticism of light and color to create for the worshiper the direct, emotional, ecstatic experience of the church as the embodiment of God's house, filled with divine light.

In all these achievements lay potential disaster. By the middle of the fourteenth century much of Europe was in crisis. Prosperity had fostered population growth, which by about 1300 began to exceed food production, and thereafter famines became increasingly common. Peasant revolts began as worsening conditions frustrated rising expectations. In 1337 a prolonged conflict known as the Hundred Years' War (1337–1453) erupted between France and England, devastating much of France. In the middle of the fourteenth century a lethal plague swept northward from Sicily, wiping out as much as 40 percent of Europe's population (see "The Black Death," page 606). By depleting the labor force, however, the plague gave surviving peasants increased leverage over their landlords and increased the wages of artisans. The Church, too, experienced great strain during the fourteenth century. In 1309 the papal court moved from Rome to Avignon, in southeastern France, where it remained until 1377. From 1378 to 1417, in what is known as the Great Schism, the papacy split, with two contending popes, one in Avignon and one in Rome, claiming legitimacy.

FRANCE The birth and initial flowering of the Gothic style took place in France against the backdrop of the growing power of the French monarchy. Louis VI (ruled 1108–1137) and Louis VII (ruled 1137–1180) consolidated royal authority over the Île-de-France and began to exert control over powerful nobles in other regions. Before succeeding to the throne, Louis VII had married Eleanor (1122–1204), heir to the region of Aquitaine (southwestern France), the largest and most prosperous feudal domain in western Europe. Eleanor of Aquitaine was one of the great figures of her age. She accompanied Louis on the Second Crusade (1147–1149), but the marriage was later annulled by papal decree. Taking her wealthy province with her, Eleanor then married Henry Plantagenet—the duke of Normandy, count of Anjou, Maine, and Touraine, and soon-to-be King Henry II of England. Their marriage created further dynastic entanglements. Henry and Eleanor together controlled more French territory than the French king, although he was technically their feudal overlord. The resulting tangle of conflicting claims was responsible for centuries of friction between England and France that culminated in the Hundred Years' War.

Eleanor was estranged from Henry in 1170 and plotted with her sons and her former husband, Louis VII, to overthrow him. When these schemes failed, Henry kept her confined for more than a decade. After his death in 1189, the dowager queen Eleanor presided over her court in Poitiers, Aquitaine, while her sons Richard the Lion-Hearted and then John were kings of England and a daughter was queen of Castile in Spain. Poitiers gained renown for its patronage of high culture and the literature of courtly love (see "Courtly Love," page 549). A woman of great courage and stamina, Eleanor had ten children, including two daughters with Louis and five sons and three daughters with Henry. She remained a formidable figure in European politics into her eighties.

The successors to Louis VII continued the consolidation of royal authority and nation building, increasing their domains and privileges at the expense of aristocrats and the Church.

Architecture and Its Decoration

The political events of the twelfth and thirteenth centuries were accompanied by a burst of church-building. It has been estimated that during the Middle Ages several million tons of stone were quarried to build some 80 cathedrals, 500 large churches, and tens of thousands of parish churches, and that within 100 years some 2,700 churches were built in the Île-de-France region alone. This staggering undertaking drew on the wealth generated by the area's agricultural products—particularly wheat and wine—and the commerce and industry of its town dwellers. Stone was but one of the expenses. In some instances, as at Chartres, the clergy already owned the quarry; in others, they bought it. Transporting the stone was sometimes a greater expense than the stone itself. Whenever possible, heavy construction material was transported by water on barges, and sometimes canals were built for this purpose. (Stone from France was often shipped by barge to England for this same reason.) When transport by land was necessary, the shortest possible route was taken, and new types of harnesses for coupling draft horses were developed. The ingenious machines created for lifting heavy materials were well documented in drawings of the time, as was scaffolding—including some suspended from above rather than resting on the ground—and spiral staircases built within the masonry. This explosion of cathedral building began at a historic abbey church on the outskirts of Paris.

Abbey Church of Saint-Denis. The Benedictine monastery of Saint-Denis, a few miles north of central Paris, had great symbolic significance for the French monarchy. It housed the tombs of French kings, regalia of the French Crown, and the relics of Saint Denis, the patron saint of France, who, according to tradition, had been the first bishop of Paris. In the 1130s, under the inspiration of Abbot Suger, construction began on the new abbey church, which is arguably Europe's first Gothic structure. Suger (c. 1081–1151) was a trusted adviser to both Louis VI and Louis VII, and he governed France as regent when Louis VII and Eleanor of Aquitaine led the crusade.

Suger described his administration of the abbey and the building of the Abbey Church of Saint-Denis in three books. His love of magnificent architecture and art brought him into conflict with the Cistercian leader, Abbot Bernard of Clairvaux (Chapter 15). As a widely traveled cleric, Suger knew all the latest developments in church building, and his design combines elements from many sources. Because the Île-de-France had great Carolingian buildings and little monumental Romanesque architecture, Suger brought in masons and sculptors from other regions. Saint-Denis became a center of artistic interchange. Unfortunately for art historians today, Suger did not record the names of the masters he employed, nor information about them and the techniques they used. The abbot took an active part in the building. He found the huge trees and stone needed by the workers on the abbey's own lands. To generate income for the rebuilding, he instituted economic reforms, receiving substantial annual payments from the town's inhabitants and establishing free villages on abbey estates to attract peasants. For additional funds, he turned to the royal coffers and even to fellow clerics.

The first part of the new structure to be completed was the west facade and narthex (1135–1140). Here Suger's masons combined Norman facade design like that at Caen (see fig. 15-27) and rib-vaulted structure like that at Durham (see fig. 15-26) with the richly sculptured portals of Burgundy. The east end represented an even more stunning change. The choir was completed in three years and three months (1140–1144), timing that Abbot Suger found auspicious. The plan of the choir (*chevet* in French) resembled that of a Romanesque pilgrimage church, with a semicircular sanctuary surrounded by an ambulatory from which radiated seven chapels of uniform size (figs. 15-3, 16-3). All the architectural elements of the choir—rib groin vaults springing from round piers, pointed arches, wall buttresses to relieve stress on the walls, and window openings—had already appeared in Romanesque buildings. The dramatic achievement of Suger's master mason was to combine these features into a fully integrated architectural whole that emphasized the open, flowing space. Sanctuary, ambulatory,

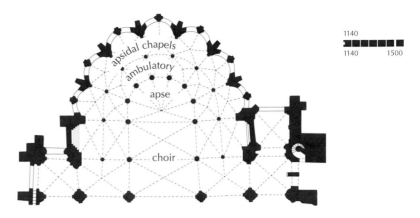

16-3. Plan of the sanctuary, Abbey Church of Saint-Denis, Saint-Denis, Île-de-France, France. 1140–44

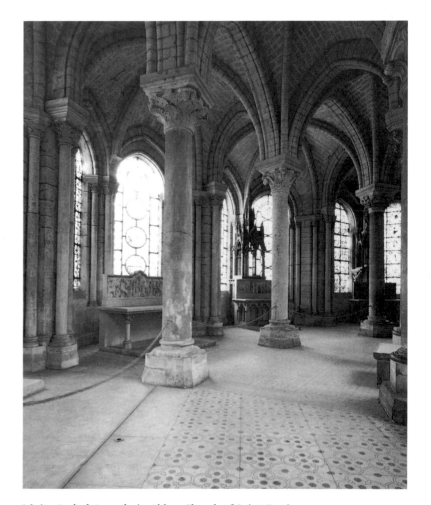

16-4. Ambulatory choir, Abbey Church of Saint-Denis

and chapels opened into one another; walls of stained glass replaced masonry, permitting the light to permeate the interior with color (fig. 16-4). To accomplish this effect, the masons relied on the systematic use of advanced vaulting techniques, the culmination of half a century of experiment and innovation (fig. 16-5; see "Elements of Architecture," page 552).

ELEMENTS OF ARCHITECTURE
Rib Vaulting

Rib vaulting was one of the chief technical contributions of Romanesque and Gothic builders. Rib vaults are a form of **groin vault** (see page 226) in which the ridges (groins) formed by the intersecting vaults may rest on and be covered by curved moldings called ribs. These ribs were usually structural as well as decorative, and they strengthened the joins and helped channel the vaults' thrusts outward and downward. The ribs were constructed first and supported the scaffolding of the vault. Ribs developed over time into an intricate masonry "skeleton" filled with an increasingly light-weight "skin," the web of the vault, or webbing. Sophisticated variations on the basic rib vault created the soaring interiors for which Gothic churches are famous.

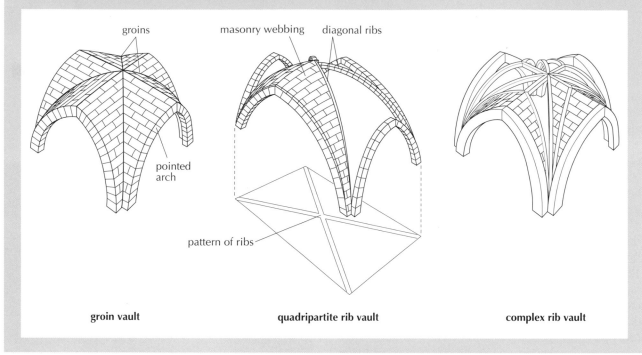

groins masonry webbing diagonal ribs

pointed arch

pattern of ribs

groin vault   **quadripartite rib vault**   **complex rib vault**

The apse of Saint-Denis represented the emergence of a new architectural aesthetic based on line and light. Citing early Christian writings, Suger saw light and color as a means of illuminating the soul and uniting it with God, a belief he shared with medieval mystics such as Hildegard of Bingen (Chapter 15). For him, the colored lights of gemstones and stained-glass windows and the glint of golden church furnishings at Saint-Denis transformed the material world into the splendor of paradise.

Louis VII and Eleanor of Aquitaine attended the consecration of the new choir on June 14, 1144. Shortly thereafter the impending Second Crusade became the primary recipient of royal resources, leaving Suger without funds to replace the old nave and transept at Saint-Denis. The abbot died in 1151, and his church remained unfinished for another century. (Saint-Denis suffered extensive damage during the French Revolution in the late eighteenth century. Its current condition is the result of nineteenth- and twentieth-century restorations and cleaning.)

The Abbey Church of Saint-Denis became the prototype for a new architecture of space and light based on a highly adaptable skeletal framework constructed from buttressed perimeter walls and an interior vaulting system of pointed-arch masonry ribs. It initiated a period of competitive experimentation in the Île-de-France and surrounding regions that resulted in ever larger churches enclosing increasingly taller interior spaces walled with ever greater expanses of colored glass (see "Notre-Dame of Paris," page 564). These great churches, with their

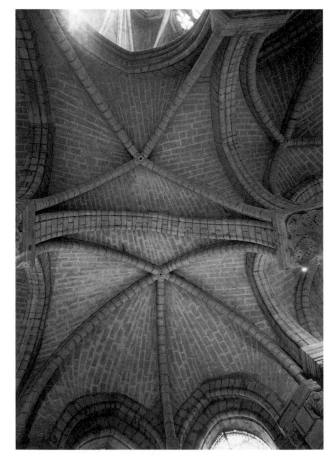

16-5. Ambulatory vaults, Abbey Church of Saint-Denis

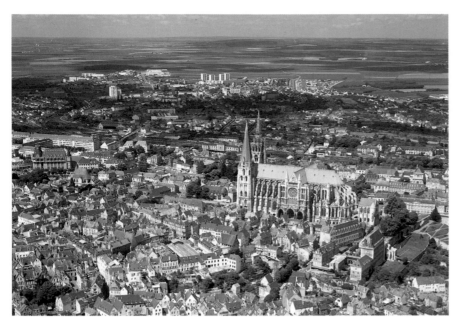

16-6. Cathedral of Notre-Dame, Chartres, Île-de-France, France. c. 1194–60; west facade begun c. 1134; north spire 1507–13. View from the southeast

Chartres was the site of a pre-Christian virgin-goddess cult and one of the oldest and most important Christian shrines in France. Its main treasure was a long piece of linen believed to have been worn by Mary—a gift from the Byzantine empress to Charlemagne, donated to the cathedral by King Charles the Bald in 876—that was on display with other relics in a huge basement crypt. The healing powers attributed to this relic and its association with Mary made Chartres a major pilgrimage destination as the cult of the Virgin grew.

unabashed decorative richness, were part of Abbot Suger's legacy to France.

Chartres Cathedral. The great Cathedral of Notre-Dame (Our Lady, the Virgin Mary) dominates the town of Chartres, southwest of Paris (fig. 16-6). For many people, Chartres Cathedral is a near-perfect embodiment of spirit in stone and glass. Constructed in several stages beginning in the mid-twelfth century and extending into the mid-thirteenth, the cathedral reflects the transition from Early to High Gothic. A fire in 1134 that damaged the western facade of an earlier cathedral on the site prompted the building of a new facade, influenced by the Early Gothic style at Saint-Denis. After another fire in 1194 destroyed most of the rest of the original structure, a papal representative convinced reluctant local church officials to undertake a massive rebuilding project. A new cathedral was built between approximately 1194 and 1260.

To erect such an enormous building required vast resources—money, raw materials, and skilled labor. Contrary to common perceptions about "the great age of cathedral building," medieval people did not always support these ambitious undertakings with devout and selfless zeal. Both nobles and ordinary people often opposed the building of cathedrals because of the burden of new taxes. Nevertheless, cathedral officials pledged all or part of their incomes for three to five years. The church's relics were sent on tour as far away as England to solicit contributions. As the new structure rose higher during the 1220s, the work grew more costly and funds dwindled. When the bishop and canons (cathedral clergy) tried to make up the deficit by raising feudal and commercial taxes, they were driven into exile for four years. The economic privileges claimed by the Church for the cathedral sparked intermittent riots by townspeople and the local nobility throughout the thirteenth century. Despite these

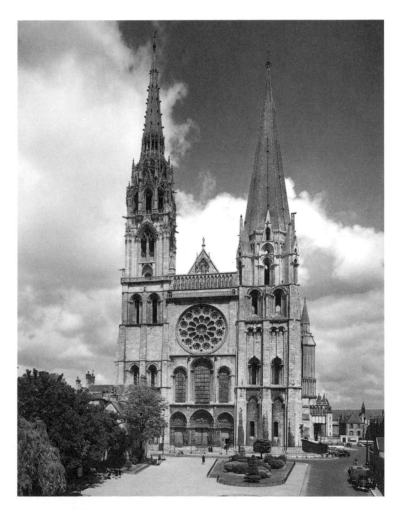

16-7. West facade, Chartres Cathedral. c. 1134–1220; south tower c. 1160; north tower 1507–13

tensions, the new cathedral emerged as a work of remarkable balance and harmony, inspiring even to nonbelievers.

From a distance the most striking features of the west facade are its prominent round **rose window** and two towers, (fig. 16-7). The spire on the north tower (left) was added in the early sixteenth century; the spire on the

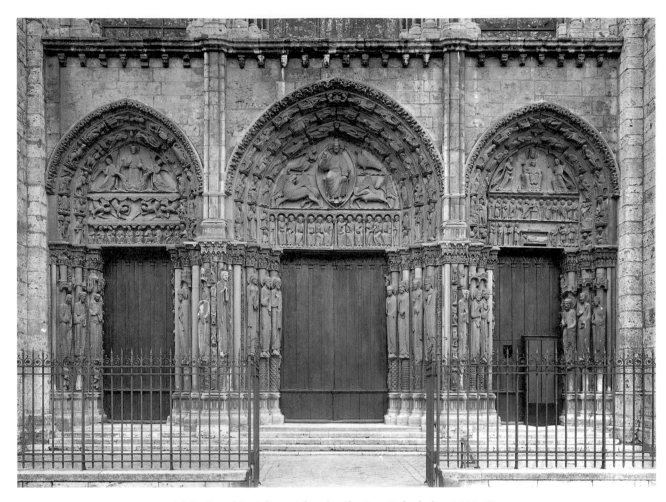

16-8. Royal Portal, west facade, Chartres Cathedral. c. 1145–55

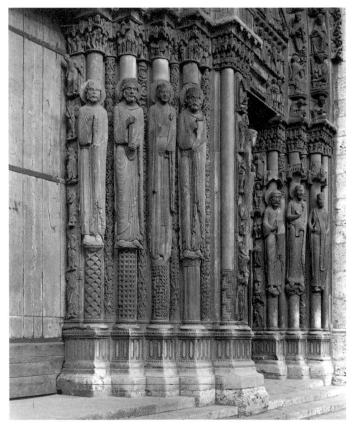

16-9. *Prophets and Ancestors of Christ*, right side, central portal, Royal Portal, Chartres Cathedral. c. 1145–55

south tower dates from the twelfth century. On closer inspection the facade's three doorways—the so-called Royal Portal—capture the attention with their sculpture (fig. 16-8). Christ Enthroned in Royal Majesty dominates the central tympanum. Flanking the doorways are monumental **column statues**, a form that originated at Saint-Denis. These column statues depict nineteen of the twenty-two original Old Testament figures who were seen as precursors of Christ (fig. 16-9). In other biblical references the builders of Gothic cathedrals identified themselves symbolically with Solomon, the builder of the first Temple in Jerusalem, and the depiction of Old Testament kings and queens evokes the close ties between the Church and the French royal house. Because of this relationship, still potent after 600 years, most such figures at other churches were smashed during the French Revolution.

Earlier sculptors had achieved dramatic, dynamic effects by compressing, elongating, and bending figures to fit them into an architectural framework. At Chartres, in contrast, the sculptors sought to pose their high-relief figures naturally and comfortably in their architectural settings. The erect, frontal column statues, with their elongated proportions and vertical drapery, echo the cylindrical shafts from which they emerge. Their heads are finely rendered with idealized features.

Calm and order prevail in the imagery of the Royal Portal, in contrast to the somewhat more crowded

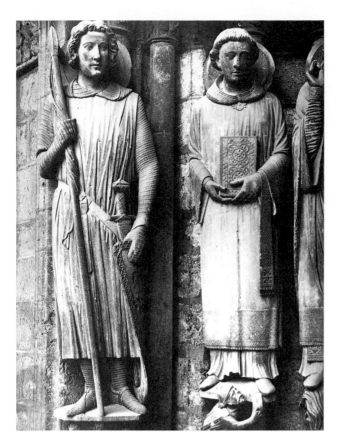

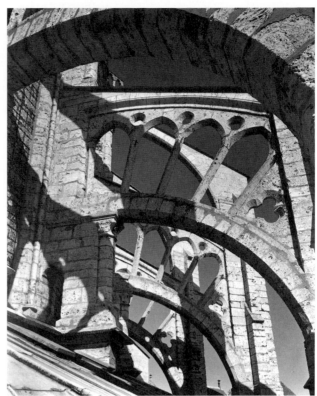

1200
1140   1500

16-10. *Saint Stephen* (right, c. 1210–20) and *Saint Theodore* (left, c. 1230–35), left side, left portal, south transept entrance, Chartres Cathedral

16-11. Flying buttresses, Chartres Cathedral. c. 1200–20

Imagery at many Romanesque churches, such as those at Moissac (see fig. 15-9) and Autun (see fig. 15-12). Christ in the central tympanum of the Royal Portal appears imposing but more benign and less terrifying than in earlier representations. The Twelve Apostles in the lintel below him and the twenty-four elders in the archivolts above him have been arranged in a hierarchy of size and location, with little narrative interaction between them. Even in narrative scenes, calm prevails, as in the Ascension of Christ in the tympanum of the left doorway and the enthroned Virgin and Child in the tympanum of the right doorway.

Column statues became standard elements of Gothic church decoration, developing from shaftlike reliefs to fully three-dimensional figures that appear to interact with one another as well as with approaching worshipers. A comparison of the column statues of the Royal Portal with those of the later north and south transept portals illustrates this transition. Figure 16-10 shows two column statues from the south transept portal. *Saint Stephen*, on the right, was made between 1210 and 1220; *Saint Theodore*, on the left, between 1230 and 1235. More lifelike than their predecessors, they seem to stand on projecting bases with carved brackets. The bases reinforce the illusion that the figures are free of the architecture to which they are attached. In another change, the dense geometric patterning and stylized foliage around the earlier statues have given way to plain stone.

Saint Stephen, still somewhat cylindrical, is more naturally proportioned than the earlier figures on the west facade. The sculptor has also created a variety of textures to differentiate cloth, embroidery, flesh, and other features. The later *Saint Theodore* reflects its sculptor's attempt to depict a convincingly "alive" figure. The saint is dressed as a contemporary crusader and stands, purposeful but contemplative, with his feet firmly planted and his hips thrust to the side (a pose often called the Gothic **S**-curve). The meticulous detailing of his expressive face and the textures of his chain mail and surcoat help create a strong sense of physical presence.

Many nearby churches built by local masons about the same time as Chartres Cathedral reflect an earlier style and are relatively dark and squat. Unlike them, Chartres was the work of artisans from areas north and northeast of the town who were accomplished practitioners of the Gothic style. In the new cathedral they brought together the hallmark Gothic structural devices for the first time: the pointed arch, ribbed groin vaulting, the **flying buttress**, and the **triforium**, now designed as a mid-level passageway (see "Elements of Architecture," page 558). The flying buttress, a gracefully arched, skeletal exterior support, counters the outward thrust of the vaulting over the nave and aisles (fig. 16-11). The Gothic triforium (which was a flat wall in the basilica church or a gallery in Byzantine and Romanesque architecture) overlooks the nave through an arcaded screen

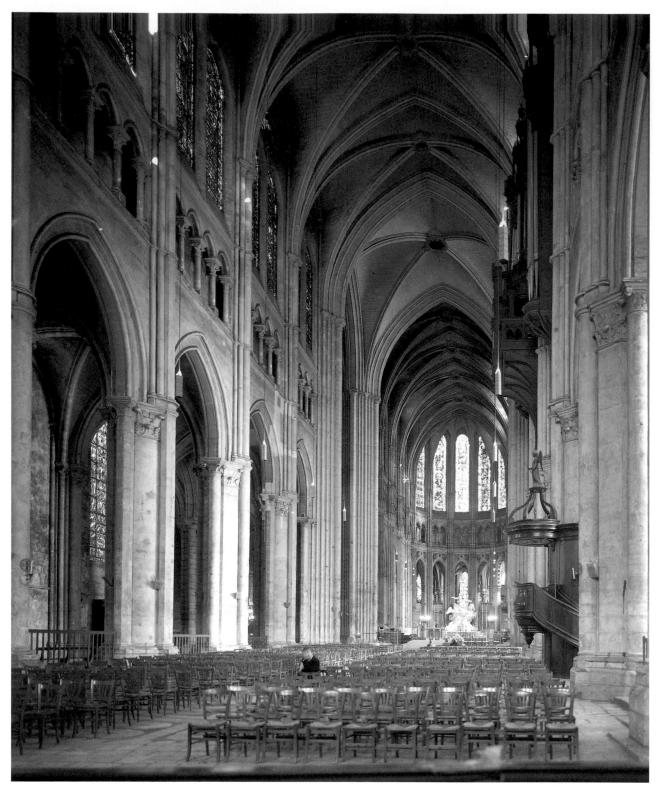

16-12. Nave, Chartres Cathedral. c. 1200–20

that contributes to the visual unity of the interior (fig. 16-12). Building on the concept pioneered at Saint-Denis of an elegant masonry shell enclosing a large open space, the masons at Chartres erected a structure with one of the widest naves in Europe and vaults that soar 118 feet above the floor. The enlarged sanctuary, another feature derived from Saint-Denis, occupies one-third of the building (fig. 16-13). Stained glass covers nearly half the clerestory surfaces. The large and luminous clerestory is filled by pairs of tall, arched windows called **lancets** surmounted by circular windows, or **oculi**. Whereas at a Romanesque pilgrimage church like Sainte-Foy (see fig. 15-4) the worshiper's gaze is drawn forward toward the apse, at Chartres it is drawn upward—to the clerestory windows and the soaring vaults overhead—as well as forward. Relatively little interior architectural decoration interrupts the visual rhythm of shafts and arches. Four-part vaulting has superseded more complex

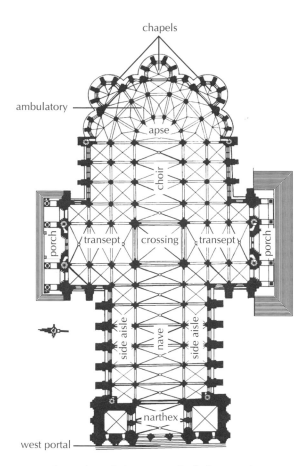

16-13. Plan of Chartres Cathedral. c. 1194–1220

systems such as that at Durham Cathedral (see fig. 15-26), and the alternating bays typical of Romanesque naves such as that at Speyer Cathedral (see fig. 15-32) have been eliminated.

At Chartres, architectural engineering went hand in hand with numerical symbolism. An equilateral triangle established the three points of the outer edges of the buttresses and the keystone of the vault in the nave. The addition of the Trinity (three) to the material world, four (the four directions, the four winds, the four seasons, the four rivers of paradise), forms the recurring number seven, the seven liberal arts, the seven gifts of the Holy Spirit. The Virgin, Notre-Dame, to whom the church is dedicated, is enthroned with Christ, who is surrounded by the Liberal Arts in the tympanum and voussoirs of the west portal. The imagery of Chartres, which stresses themes involving Mary and the Old Testament precursors of Christ, as well as the saints coming after the Incarnation, encompasses the entire program of Scholastic thought.

Chartres is unique among French Gothic buildings in that most of its stained-glass windows have survived. The light from these windows changes constantly as sunlight varies with the time of day, the seasons, and the movement of clouds. Stained glass is an expensive and difficult medium, but its effect on the senses and emotions makes the effort worthwhile (see "Stained-Glass Windows," page 559). Chartres was famous for its glassmaking workshops, which by 1260 had installed about 22,000 square feet of stained glass in 176 windows. Most of the glass dates between about 1210 and 1250, but a few earlier panels, from around 1150 to 1170, were pre-

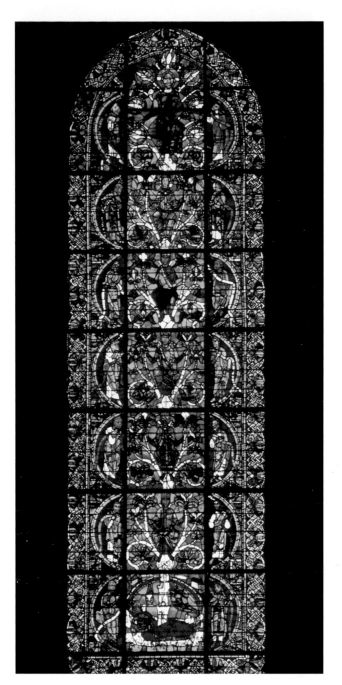

16-14. *Tree of Jesse,* west facade, Chartres Cathedral. c. 1150–70. Stained glass

served in the west facade. The iconography of the windows echoes that of the portal sculpture.

Among the twelfth-century works in the west wall of the cathedral is the *Tree of Jesse* window (fig. 16-14). The monumental treatment of this Marian subject (relating to Mary), much more complex than its depiction in an early-twelfth-century Cistercian manuscript (see fig. 15-22), was apparently inspired by a similar window at Saint-Denis. The body of Jesse lies at the base of the tree, and in the branches above him appear, first, four kings of Judaea, Christ's royal ancestors, then the Virgin Mary, and finally Christ himself. Seven doves, the seven gifts of the Holy Spirit, encircle Christ, and fourteen prophets stand in the half-moons flanking the tree.

The glass in the *Tree of Jesse* is set within a rectilinear iron armature (visible as silhouetted black lines). In a

ELEMENTS OF ARCHITECTURE

The Gothic Church

Most large Gothic churches in western Europe were built on the **Latin–cross plan**, with a projecting **transept** marking the transition from **nave** to **sanctuary**. The main entrance **portal** was generally on the west, the **choir** and **apse** on the east. A **narthex** led to the nave and **side aisles**. An **ambulatory** with radiating chapels circled the apse and facilitated the movement of worshipers through the church. Above the nave were a **triforium** passageway and windowed **clerestory**. Narthex, side aisles, ambulatory, and nave usually had **rib vaults** in the Gothic period. Church walls were decorated inside and out with **arcades** of round and pointed arches,

engaged columns and **colonnettes**, and horizontal moldings called **stringcourses**. The roof was supported by a wooden framework. A spire or **crossing** tower above the junction of the transept and nave was usually planned, though often never finished. The **apsidal chapels** ringing the apse were often visible on the exterior, as were the **buttress piers** and **flying buttresses** that countered the outward thrusts of the interior vaults. **Portal** facades were customarily marked by high, flanking towers or **gabled** porches ornamented with **pinnacles** and **finials**. Architectural sculpture covered each portal's **tympanum**, **archivolts**, and **jambs**. A magnificent stained-glass **rose window** typically formed the centerpiece of the portal facades. Stained glass filled the tall, pointed **lancets**.

1200
1140 1500

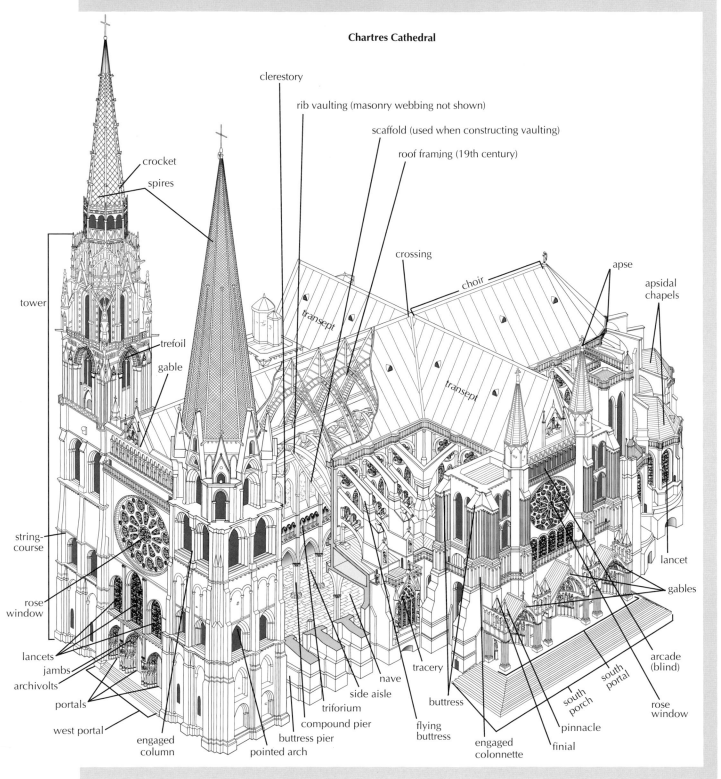

Chartres Cathedral

TECHNIQUE

STAINED-GLASS WINDOWS

The basic technique for making colored glass has been known since the days of ancient Egypt. It involves the addition of metallic oxides—cobalt for blue, manganese for red and purple—to a basic formula of sand and ash or lime that is fused at high temperature. Such "stained" glass was used on a small scale in church windows during the Early Christian period and in Carolingian and Ottonian churches. Colored glass sometimes adorned Romanesque churches, but the art form reached a height of sophistication and popularity in the cathedrals and churches of the Gothic era.

Making a stained-glass image was a complex and costly process. A designer first drew a composition on a wood panel the same size as the opening of the window to be filled, noting the colors of each of the elements in it. Glass blowers produced sheets of colored glass, and then artisans cut individual pieces from these large sheets and laid them out on the wood template. Painters then added details with enamel emulsion, and the glass was reheated to fuse the enamel. Finally, the pieces were assembled and joined together with narrow lead strips, called **cames**. The assembled pieces were set into iron frames that had been preformed to fit the window opening.

The demand for stained-glass windows stimulated technical experimentation to achieve new colors and greater purity and transparency. The colors of Romanesque glass—mainly reds and blues with touches of dark green, brown, and orange yellow—were so deep that it was nearly opaque. The Cistercians adorned their churches with **grisaille** windows, painting foliage and crosses onto a gray glass. Early uncolored glass was full of impurities, but Gothic artisans developed a clearer material onto which they could draw elaborate narrative scenes. Many new colors were discovered accidentally, such as a sunny yellow produced by the addition of silver oxide. Flashing, in which a layer of one color was fused to a layer of another color, produced an almost infinite range of colors. Blue and yellow, for example, could be combined to make green. In the same way, clear glass could be fused to layers of colored glass in varying thicknesses to produce a range of hues from light to dark. The deep colors of early Gothic stained-glass windows give them a saturated and mysterious brilliance. The richness of some of these colors, particularly blue, has never been surpassed. Pale colors and large areas of grisaille glass became increasingly popular from the mid-thirteenth century on, making the windows of later Gothic churches bright and clear by comparison.

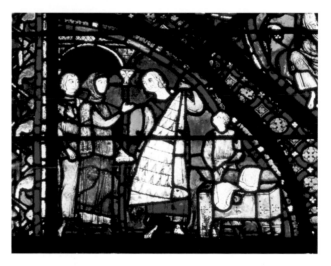

16-16. *Furrier's Shop*, detail of *Charlemagne Window*, Chartres Cathedral

This close-up shows how stained-glass artisans handled form and color. The figures have been reduced to simple shapes and their gestures kept broad to convey meaning from afar. The glass surfaces, however, are painted with fine lines that are invisible from the cathedral's floor. Forms stand out against a lustrous blue ground accented with red. Glowing clear glass serves as white, and violet-pink, green, and yellow complete the palette.

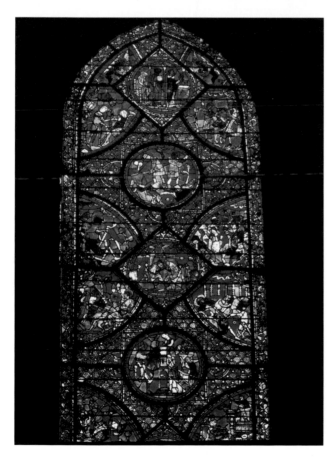

16-15. *Charlemagne Window*, ambulatory apse, Chartres Cathedral. c. 1210–36. Stained glass

This window depicts scenes from the *Song of Roland*, an epic based on events during the reign of Charlemagne; it acquired its final form sometime around 1100. The hero, Roland, was killed fighting Muslims in the Pyrenees Mountains, which lie between France and Spain. Roland is portrayed as an ideal feudal knight, devoted to his lord, his fellow knights, and his faith.

later work, the *Charlemagne Window*, the glass is set within an interlocking framework of medallions so that colored glass and **cames**, the lead strips that join the pieces of glass, work together to make the window imagery more decorative (fig. 16-15). The medallions contain narrative scenes, each surrounded by a field of stylized flowers, leaves, and geometric patterns. At the base of the *Charlemagne Window* is a scene of a customer buying a cloak in a furrier's shop (fig. 16-16). The furrier

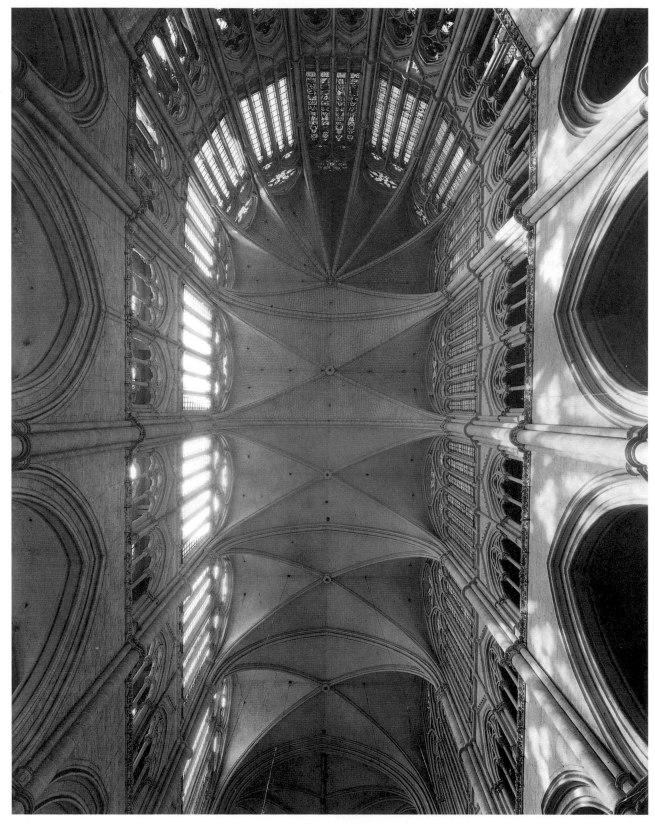

16-17. Vaults, sanctuary, Cathedral of Notre-Dame at Amiens, Île-de-France, France. 1270–88
   The light entering the windows at the left illuminates the walls at the right.

displays a large cloak made of small pelts (perhaps rabbit or squirrel) taken from the chest at the right. The potential buyer has removed one glove and reaches out, perhaps to feel the fur, perhaps to bargain. This scene is one of several at Chartres showing various tradespeople at work. Others include bakers, wheelwrights, weavers, goldsmiths, and carpenters. Similar scenes appear in other Gothic churches. They were once thought to have reflected pious donations by local guilds, but recent scholarship suggests that this was not so. The merchants and artisans of Chartres had apparently not yet been permitted to form guilds in the early thirteenth century, and they contributed to the new cathedral only through the taxes assessed on them by Church officials. The vignettes of tradespeople might thus be a form of Church propaganda, images of an ideal world in which the Church was the center of society and the focus of everyone's work.

Amiens and Reims Cathedrals.

As it continued to evolve, Gothic taste favored increasingly sculptural, ornate facades and intricate window tracery. Builders across northern France refined the geometry of church plans and elevations and found ways to engineer ever stronger masonry skeletons with ever larger expanses of stained glass.

The Cathedral of Notre-Dame at Amiens, an important trading and textile-manufacturing center north of Paris, burned in 1218, and as at Chartres, church officials devoted their resources to making its replacement as splendid as possible. Their funding came mainly from the cathedral's rural estates and from important trade fairs. Construction began in 1220 and continued for some seventy years. The result is the supreme architectural statement of elegant Gothic verticality. The nave, only 48 feet wide, soars upward 144 feet. Not only is the nave exceptionally tall, its narrow proportions create an exaggerated sense of height (figs. 16-17, 16-19).

A labyrinth, now destroyed, recorded the names of the master builders at Amiens on the inlaid floor of the nave (see "Master Builders," page 563). This practice honored the mythical Greek hero Daedalus, master builder of the first labyrinth at the palace of King Minos in Crete. The labyrinth identifies Robert de Luzarches (d. 1236) as the builder who established the overall design for the Amiens Cathedral. He was succeeded by Thomas de Cormont, who was followed by his son Renaud. The lower portions of the church were probably substantially complete by around 1240.

The plan of the cathedral of Amiens derived from that of Chartres, with some simple but critical adjustments (fig. 16-18). The narthex was eliminated, while the transept and sanctuary were expanded and the crossing brought forward. The result is a plan that is balanced east and west around the crossing. The elevation of the nave is similarly balanced and compact (fig. 16-19). Chapels of the same size and shape enhance the clarity and regularity of the design. Tracery and **colonnettes** (small columns) unite the triforium and the clerestory, which makes up nearly half the height of the nave. Evenly spaced piers with engaged half columns topped by

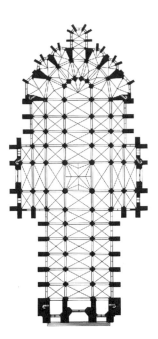

16-18. Robert de Luzarches, Thomas de Cormont, and Renaud de Cormont. Plan of Amiens Cathedral. 1220–88

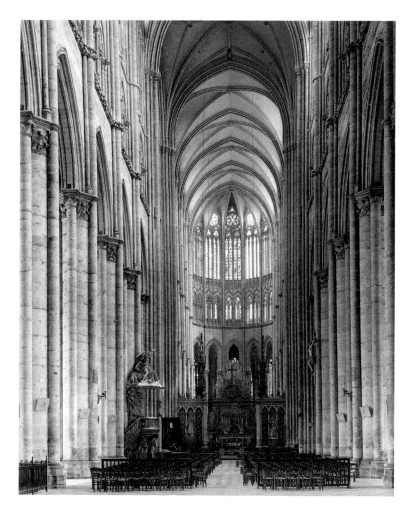

16-19. Nave, Amiens Cathedral. 1220–88

foliage capitals support the arcades. An ornate floral stringcourse below the triforium level and a simpler one below the clerestory both run uninterrupted across the otherwise plain wall surfaces and colonnettes, providing a horizontal counterpoint. The vaulting and the light-filled choir date to the second phase of construction,

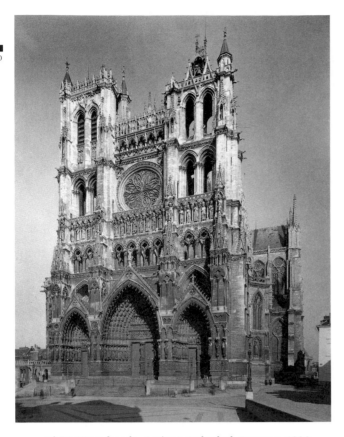

16-20. West facade, Amiens Cathedral. Begun c. 1220

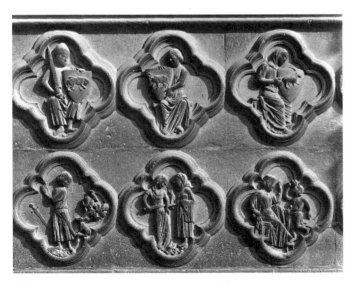

16-21. *Virtues and Vices,* central portal, west entrance, Amiens Cathedral. c. 1220–35

Quatrefoils appeared here as a framing device for the first time and soon became one of the most widespread decorative motifs in Gothic art. In the top row are the Virtues, personified as seated figures. Each holds a shield with an animal on it that symbolizes a particular virtue: the lion for Courage, the cow for Patience, and the lamb for Meekness. Below the Virtues are figures that represent the Vices that correspond to each of the Virtues: a knight dropping his sword and turning to run when a rabbit pops up (Cowardice); a woman on the verge of plunging a sword through a man (Discord); and a woman delivering a swift kick to her servant (Impatience or Injustice).

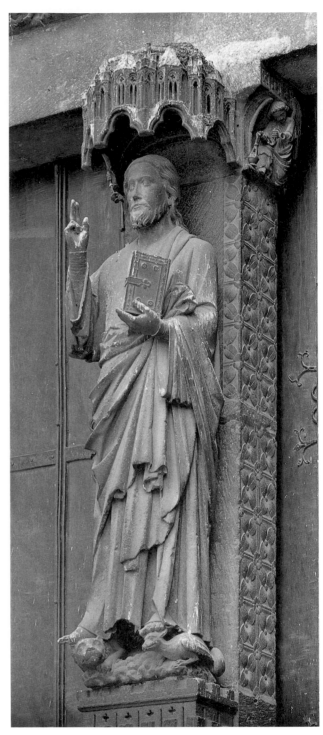

16-22. *Beau Dieu*, trumeau, central portal, west facade, Amiens Cathedral. c. 1220–35

directed by Thomas de Cormont. The choir is illuminated by large windows subdivided by tracery into slender lancets crowned by **trefoils** (three-lobed designs) and circular windows.

The west front of Amiens reflects several stages of construction (fig. 16-20). The lower levels, designed by Robert de Luzarches, are the earliest, dating to between 1220 and about 1240, but building continued over the centuries. The towers date to the fourteenth and fifteenth centuries, and the tracery in the rose window is also late. Consequently, the facade has a somewhat disjointed appearance, and all its elements do not correspond to the interior spaces behind them. Design begins to become detached from structural logic, an indication of the loosening of the traditional ties between architectural planning and the actual building process. This trend led to the elevation of architectural design—as opposed to structural engineering and construction—to a high status by the fifteenth century.

The sculptural program of the west portals of Amiens presents an almost overwhelming array of images in registers. The sculpture was produced rapidly by a large workshop in only about fifteen years (1220–c. 1235), making it stylistically more uniform than that of the cathedrals of Chartres or Reims. In the mid-thirteenth century Amiens-trained sculptors carried their style to other parts of Europe, especially Castile (Spain) and Italy.

Worshipers approaching the main entrance encountered figures of apostles and saints lined up along the door jambs and projecting buttresses, as were seen at Chartres. At Amiens something new captures the attention. On the base below the figures, at eye level, are **quatrefoils** (four-lobed medallions) containing relief sculpture illustrating Good and Evil in daily life (fig. 16-21), the seasons and labors of the months, the lives of the saints, and biblical stories. High above, in the tympanum

and archivolts of the central portal, the history of humanity ends in the Last Judgment. The left portal sculpture illustrates the life of Saint Firmin, an early bishop of Amiens and the town's patron saint; and those on the right portal are dedicated to Mary and her coronation as Queen of Heaven.

A sculpture of Christ as the *Beau Dieu* (noble, or beautiful, God), the kindly teacher-priest bestowing his blessing on the faithful (fig. 16-22), forms the **trumeau** of the central portal. This exceptionally fine sculpture may have been the work of the master of the Amiens workshop himself. The broad contours of the heavy drapery wrapped around Christ's right hip and bunched over his left arm lead the eye up to the gospel-book he holds and past it to his face, which is that of a young king. He stands on a lion and a dragonlike creature called a basilisk, which symbolizes his kingship and his triumph over evil and death. With its clear, solid forms, elegantly cascading robes, and interplay of close observation with idealization, the *Beau Dieu* embodies the Amiens style and the Gothic spirit.

In the Church hierarchy, the bishop of Amiens was subordinate to the archbishop of Reims. Politically the archbishop also had great power, for the French kings

1200
1140   1500

MASTER BUILDERS

"At the beginning of the fifth year [of the rebuilding of England's Canterbury Cathedral], suddenly by the collapse of beams beneath his feet, [master William of Sens] fell to the ground amid a shower of falling masonry and timber from . . . fifty feet or more. . . . On the master craftsman alone fell the wrath of God—or the machinations of the Devil" (Brother Gervase, Canterbury, twelfth century, cited in Andrews, page 20).

Master masons, "masters of the works," oversaw all aspects of church construction in the Middle Ages, from design and structural engineering to decoration. The job presented a formidable logistical challenge, especially at the great cathedral sites. The master mason at Chartres coordinated the work of roughly 400 people who were scattered, with their equipment and supplies, at many locations, from distant stone quarries to high scaffolding. This workforce set in place some 200 blocks a day. Master masons gained in prestige during the thirteenth century as they increasingly differentiated themselves from the laborers working under them. In the words of Nicolas de Biard, a thirteenth-century Dominican preacher,

"The master masons, holding measuring rod and gloves in their hands, say to others: 'Cut here,' and they do not work; nevertheless they receive the greater fees" (cited in Frisch, page 55). By the standards of their time they were well read; they traveled widely. They knew both aristocrats and high church officials, and they earned as much as knights. From the thirteenth century on, in what was then an exceptional honor, masters were buried, along with patrons and bishops, in the cathedrals they built. The tomb sculpture of a master mason named Hugues Libergier in the Reims Cathedral portrays him, attended by angels, as a well-dressed figure with his tools and a model of the cathedral. The names of more than 3,000 master masons are known today. In some cases their names were prominently inscribed in the labyrinths on cathedral floors.

The illustration here shows a master—right-angle and compass in hand—conferring with his royal patron while workers carve a capital, hoist stones with a winch, cut a block, level a course of masonry using a plumb, and lay dressed stones in place. Masters and their crews moved constantly from site to site, and several masters contributed to a single

building. A master's training was rigorous but not standardized, so close study of subtle differences in construction techniques can reveal the hand of specific individuals. Fewer than 100 master builders are estimated to have been responsible for all the major architectural projects in the Île-de-France during the century-long building boom there, some of them working on parts of as many as forty churches. Funding shortages and technical delays, such as the need to let mortar harden for three to six months, made construction sporadic.

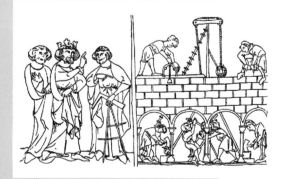

Page with *King Henry III Supervising the Works*, copy of an illustration from a 13th-century English manuscript; original in The British Library, London

NOTRE-DAME OF PARIS

Think of Gothic architecture. Chances are, the image that springs to mind is the Cathedral of Notre-Dame of Paris. Just as this structure rivals the Eiffel Tower as the symbol of Paris itself, Notre-Dame is the vision of what a Gothic cathedral should look like. In fact, the Notre-Dame we see today began as an early Gothic building that bridged the period between Abbot Suger's rebuilding of the Abbey Church of Saint-Denis and the thirteenth-century Chartres Cathedral. On this site—a small island in the Seine River called the Île de la Cité, where the Parisii people who gave the city its name first settled — Pope Alexander III set the building cornerstone in 1163. Construction was far enough along for the altar to be consecrated twenty years later.

The nave, rising to 115 feet, dates to 1180–1200, the west facade to 1200–1250. By this time, massive walls and buttresses and six-part vaults, adopted from Norman Romanesque architecture, must have seemed very old-fashioned. All the portals have figural sculpture. Tympana on the west facade and the north portal are dedicated to Mary, Notre-Dame. After 1225 new masters modernized the building by reworking the clerestory into the large double lancet and rose windows we see today. Notre-Dame had the first true flying buttresses, although those seen at the right of the photograph, rising dramatically to support the high vault of the choir, result from later Gothic remodeling. (The 290-foot spire over the crossing is the work of the nineteenth-century architect Eugène-Emmanuel Viollet-le-Duc.)

Following centuries of use as a Christian church, French Revolutionaries defamed monuments associated with deposed French nobility, transforming the cathedral temporarily into a secular Temple of Reason from 1793 to 1795. Soon thereafter Notre-Dame returned to Christian use and Napoleon crowned himself emperor at its altar in 1804. In our century the liberation of Paris from the Nazis in August 1944 was celebrated in Notre-Dame. Today, boats filled with tourists circle the Île de la Cité and drift under the Pont Neuf and other bridges, past the flower market, secluded squares, and tree-lined courtyards, to approach the beautiful cathedral. Notre-Dame so resonates with life and history that it has become more than a house of worship and work of art; it is part of the shared culture of humankind.

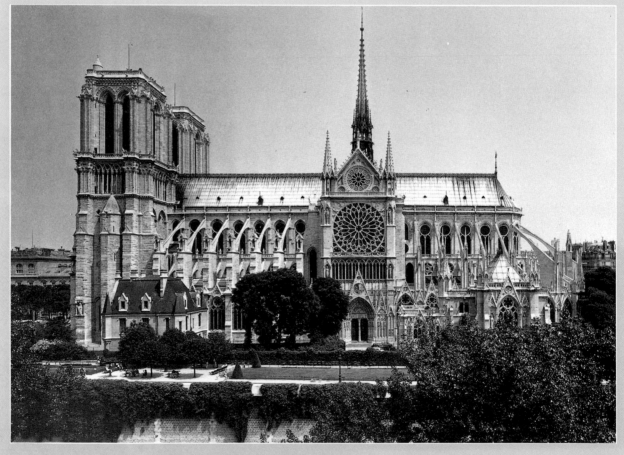

Cathedral of Notre-Dame, Paris. Begun 1163. View from the south

were crowned in his cathedral, though they were buried at Saint-Denis. Reims, like Saint-Denis, had been a cultural and educational center since Carolingian times. As at Chartres and Amiens, the community at Reims, led by the clerics responsible for the building, began to erect a new cathedral after a fire destroyed an earlier church. And as at Chartres, the expense of the project sparked local opposition, with revolts in the 1230s twice driving the archbishop and canons into exile. Construction of the cathedrals of Chartres, Amiens, and Reims overlapped, and the artisans at each site borrowed ideas from and influenced each other.

Many believe the Cathedral of Notre-Dame at Reims to be the most beautiful of all Gothic cathedrals, sur-

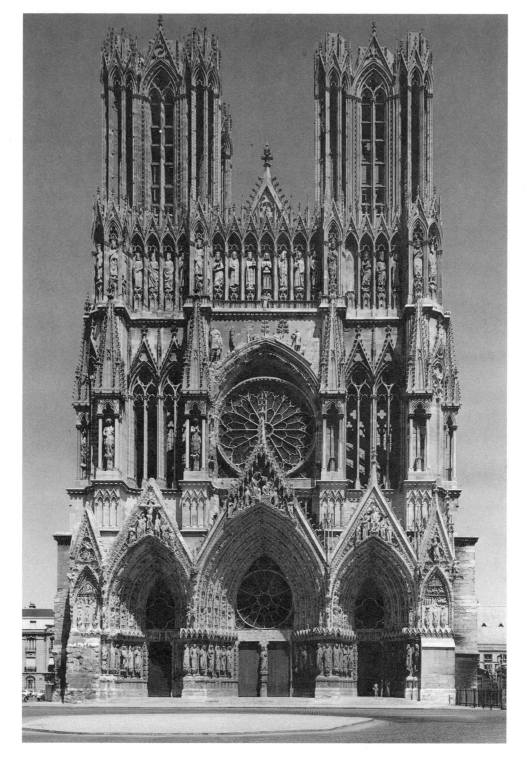

16-23. West façade, Cathedral of Notre-Dame at Reims, Île-de-France, France. 1230s–1260; towers mid-15th century

The cathedral was restored in the sixteenth century and again in the nineteenth and twentieth centuries. During World War I it withstood bombardment by some 3,000 shells, an eloquent testimony to the skills of its builders. It was recently cleaned.

passing even Chartres. Its cornerstone was laid in 1211 and work continued on it throughout the century. Its master builders, their names recorded in the cathedral labyrinth, were Jean d'Orbais, Jean le Loup, Gaucher de Reims, and Bernard de Soissons.

The magnificent west facade at Reims was built from 1255 through 1260 (fig. 16-23). Its massive gabled portals project forward, rising higher than those at Amiens. Their soaring peaks, the center one reaching to the center of the rose window, help to unify the facade. Large windows fill the portal tympana, displacing the sculpture usually found there. The deep porches are encrusted with sculpture that reflects changes in plan, iconography, and sculpture workshops. In a departure from tradition, Mar-

ian rather than Christ-centered imagery prevails in the central portal, a reflection of the growing popularity of Mary's cult. The enormous rose window, the focal point of the facade, fills the entire clerestory level. The towers were later additions, as was the row of carved figures that runs from the base of one tower to the other above the rose window. This "gallery of kings" is the only strictly horizontal element of the facade. Its subject matter is appropriate for a coronation church.

Different workshops and individuals worked at Reims over a period of several decades. Further complicating matters, a number of sculpture have been moved from their original locations, creating sometimes abrupt stylistic shifts. A group of four figures on the right jamb of

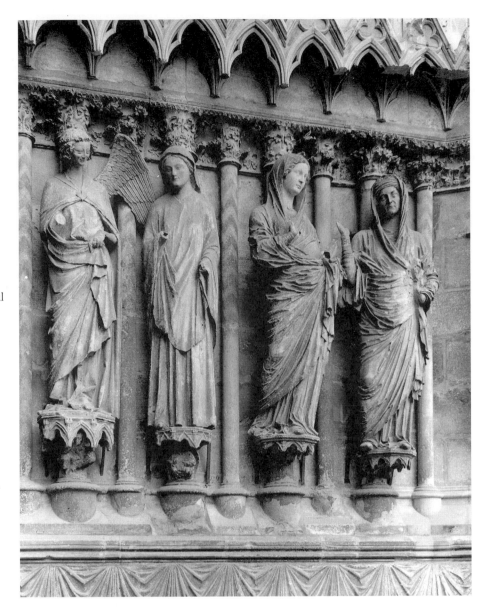

16-24. *Annunciation* (left pair: Mary c. 1245, angel c. 1255) and *Visitation* (right pair: c. 1230), right side, central portal, west facade, Reims Cathedral

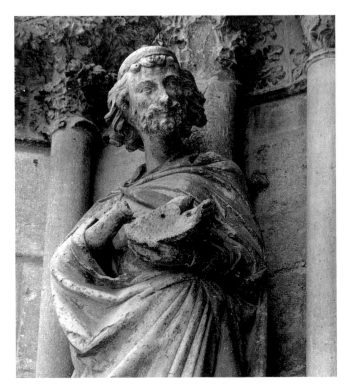

the central portal of the western front illustrates three of the Reims styles (fig. 16-24). The pair on the right is the work of the "Classical Shop," which was active beginning about 1230–1235, during the early years of construction at Reims. The subject of the pair is the Visitation, in which Mary (left), pregnant with Jesus, visits her older cousin, Elizabeth (right), who is pregnant with John the Baptist. The sculptors drew on classical sources, to which they had perhaps been exposed indirectly through earlier Mosan metalwork (see fig. 16-56) or directly in the form of local examples of ancient works (Reims had been an

16-25. *Saint Joseph*, left side, central portal, west facade, Reims Cathedral. c. 1255

On the column behind Joseph's head can be seen a "crescent moon" and four lines. These masons' marks, called setting marks, were used to position a piece of sculpture during installation. A crescent mark indicates the left side of the central doorway, and four lines indicate the fourth in a series. The work site for such an enormous project would have been filled with dressed and undressed stone blocks, sculptors carving slabs in various stages of completion, and work crews hauling and hoisting the finished pieces into place.

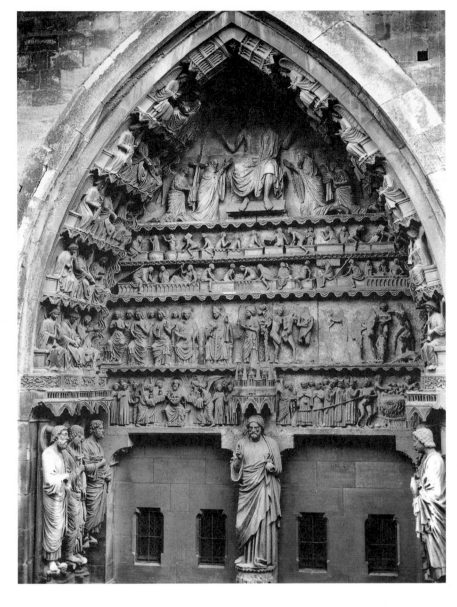

16-26. *Last Judgment* (tympanum), *Christ* (trumeau), *Apostles* (jambs), portal, north transept, Reims Cathedral. c. 1230

important Roman center). The heavy figures have the same solidity seen in Roman portrayals of noblewomen, and Mary's full face, gently waving hair, and heavy mantle recall imperial portrait statuary. The contrast between the features of the young Mary and the older Elizabeth is also reminiscent of the contrast between two Flavian portrait heads, one of a young woman and the other of a middle-aged woman (see figs. 6-43 and 6-44). The Reims sculptors used deftly modeled drapery not only to provide volumetric substance that stresses the theme of pregnancy but also to create a stance in which a weight shift with one bent knee allows the figures to seem to turn toward each other. The new freedom, movement, and sense of relationship implied in the sculpture inspired later Gothic artists toward ever greater realism.

The pair on the left of figure 16-24 illustrates the Annunciation; the archangel Gabriel (left) announces to Mary (right) that she will bear Jesus. The Mary in this pair, quiet and graceful, with a slender body, restrained gestures, and refined features, contrasts markedly with the bold tangibility of the Visitation Mary to the right. The drapery style and certain other details resemble those of

Amiens, suggesting that those who made this pair—and much of the sculpture of the west entrance as well—may also have worked at Amiens.

The figure of the angel Gabriel illustrates yet a third style, the work of a sculptor known today as the Joseph Master or the Master of the Smiling Angels. This artist created tall, gracefully swaying figures that suggest the fashionable refinement associated with the Parisian court in the 1250s (see fig. 16-36). The facial features of Gabriel—and of Saint Joseph, on the opposite side of the doorway (fig. 16-25)—are typical; small, almost triangular head with a broad brow and pointed chin has short, wavy hair; long, puffy, almond-shaped eyes under arching brows; a well-shaped nose; and thin lips curving into a slight smile. Voluminous drapery arranged in elegant folds adds to the impression of aristocratic grace. These engaging figures were imitated from Paris to Prague, and their elegance and refinement became a guiding force in later Gothic sculpture and painting.

The north transept portal sculpture show more variety. A figure of Christ stands on the trumeau with his apostles on the jambs beside him (fig. 16-26). In the

1200
1140   1500

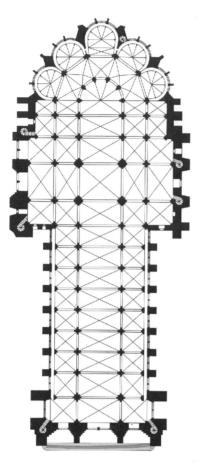

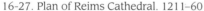

16-27. Plan of Reims Cathedral. 1211–60

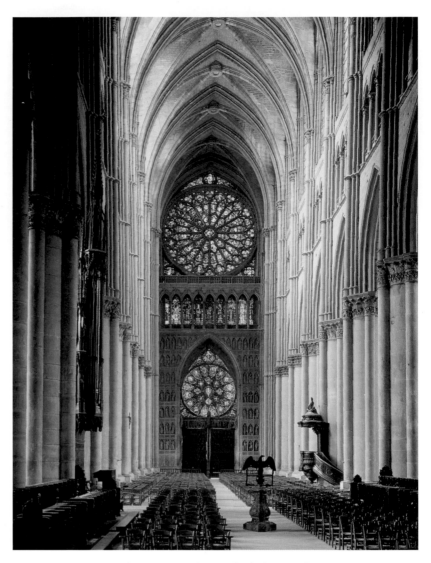

16-28. Nave, Reims Cathedral. 1211–60

tympanum, he appears again as judge in the Last Judgment. How different is this depiction of the Last Judgment from the Romanesque sculpture of Autun (see fig. 15-12). A hierarchy of scale still prevails, but Christ now seems less remote, less isolated from the figures around him. His bare, naturalistically rendered limbs emphasize his three-dimensional, physical presence. His mother and Saint John, as intercessors kneeling at his throne, indicate that he is an approachable, just judge. Humans, angels, and demons at Autun form an interlace of terror, but here at Reims they move in horizontal registers. Deep carving creates the impression of figures acting on a stage. Most of the figures at Autun are shown in profile view; those at Reims are shown from a variety of viewpoints, including some from the back, seated on the sarcophagi from which they arise to face judgment.

The architectural plan of Reims (fig. 16-27), like that of Amiens, was adapted from Chartres. The nave is longer in proportion to the choir, so the building lacks the perfect balance of Amiens. The three-part elevation and ribbed vault are familiar, too (fig. 16-28). The carvings on the capitals in the nave are notable for their variety, nat-

uralism, and quality. Unlike the idealized foliage of Amiens, the Reims carvings depict recognizable plants and figures. The remarkable sculpture and stained glass of the west wall complement the clerestory and choir. A great rose window in the clerestory, a row of lancets at the triforium level, and windows over the portals replace the stone of wall and tympana. Visually the wall "dissolves" in colored light. This great expanse of glass was made possible by **bar tracery**, a technique perfected at Reims, in which thin stone strips, called **mullions**, form a lacy matrix for the glass, replacing the older practice in which glass was inserted directly into window openings. Reims's wall of glass is anchored visually by a masonry screen around the doorway. Here ranks of carved Old Testament prophets and ancestors serve as moral guides for the newly crowned monarchs who faced them after coronation ceremonies.

The Sainte-Chapelle in Paris. In 1243 construction began on a new palace chapel to house Louis IX's prized collection of relics from Christ's Passion. The Sainte-Chapelle was finished in 1248, and soon thereafter Louis

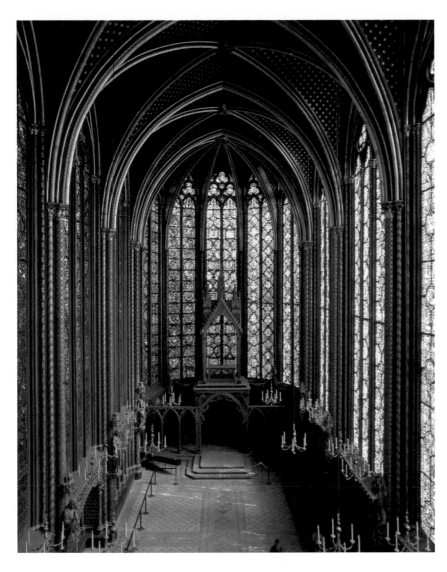

16-29. Interior, upper chapel, the Sainte-Chapelle, Paris. 1243–48

Louis IX avidly collected relics of the Passion, some of which became available in the aftermath of the Crusaders' sack of Constantinople. Those that Louis acquired were supposedly the crown of thorns that had been placed on Jesus' head before the Crucifixion, a bit of the metal lance tip that pierced his side, the vinegar-soaked sponge offered to wet his lips, a nail used in the Crucifixion, and a fragment of the True Cross. The king is depicted in the Sainte-Chapelle's stained glass walking out barefoot to demonstrate his piety and humility when his treasures arrived in Paris.

departed for Egypt on the Seventh Crusade. This exquisite structure epitomizes a new Gothic style known as Rayonnant ("radiant" or "radiating" in French) because of its radiating bar tracery, like that at Reims, or Court style because of its association with Paris and the royal court. The hallmarks of the style include daring engineering, the proliferation of bar tracery, exquisite sculptural and painted detailing, and vast expanses of stained glass.

Originally part of the king's palace and administrative complex, the Sainte-Chapelle is located in the center of Paris. Intended to house precious relics, it resembles a giant reliquary itself, one made of stone and glass instead of gold and gems. It was built in two stories, with a ground-level chapel accessible from a courtyard and a private upper chapel entered from the royal residence. The ground-level chapel has narrow side aisles, but the upper level is a single room with a western porch and a rounded east wall. Climbing up the narrow spiral stairs from the lower to the upper level is like emerging into a kaleidoscopic jewel box (fig. 16-29). The ratio of glass to stone is higher here than in any other Gothic structure, for the walls have been reduced to clusters of slender painted

colonnettes framing tall windows filled with brilliant color. Bar tracery in the windows is echoed in the blind arcading and tracery of the **dado**, the decoration on the lower walls at floor level. The dado's surfaces are richly patterned in red, blue, and gilt so that stone and glass seem to merge in the multicol-ored light. Painted statues of the Twelve Apostles stand between window sections, linking the dado and the stained glass. The windows contain narrative and symbolic scenes. Those in the curve of the sanctuary behind the altar and relics, for example, illustrate the Nativity and Passion of Christ, the Tree of Jesse, and the life of Saint John the Baptist. The story of Louis's acquisition of his relics is told in one of the bays, and the Last Judgment appeared in the original rose window on the west.

Later Gothic Architecture. Beginning in the late thirteenth century France began to suffer from overpopulation and economic decline, followed in the fourteenth century by the devastation of the Hundred Years' War and the plague (see "The Black Death," page 607). Large-scale construction gradually ceased, ending the great age of cathedral building. The Gothic style continued to

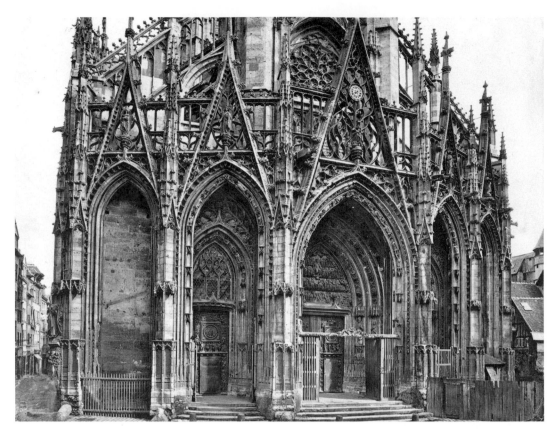

16-30. West facade, Church of Saint-Maclou, Rouen,
Normandy, France. 1436–1521

develop, however, in smaller churches, municipal and commercial buildings, and private residences. Many of these later buildings were covered with elaborate decoration in the new Flamboyant ("flaming" in French) style, named for the repeated flamelike patterns of its tracery. Flamboyant may have reflected an English architectural style known as Decorated (see fig. 16-42). New window tracery was added to many earlier churches in this period, as at Amiens (see fig. 16-20), and a Flamboyant north spire, built between 1507 and 1513, was even added to the west facade of Chartres (see fig. 16-7).

In the new style, decoration sometimes seems divorced from structure. Load-bearing walls and buttresses often have stone overlays, and traceried pinnacles, gables, and **S**-curve moldings combined with a profusion of geometric and natural ornament to dizzying effect. According to one architectural historian, the style reflects "an almost pathological dread of clarity. Ambiguity is endlessly pursued, and whereas all the elements were once integrated logically and lucidly, they are now dissolved in the shimmering air" (James, page 137).

The facade of the Church of Saint-Maclou in Rouen, begun in 1436, is an outstanding example of the new style (fig. 16-30). The projecting porch bends at the sides to enfold the facade of the church, disguising it behind a screen of openwork tracery. Sunlight on the flame-shaped openings and **crockets**—the small knoblike ornaments in the form of plants that line the steep gables and slender buttresses—casts flickering, changing shadows across the busy, intentionally complex surface.

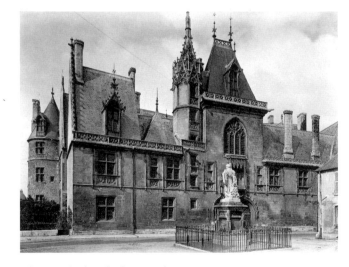

16-31. Main facade, house of Jacques Coeur, Bourges,
France. 1443–51

Illuminated manuscripts, such as that of Christine de Pisan (see fig. 20), give some indication of the interior richness of a palace or town house owned by a wealthy family. The architecture was often painted and the walls were hung with rich and colorful tapestries. Furnishings were also covered with tapestry and embroideries. Glass windows might be enriched with stained-glass inserts illustrating coats of arms.

Secular architecture and arts flourished. The house of merchant Jacques Coeur in Bourges, in central France, built at great expense between 1443 and 1451, reflects the popularity of the Flamboyant style for secular architecture (fig. 16-31). The main facade hides a rambling structure with many rooms of varying sizes on different levels—all

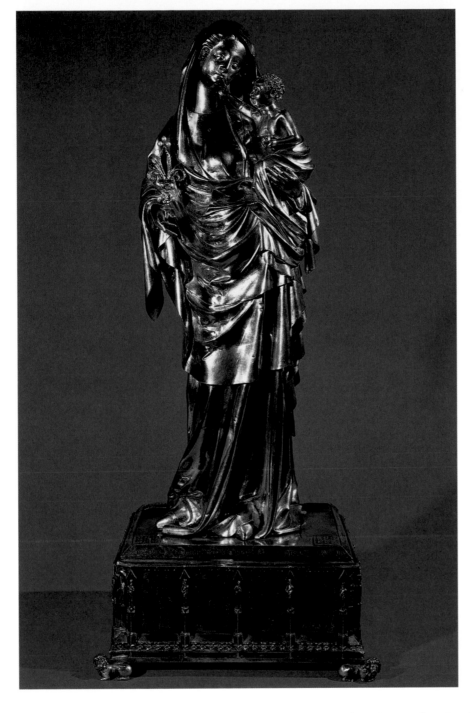

16-32. *Virgin and Child*, from the Abbey Church of Saint-Denis. c. 1339. Silver gilt and enamel, height 27⅛" (69 cm). Musée du Louvre, Paris

arranged around an open courtyard. The highest roof section covers a private chapel, and the octagonal tower, with its Flamboyant filigree crown, lights a staircase. Flamboyant detailing—the large arched window over the main entrance, the cornice balustrades and window panels, and the gable crockets—punctuates the front of the house. Among the carved decorations are puns on the patron's surname, Coeur ("heart" in French), and half-length portraits of Jacques Coeur and his wife lean from niches in the main facade to watch approaching visitors.

Independent Sculpture

Gothic sculptors found a lucrative new outlet for their work in the growing demand among wealthy patrons for small religious statues intended for homes and personal chapels or as donations to favorite churches. Busy urban workshops produced large quantities of statuettes and reliefs in wood, ivory, and precious metals, often decorated with enamel and gemstones. Much of this art was related to the cult of the Virgin Mary.

An excellent example of such works, among the treasures of the Abbey Church of Saint-Denis, is a silver-gilt image, slightly over 2 feet tall, of a standing Virgin and Child (fig. 16-32). An inscription on the base bears the date 1339 and the name of Queen Jeanne d'Evreux, wife of Charles IV of France (ruled 1322–1328). The Virgin holds her son in her left arm, her weight on her left leg, creating the graceful **S**-curve pose that was a stylistic signature of the period. Fluid drapery with the consistency of heavy silk covers her body. She holds a scepter topped with a large enameled and jeweled fleur-de-lis,

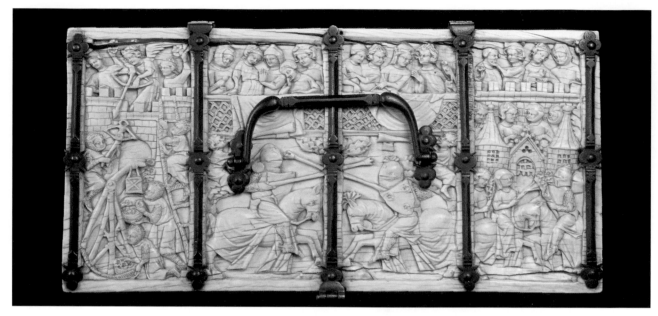

16-33. Lid of a jewelry casket, called *Attack on the Castle of Love*, from Paris. c. 1330–50. Ivory casket with iron mounts, panel 4½ x 9¹¹/₁₆" (11.5 x 24.6 cm). Walters Art Gallery, Baltimore

the heraldic symbol of French royalty, and she originally had a crown on her head. The scepter served as a reliquary for hairs said to be from Mary's head. Despite this figure's clear association with royalty, Mary's simple clothing and sweet, youthful face anticipate a type of imagery that emerged in the later fourteenth and fifteenth centuries in northern France, Flanders, and Germany: the ideally beautiful mother. The Christ Child, clutching an apple in one hand and reaching with the other to touch his mother's lips, is more babylike in his proportions and gestures than in earlier depictions. Still, prophets and scenes of Christ's Passion in enamel cover the statue's simple rectangular base, a reminder of the suffering to come.

In addition to devotional or moralizing subjects, there was also a strong market for objects with secular subjects taken from popular literature. Themes drawn from the realm of courtly love (see "Courtly Love," page 549) decorated women's jewelry boxes, combs, and mirror cases. A casket for jewelry made in a Paris workshop around 1330–1350 provides a delightful example of such a work (fig. 16-33). Its ivory panels depict scenes of love, including vignettes from the King Arthur legend. The central sections of the lid shown here depict a tournament. Such mock battles, designed to keep knights fit for war, had become one of the chief royal and aristocratic entertainments of the day. In the scene on the lid, women of the court, accompanied by their hunting falcons, watch with great interest as two jousting knights, visors down and lances set, charge to the blare of trumpets played by young boys. In the scene on the left, ardent knights assault the Castle of Love, firing roses from crossbows and a catapult. Love, in the form of a winged boy, aids the women defenders, aiming a giant "Cupid's arrow" at the attackers. The action concludes in the scene on the right,

where the tournament's victor and his lady-love meet in a playful joust of their own.

Book Arts

France gained renown in the thirteenth and fourteenth centuries not only for its new architectural style but also for its book arts. These works ranged from practical manuals for artisans to elaborate devotional works illustrated with exquisite miniatures.

Lodge books were an important tool of the master mason and his workshop, or lodge. Compiled by heads of workshops, lodge books provided visual instruction and inspiration for apprentices and assistants. Since the drawings received hard use, few have survived. One of the most famous architect's collections is the early-thirteenth-century sketchbook of Villard de Honnecourt, a well-traveled master mason who recorded a variety of images and architectural techniques. A section labeled "help in drawing figures according to the lessons taught by the art of geometry" (fig. 16-34) illustrates the use of geometric shapes to form images and how to copy and enlarge images by superimposing geometric shapes over them as guides.

The production of high-quality manuscripts flourished in Paris during the reign of Louis IX, whose royal library was renowned. Queen Blanche of Castile, Louis's mother and granddaughter of Eleanor of Aquitaine, served as regent of France (1226–1234) until he came of age. She and the teenage king appear on the dedication page (fig. 16-35) of a Moralized Bible—one in which selected passages of the Old and New Testaments are paired to give an allegorical, or moralized, interpretation. The royal pair sit against a solid gold background under trilobed arches. Below them a scholar-monk dictates to

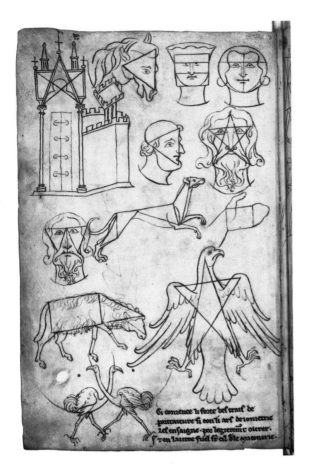

16-34. Villard de Honnecourt. Page from a sketchbook, with geometric figures and ornaments, from Paris. 1220–35. Ink on vellum, 9¼ x 6" (23.5 x 15.2 cm). Bibliothèque Nationale, Paris

a scribe. The ornate thrones of Louis and his mother and the buildings arranged atop the arches suggest that the figures are inside a royal palace, and in fact it would not have been unusual for the queen to have housed scholar, scribe, and illuminator while they were executing her commission during her regency. Interestingly, only the slightly oversized heads of the queen and king preserve a sense of hierarchical scale. The scribe, in the lower right, is working on a page with a column of roundels for illustrations. This format of manuscript illustration—used on the pages that follow the Bible's dedication page—derives from stained-glass lancets, with their columns of images in medallions (see fig. 16-29). The illuminators also show their debt to stained glass in their use of glowing red and blue and reflective gold surfaces.

The *Psalter of Saint Louis* (the king was canonized in 1297) defines the Court style in manuscript illumination. The book, containing seventy-eight full-page illuminations, was created for Louis IX's private devotions sometime between 1253 and 1270. The illustrations fall at the

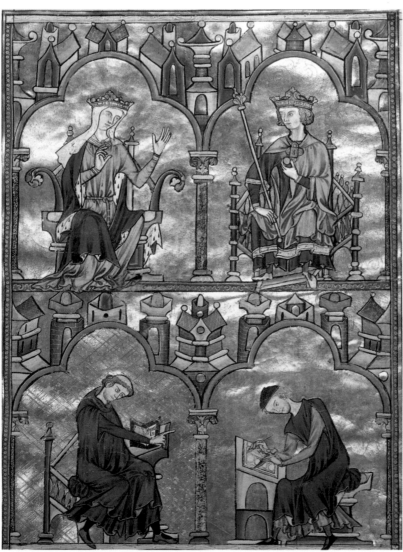

16-35. Page with *Louis IX and Queen Blanche of Castile*, Moralized Bible, from Paris. 1226–34. Ink, tempera, and gold leaf on vellum, 15 x 10½" (38 x 26.6 cm). The Pierpont Morgan Library, New York

M.240, f.8

Thin sheets of gold leaf were painstakingly attached to the vellum and then polished to a high sheen with a tool called a burnisher. Gold was applied to paintings before pigments.

back of the book, preceded by Psalms and other readings unrelated to them. Intricate scrolled borders and a background of Rayonnant architectural features modeled on the Sainte-Chapelle frame the narratives. Figures are rendered in an elongated, linear style. One page (fig. 16-36) illustrates two scenes from the Old Testament story of Abraham, Sarah, and the Three Strangers (Genesis 18). On the left, Abraham greets God, who has appeared to him as three strangers, and invites him to rest. On the right, he offers the men a meal that his wife, Sarah, standing in the doorway of their tent on the far right, has prepared. God says that Sarah will soon bear a child, and she laughs because she and Abraham are old. But God replies, "Is anything too marvelous for the Lord to do?" (18:14). She later gives birth to Isaac, whose name comes from the Hebrew word for "laughter." Christians in the Middle Ages viewed the three strangers in this story as symbols of the Trinity and believed that God's promise to Sarah was a precursor of the Annunciation to Mary.

The architectural background in this painting establishes a narrow stage space in which the story unfolds. Wavy clouds float within the arches under the gables. The imaginatively rendered oak tree establishes the location of the story and separates the two scenes. The gesture of the central haloed figure in the scene on the right and Sarah's presence in the doorway of the tent indicate that we are viewing the moment of divine promise. This new spatial sense, as well as the depiction of oak leaves and acorns, reflects a tentative move toward the representation of the natural world that will gain momentum in the following centuries.

Beginning in the late thirteenth century, more and more laypersons were literate. Private prayer books became popular among those who could afford them. Because such books contained special prayers to be recited at the eight canonical "hours" between morning and night, these books came to be called Books of Hours. The material in them was excerpted from a larger liturgical book called a breviary, which contained all the canonical offices (Psalms, readings, and prayers) used by priests in celebrating Mass. Books of Hours were most commonly devoted to the Virgin, but they could be personalized for particular patrons with prayers to other saints, a calendar of saints' feast days and other Church events, and perhaps other offices, such as that said for the dead. During the fourteenth century a richly decorated Book of Hours, like jewelry, would have been among a noble person's most important portable possessions.

A tiny, exquisite Book of Hours given by Charles IV to his queen, Jeanne d'Evreux, shortly after their marriage in 1325 is the work of an illuminator named Jean Pucelle (fig. 16-37). Instead of the intense colors used by earlier illuminators, Pucelle worked in a technique called **grisaille**—monochromatic painting in shades of gray with faint touches of color (see also "Stained-Glass Windows," page 559)—that emphasized his accomplished drawing. The book combines two narrative cycles. One, the Hours of the Virgin, juxtaposes scenes from the Infancy and Passion of Christ, a form known as the Joys and Sorrows of the Virgin. The other is a collection of scenes from the

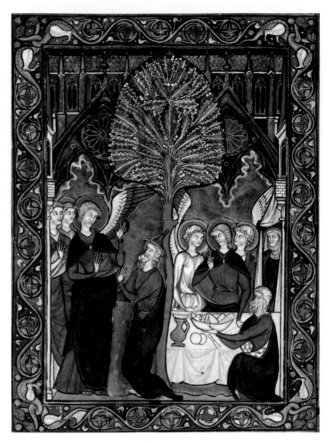

16-36. Page with *Abraham, Sarah, and the Three Strangers, Psalter of Saint Louis*, from Paris. 1253–70. Ink, tempera, and gold leaf on vellum, 5 x 3½" (13.6 x 8.7 cm). Bibliothèque Nationale, Paris

The Court style had enormous influence throughout northern Europe, spread by illuminators who flocked to Paris from other regions. There they joined workshops affiliated with the Confrérie de Saint-Jean (Guild of Saint John), supervised by university officials who controlled the production and distribution of manuscripts.

life of Saint Louis (King Louis IX), whose new cult was understandably popular at court. In the pages shown here the "Joy" of the *Annunciation* on the right is paired with the "Sorrow" of the *Betrayal and Arrest of Christ* on the left. Queen Jeanne appears in the initial below the *Annunciation*, kneeling before a lectern and reading from her Book of Hours. This inclusion of the patron in prayer within a scene, a practice that continued in monumental painting and sculpture in the fifteenth century, conveyed the idea that the scenes were "visions" inspired by meditation rather than records of historical events. In this particular case, the young queen would presumably have identified with Mary's joy at Gabriel's message.

In the *Annunciation* Mary is shown receiving the archangel Gabriel in her Gothic style home as rejoicing angels look on from windows under the eaves. The group of romping children at the bottom of the page (known as the *bas-de-page* in French) at first glance seems to echo the joy of the angels. Scholars have determined, however, that the children are playing "froggy in the middle," a game in which one child was tagged by the others (a

1260
1140   1500

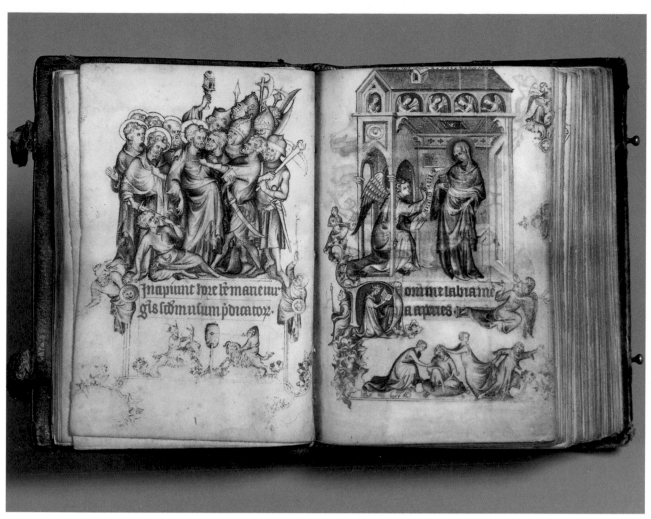

16-37. Jean Pucelle. Pages with *Betrayal and Arrest of Christ*, folio 15v. (left) and *Annunciation*, folio 16r. (right), *Petites Heures of Jeanne d'Evreux*, from Paris. c. 1325–28. Grisaille and color on vellum, each page 3½ x 2¼" (8.2 cm x 5.6 cm). The Metropolitan Museum of Art, New York

The Cloisters Collection, 1954 (54.1.2)

This book was precious to the queen, who mentioned it in her will; she named its illuminator, an unusual tribute.

symbolic reference to the Mocking of Christ). The game thus evokes a darker mood, foreshadowing Jesus' death even as his life is beginning. In the Betrayal scene on the left page, the disciple Judas Iscariot embraces Jesus, thus identifying him to the soldiers who have come to seize him and setting in motion the events that lead to the Crucifixion. Peter, on the left, realizing the danger, draws his sword to defend Jesus and slices off the ear of one of the soldiers. The *bas-de-page* on this side shows "knights" riding goats and jousting at a barrel stuck on a pole, a spoof of military training that is perhaps a comment on the valor of the soldiers assaulting Jesus.

Pucelle's work represents a sophisticated synthesis of French, English, and Italian painting traditions. From English illuminators he borrowed the merging of Christian narrative with allegory, the use of foliate borders filled with real and grotesque creatures (instead of the standard French vine scrolls), and his lively *bas-de-page* illustrations. His presentation of space, with figures placed within coherent architectural settings, apparently reflects his firsthand knowledge of developments in painting in Siena, Italy (for a slightly later example see

fig. 16-73). Pucelle also adapted to manuscript illumination the Parisian Court style in sculpture, with its softly modeled, voluminous draperies gathered around tall, elegantly curved figures with curly hair and broad foreheads. For instance, Jesus on the left page in figure 16-37 and Mary on the right stand in the swaying, S-curve pose typical of Court style works in other mediums, such as the Virgin and Child from Saint-Denis (see fig. 16-32). Similarly, the earnest face of the Annunciation archangel resembles that of the smiling Annunciation archangel at Reims (see fig. 16-24).

The thirteenth and fourteenth centuries saw the growing use of book margins for fresh and unusual images. Often drawn by illustrators who specialized in this kind of work, marginal imagery was a world of its own, interacting in unexpected ways with the main images and text, and often deliberately obscure or ambiguous. Visual puns on the main image or text abound. There are also humorous corrections of scribes' errors, pictures of hybrid monsters, erotic and scatological scenes, and charming depictions of ordinary activities and folklore that may or may not have functioned as

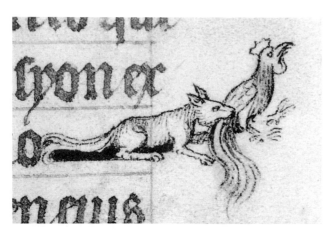

16-38. Page with *Fox Seizing a Rooster, Petites Heures of Jeanne d'Evreux.* The Metropolitan Museum of Art, New York
The Cloisters Collection, 1954 (54.1.2 f. 46)

"The Fox," according to a medieval bestiary, "never runs straight but goes on his way with tortuous windings. He is a fraudulent and ingenious animal. When he is hungry and nothing turns up for him to devour, he rolls himself in red mud so that he looks as if he were stained with blood. Then he throws himself on the ground and holds his breath. The birds, seeing that he is not breathing, think he is dead and come down to sit on him. As you can guess, he grabs them and gobbles them up. The Devil has this same nature" (cited in Schrader, page 24). Bestiaries, an English specialty, were popular compilations of animal lore that were sometimes, as here, made into Christian moral tales. Some of these fables or their characterizations survive in twentieth-century folklore, such as this familiar view of the fox as a cunning trickster.

ironic commentaries on what was going on elsewhere on the page. In addition to the *bas-de-page* scenes, the *Petites Heures of Jeanne d'Evreux* contains other minute but vivid marginalia, such as a fox capturing a rooster (fig. 16-38).

ENGLAND

The Plantagenet dynasty, founded by Henry II and Eleanor of Aquitaine in 1154, ruled England until 1485. Under Plantagenet rule, the thirteenth century was marked by conflicts between the Crown and England's feudal barons over their respective rights and the king's demands for funds. In 1215 King John, under compulsion from powerful barons, set his seal to the draft of the Magna Carta (Latin for "Great Charter"), which laid out feudal rights and dues and became an important document in the eventual development of British common law. The thirteenth century also saw the annexation of the western territory of Wales and the settlement of long-standing border disputes with Scotland. In the mid-fourteenth century the Black Death ravaged England as it did the rest of Europe. During the Hundred Years' War (1337–1453), English kings claimed the French throne and by 1429 controlled most of France, but after a number of reversals they were driven from all their holdings in France except Calais.

Late medieval England was characterized by rural villages and bustling market towns, all dominated by the great city of London. England's two universities, Oxford and Cambridge, were both founded by the thirteenth century. The Gothic period was marked by a reassertion of English cultural identity following the imposition of Norman French culture in 1066. A rich store of Middle English literature survives, including the brilliant social commentary of the *Canterbury Tales,* by Geoffrey Chaucer (c. 1342–1400). Many of the Plantagenet kings, especially Henry III, were great patrons of the arts.

Church Architecture

Gothic architecture in England was strongly influenced by Cistercian and Norman Romanesque architecture as well as by French master builders like William of Sens, who directed the rebuilding of Canterbury Cathedral between 1174 and 1178 (see "Master Builders," page 563). English cathedral builders were less concerned with height than their French counterparts, and they constructed long, broad naves, Romanesque-type galleries, and clerestory-level passageways. Walls retained a Romanesque solidity.

Salisbury Cathedral, because it was built in a relatively short period of time, has a consistency of style that makes it an ideal representative of English Gothic architecture (fig. 16-39). The cathedral was begun in 1220 and nearly finished by 1258, an unusually short period for such an undertaking. The west facade was completed by 1265. The huge crossing tower and its 400-foot spire are fourteenth-century additions, as are the flying buttresses that were added to stabilize the tower. Typically English is the parklike setting (the cathedral close) and attached cloister and chapter house for the cathedral clergy. The thirteenth-century structure hugged the earth, more akin to Fontenay, built more than a century earlier, than to the contemporary Amiens Cathedral in France.

In contrast to French cathedral facades, which suggest the entrance to paradise with their mighty towers flanking deep portals, English facades like the one at Salisbury suggest the jeweled wall of paradise itself. The small flanking towers of the west front project beyond the side walls and buttresses, giving the facade an increased width that was underscored by tier upon tier of blind tracery and arcaded niches. Lancet windows grouped in twos, threes, and fives introduce an element of vertical counterpoint.

Typical of English cathedrals, Salisbury has double projecting transepts, a square apse, and a spacious sanctuary (fig. 16-40). The interior reflects enduring Norman traditions, with its heavy walls and tall nave arcade surmounted by a short gallery and a clerestory with simple lancet windows (fig. 16-41). The emphasis on horizontal movement of the arcades, unbroken by colonnettes in the unusually restrained nave, directs worshipers' attention forward to the altar, rather than upward into the vaults. Reminiscent of Romanesque interiors is the use of color in the stonework: the shafts supporting the four-part rib vaults are made of a darker stone that contrasts with the lighter stone of the rest of the interior. The stonework was originally painted and gilded as well as carved.

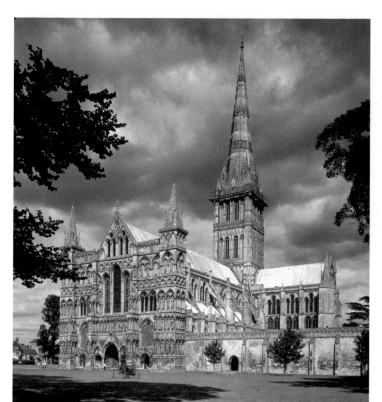

16-39. West facade, Salisbury Cathedral, Salisbury, Wiltshire, England. 1220–58; west facade 1265; spire c. 1320–30

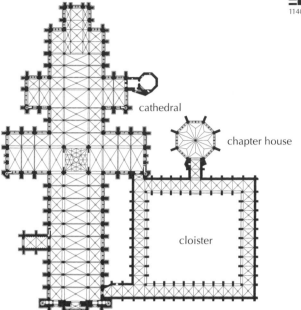

16-40. Plan of Salisbury Cathedral

cathedral

chapter house

cloister

The original cathedral had been built within the hilltop castle complex of a Norman lord. In 1217 Bishop Richard Poore petitioned the pope to relocate the church, claiming the wind howled so loudly there that the clergy could not hear themselves say Mass. A more pressing concern was probably his desire to escape the lord's control; Pope Innocent III (papacy 1198–1216) had only recently lifted a six-year ban on church services throughout England and Wales after King John (ruled 1199–1216) agreed to acknowledge the Church's sovereignty. The town of Salisbury (from the Saxon *Searisbyrig,* meaning "Caesar's burg," or town) was laid out, by the bishop himself, after the cathedral was under way. Material carted down from the old church was used in the cathedral, along with dark, fossil-silted Purbeck stone from quarries in southern England and stone from Caen. The building was abandoned and vandalized during the Protestant Reformation in England initiated by King Henry VIII (ruled 1509– 1547). In the eighteenth century the English architect James Wyatt, called the Destroyer, subjected it to radical renovations, during which the remaining stained glass and figure sculpture were removed or rearranged. Similar campaigns to refurbish medieval churches were common at the time. The motives of the restorers were complex and their results far from our late-twentieth-century notions of historical authenticity. The French architect Eugène-Emmanuel Viollet-le-Duc, the best known of these restorers, redefined the appearance of many of France's greatest twelfth- and thirteenth-century churches in the nineteenth century.

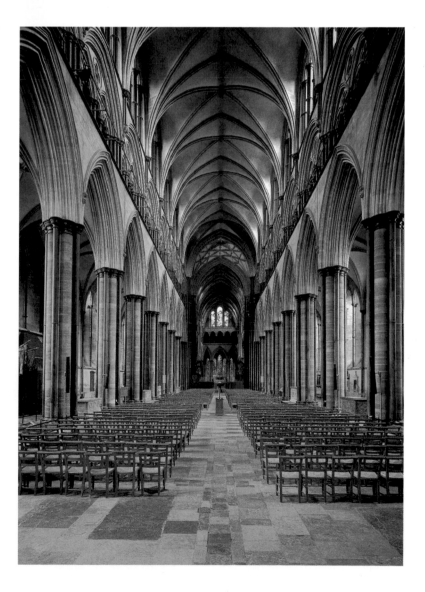

16-41. Nave, Salisbury Cathedral

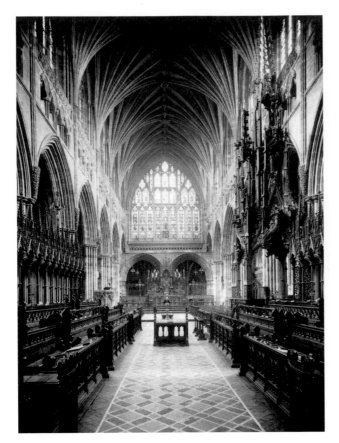

16-42. Sanctuary, Exeter Cathedral, Exeter, Devon, England. c. 1270–1366

The Gothiic choir stalls and bishop's throne illustrate the skill of the English woodcarvers and carpenters. Exeter has some of the finest still-surviving medieval furniture.

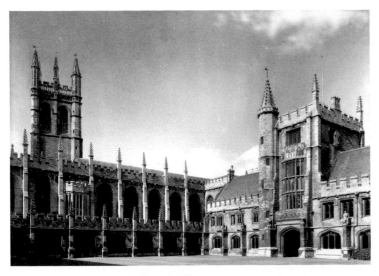

16-43. William Orchard. First Quadrangle, Magdalen College, Oxford, Oxfordshire, England. c. 1475–1500

Surviving account books reveal how much Orchard was paid for his work. For each of twenty-two cloister windows and buttresses, for example, he received 48 shillings 4 pence. In an early indication of intercollegiate rivalry, the windows were praised for being "as good as those of All Souls or better." As a final reward, the officials of Magdalen gave Orchard a lifetime lease on some college-owned land for an annual rent of one red rose, to be paid on the Feast of Saint John the Baptist.

Just as the Rayonnant style was emerging in France at mid-century, English designers were developing a new Gothic style of their own that has come to be known as the Decorated style (a nineteenth-century term). This change in taste has been credited to King Henry III's ambition to surpass his brother-in-law, Louis IX of France, as a royal patron of the arts.

A splendid example of this new style outside London is Exeter Cathedral, in southwest England. After the Norman Conquest in 1066, a Norman church replaced an earlier structure, and it, in turn, was rebuilt beginning about 1270. When the cathedral was redesigned and vaulted in the first half of the fourteenth century, its interior was turned into a dazzling stone forest of arch moldings and vault ribs (fig. 16-42). From diamond-shaped piers (partly hidden by Gothic choir stalls in the illustration), covered with colonnettes, rise massed moldings that make the arcade seem to ripple. Bundled colonnettes spring from ornate **corbels** between the arches to support conical clusters of thirteen ribs that meet at the summit of the vault, a modest 69 feet above the floor. The basic structure here is the four-part vault with intersecting cross-ribs, but the designer added purely decorative ribs, called **tiercerons**, between the supporting ribs to create a richer linear pattern. Elaborately carved knobs known as **bosses** punctuate the intersections where ribs meet. Large clerestory lancets with bar-tracery mullions illuminate the 300-foot-long nave. Unpolished gray marble shafts, yellow sandstone arches, and a white French stone used in the upper walls add color to the many-rayed space.

Secular Architecture

Although Gothic architectural style is most studied in cathedrals and other church buildings, it also is seen in such secular structures as castles, which during the turbulent Middle Ages were necessary fortress-residences. Castles evolved during the Romanesque and Gothic periods from enclosed and fortified strongholds to elaborate defended residential complexes from which aristocrats ruled their domains. Usually sited on a promontory or similar defensive height, British castles had many elements in common with continental ones (see "Elements of Architecture," opposite).

The final period of English Gothic architecture produced the Perpendicular style, another nineteenth-century term, derived from its characteristic tall, rectilinear decorative elements. The style originated in court-sponsored projects in London at the end of the thirteenth century and was close to the earlier French Rayonnant style in its emphasis on verticality and large areas of glass. As London-trained architects took commissions for work elsewhere, the style spread. Easily adapted by provincial stonemasons, the Perpendicular style appeared across England in parish churches, houses, civic buildings, and the halls, libraries, and residential colleges being added to English universities.

Magdalen College at Oxford (pronounced "maudlin" from the Middle English spelling, *Maudeleyne*) is the late-

ELEMENTS OF ARCHITECTURE

The Gothic Castle

A typical Gothic castle was a defensible, enclosed combination of fortifications and living quarters for the lord and his family and those defending them. It was built on raised ground and sometimes included a **moat** (ditch), filled with water and crossed by a bridge; **ramparts** (heavy walls), which were freestanding or built against earth embankments; **parapets**, into which towers were set; a **keep**, or **donjon**, a tower that was the most secure place within the compound; and a great hall that was where the rulers and their closest associates lived. The **bailey**, a large open courtyard in the center, contained wooden structures such as living quarters and stables, as well as a stone chapel. The castle complex was defended by a wooden **stockade**, or fence, outside the moat; inside the stockade lay **lists**, areas where knightly combats were staged. The main entrance was approached by a wide **bridge**, which passed through moat gateways called **barbicans**, ending in a **drawbridge** and then an iron **portcullis**, a grating set into the doorway. Elsewhere, small doors called **posterns** provided secret access for the castle's inhabitants. Ramparts and walls were topped by stone **battlements** designed to screen defenders standing on **parapet walks** while allowing them to repel attacks through notched **crenellations**. There were covered parapet walks, as well as miniature towers called **turrets**, along the more secure perimeter walls of the castle.

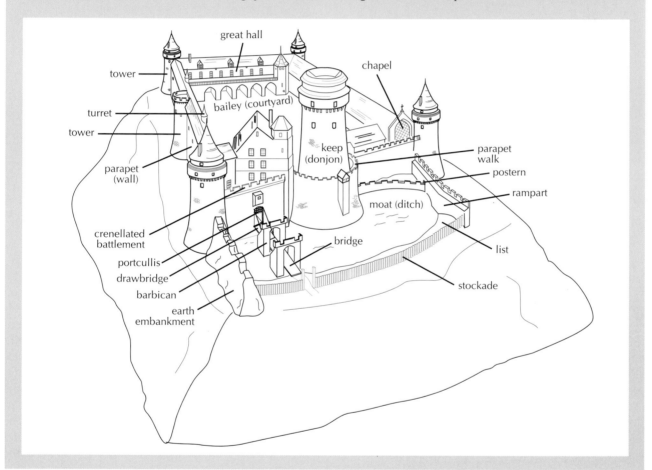

fifteenth-century work (c. 1475–1500) of a local mason, William Orchard. Laid out in an orderly way around a quadrangular courtyard similar to a monastic cloister, it has been called the ideal college, a sober and dignified setting for a life of the mind (fig. 16-43). The facades of the structures on the quadrangle exhibit a Perpendicular grid design, with the vertical lines of the arcade piers and the pinnacles rising from them intersecting the horizontal lines of the projecting stringcourses on the wall buttresses. The **crenellated** roofline—a purely decorative reference to castle battlements—completes the "perpendicular" theme.

Window and arcade openings are either rectangular or nearly so. Orchard's college is a grander version of a fortified aristocratic manor house, with a monumental gatehouse at the right and a great hall and chapel combined in the wing at the left. The turreted, crenellated tower and gatehouse serve no protective purpose but act instead as symbols of collegiate authority. The living quarters for students were built behind and above the covered walkways. A typical college apartment, or "set," accommodated four students in small individual bedrooms arranged around a common living and study room.

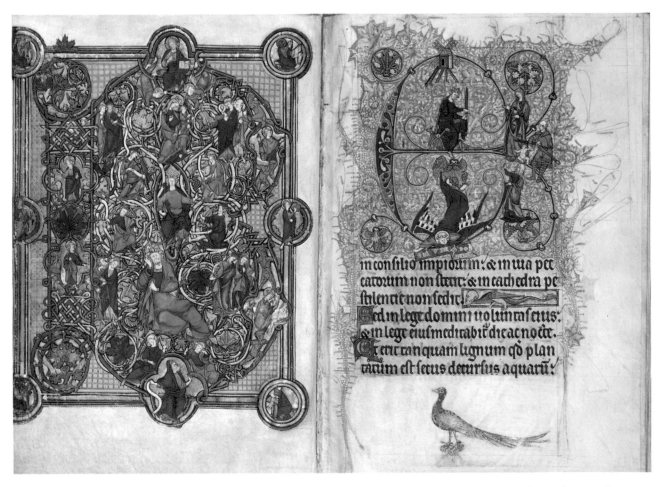

16-44. Page with *Psalm 1 (Beatus Vir)*, *Windmill Psalter*, from London. c. 1270–80. Ink pigments and gold on vellum, each page 12¾ x 8¾" (32.3 x 22.2 cm). The Pierpont Morgan Library, New York

M.102, f. lv-2

Book Arts

In France book production had become centralized in the professional **scriptoria** of Paris, and its main patrons were the universities and the court. In thirteenth-century England, by contrast, the traditional centers of production—far-flung rural monasteries that had produced such twelfth-century work as the beautiful *Winchester Psalter* (see fig. 15-29)—continued to dominate the book arts. Toward the close of the thirteenth century, however, secular workshops became increasingly active, reflecting a demand for books from newly literate landowners, townspeople, and students. These people read books, both in English and Latin, for entertainment and general knowledge as well as for prayer. The fourteenth century was a golden age of manuscript production in England, as the thirteenth century had been in France. Among the delights of English Gothic manuscripts are their imaginative marginalia (pictures in margins of pages).

The dazzling artistry and delight in ambiguities that had marked earlier Anglo-Saxon manuscript illumination reappeared in the *Windmill Psalter* (c. 1270–1290), so-called because of a windmill in the initials beginning Psalm 1 (fig. 16-44). The Psalm begins with the words *"Beatus vir qui non abiit"* ("Happy those who do not follow the counsel [of the wicked]," Psalm 1:1). A *B*, the first letter of the Psalm, fills the left page, and an *E*, the sec-

ond letter, occupies the top of the right page. The rest of the opening words appear on a banner carried by an angel at the bottom of the *E*. The *B* outlines a densely interlaced Tree of Jesse. The *E* is formed from large tendrils that escape from delicate background vegetation to support characters in the story of the Judgment of Solomon. The story, seen as a prefiguration of the Last Judgment, relates how two women (at the right) claiming the same baby came before King Solomon (on the crossbar) to settle their dispute. He ordered a guard to slice the baby in half with his sword and give each woman her share. This trick exposed the real mother, who hastened to give up her claim in order to save the baby's life.

Charming images appear among the pages' foliage, many of them visual puns on the text. For example, a large windmill at the top of the initial *E* illustrates the statement in the Psalm that the wicked would not survive the Judgment but would be "like chaff driven by the wind" (Psalm 1:4). Imagery such as this would have stimulated contemplation of the inner meanings of the text's familiar messages.

Opus Anglicanum

At least since the time of the Norman invasion and the *Bayeux Tapestry* (see fig. 15-30), the English were famous for their embroidery. From the thirteenth through the six-

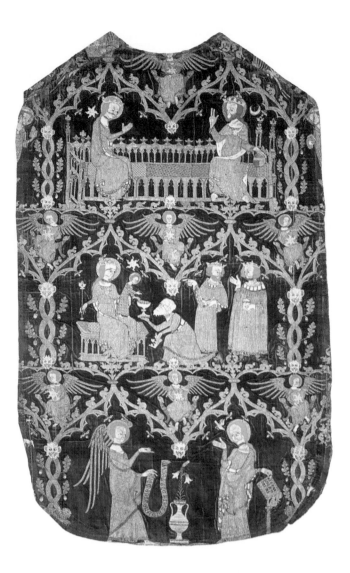

16-45. *Life of the Virgin* (Chichester-Constable chasuble back, from a set of vestments embroidered in opus anglicanum), from southern England. 1330–50. Red velvet with silk and metallic thread; length 5'6" (164 cm), width 30" (76 cm). The Metropolitan Museum of Art, New York

Fletcher Fund, 1927 (2.7 162.1)

teenth centuries the pictorial needlework in colored silk and gold thread of English embroiderers, both men and women, gained such renown that it came to be referred to by the Latin term *opus anglicanum* (English work). The pope in Rome, for instance, had more than 100 pieces of this luxurious textile art. The names of several prominent embroiderers are known, such as Mabel of Bury Saint Edmunds, who worked for Henry III, but few can be connected to specific works.

Opus anglicanum was employed for banners, court dress, and other secular uses, as well as for the liturgical vestments worn by the clergy during Mass. A mid-fourteenth-century vestment known as the Chichester-Constable chasuble (fig. 16-45) is embroidered with scenes from the Life of the Virgin—the Annunciation, the Adoration of the Magi, and the Coronation of the Virgin—arranged in three registers on its back. Cusped, crocketed **S**-shape arches, twisting branches sprouting oak leaves, seed-pearl acorns, and animal faces define each register. The star and crescent moon in the Coronation of the Virgin scene, heraldic emblems of the royal family, suggest that the chasuble may have been made under the patronage of Edward III. The embroidery was done in split stitch with fine gradations of colored silk forming the images as subtly as painting (fig. 16-46). Where

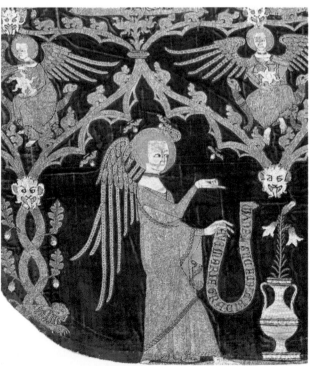

16-46. Detail, *Angel of the Annunciation*, Chichester-Constable chasuble

gold threads were laid and couched, the effect is like the burnished gold-leaf backgrounds of manuscript illuminations. During the celebration of the Mass, garments of opus anglicanum would have glinted in the candlelight amid the other treasures of the altar. So heavy did such gold and bejeweled garments become, however, that their wearers often needed help to move.

SPAIN The Christian reconquest of Muslim Spain gained momentum in the thirteenth century under Alfonso X "the Wise" (ruled 1252–1284), king of the newly unified northern realm of León and Castile. In the east, the union of Aragón with Catalonia created a prosperous realm that benefited from expanding Mediterranean trade. Christian rulers were initially tolerant of the Muslim and Jewish populations that came under their control, but in the late fifteenth century, this tolerance gave way to a drive toward religious conformity. When Spain was united under Christian rule in 1492, Jews were expelled and soon afterward Muslims were forced to convert. Like other areas of Europe, Spain was ravaged by rebellion, war, and plague in the fourteenth century.

From the twelfth century on, the art of Christian Spain reflects the growing influence of foreign styles, particularly those of France and Italy. Patrons often brought in master masons, sculptors, and painters from these regions to direct or execute important projects. The new influences, adapted by local artisans, combined with local traditions to create a recognizably Spanish Gothic style.

Architecture

While most of the great thirteenth-century churches of Castile and Leon were inspired by French Gothic architecture and some even had French masons working on their structure and sculpture, Catalonia and the Balearic Islands developed their own distinctive Catalan Gothic style. Mallorca, a major center of Mediterranean trade, had been captured from the Muslims in 1229 by James I of Aragón (ruled 1213–1276), who converted Palma's mosque into a church. His son initiated the construction of a new cathedral in 1306. The structure has an imposing, fortresslike exterior dominated by closely packed wall buttresses at the continuous line of chapels along the outer aisles. The tall nave, supported by flying buttresses (every third buttress on the exterior), soars to the amazing height of 143 feet; the side aisle vaults rise to more than 94 feet. These tall side aisles, combined with slender polygonal piers in the nave arcade, create a unified interior space. Large windows in the clerestory and both east and western nave walls flood the interior with light.

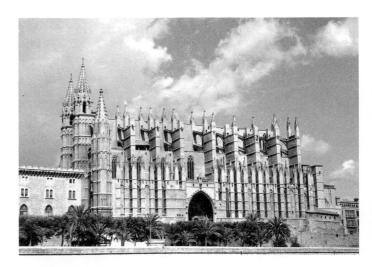

16-47. Cathedral of Palma, Mallorca, Balearic Islands, Spain. Begun 1306. View from the south

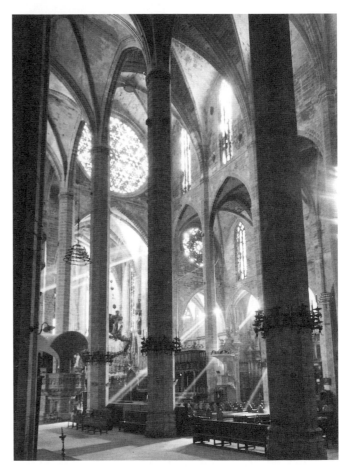

16-48. Nave and side aisle, Palma Cathedral

Book Arts

King Alfonso X of Castile was known as a patron of the arts who maintained a brilliant court of poets, scholars, artists, and musicians during the mid-thirteenth century. He promoted the use of local vernacular languages instead of Latin in his realm for everything from religious literature and history to legal codes and translations of important Arabic scientific texts. He was a poet and musician himself, compiling and setting to music a collection of poems, some of them his own, devoted to the Virgin Mary. An illustration from this manuscript, the *Cantigas de Santa María* (*Songs of Saint Mary*), shows Alfonso as poet-musician above one of his own songs

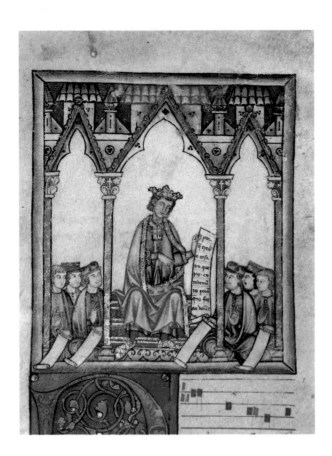

(fig. 16-49). Like Queen Blanche and King Louis in the French Court style Moralized Bible seen earlier (see fig. 16-35), Alfonso is shown seated in a Gothic building. He holds a copy of his poetry, which he presents to admiring courtiers.

Painted Altarpieces

The large-scale paintings on or just behind church altars, called **altarpieces**, began to appear in the thirteenth century and came into use throughout Europe thereafter. While manuscript illumination and stained glass, and to some extent the fiber arts of embroidery and tapestry, remained the most important forms of two-dimensional art, in the thirteenth century altarpieces, murals, and smaller paintings on wood panels became increasingly important. Professional painters worked for both individual and institutional patrons. Many were members of painting dynasties that lasted for generations, and some had wide-ranging responsibilities at court.

ALTARS AND ALTARPIECES The altar in a Christian church symbolizes both the table of the Last Supper and the tombs of Christ and the saints. Traditionally the altar is covered with a cloth, and it is usually set with candles and a cross. The reliquary of a patron saint, such as Saint Foy (see fig. 15-1), might be placed on the altar, but it might also be under or even inside the altar. Altarpieces placed behind or at the back of the altar table, the **mensa**, as well as altar frontals (**antependia**) in front of the altar tables, provide the celebrants and worshipers with images of the saints and scenes from their lives and martyrdoms. These painted, carved, or embroidered images were created to help focus meditations and prayers, but unlike Byzantine icons (see fig. 7-61) they were not intended to be conduits for prayers to saints.

The earliest altarpieces were low, fixed panels, but by the Gothic period they became increasingly large and elaborate architectonic structures filled with images and protected by movable wings that functioned like shutters. Eventually, in Spain, they grew to the full height of the building. Many altarpieces had a firm base, called a **predella**, which was also covered with images. The most common type of arrangement was the **triptych**, a central panel flanked by side panels, or wings. Polyptychs such as Duccio's *Maestà* (see fig. 16-71) consisted of many panels in a stationary frame. Wings of altarpieces were painted on both front and back because the altarpieces were kept closed most of the time and were opened on holy days to reveal special imagery.

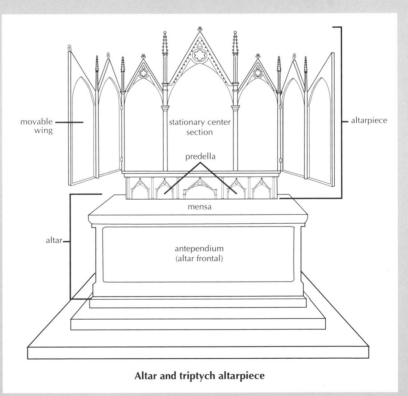

Altar and triptych altarpiece

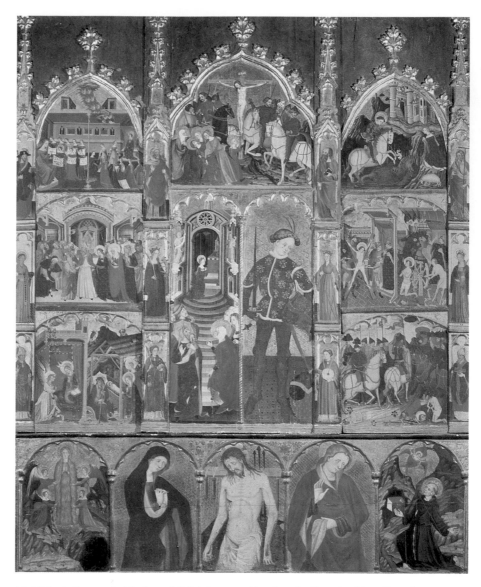

16-50. Luis Borrassá. *Virgin and Saint George*, altarpiece in Church of San Francisco, Villafrancá del Panadés, Barcelona. c. 1399. Tempera on wood

The contract for another of Borrassá's altarpieces, dated 1402, specifies its subject matter in detail as well as its dimensions and shape. The contract requires the use of high-quality materials and calls for delivery in six months, with payment at specified stages upon inspection of work in progress. It holds the painter responsible for all stages of production "according to what is customary in other beautiful [altarpieces]" (cited in Binski, page 52).

One of the major figures in late medieval Spanish painting was Luis Borrassá (1360–1426). From a Catalán family of painters, he worked for the court of Aragón early in his career, probably in the style favored by the French-born queen. Sometime during the 1380s he set up a workshop in the Catalán capital of Barcelona. Among the altarpieces attributed to him is the *Virgin and Saint George* made for the Church of San Francisco at Villafrancá del Panadés (fig. 16-50). This work is a distinctively Spanish-type altarpiece called a **retablo**, which consists of an enormous wooden framework—taking up the whole wall behind an altar—that is filled with either painted or carved narrative scenes. The depiction of space and the lively narrative scenes in the panels of the *Virgin and Saint George* reflect the influence of the paint-

ing style that had developed in Tuscany, in northern Italy, but the realistic details, elegant drawing, and rich colors are characteristically Catalán. Borrassá's synthesis of foreign artistic influences reflects the development of the courtly International Gothic style that emerged in much of Europe about the beginning of the fourteenth century.

The panel depicting the *Education of the Virgin* (fig. 16-51) shows Mary among a group of fourteenth-century Spanish girls presenting their embroidery for a teacher's approval. All except Mary have produced the assigned floral design. Mary instead has stitched the enclosed garden of Paradise where five golden-winged angels flutter around the Fountain of Life. Embroidery is such an important art that even the child Mary has learned to do it.

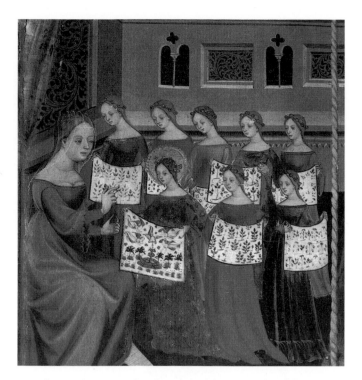

16-51. Luis Borrassá. *Education of the Virgin,* detail from *Virgin and Saint George* altarpiece

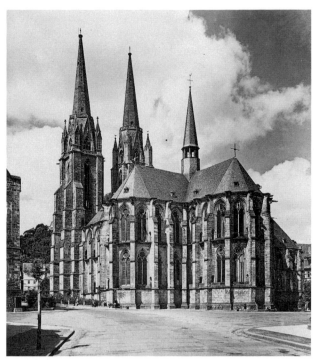

16-52. Church of Saint Elizabeth, Marburg, Germany. 1233–83

GERMANY AND THE HOLY ROMAN EMPIRE

In contrast to England and France, which were becoming strong national states, by the middle of the thirteenth century Germany had developed into a decentralized conglomeration of independent principalities, bishoprics, and "free" commercial cities The Holy Roman Empire, weakened by prolonged struggle with the papacy and with German princes, had ceased to be a significant power. Holy Roman emperors were now elected by German princes and had only nominal authority over them. Each emperor ruled from his chosen capital. Charles IV (ruled 1355–1378), for example, who was also king of Bohemia, ruled from the Bohemian city of Prague, which he helped develop into a great city. As patrons, the emperors stimulated the arts, promoting local traditions as well as the spread of the French Court style and the International Gothic style that followed it.

Architecture

A new type of church, the **hall church**, developed in thirteenth-century Germany in response to the increasing importance of sermons within church services. The hall church featured a nave and side aisles with vaults of the same height, creating a spacious and open interior that could accommodate the large crowds drawn by charismatic preachers. The flexible design of these "great halls" was also widely adopted for civic and residential buildings.

The Church of Saint Elizabeth at Marburg, near Cologne in Germany, built between 1233 and 1283, was popular as a pilgrimage site and as a funerary chapel for

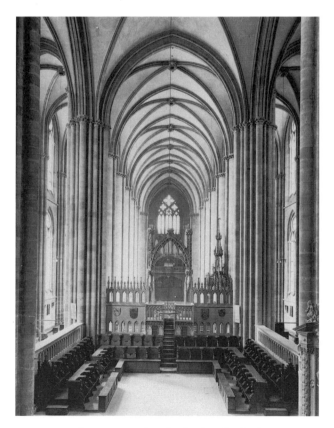

16-53. Nave, Church of Saint Elizabeth

the local nobility (fig. 16-52). The earliest example of a hall church, Saint Elizabeth has a beautiful simplicity and purity of line. Light from two stories of tall windows fills the interior, unimpeded by nave arcades, galleries, or triforia (fig. 16-53). The exterior has a similar verticality and geometric clarity.

The Gothic style was also adopted for Jewish religious structures. The oldest functioning synagogue in Europe, Prague's Altneuschul (Old-New Synagogue), was probably built in the late thirteenth or fourteenth century (fig. 16-54). One of two principal synagogues serving the Jews of Prague, it reflects the geometric clarity and regularity of Gothic architecture and demonstrates the adaptability of the Gothic hall-church design for non-Christian use (fig. 16-55). Like a hall church, the vaults of the synagogue are all the same height. Unlike a church, with its nave and side aisles, the Altneuschul has two aisles with three bays each. The bays have four-part vaulting with a decorative fifth rib.

Because of sporadic repression, Jewish communities in the cities of northern Europe tended to be small throughout the Middle Ages. Towns often imposed restrictions on the building of synagogues, requiring, for example, that they be lower than churches. Since local guilds controlled the building trades in most towns, Christian workers usually worked on Jewish construction projects.

The medieval synagogue was both a place of prayer and a communal center of learning and inspiration where men gathered to read and discuss the Torah. The synagogue had two focal points, the *aron*, or shrine for the Torah scrolls, and a raised reading platform called the *bimah*. Worshipers faced the *aron*, which was located on the east wall, in the direction of Jerusalem. The *bimah* stood in the center of the hall. The Gothic-arched *aron* of the Altneuschul can be seen in figure 16-54, partially obscured by an openwork partition around the *bimah*, which straddled the two center bays. The synagogue's single entrance was placed off-center in a corner bay at the west end. Candles along the walls and in overhead chandeliers supplemented natural light from twelve large windows. The interior was also originally adorned with murals (the large, richly decorated Torah case shown on the *bimah* table was made later). Men worshiped and studied in the principal space; women were sequestered in annexes.

Sculpture

Nicholas of Verdun, a pivotal figure in the development of early Gothic sculpture, influenced both French and German art through his work well into the thirteenth century. Born along the Meuse River between Flanders and Germany, he was heir to the great Mosan metalworking tradition (see fig. 15-35). Nicholas worked for a number of important German patrons, including the archbishop of Cologne, for whom he created a magnificent reliquary (c. 1190–c.1205–1210) to hold what were believed to be relics of the Three Magi (fig. 16-56). Called the *Shrine of the Three Kings*, the reliquary resembles a basilica, a traditional reliquary form that evolved to reflect changes in church architecture. It is made of gilded bronze and silver with gemstones and dark blue enamel that accentuate its architectonic details. Mosan classicism reached new heights in this work. Figures are fully and naturalistically modeled in gold **repoussé**. The Magi and Virgin are on the front, and figures of prophets and the apostles

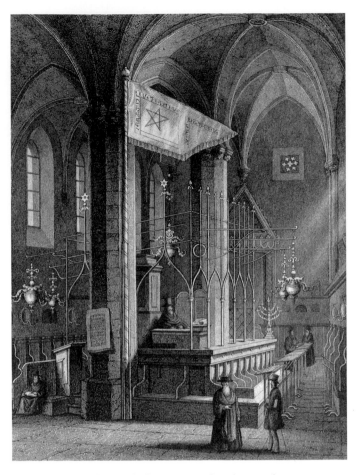

16-54. Interior, Altneuschul, Prague, Bohemia (Czech Republic). c. late 13th century; later additions and alterations. Engraving from *Das Historisches Prag in 25 Stahlstichen*, 1864

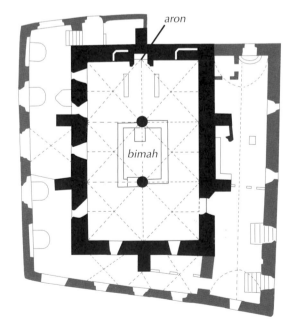

16-55. Plan of Altneuschul

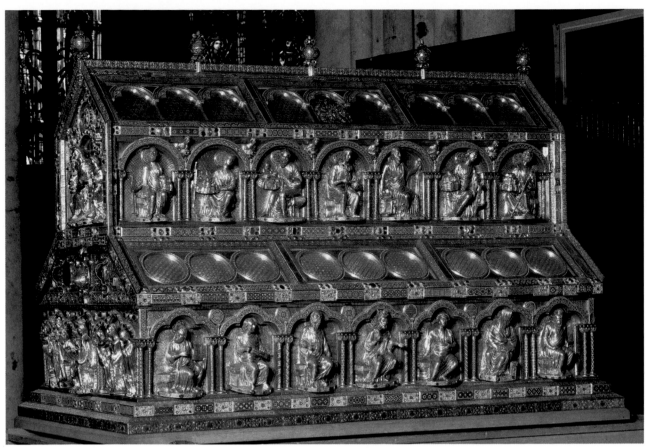

16-56. Nicholas of Verdun and workshop. *Shrine of the Three Kings*. c. 1190–c. 1205–10. Silver and bronze with enamel and gemstones, 5'8" x 6' x 3'8" (1.73 x 1.83 x 1.12 m). Cathedral Treasury, Cologne, Germany

fill the niches in the two levels of round-arched arcading on the sides. The work combines robust, expressively mobile sculptural forms with a jeweler's exquisite ornamental detailing to create an opulent, monumental setting for its precious contents.

The sculpture in the facade of Strasbourg Cathedral has a homogeneous classicizing style that reflects the influence of Nicholas of Verdun and shares features with the work produced by the "Classical Shop" at Reims (see fig. 16-24). The works on the Strasbourg facade have an emotional expressiveness, however, that is characteristic of much German medieval sculpture. A relief depicting the death and assumption of Mary, a subject known as the Dormition (Sleep) of the Virgin, fills the tympanum of the south transept portal (fig. 16-57). Mary lies on her deathbed, but Christ has received her soul, the doll-like figure in his arms, and will carry it directly to heaven, where she will be enthroned next to him. The scene is filled with dynamically expressive figures with large heads and short bodies clothed in fluid drapery that envelops their rounded limbs. Deeply undercut, the large figures stand out dramatically in the crowded scene, their grief vividly rendered.

There was a powerful naturalistic current in German Gothic sculpture, and some works—among them a famous statue from Magdeburg Cathedral of Saint Maurice, produced about 1240–1250—may have been based

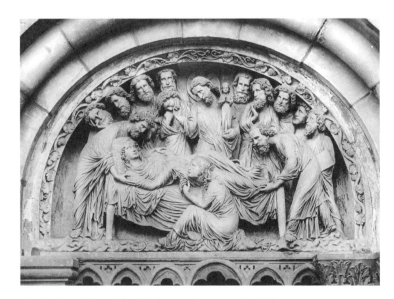

16-57. *Dormition of the Virgin*, south transept portal tympanum, Strasbourg Cathedral, Strasbourg, France. c. 1230

This sculpture is among the works traditionally attributed to a woman named Sabina, long believed to have been the daughter of the facade's designer. She is now known to have been a patron, not a sculptor. There is no evidence of women masons in medieval Europe, although a number of prominent patrons were women.

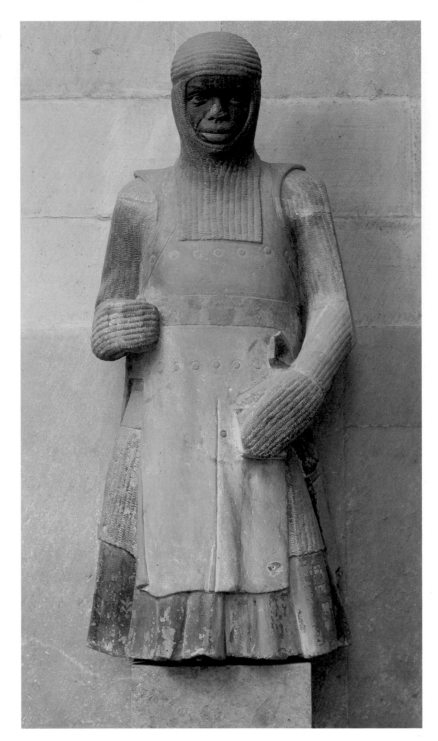

16-58. *Saint Maurice*, Magdeburg Cathedral, Magdeburg, Germany. c. 1240–50.
Dark sandstone with traces of polychromy

on living models instead of idealized types (fig. 16-58). Magdeburg Cathedral, in north-central Germany, had been built on the site of an earlier church dedicated to Saint Maurice, and his relics were preserved there. Maurice, the leader of a group of Egyptian Christians in the Roman army in Gaul, was martyred together with his troops in 286 for refusing to fight against Christian peasants. The crusading knights of the Middle Ages viewed him and other warrior-saints, such as Saint Theodore (see fig. 16-10), as models of the crusading spirit. And like Saint George, he was a favorite saint of

military aristocrats. Because he came from Egypt, Maurice was commonly portrayed with black African features. Dressed in a full suit of chain mail covered by a sleeveless coat of leather, Saint Maurice represents another ideal of warrior/manhood.

An exceptional sculptor worked for the bishop of Wettin, Dietrich II, on the decoration of a new chapel-sanctuary built at the west end of the Naumburg Cathedral about 1245–1260. Dietrich, a member of the ruling family of Naumburg, had lifesize statues of twelve ancestors who were patrons of the church placed on pedestals

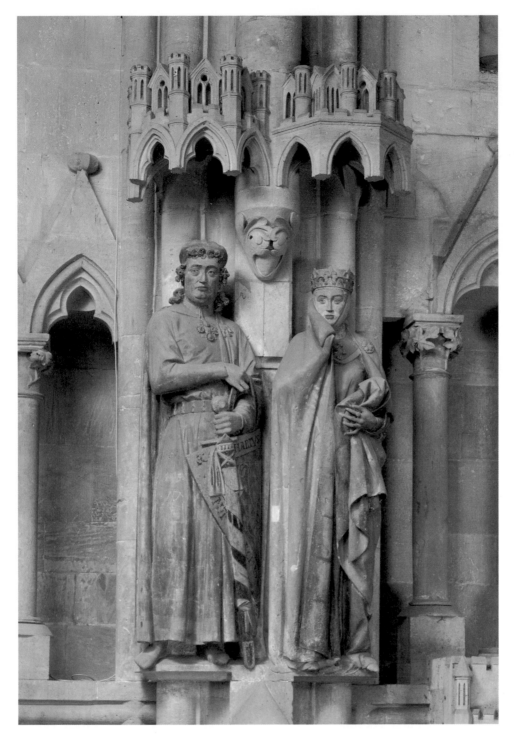

16-59. *Ekkehard and Uta*, west chapel sanctuary, Naumburg Cathedral, Naumburg, Germany.
c. 1245–60. Stone, originally polychromed, approx. 6'2" (1.88 m)

around the chapel in perpetual attendance at Mass. Among them are representations of Ekkehard of Meissen and his Polish-born wife, Uta (fig. 16-59). Although long dead when these statues were carved, they seem extraordinarily lifelike and individualized. Ekkehard appears as a proud warrior and no-nonsense administrator, while Uta, coolly elegant, artfully draws her cloak to her cheek. Traces of pigment indicate that the figures were originally painted.

The ordeals of the fourteenth century—famines, wars, and plagues—helped inspire a mystical religiosity that emphasized both ecstatic joy and extreme suffering. The joys and sorrows of Mary, from almost cloying sweetness in Nativity depictions to the excruciatingly graphic physical suffering in portrayals of the Crucifixion and the Lamentation, became important themes. Devotional images, known as *Andachtsbilder* in Germany, inspired the worshiper to contemplate Jesus' first and last hours, especially during evening prayers, vespers. Through such religious exercises, worshipers hoped to achieve understanding of the divine and union with God. In the famous example shown here

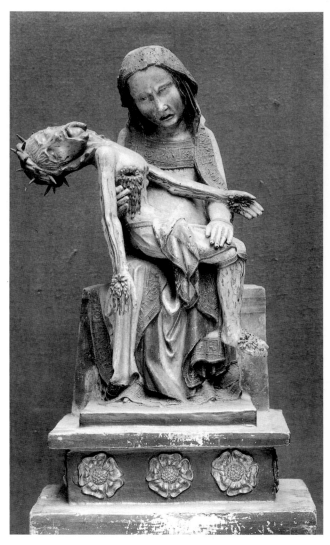

16-60. *Vesperbild*, from Middle Rhine region, Germany. c. 1330. Wood, height 34½" (88.4 cm). Landesmuseum, Bonn

In the wake of its conflict with the Holy Roman Empire, the papacy had emerged as a significant international force. But its temporal success weakened its spiritual authority and brought it into conflict with the growing power of the kings of France and England. In 1309, after the election of a French pope, the papal court moved from Rome to Avignon in southern France. During the Great Schism of 1378 to 1417, there were two rival lines of popes, one in Rome and one in Avignon.

Great wealth and a growing individualism promoted arts patronage in northern Italy. It is here that artisans begin to emerge as artists in the modern sense, both in their own eyes and the eyes of patrons. Although their methods and working conditions remained largely unchanged from before, artisans in Italy belonged to powerful urban guilds and contracted freely with wealthy townspeople and nobles and with civic and religious bodies. Their ambitious, self-aware art reflects their economic and social freedom.

Architecture

Italian Gothic architecture developed from earlier Italian Romanesque architecture in a way that only marginally reflects the influence of the French Gothic style. In the late thirteenth century, however, a new facade was erected to the Cathedral of Our Lady in Siena, Tuscany, that incorporated elements of the French style (fig. 16-61). This facade, constructed between 1284 and 1299, was the work of Giovanni Pisano (active c. 1265–1314), who may have trained or worked in France. (Giovanni Pisano was the son of the sculptor Nicola Pisano, who is discussed later in the chapter.) The new facade transformed the appearance of the cathedral. Although, in the French manner, it includes three portals and a rose window, it lacks the complex narrative sculptural programs typical of French Gothic facades. Giovanni limited his sculpture to architectural decorations like those in the portal tympana and to the huge, freestanding statues at the level of the gables and stair towers. Such freestanding statues were to become a standard feature of the Italian Gothic. As in other Italian churches, the decorative focus is on the doors themselves and, inside, on furnishings such as pulpits, tomb monuments, and baptismal fonts. The cathedral's two-tone marble banding, a hallmark of Tuscan churches, was also characteristic of Italian Gothic churches.

Siena's northern neighbor and rival, Florence, erected a colossal cathedral (duomo) in the fourteenth century that dwarfs Siena's (fig. 16-62). The building has a long and complex history. The original plan, by Arnolfo di Cambio, was approved in 1294, but political unrest brought construction to a halt until 1357. Several modifications of the design were made, and Florence Cathedral assumed much of its present appearance between 1357 and 1378. The west facade was rebuilt again in the sixteenth century. Its veneer of white and green marble coordinates with that of the nearby Baptistry of San Giovanni.

(fig. 16-60), blood gushes from the wounds of an emaciated Christ in hideous rosettes. The Virgin's face conveys the intensity of her ordeal, mingling horror, shock, pity, and grief. Such images had a profound impact on later art, both within Germany and beyond.

ITALY The thirteenth century was a period of political division and economic expansion for the Italian peninsula and its neighboring islands. With the death of Holy Roman Emperor Frederick II (ruled 1220–1250), Germany and the empire ceased to be an important factor in Italian politics and culture, and France and Spain began to vie for control of Sicily and southern Italy. The prolonged conflict between the papacy and the empire had created two factions in Italian politics: the pro-papacy Guelphs and the pro-imperial Ghibellines. Northern Italy was dominated by several independent and wealthy city-states controlled by a few powerful families. These cities were subject to chronic internal factional strife and conflict with one another.

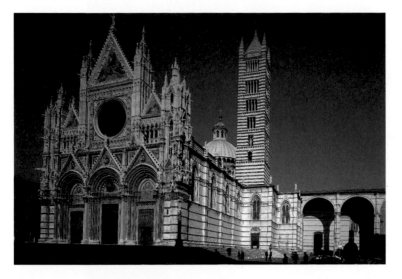

16-61. Giovanni Pisano. West facade, Cathedral of Our Lady, Siena. 1284–99; facade above gable peaks 1369–77; original sculpture removed for preservation

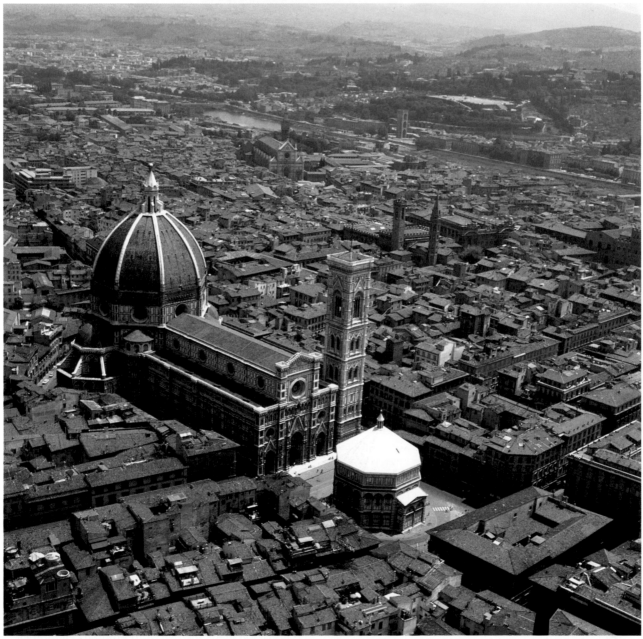

16-62. Arnolfo di Cambio, Francesco Talenti, Andrea Orcagna, and others. Florence Cathedral, Florence. Begun 1296; redesigned 1357 and 1366; drum and dome 1420–36; campanile by Giotto, Andrea Pisano, and Francesco Talenti, c.1334–50

The Romanesque Baptistry of San Giovanni stands in front of the *duomo*. In the distance, near the Arno River, is the church of Santa Croce.

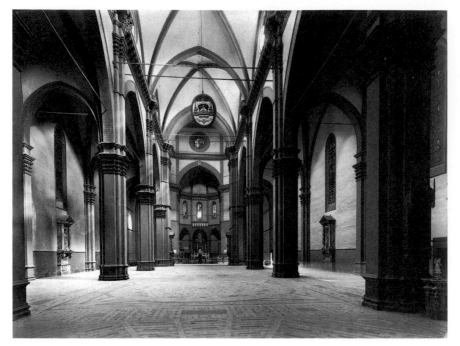

16-63. Arnolfo di Cambio, Francesco Talenti, Andrea Orcagna, and others. Nave, Florence Cathedral. 1357–78

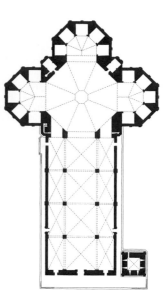

16-64. Arnolfo di Cambio, Francesco Talenti, Andrea Orcagna, and others. Plan of Florence Cathedral. 1357–78

The spacious, square-bayed nave on the interior of the cathedral (fig. 16-63) is approximately as tall as the nave at Amiens (see fig. 16-19) but is three times as wide, giving it a radically different appearance. Here well-proportioned form is more important than light. The tall nave arcade, harkening back to single-storied imperial Christian designs, has a short clerestory with a single oculus in each bay and no triforium. The regular procession of four-part ribbed vaults springing from composite piers, however, clearly reflects northern Gothic influence. When the vaults began to crack under their own weight in 1366, unsightly iron tie bars had to be installed to hold them together. Builders in northern Europe solved this problem with exterior buttressing.

Sculptors and painters rather than trained masons were often responsible for designing Italian architecture, and as the plan of Florence Cathedral reflects, they tended to be more concerned with pure design than engineering (fig. 16-64). The long nave ends in an octagonal domed crossing, as wide as the nave and side aisles, from which the apse and transept arms extend. In basic architectural terms, this is a central-plan church grafted onto a basilica-plan church. It symbolically conjoins and separates the Dome of Heaven over the crossing, where the main altar is located, and the worldly realm of the congregation in the nave. The great ribbed dome, so fundamental to this abstract conception, was structurally unrealizable when it was planned in 1365. Not until 1420 did Filippo Brunelleschi solve the engineering problems involved in constructing it.

Sculpture

In the first half of the thirteenth century, Holy Roman Emperor Frederick II fostered a classical revival at his court in southern Italy that is often compared to Charle-

magne's renaissance in the early ninth century. The revival created a trend toward greater naturalism in Italian Gothic sculpture that parallels a similar trend in the north. A leading early exemplar of the trend was Nicola Pisano (active c. 1258–1278), father of Giovanni, who came from the southern town of Apulia, where imperial patronage was strong. An inscription on a freestanding marble pulpit (fig. 16-65) in the Pisa Baptistry (see fig. 15-38) identifies it as Nicola's earliest work in northern Italy. The inscription reads: "In the year 1260 Nicola Pisano carved this noble work. May so gifted a hand be praised as it deserves." The six-sided structure is open on one side for a stairway. It is supported by columns topped with leafy Corinthian capitals and standing figures flanking Gothic trefoil arches. A center column stands on a high base carved with crouching figures and domestic animals. Every second outer column rests on the back of a shaggy-maned lion guarding its prey. The format, style, and technique of Roman sarcophagus reliefs—readily accessible in the burial ground near the cathedral—may have inspired the carving on the pulpit's upper panels. The panels illustrate New Testament subjects, each treated as an independent composition unrelated to the others.

The Nativity cycle panel (fig. 16-66) illustrates three scenes—the Annunciation, the Nativity, and the Adoration—within a shallow space. The reclining Virgin dominates the middle of the composition. In the foreground, midwives wash the infant Jesus as Joseph looks on. In the upper left is the Annunciation, with the archangel Gabriel and the Virgin. The scene in the upper right combines the Adoration with the Annunciation to the Shepherds. The composition leads the eye from group to group back to the focal point in the center, the reclining and regally detached Mother of God. The sculptural treatment of the deeply cut, full-bodied forms is quite classical, as are

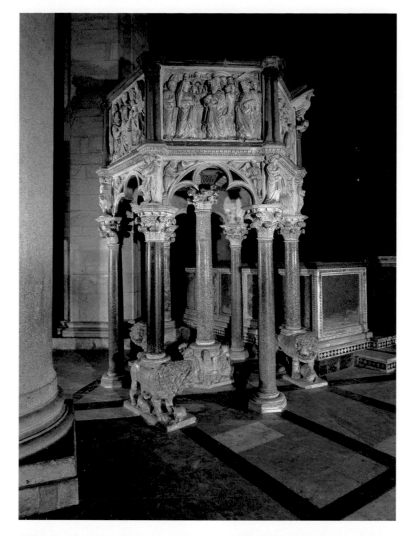

16-65. Nicola Pisano.
Pulpit, Baptistry,
Pisa. 1260.
Marble

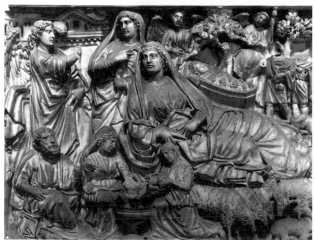

16-66. Nicola Pisano. *Nativity*, detail of pulpit, Baptistry, Pisa.
33½ x 44½" (85 x 113 cm)

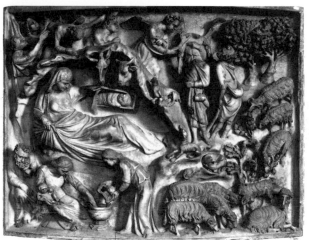

16-67. Giovanni Pisano. *Nativity*, detail of pulpit, Pisa
Cathedral, Pisa. 1302–10. Marble, 34³/₈ x 43"
(87.2 x 109.2 cm)

their heavy, placid faces; the congested layout and the use of hierarchical scale are not.

Nicola's son Giovanni, the designer of the facade of the Siena Cathedral (see fig. 16-61), assisted his father in his later projects and emerged as a versatile artist in his own right near the end of the thirteenth century. Between 1302 and 1310, Giovanni created a pulpit for Pisa Cathedral that is similar to his father's in conception and gen-

eral approach but is significantly different in style and execution. Giovanni's graceful, animated Nativity figures inhabit an uptilted, deeply carved space (fig. 16-67). In place of Nicola's impassive Roman matron, Giovanni depicts a slender young Virgin, sheltered by a shell-like niche, gazing delightedly at her baby. Below her, a midwife who doubted the virgin birth has her withered hand restored by dipping it into the baby Jesus' bathwater.

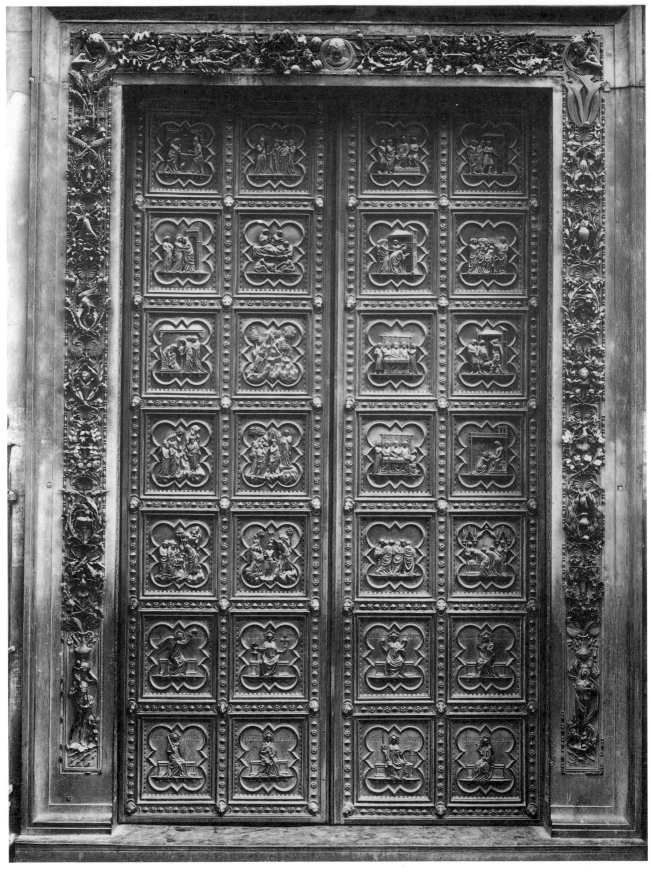

16-68. Andrea Pisano. *Life of John the Baptist*, south doors, Baptistry of San Giovanni, Florence. 1330–36. Gilded bronze

Angelic onlookers in the upper left have replaced the Annunciation. Sheep, shepherds, and announcing angels spiral up from the right, actively communicating and engaging in their surroundings. Dynamic where Nicola's was static, the scene pulses with energy.

Another Italian sculptor named Pisano (unrelated to Giovanni and Nicola), Andrea Pisano (active c. 1320s–1348), in 1330 was awarded the prestigious commission

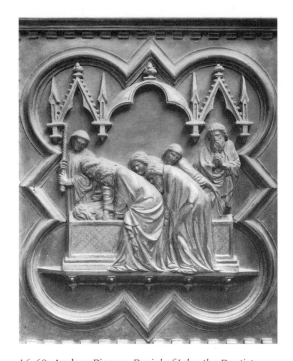

16-69. Andrea Pisano. *Burial of John the Baptist*, detail of south doors, Baptistry of San Giovanni, Florence. 9³/₄ x 17" (24.7 x 43 cm)

The death of Saint John the Baptist, described in the Gospel of Mark, has been a popular subject in art since the late Middle Ages. According to Mark's account, the ruler of Judaea, Herod Antipas, at his wife's urging, reluctantly had the preacher-saint arrested after John criticized their marriage. At a banquet, Herod's stepdaughter Salome danced so seductively that he offered to grant her any request. Prompted by her mother, she asked for the saint's head on a platter, and Herod complied. Following John's death, his disciples "came and took his body and laid it in a tomb" (Mark 6:29).

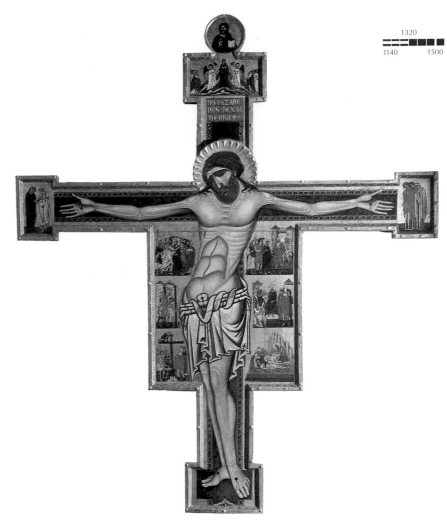

16-70. Coppo di Marcovaldo. *Crucifix*, from Tuscany, Italy. c. 1250–1300. Tempera and gold on wood, 9'7³/₈" x 8'1¹/₄" (2.93 x 2.47 m). Pinacoteca, San Gimignano, Italy

for a pair of gilded bronze doors for the Florentine Baptistry of San Giovanni. Completed within six years, the doors are decorated with twenty-eight scenes from the life of John the Baptist (San Giovanni) set in quatrefoils (fig. 16-68). Surrounding the quatrefoils are lush vine scrolls filled with flowers, fruits, and birds, cast in bronze and applied to the doorway's lintel and jambs. Within the quatrefoils are scenes with figures in the monumental classicizing style then current in Florentine painting. In the *Burial of John the Baptist* (fig. 16-69), the placement and modeling of the figures creates a remarkable illusion of three-dimensionality. The saint's body has been lowered into a sarcophagus by two heavily robed men in the foreground, who are assisted by three others nearly hidden on the far side. The bearded man praying at the right, the monkish figure holding a large candle at the left, and the pinnacled and crocketed trefoil gables of the architectonic **baldachin** provide a vertical balance to the horizontal composition.

Painting

Wall painting, common elsewhere in Europe became a preeminent art form in Italy. Painting on wood panels also surged in popularity (see "Cennini on Panel Painting," page 596). Altarpieces were commissioned not just for the main altars of cathedrals but for secondary altars, parish churches, and private chapels as well. This growing demand reflected the new sources of patronage created by Italy's burgeoning urban society. Art proclaimed a patron's status as much as it did his or her piety.

The capture of Constantinople by Crusaders in 1204 brought an influx of Byzantine art and artists to Italy, influencing Italian painters of the thirteenth and fourteenth centuries to varying degrees. This influence appears strongly in the emotionalism of a large wooden crucifix attributed to the Florentine painter Coppo di Marcovaldo and dated about 1250–1300 (fig. 16-70).

TECHNIQUE

CENNINI ON PANEL PAINTING

Cennino Cennini's *Il Libro dell' Arte* (*The Handbook of the Crafts*), a compendium of early-fifteenth-century Florentine artistic techniques, includes step-by-step instructions for making panel paintings. The wood for these paintings, he specified, should be fine-grained, free of blemishes, and thoroughly seasoned by slow drying. The first step in preparing a panel for painting was to cover its surface with clean white linen strips soaked in a **gesso** made from gypsum, a task best done on a dry, windy day. Gesso provides a ground, or surface, on which to paint. Cennini specified that at least nine layers should be applied, with a minimum of two-and-a-half days' drying time between layers, depending on the weather. The gessoed surface should then be burnished until it resembled ivory. The artist could now sketch the composition of the work with charcoal made from burned willow twigs. At this point, advised the author, "When you have finished drawing your figure, especially if it is in a very valuable [altarpiece], so that you are counting on profit and reputation from it, leave it alone for a few days, going back to it now and then to look it over and improve it wherever it still needs something . . . (and bear in mind that you may copy and examine things done by other good masters; that it is no shame to you)" (cited in Thompson, page 75). The final version of the design should be inked in with a fine squirrel-hair brush, and the charcoal brushed off with a feather. Gold leaf was to be affixed on a humid day over a reddish clay ground called bole, the tissue-thin sheets carefully glued down with a mixture of fine powdered clay and egg white, and burnished with a gemstone or the tooth of a carnivorous animal. Punched and incised patterning was to be added later.

Italian painters at this time worked in a type of paint known as **tempera**, powdered pigments mixed most often with egg yolk, a little water, and an occasional touch of glue. Apprentices were kept busy grinding and mixing paints according to their masters' recipes, setting them out for more senior painters in wooden bowls or shell dishes.

Cennini specified a detailed and highly formulaic painting process. Faces, for example, were always to be done last, with flesh tones applied over two coats of a light greenish pigment and highlighted with touches of red and white. The finished painting was to be given a layer of varnish to protect it and enhance its colors. Reflecting the increasing specialization that developed in the thirteenth century, Cennini assumed that an elaborate frame would have been produced by someone else according to the painter's specifications and brought fully assembled to the studio.

Cennini claimed that panel painting was a gentleman's job, but given its laborious complexity, that was wishful thinking. The claim does, however, reflect the rising social status of painters.

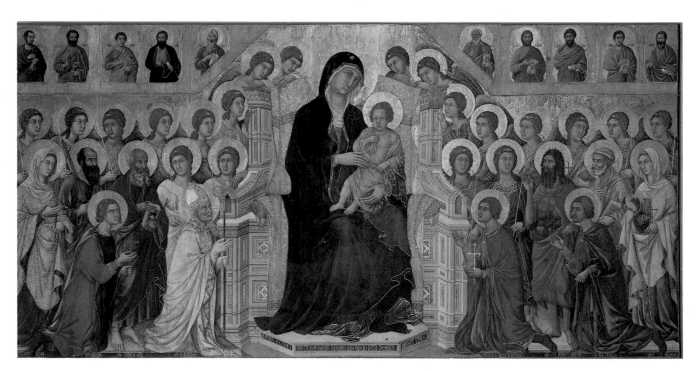

16-71. Duccio di Buoninsegna. *Virgin and Child in Majesty (Maestà)*, main panel of *Maestà Altarpiece*, from Siena Cathedral. 1308–11. Tempera and gold on wood, 7' x 13'6¼" (2.13 x 4.12 m). Museo dell'Opera del Duomo, Siena

"On the day that it was carried to the [cathedral] the shops were shut, and the bishop conducted a great and devout company of priests and friars in solemn procession, accompanied by . . . all the officers of the commune, and all the people, and one after another the worthiest with lighted candles in their hands took places near the picture, and behind came the women and children with great devotion. And they accompanied the said picture up to the [cathedral], making the procession around the Campo [square], as is the custom, all the bells ringing joyously, out of reverence for so noble a picture as is this" (Holt, page 69).

Instead of the *Christus triumphans* type common in earlier Italo-Byzantine painting, Coppo has represented the *Christus patiens*, or suffering Christ, with closed eyes and bleeding, slumped body (see fig. 14-30). The six scenes at the sides of Christ's body tell the Passion story. Such historiated crucifixes were mounted on the **rood screens** (partitions) that hid sanctuary rituals from worshipers (see fig. 16-79). Some were painted on the back, too, suggesting that they were carried in religious processions.

The two most important schools of Italian Gothic painting emerged in Siena and Florence, rivals in this as in everything else. Siena's foremost painter was Duccio di Buoninsegna (active 1278–1318), whose synthesis of Byzantine and northern Gothic influences transformed the tradition in which he worked. Duccio and his studio painted the grand *Maestà* (Majesty) *Altarpiece* for the main altar of the Siena Cathedral—dedicated, like the town itself, to the Virgin—between 1308 and 1311. Creating this altarpiece was an arduous undertaking. The work was large—the central panel alone was 7 by 13 feet—and it had to be painted on both sides because the main altar stood in the center of the sanctuary (fig. 16-71).

Because the *Maestà* was broken up in the eighteenth century, the power and beauty of Duccio's original work must be imagined today from its scattered parts (fig. 16-72). The main scene, depicting the *Virgin and Child in Majesty*, was once accompanied above and below by narrative scenes from the Life of the Virgin and the Infancy of Christ. On the back were scenes from the Life and Passion of Christ. The brilliant palette and ornate **punchwork**-tooled designs in gold leaf are characteristically Sienese. Duccio has combined a softened Italo-Byzantine figure style with the linear grace and the easy relationship between figures and their settings characteristic of the north-

ern High Gothic style. This subtle blending of northern and southern elements can be seen in the haloed ranks around Mary's architectonic throne (which represents both the Church and its specific embodiment, the Siena Cathedral). The central, most holy figures retain an iconic Byzantine solemnity and immobility, but those adoring them reflect a more naturalistic, courtly style which became the hallmark of the Sienese school for years to come.

Simone Martini, a practitioner (active 1315–1344) of the style pioneered by Duccio, may have been among Duccio's assistants on the *Maestà*. One of Martini's outstanding works, an altarpiece depicting the Annunciation (fig. 16-73), was painted in 1333 for the Siena Cathedral. This exquisite work, with its lavish punchwork, reflects a love of ornamental detail. The elegant figures, robed in fluttering draperies and silhouetted against a flat gold ground, seem weightless. Reflecting the Marian literature of his day, the painter has focused on the psychological impact of the Annunciation on a young and very human Mary. Gabriel has just appeared, his plaid-lined cloak swirling about him as he kneels in front of the Virgin. The words of his salutation—"Hail, favored one! The Lord is with you"—run from his mouth to her ear. Interrupted while reading the Bible in her room, Mary recoils in shock

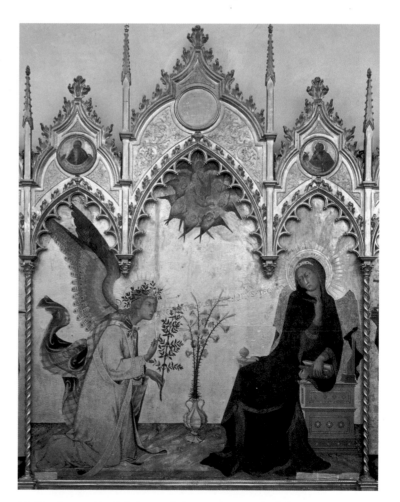

16-73. Simone Martini. *Annunciation*, center panel of altarpiece from Siena Cathedral. 1333. Tempera and gold on wood; 19th-century frame, 10' x 8' 9" (3.05 x 2.67 m). Galleria degli Uffizi, Florence. Side panels with standing prophets by Lippo Memmi not shown

16-72. Diagram, front side of *Maestà Altarpiece.* Panels seen in figure 16-71 are shaded.

Duccio's *Maestà Altarpiece* was removed from the cathedral's main altar in 1505. In 1771 the altarpiece was cut up to make it salable. Over the years, sections were dispersed, appearing later at auctions or in museums and private collections. The value of the panels remaining in Siena was finally recognized, and they were placed in the cathedral museum there in 1878.

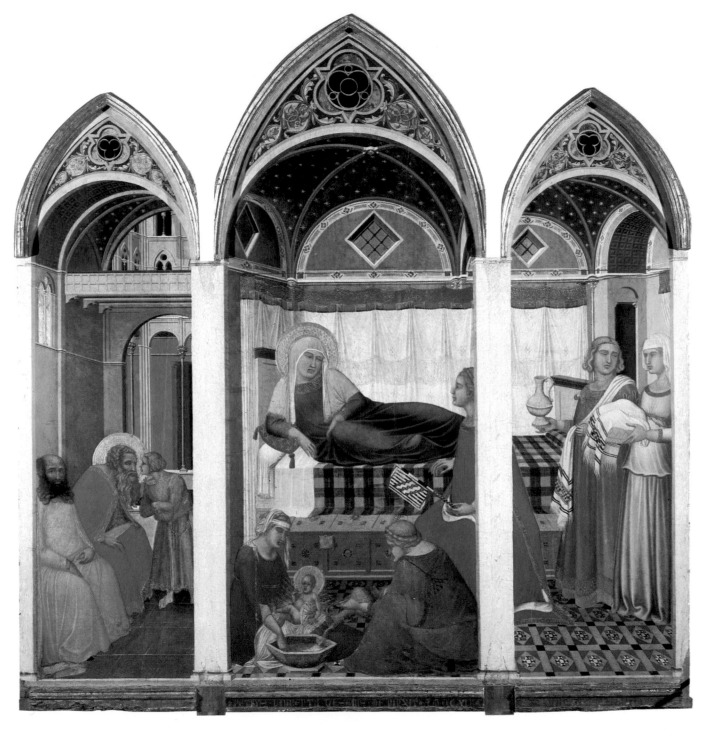

16-74. Pietro Lorenzetti. *Birth of the Virgin*, from Siena Cathedral. 1342. Tempera and gold on wood; frame partially replaced, 6'1½" x 5'11½" (1.88 x 1.82 m). Museo dell'Opera del Duomo, Siena

BUON FRESCO

Buon ("true") fresco ("fresh") wall painting on wet plaster was an Italian specialty, derived from Byzantine techniques and distinguished from fresco secco ("dry" fresco). The two methods were commonly used together in Italy.

The advantage of buon fresco was its durability. A chemical reaction occurred as the painted plaster dried that bonded the pigments into the wall surface. Fresco secco, in contrast, tended to flake off over time. The chief disadvantage of buon fresco was that it had to be done quickly and in sections. The painter plastered and painted only as much as could be completed in a day. Each section was thus known as a **giornata**, or day's work. The size of a giornata varied according to the complexity of the painting within it. The Virgin's face, for instance, could occupy an entire day, whereas large areas of sky could be painted quite rapidly. A wall to be frescoed was first prepared with a rough, thick undercoat of plaster. When this was dry, assistants copied the artist's composition onto it with sticks of charcoal, and he made any necessary adjustments. These drawings, known as **sinopia**, were often beautifully executed. Painting proceeded in irregularly shaped sections conforming to the contours of major figures and objects, with painters working from the top down so that drips fell on unfinished portions. Assistants covered one section at a time with a fresh, thin coat of very fine plaster over the sinopia, and when this was "set" but not dry, pigments mixed with water were painted on. Blue areas, as well as details, were usually painted afterward in tempera using the fresco secco method.

and fear from this gorgeous apparition. Only essential elements occupy the emotionally charged space. In addition to the two figures, these include Gabriel's olive-branch crown and scepter (emblems of triumph and peace), Mary's thronelike seat (an allusion to her future status as Queen of Heaven), the vase of white lilies (a symbol of her purity), and the dove of the Holy Spirit surrounded by cherubim. Mary's face harks back to Byzantine conventions, but the stylized elegance of her body, seen in the deft curve of her recoiling form, the folds of her rich robe, and her upraised right hand, are characteristic of the Italian Gothic court style. Soon after finishing the Annunciation, Simone Martini was summoned to southern France to head a workshop at the papal court in Avignon (he had worked earlier for the French king of Sicily and Naples). His Sienese reformulation of the French Gothic style contributed to the development of the International Gothic style at the turn of the century.

The Lorenzetti brothers, Pietro (active c. 1306–1345) and Ambrogio (active c. 1319–1347), worked in a more robust style that dominated Sienese painting during the second quarter of the fourteenth century. One of Pietro's outstanding works was a **triptych**, the Birth of the Virgin (fig. 16-74), painted in 1342 for one of the cathedral's secondary altars. In striking contrast to the Annunciation, Pietro's ample figures people a well-furnished scene. The only supernatural elements here are the gold halos identifying the baby Mary and her parents, Anna and Joachim. The painter has attempted to create the illusion of an interior space seen through the "windows" of a triple-arched frame. The center and right windows open into a single room, and the left window opens into an antechamber. Although the figures and the architecture are on different scales, Pietro has conveyed a convincing sense of space through an intuitive system of perspective. The lines of floor tiles, the chest, and the plaid bedcover, for example, appear to converge as they recede. Thematically, the Virgin's birth is depicted as a forerunner of Jesus, with elements that echo those of Nativity scenes: the mother reclines on a bed, midwives bathe the newborn, the elderly father sits off to one side, and three people bearing gifts appear at the right. The gift bearers are local women with simple offerings of bread and wine (an allusion to the Eucharist) instead of kings bearing treasures. Anna wears the royal color purple, and gold-starred vaulting forms a heavenly canopy.

A few years earlier, in 1338, the Siena city council commissioned Pietro's brother Ambrogio to paint in fresco (see "Buon Fresco," above) a room called the Sala della Pace (Chamber of Peace) in the Palazzo Pubblico (city hall). The allegorical theme chosen for the walls was the contrast between the effects of good and bad government on people's lives (fig. 16-75; see also fig. 16-2, a detail of the same work). For the Allegory of Good Government in the City, and in tribute to his patrons, Ambrogio created an idealized but recognizable portrait of Siena and its immediate environs. The cathedral dome and the distinctive striped **campanile** are visible in the upper left-hand corner (compare fig. 16-61). The statue of the wolf suckling Romulus and Remus, the legendary founders of Rome, perched above the portal of the gateway identifies it as Siena's Porta Romana. An allegory of Security as a woman clad only in a wisp of transparent drapery hovers outside the gate, a scroll in one hand and a miniature gallows complete with a hanged man in the other. The scroll bids those entering the city to come in peace, and the gallows is a reminder of the consequences of not doing so.

Ambrogio's achievement in this fresco was twofold. First, he maintained an overall visual coherence despite the shifts in vantage point and scale that help keep all parts of the flowing composition intelligible. Second, he created

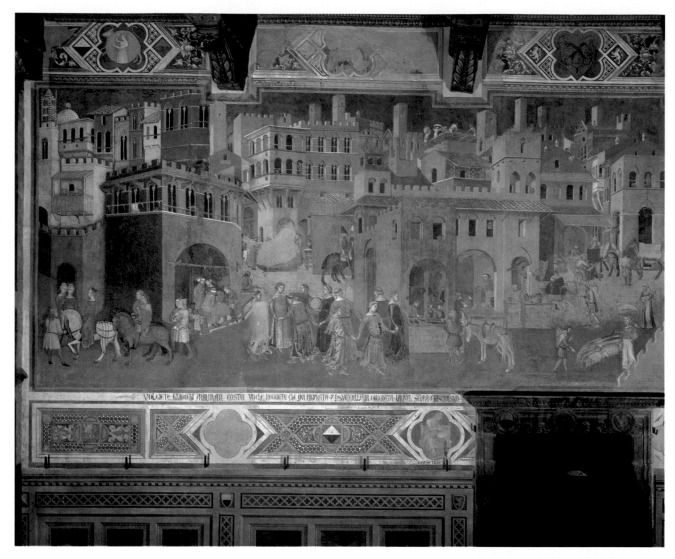

16-75. Ambrogio Lorenzetti. *Allegory of Good Government
in the City* and *Allegory of Good Government in
the Country*, frescoes in the Sala della Pace, Palazzo
Pubblico, Siena. 1338–39

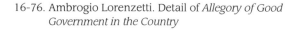

a feeling of natural scale in the relationship between figures and environment. From the women dancing to a tam-
bourine outside a shoemaker's shop (see fig. 16-2) to the
contented peasants tending fertile fields and lush vineyards (fig. 16-76), the work conveys a powerful vision of an
orderly society, of peace and plenty at this particular time
and place. Sadly, famine, poverty, and disease overcame
Siena just a few years after this work was completed.

In Florence, the transformation of the Italo-Byzantine
style began somewhat earlier than in Siena. Duccio's Florentine counterpart was an older painter named Cenni di
Pepi (active c. 1272–1302), better known by his nickname,
Cimabue. He is believed to have painted the *Virgin and*

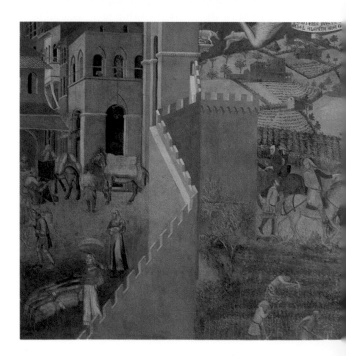

16-76. Ambrogio Lorenzetti. Detail of *Allegory of Good
Government in the Country*

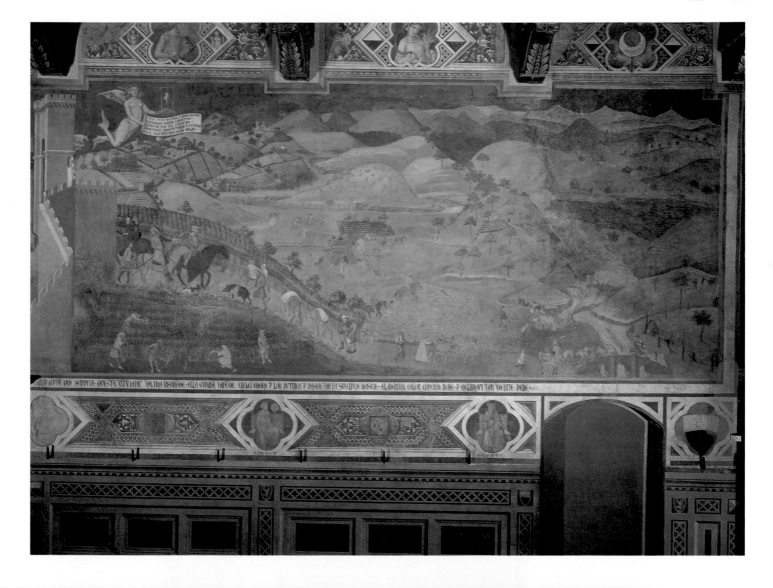

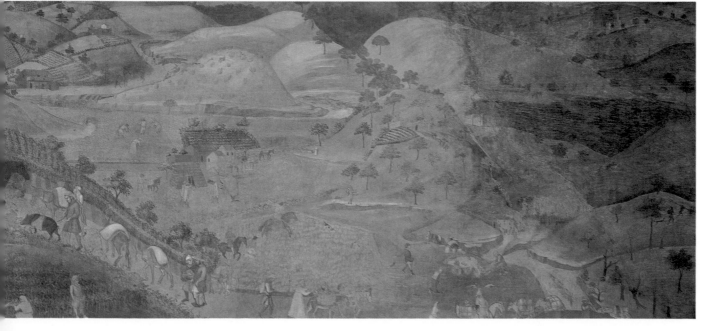

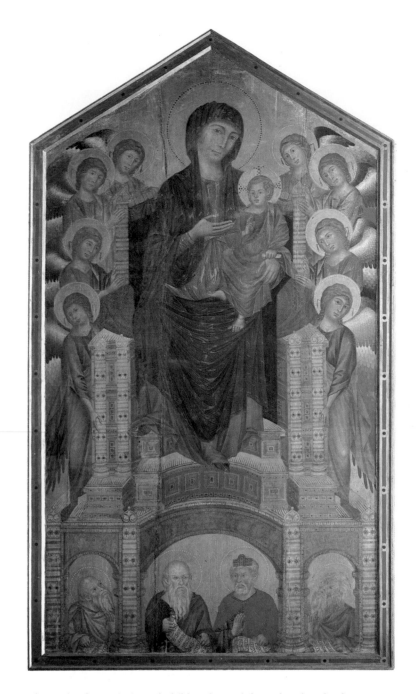

16-77. Cimabue. *Virgin and Child Enthroned*, from the Church of
Santa Trinità, Florence. c. 1280. Tempera and gold on wood,
12'7½" x 7'4" (3.9 x 2.2 m). Galleria degli Uffizi, Florence

Child Enthroned (fig. 16-77) in about 1280 for the main altar of the Church of Santa Trinità (Holy Trinity) in Florence. At more than 11½ feet high, this enormous panel painting seems to have set a precedent for monumental altarpieces. In it, Cimabue follows the Byzantine iconography of the Virgin Pointing the Way. The Virgin sits surrounded by saints, angels, and Old Testament prophets. She holds the infant Jesus in her lap and points to him as the path to salvation.

Cimabue employed Byzantine formulas in determining the proportions of his figures, the placement of their features, and even the tilts of their haloed heads. Mary's

huge throne, painted to resemble gilded bronze with inset enamels and gems, provides an architectural framework for the figures. To render her drapery and that of the infant Jesus, Cimabue used the Italo-Byzantine technique of highlighting drapery with thin lines of gold to indicate divinity, as in Mary's blue cloak. The vantage point suspends the viewer in space in front of the image, simultaneously looking down on the projecting elements of the throne and Mary's lap while looking straight on at the prophets at the base of the throne and the splendid angels at each side. These interesting spatial ambiguities, as well as subtle asymmetries throughout the com-

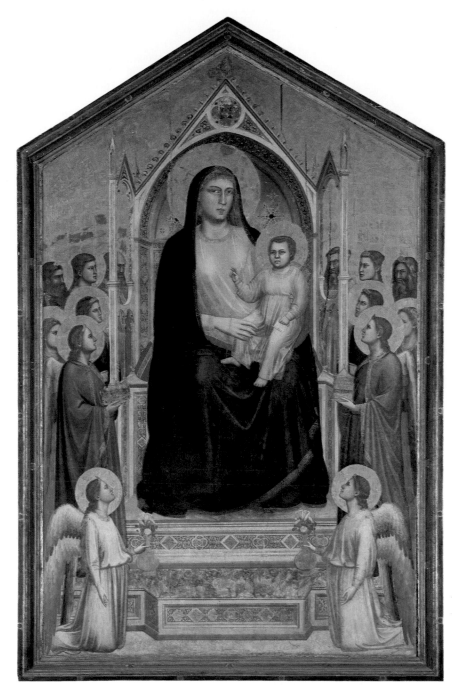

16-78. Giotto di Bondone. *Virgin and Child Enthroned*, from the Church of the Ognissanti, Florence. c. 1310. Tempera and gold on wood, 10'8" x 6'8¼" (3.53 x 2.05 m). Galleria degli Uffizi, Florence

position, the Virgin's thoughtful, engaging gaze, and the well-observed faces of the old men are all departures from tradition that enliven the picture. Cimabue's concern for spatial volumes, solid forms, and warmly naturalistic human figures contributed to the course of later Italian painting.

According to the sixteenth-century Renaissance chronicler Vasari, Cimabue discovered a talented shepherd boy, Giotto di Bondone, and taught him how to paint. Then, "Giotto obscured the fame of Cimabue, as a great light outshines a lesser." Vasari also credited Giotto (active c. 1300–1337) with "setting art upon the path

that may be called the true one[, for he] learned to draw accurately from life and thus put an end to the crude Greek [i.e., Italo-Byzantine] manner" (cited in Barroughs, page 97). The painter and commentator Cennino Cennini (c. 1370–1440), writing in the late fourteenth century, was struck by the accessibility and modernity of Giotto's art, which, though it retained traces of the "Greek manner," was moving toward the depiction of a humanized world anchored in three-dimensional form.

Compared to Cimabue's *Virgin and Child Enthroned*, Giotto's 1310 painting of the same subject (fig. 16-78) for the Church of the Ognissanti (All Saints) in Florence,

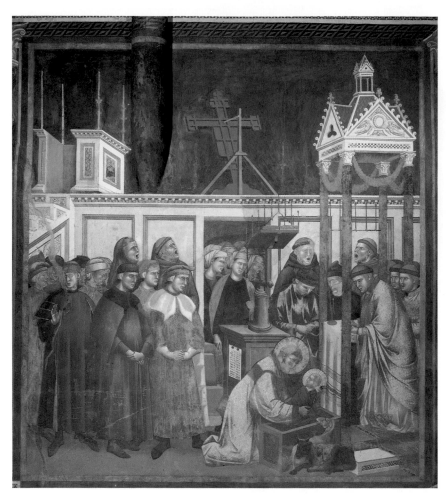

16-79. Saint Francis Master. *Miracle of the Crib of Greccio*, fresco in Upper Church of San Francesco, Assisi, Umbria, Italy. c. 1295–1301/30

Saint Francis, born Giovanni Bernadone (c. 1181–1226), was the educated son of a rich cloth merchant. After an early career as a soldier, he dedicated himself to God. Embracing poverty, he lived as a wandering preacher. The Franciscan order began after he and his followers gained the recognition of the pope. Contemporaries described him as an innocent eccentric. Two years before his death he experienced the stigmata, wounds in his hands and feet like those of the crucified Christ.

This panel, on a lower nave wall, survived the disastrous earthquake of September 26, 1997.

while retaining certain of Cimabue's conventions, exhibits a groundbreaking spatial consistency and sculptural solidity. The central and largely symmetrical composition, the rendering of the angels' wings, and Mary's Byzantine facial type all reflect Cimabue's influence. Gone, however, are her modestly inclined head and delicate gold-lined drapery. This colossal and mountain-like Mary seems to burst forth from her slender Gothic baldachin. Giotto has imbued the picture with an unprecedented physical immediacy, despite his retention of hierarchical scale, the formal, enthroned image type, and a flat-gold ground. By rendering the play of light and shadow across their substantial forms, he has created the sense that his figures are fully three-dimensional beings inhabiting real space.

Giotto may have collaborated on murals at the prestigious Church of San Francesco in Assisi, the home of Saint Francis, the founder of the new Franciscan order, which was gaining followers throughout western Europe. Saint Francis's message of simple, humble devotion, direct experience of God, and love for all his creatures had a powerful impact on thirteenth-century Italian literature and art. The Church of San Francesco, the Franciscans' mother church, was consecrated by the pope in 1253, and the Franciscans commissioned many works to adorn it. Among those who worked there were Simone Martini, Pietro Lorenzetti, and Cimabue.

The *Life of Saint Francis*, in the upper church at San Francesco, was apparently among the last of the fresco cycles to be completed there. Scholars differ on whether

they were painted by the young Giotto as early as 1295–1301 or by his followers as late as 1330; many have adopted the neutral designation of the artist as the Saint Francis Master. One scene, the *Miracle of the Crib at Greccio* (fig. 16-79), shows Saint Francis making the first crèche, a Christmas tableau representing the birth of Jesus, according to legend, in the church at Greccio. The artist of this scene has made great strides in depicting a convincing space with freely moving solid figures. The fresco documents the way the sanctuary of an early Franciscan church looked and the observances that took place within it. A large wooden historiated crucifix similar to the one by Coppo di Marcovaldo (see fig. 16-70) has been suspended from a stand on top of the rood screen. It has been reinforced by cross-bracing on the back and tilted forward to hover over worshipers in the nave. A high pulpit with candlesticks at its corners rises over the screen at the left. Other small but telling touches include a seasonal liturgical calendar posted on the lectern, foliage swags decorating a Gothic baldachin, and the singing monks. Saint Francis, in the foreground, reverently places a statue of the Holy Infant in a plain, boxlike crib next to representations of various animals that might have been present at his birth. Richly dressed people—presumably patrons of the church—stand at the left, while Franciscan nuns, apparently excluded from the sanctuary, look on through an opening in the screen.

Giotto's masterpiece is the frescoed interior of another church, the Arena Chapel in Padua (fig. 16-80), painted about 1305. While working at the Church of

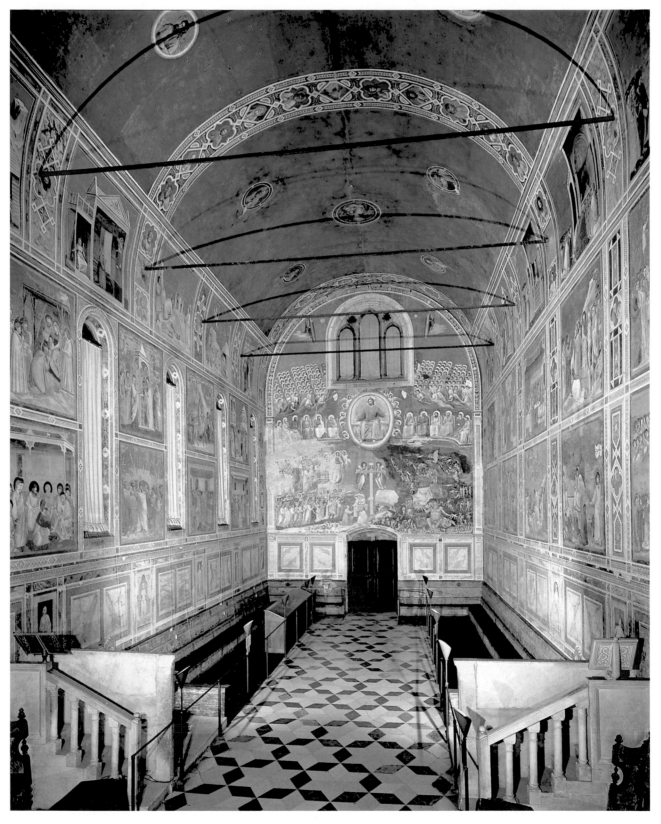

16-80. Giotto di Bondone. *Last Judgment* and frescoes on west wall of Arena Chapel, Padua. 1305–6

THE BLACK DEATH

In the early 1340s rumors began to circulate in Europe of a deadly plague spreading by land and sea from Asia. By 1348 the plague had reached Constantinople, Italy, and France; by the next winter it had struck the British Isles; and by 1350 it had swept across Germany, Poland, and Scandinavia. Successive waves struck again in 1362, 1374, 1383, 1389, and 1400, and new outbreaks continued sporadically for the next 300 years, culminating in England's Great Plague of 1665. As much as half the urban population of Florence and Siena died in the summer of 1348, including many promising artists. England was similarly hard hit.

The plague, known as the Black Death, took two forms, both of which killed rapidly. The bubonic form was spread by fleas from rats, the pneumonic form through the air from the lungs of infected victims. To people of the time, ignorant of its causes and powerless to prevent it, the Black Death was a catastrophe. The fourteenth-century Italian writer Gio-vanni Boccaccio described how "the calamity had instilled such terror in the hearts of men and women that . . . fathers and mothers shunned their children, neither visiting them nor helping them" (cited in Herlihy, page 355). In their panic, some people turned to escapist pleasure seeking, others to religious fanaticism. Many, seeking a scapegoat, turned against Jews, who were massacred in several cities.

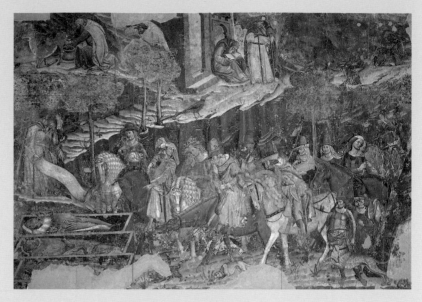

Francesco Traini. *Triumph of Death*, detail of a fresco in the Campo Santo, Pisa. 1325-50

Saint Anthony in Padua, Giotto was approached by a local merchant to decorate a new family chapel. The chapel, named for a nearby ancient Roman arena, is a simple, barrel-vaulted room. Giotto covered the entrance wall with a scene of the Last Judgment. He subdivided the side walls with a dado of allegorical grisaille paintings of the Virtues and Vices, from which rise vertical bands containing quatrefoil portrait medallions. The medallions are set within a framework painted to resemble marble inlay and carved relief. The central band of medallions spans the vault, crossing a brilliant lapis-blue, star-spangled sky in which large portrait disks float like glowing moons. Set into this framework are rectangular narrative scenes juxtaposing the life of the Virgin with that of Jesus. Both the individual scenes and the overall program display Giotto's genius for distilling a complex narrative into a coherent visual experience. Among Giotto's achievements was his ability to model form with color. He rendered his bulky figures as pure color masses, painting the deepest shadows with the most intense hues and highlighting shapes with lighter shades mixed with white. These sculpturally modeled figures enabled Giotto to convey a sense of depth in landscape settings without relying on the traditional convention of an architectural framework, although he did make use of that convention.

In the moving *Lamentation* (fig. 16-81), in the lowest register of the Arena Chapel, Giotto focused the composition for maximum emotional effect off-center on the faces of Mary and the dead Jesus. A great downward-swooping ridge—its barrenness emphasized by a single dry tree, a medieval symbol of death—carries the psychological weight of the scene to its expressive core. Mourning angels hovering overhead mirror the anguish of Jesus' followers. The stricken Virgin communes with her dead son with mute intensity, while John the Evangelist flings his arms back in convulsive despair and other figures hunch over the corpse. Instead of symbolic sorrow, Giotto conveys real human suffering, drawing the viewer into the circle of personal grief. The direct, emotional appeal of his art, as well as its deliberate plainness, embodies Franciscan values.

While Sienese painting was a key contributor to the development of the International Gothic style, Florentine painting in the style originated by Giotto and kept alive by his pupils and their followers was fundamental to the development of Italian Renaissance art over the next two centuries. Before these movements, however, came the disastrous last sixty years of the fourteenth century, in which the world of the Italian city-states—which had seemed so full of promise in Ambrogio Lorenzetti's *Good Government* frescoes—was transformed into a world of

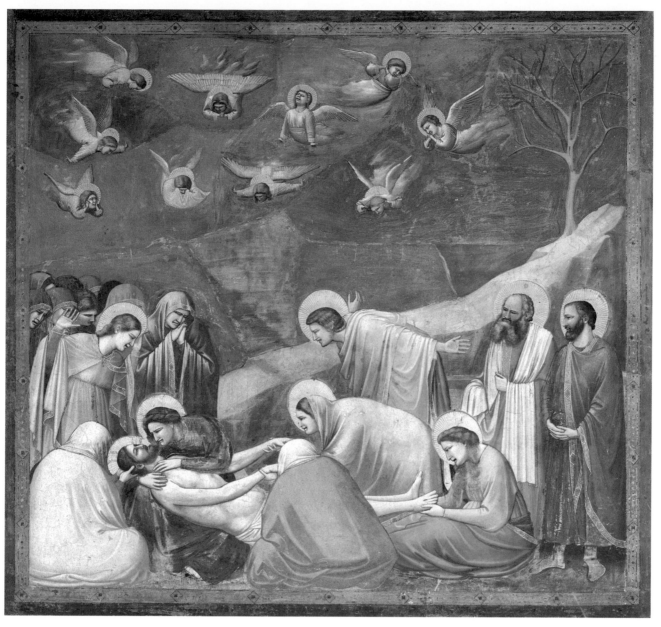

16-81. Giotto di Bondone. *The Lamentation*. 1305–6. Fresco in the Arena Chapel

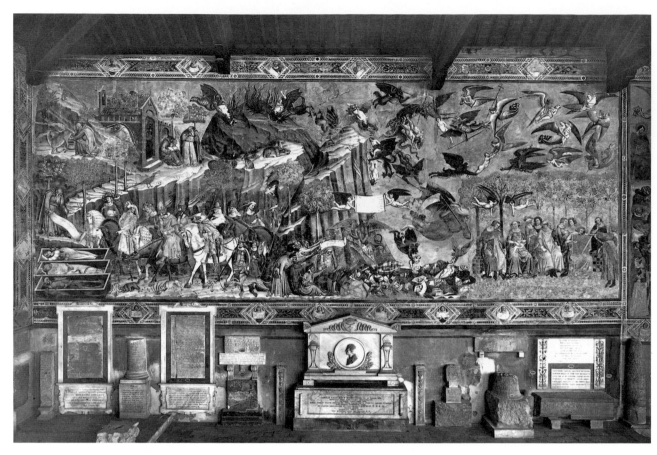

16-82. Francesco Traini. *Triumph of Death*, fresco in Campo Santo, Pisa. Mid-14th century
The fresco was damaged by American shells during World War II and has been detached from the wall to preserve it.

uncertainty, and desolation by epidemics of the plague.

The horror and the terror of impending death are vividly depicted in the *Triumph of Death* (fig. 16-82). This much-copied fresco was painted by a Pisan named Francesco Traini (active c. 1321–1363) in the Campo Santo, the funerary structure on the grounds of Pisa Cathedral. It shows the encounter between the Three Living (aristocrats leading a hunt) and the Three Dead (corpses in varying stages of decomposition), a grim theme popular in plague-wracked Europe in the mid-fourteenth century. A crowned woman in the center of the leading group of riders recoils at the sight of her dead counterpart, the crowned man in the middle coffin. One of her courtiers covers his nose, gagging at the smell, while his wild-eyed horse cranes its neck forward. The animal's

neck and the diagonal, Giottoesque cliff above lead the eye inexorably to the bloated, worm-riddled body in the top coffin. A stern old man unrolls a scroll, symbolically delivering the message of the scene: neither youth nor beauty, wealth nor power, but only piety like that of the hermits on the cliff above provides protection from the wrath of God. It was as if the self-confident hunting party in *Lorenzetti's Allegory of Good Government in the Country* fresco had set forth in sunshine only to return in shadow.

Yet as dark as it must have seemed to the men and women living through those times, beneath the surface profound, unstoppable changes were underway. In a relatively short moment of history, the European Middle Ages gave way to what is known as the Renaissance.

Glossary

abacus The flat, usually square slab forming the top of a **capital**, directly under the **entablature**.

absolute dating A method of assigning a precise historical date to ancient periods and objects based on known and recorded events in the region as well as technically extracted physical evidence (such as carbon-14 disintegration). *See also* **radiometric dating**, **relative dating**.

abstract, abstraction Any art that does not represent observable aspects of nature or transforms visible **forms** into a pattern resembling the orignal model. Also: the formal qualities of this process.

academy, academician An academy is an institutional group established for the training of artists. Most academies date from the Renaissance and after; they were particularly powerful state-run institutions in the seventeenth and eighteenth centuries. In general, academies replaced **guilds** as the venue where students learned the craft of art and were also provided with a complete education, including art theory and artistic rules. The academies helped artists be seen as trained specialists, rather than craftspeople, and promoted the change in the social status of the artist. An academician is an official academy-trained artist, whose work conforms to the accepted **style** of the day.

acanthus A plant whose foliage inspires a leaflike architectural ornamentation used in the **Corinthian** and **Composite orders**.

acropolis The **citadel** of an ancient Greek city, located at its highest point and consisting of temples, a **treasury**, and sometimes a royal palace. The most famous is the Acropolis in Athens, where the ruins of the Parthenon can be found.

acrylic A fast-drying synthetic paint popular since the 1950s.

adobe Sun-baked blocks made of clay mixed with straw. Also: the buildings made with this material.

adyton The innermost **sanctuary** of a Greek temple. If a temple with an **oracle**, the place where the **oracles** were delivered. More generally, a very private space or room.

aedicula (aediculae) A type of decorative architectural frame, usually found around a **niche**, door, or window. An aedicula is made up of a **pediment** and **entablature** supported by **columns** or **pilasters**.

aesthetics The philosophic theories relating to the concept of beauty in art and, by extension, to the history of art appreciation and taste.

agora An open space in a Greek town used as a central gathering place or market. In Roman times, called a **forum**.

album A book consisting of blank pages (leaves) on which typically an artist may sketch, draw, or paint.

album leaves *See* **album**.

alignment In prehistoric architecture, an arrangement of **menhirs** in straight rows.

allegory The representation in a work of art of an abstract concept or idea using specific objects or human figures.

altar A tablelike structure where religious rites are performed. In Christian churches, the **altar** is the site of the rite of the **Eucharist**.

altarpiece A painted or carved panel or **winged** structure placed at the back of or behind an **altar**. Contains religious imagery, often specific to the place of worship for which it was made.

amalaka In Hindu architecture, the circular or square-shaped element on top of a **shikhara**, often crowned with a **finial**, symbolizing the cosmos.

ambulatory The passage walkway around the **apse** in a basilican church or around the central space in a centrally planned building.

amphiprostyle Term describing a building, usually a temple, with **porticoes** at each end but without **columns** along the other two sides.

amphora An ancient Greek jar for storing oil or wine, with an egg-shaped body and two curved handles.

Andachtsbild (Andachtsbilder) Literally "devotional image," a painting or sculpture that depicts themes of Christian grief and suffering, such as the **pietà**, intended to encourage meditation.

aniconic A term describing a representation without images of human figures, often found in Islamic cultures.

animal interlace Decoration made up of interwoven animal or serpent **forms**, often found in Celtic and northern European art of the medieval period.

animal style A type of imagery popular in Europe and western Asia during the ancient and medieval periods, characterized by **linear**, animal-like **forms** arranged in intricate patterns or combats.

ankh A **hieroglyph** signifying life, used by ancient Egyptians.

anta (antae) A rectangular **pier** or **pilaster** found at the ends of the framing walls of a recessed **portico**.

antependium (antependia) The front panel of a **mensa** or **altar** table.

anticlassical A term designating any image, idea, or **style** that opposes the **classical** norm.

apex A peak or top point.

apotheosis Deification of an individual. In painting, often shown as an ascent to Heaven, borne by angels or **putti**.

appliqué A piece of any material applied as decoration on another.

apprentice A student artist or craftsperson in training. In a system of artistic training established under the **guilds** and still in use today, master artists took on apprentices (who usually lived with the master's family) for several years. The apprentice was taught every aspect of the artist's craft, and he or she participated in the master's workshop or **atelier**.

appropriation Term used to describe an artist's practice of borrowing from another source for a new work of art. While in previous centuries artists often copied one another's figures, **motifs**, or **compositions**, in modern times the sources for appropriation extend from material culture to works of art.

apse, apsidal A large semicircular or polygonal (and usually **vaulted**) **niche** protruding from the end wall of a building. In the Christian church, it contains the **altar**. Apsidal is an adjective describing the condition of having such a semicircular or polygonal space.

aquamanile A vessel used for washing hands, whether during the celebration of the Catholic Mass or before eating at a secular table. An aquamanile is often formed in the shape of a human figure or a grotesque animal.

aquatint A type of **intaglio** printmaking developed in the eighteenth century that produces an area of even **tone** without laborious **cross-hatching**. Basically similar in technique to an **etching**, the aquatint is made through use of a porous resin coating of a metal plate, which when immersed in acid allows an even, allover biting of the plate. When printed, the end result has a granular, textural effect.

aqueduct A trough to carry flowing water, if necessary, supported by **arches**. Under the Romans, built over long distances at a gradually decreasing incline.

arabesque A type of **linear** surface decoration based on foliage and calligraphic **forms**, usually characterized by flowing lines and swirling shapes.

arcade A series of **arches**, carried by **columns** or **piers** and supporting a common wall or **lintel**. In a blind arcade, the **arches** and supports are engaged (attached to the background wall) and have a decorative function.

arch In architecture, a curved structural element that spans an open space. Built from wedge-shaped stone blocks called **voussoirs**, which, when placed together and held at the top by a trapezoidal **keystone**, form an effective weight-bearing unit. Requires **buttresses** for support at either side to contain outward thrust of structure. Found in a variety of shapes and sizes, depending upon **style** of period. **Corbel arch**: arch or **vault** formed by **courses** of stones, each of which projects beyond the lower **course** until the space is enclosed; usually finished with a **capstone**. **Horseshoe arch**: an arch with a rounded horseshoe shape; the standard arch **form** in western Islamic architecture. **Ogival arch**: a pointed arch created by **S** curves. **Relieving arch**: an arch built into a heavy wall just above a **post-and-lintel** structure (such as a gate, door, or window) to help support the wall above. Relieves some of the weight on the **lintel** by transferring the load to the side walls.

Archaic smile The curved lips of an ancient Greek statue, usually interpreted as a half-smile.

architectonic Resembling or relating to the spatial or structural aspects of architecture.

architectural interior A subject in **genre painting** particularly popular in Holland in the seventeenth century, depicting the interiors of churches and other important civic buildings, usually with small figures going about ordinary activities.

architrave The bottom layer of an **entablature**, beneath the **frieze** and the **cornice**.

ashlar *See* **dressed stone**.

assemblage An artwork created by gathering and manipulating found objects and other three-dimensional items. The technique of assemblage was especially popular in the first half of the twentieth century.

astragal A thin convex decorative **molding**, often found on **Classical entablatures**, and usually decorated with a continuous row of beadlike circles.

atelier The studio or workshop of a master artist or craftsperson, usually consisting of junior associates and **apprentices**.

atmospheric perspective *See* **perspective**.

atrial cross The cross placed in the **atrium** of a church. In Colonial America, used to mark a gathering and teaching place. Atrial crosses were often carved by native sculptors in local styles.

atrium An unroofed interior coutyard or room in a Roman house, sometimes having a pool or garden. Also: the open courtyard in front of a Christian church, or an entrance area in modern architecture.

attached column *See* **column**.

attic story The top story of a building. In **classical** architecture, the level above the **entablature**, often decorated or carrying an inscription.

attribute The symbolic object or objects that identify a particular deity, saint, or personification in art.

automatism A technique whereby the usual intellectual control of the artist over his or her brush or pencil is foregone. The artist's aim is to allow the subconscious to create the artwork without rational interference. Also called automatic writing, automatism was developed by the Surrealists in the 1910s, and it was influential for later movements such as Abstract Expressionism.

avant-garde A term derived from the French military word meaning "before the group," or "vanguard." Avant-garde denotes those artists or concepts of a strikingly new, experimental, or radical nature for the time.

axial Term used to describe a **plan** or design that is based on a symmetrical, **linear** arrangement of elements.

axis mundi A concept of an axis of the world, which denotes important sacred sites and provides a link between the human and celestial realms. For example, in Buddhist art, the axis mundi can be marked by **monumental** free-standing decorated **pillars**.

background Within the depicted space of an artwork, the area of the image at the greatest distance from the **picture plane**.

backstrap loom A type of loom common among the indigenous peoples of Asia and the Americas in which the **warp** threads are wound between two bars, one attached to an object such as a pole or tree and the other to the weaver's waist. Also called a body-tensioned loom.

bailey The outermost walled courtyard of castle fortifications. Usually the first line of defense, the bailey was bounded on the outer side by a defensive wall such as a palisade.

baldachin A canopy (whether suspended from the ceiling, projecting from a wall, or supported by **columns**) placed over an honorific or sacred space such as a throne or church **altar**.

balustrade A series of short circular posts (called balusters), with a rail on top. Sometimes balusters are replaced by decorated panels or ironwork under the rail.

baptismal font A large open vessel, usually made of stone, containing water for the Christian ritual of baptism.

baptistry A building used for the Christian ritual of baptism. It is usually separate from the main church and often octagonal or circular in shape.

barbican A defensive structure located at the gate to a city or castle, attached to the exterior wall. A barbican is usually heavily fortified.

bargeboard A wooden board, often carved in a decorative manner, affixed to the sloping sides of a roof **gable** to conceal or protect the end of the roof timbers.

barrel vault *See* **vault.**

bar tracery *See* **tracery.**

base A slab of masonry supporting a statue or the **shaft** of a **column** (also called a **plinth**).

basilica A large rectangular building. Often built with a **clerestory** and side aisles separated from the center **nave** by **colonnades**. Used in Roman times as centers for administration or justice and later adapted to Christian church use. A basilica-plan structure incorporates the essential elements of this plan.

basilica plan *See* **basilica.**

bas-relief *See* **relief sculpture.**

battered A building technique used in the construction of stone walls. For stability, a battered wall is built with a distinct inward slope at the top.

battlement The uppermost, fortified sections of a building or **parapet**, used for military purposes, usually including **crenellated** walls and other defensive structures.

bay One unit of a construction system of a building. Bays divide the space of a building into regular spatial units marked by elements such as **columns**, **piers**, **buttresses**, windows, or **vaults**.

beadwork Any decorative element created with beads. Also: a type of **molding** made from convex circles, often found in **classical** architecture and decoration.

beehive tomb A **corbel vaulted** tomb, conical in shape like a beehive, and covered by an earthen mound.

Benday dots In modern printing and typesetting, the individual dots which, together with many others, make up lettering and images. Often machine- or computer-generated, the dots are very small and closely spaced to give the effect of density and richness of **tone**.

bestiary A book of moralizing tales about real and imaginary animals especially popular during the Middle Ages in western Europe.

bevel, beveling A cut made at any angle except a right angle. Also: the technique of cutting at a slant, which creates shadows. Used in architecture, carpentry, printmaking, metalwork, and sculpture.

bi A jade disk with a hole in the center used in China for the ritual worship of the sky. Also: a badge indicating noble rank.

bird's-eye view Painting, drawing, or print that incorporates high-level **perspective**.

black-figure A decorative **style** of ancient Greek pottery in which black figures are painted on a red clay background.

blackware An ancient ceramic technique that produced pottery with a primarily black surface. As rediscovered and adapted by Maria Montoya Martinez, a Native American potter in the United States, blackware exhibits alternating **matte** and glossy patterns on the black surfaces of the objects.

blind arcade *See* **arcade**.

blind window The outlining elements of a window applied to a solid wall, often to help create symmetry on a **facade**, but without the actual window opening.

block book A book printed from carved wooden blocks. Block books were superseded by the invention, about 1450, of printing from movable type. *See also* **movable-type printing, wood-block print**.

block printing A printed image, such as a **woodcut** or wood **engraving**, made from a carved wooden block.

bobbin A cylindrical reel around which a material such as yarn or thread is wound when spinning, sewing, or weaving.

bodhisattva A deity that is far advanced in the long process of transforming itself into a buddha. While seeking enlightenment or emancipation from this world (nirvana), bodhisattvas help others attain this same liberation.

boiserie Wood paneling or wainscotting, usually applied to seventeenth- and eighteenth-century French interiors, where it was often decorated with painting and **relief carving**.

boss A decorative knoblike element. Bosses can be found in many places, such as at the intersection of a Gothic ceiling or **vault** rib (and, similarly, at the end of a **molding**). Also: buttonlike projections in medieval decorations and metalwork.

bracket, bracketing An architectural element that projects from a wall, and that often helps support a horizontal part of a building, such as beams or the eaves of a roof.

breakfast piece A painting depicting a **still life** of plates and food. The breakfast piece was popular in Dutch seventeenth-century painting and may have had a *vanitas* significance.

broken pediment *See* **pediment.**

bronze A metal made from copper alloy, usually mixed with tin. Also: any sculpture or object made from this substance.

bulwark A raised promontory built for purposes of defense.

buon fresco *See* **fresco**.

burin A metal instrument used in the making of **engravings** to cut lines into the metal plate. The sharp end of the burin is trimmed to give a diamond-shaped cutting point, while the other end is finished with a wooden handle that fits into the engraver's palm.

bust A portrait sculpture depicting only the head and shoulders of the subject.

buttress, buttressing A type of architectural support. Usually consists of massive masonry with a wide base built against an exterior wall to brace the wall and strengthen the **vaults**. Acts by transferring the weight of the building from a higher point to the ground. Flying buttress: An **arch** built on the exterior of a building that transfers the thrust of the roof vaults at important stress points through the wall to a detached buttress **pier** leading to the wall buttress.

cabinet piece A term often applied to seventeenth-century Dutch art, meaning a small-scale painting executed with a luscious surface and finest detail. The cabinet piece carries the associations of a precious object meant for close scrutiny and leisured appreciation.

caduceus In Classical mythology, the staff carried by the god Hermes. It possessed various powers, including the guarantee of safe passage by any messenger. The caduceus is shaped like a wand with two wings at the top and snakes intertwined around the **shaft**. Also: the modern symbol of medicine.

cairn A pile of stones or earth and stones that served both as a prehistoric burial site and as a marker of underground tombs.

calligraph A **form** of writing with pictures, as in the Chinese language.

calligraphy The art of highly ornamental handwriting.

calotype The first photographic process utilizing negatives and paper positives. It was invented by William Henry Fox Talbot in the late 1830s.

calyx krater *See* **krater**.

came (cames) A lead strip used in the making of leaded or **stained-glass** windows. Cames have an indented vertical groove on the sides into which the separate pieces of glass are fitted to hold the design together.

cameo Gemstone, clay, glass, or shell having layers of color, carved in **low relief** to create an image and ground of diffent colors.

camera obscura An early cameralike device used in the Renaissance and later for capturing images of nature. Made from a dark box (or room) with a hole in one side (sometimes fitted with a lens), the camera obscura operates when bright light shines through the hole, casting an upside-down image of an object outside onto the inside wall of the box. This image then can be traced.

campanile The campanile, from the Italian word meaning "bell tower," is usually a freestanding structure.

canon of proportions A set of ideal mathematical ratios in art, especially sculpture, originally applied by the Egyptians and later the ancient Greeks to measure the various parts of the human body in relation to each other.

capital The sculpted block which tops a **column**. According to the conventions of the **orders**, capitals include different decorative elements. *See* **order**. Also: a historiated capital in Medieval art is a capital displaying a narrative.

capriccio A painting or print of a fantastic, imaginary landscape, usually with architecture.

capstone The final, topmost stone in a **corbel arch** or **vault**, which joins the sides and completes the structure.

Caravaggism A **style** of painting based on the example of the Italian seventeenth-century painter Michelangelo da Caravaggio and popular throughout Europe around 1600–1620. Caravaggist painters are marked by, among other elements, the use of **realism**, strong **chiaroscuro**, and lower-class types for subjects.

caricature An artwork that exaggerates a person's features or individual peculiarities, usually with humorous or satirical intent.

Caroline minuscule The clear and legible script developed in Carolingian times.

cartoon A full-scale drawing used to transfer the outline of a design onto a surface (such as a wall, canvas, or panel) to be painted.

cartouche A frame for a **hieroglyphic** inscription formed by a rope design surrounding an oval space. Used to signify a sacred or honored name. Also: in architecture, a decorative device or plaque, usually with plain center and rolled or sculpted edges, used for inscriptions or epitaphs.

caryatid A sculpture of a draped female figure acting as a **column** that supports an **entablature**.

catacomb An underground cemetery; also called a **hypogeum**. Urns and busts of the dead were placed in **niches** along the tunnels, which crisscrossed the area under an existing cemetery and often incorporated rooms (cubiculae) and several different levels.

cella The principal interior structure at the center of a Greek or Roman temple within which the cult statue was usually housed. Also called the **naos**.

cenotaph A funerary monument commemorating an individual or group buried elsewhere.

centaur In Greek mythology, a creature with the head, arms, and torso of a man and the legs and hind quarters of a horse.

centering A temporary structure which supports the **vault**, **arch**, or **dome** during construction until the mortar is fully dried and the **arch** is self-sustaining.

central-plan building Any structure designed with a primary central space surrounded by symmetrical areas on each side. For example, **Greek-cross plan** (equal armed cross).

Chacmool In Mayan sculpture, a half-reclining figure, often **monumental** in scale and carved in a blocky **style**. Probably representing offering bearers. Chacmools can be found at Chichen Itza.

chaitya A type of Buddhist temple found in India. Built in the **form** of a hall or basilica, a chaitya hall is highly decorated with sculpture, and usually carved from a cave or natural rock location. It houses the sacred shrine or **stupa** for worship.

chamfer The slanted surface produced when an angle is trimmed or beveled, common in building and metalwork.

château (châteaux) The country house or castle of a French aristocrat. Usually built on a grand scale, châteaux are luxurious homes intended for an elegant lifestyle (although many do incorporate defensive fortifications such as **moats** and towers).

chattri (chattra) A decorative pavilion with an umbrella-shaped **dome** common in Indian architecture.

cherub (cherubim) The second highest order of angels (*see* **seraph**). Popularly, an idealized small child, usually depicted naked and with wings.

chevet The easternmost end of an oriented church, including the **crossing** (such as the **apse**, **ambulatory**, and radiating apsidal chapels).

chevron A decorative **motif** made up of repeated inverted Vs.

chiaroscuro An Italian word designating the relative contrast of dark and light in a painting, drawing, or print. Artists use chiaroscuro to create spatial depth and **volumetric forms** through slight gradations in the intensity of light and shadow.

chinoiserie The imitation of Chinese art and **style** common in the eighteenth century, and related to the lighthearted art of the Rococo period.

chip carving A type of decorative incision on wood, usually made with a knife or chisel, characterized by small **geometric** patterns and often found on furniture.

chiton A thin sleeveless garment, fastened at waist and shoulders, worn by men and women in ancient Greece.

choir The section of a church, usually between the **crossing** and the **apse**, where the clergy officiate.

chromolithography A type of **lithographic** process utilizing color. A new stone is made for each color, and all are printed onto the same piece of paper to create a single, colorful lithographic image.

chronophotography In the mid-nineteenth century, the development of the camera to the point where quick shutter speeds allowed the freezing of motion, enabling photographers to use multiple-exposure photographs to analyze movement. Chronophotographs, such as those by Eadward Muybridge, showed the subject against a black background performing a particular action, each frame depicting a different moment in the movement.

churrigeresque A showy, **painterly style** of Baroque architecture and ornament seen in Spain, Portugal, and Latin America, named after the Spanish architect José Benito de Churriguera (1665–1725).

ciborium An honorific pavilion erected in Christian churches to mark places of particularly sacred significance, such as an **altar**. The ciborium usually consists of a domed roof supported by **columns**, all highly decorated. Also: the receptacle for the **Eucharist** in the Catholic Mass. *See* baldachin.

circus An oval arena built by ancient Romans and usually enclosed by raised seats for spectators.

citadel An area of a fortress or defended city placed in a high, commanding spot.

clapboard Horizontal planks used as protective siding for buildings, particularly houses in North America.

Classical A term referring to the art and architecture of the ancient Greeks and Romans.

classical, classicism Any aspect of later art or architecture reminiscent of the rules, canons, and examples of the art of ancient Greece and Rome. Also: in general, any art aspiring to the qualities of restraint, balance, and rational **order** exemplified by the ancients.

Classical orders See order.

clerestory The topmost zone of a wall with windows (especially of a church or temple), when it extends above any abutting aisles or secondary roofs. Provides direct light into the central interior space.

cloison *See* **cloisonné**.

cloisonné A technique in **enameled** decoration of metal involving metal wire (**filigree**) that is affixed to the surface in a design. The resulting areas (**cloisons**) are filled with decorative enamel.

cloister An open space, part of a monastery or church, surrounded by an arcaded or **colonnaded** walkway, often having a fountain and garden, and dedicated to non-liturgical activities and the secular life of the religious. Members of a cloistered order do not interact with outsiders.

cloth of honor A piece of fabric, usually rich and highly decorated, hung behind a person of great rank on ceremonial occasions. Signifying the exalted status of the space before it, cloths of honor can be found behind thrones as well as **altars**, or behind representations of holy figures.

codex (codices) A book, or a group of **manuscript** pages, held together by stitching or other binding on one side.

codex style A **style** of vase painting derived from the fluid and elegant script of **manuscripts**.

coffer A recessed decorative panel that, with many other similar ones, is used to decorate ceilings or **vaults**. The use of coffers is called coffering.

coiling A technique in basketry. Coiled baskets are made from a spiraling structure to which another material is sewn.

collage A technique in which cutout paper forms (often painted or printed) are pasted onto another surface in a **composition**. Also: an image created using this technique.

colonnade A sequence or row of **columns**, supporting a straight **lintel** (as in a **porch** or **portico**) or a series of **arches** (an arcade).

colonnette A small **column**like vertical element, usually found attached to a **pier**. Colonnettes are decorative features, and they can reach into the **vaulted** sections of the building, contributing to the vertical effect of a Gothic cathedral.

colophon The data placed at the end of a book, especially a late medieval **manuscript**, listing the book's author, publisher, illuminator, and other information related to its production.

colossal order *See* **order**.

column An architectural element used for support and/or decoration. Consists of a rounded vertical **shaft** placed on a block (base) topped by a larger, usually decorative block (**capital**). Usually built in accordance with the rules of one of the architectural **orders**. Although usually freestanding, **columns** can be attached to a background wall (**engaged**).

column statue A carved **column**, depicting usually a religious person but also **allegorical** or mythological themes.

complementary color The primary and secondary colors across from each other on the color wheel (red and green, blue and orange, yellow and purple). When juxtaposed, the intensity of both colors increase.

Composite order *See* **order**.

composition The arrangement of elements in an artwork.

compound pier Typically found in a Romanesque or Gothic church, a compound pier is a **pier** or large **column** with multiple **shafts**, **pilasters**, or **colonnettes** attached to it on one or all sides.

conch A semicircular recess, such as an **apse** or **niche**, with a half-dome **vault**.

concrete A building material invented by the Romans, which is easily poured or molded when wet, and hardens into a particularly strong and durable stonelike substance. Made primarily from lime, sand, cement, and rubble mixed with water.

cone mosaic An early type of surface decoration created by pressing colored cones of baked clay into prepared wet plaster; associated with Sumerian architecture.

cong A square or octagonal tube made of jade with a cylindrical hole in the center. A symbol of the earth, it was used for ritual worship and astronomical observations in ancient China.

connoisseurship A term derived from the French word connoisseur, meaning "an expert," and signifying the practice of art history based primarily on formal, visual, and stylistic analysis. A connoisseur studies the **style** and technique of an object to deduce its relative quality and possible maker. This is done through visual association with other, similar objects and styles the connoisseur has seen in his or her study. *See also* **contextualism, formalism**.

content When discussing a work of art, the term can include all of the following: its subject matter; the ideas contained in the work; the artist's intention; and even its meaning for the beholder.

contextualism A methodological approach in art history which focuses on the cultural background of an art object. Unlike **connoisseurship**, contextualism utilizes the literature, history, economics, and social developments (among others) of a period, as well as the object itself, to explain the meaning of an artwork. *See also* **connoisseurship**.

contrapposto A way of representing the human body so that its weight appears to be borne on one leg. Contrapposto first appears in sculpture from the ancient Greece, when sculptors adopted a great degree of **naturalism** in their works.

corbel, corbeling Early roofing and **arching** technique in which each **course** of stone projects inward and slightly beyond the previous layer (a corbel) until the uppermost cobels meet. Results in a high, narrowly pointed **arch** or **vault**. A corbel table is a table supported underneath by corbels.

corbel arch *See* **arch**.

corbel vault *See* **vault**.

Corinthian order *See* **order**.

cornice The uppermost section of a **Classical entablature**. More generally, any horizontally projecting element of a building, usually found at the top of a wall or a **pedestal**. A raking cornice is formed by the junction of two slanted cornices, most often found in **pediments**.

course A horizontal layer of stone used in building.

cove A concave **molding** or area of ceiling where a wall and ceiling converge. A cove ceiling incorporates such moldings on all sides.

cove ceiling *See* **cove**.

crenellation A pattern of open notches built into the top **parapets** and battlements of many fortified buildings for the purposes of defense.

crocket A leaflike decorative element found in Gothic architecture, often on **pinnacles** and

gables. A crocket is shaped like an open leaf that gently curves outward, its edges curling up.

cromlech In prehistoric architecture, a circular arrangement of **menhirs**.

cross vault *See* **vault**.

cross-hatching A technique primarily used in printmaking and drawing, in which a set of parallel lines (hatching) is drawn across a previous set, but from a differing (usually right) angle. Cross-hatching gives a great density of **tone**, and allows the artist to create the illusion of shadows efficiently.

crossing The part of a cross-shaped church where the **nave** and the **transept** meet, often marked on the exterior by a tower or **dome**.

cruciform A term describing anything that is cross-shaped, as in the cruciform **plan** of a church.

crypt The **vaulted** underground space beneath the floor of a church, usually under the sanctuary which may contain tombs and relics.

cubiculum (cubicula) A private chamber for burial in the **catacombs**. The **sarcophagi** of the affluent were housed there in **arched** wall **niches**.

cuneiform writing An early form of writing with wedge-shaped marks; impressed into wet clay with a **stylus**, primarily by ancient Mesopotamians.

curtain wall A wall in a building that does not support any of the weight of the structure. Also: the freestanding outer wall of a castle, usually encircling the inner **bailey** and **keep**.

cycle A series of paintings, **frescoes**, or **tapestries** depicting a single story or theme intended to be displayed together.

cyclopean construction A prehistoric method of building, utilizing megalithic blocks of rough-hewn stone. Any large-scale, **monumental** building project that impresses by sheer size. Named after one-eyed giants of legendary strength from Greek myths.

cylinder seal A small cylindrical stone decorated with **incised** patterns. When rolled across soft clay or wax, a raised pattern or design (relief) is made, which served in Mesopotamian and Indus Valley cultures as an identifying signature.

dado (dadoes) The lower part of a wall, differentiated in some way (by a **molding** or different color) from the upper section. Also: the part of a **pedestal** between the base and the **cornice**, usually constructed of plain stone without decoration.

daguerrotype An early photographic process invented and marketed in 1839 by Louis-Jacques Mondé Daguerre. The first practically possible photographic system, a daguerrotype was a positive print made on a light-sensitized copperplate.

Day-Glo A trademark name for fluorescent painted materials.

Deesis In Byzantine art, the representation of Christ flanked by the Virgin Mary and Saint John the Baptist.

demotic writing An informal script developed by the ancient Greeks in about the eighth century BCE, and used exclusively for nonsacred texts.

dentil Small, toothlike blocks arranged in a continuous band to decorate a **Classical entablature**.

diorama A large painting made to create an environment, giving the viewer an impression of being at the site depicted. Usually hung on several walls of a room and specially lit, the diorama was a popular attraction in the nineteenth century, and was sometimes exhibited with sculpted figures.

dipteral A term that describes a building with a double **peristyle**, that is, surrounded by two rows of **columns**.

diptych Two panels of equal size (usually decorated with paintings or reliefs) hinged together.

dogu Small human figurines made in Japan during the Jomon period. Shaped from clay with exaggerated expressions and in contorted poses, dogu were probably used in religious rituals.

dolmen A prehistoric structure made up of two or more large (often upright) stones supporting a large, flat, horizontal slab or slabs (called **capstones**).

dome A **round vault**, usually over a circular space. Consists of the supporting vertical wall (**drum**), from which the **vault** springs, and a curved masonry **vault** of shapes and cross sections that can vary from hemispherical to bulbous to **ovoidal**. May be crowned by an open space (**oculus**) and/or an exterior **lantern**. When a dome is built over a square space, an intermediate element is required to make the transition to a circular drum. There are two types: A dome on **pendentives** (spherical triangles) incorporates **arch**ed, sloping intermediate sections of wall that carry the weight and thrust of the dome to heavily **buttressed** supporting **piers**. A dome on **squinches** uses an **arch** built into the wall (squinch) in the upper corners of the space to carry the weight of the dome across the corners of the square space below.

donjon See **keep**.

Doric order *See* **order**.

dormer A vertical window built into a sloping roof. A dormer window has its own roof and side walls that adjoin the body of the roof proper.

dressed stone A highly finished, precisely cut block of stone. When laid with others in even **courses**, dressed stone creates a uniform face with fine joints. Most often used as a facing on the visible exterior of a building, especially as a **veneer** for the **facade**. Also called ashlar.

drillwork The technique of using a drill for the creation of certain effects in sculpture.

drum The wall that supports a **dome**. Also: a segment of the circular **shaft** of a **column**.

drypoint An **intaglio** printmaking process by which a metal (usually copper) plate is directly inscribed by means of a pointed instrument (**stylus**). The resulting design of scratched lines is inked, wiped, and printed. Also: the print made by this process.

earthworks Artwork and/or sculpture, usually on a large scale, created by manipulating the natural environment. Also: the earth walls of a fort.

easel painting Any painting of small to intermediate size that can be executed on an artist's easel.

echinus A cushionlike circular element found below the **abacus** of a **Doric capital**. Also: a similarly shaped **molding** (usually with **egg-and-dart motifs**) underneath the **volutes** of an **Ionic capital**.

edition A single printing of a book or print. An edition can be of differing numbers but includes only what is printed at a particular moment, usually pulled from the same press by the same publisher.

egg-and-dart A decorative **molding** made up of an alternating pattern of round (egg) and downward-pointing, tapered (dart) elements.

elevation The arrangement, proportions, and details of any vertical side or face of a building. Also: an architectural drawing showing an exterior or interior wall of a building. A building's main elevation is usually its **facade**.

emblema (emblemata) In a **mosaic**, the elaborate central **motif** on a floor, usually a self-contained unit done in a more refined manner, with smaller **tesserae** of both marble and semiprecious stones. Also: an object or action represented in painting, prints, and drawings as a symbol for an idea, action, or other subject (as in an **allegory**). Emblemata are commonly associated with seventeenth-century Dutch art.

emblem book A collection of individual symbolic images, often concerning a single theme, and published with texts or verse. These books were sometimes used by artists as a source of inspiration. They were especially popular as literature in the Netherlands and England during the sixteenth and seventeenth centuries.

embossing *See* **repoussé**.

embroidery The technique in needlework of decorating fabric by stitching designs and figures of colored threads of fine material (such as silk) into another material (such as cotton, wool, leather, or paper). Also: the material produced by this technique.

emotionalism Any aspect of art that appeals overtly to sentimentality, melodrama, excitement, or other strong emotion.

enamel A technique in which powdered glass is applied to a metal surface in a decorative design. After firing, the glass forms an opaque or transparent substance that is fixed to the metal background. Also: an object created with enamel technique.

encaustic A type of painting technique utilizing pigments mixed with a **medium** of hot wax. Encaustic paintings were typically made in ancient times, particularly in Egypt, Greece, and Rome.

engaged column *See* **column**.

engraving An **intaglio** printmaking process of inscribing an image, design, or letters onto a metal or wood surface from which a print is made. An engraving is usually drawn with a sharp implement (burin) directly onto the surface of the plate. Also: the print made from this process.

entablature In the **Classical orders**, the horizontal elements above the **columns** and **capitals**. The entablature consists of, from top to bottom, a **cornice**, **frieze**, and **architrave**.

entasis A slight bulge built into the **shaft** of a Greek **column**. The optical illusion of entasis makes the **column** appear from afar to be straight.

etching An **intaglio** printmaking process, in which a metal plate is coated with acid-resistant resin and then inscribed with a **stylus** in a design, revealing the plate below. The plate is then immersed in acid, and the design of exposed metal is eaten away by the acid. The resin is removed, leaving the design etched permanently into the metal and the plate ready to be inked, wiped, and printed.

Eucharist The central rite of the Christian church, from the Greek word "thanksgiving." Also known as the Mass or Holy Communion, it is based on the Last Supper. According to traditional Catholic Christian belief, consecrecrated bread and wine become the body and blood of Christ; in Protestant belief, bread and wine symbolize body and blood.

exedra (exedrae) In architecture, a semicircular **niche**. On a small scale, often used as decoration, whereas larger exedrae can form interior spaces (such as an **apse**).

expressionism, expressionistic Terms describing a work of art in which **forms** are created primarily to evoke subjective emotions rather than to portray objective reality.

extrados The upper, curving surface of a **vault** or **arch**. *See also* **intrados**.

facade The face or front wall of a building.

faience A **glazing** technique for ceramic vessels, utilizing a glass paste that, upon firing, acquires a lustrous shine and smooth texture.

faktura An idea current among Russian Constructivist artists and other Russian artists of the early twentieth century that referred to the inherent **forms** and colors suitable to different materials. Used primarily in their mixed-**medium** constructions of a **nonrepresentational** type, faktura focused the artists' attention on the manner in which different materials create a variety of effects.

fang ding A square or rectangular bronze vessel with four legs. The *fang ding* was used for ritual offerings in ancient China during the Shang dynasty.

fête galante A subject in painting depicting well-dressed people at leisure in a park or country setting. It is most often associated with eighteenth-century French Rococo painting and the work of Antoine Watteau.

filigree Delicate, lacelike ornamental work of interwined wire.

finial A knoblike architectural decoration usually found at the top point of a spire, **pinnacle**, canopy, or **gable**. Also found on furniture.

flower piece Any painting with flowers as the primary subject. **Still lifes** of flowers became particularly popular in the seventeenth century in the Netherlands and Flanders.

fluting In architecture, evenly spaced parallel vertical grooves **incised** on **shafts** of **columns** or columnar elements (such as **pilasters**).

flying buttress *See* **buttress**.

folio A large sheet of paper, which, when folded and cut, becomes four separate or **parchment** pages in a book. Also: a page or leaf in a **manuscript** or book; more generally, any large book.

foreground Within the depicted space of an artwork, the area that is closest to the **picture plane**.

foreshortening The illusion created on a flat painted or drawn surface in which figures and objects appear to recede or project sharply into space. Often accomplished according to the rules of **perspective**.

form In speaking of a work of art or architecture, the term refers to purely visual components: line, color, shape, texture, mass, spatial qualities, and **composition**—all of which are called formal elements.

formal elements *See* **form**.

formalism, formalist An approach to the understanding, appreciation, and valuation of art based almost solely on considerations of **form**. This approach tends to regard an artwork as independent of its time and place of making.

formline In Native American works of art, a line that defines a space or **form**.

forum The central square of a Roman town, often used as a market or gathering area for the citizens. Site of most community temples and administrative buildings.

freestanding column *See* **column**.

fresco A painting technique in which water-based pigments are applied to a surface of wet plaster (called *buon fresco*). *Fresco secco* is created by painting on dried plaster. **Murals** made by both these techniques are called frescoes.

fresco secco *See* **fresco**.

frieze The middle element layer of an **entablature**, between the **architrave** and the **cornice**. Usually decorated with sculpture, painting, or **moldings**. Also: any continuous flat band with **relief sculpture** or painted decorations.

fritware A type of pottery made from a mix of white clay, quartz, and other chemicals that, when fired, produces a highly brittle substance.

frontispiece An illustration opposite or preceding the title page of a book. Also: the primary **facade** or main entrance bay of a building.

frottage A design produced by laying a piece of paper over a relief or **incised** pattern and rubbing with charcoal or other soft **medium**.

fusuma Sliding doors covered with paper, used in an East Asian house. Fusuma are often highly decorated with paintings and colored backgrounds.

gable The triangular wall space found on the end wall of a building between the two sides of a pitched roof. Also: a triangular decorative panel that has a gablelike shape.

gadrooning A form of decoration on architecture and in metalwork; characterized by sequential convex **moldings** that curve around a circular surface.

galleria In church architecture, the story found above the side aisles of a church, usually open to and overlooking the **nave**. Also: in secular architecture, a long room, usually above the ground floor in a private house or a public building, used for entertaining, exhibiting pictures or promenading. In English, gallery.

garbhagriha From the Sanskrit word meaning "womb chamber," a small room or shrine in a Hindu temple containing a holy image.

genre A type or category of artistic form, subject, technique, **style**, or **medium**. *See also* **genre painting**.

genre painting A term used to loosely categorize paintings depicting scenes of everyday life, including (among others) domestic interiors, merry companies, inn scenes, and street scenes.

geoglyphs Earthen designs on a colossal scale, often created in a landscape as if to be seen from an aerial viewpoint.

geometric A term describing Greek art, especially pottery, from about 1100 to 600 bce and characterized by patterns of rectangles, squares, and other **abstract** shapes. Also: any **style** or art using primarily these shapes.

gesso A thick **medium** usually made from glue, gypsum, and/or chalk and often forming the ground, or priming layer, of a canvas. A gesso ground gives a smooth surface for painting and seals the absorbency of the canvas.

gesturalism The motivation behind painting and drawing in which the brushwork or line visibly records the artist's physical gesture at the moment the paint was applied or the lines laid down. Associated especially with expressive **styles**, such as European Baroque, Zen painting, and Abstract Expressionism.

gilding The application of paper-thin **gold leaf** to an object made from another **medium** (for example, a sculpture or painting). Usually used as a decorative finishing detail.

giornata Adopted from the Italian term meaning "a day's work," a giornata is the section of a **fresco** plastered and painted in a single day.

glaze *See* **glazing**.

glazing In ceramics, a method of treating earthenwares with an outermost layer of vitreous liquid (glaze) that, upon firing, renders a waterproof and decorative surface. In painting, a technique particularly used with oil **mediums** in which a transparent layer of paint (glaze) is laid over another, usually lighter, painted or glazed area.

gloss A type of clay **slip** used in ceramics by ancient Greeks and Romans that, when fired, imparts a colorful sheen to the surface.

gold leaf Paper-thin sheets of hammered gold that are used in **gilding**. In some cases (such as Byzantine **icons**), also used as a ground for paintings.

golden section A **linear** measurement said to be of ideal proportions, supposedly discovered by the ancient Greeks. When the measurement is divided into two, the smaller part is the same proportion to the larger as the larger is to the whole.

Good Shepherd A man carrying a sheep or with a sheep at his side. In **Classical** art, the god Hermes; in Christian art, Jesus Christ (an image inspired by the Old Testament 23rd Psalm or the New Testament parable of the Good Shepherd).

gopura The towering gateway to an Indian Hindu **temple complex**. A temple complex can have several different gopuras.

gouache A type of opaque watercolor that has a distinctive, chalky effect.

graffiti Imposed on public structures by anonymous persons, graffiti usually consists of drawings and/or text of an obscene, political, or violent nature, and can be found in all periods and all **mediums**.

Grand Manner A grand and elevated **style** of painting popular in the Neoclassical period of the eighteenth century. An artist working in the Grand Manner looked to the ancients and to the Renaissance for inspiration; for portraits as well as **history painting**, the artist would adopt the poses, **compositions**, and attitudes of Renaissance and antique models.

granulation A technique for decorating gold in which tiny balls of the precious metal are fused to the main surface in a pattern.

graphic arts A term referring to those branches of the arts that utilize paper as primary support. The graphic arts, whether drawn, typeset, or printed, often have a heavy emphasis on **linear** means of expression.

graphic design A concern in the visual arts for shape, line, and two-dimensional patterning, often especially apparent in works including typography and lettering.

Greek-cross plan *See* **central-plan building**.

Greek-key pattern *See* **meander**.

grid A system of regularly spaced horizontally and vertically crossed lines that gives regularity to an architectural **plan**. Also: in painting, a grid enables designs to be enlarged or transferred easily.

griffin A creature with the head, wings, and claws of an eagle and the body and hind legs of a lion.

grisaille A painting executed primarily in various **tones** of gray.

groin vault *See* **vault**.

groundline The solid baseline that indicates the ground plane of an image on which the figure stands. In ancient representations, such as those of the Egyptian, the figures and the objects are placed on the groundline without reference to their actual spatial relationships.

grout A soft cement placed between the **tesserae** of a **mosaic** to hold the design together. Also used in tiling.

guild An association of craftspeople. The medievalguild had great political power, as it controlled the selling and marketing of its members' products, and it provided economic protection, political solidarity, and training in the craft to its members. An artists' guild was usually dedicated to Saint Luke, the patron saint of artists.

half-barrel vault *See* **vault**.

half-timber construction A method of building, particularly in heavily timbered northern European areas, for vernacular structures. Beginning with a timber framework built in the post-and-lintel manner, the builder constructed walls between the timbers with bricks, mud, or wattle. The exterior could then be faced with plaster or other material.

hall church A church (typified by those in the Gothic style in Germany), with a **nave** and aisles that are all the same height, giving the impression of a large, open hall.

halos An outdoor pavement used by ancient Greeks for ceremonial dancing.

handscroll A long, narrow, horizontal painting or text (or combination thereof) common in Chinese and Japanese art, and of a size intended for individual use. A handscroll is stored wrapped tightly around a wooden pin and is unrolled for viewing or reading.

hanging scroll In Chinese and Japanese art, a vertically oriented painting or text mounted within sections of silk. At the top is a semicircular rod; at the bottom is a round dowel. Hanging scrolls are kept rolled and tied except for special occasions, when they are hung for display, contemplation, or commemoration.

haniwa Pottery figures that were placed on top of Japanese tombs or burial mounds.

happening A type of art form incorporating performance, theater, and visual images developed in the 1960s. A happening was organized without a specific narrative or intent; with audience participation, the event proceeded according to chance and individual improvisation.

header In building, a brick laid so that its end, rather than its side, faces out.

heliograph A type of early photograph created by the exposure to sunlight of a plate coated with light-sensitive asphalt.

hemicycle A semicircular interior space or structure.

henge A circular area enclosed by stones or wood posts set up by Neolithic peoples. It is usually bounded by a ditch and raised embankment.

herm A statue that has the head and torso of a human, but the lower part of which is a plain, tapering **pillar** of rectangular shape. Used primarily for architectural decoration.

hieratic In painting and sculpture, when the concern to communicate spiritual values results in a formalized, grand **style** for representing rulers, or sacred or priestly figures. Can also be seen in the use of different scales for holy figures and those of the everyday world.

hieratic scale The larger the figure, the greater the importance.

hieroglyphic Picture writing signs rendered in the form of pictorial symbols, utilized primarily for sacred names and ceremonial inscriptions (**cartouches**) by the ancient Egyptians.

high relief *See* **relief sculpture**.

himation In ancient Greece, a garment wrapped around the body, with a rectangular piece of cloth thrown over the shoulder. Worn by both men and women.

historicism A nineteenth-century consciousness of and attention to the newly available and accurate knowledge of the past, made accessible by historical research, textual study, and archeology.

history painting The term used to denote those paintings that include figures in any kind of historical, mythological, or biblical narrative. Considered since the Renaissance (until the twentieth century) as the noblest form of art, history paintings generally convey a high moral or intellectual idea, and often painted in a grand pictorial **style**.

hollow-casting *See* **lost-wax casting**.

horizon line A horizontal "line" formed by the actual or implied meeting point of earth and sky. In **linear perspective**, the **vanishing point** or points are located on this line.

horseshoe arch *See* **arch**.

house-church In early Christian times, any small and relatively secret church located in a private home.

house-synagogue A Jewish place of worship located in a private home.

hue Pure color. The saturation or intensity of the hue depends on the purity of the color. Its **value** depends in its lightness or darkness.

hydria A large ancient Greek and Roman jar with three handles (horizontal ones at both sides and one vertical at the back), used for storing water.

hypogeum (hypogea) *See* **catacomb**.

hypostyle hall Marked by numerous rows of tall, closely spaced **columns**. In ancient Egyptian architecture, a large interior room of a **temple complex** preceding the **sanctuary**.

icon A painted, **low relief** or **mosaic** image representing a sacred figure or event in the Byzantine, and later the Orthodox, church. Icons were venerated by the faithful who believed them to have miraculous powers.

iconoclasm The banning or destruction of **icons** and religious art. Iconoclasm in eighth and ninth century Byzantium and sixteenth and seventeenth century Protestant territories arose from differing beliefs about the power, meaning, function and purpose of imagery in religion.

iconography In the visual arts, the study of the **subject matter** of a representation and its meaning.

iconology The study of the significance and interpretation of the **subject matter** of art. Iconology often incorporates contextual evidence regarding traditions of representation of specific subjects to aid in understanding.

iconostasis The wall or screen in an Early Christian, Byzantine or Greek Orthodox church between the **sanctuary** (where the Mass is performed) and the body of the church (where the congregation assembles). The iconostasis was usually hung with **icons**.

idealization A process in art through which artists strive to make their forms and figures attain perfection, based on pervading cultural values or their own mental image of what the ideal is.

ideograph A **motif** or written character that expresses an idea or symbolizes an action in the world. It is distinct from a **pictograph**, which symbolizes or represents an actual object, person, or thing. Egyptian hieroglyphs and Chinese calligraphs are examples of writing which consist of both ideographs and pictographs.

illumination A painting on paper or **parchment** used as illustration and/or decoration for **manuscripts** or **albums**. Usually done in rich colors, often supplemented by gold and other precious materials. The illustrators are referred to as illuminators. Also: the technique of decorating manuscripts with such paintings.

illusionism, illusionistic An appearance of reality in art created by the use of certain pictorial means, such as **perspective** and **foreshortening**. Also: the quality of having this type of appearance.

impost, impost block A block, serving to concentrate the weight above, imposed between the **capital** of a **column** and the springing of an **arch** above.

impression Any single printing of an **intaglio** print (**engraving, drypoint** or **etching**). Each and every impression of a print is by nature different, given the possibilities for variation inherent in the printing process, which requires the plate to be inked and wiped between every impression.

in antis Term used to describe the position of **columns** set between two walls, as in a **portico** or a **cella**.

incising A technique in which a design or inscription is cut into a hard surface with a sharp instrument.

ink painting A **style** of painting developed in China using only monochrome colors, usually black ink with gray washes. Ink painting was often used by artists of the **literati painting** tradition and is connected with Zen Buddhism.

inlay A decorative process in which pieces of one material are set into the surface of an object fashioned from a different material.

intaglio Term used for a technique in which the design is carved out of the surface of an object, such an engraved seal stone. In the **graphic arts**, intaglio includes **engraving**, **etching**, and **drypoint**—all processes in which ink transfers to paper from **incised**, ink-filled lines cut into a metal plate.

intarsia The decoration of wood surfaces with **inlaid** designs created of contrasting materials such as metal, shell, and ivory.

interlace A type of **linear** decoration particularly popular in early medieval art, in which ribbon-like bands are **illusionistically** depicted as if woven under and over one another.

intrados The curving inside surface of an **arch** or **vault**. *See also* **extrados**.

intuitive perspective *See* **perspective**.

Ionic order *See* **order**.

isometric projection A building diagram that represents graphically the parts of a building. Isometric projections have all planes of the building parallel to two established vertical and horizontal axes. The vertical axis is true, while the horizontal is drawn at an angle to show the effect of recession. All dimensions in an isometric drawing are proportionally correct. *See also* **plan**, **section**.

iwan A large, **vaulted** chamber in a **mosque** with a **monumental arched** opening on one side.

jamb In architecture, the vertical element found in pairs on both sides of an opening in a wall, such as a door or window.

japonisme A **style** in French and American nineteenth-century art that was highly influenced by Japanese art, especially prints.

joined-wood sculpture A method of constructing large-scale wooden sculpture developed in Japan. The entire work is constructed from smaller hollow blocks, each individually carved, and assembled when complete. The joined-wood technique allowed the production of larger sculpture, as the multiple joints alleviate the problems of drying and cracking found with sculpture carved from a single block.

ka The name given by ancient Egyptians to the human life force, or spirit.

kantharos A type of Greek vase or goblet with two large handles and a wide mouth.

keep The most heavily fortified defensive structure in a castle, a tower located at the heart of the castle complex.

kente A woven cloth made by the Ashanti peoples of Africa. *Kente* cloth is woven in long, narrow pieces in complex and colorful patterns, which are then sewn together.

key block A key block is the master block in the production of a colored **woodcut**, which requires different blocks for each color. The key block is a flat piece of wood with the entire design carved or drawn on its surface. From this, other blocks with partial drawings are made for printing the areas of different colors.

keystone The topmost **voussoir** at the center of an **arch**, usually the last block to be placed. The pressure of this block holds the arch together. Often of a larger size and/or highly decorated.

kiln An oven designed to produce enough heat for the baking, or firing, of clay.

kiva Structure in a Native American pueblo used for community gatherings and rituals.

kondo The main hall inside a Japanese Buddhist temple where the images of Buddha are housed.

kore An archaic Greek statue of a young woman.

kouros An archaic Greek statue of a young man or boy.

krater An ancient Greek vessel for mixing wine and water, with many subtypes that each have a distinctive shape. **Calyx krater**: a bell-shaped vessel with handles near the base that resemble a flower calyx. **Volute krater**: a type of krater with handles shaped like scrolls.

kylix A shallow Greek vessel or cup, used for drinking, with a wide mouth and small handles near the rim.

lacquer A type of hard, glossy surface varnish used on objects in East Asian cultures. Lacquer can be layered and manipulated or combined with pigments and other materials for various decorative effects.

lakshana Term used to designate the thirty-two marks of the Buddha. These characteristics of the historical Buddha have come to be part of the **iconography** of the Buddha in general. The *lakshana* include, among others, the Buddha's golden body, his long arms, the wheel impressed on his palms and the soles of his feet, and his elongated earlobes.

lancet A tall narrow window crowned by a sharply pointed **arch**, typically found in Gothic architecture.

landscape architecture Any design for an outdoor space.

landscape painting A painting in which a natural outdoor scene or vista is the primary subject.

lantern A cylindrical **turret**like structure situated on top of a **dome**, with windows that allow light into the space below.

Latin-cross plan A cross-shaped building plan, incorporating one longer arm (**nave**) and three arms of equal length.

lectionary An ecclesiastical book containing readings from Christian Scripture. It is the book from which the officiant reads to the congregation during holy services.

lekythos A slim Greek oil vase with one handle and a narrow mouth.

limner The name used to denote an artist, particularly a portrait painter, in England during the sixteenth and seventeenth centuries and in New England during the eighteenth and nineteenth centuries.

linear, linearity A descriptive term indicating an emphasis on line, as opposed to mass or color, in art.

linear perspective *See* **perspective**.

lingam shrine A place of worship centered on an object or representation in the form of a phallus (the lingam), which symbolizes the power of the Hindu god Shiva.

lintel A horizontal element of any material carried by two or more vertical supports to form an opening.

list An open section of the grounds of a fortified building or castle, usually in the bailey, that was set aside for knightly combat.

literary illustration An image or artwork with a subject or **content** drawn from a literary source.

literati *See* **literati painting**.

literati painting A **style** of painting that reflects the taste of the educated class of East Asian intellectuals and scholars. Aspects include an appreciation for the antique, smaller scale, and an intimate connection between maker and audience.

lithograph A print made from a design drawn on a flat stone block with greasy crayon. Ink is applied to the stone, and when printed, adheres only to the open areas of the design. *See also* **chromolithography**.

loculus (loculi) A **niche** in a tomb or **catacomb** in which a **sarcophagus** was placed.

loggia Italian term for a covered open-air gallery. Often used as a corridor between buildings or around a courtyard, loggia usually have arcades or **colonnades** and an upper story.

lost-wax casting A method of casting metal, such as bronze, by a process in which a wax mold is covered with clay and plaster, then fired, melting the wax and leaving a hollow **form**. Molten metal is then poured into the hollow space and slowly cooled. When the hardened clay and plaster exterior shell is removed, a solid metal form remains to be smoothed and polished.

low relief *See* **relief sculpture**.

lozenge A decorative **motif** in the shape of a diamond.

lunette A semicircular wall area, framed by an **arch** over a door or window. Can be either plain or decorated.

lusterware A type of ceramic pottery decorated with **glazes**.

madrasa An Islamic institution of higher learning, where teaching is focused on theology, law, and the sciences.

maenad In ancient Greece, a female devotee of the wine god Dionysos who participated in orgiastic rituals. She is often depicted with swirling drapery. (Also called a Bacchante, after Bacchus, the Roman name of Dionysos.)

majolica Pottery painted with a tin **glaze** that, when fired, gives a lustrous and colorful surface.

maki-e In Japanese art, the effect achieved by sprinkling gold or silver powder on successive layers of **lacquer** before each layer dries.

mandala An image of the cosmos represented by an arrangement of circular or concentric **geometric** shapes containing diagrams or images. Used for meditation and contemplation, mandalas are most often found in Buddhist places of worship.

mandapa In a Hindu temple, an open hall dedicated to ritual worship.

mandorla An almond-shaped area in which a sacred figure, such as Christ, is represented.

manifesto A written declaration of an individual or group's ideas, purposes, and intentions.

manuscript A handwritten book or document.

maqsura A separate enclosure in a Muslim **mosque** near the **mihrab**, designated for dignitaries.

martyrium (martyria) In Christian architecture, a church, chapel, or shrine built over the grave of a martyr or the site of a great miracle.

mastaba A flat-topped, one-story building with slanted walls. Invented by the ancient Egyptians to mark a part of underground tombs.

mathematical perspective *See* **perspective**.

matte A surface that is smooth but without shine or luster.

mausoleum A **monumental** building used as a tomb. Named after the tomb of Mausolos erected at Halikarnassos around 350 BCE

meander A type of two-dimensional ornament made up of continuous **geometric motifs** and often used as a decorative border. Also called Greek-key pattern.

medallion In architecture, any round ornament or decoration. Also: a large medal.

medium (mediums, media) In general, the material from which any given object is made. In painting, the liquid substance in which pigments are suspended.

megaron The main hall of a Mycenaean palace or grand house. Usually of a rectangular shape and sometimes subdivided into two unequal spaces by **columns**.

memento mori From Latin terms meaning "reminder of death." An object, such as a skull or extinguished candle, typically found in a *vanitas* image, symbolizing the transience of life.

menhir A megalithic stone block, placed by prehistoric peoples in an upright position.

menorah A Jewish lamp, usually in the form of a candelabrum, divided into seven or nine branches; the nine-branched menorah is used during the celebration of Hanukkah. Representations of the seven-branched menorah, once used in the Temple of Jerusalem, became in general a symbol of Judaism.

mensa The blocklike table serving as the **altar** in a Christian church.

metope The rectangular spaces, sometimes decorated but often plain, between the triglyphs of a **Doric frieze**.

mezzanine Any intermediate story of a building inserted between two stories of regular size.

middle ground Within the depicted space of an artwork, the area that takes up the middle distance of the image. *See also* **foreground**.

mihrab A recess or **niche** that distinguishes the wall oriented toward Mecca (**qibla**) in a **mosque**.

minaret A tall slender tower on the exterior of a **mosque** from which believers are called to prayer.

minbar A high platform or pulpit in an Islamic **mosque**.

miniature A small-scale painting. Miniatures have a variety of uses, from illustrations within **albums** or **manuscripts** to intimate portraits.

mirador In Spanish and Islamic palace architecture, a room with windows and sometimes balconies on three sides overlooking gardens and courtyards.

mithuna The amorous male and female couples in Buddhist sculpture, usually found at the entrance to a sacred building. The *mithuna* symbolize the harmony and fertility of life.

moat A large ditch or canal dug around a castle or fortress for military defense. When filled with water, the moat protects the walls of the building from direct attack.

modeling In painting, the process of creating the illusion of three-dimensionality on a two-dimensional surface by use of light and **shade**. In sculpture, the process of molding a three-dimensional form out of a malleable substance.

module A segment or portion of a repeated design.

molding A shaped or sculpted strip with varying contours and patterns. Used as decoration on architecture, furniture, frames, and other objects.

monolith A single stone, often very large. Monoliths may be set up as focal points for rituals or to define a ritual space.

Monophysitism The Christian doctrine stating that Jesus Christ has only one nature, both divine and human. Declared a heresy in the fifth century.

monoprint A single print pulled from a hard surface (such as a blank plate or stone) that has been prepared with a painted design. Each print is an individual artwork, as the original design is a transient one, lost in the printing process.

monumental A term used to designate a project or object that, whatever its physical size, gives an impression of grandeur and excellence.

mortise-and-tenon joint A method of joining two elements. A projecting pin (tenon) on one element fits snugly into a hole designed for it (mortise) on the other. Such joints are very strong and flexible.

mosaic Images formed by small colored stone or glass pieces (**tesserae**), affixed to a hard, stable surface.

mosque An edifice used for communal Muslim worship.

motif Any recurring element of a design or **composition**. Also: a recurring theme or subject in artwork, often referring to those that can be easily separated from the whole for the purposes of copying or study.

movable-type printing A method of printing text in which the individual letters, cast on small pieces of metal (die), are assembled into words on a mechanical press. When each **edition** was complete, the type could be reused for the next project. Movable-type printing, invented around 1450, revolutionized the printing industry in Europe and allowed the large-scale dissemination of affordable books.

mudra A symbolic hand gesture in Indian art. The many different mudras each denote certain behaviors, actions, or feelings.

mullion A slender vertical element or **colonnette** that divides a window into subsidiary sections.

multiculturalism Recognition of all cultures and ethnicities in a society or civilization.

multiple-point perspective *See* **perspective**.

muqarna The **geometric** patterning used in Islamic architecture to smooth the transition between decorative flat and rounded surfaces; usually found on the **vault** of a **dome**.

mural A large painting or decoration, done either directly on the wall or separately and affixed to it.

naos In ancient art, *See* **cella**. In a Byzantine church, the **nave** and **sanctuary**.

narthex The rectangular vestibule at the main (usually western) entrance of a church. In Early Christian architecture, it can also be an entrance **porch** with **columns** on the outside of a church.

naturalism, naturalistic A **style** of depiction in which the physical appearance of the rendered image in nature is the primary inspiration. A naturalistic work appears to resemble visible nature.

nave The rectangular central aisle of a basilica, two or three stories high and flanked by aisles.

necking The **molding** at the top of the **shaft** of the **column**.

necropolis A large cemetery or burial area.

negative space Empty or open space within or bounding a painting, sculpture, or architectural design. Negative space emphasizes the overall **form** of the work.

niche A hollow or recess in a wall or other solid architectural element. Niches can be of varying size and shape, and may be intended for many different uses, from display of objects to housing of a tomb.

niello An **inlay** technique in which a black sulphur alloy is rubbed into fine lines engraved into a metal (usually gold or silver). The alloy becomes fused with the surrounded metal when heated, and provides contrasting detail.

nishiki-e A multicolored and ornate Japanese print.

nocturne A night scene in painting, usually lit by artifical illumination.

nonrepresentational A term describing any artwork of an **abstract** nature. Nonrepresentational art does not attempt to reproduce the appearance of the natural world.

obelisk A tall stone **shaft** of four-sided rectangular shape, hewn from a single block, that tapers at the top and is completed by a **pyramidion**. Erected by the ancient Egyptians in ceremonial spaces (such as entrances to **temple complexes**). Today used as commemorative monuments and sun symbols.

oblique perspective *See* **perspective**.

oculus (oculi) In architecture, a circular opening. Oculi are usually found either as windows or at the apex of a **dome**. When at the top of a **dome**, an oculus is either open to the sky or covered by a decorative exterior **lantern**.

odalisque A subject in painting of a reclining female nude, usually shown among the accoutrements of an exotic, haremlike environment.

ogival arch *See* **arch**.

oil painting Any painting executed with the pigments floating in a **medium** of oil. Oil paint has particular properties that allow for greater ease of working (among others, a slow drying time, which allows for corrections, and a great range of relative opaqueness of paint layers, which permits a high degree of detail and luminescence). It was adopted on a wide scale in Europe after about 1450.

oil sketch An **oil painting**, usually on a small scale, intended as a preliminary stage for the production of a larger work. Oil sketches are often very **painterly** in technique.

oinoche A Greek wine jug with a round mouth and a curved handle.

olpe Any Greek vase or jug without a spout.

one-point perspective *See* **perspective**.

openwork Decoration, such as **tracery**, with open spaces incorporated into the pattern. Also: a needlework technique in which some of the fabric support is left visible within the design.

oracle A person, usually a priest or priestess, who acts as a conduit for divine information. Also: the information itself or the place at which this information is communicated.

orant The representation, usually in ancient or Early Christian art, of a standing figure praying with outstretched arms.

order A system of proportions in **Classical** architecture. **Doric**: the **column shaft** of the Doric order can be **fluted** or smooth-surfaced and has no **base**. The Doric **capital** consists of an undecorated **echinus** and **abacus**. The Doric **entablature** has a plain **architrave**, a **frieze** with **metopes** and **triglyphs**, and a simple **cornice**. **Tuscan**: a variation of Doric characterized by a smooth-surfaced column shaft with a base, a plain architrave, and an undecorated frieze. **Ionic**: the column of the Ionic order has a base, a fluted shaft and a capital decorated with **volutes**. The Ionic entablature consists of an architrave of two panels and **moldings**, a frieze usually containing sculpted **relief** ornament, and a cornice with **dentils**. **Corinthian**: the most ornate of the orders, the Corinthian includes a base, a fluted column shaft with a capital elaborately decorated with **acanthus** leaf carvings. Its entablature consists of an architrave decorated with moldings, a frieze often containing sculptured reliefs, and a cornice with dentils. **Composite**: a combination of the Ionic and the Corinthian orders. The capital combines acanthus leaves with volute scrolls. A **colossal** order is any of the above built on a large scale, rising through several stories in height and often raised from the ground by a **pedestal**.

orthogonal Any line running back into the represented space of a picture perpendicular to the imagined **picture plane**. In **linear perspective**, all orthogonals converge at a single **vanishing point** in the picture and are the basis for a **grid** that maps out the internal space of the image. An orthogonal **plan** is any plan for a building or city that is based exclusively on right angles, such as the grid plan of many modern cities.

orthogonal plan *See* **orthogonal**.

ovoid An adjective describing a rounded oval object or shape. Also: a characteristic **form** in

Native American art, consisting of a rectangle with bent sides and rounded corners.

pagoda An East Asian temple in the **form** of a tower built with successively smaller, repeated stories. Each story is usually marked by an elaborate projecting roof.

painterly A **style** of painting, that emphasizes the techniques and surface effects of brushwork (also light and **shade**).

palace complex A group of buildings used for living and governing by a particular ruler, usually located in a fortress or **citadel**.

palette A handheld support used by artists for the storage and mixing of paint during the process of painting. Also: the choice of a range of colors made by an artist in a particular work, or typical of his or her **style**.

Palladian An adjective describing a style of architecture, or an architectural detail, reminiscent of the classicizing work of the sixteenth-century Italian architect Andrea Palladio.

palmette A fan-shaped ornament with radiating leaves.

panel painting Any painting executed on a wood support. The wood is usually planed to provide a smooth surface. A panel can consist of several boards joined together.

papyrus A native Egyptian riverine plant from the stems of which ancient Egyptians produced an early form of paper. The papyrus plant was a popular decorative element in Egyptian architecture.

parapet A low wall at the edge of a balcony, bridge, roof, or other place from which there is a steep drop, built for the safety of onlookers. A parapet walk is the passageway, usually open, immediately behind the uppermost exterior wall or battlement of a fortified building.

parapet walk *See* **parapet**.

parchment A writing surface made from treated skins of animals and used during antiquity and the Middle Ages.

Paris Salon The annual display of art by French artists in Paris during the eighteenth and nineteenth centuries. Established in the seventeenth century as a venue to show the work of members of the French **Academy**, the Salon and its judges established the accepted official **style** of the time.

parterre An ornamental, highly regimented flower bed. Parterres became a crucial element of the ornate gardens of seventeenth-century palaces and châteaux.

passage In painting, passage refers to any particular area within a work, often those where **painterly** brushwork or color changes exist. Also: a term used to describe Paul Cézanne's technique of blending adjacent shapes.

passage grave A prehistoric tomb under a cairn, reached by a long, narrow, slab-lined access passageway or passageways.

pastel Dry pigment, chalk, and gum in stick or crayon form.

pedestal A platform or base supporting a sculpture or other monument. Also: the block found below the base of a **Classical column** (or **colonnade**), serving to raise the entire element off the ground.

pediment A triangular **gable** found over major architectural elements such as **Classical** Greek **porticoes**, windows, or doors. Formed by an **entablature** and the ends of a sloping roof or a **raking cornice**. A similar architectural element is often used decoratively above a door or window, sometimes with a curved upper **molding**. A broken pediment is a variation on the traditional pediment, with an open space at the center of the topmost angle and/or the horizontal **cornice**. Often filled with a decorative element, such as a **cartouche**.

pendentive The concave triangular section of a wall that forms the transition between a square or polygonal space and the circular base of a **dome**.

pendentive dome *See* **dome**.

peplos A loose outer garment worn by women of ancient Greece. Belted below the bust or at the hips.

performance art An artwork based on a live, sometimes theatrical performance by the artist.

peripteral A term used to describe any building (or room) that is surrounded by a single row of **columns**. When such columns are engaged instead of freestanding, called pseudo-peripteral.

peristyle A surrounding **colonnade** in Greek architecture. A peristyle building is surrounded on the exterior by a colonnade. Also: a peristyle court is an open colonnaded courtyard, often having a pool and garden.

perspective A system for representing three-dimensional space on a flat surface. **Atmospheric perspective**: A method of rendering the effect of spatial distance on a two-dimensional plane by subtle variations in color and clarity of representation. **One-point** and **multiple-point perspective** (also called **linear**, scientific, or **mathematical perspective**): A method of creating the illusion of three-dimensional space on a two-dimensional surface by delineating a **horizon line** and multiple **orthogonal** lines. These recede to meet at one or more points on the horizon (called **vanishing points**), giving the appearance of spatial depth. Called scientific or mathematical because its use requires some knowledge of geometry and mathematics, as well as optics. **Intuitive perspective**: A method of representing three-dimensional space on a two-dimensional surface by the use of **formal elements** that act to give the impression of recession. This impression, however, is achieved by visual instinct, not by the use of an overall system or program (usually involving scientific principles or mathematics) for depicting the appearance of spatial depth. **Oblique perspective**: An intuitive spatial system used in painting, in which a building or room is placed with one corner in the **picture plane**, and the other parts of the structure all recede to an imaginary vanishing point on its other side. Oblique perspective is not a comprehensive, mathematical system. **Reverse perspective**: A Byzantine perspective theory in which the orthogonals or rays of sight do not converge on a vanishing point in the picture, but are thought to originate in the viewer's eye in front of the picture. Thus, in reverse perspective the image is constructed with orthogonals that diverge, giving a slightly tipped aspect to objects.

photomontage A photographic work created from many smaller photographs arranged (and often overlapping) in a **composition**.

piazza The Italian word for an open city square.

pictograph A highly stylized depiction serving as a symbol for a person or object. Also: a type of writing utilizing such symbols.

picture plane The theoretical spatial plane corresponding with the actual surface of a painting (usually vertical).

picture stone A stone used in medieval northern Europe as a commemorative monument, which is carved or inscribed with representations of human figures or symbolic **forms**.

picturesque A term describing the taste for the familiar, the pleasant, and the pretty, popular in the eighteenth and nineteenth centuries in Europe. When contrasted with the **sublime**, the picturesque stood for all that was ordinary but pleasant.

piece-mold casting A casting technique in which the mold consists of several sections that are connected during the pouring of molten metal, usually bronze. After the cast form has hardened, the pieces of the mold are then disassembled, leaving the completed object. Because it is made in pieces, the mold can be reused.

pier A masonry support made up of many stones, or rubble and **concrete** (in contrast to a **column shaft** which is formed a single stone or a series of drums), often square or rectangular in **plan**, and capable of carrying very heavy architectural loads. *See also* **compound pier**.

pietà A devotional subject in Christian religious art. After the Crucifixion the body of Jesus was laid across the lap of his grieving mother, Mary. When others are present the subject is called the Lamentation.

pietra dura (pietre dure) A type of **mosaic** made in relief from semiprecious stones. Popular among the Florentine nobility of the seventeenth century, pietre dure often depicted ornamental designs such as flowers or fruit.

pietra serena The gray Tuscan limestone used in Florence.

pilaster An engaged **columnar** element that is rectangular in format and used for decoration in architecture.

pillar In architecture, any large, freestanding vertical element. Usually functions as an important weight-bearing unit in buildings.

pinnacle In Gothic architecture, a steep pyramid decorating the top of another element such as a **buttress**.

plaiting In basketry, the technique of weaving strips of fabric or other flexible substances under and over each other.

plan A graphic convention for representing the arrangement of the parts of a building.

plasticity The three-dimensional quality of an object, or the degree to which any object can be modeled, shaped, or altered.

plinth The slablike base or **pedestal** of a **column**, statue, wall, building, or piece of furniture.

pluralism A social structure or goal that allows members of diverse ethnic, racial, or other groups to exist within the society while continuing to practice the customs of their own divergent cultures. Also: an adjective describing the state of having many valid contemporary **styles** available at the same time to artists.

podium A raised platform that acts as the foundation for a building. Most often used for Etruscan, Greek, and Roman temples.

polychromy The multicolored painted decoration applied to any part of a building, sculpture, or piece of furniture.

polyptych An **altarpiece** constructed from multiple panels, sometimes with hinges to allow for movable **wings**.

popular culture The elements of society that are recognized by the general public. Popular culture has the associations of something cheap, fleeting, and accessible to all.

porcelain A type of extremely hard and fine ceramic made from a mixture of kaolin and other minerals. Porcelain is fired at a very high heat, and the final product has a translucent surface.

porch The covered entrance on the exterior of a building. With a row of **columns** or **colonnade**, also called a **portico**.

portal A grand entrance, door, or gate, usually to an important public building, and often decorated with sculpture.

portcullis A fortified gate, constructed to move vertically and often made of metal bars, used for the defense of a city or castle.

portico In architecture, a projecting roof or **porch** supported by **columns**, often marking an entrance.

post-and-lintel construction An architectural system of construction with two or more vertical elements (posts) supporting a horizontal element (**lintel**).

postern A side entrance to a fortified city or castle, usually on a much smaller scale than the main gates.

potsherd A broken piece of ceramic **ware**.

predella The lower zone, or base, of an **altarpiece**, decorated with painting or sculpture related to the main iconographic theme of the altarpiece.

primary colors Blue, red, and yellow, the three colors from which all others are derived.

Prix de Rome A prestigious scholarship offered by the French **Academy** at the time of the establishment of its Roman branch in 1666. The scholarship allowed the winner of the prize to study in Rome for four years at the expense of the state. Originally intended only for painters and sculptors, the prize was later expanded to include printmakers, architects, and musicians.

pronaos The enclosed vestibule of a Greek or Roman temple, found in front of the **cella** and marked by a row of **columns** at the entrance.

propylon (propylaia) A large, often elaborate gateway to a temple or other important building.

proscenium The stage of an ancient Greek or Roman theater. In modern theater, the area of the stage in front of the curtain. Also: the framing **arch** which separates a stage from the audience.

prostyle A term used to describe a **Classical** temple with a **colonnade** placed across the entrance.

provenance The history of ownership of a work of art from the time of its creation to the present.

pseudo-kufic Designs intended to resemble the script of the Arabic language.

pseudo-peripteral *See* **peripteral**.

punchwork Decorative designs that are stamped onto a surface, such as metal or leather, using a punch (a handheld metal implement).

putto (putti) A divine creature in the **form** of a plump, naked little boy, often with wings. In **classical** art, called a cupid or **cherub** (secular).

pylon A massive gateway formed by a pair of tapering walls of oblong shape. Erected by ancient Egyptians to mark the entrance to a **temple complex**.

pyramidion A pyramid-shaped block set as the finishing element atop an **obelisk**.

qibla The **mosque** wall oriented toward Mecca that includes the **mihrab**.

quadrant vault *See* **vault**.

quatrefoil A four-lobed decorative pattern common in Gothic art and architecture.

quillwork A Native American decorative craft technique. The quills of porcupines and bird feathers are dyed, woven together in patterns, and attached to fabric, birch bark, or other material.

quincunx A building in which five equal domed bays are arranged within a square, with a central unit and four corner units. (Note: When the central unit has similar units extending from each side, the **form** becomes a Greek cross).

quoin A stone, often extra large or decorated for emphasis, forming the corner of two walls.

radiometric dating A method of dating prehistoric works of art made from organic materials, based on the rate of degeneration of radiocarbons in these materials. *See also* **relative dating**, **absolute dating**.

raigo A painted image that depicts the Amida Buddha and other Buddhist deities guiding the soul of a dying worshiper to paradise.

raking cornice *See* **cornice**.

raku A type of ceramic pottery made by hand, coated with a thick, dark **glaze**, and fired at a low heat. The resulting vessels are irregularly shaped and glazed, and are highly prized. Raku **ware** is used in the Japanese tea ceremony.

rampart The raised walls or embankments used as primary protection in the fortification of a city or castle. Ramparts may be of different heights or thicknesses, and are usually surmounted by a **parapet**.

readymade An object from popular or material culture presented without further manipulation as an artwork by the artist.

realism A term first used in Europe around 1850 to designate a kind of **naturalism** with a social or political message, which soon lost its didactic import and became synonymous with naturalism.

recto The right-hand page in the opening of a book or **manuscript**. Also: the principal or front side of a leaf of paper, as in the case of a drawing.

red-figure A **style** of ancient Greek vase painting made in the sixth and fifth century BCE. Characterized by red clay-colored figures on a black background.

refectory The dining hall for monks or nuns in a monastery or convent.

register A device used in systems of spatial definition. In painting, a register indicates the use of differing groundlines to differentiate layers of space within an image. In sculpture, the placement of self-contained bands of reliefs in a vertical arrangement. In printmaking, the marks at the edges used to align the print correctly on the page, especially in multiple-block color printing.

reintegration The process of adaptation and transformation of European techniques and **styles** by artists in colonial areas.

relative dating A method of dating ancient artifacts by their relation to other objects, not to a historical moment. *See also* **radiometric dating**, **absolute dating**.

relief sculpture A sculpted image or design whose flat background surface is carved away to a certain depth, setting off the figure. Called high or low (bas) depending upon the extent of projection of the image from the background. Called sunken relief when the image is modeled below the original surface of the background, which is not cut away.

relieving arch *See* **arch**.

reliquary A container, often made of precious materials, used as a repository for sacred relics.

replica A very close copy of a painting or sculpture, sometimes done by the same artist who created the original.

repoussé A technique by which metal reliefs are created. Thin sheets of metal are gently hammered from the back to create a protruding image. More elaborate reliefs are created with wooden **forms** against which the metal sheets are pressed.

representational Any art that attempts to depict an aspect of the external, natural world in a visually understandable way.

reredos A decorated wall behind the **altar** of a church.

retablo The screen placed behind an **altar**. Often built on a large scale, with multiple painted panels and successive stories is a **form** of **altarpiece**. Retablos are most commonly found in Spain or in Spanish-influenced areas such as Latin America.

reverse perspective *See* **perspective**.

revetment A covering of cut stone, fine brick, or other solid facing material over a wall built of coarser materials. Also: surface covering used to reinforce a retaining wall, such as an embankment.

revivalism The practice of using older **styles** and modes of expression in a conscious manner. Revivalism does not usually entail the same academic and historical interest as **historicism**.

rhyton A vessel in the shape of a figure or an animal, used for drinking or pouring liquids on special occasions.

ribbon interlace A **linear** decoration made up of interwoven bands, often found in Celtic and northern European art of the medieval period.

rib vault *See* **vault**.

ridge rib A rib running the length of the **vault**.

ring wall Any wall surrounding a building, town, or fortification, intended to separate and protect the enclosed area.

rock-cut tomb Ancient Egyptian multichambered burial site, hewn from solid rock and often hidden.

rood screen In a church, a screen that separates the public **nave** from the private and sacred area of the **choir**. The screen supports a rood (sculpted crucifix).

roof comb In a Mayan building, a masonry wall along the apex of a roof that is built above the level of the roof proper. Roof combs support the highly decorated false **facades** that rise above the height of the building at the front.

rosette A round or oval ornament resembling a rose.

rose window A round window, often filled with **stained glass**, with **tracery** patterns in the form of wheel spokes. Large, elaborate, and finely crafted, rose windows are usually a central element of the **facade** of French Gothic cathedrals.

rotulus (rotuli) A scroll or **manuscripts** rolled in a tubular **form**.

rotunda Any building (or part thereof) constructed in a circular (or sometimes polygonal) shape, usually producing a large open space crowned by a **dome**.

roundel Any element with a circular format, often placed as a decoration on the exterior of architecture.

round vault *See* **vault**.

rune stone A stone used in early medieval northern Europe as a commemorative monument, which is carved or inscribed with ancient German or Scandinavian writing, runes.

running spirals A decorative **motif** based on the shape formed by a line making a continuous spiral.

rustication In building, the rough, irregular, and unfinished effect deliberately given to the exterior facing of a stone edifice. Rusticated stones are often large and used for decorative emphasis around doors or windows, or across the entire lower floors of a building, probably deriving from fortifications.

sacristy In a Christian church, the room in which the priest's robes and the sacred vessels are housed. Sacristies are usually located close to the **sanctuary** and often have a place for ritual washing as well as a private door to the exterior.

sahn The central courtyard of a Muslim **mosque**.

sanctuary In Greek architecture, a sacred or holy enclosure used for worship consisting of one or more temples and an **altar**. Also: the space around the altar in a church, usually at the east end (also called the chancel or presbytery).

sand painting Ephemeral religious designs created with different colored sands by Native Americans of North America, Australian Aborigines, and other peoples in Japan and Tibet.

sanghati The robe worn by a Buddhist monk. Draped over the left shoulder, the robe is made from a single piece of cloth wrapped around the body.

sarcophagus (sarcophagi) A rectangular stone coffin. Often decorated with **relief sculpture**.

scarification Ornamental marks, scars, or scratches made on the human body.

school of artists An art historical term describing a group of artists, usually working at the same time and sharing similar **styles**, influences, and ideals. The artists in a particular school may not necessarily be directly associated with one another, unlike in a workshop or atelier.

scientific perspective *See* **perspective**.

scriptorium (scriptoria) A room in a monastery for writing or copying **manuscripts**.

scroll painting A painting executed on a rolled support. Rollers at either end permit the horizontal scroll to be unrolled as it is studied or the vertical scroll to be hung for contemplation or decoration.

sculpture in the round Three-dimensional sculpture that is carved free of any attaching background or block.

section A method of representing the three-dimensional arrangement of a building in a graphic manner. A section is produced when an imaginary vertical plane intersects with a building, laying bare all the elements that make up the structure at that point. Also: a view of an element of object as if sliced through.

segmental pediment A **pediment** formed when the upper **cornice** is a shallow arc.

sepia An ink **medium** often used in drawing that has an extremely rich, dark **tone** of brownish color.

seraph (seraphim) An angel of the highest rank in the Christian hierarchy.

serdab In Egyptian tombs, the small room in which the **ka** statue was placed.

sesto The curve of an **arch**.

sfumato In painting, the effect of haze in an image. Resembling the color of the atmosphere at dusk, sfumato gives a smoky effect.

shade Any area of an artwork that is shown through various technical means to be in shadow. Also: the technique of making such an effect.

shaft The main vertical section of a **column** between the **capital** and the base, usually circular in cross **section**.

shater A type of roof or **dome** used in Russia and the Near East with a steep pitch and tentlike shape.

shikhara In the architecture of northern India, a conical (or pyramidal) spire found atop a Hindu temple and often crowned with an **amalaka**.

shoin The architecture of the aristocracy and upper classes in Japan, built in traditional asymmetrical fashion and incorporating the traditional elements of residences, such as the *tokonoma* and **shoji** screens.

shoji A standing Japanese screen covered in translucent rice paper and used in interiors.

sinopia The preparatory design or underdrawing of a **fresco**. Also: a reddish chalklike earth pigment.

site-specific sculpture A sculpture commissioned and designed for a particular spot. Most site-specific sculpture requires the location for which it was designed in order to be complete.

slip A mixture of clay and water applied to a ceramic object as a final decorative coat. Also: a

solution that binds different parts of a vessel together, such as the handle and the main body.

spandrel The area of wall adjoining the exterior curve of an **arch** between its springing and the **keystone**, or the area between two arches, as in an **arcade**.

speech scroll A scroll painted with words indicating the speech or song of a depicted figure.

squinch An arch or **lintel** built over the upper corners of a square space, allowing a circular or polygonal **dome** to be more securely set above the walls.

stadium In ancient Greece, race track with tiers of seats for spectators.

stained glass A decorative process in glass-making by which glass is given a color (whether intrinsic in the material or painted onto the surface). Stained glass is most often used in windows, for which small pieces of differently colored glass are precisely cut and assembled into a design, held together by **cames**.

stela (stelae) A stone slab placed vertically and decorated with inscriptions or reliefs. Used as a grave marker or memorial.

stigmata Marks resembling the wounds of Christ; said to appear on the bodies of certain holy persons.

still life A type of painting that has as its subject inanimate objects (such as food, dishes, fruit, or flowers).

stoa In Greek architecture, a **portico** or promenade with long rows of **columns** used as a meeting place.

stockade A defensive fencelike wood fortification built around a village, house, or other enclosed area.

stretcher The wooden framework on which an artist's canvas is attached, usually with tacks, nails, or staples. Also: a reinforcing horizontal brace between the legs of a piece of furniture, such as a chair. Also: in building, a brick laid so that its longer edge is parallel to the wall.

stringcourse A continuous horizontal band, such as a **molding**, decorating the face of a wall.

stucco A mixture of lime, sand, and other ingredients into a material that can be easily molded or modeled. When dry, produces a very durable surface used for covering walls or for architectural sculpture and decoration.

stupa In Buddhist architecture, a bell-shaped or pyramidal religious monument, made of piled earth or stone, and containing sacred relics.

style A particular manner, form, or character of representation, construction, or expression typical of an individual artist or of a certain school or period.

stylization A manner of representation that conforms to an intellectual or artistic idea rather than to **naturalistic** appearances.

stylobate In **Classical** architecture, the stone foundation on which a temple **colonnade** stands.

stylus An instrument with a pointed end (used for writing and printmaking), which makes a delicate line or scratch. Also: a special writing tool for **cuneiform writing** with one pointed end and one triangular wedge end.

subject matter *See* **content**.

sublime A concept, thing, or state of exceptional and awe-inspiring beauty and moral or intellectual expression. The sublime was a goal to which many nineteenth-century artists aspired in their artworks.

sunken relief *See* **relief sculpture**.

swag A decorative device in architecture or interior ornament (and in paintings), in which a loosely hanging garland is made to look as if constructed of flowers or gathered cloth.

syncretism In religion or philosophy, the union of different ideas or principles.

talud-tablero A design characteristic of Mayan architecture at Teotihuacan in which a sloping talud at the base of a building supports a wall-like tablero, where ornamental painting and sculpture are usually placed.

taotie A mask with a dragon or animal-like face common as a decorative **motif** in Chinese art.

tapa A cloth made in Polynesia by pounding the bark of a tree, such as the paper mulberry. It is also known as bark cloth.

tapestry Pictorial or decorative weaving meant to be hung on a wall or placed on furniture.

tatami Mats of woven straw used in Japanese houses as a floor covering.

temenos A sacred enclosure. In **classical** architecture, includes temples, treasuries, **altar**s and other buildings and spaces for ritual activities.

tempera A painting **medium** made by blending egg yolks with water, pigments, and occasionally other materials, such as glue. The technique was often used during the fourteenth and fifteenth centuries to paint **frescoes** and **panel paintings**.

temple complex A group of buildings dedicated to a religious purpose, usually located close to one another in a **sanctuary**.

tenebrism A term signifying the prevalent use of dark areas in a painting. A tenebrist **style**, such as Caravaggism, uses strong **chiaroscuro** and artificially illuminated areas to create a dramatic contrast of light and dark.

tepee A dwelling constructed from hides stretched on a structure of poles set at the base in a circle and leaning against one another at the top. Tepees were typically found among the nomadic Native Americans of the North American plains.

terminal Any element of sculpture or architecture that functions as decorative closure. Terminals are usually placed in pairs at either end of an object (such as furniture) or **facade** (as on a building) to help frame the **composition**.

terra-cotta A **medium** made from clay fired over a low heat and usually left unglazed. Also: the orange-brown color typical of this medium.

tessera (tesserae) The small piece of stone, glass, or other object that is pieced together with many others to create a **mosaic**.

tholos A small, round building. Sometimes built underground, as in a Mycenaean tomb.

tierceron In **vault** construction, a secondary rib that arcs from a springing point to the rib that runs lengthwise through the **vault**, called the **ridge rib**.

tint The dominant color in an object, image, or pigment.

tokonoma A **niche** for the display of an art object (such as a scroll or flower arrangement) in a Japanese tearoom.

tomb effigy A sculpted portraitlike image on a tomb or **sarcophagus** that represents a deceased individual.

tondo A painting or relief of circular shape.

tone The overall degree of brightness or darkness in an artwork. Also: saturation, intensity, or **value** of color and its effect.

torana In Indian architecture, an ornamented gateway **arch** in a temple, usually leading to the **stupa**.

torii The ceremonial entrance gate to a Shinto temple.

toron In West African **mosque** architecture, the wooden beams that project from the walls. Torons are used as support for the scaffolding erected annually for the replastering of the building.

torque A neckpiece, especially favored by the Celts, fashioned as a twisted metal collar.

tracery The thin stone or wooden bars in a Gothic window, screen, or panel, which create an elaborate decorative matrix or pattern.

transept The arm of a **cruciform** church, perpendicular to the **nave**. The point where the nave and transept cross is called the **crossing**. Beyond the crossing lies the **sanctuary**, whether **apse**, **choir**, or **chevet**.

travertine A mineral building material similar to limestone, typically found in central Italy.

treasury A building or room, for keeping holy (and often highly valuable) objects.

trefoil An ornamental design made up of three rounded lobes placed adjacent to one another.

triforium The element of the interior **elevation** of a church, found directly below the **clerestory** and consisting of a series of **arched** openings. The triforium can be made up of openings from a passageway or gallery, or can be a purely decorative device built into the wall.

triglyph Rectangular blocks between the **metopes** of a **Doric frieze**. Identified by the three carved vertical grooves, which approximate the appearance of the ends of wooden beams.

triptych An artwork made up of three panels. The panels are often hinged together so the side segments (**wings**) fold over the central area.

triumph In Roman times, a celebration of a particular military victory, usually granted to the commanding general upon his return to Rome. Also: in later times, any depiction of a victory.

triumphal arch A freestanding, massive stone gateway with a large central **arch**, built as urban ornament and/or to celebrate military victories (as by the Romans).

trompe l'oeil A manner of representation in which the appearance of natural space and objects is re-created with the express intention of fooling the eye of the viewer, who may be convinced that the subject actually exists as three-dimensional reality.

trophy Captured military objects such as armor

and weapons that Romans displayed in an upheld pole or tree to celebrate victory. Also: a similar grouping that recalls the Roman custom of displaying the looted armor of a defeated opponent.

trumeau A **column**, **pier**, or post found at the center of a large **portal** or doorway, supporting the **lintel**.

tugra The calligraphic imperial monograms used in Ottoman courts.

tunnel vault *See* **vault**.

turret A tall and slender tower.

Tuscan order *See* **order**.

twining A basketry technique in which short rods are sewn together vertically. The panels are then joined together to form a vessel.

tympanum In **Classical** architecture, the vertical panel of the **pediment**. In medieval and later architecture, the area over a door enclosed by an **arch** and a **lintel**, often decorated with sculpture or **mosaic**.

typology The study of symbolic types of representation in art history, especially of Old Testament events of the Bible as they prefigure those of the New Testament.

ukiyo-e A Japanese term for a type of popular art that was favored from the sixteenth century, particularly in the **form** of color **woodblock prints**. Ukiyo-e prints often depicted the world of the common people in Japan, such as courtesans and actors, as well as landscapes and myths.

undercutting A technique in sculpture by which a **form** is carved to project outward, then under. Undercutting gives a highly three-dimensional effect with deep shadows behind the form.

underglaze Color or decoration applied to a ceramic piece before **glazing**.

urna In Buddhist art, the curl of hair on the forehead that is a characteristic mark of a Buddha. The urna is a symbol of divine wisdom.

ushnisha In Asian art, a round turban or tiara symbolizing royalty and, when worn by a Buddha, enlightenment.

value The darkness or lightness of a color (**hue**).

vanishing point In a **perspective** system, the point on the **horizon line** at which **orthogonals** meet. A complex system can have multiple vanishing points.

vanitas An image, especially popular in Europe during the seventeenth century, in which all the objects symbolize the transience of life. *Vanitas* paintings are usually of **still lifes** or **genre** subjects.

vault An **arched** masonry structure covering that spans an interior space. In different shapes, called by different names. **Barrel or tunnel vault**: a continuous semicircular vault. **Corbel vault**: a vault made by the technique of **corbeling**. **Groin or cross vault**: a vault created by the intersection of two barrel vaults of equal size. **Rib vault**: a rib vault is found when the joining of curved sides of a groin vault is demarcated by a raised rib. **Quadrant or half-barrel vault**: a vault with two diagonally crossed ribs, which creates four side compartments of equal size and shape.

veduta (vedute) A term derived from the Italian

word for a vista, or view. Paintings, drawings or prints often of expansive city scenes or of harbors.

vellum A fine animal skin prepared for writing and painting. *See* **parchment**.

veneer In architecture, the exterior facing of a building, often in decorative patterns of fine stone or brick. In decorative arts, a thin exterior layer for decoration laid over wooden objects or furniture. Made of fine materials such as rare wood, ivory, metal, and semiprecious stones.

verism A **style** in which artists concern themselves with capturing the exterior likeness of an object or person, usually by rendering its visible details in a finely executed, meticulous manner.

verso The (reverse) left-hand page of the opening of a book or **manuscript**. Also: the subordinate or back side of a leaf of paper, as in the case of drawings.

vignette A small **motif** or scene that has no established border.

vihara From the Sanskrit term meaning "for wanderers." A vihara is, in general, a Buddhist monastery in India. It also signifies the monks' cells and gathering places in such a monastery.

vimana The main element of a Southern Indian Hindu temple, usually in the shape of a pyramidal or tapering tower raised on a **plinth**.

volumetric A term indicating the concern for rendering the impression of three-dimensional volumes in painting, usually achieved through **modeling** and the manipulation of light and shadow (**chiaroscuro**).

volute A spiral scroll, most often decoration on an **Ionic capital**.

volute krater *See* **krater**.

votive figure An image created as a devotional offering to a god or other deity.

voussoirs The oblong, wedge-shaped stone blocks used to build an **arch**. The topmost voussoir is called a **keystone**.

wall painting *See* **mural**.

ware A general term designating the different techniques by which pottery is produced and decorated. Different wares utilize different procedures to achieve different decorative results. *See also* **black-figure**, **red-figure**, and **white-ground**.

warp The vertical threads in a weaver's loom. Warp threads make up a fixed framework that provides the structure for the entire piece of cloth, and are thus often thicker than weft threads. *See also* **weft**.

wash A diluted watercolor. Often washes are applied to drawings or prints to add **tone** or touches of color.

watercolor A type of painting using water-soluble pigments that are floated in a water **medium** to make a transparent paint. The technique of watercolor is most suited to a paper support.

wattle and daub A wall construction method combining upright branches, woven with twigs (wattles) and plastered or filled with clay or mud (daub).

weft The horizontal threads in a woven piece of cloth. Weft threads are woven at right angles to and through the **warp** threads to make up the bulk of the decorative pattern. In carpets, the weft is often completely covered or formed by the rows of trimmed knots that form the carpet's soft surface.

westwork The **monumental**, west-facing entrance section of a Carolingian, Ottonian, or Romanesque church. The exterior consists of multiple stories between two towers; the interior includes an entrance vestibule, a chapel, and a series of galleries overlooking the **nave**.

white-ground A type of ancient Greek pottery **ware** in which the background color of the object is painted with a type of **slip** that turns white in the firing process. Figures and details were added by painting on or **incising** into this slip. White-ground wares were popular in the High **Classical** period as funerary objects.

wing A side panel of a **triptych** or **polyptych** (usually found in pairs), which was hinged to fold over the central panel. Wings often held the depiction of the donors and/or subsidiary scenes relating to the central image.

woodblock print A print made from a block of wood that is carved in relief or **incised**.

woodcut A type of print made by carving a design into a wooden block. The ink is applied to the plate with a roller. As the ink remains only on the raised areas between the carved-away lines, these carved-away areas and lines provide the white areas of the print. Also: the process by which the woodcut is made.

x-ray style In aboriginal art, a manner of representation in which the artist depicts a figure or animal by illustrating its outline as well as essential internal organs and bones.

yaksha, yakshi The male (yaksha) and female (yakshi) nature spirits that act as agents of the Hindu gods. Their sculpted images are often found on Hindu temples and other sacred places, particularly at the entrances.

zeitgeist From the German word for "spirit of the time," the term means cultural and intellectual aspects of a time period that pervade human experience and are expressed in all creative and social endeavors.

ziggurat In Mesopotamia, a man-made mountain; a tall stepped tower of earthen materials, often supporting a shrine.

Bibliography

Susan Craig

This bibliography is composed of books in English that are appropriate "further reading" titles. Most items on this list are available in good libraries, whether college, university, or public institutions. There are three classifications of listings: general surveys and art history reference tools, including journals; surveys of large periods (ancient art in the Western tradition, European medieval art, European Renaissance through eighteenth-century art, modern art in the West, Asian art, and African and Oceanic art and art of the Americas); and books for individual Chapters 1 through 29. Sources of quotations cited in short form in the text will also be found in this bibliography.

General Art History Surveys and Reference Tools

Adams, Laurie. *A History of Western Art*. Madison: Brown and Benchmark, 1994.

Bazin, Germain. *A Concise History of World Sculpture*. London: David & Charles, 1981.

Brownston, David M., and Ilene Franck. *Timelines of the Arts and Literature*. New York: HarperCollins, 1994.

Bull, Stephen. *An Historical Guide to Arms and Armor*. Ed. Tony North. New York: Facts on File, 1991.

Chadwick, Whitney. *Women, Art, and Society*. New York: Thames and Hudson, 1990.

Cole, Bruce, and Adelheid Gealt. *Art of the Western World: From Ancient Greece to Post-Modernism*. New York: Summit, 1989.

Crofton, Ian, comp. *A Dictionary of Art Quotations*. New York: Schirmer, 1989.

Crouch, Dora P. *A History of Architecture: Stonehenge to Skyscrapers*. New York: McGraw-Hill, 1985.

Dictionary of Art, The. 34 vols. New York: Grove's Dictionaries, 1996.

Encyclopedia of World Art. 16 vols. New York: McGraw-Hill, 1972–83.

Fleming, John, Hugh Honour, and Nikolaus Pevsner. *The Penguin Dictionary of Architecture*. 4th ed. New York: Penguin, 1991.

Fletcher, Banister. *Sir Banister Fletcher's A History of Architecture*. 19th ed. Ed. John Musgrove. London: Butterworths, 1987.

Gardner, Helen. *Gardner's Art through the Ages*. 9th ed. Ed. Horst de la Croix, Richard G. Tansey, and Diana Kirkpatrick. San Diego: Harcourt Brace College, 1991.

Hall, James. *Dictionary of Subjects and Symbols in Art*. Rev. ed. New York: Harper & Row, 1979.

Hartt, Frederick. *Art: A History of Painting, Sculpture, Architecture*. 4th ed. New York: Abrams, 1993.

Heller, Nancy G. *Women Artists: An Illustrated History*. New York: Abbeville, 1987.

Holt, Elizabeth Gilmore, ed. *A Documentary History of Art*. 3 vols. New Haven: Yale Univ. Press, 1986.

Honour, Hugh. *The Visual Arts: A History*. 3rd ed. New York: Abrams, 1991.

Janson, H. W. *History of Art*. 5th ed. Rev. and exp. Anthony F. Janson. New York: Abrams, 1995.

Jervis, Simon. *The Penguin Dictionary of Design and Designers*. London: Lane, 1984.

Jones, Lois Swan. *Art Information: Research Methods and Resources*. 3rd ed. Dubuque: Kendall/Hunt, 1990.

Kostof, Spiro. *A History of Architecture: Settings and Rituals*. New York: Oxford Univ. Press, 1985.

Kurtz, Bruce D. *Visual Imagination: An Introduction to Art*. Englewood Cliffs, N.J.: Prentice-Hall, 1987.

Lindemann, Gottfried. *Prints and Drawings: A Pictorial History*. Trans. Gerald Onn. Oxford: Phaidon, 1976.

Mair, Roslin. *Key Dates in Art History: From 600 BC to the Present*. Oxford: Phaidon, 1979.

Mayor, A. Hyatt. *Prints and People: A Social History of Printed Pictures*. New York: Metropolitan Museum of Art, 1971.

McConkey, Wilfred J. *Klee as in Clay: A Pronunciation Guide*. Lantham, Md.: Univ. Press of America, 1985.

Myers, Bernard, ed. *McGraw-Hill Dictionary of Art*. 5 vols. New York: McGraw-Hill, 1969.

Rothberg, Robert I., and Theodore K. Rabb, eds. *Art and History: Images and Their Meaning*. Cambridge: Cambridge Univ. Press, 1988.

Stangos, Nikos. *The Thames and Hudson Dictionary of Art and Artists*. Rev ed. World of Art. New York: Thames and Hudson, 1994.

Steer, John, and Antony White. *Atlas of Western Art History: Artists, Sites and Movements from Ancient Greece to the Modern Age*. New York: Facts on File, 1994.

Thacker, Christopher. *The History of Gardens*. Berkeley: Univ. of California Press, 1979.

Trachtenberg, Marvin, and Isabelle Hyman. *Architecture, from Prehistory to Post-Modernism: The Western Tradition*. New York: Abrams, 1986.

Tufts, Eleanor. *Our Hidden Heritage: Five Centuries of Women Artists*. New York: Paddington, 1974.

Wilkins, David G., Bernard Schultz, and Katheryn M. Linduff. *Art Past/Art Present*. 2nd ed. New York: Abrams, 1994.

The World Atlas of Architecture. Boston: Hall, 1984.

Art History Journals: A Selected List

African Arts. Quarterly. Los Angeles, Calif.

American Art. Quarterly. Washington, D.C.

American Journal of Archaeology. Quarterly. Boston, Mass.

Antiquity. Quarterly. Oxford

Apollo. Monthly. London

Architectural History. Annually. London

Archives of American Art Journal. Quarterly. Washington, D.C.

Archives of Asian Art. Annually. New York

Ars Orientalis. Ann Arbor, Mich.

Art Bulletin. Quarterly. New York

Artforum. Monthly. New York

Art History. Quarterly. Oxford

Art in America. Monthly. New York

Art Journal. Quarterly. New York

Art News. Monthly. New York

Arts and the Islamic World. Annually. London

Asian Art and Culture. Triannually. New York

Burlington Magazine. Monthly. London

Flash Art. Bimonthly. New York

Gesta. Semiannually. New York

History of Photography. Quarterly. London

Journal of Egyptian Archaeology. Quarterly. London

Journal of Hellenic Studies. Annually. London

Journal of Roman Archaeology. Annually. Ann Arbor, Mich.

Journal of the Society of Architectural Historians. Quarterly. Philadelphia

Journal of the Warburg and Courtauld Institutes. Annually. London

Marg. Quarterly. Bombay, India

Oriental Art. Quarterly. Richmond, Surrey, England

Oxford Art Journal. Semiannually. Oxford

Simiolus. Quarterly. Apeldoorn, Netherlands

Textile History. Semiannually, London

Woman's Art Journal. Semiannually, Laverock, Penn.

Ancient Art in the Western Tradition, General

Adam, Robert. *Classical Architecture: A Comprehensive Handbook to the Tradition of Classical Style*. New York: Abrams, 1991.

Amiet, Pierre. *Art in the Ancient World: A Handbook of Styles and Forms*. New York: Rizzoli, 1981.

Becatti, Giovanni. *The Art of Ancient Greece and Rome, from the Rise of Greece to the Fall of Rome*. New York: Abrams, 1967.

Ehrich, Robert W., ed. *Chronologies in Old World Archaeology*. 3rd ed. Chicago: Univ. of Chicago Press, 1992.

Groenewegen-Frankfort, H. A., and Bernard Ashmole. *Art of the Ancient World: Painting, Pottery, Sculpture, Architecture from Egypt, Mesopotamia, Crete, Greece, and Rome*. Library of Art History. Englewood Cliffs, N.J.: Prentice-Hall, 1972.

Huyghe, René. *Larousse Encyclopedia of Prehistoric and Ancient Art*. Art and Mankind. New York: Prometheus, 1966.

Laing, Lloyd Robert, and Jennifer Laing. *Ancient Art: The Challenge to Modern Thought*. Dublin: Irish Academic, 1993.

Lloyd, Seton, and Hans Wolfgang Muller. *Ancient Architecture*. New York: Rizzoli, 1986.

Oliphant, Margaret. *The Atlas of the Ancient World: Charting the Great Civilizations of the Past*. New York: Simon & Schuster, 1992.

Powell, Ann. *Origins of Western Art*. London: Thames and Hudson, 1973.

Saggs, H. W. F. *Civilization before Greece and Rome*. New Haven: Yale Univ. Press, 1989.

Scranton, Robert L. *Aesthetic Aspects of Ancient Art*. Chicago: Univ. of Chicago Press, 1964.

Smith, William Stevenson. *Interconnections in the Ancient Near East: A Study of the Relationships between the Arts of Egypt, the Aegean, and Western Asia*. New Haven: Yale Univ. Press, 1965.

Stillwell, Richard, ed. *Princeton Encyclopedia of Classsical Sites*. Princeton: Princeton Univ. Press, 1976.

European Medieval Art, General

Calkins, Robert C. *Monuments of Medieval Art*. New York: Dutton, 1979.

Duby, Georges. *Sculpture: The Great Art of the Middle Ages from the Fifth to the Fifteenth Century*. New York: Skira/Rizzoli, 1990.

Hurlimann, Martin, and Jean Bony. *French Cathedrals*. Boston: Houghton Mifflin, 1951.

Kenyon, John. *Medieval Fortifications*. Leicester: Leicester Univ. Press, 1990.

Labarge, Margaret Wade. *A Small Sound of the Trumpet: Women in Medieval Life*. London: Hamilton, 1990.

Larousse Encyclopedia of Byzantine and Medieval Art. London: Hamlyn, 1963.

Mâle, Emile. *Religious Art in France: The Late Middle Ages: A Study of Medieval Iconography and Its Sources*. Princeton: Princeton Univ. Press, 1986.

Murphey, Cecil B., comp. *Dictionary of Biblical Literacy*. Nashville: Oliver-Nelson, 1989.

Snyder, James. *Medieval Art: Painting-Sculpture-Architecture, 4th–14th Century*. New York: Abrams, 1989.

Stoddard, Whitney. *Art and Architecture in Medieval France: Medieval Architecture, Sculpture, Stained Glass, Manuscripts*. The Art of the Church Treasuries. New York: Harper & Row, 1972.

Stokstad, Marilyn. *Medieval Art*. New York: Harper & Row, 1986.

Zarnecki, George. *The Art of the Medieval World: Architecture, Sculpture, Painting, the Sacred Arts*. New York: Abrams, 1975.

European Renaissance through Eighteenth-Century Art, General

Art and Politics in Late Medieval and Early Renaissance Italy, 1250–1500. South Bend, Ind.: Univ. of Notre Dame Press, 1990.

Black, C. F., et al. *Cultural Atlas of the Renaissance*. New York: Prentice Hall, 1993.

Blunt, Anthony. *Art and Architecture in France, 1500 to 1700*. Pelican History of Art. Harmondsworth, Eng.: Penguin, 1957.

Circa 1492: Art in the Age of Exploration. Washington, D.C.: National Gallery of Art, 1991.

Cole, Bruce. *Italian Art, 1250–1550: The Relation of Renaissance Art to Life and Society*. New York: Harper & Row, 1987.

Cuttler, Charles D. *Northern Painting from Pucelle to Bruegel: Fourteenth, Fifteenth and Sixteenth Centuries*. New York: Holt, Rinehart and Winston, 1973.

Evers, Hans Gerhard. *The Modern Age: Historicism and Functionalism*. Art of the World. London: Methuen, 1970.

Hartt, Frederick. *History of Italian Renaissance Art: Painting, Sculpture, Architecture*. 3rd ed. New York: Abrams, 1987.

Heydenreich, Ludwig Heinrich. *Architecture in Italy, 1400 to 1600*. Pelican History of Art. Harmondsworth, Eng.: Penguin, 1966.

Huizinga, Johan. *Waning of the Middle Ages: A Study of the Forms of Life, Thought, and Art in France and the Netherlands in the XIVth and XVth Centuries*. Garden City, N.Y.: Doubleday, 1954.

Husband, Timothy. *Wild Man: Medieval Myth and Symbolism*. New York: Metropolitan Museum of Art, 1980.

Huyghe, René. *Larousse Encyclopedia of Renaissance and Baroque Art*. Art and Mankind. New York: Prometheus, 1964.

Kubler, George, and Martin Soria. *Art and Architecture in Spain and Portugal and Their American Dominions, 1500–1800*. Pelican History of Art. Harmondsworth, Eng.: Penguin, 1959.

Levey, Michael. *Early Renaissance*. Harmondsworth, Eng.: Penguin, 1967.

Murray, Peter. *Renaissance Architecture*. History of World Architecture. Milan: Electa, 1985.

———, and Linda Murray. *The Art of the Renaissance*. World of Art. London: Thames and Hudson, 1963.

Stechow, Wolfgang. *Northern Renaissance, 1400–1600: Sources and Documents*. Englewood Cliffs, N.J.: Prentice-Hall, 1966.

Waterhouse, Ellis K. *Painting in Britain: 1530 to 1790*. 4th ed. Pelican History of Art. Harmondsworth, Eng.: Penguin, 1978.

Whinney, Margaret Dickens. *Sculpture in Britain: 1530–1830*. 2nd ed. Rev. by John Physick. Pelican History of Art. London: Penguin, 1988.

Modern Art in the West, General

Arnason, H. H. *History of Modern Art: Painting, Sculpture, Architecture, Photography*. 3rd ed. rev. New York: Abrams, 1986.

Bearden, Romare. *A History of African American Artists: From 1792 to the Present*. New York: Pantheon, 1993.

Brown, Milton W. *American Art: Painting, Sculpture, Architecture, Decorative Arts, Photography*. New York: Abrams, 1979.

Canaday, John. *Mainstreams of Modern Art*. 2nd ed. New York: Holt, Rinehart and Winston, 1981.

Chipp, Herschel Browning. *Theories of Modern Art: A Source Book by Artists and Critics*. California Studies in the History of Art. Berkeley: Univ. of California Press, 1984.

Craven, Wayne. *American Art: History and Culture*. New York: Abrams, 1994.

Eitner, Lorenz. *An Outline of Nineteenth Century European Painting: From David to Cezanne*. 2 vols. New York: Harper & Row, 1987.

Ferebee, Ann. *A History of Design from the Victorian Era to the Present*. New York: Van Nostrand Reinhold, 1980.

Ferrier, Jean Louis, ed. *Art of Our Century: The Chronicle of Western Art, 1900 to the Present*. New York: Prentice Hall, 1989.

Frampton, Kenneth. *Modern Architecture: A Critical History*. World of Art. New York: Oxford Univ. Press, 1980.

Hamilton, George Heard. *19th and 20th Century Art: Painting, Sculpture and Architecture*. Library of Art History. New York: Abrams, 1972.

Hammacher, A. M. *Modern Sculpture: Tradition and Innovation*. Enlg. ed. New York: Abrams, 1988.
Handlin, David P. *American Architecture*. World of Art. London: Thames and Hudson, 1985.
Harris, Ann Sutherland, and Linda Nochlin. *Women Artists: 1550–1950*. Los Angeles: Los Angeles County Museum of Art, 1976.
Harrison, Charles, and Paul Wood, eds. *Art in Theory, 1900–1990: An Anthology of Changing Ideas*. Cambridge: Blackwell, 1992.
Hitchcock, Henry Russell. *Architecture: Nineteenth and Twentieth Centuries*. 4th ed. Pelican History of Art. Harmondsworth, Eng.: Penguin, 1977.
Hunter, Sam, and John Jacobus. *American Art of the 20th Century: Painting, Sculpture, Architecture*. New York: Abrams, 1973.
———. *Modern Art: Painting, Sculpture, Architecture*. 3rd ed. New York: Abrams, 1992.
Jeffrey, Ian. *Photography: A Concise History*. London: Thames and Hudson, 1981.
Lynton, Norbert. *The Story of Modern Art*. 2nd ed. Oxford: Phaidon, 1989.
McCoubrey, John W. *American Art, 1700–1960: Sources and Documents*. Englewood Cliffs, N.J.: Prentice-Hall, 1965.
Newhall, Beaumont. *The History of Photography: From 1839 to the Present*. Rev. ed. New York: Museum of Modern Art, 1982.
Pevsner, Nikolaus, Sir. *The Sources of Modern Architecture and Design*. World of Art. New York: Oxford Univ. Press, 1968.
Read, Herbert. *A Concise History of Modern Painting*. London: Thames and Hudson, 1974.
———. *A Concise History of Modern Sculpture*. World of Art. New York: Praeger, 1964.
Rosenblum, Naomi. *A World History of Photography*. Rev. ed. New York: Abbeville, 1989.
Rosenblum, Robert. *19th Century Art*. New York: Abrams, 1984.
Schapiro, Meyer. *Modern Art: 19th and 20th Century Art*. New York: Braziller, 1978.
Selz, Peter. *Art in Our Times: A Pictorial History 1890–1980*. New York: Abrams, 1981.
Sparke, Penny. *Introduction of Design and Culture in the Twentieth Century*. New York: Harper & Row, 1986.
Stangos, Nikos, ed. *Concepts of Modern Art*. 3rd ed. World of Art. New York: Thames and Hudson, 1994.
Tafuri, Manfredo. *Modern Architecture*. 2 vols. History of World Architecture. New York: Electa/Rizzoli, 1986.
Tuchman, Maurice. *The Spiritual in Art: Abstract Painting 1890–1985*. Los Angeles: Los Angeles County Museum of Art, 1986.
Weaver, Mike, ed. *The Art of Photography, 1939–1989*. London: Royal Academy of Arts, 1989.
Wilmerding, John. *American Art*. Pelican History of Art. Harmondsworth, Eng.: Penguin, 1976.

Asian Art, General

Akiyama, Terukazu. *Japanese Painting*. Treasures of Asia. Geneva: Skira, 1961.
Arts of China. 3 vols. Tokyo: Kodansha International, 1968–70.
Blunden, Caroline, and Mark Elvin. *Cultural Atlas of China*. New York: Facts on File, 1983.
Bussagli, Mario. *Oriental Architecture*. 2 vols. History of World Architecture. New York: Electa/Rizzoli, 1989.
Chang, Leon Long-Yien, and Peter Miller. *Four Thousand Years of Chinese Calligraphy*. Chicago: Univ. of Chicago Press, 1990.
Collcutt, Martin, Marius Jansen, and Isao Kumakura. *Cultural Atlas of Japan*. New York: Facts on File, 1988.
Craven, Roy C. *Indian Art: A Concise History*. World of Art. New York: Thames and Hudson, 1985.
Fisher, Robert E. *Buddhist Art and Architecture*. World of Art. New York: Thames and Hudson, 1993.
Frankfort, Henri. *Art and Architecture of the Ancient Orient*. 4th ed. Pelican History of Art. Harmondsworth, Eng.: Penguin, 1970.
Goetz, Hermann. *The Art of India: Five Thousand Years of Indian Art*. 2nd ed. Art of the World. New York: Crown, 1964.
Harle, James C. *Art and Architecture of the Indian Subcontinent*. Pelican History of Art. Harmondsworth, Eng.: Penguin, 1987.
Lee, Sherman E. *A History of Far Eastern Art*. 4th ed. New York: Abrams, 1982.
Loehr, Max. *The Great Painters of China*. New York: Harper & Row, 1980.
Martynov, Anatolii Ivanovich. *Ancient Art of Northern Asia*. Urbana: Univ. of Illinois Press, 1991.
Mason, Penelope. *History of Japanese Art*. New York: Abrams, 1993.
Medley, Margaret. *Chinese Potter: A Practical History of Chinese Ceramics*. 3rd ed. Oxford: Phaidon, 1989.
Michell, George. *The Penguin Guide to the Monuments of India*. 2 vols. New York: Viking, 1989.
Mikami, Tsugio. *Art of Japanese Ceramics*. Trans. Ann Herring. Heibonsha Survey of Japanese Art, vol. 29. New York: Weatherhill, 1972.
Nakata, Yujiro. *Art of Japanese Calligraphy*. Trans. Alan Woodhull. Heibonsha Survey of Japanese Art, vol. 27. New York: Weatherhill, 1973.
Paine, Robert Treat, and Alexander Soper. *Art and Architecture of Japan*. 3rd ed. Pelican History of Art. Harmondsworth, Eng.: Penguin, 1981.
Rowland, Benjamin. *Art and Architecture of India: Buddhist, Hindu, Jain*. Pelican History of Art. Harmondsworth, Eng.: Penguin, 1977.
Seckel, Dietrich. *Art of Buddhism*. Art of the World. New York: Crown, 1964.
Sickman, Lawrence, and Alexander Soper. *Art and Architecture of China*. Pelican History of Art. Harmondsworth, Eng.: Penguin, 1971.
Speiser, Werner. *The Art of China: Spirit and Society*. Art of the World. New York: Crown, 1961.
Stanley-Baker, Joan. *Japanese Art*. World of Art. New York: Thames and Hudson, 1984.
Stutley, Margaret. *Harper's Dictionary of Hinduism: Its Mythology, Folklore, Philosophy, Literature and History*. New York: Harper & Row, 1977.
Tregear, Mary. *Chinese Art*. World of Art. New York: Oxford Univ. Press, 1980.
Vainker, S. J. *Chinese Pottery and Porcelain: From Prehistory to the Present*. London: British Museum, 1991.
Varley, H. Paul. *Japanese Culture*. 3rd ed. Honolulu: Univ. of Hawaii Press, 1984.
Yoshikawa, Itsuji. *Major Themes in Japanese Art*. Trans. Armins Nikovskis. Heibonsha Survey of Japanese Art, vol. 1. New York: Weatherhill, 1976.

African and Oceanic Art and Art of the Americas, General

Anderson, Richard L. *Art in Small-Scale Societies*. 2nd ed. Englewood Cliffs, N.J.: Prentice Hall, 1989.
Berlo, Janet Catherine, and Lee Ann Wilson. *Arts of Africa, Oceania, and the Americas: Selected Readings*. Englewood Cliffs, N.J.: Prentice Hall, 1993.
Blocker, H. Gene. *The Aesthetics of Primitive Art*. Lantham, Md.: Univ. Press of America, 1994.
Coote, Jeremy, and Anthony Shelton, eds. *Anthropology, Art, and Aesthetics*. New York: Oxford Univ. Press, 1992.
D'Azevedao, Warren L. *The Traditional Artist in African Societies*. Bloomington: Indiana Univ. Press, 1989.
Drewal, Henry, and John Pemberton III. *Yoruba: Nine Centuries of African Art and Thought*. New York: Center for African Art, 1989.
Guidoni, Enrico. *Primitive Architecture*. Trans. Robert Eric Wolf. History of World Architecture. New York: Rizzoli, 1987.
Leiris, Michel, and Jacqueline Delange. *African Art*. Arts of Mankind. London: Thames and Hudson, 1968.
Leuzinger, Elsy. *Africa: The Art of the Negro Peoples*. 2nd ed. Art of the World. New York: Crown, 1967.
Mbiti, John S. *African Religions and Philosophy*. 2nd ed. Oxford: Heinemann, 1990.
Mexico: Splendors of Thirty Centuries. New York: Metropolitan Museum of Art, 1990.
Murray, Jocelyn, ed. *Cultural Atlas of Africa*. New York: Facts on File, 1981.
Price, Sally. *Primitive Art in Civilized Places*. Chicago: Univ. of Chicago Press, 1989.
Willett, Frank. *African Art: An Introduction*. Rev ed. World of Art. New York: Thames and Hudson, 1993.

Chapter 1 Prehistory and Prehistoric Art in Europe

Anati, Emmanuel. *Camonica Valley: A Depiction of Village Life in the Alps from Neolithic Times to the Birth of Christ, as Revealed by Thousands of Newly Found Rock Carvings*. Trans. Linda Asher. New York: Knopf, 1961.
Bandi, Hans-Georg, et al. *Art of the Stone Age: Forty Thousand Years of Rock Art*. 2nd ed. Trans. Ann E. Keep. Art of the World. London: Methuen, 1970.
Beltrán Martínez, Antonio. *Rock Art of the Spanish Levant*. Trans. Margaret Brown. Cambridge: Cambridge Univ. Press, 1982.
Castleden, Rodney. *The Making of Stonehenge*. London: Routledge, 1993.
Chippindale, Christopher. *Stonehenge Complete*. New York: Thames and Hudson, 1994.
Freeman, Leslie G. *Altamira Revisited and Other Essays on Early Art*. Chicago: Institute for Prehistoric Investigation, 1987.
Gowlett, John A. J. *Ascent to Civilization: The Archaeology of Early Humans*. 2nd ed. New York: McGraw-Hill, 1993.
Graziosi, Paolo. *Paleolithic Art*. New York: McGraw-Hill, 1960.
Leroi-Gourhan, André. *The Dawn of European Art: An Introduction to Paleolithic Cave Painting*. Trans. Sara Champion. Cambridge: Cambridge Univ. Press, 1982.
———. *Treasures of Prehistoric Art*. New York: Abrams, 1967.
Lewin, Roger. *The Origins of Modern Humans*. New York: Scientific American Library, 1993.
Lhote, Henri. *The Search for the Tassili Frescoes: The Story of the Prehistoric Rock-Paintings of the Sahara*. 2nd ed. Trans. Alan Houghton Brodrick. London: Hutchinson, 1973.
Marshack, Alexander. *The Roots of Civilization: The Cognitive Beginnings of Man's First Art, Symbol, and Notation*. New York: McGraw-Hill, 1971.
Moscati, Sabatino, ed. *The Phoenicians*. New York: Abbeville, 1988.
O'Kelly, Michael J. *Newgrange: Archaeology, Art, and Legend*. New Aspects of Antiquity. London: Thames and Hudson, 1982.
Powell, T. G. E. *Prehistoric Art*. World of Art. New York: Oxford Univ. Press, 1966.
Price, T. Douglas, and Gray M. Feinman. *Images of the Past*. Mountain View, Calif.: Mayfield, 1993.
Renfrew, Colin, ed. *The Megalithic Monuments of Western Europe*. London: Thames and Hudson, 1983.
Ruspoli, Mario. *The Cave of Lascaux: The Final Photographs*. New York: Abrams, 1987.
Sandars, N. K. *Prehistoric Art in Europe*. 2nd ed. Pelican History of Art. Harmondsworth, Eng.: Penguin, 1985.
Sieveking, Ann. *The Cave Artists*. Ancient People and Places, vol. 93. London: Thames and Hudson, 1979.
Soffer, Olga. *The Upper Paleolithic of the Central Russian Plain*. Studies in Archaeology. Orlando, Fla.: Academic, 1985.
Torbrugge, Walter. *Prehistoric European Art*. Trans. Norbert Guterman. Panorama of World Art. New York: Abrams, 1968.
Ucko, Peter J., and Andree Rosenfeld. *Paleolithic Cave Art*. New York: McGraw-Hill, 1967.

Chapter 2 Art of the Ancient Near East

Akurgal, Ekrem. *The Art of the Hittites*. Trans. Constance McNab. New York: Abrams, 1962.
Amiet, Pierre. *Art of the Ancient Near East*. Trans. John Shepley and Claude Choquet. New York: Abrams, 1980.
Baring, Anne, and Jules Cashford. *The Myth of the Goddess: Evolution of an Image*. London: Viking Arkana, 1991.
Bottero, Jean. *Mesopotamia: Writing, Reasoning, and the Gods*. Trans. Zainab Bahrani and Marc Van De Mieroop. Chicago: Univ. of Chicago Press, 1992.
Collon, Dominque. *First Impressions: Cylinder Seals in the Ancient Near East*. Chicago: Univ. of Chicago Press, 1987.
Ferrier, R. W., ed. *Arts of Persia*. New Haven: Yale Univ. Press, 1989.
Ghirshman, Roman. *The Arts of Ancient Iran from Its Origins to the Time of Alexander the Great*. Trans. Stuart Gilbert and James Emmons. Arts of Mankind. New York: Golden, 1964.
Giedion, Sigfried. *The Eternal Present: A Contribution on Constancy and Change*. 2 vols. New York: Pantheon, 1962–64.
Harper, Prudence, Joan Arz, and Françoise Tallon, eds. *The Royal City of Susa: Ancient Near Eastern Treasures in the Louvre*. New York: Metropolitan Museum of Art, 1992.
Kramer, Samual Noah. *History Begins at Sumer: Thirty-Nine Firsts in Man's Recorded History*. 3rd rev. ed. Philadelphia: Univ. of Pennsylvania Press, 1981.
———. *The Sumerians, Their History, Culture, and Character*. Chicago: Univ. of Chicago Press, 1963.
Lloyd, Seton. *Ancient Turkey: A Traveller's History of Anatolia*. Berkeley: Univ. of California Press, 1989.
Mellaart, James. *The Earliest Civilization of the Near East*. London: Thames and Hudson, 1965.
Oppenheim, A. Leo. *Ancient Mesopotamia: Portrait of a Dead Civilization*. Rev. ed. completed by Erica Reiner. Chicago: Univ. of Chicago Press, 1977.
Parrot, André. *The Arts of Assyria*. Trans. Stuart Gilbert and James Emmons. Arts of Mankind. New York: Golden, 1961.
———. *Sumer: The Dawn of Art*. Trans. Stuart Gilbert and James Emmons. Arts of Mankind. New York: Golden, 1961.
Porada, Edith. *The Art of Ancient Iran: Pre-Islamic Cultures*. Art of the World. New York: Crown, 1965.
Roaf, Michael. *Cultural Atlas of Mesopotamia and the Ancient Near East*. New York: Facts on File, 1990.
Roux, Georges. *Ancient Iraq*. 3rd ed. London: Penguin, 1992.
Russell, John Malcolm. *Sennacherib's Palace without Rival at Nineveh*. Chicago: Univ. of Chicago Press, 1991.
Saggs, H. W. F. *Everyday Life in Babylonia and Assyria*. New York: Dorset, 1987.
———. *Civilization before Greece and Rome*. New Haven: Yale Univ. Press, 1989.
Wolkstein, Dianne, and Samuel Noah Kramer. *Inanna: Queen of Heaven and Earth*. New York: Harper & Row, 1983.
Woolley, Leonard. *The Art of the Middle East including Persia, Mesopotamia and Palestine*. Trans. Ann E. Keep. Art of the World. New York: Crown, 1961.

Chapter 3 Art of Ancient Egypt

Aldred, Cyril. *Akenaten and Nefertiti*. New York: Brooklyn Museum, 1973.
———. *Egyptian Art in the Days of the Pharaohs, 3100–320 B.C.* World of Art. London: Thames and Hudson, 1980.
Andrews, Carol. *Ancient Egyptian Jewelry*. New York: Abrams, 1991.
Baines, John, and Jaromír Málek. *Atlas of Ancient Egypt*. New York: Facts on File, 1980.
Bierbrier, Morris. *Tomb-Builders of the Pharaohs*. London: British Museum, 1982.
Breasted, James Henry. *A History of Egypt from the Earliest Times to the Persian Conquest*. New York: Scribner's, 1909.
Brier, Bob. *Egyptian Mummies*. New York: Morrow, 1994.
David, A. Rosalie. *The Pyramid Builders of Ancient Egypt: A Modern Investigation of Pharaoh's Workforce*. London: Routledge, 1986.

Edwards, I. E. S. *The Pyramids of Egypt*. Rev. ed. Harmondsworth, Eng.: Penguin, 1985.

The Egyptian Book of the Dead: The Book of Going Forth by Day: Being the Papyrus of Ani (Royal Scribe of the Divine Offerings). Trans. Raymond O. Faulkner. San Francisco: Chronicle, 1994.

Grimal, Nicolas. *A History of Ancient Egypt*. Trans. Ian Hall. Oxford: Blackwell, 1992.

James, T. G. H. *Egyptian Painting*. London: British Museum, 1985.

———, and W. V. Davies. *Egyptian Sculpture*. Cambridge: Harvard Univ. Press, 1983.

Kozloff, Arielle P., and Betsy M. Bryan. *Egypt's Dazzling Sun: Amenhotep III and His World*. Cleveland: Cleveland Museum of Art, 1992.

Manniche, Lise. *City of the Dead: Thebes in Egypt*. Chicago: Univ. of Chicago Press, 1987.

Martin, Geoffrey Thorndike. *The Hidden Tombs of Memphis: New Discoveries from the Time of Tutankhamun and Ramesses the Great*. London: Thames and Hudson, 1991.

Montet, Pierre. *Everyday Life in Egypt in the Days of Ramesses the Great*. Trans. A. R. Maxwell-Hysop and Margaret S. Drower. Philadelphia: Univ. of Pennsylvania Press, 1981.

Pemberton, Delia. *Ancient Egypt*. Architectural Guides for Travelers. San Francisco: Chronicle, 1992.

Reeves, C. N. *The Complete Tutankhamun: The King, the Tomb, the Royal Treasure*. London: Thames and Hudson, 1990.

Russmann, Edna R. *Egyptian Sculpture: Cairo and Luxor*. Austin: Univ. of Texas Press, 1989.

Smith, W. Stevenson. *The Art and Architecture of Ancient Egypt*. Rev. ed. Pelican History of Art. Harmondsworth, Eng.: Penguin, 1981.

Strouhal, Eugen. *Life of the Ancient Egyptians*. Norman: Univ. of Oklahoma Press, 1992.

Treasures of Tutankhamun. New York: Ballantine, 1976.

Wilkinson, Charles K. *Egyptian Wall Paintings: The Metropolitan Museum of Art's Collection of Facsimiles*. New York: Metropolitan Museum of Art, 1983.

Winstone, H. V. F. *Howard Carter and the Discovery of the Tomb of Tutankhamun*. London: Constable, 1991.

Woldering, Irmgard. *The Art of Egypt: The Time of the Pharaohs*. Trans. Ann E. Keep. Art of the World. New York: Crown, 1963.

Chapter 4 Aegean Art

Barber, R. L. N. *The Cyclades in the Bronze Age*. Iowa City: Univ. of Iowa Press, 1987.

Castleden, Rodney. *The Knossos Labyrinth: A New View of the "Palace of Minos" at Knossos*. London: Routledge, 1990.

Demargne, Pierre. *The Birth of Greek Art*. Trans. Stuart Gilbert and James Emmons. Arts of Mankind. New York: Golden, 1964.

Doumas, Christos. *The Wall-Paintings of Thera*. Trans. Alex Doumas. Athens: Thera Foundation, 1992.

Fitton, J. Lesley. *Cycladic Art*. Cambridge: Harvard Univ. Press, 1990.

Higgins, Reynold. *Minoan and Mycenean Art*. Rev. ed. World of Art. New York: Oxford Univ. Press, 1981.

Immerwahr, Sara Anderson. *Aegean Painting in the Bronze Age*. University Park: Pennsylvania State Univ. Press, 1990.

Marinatos, Nanno. *Art and Religion in Thera: Reconstructing a Bronze Age Society*. Athens: Mathioulakis, 1984.

Marinatos, Spyridon, and Max Hirmer. *Crete and Mycenae*. New York: Abrams, 1960.

Matz, Friedrich. *The Art of Crete and Early Greece: Prelude to Greek Art*. Trans. Ann E. Keep. Art of the World. New York: Crown, 1962.

Morgan, Lyvia. *The Miniature Wall Paintings of Thera: A Study in Aegean Culture and Iconography*. Cambridge: Cambridge Univ. Press, 1988.

Pellegrino, Charles R. *Unearthing Atlantis: An Archaeological Survey*. New York: Random House, 1991.

Chapter 5 Art of Ancient Greece

Akurgal, Ekrem. *The Art of Greece: Its Origins in the Mediterranean and Near East*. Trans. Wayne Dynes. Art of the World. New York: Crown, 1968.

Andrewes, Antony. *The Greeks: History of Human Society*. New York: Knopf, 1967.

Arafat, K. W. *Classical Zeus: A Study in Art and Literature*. Oxford: Clarendon, 1990.

Arias, Paolo. *A History of 1000 Years of Greek Vase Painting*. New York: Abrams, 1962.

Ashmole, Bernard. *Architect and Sculptor in Classical Greece*. Wrightsman Lectures. New York: New York Univ. Press, 1972.

Avery, Catherine, ed. *The New Century Handbook of Greek Mythology and Legend*. New York: Appleton-Century-Crofts, 1972.

Berve, Helmut, and Gottfried Gruben. *Greek Temples, Theatres, and Shrines*. New York: Abrams, 1963.

Biers, William. *The Archaeology of Greece: An Introduction*. Rev. ed. Ithaca: Cornell Univ. Press, 1987.

Blumel, Carl. *Greek Sculptors at Work*. 2nd ed. Trans. Lydia Holland. London: Phaidon, 1969.

Boardman, John. *Greek Art*. Rev. ed. World of Art. New York: Oxford Univ. Press, 1973.

———. *Greek Sculpture: The Archaic Period: A Handbook*. World of Art. New York: Oxford Univ. Press, 1978.

———. *Greek Sculpture: The Classical Period: A Handbook*. London: Thames and Hudson, 1985.

———. *Oxford History of the Classical World*. Oxford: Oxford Univ. Press, 1986.

———. *The Parthenon and Its Sculptures*. Austin: Univ. of Texas Press, 1985.

Branigan, Keith, and Michael Vickers. *Hellas: The Civilizations of Ancient Greece*. New York: McGraw-Hill, 1980.

Camp, John M. *The Athenian Agora: Excavations in the Heart of Classical Athens*. New York: Thames and Hudson, 1986.

Carpenter, Thomas H. *Art and Myth in Ancient Greece: A Handbook*. World of Art. London: Thames and Hudson, 1991.

Charbonneaux, Jean, Robert Martin, and François Villard. *Archaic Greek Art (620–480 B.C.)*. Trans. James Emmons and Robert Allen. Arts of Mankind. New York: Braziller, 1971.

———. *Classical Greek Art (480–330 B.C.)*. Trans. James Emmons. Arts of Mankind. New York: Braziller, 1972.

———. *Hellenistic Art (330–50 B.C.)*. Trans. Peter Green. Arts of Mankind. New York: Braziller, 1973.

Chitham, Robert. *The Classical Orders of Architecture*. New York: Rizzoli, 1985.

Finley, Moses. *The Ancient Greeks: An Introduction to Their Life and Thought*. New York: Viking, 1963.

Francis, E. D. *Image and Idea in Fifth-Century Greece: Art and Literature after the Persian Wars*. London: Routledge, 1990.

Havelock, Christine Mitchell. *Hellenistic Art: The Art of the Classical World from the Death of Alexander the Great to the Battle of Actium*. 2nd ed. New York: Norton, 1981.

Homann-Wedeking, Ernst. *The Art of Archaic Greece*. Trans. J. R. Foster. Art of the World. New York: Crown, 1968.

Hood, Sinclair. *Arts in Prehistoric Greece*. Pelican History of Art. Harmondsworth, Eng.: Penguin, 1978.

Hopper, Robert John. *The Acropolis*. London: Weidenfeld and Nicolson, 1971.

Hurwit, Jeffrey M. *The Art and Culture of Early Greece 1100–480 B.C.* Ithaca: Cornell Univ. Press, 1985.

Jenkins, Ian. *The Parthenon Frieze*. Austin: Univ. of Texas Press, 1994.

Kagan, Donald. *The Outbreak of the Peloponnesian War*. Ithaca: Cornell Univ. Press, 1969.

Lawrence, A. W. *Greek Architecture*. 4th ed. Pelican History of Art. Harmondsworth, Eng.: Penguin, 1983.

Lullies, Reinhart, and Max Hirmer. *Greek Sculpture*. Rev. ed. Trans. Michael Bullock. New York: Abrams, 1957.

Martin, Roland. *Greek Architecture: Architecture of Crete, Greece, and the Greek World*. History of World Architecture. New York: Electa/Rizzoli, 1988.

Morg, Catherine. *Athletes and Oracles: The Transformation of Olympia and Delphi in the Eighth Century B.C.* Cambridge: Cambridge Univ. Press, 1990.

Onians, John. *Art and Thought in the Hellenistic Age: The Greek World View 350–50 B.C.* London: Thames and Hudson, 1979.

Papaioannou, Kostas. *The Art of Greece*. Trans. I. Mark Paris. New York: Abrams, 1989.

Pedley, John Griffiths. *Greek Art and Archaeology*. New York: Abrams, 1993.

Pollitt, J. J. *Art in the Hellenistic Age*. Cambridge: Cambridge Univ. Press, 1986.

———. *The Art of Ancient Greece: Sources and Documents*. Cambridge: Cambridge Univ. Press, 1990.

Ridgway, Brunilde Sismondo. *Fifth Century Styles in Greek Sculpture*. Princeton: Princeton Univ. Press, 1981.

———. *Hellenistic Sculpture I: The Styles of ca. 331–200 B.C.* Wisconsin Studies in Classics. Madison: Univ. of Wisconsin Press, 1990.

Robertson, Martin. *Greek Painting: The Great Centuries of Painting*. Geneva: Skira, 1959.

Roes, Anna. *Greek Geometric Art: Its Symbolism and Its Origin*. London: Oxford Univ. Press, 1933.

Schefold, Karl. *Classical Greece*. Trans. J. R. Foster. Art of the World. London: Methuen, 1967.

Schmidt, Evamaria. *The Great Altar of Pergamon*. Trans. Lena Jack. Leipzig: VEB Edition Leipzig, 1962.

Scully, Vincent. *The Earth, the Temple, and the Gods: Greek Sacred Architecture*. Rev. ed. New Haven: Yale Univ. Press, 1979.

Smith, R. R. R. *Hellenistic Sculpture: A Handbook*. World of Art. New York: Thames and Hudson, 1991.

Stewart, Andrew F. *Greek Sculpture: An Exploration*. 2 vols. New Haven: Yale Univ. Press, 1990.

———. *Skopas of Paros*. Park Ridge: Noyes, 1977.

Webster, T. B. L. *The Art of Greece: The Age of Hellenism*. Art of the World. New York: Crown, 1966.

Whitley, A. James M. *Style and Society in Dark Age Greece: The Changing Face of a Pre-literate Society, 1100–700 B.C.* New Studies in Archaeology. Cambridge: Cambridge Univ. Press, 1991.

Chapter 6 Etruscan Art and Roman Art

Andreae, Bernard. *The Art of Rome*. Trans. Robert Erich Wolf. New York: Abrams, 1977.

Aries, Philippe, and Georges Duby, eds. *A History of Private Life*. Vol. 1: *From Pagan Rome to Byzantium*. Trans. Arthur Goldhammer. Cambridge, Mass.: Belknap, 1987.

Balsdon, J. P. V. D. *Roman Women: Their History and Habits*. London: Bodley Head, 1962.

Bianchi Bandinelli, Ranuccio. *Rome: The Centre of Power: Roman Art to A.D. 200*. Trans. Peter Green. Arts of Mankind. London: Thames and Hudson, 1970.

———. *Rome: The Late Empire: Roman Art A.D. 200–400*. Trans. Peter Green. Arts of Mankind. New York: Braziller, 1971.

Bloch, Raymond. *Etruscan Art*. Greenwich, Conn.: New York Graphic Society, 1965.

Boardman, John. *Oxford History of the Classical World*. Oxford: Oxford Univ. Press, 1986.

Boethius, Axel, and J. B. Ward-Perkins. *Etruscan and Early Roman Architecture*. 2nd ed. Pelican History of Art. Harmondsworth, Eng.: Penguin, 1978.

Breeze, David John. *Hadrian's Wall*. London: Allen Lane, 1976.

Brendel, Otto J. *Etruscan Art*. Pelican History of Art. Harmondsworth, Eng.: Penguin, 1978.

Brilliant, Richard. *Roman Art from the Republic to Constantine*. London: Phaidon, 1974.

Brown, Peter. *The World of Late Antiquity: A.D. 150–750*. New York: Norton, 1989.

Buranelli, Francesco. *The Etruscans: Legacy of a Lost Civilization from the Vatican Museums*. Memphis: Lithograph, 1992.

Christ, Karl. *The Romans: An Introduction to Their History and Civilisation*. Berkeley: Univ. of California Press, 1984.

Cornell, Tim, and John Matthews. *Atlas of the Roman World*. New York: Facts on File, 1982.

Guilland, Jacqueline, and Maurice Guilland. *Frescoes in the Time of Pompeii*. New York: Potter, 1990.

Heintze, Helga von. *Roman Art*. New York: Universe, 1990.

Henig, Martin, ed. *A Handbook of Roman Art: A Comprehensive Survey of All the Arts of the Roman World*. Ithaca: Cornell Univ. Press, 1983.

Kahler, Heinz. *The Art of Rome and Her Empire*. Trans. J. R. Foster. Art of the World. New York: Crown, 1963.

Ling, Roger. *Roman Painting*. Cambridge: Cambridge Univ. Press, 1991.

L'Orange, Hans Peter. *The Roman Empire: Art Forms and Civic Life*. New York: Rizzoli, 1985.

MacDonald, William L. *The Architecture of the Roman Empire: An Introductory Study*. Rev. ed. 2 vols. Yale Publications in the History of Art. New Haven: Yale Univ. Press, 1982.

———. *The Pantheon: Design, Meaning, and Progeny*. Cambridge: Harvard Univ. Press, 1976.

Maiuri, Amedeo. *Roman Painting: The Great Centuries of Painting*. Trans. Stuart Gilbert. Geneva: Skira, 1953.

Mansuelli, G. A. *The Art of Etruria and Early Rome*. Art of the World. New York: Crown, 1965.

Pollitt, J. J. *The Art of Rome, c. 753 B.C.–337 A.D.: Sources and Documents*. Englewood Cliffs, N.J.: Prentice-Hall, 1966.

Quennell, Peter. *The Colosseum*. New York: Newsweek, 1971.

Ramage, Nancy H., and Andrew Ramage. *Roman Art: Romulus to Constantine*. New York: Abrams, 1991.

Rediscovering Pompeii. Rome: L'Erma di Bretschneider, 1990.

Sprenger, Maja, and Bartolini, Gilda. *The Etruscans: Their History, Art, and Architecture*. New York: Abrams, 1983.

Strong, Donald. *Roman Art*. 2nd ed. Pelican History of Art. Harmondsworth, Eng.: Penguin, 1988.

Ward-Perkins, J. B. *Roman Architecture*. History of World Architecture. New York: Electa/Rizzoli, 1988.

Wheeler, Robert Eric Mortimer, Sir. *Roman Art and Architecture*. World of Art. New York: Oxford Univ. Press, 1964.

Wilkinson, L. P. *The Roman Experience*. New York: Knopf, 1974.

Chapter 7 Early Christian, Jewish, and Byzantine Art

Age of Spirituality: Late Antique and Early Christian Art, Third to Seventh Century. New York: Metropolitan Museum of Art, 1979.

Beckwith, John. *The Art of Constantinople: An Introduction to Byzantine Art 330–1453*. 2nd ed. London: Phaidon, 1968.

———. *Early Christian and Byzantine Art*. 2nd ed. Pelican History of Art. Harmondsworth, Eng.: Penguin, 1979.

Boyd, Susan A. *Byzantine Art*. Chicago: Univ. of Chicago Press, 1979.

Buckton, David, ed. *The Treasury of San Marco, Venice*. Milan: Olivetti, 1985.

Carr, Annemarie Weyl. *Byzantine Illumination, 1150–1250: The Study of a Provincial Tradition*. Chicago: Univ. of Chicago Press, 1987.

Christe, Yves. *Art of the Christian World, A.D. 200–1500: A Handbook of Styles and Forms*. New York: Rizzoli, 1982.

Cutler, Anthony. *The Hand of the Master: Craftsmanship, Ivory, and Society in Byzantium (9th–11th Centuries)*. Princeton: Princeton Univ. Press, 1994.

Demus, Otto. *Byzantine Art and the West*. Wrightsman Lectures. New York: New York Univ. Press, 1970.

———. *Byzantine Mosaic Decoration: Aspects of Monumental Art in Byzantium*. New Rochelle: Caratzas, 1976.

———. *The Church of San Marco in Venice: History, Architecture, Sculpture*. Washington, D.C.: Dumbarton Oaks, 1960.

Ferguson, George Wells. *Signs and Symbols in Christian Art*. New York: Oxford Univ. Press, 1967.

Gough, Michael. *Origins of Christian Art*. World of Art. London: Thames and Hudson, 1973.

Grabar, André. *The Art of the Byzantine Empire: Byzantine Art in the Middle Ages*. Trans. Betty Forster. Art of the World. New York: Crown, 1966.

———. *Early Christian Art: From the Rise of Christianity to the Death of Theodosius*. Trans. Stuart Gilbert and James Emmons. Arts of Mankind. New York: Odyssey, 1969.

———. *The Golden Age of Justinian from the Death of Theodosius to the Rise of Islam*. Trans. Stuart Gilbert and James Emmons. Arts of Mankind. New York: Odyssey, 1967.
Hubert, Jean, Jean Porcher, and W. F. Volbach. *Europe of the Invasions*. Trans. Stuart Gilbert and James Emmons. Arts of Mankind. New York: Braziller, 1969.
Kitzinger, Ernst. *Byzantine Art in the Making: Main Lines of Stylistic Development in Mediterranean Art, 3rd–7th Century*. Cambridge: Harvard Univ. Press, 1977.
Krautheimer, Richard. *Early Christian and Byzantine Architecture*. 4th ed. Pelican History of Art. Harmondsworth, Eng: Penguin, 1986.
Lane Fox, Robin. *Pagans and Christians*. Harmondsworth, Eng.: Viking, 1986.
Mainstone, R. J. *Hagia Sophia: Architecture, Structure and Liturgy of Justinian's Great Church*. London: Thames and Hudson, 1988.
Mango, Cyril. *Art of the Byzantine Empire, 312–1453: Sources and Documents*. Englewood Cliffs, N.J.: Prentice-Hall, 1972.
———. *Byzantine Architecture*. History of World Architecture. New York: Rizzoli, 1985.
Manicelli, Fabrizio. *Catacombs and Basilicas: The Early Christians in Rome*. Florence: Scala, 1981.
Mathew, Gervase. *Byzantine Aesthetics*. London: J. Murray, 1963.
Milburn, R. L. P. *Early Christian Art and Architecture*. Berkeley: Univ. of California Press, 1988.
Oakshott, Walter Fraser. *The Mosaics of Rome: From the Third to the Fourteenth Centuries*. London: Thames and Hudson, 1967.
Rice, David Talbot. *Art of the Byzantine Era*. New York: Praeger, 1963.
———. *Byzantine Art*. Harmondsworth, Eng.: Penguin, 1968.
Schapiro, Meyer. *Late Antique, Early Christian, and Mediaeval Art*. New York: Braziller, 1979.
Simson, Otto Georg von. *Sacred Fortress: Byzantine Art and Statecraft in Ravenna*. Chicago: Univ. of Chicago Press, 1948.
Snyder, James. *Medieval Art: Painting, Sculpture, Architecture, 4th–14th Century*. Englewood Cliffs, N.J.: Prentice-Hall, 1989.
Stevenson, James. *The Catacombs: Rediscovered Monuments of Early Christianity*. Ancient Peoples and Places. London: Thames and Hudson, 1978.
Weitzmann, Kurt. *Late Antique and Early Christian Book Illumination*. New York: Braziller, 1977.
———. *Place of Book Illumination in Byzantine Art*. Princeton: Art Museum, Princeton Univ., 1975.
Wharton, Annabel Jane. *Art of Empire: Painting and Architecture of the Byzantine Periphery: A Comparative Study of Four Provinces*. University Park: Pennsylvania State Univ. Press, 1988.

Chapter 8 Islamic Art

Akurgal, Ekrem, ed. *The Art and Architecture of Turkey*. New York: Rizzoli, 1980.
Al-Faruqi, Ismail R, and Lois Lamya'al Faruqi. *Cultural Atlas of Islam*. New York: Macmillan, 1986.
Aslanapa, Oktay. *Turkish Art and Architecture*. London: Faber, 1971.
Atasoy, Nurhan. *Splendors of the Ottoman Sultans*. Ed. and Trans. Tulay Artan. Memphis, Tenn.: Lithograph, 1992.
Atil, Esin. *The Age of Sultan Suleyman the Magnificent*. Washington, D.C.: National Gallery of Art, 1987.
———. *Art of the Arab World*. Washington, D.C.: Smithsonian Institution, 1975.
———. *Islamic Art and Patronage: Treasures from Kuwait*. New York: Rizzoli, 1990.
———. *Renaissance of Islam: Art of the Mamluks*. Washington, D.C.: Smithsonian Institution, 1981.
Blair, Sheila S., and Jonathan M. Brown. *The Art and Architecture of Islam 1250–1800*. New Haven: Yale Univ. Press, 1994.
Brend, Barbara. *Islamic Art*. Cambridge: Harvard Univ. Press, 1991.
Dodds, Jerrilynn D., ed. *Al-Andalus: The Art of Islamic Spain*. New York: Metropolitan Museum of Art, 1992.
Ettinghausen, Richard, and Oleg Grabar. *The Art and Architecture of Islam: 650–1250*. Pelican History of Art. Harmondsworth, Eng.: Penguin, 1987.
Falk, Toby, ed. *Treasures of Islam*. London: Sotheby's, 1985.
Ferrier, R. W., ed. *Arts of Persia*. New Haven: Yale Univ. Press, 1989.
Frishman, Martin, and Hasan-Uddin Khan. *The Mosque: History, Architectural Development and Regional Diversity*. London: Thames and Hudson, 1994.
Glasse, Cyril. *The Concise Encyclopedia of Islam*. San Francisco: Harper & Row, 1989.
Grabar, Oleg. *The Alhambra*. Cambridge: Harvard Univ. Press, 1978.
———. *The Formation of Islamic Art*. Rev. ed. New Haven: Yale Univ. Press, 1987.
———. *The Great Mosque of Isfahan*. New York: New York Univ. Press, 1990.
———. *The Mediation of Ornament*. A. W. Mellon Lectures in the Fine Arts. Princeton: Princeton Univ. Press, 1992.
Grube, Ernest J. *Architecture of the Islamic World: Its History and Social Meaning*. Ed. George Mitchell. New York: Morrow, 1978.
Hoag, John D. *Islamic Architecture*. History of World Architecture. New York: Abrams, 1977.
Jones, Dalu, and George Mitchell, eds. *The Arts of Islam*. London: Arts Council of Great Britain, 1976.
Khatibi, Abdelkebir, and Mohammed Sijelmassi. *The Splendour of Islamic Calligraphy*. New York: Rizzoli, 1977.
The Koran. Rev. ed. Trans. N. J. Dawood. London: Penguin, 1993.
Lentz, Thomas W., and Glenn D. Lowry. *Timur and the Princely Vision: Persian Art and Culture in the Fifteenth Century*. Los Angeles: Los Angeles County Museum of Art, 1989.
Papadopoulo, Alexandre. *Islam and Muslim Art*. Trans. Robert Erich Wolf. New York: Abrams, 1979.
Petsopoulos, Yanni, ed. *Tulips, Arabesques and Turbans: Decorative Arts from the Ottoman Empire*. New York: Abbeville, 1982.
Raby, Julian, ed. *The Art of Syria and the Jazira, 1100–1250*. Oxford Studies in Islamic Art. Oxford: Oxford Univ. Press, 1985.
Rice, David Talbot. *Islamic Art*. World of Art. New York: Thames and Hudson, 1965.
Schimmel, Annemarie. *Calligraphy and Islamic Culture*. New York: New York Univ. Press, 1983.
Sharma, Arvind, ed. *Our Religions*. San Francisco: HarperSanFrancisco, 1993.
Ward, R. M. *Islamic Metalwork*. New York: Thames and Hudson, 1993.
Welch, Anthony. *Calligraphy in the Arts of the Muslim World*. Austin: Univ. of Texas Press, 1979.

Chapter 9 Art of India before 1100

Berkson, Carmel. *Elephanta: The Cave of Shiva*. Princeton: Princeton Univ. Press, 1983.
Chandra, Pramod. *The Sculpture of India, 3000 B.C.–1300 A.D.* Washington, D.C.: National Gallery of Art, 1985.
Coomaraswamy, Ananda K. *Yaksas: Essays in the Water Cosmology*. Rev. ed. Ed. Paul Schroeder. New York: Oxford Univ. Press, 1993.
Czuma, Stansilaw J. *Kushan Sculpture: Images from Early India*. Cleveland: Cleveland Museum of Art, 1985.
De Bary, William, ed. *Sources of Indian Tradition*. New York: Columbia Univ. Press, 1958.
Dehejia, Vidya. *Art of the Imperial Cholas*. New York: Columbia Univ. Press, 1990.
———. *Early Buddhist Rock Temples*. Ithaca: Cornell Univ. Press, 1972.
Dessai, Vishakha N., and Darielle Mason. *Gods, Guardians, and Lovers: Temple Sculptures from North India, A.D. 700–1200*. New York: Asia Society Galleries, 1993.
Dimmitt, Cornelia. *Classical Hindu Mythology*. Philadelphia: Temple Univ. Press, 1978.
Eck, Diana L. Darsan. *Seeing the Divine Image in India*. 2nd rev. ed. Chambersburg, Penn.: Anima, 1985.
Errington, Elizabeth, and Joe Cribb, eds. *The Crossroads of Asia: Transformation in Image and Symbol in the Art of Ancient Afghanistan and Pakistan*. Cambridge, Eng.: Ancient India and Iran Trust, 1992.
Goswamy, B. N. *An Early Document of Indian Art: The Citralak-sa-na of Nagnajit*. New Delhi: Manohar Book Service, 1976.
Harle, James C. *Art and Architecture of the Indian Subcontinent*. Pelican History of Art. Harmondsworth, Eng.: Penguin, 1987.
———. *Gupta Sculpture*. Oxford: Clarendon, 1974.
Huntington, Susan L. *Art of Ancient India*. New York: Weatherhill, 1985.
———. *Leaves from the Bodhi Tree: The Art of Pala India (8th–12th Centuries) and Its International Legacy*. Dayton: Dayton Art Institute, 1990.
Hutt, Michael. *Nepal: A Guide to the Art and Architecture of the Kathmandu Valley*. Boston: Shambala, 1995.
Johnston, E. H. *Buddhacharita, or Acts of the Buddha*. 2nd ed. New Delhi: Oriental Books Reprint, 1972.
Knox, Robert. *Amaravati: Buddhist Sculpture from the Great Stupa*. London: British Museum, 1992.
Kramrisch, Stella. *The Art of Nepal*. New York: Abrams, 1964.
———. *The Hindu Temple*. 2 vols. Calcutta: Univ. of Calcutta, 1946.
———. *Presence of Siva*. Princeton: Princeton Univ. Press, 1981.
———. *Vichnudharmottara, Part III: A Treatise on Indian Painting and Image-Making*. 2nd rev. ed. Calcutta: Calcutta Univ. Press, 1928.
Meister, Michael, ed. *Discourses on Siva: On the Nature of Religious Imagery*. Philadelphia: Univ. of Pennsylvania Press, 1984.
O'Flaherty, Wendy. *Hindu Myths*. Harmondsworth, Eng.: Penguin, 1975.
Pal, Pratapaditya, ed. *Aspects of Indian Art*. Leiden: Brill, 1972.
———. *The Ideal Image: The Gupta Sculptural Tradition and Its Influence*. New York: Asia Society, 1978.
Peterson, Indira Vishnvanathan. *Poems to Shiva: The Hymns of the Tamil Saints*. Princeton: Princeton Univ. Press, 1989.
Possehl, Gregory, ed. *Ancient Cities of the Indus*. Durham: Carolina Academic, 1979.
———. *Harappan Civilization: A Recent Perspective*. 2nd ed. New Delhi: American Institute of Indian Studies, 1993.
Poster, Amy G. *From Indian Earth: 4,000 Years of Terracotta Art*. Brooklyn: Brooklyn Museum, 1986.
Rosenfeld, John M. *The Dynastic Arts of the Kushans*. California Studies in the History of Art. Berkeley: Univ. of California Press, 1967.
Shearer, Alistair. *Upanishads*. New York: Harper & Row, 1978.
Singh, Madanjeet. *The Cave Paintings of Ajanta*. London: Thames and Hudson, 1965.
Skelton, Robert, and Mark Francis. *Arts of Bengal: The Heritage of Bangladesh and Eastern India*. London: Whitechapel Gallery, 1979.
Smith, Bardwell L., ed. *Essays in Gupta Culture*. Delhi: Motilal Banarsidass, 1983.
Thapar, Romila. *Asoka and the Decline of the Mauryas*. 2nd ed. Delhi: Oxford, 1973.
———. *History of India*. Harmondsworth, Eng.: Penguin, 1972.
Weiner, Sheila L. *Ajanta: Its Place in Buddhist Art*. Berkeley: Univ. of California Press, 1977.
Williams, Joanna G. *Art of Gupta India, Empire and Province*. Princeton: Princeton Univ. Press, 1982.
Zimmer, Heinrich Robert. *Myths and Symbols in Indian Art and Civilization*. ed. Joseph Campbell. Bollingen Series. New York: Pantheon, 1946.

Chapter 10 Chinese Art before 1280

Ackerman, Phyllis. *Ritual Bronzes of Ancient China*. New York: Dryden, 1945.
The Art Treasures of Dunhuang. Hong Kong: Joint, 1981.
Arts of China. 3 vols. Tokyo: Kodansha International, 1968–70.
Barnhart, Richard. *Along the Border of Heaven: Sung and Yuan Painting from the C. C. Wang Family Collection*. New York: Metropolitan Museum of Art, 1983.
Billeter, Jean François. *The Chinese Art of Writing*. New York: Skira/Rizzoli, 1990.
Blunden, Caroline, and Mark Elvin. *Cultural Atlas of China*. New York: Facts on File, 1983.
Cahill, James. *Art of Southern Sung China*. New York: Asia Society, 1962.
———. *Chinese Painting*. Treasures of Asia. Geneva: Skira, 1960.
———. *Index of Early Chinese Painters and Paintings: T'ang, Sung, and Yuan*. Berkeley: Univ. of California Press, 1980.
Cleary, Thomas, trans. *The Essential Tao: An Initiation into the Heart of Taoism through the Authentic Tao Te Ching and the Inner Teachings of Chuang Tzu*. San Francisco: HarperSanFrancisco, 1991.
De Silva, Anil. *The Art of Chinese Landscape Painting: In the Caves of Tun-huang*. Art of the World. New York: Crown, 1967.
Fong, Wen, ed. *Beyond Representation: Chinese Painting and Calligraphy, 8th–14th Century*. Princeton Monographs in Art and Archaeology. New York: Metropolitan Museum of Art, 1992.
———. *The Great Bronze Age of China: An Exhibition from the People's Republic of China*. New York: Metropolitan Museum of Art, 1980.
Fong, Wen, and Marilyn Fu. *Sung and Yuan Paintings*. New York: New York Graphic Society, 1973.
Gridley, Marilyn Leidig. *Chinese Buddhist Sculpture under the Liao: Free Standing Works in Situ and Selected Examples from Public Collections*. New Delhi: International Academy of Indian Culture, 1993.
Ho, Wai-kam, et al. *Eight Dynasties of Chinese Painting: The Collections of the Nelson Gallery-Atkins Museum, Kansas City, and the Cleveland Museum of Art*. Cleveland: Cleveland Museum of Art, 1980.
Juliano, Annette L. *Art of the Six Dynasties: Centuries of Change and Innovation*. New York: China House Gallery, 1975.
Lawton, Thomas. *Chinese Art of the Warring States Period: Change and Continuity, 480–222 B.C.* Washington, D.C.: Freer Gallery of Art, Smithsonian Institution, 1982.
———. *Chinese Figure Painting*. Washington, D.C.: Smithsonian Institution, 1973.
Lim, Lucy. *Stories from China's Past: Han Dynasty Pictorial Tomb Reliefs and Archaeological Objects from Sichuan Province, People's Republic of China*. San Francisco: Chinese Culture Foundation, 1987.
Medley, Margaret. *Chinese Potter: A Practical History of Chinese Ceramics*. 3rd ed. Oxford: Phaidon, 1989.
Munakata, Kiyohiko. *Sacred Mountains in Chinese Art*. Champaign: Krannert Art Museum, Univ. of Illinois, 1991.
Paludan, Ann. *Chinese Spirit Road: The Classical Tradition of Stone Tomb Sculpture*. New Haven: Yale Univ. Press, 1991.
———. *Chinese Tomb Figurines*. Hong Kong: Oxford Univ. Press, 1994.
Powers, Martin J. *Art and Political Expression in Early China*. New Haven: Yale Univ. Press, 1991.
Rawson, Jessica. *Ancient China: Art and Archaeology*. London: British Museum, 1980.
Sickman, Lawrence, and Alexander Soper. *Art and Architecture of China*. Pelican History of Art. Harmondsworth, Eng.: Penguin, 1971.
Speiser, Werner. *The Art of China: Spirit and Society*. Art of the World. New York: Crown, 1961.
Tregear, Mary. *Chinese Art*. World of Art. New York: Oxford Univ. Press, 1980.
Vainker, S. J. *Chinese Pottery and Porcelain: From Prehistory to the Present*. London: British Museum, 1991.
Watson, William. *Art of Dynastic China*. New York: Abrams, 1981.
Weidner, Marsha, ed. *Latter Days of the Law: Images of Chinese*

Buddhism, 850–1850. Lawrence: Spencer Museum of Art, Univ. of Kansas, 1994.

Whitfield, Roderick, and Anne Farrer. *Caves of the Thousand Buddhas: Chinese Art from the Silk Route*. London: British Museum, 1990.

Chapter 11 Japanese Art before 1392

Bethe, Monica. *Bugaku Masks*. Japanese Arts Library, vol. 5. New York: Kodansha International, 1978.

Egami, Namio. *The Beginnings of Japanese Art*. Trans. John Bester. Heibonsha Survey of Japanese Art, vol. 2. New York: Weatherhill, 1973.

Elisseeff, Danielle, and Vadime Elisseeff. *Art of Japan*. Trans. I. Mark Paris. New York: Abrams, 1985.

Fujioka, Ryoichi. *Shino and Oribe Ceramics*. Trans. Samuel Crowell Morse. Japanese Arts Library, vol. 1. New York: Kodansha International, 1977.

Fukuyama, Toshio. *Heian Temples: Byudo-in and Chuson-ji*. Trans. Ronald K. Jones. Heibonsha Survey of Japanese Art, vol. 9. New York: Weatherhill, 1976.

Hashimoto, Fumio, ed. *Architecture in the Shoin Style: Japanese Feudal Residences*. Trans. and adapted by H. Mack Horton. Japanese Arts Library, vol. 10. New York: Kodansha International, 1981.

Hayashi, Ryoichi. *Silk Road and the Shoso-in*. Trans. Robert Ricketts. Heibonsha Survey of Japanese Art, vol. 6. New York: Weatherhill, 1975.

Ienaga, Saburo. *Japanese Art: A Cultural Appreciation*. Trans. Richard L. Gage. Heibonsha Survey of Japanese Art, vol. 30. New York: Weatherhill, 1979.

———. *Painting in the Yamato Style*. Trans. John M. Shields. Heibonsha Survey of Japanese Art, vol. 10. New York: Weatherhill, 1973.

Ishida, Hisatoyo. *Esoteric Buddhist Painting*. Trans. and adapted by E. Dale Saunders. Japanese Arts Library, vol. 15. New York: Kodansha International, 1987.

Itoh, Teiji. *Traditional Domestic Architecture of Japan*. Trans. Richard L. Gage. Heibonsha Survey of Japanese Art, vol. 21. New York: Weatherhill, 1972.

Kidder, J. Edward. *Early Buddhist Japan*. Ancient People and Places. New York: Praeger, 1972.

———. *Early Japanese Art: The Great Tombs and Treasures*. Princeton: Van Nostrand, 1964.

———. *Japanese Temples: Sculpture, Paintings, Gardens, and Architecture*. London: Thames and Hudson, 1964.

———. *Prehistoric Japanese Arts: Jomon Pottery*. Tokyo: Kodansha International, 1968.

Kobayashi, Takeshi. *Nara Buddhist Art: Todai-ji*. Trans. and adapted by Richard L. Gage. Heibonsha Survey of Japanese Art, vol. 5. New York: Weatherhill, 1975.

Kurata, Bunsaku. *Horyu-ji, Temple of the Exalted Law: Early Buddhist Art from Japan*. New York: Japan Society, 1981.

Miki, Fumio. *Haniwa*. Trans. and adapted by Gino Lee Barnes. Arts of Japan, 8. New York: Weatherhill, 1974.

Miner, Earl, Hiroko Odagiri, and Robert E. Morrell. *The Princeton Companion to Classical Japanese Literature*. Princeton: Princeton Univ. Press, 1985.

Mino, Yutaka. *The Great Eastern Temple: Treasures of Japanese Buddhist Art from Todai-ji*. Chicago: Art Institute of Chicago, 1986.

Mizuno, Seiichi. *Asuka Buddhist Art: Horyuji*. Trans. Richard L. Gage. Heibonsha Survey of Japanese Art, vol. 4. New York: Weatherhill, 1974.

Mori, Hisashi. *Japanese Portrait Sculpture*. Trans. Widayati Roesijadi. Japanese Arts Library, vol. 2. New York: Kodansha International, 1977.

———. *Sculpture of the Kamakura Period*. Trans. Katherine Eickman. Heibonsha Survey of Japanese Art, vol. 11. New York: Weatherhill, 1974.

Murase, Miyeko. *Iconography of the Tale of Genji: Genji Monogatari Ekotoba*. New York: Weatherhill, 1983.

Nakagawa, Sensaku. *Kutani Ware*. Trans. and adapted by John Bester. Japanese Arts Library, vol. 7. New York: Kodansha International, 1979.

Nishiwara, Kyotaro, and Emily J. Sano. *The Great Age of Japanese Buddhist Sculpture, A.D. 60–1300*. Fort Worth, Tex.: Kimbell Art Museum, 1982.

Okazaki, Joji. *Pure Land Buddhist Painting*. Trans. Elizabeth ten Grutenhuis. Japanese Arts Library, vol. 4. New York: Kodansha International, 1977.

Okudaira, Hideo. *Narrative Picture Scrolls*. Trans. Elizabeth ten Grutenhuis. Arts of Japan, 5. New York: Weatherhill, 1973.

Ooka, Minoru. *Temples of Nara and Their Art*. Trans. Dennis Lishka. Heibonsha Survey of Japanese Art, vol. 7. New York: Weatherhill, 1973.

Pearson, Richard J. *Ancient Japan*. Washington, D.C.: Sackler Gallery, 1992.

Rosenfield, John M., Fumiko E. Cranston, and Edwin A. Cranston. *The Courtly Tradition in Japanese Art and Literature: Selections from the Hofer and Hyde Collections*. Cambridge: Fogg Art Museum, Harvard Univ., 1973.

———. *Japanese Arts of the Heian Period: 794–1185*. New York: Asia Society, 1967.

Sato, Kanzan. *Japanese Sword*. Trans. and adapted by Joe Earle. Japanese Arts Library, vol. 12. New York: Kodansha International, 1983.

Sawa, Takaaki. *Art in Japanese Esoteric Buddhism*. Trans.

Richard L. Gage. Heibonsha Survey of Japanese Art, vol. 8. New York: Weatherhill, 1972.

Soper, Alexander Coburn. *Evolution of Buddhist Architecture in Japan*. Princeton Monographs in Art and Archaeology, no. 22. New York: Hacker Art, 1978.

Sugiyama, Jiro. *Classic Buddhist Sculpture: The Tempyo Period*. Trans. and adapted by Samuel Crowell Morse. Japanese Arts Library, vol. 11. New York: Kodansha International, 1982.

Suzuki, Kakichi. *Early Buddhist Architecture in Japan*. Trans. and adapted by Mary Neighbor Parent and Nancy Shatzman Steinhardt. Japanese Arts Library, vol. 9. New York: Kodansha International, 1980.

Swann, Peter. *The Art of Japan: From the Jomon to the Tokugawa Period*. Art of the World. New York: Crown, 1966.

Tanaka, Ichimatsu. *Japanese Ink Painting: Shubun to Sesshu*. Trans. Bruce Darling. Heibonsha Survey of Japanese Art, vol. 12. New York: Weatherhill, 1972.

Varley, H. Paul. *Japanese Culture*. 3rd ed. Honolulu: Univ. of Hawaii Press, 1984.

Watanabe, Yasutada. *Shinto Art: Ise and Izumo Shrines*. Trans. Robert Ricketts. Heibonsha Survey of Japanese Art, vol. 3. New York: Weatherhill, 1974.

Yamane, Yuzo. *Momoyama Genre Painting*. Trans. John M. Shields. Heibonsha Survey of Japanese Art, vol. 17. New York: Weatherhill, 1973.

Yonezawa, Yoshiho, and Chu Yoshizawa. *Japanese Painting in the Literati Style*. Trans. and adapted by Betty Iverson Monroe. Heibonsha Survey of Japanese Art, vol. 23. New York: Weatherhill, 1974.

Chapter 12 Art of the Americas before 1300

Abel-Vidor, Suzanne. *Between Continents/Between Seas: Precolumbian Art of Costa Rica*. New York: Abrams, 1981.

Abrams, Elliot Marc. *How the Maya Built Their World: Energetics and Ancient Architecture*. Austin: Univ. of Texas Press, 1994.

Alcina Franch, José. *Pre-Columbian Art*. Trans. I. Mark Paris. New York: Abrams, 1983.

Anton, Ferdinand. *Art of the Maya*. Trans. Mary Whitall. London: Thames and Hudson, 1970.

Berlo, Janet Catherine, ed. *Art, Ideology, and the City of Teotihuacan: A Symposium at Dumbarton Oaks*. Washington, D.C.: Dumbarton Oaks, 1992.

Berrin, Kathleen, ed. *Feathered Serpents and Flowering Trees: Reconstructing the Murals of Teotihuacan*. San Francisco: Fine Arts Museums of San Francisco, 1988.

———, and Esther Pasztory. *Teotihuacan: Art from the City of the Gods*. New York: Thames and Hudson, 1993.

Brody, J. J. *The Anasazi: Ancient Indian People of the American Southwest*. New York: Rizzoli, 1990.

———. *Anasazi and Pueblo Painting*. Albuquerque: Univ. of New Mexico Press, 1991.

Clewlow, C. William. *Colossal Heads of the Olmec Culture*. Contributions of the Univ. of California Archaeological Research Facility. Berkeley: Archaeological Research Facility, Univ. of California, 1967.

Coe, Michael D. *The Jacquar's Children: Pre-Classical Central Mexico*. New York: Museum of Primitive Art, 1965.

Coe, Ralph T. *Sacred Circles: Two Thousand Years of North American Indian Art*. London: Arts Council of Great Britain, 1976.

Donnan, Christopher B. *Ceramics of Ancient Peru*. Los Angeles: Fowler Museum of Cultural History, Univ. of California, 1992.

———. *Moche Art of Peru: Pre-Columbian Symbolic Communication*. Rev. ed. Los Angeles: Museum of Cultural History, Univ. of California, 1978.

Fash, William Leonard. *Scribes, Warriors, and Kings: The City of Copan and the Ancient Maya*. London: Thames and Hudson, 1991.

Fewkes, Jesse Walter. *The Mimbres: Art and Archaeology*. Albuquerque: Avanyu, 1989.

Fitzhugh, William, and Aron Crowell, eds. *Crossroads of Continents: Cultures of Siberia and Alaska*. Washington, D.C.: Smithsonian Institution, 1988.

Frazier, Kendrick. *People of Chaco: A Canyon and Its Culture*. New York: Norton, 1986.

Herreman, Frank. *Power of the Sun: The Gold of Colombia*. Antwerp: City of Antwerp, 1993.

Heyden, Doris, and Paul Gendrop. *Pre-Columbian Architecture of Mesoamerica*. Trans. Judith Stanton. History of World Architecture. New York: Electa/Rizzoli, 1988.

Korp, Maureen. *The Sacred Geography of the American Mound Builders*. Native American Studies. Lewiston, N.Y.: Mellen, 1990.

Kubler, George. *The Art and Architecture of Ancient America: The Mexican, Maya, and Andean Peoples*. 2nd ed. Pelican History of Art. Harmondsworth, Eng.: Penguin, 1975.

———. *Esthetic Recognition of Ancient Amerindian Art*. Yale Publications in the History of Art. New Haven: Yale Univ. Press, 1991.

Miller, Arthur G. *The Mural Painting of Teotihuacan*. Washington, D.C.: Dumbarton Oaks, 1973.

Miller, Mary Ellen. *The Art of Mesoamerica: From Olmec to Aztec*. World of Art. New York: Thames and Hudson, 1986.

———, and Karl Taube. *The Gods and Symbols of Ancient Mexico and the Maya: An Illustrated Dictionary of*

Mesoamerican Religion. New York: Thames and Hudson, 1993.

Moseley, Michael. *The Incas and Their Ancestors: The Archaeology of Peru*. London: Thames and Hudson, 1992.

Pang, Hildegard Delgado. *Pre-Columbian Art: Investigations and Insights*. Norman: Univ. of Oklahoma Press, 1992.

Paul, Anne. *Paracas Art and Architecture: Object and Context in South Coastal Peru*. Iowa City: Univ. of Iowa Press, 1991.

Schele, Linda, and David Freidel. *A Forest of Kings: The Untold Story of the Ancient Maya*. New York: Morrow, 1990.

Schele, Linda, and Mary Ellen Miller. *The Blood of Kings: Dynasty and Ritual in Maya Art*. New York: Braziller, 1986.

Stone-Miller, Rebecca. *To Weave for the Sun: Andean Textiles in the Museum of Fine Arts, Boston*. Boston: Museum of Fine Arts, 1992.

Townsend, Richard, ed. *The Ancient Americas: Art from Sacred Landscapes*. Chicago: Art Institute of Chicago, 1992.

———. *The Aztecs*. Ancient Peoples and Places. London: Thames and Hudson, 1992.

Wuthenau, Alexander von. *The Art of Terracotta Pottery in Pre-Columbian Central and South America*. Art of the World. New York: Crown, 1970.

Chapter 13 Art of Ancient Africa

Bassani, Ezio, and William Fagg. *Africa and the Renaissance: Art in Ivory*. New York: Center for African Art, 1988.

Ben-Amos, Paula. *The Art of Benin*. London: Thames and Hudson, 1980.

———, and Arnold Rubin. *The Art of Power, the Power of Art: Studies in Benin Iconography*. Monograph Series, no. 19. Los Angeles: Museum of Cultural History, Univ. of California, 1983.

Cole, Herbert M. *Igbo Arts: Community and Cosmos*. Los Angeles: Museum of Cultural History, Univ. of California, 1984.

Connah, Graham. *African Civilizations: Precolonial Cities and States in Africa: An Archaeological Perspective*. Cambridge: Cambridge Univ. Press, 1987.

Eyo, Ekpo, and Frank Willett. *Treasures of Ancient Nigeria*. Ed. Rollyn O. Kirchbaum. New York: Knopf, 1980.

Ezra, Kate. *Royal Art of Benin: The Perls Collection in the Metropolitan Museum of Art*. New York: Metropolitan Museum of Art, 1992.

Fagg, Bernard. *Nok Terracottas*. Lagos: Ethnographica, 1977.

Garlake, Peter S. *Great Zimbabwe*. London: Thames and Hudson, 1973.

———. *The Painted Caves: An Introduction to the Prehistoric Art of Zimbabwe*. Harare: Modus, 1987.

Huffman, Thomas N. *Symbols in Stone: Unravelling the Mystery of Great Zimbabwe*. Johannesburg: Witwatersrand Univ. Press, 1987.

Lhote, Henri. *The Search for the Tassili Frescoes: The Story of the Prehistoric Rock-Paintings of the Sahara*. 2nd ed. Trans. Alan Houghton Brodrick. London: Hutchinson, 1973.

Shaw, Thurstan. *Unearthing Igbo-Ukwu: Archaeological Discoveries in Eastern Nigeria*. New York: Oxford Univ. Press, 1977.

Willcox, A. R. *The Rock Art of Africa*. London: Croon Helm, 1984.

Willett, Frank. *Ife in the History of West African Sculpture*. New York: McGraw-Hill, 1967.

Chapter 14 Early Medieval Art in Europe

Alexander, J. J. G. *Medieval Illuminators and Their Methods of Work*. New Haven: Yale Univ. Press, 1992.

Backes, Magnus, and Regine Dolling. *Art of the Dark Ages*. Trans. Francisca Garvie. Panorama of World Art. New York: Abrams, 1971.

Backhouse, Janet, D. H. Turner, and Leslie Webster. *The Golden Age of Anglo-Saxon Art, 966–1066*. Bloomington: Indiana Univ. Press, 1984.

Beckwith, John. *Early Medieval Art: Carolingian, Ottonian, Romanesque*. World of Art. New York: Oxford Univ. Press, 1974.

Calkins, Robert G. *Illuminated Books of the Medieval Ages*. Ithaca: Cornell Univ. Press, 1983.

Cirrker, Blanche, ed. *The Book of Kells: Selected Plates in Full Color*. New York: Dover, 1982.

Conant, Kenneth John. *Carolingian and Romanesque Architecture, 800–1200*. 3rd ed. Pelican History of Art. Harmondsworth, Eng.: Penguin, 1973.

Davis-Weyer, Caecilia. *Early Medieval Art, 300–1150: Sources and Documents*. Englewood Cliffs, N.J.: Prentice-Hall, 1971.

Dodds, Jerrilynn D. *Architecture and Ideology in Early Medieval Spain*. University Park: Pennsylvania State Univ. Press, 1990.

Dodwell, C. R. *The Pictorial Arts of the West, 800–1200*. Pelican History of Art. New Haven: Yale Univ. Press, 1993.

Evans, Angela Care. *The Sutton Hoo Ship Burial*. London: British Museum, 1986.

Fernie, E. C. *The Architecture of the Anglo-Saxons*. London: Batsford, 1983.

Henderson, George. *Early Medieval*. Style and Civilization. Harmondsworth, Eng.: Penguin, 1972.

———. *From Durrow to Kells: The Insular Gospel-Books, 650–800*. London: Thames and Hudson, 1987.

Horn, Walter W., and Ernest Born. *Plan of Saint Gall: A Study of the Architecture and Economy of and Life in a Paradigmatic*

Carolingian Monastery. 3 vols. California Studies in the History of Art. Berkeley: Univ. of California Press, 1979.
Hubert, Jean, Jean Porcher, and W. F. Volbach. *Carolingian Renaissance*. Arts of Mankind. New York: Braziller, 1970.
Laing, Lloyd. *Art of the Celts*. World of Art. New York: Thames and Hudson, 1992.
Lasko, Peter. *Ars Sacra, 800–1200*. Pelican History of Art. Harmondsworth, Eng.: Penguin, 1972.
Mayr-Harting, Henry. *Ottonian Book Illumination: An Historical Study*. 2 vols. New York: Oxford Univ. Press, 1991.
Megaw, Ruth, and Vincent Megaw. *Celtic Art: From Its Beginnings to the Book of Kells*. New York: Thames and Hudson, 1989.
New American Bible. New York: Catholic, 1992.
Nordenfalk, Carl Adam Johan. *Early Medieval Book Illumination*. New York: Rizzoli, 1988.
Palol, Pedro de, and Max Hirmer. *Early Medieval Art in Spain*. Trans. Alisa Jaffa. London: Thames and Hudson, 1967.
Richardson, Hilary, and John Scarry. *An Introduction to Irish High Crosses*. Dublin: Mercier, 1990.
Treasures of Irish Art, 1500 B.C. to 1500 A.D.: From the Collections of the National Museum of Ireland, Royal Irish Academy, Trinity College, Dublin. New York: Metropolitan Museum of Art, 1977.
Verzone, Paola. *The Art of Europe: The Dark Ages from Theodoric to Charlemagne*. Art of the World. New York: Crown, 1968.
Williams, John. *Early Spanish Manuscript Illumination*. New York: Braziller, 1977.
Wilson, David M. *Anglo-Saxon Art: From the Seventh Century to the Norman Conquest*. London: Thames and Hudson, 1984.
———, and Ole Klindt-Jensen. *Viking Art*. 2nd ed. Minneapolis: Univ. of Minnesota Press, 1980.

Chapter 15 Romanesque Art

Armi, C. Edson. *Masons and Sculptors in Romanesque Burgundy: The New Aesthetics of Cluny III*. 2 vols. University Park: Pennsylvania State Univ. Press, 1983.
Busch, Harald, and Bernd Lohse. *Romanesque Sculpture*. London: Batsford, 1962.
Cahn, Walter. *Romanesque Bible Illumination*. Ithaca: Cornell Univ. Press, 1982.
Evans, Joan. *Cluniac Art of the Romanesque Period*. Cambridge: Cambridge Univ. Press, 1950.
Focillon, Henri. *The Art of the West in the Middle Ages*. 2 vols. Ed. Jean Bony. Trans. Donald King. London: Phaidon, 1963.
Forsyth, Ilene H. *The Throne of Wisdom: Wood Sculptures of the Madonna in Romanesque France*. Princeton: Princeton Univ. Press, 1972.
Gantner, Joseph, and Marvel Pobe. *Romanesque Art in France*. London: Thames and Hudson, 1956.
Grape, Wolfgang. *The Bayeux Tapestry: Monument to a Norman Triumph*. New York: Prestel, 1994.
Hearn, M. F. *Romanesque Sculpture: The Revival of Monumental Stone Sculptures in the Eleventh and Twelfth Centuries*. Ithaca: Cornell Univ. Press, 1981.
Holt, Elizabeth Gilmore. *A Documentary History of Art*. 3 vols. Princeton: Princeton Univ. Press, 1982.
Jacobs, Michael. *Northern Spain: The Road to Santiago de Compostela*. Architectural Guides for Travelers. San Francisco: Chronicle, 1991.
Kennedy, Hugh. *Crusader Castles*. Cambridge: Cambridge Univ. Press, 1994.
Kubach, Hans Erich. *Romanesque Architecture*. History of World Architecture. New York: Electa/Rizzoli, 1988.
Kuhnel, Biana. *Crusader Art of the Twelfth Century: A Geographical, and Historical, or an Art Historical Notion?* Berlin: Gebr. Mann, 1994.
Kunstler, Gustav. *Romanesque Art in Europe*. Greenwich, Conn.: New York Graphic Society, 1969.
Little, Bryan D. G. *Architecture in Norman Britain*. London: Batsford, 1985.
Mâle, Emile. *Religious Art in France, the Twelfth Century: A Study of the Origins of Medieval Iconography*. Bollingen Series. Princeton: Princeton Univ. Press, 1978.
Nebosine, George A. *Journey into Romanesque: A Traveller's Guide to Romanesque Monuments in Europe*. Ed. Robyn Cooper. London: Weidenfeld and Nicolson, 1969.
Norton, Christopher, and David Park. *Cistercian Art and Architecture in the British Isles*. Cambridge: Cambridge Univ. Press, 1986.
Radding, Charles M., and William W. Clark. *Medieval Architecture, Medieval Learning: Builders and Masters in the Age of Romanesque and Gothic*. New Haven: Yale Univ. Press, 1992.
Rollason, David, Margaret Harvey, and Michael Prestwich, eds. *Anglo-Norman Durham: 1093–1193*. Rochester, N.Y.: Boydell, 1994.
Schapiro, Meyer. *Romanesque Art*. New York: Braziller, 1977.
———. *The Romanesque Sculpture of Moissac*. New York: Braziller, 1985.
Swarzenski, Hanns. *Monuments of Romanesque Art: The Art of Church Treasures of North-Western Europe*. 2nd ed. Chicago: Univ. of Chicago Press, 1967.
Tate, Robert Brian, and Marcus Tate. *The Pilgrim Route to Santiago*. Oxford: Phaidon, 1987.
Theophilus. *On Divers Arts: The Treatise of Theophilus*. Trans. John G. Hawthorne and Cyril Stanley Smith. Chicago: Univ. of Chicago Press, 1963.
Wilson, David M. *The Bayeux Tapestry: The Complete Tapestry in Color*. New York: Random House, 1985.
The Year 1200. 2 vols. New York: Metropolitan Museum of Art, 1970.
Zarnecki, George. *Romanesque Art*. New York: Universe, 1971.
———, Janet Holt, and Tristam Holland. *English Romanesque Art, 1066–1200*. London: Weidenfeld and Nicolson, 1984.

Chapter 16 Gothic Art

Alexander, Jonathan, and Paul Binski, eds. *Age of Chivalry: Art in Plantagenet England, 1200–1400*. London: Royal Academy of Arts, 1987.
Andrews, Francis B. *The Mediaeval Builder and His Methods*. New York: Barnes & Noble, 1993.
Armi, C. Edson. *The "Headmaster" of Chartres and the Origins of "Gothic" Sculpture*. University Park: Pennsylvania State Univ. Press, 1994.
Aubert, Marcel. *The Art of the High Gothic Era*. Rev. ed. Art of the World. New York: Greystone, 1966.
Binski, Paul. *Medieval Craftsmen: Painters*. London: British Museum, 1991.
Bogin, Magda. *Gothic Cathedrals of France and Their Treasures*. London: Kaye, 1959.
———. *The Women Troubadours*. New York: Norton, 1980.
Bony, Jean. *French Gothic Architecture of the 12th and 13th Centuries*. California Studies in the History of Art. Berkeley: Univ. of California Press, 1983.
Borsook, Eve, and Fiorella Superbi Gioffredi. *Italian Altarpieces, 1250–1550: Function and Design*. Oxford: Clarendon, 1994.
Bottineau, Yves. *Notre-Dame de Paris and the Sainte Chapelle*. Trans. Lovett F. Edwards. London: Allen, 1967.
Branner, Robert. *Manuscript Painting in Paris during the Reign of Saint Louis: A Study of Styles*. California Studies in the History of Art. Berkeley: Univ. of California Press, 1977.
Chiellini, Monica. *Cimabue*. Trans. Lisa Pelletti. Florence: Scala, 1988.
Coe, Brian. *Stained Glass in England, 1150–1550*. London: Allen, 1981.
Cole, Bruce. *Giotto and Florentine Painting, 1280–1375*. New York: Harper & Row, 1975.
Crosby, Sumner McKnight. *The Royal Abbey of Saint-Denis from Its Beginnings to the Death of Suger, 475–1151*. Yale Publications in the History of Art. New Haven: Yale Univ. Press, 1987.
Erlande-Brandenburg, Alain. *Gothic Art*. Trans. I. Mark Paris. New York: Abrams, 1989.
Favier, Jean. *The World of Chartres*. Trans. Francisca Garvie. New York: Abrams, 1990.
Franklin, J. W. *Cathedrals of Italy*. London: Batsford, 1958.
Frisch, Teresa G. *Gothic Art, 1140–c. 1450: Sources and Documents*. Englewood Cliffs, N.J.: Prentice-Hall, 1971.
Grodecki, Louis. *Gothic Architecture*. Trans. I. Mark Paris. History of World Architecture. New York: Electa/Rizzoli, 1985.
———, and Catherine Brisac. *Gothic Stained Glass, 1200–1300*. Ithaca: Cornell Univ. Press, 1985.
Herlihy, David. *Medieval Households*. Cambridge: Harvard Univ. Press, 1985.
Jantzen, Hans. *High Gothic: The Classic Cathedrals of Chartres, Reims, Amiens*. Trans. James Palmes. New York: Pantheon, 1962.
Katzenellenbogen, Adolf. *The Sculptural Programs of Chartres Cathedral: Christ, Mary, Ecclesia*. New York: Norton, 1964.
Mâle, Emile. *Chartres*. Trans. Sarah Wilson. New York: Harper & Row, 1983.
———. *Religious Art in France, the Thirteenth Century: A Study of Medieval Iconography and Its Sources*. Princeton: Princeton Univ. Press, 1984.
Martindale, Andrew. *Gothic Art*. World of Art. London: Thames and Hudson, 1967.
McIntyre, Anthony. *Medieval Tuscany and Umbria. Architectural Guides for Travellers*. San Francisco: Chronicle, 1992.
Moskowitz, Anita Fiderer. *The Sculpture of Andrea and Nino Pisano*. Cambridge: Cambridge Univ. Press, 1986.
Panofsky, Erwin. *Abbot Suger on the Abbey Church of St.-Denis and Its Art Treasures*. 2nd ed. Ed. Gerda Panofsky-Soergel. Princeton: Princeton Univ. Press, 1979.
———. *Gothic Architecture and Scholasticism*. Latrobe, Penn.: Archabbey, 1951.
Pevsner, Nikolas, and Priscilla Metcalf. *The Cathedrals of England*. 2 vols. Harmondsworth, Eng.: Viking, 1985.
Pope-Hennessy, John. *Italian Gothic Sculpture*. 3rd ed. Oxford: Phaidon, 1986.
Sauerlander, Willibald. *Gothic Sculpture in France, 1140–1270*. Trans. Janet Sandheimer. London: Thames and Hudson, 1972.
Simson, Otto Georg von. *The Gothic Cathedral: Origins of Gothic Architecture and the Medieval Concept of Order*. 3rd ed. Bollingen Series. Princeton: Princeton Univ. Press, 1988.
Smart, Alastair. *The Dawn of Italian Painting, 1250–1400*. Ithaca: Cornell Univ. Press, 1978.
White, John. *Art and Architecture in Italy, 1250 to 1400*. 3rd ed. Pelican History of Art. Harmondsworth, Eng.: Penguin, 1993.
———. *Duccio: Tuscan Art and the Medieval Workshop*. New York: Thames and Hudson, 1979.
Wieck, Roger S. *Time Sanctified: The Book of Hours in Medieval Art and Life*. New York: Braziller, 1988.
Wilson, Christopher. *The Gothic Cathedral: The Architecture of the Great Church, 1130–1530*. New York: Thames and Hudson, 1990.

Chapter 17 Early Renaissance Art in Europe

Ainsworth, Maryan Wynn. *Petrus Christus: Renaissance Master of Bruges*. New York: Metropolitan Museum of Art, 1994.
Baxandall, Michael. *Painting and Experience in Fifteenth-Century Italy: A Primer in the Social History of Pictorial Style*. Oxford: Clarendon, 1972.
Blum, Shirley. *Early Netherlandish Triptychs: A Study in Patronage*. California Studies in the History of Art. Berkeley: Univ. of California Press, 1969.
Borsi, Franco. *Leon Battista Alberti: The Complete Works*. New York: Electa/Rizzoli, 1989.
———, and Stefano Borsi. *Paolo Uccello*. Trans. Elfreda Powell. New York: Abrams, 1994.
Campbell, Lorne. *Renaissance Portraits: European Portrait-Painting in the 14th, 15th, and 16th Centuries*. New Haven: Yale Univ. Press, 1990.
Chastel, André. *The Flowering of the Italian Renaissance*. Trans. Jonathan Griffin. Arts of Mankind. New York: Odyssey, 1965.
———. *Studios and Styles of the Italian Renaissance*. Trans. Jonathan Griffin. Arts of Mankind. New York: Odyssey, 1966.
Christianity and the Renaissance: Image and Religious Imagination in the Quattrocento. Syracuse. N.Y.: Syracuse Univ. Press, 1990.
Christiansen, Keith. *Andrea Mantegna: Padua and Mantua*. New York: Braziller, 1994.
———, Laurence B. Kanter, and Carl Brandon Strehlke. *Painting in Renaissance Siena, 1420–1500*. New York: Metropolitan Museum of Art, 1988.
Cole, Bruce. *Masaccio and the Art of Early Renaissance Florence*. Bloomington: Indiana Univ. Press, 1980.
Davies, Martin. *Rogier van der Weyden: An Essay, with a Critical Catalogue of Paintings Assigned to Him and to Robert Campin*. London: Phaidon, 1972.
de Pisan, Christine. *Le Livre de la Cité des Dames (The Book of the City of Ladies)*. Trans. Earl J. Richards. New York: Persea, 1982.
Dhanens, Elisabeth. *Van Eyck: The Ghent Altarpiece*. New York: Viking, 1973.
Flanders in the Fifteenth Century: Art and Civilization. Detroit: Detroit Institute of Arts, 1960.
Freeman, Margaret B. *The Unicorn Tapestries*. New York: Metropolitan Museum of Art, 1976.
Gilbert, Creighton, ed. *Italian Art, 1400–1500: Sources and Documents*. Evanston: Northwestern Univ. Press, 1992.
Goffen, Rona. *Giovanni Bellini*. New Haven: Yale Univ. Press, 1989.
Goldwater, Robert, and Marco Treves. *Artists on Art: From the XIV to the XX Century*. New York: Random House, 1945.
Hind, Arthur M. *An Introduction to a History of Woodcut*. New York: Dover, 1963.
Joannides, Paul. *Masaccio and Masolino: A Complete Catalogue*. London: Phaidon, 1993.
Krautheimer, Richard. *Ghiberti's Bronze Doors*. Princeton: Princeton Univ. Press, 1971.
Lane, Barbara G. *The Altar and the Altarpiece: Sacramental Themes in Early Netherlandish Painting*. New York: Harper & Row, 1984.
Lightbown, Ronald. *Piero della Francesca*. New York: Abbeville, 1992.
———. *Sandro Botticelli: Life and Work*. New ed. New York: Abbeville, 1989.
Lloyd, Christopher. *Fra Angelico*. Rev. ed. London: Phaidon, 1992.
Meiss, Millard. *French Painting in the Time of Jean de Berry: The Limbourgs and Their Contemporaries*. New York: Braziller, 1974.
Muller, Theodor. *Sculpture in the Netherlands, Germany, France, and Spain: 1400–1500*. Trans. Elaine and William Robson Scott. Pelican History of Art. Harmondsworth, Eng.: Penguin, 1966.
Pacht, Otto. *Van Eyck and the Founders of Early Netherlandish Painting*. Ed. Maria Schmidt-Dengler. Trans. David Britt. London: Miller, 1994.
Panofsky, Erwin. *Early Netherlandish Painting: Its Origins and Character*. 2 vols. Cambridge: Harvard Univ. Press, 1966.
Plummer, John. *The Last Flowering: French Painting in Manuscripts, 1420–1530, from American Collections*. New York: Pierpont Morgan Library, 1982.
Pope-Hennessy, Sir John. *Donatello: Sculptor*. New York: Abbeville, 1993.
Saalman, Howard. *Filippo Brunelleschi: The Buildings*. University Park: Pennsylvania State Univ. Press, 1993.
Seymour, Charles. *Sculpture in Italy, 1400–1500*. Pelican History of Art. Harmondsworth, Eng.: Penguin, 1966.
Snyder, James. *Northern Renaissance Art: Painting, Sculpture, the Graphic Arts from 1350 to 1575*. New York: Abrams, 1985.
Vos, Dirk de. *Hans Memling: The Complete Works*. Ghent: Ludion, 1994.

Chapter 18 Renaissance Art in Sixteenth-Century Europe

Ackerman, James S. *The Architecture of Michelangelo*. Rev ed. Studies in Architecture. London: Zwemmer, 1966.
Baldini, Umberto. *The Sculpture of Michelangelo*. Trans. Clare Coope. New York: Rizzoli, 1982.
Baxandall, Michael. *The Limewood Sculptors of Renaissance Germany*. New Haven: Yale Univ. Press, 1980.
Beck, James H. *Raphael*. New York: Abrams, 1994.
Bier, Justus. *Tilman Riemenschneider, His Life and Work*. Lexington: Univ. of Kentucky Press, 1989.
Blunt, Anthony. *Art and Architecture in France: 1500–1700*. 4th ed. Pelican History of Art. Harmondsworth, Eng.: Penguin, 1981.
Bosquet, Jacques. *Mannerism: The Painting and Style of the Late Renaissance*. Trans. Simon Watson Taylor. New York: Braziller, 1964.
Boucher, Brude. *Andrea Palladio: The Architect in His Time*. New York: Abbeville, 1994.
Bronstein, Leo. *El Greco (Domenicos Theotocopoulos)*. New York: Abrams, 1990.
Brown, Jonathan. *The Golden Age of Painting in Spain*. New Haven: Yale Univ. Press, 1991.
Bruschi, Arnaldo. *Bramante*. London: Thames and Hudson, 1977.
Chastel, André. *The Age of Humanism: Europe, 1480–1530*. Trans. Katherine M. Delavenay and E. M. Gwyer. London: Thames and Hudson, 1963.
Ettlinger, Leopold D., and Helen S. Ettlinger. *Raphael*. Oxford: Phaidon, 1987.
Farmer, John David. *The Virtuoso Craftsman: Northern European Design in the Sixteenth Century*. Worcester, Mass.: Worcester Art Museum, 1969.
Foote, Timothy. *The World of Bruegel, c. 1525–1569*. New York: Time-Life, 1968.
Freedberg, S. J. *Painting in Italy, 1500 to 1600*. 3rd ed. Pelican History of Art. New Haven: Yale Univ. Press, 1993.
Gibson, Walter. *Hieronymus Bosch*. World of Art. New York: Oxford Univ. Press, 1973.
Goldschneider, Ludwig. *Leonardo da Vinci: Life and Work, Paintings and Drawings*. 7th ed. London: Phaidon, 1964.
Hartt, Frederick. *Michelangelo*. New York: Abrams, 1984.
Hayum, André. *The Isenheim Altarpiece: God's Medicine and the Painter's Vision*. Princeton Essays on the Arts. Princeton: Princeton Univ. Press, 1989.
Heydenreich, Ludwig H. *Leonardo—"The Last Supper."* Art in Context. London: Allen Lane, 1974.
Hollingsworth, Mary. *Patronage in Renaissance Italy: From 1400 to the Early Sixteenth Century*. London: Murray, 1994.
Howard, Deborah. *Jacopo Sansovino: Architecture and Patronage in Renaissance Venice*. New Haven: Yale Univ. Press, 1975.
Huse, Norbert, and Wolfgang Wolters. *Art of Renaissance Venice: Architecture, Sculpture and Painting, 1460–1590*. Trans. Edmund Jephcott. Chicago: Univ. of Chicago Press, 1990.
Jones, Roger, and Nicholas Penny. *Raphael*. New Haven: Yale Univ. Press, 1983.
Klein, Robert, and Henri Zerner. *Italian Art, 1500–1600: Sources and Documents*. Englewood Cliffs, N.J.: Prentice-Hall, 1966.
Kubler, George. *Building the Escorial*. Princeton: Princeton Univ. Press, 1982.
Landau, David, and Peter Parshall. *The Renaissance Print: 1470–1550*. New Haven: Yale Univ. Press, 1994.
Langdon, Helen. *Holbein*. 2nd ed. London: Phaidon, 1993.
Lazzaro, Claudia. *The Italian Renaissance Garden: From the Conventions of Planting, Design, and Ornament to the Grand Gardens of Sixteenth-Century Central Italy*. New Haven: Yale Univ. Press, 1990.
Lieberman, Ralph. *Renaissance Architecture in Venice, 1450–1540*. New York: Abbeville, 1982.
Linfert, Carl. *Hieronymus Bosch*. Masters of Art. New York: Abrams, 1989.
Martineau, Jane, and Charles Hope. *The Genius of Venice, 1500–1600*. New York: Abrams, 1984.
McCorquodale, Charles. *Bronzino*. New York: Harper & Row, 1981.
McMullen, Roy. *Mona Lisa: The Picture and the Myth*. Boston: Houghton Mifflin, 1975.
Murray, Linda. *The High Renaissance*. World of Art. New York: Praeger, 1967.
———. *Late Renaissance and Mannerism*. World of Art. London: Thames and Hudson, 1967.
———. *Michelangelo*. World of Art. New York: Oxford Univ. Press, 1980.
Olson, Roberta J. M. *Italian Renaissance Sculpture*. World of Art. New York: Thames and Hudson, 1992.
Osten, Gert von der, and Horst Vey. *Painting and Sculpture in Germany and the Netherlands, 1500–1600*. Pelican History of Art. Harmondsworth, Eng.: Penguin, 1969.
Perlingieri, Ilya Sandra. *Sofonisba Anguissola: The First Great Woman Artist of the Renaissance*. New York: Rizzoli, 1992.
Pietrangeli, Carlo, et al. *The Sistine Chapel: The Art, the History, and the Restoration*. New York: Harmony, 1986.
Pignatti, Terisio. *Giorgione*. New York: Phaidon, 1971.
Pope-Hennessy, Sir John. *Cellini*. New York: Abbeville, 1985.
———. *Italian High Renaissance and Baroque Sculpture*. 3rd ed. Oxford: Phaidon, 1986.
———. *Italian Renaissance Sculpture*. 3rd ed. Oxford: Phaidon, 1986.
Rearick, William R. *The Art of Paolo Veronese, 1528–1588*. Washington, D.C.: National Gallery of Art, 1988.
Rosand, David. *Painting in Cinquecento Venice: Titian, Veronese, Tintoretto*. New Haven: Yale Univ. Press, 1982.
Russell, Francis. *The World of Dürer, 1471–1528*. New York: Time-Life, 1967.
Settis, Salvatore. *Giorgione's Tempest: Interpreting the Hidden Subject*. Trans. Ellen Bianchini. Chicago: Univ. of Chicago Press, 1990.
Shearman, John. *Mannerism*. Harmondsworth, Eng.: Penguin, 1967.
Smith, Jeffrey Chipps. *Nuremberg, a Renaissance City, 1500–1618*. Austin: Huntington Art Gallery, Univ. of Texas, 1983.
Stechow, Wolfgang. *Pieter Bruegel the Elder*. Masters of Art. New York: Abrams, 1990.
Strong, Roy C. *Artists of the Tudor Court: The Portrait Miniature Rediscovered, 1520–1620*. London: Victoria and Albert Museum, 1983.
Summerson, John. *Architecture in Britain: 1530 to 1830*. 7th ed. Pelican History of Art. Harmondsworth, Eng.: Penguin, 1983.
Tavernor, Robert. *Palladio and Palladianism*. World of Art. New York: Thames and Hudson, 1991.
Valcanover, Francesco. *Tintoretto*. Trans. Robert Erich Wolf. Library of Great Painters. New York: Abrams, 1985.
Vasari, Giorgio. *The Lives of the Artists*. Trans. Julia Conaway Bondanella and Peter Bondanella. New York: Oxford Univ. Press, 1991.
Verheyen, Egon. *The Paintings in the Studiolo of Isabella d'Este at Mantua*. Monographs on Archaeology and Fine Arts. New York: New York Univ. Press, 1971.
Vitruvius Pollio. *Vitruvius: The Ten Books on Architecture*. Trans. Morris Hicky Morgan. New York: Dover, 1960.
Whiting, Roger. *Leonardo: A Portrait of the Renaissance Man*. London: Barrie and Jenkins, 1992.

Chapter 19 Baroque, Rococo, and Early American Art

Ackley, Clifford S. *Printmaking in the Age of Rembrandt*. Boston: Museum of Fine Arts, 1981.
The Age of Caravaggio. New York: Metropolitan Museum of Art, 1985.
Bazin, Germain. *Baroque and Rococo*. Trans. Jonathan Griffin. World of Art. New York: Praeger, 1964.
Berger, Robert W. *The Palace of the Sun: The Louvre of Louis XIV*. University Park: Pennsylvania State Univ. Press, 1993.
———. *Versailles: The Chateau of Louis XIV*. Monographs on the Fine Arts. University Park: Pennsylvania State Univ. Press, 1985.
Blankert, A. *Vermeer of Delft*. Oxford: Phaidon, 1978.
Blunt, Anthony, et al. *Baroque and Rococo Architecture and Decoration*. New York: Harper & Row, 1982.
Boucher, François. *François Boucher, 1703–1770*. New York: Metropolitan Museum of Art, 1986.
Brown, Christopher. *Scenes of Everyday Life: Dutch Genre Painting of the Seventeenth Century*. London: Faber & Faber, 1984.
Brown, Dale. *The World of Velázquez, 1599–1660*. New York: Time-Life, 1969.
Brown, Jonathan. *The Golden Age of Painting in Spain*. New Haven: Yale Univ. Press, 1991.
———. *Velázquez, Painter and Courtier*. New Haven: Yale Univ. Press, 1986.
Domingues Ortiz, Antonio, Alfonso E. Perez Sanchez, and Julian Gallego. *Velázquez*. New York: Metropolitan Museum of Art, 1989.
Enggass, Robert, and Jonathan Brown. *Italy and Spain 1600–1750: Sources and Documents*. Englewood Cliffs, N.J.: Prentice-Hall, 1970.
Frankenstein, Alfred Victor. *The World of Copley, 1738–1815*. New York: Time-Life, 1970.
Fuchs, R. H. *Dutch Painting*. World of Art. New York: Oxford Univ. Press, 1978.
Gerson, Horst, and E. H. ter Kuile. *Art and Architecture in Belgium, 1600–1800*. Pelican History of Art. Baltimore: Penguin, 1960.
———. *Rembrandt Paintings*. Trans. Heinz Norden. Ed. Gary Schwartz. New York: Reynal, 1968.
Grasselli, Margaret Morgan, and Pierre Rosenberg. *Watteau, 1684–1721*. Washington, D.C.: National Gallery of Art, 1984.
Grimm, Claus. *Frans Hals—The Complete Work*. Trans. Jurgen Riehle. New York: Abrams, 1990.
Haak, Bob. *The Golden Age: Dutch Painters of the Seventeenth Century*. Trans. and ed. Elizabeth Willems-Treeman. New York: Abrams, 1984.
Held, Julius Samuel, and Donald Posner. *17th and 18th Century Art: Baroque Painting, Sculpture, Architecture*. Library of Art History. New York: Abrams, 1971.
Hempel, Eberhard. *Baroque Art and Architecture in Central Europe: Germany, Austria, Switzerland, Hungary, Czechoslovakia, Poland. Painting and Sculpture: 17th and 18th Centuries. Architecture: 16th to 18th Centuries*. Trans. Elisabeth Hempel and Marguerite Kay. Pelican History of Art. Harmondsworth, Eng.: Penguin, 1965.
Jacobson, Dawn. *Chinoiserie*. London: Phaidon, 1993.
Kalnein, Wend, and Michael Levey. *Art and Architecture of the Eighteenth Century in France*. Pelican History of Art. Harmondsworth, Eng.: Penguin, 1972.
Köning, Hans. *The World of Vermeer, 1632–1675*. New York: Time-Life, 1967.
Lagerlof, Margaretha Rossholm. *Ideal Landscape: Annibale Caracci, Nicolas Poussin, and Claude Lorrain*. New Haven: Yale Univ. Press, 1990.
Martin, John Rupert. "The Baroque from the Viewpoint of the Art Historian." *Journal of Aesthetics and Art Criticism* 15(2): 164–70.
Moir, Alfred. *Anthony Van Dyck*. New York: Abrams, 1994.
———. *Caravaggio*. Library of Great Painters. New York: Abrams, 1982.
Montagu, Jennifer. *Roman Baroque Sculpture: The Industry of Art*. New Haven: Yale Univ. Press, 1989.
Norberg-Schulz, Christian. *Baroque Architecture*. New York: Rizzoli, 1986.
———. *Late Baroque and Rococo Architecture*. History of World Architecture. New York: Rizzoli, 1985.
Rosenberg, Jakob, Seymour Slive, and E. H. ter Kuile. *Dutch Art and Architecture, 1600 to 1800*. 3rd ed. Pelican History of Art. Harmondsworth, Eng.: Penguin, 1977.
———. *Fragonard*. New York: Metropolitan Museum of Art, 1988.
Russell, H. Diane. *Claude Lorrain, 1600–1682*. Washington, D.C.: National Gallery of Art, 1982.
Schwartz, Gary. *Rembrandt, His Life, His Paintings*. New York: Penguin, 1991.
Scribner, Charles, III. *Gianlorenzo Bernini*. Masters of Art. New York: Abrams, 1991.
———. *Peter Paul Rubens*. Masters of Art. New York: Abrams, 1989.
Slive, Seymour, et al. *Frans Hals*. London: Royal Academy of Arts, 1989.
Stechow, Wolfgang. *Dutch Landscape Painting of the Seventeenth Century*. 3rd ed. Oxford: Phaidon, 1981.
Summerson, John. *Architecture of the Eighteenth Century*. World of Art. New York: Thames and Hudson, 1986.
———. *Inigo Jones*. Harmondsworth, Eng.: Penguin, 1966.
Sutton, Peter. *The Age of Rubens*. Boston: Museum of Fine Arts, 1993.
Wallace, Robert. *The World of Bernini, 1598–1680*. New York: Time-Life, 1970.
Temple, R. C., ed. *The Travels of Peter Mundy in Europe and Asia, 1608–1667*. London: n.p., 1925.
Wedgwood, C. V. *The World of Rubens, 1577–1640*. New York: Time-Life, 1967.
Welu, James A., and Pieter Biesboer, eds. *Judith Leyster: A Dutch Master and Her World*. New York: Yale Univ. Press, 1993.
Wheelock, Arthur K., Jr. *Jan Vermeer*. New York: Abrams, 1988.
———, Susan J. Barnes, and Julius S. Held. *Anthony Van Dyck*. Washington, D.C.: National Gallery of Art, 1990.
White, Christopher. *Peter Paul Rubens: Man & Artist*. New Haven: Yale Univ. Press, 1987.
———. *Rembrandt*. World of Art. London: Thames and Hudson, 1984.
Wittkower, Rudolf. *Art and Architecture in Italy, 1600 to 1750*. 3rd ed. Pelican History of Art. Harmondsworth, Eng.: Penguin, 1982.

Chapter 20 Art of India after 1100

Asher, Catherine B. *Architecture of Mughal India*. New York: Cambridge Univ. Press, 1992.
Beach, Milo Cleveland. *Grand Mogul: Imperial Painting in India, 1600–1660*. Williamstown: Sterling and Francine Clark Art Institute, 1978.
———. *Imperial Image, Paintings for the Mughal Court*. Washington, D.C.: Freer Gallery of Art, Smithsonian Institution, 1981.
———. *Mughal and Rajput Painting*. New York: Cambridge Univ. Press, 1992.
Blurton, T. Richard. *Hindu Art*. Cambridge: Harvard Univ. Press, 1993.
Davies, Philip. *Splendours of the Raj: British Architecture in India, 1660 to 1947*. London: Murray, 1985.
Desai, Vishakha N. *Life at Court: Art for India's Rulers, 16th–19th Centuries*. Boston: Museum of Fine Arts, 1985.
Losty, Jeremiah P. *The Art of the Book in India*. London: British Library, 1982.
Miller, Barbara Stoller. *Love Song of the Dark Lord: Jayadeva's Gitagovinda*. New York: Columbia Univ. Press, 1977.
Mitchell, George. *The Royal Palaces of India*. London: Thames and Hudson, 1994.
Nou, Jean-Louis. *Taj Mahal*. Text by Amina Okada and M. C. Joshi. New York: Abbeville, 1993.
Pal, Pratapaditya. *Court Paintings of India, 16th–19th Centuries*. New York: Navin Kumar, 1983.
———, et al. *Romance of the Taj Mahal*. Los Angeles: Los Angeles County Museum of Art, 1989.
Tillotson, G. H. R. *Mughal India*. Architectural Guides for Travelers. San Francisco: Chronicle, 1990.
———. *The Tradition of Indian Architecture: Continuity, Controversy and Change since 1850*. New Haven: Yale Univ. Press, 1989.
Welch, Stuart Cary. *The Emperors' Album: Images of Mughal India*. New York: Metropolitan Museum of Art, 1987.
———. *India: Art and Culture 1300–1900*. New York: Metropolitan Museum of Art, 1985.

Chapter 21 Chinese Art after 1280

Andrews, Julia Frances. *Painters and Politics in the People's Republic of China, 1949–1979*. Berkeley: Univ. of California Press, 1994.

Barnhart, Richard M. *Painters of the Great Ming: The Imperial Court and the Zhe School*. Dallas: Dallas Museum of Art, 1993.

———. *Peach Blossom Spring: Gardens and Flowers in Chinese Painting*. New York: Metropolitan Museum of Art, 1983.

———, et al. *The Jade Studio: Masterpieces of Ming and Qing Painting and Calligraphy from the Wong Nan-p'ing Collection*. New Haven: Yale Univ. Art Gallery, 1994.

Beurdeley, Michael. *Chinese Furniture*. Trans. Katherine Watson. Tokyo: Kodansha International, 1979.

Billeter, Jean François. *The Chinese Art of Writing*. New York: Skira/Rizzoli, 1990.

Bush, Susan, and Hsui-yen Shih, eds. *Early Chinese Texts on Painting*. Cambridge: Harvard Univ. Press, 1985.

Cahill, James. *The Compelling Image: Nature and Style in Seventeenth-Century Chinese Painting*. Charles Norton Lectures 1978–79. Cambridge: Harvard Univ. Press, 1982.

———. *The Distant Mountains: Chinese Painting in the Late Ming Dynasty, 1580–1644*. New York: Weatherhill, 1982.

———. *Hills beyond a River: Chinese Painting of the Y'uan Dynasty, 1279–1368*. New York: Weatherhill, 1976.

———. *Parting at the Shore: Chinese Painting of the Early and Middle Ming Dynasty, 1368–1580*. New York: Weatherhill, 1978.

Chan, Charis. *Imperial China*. Architectural Guides for Travelers. San Francisco: Chronicle, 1992.

Fontein, Jan, and Money Hickman. *Zen Painting and Calligraphy: An Exhibition of Works of Art Lent by Temples, Private Collectors, and Public and Private Museums in Japan*. Boston: Museum of Fine Arts, 1971.

Ho, Wai-Kam, ed. *The Century of Tung Ch'i-Chiang*. 2 vols. Kansas City: Nelson-Atkins Museum of Art, 1992.

In Pursuit of the Dragon: Traditions and Transitions in Ming Ceramics: An Exhibition from the Idemitsu Museum of Arts. Seattle: Seattle Art Museum, 1988.

Jenyns, Soame. *Later Chinese Porcelain: The Ch'ing Dynasty, 1644–1912*. 4th ed. London: Faber & Faber, 1971.

Keswick, Maggie. *The Chinese Garden: History, Art and Architecture*. New York: Rizzoli, 1978.

Knapp, Ronald G. *China's Vernacular Architecture: House Form and Culture*. Honolulu: Univ. of Hawaii Press, 1989.

Lee, Sherman, and Wai-Kam Ho. *Chinese Art under the Mongols: The Y'uan Dynasty, 1279–1368*. Cleveland: Cleveland Museum of Art, 1968.

Li, Chu-tsing. *The Autumn Colors on the Ch'iao and Hua Mountains: A Landscape by Chao Meng-fu*. Artibus Asiae, supplementum 21. Ascona: Artibus Asiae, 1965.

Lim, Lucy. *Contemporary Chinese Painting: An Exhibition from the People's Republic of China*. San Francisco: Chinese Culture Foundation of San Francisco, 1983.

———, ed. *Wu Guanzhong: A Contemporary Chinese Artist*. San Francisco: Chinese Culture Foundation, 1989.

Liu, Laurence G. *Chinese Architecture*. New York: Rizzoli, 1989.

Ng, So Kam. *Brushstrokes: Styles and Techniques of Chinese Painting*. San Francisco: Asian Art Museum of San Francisco, 1993.

Polo, Marco. *The Travels of Marco Polo*. Trans. Teresa Waugh and Maria Bellonci. New York: Facts on File, 1984.

Shih-t'ao. *Returning Home: Tao-chi's Album of Landscapes and Flowers*. Commentary by Wen Fong. New York: Braziller, 1976.

Sullivan, Michael. *Symbols of Eternity: The Art of Landscape Painting in China*. Stanford: Stanford Univ. Press, 1979.

Tregear, Mary. *Chinese Art*. World of Art. New York: Oxford Univ. Press, 1980.

Tsu, Frances Ya-sing. *Landscape Design in Chinese Gardens*. New York: McGraw-Hill, 1988.

Vainker, S. J. *Chinese Pottery and Porcelain: From Prehistory to the Present*. London: British Museum, 1991.

Walters, Derek. *Feng Shui: The Chinese Art of Designing a Harmonious Environment*. New York: Simon & Schuster, 1988.

Yu Zhuoyun, comp. *Palaces of the Forbidden City*. Trans. Ng Mau-Sang, Chan Sinwai, and Puwen Lee. New York: Viking, 1984.

Chapter 22 Japanese Art after 1392

Addiss, Stephen. *The Art of Zen: Painting and Calligraphy by Japanese Monks, 1600–1925*. New York: Abrams, 1989.

———. *Zenga and Nanga: Paintings by Japanese Monks and Scholars, Selections from the Kurt and Millie Gitter Collection*. New Orleans: New Orleans Museum of Art, 1976.

Baekeland, Frederick, and Robert Moes. *Modern Japanese Ceramics in American Collections*. New York: Japan Society, 1993.

Doi, Tsugiyoshi. *Momoyama Decorative Painting*. Trans. Edna B. Crawford. Heibonsha Survey of Japanese Art, vol. 14. New York: Weatherhill, 1977.

Forrer, Matthi. *Hokusai*. New York: Rizzoli, 1988.

Hayakawa, Masao. *The Garden Art of Japan*. Trans. Richard L. Gage. Heibonsha Survey of Japanese Art, vol. 28. New York: Weatherhill, 1973.

Hayashiya, Tatsusaburo, Masao Nakamura, and Seizo Hayashiya. *Japanese Arts and the Tea Ceremony*. Trans. and adapted by Joseph P. Macadam. Heibonsha Survey of Japanese Art, vol. 15. New York: Weatherhill, 1974.

Hinago, Motoo. *Japanese Castles*. Trans. and adapted by William H. Coaldrake. Japanese Arts Library, vol. 14. New York: Kodansha International, 1986.

Hirai, Kiyoshi. *Feudal Architecture of Japan*. Trans. Hiroaki Sato and Jeannine Ciliotta. Heibonsha Survey of Japanese Art, vol. 13. New York: Weatherhill, 1973.

Hosono, Masanobu. *Nagasaki Prints and Early Copperplates*. Trans. and adapted by Lloyd R. Craighill. Japanese Arts Library, vol. 6. New York: Kodansha International, 1978.

Leach, Bernard. *Kenzan and His Tradition: The Lives and Times of Koetsu, Sotatsu, Korin and Kenzan*. London: Faber, 1966.

Kanazawa, Hiroshi. *Japanese Ink Painting: Early Zen Masterpieces*. Trans. and adapted by Barbara Ford. Japanese Arts Library, vol. 8. New York: Kodansha International, 1979.

Kawahara, Masahiko. *The Ceramic Art of Ogata Kenzan*. Trans. and adapted by Richard L. Wilson. Japanese Arts Library, vol. 13. New York: Kodansha International, 1985.

Kawakita, Michiaki. *Modern Currents in Japanese Art*. Trans. and adapted by Charles S. Terry. Heibonsha Survey of Japanese Art, vol. 24. New York: Weatherhill, 1974.

Meech-Pekarik, Julia. *The World of the Meiji Print: Impressions of a New Civilization*. New York: Weatherhill, 1986.

Merritt, Helen. *Modern Japanese Woodblock Prints: The Early Years*. Honolulu: Univ. of Hawaii Press, 1990.

Michener, James A. *The Floating World*. New York: Random House, 1954.

Mizuo, Hiroshi. *Edo Painting: Sotatsu and Korin*. Trans. John M. Shields. Heibonsha Survey of Japanese Art, vol. 18. New York: Weatherhill, 1972.

Muraoka, Kageo, and Kichiemon Okamura. *Folk Arts and Crafts of Japan*. Trans. Daphne D. Stegmaier. Heibonsha Survey of Japanese Art, vol. 26. New York: Weatherhill, 1973.

Murase, Miyeko. *Emaki, Narrative Scrolls from Japan*. New York: Asia Society, 1983.

———. *Masterpieces of Japanese Screen Painting: The American Collections*. New York: Braziller, 1990.

———. *Tales of Japan: Scrolls and Prints from the New York Public Library*. Oxford: Oxford Univ. Press, 1986.

Noma, Seiroku. *Japanese Costume and Textiles Arts*. Trans. Armins Nikoskis. Heibonsha Survey of Japanese Art, vol. 16. New York: Weatherhill, 1974.

Oka, Isaburo. *Hiroshige: Japan's Great Landscape Artist*. Trans. Stanleigh H. Jones. Tokyo: Kodansha International, 1992.

Okakura, Kakuzo. *The Book of Tea*. Ed. Everett F. Bleiler. New York: Dover, 1964.

Okamoto, Yoshitomo. *The Namban Art of Japan*. Trans. Ronald K. Jones. Heibonsha Survey of Japanese Art, vol. 19. New York: Weatherhill/Heibonsha, 1972.

Okawa, Naomi. *Edo Architecture: Katsura and Nikko*. Trans. Alan Woodhull and Akito Miyamoto. Heibonsha Survey of Japanese Art, vol. 20. New York: Weatherhill, 1975.

Okyo and the Maruyama-Shijo School of Japanese Painting. Trans. Miyeko Murase and Sarah Thompson. St. Louis: St. Louis Art Museum, 1980.

Takahashi, Seiichiro. *Traditional Woodblock Prints of Japan*. Trans. Richard Stanley-Baker. Heibonsha Survey of Japanese Art, vol. 22. New York: Weatherhill, 1972.

Takeda, Tsuneo. *Kano Eitoku*. Trans. Catherine Kaputa. Japanese Arts Library, vol. 3. New York: Kodansha International, 1977.

Takeuchi, Melinda. *Taiga's True Views: The Language of Landscape Painting in Eighteenth-Century Japan*. Stanford: Stanford Univ. Press, 1992.

Terada, Toru. *Japanese Art in World Perspective*. Trans. Thomas Guerin. Heibonsha Survey of Japanese Art, vol. 25. New York: Weatherhill, 1976.

Thompson, Sarah E., and H. D. Harpptunian. *Undercurrents in the Floating World: Censorship and Japanese Prints*. New York: Asia Society Gallery, 1992.

Wilson, Richard L. *The Art of Ogata Kenzan: Persona and Production in Japanese Ceramics*. New York: Weatherhill, 1991.

Yamane, Yuzo. *Momoyama Genre Painting*. Trans. John M. Shields. Heibonsha Survey of Japanese Art, vol. 17. New York: Heibonsha, 1973.

Chapter 23 Art of the Americas after 1300

Archuleta, Margaret, and Rennard Strickland. *Shared Visions: Native American Painters and Sculptors in the Twentieth Century*. Phoenix: Heard Museum, 1991.

Baquedano, Elizabeth. *Aztec Sculpture*. London: British Museum, 1984.

Berdan, Frances F. *The Aztecs of Central Mexico: An Imperial Society*. New York: Holt, 1982.

Bringhurst, Robert. *The Black Canoe: Bill Reid and the Spirit of Haida Gwaii*. Seattle: Univ. of Washington Press, 1991.

Broder, Patricia Janis. *American Indian Painting and Sculpture*. New York: Abbeville, 1981.

Coe, Ralph. *Lost and Found Traditions: Native American Art 1965–1985*. Ed. Irene Gordon. Seattle: Univ. of Washington Press, 1986.

Conn, Richard. *Circles of the World: Traditional Art of the Plains Indians*. Denver: Denver Art Museum, 1982.

Dockstader, Frederick J. *The Way of the Loom: New Traditions in Navajo Weaving*. New York: Hudson Hills, 1987.

Feest, Christian F. *Native Arts of North America*. Updated ed. World of Art. New York: Thames and Hudson, 1992.

Haberland, Wolfgang. *Art of North America*. Rev. ed. Art of the World. New York: Greystone, 1968.

Hawthorn, Audrey. *Art of the Kwakiutl Indians and Other Northwest Coast Tribes*. Vancouver: Univ. of British Columbia Press, 1967.

Hemming, John. *Monuments of the Incas*. Boston: Little, Brown, 1982.

Highwater, Jamake. *The Sweet Grass Lives On: Fifty Contemporary North American Indian Artists*. New York: Lippincott and Crowell, 1980.

Jonaitis, Aldona. *Art of the Northern Tlingit*. Seattle: Univ. of Washington Press, 1986.

———, ed. *Chiefly Feasts: The Enduring Kwakiutl Potlatch*. Seattle: Univ. of Washington Press, 1991.

Kahlenberg, Mary Hunt, and Anthony Berlant. *The Navajo Blanket*. New York: Praeger, 1972.

Levi-Strauss, Claude. *Way of the Masks*. Trans. Sylvia Modelski. Seattle: Univ. of Washington Press, 1982.

MacDonald, George F. *Haida Monumental Art: Villages of the Queen Charlotte Islands*. Vancouver: Univ. of British Columbia Press, 1983.

Maurer, Evan M. *Visions of the People: A Pictorial History of Plains Indian Life*. Minneapolis: Minneapolis Institute of Arts, 1992.

McNair, Peter L., Alan L. Hoover, and Kevin Neary. *Legacy: Tradition and Innovation in Northwest Coast Indian Art*. Vancouver: Douglas and McIntyre, 1984.

Nicholson, H. B., and Eloise Quinones Keber. *Art of Aztec Mexico: Treasures of Tenochtitlan*. Washington, D.C.: National Gallery of Art, 1983.

Parezo, Nancy J. *Navajo Sandpainting: From Religious Act to Commercial Art*. Tucson: Univ. of Arizona Press, 1983.

Pasztory, Esther. *Aztec Art*. New York: Abrams, 1983.

Penney, David. *Art of the American Indian Frontier: The Chandler-Pohrt Collection*. Detroit: Detroit Institute of Arts, 1992.

Peterson, Susan. *The Living Tradition of Maria Martinéz*. Tokyo: Kodansha International, 1977.

Smith, Jaune Quick-to-See, and Harmony Hammond. *Women of Sweetgrass: Cedar and Sage*. New York: American Indian Center, 1984.

Stewart, Hilary. *Totem Poles*. Seattle: Univ. of Washington Press, 1990.

Stierlin, Henri. *Art of the Aztecs and Its Origins*. New York: Rizzoli, 1982.

———. *Art of the Incas and Its Origins*. New York: Rizzoli, 1984.

Trimble, Stephen. *Talking with the Clay: The Art of Pueblo Pottery*. Santa Fe: School of American Research Press, 1987.

Wade, Edwin, and Carol Haralson, eds. *The Arts of the North American Indian: Native Traditions in Evolution*. New York: Hudson Hills, 1986.

Walters, Anna Lee. *Spirit of Native America: Beauty and Mysticism in American Indian Art*. San Francisco: Chronicle, 1989.

Wood, Nancy C. *Taos Pueblo*. New York: Knopf, 1989.

Chapter 24 Art of Pacific Cultures

Allen, Louis A. *Time before Morning: Art and Myth of the Australian Aborigines*. New York: Crowell, 1975.

Barrow, Terrence. *The Art of Tahiti and the Neighbouring Society, Austral and Cook Islands*. New York: Thames and Hudson, 1979.

———. *An Illustrated Guide to Maori Art*. Honolulu: Univ. of Hawaii Press, 1984.

Buhler, Alfred, Terry Barrow, and Charles P. Montford, *The Art of the South Sea Islands, including Australia and New Zealand*. Art of the World. New York: Crown, 1962.

Caruana, Wally. *Aboriginal Art*. World of Art. New York: Thames and Hudson, 1993.

Craig, Robert D. *Dictionary of Polynesian Mythology*. New York: Greenwood, 1989.

Gauguin, Paul. *Intimate Journals*. Trans. Van Wyck Brooks. Bloomington: Indiana Univ. Press, 1958.

Gell, Alfred. *Wrapping in Images: Tattooing in Polynesia*. Oxford Studies in Social and Cultural Anthropology. New York: Oxford Univ. Press, 1993.

Greub, Suzanne, ed. *Art of Northwest New Guinea: From Geelvink Bay, Humboldt Bay, and Lake Sentani*. New York: Rizzoli, 1992.

Guiart, Jean. *The Arts of the South Pacific*. Trans. Anthony Christie. Arts of Mankind. New York: Golden, 1963.

Hammond, Joyce D. *Tifaifai and Quilts of Polynesia*. Honolulu: Univ. of Hawaii Press, 1986.

Hanson, Allan, and Louise Hanson. *Art and Identity in Oceania*. Honolulu: Univ. of Hawaii Press, 1990.

Heyerdahl, Thor. *The Art of Easter Island*. Garden City, N.Y.: Doubleday, 1975.

Jone, Stella M. *Hawaiian Quilts*. Rev. 2nd ed. Honolulu: Daughters of Hawaii, 1973.

Layton, Robert. *Australian Rock Art: A New Synthesis*. New York: Cambridge Univ. Press, 1992.

Leonard, Anne, and John Terrell. *Patterns of Paradise: The Style and Significance of Bark Cloth around the World*. Chicago: Field Museum of Natural History, 1980.

Mead, Sydney Moko, ed. *Te Maori: Maori Art from New Zealand Collections*. New York: Abrams, 1984.

Morphy, Howard. *Ancestral Connections: Art and an Aboriginal System of Knowledge.* Chicago: Univ. of Chicago Press, 1991.

People of the River, People of the Trees: Change and Continuity in Sepik and Asmat Art. St. Paul: Minnesota Museum of Art, 1989.

Rabineau, Phyllis. *Feather Arts: Beauty, Wealth, and Spirit from Five Continents.* Chicago: Field Museum of Natural History, 1979.

Scutt, R. W. B., and Christopher Gotch. *Art, Sex, and Symbol: The Mystery of Tattooing.* 2nd ed. New York: Cornell Univ. Press, 1986.

Serra, Eudaldo, and Alberto Folch. *The Art of Papua and New Guinea.* New York: Rizzoli, 1977.

Sutton, Peter, ed. *Dreamings, the Art of Aboriginal Australia.* New York: Braziller, 1988.

Wardwell, Allen. *Island Ancestors: Oceania Art from the Masco Collection.* Seattle: Univ. of Washington Press, 1994.

Chapter 25 Art of Africa in the Modern Era

Abiodun, Rowland, Henry J. Drewal, and John Pemberton III, eds. *The Yoruba Artist: New Theoretical Perspectives on African Arts.* Washington, D.C.: Smithsonian Institution, 1994.

Adler, Peter, and Nicholas Barnard. *African Majesty: The Textile Art of the Ashanti and Ewe.* New York: Thames and Hudson, 1992.

Astonishment and Power. Washington, D.C.: National Museum of African Art, Smithsonian Institution, 1993.

Barley, Nigel. *Foreheads of the Dead: An Anthropological View of Kalabari Ancestral Screens.* Washington, D.C.: National Museum of African Art, Smithsonian Institution, 1988.

———. *Smashing Pots: Feats of Clay from Africa.* London: British Museum, 1994.

Biebuyck, Daniel P. *Lega Culture: Art, Initiation, and Moral Philosophy among a Central African People.* Berkeley: Univ. of California Press, 1973.

Brincard, Marie-Therese, ed. *The Art of Metal in Africa.* Trans. Evelyn Fischel. New York: African-American Institute, 1984.

Cole, Herbert M., ed. *I Am Not Myself: The Art of African Masquerade.* Los Angeles: Museum of Cultural History, Univ. of California, 1985.

———. *Icons: Ideals and Power in the Art of Africa.* Washington, D.C.: National Museum of African Art, Smithsonian Institution, 1989.

———. *Mbari, Art and Life among the Owerri Igbo.* Bloomington: Indiana Univ. Press, 1982.

Drewal, Henry John. *African Artistry: Technique and Aesthetics in Yoruba Sculpture.* Atlanta: High Museum of Art, 1980.

———, and Margaret Thompson Drewal. *Gelede: Art and Female Power among the Yoruba.* Bloomington: Indiana Univ. Press, 1983.

Fagg, William Buller, and John Pemberton III. *Yoruba Sculpture of West Africa.* Ed. Bryce Holcombe. New York: Knopf, 1982.

Gilfoy, Peggy S. *Patterns of Life: West African Strip-Weaving Traditions.* Washington, D.C.: National Museum of African Art, Smithsonian Institution, 1992.

Glaze, Anita. *Art and Death in a Senufo Village.* Bloomington: Indiana Univ. Press, 1981.

Heathcote, David. *The Arts of the Hausa.* Chicago: Univ. of Chicago Press, 1976.

Kennedy, Jean. *New Currents, Ancient Rivers: Contemporary Artists in a Generation of Change.* Washington, D.C.: Smithsonian Institution, 1992.

Laude, Jean. *African Art of the Dogon: The Myths of the Cliff Dwellers.* Trans. Joachim Neugroschell. New York: Brooklyn Museum, 1973.

Martin, Phyllis, and Patrick O'Meara, eds. *Africa.* 2nd ed. Bloomington: Indiana Univ. Press, 1986.

McEvilley, Thomas. *Fusion: West African Artists at the Venice Biennale.* New York: Museum for African Art, 1993.

McNaughton, Patrick R. *The Mande Blacksmiths: Knowledge, Power and Art in West Africa.* Bloomington: Indiana Univ. Press, 1988.

Neyt, François. *Luba: To the Sources of the Zaire.* Trans. Murray Wyllie. Paris: Editions Dapper, 1994.

Perrois, Louis, and Marta Sierra Delage. *The Art of Equatorial Guinea: The Fang Tribes.* New York: Rizzoli, 1990.

Picon, John, and John Mack. *African Textiles.* New York: Harper & Row, 1989.

Roy, Christopher D. *Art of the Upper Volta Rivers.* Meudon, France: Chaffin, 1987.

Schildkrout, Enid, and Curtis A. Keim. *African Reflections: Art from Northeastern Zaire.* Seattle: Univ. of Washington Press, 1990.

Sieber, Roy. *African Furniture and Household Objects.* Bloomington: Indiana Univ. Press, 1980.

———. *African Textiles and Decorative Arts.* New York: Museum of Modern Art, 1972.

———, and Roslyn Adele Walker. *African Art in the Cycle of Life.* Washington, D.C.: National Museum of African Art, Smithsonian Institution, 1987.

Thompson, Robert Farris, and Joseph Cornet. *The Four Moments of the Sun: Kongo Art in Two Worlds.* Washington, D.C.: National Gallery of Art, 1981.

Vogel, Susan. *Africa Explores: 20th Century African Art.* New York: Center for African Art, 1991.

Chapter 26 Neoclassicism and Romanticism in Europe and the United States

Abrams, Ann Uhry. *The Valiant Hero: Benjamin West and Grand-Style History Painting.* Washington, D.C.: Smithsonian Institution, 1985.

Age of Neoclassicism. London: Arts Council of Great Britain, 1972.

Bindman, David. *William Blake: His Art and Time.* New Haven: Yale Center for British Art, 1982.

Boime, Albert. *Art in an Age of Bonapartism, 1800–1815.* Chicago: Univ. of Chicago Press, 1990.

———. *Art in an Age of Revolution, 1750–1800.* Chicago: Univ. of Chicago Press, 1987.

Braham, Allan. *The Architecture of the French Enlightenment.* Berkeley: Univ. of California Press, 1980.

Brion, Marcel. *Art of the Romantic Era: Romanticism, Classicism, Realism.* World of Art. New York: Praeger, 1966.

Byson, Norman. *Tradition and Desire: From David to Delacroix.* New York: Cambridge Univ. Press, 1984.

Clark, Kenneth. *The Romantic Rebellion: Romantic versus Classic Art.* New York: Harper & Row, 1973.

Cooper, Wendy A. *Classical Taste in America 1800–1840.* Baltimore: Baltimore Museum of Art, 1993.

Eitner, Lorenz. *Neoclassicism and Romanticism, 1750–1850: An Anthology of Sources and Documents.* New York: Harper & Row, 1989.

French Painting 1774–1830: The Age of Revolution. Detroit: Wayne State Univ. Press, 1975.

Harris, Enriqueta. *Goya.* Rev. ed. London: Phaidon, 1994.

Honour, Hugh. *Neo-Classicism.* Harmondsworth, Eng.: Penguin, 1968.

———. *Romanticism.* London: Allen Lane, 1979.

Kroeber, Karl. *British Romantic Art.* Berkeley: Univ. of California Press, 1986.

Lindsay, Jack. *Death of the Hero: French Painting from David to Delacroix.* London: Studio, 1960.

Manners and Morals: Hogarth and British Painting 1700–1760. London: Tate Gallery, 1987.

Mayoux, Jean-Jacques. *English Painting.* Trans. James Emmons. New York: Grove, 1975.

Middleton, Robin, and David Watkin. *Neoclassical and 19th Century Architecture.* 2 vols. History of World Architecture. New York: Electa/Rizzoli, 1987.

Novotny, Fritz. *Painting and Sculpture in Europe, 1780–1880.* Pelican History of Art. Harmondsworth, Eng.: Penguin, 1980.

Paulson, Ronald. *The Art of Hogarth.* London: Phaidon, 1975.

Perez Sanchez, Alfonso E., and Eleanor A. Sayre. *Goya and the Spirit of Enlightenment.* Boston: Museum of Fine Arts, 1989.

Powell, Earl A. *Thomas Cole.* New York: Abrams, 1990.

Prideaux, Tom. *World of Delacroix, 1798–1863.* New York: Time-Life, 1966.

Roberts, Warren E. *Jacques-Louis David, Revolutionary Artist: Art, Politics, and the French Revolution.* Chapel Hill: Univ. of North Carolina Press, 1989.

Rosenberg, Pierre. *Chardin, 1699–1779.* Trans. Emilie P. Kadish and Ursula Korneitchouk. Ed. Sally W. Goodfellow. Cleveland: Cleveland Museum of Art, 1979.

Rosenblum, Robert. *Jean-Auguste-Dominique Ingres.* Masters of Art. New York: Abrams, 1990.

Rousseau, Jean-Jacques. *Emile.* Ed. F. and P. Richard. New York: French & European, 1962.

Roworth, Wendy Wassyng. *Angelica Kauffman: A Continental Artist in Georgian England.* London: Reaktion, 1992.

Rykwert, Joseph, and Anne Rykwert. *Robert and James Adam: The Men and the Style.* New York: Rizzoli, 1985.

Shapiro, Michael Edward. *George Caleb Bingham.* New York: Abrams, 1993.

Turner, Roger. *Capability Brown and the Eighteenth Century English Landscape.* London: Weidenfeld and Nicolson, 1985.

Vaughan, William. *German Romantic Painting.* New Haven: Yale Univ. Press, 1980.

———. *Romanticism and Art.* World of Art. New York: Thames and Hudson, 1994.

Walker, John. *John Constable.* New York: Abrams, 1991.

Wilton, Andrew. *Turner in His Time.* New York: Abrams, 1987.

Wolf, Bryan Jay. *Romantic-Revision: Culture and Consciousness in Nineteenth-Century American Painting and Literature.* Chicago: Univ. of Chicago Press, 1986

Chapter 27 Realism to Impressionism in Europe and the United States

Adams, Steven. *The Barbizon School and the Origins of Impressionism.* London: Phaidon, 1994.

Art of the July Monarchy: France, 1830 to 1848. Columbia: Univ. of Missouri Press, 1989.

Ashton, Dore. *Rosa Bonheur: A Life and a Legend.* New York: Viking, 1981.

Barger, M. Susan, and William B. White. *The Daguerreotype: Nineteenth-Century Technology and Modern Science.* Washington, D.C.: Smithsonian Institution, 1991.

Baudelaire, Charles. *The Painter of Modern Life, and Other Essays.* Trans. and ed. Jonathan Mayne. London: Phaidon, 1964.

Boime, Albert. *The Academy and French Painting in the Nineteenth Century.* London: Phaidon, 1971.

Cachin, Françoise, Charles S. Moffett, and Michel Melot, eds. *Manet, 1832–1883.* New York: Metropolitan Museum of Art, 1983.

Clark, T. J. *The Absolute Bourgeois: Artists and Politics in France, 1848–1851.* London: Thames and Hudson, 1973.

———. *Image of the People: Gustave Courbet and the 1848 Revolution.* London: Thames and Hudson, 1973.

Clarke, Michael. *Corot and the Art of Landscape.* London: British Museum, 1991.

Cumming, Elizabeth, and Wendy Caplan. *Arts and Crafts Movement.* World of Art. New York: Thames and Hudson, 1991.

Denvir, Bernard. *The Thames and Hudson Encyclopedia of Impressionism.* World of Art. New York: Thames and Hudson, 1990.

Faxon, Alicia Craig. *Dante Gabriel Rossetti.* Oxford: Phaidon, 1989.

Fried, Michael. *Courbet's Realism.* Chicago: Univ. of Chicago Press, 1982.

Gordon, Robert, and Andrew Forge. *Degas.* Trans. Richard Howard. New York: Abrams, 1988.

Harding, James. *Artistes Pompiers: French Academic Art in the 19th Century.* New York: Rizzoli, 1979.

Hargrove, June, ed. *The French Academy: Classicism and Its Antagonists.* Newark: Univ. of Delaware Press, 1990.

Hendricks, Gordon. *Albert Bierstadt: Painter of the American West.* New York: Abrams, 1974.

Higonnet, Anne. *Berthe Morisot's Images of Women.* Cambridge: Harvard Univ. Press, 1992.

Hilton, Timothy. *Pre-Raphaelites.* World of Art. London: Thames and Hudson, 1970.

Homer, William Innes. *Thomas Eakins: His Life and Art.* New York: Abbeville, 1992.

Mathews, Nancy Mowll. *Mary Cassatt.* Library of American Art. New York: Abrams, 1987.

McKean, John. *Crystal Palace: Joseph Paxton and Charles Fox.* Architecture in Detail. London: Phaidon, 1994.

Mead, Christopher Curtis. *Charles Garnier's Paris Opera: Architectural Empathy and the Renaissance of French Classicism.* Cambridge: MIT Press, 1991.

Murphy, Alexandra R. *Jean-François Millet.* Boston: Museum of Fine Arts, 1984.

Needham, Gerald. *19th-Century Realist Art.* New York: Harper & Row, 1988.

Nochlin, Linda. *Impressionism and Post-Impressionism, 1874–1904: Sources and Documents.* Englewood Cliffs, N.J.: Prentice-Hall, 1966.

———. *Realism and Tradition in Art, 1848–1900: Sources and Documents.* Englewood Cliffs, N.J.: Prentice-Hall, 1966.

Pissarro, Joachim. *Camille Pissarro.* New York: Abrams, 1993.

Pool, Phoebe. *Impressionism.* World of Art. New York: Praeger, 1967.

The Pre-Raphaelites. London: Tate Gallery, 1984.

Prideaux, Tom. *The World of Whistler, 1834–1903.* New York: Time-Life, 1970.

Rewald, John. *The History of Impressionism.* 4th rev. ed. New York: Museum of Modern Art, 1973.

Rouart, Denis. *Renoir.* New York: Skira/Rizzoli, 1985.

Schaaf, Larry J. *Out of the Shadows: Herschel, Talbot and the Invention of Photography.* New Haven: Yale Univ. Press, 1992.

Schneider, Pierre. *The World of Manet, 1832–1883.* New York: Time-Life, 1968.

Spate, Virginia. *Claude Monet: Life and Work.* New York: Rizzoli, 1992.

Stansky, Peter. *Redesigning the World: William Morris, the 1880s, and the Arts and Crafts.* Princeton: Princeton Univ. Press, 1985.

Touissaint, Hélène. *Gustave Courbet, 1819–1877.* London: Arts Council of Great Britain, 1978.

Triumph of Realism. Brooklyn: Brooklyn Museum, 1967.

Valkenier, Elizabeth Kridl. *Ilya Repin and the World of Russian Art.* New York: Columbia Univ. Press, 1990.

Wagner, Anne Middleton. *Jean-Baptiste Carpeaux: Sculptor of the Second Empire.* New Haven: Yale Univ. Press, 1986.

Walker, John. *James McNeill Whistler.* Library of American Art. New York: Abrams, 1987.

Weisberg, Gabriel P. *The European Realist Tradition.* Bloomington: Indiana Univ. Press, 1982.

Wilmerding, John, et al. *American Light: The Luminist Movement, 1850–1875: Paintings, Drawings, Photographs.* Washington, D.C.: National Gallery of Art, 1980.

Chapter 28 The Rise of Modernism in Europe and America

Ades, Dawn. *Photomontage.* Rev ed. World of Art. New York: Thames and Hudson, 1986.

Alexandrian, Sarane. *Surrealist Art.* World of Art. London: Thames and Hudson, 1970.

Art into Life: Russian Constructivism, 1914–32. New York: Rizzoli, 1990.

Baigell, Matthew. *The American Scene: American Painting of the 1930's.* New York: Praeger, 1974.

Banham, Reyner. *Theory and Design in the First Machine Age.* 2nd ed. Cambridge: MIT Press, 1980.

Barr, Alfred H., Jr. *Cubism and Abstract Art: Painting, Sculpture, Constructions, Photography, Architecture, Industrial Arts, Theatre, Films, Posters, Typography.* Cambridge, Mass.: Belknap, 1986.

Barron, Stephanie, ed. *Degenerate Art: The Fate of the Avant-*

Garde in Nazi Germany. Los Angeles: Los Angeles County Museum of Art, 1991.
Bayer, Herbert, Walter Gropius, and Ise Gropius. *Bauhaus, 1919–1928*. New York: Museum of Modern Art, 1975.
Brown, Milton. *Story of the Armory Show: The 1913 Exhibition That Changed American Art*. 2nd ed. New York: Abbeville, 1988.
Champigneulle, Bernard. *Rodin*. World of Art. New York: Oxford Univ. Press, 1980.
Cowling, Elizabeth. *Picasso: Sculptor/Painter*. London: Tate Gallery, 1994.
Curtis, James. *Mind's Eye, Mind's Truth: FSA Photography Reconsidered*. Philadelphia: Temple Univ. Press, 1989.
Curtis, William J. R. *Le Corbusier: Idea and Forms*. New York: Rizzoli, 1986.
Dachy, Marc. *The Dada Movement, 1915–1923*. New York: Skira/Rizzoli, 1990.
Davidson, Abraham A. *Early American Modernist Painting, 1910–1935*. New York: Harper & Row, 1981.
Denvir, Bernard. *Post-Impressionism*. World of Art. New York: Thames and Hudson, 1992.
———. *Toulouse-Lautrec*. World of Art. New York: Thames and Hudson, 1991.
Doherty, Robert J., ed. *The Complete Photographic Work of Jacob A. Riis*. New York: Macmillan, 1981.
Dube, Wolf-Dieter. *Expressionism*. Trans. Mary Whittall. World of Art. New York: Praeger, 1973.
Duncan, Alastair. *Art Nouveau*. World of Art. New York: Thames and Hudson, 1994.
Eldredge, Charles C. *Georgia O'Keeffe*. Library of American Art. New York: Abrams, 1991.
Freeman, Judi. *The Fauve Landscape*. Los Angeles: Los Angeles County Museum of Art, 1990.
Fry, Edward. *Cubism*. New York: McGraw-Hill, 1966.
Gay, Peter. *Art and Act: On Causes in History—Manet, Gropius, Mondrian*. New York: Harper & Row, 1976.
Gerdts, William H. *American Impressionism*. New York: Abbeville, 1984.
Glackens, Ira. *William Glackens and the Ashcan Group: The Emergence of Realism in American Art*. New York: Crown, 1957.
Golding, John. *Cubism: A History and an Analysis, 1907–1914*. Cambridge, Mass.: Belknap, 1988.
Gordon, Donald E. *Expressionism: Art and Idea*. New Haven: Yale Univ. Press, 1987.
Gowing, Lawrence. *Matisse*. World of Art. New York: Oxford Univ. Press, 1979.
Gray, Camilla. *Russian Experiment in Art, 1863–1922*. New York: Abrams, 1970.
Hahl-Koch, Jelena. *Kandinsky*. New York: Rizzoli, 1993.
Haiko, Peter, ed. *Architecture of the Early XX Century*. Trans. Gordon Clough. New York: Rizzoli, 1989.
Hamilton, George Heard. *Painting and Sculpture in Europe, 1880–1940*. 2nd ed. Pelican History of Art. Harmondsworth, Eng.: Penguin, 1981.
Harrison, Charles, Francis Frascina, and Gill Perry. *Primitivism, Cubism, Abstraction: The Early Twentieth Century*. New Haven: Yale Univ. Press, 1993.
Herbert, James D. *Fauve Painting: The Making of Cultural Politics*. New Haven: Yale Univ. Press, 1992.
Herrera, Hayden. *Frida Kahlo: The Paintings*. New York: HarperCollins, 1991.
Hilton, Timothy. *Picasso*. World of Art. New York: Praeger, 1975.
Holt, Elizabeth Gilmore, ed. *The Expanding World of Art, 1874–1902*. New Haven: Yale Univ. Press, 1988.
Homer, William Innes. *Alfred Stieglitz and the American Avant-Garde*. Boston: New York Graphics Society, 1977.
Hulsker, Jan. *The Complete Van Gogh: Paintings, Drawings, Sketches*. New York: Abrams, 1980.
Hulten, Pontus. *Futurism and Futurisms*. New York: Abbeville, 1986.
Jaffe, Hans L. C. *De Stijl, 1917–1931: The Dutch Contribution to Modern Art*. Cambridge, Mass.: Belknap, 1986.
Kuenzli, Rudolf, and Francis M. Naumann. *Marcel Duchamp: Artist of the Century*. Cambridge: MIT Press, 1989.
Lane, John R., and Susan C. Larsen. *Abstract Painting and Sculpture in America 1927–1944*. Pittsburgh: Museum of Art, Carnegie Institute, 1984.
Larkin, David, and Bruce Brooks Pfeiffer. *Frank Lloyd Wright: The Masterworks*. New York: Rizzoli, 1993.
Lloyd, Jill. *German Expressionism: Primitivism and Modernity*. New Haven: Yale Univ. Press, 1991.
McQuillan, Melissa. *Van Gogh*. World of Art. New York: Thames and Hudson, 1989.
Milner, John. *Vladimir Tatlin and the Russian Avant-Garde*. New Haven: Yale Univ. Press, 1983.
Norman, Dorothy. *Alfred Stieglitz, an American Seer*. New York: Aperture, 1990.
O'Gorman, James F. *Three American Architects: Richardson, Sullivan, and Wright, 1865–1915*. Chicago: Univ. of Chicago Press, 1991.
Overy, Paul. *De Stijl*. World of Art. New York: Thames and Hudson, 1991.
Picon, Gaetan. *Surrealists and Surrealism, 1919–1939*. Trans. James Emmons. New York: Rizzoli, 1977.
Post-Impressionism: Cross-Currents in European and American Painting, 1880–1906. Washington, D.C.: National Gallery of Art, 1980.
Rewald, John. *Post-Impressionism: From Van Gogh to Gauguin*. 3rd ed. New York: Museum of Modern Art, 1978.
Rosenblum, Robert. *Cubism and Twentieth-Century Art*. Rev. ed. New York: Abrams, 1984.
Rubin, William, ed. *Pablo Picasso, a Retrospective*. New York: Museum of Modern Art, 1980.
———, comp. *Picasso and Braque: Pioneering Cubism*. New York: Museum of Modern Art, 1989.
Russell, John. *Seurat*. World of Art. London: Thames and Hudson, 1965.
———. *The World of Matisse, 1869–1954*. New York: Time-Life, 1969.
Spate, Virginia. *Orphism: The Evolution of Non-Figurative Painting in Paris, 1910–1914*. Oxford Studies in the History of Art and Architecture. Oxford: Clarendon, 1979.
Stich, Sidra. *Anxious Visions: Surrealist Art*. New York: Abbeville, 1990.
Sutter, Jean, ed. *The Neo-Impressionists*. Greenwich, Conn.: New York Graphic Society, 1970.
Thomson, Belinda. *Gauguin*. World of Art. New York: Thames and Hudson, 1987.
Tisdall, Caroline, and Angelo Bozzolla. *Futurism*. World of Art. New York: Oxford Univ. Press, 1978.
Verdi, Richard. *Cezanne*. World of Art. New York: Thames and Hudson, 1992.
Weiss, Jeffrey S. *The Popular Culture of Modern Art: Picasso, Duchamp, and Avant-Gardism*. New Haven: Yale Univ. Press, 1994.
Whitford, Frank. *Bauhaus*. World of Art. London: Thames and Hudson, 1984.
Wilkin, Karen. *Georges Braque*. New York: Abbeville, 1991.
Zhadova, Larissa A. *Malevich: Suprematism and Revolution in Russian Art*. Trans. Alexander Lieven. London: Thames and Hudson, 1982.

Chapter 29 Art in the United States and Europe since World War II

Alloway, Lawrence. *Roy Lichtenstein*. New York: Abbeville, 1983.
Andersen, Wayne. *American Sculpture in Process, 1930–1970*. Boston: New York Graphic Society, 1975.
Anfam, David. *Abstract Expressionism*. World of Art. New York: Thames and Hudson, 1990.
Ashton, Dore. *American Art since 1945*. New York: Oxford Univ. Press, 1982.
———. *The New York School: A Cultural Reckoning*. Harmondsworth, Eng.: Penguin, 1979.
Atkins, Robert. *Artspeak: A Guide to Contemporary Ideas, Movements, and Buzzwords*. New York: Abbeville, 1990.
Baker, Kenneth. *Minimalism: Art of Circumstance*. New York: Abbeville, 1988.
Battcock, Gregory. *Idea Art: A Critical Anthology*. New York: Dutton, 1973.
———. *Minimal Art: A Critical Anthology*. New York: Dutton, 1968.
———, and Robert Nickas. *The Art of Performance: A Critical Anthology*. New York: Dutton, 1984.
Beardsley, John. *Earthworks and Beyond: Contemporary Art in the Landscape*. New York: Abbeville, 1984.
Berger, Maurice. *Labyrinths: Robert Morris, Minimalism, and the 1960s*. New York: Harper & Row, 1989.
Blake, Peter. *No Place Like Utopia: Modern Architecture and the Company We Kept*. New York: Knopf, 1993.
Bolton, Richard, ed. *Culture Wars: Documents from the Recent Controversies in the Arts*. New York: New, 1992.
Bourdon, David. *Warhol*. New York: Abrams, 1989.
Broude, Norma, and Mary D. Garrard. *The Power of Feminist Art: The American Movement of the 1970s, History and Impact*. New York: Abrams, 1994.
Castleman, Riva, ed. *Art of the Forties*. New York: Museum of Modern Art, 1991.
Cernuschi, Claude. *Jackson Pollock: Meaning and Significance*. New York: Icon Editions, 1992.
Chase, Linda. *Hyperrealism*. New York: Rizzoli, 1975.
Collins, Michael, and Andreas Papadakis. *Post-Modern Design*. New York: Rizzoli, 1989.
Deutsche, Rosalyn, et al. *Hans Haacke, Unfinished Business*. Ed. Brian Wallis. Cambridge: MIT Press, 1986.
Dormer, Peter. *Design since 1945*. World of Art. New York: Thames and Hudson, 1993.
Endgame: Reference and Simulation in Recent Painting and Sculpture. Boston: Institute of Contemporary Art, 1986.
Ferguson, Russell, ed. *Discourses: Conversations in Postmodern Art and Culture*. Documentary Sources in Contemporary Art. Cambridge: MIT Press, 1990.
Goldberg, Rose Lee. *Performance Art: From Futurism to the Present*. Rev. ed. New York: Abrams, 1988.
Green, Jonathan. *American Photography: A Critical History since 1945 to the Present*. New York: Abrams, 1984.
Greenough, Sarah, and Philip Brookman. *Robert Frank*. Washington, D.C.: National Gallery of Art, 1994.
Grundberg, Andy. *Photography and Art: Interactions since 1945*. New York: Abbeville, 1987.
Hays, K. Michael, and Carol Burns, eds. *Thinking the Present: Recent American Architecture*. New York: Princeton Architectural, 1990.
Henri, Adrian. *Total Art: Environments, Happenings, and Performance*. World of Art. New York: Oxford Univ. Press, 1974.
Hertz, Richard. *Theories of Contemporary Art*. 2nd ed. Englewood Cliffs, N.J.: Prentice Hall, 1993.
Hobbs, Robert Carleton, and Gail Levin. *Abstract Expressionism: The Formative Years*. Ithaca: Cornell Univ. Press, 1981
Hoffman, Katherine. *Explorations: The Visual Arts since 1945*. New York: HarperCollins, 1991.
Jencks, Charles. *Architecture Today*. 2nd ed. London: Academy, 1993.
———. *The New Moderns from Late to Neo-Modernism*. New York: Rizzoli, 1990.
———. *Post-Modernism: The New Classicism in Art and Architecture*. New York: Rizzoli, 1987.
———. *What Is Post-Modernism?* 3rd rev. ed. London: Academy Editions, 1989.
Joachimedes, Christos M., Norman Rosenthal, and Nicholas Serota, eds. *New Spirit in Painting*. London: Royal Academy of Arts, 1981.
Johnson, Ellen H., ed. *American Artists on Art from 1940 to 1980*. New York: Harper & Row, 1982.
Kaprow, Allan. *Assemblage, Environments & Happenings*. New York: Abrams, 1965.
Kingsley, April. *The Turning Point: The Abstract Expressionists and the Transformation of American Art*. New York: Simon & Schuster, 1992.
Kramer, Hilton. *The Age of the Avant-Garde: An Art Chronicle of 1956–1972*. New York: Farrar, Straus & Giroux, 1973.
Kuspit, Donald B. *Clement Greenberg, Art Critic*. Madison: Univ. of Wisconsin Press, 1979.
Levick, Melba. *The Big Picture: Murals of Los Angeles*. Boston: Little, Brown, 1988.
Lewis, Samella S. *African American Art and Artists*. Rev. ed. Berkeley: Univ. of California Press, 1994.
Lippard, Lucy. *Pop Art*. World of Art. New York: Praeger, 1966.
Livingstone, Marco. *Pop Art: A Continuing History*. New York: Abrams, 1990.
Lucie-Smith, Edward. *Art in the Eighties*. Oxford: Phaidon, 1990.
———. *Art in the Seventies*. Ithaca: Cornell Univ. Press, 1980.
———. *Art Today: From Abstract Expressionism to Superrealism*. 3rd ed. Oxford: Phaidon, 1989.
———. *Movements in Art since 1945*. Rev. ed. World of Art. London: Thames and Hudson, 1984.
———. *Super Realism*. Oxford: Phaidon, 1979.
Manhart, Marcia, and Tom Manhart, eds. *The Eloquent Object: The Evolution of American Art in Craft Media since 1945*. Tulsa: Philbrook Museum of Art, 1987.
Meisel, Louis K. *Photo-Realism*. New York: Abrams, 1989.
Morgan, Robert C. *Conceptual Art: An American Perspective*. Jefferson, N.C.: McFarland, 1994.
Nash, Steven A. *Arneson and Politics: A Commemorative Exhibition*. San Francisco: Fine Arts Museums of San Francisco, 1993.
Risatti, Howard, ed. *Postmodern Perspectives: Issues in Contemporary Art*. Englewood Cliffs, N.J.: Prentice Hall, 1990.
Rosen, Randy, and Catherine C. Brawer, comps. *Making Their Mark: Women Artists Move into the Mainstream, 1970–85*. New York: Abbeville, 1989.
Russell, John. *Pop Art Redefined*. New York: Praeger, 1969.
Sandler, Irving. *American Art of the 1960's*. New York: Harper & Row, 1988.
———. *The New York School: The Painters and Sculptors of the Fifties*. New York: Harper & Row, 1978.
———. *The Triumph of American Painting: A History of Abstract Expressionism*. New York: Harper & Row, 1976.
Sayre, Henry M. *The Object of Performance: The American Avant-Garde since 1970*. Chicago: Univ. of Chicago Press, 1989.
Shapiro, David, and Cecile Shapiro. *Abstract Expressionism: A Critical Record*. New York: Cambridge Univ. Press, 1990.
Slivka, Rose. *Peter Voulkos: A Dialogue with Clay*. Boston: New York Graphic Society, 1978.
Smith, Paul J., and Edward Lucie-Smith. *Craft Today: Poetry of the Physical*. New York: American Craft Museum, 1986.
Spaeth, David A. *Mies Van Der Rohe*. New York: Rizzoli, 1985.
Stich, Sidra. *Made in USA: An Americanization in Modern Art, the '50s & '60s*. Berkeley: Univ. of California Press, 1987.
Taylor, Paul, ed. *Post-Pop Art*. Cambridge: MIT Press, 1989.
Vaizey, Marina. *Christo*. New York: Rizzoli, 1990.
Waldman, Diane. *Collage, Assemblage, and the Found Object*. New York: Abrams, 1992.
———. *Jenny Holzer*. New York: Abrams, 1989.
———. *Transformations in Sculpture: Four Decades of American and European Art*. New York: Solomon R. Guggenheim Foundation, 1985.
———. *Willem de Kooning*. Library of American Art. New York: Abrams, 1988.
Wallis, Brian, ed. *Art after Modernism: Rethinking Representation*. Documentary Sources in Contemporary Art. New York: New Museum of Contemporary Art, 1984.
Wheeler, Daniel. *Art since Mid-Century: 1945 to the Present*. Englewood Cliffs, N.J.: Prentice Hall, 1991.
Word as Image: American Art, 1960–1990. Milwaukee: Milwaukee Art Museum, 1990.

Website Directory of Museums

This directory is comprised mainly of the museums that holds works of art illustrated in this book. A few additional institutions are also listed. We have made every effort to provide up-to-date addresses, phone numbers, and websites as of the date of printing.

UNITED STATES

ARIZONA

Center for Creative Photography,
University of Arizona, 843 E. University Blvd., Tuscon 85721. (520)621–7968.
www.ccp.arizona.edu

The Heard Museum,
22 E. Monte Vista Rd., Phoenix 85004.
(602)252–8840.
hanksville.phast.umass.edu/defs/
independent/Heard/Heard.html

Phoenix Art Museum,
1625 N. Central Ave., Phoenix 85004.
(602)257–1880.
www.azcentral.com/community/phxart/home.
html

CALIFORNIA

Crocker Museum of Art,
216 O St., Sacramento 95814. (916)264–5423.
www.sacti.org/crocker/

The Fine Arts Museums of San Francisco:
California Palace of the Legion of Honor,
Lincoln Park, near 34th Ave. and Clement St., San Francisco 94121. (415)863–3330;
M. H. de Young Memorial Museum,
Golden Gate Park, San Francisco 94118.
(415)221–4811.
www.famsf.org

Frederick S. Wright Art Gallery,
University of California, Los Angeles, 405 Hilgard Ave., Los Angeles 90024. (213)825–1461

Huntington Library, Art Collections, and Botanical Gardens,
1151 Oxford Rd., San Marino 91108.
(818)405–2141.
www.huntington.org/ArtDiv/HEHARTHOME.
html

The J. Paul Getty Museum,
17985 Pacific Coast Hwy., Malibu 90265.
(310)458–2003.
www.getty.edu/museum

Los Angeles County Museum of Art,
5905 Wilshire Blvd., Los Angeles 90036.
(213)857–6111.
www.lacma.org

Museum of Contemporary Art, San Diego,
1001 Kettner Blvd., San Diego 92101,
700 Prospect St., La Jolla 92037. (619)454–3541.
www.sddt.com/features/mca/mcainfo.html

The Museum of Contemporary Art, Los Angeles, 250 S. Grand Ave. at California Plaza, Los Angeles 90012. (213)382–6622, 621–2766.
www.MOCA-LA.org

Norton Simon Museum,
411 W. Colorado Blvd., Pasadena 91105.
(818)449–6840; 449–3730.
www.citycet.com/CCC/nsmuseum.htm

San Diego Museum of Art,
Balboa Park, 1450 El Prado, San Diego 92101.
(619)232–7931.
www.sddt.com/sdma.html

San Francisco Museum of Modern Art,
151 3rd St., San Francisco 94103. (415)357–4000.
www.sfmoma.org

San Jose Museum of Art,
110 S. Market St., San Jose 95113.
(408)294–2787.
www.sjmusart.org

Santa Barbara Museum of Art,
1130 State St., Santa Barbara 93101.
(805)963–4364.
www.artdirect.com/sbma/

Stanford University Museum and Art Gallery,
Lomita Dr. & Museum Way, Palo Alto 94305.
(415)725–4177.
www-leland.stanford.edu/dept/SUMA/

University Art Museum and Pacific Film Archive,
University of California, 2626 Bancroft Way, Berkeley 94704. (510)642–0808.
www.uampfa.berkeley.edu

COLORADO

Colorado Springs Fine Arts Center,
30 W. Dale St., Colorado Springs 80903.
(719)634–5581.
vanbriggle.com/Pikes-Peak/FineArts/

The Denver Art Museum,
100 W. 14th Ave. Pkwy., Denver 80204.
(303)640–2793.
www.denverartmuseum.org

Connecticut

Wadsworth Atheneum,
600 Main St., Hartford 06103. (203)278–2670.
www.hartfordct.com/wad.html

Yale Center for British Art,
1080 Chapel St., New Haven 06520.
(203)432–2800.
www.yale.edu/ycba/

Yale University Art Gallery,
1111 Chapel St. at York, New Haven 06520.
(203)432–0600.
www.yale.edu/yups/yuag/index.html

DELAWARE

Delaware Art Museum,
2301 Kentmere Pkwy., Wilmington 19806.
(302)571–9590.
www.udel.edu/delart/

District of Columbia

The Corcoran Gallery of Art,
500 17th St. NW, 20006. (202)638–1903.
www.corcoran.org

Freer Gallery of Art, Smithsonian Institution,
Jefferson Dr. at 12th St. SW, 20560.
(202)357–4880.
www.si.edu/organiza/museums/freer/start.htm

Hirshhorn Museum and Sculpture Garden, Smithsonian Institution, Independence Ave. at 7th St. SW, 20560. (202)357–2700.
www.si.edu/organiza/museums/hirsh/start.htm

National Gallery of Art,
4th St. at Constitution Ave. NW, 20565.
(202)737–4215; (202)842–6176 (TDD).
www.nga.gov

National Museum of American Art,
8th and G Sts., 20560; **Renwick Gallery,**
Pennsylvania Ave. at 17th St. NW, 20006.
(202)357–2700.
www.nmaa.si.edu

National Museum of Women in the Arts,
1250 New York Ave. NW, 20005, (202) 783–5000.
www.nmwa.org

National Portrait Gallery,
8th and F Sts. NW, 20560. (202)357–2700.
www.npg.si.edu

The Phillips Collection,
1600 21st St. NW, 20009. (202)387–0961

FLORIDA

John and Mable Ringling Museum of Art,
5401 Bay Shore Rd., Sarasota 34243.
(813)359–5700.
www.ringling.org

Lowe Art Museum,
University of Miami, 1301 Stanford Dr., Coral Gables 33124. (305)284–3535.
www.flamuseums.org/fam/flamuseums/
pages/185.htm

Museum of Fine Arts, Saint Petersburg, Florida,
255 Beach Dr. NE, Saint Petersburg 33701.
(813)896–2667.
www.fine-arts.org

GEORGIA

Georgia Museum of Art, University of Georgia,
Jackson St., North Campus, Athens 30602.
(706)542–GMOA or 4662

High Museum of Art,
1280 Peachtree St. NE, Atlanta 30309.
(404)733–HIGH or 4444.
www.high.org

HAWAII

Honolulu Academy of Arts,
900 S. Beretania St., Honolulu 96814.
(808)532–8700; 532–8701.

Illinois

The Art Institute of Chicago,
111 S. Michigan Ave. at Adams St., Chicago 60603. (312)443–3600; 443–3500.
www.artic.edu

Krannert Art Museum, University of Illinois,
500 E. Peabody Dr., Champaign 61820.
(217)333–1861.
www.art.uiuc.edu/kam/

Museum of Contemporary Art,
220 E. Chicago Ave., Chicago 60611.
(312)280–2660; 280–5161.
www.mcachicago.org

Oriental Institute Museum, The University of Chicago, 1155 E. 58th St., Chicago 60637.
(773)702–9521.
www-oi.uchicago.edu/OI/MUS/OI-Museum.html

Terra Museum of American Art,
666 N. Michigan Ave., Chicago 60611.
(312)664–3939

INDIANA

Indianapolis Museum of Art,
1200 W. 38th St., Indianapolis 46208.
(317)923–1331.
web.ima-art.org/ima

IOWA

Des Moines Art Center,
4700 Grand Ave.,
Des Moines 50312. (515)277–4405

University of Iowa Museum of Art,
150 N. Riverside Dr., Iowa City 52242.
(319)335–1727

KANSAS

Spencer Museum of Art, University of Kansas,
1301 Mississippi St., Lawrence 66045.
(913)864–4710.
www.ukansas.edu/~sma

Wichita Art Museum,
619 Stackman Dr., Wichita, 67203. (316)268–4921.
www.feist.com/~wam

KENTUCKY

J. B. Speed Art Museum,
2035 S. 3rd St., Louisville 40208. (502)636–2920.
www.speedmuseum.org

LOUISIANA

New Orleans Museum of Art,
1 Collins Diboll Circle, City Park, New Orleans
70124. (504)488–2631.
www.noma.org

MAINE

Bowdoin College Museum of Art,
Walker Art Building, Brunswick 04011.
(207)725–3275. www.bowdoin.edu

Portland Museum of Art,
7 Congress Sq., Portland 04101. (207)775–6148.
www.portlandmuseum.org

MARYLAND

The Baltimore Museum of Art,
Art Museum Dr. at North Charles and 31st Sts.,
Baltimore 21218. (410)396–7100.

Walters Art Gallery,
600 N. Charles St., Baltimore 21201.
(410)547–9000; 547–ARTS.
www.thewalters.org

MASSACHUSETTS

Addison Gallery of American Art, Phillips Academy,
Andover 01810. (508)749–4015.
www.andover.edu/addison/home.html

Davis Museum and Cultural Center, Wellesley College,
106 Central St., Wellesley 02181. (617)283–2051.
www.wellesley.edu/DavisMuseum/
davismenu.html

Harvard University Art Museums,
Cambridge 02138. (617)495–9400
www.fas.harvard.edu/~artmuseums/:
Busch-Reisinger Museum, 32 Quincy St.;
Fogg Art Museum, 32 Quincy St.; The Arthur M.
Sackler Museum, 485 Broadway

Isabella Stewart Gardner Museum,
280 The Fenway, Boston 02115. (617)566–1401.
www.boston.com/gardner

Mead Art Museum, Amherst College,
Amherst 01002. (413)542–2335.
www.amherst.edu/~mead

Mount Holyoke College Art Museum,
South Hadley 01075. (413)538–2245.
www.myholyoke.edu/offices/artmuse/
general.html

Museum of Fine Arts, Boston,
465 Huntington Ave., Boston 02115.
(617)267–9300.
www.mfa.org

Peabody Essex Museum,
East India Sq., Salem 01970. (508)745–1876.
www.pem.org

Rose Art Museum, Brandeis University,
415 South St., Waltham 02254. (617)736–3434.
www.brandeis.edu/rose/index.html

Smith College Museum of Art,
Elm St. at Bedford Terrace, Northampton 01063.
(413)585–2760.
www.smith.edu/artmuseum/

Sterling and Francine Clark Art Institute,
225 South St., Williamstown 01267.
(413)458–9545.
www.clark.williams.edu

Williams College Museum of Art,
Main St., Williamstown 01267. (413)597–2429.
www.williams.edu/WCMA/

Worcester Art Museum,
55 Salisbury St., Worcester 01609.
(508)799–4406.
www.worcesterart.org

MICHIGAN

The Detroit Institute of Arts,
5200 Woodward Ave., Detroit 48202.
(313)833–7900.
www.dia.org

Grand Rapids Art Museum,
155 Division North, Grand Rapids 49503.
(616)459–4677.
www.grandrapids.org/artmuseum/

The University of Michigan Museum of Art,
525 S. State St., Ann Arbor 48109.
(313)764–0395.
www.umich.edu/~umma

MINNESOTA

The Minneapolis Institute of Arts,
2400 3rd Ave. S., Minneapolis 55404.
(612)870–3131; 870–3200.
www.artsMIA.org

Walker Art Center,
Vineland Pl., Minneapolis 55403.
(612)375–7622.
www.walkerart.org

MISSOURRI

The Nelson-Atkins Museum of Art,
4525 Oak St., Kansas City 64111.
(816)561–4000.
www.nelson-atkins.org

The Saint Louis Art Museum,
1 Fine Arts Dr., Forest Park, St. Louis 63110.
(314)721–0072. www.slam.org

NEBRASKA

Joslyn Art Museum,
2200 Dodge St., Omaha 68102. (402)342–3300.
www.joslyn.org

University of Nebraska-Lincoln/Sheldon Memorial Art Gallery and Sculpture Garden,
12th and R Sts., Lincoln 68588. (402)472–2461.
sheldon.unl.edu

NEW HAMPSHIRE

Hood Museum of Art, Dartmouth College,
Wheelock St., Hanover 03755. (603)646–2808.
gopher://gopher.dartmouth.edu/II/HopHood

NEW JERSEY

The Art Museum, Princeton University,
Princeton 08544. (609)258–3788

Jane Zimmerli Art Museum,
Rutgers The State University of New Jersey,
Hamilton and George Sts., New Brunswick
08903 (732)932–7237.
www-rci.rutgers.edu/~zamuseum/

The Montclair Art Museum,
3 S. Mountain Ave. at Bloomfield Ave.,
Montclair 07042. (973)746–5555.
www.montclair-art.com

The Newark Museum,
49 Washington St., Newark 07101.
(973)596–6550

NEW MEXICO

Millicent Rogers Museum,
1504 Millicent Rogers Rd., Taos 87571.
(505)758–2462

NEW YORK

Albright-Knox Art Gallery,
1285 Elmwood Ave., Buffalo 14222.
(716)882–8700.
www.albright-knox.org

American Craft Museum,
40 W. 53rd St., New York 10019. (212)956–3535

The Brooklyn Museum,
200 Eastern Pkwy., Brooklyn 11238.
(718)638–5000.
www.brooklynart.com

The Cloisters,
Fort Tryon Park, New York 10040.
(212)923–3700.
www.metmuseum.org/htmlfile/gallery/
cloister/cloister.html

Cooper-Hewitt National Museum of Design,
Smithsonian Institution, 2 E. 91st St., New York
10128. (212) 860–6868.
www.si.edu/organiza/museums/design/home/
home.htm

Everson Museum of Art of Syracuse and Onondaga County,
401 Harrison St., Syracuse 13202.
(315)474–6064.
www.everson.org

The Frick Collection,
1 E. 70th St., New York 10021. (212)288–0700

George Eastman House/International Museum of Photography and Film,
900 E. Ave., Rochester 14607. (716)271–3361.
www.eastman.org

The Grey Art Gallery and Study Center, New York University Art Collection,
33 Washington Pl., New York 10003.
(212)998–6780.
www.nyu.edu/greyart

Guggenheim Museum SoHo,
575 Broadway, New York 10012. (212)423–3500.
www.guggenheim.org/soho.html

Herbert F. Johnson Museum of Art, Cornell University,
Ithaca 14853. (607)255–6464.
www.museum.cornell.edu

The Hudson River Museum of Westchester,
511 Warburton Ave., Yonkers 10701.
(914)963–4550.
www.hrm.org

International Center of Photography:
1130 5th Ave., New York 10028. (212)860–1777;
Midtown, 1133 6th Ave., New York 10036.
(212)860–1783.
www.icp.org

The Jewish Museum,
1109 5th Ave., New York, 10128.
(212)423–3200
www.jewishmuseum.org

Memorial Art Gallery of the University of Rochester,
500 University Ave., Rochester, NY 14607.
(716)473–7720.
www.cc.rochester.edu/MAG

The Metropolitan Museum of Art,
5th Ave. at 82nd St., New York 10028.
(212)879–5500. www.metmuseum.org

The Museum of Modern Art,
11 W. 53rd St., New York 10019. (212)708–9400.
www.moma.org

Munson-Williams-Proctor Institute Museum
of Art, 310 Genesee St., Utica 13502.
(315)797–0000

Neuberger Museum of Art, Purchase College,
State University of New York at Purchase,
735 Anderson Hill Rd., Purchase 10577.
(914)251–6133.
www.neuberger.org

The New Museum of Contemporary Art,
583 Broadway, New York 10012. (212)219–1222.
www.newmuseum.org

The Pierpont Morgan Library, 29 E. 36th St.,
New York 10016. (212)685–0008

Solomon R. Guggenheim Museum,
1071 5th Ave., New York 10128. (212)423–3500.
www.guggenheim.org/srgm.html

The Studio Museum in Harlem,
144 W. 125th St., New York 10027.
(212)864–4500.
www.studiomuseuminharlem.org

Storm King Art Center,
Old Pleasant Hill Rd., Mountainville 10953.
(914)534–3115.
www.skac.org

Whitney Museum of American Art,
945 Madison Ave., New York 10021.
(212)570–3676.
www.echonyc.com/~whitney

NORTH CAROLINA
The Ackland Art Museum, University of North
Carolina, Chapel Hill,
Columbia and Franklin Sts., Chapel Hill 27599.
(919)966–5736.
www.unc.edu/depts/ackland/frontpage.htm

Duke Univerisity Museum of Art,
Buchanan Blvd. at Trinity, East Campus,
Durham 27708. (919)684–5135.
www.duke.edu/web/duma/

North Carolina Museum of Art,
2110 Blue Ridge Rd., Raleigh 27607.
(919)839-6262.
www.ncsu.edu/NCMA/

Weatherspoon Art Gallery, University of
North Carolina, Greensboro,
Spring Garden and Tate Sts., Greensboro 27412.
(910)334–5770.
www.uncg.edu/wag/

OHIO
Allen Memorial Art Museum, Oberlin College,
87 N. Main St., Oberlin 44074. (216)775–8665.
www.oberlin.edu/wwwmap/allen_art.html

The Butler Institute of America,
524 Wick Ave., Youngstown 44502.
(216)743–1711.
www.butlerart.com

Cincinnati Art Museum, Eden Park,
Cincinnati 45202. (513)721–5204.
www.cincinnatiartmuseum.org

The Cleveland Museum of Art,
11150 E. Blvd., Cleveland 44106.
(216)421–7340.
www.clemusart.com

The Columbus Museum of Art,
480 E. Broad St., Columbus 43215.
(614)221–6801

Dayton Art Institute,
456 Belmonte Park North, Dayton 45405.
(513)223–5277.

The Taft Museum,
316 Pike St., Cincinnati 45202. (513)241–0343.
www.taftmuseum.org

The Toledo Museum of Art,
2445 Monroe St., Toledo 43620. (419)255–8000;
(800)644–6862.
www.toledomuseum.org

Wexner Center for the Arts, The Ohio State
University,
North High St. at 15th Ave., Columbus 43210.
(614)292–3535.
web.cgrg.ohio-state.edu/Wexner

OKLAHOMA
Gilcrease Museum,
1400 Gilcrease Museum Rd., Tulsa 74127.
(918)596–2700

The Philbrook Museum of Art,
2727 S. Rockford Rd., Tulsa 74114.
(918)749–7941.

OREGON
Portland Art Museum,
1219 SW Park Ave, Portland 97205.
(503)226–2811.
www.pam.org

PENNSYLVANIA
The Andy Warhol Museum,
117 Sandusky St., Pittsburgh 15212.
(412)237–8300.
www.warhol.org/warhol/

Barnes Foundation,
300 North Natch's Ln., Merion Station 19066.
(610)667–0290

Brandywine River Museum, Brandywine
Conservancy,
Rt. 1 at PA Rt. 100, Chadds Ford 19317.
(610)388–2700.
www.brandywinemuseum.org

The Carnegie Museum of Art,
4400 Forbes Ave., Pittsburgh 15213.
(412)622–3131.
www.warhol.org/moa

The Frick Art Museum,
7227 Reynolds St., Pittsburgh 15208.
(412)371–0600

Institute of Contemporary Art, University
of Pennsylvania,
118 S. 36th St., Philadelphia 19104.
(215)898–7108.
www.upen.edu/ica/

Museum of American Art of the Pennsylvania
Academy of the Fine Arts,
118 N. Broad St., Philadelphia 19102.
(215)972–7600.
www.pond.com/~pafa

Philadelphia Museum of Art,
26th St. and Benjamin Franklin Pkwy.,
Philadelphia 19130. (215)763–8100.
www.philamuseum.org

University of Pennsylvania Museum of
Archaeology and Anthropology,
33rd and Spruce Sts., Philadelphia 19104.
(215)898–4000,4001.
www.upenn.edu/museum

RHODE ISLAND
Museum of Art, Rhode Island School of Design,
224 Benefit St., Providence 02903.
(401)454–6500.
www.risd.edu/museum.html

SOUTH CAROLINA
Greenville County Museum of Art,
420 College St., Greenville 29601. (803)271–7570

TENNESSEE
Knoxville Museum of Art,
410 10th Ave., World's Fair Park,
Knoxville 37916. (615)525–6101.
www.esper.com/kma/index.html

Memphis Brooks Museum of Art,
Overton Park, 1934 Poplar, Memphis 38104.
(901)722–3500.
www.memphisguide.com/Brooks.html

Texas
Amon Carter Museum,
3501 Camp Bowie Blvd., Fort Worth 76107.
(817)738–1933.
www.cartermuseum.org

Contemporary Arts Museum,
5216 Montrose Blvd., Houston 77006.
(713)526–0773. www.camh.org

Dallas Museum of Art,
1717 N. Harwood, Dallas 75201. (214)922–1200.
www.unt.edu/dfw/dma/

Kimbell Art Museum,
3333 Camp Bowie Blvd., Fort Worth 76107.
(817)332–8451.
www.kimbellart.org

Marion Koogler McNay Art Museum,
6000 N. New Braunfels Ave., San Antonio 78209.
(210)824–5368

The Menil Collection,
1515 Sul Ross, Houston 77006.
www.menil.org/~menil

Modern Art Museum of Fort Worth,
1309 Montgomery St. at Camp Bowie Blvd.,
Fort Worth 76107. (817)738–9215

The Museum of Fine Arts, Houston,
1001 Bissonnet St., Houston 77005.
(713)639–7300.
mfah.org

Rothko Chapel,
1409 Sul Ross, Houston 77006. (713)524–9839.
www.menil.org/rothko.html

San Antonio Museum of Art,
200 W. Jones St., San Antonio 78215.
(210)978–8100.
www.samuseum.org

VIRGINIA
The Chrysler Museum,
245 W. Olney Rd.,
Norfolk 23510. (804)664–6200.
www.whro.org/cl/cmhh

Hampton University Museum,
Hampton 23668. (757)727–5308.
www.hamptonu.edu/HUMUS/HUMUS.htm

Monticello,
P. O. Box 316, Charlottesville 22902.
(804)984-9822.
www.monticello.org

Virginia Museum of Fine Arts,
2800 Grove Ave., Richmond 23221.
(804)367–0844.
xroads.virginia.edu/~VAM/VMFA

WASHINGTON
Seattle Art Museum,
100 University St., Seattle 98101. (206)625–8900;
654–3100.
www.sam.tripl.org

Tacoma Art Museum,
1123 Pacific Ave., Tacoma 98402. (206)272–4258.
www.tamart.org

WISCONSIN
Milwaukee Art Museum,
750 N. Lincoln Memorial Dr., Milwaukee 53202.
(414)224–3200.
www.mam.org

OUTSIDE THE UNITED STATES

AUSTRIA
Graphische Sammlung Albertina,
A-1010 Wien, Augustinerstrße 1. (0222)534830.
www2.telecom.at/albertina/welcome1.html

Kunsthistoriches Museum,
A-1010 Wien, Burgring 5.
(0222)525240

Österreichische Galerie Belvedere,
1037 Wien, Prinz-Eugen-Str. 27. (01)79570

BELGIUM
Musée Royaux d'Art et d'Histoire,
Parc du Cinquantenaire 10, 1000 Brussels.
(02)7417211

Musées Royaux des Beaux-Arts de Belgique,
9, Rue de Musée, 1000 Brussels.
(02)5139630.
www.fine-art-museum.be

CANADA
Art Gallery of Ontario, 317 Dundas St. W.,
Toronto, Ontario M5T 1G4. (416)977–6648.
www.ago.net

Canadian Center for Archictecture,
1920, rue Baile, Montréal, Quebec H3H 2S6.
(514)939–7000; 939–7026.
cca.qc.ca

Edmonton Art Gallery,
2 Sir Winston Churchhill Sq., Edmonton,
Alberta T5J 2C1. (403)422–6223

Glenbow,
130 9th Ave., Southeast, Calgary,
Alberta T2G 0P3. (403)268–4100.
www.glenbow.org

Montréal Museum of Fine Arts,
1379-80 Sherbrook St. W., Montréal,
Quebec H36 2T9.
(514)285–1600; 285–2000.
www.mmfa.qc.ca

National Gallery of Canada,
380 Sussex Dr., Ottawa, Ontario K1N 9N4.
(800)319–ARTS; (613)990–1985.
national.gallery.ca

Royal Ontario Museum,
100 Queen's Park, Toronto, Ontario M5S 2C6.
(416)586–5551.
www.rom.on.ca

Vancouver Art Gallery,
750 Hornby St., Vancouver,
British Columbia V6Z 2H7.
(604)682–4668.
www.vanartgallery.bc.ca

CZECH REPUBLIC
National Gallery in Prague,
Hradcanské námesti 15, Prague. (02)536867

DENMARK
Louisiana Museum of Modern Art,
GI Strandvej 13, 3050 Humlebæk. 42190719.
www.louisiana.dk

Ny Carlsberg Glyptotek,
Dantes Plads 7, 1556 Copenhagen. 33418141.
www.kulturnet.dk/homes/ncg/

EGYPT
Egyptian Museum,
Cairo University. Midan el Tahrir,
Cairo. (2)760390.
www.idsc.gov.eg/culture/egy_mus.htm

ENGLAND
Ashmolean Museum of Art and Archaeology,
Beaumont St., Oxford OX1 2PH. (01865)278000.
www.ashmol.ox.ac.uk

Banqueting House, Whitehall,
London SW1 2ER. (0171)8398919

Birmingham Museum and Art Gallery,
Chamberlain Sq., Birmingham B3 3DH.
(0121)2352834

Blenheim Palace,
Woodstock OX7 1PX. (01993)811325

British Library Exhibition Galleries,
Great Russell St., London WC1B 3DG.
(0171)4127595

British Museum,
Great Russell St., London WC1B 3DG.
(0171)6361555.
www.british-museum.ac.uk

Courtauld Institute Galleries,
Somerset House, Strand, London WC2R ORN.
(0171)8732526

Durham Cathedral,
Durham DH1 3EH. (0191)3844854

The National Gallery,
Trafalgar Sq., London WC2N 5DN. (0171)7472885.
www.nationalgallery.org.uk

Royal Academy of Arts,
Burlington House, Piccadilly, London W1V 0DS.
(0171)4397438.
www.royalacademy.org.uk

Sir John Soane's Museum,
13 Lincoln's Inn Fields, London WC2A 3BP.
(0171)4052107.
www.demon.co.uk/heritage/soanes/

Tate Gallery,
Millbank, London SWIP 4RG. (0171)8878000.
www.tate.org.uk

Victoria and Albert Museum,
Cromwell Rd., South Kensington,
London SW7 2RL. (0171)9388500.
www.vam.ac.uk

Wellington Museum,
Apsley House, 149 Piccadilly, Hyde Park Corner,
London W1V 9FA. (0171)4995676.
www.vam.ac.uk/apsley/

Westminster Abbey,
London SW1P 3PA. (0171) 2225152

FRANCE
Bibliothèque Nationale de France,
58 Rue de Richelieu, Paris 75002. (1)47038126.
www.bnf.fr

Château de Versailles,
Versailles 78000. (1)30847400.
www.chateauversailles.fr

Chauvet cave,
Vallon-Pont-d'Arc.
www.culture.gouv.fr/culture/arcnat/chauvet/
en/gvpda-d.htm

**Galeries Nationales d'Exposition du Grand
Palais,**
Avenue du Général Eisenhower, Paris 75008.
(1)42895410

Musée Auguste Rodin,
77 Rue de Varenne, Paris 75007. (1)47050134.
www.paris.org/Musee/Rodin

Musée Claude Monet,
Rue Claude Monet, Giverny 27620. 32512821.
giverny.org/monet/welcome.htm

Musée des Antiquités Nationales,
Château de Saint-Germaine-en-Laye, Saint-
Germain-en-Laye 78100. (1)34515365

Musée des Beaux-Arts de Lyon,
Palais St. Pierre, 20 Place des Terreaux, 69001
Lyon. 78280766

Musée du Louvre,
34-36 Quai Louvre, Paris 75058. (1)40205009.
www.Louvre.fr

**Musée National d'Art Moderne—Centre
National d'Art et de Culture Georges
Pompidou,**
19 Rue du Renard, Paris 75191. (1)44781233.
www.cnac-gp.fr

**Musée National du Château de
Fontainebleau,**
Fontainebleau 77300. (1)60715070

Musée d'Orsay,
1 Rue de Bellechasse, Paris 75007. (1)40494814.
www.musee-orsay.fr

Musée Picasso,
Hôtel Salé, 5 Rue de Thorigny, Paris 75003.
(1)42712521

Musée d'Unterlinden,
1 Rue des Unterlinden, Colmar 68000. 89201550

GERMANY
**Ägyptisches Museum und Papyrussammlung,
Staatliche Museeun zu Berlin-Preussischer**
Preußischer Kulturbesitz, Schlossstr. 70,
Berlin 14059. (030)32091261.
userpage.hu-berlin.de/~kurtwagn/gendir/
aegy-pap/aegychar.html

**Alte Pinakothek, Bayerische
Staatsgemäldesammlungen,**
Barer Str. 27, Munich 80333.
(089)23805216.

Brücke-Museum,
Bussardsteig 9, Berlin 14195. (030)8312029.
www/dhm.de/museen/bruecke/

Hamburger Kunsthalle,
Glockengießerwall, Hamburg 20095.
(040)24862612.
www.hamburg.de/Behoerden/Museen/kh/

Museum Ludwig,
Bischofsgartenstr. 1, Cologne 50667.
(0221)2212370.
www.museenkoeln.de/ludwig/

Schloss Charlottenburg,
Luisenplatz, Berlin 14059.

Staatliche Kunsthalle,
Hans-Thoma-Str. 2-6, Karlsruhe 76133.
(0721)9263355.
www.rz.uni- karlsruhe.de/Nick/Karlsruhe/

Staatliche Antikensammlungen und Glyptothek,
Königspl 1–3, Munich 80333. (089)598359

Staatliche Graphische Sammlung,
Meiserstr. 10, Munich 80333. (089)5591490

Gemäldegalerie, Staatliche Museen zu Berlin-Preussischer Kulturbesitz,
Arnimallee 23-27, Berlin 14195. (030)8301217

Staatsgalerie Stuttgart,
Konrad-Adenauer Str. 30-32, Stuttgart 70182. (0711) 2124050.

Städelsches Kunstinstitut und Städtische Galerie,
Schaumainkai 63, Frankfurt 60596. (069)6050980.

GREECE
Acropolis Museum,
2-3 Makriyianni, Athens 117 42. (01)9238724. www.culture.gr

Archaeological Museum,
Delphi 33054. (0265)82313.

Archaeological Museum,
Iera Odos, 2, Elefsis (Eleusis) 19200. (01)5546019

National Archaeological Museum,
Od Tosita 1, Athens 10682. (01)8217717.

HUNGARY
Szépmüvészeti Múzeum, Dózsa György út 41, Budapest 1146. (01)429759. origo.hnm.hu

IRAN
Iran Bastan Museum,
Khiaban-e Imam Khomeini, Khiaban-e Siume Tir, Teheran 11364. (021)672061-6

IRAQ
Iraq Museum,
Karkh Museum Sq., Baghdad. 361215

IRELAND
National Gallery of Ireland,
Merrion Sq. West, Dublin 2. (01)6615133. indigo.ie/~nmi1/museum/index.htm

ITALY
Galleria Borghese,
Piazzale Scipione Borghese 5, Rome 00197. (06)858577.
www.thais.it/scultura/rgb.htm

Galleria degli Uffizi,
Piazza degli Uffizi , Florence 50122. (055)2388651/2.
www.uffizi.firenze.it

Galleria dell'Accademia,
Via Ricasoli 60, Florence 50122. (055)214375

Galleria dell'Accademia,
Campo della Carità, Venice 30121. (041)22247

Galleria Nazionale d'Arte Antica,
Via delle Quattro Fontane 13, Rome 00184. (06)4824184

Musei Capitolini,
Piazza del Campidoglio, Rome 00186. (06)67102475

Museo Archeologico Nazionale,
Via Museo 19, Naples 80135. (081)440166

Museo Archeologico Nazionale,
Via Aquilia, Paestum 84063. (0828)811023

Museo Archeologico Nazionale du Firenze,
Via della Colonna 38, Florence 50121. (055)23575

Museo Civico Archeologico,
Via dell'Archiginnasio 2, Bologna 40124. (051)233849.
www.commune.bologna.it/bologna/Musei/Archeologico/l

Museo Civico Cristiano,
Via Musei, 81, Brescia 25100. (030)44327

Museo dei Conservatori,
Piazza del Campidoglio, Rome 00186. (06)67102475

Museo di Antichità Etrusche e Italiche,
Istituto Etruscologia e Antichità Italiche, Facoltà di Lettere Università di Roma La Sapienza, Piazzale Aldo Moro, Rome 00185

Museo e Gallerie Nazionale di Capodimonte,
Palazzo di Capodimonte, Naples 80136. (081)7410801.
capodimonte.selfin.net

Museo Etrusco,
Piazza della Cattedrale, Chiusi Città 53043

Museo Nazionale del Bargello,
Via del Proconsolo 4, Florence 50122. (055)210801

Museo Nazionale di Villa Giulia,
Piazza di Villa Giulia 9, Rome 00195. (06)350719

Palazzo della Farnesina,
Via della Lungara 230, Rome 00165. (06)651629

Peggy Guggenheim Collection,
Palazzo Venier dei Leoni, 701 Dorsoduro, Venice 30123. (041)5206288.
www.guggenheim.org/venice.html

Vatican Museums,
Viale Vaticano, Città del Vaticano 00120, Rome. (06)698833.
www.christusrex.org/www1/vaticano/0-Musei.html

JORDAN
Jordan Archaeological Museum,
Amman Citadet, P.O.Box 88, Amman. 638795

THE NETHERLANDS
Centraal Museum Utrecht,
Agnietenst. 1, Utrecht 3500 GC. (030)362362.

Frans Halsmuseum,
Groot Heiligland 62, Haarlem 2001 DJ. (023)164200.

Kröller-Müller Museum,
Postbus 1, Otterlo 6730 AA. (08382)1241

Museum Boijmans-van Beuningen,
Museumpark 18-20, Rotterdam 3015 CK. (010)441400.
www.boijmans.rotterdam.nl

Rijksmuseum,
Stadhouderskade 42, Postbus 74888, Amsterdam 1070 DN. (020)6732121.

Rijksmuseum Vincent van Gogh,
Paulus Potterstr. 7, Postbus 75366, Amsterdam 1070 AJ. (020)5705200.

Stedelijk Museum of Modern Art,
Paulus Potterstr. 13, Postbus 75082, Amsterdam 1070 AB. (020)5732911.
art.cwi.nl

NORWAY
Nasjonalgalleriet,
Universitestsgaten 13, Oslo 0033. 22200404.
www.museumsnett.no/nasjonalgalleriet/eng/

ROMANIA
National Museum of Art,
Str. Stirbei Vida, nr. 1–3, Bucharest 70733. (01)6155193

RUSSIA
Hermitage Museum,
Dworzowaja Nabereshnaja 34-36, Saint Petersburg 191065, (212)9545.
www.hermitage.ru

Pushkin Museum of Fine Arts,
Ul. Volkhonka 12, Moscow. (095)2037412.
www.rosprint.ru/art/museum/pushkin

SCOTLAND
National Gallery of Scotland,
The Mound, Edinburgh EH2 2EL. (0131)5568921.
www.nms.ac.uk

SPAIN
Museo Nacional Centro de Arte Reina Sofía,
Santa Isabel 52, Madrid 28012. (91)4675062

Museo Nacional del Prado,
Paseo del Prado, Madrid 28014. (91)4680950.
museoprado.mcu.es

SWEDEN
Moderna Museet,
Spårvagnshallarna, Box 16382, Stokholm 103 27. (08)6664250.
www.modernamuseet.se

Nationalmuseum,
S. Blasieholmshamnen, Box 16176, Stockholm 103 24. (08)6664250.
www.nationalmuseum.se

University Art Gallery, Uppsala University,
Domkyrkoplam 7, Uppsala 752 20. (018)155400

SWITZERLAND
Kunstmuseum Basel und Museum für Gegenwartskunst, St. Alban-Graben 16, Basel 4010. (061)2710828.
www.kunstmuseumbasel.ch

Kunstmuseum Bern,
Hodlerstr. 8-12, Bern CH-3000. (031)3110944

Musée d'Art et d'Histoire,
2 Rue Charles Galland, Geneva 1211. (022)3114340

TURKEY
Archaeological Museum of Istanbul,
Gülhane Sultanahmet, Istanbul 34400. (520)7742.
www.exploreturkey.com/ist_arch.htm

Index

D

Neo-Babylonia, 63, 81–83
Neo-Confucianism, 415–16; "School of the Mind", 419
Neolithic period, 37; Aegean, 128–29; China, 57, 397–99; Egypt, 93–94; Europe, 47–58; Near East, 63–85
Neon, Bishop, 304
Nepal, 366
Nephthys, 96, 125
Nerezi (near Skopje), Macedonia, Saint Panteleimon church, 328; *Lamentation*, 328, *328*
Nero, 252
Nerva, 259
Newgrange, Ireland: passage grave, 144; tomb interior, *52*, 53
Ngongo ya Chintu, 470
Nicaea: First Council of, 290, 304; Second Council of, 322
niche, muqarnas-filled, *347*
Nicholas of Verdun, 586, 587; *Shrine of the Three Kings* (reliquary), 566, 586–87, *587*
niello, 58, 137, 149, 537
Night Attack on the Sanjo Palace (scroll), Kamakura period, Japan, 437–38, *437*
Nike, 156
Nike (Victory), Samothrace, Macedonia, *214*, 215
Nike (Victory) Adjusting Her Sandal (relief sculpture), Athens, Temple of Athena Nike, 193, *194*, 202, 219, 247
Nile River, 93
Nîmes, France, 243; Maison Carrée, *242*, 243; Pont du Gard, 241–43, *241*
Nineveh (modern Kuyunjik, Iraq), 80; *Assurbanipal and His Queen in the Garden*, 80, *80*; sculpted head of a man, 74, *74*
Nishapur, Iran, 348
Nizami, *Khamsa* (Five Poems), 362
Nok culture (Nigeria), 468–69
Noli Me Tangere (in Christian art), 307
nonrepresentational (nonobjective) style, 29
Normandy, France, 481; Romanesque period, 530–35
Normans, 327
   architecture of, influence on English, 576
   conquest of Britain, 509, 530; tapestry depiction of, 534–35
Norse peoples, 481, 483
North Acropolis, Tikal, 452
North America, 460–63
Northern Song dynasty, 415, 416
Northern Wei dynasty, 409
Notre-Dame Cathedral. *See* Amiens; Paris, France; Reims, France; Île-de-France, France
nudes, in Greek sculpture, 169–70, 201–2
numerical symbolism, Gothic, 557
Nut, 96

O

oba (Benin royalty), 471–74
obelisk, 116
Obembe Alaye (African artist), 470
ocher, 38, 39
Octavian. *See* Augustus Caesar
Octopus Flask, Palaikastro, Crete, *139*, 139
oculus, 226, 264, 310, 556
Odo, bishop of Bayeux in Normandy, 534
Odysseus, 156
Odyssey, 143, 216
ogival arch, *347*, 347, 354
oinochoe (wine pitcher), 161
O'Keeffe, Georgia, 22; *Portrait of a Day, First Day*, 22, *22*
Olbrechts, Frans, 470
Old Saint Peter's, Rome, Italy, 297–99, *297*, 492
Old Testament Trinity, The (Three Angels Visiting Abraham) (icon), Rubiyov, Andrey, 335, *335*, 583
Olmec culture, 447–48; influence on Mayan, 451
olpe (wide-mouthed pitcher), 161
Olympia, Greece
   Man and Centaur (statuette), 160, *160*
   Sanctuary of Hera and Zeus, 153, 155–57, 178
   Temple of Hera, 201
   Temple of Zeus, pediment sculpture, 178–79, *178*, *179*, 189, 202; *Athena, Herakles, and Atlas*, 178, *179*, 196, 202
Olympian/ic Games, 153, 157, 179
Olympias (artist), 207
Olympos, Mount, 155, 156
omega symbol, 525
one-point perspective. *See* perspective
oni (Yoruba royalty), 469–71
opet festival (Egypt), 96
opus anglicanum, 580–82
opus incertum, 236, *236*
opus reticulatum, 236, *236*
opus testaceum, 236, *236*

oracle, 157
oracle bones, 400
Orange, France, Roman theater at, *242*, 243
orant figures, 291, 293, 295
Orchard, William, 578, 579; Magdalen College, Oxford, 578–79, *578*
orders of architecture. *See* classical orders
Orientalizing period, Greek, 158, 161–62, 174
Orthodox Church (Eastern), 290, 291, 323–24
orthogonal, 30, 198
orthogonal plan, 198–99
Oseberg, Norway, burial ship (Viking), 480, *480*, 483; post with animal figures, 483, *484*, 519
Osiris, 95, 96, 124, 125, 235
Osman, 350
Ostia, Italy, Trajan's Harbor, 268–70
Ostrava Petrkovice, Czech Republic, *Woman* (figurine), 39, *39*
Ostrogoths, 302, 313
Otto I, Emperor, 498, 499
Otto I Presenting Magdeburg Cathedral to Christ (plaque), from *Magdeburg Ivories* (German), 499–501, *499*
Otto II, Emperor, 498
Otto III, Emperor, 498, 501, 503
Otto III Enthroned, page from *Liuthar (Aachen) Gospels* (Ottonian manuscript), 503, *503*
Ottoman Empire, 350, 354
Ottoman Turks, 290, 323, 350, 363; art, 345, 363
Ottonian art, 498–505; influence on Romanesque, 535; stained-glass windows, 559
overlapping, 30
Ovid, 259
ox (Christian symbol), 294
Oxford, Oxfordshire, England: Magdalen College, 578–79, *578*; Oxford University, 576

P

Pacal, Lord, 453–54
Padua, Italy, Arena Chapel, frescoes, Giotto, 604–7, *605*, *606*, *607*
Paestum, Italy, 163; Temple of Hera I, 163–64, *163*
paganism, late Roman Empire, 284
pagoda, 413, 414, *414*; Japan, 426; stone, 414; wooden, 414
Painted Pottery cultures (Neolithic China), 398–99
Painted Stoa, 186
Painter in Her Studio (tomb relief, Rome), *259*
painterly style, 29
painting, 30; Buddhist, 430, 440; Chinese, 407–8, 414; early Christian, 291–95; Egyptian, 110; figure, 414; Greek, 205–6; Indian, 383; Indus Valley, 370; Italian Gothic, 595–608; Japanese, 428–29, 430, 435–37, 441; Judaic, 291–95; Mayan, 455, 456; Peruvian, 459; prehistoric, 41–46; Roman (ancient), 278–80
Pakistan, 366
Palace Chapel of Charlemagne, Aachen (Aix-la-Chapelle), Germany, 492–93, *493*
palace complex: Aegean, 128; Assyrian, 79; Mesopotamian, 77; Minoan, 131–34
Palace of Assurnasirpal II, Kalhu (modern Nimrud, Iraq), *Assurnasirpal II Killing Lions*, 78, 79
Palace of Diocletian, Split, Dalmatia, 275–76, *275*
Palace of the Lions, Granada, Spain, Alhambra, 347, *350*, 351–52, *351*, 360
Palace of Zimrilim, Mari (modern Tell Hariri, Iraq), 131
Palaikastro, Crete, *Octopus Flask*, 139, *139*
Palatine Chapel, Palermo, Sicily, Italy, *Nativity*, 328, *328*
Palenque, Mexico, 453–54
   palace, 453, *453*
   Temple of the Inscriptions, 453, *453*; portrait of Lord Pacal, 454, *454*; sarcophagus lid from tomb of Lord Pacal, 454, *454*
Paleolithic period: Americas, 445; Europe, 37–47
Palermo, Sicily, Italy, Palatine Chapel, 328; *Nativity*, 328, *328*
Palestine, 289, 291, 339
Palestrina, Italy, Sanctuary of Fortuna, *236*, 237, *237*
palette (utensil for mixing colors), 96
Palette of Narmer, Hierakonpolis, Egypt, 96–97, *97*, 98
Pallavas dynasty, 388
Palma, Mallorca, Spain, Cathedral, 582, *582*
palmette, 176
Pan, 156
Panathenaic Way, Athens, Greece, 185
panel painting: Byzantine, 318–22; Italian Gothic, 595–97
Pan Painter, 183–84; *Artemis Slaying Actaeon* (vase painting), 184, *184*
Pantheon, Rome, Italy, 145, 226, 263–64, *264*, *265*, 298, 310
Pantokrator, Romanesque interpretation of, 525, 529
papyrus, 96, 101–2, 104, 319

Paracas culture (Peru), 457–58
parapet, 579, *579*
parchment, 319, 486, 490
Paris, France: Île-de-la-Cité, 564; Notre-Dame Cathedral, 564, *564*; *see also* Saint-Denis abbey church; Sainte-Chapelle
Paris (hero), 156
Paris Psalter (manuscript), *David the Psalmist* from, 333–34, *333*
parodos, 210
Paros, Greek island, 130, 169; *Little Girl with a Bird* (stela), 196–97, *196*
Parthenon, Athens, Greece, Acropolis, *164*, 186, 187–90, *188*
   friezes, 190, *190*; *Horsemen*, detail of *Procession*, 190, *190*; *Marshals and Young Women*, detail of *Procession*, 190, *191*, 246
   metopes sculpture, *Lapith Fighting a Centaur*, 189, *189*, 190
   pediment sculpture, 84, 188–89, *189*; *Three Seated Goddesses*, 188–89, *189*
Parthians, 248
Parting of Lot and Abraham, Rome, Italy, Santa Maria Maggiore, 300, *300*, 495
passage graves, 51, *52*, 53, *53*, 144
Passion Cycle (in Christian art), 306
Passover seder, 289
patriarch, 291
Patroclus, 156
patronage of art, 25–26; Africa, 470; Europe, 481, 548, 590, 595; religious, 548
Paul (Saul), Saint, 290, 291
Pausanias, 201
Pausias, 207, 273
Pax Romana, 235, 245
Pech-Merle Cave, France, *Spotted Horses and Human Hands* (cave painting), 41–42, *41*, 42
Pedanius Dioscorides, 319
pedestal, 166, 227, *227*, 517, *517*
pediment, 163, *165*, 243
Peisistratos, 155
Peloponnesian Wars, 184–85
pendentive, 309, 310, 324; dome on, 302, *310*
Pentecost, page from *Cluny Lectionary* (Romanesque manuscript), *528*, 529
Pepi, Cenni di. *See* Cimabue
peplos, 171
Peplos Kore, Athens, Greece, Acropolis, sculpture, 171, *171*
Pepy II, 106
Pepy II and His Mother, Queen Merye-ankhnes (Egyptian), 106, *106*
Pergamene Style, 211–16
Pergamon, Asia Minor (in modern Turkey), 211
   Altar of Zeus, 212–13, *213*, 237; frieze sculpture, *Athena Attacking the Giants*, 212, *213*, 246
   sculptural style of, 219
Perikles, 185–86, 187, 191
period, 29, 31
peripteral temple, 163, 164, *164*, 187, 238
peristyle, 163, 164
peristyle court, 116, 241, 275–76
peristyle garden, 240
Perpendicular style (English Gothic), 578–79
Persephone, 156, 171
Persepolis, Persia (modern Iran), 86–88
   ceremonial complex: Apadana of Darius and Xerxes, 86–87, *86*; column from, 87, *87*; detail of, *Darius and Xerxes Receiving Tribute*, 87–88, *87*; Hall of 100 Columns, 87; plan, 86, *86*
Perseus, 156, 166
Persia (modern Iran), 62, 63, 85–89, 101, 177–78, 349; Daric (coin) from, 88, *89*; Seleucid, 209
Persian knot, *359*
Persian War, 88, 177–78, 184
perspective: atmospheric (aerial), 30, 258, 334; Chinese landscape, 417; diagonal, 30; divergent, 30; intuitive, 30, 251, 599; linear (scientific, mathematical, one-point), 30; reverse, 316; two-point, *30*; vertical, 30
Peru, 457–60
Perugia, Italy, Porta Augusta, 225, *225*, 253
Peter, Saint, 297
Petites Heures of Jeanne d'Evreux (manuscript), Jean Pucelle, pages from: *Annunciation*, 574–75, *575*; *Betrayal and Arrest of Christ*, 574–75, *575*; *Fox Seizing a Rooster*, 576, *576*
Phaistos, Crete: Kamares Ware jug, 139, *139*; palace complex, 133
pharaoh (title), 114
Pheidias, 186, 187–88, 190, 201; Zeus, statue of, at Olympia, 102

Credits

Credits and Copyrights

The author and publisher wish to thank the galleries, libraries, museums, and private collectors named in the picture captions for permitting the reproduction of works of art in their collections and for supplying the necessary photographs. Photographs from other sources are gratefully acknowledged below.

Adros Studio, Rome: 7-16, 7-17, 15-17, 15-18, 16-41; Aerofilms, Borehamwood, Herts, England: pages 34–35, 1-21, 8-8; Mark Horton, Aga Kahn Program Visual Archives, Massachusetts Institute of Technology, Cambridge, MA, 1981: 13-9; Alexandria Press, London: 8-25; Archivi Alinari, Florence: 5-54, 5-70, 5-79, 5-87, 6-2, 6-20, 6-40, 6-41, 6-42, 6-43, 6-44, 6-46, 6-51, 6-52, 6-66, 6-67, 6-71, 6-73, 6-76, 6-77, 6-78, 6-84, 6-85, 6-87, 15-40, 16-63, 16-67, 16-68, 16-69, 16-80, 16-82; American Institute of Indian Studies, Ram Nagar, India: 9-5, 9-18, 9-25; Alison Frantz Collection, American School of Classical Studies, Athens: 4-9, 4-20, 5-50, 5-52, 7-42; Pierre Amiet, *The Art of the Ancient Near East*, New York, Harry N. Abrams, Inc./Paris, Citadelles & Mazenod, 1980, fig. 680: 2-33; Ronald Sheridan's Ancient Art & Architecture Collection, London: 7-50, 8-15; Fred Anderegg, reprinted by permission of Princeton University Press: 7-8; Francis B. Andrews, *The Mediaeval Builder and His Methods*, New York, Barnes & Noble Books, 1993, fig. 1: page 564; Sören Hallgren, 1965 © Antikvarisk-Topografiska Arkivet (ATA), Stokholm: 14-3; Archeological Survey of India, Government of India, Calcutta: 9-19; Archiv für Kunst und Geschichte, Berlin, Germany: 7-46, 7-54, 15-32; Philippe Ariès and Georges Duby, *A History of Private Life, Vol. I. From Pagan Rome to Byzantium*, Cambridge MA and London, The Belknap Press of Harvard University Press, © 1987: page 259; © 1995 The Art Institute of Chicago, All Rights Reserved: 11-17, 12-17; *Art of Ancient India* (exhibition catalogue), plate 155, courtesy Marylin Rhie: 9-15; Art Resource, New York: 2, 11, 16; Bildarchiv Foto Marburg/Art Resource, New York: 14-24, 14-26, 14-29, 16-8, 16-31, 16-42, 16-52, 16-53, 16-57; Erich Lessing/Art Resource, New York: pages 464-65, 13-1, 15-43; Scala/Art Resource, New York: 5-38, 7-1, 7-3, 7-32, 7-34, 7-60, 16-2, 16-75, 16-76, 16-79; Werner Forman Archive, London/Art Resource, New York: page 110 below; Asian Art Archives, University of Michigan, photo by Dr. Michael Meister, University of Pennsylvania: 9-24; Asian Art Archives, University of Michigan: pages 364-65, 9-9, 9-11, 9-20, 9-22, 9-23; James Austin, Cambridge, England: 15-2, 15-27, 16-23; Avery Architectural and Fine Arts Library, Columbia University in the City of New York: 16-54; © Dirk Bakker, courtesy The Detroit Institute of Arts: 13-2, 13-3, 13-4, 13-7; Bernard Beaujard, Martignargues, France: 6-24, 16-6; Benoy K. Behl, Bombay, courtesy Indira Gandhi National Centre for the Arts, New Delhi: 9-16, 9-26; Raffaello Bencini, Florence: 8-6, 8-7; Jacques Bendien, Naples: 6-47; Benrido, Tokyo: 11-6, 11-8, 11-9; Jean Bernard, Aix-en-Provence, France: 16-1, 16-14, 16-29; Constantin Beyer, Weimar, Germany: 15-33, 16-58, 16-59; Bibliothèque Nationale, Paris, France: 14-21; Bildarchiv Preussischer Kulturbesitz, Berlin: 2-27, 3-36, 3-37, 3-38, 5-22, 5-32, 5-80, 5-81, 6-62, 6-69, 6-79, 8-5; Montserrat Blanch, *Arte Gortico en Espagñe*, Barcelona, Ediciones Poligrafa, 1972: 16-51; Blaser, Hannaford & Stucky, *Drawings of Great Buildings*, Basel, Birkhäuser Verlag AG, © 1993: 15-41 (page 60, Joseph Weber), 16-13 (page 80, Alex Sims), 16-18 (page 82, James McCahon), 16-27 (page 81, Charles Young), 16-40 (page 93, Peter Blinn), 16-64 (page 108, Raymond Krebs); Jon Blumb, Lawrence, KS: 18; Axel Boëthius and J. B. Ward-Perkins, *Etruscan and Roman Architecture*, Penguin Books, © 1970, fig. 96: 6-53; Erwin Böhm, Mainz, Germany: 2-5; Boltin Picture Library, Croton-on-Hudson, NY: 5-72; The British Museum, London: 5-61; Percy Brown, *Indian Architecture, Vol. I*, Bombay Taraporevale Sons & Co., 1965 (reprint), plate XIX: 9-10; Diana Buitron-Oliver, *The Greek Miracle, Classical Sculpture from the Dawn of Democracy: The Fifth Century B.C.*, Washington, D.C., National Gallery of Art, © 1992 Board of Trustees, pages 154-55 below: 5-18; Photographie Bulloz, Paris, France: 15-12, 15-13; © Dr. Brian Byrd, University of California, San Diego and Dr. E. B. Banning, University of Toronto, drawn by Jonathan Mabry: 2-1; Caisse Nationale des Monuments Historiques et des Sites, Paris © Arch.phot.Paris/SPADEM: 1-12, 15-4, 15-7, 15-11, 16-7, 16-10, 16-21, 16-26; Calveras/Sagristà, Barcelona: 15-19; Cambridge University Collection of Air Photographs, copyright reserved, Cambridge, England: 15-23; Canali Photobank, Capriolo, Italy: 5-1, 5-13, 5-27, 6-5, 6-16, 6-25, 6-36, 6-38, 6-58, 7-12, 7-13, 7-14, 7-19, 7-20, 7-21, page 319, 15-39, 15-42, 16-65, 16-70, 16-71, 16-73, 16-74, page 607; Piero Codato courtesy Canali Photobank, Capriolo, Italy: 16-81; Luciano Pedicini courtesy Canali Photobank, Capriolo, Italy: 6-55; Paul Caponigro: 1-23; Mario Carrieri, Milan: 7-57, 8-18; Casement Collection Photo Library, London: 13-10; Centre d'Etudes et Documentation sur l'Art Chretien Oriental, Estampes, France: 7-41; Chamberlain, Marblehead, MA: 16-9; China Pictorial Publications, Beijing: 10-1; University of Cincinnati Department of Classics, reproduced by permission of Princeton University Press: 4-25; Jean Mazenod, Éditions Citadelles & Mazenod, Paris: 2-10; Éditions Citadelles & Mazenod, Paris: 6-15; Peter Clayton: 3-33; © 1995 The Cleveland Museum of Art: 11-18, page 458 left, 12-7; drawing by Stephen Conlin, from Margaret Oliphant, *The Atlas of the Ancient World*, New York, Simon & Schuster, © 1992, page 95, courtesy Marshall Editions, London: 4-4; The Conway Library, Courtauld Institute of Art, London: 4-22; David A. Loggie, photographer, *Corpus Christianorum Continuatio Mediaevalis 43-43A: Hildegardis Scivias,* Turnhout, Brepols Publishers, © 1978: 15-36; Cultural Relics Publishing House, Beijing: 10-3, 10-6, 10-7, 10-8, 10-14, 10-15, 10-16, 10-17; Nina M. Davis, *Ancient Egyptian Paintings, Volume I*, University of Chicago/Oxford University Press, 1936, Plate VII: 3-23; Deutsches Archäologisches Institut, Athens: 5-14, 5-15, 5-65, 5-77; Deutsches Archaeologisches Institut, Rome: 5-78, 6-12, 6-31, 6-57, 6-86; Laboratoires Photographiques Devos, Boulogne-sur-Mer: 5-29; Frank Tomio, Dom- und Diözesanmuseum Hildesheim, Germany: 14-28; © Domkapitel Aachen (Foto Münchow), Aachen, Germany: 14-31; Christos Doumas, *The Wall-Paintings of Thera*, Athens, The Thera Foundation, 1992, page 56; Hugues Dubois, Brussels/Paris: 13-6; Dumbarton Oaks, Washington, D.C. © Byzantine Visual Resources: 7-47, 7-48, 7-53; Nikos Kontos, courtesy Ekdotike Athenon, Athens: 7-28, 7-40; Fotocielo, Rome: 6-37, 7-33; Fototeca Unione, American Academy, Rome: 6-14, 6-28, 6-29, 6-39, 6-49, 6-54, 6-60, 6-65, 6-81; Fotowerkstatte, Cologne, Germany: 14-19; Susan Einstein, Fowler Museum of Cultural History, University of California, Los Angeles: 12-18; Gabinetto Fotografico Nazionale, Rome: 6-11; Gabinetto Fotografico, Pisa: 16-66; Gayle Garrett, Washington, D.C.: page 359; GEKS, New York: 7-25; Georg Gerster, Comstock, Inc., New York: 12-3, 12-16; Getty Conservation Institute, Marina del Rey, CA: 3-43, page 124; Photographie Giraudon, Paris: 15-10, 16-30; Erwin R. Goodenough, *Jewish Symbols in the Greco-Roman Period*, Bollingen Series 37, vol. II: Symbolism in the Dura Synagogue, © 1964, Princeton University Press (photographs by Fred Anderegg), reprinted by permission of Princeton University Press:7-8; Oleg Grabar, *The Formation of Islamic Art*, New Haven and London, © Yale University Press, 1973, fig. 66: 8-4; The Green Studio Limited, Dublin: 14-8, 14-9; Griffith Institute, Ashmolean Museum, Oxford: 3-1; Gulf International (U.K.) Ltd, London: 8-21; Dr. Reha Günay, Istanbul: 7-51; Sonia Halliday Photographs, Weston Turville, Bucks, England: 8-16; Photo Hassia: 4-7; Françoise Henry, *Irish Art in the Early Christian Period*, Ithaca, Cornell University, 1965: 14-10; Brian Brake, John Hillelson Agency, London: 6-63; Hirmer Fotoarchiv, Munich: 9, 2-8, 3-12, 3-13, 3-18, 4-5, 4-6, 4-14, 4-27, 4-28, 5-2, 5-8, 5-11, 5-17, 5-25, 5-34, 5-35, 5-36, 5-44, 5-45, 5-46, 5-49, 5-51, 5-55, 5-63, 6-67, 5-68, 5-82, 6-7, 6-8, 6-9, 7-18, 7-22, 7-23, 7-24, 7-31, pages 544-45, page 554, 16-22, 16-56; Ove Holst, Oslo: 14-4; *The Human Figure in Early Greek Art*, 1988, Greek Ministry of Culture/National Gallery of Art, Washington, page 58: 5-4; Martin Hürlimann, *India: The Landscape, the Monuments and the People*, New York, B. Westermann, 1928, fig. 131: 9-21; The Hutchison Library, London: 6-61; The Image Bank, New York: pages 90–91, 3-8, 3-10, 3-14, 3-35; (former) Imperial Embassy of Iran, Washington, D.C.: 8-13; Japan National Tourist Organization, New York: 11-10; © Wolfgang Kaehler, Bellevue, WA: 10-12; Justin Kerr, New York: pages 442-43, 12-8, 12-12; A. F. Kersting, London: 8-2, 8-17, 15-26; © Kodansha Ltd, Tokyo: 3-2; © Studio Kontos, Athens: 4-1, 4-3, 4-8, 4-11, 4-13, 4-15, 4-16, 4-19, 4-26, 4-29, 5-21, 5-23, 5-24, 5-37, 5-42, 5-69; Laboratoire Photographique Blow Up, Dijon, France: 15-22; Kurt Lange, Oberstdorf/Allgäu, Germany: 3-4; Michael Larvey, Austin, TX: 6-21, 6-27, 6-33, 6-45, 6-68; Fanny Broadcast, Liason International, New York: 1-1; © Tony Linck, Fort Lee, NJ: 12-1; Gene Markowski: 9-8; Arxiu MAS, Barcelona: 1-16, 8-11, 8-22, 16-47, 16-48, 16-49; Junkichi Mayuyama, Tokyo: 11-5; All rights reserved, The Metropolitan Museum of Art: 2-13, 3-32, 5-6, 5-20, 5-56, 5-84, 5-85, 6-35, 6-75, 16-38; Copyright © By The Metropolitan Museum of Art: 3-20 (1993), 3-25 (1983), 3-26 (1983), 3-42 (1978), 5-5 (1978), 5-7 (1985), 5-31 (1986), 5-73 (1990), 5-74 (1993), 6-1 (1986), 6-34 (1986), 8-1 (1994), 8-14 (1982), 8-27 (1986), 12-2 (1990), 12-9 (1990), 14-13 (1994), 14-27 (1986), 15-15 (1982), 16-37 (1985), 16-45 (1981), 16-46 (1981); Schecter Lee, © 1986 By The Metropolitan Museum of Art: 13-8; Kazimierz Michalowski, *Art of Ancient Egypt*, Paris, Éditions d'Art Lucien Mazenod/New York, Harry N. Abrams, Inc., fig. 476: 3-41; Ministry of Culture/Archaeological Receipts Fund (TAP Service), Athens: pages 126-127, 4-1, 4-18, 5-53; Ministry of Public Buildings and Works, Edinburgh. Crown Copyright Reserved: 1-18; Monumenti Musei e Gallerie Pontificie, Vatican City (Rome): 5-64, 5-66, 5-83, pages 220–221, 6-13, 6-30, 6-70; Roger Moss, Cornwall, England: 16-12; Foto Ann Münchow, Aachen, Germany: 14-17; Joan Myers, Tesuque, NM: 17; © 1995 Board of Trustees, National Gallery of Art, Washington, D.C.: 4; Sisse Brimberg, National Geographic Society Image Collection: 1-6, 1-9, 1-11; National Monuments Record Center, Swindon, England: 16-43; National Museum, Copenhagen: 1-28; National Park Service, U.S. Department of the Interior, Washington, D.C.: 12-22; Archive Jean-Louis Nou, Paris: 9-2, 9-3, 9-6, 9-17; Office of Public Works, Dublin: 1-19; Courtesy The Oriental Institute, The University of Chicago: 2-9, 2-22, 2-32, 2-34; Oroñoz, Madrid, Spain: 14-14, 16-50; K. Papaioannou, *The Art of Greece*, New York, Harry N. Abrams, Inc., 1989/Éditions Mazenod, Paris, 1972, pages 400-401 top: 5-43; André Parrot, Sumer, *The Dawn of Art*, New York, Golden Press, 1961, fig. 346: 2-19, 2-20; Donato Pineider, Florence: 7-38, 7-39; Nicholas Platon, *Zakros: The Discovery of a Lost Palace of Ancient Crete*, New York, Charles Scribner's Sons, 1971, page 46 below: 4-12; Pontificia Commissione di Archeologia Sacra, Rome: 7-2, 7-3, 7-4, 7-5, 7-6; Studio Mario Quattrone, Florence: 16-77, 16-78; Archivio e Studio Folco Quilici, Rome: 6-6, 15-38, 16-62; Stephen Quirke and Carol Andrews, *The Rosetta Stone, Facsimile Drawing with an Introduction and Translation*, New York, Harry N. Abrams, Inc., 1989, © 1988 The Trustees of the British Museum: page 113; Fotostudio Rapuzzi, Brescia, Italy: 6-80; Rheinisches Landesmuseum Trier: 6-83; Réunion des Musées Nationaux, Paris: 1-7, 1-15, 2-16, 2-17, 2-18, 2-29, 2-30, 2-35, 3-17, pages 150-51, 5-48, 5-86, 6-26, 7-56, 8-9, 8-10, 16-32; Rheinisches Bildarchiv, Cologne: 14-30, 16-60; Merle Greene Robertson © 1976: 12-10; Peter Dorrell and Stuart Laidlaw, courtesy University of London, Institute of Archaeology, © Dr. Gary Rollefson 'Ain Ghazal Research Institute, Ober-Ramstadt, Germany: 2-2; Jean Roubier, Paris: 15-14; 16-19; Royal Smeets Offset, Amsterdam: 9-1; Sakamoto Manschichi Photo Research Library, Tokyo: 11-11; 11-14; Peter Sanders Photography, Chesham, Bucks, England: pages 336-37, 8-12; Reconstruction drawing by J. V. Schaubild, *Der heilige Bezirk von Delphi*, published 1913: 5-3; *Dr. Schliemann's Houses and Magazine*, Plan of Troy and Hellespont, Plate X, page 287: page 143; Fotoarchiv Helga Schmidt-Glassner, © Callweyverlag, Munich: 6-23; Ann Pearce, "Heroic Bronzes of Fifth Century B.C. Regain Old Splendor," *Smithsonian Magazine*, Volume 12, No. 8, November 1981, page 130, top left: page 182; Susan Dirk, © Seattle Art Museum: 24; Soprintendenza Archeologica all'Etruria Meridionale, Tarquinia, Italy: 6-10; Sovfoto/ Eastfoto, New York: 7-61; Spectrum